MW00994070

Psychology and Our Curious World

The author team dedicates this book to our families and students, who made this project possible and who continue to inspire us.

The authors are donating a portion of their royalties to charities close to their hearts.

Wind is supporting two charities. One is the Wounded Warrior Project, which provides services to U.S. military veterans. The other is the Trevor Project, the leading suicide prevention organization for LGBTQ+ youth.

Gary is supporting the Make-A-Wish Foundation. Their mission is to bring joy, strength, and hope to children with critical illnesses and their families through the granting of transformative wishes.

Charity is supporting the Thurgood Marshall College Fund. It provides scholarships, innovative programs, and strategic partnerships to Historically Black Colleges and Universities.

Tom is supporting GlassRoots. They are an entrepreneurial community organization dedicated to building business skills and inclusivity through glass art.

As a global academic publisher, Sage is driven by the belief that research and education are critical in shaping society. Our mission is building bridges to knowledge—supporting the development of ideas into scholarship that is certified, taught, and applied in the real world.

Sage's founder, Sara Miller McCune, transferred control of the company to an independent trust, which guarantees our independence indefinitely. This enables us to support an equitable academic future over the long term by building lasting relationships, championing diverse perspectives, and co-creating social and behavioral science resources that transform teaching and learning.

Psychology and Our Curious World

Wind Goodfriend

Buena Vista University
Storm Lake, Iowa

Gary W. Lewandowski Jr.

Monmouth University
West Long Branch, New Jersey

Charity Brown Griffin

Winston-Salem State University
Winston-Salem, North Carolina

Thomas Heinzen

William Paterson University
Wayne, New Jersey

FOR INFORMATION:

2455 Teller Road
Thousand Oaks, California 91320
E-mail: order@sagepub.com

1 Oliver's Yard
55 City Road
London EC1Y 1SP
United Kingdom

Unit No 323-333, Third Floor, F-Block
International Trade Tower Nehru Place
New Delhi 110 019
India

18 Cross Street #10-10/11/12
China Square Central
Singapore 048423

Acquisitions Editor: Mary Dudley
Content Development Editor: Ivey Mellem
Production Editor: Tracy Buyan
Copy Editor: Gillian Dickens
Proofreader: Barbara Coster
Typesetter: C&M Digitals (P) Ltd.
Indexer: Integra
Cover Designer: Scott Van Atta
Marketing Manager: Victoria Velasquez

Copyright © 2026 by Sage.

All rights reserved. Except as permitted by U.S. copyright law, no part of this work may be reproduced or distributed in any form or by any means, or stored in a database or retrieval system, without permission in writing from the publisher.

All third-party trademarks referenced or depicted herein are included solely for the purpose of illustration and are the property of their respective owners. Reference to these trademarks in no way indicates any relationship with, or endorsement by, the trademark owner.

Printed in the United States of America

Library of Congress Control Number: 2024939977

ISBN 9781544380490 (paperback) | ISBN 9781544380476 (loose-leaf) | ISBN 9781544380513 (epub) | ISBN 9781544380506 (epub) | 9781544380483 (Web PDF)

This book is printed on acid-free paper.

FSC
www.fsc.org
100%
Paper from well-managed forests

24 25 26 27 28 10 9 8 7 6 5 4 3 2 1

BRIEF CONTENTS

DETAILED CONTENTS

iStock.com/Natali_Mis

iStock.com/Kenneth Cheung

iStock.com/miodrag ignjatovic

REUTERS/Mike Blake

iStock.com/SeanZeroThree

CHAPTER 4. Identity, Sex, and Gender

CHAPTER 5. Stress, Health, and Happiness

iStock.com/gparusnikov

iStock.com/Oleksii Didok

CHAPTER 6. Sensation and Perception 155

CHAPTER 7. Consciousness 191

iStock.com/PatriciaPix

iStock.com/PeopleImages

CHAPTER 8. Human Development

iStock.com/-id-art

Jeffrey Isaac Greenberg 12+/Alamy Stock Photo

iStock.com/fcafotodigital

iStock.com/Anna Frank

CHAPTER 11. Motivation and Emotion 327

iStock.com/piovesempre

iStock.com/kalig

iStock.com/Kerkez

iStock.com/Image Source

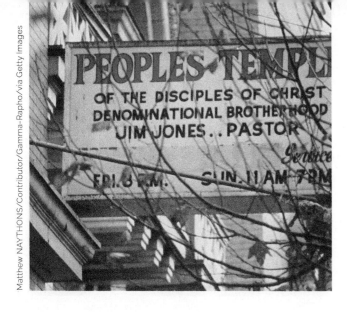

Matthew NAYTHONS/Contributor/Gamma-Rapho/via Getty Images

Bob Daemmrich/Alamy Stock Photo

Courtesy of Lisa Rinzler

iStock.com/Daisy-Daisy

CHAPTER 16. Mental Health: Therapy and Treatment 497

PREFACE

Dear Student,

The world has never seen a diverse group of individuals like you before.

In college, people of all ages pursue education and bring a wealth of experiences and dreams to the classroom. Whether you were born between 1997 and 2012 (making you a member of Generation Z) or fall before or after that range, your journey is unique to you. You've navigated through social media, cell phones, a pandemic, and global economic and environmental crises that previous generations left for you to solve. At every step of the way, you defy expectations.

People of different age groups collectively hold common aspirations. However, behavioral trends, research surveys, and current events indicate that Generation Z embraces five ideals (Nemeth, 2022):

1. More than money: Generation Z values pure salary at work less than any previous generation, putting benefits like flexible hours, vacation time, and a healthy lifestyle as more important.

2. Personal values: Your generation prioritizes personal values and cares whether their career and consumer choices align with what they believe in. You refuse to sacrifice work–life balance.

3. Screen time: While completely comfortable with screen time, your generation is very aware that virtual meetings lack the intimacy of in-person meetings. A mixture of both is preferred.

4. Embrace innovation: More than any other generation, you are used to exploring and experimenting with technology and expect it from others.

5. Everyone is unique: Even though we just made a list of what people in your generation have in common, you don't necessarily like labels or assumptions about who you are.

No matter what your college major or career goals might be, psychology is fundamental to every judgment, preference, memory, decision, and interaction in your life. The goals and priorities of your generation signal that you are fundamentally interested in creating a future centered on a healthy mental well-being, positive social interactions, altruism and equity, innovative and creative solutions for current problems, and decreased stereotypes and prejudice. These are the same goals that the field of psychology has.

In this book, we use the theme of natural curiosity to guide you through each major topic. Our hope was to write a book you would actually enjoy reading—one that had an engaging, friendly tone. We don't have room to cover every topic in an introductory book, so we chose to discuss concepts that are either the most famous or what we simply thought you would enjoy the most—like how to take the most efficient naps, whether it's possible to remember something that never actually happened to you, and why some people are afraid of clowns. Because everyone loves a good story, we craft each chapter around a compelling theme or case study we hope you find compelling.

Curiosity is a key component of a great life; people who are more curious report greater life satisfaction, flourishing, and happiness (Lydon-Staley et al., 2020). If you're curious, you'll never stop learning and growing. We hope this book piques your curiosity and begins your lifelong love of psychological science.

Wind, Gary, Charity, and Tom

REFERENCES

Lydon-Staley, D. M., Zurn, P., & Bassett, D. S. (2020). Within-person variability in curiosity during daily life and associations with well-being. *Journal of Personality, 88*(4), 625–641. https://doi.org/10.1111/jopy.12515

Nemeth, D. (2022, August). Authentically Gen Z: The values, aspirations & drivers that will re-define the future of work. *Work Design Magazine.* https://www.workdesign.com/2022/08/authentically-gen-z-the-values-aspirations-drivers-that-will-re-define-the-future-of-work/

Dear Instructor,

You may wonder: Why do we need another introduction to psychology textbook? Well, if it's just like all the others, frankly we don't. What makes *Psychology and Our Curious World* special, and therefore appealing to students and instructors? Allow us to share the key principles that guide our approach.

(1) ***Curiosity Builds Competence: Now and in the Future***

Learning is not about one semester, one year, or one degree. Rather, it's about helping students become more sophisticated in the way they think about the world. We do that by cultivating their curiosity. In this view, a textbook isn't just a way to deliver information, but a tool to stimulate students' interest. Psychology should be inherently interesting and applicable; the moment it's not, we've failed.

(2) ***Forthright Candor***

Students deserve our respect. We do not communicate with them as if they are naive, lack a sense of humor, or are unaware of modern concerns in the world today. Psychology is needed to address these concerns, which is one of the reasons this book and the accompanying course matter in their lives. We are unapologetic about how the material relates to relevant issues today. Importantly, we unapologetically embrace diversity and support the idea of intersectionality as affecting the human experience. We also point out that some aspects of the history of psychology have been affected by prejudice, that some conclusions are limited by WEIRD samples, and that culture matters. As an author team, we ourselves represent diversity in terms of age, race, sexual orientation, religious background, region, and academic setting. People vary—and that's a good thing.

(3) ***Everyone Loves a Good Story***

Students light up with interest when their professors break away from PowerPoints to share stories; it makes the content come alive. These are the tidbits students somehow seem to remember years later. How can a textbook capture our instinct to become immersed in stories—how can our content be as captivating? We use a storytelling approach in each chapter, centering the content on a central theme or case study. Following the course of someone's life, getting out of an escape room, or watching the disastrous dynamics of a cult to the tragic end helps students place concepts in a memorable and "sticky" context.

(4) ***Written by Award-Winning Teachers***

The authors of this book are award-winning instructors of undergraduates who have taught introduction to psychology many times. We actually teach these concepts every day—so we've written the book the way we explain the concepts to actual people. We also include concepts our students care about that most books skip over, based on the questions we get in class. Students care about naps, the fear of clowns, and social media. Our book highlights the psychology of everyday life.

(5) *A Book That's "Just Right"*

Psychology and Our Curious World follows a "just right" principle: not "too overwhelming" and not "too brief." Rather, it's "just right." For us, "just right" means

- leaning into students' natural curiosity to build excitement and facilitate learning;
- chapters with engaging themes from students' lives with curiosity-inducing "big questions" to move students beyond basic understanding to higher levels of thinking;
- providing enough scaffolding to move students along Bloom's taxonomy from simple memorization to application and analysis;
- beautifully written paragraphs that deliver plenty of memorable examples, without unnecessary words;
- chapter lengths that respect students' time and intellect by hitting that "just right" spot between being impossibly long and superficially brief;
- personal authenticity and conversational writing from teachers who know how to connect with their students;
- building psychological literacy through practical insights and encouragement of critical thinking and evidence-based decisions;
- respecting students as individuals and recognizing the value in greater inclusion of diverse perspectives;
- recognizing that diverse voices and perspectives have been stifled in the past and that these injustices must be acknowledged and rectified moving forward;
- fostering psychological literacy by persuading students that critical thinking improves their lives;
- carefully crafted ancillaries that recognize that engagement is a necessary teaching technique; and
- novel assessments that capture the information trails left behind by authentic learning.

We hope our "just right" approach means a book that provides students with tools and skills that will make them lifelong learners and fans of psychology.

INNOVATIVE FEATURES AND ANDRAGOGY

Chapter 1 explicitly shares the APA's Introductory Psychology Initiative 3.0 with students. The learning outcomes and integrative themes are covered, so students can understand the field's current direction. For you (the instructor), note that this book's supplemental materials are designed to help you assess your students along the learning objectives and integrative themes as well.

After that, *Psychology and Our Curious World* has purposeful features in every chapter that have been vetted by expert focus groups and used successfully in the authors' social psychology text. Instead of chasing trendy gimmicks, these features offer genuinely important ways for students to connect to the material in meaningful ways. Each chapter features the following:

- *Career Corner:* Many psychology careers require graduate degrees—but what about psychology careers students can explore immediately after earning a bachelor's degree? Every chapter features a brief interview of a real person who started a career by majoring in psychology. This feature is key to helping students understand the variety of career options and to know they have choices that don't require years of additional schooling (and possible debt).

- *Spotlight on Research Methods:* While there is a dedicated chapter on research methods and basic statistics within psychology, most books isolate this topic into a chapter and then never explicitly return to it. Our book features a "box" feature called *Spotlight on Research Methods* that explicitly goes through the methods and statistics of a famous or important study relevant to that chapter. This emphasis reminds students that psychology uses a scientific, evidence-based approach and that *what* we know is connected to *how* we learned it.

- *What's My Score?* Each chapter has at least one self-report scale students can take to calculate their own score on a construct relevant to that chapter. With the popularity of "personality tests" on social media, students enjoy engaging in self-discovery tasks. From an andragogic perspective, though, this feature shows students how research studies operationalize abstract constructs, another reminder of the scientific approach within psychology.

- *Psychology and Our Curious World:* From documentaries to Marvel Comics Universe movies, psychology has a presence in popular movies, songs, and literature. By linking concepts to what students enjoy in their spare time, we can remind them that psychology can be seen in almost every setting. Students also find concepts easier to understand when they apply to familiar experiences (e.g., "Do video games stigmatize mental illness?"). Enjoyment, engagement, relevance, and retention are the happy by-products of connecting psychology to popular culture.

- *Critical Thinking Questions:* As depth of processing theory (Craik & Lockhart, 1972) suggests, students retain information better if they cognitively process it on a deep level. Critical thinking is a skill that all college and university students should practice so they can apply these tools to global citizenship, community engagement, and personal life decisions. Thus, every chapter ends with several critical thinking and discussion questions. Instructors can use these as written homework assignments or as discussion prompts for "flipped" classroom time.

SAGE VANTAGE

This text is available in Sage Vantage—an intuitive learning platform you and your students will actually love.

9 out of 10 of your colleagues using Sage Vantage would recommend it!

Sage Vantage for *Psychology and Our Curious World* integrates all the textbook content with assignable multimedia activities and auto-graded assessments to drive student engagement and ensure accountability. Unparalleled in its ease of use and built for dynamic teaching and learning, Vantage offers customizable LMS integration and best-in-class support.

Vantage Learning Platform ISBN: 978-1-0719-4141-6

See why you'll love Sage Vantage at **collegepublishing.sagepub.com/vantage**.

Faculty and Students Approve

"**Student performance after implementing Vantage is incredible.**... We know that reading increases performance, but this is a really tangible way to see that."

—Karen Deeming, Instructor, Merced College

"With Vantage, **I set up my course in under 10 minutes.**... I love Vantage!"

—Karin Machluf, Instructor, Penn State Scranton

"**Interactive, engaging and simple to use.**"

—Alyssa Salazar, Student, University of North Texas

"It really **helps you wrap your head around what you're learning** and come to a complete understanding of the course material."

—Aubrey Akins, Student, St. Bonaventure University

"This is the **smoothest student onboarding process** I have ever experienced."

—Echo Leaver, Instructor, Salisbury University

Video and Analytic Skill-Building

Assignable video activities in Vantage align with learning objectives, reinforcing fundamental concepts in every chapter. With automatic assessment integration into your gradebook, these resources provide an ideal platform for students to hone their analytical and application skills by applying chapter concepts to real-world scenarios.

Video Activities for *Psychology and Our Curious World*

1.1: Careers in Psychology

1.2: Diverse Voices in the History of Psychology

2.1: The Open Science Movement

2.2: Twin Studies

3.1: The Brain's Lobes

3.2: Advances in Neuroscience

4.1: The Difference Between Sex and Gender

4.2: Defining Intersectionality

5.1: Stress

5.2: The PERMA Model of Happiness

6.1: Sensation vs. Perception

6.2: Perceptual Illusions

7.1: Improving Sleep

7.2: Cannabis

8.1: Erikson's Eight Stages of Identity Development

8.2: Piaget's Four Stages of Cognitive Development

9.1: Pavlov and His Dogs

9.2: Reinforcement vs. Punishment

10.1: The Keys to Better Memory

What Are the Benefits of Vantage?

Enables Easy, 3-Step Course Creation. Our simple interface enables you to create your course in minutes so you can focus on content. Just enter your course information, select your assignments and grading preferences, and review your settings.

Drives Student Engagement. An evidence-based learning design integrates text content with frequent multimedia activities and learning assessments to facilitate better student preparation, engagement, and learning retention.

Ensures Student Accountability. Auto-graded assignments feed your gradebook while instructor reports complement your ability to track student activity, assignment completion, and learning objective mastery. These real-time analytics provide quick insights into individual and class performance for tailoring course instruction to help you address the needs of struggling students.

Delivers First-day-of-class Access and Flexibility. With our 2-week grace period access, all students can use Vantage on the very first day of class. The flexibility to use Vantage on mobile, desktop, or tablet devices means your dynamic Vantage content will consistently be available to learners any time they need it.

Offers Best-in-class Technical Support and Training. Our personalized support for instructors, students, and LMS administrators facilitates an easy transition to Vantage and the quality service you've come to expect from Sage.

collegepublishing.sagepub.com/vantage

TEACHING RESOURCES

This text includes an array of instructor teaching materials designed to save you time and to help you keep students engaged. To learn more, visit **collegepublishing.sagepub.com** or contact your Sage representative at **collegepublishing.sagepub.com/findmyrep.**

- **Course management system integration** makes it easy for student test results and graded assignments to seamlessly flow into the instructor's gradebook.

- **Test banks,** aligned to Bloom's Taxonomy, provide a diverse range of 150 test items per chapter, including multiple choice, true/false, and essay.

- **Respondus® test generator** is an alternate solution for delivering digital or printed tests built from the standard test bank.

- **Instructor's manual,** authored by Dr. Natalie Dove at Eastern Michigan University, offers a wide range of customizable teaching and learning content for all chapters, including:
  - Correlation grids that align assessment questions to each learning objective
  - Discussion topics, activities, and questions
  - Critical thinking activities
  - Essay and research paper topics
  - Career activities
  - APA IPI learning activities that allow instructors to easily assess and report out on the APA IPI outcomes
  - Concept highlights
  - Suggested grading rubrics

- **Lecture notes** provide instructors an outline and the key concepts in each chapter to aid in lecture preparation

- **PowerPoint® slides** offer a flexible, accessible, and customizable solution for creating multimedia lectures

- **Curious Conversations PowerPoint® slides** provide in-class and online discussion topics aligned to the textbook's "Have You Ever Wondered" questions and learning objectives, piquing students' curiosity and increasing their engagement

- **Figures and tables from the book** are available to support lecture preparation and class discussions

- **Sample course syllabi** include suggested models for structuring your course

REFERENCE

Craik, F. I., & Lockhart, R. S. (1972). Levels of processing: A framework for memory research. *Journal of Verbal Learning & Verbal Behavior, 11*(6), 671–684. https://doi.org/10.1016/S0022-5371(72)80001-X

ACKNOWLEDGMENTS

Sage and the authors gratefully acknowledge the following reviewers for providing feedback on drafts of the first edition:

Molly Beth Alvaro, Potomac State College of West Virginia University
Jennifer C. Arasmith, Avila University
O. Binkley-Webb, Restoration Life Project
Stefanie S. Boswell, University of the Incarnate Word
Pamela C. Bradley, Sandhills Community College Pinehurst, NC
Silas E. Burris, Montgomery College
Jennifer Butler, Case Western Reserve University
R. Canter, Wheeling University
Eliann R. Carr, Yakima Valley College
Herb Coleman, Austin Community College
Mike Corcoran, Widener University
Marc Coutanche, University of Pittsburgh
Theresa DiDonato, Loyola University Maryland
Stephanie B. Ding, Del Mar College
John E. Edlund, Rochester Institute of Technology
Matthew Eisenhard, Rowan University
Rebecca Ewing, Western New Mexico University
Christopher J. Ferguson, Stetson University
Johnathan D. Forbey, Ball State University
Frank R. George, Kent State University
Catherine Graney, Sussex County Community College
Shelia P. Greenlee, Christopher Newport University
Mario E. Herrera, University of North Carolina Asheville
Cindy J. Lahar, University of South Carolina Beaufort
Brenda A. Lederach, Ursinus College
Melissa Lemons, Wilmington University
Jerome A. Lewis, Bellevue University
Manyu Li, University of Louisiana at Lafayette
Salvador Macias III, University of South Carolina Sumter
Scott D. Martin, Brigham Young University–Idaho
Eva McGuire, Guilford College
Aradhana Mehta, Rhode Island College, Providence
Tifany T. Moreira, Riverside City College
Steven Neese, Cornell College
Yea Won Park, West Virginia University
Christina Pedram, Arizona State University
Adam Prus, Northern Michigan University
Darrell Rudmann, Shawnee State University
Beverly Salzman, University of St. Joseph
Jeannine Stamatakis-Amess, Lincoln University
Eric C. Stephens, University of the Cumberlands
Glenn Sullivan, Virginia Military Institute

Rachelle Tannenbaum, Anne Arundel Community College
Melissa S. Terlecki, Cabrini University
Abbie Thompson, Valparaiso University
Benjamin White, University of Tennessee–Knoxville
Autumn Willard, Macomb Community College
Manda Williamson, University of Nebraska–Lincoln
Marc Wolpoff, Riverside City College
Roger Young, University of South Florida

ABOUT THE AUTHORS

Dr. Wind Goodfriend has been named Faculty of the Year three times in her 19 years as a professor at Buena Vista University. This distinction is the result of an all-student vote, and her General Psychology course was chosen as the "Most Recommended" individual class in the entire university by the BVU newspaper. She has also won the Wythe Award, one of the largest collegiate teaching prizes in the nation. She has written over a dozen book chapters about psychology in pop culture, four textbooks for Sage, three Audible audiobooks about psychology, dozens of peer-reviewed journal articles, and has published over 30 journal articles featuring her undergraduate students as the first author. She also wrote and "starred" in a docuseries about the psychology of cult manipulation for The Great Courses. Wind won the 2023 Undergraduate Teaching & Mentoring Award from the Society for Personality and Social Psychology.

Dr. Gary W. Lewandowski Jr. started college right after high school and loved it so much he never left. As a professor at Monmouth University, he has published over 70 academic books/articles/chapters and given over 120 conference presentations (most with student coauthors). He is a nationally recognized teacher who the Princeton Review counted as its Best 300 Professors from an initial list of 42,000. He has won teaching awards everywhere he has taught. He has given a TEDx talk, *Break-ups Don't Have to Leave You Broken,* which has over 2.6 million views, and has written over 150 articles for mass media outlets that have been enjoyed by over 8 million readers. He has also written a research methods textbook and authored *Stronger Than You Think: The 10 Blind Spots That Undermine Your Relationship . . . and How to See Past Them.*

Dr. Charity Brown Griffin has a passion for teaching first-generation and racially marginalized undergraduate students as an Associate Professor of Psychological Sciences at Winston-Salem State University (WSSU), a historically Black university. She also engages in practice work as a Nationally Certified School Psychologist (NCSP) and Licensed Psychologist and serves as a content consultant for numerous children's media programming. During her tenure at WSSU, she has received numerous awards and honors, including the Bill Sheppard Master Teacher Award, the Wilveria B. Atkinson Distinguished Research Award, and student choice Advisor of the Year award for her mentorship of Psychology Club. Her research focused on schooling experiences and positive youth development has received over 2.2 million dollars in grant funding, has resulted in over 30 peer-reviewed publications and over 50 conference presentations, and has been featured in popular media and news outlets such as *Successful Black Parenting Magazine,* CNN, and PBS Kids.

Dr. Thomas Heinzen, at William Paterson University of New Jersey, is proudest that he has mentored more than 60 student presentations and published research. He has been a keynote speaker at a variety of teaching-related conferences, including NITOP, Rocky Mountain Teaching of Psychology, and the Association for Psychological Science about his book on Clever Hans and facilitated communication. He has been elected as a fellow to the Eastern Psychological Association, to the Association for Psychological Science, and to Division 1 of the American Psychological Association. He has also been an invited speaker at several technology conferences to discuss how to apply principles of game design to social problems such as improving rates of college completion. Students have honored him with a variety of awards that range from being the winning lab in an egg-tossing contest to numerous recognitions from the Psychology Club.

STUDENT SUCCESS GUIDE

Suppose you are taking a college course for the first time. You purchase your course material and begin to peruse its contents. Within moments you realize that there is a lot of information to learn. You wonder how you are going to understand all this material by the end of the course. You might feel a mix of emotions, from intimidated to overwhelmed to excited. These emotions are all quite common among college students. Learning is a process of growth, and growth is not always comfortable. One reason is that learning is similar to exercising. You exercise to become stronger, faster, and more agile. Your goal is to be healthier, and this does not come without times of being tired or exhausted. But you work through it so that you can reach your goal of being healthier. Similarly, as a student, you learn to become more knowledgeable and capable, and to be smarter, and this also does not come without times of being tired or exhausted. But you work through it so that you can reach your goal of being educated. This parallel brings to light a key to your success in college: to set goals. Setting goals helps you to stay focused and motivated to "work through" the challenging times. Of course, it is also helpful to have a plan or guide that can help you achieve your goals. For this reason, we have prepared the following guide to help you achieve your academic goals and to support your success.

TIPS AND TRICKS FOR STUDENT SUCCESS: THE BASICS

Textbooks typically do not provide a "How-to-Rock-This-Class Manual," yet every student would love to have one. How do you study efficiently? How do you know what to say to your professors? Who can you reach out to for help? What strategies can you use to be a successful student? If these types of questions are what students seek answers for, then this guide is a great place to start. So, let's start at the very beginning—the basics:

- It is important to want to be a great student. Being a great student does not mean getting straight As, but it does mean that you are truly committed to learning. As a student, you should embrace the opportunity to learn, be genuinely curious about the information being taught, and take the time to study it, question it, and think critically about it. This perspective captures the spirit of what it means to be a great student.

- Take the time on the first day of class to introduce yourself to your professor and teaching assistants (if applicable). Whether your class is online, in person, or a hybrid course, go out of your way to introduce yourself.

Your professors are more than just teachers. They are experts in their fields of study, and this makes them excellent people to connect with. Additionally, getting to know your professors can benefit your learning in class and even into your career as possible people you can reach out to for a professional recommendation.

- Attend each class session if it is in a synchronous or face-to-face format. What is taught in class is very often the bulk of the material that is tested and/or assessed. Not only are you putting your best foot forward by attending each class session, but you are also doing your due diligence to be a great student and setting yourself up for success. If your class is asynchronous (fully online), then make sure you watch each lecture. Professors who teach asynchronous classes offer good information in the recorded lectures, and it is important to watch the full lecture—from beginning to end—so that you are not missing important information.

- Be prepared—have your materials ready, put your distracting technology away, and read before attending class. If you are in a fully online class, the same rules apply. When you are ready to watch your lecture, put the technology away. Research has demonstrated that being distracted because of multitasking—specifically by looking at your phone at the same time you are listening to a lecture—lowers your performance and retention. Students often think they are good at multitasking, but the science says that's not accurate.

GETTING THE MOST OUT OF YOUR COURSE

On the first day, the professor is going to give you the owner's manual to the class: the **syllabus**. This document will give you all the information you need for the class. In general, the first bit of information you see on the syllabus is your professor's contact information. This information generally includes the professor's email address, office hours, office location (if applicable), and availability. When it comes to professors, there are a few things to remember:

- Be respectful when you email. This is a professional communication. Start the email with "Dear Professor _____."

- When you do email, make sure it does not sound like a text. You are conducting a formal business-like exchange.

- Use correct grammar and punctuation.

- Always let professors know what class you are in by typing it in the subject header, so that they can appropriately answer your questions—most professors teach multiple classes.

- Allow for at least 24–48 hours for a response from your professor. Allow a bit more time if you email on a Friday or the weekend.

- Ask questions. If you have questions, other students likely do too!

- If you have a few questions, consider making an appointment with your professor to meet during office hours. Having a conversation with your professor might answer many questions in one sitting; and, as most of us know, sometimes answers can be lost in translation in an email.

- Just a reminder: Teachers love to teach, and they appreciate enthusiastic students. So, make an appointment with your professors and say hello.

Next, you need to sit down and *read all of the syllabus*. The syllabus is like your road map. You will be able to find *exactly* which textbook to obtain (never assume an older edition is going to be "good enough") and any other course requirements. Additionally, the syllabus will include course policies, course materials, a course calendar, and grading and assessment policies.

Helpful tip: Note in your calendar when you should start each assignment and when it is due. That will make it easier to keep on track (in other words, put it in your calendar RIGHT NOW). Multiple research studies have found that 80 to 95 percent of college students put off doing their work and studying on "a regular basis." Procrastination is not your friend, so start projects and assignments as early as possible. Life happens, and you do not want to turn in work late. Plan to start working on written work at least two weeks in advance if assignments are available to you that far in advance.

Also add to your calendar the dates for all quizzes and exams. A general rule of thumb is to start studying for quizzes and exams one week in advance. Never, ever cram. And get good sleep.

Many students color-code their schedules to keep all of their classes organized. This might sound like a lot of work, but you will be glad you did it!

FIGURE 1

Professional Communication

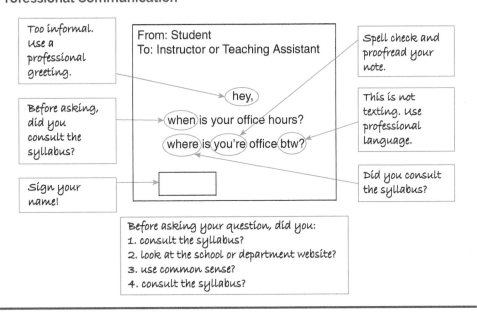

COURSE MATERIALS

It's important to have a plan—and to use science to help you out. Researchers have found that certain strategies work well for learning, particularly when it comes to reading the textbook. So, use them! For starters, many students do not read before class, and they often try to start reading without any real plan for reading a textbook efficiently. *Helpful tip:* Read BEFORE CLASS. It will save you time and improve your grades. Research has shown that if you have no idea what the professor is going to teach about, and then you sit down and try to take notes and listen, your brain will literally put you in a "time out." It is too much! *You will have cognitive overload.* So, be fair to your brain and give yourself the information you need to be able to absorb the material.

As part of your plan, figure out how to tackle your weekly reading, which is often approximately 40 pages of generally dense material. Use tools that will help you want to keep going rather than stop before you have even begun. So, make a plan of action:

- First, skim over the chapter that you are preparing to read. Whether your book is in a hardcopy format or a digital ebook, it's important to get a sense of the formatting of the book such as the illustrations, applied sections, questions, summaries, and text size. If this is your first time using an ebook, spend some extra time familiarizing yourself with the basics such as how to "turn" pages and enlarge the font if needed, as well as the general format of the book. Many students prefer digital ebooks, but if this is your first one, it can be a very different experience for you. It may take a bit of adjusting on your part. Also, no matter the format, get familiar with the interactive elements that are often included with the book.

- When you are ready to start working on a specific chapter, consider starting at the back of the chapter. The end of the chapter will give you a clear and concise **summary** of the chapter. You can also review **key words**, which will acquaint you with what the professor is going to discuss in class.

- Read over any **thought questions** at the end of each chapter. Obviously, you will not know the answers, but it'll give you an idea of what is important.

- When you begin a chapter, peruse the first page. Read the **chapter outline**, or scan the **section headings**, and, if present, review the **learning objectives**. The learning objectives state what you should be able to accomplish when you truly learn the material. They'll also give insight into the chapter.

- Divide your reading into reasonable portions. Researchers recommend setting a timer for 20–30 minutes (approximately 7–10 pages) to serve as a reminder to take a break. When the timer goes off, take a moment or two to stretch and move around a little. It is also recommended that you not have your phone close by or that you put it on silent mode, so that random alerts and messages won't interrupt you and break your flow.

- **Learning is not about being fast. Learning is about appropriately retaining important information.** When you read those 7–10 pages, try to understand the *main points*, not every point. Do not take notes initially. You don't want to break your cognitive flow. As you go back and review the pages you've read, notetaking can be beneficial. Research has shown that taking notes (pen-to-paper notetaking) can help students understand and retain the material better. *Helpful tip*: Paraphrase what the authors are saying and write it in your notes. This will help you articulate, and therefore understand, the material better. We call this approach *deep processing*, compared to memorizing, which is *surface processing*.

- It is highly recommended that you create a learning community (aka a study group) and then discuss the chapters with that group. This will help you with deep processing, and you are more likely to remember the material. *Helpful tip*: If you are unsure how to go about creating a learning community, consider discussing this with your professor. Professors can make announcements in class, start an online forum for the class, or offer you and your classmates other ways to connect. Many study groups create their own Google Docs so that they can exchange notes with others or post questions. Other study groups may use social media as a way to connect. No matter how you do it, be sure to do it *early* in the term. The sooner you have a study support team, the better.

STUDYING: NOW THAT YOU KNOW HOW TO READ THE MATERIAL, HOW DO YOU STUDY IT?

General Studying

We have talked about ways to tackle the book, but studying involves more than that. Reading, paraphrased notetaking, time with a learning community—all of those are great strategies, but sometimes (to quote a common saying) "you don't know what you don't know." Well, how are you ever going to *know* what you are supposed to *know*, then? Again, let's turn back to science for help. The cognitive psychologist Regan Gurung posits that, based on his extensive research, the ways people try to learn are not necessarily helpful. Yes, highlighting helps and rereading is good, but if you want GREAT results, start paying attention to what science is saying!

Gurung suggests three things you need to keep in mind if you want the best learning outcomes:

1. What do you **NEED** to know? This requires reviewing the syllabus.

2. What **DO** you know? This requires testing yourself and reviewing those tests.

3. What do you **NOT** know? Again, review the tests. Many books offer sets of knowledge checks and flashcards to help you in this process.

It is important for you to fully understand the professor's learning objectives. In other words, what exactly does the professor want you to know? Between the syllabus and the learning objectives in the textbook, you should have a pretty good idea what you need to know. If it's still not clear to you, ask your study group. At that point you should have it figured out, but if not, that is okay. *Helpful tip:* Do not spend more time trying to figure it out. It's time to write to the teaching assistant, or TA, if there is one. TAs are good "first contacts." If you're still unclear or there isn't a TA, then ask the professor. Do not be shy to ask questions. If you can't figure it out, many other students probably can't either. There are great webinars and free materials available online from some of the best researchers out there, too. Search for reputable online resources on studying, notetaking, and test preparation.

Prepping for a Test

Never, ever, ever cram for a test! Cramming is bad in a multitude of ways:

- Cramming is associated with anxiety and stress, which results in lower scores.

- You will have cognitive overload, which means your brain is overworked.

- Learning takes *time*, and one night of cramming will not help you learn.

- Lack of sleep results in lower test scores.

You get the idea. Do not cram for a test. Here are a few scientifically supported practices for prepping for a test. Recent research by John Dunlosky and colleagues found that a key component for doing well on exams is **spaced practicing**:

- The idea of spaced practicing is to study the same content on different occasions. Think of it like this: If you were a softball player, you might practice catching and throwing three of the five days of the week (the same drill on different days). You would schedule these specific days and times to practice your throwing and catching. *Practicing the same thing over and over embeds it into your memory and recall.* It works for softball, and it works for psychology exams!

Next, work on retrieval practicing:

- Retrieval practicing involves bringing key information to mind to increase learning and retention.

- Test yourself frequently to make sure you know what you need to know.

- This can be done by using the flashcards and practice tests that go with your textbook. Many researchers believe that practice tests are the most underutilized resource that students have.

- Often, textbook authors work hard to provide the student resources to use in retrieval practicing. If you have them available, be sure to use them.

WHAT ABOUT YOU?
SCHOOL-WORK-FAMILY BALANCE

Research has demonstrated that there is no simple, easy answer to balancing multiple roles such as being a student, an employee, a parent, a friend, a partner, and a family member, to name just a few roles. In fact, many psychologists have suggested that "balancing" these roles isn't the correct way to think about them. Is your life ever really balanced? And with one more major life role added to the list—student—it is important to keep expectations in check. This is going to be difficult, but that's okay. It can be done if you use the resources you have around you ... and science:

- Time management is key to reducing stress and anxiety. Plan out your day and week, and stick to a schedule. *Helpful tip*: It's easy to lose track of time, so setting reminders on your phone or watch will help you to keep track of what you need to be doing and when you should be doing it. Set a timer when you are studying so that you remember to get up and move and take a break, but also set a timer to remind yourself to get back to studying.

- Pick your method of tracking (e.g., when assignments are due, when you should start studying for a test) and stick to it. Many people like to use paper calendars so that they can check off what they've done and color-code what needs to be done. If you choose this method, pick a calendar that fits in your bag and take it everywhere.

- You may choose to use an online calendar. That's a great method, too. You certainly can color-code assignments, due dates, and deadlines, as well as prioritize activities and set alerts. The key to using a calendar (electronic or paper) is to *remember to look at it ... every day.* Without exception. Do not rely on your memory.

- Prioritize sleeping and exercising. These two activities go together; research has demonstrated that the relationship between sleep and exercise is bidirectional. More specifically, exercise helps you sleep better. And when you sleep better, you are more likely to exercise. Also, research has shown that increasing both activities increases recall. That is a win-win-win! You might think that it's more important to study than to sleep for a full 7 or 8 hours, or take a brisk walk, but that is a myth. The less sleep you get, the less efficient your brain will be. The same goes for exercise. Your brain needs oxygen to function at its best, and there is no better way to get oxygen to your brain than through exercise.

- Ask your academic advisor about your school's counseling center. The transition to college can be difficult. It's always a great idea to build a support system as early as possible, and counselors are trained to provide exactly that. They can also direct you to support groups on and off campus.

- You might be a first-generation college student or a student who is a caretaker of others. There will be times when you might feel pulled in different directions, or times when your family will not understand why you need to spend so many hours on your studies. *Helpful tip*: Keep the lines of communication open with your family, which will help them get a better grasp of what you need to succeed. If you must be in a quiet room for 3 hours a day to study, let them know. If you need to be on campus late that week to prepare for a big project, tell them! Many students who try to balance school and family have found that discussing needs and responsibilities can create a supportive environment.

- Practice mindfulness throughout the day. Many smartphone apps are available that provide guided meditation. Also, many smartwatches have a 2-minute mindfulness activity. For some, it might be praying. For others, it could just be sitting still and being fully present in the moment. There are many ways to practice mindfulness. Pick a technique that works for you and practice consistently. *Helpful tip*: Schedule "mindfulness moments" into your day.

EFFECTIVE DISTANCE LEARNING

More and more people are deciding to become distance learners, and they need a game plan, too. Not attending college in a more traditional manner can make students feel isolated and not connected to their peers or professors. There are ways to address those issues, many of which have already been mentioned. But here's a refresher:

- Ideally, try to designate a specific area for studying. Keep it organized and clean so that when you are ready to study, your study space is prepared. If you cannot do this, make sure you are studying in a nondistracting environment that has all the "tools" (e.g., computer, paper, pen) that you need for studying.

- Create a study community. If you are unsure how to go about it, talking to your professor is a great place to start.

- Study groups give you the opportunity to articulate what you are learning (paraphrasing the content), which helps with deep processing.

- Study groups allow you to test each other on the content.

- Because many people are deciding to take classes from home, try to keep distractions to a minimum when studying and testing. It's easy to get distracted when laundry and other chores need to be done. Also, other family members can be a distraction, so try to communicate what you need and how long you need it to the others in your home. Communication is key when it comes to keeping the distractions at bay.

SECRET WEAPONS

Sometimes it may feel that being a student is a solitary endeavor, but it should not be. A wealth of resources are available to you. Here are a few:

- **Teaching Assistants.** They know so much about the inner workings of the department, faculty, university, and your specific class. They are an amazing resource! If your class is not face-to-face, TAs will often have virtual office hours. Be sure to schedule a short appointment to introduce yourself, and if you have questions, come prepared. *Helpful tip*: Write down all your questions ahead of time so that you can use your time efficiently.

- **Librarians.** Get to know those wonderful people! They can help you in so many ways. If you're not able to meet with them on campus, you can email them and ask for a quick phone call to introduce yourself. Or you can ask for an online video session to say hello and ask for any resources that you may need. Again, be prepared for the meeting.

- **Writing Center.** The people who work at your school's writing center are focused on helping students. Many writing centers are set up to help students by subject area, and then there are more "generalists" (people who can help in any discipline). Commonly, it is recommended that students go to subject-specific tutors, if possible. Be sure to bring your assignment with you. Writing center tutors do not know every assignment for every class, but they are great with helping you understand the writing component. Keep in mind that if you do not live on campus, most writing centers have evening hours, and most universities offer online sessions.

- **Other Students.** So many students are struggling with school-work-family balance, so creating a support and study group can be extremely beneficial. If you can't find one, ask your TA or professor. Research suggests that the more connections you have, the better you will do in school.

ATTEND OFFICE HOURS

One of the first things students should do at the beginning of the term is to attend their professors' office hours (whether in person or virtually). For many students, the idea of attending office hours can be a scary prospect, but that one-on-one time with the professor is priceless. Specifically, you can ask questions you might not want to ask in class. Additionally, it is a chance for you to find out how nice and caring your professors really are! To make the most of the time with your professors, do the following:

- Read the syllabus before you go and think about any questions you have.

- Write down your questions before you go. This will help you use the time effectively.

- Do not be late.

- Discuss "best practices" with your professor. This means, ask what your professor believes are the best study methods for the class and how long it might take to properly prepare for exams.

- Inquire about any additional resources. It never hurts to ask.

- If you have questions about a grade, now is the time to ask for clarity.

- Take notes during your meeting because you might be covering a lot of ground and you do not want to rely on your memory.

- If you are unsure about what the professor suggested or said, do not hesitate to ask for clarification. Professors appreciate it when you are honest about not understanding an explanation. They would rather clarify during this one-on-one time rather than you leave confused.

- Lastly, thank your professors for their time. That's the best way to leave your appointment.

FIGURE 2
_____

Advice From an Undergraduate Advisor

- It is not recommended that students take classes back-to-back. It's better to have some time to absorb what you just learned, and then maybe write down a few more thoughts.

- If possible, do not take classes at times when you know you cannot do your best. For example, if you are not an 8 a.m. person, do not take a class first thing in the morning.

- Make sure you are a good fit for the instructor. Ask other students about the instructor and visit the instructor during office hours.

- Do not overload your schedule. You are in college to learn, not to stress yourself out. Be realistic with what you can do.

- We want you to be successful!

LIMIT MEDIA EXPOSURE

Being a student is stressful. If you add in personal or global events, it can be downright unmanageable. It is important that you take care of yourself so that you can prosper as a student, friend, family member, and community member. To help manage stress today, the American Psychological Association offers some great tips. One of the best tips is to limit media exposure. Media are there to keep you interested, so they often focus on the negative so that viewers will have a more visceral reaction. Keep that in mind...and limit the amount of time you spend on social media and news outlets.

SUMMARY OF HELPFUL TIPS

- **Planning.** Note in your calendar when you should be starting assignments and when they are due.

- **Reading.** Read *before* class. It will save you time and improve your grades.

- **Studying.** Paraphrase what the authors are saying and write it in your notes.

- **Study group.** If you are unsure how to go about creating a learning community, discuss it with your professor or teaching assistant.

- **Course goals.** If you do not fully understand what the course learning goals are, write to the teaching assistant (if there is one) or the professor (if there is no teaching assistant).

- **Reminders.** Setting reminders on your phone or watch will help remind you what you need to be doing and when you should be doing it.

- **Communication.** Keep the lines of communication open with your family and/or roommates to help them get a better grasp of what you need to succeed.

- **Take a moment.** Schedule mindfulness moments into your day.

- **Questions.** Write down all of your questions for instructors, teaching assistants, or study groups ahead of time so that you can use your time efficiently.

College is an exciting time in a person's life, but it can be stressful at times. By practicing good study habits and connecting to your college community—online or in person—you will be well suited to handle any bumps in the road!

MOMENTS IN PSYCHOLOGY
AROUND THE WORLD

DATE	MILESTONE
BCE	
387	Plato (Greece) argues that the brain is the center of mental process.
335	Aristotle (Greece) argues that the heart is the center of mental process.
CE	
1637	René Descartes (France) publishes *A Discourse on Method*. Descartes asserts that ideas are innate to humans from birth.
1690	John Locke (England) publishes *An Essay Concerning Human Understanding*. Locke asserts that ideas come from experience and the human ability to reason.
1774	Franz Mesmer (Austria) presents a treatment for mental illnesses, originally called mesmerism and now known as hypnosis.
1794	Philippe Pinel (France) publishes *Memoir on Madness*. It argues for humane treatment of mentally ill patients. Pinel made significant contributions to the classification of mental disorders.
1808	Franz Joseph Gall (Germany) proposes the idea of phrenology, the belief that the shape of a person's skull reveals personality traits.
1848	Phineas Gage (United States) suffers massive brain damage when his brain is pierced by a large iron rod. This leaves his intellect intact, but his personality is changed. From this, researchers study how areas in the brain play a role in personality.
1856	Hermann von Helmholtz (Germany) publishes *Handbook of Physiological Optics*. His many works make important contributions, including reports on the physiology of vision and hearing, and measurement of nerve impulse speed.
1859	Charles Darwin (England) publishes *On the Origin of Species*. Darwin asserts that species evolve, and that living beings all share a common ancestor.
1861	Paul Broca (France) presents his findings regarding the area in the left frontal lobe of the brain that is critical for the production of spoken language. This is now called Broca's area.
1869	Francis Galton (England) publishes *Hereditary Genius*. He asserts that intelligence is inherited. Galton is credited with the expression "nature and nurture" and associated with the racist eugenics movement.
1874	Carl Wernicke (Germany) presents his findings that damage to a specific area in the left temporal lobe damages the ability to comprehend or produce language. This is now called Wernicke's area.
1879	Wilhelm Wundt (Germany) founds the first formal laboratory for psychological study at the University of Leipzig. Wundt, the first person to refer to himself as a psychologist, helped to establish psychology as an independent field of study.
1883	The first formal U.S. psychology laboratory is established at Johns Hopkins University.
1885	Hermann Ebbinghaus (Germany) publishes *On Memory*. Ebbinghaus made numerous contributions to the areas of learning and memory.
1887	G. Stanley Hall (United States) founds the *American Journal of Psychology*. Hall was the first North American to receive a PhD in psychology.
1890	William James (United States) publishes *Principles of Psychology*. His research contributes to the study of functionalism. He is also the first person to teach a psychology course in the United States.

(Continued)

(Continued)

DATE	MILESTONE
CE	
1892	The American Psychological Association (APA) is organized by G. Stanley Hall. The APA's stated mission is to promote the advancement, communication, and application of psychological science and knowledge to benefit society and improve lives.
1894	Margaret Floy Washburn (United States) is the first woman to receive a PhD in psychology. She made contributions in the fields of animal behavior and motor theory development.
1896	John Dewey (United States) publishes *The Reflex Arc Concept in Psychology*. He focused on the areas of education and helped develop the psychological philosophy of functionalism.
1898	Edward Thorndike (United States) publishes *Animal Intelligence*. His work proposes that animals and humans learn similarly and leads to the development of operant conditioning.
1900	Sigmund Freud (Austria, England) publishes *The Interpretation of Dreams*. Freud is considered the founder of psychoanalysis.
1901	Mary Whiton Calkins (United States) publishes *An Introduction to Psychology*. In 1905, she is the first woman elected as president of the American Psychological Association.
1903	Alfred Binet (France) publishes *Experimental Studies of Intelligence*. Binet made contributions to the study of intelligence, including the creation, along with colleague Theodore Simon, of the Binet-Simon intelligence scale.
1906	Ivan Pavlov (Russia) publishes his first studies on classical conditioning.
1912	Carl Jung (Switzerland) publishes *Psychology of the Unconscious*. Jung is considered the founder of analytical psychology.
1912	Tsuruko Haraguchi (Japan) receives a PhD in psychology. She is the first Japanese woman to receive a PhD in any subject.
1913	John Watson (United States) publishes *The Behaviorist Manifesto*. This puts forth a new area called behaviorism. In 1920, he and Rosalie Raynor conducted the controversial "Little Albert" experiment.
1920	Francis Cecil Sumner (United States) receives a PhD in psychology. He is the first African American person to earn a PhD in psychology. His work focuses on race psychology and education reform.
1921	Hermann Rorschach (Switzerland) publishes *Psychodiagnostik*. This work introduces the Rorschach Inkblot Test.
1923	Jean Piaget (Switzerland) publishes *The Language and Thought of the Child*. Piaget contributed in the area of child development, and championed child education.
1926	Leta Stetter Hollingworth (United States) publishes *Gifted Children*. Her work in the psychology of women helped to dispel myths that had been used to argue against women's rights.
1927	Anna Freud (Austria, England), the sixth and youngest child of Sigmund Freud, publishes *Introduction to the Technique of Child Analysis*. Freud developed the field of child psychoanalysis.
1929	Christine Ladd-Franklin (United States) publishes *Color and Color Theories*. Ladd-Franklin makes contributions in the field of color vision, in addition to other fields.
1929	Wolfgang Köhler (Germany) publishes *Gestalt Psychology*. This work criticizes behaviorism.
1932	Walter B. Cannon (United States) publishes *The Wisdom of the Body*. This work introduces the term *homeostasis* and discusses the fight-or-flight response.
1933	Inez Beverly Prosser (United States) becomes the first African American woman to receive a doctoral degree in psychology from a U.S. institution.

DATE	MILESTONE
CE	
1936	Anna Freud (Austria, England) publishes her influential book, *The Ego and the Mechanisms of Defense*.
1936	Egas Moniz (Portugal) publishes work on the first human frontal lobotomies.
1936	Herman George Canady (United States) publishes *The Effect of "Rapport" on the I.Q.: A New Approach to the Problem of Race Psychology*. He was the first psychologist to examine the role of the examiner's race as a bias factor in IQ testing. His work provided suggestions for establishing a more equal testing environment.
1938	Ugo Cerletti (Italy) and Lucio Bini (Italy) use electroshock treatment on a human patient.
1939	David Wechsler (Romania, United States) publishes the Wechsler-Bellevue intelligence test, which will later evolve into the Wechsler Intelligence Scale for Children (WISC) and the Wechsler Adult Intelligence Scale (WAIS).
1940	George I. Sanchez (United States) publishes *Forgotten People: A Study of New Mexicans*. Also in 1940, he receives a tenured, full professorship at the University of Texas, where he becomes the first professor of Latin American Studies.
1943	Starke Hathaway (United States) and J. Charnley McKinley (United States) publish the Minnesota Multiphasic Personality Inventory (MMPI).
1945	Karen Horney (Germany, United States) publishes *Our Inner Conflicts*. Her work criticizes Freud's theory of female sexual development.
1946	Mamie Phipps Clark (United States) founds the Northside Center for Child Development. The first program of its kind in Harlem, it offers necessary therapy and assistance to children and families.
1948	Alfred Kinsey (United States) publishes *Sexual Behavior in the Human Male,* and then *Sexual Behavior in the Human Female* in 1953 with colleagues.
1948	B. F. Skinner (United States) publishes *Walden Two*. It describes a utopian community based on positive reinforcement and an experimental attitude. The book encourages the application of psychological principles to everyday life.
1949	Donald O. Hebb (Canada) publishes *The Organization of Behavior: A Neuropsychological Theory*. It offers a new and influential conceptualization about how the nervous system functions.
1950	Erik Erikson (Germany, United States) publishes *Childhood and Society*. He made contributions that advanced the study of human development across the lifespan.
1951	Carl Rogers (United States) publishes *Client-Centered Therapy*. His work advanced the humanist movement.
1952	The American Psychiatric Association publishes the first *Diagnostic and Statistical Manual of Mental Disorders (DSM)*, an influential text that is updated periodically.
1953	Janet Taylor Spence (United States) publishes her Taylor Manifest Anxiety Scale in the *Journal of Abnormal Psychology*. Her contributions advance the fields of anxiety and gender studies.
1954	Abraham Maslow (United States) publishes *Motivation and Personality*. It proposes a hierarchy of needs, ranging from physiological needs to self-actualization.
1954	Gordon Allport (United States) publishes *The Nature of Prejudice*. He was one of the first psychologists to study personality.
1955	Kenneth Clark (United States) publishes *Prejudice and Your Child*. His earlier research and experiments with his colleague and wife, Mamie Phipps Clark, explored issues of race for African American children. The findings of that research were included as evidence in the Supreme Court decision *Brown v. Board of Education* (1954) by proving that segregation psychologically harms children.
1957	B. F. Skinner (United States) publishes *Schedules of Reinforcement*. He contributed in the areas of behavior analysis and the experimental analysis of behavior.

(Continued)

(Continued)

DATE	MILESTONE
CE	
1957	Leon Festinger (United States) proposes his theory of cognitive dissonance; in 1959, he and his colleague James Carlsmith conduct a landmark experiment to test this theory at Stanford University.
1958	Lawrence Kohlberg (United States) proposes his theory of moral development.
1960	Beatrice Ann Wright (United States) publishes *Physical Disability: A Psychological Approach*. Her contributions include developing appropriate and culturally relevant ways of working with differently abled people.
1961	Aaron Beck (United States) creates the Beck Depression Inventory, which is still used widely. Beck's contributions include the development of cognitive therapy and cognitive-behavioral therapy, along with making advances in the study of clinical depression and anxiety disorders.
1962	Martha E. Bernal (United States) becomes the first Hispanic woman to earn a PhD in psychology from a U.S. institution. She is later outspoken about underrepresentation in the field of counseling, helping influence the APA to form the Board of Ethnic Minority Affairs.
1967	Zing-Yang Kuo (China) publishes *The Dynamics of Behavior in Development*. He contributed in the areas of animal and comparative psychology.
1967	Raymond Cattell (England, United States) publishes *Objective Personality and Motivation Tests*. He made contributions in the field of personality, putting forth a taxonomy of 16 different personality traits that could explain differences in people's personalities.
1969	Eleanor Gibson (United States) publishes *Principles of Perceptual Learning and Development*. With colleague Richard Walk (United States), Gibson conducts research on infant depth perception, known as "The Visual Cliff."
1971	Phillip Zimbardo (United States) conducts the Stanford Prison Experiment in the basement of an academic hall to examine the effects of authority in a prison environment.
1971	Albert Bandura (Canada, United States) publishes *Social Learning Theory*. His contributions advance the field of social cognitive psychology, and he is well known for his experiments regarding aggression.
1972	Elliot Aronson (United States) publishes *The Social Animal*. His contributions lead to advances in the theory of cognitive dissonance and explore the importance of situational factors on behavior.
1974	Eleanor Maccoby (United States) and Carol Jacklin (United States) publish *The Psychology of Sex Differences*. Their contributions lead to advances in the fields of gender studies and developmental psychology.
1974	Stanley Milgram (United States) publishes *Obedience to Authority: An Experimental View*. Milgram may be best known for his controversial experiments on obedience, which researched to what extent people would obey orders, even if the orders were dangerous or immoral.
1976	Robert V. Guthrie (United States) publishes *Even the Rat Was White*, the first history of African American psychologists in the United States.
1979	James J. Gibson (United States) publishes *The Ecological Approach to Visual Perception*. His contributions lead to advances in the field of visual perception.
1979	Elizabeth Loftus (United States) publishes *Eyewitness Testimony*. Her contributions lead to advances in the field of memory, misinformation, and eyewitness memory.
1983	Howard Gardner (United States) publishes *Frames of Mind*. This work outlines his theory of multiple intelligences.
1984	Hiroshi Azuma (Japan) publishes "Psychology in a Non-Western Country" in the *International Journal of Psychology*. He made contributions in the areas of cross-cultural psychology.

DATE	MILESTONE
CE	
1986	Durganand Sinha (India) publishes *Psychology in a Third World Country: The Indian Experience*. He studied indigenous psychology; self, family, and social values; and human and socioeconomic development. He was central to the modern development of psychology from an Indian perspective.
1987	Marius Romme (Amsterdam) founds the Hearing Voices Network with Sandra Escher, a science journalist, and Patsy Hage, a person who hears voices. The network serves as a peer-mentor organization for persons who have auditory hallucinations and their supporters. The network soon spreads across the world.
1988	Muzafer Sherif (Turkey, United States) publishes *The Robbers Cave Experiment* with colleagues. One of the founders of modern social psychology, he advanced the fields of social judgment theory and realistic conflict theory.
1988	The Association for Psychological Science (APS), previously the American Psychological Society, is founded. Its stated mission is to promote, protect, and advance the interests of scientifically oriented psychology in research, application, teaching, and the improvement of human welfare.
1989	Kimberlé Williams Crenshaw (United States) publishes the paper "Demarginalizing the Intersection of Race and Sex." She is one of the founders of critical race theory, developing the theory of intersectionality.
1990	Reiko True (Japan, United States) publishes "Psychotherapeutic Issues With Asian American Women" in the journal *Sex Roles*. Her work has advanced mental health services for Asian Americans and other minorities.
1991	Martin Seligman (United States) publishes *Learned Optimism*. This work introduces the field of positive psychology.
1991	Qicheng Jing (China) publishes *Landmarks of Psychology: Contemporary Great Masters in Psychology*. He made contributions in highlighting the international aspect of psychology, advancing the exchange of international psychology, and lifting Chinese psychology onto the world stage.
1997	Beverly Daniel Tatum (United States) publishes *Why Are All the Black Kids Sitting Together in the Cafeteria?* This work examines the development of racial identity.
1997	U.S. president Bill Clinton apologizes for the Tuskegee Syphilis Study, an infamous study that violated human participant rights and led to the publishing of the Belmont Report in 1979, a U.S. code of ethics for human participants in research.
2003	Kuo-Shu Yang (China, Taiwan) publishes *Progress in Asian Social Psychology* with colleagues. A pioneer in indigenous Chinese and Taiwanese psychology, he also devoted his life to social reform in Taiwan.
2007	Alice Eagly (United States) publishes *Through the Labyrinth: The Truth About How Women Become Leaders* with colleague Linda Carli (United States). Her contributions have advanced the understanding of prejudice, sex differences, leadership styles, feminism, and stereotypes.
2008	U.S. president George W. Bush signs Mental Health Parity Act, requiring insurance to equally cover both mental and physical health.
2008	Lisa Diamond publishes *Sexual Fluidity: Understanding Women's Love and Desire*. Her research has advanced the understanding of sexual identity, sexual orientation development, and human bonding.
2010	Derald Wing Sue (United States) publishes *Microaggressions in Everyday Life: Race, Gender, and Sexual Orientation*. His contributions have advanced the fields of multicultural counseling and research.
2010	Claude Steele (United States) publishes *Whistling Vivaldi and Other Clues to How Stereotypes Affect Us*. He has advanced the areas of stereotype threat and its impact on the academic performance of minority students.
2010	The replication controversy impacts how a variety of disciplines, including psychology, validate existing studies.

(Continued)

(Continued)

DATE	MILESTONE
CE	
2011	Michael Gazzaniga (United States) publishes *Who's in Charge? Free Will and the Science of the Brain*. His studies advance understanding of the functions of each brain hemisphere, and how they work independently and in collaboration.
2011	Daniel Kahneman (Israel) publishes *Thinking, Fast and Slow*. His contributions have advanced the fields of judgment and decision making. With colleague Amos Tversky (Israel), Kahneman has established a cognitive basis for common human errors that arise from heuristics and biases.
2013	*DSM-5* is published by the American Psychiatric Association.
2014	A radio soap opera, "Musekeweya," is created by clinical psychologist Ervin Staub (Hungary, United States) and disseminated to Rwandan listeners to counteract hate speech and intolerance.
2015	The American Psychological Association bans psychologist participation in national security interrogations.
2015	Mona Amer (Egypt) and Germine Awad (United States) publish *The Handbook of Arab American Psychology*. It is the first major publication to comprehensively discuss the Arab American experience from a primarily psychological lens.
2015	David Trafimow (United States) bans null hypothesis significance testing for the journal *Basic and Applied Social Psychology*. This begins the debate about how to better determine if a hypothesis is supported or rejected.
2016	U.S. president Barack Obama signs the 21st Century Cures Act, which provides essential prevention services and treatments for populations in need and support.
2016	Mahzarin Banaji (India, United States) publishes *Blindspot: Hidden Biases of Good People* with colleague Anthony Greenwald (United States). Her work has advanced awareness of implicit or unconscious bias.
2017	Arkansas (United States) opens the first intimate partner violence shelter for men in the United States. The shelter also runs a domestic violence hotline for men.
2018	Mental Health at Work (United Kingdom) is launched by The Royal Foundation. The nonprofit provides support to employers and employees to help them improve well-being in their workplace and encourage conversations about mental health.
2019	Jennifer Eberhardt (United States) publishes *Biased: Uncovering the Hidden Prejudice That Shapes What We See, Think, and Do*. Her research advances the fields of race, bias, and inequality.
2020	In Mexico, a mental health bill that would have removed a person's right to consent to treatment was stopped by human rights activists.
2020	Telemental health availability broadens treatment options during the coronavirus pandemic.
2021	American Psychological Association apologizes for contributions to systemic racism, and vows to achieve the social equality, health equity, and fairness that all human beings deserve.

iStock.com/Natali_Mis

1

Introduction to Psychology

Are you curious?

We hope so. We also hope you enjoy a good story. Those are the two themes—curiosity and storytelling—that we've used to write this book. All four of us (the book's authors) truly *love* psychology. We want you to love it too. We think you will, because psychology answers questions your curiosity has naturally led you to ask about why people think, feel, and act the way we do.

Psychology is a comprehensive and diverse scientific field, with a tremendous number of subspecialties and applications. Every conversation you have—with every person, every day—is steeped in psychology. No matter what career you choose, every job path benefits from a foundational understanding of behavior. This book discusses just a tiny fraction of what psychologists are working on right now. We hope that these chapters are an appetizer that makes your curiosity and hunger for understanding grow.

We're excited—so let's get started.

After reading this chapter, you will get answers to several questions you've been curious about:

Have You Ever Wondered?

1.1	What is psychology?
1.2	How has psychology grown and changed over time?
1.3	How has diversity helped psychology?
1.4	How should I use this book?

Learning Objectives

LO 1.1	Define psychology and explain the American Psychological Association's Introductory Psychology Initiative.
LO 1.2	Explain important historical figures and approaches to psychological inquiry.
LO 1.3	Discuss the history of prejudice in psychology and identify key diverse voices in the field over time.
LO 1.4	Analyze how the ideas in this book can relate to you, personally.

STARTING YOUR PSYCHOLOGY JOURNEY

? Have You Ever Wondered?
1.1 What is psychology?

>> **LO 1.1   Define psychology and explain the American Psychological Association's Introductory Psychology Initiative.**

Are you curious about what is in this book?

If you're reading as part of an introduction to psychology course at a college or university, you're not alone. Over a million students take that course *every year* in the United States alone (Steuer & Ham, 2008). It's the second most popular college course in the nation, following only intro to English composition (Adelman, 2004). You probably have a general idea of "psychology"—but you may also harbor some misconceptions. Many new students of psychology, for example, are surprised to learn that mental disorders, counseling, and therapy are just one part of a much larger science studying the entire human experience.

Defining Psychology

You're using psychology right now.

One of your amazing abilities is perceiving marks on a page as letters, turning them into sounds, transforming those patterns into words, and then combining them into sentences and meaningful ideas (in other words, sensation and perception). Psychology is also about making decisions, learning from mistakes, remembering information, managing difficult relationships, developing a personality, dreaming, using (and misusing) your brain, and analyzing whether people are inherently good, evil, or somewhere in between. One of the people we interview about careers in psychology may have said it best: "A degree in psychology is a degree without limits."

More formally, psychology is the scientific study of mental processes and behaviors. "Mental processes" include perceptions, thoughts, feelings, and decisions we make at every point in life. Psychology has only been an official, separate science since the late 1800s (American Psychological Association [APA], 2014; Shaughnessy et al., 2009). Before that, mostly either philosophers or physiologists addressed mental processes and behaviors. So as sciences go, psychology is a relatively "young" field but with deep historical roots.

Humans are complicated. We sometimes make decisions that turn out to be bad for us—or good for us (in a selfish way), but bad for society overall. However, human history is also filled with simple, selfless acts of heroism by people sacrificing their own well-being to save others. Psychology studies the best and the worst parts of living in a social world. What could be more interesting and important? Many modern psychologists spend their careers trying to apply their knowledge to make the world a better place, and there are hundreds of career opportunities, both with and without graduate training. You'll learn about many of those careers throughout this book.

Psychology: The scientific study of mental processes (perceptions, thoughts, and feelings) and behaviors.

The American Psychological Association

The diversity of research topics in psychology might amaze you.

While wandering door to door around one graduate department, one of your authors met people studying the tongue and taste perception, what makes people laugh, how to treat social anxiety, using GPS systems in smartphones to map the prevalence of mental disorders, interventions for the fear of failing, neural paths in the brain for empathy, whether animals have a sense of self, and predictors of interpersonal attraction. If you're curious, then having access to psychology insights might make you feel like a kid in a candy store.

To embrace that diversity of information, there's a large group of professional psychologists called the American Psychological Association, or APA for short. The APA has over 130,000 members in North America and calls itself the "leading scientific and professional organization representing psychology" (at least, on this continent; see www.apa.org). Members of the APA can join the overall organization and/or join subdivisions or interest groups aligned with their specialty, such as "military psychology," "clinical neuropsychology," and "addiction psychology." Many other subdivisions match the names of this book's chapters (such as developmental or social psychology). Table 1.1 is a full list of their divisions and research subfields. Which look the most interesting to you?

American Psychological Association: The largest professional organization for psychologists in North America, including over 50 subdivisions or interest groups.

TABLE 1.1

American Psychological Association Divisions

General Psych	Teaching of Psych
Experimental Psych and Cognitive Science	Quantitative and Qualitative Methods
Behavioral Neuroscience & Comparative Psych	Developmental Psych
Personality and Social Psych	Psych of Social Issues
Psych of Aesthetics, Creativity, and Arts	Clinical Psych
Consulting Psych	Industrial and Organizational Psych
Educational Psych	School Psych
Counseling Psych	Psychologists in Public Service
Military Psych	Adult Development and Aging
Engineering Psych	Rehabilitation Psych
Consumer Psych	Theoretical and Philosophical Psych
Behavior Analysis	History of Psych
Community Psych	Psychopharmacology and Substance Abuse
Psychotherapy	Society of Psychological Hypnosis
State, Provincial, and Territorial Psych	Society for Humanistic Psych
Intellectual/Developmental Disabilities	Environmental Psych
Psych of Women	Psych of Religion and Spirituality
Child and Family Policy and Practice	Health Psych
Psychoanalytic Psych	Clinical Neuropsych
American Psych-Law Society	Psychologists in Independent Practice
Couple and Family Psych	Psych of Sexual Orientation and Gender Diversity
Psych of Culture, Ethnicity, and Race	Media Psych and Technology
Sport, Exercise, and Performance Psych	Peace, Conflict, and Violence: Peace Psych Division
Group Psych Psychotherapy	Addiction Psych
Psych of Men and Masculinities	International Psych
Clinical Child and Adolescent Psych	Pediatric Psych
Prescribing Psych	Trauma Psych

There are a wide variety of subfields within psychology.

Source: Adapted from https://www.apa.org/about/division.

The Introductory Psychology Initiative

Psychologists often gather at conferences to share their cutting-edge research and teaching innovations. One of these meetings resulted in an initiative to create guiding principles for high-quality teaching of introductory psychology courses at the college and university level. Over the years, many individuals and task forces have contributed to that goal, which the field refers to as the **Introductory Psychology Initiative** (APA, 2014, 2023). The vision statement of the most recent version (from 2023) of that initiative is that "psychological science will be recognized as a high-impact undergraduate major that empowers people from all backgrounds to make a difference in their lives and communities."

The initiative suggests that introduction to psychology courses have learning goals around five major topics:

1. *Content knowledge and applications:* Identify key concepts, subfields, and aspects of psychology's history; apply content to solve problems; and provide examples of integrative themes.

2. *Scientific inquiry and critical thinking:* Exercise scientific reasoning; interpret, design, and evaluate research; incorporate sociocultural factors; and use statistics to evaluate findings.

3. *Values in psychological science:* Employ ethical standards and values to psychological inquiry, practice interpersonal and intercultural responsiveness, strengthen the community, and improve quality of life.

4. *Communication, psychological literacy, and technology skills:* Interact effectively with others, write and present effectively, show psychological literacy, and exhibit tech skills.

5. *Personal and professional development:* Exhibit self-regulation, refine management skills, display effective judgment, cultivate collaboration skills, demonstrate tech skills, and develop direction for life after graduation.

Each goal also has subgoals. These goals run throughout every chapter of this entire book, and we encourage you to keep them in mind as your knowledge grows and you're able to make connections from one concept to the next.

The initiative also suggests that instructors should teach content using an approach represented in Figure 1.1. It has three components; we'll briefly describe each of them for you.

The Five Pillars

The vertical lines in Figure 1.1 are the five "pillars" of the APA's Introductory Psychology Initiative (APA, 2014, 2023). They represent five major subfields: biological, cognitive, developmental, social and personality, and mental and physical health. As you saw in Table 1.1, we can get much more detailed if we want, but these five large categories cover enough to give new students a good overview of the field for an initial course.

When you look at this book's table of contents, you'll notice that we follow the pillar model, with two bonus features (like secret levels you've unlocked in a video game!). First, you'll see chapters that fit nicely into each of the five main pillars:

- Biological: *Biological psychology* is a complex subfield covering a wide variety of topics. Mostly, biological aspects of psychology will be a focus in the chapters titled "Biology and Your Brain" (Chapter 3), "Sensation and Perception" (Chapter 6), and "Consciousness" (Chapter 7).

- Cognitive: *Cognitive psychology* is the study of thought, learning, memory, and perception. These topics are most clearly the focus of the chapters titled "Learning" (Chapter 9), "Memory" (Chapter 10), "Motivation and Emotion" (Chapter 11), and "Cognition and Intelligence" (Chapter 12).

Introductory Psychology Initiative: The APA's suggested approach to teaching high-quality initial, general psychology courses for the college level.

FIGURE 1.1

A Structure for the Undergraduate Introductory Psychology Course

The American Psychological Association suggests that Intro Psych books and courses include five "pillars" or subfields, guided by integrative themes and a foundation of research methods.

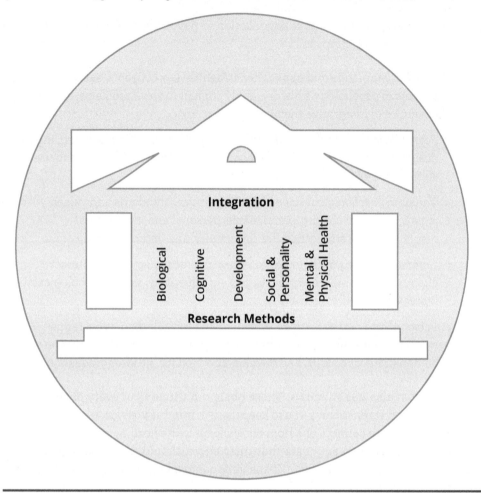

Source: American Psychological Association. (2014). *Strengthening the common core of the introductory psychology course.* Washington, DC: American Psychological Association, Board of Educational Affairs. Retrieved from https://www.apa.org/ed/governance/bea/intro-psych-report.pdf.

- Development: *Developmental psychology* is the study of how we change and grow over our lifetime. This pillar is highlighted in the chapter titled "Human Development" (Chapter 8).

- Social and personality: *Social psychology* is the study of how we interact with other people, while *personality psychology* studies how we tend to act consistently across different situations and over time. The chapters titled "Personality" (Chapter 13) and "Social Psychology" (Chapter 14) are devoted most closely to this pillar.

- Mental and physical health: The last pillar aligns with the last two chapters of the book, which are titled "Psychological Disorders" (Chapter 15) and "Mental Health: Therapy and Treatment" (Chapter 16). Generally, subfields related to mental health are called either *clinical psychology* (which usually focuses on more severe or biologically based illnesses) or *counseling psychology* (which usually focuses on social or psychologically based illnesses and challenges).

The pillars are a traditional way of thinking about psychology, and they guide most of the book. After this chapter, Chapter 2 provides a foundation of research methods and Chapter 3 establishes important concepts regarding neurobiology and the brain. But then, we diverge from the pillars with two chapters that allow you to explore the exciting part of *why* psychology really matters in our curious world.

The next two chapters are applied topics that allow you to think about the APA's five learning goals. The topics are (1) identity and intersectionality and (2) health and positive psychology. *Intersectionality* is an exciting new area of psychology (borrowed from its original home, legal studies) that emphasizes how the human experience changes based on diversity issues. *Health psychology* is the study of how mental processes and behaviors affect both psychological and physical health, while *positive psychology* is the study of happiness and fulfilling our potential.

After exploring these very applied topics, we go back to the traditional pillar model.

A Foundation of Research Methods

Psychology is interesting because it's all around us. Chances are that you've recently encountered psychological ideas in the last week, whether it was something you read online, an item you saw in a magazine, or a theory you learned about on TikTok. However, what sets this course and textbook apart is like the pillars shown in Figure 1.1: Everything we share with you here stands on research methods. This is important, because it gives us more confidence in the information.

Psychology is a *science*, meaning that ideas, theories, and evidence-based therapies advance through the scientific method. Chapter 2 focuses on how to study humans and other animals while maintaining ethical standards. Psychology is a particularly difficult science because many concepts are abstract and hard to directly measure (such as bias, memory, or decision-making) and because ethics are paramount.

Over the years, many popular ideas have been rejected because scientific testing could not validate them. Psychology has also been in the news for the past few years because several famous studies from the 1960s and 1970s were tried again—a scientific technique called *replication*—and they failed to show the same results. We discuss this "scandal" in the chapter and what it has meant (and continues to mean) for the field. Humans are flawed and science is a human endeavor, so it's critical that we acknowledge any potential biases we have if we want to improve.

Author, anthropologist, and filmmaker Zora Neale Hurston was a master storyteller. Known best for her novel *Their Eyes Were Watching God,* Hurston wrote about prejudice in the American South, religion, struggle, and science. We appreciate her love of curiosity when she noted, "Research is formalized curiosity. It is poking and prying with a purpose." One of the things that has made teaching psychology and writing this textbook so fun for us is all the poking and prying we've done into so many interesting topics.

Zora Neale Hurston, American author and anthropologist, said, "Research is formalized curiosity."

Historical/Corbis Historical/via Getty Images

Consider global issues like pollution. How do different subfields in psychology all contribute to help understand—and hopefully solve—this problem?

iStock.com/Hramovnick

Integrative Themes

All the subfields of psychology work together (APA, 2023). To show that, the word *integration* also appears across the top of Figure 1.1. The initiative's seven guiding integrative themes are the following:

1. Psychological science relies on empirical evidence and adapts as new data develop.

2. Psychological science explains general principles that govern behavior while recognizing individual differences.

3. Psychological, biological, social, and cultural factors influence behavior and mental processes.

4. Psychological science values diversity, promotes equity, and fosters inclusion in pursuit of a more just society.

5. Our perceptions and biases filter our experiences of the world through an imperfect personal lens.

6. Applying psychological principles can change our lives, organizations, and communities in positive ways.

7. Ethical principles guide psychological science research and practice.

The reason integration matters is because all of us live in a world where our goals and decisions affect each other. For example, when you consider major global problems such as pollution, resource depletion, poverty, climate change, pandemics, crime, and terrorism, solutions can't be found without collaboration. Psychologists are needed to change people's motivations and behaviors. In addition, we must find solutions that respect everyone's needs and that work with people from other relevant fields, like communication, biology, physics, chemistry, political science, and business (APA, 2014). This kind of integration means that unlike some other academic fields, most research papers in psychology are published with multiple authors who take a team approach.

Sage Vantage   Practice what you learn in **Knowledge Check 1.1**

A BRIEF HISTORY OF PSYCHOLOGY IN EUROPE AND THE UNITED STATES

?

Have You Ever Wondered?
1.2 How has psychology grown and changed over time?

>> LO 1.2 **Explain important historical figures and approaches to psychological inquiry.**

Are you curious about how psychology got started?

Like all epic tales, psychology has an origin story. It all began when innovative minds connected and applied different methods and theories about knowledge to create a new science. Philosophers and other scholars had been debating about mental processes and explanations for behavior for hundreds of years without considering it "psychology." For example, in the personality chapter of this book (Chapter 13), you'll learn about how ancient Greeks believed liquids in your body influence your tendencies—but that theory wasn't tested in any kind of scientific way. Psychology didn't become what it is today until the scientific method became its most fundamental principle.

European Psychology's Origin Story: Wilhelm Wundt

Picture Germany in the late 1800s.

Philosophers, medical doctors, some biologists, and others had considered mental processes and behaviors for years. But there wasn't a clear devoted area of scientific study just for those questions. The person now considered the founder of psychology as a separate science was a physiologist named Wilhelm Wundt (pronounced VILL-helm Vunt).

In 1874, he wrote a textbook called *Principles of Physiological Psychology*. In it, he argued that psychology should be a separate field of study, using scientific experiments to understand thoughts and behaviors. Just a few years later, in 1879, he established the first psychology lab at the University of Leipzig in Germany (Kohls & Benedikter, 2010). He was also the first person to officially call himself a psychologist. Wundt gained international recognition as thousands of people traveled to hear his lectures on this exciting new science (Blumenthal, 1998).

Wundt studied sensation and perception with simple but groundbreaking experiments. Many of them focused on reaction time. Back then, that was cutting-edge science. For example, he asked people to press a button when they saw a white circle on a screen or when they heard a dropped ball hit a platform (Hunt, 1993). How quickly and accurately could they do these tasks? How many mistakes would they make? He concluded there was a fraction of a second between when the visual or auditory stimulus actually *happened* and when we *perceive* that it happened (Fancher & Rutherford, 2012). The study of sensation and perception—and of the difference between the two—was born as one small part of what would evolve into modern psychology.

Wilhelm Wundt (1832–1920), who many people today consider the founder of psychology.

Bildagentur-online/Universal Images Group/via Getty Images

Wilhelm Wundt: Considered by many to be the founder of psychology as a separate scientific field of study.

Famous Names and Approaches to Psychology

Wundt is where we start.

The men in Figure 1.2 were integral to psychology's growth over the past 150 years or so. This part of the chapter briefly explains each person's valuable contribution. In later chapters, we'll come back to these ideas in further detail, in the context of the relevant subfield and topic.

But for now, please note what these classic figures all have in common: They are all White men. That's not meant as a value judgment, simply as a statement of fact. Psychology wouldn't have progressed the way it did without them, and we need to acknowledge their important contributions. We also need to acknowledge that their own backgrounds shaped, and may have limited, their perspectives (just as anyone's perspective is limited, no matter who they are). That's not a slight on them, but an honest recognition of the reality of how culture influences the development of science. So in the next section, we'll explicitly address psychology's history of systemic prejudices not to assign blame, but to recognize and celebrate how diverse voices are now enlarging psychology and making it better.

FIGURE 1.2

Some Famous Historical Figures in Psychology

In addition to Wundt, here are some important people in the history of the field. Notice, however, what they all have in common and read the next section for more diversity.

Edward Titchener (1867–1927)

William James (1842–1910)

Ivan Pavlov (1849–1936)

Sigmund Freud (1856–1939)

John Watson (1878–1958)

Kurt Lewin (1890–1947)

Carl Rogers (1902–1987)

Daniel Kahneman (1934–2024)

Fotosearch/Stringer/Archive Photos/via Getty Images; Stock Montage/Contributor/Archive Photos/via Getty Images; Bettmann/Contributor/Bettmann/via Getty Images; Hans Casparius/Stringer/Hulton Archive/via Getty Images; Bettmann/Contributor/Bettmann/via Getty Images; Album/Fine Art Images/Newscom; Bettmann/Contributor/Bettmann/via Getty Images; Andreas Rentz/Staff/Getty Images News/via Getty Images

Wundt, Titchener, and Structuralism

Wilhelm Wundt's general approach assumed that sensation and perception could be broken down into smaller experiences. In chemistry, a "compound" is a substance made up of smaller elements (like how water is a combination of hydrogen and oxygen). Wundt wanted people to use *introspection*, inner observation and analysis of personal mental experiences, to break down thoughts in the same way (Fancher & Rutherford, 2012).

Wundt and his student Edward Titchener developed their ideas into an approach now known as **structuralism**, the idea that complex mental experiences can be broken down into smaller parts. Imagine you are in a lab and a scientist puts a rose in front of you. You might notice the smell, the color, the feeling when you touch the thorns, and any memories or associations you have with roses from your past (Titchener, 1896/2009). Listing each component of your experience is the process of introspection.

Structuralism: An early approach to psychology in which people attempted to break down sensation and perception experiences into their smaller parts.

Wundt was aware that introspection was tricky, unverifiable, and unreliable. Two people confronted with a rose might have very different inner experiences, and neither could really be measured. There were other problems, too. For example, introspection isn't going to work very well when you're trying to understand the psychology of animals or children, who can't fill out surveys or verbalize their experiences. Wundt also knew that our perceptions are full of biases and mistakes. These realizations led to a drop in the popularity of structuralism and made way for different approaches.

James and Functionalism

Philosopher William James taught the first-ever psychology course in the United States at Harvard University in 1875. While James was inspired by Wundt's ideas about psychology being a separate science, he wasn't very impressed with structuralism. James and his student Edward Thorndike developed their own approach called functionalism.

Functionalism emphasized the *purpose* of thought, sensation, perception, memory, and so on (Fancher & Rutherford, 2012). So, while structuralism asked, "How does perception work?" functionalism asked, "Why does it work like that?" James, Thorndike, and their fans relied less on introspection as a research method and instead favored observation and measurement of behaviors, often in animals. Thorndike conducted a series of studies measuring how quickly cats could get out of puzzle boxes—which are basically little feline escape rooms (Thorndike, 1911).

Functionalism: Studying psychology by focusing on the purpose of mental processes and behaviors.

Functionalism appealed to many early psychologists because it seemed more scientific than the methods used in structuralism. Still, changing times brought even more new ideas that helped shape the field.

Pavlov and the Biological Approach

One of the biggest bombshells in the history of science was Darwin's 1859 book *On the Origin of Species*. If animals evolved slowly through natural and sexual selection, that also includes humans. Many psychologists started using animals in their lab studies, and that helped connect biologists and physiologists with psychologists.

For example, the Russian physiologist Ivan Pavlov was studying how digestion reflexes worked in dogs (Pavlov, 1927). But he quickly realized that the dogs would pick up on environmental cues that indicated that they were about to get fed, and the dogs would respond with anticipation, such as salivating. This kind of scholarly crossover influenced psychology's **biological approach** that explores, for example, how hormones, genetics, and neurotransmitters influence thoughts, feelings, and behaviors.

Biological approach: Studying psychology in terms of how thoughts and behaviors are influenced by biological factors in the body (genes, hormones, etc.).

Freud and the Psychodynamic Approach

No history of psychology would be complete without mentioning Sigmund Freud. Freud is certainly not the "founder" or "father" of the science of psychology—that's Wundt—but many do consider Freud to be the pioneer of therapy and counseling. His **psychodynamic approach** proposed that our childhood experiences, along with our hidden hopes and fears, drive our thoughts, feelings, and behaviors.

Even while alive, Freud was controversial. Many early psychologists (like Wundt and James) were doing research in the lab with scientific methods, but Freud was more interested in the individual patients' mental health. Trained as a medical doctor, Freud realized that talking about issues and tracing them back to when they began, often in childhood, could treat at least some mental illness symptoms (Freud, 1920/1966, 1933). Despite his claims, Freud's approach was not particularly scientific or objective. Many of his ideas were based on case studies and even secondhand reports about particular patients, friends, or family members. His interpretations reflected his culture, personal upbringing, and life experiences.

But it's undeniable that Freud's work greatly influenced psychotherapy. Many of his ideas still inform psychology today, although usually in a modified and updated form.

Watson and the Behaviorist Approach

Wundt's introspection fell out of favor as a scientific methodology because it was inherently biased and inconsistent. Similarly, many people criticized Freud's approach to psychology as untestable and, frankly, sexist. Many people loved the growing field of psychology but wanted to emphasize that it should, above all else, be a *science*.

In the first half of the 1900s, especially in the United States, many psychologists embraced an approach called behaviorism, or the **behaviorist approach**. Behaviorism recognized that "thoughts," "perceptions," and "feelings" existed and were important but that they couldn't be directly measured, which made them less scientific. Behaviorists believe the only way to be objective and scientific is to focus on observable *behaviors* (Skinner, 1954; Watson, 1913).

John Watson is credited with officially starting the behaviorist approach in 1913. He explicitly criticized introspection, asserting that psychology was "a purely objective experimental branch of natural science" (Watson, 1913, p. 158) and that there was absolutely no difference between the mental processes of humans and other animals. He believed that psychology should predict and control behaviors rather than describe or explain mental processes (Fancher & Rutherford, 2012). Watson later became infamous for an extremely controversial and unethical study in which he and his student, who later became his wife, created fear in a human baby (we'll talk about this study in the chapter on learning, Chapter 9; Watson & Rayner, 1920).

Lewin and the Sociocultural Approach

The history of psychology we've discussed so far has focused on three general subjects: (1) human sensation and perception (Wundt, James), (2) animal research (Pavlov, Watson), and (3) the start of psychological therapy (Freud). These are still important topics, but psychology is also about falling in love, starting friendships, creating memories, aggression, prejudice, career development, leadership, social cooperation, and every other part of living in a social world.

In the period between World Wars I and II, Kurt Lewin immigrated to the United States to escape the rapidly escalating anti-Semitism in Europe that would climax in the Holocaust. Lewin joined many other psychologists studying aggression, prejudice,

Psychodynamic approach: Studying psychology by focusing on how our mental processes are affected by childhood and by thoughts and fears (which we are often unaware of).

Behaviorist approach: Studying psychology with the belief that the only truly scientific approach to the field is to measure only objective, observable behaviors in humans and other animals.

and topics relevant to world events and people's lives. Lewin particularly called for what he labeled *action research,* the application of psychology to solving problems and making the world a better place, including promoting independence, respect, and cooperation (Lewin, 1946; see also Adelman, 1993).

The sociocultural approach in modern psychology echoes and incorporates Lewin's ideas by focusing on the social dynamics of interaction, including the influence of culture. Specific topics like conformity, identity, religious rituals and practices, aggression and altruism, and prejudice all fall within this approach to understanding mental processes and behaviors.

Sociocultural approach: Studying psychology by considering how social dynamics and culture interact in our everyday lives.

Rogers and the Humanistic Approach

After World War II, psychology was more popular than ever—and cultural values were changing. Civil rights were on everyone's mind as people started to demand equal treatment across the board for historically marginalized groups (such as women, people of color, people with disabilities, and so on). Psychology responded in kind.

The humanistic approach of psychology focused on helping people achieve their own personal best potential and positive self-esteem. One of the leaders of the movement was Carl Rogers, a therapist who developed a new system of counseling that helped people feel respected and accepted, no matter what (Rogers, 1957). Humanism still guides many therapists and has been reinvigorated through the positive psychology movement, which emphasizes how people move from simply surviving to thriving.

Humanistic approach: Studying psychology by exploring how individuals can achieve their personal potential and positive self-esteem.

Kahneman and the Cognitive Approach

At about the same time the humanistic perspective was ramping up, so was the final approach we're going to discuss. Psychologists trained by the behaviorists in the first half of the 1900s were now scholars and professors themselves. Many now wanted to focus more on studying internal mental processes (not just behaviors). The cognitive approach did just that, studying topics such as memory, motivation, problem-solving, and thinking in general.

Cognitive approach: Studying psychology with a focus on inner mental processes such as memory, decision-making, and thought structures.

FIGURE 1.3

Some Important Moments in the History of Psychology

Psychology grew and changed over time; here are some classic names in the history of psychology (but note that more diversity is discussed in the next section of this book).

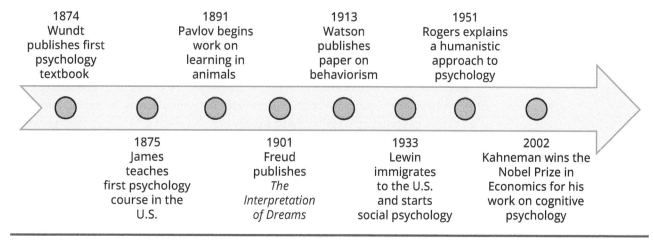

1874 Wundt publishes first psychology textbook

1891 Pavlov begins work on learning in animals

1913 Watson publishes paper on behaviorism

1951 Rogers explains a humanistic approach to psychology

1875 James teaches first psychology course in the U.S.

1901 Freud publishes *The Interpretation of Dreams*

1933 Lewin immigrates to the U.S. and starts social psychology

2002 Kahneman wins the Nobel Prize in Economics for his work on cognitive psychology

One of the most famous scholars within the cognitive perspective is Daniel Kahneman. His career was spent researching mistakes that people often make when they process information and make decisions (Kahneman, 2011). Often our thinking leads to mistakes because we rely too much on intuition or on logic; we need a healthy balance of both. Kahneman's fascinating series of studies and applications to consumer behaviors led to his winning the Nobel Prize in Economic Sciences in 2002.

Sage Vantage⤳   Practice what you learn in **Knowledge Check 1.2**

THE BEAUTY OF DIVERSITY

?
Have You Ever
Wondered?
1.3 How has diversity
helped psychology?

>> LO 1.3   Discuss the history of prejudice in psychology and identify key diverse voices in the field over time.

Are you curious about other perspectives in psychology?

Everyone lives with some combination of social and cultural advantages and disadvantages; it's simply part of being human. Admitting our personal biases is a big step toward overcoming them. Academic scholarship is guided by flawed humans with these biases, so acknowledging how our field has been affected is important and is, again, a needed step toward doing better.

In this section, we emphasize three things. First, we need to honestly acknowledge when the field has fallen short of our ideals for equality and respect, so we can learn from our mistakes. Second, we recognize neglected contributions by honoring ideas and innovations from women, people of color, people from the LGBTQIA2S+ population, people with disabilities, and so on. Third, we'll summarize how psychology has become committed to a better future.

A History of Prejudice

Prejudice comes in many forms.

You have probably encountered sexism, homophobia, transphobia, discrimination against people due to their size, disabilities, immigration status, mental health status, and so on. You might not expect those prejudices in a scientific field—but it has happened many times.

For example, in 1962, three men received the Nobel Prize for discovering the double-helix structure of DNA (Watson, Crick, and Wilkins). But their "discovery" came after going through the research diagrams of Rosalind Franklin—without her permission—in which she clearly laid out the double helix. They essentially stole her work. In Watson's book, he admitted that Franklin had no idea they were going over her materials and that she had to either "go or be put in her place" (Watson, 1968; see also Maddox, 2003). Many people looking back now believe it was Franklin who should have received credit for this landmark discovery.

Psychology, like all human endeavors, has a history of *systemic prejudice* (also known as structural or institutional prejudice). Sexism, racism, heterosexism, and other forms of prejudice have affected theory development and unethical treatment of participants in studies. There are many examples, and we will mention some throughout this book in the context of their subject area.

In October 2021, the American Psychological Association published a formal apology for contributing to racist ideas, theories, policies, or any other aspect of a racist society (APA, 2021). The opening paragraph reads,

The American Psychological Association failed in its role leading the discipline of psychology, was complicit in contributing to systemic inequities, and hurt many through racism, racial discrimination, and denigration of people of color, thereby falling short on its mission to benefit society and improve lives. APA is profoundly sorry, accepts responsibility for, and owns the actions and inactions of APA itself, the discipline of psychology, and individual psychologists who stood as leaders for the organization and field. (p. 1)

One year later, in October 2022, they sponsored another paper titled, "Historical Chronology: Examining Psychology's Contributions to the Belief in Racial Hierarchy and Perpetuation of Inequality for People of Color in the U.S." (Cummings & Cummings, 2022). This follow-up again acknowledged psychology's contributions to systemic prejudice and offered a list of specific examples. Overall, the type of things discussed are

- theories and hypotheses that assume "race" is a biological, innate difference among people instead of a social construct;

- studies comparing races that treat White people as the default or standard, therefore biasing interpretations favoring any differences as somehow "inferior";

- standardizing tests using White people as the norm, such that questions use references based on cultural norms more likely to be familiar with people from certain subcultures and therefore giving those populations advantages;

- failing to study negative effects of international policies like colonization or assimilation of language and culture; and

- research studies that assume findings are true of "people" in general, even when the participants really only represent a small portion of people (e.g., they are very limited in terms of their ages, ethnicities, language spoken, socioeconomic status, or education).

A Chronology of Racist Research and Theory

Although most of psychology is not racist, the field hasn't always gotten it right. The APA-sponsored paper offers examples of when and where psychology has shown bias and contributed to prejudice, organized as a timeline (Cummings & Cummings, 2022). Here is a sample that you can map onto the timeline in Figure 1.3.

_1850–1900:_

- The American Psychological Association is founded in 1892. It has a White male president (G. Stanley Hall, whom William James mentored) and 31 White male members.

- A paper is published in 1895 with findings that Black and Native American people have better "primitive" reflexes like reaction time but that White Americans have more intelligence (Bache, 1895).

- A study compares Black and White children on a memory task. When the Black children did better, the author concluded it was because memory is needed in "primitive brains" (Stetson, 1897).

1900–1925:

- G. Stanley Hall (first APA president) writes a textbook in which he describes Native American people as childlike. He supports programs designed to "civilize" them such as forcing them to change their languages and religions (Hall, 1904, 1905).

- In 1910, the Eugenics Record office is established. It advocates for designer human reproduction, segregation of races, and forced sterilization of "unfit and inferior races" (Brigham, 1923). In the years from 1892 tó 1947, 31 different APA presidents support eugenics organizations. By 1930, 35,000 people have been sterilized due to being labeled socially or biologically unfit; the majority of them are immigrants, people of color, poor people, and/or people with disabilities (Greenwood, 2017; Kevles, 1968).

- The "mulatto hypothesis" becomes popular; it's the idea that for mixed-ethnicity individuals, positive traits such as reasoning, memory, and intelligence go up the lighter their skin color is (Ferguson, 1916; see also Guthrie, 2004).

- The U.S. military starts giving all recruits intelligence tests with culturally biased questions. Eighty-nine percent of Black recruits are labeled "morons" (Yerkes, 1921). These tests serve as the foundation for later standardized tests like the Scholastic Aptitude Test (SAT).

1925–1975:

- Belief in eugenics and biological differences based on race/ethnicity continues. For example, psychologist Raymond Cattell writes about the evils of "mixture of blood between racial groups" (Cattell, 1933, p. 155). He continues to publish this opinion at least through the 1990s (e.g., Cattell, 1972).

- Several Black psychologists publish studies that counter the results from previously published White psychologists. These studies are largely discounted or ignored (Guthrie, 2004).

- Several prominent psychologists participate in explicitly racist groups such as those supporting the Nazi agenda and White nationalists (cf. Jackson & Winston, 2021). Others argue in favor of keeping public schools segregated by race (Winston, 1998).

- In 1968, the Association of Black Psychologists is created. Seventy-five Black psychologists resign membership in the APA, calling for the organization to stop endorsing racist standardized tests (Nelson, 1968). The APA responds by saying any problems are due to misuse of the tests, not the tests themselves.

1975–Present Day:

- Two Chicana Studies professors publish a book arguing that very little research has been done on counseling techniques specifically validated within communities of color (Vásquez & Gold, 1981). Similarly, another paper notes that Puerto Rican and Black individuals are more likely to be diagnosed with mental illnesses than people from other ethnicities (Rogler, 1983).

- A paper published in 1988 reviews over 150 studies comparing White, Black, and Asian participants (Rushton, 1988). Some conclusions are that Asian people are the most restrained and highest achieving, while Black people are the most sexual and criminal. The author notes that these conclusions are often based on biased methodologies and interpretations, perpetuating stereotypes.

- In 1998, psychologist Glayde Whitney writes the foreword to the autobiography of KKK leader David Duke. Whitney writes that the "truth" about racial differences has been suppressed by "organized Jewry."

- By the year 2000, people of color make up 26.3% of the U.S. population but only 5.8% of APA's members. By 2017, White people make up 60% of APA membership (APA, 2017).

- From 1974 to 2018, only 5% of editors of the top six professional psychology journals have been people of color (Cummings & Cummings, 2022).

Diverse Voices in Psychology

Well, that was depressing—especially since it only focused on one form of prejudice (racism) within psychology.

But the point of acknowledging the bias is that we have to admit problems if we want to do better. We all want to do better. Despite these significant challenges, inspiring pioneers overcame systemic discrimination by becoming leaders, publishing papers, and participating in professional organizations. Such representations matter; seeing people who look like us makes us feel welcome and validated (Hewer, 2015). For example, college students who feel like they belong, either within their major or within college overall, are more likely to persist through graduation (Tinto, 2017).

If implicit biases in psychology as a field seep into intro to psychology courses, it might hurt marginalized students who don't feel that they belong. Junior and senior psychology majors at one university reviewed a list of 42 pioneers in psychology that included 21 women and 9 people of color (Cramblet Alvarez et al., 2019). This rising generation of psychologists were much more likely to recognize the names of White men on the list. This means that most curricula are emphasizing the names you saw earlier in this chapter, such as Wundt, James, and Freud.

Let's emphasize just a few examples of some of the other important voices, who don't always get the recognition they deserve.

Yūjirō Motora

One of the first people to bring psychology to Japan was Yūjirō Motora (1858–1912). After a childhood in Japan, he earned degrees at Boston University and at Johns Hopkins University before returning home and becoming a professor at the University of Tokyo. Motora studied physiological psychology and published work on sensation and perception with G. Stanley Hall in the very first edition of *The American Journal of Psychology* (Hall & Motora, 1887). He translated important writings by Wilhelm Wundt and William James to give them a broader audience, despite personally disagreeing with some of their conclusions.

Yūjirō Motora (1858–1912).

He is also known for his own unique contributions. He created the first scientific psychology lab in Japan (Sato & Sato, 2005). As a practitioner of Zen Buddhism, Motora challenged the idea that students should accept whatever their teachers said. Instead, he argued that students should interpret what was important themselves. He also published ideas about how religion and science can be complementary friends, not enemies (Motora, 1905).

Perhaps most important, some of his research focused on troubled schoolchildren. Instead of blaming or giving up on them, he recognized and described challenges that would later be identified as attention-deficit/hyperactivity disorder (ADHD) (Takeda et al., 2015).

Mary Whiton Calkins (1863–1930).

Mary Whiton Calkins

Mary Whiton Calkins (1863–1930) was born during the American Civil War. She fought hard to study psychology at Harvard—despite a formal policy blocking women from enrolling. She eventually completed all of Harvard's requirements to earn a doctorate, but they still refused to give her one. She became the first woman president of the APA and of the American Philosophical Association. She published four books and over 100 research papers on memory, dreams, and identity. She also established the first psychology laboratory specifically studying women (e.g., Calkins, 1893). She reset expectations about what women could achieve within psychology.

Mamie Phipps Clark (1917–1983) and her husband, Kenneth Clark (1914–2005).
Library of Congress

Mamie Phipps Clark and Kenneth Clark

Mamie Phipps Clark (1917–1983) and Kenneth Clark (1914–2005) were a married African American couple who played an important role in social justice. Phipps Clark's master's thesis started the basic research that influenced one of the most famous Supreme Court cases (Clark & Clark, 1939). The case of *Brown v. Board of Education* ended segregation of public schools—and the justices cited her work as evidence in their decision. She and her husband were the first African Americans to earn PhDs in psychology from Columbia University (see Benjamin & Crouse, 2004).

Their famous "doll studies" vividly demonstrated the harmful effects of internalized racism on children. (You can search YouTube for the visual record of some of their interviews with children, as well as more modern replications.) In these studies, children playing with brown-skinned and white-skinned dolls preferred the white-skinned dolls, even when the children were African American themselves. Kenneth Clark later became the first African American president of the APA.

Robert Lee Williams II (1930–2020).
Reprinted by permission of the Arkansas Black Hall of Fame

Robert Lee Williams II

Robert Lee Williams II (1930–2020) was a leader in establishing the Black Studies department at Washington University and in organizing their African and Afro-American Studies programs. Many other universities followed his lead. Williams devoted many years to criticizing standardized tests, doing research studies establishing that they were culturally biased and that they disadvantaged people without privileged access to education.

Williams is also known for coining the term *Ebonics* (a combination of the words *ebony* and *phonics*), referring to common phrasing and slang terms used by some African Americans (Williams, 1975). He argued that Ebonics should be accepted as a regional dialect just like any other dialect in the country and that using it should not have a negative connotation.

Martha Bernal

Martha Bernal (1931–2001) grew up in Texas with parents who were immigrants from Mexico. When her elementary school banned her from speaking any Spanish, she felt shame about her family and ethnicity (see Vasquez & Lopez, 2002). She didn't let that stop her, though; she became the first Latina woman to earn a PhD in psychology in the United States (from Indiana University Bloomington). After years of struggling to find a university that would hire her as part of the faculty, Bernal got a job at Arizona State University and spent a career devoted to studying identity development and ethnicity in Mexican American children. She helped develop interventions for community resources and groups that served hundreds of children. The APA later gave her a Distinguished Life Achievement Award, and she became the second president of the National Latino Psychological Association.

Martha Bernal (1931–2001).
John Sunderland/Contributor/Denver Post/via Getty Images

Mahzarin Banaji

Born in India, Mahzarin Banaji is an experimental psychologist who has taught at Yale and is currently at Harvard University. She has received numerous recognitions for her work including election to the National Academy of Sciences, the William James Fellow Award from APS (an organization of which she was also president), and APS's Distinguished Scientific Contribution Award. Banaji and colleagues coined the term *implicit bias* to examine forms of discrimination of which we are not aware. These ideas are spelled out in a popular co-authored book *Blindspot: Hidden Biases of Good People*. At present Banaji is focused on public teaching found at www.outsmartingimplicitbias.org.

Mahzarin Banaji.
Courtesy of Mahzarin Banaji

Laura King

Laura King, as part of the LGBTQ+ community, has broken through professional barriers. She became the first woman editor of the *Journal of Personality and Social Psychology: Personality Processes and Individual Differences*, the leading outlet for research on personality psychology. She has published over 100 articles and book chapters on her own work, which investigates individual well-being and happiness, often within the LGBTQ+ community. She promotes positive psychology and how to make meaning from life events, even when (and maybe especially when) we experience difficult times (e.g., King, 2001; King & Smith, 2004). She is a popular professor of psychology producing important work right now.

Laura King.
Courtesy of Laura A. King, PhD

Alette Coble-Temple

Did you know about the Ms. Wheelchair America pageant? In 2016, Alette Coble-Temple, who is a clinical and sport psychologist, earned the title Ms. Wheelchair America, where she spent a year advocating across the United States for "PRIDE - Parental Rights Include Disability Equality!" In her role as faculty member and program director, she embraces her cerebral palsy, especially her "CP accent," to transform the perception of disability within society and dismantle ableism across academia, healthcare, and legal systems. She also uses her clinical expertise to assist the state of California in determining parole eligibility for convicted individuals. Additionally, she routinely serves in leadership positions on APA boards and committees connected to advancing women's rights, and she frequently delivers keynote addresses at conventions and business trainings on disability research, policy, law, and counseling.

Alette Coble-Temple.
Reprinted by permission of Rick Guidotti

Building a Better Future

Now, we need to do better. How?

The American Psychological Association started by sincerely apologizing and admitting its mistakes of the past. Resolutions have now been passed that formalize how the field is explicitly working to improve. The APA is implementing these tactics in part through grant funding of over a million dollars to support the effort (APA, 2022). In short, grants prioritize scholarship that

- promotes research on cultural diversity and education about systemic prejudice,

- provides training and opportunities for students of all backgrounds in terms of graduate school and career paths (such as being editors for scientific journals, support for new professors, etc.),

- prioritizes efforts to address diversity in clinical and health practices (including trauma-informed mental health care), and

- shares data and progress on improvements.

Psychology undeniably has a checkered past. Though we can't change the past, we can learn from it, and the field is honestly trying to do better.

Sage Vantage   Practice what you learn in **Knowledge Check 1.3**

HOW TO USE THIS BOOK

? Have You Ever Wondered?
1.4 How should I use this book?

>> **LO 1.4**   **Analyze how the ideas in this book can relate to you, personally.**

Are you curious about how psychology applies to you?

We wrote every chapter with three objectives: to stimulate, satisfy, and enhance your curiosity about human behavior. In every chapter, you'll see a table on the first page with two columns. Column 1 shows curiosity questions we hope you ask (or have already asked about human nature), and column 2 matches those questions with specific learning objectives in the chapter. The rows in the starting table tell you how many major sections you'll see in that chapter (one row per major section).

We bring the material to life through storytelling. At the start of each chapter, you'll be introduced to a narrative—some fictional, some nonfictional, some theoretical—that will carry you through from start to finish. We conclude with a summary of the main ideas, followed by some critical thinking questions. Your instructor might use these to help you apply what you've learned, or we encourage you to ponder them yourself.

Beyond these basics, how do we hope you use this book?

Four Features

Don't skip the features.

We specifically designed them to help you experience and achieve all five of the APA Introductory Psychology Initiative goals. Sure, each chapter's main content is like your meal at a feast; it's what most introductory books cover. But this book offers you a figurative dessert with the four special features we're excited to share with you.

Feature 1 is the *Spotlight on Research Methods*. You'll learn about research designs and statistical analyses in the very next chapter (Chapter 2). But remember from Figure 1.1 that research methods are the foundation of our science, so we remind you of that importance throughout. Each chapter takes a deep dive into one or two studies to explain not just the results, but *how* we know what we know.

Feature 2 is *Psychology and Our Curious World*. Do you like movies about superheroes and supervillains? What's your favorite type of music or literature? Psychology should come alive for you both as you observe your own life and when you relax with popular culture. Several of your authors are dedicated fans of blockbuster franchises (Marvel Cinematic Universe vs. DC Universe? The Mandalorian vs. Boba Fett?), and we want to show you how to find psychology everywhere you look.

Next, check out Feature 3: *What's My Score?* If you enjoy Buzzfeed quizzes, we think you'll love taking this survey in each chapter. These show you a real self-report questionnaire that's been developed by qualified psychologists to measure a personality trait or another variable relevant to each chapter. By filling them out, you'll not only have a better understanding of how researchers measure these concepts in real studies but also be better able to apply the ideas to yourself.

Finally, Feature 4 is the *Career Corner*. Lots of people get excited about psychology when they take an introductory course, but they're not clear what career options exist beyond therapists or counselors. The *Career Corner* features real people who majored in psychology and went on to get a wide variety of jobs immediately after graduating—*without* going to graduate school. Being a counselor and/or going to graduate school is a fantastic aspiration, but there are so many more options to consider. This feature might help you brainstorm and find your own passion.

Applying Psychology to You

Be curious (please).

Even if you never take another psychology course, psychology is everywhere around you. Applying each concept throughout this book will help you both do better in terms of your grade (yay!), but it will also help you answer many of life's questions about human interactions, everyday decisions, mistakes we make along the way, and how we overcome obstacles. The next time you wonder, "Why did they do that?" we hope you'll turn to one of the chapters in this book.

We could spend a lot more time in this opening chapter talking to you about why psychology matters and about its history—but we don't want to waste your time. We want to get to the good stuff, and we're going to assume that if you're reading this, you're already hooked. So let's get started. ●

CHAPTER SUMMARY

Learning Objectives Summary

1.1   What is psychology?

>> LO 1.1   Define psychology and explain the American Psychological Association's Introductory Psychology Initiative.

Psychology is the scientific study of mental processes and behaviors. The American Psychological Association (APA) is the leading professional organization in North America, and the Introductory Psychology Initiative suggests that initial courses to the field emphasize research methods, integrative themes, and five "pillars" or major subfields: biological, cognitive, developmental, social/personality psychology, and mental/physical health.

1.2   How has psychology grown and changed over time?

>> LO 1.2   Explain important historical figures and approaches to psychological inquiry.

Many people consider Wilhelm Wundt to be the "founder" of psychology; he started the first scientific lab devoted to human sensation and perception in Germany in the late 1800s. Other important people in the history of psychology include Edward Titchener, William James, Ivan Pavlov, Sigmund Freud, John Watson, Kurt Lewin, Carl Rogers, and Daniel Kahneman (their work is discussed in future chapters).

1.3   How has diversity helped psychology?

>> LO 1.3   Discuss the history of prejudice in psychology and identify key diverse voices in the field over time.

Note that all the people listed in the previous section were White men. The APA has acknowledged years of systemic prejudice, including racism and sexism. Examples of important pioneers in helping advance diversity in psychology are Yūjirō Motora, Mary Whiton Calkins, Mamie Phipps Clark and Kenneth Clark, Robert Lee Williams II, Martha Bernal, Mahzarin Banaji, Laura King, and Alette Coble-Temple. Their work is very briefly summarized in this section.

1.4   How should I use this book?

>> LO 1.4   Analyze how the ideas in this book can relate to you, personally.

The APA provides grant funding to help research efforts devoted to improving the global community through scientific inquiry, ending systemic prejudice, and promoting equality.

This book believes in the same goals. Each chapter highlights curiosity and storytelling, including use of four special features (*Spotlight on Research Methods, Psychology in Your Curious World, What's My Score?* and *Career Corner*). The material will be more memorable if you apply it to your own life.

CRITICAL THINKING QUESTIONS

1.   Go to https://www.apa.org/about/division to learn more about the APA subdivisions. Choose three of the divisions you find particularly interesting and click on the links provided by the website to investigate details. Then, share at least two things you learned about each division you picked. Why do you find these divisions interesting or important to psychology? Can you think of any divisions not currently on the list you think will be added in the future?

2.   Consider the timeline of the history of psychology shown in Figure 1.3. Besides wars, think of at least two important national or international events that occurred between 1870 and present day that might have influenced culture and/or scientific thinking in psychology. Explain how each event may have had an impact on psychological theory or research.

3.   Pick three of the people listed as influential in the history of psychology from this chapter (make sure at least one is from the "diverse voices" section). Find three additional pieces of information about each person's life or contribution to psychology. Then, find one person not listed in this chapter and discuss why they are also important to the growth of psychology over time.

4.   Look again at the five goals the APA identified for introductory psychology courses. Rank order the goals in terms of how important they are for you, personally, and for what you hope to get out of this book and/or course. Explain why you put the goals in the order you did.

American Psychological
   Association, 3
Behaviorist approach, 12
Biological approach, 11
Cognitive approach, 13
Functionalism, 11
Humanistic approach, 13

Introductory Psychology Initiative, 5
Psychodynamic approach, 12
Psychology, 3
Sociocultural approach, 13
Structuralism, 11
Wilhelm Wundt, 9

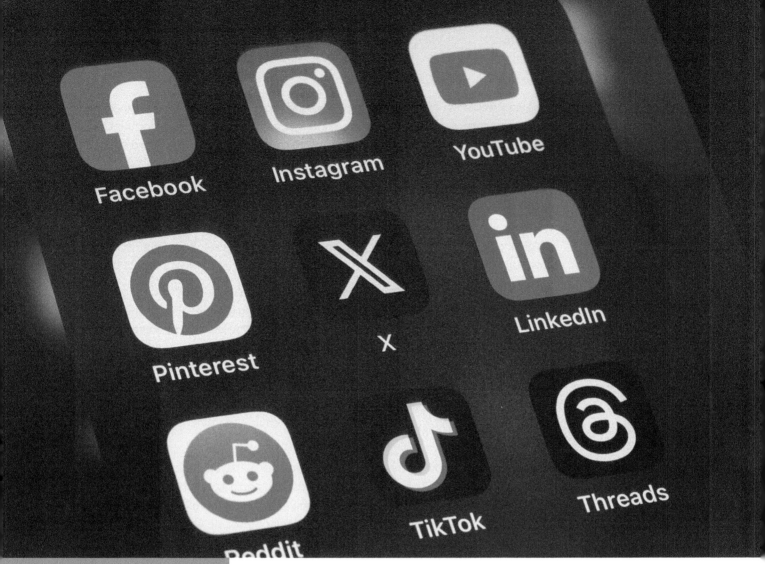

iStock.com/Kenneth Cheung

2

The Science of Psychology

Research Methods and Statistics

Is social media ruining the world?

If it is, how would we know? Psychology's methods and statistics empower us to find out. We (your authors) use social media and are willing to bet that many of you taking this course also use at least one form of it. But is social media making our lives better, or worse?

There must be some benefits, or we wouldn't spend so much time posting and scrolling through the apps. In fact, research shows that social media helps people keep up with trends, read the news, share opinions and photos with friends and family, find communities of people with similar interests, and indulge in hours of distraction when we just don't feel like getting our homework done (or grading papers; e.g., Khan et al., 2014; Pinter et al., 2021; Uhls et al., 2017).

But many people worry about social media's potential negative side effects, ranging from car accidents, cyberbullying, gambling, and even promoting terrorism (Hashash et al., 2019; Juergensmeyer, 2017; Khan et al., 2014; Pinter et al., 2021; Uhls et al., 2017; Weimann, 2016). People with high levels of anxiety also worry about how they use social media, sometimes worrying about if they're addicted (Bhandarkar et al., 2021; Bowden-Green et al., 2021; Praveen et al., 2020; Zhong et al., 2021). This list of anxieties could be a lot longer, but you get the idea. Research indicates that social media can have both positive and negative effects. But it's unclear whether using social media causes these negative outcomes or if these variables simply are related for other reasons.

How do scientists know all this information—and how do psychological studies work in general? You can form your own opinion about social media, or anything else, with more ease and confidence when you understand research on both sides of a debate. Even if you never do research yourself, being a good consumer of research will help you know that your opinions are based on solid, scientific evidence. It will also help you see how hard psychologists work to make sure psychological ideas are tested with real data from real people, all over the world.

After reading this chapter, you will get answers to several questions you've been curious about:

Have You Ever Wondered?

2.1   How is psychology a science?

2.2   How do psychologists design studies?

2.3   What are correlations?

2.4   How are the results of experiments analyzed?

2.5   How can I tell if a study is done well?

2.6   What is the open science movement?

2.7   How do ethics guide psychological research?

Learning Objectives

LO 2.1   Explain how the scientific method is used in psychological science.

LO 2.2   Compare and contrast research methodologies.

LO 2.3   Explain how we show relationships between variables and why correlation doesn't imply causation.

LO 2.4   Compare and contrast t-tests and ANOVAs.

LO 2.5   Summarize how studies can be analyzed for quality.

LO 2.6   Explain how the open science movement is addressing the replication crisis in psychology.

LO 2.7   Describe ethical considerations for research with humans and animals.

ELEMENTS OF THE SCIENTIFIC METHOD

>> **LO 2.1**   **Explain how the scientific method is used in psychological science.**

How is psychology a science?

Your high school memories of science and scientists may include learning about rocks and minerals, perhaps using a Bunsen burner or a microscope, and applying equations that describe force and acceleration. You might be familiar with famous scientists like the pioneering chemist Marie Curie, or maybe Katherine Johnson, the lunar landing mathematician whose life was dramatized in the film *Hidden Figures*. Or maybe a documentary from astrophysicist and science communicator Neil DeGrasse Tyson stirred your interest in the cosmos. How well does psychology fit with these other sciences?

? Have You Ever Wondered?
2.1 How is psychology a science?

(a)
Bettmann/Contributor/Bettmann/
via Getty Images

(b)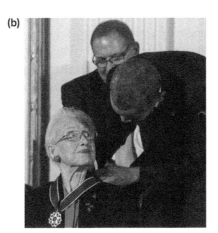
NICHOLAS KAMM/AFP/via Getty Images

(c)
Amanda Edwards/Getty Images
Entertainment/via Getty Images

(a) Two-time Nobel Prize–winning physicist and chemist Marie Curie said, "Nothing in life is to be feared, it is only to be understood. Now is the time to understand more, so that we may fear less."

(b) Katherine Johnson, lunar landing mathematician, noted, "I tried to go to the root of the question."

(c) Neil DeGrasse Tyson, astrophysicist and science communicator, explained, "Knowing how to think empowers you far beyond knowing what to think."

Katherine Johnson had to understand the changing gravitational mathematics of outer space to calculate the lunar landing. The scientific approach to physics and math is objective—and gravity never gets bored, misunderstands instructions, or lies on surveys about personal needs. In contrast, the science of psychology is challenging because understanding human and animal thought and behavior requires essential considerations for ethics. In addition, many abstract ideas—like love and prejudice—can be defined and measured in a wide variety of ways. Some psychologists in the past didn't use scientific methods by today's standards.

For example, Sigmund Freud was an original thinker and highly influential. But while Freud's ideas "contain most interesting psychological suggestions," observed the science philosopher Karl Popper, they were not presented "in a testable form" (Popper, 1963, pp. 33–39). Modern psychologists pride themselves on doing things differently. Theories need to be stringently tested multiple times before we can start to feel confident that we understand something. Doing scientific studies with humans and animals is, in a lot of ways, more challenging than mixing acids together or measuring how quickly an apple falls from a tree. People are complicated, and any research must be ethical. How does all of that happen?

The Cycle of Science

Science never ends—it's a cycle that constantly evolves.

Any discipline or field of study—physics, chemistry, biology, psychology—can only claim to be a science if those who practice it use the **scientific method**. It's a general approach to forming and testing ideas using an objective framework. The scientific method uses evidence to determine whether an idea has merit, needs to be changed and refined, or should just be discarded altogether. It's a framework that proposes ideas tested with methods that are *reliable*, *observable*, *testable*, and *valid*. (Memory helper: Think of them as the ROTV requirements.)

The scientific method relies on "ROTV" evidence to evaluate how a hypothesis needs to be changed, refined, or rejected in service of the next, better question. It's a series of steps, displayed in Figure 2.1.

The scientific method usually starts when people perceive some pattern and become curious. That curiosity leads to a **hypothesis**, a specific statement about the study's expected outcome. For example, imagine a professor notices that some students seem to be checking social media during class instead of taking notes—and that those same students are struggling with their grade (a pattern has been observed). The professor forms the hypothesis that the more time students spend on social media in class, the worse their grades are.

Once a hypothesis is generated, the scientist can choose some way to use the ROTV requirements to test the hypothesis. There are dozens of different ways that might happen, and many of those options will be explained in this chapter. For now, imagine the professor used a survey asking students to estimate how many minutes per hour in class they spend looking at social media (instead of paying attention and taking notes). The professor might then compare each person's estimate with their grade, testing for the hypothesized pattern.

Scientific method: A series of objective steps for empirically testing an idea.

Hypothesis: A specific statement about the expected outcome of a study.

FIGURE 2.1

The Scientific Method

The scientific method starts by noticing interesting patterns and generating hypotheses regarding those patterns. Then, evidence is gathered that either supports or refutes the hypothesis. Those results help us refine hypotheses and keep testing them as we learn more.

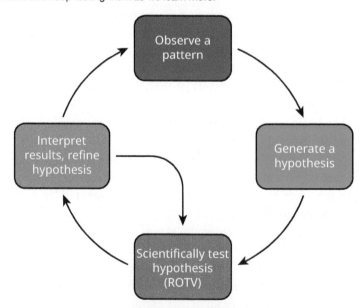

However, even if the data support the hypothesis, the professor won't fully believe it because the class may be a unique case, and there are alternative explanations. If the hypothesis seems right, the professor might want to double- and triple-check with other classes to see if the same pattern holds up. From there, they could keep going by adding to the hypothesis, making it more complicated or focused, or testing it in a variety of ways. That would inspire more research studies—and the process keeps going.

The Path to Precision: Defining and Measuring Constructs

You can't take an X-ray of self-esteem or anxiety.

Psychological concepts are often abstract and invisible; these features make the path to scientific precision more challenging. On the other hand, gravity is also invisible—but that never stopped Katherine Johnson from measuring its effects. So, imagine this hypothesis: Greater use of social media is associated with greater anxiety. That's a good hypothesis, and many studies have found evidence supporting it (e.g., Dobrean & Păsărelu, 2016; Keles et al., 2020; Vannucci et al., 2017). But what exactly is meant by "anxiety"? For that matter, what counts as "use of social media"?

Science requires precision. Hypotheses identify variables of interest, and in psychology, these variables might be concepts like anxiety, personality, intelligence, love, conformity, and so on. Abstract concepts or variables of interest like these are called **constructs**, which is a useful term because it reminds us that we have built a concept (like a construction crew) into something we can measure using the ROTV requirements.

The first step in building the construct is performing **operationalization**, which is specifying how we are going to define and measure a particular variable.

Researchers might operationalize anxiety differently:

- One researcher might measure "anxiety" through physiological measures like heart rate and sweaty palms after asking a person to imagine being rejected by friends.

- Another might use surveys or checklists of anxiety symptoms, such as nervousness or sleep difficulties.

- A third approach might test how well people can concentrate under time pressure by asking them to remember lists of random letters or words.

If you think these multiple ways of testing anxiety complicate things, then you are correct. In a paper that reviewed the connections between social media use and anxiety, researchers noted that these different methods made it more complicated and difficult to know what to believe (Keles et al., 2020).

However, it's not necessarily a bad thing to rely on various definitions and measurements. If different measurement approaches find similar connections between social media use and anxiety, then we are more confident that the connection is real. It's like the old example of people who can't see—they can only feel—trying to describe an elephant. One is holding the tail, another the trunk, and a third an enormous foot; they all get different impressions of the same animal. They have good reasons to disagree, but each of their measurements or observations have merit. Only by combining their information do we form an accurate overall picture.

When you start doing your own studies, one of your first jobs is to operationalize your variables. Once you have established the hypothesis, the variables, and how to define and measure them, you can select a research methodology.

Construct: An abstract concept or variable within a research study.

Operationalization: Specifying how a construct will be defined and measured in a given study.

TYPES OF RESEARCH

Have You Ever Wondered?
2.2 How do psychologists design studies?

>> **LO 2.2   Compare and contrast research methodologies.**

How do psychologists set up research studies?

You will learn about the many creative ways psychologists test hypotheses during this course. This chapter focuses on the strengths and weaknesses of four common methods: archival studies, naturalistic observation, surveys, and experiments. There will be examples of each in this chapter, but as you progress through the course, consider the methodology chosen by the researchers and whether it was the best choice—and why.

The options covered here are summarized for you in Table 2.1. Note that in addition to these specific choices, researchers also have to decide whether to do a quantitative or qualitative design. Again, there are advantages and disadvantages to each choice. *Qualitative* research is usually (but not always) done with surveys or interviews, and the results are in nonnumerical form. The researcher will identify patterns or themes across people's answers. A big advantage of qualitative designs is that it honors the personal voices and experiences of the participants; it also provides deeper insights into individual lives. But a disadvantage is that the results generally can't be analyzed with most statistics. In contrast, *quantitative* methods are any for which the results are in numerical form—and therefore, patterns can emerge through mathematical, statistical analyses.

Archival Studies

The first option might be the most convenient way to test hypotheses.

Archival studies analyze materials that were originally gathered, produced, or published for some other purpose. Patterns can be observed in newspapers, census data, police reports, college transcripts, and—increasingly—on the Internet. Data for archival studies can be found anywhere that has stored information.

Archival studies: Research using materials originally created for some other purpose, like police records or social media posts.

TABLE 2.1

Pros and Cons of Methodology Options

Archival Studies	Pro: Data are publicly available and usually inexpensive
	Con: Data are limited to what already exists
Naturalistic Observation	Pro: Behavior is authentic and honest
	Con: Reactivity and uncontrolled environment
Surveys	Pro: Large samples can be gathered relatively quickly
	Con: Answers may not be honest; conclusions may be only correlational in nature
Experiments	Pro: Random assignment to condition allows for causal conclusions
	Con: Relatively expensive, time-consuming, and/or slow

Every methodological option has advantages and disadvantages.

Studies on social media commonly use archival data because social media users produce so much material to be analyzed! One study investigated if there was a difference between what men and women posted to Facebook (Park et al., 2016). Do the topics, and even the words, used on status updates differ? They found that girls and women were more likely to post things related to social relationships (such as their close friends and family) and emotions. In contrast, boys and men were more likely to focus on specific activities (like sports or jobs) and objects (like computers).

Another study analyzed posts from college students during a presidential election (Carlisle & Patton, 2013). The researchers examined each profile for 50 different characteristics, such as political opinions or support for a certain candidate. Not surprisingly, political posts increased as the election got closer. A more interesting finding was that having more online "friends" predicted fewer political postings. Keep in mind that even when a study answers one question, it may create others such as: Why might having more friends discourage political posts? Every study can inspire more.

There are pros and cons to archival studies. One big advantage is that the data sources already exist and are ready to be analyzed (often, for free!). But a major disadvantage is that the information available is limited, and its availability can't be controlled. So, researchers often also consider other methodology options.

Naturalistic Observation

Have you ever sat and done some "people watching" over a cup of coffee? **Naturalistic observation** is a bit like that, but if you also systematically recorded the behaviors you witnessed. This technique observes people in their natural environments—where they would have been anyway. We can observe littering in parking lots, how shoppers navigate the aisles in grocery stores, and how much time men versus women need to complete ATM transactions. Anywhere public will do. Researchers choose a particular spot where they can test a hypothesis or research question in an authentic way, because (ideally) the people being watched have no idea they're part of the study at all.

Naturalistic observation: Watching and recording people's behaviors where they would have happened anyway, but for research purposes.

One observational study offered some archival value after the COVID-19 pandemic. Researchers wanted to observe hand hygiene among medical students (Kwok et al., 2015). To observe their behavior, the scientists videotaped 26 medical students in a classroom and watched how often they touched their faces, which was an average of 23 times per hour. Of those times, 44% of the touches were to mucous membrane areas of the face: eyes, nose, and mouth. Observation is important here, because it is likely many of the students had no idea how much face-touching they were doing—so asking them to report it in a survey wouldn't have produced accurate results.

A clever example of naturalistic observation and social media studied how romantic couples act when one of them starts "phubbing" the other in public (Franz, 2014). What's phubbing? It's "phone snubbing"—when the person you're with is more interested in their phone than they are in talking and looking at you. Rude, right? To study this, the researcher walked through local farmers markets looking for people who appeared to be couples—then waited until one or the other started using their phone for (apparently) checking or posting to social media.

How would the other person react? Three common responses were observed:

(1) Indifference: Ignoring what was happening and looking away.

(2) Collaboration: Participating by also looking at the device and talking about whatever was on the screen.

(3) Assertiveness: This included purposely walking away to show annoyance or even taking the device away from the other person.

Women were more likely to collaborate; men were more likely to show indifference or be assertive about not liking what was happening. Note a disadvantage to this study: The people who shop at a farmers market might act differently in that situation than in others (say, at home). And the results might vary among people with different backgrounds, experiences, cultures, ages, and so on. Maybe behavior at farmers markets in California are different from those in Ohio. Researchers can't control all of these variables, so it's important to know the limitations.

There are both advantages and disadvantage to naturalistic observation. We get to see how people really act in the "real world." Their behaviors are authentic and honest because they don't realize they're being watched. In addition to the problems noted in the previous paragraph, there are also potential ethical problems because participants have not given their permission to being observed for research purposes.

Here's another problem: What if the people being observed *do* suspect that they are being observed? **Reactivity** occurs when people change their behavior when they believe they're being watched—so the behavior is no longer authentic. How can researchers get around the problem of reactivity? **Participant observation** is one solution; it's when researchers, like spies, go "undercover" pretending to be part of the natural environment. In the phubbing study, they chose the farmers market because it was a busy place and easy to remain unobtrusive (Franz, 2014). I'm not watching you; I'm just looking for good deals on pickles and berries!

Reactivity: When people change their behaviors because they realize they're being watched.

Participant observation: A technique used during naturalistic observation where researchers covertly disguise themselves as people belonging in an environment.

(a)

(b)

In the movie *21 Jump Street* (a), two young police officers go undercover pretending to be high school students. In *Imperium* (b), Daniel Radcliffe's character works for the FBI to infiltrate a White supremacist group. If any of them had been psychologists doing research with this undercover technique, it would have been called participant observation.

COLUMBIA PICTURES/Album/Newscom; ATOMIC FEATURES/GREEN-LIGHT INT/GRINSTONE ENT/SCULPTOR MEDIA/Album T51/Newscom

Surveys

Just ask.

Probably the most common research methodology in psychology is the **survey**, where information is collected as participants answer direct questions. Surveys can be an efficient method to collect data, especially if constructs are measured in a reliable, valid way. Surveys are often the only way to access people's private thoughts and behaviors. If the survey is convenient (for example, online) and people are compensated for their time (maybe with money or extra credits in a class), then data can be gathered from hundreds of people in just a few hours.

This course is full of examples of survey studies. But to stay with the social media theme, consider a study that explored whether posting "selfies" to social media signals a narcissistic personality (Barry et al., 2017). The researchers operationalized narcissism by asking 128 college students to rate themselves on statements such as "I am apt to show off when I get the chance" on a scale of 1 to 7, with 1 being *not true at all* and 7 being *very true*. This particular scale measured both "grandiose narcissism" (which involves exploiting others; the individual enhances how others see them) and "vulnerable narcissism" (which involves constantly seeking validation from others).

Survey: Asking questions directly to participants in order to collect information.

Participants also gave researchers access to their Instagram accounts so researchers could count and analyze their posted selfies.

Results indicated that people who scored high in grandiose narcissism (exploiting others) tended to post more selfies showing them surrounded by friends and having fun (Barry et al., 2017). People who scored high in vulnerable narcissism (wanting validation) tended to post selfies highlighting their attractive physical appearance. However, before you label yourself a narcissist for posting a selfie, their general finding was that almost everyone on Instagram posts selfies. Again, the research cycle generates new questions further research could explore: Does Instagram tend to attract narcissists?

There's a catch, or a disadvantage to surveys, and it's a big one. For the research to be valid, people must be honest. Social desirability influences people to respond with what they think is socially expected or what they think the researcher wants to hear. The "just ask" approach that makes surveys convenient assumes that people can and will tell the truth about themselves. But people often fib or stretch the truth when it might make them look bad.

On the other hand, don't underestimate the creativity of a motivated researcher! To counter social desirability, researchers sometimes embed "liar scales" in surveys. These items typically ask people to self-report common but socially disapproved behaviors—like littering or gossiping. Since many people do these things, not admitting to them may be a sign that people are stretching the truth to make themselves look good. So, would you admit to these behaviors on a scientific survey? You can try it yourself in the *What's My Score?* feature. This time, you'll have to simply choose "true" or "false" for each statement to get your score.

Social desirability: The tendency for participants to provide dishonest survey answers because they want to look good to the researchers or to themselves.

WHAT'S MY SCORE?

Measuring Social Desirability

Instructions: Social desirability scales are sometimes included in survey research to see if people are being honest. This scale includes several statements concerning personal attitudes and traits.

Read each item and decide whether the statement is true or false as it pertains to you.

Circle "T" for true statements and "F" for false statements.

T F   1. Before voting I thoroughly investigate the qualifications of all the candidates.

T F   2. I never hesitate to go out of my way to help someone in trouble.

T F   3. I sometimes feel resentful when I don't get my way.

T F   4. I am always careful about my manner of dress.

T F   5. My table manners at home are as good as when I eat out in a restaurant.

T F   6. I like to gossip at times.

T F   7. I can remember "playing sick" to get out of something.

T F   8. There have been occasions when I took advantage of someone.

T F   9. I'm always willing to admit it when I make a mistake.

T F   10. There have been occasions when I felt like smashing things.

T F   11. I am always courteous, even to people who are disagreeable.

T F   12. At times I have really insisted on having things my own way.

Scoring: Give yourself 1 point if you said TRUE for 1, 2, 4, 5, 9, or 11. Then, give yourself 1 point if you said FALSE for 3, 6, 7, 8, 10, or 12. Then, add your points. Higher scores indicate more attempts to manage your impression on others, or a higher tendency toward socially desirable responding on self-report scales. This means you might change your answers in psychology studies to look good to the researchers (or maybe to yourself). ●

Source: Crowne and Marlowe (1960).

Experiments: Research designs in which researchers compare two or more groups to see how groups differ by the end of the study.

Quasi-experiments: Research designs that compare preexisting groups to see how or if they differ in response to something in the study.

True experiments: Research designs that compare groups created by the researcher using random assignment.

Random assignment: Putting participants into experimental groups by a purely chance method (like flipping a coin).

Experiments

Don't psychologists do experiments?

Yes! In fact, for many scientists in psychology, experiments are the preferred method of research. **Experiments** are research designs in which two or more groups are compared to see how they differ by the end of the study. In psychology, there are generally two kinds of experiments—quasi and true.

Quasi-Experiments

Quasi-experiments compare preexisting groups. Quasi-experiments are necessary when researchers want to compare groups in interesting ways but can't create the groups because they have already formed themselves. If you compared boys to girls, or psychology majors to education majors, or basketball players to tennis players, you'd potentially be doing a quasi-experiment. In quasi-experiments, each group usually goes through the same experimental procedure, and the researchers are interested in whether people in the groups respond differently compared to each other.

For example, one study wanted to discover what influences children's ability to identify fake news on social media. The researchers compared how well children from two different countries—the Netherlands and Romania—could detect fake news on social media (Dumitru, 2020). Researchers showed schoolchildren fake websites from the environmental group Greenpeace supposedly fundraising to save fictitious endangered animals like the tree octopus and the jackalope. Few children from either country realized the animals were not real, which suggests a lack of critical thinking when scrolling through social media. Here, the two groups (children from each country) responded similarly to each other.

The problem with quasi-experiments is that even if the two groups *do* respond differently, it's not always clear exactly *why*. If children in two countries are different, for example, is it due to their culture, or the different kinds of TV shows and advertising they see, or food, or religion, or maybe how their school system is structured? There are so many variables involved, we can never be sure—which is why we need true experiments.

"Rare photo of the endangered jackalope!" If you saw this photo on your social media feed, would you realize it was fake?

Found Image Holdings Inc/Contributor/ Corbis Historical/via Getty Images

True Experiments

True experiments help definitively answer the "why" question by comparing two or more groups that have been made equivalent at the start of the experiment. They are usually made equivalent by **random assignment**, which first involves identifying everyone who will be in the experiment and then gives each participant an equal chance of being put in any of the experimental conditions. Flipping a coin would work; so would pulling names out of a hat. Usually, we just ask a computer to do the job.

In a true experiment, assuming there is a large sample, the people in the different groups are close to identical. *Then,* each group goes through a different experience that's controlled by the researcher (their experimental "condition"). In pharmaceutical trials, one group gets the real drug while the other group gets a *placebo*, or a treatment the participant believes is real but is not. All participants are "blind," or unaware of, their experimental condition, which means they have no idea which group they're in. Later, the researcher will compare the groups' symptoms and side effects to help determine whether the drug was effective.

A true experiment about social media investigated how people evaluate each other's profiles (Antheunis & Schouten, 2011). The researchers created fictitious profiles that differed in terms of (1) how many "friends" the fake person had, (2) how physically attractive those "friends" were, and (3) whether the posts on the profile were positive or negative. Over 500 high school students were randomly assigned to read just one of the 12 fictional profiles. The results showed that the high schoolers didn't care about how many friends someone had, but their ratings of the fictional person in the profile went up if the person had conventionally more attractive friends and positive posts on their profile.

Note that there are two ways you could set up a true experiment. The example just described is what researchers call *between-participants* designs. This means that you have multiple groups, and each group receives a different treatment. For example, half of the participants view and react to social media Profile A while the other half view and react to social media Profile B. There is another option, which comes in handy if you have a limited number of participants.

You could instead do a *within-participants* design. Here, you have a single group of people who experience multiple treatments or conditions—then you compare their reaction to each condition. You might have the same group of people first react to Profile A, then react to Profile B. It's still an experiment, just all within the same group. Here, you'd have a few other things to worry about, such as whether the viewing order would matter in forming impressions of profiles. So, you might want to randomly assign some people to see Profile A first while others see Profile B first. Now, the random assignment is about *order* of conditions for each person, instead of *which* condition each person will experience.

Either way, experiments allow for comparisons between and across conditions that no other methodology can provide. They are the only method that allows researchers to make cause-and-effect conclusions.

Experimental Groups and Variable Types

You already know that experiments compare groups or conditions. Many (but not all) true experiments compare two specific types of groups. In the **control group**, participants are essentially left alone to serve as a neutral or baseline group. In drug trials, those who get the placebo are the control group. In contrast, in the **experimental group**, the participants get some intervention or change in the environment. In drug trials, those who receive the actual drug are the experimental group.

There are also different types of variables. The **independent variable** is the influencing variable at the *beginning* of a study that, according to the hypothesis, may cause the two (or more) groups to differ from each other by the end of the study. It is what is changed and controlled in a study. The independent variable is what differentiates Group 1 from Group 2 (and Group 3, and so on). In a drug experiment, the independent variable is whether the participant receives the drug or the placebo. In the social media experiment described earlier, the independent variables were the number of friends, attractiveness of friends, and positive or negative posts on social media profiles they viewed (so, three independent variables). They are called "independent" because they cannot be influenced by the other variables in the study.

Control group: A neutral or baseline group in a study, used as a comparison to what is being tested.

Experimental group: The group (or groups) in a study that experiences an intervention or change, to see how that change affects the participants.

Independent variable: A variable that's manipulated at the beginning of the study, creating groups that will be compared to each other.

TABLE 2.2

Independent and Dependent Variables in Experiments

STUDY BASICS	INDEPENDENT VARIABLE	DEPENDENT VARIABLE
Students listen to either classical or rock music while they study, to see if music affects their memory on a test later.	Type of music (classical or rock)	Performance on the memory test
People write an essay about either death or puppies, then rate how much anger they feel.	Essay topic (death or puppies)	Level of anger
Children watch a commercial with dolls or with trucks, then are rated on how aggressively they play with clay and crayons.	Commercial topic (dolls or trucks)	Level of aggression
Sports fans see images of athletes wearing black jerseys or green jerseys and are asked to rate how well they expect each player to do that year.	Jersey color (black or green)	Expectations of players' performance

Dependent variable: The measured outcome at the end of a study, to see how the groups in an experiment had different results.

The **dependent variable** is the outcome at the *end* of the study that is measured. It's what the hypothesis suggests will be the result of being randomly assigned to a particular group. The dependent variable in the drug experiment is whether the drug worked. In the social media experiment, the dependent variable is how attractive the participants found the person in the fake profile. It is called a *dependent* variable because it is the outcome that, hypothetically, depends on the participant's group placement (which condition they were in).

Table 2.2 summarizes independent and dependent variables; you will grow more comfortable with these terms as you use and encounter them in each chapter.

Confounding variables: Other explanations for why the outcome of study happened, besides what the researcher is testing.

Finally, **confounding variables** are alternative explanations for the outcomes in an experiment. They are anything that resulted in group differences besides the independent variable. In experiments, it is important to control confounding variables because they confuse the logic of cause–effect that experiments hope to reveal. Quasi-experiments have more confounding variables than true experiments, which is why true experiments are preferred. Ideally, if all the groups in a true experiment really were as equivalent as possible at the start of a study—and the *only* real difference was the independent variable—then any differences in the dependent variable must have been due to experimental condition. At least, that's the goal.

Sage Vantage   Practice what you learn in **Knowledge Check 2.2**

CORRELATIONAL ANALYSES

Have You Ever Wondered?
2.3 What are correlations?

≫ LO 2.3   Explain how we show relationships between variables and why correlation doesn't imply causation.

Do you think that more time on social media is associated with worse grades in college?

Once a study has been designed and the data are gathered, it's time to analyze the results.

Many psychological studies gather all their data from just one group of people. Unlike experiments that compare people in two or more groups, correlational research collects a lot of data from every person in the study, often based on multiple constructs.

For example, one survey asked participants to provide information about their time on social media as well as several other variables related to college life (Nwosu et al., 2020). The researchers found that simply measuring time on a computer didn't have anything to do with college success—because what matters is what people are *doing* on their computer. Time spent on the computer studying or doing homework was fine—but if students were spending that time on social media to procrastinate, then more time on the computer was associated with worse academic performance.

A correlation analysis tests whether two constructs (or variables) you're measuring are systematically tied to each other. Note that with correlations, you don't manipulate anything—you just measure. Knowing the score on one variable makes it possible to predict a score based on the other variable. Most correlational variables are continuous, meaning they're measured on a continuum or range. Let's imagine that both your time on social media and time spent studying have a range of possible data points between 0 and 24 hours per day. Similarly, someone's cumulative GPA could be measured continuously, but this time on the traditional range from 0.0 to 4.0.

Correlation analysis: Statistical analyses testing whether two variables are systematically tied to each other.

Scatterplots

Visualizing a data story can save lives.

Before Francis Galton devised the mathematical formula for a correlation (in 1888), English physician John Snow drew a map showing how two ideas were associated with each other (Figure 2.2) that helped explain London's terrifying cholera epidemic of 1854 (Brody et al., 2000; Stigler, 1989). The map demonstrated that there were more cholera deaths among families living closer to a certain water well on Broad Street. Each dot represents a real person who died after drinking water from that specific well, which helped Londoners realize how cholera was being spread through the community. Though a bunch of dots may seem trivial, don't underestimate the power of a data story effectively told with a well-designed picture, image, or graph.

FIGURE 2.2

John Snow's Map of the Cholera Epidemic

Creation of a map showing locations affected by the cholera epidemic of 1854 in London helped people identify the cause and how the illness was spread through water.

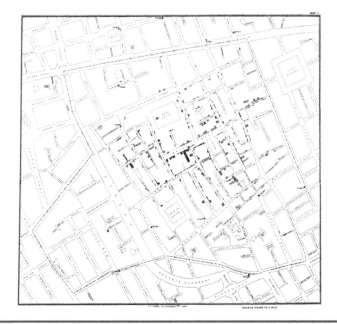

Source: Snow (1854).

Scatterplot: A graph used to show a pattern between two continuous variables (a correlation).

Graphs used to show patterns between two continuous variables are called scatterplots. So, scatterplots are visual representations of a correlation. Figure 2.3 demonstrates a correlational data story framed within a horizontal x-axis and a vertical y-axis. The orange line summarizes the group's overall data story: As study hours increase, so does GPA.

Like John Snow's map, each dot represents two pieces of information about a real person. The line shows a general pattern and is called the "line of best fit." The overall pattern is that more studying is usually associated with better grades. The people far away from the line are called *outliers*, or cases that are substantially different from the overall pattern. Find the person in Figure 2.3 who rarely studies yet has a 3.5 GPA—and then find the student who studies about 25 hours per week to earn similar grades. A visual correlation shows both what is typical and that there are exceptions due to a variety of potentially interesting factors. Creating a scatterplot is usually the first step to correlational analysis.

Positive and Negative Correlations

There are two types of correlations.

Correlations in which both variables move in the same direction are called *positive correlations*. As one goes up, so does the other—and vice versa. For most students, more time studying predicts higher grades (measured as GPA). Positive correlations such as Figure 2.4 display a line rising from the lower left to the upper right. In a *negative correlation,* that line moves downward from upper left to lower right because the two variables move in *opposite* directions. As the hours spent procrastinating on social media increase, GPA goes down (Nwosu et al., 2020).

Correlations can be summarized as a number ranging from negative −1.00 to positive +1.00:

- If every data point falls exactly on the line, then there is "perfect" correlation between the two variables.

FIGURE 2.3 ─────────────────────────────

Sample Scatterplot

In this graph, each dot represents one person. For each person, study hours per week fall on the *x*-axis, and grade point average (GPA) falls on the *y*-axis. By looking at the general pattern, we can determine whether the two variables are correlated.

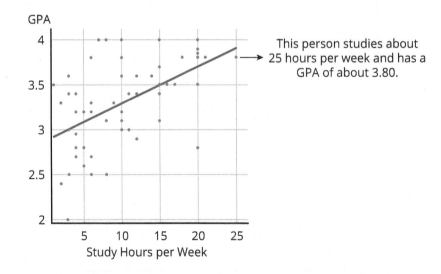

This person studies about 25 hours per week and has a GPA of about 3.80.

- The number summarizing that correlation will be positive if the line is rising upward from left to right and negative if moving downward from left to right.

- As the number gets closer to zero (such as −.01 or +.01), the dots look more like a cloud with no clear pattern—there is no apparent correlation between the two variables.

Figure 2.4 shows examples of how you can think about correlations at different strengths.

A Warning About Correlations and Causation

There are three things to understand when evaluating if two related variables are associated with each other.

Caution 1: *Correlation does not imply causation.* If two things keep happening at the same time, it does not mean that one is causing the other. A third variable could also be the cause. In the case of a student who spends many hours studying and has a very good GPA, both outcomes might have been caused by the student's (1) motivation to do well, (2) level of pressure from parents, (3) amount of enjoyment of class subjects, or (dare we hope) (4) the skill and engagement of talented professors.

FIGURE 2.4

Correlation in Graphs

Correlations always range from –1.00 to +1.00. The sign (positive or negative) indicates whether the two variables move in the same direction or in opposite directions.

The number (from 0.0 to 1.0) tells you how well each data point fits onto a general pattern. If a correlation is zero, it means there is no pattern or association between the two variables.

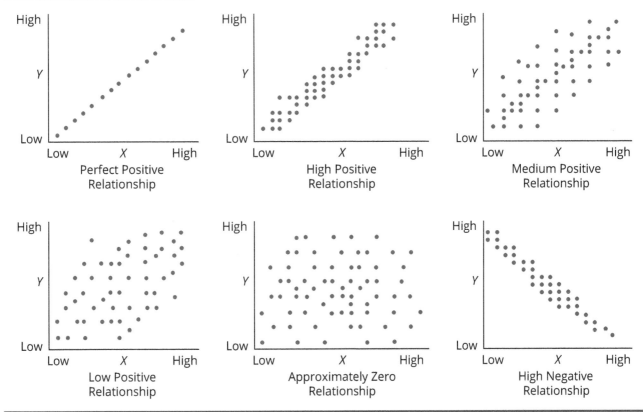

Caution 2: *Cause and effect can occur in either direction.* Sure, it seems logical that if someone spends all their time on social media, that might cause their grades to go down. But it could work in the other direction. Their grades might go down first, which the student finds so discouraging that they then escape into the distracting comforts of social media. In this scenario, poor grades were the cause and more time on social media the effect.

Caution 3: *Spurious correlations are common.* Many millions of things are happening in our world at any given time. Consequently, there are unlimited combinations of spurious, or false, correlations where variables appear related but actually represent meaningless patterns. Tyler Vigen (2015) has some fun with this insight by reporting ridiculous, spurious correlations, such as the correlation between the number of Nicholas Cage films in a given year and how many people drowned in swimming pools the same year ($r = +0.66$), or letters in the final word of a Scripps spelling bee and deaths from venomous spiders that year ($r = +0.81$). It's pretty unlikely these variables are actually tied to each other in any meaningful way, despite relatively high correlations.

Remember—spurious correlations can trick you into believing that outlandish conspiracy theory reflects reality. Two things happening at the same time does not mean that one is causing the other. *You* need to be the critical thinker—sometimes correlations are life-saving clues that can help save lives from terrifying epidemics. Other times, they're just coincidences.

Because of these important cautions, some researchers prefer to set up experimental methods and analyses—the topic of our next section.

Sage Vantage   Practice what you learn in **Knowledge Check 2.3**

EXPERIMENTAL ANALYSES

Have You Ever Wondered?
2.4 How are the results of experiments analyzed?

>> **LO 2.4**   **Compare and contrast *t*-tests and ANOVAs.**

Unlike correlations, true experiments provide solid evidence about cause and effect.

Remember that a true experiment relies on random assignment to groups because it makes each experimental condition equal before the experiment begins. The *only* possible difference in the outcome between competing groups is the independent variable.

Imagine you are conducting an experiment that tests students' multitasking ability by listening to a lecture while browsing their favorite social media. How do you discover whether spending more time on social media during a lecture (the cause, the independent variable) influenced exam scores (the outcome, the dependent variable)?

- Each student will be tested on the content of the lecture at the end of class.

- You recruit 100 students and randomly assign 50 to look at social media for 30 minutes during the lecture, while the other 50 look for 10 minutes.

We have Guinness to thank for the statistic known as the *t*-test.

iStock.com/WaraJenny

You've got the data; now you must analyze the results. But first, let's take a break for a mental beer.

Comparing Two Groups: The *t*-Test Statistic

For the rest of your life, whenever you think of beer, think also of the *t*-test.

Think of Guinness ale, to be specific. You don't have to drink alcohol or like beer to understand why the creation of the *t*-test was a such a powerful industrial secret. The *t*-test is statistical analysis that compares averages and ranges of two groups, to see if they are different from each other. William Sealy Gossett, a chemist and statistician who also happened to be the head brewer at the Guiness brewery in Dublin, Ireland, developed the *t*-test to monitor the quality of morning versus afternoon productions of Guinness without having to sample every keg (Mankiewicz, 2000). It would not be good for Guinness's business if the morning batch tasted different from the afternoon batch. #thanksbeer!

t-test: Statistical analysis that compares the outcomes of two groups, to see if they are different from each other.

There were two critical components to Gossett's statistical invention:

1. The samples of beer each morning and afternoon had to be random (to avoid bias).
2. The number of samples had to be big enough to fairly represent all beer casks Guinness made during a production run.

Since other manufacturers faced similar challenges to quality, Gossett was prohibited from sharing his powerful industrial secret that ensured quality control of the manufacturing process. But he published it anyway, under the anonymous penname of "Student"—and without mentioning beer. Statisticians and some textbooks still refer to it as "Student's *t*." It would be kinder to call it "Gossett's *t*."

Let's go back to your social media and multitasking experiment: Half the class pays attention to social media for 30 minutes, the other half for 10 minutes. The test scores of all participants are visualized in Figure 2.5 and organized into the two

---

FIGURE 2.5

t-Tests and ANOVAs to Compare Groups

One way social scientists look for patterns is by comparing average scores within different groups of participants. When we compare two groups, as here, we use a *t*-test. When we compare three or more groups, we do an analysis of variance, or "ANOVA."

(a)

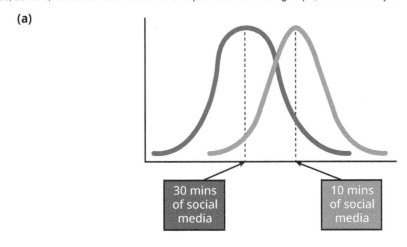

30 mins of social media

10 mins of social media

(b)

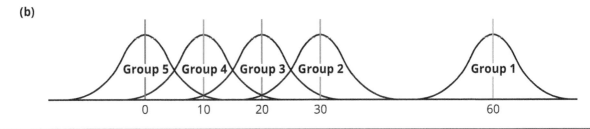

Group 5 Group 4 Group 3 Group 2   Group 1

0   10   20   30   60

groups: 30 minutes in blue, 10 minutes in green. Note that overall, the green group (10 minutes) did better on the test than the blue group (30 minutes).

Comparing Three or More Groups: Analysis of Variance

What if you have more than two groups that you want to compare?

In the example experiment, you might have set it up with five groups: one with no time at all on social media during the lecture (a control group), a group allowed 10 minutes, another group that used social media for 20 minutes, one who used social media for 30 minutes, and another that was on social media for the entire class. To analyze the results of an experiment with more than two groups, the same logic as the *t*-test applies, but the mathematics are slightly different. **Analysis of variance (ANOVA)** compares three or more groups and tells us if one group is significantly different than the others (see Figure 2.5). If so, we must dig further to find out which group(s) stand out.

Analysis of variance: Statistical analysis that compares the outcomes of three or more groups, to see if they are different from each other.

ANOVA: See *analysis of variance.*

SageVantage✹   Practice what you learn in **Knowledge Check 2.4**

ANALYZING THE QUALITY OF RESEARCH

?

Have You Ever Wondered?
2.5 How can I tell if a study is done well?

>> LO 2.5   Summarize how studies can be analyzed for quality.

How can you tell if a study is done well?

Evaluating research is like buying a car. Quality control matters, and it's important to ask educated questions. As you encounter research studies during this course, ask the same questions you would when buying a car. Does it get reliable ratings from reviewers? Are the people selling it trustworthy? Does it sound too good to be true? Are you vulnerable because you are desperate to believe in some key feature?

The history of science tells us that sometimes great ideas are ignored and terrible ideas embraced with dangerous enthusiasm. Whether it's a used car, a potential romantic partner, or a scientific study, the key to making a good evaluation is an attitude of hopeful but healthy skepticism. There are three important questions you should ask when evaluating research.

Random Sampling—Don't Be WEIRD

Who were the participants?

All published studies have a section describing who or what was in the study. Researchers start by identifying their population of interest, the group of people they want to know about. It might be people who have a certain mental disorder, people of a certain age, or students at a specific school. It's unlikely that *every* person in the population will participate. So, the "sample" refers to just the portion of the population that participates in the study.

Random sampling: Method of choosing who will participate in a study from the larger group of interest in an unbiased, random way.

The best way to avoid a biased sample is by **random sampling** from the population (*not* the same thing as random assignment to groups). Random sampling means that the people in the study were randomly chosen from the larger population of interest—everyone has an equal chance of being selected. This is often accomplished by a computer generating a random sublist of names.

Random sampling is the ideal because the sample will be a miniature version of the population. For example, if the larger population is 25% business majors, 25% education majors, 25% science majors, and 25% humanities majors, a truly random sample will produce very close to the same percentages. When the sample represents the population, then the results from the sample are generalizable—or probably true, in *general,* for the larger group.

But the real world of research often falls short of the ideal. Psychologists often resort to a convenient sample by simply asking for volunteers or offering an incentive like extra credit to students. Thousands of studies in psychology rely on people between 18 and 22 years old who are attending colleges in the United States. That may limit how generalizable the studies are. Can these results apply to younger people, older people, people without the privilege of going to college, or people in other countries?

This problem is sometimes known by the acronym WEIRD. WEIRD samples are those where the participants are:

- "Western" (from places like the United States),

- Educated, and from

- Industrialized,

- Rich,

- Democratic cultures.

We know less about other kinds of people—the diversity in participants is sometimes lacking. This is one reason cross-cultural research is so valuable to psychology and why researchers work hard to increase the diversity among participants. Limited diversity in a sample is also why a study might not replicate when tried again. This is one reason to consider the ideas in the next section— Reliability and Validity.

This family appears to be "Western," Educated, and from the United States (an Industrialized nation). They also appear to be relatively Rich and from a Democratic country. That means the acronym "WEIRD" applies to them. If they were the only people used in psychology studies, then we'd know a lot about WEIRD people but very little about most of the other people living in the world.

iStock.com/ljubaphoto

Generalizable: A term describing studies in which the sample of participants represents the diversity in the larger population of interest.

Reliability and Validity

Was everything in the study done correctly?

Always ask about the reliability and validity of the study. Reliability refers to whether the measurements were consistent. Over time or across multiple tests, would participants get the same score (on a variable assumed to be stable)? If there are strange fluctuations in how the constructs were operationalized (defined and measured), then the results might be questionable.

Several kinds of validity ensure a study stays focused on what it was intended to study in the first place. Let's consider three important kinds:

- Internal validity means the internal structure of the study was set up correctly; the results mean what we think they mean. Are we measuring social media use, specifically, or just time looking at the phone? Methods like random assignment to groups increases internal validity—and our

Reliability: Whether the measures in a study are consistent over time and place.

Internal validity: Confidence that a study was designed correctly and the results mean what we think they mean.

confidence in the connections between the independent and the dependent variables—because it helps rule out alternate explanations.

Construct validity: The degree to which tests, surveys, and so on chosen for a study really measure what we think they're measuring.

- **Construct validity** is whether methods are measuring the concept that we started with. A poorly written survey might confuse participants; a lie detector measuring palm sweating might only measure nervousness. Those problems would decrease confidence that we were measuring what we intended to assess.

External validity: The extent to which results of any single study could apply to other people or settings (see *generalizability*).

- **External validity** refers to whether the results apply to other people or settings. For example, the results from using a convenient sample of college students to study recognition of famous hip-hop music probably would not apply to people older than 70 who live in a culture that doesn't listen to much hip-hop. External validity can also be questionable if the study is so artificial or strange that it doesn't apply to behaviors outside of the lab. It would be strange if a researcher asked you to scroll through social media while riding an elephant, listening to a K-pop band on headphones, and counting the number of times you chew your food before swallowing. It's unlikely to have much meaning or usefulness to psychology (or any other science).

The CRAAP Test

Is this study CRAAP?

The CRAAP test is an efficient (and memorable) way to evaluate any study. The guidelines in Table 2.3 were first suggested by librarian Sarah Blakeslee (2004).

The CRAAP test can help you assess blogs on social media (Wichowski & Kohl, 2013). For example, you could consider its purpose in the context of its content—whether the blog is a personal story to help others, informal journalism, fame-enhancing, or sharing scientific advances with the public. In a world of malicious "fake news," a CRAAP test can help you evaluate whatever is popping up on your screen.

TABLE 2.3

The CRAAP Test

CRAAP	QUESTION
Currency	When was the information published? Is it current and still relevant to people today?
Relevance	Does this relate to your topic of interest? Who is the intended audience for the published paper?
Authority	What are the researchers' credentials? Is contact information available? Is the publisher reputable?
Accuracy	Are the conclusions supported by the results, or are they a bit of a stretch? Are the conclusions free of bias or emotion? Has the study been reviewed by other scholars in the field (a process called "peer review")?
Purpose	Is the purpose of the study science, or it is promoting a product to sell? Is it fact, or propaganda? Are there political, religious, or personal biases in how the researchers suggest the results should be used?

THE OPEN SCIENCE MOVEMENT

>> **LO 2.6** **Explain how the open science movement is addressing the replication crisis in psychology.**

Psychology has evolved.

Early psychologists did many things now considered unscientific or unethical. Unfortunately, so have some recent psychologists. If psychology is to make any progress, then the rising generation (you!) needs to be open, honest, unbiased, and ethical. A recent controversy rocked the psychology world so hard that some people quit the field entirely.

The Replication Crisis

Were the studies a bunch of lies?

In addition to reliability and validity, science relies on **replication**: getting the same findings over and over again. If a psychological principle is strong and real, then we should see the same outcomes across different settings—especially in studies conducted by *other scientists*.

Over 250 psychologists tested the replicability of 100 classic studies (Camerer et al., 2018; Diener & Biswas-Diener, 2019; Edlund et al., in press; Open Science Collaboration, 2017; Yong, 2018).

They found a bombshell: They could replicate only 40% of the findings from the original studies. This problem was quickly labeled the **replication crisis** in psychology. Psychology is not the only discipline confronting this issue, but our troubles got the most attention. How could this have happened?

Some blamed elements of academic culture, such as the pressure for professors to publish their research results to keep their jobs. Others accused specific psychologists of shoddy work (at best) or outright lying (at worst). Still others identified issues such as publication bias from academic journals or private companies paying for studies that might promote their products. A few researchers quit psychology, others lost their jobs, some received death threats, and others started a crusade to weed out dishonest researchers (Cairo et al., 2020; Lilienfeld, 2017; Renkewitz & Heene, 2019; Singal, 2017).

Bullying and death threats are not appropriate responses to any situation. What might help is critical thinking about ways to make psychology better (Schooler, 2014). First, there are some reasonable explanations for low replication rates. Cultures change, so results from studies performed in 1970 might not be the same if the same studies were performed today. Another explanation is that slight differences in a study's setting may affect participants without the researchers' knowledge (e.g., Mischel, 2014; Mischel & Ebbesen, 1970; Watts et al., 2018). That doesn't necessarily mean the original study wasn't valid at the time or poorly done. But it does mean we should ask better questions. A failed replication might directly affect your life in college. To see how, check out the *Spotlight on Research Methods* feature.

Replication: Getting the same findings over and over again, with different participants, in different settings, and with different researchers.

Replication crisis: The controversial finding that only 40% of several classic psychology studies replicated years later.

Does it matter if you take notes on a laptop or in a paper notebook? See the *Spotlight on Research Methods* to learn about some research over this question.

iStock.com/fizkes

Have You Ever Wondered?
2.6 What is the open science movement?

Understanding Replication: Should You Take Notes by Hand?

As scientists, we obsess about getting it right. This impulse is not entirely about being right in the sense of seeing hypotheses supported (though that is nice) but more about getting the facts straight—even if we don't like those facts.

Lots of college and university professors were thrilled when a study claimed that memory for classroom material was far greater when students took notes by hand—with a pencil or pen, on actual paper—than by typing (Mueller & Oppenheimer, 2014). No more annoying typing noises in class! No more temptation to check your social media or go shopping. Simply go "old school" and take notes on a piece of paper and learn more along the way.

In the study, students were showed five TED talks:

- The students took notes either on laptops or paper notebooks.

- Next, the students did distracting tasks for 30 minutes.

- Finally, they were tested on their understanding of the TED talks.

Results showed that both note-taking groups performed well on basic memory questions (no difference there). On harder conceptual and application types of questions, people who took notes on paper tested significantly better. The authors (Mueller & Oppenheimer, 2014) wanted to be confident with their results, so they did three studies—and each showed the same pattern.

But wait. A few years later, another paper questioned those results. In a direct replication of the original study's method, new researchers showed that for their participants, taking notes via typing or longhand writing just didn't really matter (Urry et al., 2021). They also pointed out eight other studies showing no real difference. They even called their study, "Don't ditch the laptop just yet."

So, do you believe the results from the original study? They failed to replicate—does that mean it doesn't really matter how you take notes? Or is there more to the story? Only additional research will be able to tell us for sure. ●

Regardless of where people fall on their view of the replication crisis, it was an opportunity for psychology to do better. Just in the past decade or so, the field has majorly changed how many studies are conducted and published. The goal is to make psychological research as open and honest as possible.

The Open Science Movement

How can we make psychological science even better?

Open science is a movement to make scientific research transparent, accessible, cooperative, reproducible, and honest. The aim is to remove any barriers in the study's creation, analysis of the data, sharing of the results, or understanding of the conclusions. Open science is a way of asking other scientists to form a team together in a transparent, honest environment. One specific goal is to increase the number of studies focused on replication of previous work, so we can be confident in the conclusions we make and in the theories we teach in classes and textbooks (like this one!).

There are three practical consequences for psychology resulting from the open science movement: preregistration, results-blind peer review, and publication badges. Find out more about this exciting trend by searching online for:

- The Center for Open Science

- The Open Science Framework

- OpenScience

Open science: A movement to make science more transparent, cooperative, reproducible, and honest.

- ORION Open Science

- The FOSTER Portal

Preregistration

Exploratory research occurs when a scientist doesn't have a hypothesis—they're just curious about some variables that might be related. However, scientists could publish such studies and pretend they had predicted the outcomes from the beginning. They look super smart! But it's not honest.

Open science's solution to this form of playing pretend is *preregistration,* or sharing hypotheses, procedures, and statistical plan for analyses in advance of collecting data (see Nosek et al., 2017). Several preregistration templates help researchers through this process; independent websites allow researchers to publicly declare the details of their studies beforehand.

This practical solution also has some practical problems. You might commit to having 100 participants but can only get 75, or participants can misunderstand procedures despite being presented with well-articulated plans. A typo may change the meaning of the instructions. These practical problems also have another practical solution: honesty. Document and report your mistakes and judgment calls, explain why you made them, and discuss how you addressed them.

Results-Blind Peer Review

Every research field has professional journals (like magazines), where researchers publish their results. Most journals are peer-reviewed—experts in the field evaluate each study prior to possible publication. Peer reviewers give anonymous feedback to the authors, suggest changes, and make recommendations—including whether to publish the article.

Prior to the open science movement, all this reviewing happened *after* a study was completed. Peer reviewers knew how the research story ended, which invited biases. For example, a researcher may prefer (and review more positively) studies based on a theory they favor—or vice versa. A more common, but hidden, problem was well-conducted studies that never appeared online or in print because they didn't find any differences among groups, an issue known as the *file drawer problem* (because the study went nowhere except in a file inside the researcher's office). When these unpublished studies were failed replications, it made it impossible for the field to update its knowledge.

The open science movement proposed a solution: the results-blind peer review described in Figure 2.6. Peer reviewers assess a study's procedures *before* it is

---

FIGURE 2.6

The Results-Blind Peer Review Process

When an article goes through the "results-blind peer review" process, outside experts give feedback about the quality and importance of an article before the data are actually collected. Then, they review a second time, focusing on whether the study followed the original design plan.

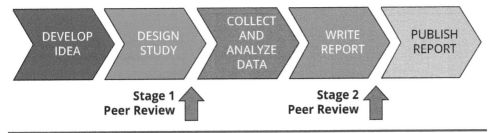

Source: Center for Open Science (2021). Retrieved from https://cos.io/rr/. Licensed under CC BY 4.0.

conducted—if they agree it has merit, then they accept it for publication. Reviewers will also provide feedback after the results are known—but now they comment on whether the study followed the preregistration plan and interpreted everything correctly. That way, even if the results surprise everyone, the study still gets published.

Publication Badges

Doing good science is its own reward. There are also extrinsic incentives for participating in the open science movement. Badges are visual icons that signal researchers' participation in these practices. You can see some of the badges in Figure 2.7.

Over 50 journals now use the badge system, and early trends indicate that they do increase the number of scientists who participate in open science (Kidwell et al., 2016; Rowhani-Farid et al., 2017). More important is that the open science movement provides ethical guard rails that limit the human tendency toward self-deception and help science stay in the lane of objectivity and transparency.

FIGURE 2.7

Examples of Open Science Badges

Professional journals are increasingly marking studies with these images, called "badges," when they follow open science guidelines. These examples are from the Center for Open Science.

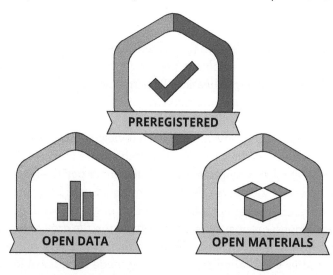

Source: Center for Open Science (2021). Retrieved from https://cos.io/our-services/open-science-badges/. Licensed under CC BY 4.0.

SageVantage   Practice what you learn in **Knowledge Check 2.6**

ETHICAL CONSIDERATIONS

Have You Ever Wondered?
2.7 How do ethics guide psychological research?

>> **LO 2.7   Describe ethical considerations for research with humans and animals.**

Ethical guidelines change over time.

The open science movement highlights ethical concerns that psychology has only focused on recently. And 100 years from now, future students and scientists might scratch their heads and wonder about us, "What were they thinking!?" The core of ethics in psychology is an attempt to avoid both short-term and long-term harm to the human and nonhuman animals in our studies. Let's start with what *not* to do.

Unethical Studies

Unfortunately, there are some ethically embarrassing studies in psychology's history.

You'll be learning the details of some particularly bad ones as they come up in future chapters. There's a range or continuum for just *how* unethical a study might be. For example, causing someone to feel sad for an hour is a violation, but it's not as harmful as causing someone a permanent physical or mental issue. Table 2.4 shows (in chronological order) studies that would be considered unethical by today's standards.

TABLE 2.4

Some Examples of Unethical Psychology Studies

These studies would all be considered relatively unethical by modern psychological standards.

REFERENCE	GOAL	STUDY DESCRIPTION
Landis (1924)	Studying facial expression of various emotions.	To get authentic expressions, the researcher • surprised them with a lit firecracker under their chair, • showed them pornography, and • asked them to put their hand in a bucket—without telling them the bucket contained live frogs. • To end, he handed them a butcher knife and a live rat and asked them to behead it. If they refused, he did it for them while they watched.
The Tuskegee Syphilis Study (1930s)	Studying the effects of untreated syphilis.	Over a 40-year span, African American men with syphilis were told they were getting treatment. Really, they were misled and medicine was purposely withheld.
Henle and Hubbell (1938)	Observing natural conversations between adults to analyze topics of discussion.	To ensure the people being observed didn't realize it, the researchers • eavesdropped in the bathroom, • secretly listened in on telephone conversations and even hid under beds in college students' rooms during parties.
Johnson et al. (1959)	Testing what causes stuttering in children.	Researchers selected six orphans of varying ages: • The children were told they were stutterers (even though they were not at the start of the study). • The label was reinforced multiple times for a few months, until eventually all six children started stuttering (see Silverman, 1988).
Humphreys (1970)	Studying casual sexual interactions among gay men.	• The researcher went to public parks and observed people who met there to have anonymous sex in the bathrooms. • The people knew they were being watched, but not that it was for a research study.
Piliavin and Piliavin (1972)	Testing when people will help in what appears to be an emergency.	• An experimenter collapsed on a moving subway car multiple times, varying whether they had fake blood coming out of their mouth or not. • Other experimenters on the same subway car then observed how many people tried to help (again, without knowing they were in a study).
Rekers and Lovaas (1974)	Testing whether gender-typical behaviors can be modified in children.	A 5-year-old boy expressing a desire to be a girl was trained by researchers and his mother: • They attempted to suppress any "feminine" behaviors and reinforce "masculine" behaviors with verbal praise, candy, and other rewards over about a year. • The researchers declared successful "treatment" when the child's behaviors were "normalized" (p. 181).
Middlemist et al. (1976)	Testing if invasion of personal space affected men who tried to urinate in public bathrooms.	• They found that men forced to urinate immediately next to another man (at the adjacent urinal) had trouble in terms of delay and flow. • The participants were timed without their knowledge as another researcher watched them via a hidden periscope in a nearby stall.
Kramer et al. (2014)	Studying how social media usage might affect mood.	Without users' knowledge, Facebook researchers manipulated over 600,000 people's newsfeeds: • For half, Facebook hid positive messages from friends; for the other half, negative messages from friends were hidden. • After doing this for a week, the researchers measured the users' own messages for positivity versus negativity and did find "emotional contagion."

Just as one example—and keeping with the social media theme for this chapter—consider a study created by the staff at Facebook (Kramer et al., 2014, in Table 2.4). They decided to manipulate users' newsfeeds for a week:

- Facebook staff purposely hid posts in the feeds of half the people in the study (who were unknowing participants) that contained happy, positive messages. For the other half of people, Facebook purposely hid negative messages.

- At the end of the week, the researchers coded the users' own posts in terms of emotional content.

As they expected, users who had been deprived of positive messages from friends over the week produced fewer positive posts themselves—and the same pattern emerged for negative messages. Again, users never realized they were in the study at all (and probably still have no idea that Facebook manipulated their experience).

APA Ethical Guidelines

What should you expect if you participate in a psychology study?

Notice first that several of the studies in Table 2.4 were done in the 1970s, when ethics debates were heating up across the sciences. In 1979, the National Commission for the Protection of Human Subjects of Biomedical and Behavioral Research published a report, called the Belmont Report, with strict ethical guidelines that are still followed today. These guidelines will affect you very personally if you are given the opportunity to participate in research.

The specific guidelines for ethical research in psychology come from both the Belmont Report and from the American Psychological Association (APA), an organization of thousands of professionals in the field. The APA lists several rights for participants of research studies. The most important of which is that someone can stop participating in any study for any reason at any time. Some of the rights recognized by the APA include:

- Informed consent: Participants should be told what they will be asked to do and whether there are any potential dangers or risks.

- Anonymity: Personal information will be as anonymous as possible to the researchers and a participant's identity will not be published in any reports.

- Deception: Participants should be told the purpose and nature of the study. Deception is *only* allowed when knowing the truth would change how participants responded.

- Right to withdraw: Participants have the right to withdraw from the study at any time, for any reason, or to skip any uncomfortable questions.

- Debriefing: After the study, all participants can ask about the hypotheses, see the results, understand any deceptions, and receive contact information for their local ethics committee if they want to report concerns or ask questions.

Ethics, Nature, and Nurture: Three Identical Strangers

Album/Alamy Stock Photo

"Nature versus nurture" is a classic debate in psychology.

Twin studies is one of the interesting methods to study this question. If we can compare twins—especially identical twins separated at birth—we can see how they are similar and different. Any differences must be due to their environment, or nurture, since they share the exact same genetics, or nature. But it's rare to find twins separated at birth and even rarer to get everyone involved to consent to being in a study. What would happen if a researcher *created* this scenario without anyone's knowledge?

This incredible situation plays out in the documentary *Three Identical Strangers* (Read et al., 2018). Identical triplet infants were adopted by three different families— one blue collar, one middle class, and one affluent. None of the adoptive parents knew there were two other boys. The truth was that it was a secret research study planned by clinical psychiatrist Peter Neubauer. He did it to several sets of twins as well—ripping families apart to study how it would affect them.

When the triplets found each other by sheer coincidence at the age of 19, they had amazing similarities. They wore the same kinds of clothes and had similar personalities. They had all wrestled in junior high or high school, all smoked Marlboro cigarettes, and all preferred older women. And they also all suffered from mental illness. As they grew up, the boys started to show important differences as well, including how each responded to their unusual situation after it was discovered. When they contacted the adoption agency and Yale University, which had boxes and boxes of information about the secret study, they were barred from access to any of the information. And the researchers never even published their findings.

This strange—and highly unethical—case is captivating to watch in the documentary. No spoilers, but things did not go well for everyone. One of the boy's aunts poignantly summarized what happened like this: "When you play with humans, you do something very wrong. These three boys did not have happy endings." For more about the ethics involved in this study, read Hlavinka (2019). ●

Animal Research

What about research with animals?

There are also some sad stories in psychology's history that are now considered animal abuse. Modern standards are much stricter. The APA maintains a hotline to report abuses. Some of the critical guidelines for working with animals include:

- Justification: Research should have a clear purpose and provide results that will increase understanding of the species and/or benefit humans or other animals. The welfare of the animals must be monitored throughout the study.

- Care and housing: Animals should be housed in clean, working facilities and treated with care. No unnecessary stress should be imposed.

- Procedures: Experiments should minimize discomfort; if surgery is needed, animals must be given anesthesia. If animals are observed in their natural field environments, researchers should take care not to disturb the area.

Meet Angie, Clinical Site Manager

What is your career?

I help monitor clinical trials from start to finish at a Clinical Research Organization (CRO). This includes making sure medical doctors at universities and standing research sites are well trained, follow guidelines, correctly execute trial procedures, and clean data before analyzed. I write reports on whether they're doing what they are supposed to do.

How was studying psychology important for success in this career?

Psychology helped me understand research methods and statistics and *why* clinical trials require certain procedures. For example, it helped me understand the importance of informed consent in all research. Studying psychology also assisted in understanding why certain clinical trials choose from certain demographics, certain ages, and even certain geographic regions.

How do concepts from this chapter help in this career?

I train teams weekly on the importance of informed consent. I learned what items need to be present on consent forms while studying psychology. I also train

and educate medical doctors and study coordinators on the importance of following the protocol, which outlines the study design. When sites do not follow the protocol, I record it as a protocol deviation. Sometimes data need to be eliminated because the doctor didn't follow the procedure.

Is this the career you always planned to have after college?

I knew I always wanted to do research, but I didn't know the route to take. I originally started as a biology major but knew I didn't want to be in a lab or become a doctor, so I switched my major to psychology. It was a great decision for me. While I was a psychology major, I completed an internship with an epidemiologist who analyzed colorectal cancer rates based on geographical region around my home state. It was a great segue into clinical research. I now work with epidemiologists daily with study design.

If you could give current college students one sentence of advice, what would it be?

The sooner you learn how to grind and have grit, the sooner you'll reach your professional and personal goals. ●

Institutional Review Boards

Researchers are held accountable to protect participants.

All organizations sponsoring research with humans or animals—including colleges and universities—have committees that monitor the studies' ethics. There are generally two types of committees:

1. Institutional review boards (IRBs) review proposed studies with human participants.

2. The institutional animal care and use committee (IACUC) reviews proposed studies with nonhuman animals.

Each committee is made up of representatives from different departments at the organization. Your college or university's IRB probably includes faculty from the arts, sciences, humanities, and social sciences. In addition, there is often a lawyer and a nonresearcher from the community to give a layperson's perspective.

Psychologists planning a study must first get approval from their university's IRB or IACUC. This usually involves filling out lots of forms with detailed explanations of the exact purpose of the study, procedure, who the participants will be, whether they will be compensated for their time, projected benefits, and any possible harm that the participants might experience. The committee may ask the researcher questions, and they might even require modifications to the study if they have any concerns.

Modern psychology really cares about two basic things: doing science well and doing science ethically. If it were any other way, we (your authors) wouldn't be so proud to be in this fascinating, challenging, and rewarding field of science. ●

Practice what you learn in **Knowledge Check 2.7**   Sage Vantage

---

Learning Objectives Summary

2.1   How is psychology a science?

>> LO 2.1   **Explain how the scientific method is used in psychological science.**

Psychology is a science because it uses the scientific method. The scientific method is a series of objective steps for empirically testing an idea. Psychologists use the scientific method to advance the field by observing patterns, generating hypotheses, testing them with research studies, and continuing the cycle. In psychology, abstract concepts called "constructs" must be operationalized, which means specifying how they will be defined and measured.

2.2   How do psychologists design studies?

>> LO 2.2   **Compare and contrast research methodologies.**

Five methodological options for research studies are archival studies, naturalistic observation, surveys, quasi-experiments, and true experiments. Each method has advantages and disadvantages, shown in Table 2.1.

2.3   What are correlations?

>> LO 2.3   **Explain how we show relationships between variables and why correlation doesn't imply causation.**

Correlations are statistical analyses testing whether two variables are systematically tied to each other. A "positive" correlation means the variables move together in the same direction, while a "negative" correlation means they move in opposite directions. Importantly, just because two things appear to be correlated doesn't mean we know if one causes the other.

2.4   How are the results of experiments analyzed?

>> LO 2.4   **Compare and contrast *t*-tests and ANOVAs.**

Experiments involve comparing two or more groups. If two groups are used, the results are analyzed with a *t*-test; three or more groups are analyzed with an analysis of variance (or ANOVA for short).

2.5   How can I tell if a study is done well?

>> LO 2.5   **Summarize how studies can be analyzed for quality.**

Quality of research can be assessed by considering several criteria, such as (1) were the participants found through random sampling, (2) is the sample generalizable to the population, and (3) does the study have good reliability and validity? The "CRAAP" test also asks about a study's currency, relevance, authority, accuracy, and purpose.

2.6   What is the open science movement?

>> LO 2.6   **Explain how the open science movement is addressing the replication crisis in psychology.**

Psychology suffered from the "replication crisis" when researchers repeated a large portion of classic studies and did not receive similar results. The open science movement is an attempt to improve how research is done by increasing honesty and transparency in each step of the research process.

2.7   **How do ethics guide psychological research?**

>> LO 2.7   **Describe ethical considerations for research with humans and animals.**

While some studies in psychology's history have been highly unethical, today's standards are fairly strict when it comes to research using humans and other animals. Colleges and universities have committees that consider the ethics of any study before it is done.

CRITICAL THINKING QUESTIONS

1. Now that you've learned more about scientific studies on using social media, has it affected your opinions or behaviors about your own usage? Why or why not?

2. Find a psychological study that investigated the effects of social media. Identify the following aspects of the study: (1) What was their hypothesis? (2) How did they operationalize the variables in their hypothesis? (3) What method did they use to test their hypothesis?

3. This chapter mentioned one paper that reviewed three studies showing better memory if students take notes by hand on paper, compared to if they type notes. But another paper showed that this finding failed to replicate. Think about your own preference for note-taking and explore two ideas for a study that might provide additional information. What other variables might matter? For example, do the results depend on student interest in the material? Or student personality? Or how quickly students can write or type? Generate two original hypotheses and explain how you would test them in a study.

4. Think a bit more about the studies described in Table 2.4. Rank order them from most to least ethical (knowing that they are all relatively unethical by today's standards in psychology). Then, explain why you came up with the order you did. What criteria did you use to make your judgments?

KEY TERMS

Analysis of variance, 42
ANOVA, 42
Archival studies, 30
Confounding variables, 36
Construct, 29
Construct validity, 44
Control group, 35
Correlation analysis, 37
Dependent variable, 36
Experimental group, 35
Experiments, 34
External validity, 44
Generalizable, 43
Hypothesis, 28
Independent variable, 35
Internal validity, 43
Naturalistic observation, 31

Open science, 46
Operationalization, 29
Participant observation, 32
Quasi-experiments, 34
Random assignment, 34
Random sampling, 42
Reactivity, 32
Reliability, 43
Replication, 45
Replication crisis, 45
Scatterplot, 38
Scientific method, 28
Social desirability, 33
Survey, 32
True experiments, 34
t-test, 41

iStock.com/miodrag ignjatovic

3

Biology and Your Brain

As a young Black girl, one of your authors [Charity] had a Saturday tradition: Her mom washed and styled her hair in the kitchen. Her mom used a hot comb hair straightener to give a different look than her natural curls. If you are unfamiliar, a hot comb hair straightener is a metal comb that you heat on a kitchen stove that straightens curly hair from the roots. Every time the hot comb approached her hair's roots, she flinched. Once, her mom accidently let the hot comb touch her scalp and she quickly pulled her head away to avoid what certainly would have been a nasty burn!

You may have had a similar experience when you knowingly (or unknowingly!) anticipated something would hurt you and quickly reacted by jolting away. These reactions are not happenstance. Rather, they are the product of an entire nervous system composed of cells, chemicals, and organs that send the messages that enable us to act, think, and react. Every thought and behavior we have is because of our curious and beautiful brain.

After reading this chapter, you will get answers to several questions you've been curious about:

Have You Ever Wondered?

3.1   How do neurons communicate with each other and the body?

3.2   What are neurotransmitters, and how do they relate to drugs and disorders?

3.3   What are the different structures of the brain and what do they do?

3.4   How do we understand the location and/or function of different structures of the brain?

3.5   What is the endocrine system?

Learning Objectives

LO 3.1   Explain the nervous system, types of neurons, and their structure.

LO 3.2   Compare and contrast how different neurotransmitters and drugs affect the brain.

LO 3.3   Identify major parts of the brain and their functions.

LO 3.4   Compare and contrast different brain neuroimaging techniques.

LO 3.5   Compare and contrast the nervous and endocrine systems and how they each affect behavior.

YOUR UNIQUE BRAIN: THE NERVOUS SYSTEM AND NEURONS

>> **LO 3.1   Explain the nervous system, types of neurons, and their structure.**

Your brain is unique.

Neurodiversity is the concept that there are a variety of ways that people's brains process information, function, and present behaviorally. Being neurodivergent means having a brain that works differently from the average or "neurotypical" person. This may be differences in social preferences, ways of learning, ways of communicating, and/or ways of perceiving the environment. But rather than thinking there is something wrong or problematic when a person's brain operates differently, neurodiversity embraces difference.

Neurodivergence manifests in different ways. You may be familiar with more common examples of neurodivergence such as autism, attention-deficit/hyperactivity disorder (ADHD), and dyslexia. This list is not exhaustive. There are many forms of neurodivergence—and many are an innate part of how the brain develops and functions (Lohani & Rana, 2023). The nervous system of neurodivergent people may cause them to experience the world differently.

Have You Ever Wondered?
3.1 How do neurons communicate with each other and the body?

Neurodiversity: The idea that there are a variety of ways people's brains process information, function, and lead to behaviors.

FIGURE 3.1

The Two-Part Nervous System

This chart represents the two-part organization of the nervous system, with multiple interconnected subsystems.

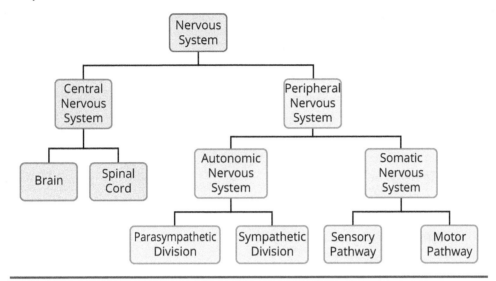

For example, neurodivergent people may be especially sensitive to sound and touch. They may be unable to go to a rap concert because of the loud noise. Tactile needs may require a neurodivergent person to wear clothes made of certain types of fabric or without tags that might rub against their skin. Other neurodivergent people may have movement needs that require teachers or work supervisors to allow the use of fidget toys, extra movement breaks, and flexible seating, such as a use of a yoga ball rather than a chair. It is normal, acceptable, and advantageous for society when our members have brains that function differently.

Your nervous system's speed is superior to the Internet, its reliability better than any mail service, and its content far more trustworthy. Such a delivery service requires the organization of millions of employees. The nervous system's employees are called neurons. **Neurons** are the messenger cells that receive, integrate, and transmit information using electrical impulses and chemical signals. They interact with each other and the brain through the central and peripheral systems (Figure 3.1).

Neurons: Messenger cells that receive, integrate, and transmit information through the body.

The Central Nervous System

Imagine a vertical line through the middle of your body.

The **central nervous system** (CNS) is the "center" line of your body: your brain and spinal cord. More than 99% of our nerve cells are in the central nervous system. The brain processes information received from the senses, makes decisions, and sends commands out to the rest of the body. The spinal cord is a long bundle of nerves about as thick as a pencil running down the length of the back. It is the primary path the brain uses to process messages with the rest of the body.

Central nervous system: The brain and the spinal cord.

The spinal cord is more than a message "pipeline." It also processes simple, potentially life-saving information without any help from the brain. Remember that way Charity automatically jumped away from the intense heat of that hot comb? The same response occurs when the knee is tapped with a rubber hammer. These behaviors are *reflexes*—automatic, involuntary responses to a stimulus. Having this *reflex arc* controlled by the spinal cord alone, without the brain, allows for a very quick response time (see Figure 3.2). Although neurons in the spinal cord direct the initial withdrawal, the pain message does eventually get to the brain that will likely trigger other motor responses such as "Ouch, [insert profanity here]!"

FIGURE 3.2

The Reflex Arc

This figure illustrates a neural pathway that controls a reflex response to a heat stimulus that does not involve the brain. The flame stimulates pain receptors (sensory neurons) that excite interneurons (or relay neurons) in the spinal cord. When receiving the signal from the interneurons, motor neurons in the muscle of the arm respond automatically, removing the hand from the flame before you've had time to think about it.

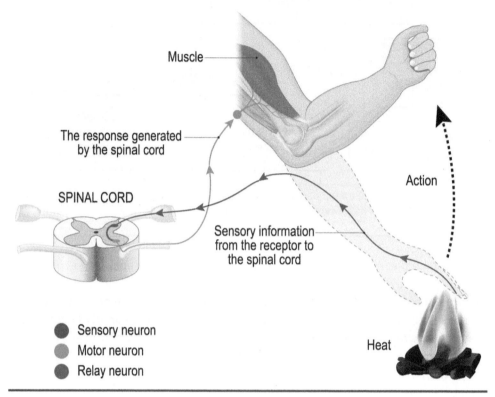

iStock.com/ttsz

The Peripheral Nervous System

Stare straight ahead of you.

Even though most of what you see might be straight ahead, you can still see some things out to the side using just as your "peripheral" vision. Similarly, your **peripheral nervous system** consists of neurons that form the communication network between the central nervous system and the body parts.

Peripheral nervous system: All the nerve cells in the body outside the central nervous system.

The peripheral nervous system has two major systems: (1) the somatic nervous system, which consists of nerves that control *voluntary* muscles, and (2) the autonomic nervous system, which consists of nerves that control *involuntary* muscles, organs, and glands.

The Somatic Nervous System

Somatic nervous system: Part of the peripheral nervous system that controls voluntary movements through sensory and motor pathways.

The **somatic nervous system** controls parts of the body responsible for voluntary movements, such as the motion of the eyes to read this sentence or twerking to the newest Drake record. The term *somatic* is drawn from soma, which means "body"—appropriate for the system that connects information between the body and the central nervous system. Information is transmitted from sensory organs back to the central nervous system and to the motor neurons that carry messages from muscles back to the central nervous system. These muscles are called "voluntary" because they can move at will but are not limited to only that kind of movement. Like reflexes, they can move involuntarily when necessary.

The Autonomic Nervous System

The **autonomic nervous system**, as the name implies, means that the functions of this system are automatic. Many parts of the body keep us alive without our awareness such as the heart, blood vessels, glands, and lungs. These organs are controlled by neurons located *on* or *near* the spinal cord (remember, neurons *inside* the spinal cord are part of the central nervous system, not the peripheral nervous system). So, as you're reading this sentence, the autonomic nervous system controls processes such as your breathing, heart rate, and digestion.

The autonomic nervous system also plays a critical role in emergencies. Imagine you suddenly hear a repeated loud banging noise, like gunshots, coming closer. If you are like most people, your body begins to react on a physiological level: sweating hands, a rapid heart rate, chills in your body, and a pounding inside your chest. These physiological changes are a result of the **sympathetic division** of the nervous system that prepares your body to deal with stress by running away ("flight"), confronting the threat ("fight"), or stopping in your tracks ("freeze").

In contrast, the **parasympathetic division** calms the body after the emergency. When you find, for instance, that the loud bang was a fireworks show in celebration of a special occasion at a nearby park, your parasympathetic division begins to stop your sweating, lower your heart rate, and return your body to a less active, less stressful state. In general, the parasympathetic division is important in supporting *homeostasis*—maintaining stability and balance to survive (Figure 3.3).

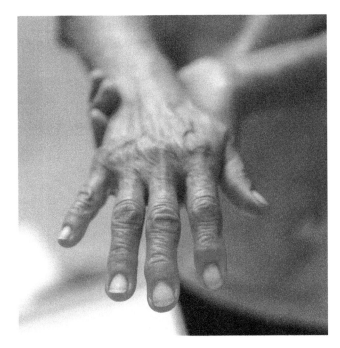

Diseases that impact the nerve fibers of the somatic nervous system can lead to peripheral neuropathy. The result is pain and numbness in the legs, feet, and hands. Diabetes is one of the most common causes of peripheral neuropathy, when high blood sugar (glucose) injures nerves throughout the body. Peripheral neuropathy can also be caused by autoimmune conditions, infectious diseases, and trauma.

iStock.com/Chinnapong

Types of Neurons

Neurons are, in the words of the famous DJ Khaled, #majorkey in the nervous system.

There are billions of neurons in the human nervous system (Lent et al., 2012) busily making an estimated 10 quadrillion (10,000,000,000,000,000) connections in your brain (John et al., 2018)—a number so big that it's hard to wrap our minds around it. Think of neurons as chains of gossip that distribute vital information, but only to selected groups. Scientists classify neurons into three broad types:

- *Sensory neurons*, also known as afferent neurons, detect and respond to stimuli in our environment (like hot combs!) and relay that information to the spinal cord.

- *Motor neurons*, also known as efferent neurons, carry messages from the brain to the muscles. Charity's motor neurons contacted the muscles of her neck, which led to an automatic response: pulling away from that hot comb!

- *Interneurons*, also known as relay neurons, lie between sensory and motor neurons. Interneurons in Charity's spinal cord received the "heat" message from sensory neurons on her scalp and passed it along to motor neurons.

Autonomic nervous system: Part of the peripheral nervous system that controls involuntary muscles, organs, and glands that support processes such as breathing, heart rate, and digestion.

Sympathetic division: Part of the autonomic system that responds to stress and arouses the body for action in response to threats.

Parasympathetic division: Part of the autonomic nervous system that calms the body.

One of the great research stories began in a primate lab where researchers were monitoring brain activity in macaque monkeys. Researchers noticed particular areas of neural activity in the monkeys when they observed the researchers picking up a peanut (Rizzolatti et al., 1996; Winerman, 2005). It seemed the monkeys' neurons

FIGURE 3.3

The Sympathetic and Parasympathetic Nervous Systems

The sympathetic division responds to stress and arouses the body for action in response to threats, whereas the parasympathetic division calms the body and returns it back to rest.

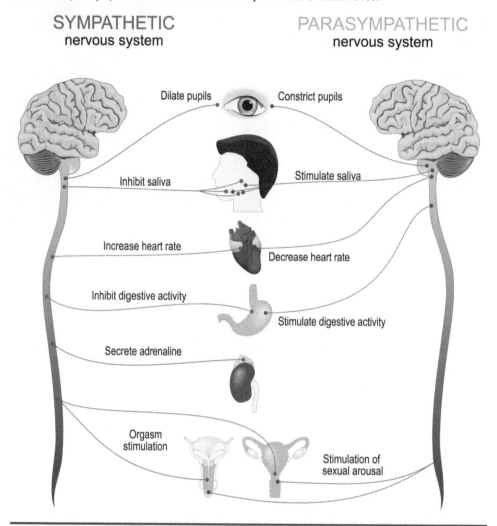

iStock.com/ttsz

were mirroring or mimicking what they saw. These *mirror neurons* may help explain observational learning, such as a younger child imitating an older sibling (Bonini et al., 2022). Mirror neurons are seen by some as a distinct (fourth) type of neuron, but they can also be classified as a type of motor neuron.

Importantly, *mirror neurons* also appear to help explain *empathy*, our ability to understand and share feelings with others (Bekkali et al., 2021; Praszkier, 2016). There's a lot more to learn about this relatively new (and somewhat controversial) development in neuroscience. The excitement of research is not knowing where the next discovery might lead and why curiosity is built into science.

Neurons and Glial Cells: Working Together

Passing messages requires cooperation.

Expecting the touch of a hot comb evokes a thought about potential pain; that anticipated sensation quickly triggered a reaction of pulling away. And it all happens in an instant. To pull that off, there have to be specialized cells with specialized structures, helping bring it all together.

Neuron Structure

The neuron has four structures that allow it to share information with other neurons: dendrites, a soma, an axon, and axon terminals (see Figure 3.4). **Dendrites** look like the branches of a tree and receive messages from other neurons. Received messages are processed in the **soma**, the main body of the cell. The soma contains nucleus, which controls the cell's growth and maintenance. An **axon**, which looks like a tree trunk, is attached to the soma and transmits a message along its entire length using an electrical impulse. Axons are thinner than a human hair but can extend more than 3 feet. At the end of the long "trunk" are **axon terminals** (also called *terminal buttons*). These sac-like bulges contain neurotransmitters that send chemical signals to other neurons.

The Role of Glial Cells

Neuronal structures are obviously important, but messages would not get communicated without glial cells. *Glial* is related to the word *glue*, and holding neurons together was one of the first recognized purposes of glial cells. Glial cells are the backroom janitorial, maintenance, and administrative staff that make it possible for neurons to do their important work. For example, glial cells help physically hold neurons in place to create *nerves*, a bundle of neurons wrapped in connective tissue.

Specialized glial cells called *Schwann cells* form the **myelin sheath**, a protective coat of fat and protein that surrounds the axons of many neurons. The myelin sheath insulates the axon, similar to the plastic or rubber coating around the electrical wire that turns on your computer. There are intermittent gaps in the myelin sheath known as the *nodes of Ranvier*. They speed up and regulate the pace of neural messages by jumping from node to node, like Spiderman swinging from building to building (Arancibia-Cárcamo et al., 2017).

Activity Inside Neurons

The Saturday hair wash and styling always happened in the same predictable order.

Neurons also have a predictable and consistent communication flow, but it all happens in milliseconds. The electrical energy flows from dendrites to the soma to the axon to the axon terminals (see Figure 3.5). Communication across these structures relies on a two-step process: (1) action potentials and (2) neurotransmitters. Let's talk about each step.

Dendrites: Thick treelike fibers that receive messages from other neurons.

Soma: The main body of a neuron cell.

Axon: Part of the neuron that the electrical impulse travels through.

Axon terminals: Small sacs at the end of the neuron that contain chemicals that communicate with other neurons.

Myelin sheath: The coating of fat and protein surrounding axons that protects and speeds communications.

FIGURE 3.4

Parts of a Neuron

Structure of the neuron, the messenger cells of the nervous system.

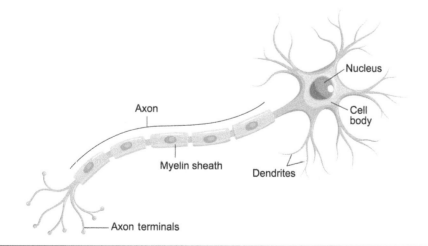

iStock.com/Vitalii Dumma

FIGURE 3.5

Neuron Communication Flow

Communication inside a neuron has a predictable flow, always in this order.

Resting Potential: Before the Action Potential

Similar to human skin that protects but can be punctured, the semipermeable membrane that covers the neuron allows certain substances to pass through it but not others. Electrically charged groups of atoms called *ions* can pass in and out of neurons. That membrane also allows a neuron to hold an electrical charge even when it is resting and ions are not moving through it—the membrane is said to be *polarized*.

At **resting potential**, a neuron is not transmitting information. Positively charged sodium ions are outside of the cell; negatively charged potassium ions are mostly inside. The arrangement of these ions creates a stable, negative electrical charge of about −70 millivolts within the cell.

But neurons don't stay at rest! An incoming impulse—which may be triggered by heat from a hot comb (boo) or a touch from a loved romantic partner (yay)—can temporarily change the balance or potential. Let's explore how a romantic partner's soft touch triggers an electrical impulse. Dendrites from sensory neurons in the skin change the permeability of the cell membrane, allowing positively charged sodium ions to rush inside the neuron's cell body (or soma). Pretty sexy, right? Well, OK ... not yet.

Action Potential: The Neuron Is Firing

The neuron's only job is to communicate information, so the romantic touch triggers the same process in the neurons as the hot comb. The sudden arrival of the positive sodium ions while negative potassium ions are pushed out momentarily reverses the charge of the cell from negative (−70 millivolts) to positive (+40 millivolts), which is known as an **action potential** and the cell is said to be *depolarized*. When the positive charge reaches a certain minimum level, or threshold, an electrical charge is released and travels down the axon. At that point, the neuron "fires."

Neurons operate on an *all-or-nothing principle*. A neuron either fires or it doesn't—depending on whether or not the charge in the cell body reaches the threshold. Like a light switch, once the electrical charge reaches the needed threshold, it fires and moves along the axon without losing any intensity. The movement of this charge along the axon is called an electrical impulse. The cycle of depolarization and repolarization that is the action potential is extremely rapid, taking only about 2 milliseconds (0.002 seconds) and thus allows neurons to fire action potentials in rapid bursts.

The action potential only moves in one direction. The sodium channels in the neuron membrane are opened in response to a small depolarization of the membrane potential. So when an action potential depolarizes the membrane, the leading edge activates other adjacent sodium channels. This leads to another spike of depolarization, the leading edge of which activates more adjacent sodium channels ... etc. Thus, a wave of depolarization spreads from the point of initiation.

In neurons with myelin sheaths, ions flow across the membrane only at the nodes between sections of myelin. As a result, the action potential jumps along the axon membrane from node to node, rather than spreading smoothly along the entire membrane. This increases the speed at which it travels.

Resting potential: The state when a neuron is not transmitting information; positively charged sodium ions are outside of the cell and negatively charged potassium ions are largely contained inside.

Action potential: The sudden arrival of positive ions that reverses the charge of the cell from negative to positive, abiding by the all-or-nothing principle.

The Refractory Period: After the Action Potential

As shown in Figure 3.6, when an impulse arrives at a neuron, sodium channels open briefly (about 1/1,000 of a second). When the sodium channels close, the negatively charged potassium ions reenter the neuron, the positively charged sodium ions are pumped out, and the neuron returns to its resting state of –70 millivolts: ready for the next action potential.

After an action potential has passed through a section of an axon, the cell membrane in that region can no longer admit positive sodium ions again for a few milliseconds. The cell membrane becomes super negatively charged and cannot fire again no matter how much stimulation it receives. This brief span of time when a neuron cannot fire is called the **refractory period**.

Refractory period: The brief span of time a neuron cannot fire immediately after an action potential.

FIGURE 3.6

Action Potentials

This figure illustrates the electrical impulse during an action potential (also called an "impulse" or "firing"). The sodium channels in the cell membrane open briefly and positive sodium cells surge into the cell. When they close, negatively charged potassium ions reenter the cell, returning it to a resting state—ready for the next action potential.

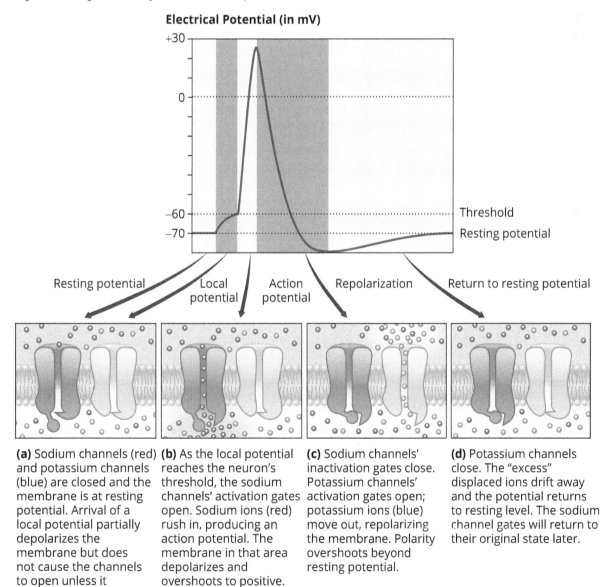

(a) Sodium channels (red) and potassium channels (blue) are closed and the membrane is at resting potential. Arrival of a local potential partially depolarizes the membrane but does not cause the channels to open unless it reaches threshold.

(b) As the local potential reaches the neuron's threshold, the sodium channels' activation gates open. Sodium ions (red) rush in, producing an action potential. The membrane in that area depolarizes and overshoots to positive.

(c) Sodium channels' inactivation gates close. Potassium channels' activation gates open; potassium ions (blue) move out, repolarizing the membrane. Polarity overshoots beyond resting potential.

(d) Potassium channels close. The "excess" displaced ions drift away and the potential returns to resting level. The sodium channel gates will return to their original state later.

Source: Garrett and Hough (2022).

How is a crowd doing "the wave" similar to neural communication in the brain?

iStock.com/simonkr

Some neurons have short axons and communicate with nearby neurons. Others have long axons and distant communications. Neural communications occur at variable speeds estimated from 2 to 225 miles per hour (Micheva et al., 2016). It's quite remarkable when you think about it—any piece of information (a startling loud noise, reacting to a hot comb, or experiencing a romantic touch) is the product of millions of neural connections collectively firing electrical impulses (Senan et al., 2017).

Sage Vantage❯   Practice what you learn in **Knowledge Check 3.1**

YOUR ELECTROCHEMICAL BRAIN: NEUROTRANSMITTERS AND DRUGS

? **Have You Ever Wondered?** 3.2 What are neurotransmitters, and how do they relate to drugs and disorders?

>> **LO 3.2**   **Compare and contrast how different neurotransmitters and drugs affect the brain.**

If you've been to a sports stadium, you've probably seen or been part of a "wave."

An electrical impulse's movement in a neuron is like fans doing a wave in their seats. The movement flows seamlessly but sometimes comes to a halt at the stadium aisle. The gap at the aisle is like the gap between neurons, which do not touch each other directly. The nervous system fills that gap with a chemical bridge of neurotransmitters that enables information to keep moving forward.

Neurotransmitters: The Chemical Messengers

There's a very tiny space between nearby neurons.

The space is called a **synapse** (also called the *synaptic cleft* or *synaptic gap*). When an electrical impulse reaches a neuron's axon terminals, those sacs (also called *vesicles*) release **neurotransmitters** into the synaptic gap. These chemical substances flood the synaptic gap, trying to bind to the dendrites of the next neuron in line, called the postsynaptic neuron.

Synapse: The tiny gap where the axon of a presynaptic neuron communicates with the dendrite of a postsynaptic neuron.

Neurotransmitters: Chemical substances that are stored in tiny synaptic sacs and allow neurons to communicate with each other throughout the body.

Bridging the Synaptic Gap

Neurotransmitters and dendrite receptors act like a system of locks and keys.

As illustrated in Figure 3.7, only specific neurotransmitters (the keys) can bind to specific dendrite receptors (the locks). When a key fits a lock, neurotransmitters found at synapses around the nervous system trigger a cascade of chemical events—either excitatory, inhibitory, or both.

Excitatory messages (or effects) increase the likelihood the receiving neuron will reach the threshold and fire. *Inhibitory* messages (or effects) decrease the likelihood that the receiving neuron will fire. Some neurotransmitters have both excitatory and inhibitory effects (Boto & Tomchik, 2019). The binding of one neurotransmitter to a dendrite receptor is generally not enough to push a cell to the threshold. When a sufficient number of excitatory neurotransmitters "lock" into position, the neuron fires. When a sufficient number of inhibitory neurotransmitters "lock" into position, neurons don't fire.

FIGURE 3.7

Communication Between Neurons

Like a lock and key, a neurotransmitter (the key) binds to a specific receptor (the lock) located in the dendrite membrane of another neuron on the opposite side of the synaptic cleft.

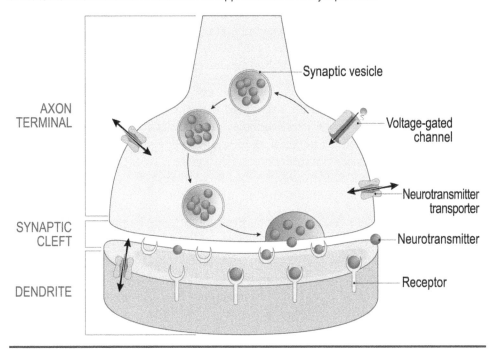

iStock.com/ttsz

Many competing neurons may be simultaneously releasing different neurotransmitters into the synaptic gaps between the single neurons at any given time. There's a bit of a Goldilocks phenomenon at play in which neurotransmitters influence behavior when they are *"just right."* That is, optimal functioning usually involves the "just right" amount of the "just right" neurotransmitters at the "just right" moments. When the neurotransmitter work is completed, it is reabsorbed back into the cell that previously released it (instead of moving along to the next neuron) in a process called *reuptake*.

Types of Neurotransmitters

There may be more than 100 chemically unique neurotransmitters. Those we know the most about are summarized in Table 3.1.

TABLE 3.1

Major Neurotransmitters: Their Location and Function

NEUROTRANSMITTER	LOCATION	EXCITATORY OR INHIBITORY?	FUNCTION
Acetylcholine	Brain, spinal cord, and peripheral nervous system	Excitatory or inhibitory	Muscle movement, arousal, attention, memory
Norepinephrine	Brain, spinal cord	Excitatory	Increases alertness
Dopamine	Brain	Excitatory or inhibitory	Control of movement and sensations of pleasure and reward
Serotonin	Brain, spinal cord	Excitatory or inhibitory	Sleep, mood, anxiety, and appetite
Gaba-aminobutyric acid, or GABA	Brain, spinal cord	Inhibitory	Slows central nervous system function
Glutamate	Brain, spinal cord	Excitatory	Learning and memory
Endorphins	Brain, spinal cord	Inhibitory	Pain relief, pleasurable feelings
Oxytocin	Brain, spinal cord	Excitatory or inhibitory	Love, emotional bonding, lactation

Rev. Jesse Jackson, the influential and outspoken 1960s civil rights leader who marched alongside Dr. Martin Luther King Jr., announced his diagnosis with Parkinson's disease in 2017. The low levels of dopamine are related to tremors, stiffness, and difficulty balancing, walking, and coordinating movement.

LUDOVIC MARIN/Contributor/AFP/via Getty Images

Acetylcholine. Acetylcholine influences physical movement because it releases at the synapses between neurons and muscle cells. Want another reason to hate spiders? If you get bitten by a black widow spider, its venom triggers a flood of acetylcholine into the synapses between the spinal cord and skeletal muscles, causing spasms and possible death. Neurotransmitters are often multipurpose. For example, acetylcholine also influences learning and memory (Yoder et al., 2017). People with Alzheimer's disease experience acetylcholine deficiency (Ma & Qian, 2019; Yi et al., 2020).

Norepinephrine. Norepinephrine is a hormone *and* a neurotransmitter associated with the "fight-or-flight" response to perceived danger. Ever been stressed out about how you're going to pay a bill or nervous about giving a speech? Stress stimulates the release of norepinephrine (Tillage et al., 2021; Wood & Valentino, 2017). The increased arousal brought about by norepinephrine may increase heart rate and blood pressure.

Dopamine. Dopamine is associated with varied effects. Positive effects include feelings of pleasure (Flack et al., 2019; Zald & Treadway, 2017) such as savoring a good meal, passing a difficult test, or enjoying a romantic touch. Negative effects of too much dopamine in particular areas of the brain are associated with serious mental disorders such as schizophrenia (McCutcheon et al., 2019). Low levels of dopamine are associated with Parkinson's disease and its uncontrollable body movements (Kaasinen et al., 2021; Latif et al., 2021). Remember the Goldilocks effect.

Serotonin. Serotonin helps regulate sleep, eating, mood, and pain. Those who experience depression or anxiety may have low levels of serotonin (Borroto-Escuela et al., 2021). Antidepressants, such as Prozac, increase serotonin by blocking its reuptake at the synapses (Hengartner et al., 2021; Sørensen et al., 2022). When it's difficult for a neuron to reabsorb a neurotransmitter, that amplifies the neurotransmitter's effect. Serotonin-related genes may increase the family risk for depression (Maruta et al., 2021; Soga et al., 2021).

Gaba-aminobutyric acid, or GABA. GABA inhibits neurotransmitters by telling the postsynaptic neurons (the next neurons in line) not to fire. GABA is the brain's brake pedal that helps regulate neural activity. Low GABA levels are linked with anxiety. Antianxiety drugs, such as Valium, increase GABA's inhibiting effects (Cheng et al., 2018). GABA may not function the same for people with epilepsy, and stress appears to increase GABA (Lee & Kim, 2021; Sarlo & Holton, 2021).

Glutamate. Unlike GABA, the neurotransmitter glutamate tells the postsynaptic neuron to fire. It affects learning and memory (Zhu et al., 2018). Too much glutamate overstimulates the brain to trigger migraines or even seizures. Glutamate is implicated across a variety of mental illnesses (de la Rubia Ortí et al., 2021; Duman et al., 2019; Iovino et al., 2020; Nasir et al., 2020).

Endorphins. Have you ever injured yourself but kept pushing through the pain? Your behavior was likely impacted by endorphins. Similar to painkilling drugs such as morphine, endorphins shield the body from pain and elevate feelings of pleasure. They may help explain why harmless pills or treatments (called placebos) relieve real symptoms. The patient's belief in the treatment may release endorphins leading to pain reduction (Micozzi, 2018).

Oxytocin. At last: the famous "love" hormone. Oxytocin is a neurotransmitter *and* a hormone that promotes the experience of love and increases social bonding. At childbirth, a powerful surge of oxytocin is released in birthing parents that promotes lactation (UvnäsMoberg et al., 2020). Oxytocin is not just for birth mothers; fathers' interactions with their children also raise their oxytocin levels (Feldman & Bakermans-Kranenburg, 2017). Oxytocin promotes emotional bonds and can increase pleasure during sexual orgasms (Cera et al., 2021).

Study Tip: Eggos and Pie, Ma'am

Trying to remember the eight key neurotransmitters and function? Use this fun *"Eggos and Pies Ma'am"* mnemonic device developed by Jason Spiegelman, a professor of psychology at the Community College of Baltimore County, and further adapted by Andrea Golden Atkins and her students to include oxytocin.

Write EGGOSAND in the first column and PIESMAAM in the second column. Then, fill in as shown here. The first column can remind you of the names of some important neurotransmitters, and the second column reminds you of at least one of that neurotransmitter's functions:

E = Endorphins	**P** = Pain reduction
G = GABA	**I** = Inhibitory
G = Glutamate	**E** = Excitatory
O = Oxytocin	**S** = Social
S = Serotonin	**M** = Mood
A = Acetylcholine	**A** = Arouse
N = Norepinephrine	**A** = Activate
D = Dopamine	**M** = Movement

Recreational Drugs and Disorders: Changing the Locks and Keys

Recreational drugs alter the lock and key mechanisms of neurotransmitters.

Recreational drugs, whether consumed by swallowing, smoking, snorting, or injecting, alter how neurotransmitters fit into receptor sites. Drugs that mimic neurotransmitters' effects are **agonists** and drugs that block neurotransmitters' effects are **antagonists**.

Agonists: Recreational drugs that mimic neurotransmitters' effects.

Antagonists: Recreational drugs that block neurotransmitters' effects.

Agonists increase the presence of neurotransmitters by limiting their reuptake, how well a neuron reabsorbs a particular neurotransmitter. They remind your author of some real-life neighbors who had five small children. They had a big yard in a safe neighborhood, so the exhausted mother would sometimes tell them to "go outside and play" and actually lock them out of the house for an hour or so. She was limiting their reuptake.

Below we discuss several recreational drugs and how they act on neurotransmitter receptors. Therapeutic drugs, like selective serotonin reuptake inhibitors (SSRIs) are typically used as antidepressants and also act on neurotransmitter receptors but are discussed in another chapter.

Cocaine, Ecstasy, and Hallucinogens

Cocaine blocks the reuptake of the "feel-good" neurotransmitter dopamine. Consequently, dopamine remains in the synapse longer before binding to receptors in other neurons (Clare et al., 2021). The result is a feeling of alertness, decreased fatigue, and elevated mood. Ecstasy or molly (a slang term for the synthetic drug 3,4-methylenedioxy-methamphetamine [MDMA]) is also an agonist that stimulates extremely high levels of serotonin, which makes people temporarily feel euphoria, love, pleasure, and sexual arousal.

**Eggos and pies, anyone?
Shown here are three of
Charity's [one of your authors]
children.**

Charity Brown Griffin

But keep the "just right" effect in mind. You really want the "just right" amount of such neurotransmitters in your system. Ecstasy ultimately interferes with the brain's ability to produce serotonin. The ironic effect of this feel-good drug is depression, a serious side effect (Parrott, 2013).

Hallucinogenic drugs, such as psilocybin (or "magic") mushrooms and LSD (lysergic acid diethylamide), also produce changes in a person's state of awareness, activate serotonergic systems (Basedow et al., 2021), and generate hallucinations and distortions of perception that resemble psychoses.

Alcohol and Tobacco

While alcohol (another agonist) may not be an illegal recreational drug, it is a depressant and affects our brain by increasing GABA activity. This is why that glass of wine in the evening is so relaxing. But the Goldilocks principle reminds us that moving past a "just right" amount by having too many glasses of wine can lead to a lack of coordination—and more serious problems.

GABA inhibits much of the central nervous system activity that keeps us conscious, alert, and able to form memories. Large amounts of alcohol—let's say, the 21 shots someone might unwisely attempt to drink to celebrate their 21st birthday—can lead to memory lapses, blackouts, loss of consciousness, and even death (Hermens & Lagopoulos, 2018; Miller et al., 2018).

In contrast, the stimulating effects of nicotine in tobacco come from glutamate synapses (Chawla & Garrison, 2018). Emerging treatments for tobacco addiction engage both agonists and antagonist neurotransmitters. A nicotine-like agonist reduces craving, and a nicotine-blocking antagonist competes with inhaled nicotine during a relapse (Rollema & Hurst, 2018).

Marijuana

Marijuana, known to some as "weed," "pot," "bud," "the Devil's lettuce," "dope," and "Mary Jane," is one of several drugs that can have both agonist and antagonist effects, influenced by other factors such as dose (Fudin, 2018). Marijuana affects both excitatory (mainly glutamatergic) and inhibitory (mainly GABAergic) receptors. Putting the brakes on a glutamate neuron slows things down, but inhibiting a GABA neuron reduces inhibition, so it speeds things up.

Some researchers think that this dual effect helps to explain the contradictory psychoactive effects of marijuana (Metrik et al., 2011). It can cause both drowsiness and enhanced sensory experiences; it can decrease anxiety at low doses but worsen it at higher doses.

Marijuana is becoming a popular option for relieving pain resulting from nerve damage.

iStock.com/Charles Wollertz

Marijuana's impairment of short-term memory is likely due to THC (the main active ingredient in marijuana) slowing down neurotransmission in the hippocampus, where we normally create memories. There are no cannabinoid receptors in the brainstem, which is responsible for respiration. Consequently, high doses of marijuana do not cause respiratory depression and death (unlike opioid overdoses). However, constant use of marijuana *or* use at critical periods of brain development, such as early adolescence, could spark long-term effects such as poorer motivation and difficulty learning and remembering information (Becker et al., 2018; Volkow et al., 2016).

The story doesn't end there. Marijuana has documented medicinal use. THC can mimic some neurotransmitters and bind to dendrite receptors that inhibit messages associated with feeling pain. Consequently, medical marijuana is primarily used for pain management—though also for nausea (Bao et al., 2023). For example, marijuana may help alleviate chronic pain from illnesses such as multiple sclerosis by influencing neural transmission in the spinal cord.

Glial Cells and Neurological Differences

Is your brain like a garden?

"Errant gardeners" is one of the helpful metaphors that describe how malfunctioning glial cells are associated with neurological disorders (Neniskyte & Gross, 2017). Normal brain development requires *pruning* (also a gardening term) or removal of unwanted parts. Actual trees become healthier when dead limbs are properly pruned (just above the joint). *Synaptic pruning* is the job of glial cells that target synapses that "have to be removed in a controlled and timely manner" to mature (Neniskyte & Gross, 2017, p. 658). Specific types of glial cells (microglia and astrocytes) identify and prune excessive synapses at particular stages of development. Too many synapses or too much pruning may be associated with autism, schizophrenia, and epilepsy.

Montel Williams, former talk show host, went public with his multiple sclerosis (MS) diagnosis in 1999 and started a foundation to advance MS research. Williams advocates for use of medical marijuana.

iStock.com/Roberto Galan

Damaged glial cells are less able to protect and nourish neurons (Hughes, 2021; Micheva et al., 2016). For example, multiple sclerosis (MS; see Figure 3.8) appears to be the result of damage to the myelin sheath (Wilbanks et al., 2019). When your myelin sheath on nerve cells is damaged, the electrical signal is slowed or stopped. Without efficient neural communication, people with MS, such as Montel

FIGURE 3.8

FIGURE 3.8

Multiple Sclerosis

Multiple sclerosis (MS) is the most common demyelinating disease of the central nervous system. The immune system attacks the myelin sheath, resulting in loss of muscle control, vision, and balance.

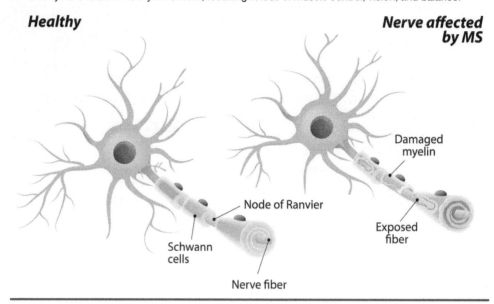

iStock.com/ttsz

Williams—former talk show host and marijuana activist—may experience sensory and motor impairment.

Researchers are probing the role of glial cells in other neurodegenerative diseases such as amyotrophic lateral sclerosis (ALS), Parkinson's disease, Alzheimer's disease, and Huntington's disease. The symptoms vary but there are similarities in the damage done to the myelin sheath. Good gardening of glial cells is critical to healthy neurons.

SPOTLIGHT ON RESEARCH METHODS

Runner's High

iStock.com/gradyreese

Have you experienced it—that strong sense of well-being after a good run? Some people call it a "runner's

high." Runner's high is a feeling of relaxed euphoria and for decades was attributed to a burst of endorphins released during exercise. But is that truly an endorphin rush you're feeling or something else? Anandamide, a little-known brain chemical that's been called the "bliss molecule," might provide the explanation.

Anandamide produces feelings of happiness and can move easily through the cellular barrier separating the bloodstream from the brain. When this chemical increases during exercise, it activates neurons' cannabinoid receptors—the same ones activated when THC or other chemicals from marijuana are in the bloodstream, to promote short-term psychoactive effects such as reduced anxiety and feelings of calm.

To test anandamide's effects, researchers (Fuss et al., 2015) didn't rely on human subjects—but, instead, mice!

Thirty-two mice were trained to run on a wheel over the course of 3 days. Half the mice would run for 5 hours per day, while the others would not run. They found that the mice that had been running responded with less anxiety to stress tests and were less sensitive to pain when put on a hot plate.

Two days later, the researchers conducted the same tests on two groups of mice: One group was given drugs that blocked only endorphins, while the other group was given drugs to block only anandamide (Fuss et al., 2015). The group of mice that had only their endorphins blocked—but could still produce anandamide—showed less stress and sensitivity to pain when compared to the group that had the anandamide blocked.

Research with mice helped to answer a basic question about the human brain and behavior. Unfortunately, the researchers could not determine if the mice felt euphoria because "euphoria is a highly subjective feeling that may be difficult to model in mice" (Fuss et al., 2015, p. 13105). Still, this study was groundbreaking because strongly suggested that cannabinoids, and not endorphins, are responsible for a runner's high. So essentially, to your brain, a runner's high might look a lot like a marijuana high.

In what ways can this research be used to develop new treatments for chronic pain or anxiety conditions? How could you use this research to convince someone that exercise comes with benefits beyond physical health? ●

Practice what you learn in **Knowledge Check 3.2**   **Sage** Vantage➤

YOUR ORGANIZED BRAIN: MAJOR PARTS AND FUNCTIONS

>> LO 3.3   Identify major parts of the brain and their functions.

The teenage brain has long been a puzzle to psychologists.

It annoys new young car owners to learn that their insurance rates are so high. But insurers are guided by statistical realities (Jensen, 2015). The cost curve in Figure 3.9 reflects the same risk assessment: Teenage drivers get in lots of accidents. It's a bit counterintuitive, because teenagers probably have quicker reaction times than their parents. So, why do so many smart teenagers do really dumb things (like texting while driving)—and not just when they are driving?

Think of the brain as a great athletic team. All the parts must work together, but each part has its own special contribution to the whole. Your developing brain can be divided into three major regions: the hindbrain, the midbrain, and the forebrain (Figure 3.10). The various parts don't start playing as a team until, well, about the same age as when your auto insurance rates decline. Teenagers have the brain power, but they don't have completed neural connections. Until we're about 25 years old, powerful, ancient hindbrain impulses more easily override reasoning and wise decision-making. Teenagers have potential—they just need a bit more emotional and neural maturity.

Have You Ever Wondered?
3.3 What are the different structures of the brain and what do they do?

The Hindbrain

Your hindbrain is at the top of your spinal cord.

It's the oldest part of the human brain in terms of our species' evolution, and it develops first during gestation—about 4 to 6 weeks into pregnancy. The hindbrain coordinates the many automatic behaviors your body *must* do to survive. For example, the hindbrain connects the brain to the spinal cord, so messages can be sent from the brain, down the spinal cord, to the rest of the body. It includes the medulla oblongata, pons, and cerebellum.

FIGURE 3.9

Average Auto Insurance Costs by Age of Driver

As we get older, our car insurance gets cheaper. This is because insurance companies know that teenagers get in a lot of car accidents (Jensen, 2015).

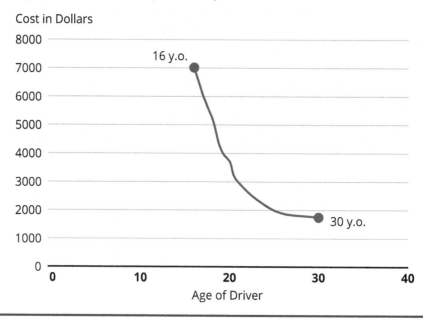

Medulla oblongata: A structure of the hindbrain that controls processes such as breathing, blood pressure, and heart rate.

The **medulla oblongata** begins where the spinal cord enters the skull and controls the automatic processes of the autonomic nervous system, such as breathing, blood pressure, and heart rate. It also regulates our reflexes—like jerking away from a potentially scalding hot comb! Because this part of the brain controls these life-sustaining functions, it is the part of the brain that a person would least want to have damaged.

Pons: A structure of the hindbrain that transmits information to coordinate motor movements.

"Pons" means bridge, and the pons does just that by serving as a bridge between the lower and upper parts of the brain. The **pons** coordinates motor movements from the right and left sides of the body. The pons is also involved in sleep and arousal (Scammell et al., 2017). While you're sleeping, the pons sends signals to your muscles to rest. This, in turn, prevents you from acting out on your dreams, which can happen if your pons stops functioning properly.

Cerebellum: A structure of the hindbrain that controls movement, balance, and coordination.

The **cerebellum** contains about half of the brain's neurons and controls movement, balance, and coordination. The cerebellum is important for athleticism and motor skills required for everyday tasks like texting on your phone or simply walking in a straight line. Consuming alcohol weakens activity in the cerebellum, leading to the clumsy movements typical of a drunk person (who can't walk in a straight line). Like an athlete who excels at more than one position, the cerebellum is also involved with cognition, emotional processing, and social behavior (Hoche et al., 2016).

The Midbrain

Your midbrain, located just above the hindbrain, was the next region to evolve in humans.

This tiny (just 2 centimeters!) but mighty structure processes information related to hearing, vision, and movement. The midbrain, the medulla oblongata, and the pons together are called the brainstem. The *brainstem* connects the cerebrum (a structure of the forebrain we examine later) to the spinal cord and cerebellum. The brainstem

FIGURE 3.10

Major Parts of the Human Brain

The brain consists of many important areas and can generally be thought of as a hindbrain, midbrain, and forebrain.

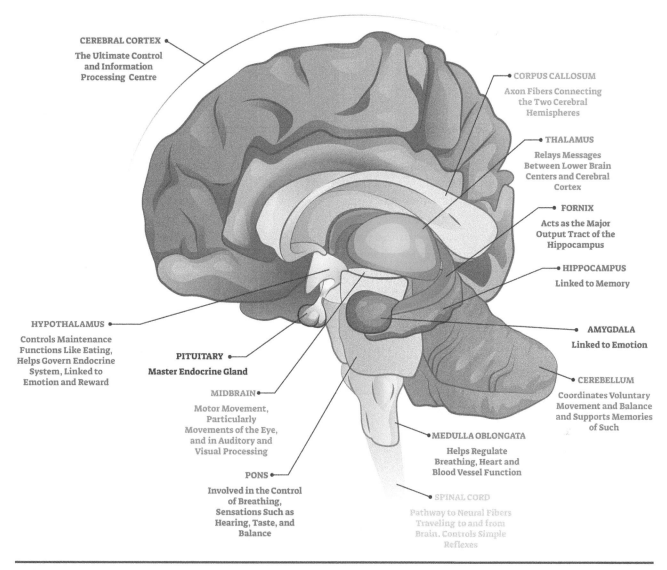

CEREBRAL CORTEX
The Ultimate Control and Information Processing Centre

CORPUS CALLOSUM
Axon Fibers Connecting the Two Cerebral Hemispheres

THALAMUS
Relays Messages Between Lower Brain Centers and Cerebral Cortex

FORNIX
Acts as the Major Output Tract of the Hippocampus

HIPPOCAMPUS
Linked to Memory

HYPOTHALAMUS
Controls Maintenance Functions Like Eating, Helps Govern Endocrine System, Linked to Emotion and Reward

AMYGDALA
Linked to Emotion

PITUITARY
Master Endocrine Gland

CEREBELLUM
Coordinates Voluntary Movement and Balance and Supports Memories of Such

MIDBRAIN
Motor Movement, Particularly Movements of the Eye, and in Auditory and Visual Processing

MEDULLA OBLONGATA
Helps Regulate Breathing, Heart and Blood Vessel Function

PONS
Involved in the Control of Breathing, Sensations Such as Hearing, Taste, and Balance

SPINAL CORD
Pathway to Neural Fibers Traveling to and from Brain. Controls Simple Reflexes

iStock.com/VectorMine

indeed looks like a stem and is one of the oldest parts of the brain, evolving more than 500 million years ago (Carter, 1998)!

A network of nerves in the midbrain called the **reticular formation** runs through the hindbrain and midbrain. The reticular formation regulates our sleep–wake cycle and plays a major role in alertness, fatigue, and motivation—and may control some 25 specific and mutually exclusive behaviors: sleep, walking, eating, urination, defecation, and sexual activity.

The reticular formation may influence two important character traits: introversion and extroversion (Bullock & Gilliland, 1993). The reticular formation of introverted people is more easily stimulated, resulting in a diminished desire to seek out stimuli. Extroverted people, however, have a less easily stimulated reticular formation, resulting in the need for more stimulation to maintain brain activity.

Reticular formation: A network of nerves in the midbrain that regulates the sleep–wake cycle and plays a major role in alertness, fatigue, and motivation to perform various activities.

The Forebrain

Think you're doing a good job of understanding all these parts of the brain?

Are you highly motivated to complete college, start your career, build your own company, or just get on with your life? All these different thoughts and feelings are possible because of the forebrain, the largest part of the brain and the last major region to evolve for humans. Most forebrain structures are bilateral: There is one on each side of the brain. The most important include the limbic system, thalamus, hypothalamus, cerebral cortex, and cerebrum. Let's cover each.

The Limbic System

The *limbic system* is involved in processing emotion, motivation, and memory. There are different opinions about what structures are included in the system and what interacts closely with it (Rajmohan & Mohandas, 2007). However, there are two widely accepted structures of the limbic system: the hippocampus and the amygdala.

The **hippocampus**, named for its similar appearance to a seahorse (hippocampus is the Greek word for "seahorse"), is located just above each ear. The hippocampus is involved with the formation and storage of memories. The neurotransmitter acetylcholine, which is involved in muscle control, is also involved in the memory function of the hippocampus.

A loud bang!

The **amygdala** is activated. This almond-shaped structure located near the hippocampus processes the fear you might experience from a gun like sound, even if you live in a small, historically safe town in the United States. You try to gather more information from your senses that gets routed to the amygdala *before* it goes to other parts of the brain. This is why people can respond to danger quickly, sometimes before they can identify the source or type of threat. While the amygdala is involved in memory of fear, it is unknown if memories are stored here (Squire & Kandel, 2009).

Hippocampus: A structure of the limbic system responsible for formation and storage of memories.

Amygdala: A structure of the limbic system involved in fear responses.

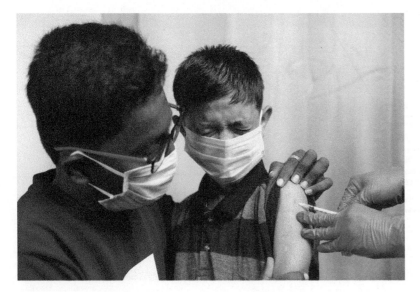

Because this child has a fear of needles, his amygdala is involved in producing this fear response.

iStock.com/lakshmiprasad S

Thalamus: The "triage" system of the brain that processes sensory information before sending it on to the part of the forebrain that deals with that kind of sensation.

Hypothalamus: A structure of the brain that maintains homeostasis and regulates hunger, thirst, temperature, and sexual desires.

The Thalamus

Triage nurses develop specialized skills. They assess patients, prioritize who gets treated first, and route patients to specialists according to the urgency of need. In many ways, the thalamus is like a triage nurse. The **thalamus** processes a variety of sensory information—hearing, sight, touch, or taste—and routes it to the part of the right part of the forebrain (Stafford & Huberman, 2017). Interestingly, smell does not pass through the thalamus; olfactory bulbs in the forebrain receive and direct neural input about odors detected by cells in the nasal cavity.

You'll learn more about how the senses work in the chapter on sensation and perception.

The Hypothalamus

Your **hypothalamus**, a structure located just below the thalamus, acts as your body's coordinating center. Its main function is to maintain homeostasis (maintaining stability to survive), regulating hunger, thirst, temperature, and sexual desires. The hypothalamus does its job by directly influencing your autonomic nervous system or by managing hormones through its control of the pituitary gland.

The Cerebral Cortex

What is your mental image of a brain?

You probably envision the *cerebral cortex*, the gray, thin (about 1/10 inch) outer layer of the cerebrum—that "gray matter" on the outermost layer of the brain. It is made up of deep folds and wrinkles that can pack a lot of brain into the skull's small space. A standard sheet of paper laid flat could not fit inside your closed fist—until you balled it up. If the cerebral cortex were ironed flat, it would be about 2 to 3 square feet—and your skull would have to be very large and very flat! *Corticalization* describes this prebirth brain-wrinkling process that allows for a lot of brain in a small space.

The Largest Part of the Forebrain: Cerebrum

There's one more part of the brain to know.

The gray cerebral cortex surrounds the *cerebrum*, the largest and uppermost portion of the brain. It consists of two roughly mirror-image halves called *hemispheres*. One hemisphere, usually the left, controls language and speech. The left hemisphere also processes information sequentially, one bit at a time (Gotts et al., 2013). The right hemisphere interprets visual and spatial information (for example, patterns and drawings, music, and emotional expression). This hemisphere also tends to process information in a broader manner, considering it as a whole (Longo et al., 2015).

Despite the different strengths of the two hemispheres, they function collaboratively, such as that people are not either "right-brained" or "left-brained" (#fakenews). The two hemispheres work simultaneously and together to help us interpret and interact with the world around us. The two hemispheres talk to each other through a thick band of white matter called the *corpus callosum*. Interesting research on "split brain" patients was done when some people with epilepsy had their corpus callosum cut, severing the two hemispheres (e.g., Gazzaniga et al., 1962). These studies helped clarify the distinctive processing that occurs in each hemisphere: verbal on the left and spatial on the right (see Figure 3.11).

Perhaps it is just one of those curious features of evolution, but each hemisphere is responsible for the opposite side of the body. If you write with your right hand, the motor cortex in the left hemisphere is responsible for controlling those movements. Keep in mind that information from our body can be transmitted to both sides of the brain, such as with hearing and vision, or to only one side of the brain, as with taste and olfaction.

The cerebrum is divided into four sections called *lobes:* the frontal, temporal, parietal, and occipital (Figure 3.12). Each lobe is associated with specific functions, although behavior is typically influenced simultaneously by several areas within the brain.

The Occipital Lobes

The **occipital lobes** are at the back of the brain and are responsible for processing visual information. When we see something with our eyes, electrical signals travel to the optic nerve from the eye to the thalamus and then to the *primary visual cortex* in the occipital lobes. These lobes also contain the *visual association cortex*, which helps us interpret aspects of the visual stimuli such as color, shape, and motion. Our eyes alone do not see but instead detect and transport information that must be processed in the occipital lobes for us to be able to truly see it. An injury to the occipital lobe can cause vision impairment or visual distortions.

Occipital lobes: Lobes located in the back of the brain and are responsible for processing visual information.

FIGURE 3.11

Split Brain Research

When patients have corpus callosum severed, usually to treat severe epilepsy, the two hemispheres can't talk to each other. Adapted from Gazzaniga et al. (1962).

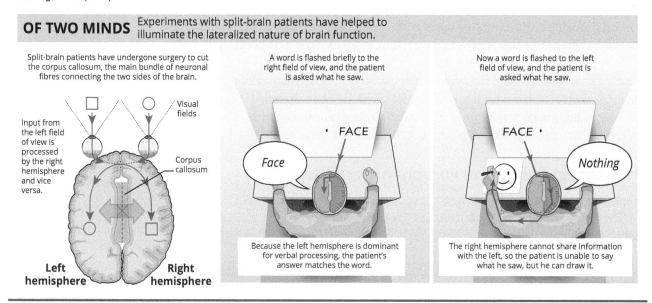

OF TWO MINDS Experiments with split-brain patients have helped to illuminate the lateralized nature of brain function.

Split-brain patients have undergone surgery to cut the corpus callosum, the main bundle of neuronal fibres connecting the two sides of the brain.

Visual fields

Input from the left field of view is processed by the right hemisphere and vice versa.

Corpus callosum

Left hemisphere   **Right hemisphere**

A word is flashed briefly to the right field of view, and the patient is asked what he saw.

FACE

Face

Because the left hemisphere is dominant for verbal processing, the patient's answer matches the word.

Now a word is flashed to the left field of view, and the patient is asked what he saw.

FACE

Nothing

The right hemisphere cannot share information with the left, so the patient is unable to say what he saw, but he can draw it.

Source: Wolman (2012).

FIGURE 3.12

The Brain's Main Lobes

The cerebrum is divided into four sections called lobes (frontal, temporal, parietal, and occipital) which are located on both the left and right sides of the brain and handle specific functions.

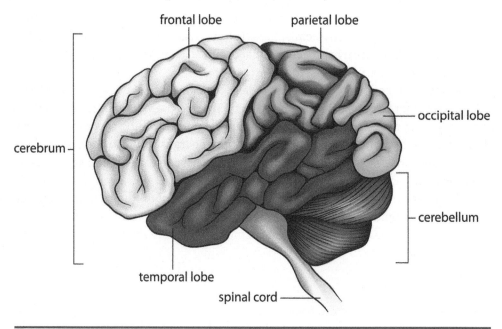

frontal lobe   parietal lobe

occipital lobe

cerebrum

cerebellum

temporal lobe

spinal cord

iStock.com/blueringmedia

The Temporal Lobes

Temporal lobes: Lobes located right behind the ears and are responsible for processing auditory information.

Right behind the ears are the second largest lobes, the **temporal lobes**. The temporal lobes have multiple functions but the main one is processing hearing. They contain the *primary auditory cortex* and *auditory association area*. Researchers have found that specific areas within the auditory association area respond to different pitches (Anderson et al., 2017). For most people, there is an area in the left temporal lobe that is involved with language, which will be discussed later.

The Parietal Lobes

At the top/back of the head are the **parietal lobes**, which are involved in understanding body position and movement (also called proprioception; Daprati et al., 2010). The parietal lobes are activated whenever you must draw on sensations and perceptions to judge how far to throw or kick a ball, how much to bend when sitting down in a chair, or how quickly to pull away when a hot comb approaches your scalp.

The frontmost portion of the parietal lobes includes the *somatosensory area*, which is important for processing and interpreting perception of touch, as well as temperature, body position, and pain. The somatosensory area in the parietal lobe has specific locations associated with the ability to perceive touch and pressure in a particular part of the body—including the fingertips, limbs, and genitalia. Our fingertips are very sensitive to touch and therefore have a larger corresponding portion of brain tissue in the somatosensory area.

Parietal lobes: Lobes located at the top/back of the brain and are responsible for understanding body position and movement as well as sensation and perception of touch.

Frontal lobes: Lobes located in the front of the brain and are responsible for higher-order functions such as attention, planning, impulse control, problem solving, creativity, social interaction, and motor function.

The Frontal Lobes

More than any other part of the brain, the **frontal lobes** (at the front part of the brain) are what makes humans, human. They are responsible for higher-order functions such as attention, planning, impulse control, problem solving, creativity, social interaction, and motor function. For most people, an area in the left hemisphere of the frontal lobe is devoted to language. The frontal lobes are closely interconnected with other brain regions. For example, the frontal lobes work with the hippocampus and temporal lobes to help you with memory and language tasks.

As the last section to fully develop in each of us (Leisman & Melillo, 2012), we can better understand why children, teenagers, and even some young adults continue to follow foolish impulses (Welsh & Pennington, 1988)! If your brain is an athletic team, the arrival of the frontal lobes can finally transform a good team into a great team. It's like the star player, who just showed up a little late to the game.

The most forward part of the frontal lobes is the *prefrontal cortex*. You can think of the prefrontal cortex as the executive director of your brain. It is involved in *executive functioning*, which includes abilities such as planning, goal setting, reasoning, and organization (Duverne & Koechlin, 2017; Miller & Cummings, 2017). It's like the captain of the team.

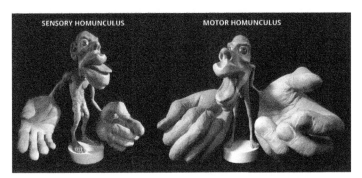

If brain tissue were mapped out in a sculpture shaped like a small person—a homunculus—there could be two options. The sensory homunculus shows larger body parts depending on how sensitive they are. The motor homunculus shows how we use our body to interact with the world—for example, very large hands for the complex range of motion involved in activities like typing or grasping an object.

The Natural History Museum, London/Science Source

Skills like typing require a huge amount of brain processing in the motor area of the frontal lobes.

iStock.com/lka84

The frontal lobes also contain the *motor area*, which is largely responsible for the body's voluntary movement, such as jumping, running, walking, handwriting, or texting. Just as with the somatosensory area, each part of the motor area corresponds to a specific location in the body. As an illustration of this, if someone were to use an electrode to apply mild electrical stimulation to a specific part of the motor area, there would be involuntary movement in that corresponding part of the body.

Brain Myths and "Lucy"

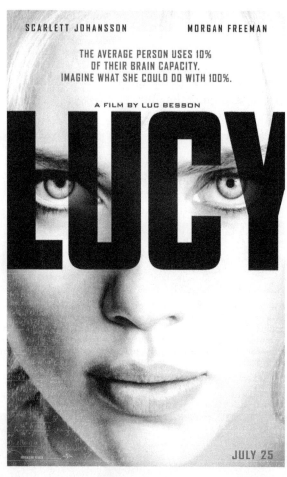

SilverScreen/Alamy Stock Photo

True or False?

- People fall into one of three learning styles: visual, auditory, or tactile/kinesthetic.
- Men's brains are wired for reasoning and action, whereas women's brains are wired for intuition and empathy.
- Some people (such as artists) tend to use the right hemisphere of their brain more, while others (such as scientists) tend to use the left side more.
- Most humans only use 10% of their brain.

Psychology research tells us: They're all false.

These myths about how our brains work have gained popular appeal for many . . . but they simply aren't true. Despite what your high school teachers might have taught you, "learning styles" are simply not a thing (Westby, 2019). The simplification of learning styles distorts the fact that all of us learn in all ways, though some of us have an easier time with some approaches and need accessibility provisions. We generally learn better when we process information in a variety of ways (such as *both* reading an explanation of trends and seeing a chart or graph) and when we learn in the same way that we'll be tested. For example, if you need to learn how to change a tire, actually doing it (kinesthetic) is better than seeing pictures of how it's done (visual).

The belief that men's brains are "rational" while women's brains are "intuitive" or "emotional" promotes sexist stereotypes that are socially constructed, rather than based on scientific evidence (Eliot, 2019). Most kinds of thought, including art and scientific reasoning, are done in both hemispheres (Hines, 1987), and people being "left-brained" or "right-brained" is, again, not backed up by science (Lilienfeld et al., 2009).

And if you really want to annoy your psychology professor, stick with the "we only use 10% of our brains" myth. Hopefully after reading this chapter, you realize how that idea simply isn't true. Unfortunately, one reason people continue to believe these myths might be because they're perpetuated by popular culture. The 2014 movie *Lucy* featured a main character who is forced to be a drug mule by her boyfriend until the drugs in her body are released. The plot focuses on how the drugs allow her to have new physical and mental powers because she can now use 100% of her brain. She's a psychic, has telekinesis, and is capable of mental time travel (also not a thing). While the movie has some appeal in terms of action shots and female empowerment, it's not based on any kind of science. ●

YOUR BEAUTIFUL BRAIN: NEUROIMAGING TECHNIQUES

>> **LO 3.4**   **Compare and contrast different brain neuroimaging techniques.**

Have You Ever Wondered?
3.4 How do we understand the location and/or function of different structures of the brain?

Your curious brain is beautiful.

We know that because modern technology allows us to take pictures of it. But research on brain functioning starts with a brutal accident in 1848. An explosion drove a 3-foot-long iron bar completely through the skull of Phineas Gage, a man working for the railroad. Yet a few minutes later he seemed to be fine! This was despite the fact that his doctor could physically press on the wound with one hand from the entry point below Gage's left eye and with the other hand from the exit point in his scalp above his left frontal lobe and touch his two hands together.

Over the next few weeks of his recovery, it became obvious that Gage's injury significantly affected his personality. The well-liked, competent railway foreman became crude, obstinate, and strangely indifferent to money. The effects on his personality were so profound that he was described as "no longer Gage" by people who knew him before the accident. All was not lost, however. Phineas Gage was still able to hold a job, drive a six-horse stagecoach in Chile, tell tall tales to his nephews, and work well with animals (Macmillan, 2002). This interesting case sparked new ideas in the study of the brain, with researchers hypothesizing a connection between the frontal lobe and personality.

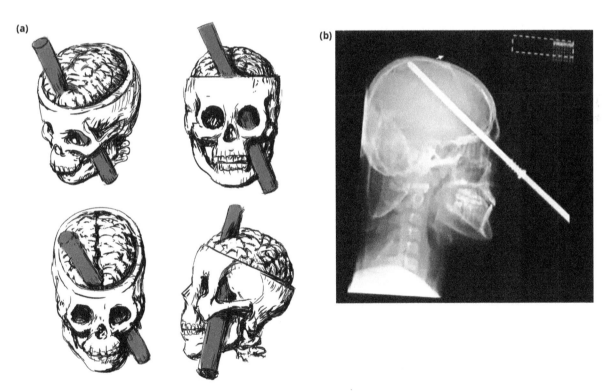

These images show traumatic brain injuries experienced by Phineas Gage in 1848 in Cavendish, Vermont (a), and Devon White in 2018 near Rome, Italy (b).

(a) Science History Images/Alamy Stock Photo; (b) San Camillo Hospital

Brain-Imaging Techniques

We've come a long way since Phineas Gage.

Since that famous case in 1848, new technology has developed providing many more insights. Current brain-imaging techniques allow us to observe living, active brains. This section looks at various technologies and what we learning from them.

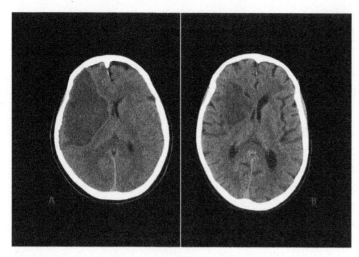

The red in these computed tomography (CT) scans indicates a stroke caused by a loss of blood supply to the brain.

Science Source

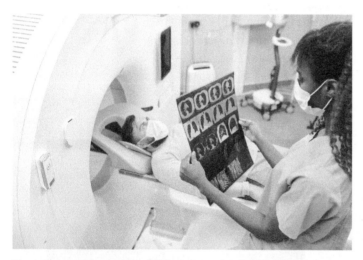

Magnetic resonance imaging (MRI) produces detailed images of brain structures and other soft tissues. MRI scans are helping us understand how COVID-19 damages the brain.

iStock.com/shironosov

During an electroencephalograph (EEG) test, electrodes are attached to the head. They record electrical activity from different parts of the brain as they react to visual or auditory stimuli.

AJPhoto/Science Source

Computed Tomography (CT)

Computed tomography (CT) takes X-ray images from different angles and uses software to create cross-sectional images (slices) that map the structure of the brain. A CT scan can show stroke damage, tumors, skull fractures, and abnormal brain structures, as well as examine metal (such as a bullet) inside the brain. The CT scan shown here indicates a stroke occurred. Depending on the affected brain region, symptoms often include an inability to move one or more limbs on one side of the body, failure to understand or formulate speech, or vision impairment. COVID-19 is a risk factor for stroke (Nannoni et al., 2021). One disadvantage of a CT scan is that it cannot show very small details within the brain.

Magnetic Resonance Imaging (MRI)

Unlike a CT scan, *magnetic resonance imaging (MRI)* shows small details that help identify the effects of small strokes. During an MRI, a person lies on a bed that slides into a tube surrounded by a circular magnet. The magnet, along with radio waves, creates detailed images of the brain but does not record brain activity.

In one study, participants exposed to COVID-19 found loss of gray matter in the cortex equivalent to nearly 10 years of aging (Douaud et al., 2022). People who experienced no or mild symptoms of COVID-19 displayed brain damage involving smell dysfunction regardless of disease severity, age, or sex. Whether the brain damage can be partially reversed, or whether these effects will persist in the long term, remains to be investigated with additional follow-up.

Electroencephalography (EEG)

Electroencephalography (EEG) measures ongoing electrical functioning in the brain by placing electrodes (metal disks attached to wires) on the scalp. It's not painful—nothing like a hot comb! The EEG is better at showing *when* electrical activity occurs (rather than where). An EEG can help detect and identify types of epilepsy. For example, Wind [one of your authors] got an EEG twice—once as a sophomore in college, then again 15 years later—to help explain why she sometimes has small seizures.

There are a lot of purposes for an EEG test. EEGs were recently used to compare learning from physical writing, digital key tapping, and drawing among 12-year-olds and young adults. That study concluded that writing or drawing by hand, as opposed to typing, optimized learning (Ose Askvik et al., 2020). The EEG showed that when writing or drawing (not typing), important brain areas were activated that are tied to memory and encoding of new information. Some researchers believe this is why handwriting notes in class might be better for encoding memory than typing notes.

Positron Emission Tomography (PET)

Positron emission tomography (PET) measures blood flow to active areas in the brain. PET involves injecting a person with a safe form of radioactive glucose (a kind of sugar). The computer detects brain activity by looking at which neurons are using up the radioactive glucose. It then projects those active images onto the monitor using colors to indicate what regions of your brain are active during a particular task. PET scans have been used to evaluate brain tumors (Herholz et al., 2012), memory (Zwan et al., 2017), and alcohol abuse (Vijay et al., 2018), among other things.

   While the risks due to the injection of radioactive substances during a PET scan are low, functional MRI (fMRI) is an even safer way to image the brain.

Functional MRI (fMRI)

Functional MRI (fMRI) is a variation on MRI that indicates brain activity. fMRI does not provide a direct measure of neural activity. Instead, it uses magnets to generate a detailed, three-dimensional computer image of brain structures *and* activity based on how the brain uses oxygen. fMRIs tend to be clearer than PET scans and avoid exposing brain cells to radiation. One of the promises of fMRI is early detection of Alzheimer's disease, which typically reduces activity in certain brain regions (Guo & Zhang, 2020).

Cultural Neuroscience: Understanding Our Bio-sociocultural Brain

Some brains are studied more than others.

   We learn more when we leverage many perspectives. Currently, about 90% of brain visualizations come from countries of "Western" origin—countries that represent only 12% of the

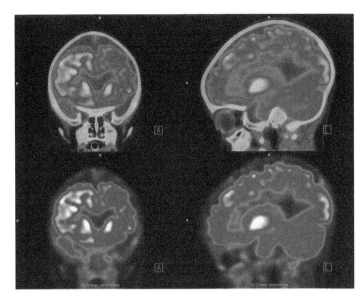

Positron emission tomography (PET) involves injecting a radioactive glucose into the bloodstream; three-dimensional images are then constructed by computer analysis. Lighter colors indicate greater brain activity.

iStock.com/wenht

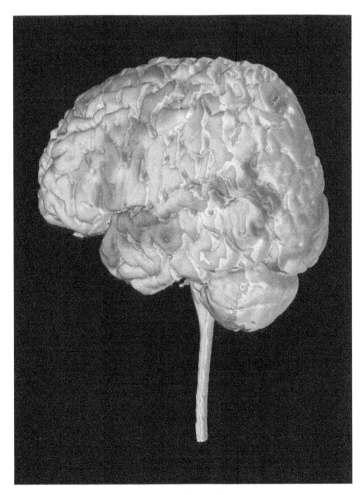

This functional magnetic resonance imaging (fMRI) scan overlapped on a model of the brain shows areas of the brain with increased activity during tasks. This scan shows the results of a visual sentence completion task.

K H FUNG/Science Source

Cultural neuroscience provides insight into how much the brain can be shaped by the environment. Research from Northwestern University psychologist Dr. Joan Chiao suggests that Eastern collectivist cultures may buffer against depression.

iStock.com/PamelaJoeMcFarlane

Motor vehicle accidents like that of famous comedian Tracy Morgan are one of the most common causes of TBI. Left with permanent brain damage after a driver crashed a tractor-trailer into his limousine van, Morgan continues to perform standup comedy.

Bobby Bank/Contributor/Getty Images Entertainment/via Getty Images

Neuroplasticity: The brain's ability to adopt new functions, reorganize itself, or make new neural connections as a function of experience.

world population (Arnett, 2009). Looking at brain imaging of individuals from other countries provides new insights. For example, Joan Chiao (2009) found that people from East Asian collectivist cultures are more likely to have a gene that buffers them from depression than people from Western cultures. The field of cultural neuroscience is an interdisciplinary approach that allows us to understand the interaction between genes, the brain, and social and cultural factors. Thanks to this new field, we are beginning to understand beautiful differences in neural mechanisms within and across different cultures.

Brain Damage and Plasticity

Phineas Gage is not the only person to suffer brain injury and survive.

In June 2018, 14-year-old Devon White was with his family on a boat and was loading a harpoon, a long spear-like tool used to catch large fish. Accidentally, the lethal razor-sharp harpoon went off and struck White in the left eye at more than 60 miles per hour. He was airlifted 100 miles to the hospital to have the bolt removed from his head. Surprisingly, surgeons expected he would recover.

What allowed White and Gage to recover so remarkably? The brain has the potential to rewire itself, to some degree, even after such profound injuries. People who have endured other *traumatic brain injuries (TBIs)* have shown remarkable capacity for the brain to change and heal. TBIs can range from relatively mild concussions to repeated injuries to the brain that lead to catastrophic mental breakdowns. Even milder TBIs can lead to major brain damage when they occur repeatedly, leading to concerns for athletes in contact sports like football, hockey, and boxing.

Thankfully, the brain can move critical functions from a damaged area to a healthy one or re-create connections that were lost. **Neuroplasticity** is the brain's ability to adopt new functions, reorganize itself, or make new neural connections as a function of experience. Brain plasticity varies with age, being strongest in infancy and early childhood and gradually decreasing with age.

Almost every major structure of the neuron is capable of experience-based change, which can occur in *all* stages of life. This means that we can form new neurons (called *neurogenesis*) and that interconnections between neurons can become more complex even during adulthood, especially in areas like the hippocampus (Apple et al., 2017; Pons-Espinal et al., 2019).

Your mind and body can reshape your brain. Aerobic activity and meditation can support lasting changes in plasticity and connectivity (Chételat et al., 2018).

iStock.com/YakobchukOlena

Meet Kathia, Neuropsychometrist

What is your career?

I am a neuropsychometrist at a hospital. My team works on head trauma, spinal cord injuries, chronic pain management, adjustments to disabilities, abnormal illness behaviors, and dementia. I administer over 75 different cognitive tests designed to assess individuals' cognitive functioning following injury-causing head accidents. After I test the patients, I report the results to the neuropsychologist who uses that information to make diagnoses and interpretations.

How was studying psychology important for success in this career?

Studying psychology helped me understand that different behaviors come from a variety of areas of the brain. Learning the functions of all the lobes really helped me. Within my job now, one element is to understand test methods and what the results mean. Studying psychology, I had opportunities to participate in conducting psychological research projects in which I learned a lot about statistics and results.

How do concepts from this chapter help in this career?

When I see patients, I read their charts and it will tell me what lobes their injury impacted and from

that I know what to expect when they come in for appointments. Sometimes, depending on the area that is injured, people can become inhibited and/or unaware of how they are to others. I keep that in mind when they come to see me so I understand why they may act the way they do. Understanding various cognitive disorders is also beneficial because that helps me understand why specific tests are given to certain patients.

Is this the career you always planned to have after college?

Graduating college, I really was not sure what exactly I wanted to do, but I had always been very interested in the concepts of the brain and how it influences behaviors. I simply searched for jobs relating to the brain. I developed a passion for learning about traumatic brain injuries. I saw that the individuals I was working with used to have much different lives and suddenly everything they had looked forward to in life was essentially nonexistent depending on the severity of their situation.

If you could give current college students one sentence of advice, what would it be?

Find something you are passionate about and follow it. ●

One of the most powerful ways to stimulate neuroplasticity in the brain is physical activity. Aerobic exercise helps the brain as much as the heart by releasing brain-derived neurotropic factor (BDNF). This substance sets in motion the growth of new synaptic connections and bolsters the strength of signals transmitted from neuron to neuron.

Although concussion injuries are a major concern in sports, there is some evidence suggesting sports have the potential to support brain health. Researchers say that if an athlete avoids head injuries, their brain is likely healthier than a nonathlete's because playing a variety of sports can tune the brain to better understand one's sensory environment (Krizman et al., 2020).

SageVantage🐦   Practice what you learn in **Knowledge Check 3.4**

YOUR COMPLICATED BRAIN: THE ENDOCRINE SYSTEM

?

Have You Ever Wondered?
3.5 What is the endocrine system?

Endocrine system: A complex network of glands and organs that release chemicals directly into the bloodstream to communicate messages that influence biological functioning *and* behavior.

Hormones: Chemical messengers released in the endocrine system.

>> **LO 3.5**   **Compare and contrast the nervous and endocrine systems and how they each affect behavior.**

Neurons are not the only means of communication within the body.

The **endocrine system** is a network of glands and organs that release chemicals directly into the bloodstream to communicate messages that influence biological functioning *and* behavior (Figure 3.13). The chemicals released in the endocrine system are called **hormones**. Insulin, cortisol, testosterone, estrogen, and melatonin are hormones you may have heard of.

Hormones are quite different from neurotransmitters in terms of their speed and mode of transmission. For example, neurotransmitters send messages almost immediately, whereas hormonal messages may take minutes to reach their destination, and the behaviors and responses affected may not occur until quite a while later.

Also, neurotransmitters move through neurons along a line like a signal carried by a wire along a cellphone tower. However, hormones travel outward in different directions through the body in the bloodstream like radio waves that only respond when the radio is tuned to the correct station. Hormones' molecules fit into the receptor sites of the organs, which allows hormones to fulfill their function and affect behavior, such as controlling and coordinating your body's metabolism, energy level, reproduction, growth and development, response to injury, stress, and mood. Briefly consider each gland as we get to the end of this chapter.

The Pituitary Gland

The *pituitary gland* is a pea-sized gland just beneath the hypothalamus.

This gland is seen as *the* major gland of the body because it controls functioning across the entire endocrine system. The pituitary gland does this by acting as a commander sending messages to other

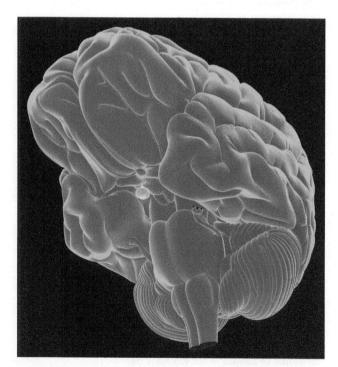

The pituitary gland is a major endocrine gland important for controlling growth and development and the functioning of the other endocrine glands.

iStock.com/SciePro

FIGURE 3.13

The Endocrine System

The endocrine system is another messenger system made up of eight glands. The endocrine glands secrete hormones directly into the bloodstream, which carries them to the target organs of the body to communicate messages that influence biological functioning and behavior.

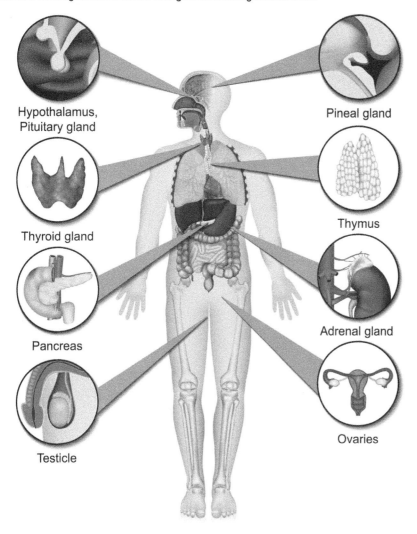

Hypothalamus, Pituitary gland

Thyroid gland

Pancreas

Testicle

Pineal gland

Thymus

Adrenal gland

Ovaries

iStock.com/medicalstocks

glands and organs. For example, a part of the pituitary gland secretes a growth hormone that regulates how tall children grow from infancy to childhood. The pituitary gland also directly controls important functions involved in pregnancy and levels of water in the body (Woodmansee, 2019).

The Thyroid Gland

The *thyroid gland* is a butterfly-shaped gland at the base of your neck.

This gland releases hormones that control metabolism—the way your body uses energy and regulates vital body functions such as body weight, body temperature, cholesterol levels, and much more. The thyroid gland uses iodine from the foods you eat to make two main hormones: triiodothyronine (T3) and thyroxine (T4). It is important that T3 and T4 levels are neither too high nor too low.

Symptoms of *too much* T3 and T4 in your body (i.e., *hyper*thyroidism) can include anxiety, irritability, nervousness, sweating or sensitivity to high temperatures, hand

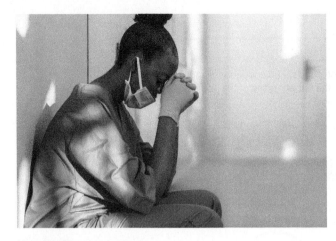

Many health care professionals continue to experience physical and psychological stress because of working extra hours due to the COVID-19 pandemic. How might the endocrine system be involved in responding to this prolonged stress?

iStock.com/insta_photos

trembling (shaking), hair loss, or missed or light menstrual periods. In contrast, symptoms of *too little* T3 and T4 in your body (i.e., *hypo*thyroidism) can include trouble sleeping; tiredness and fatigue; difficulty concentrating; dry skin and hair; depression; sensitivity to cold temperature; frequent, heavy periods; and joint and muscle pain.

The Adrenal Glands

The *adrenal glands* are small, triangular-shaped glands located on top of both kidneys.

Adrenal glands produce hormones that help regulate mood and energy and respond to stress. Each adrenal gland secretes epinephrine (also known as adrenaline) and norepinephrine (also known as noradrenaline).

We already learned that norepinephrine also functions as a neurotransmitter when released by neurons (conveying information to neurons). But in the adrenal glands, *norepinephrine* is released as a hormone (conveying information to glands). Unlike most hormones, epinephrine and norepinephrine act quickly to activate the autonomic nervous system when you are under stress.

Cortisol is another adrenal hormone that maintains the activation of bodily systems during prolonged stress. Your body releases cortisol when you experience physical stress (such as illness, surgery, or extreme heat or cold) and psychological stress (such as an emotionally traumatic event).

WHAT'S MY SCORE?

How Stressed Are You?

The nervous and endocrine systems are involved in stress responses. Many studies rely on self-report measures to understand how stress impacts the body. The Perceived Stress Scale (PSS) measures how much situations in your life affect your stress (Cohen & Williamson, 1988). How do you score?

Instructions: For each question, rate how you felt or thought a certain way *within the past month*. Use the following scale for each question:

0	1	2	3	4
Never	Almost Never	Sometimes	Fairly Often	Very Often

1. How often have you been upset because of something that happened unexpectedly?

2. How often have you felt that you were unable to control the important things in your life?

3. How often have you felt nervous and "stressed"?

4. How often have you felt confident about your ability to handle your personal problems?

5. How often have you felt that things were going your way?

6. How often have you found that you could not cope with all the things that you had to do?

7. How often have you been able to control irritations in your life?

8. How often have you felt that you were on top of things?

9. How often have you been angered because of things that were outside of your control?

10. How often have you felt difficulties were piling up so high that you could not overcome them?

Scoring Instructions: Your final score will range from 0 to 40, with higher scores suggesting greater perceived stress.

When you consider your score, how stressed were you in the past month? In what ways do you think your nervous and endocrine systems were impacted? ●

Source: Cohen and Williamson (1988).

The Pineal Gland, Pancreas, Thymus, and Gonads

The *pineal gland* is a small, pea-shaped gland in the brain.

Though its function isn't fully understood, researchers do know that it receives information about the state of the light–dark cycle from the environment and conveys this information to produce and secrete the hormone melatonin (Aulinas, 2019). Melatonin is best known for the role it plays in regulating sleep patterns (also called circadian rhythms).

The *pancreas* is an organ located in the abdomen and is involved in digestion and endocrine functions. As part of the endocrine system, the pancreas regulates blood sugar by secreting insulin and glucagon. If the pancreas secretes *too little* insulin, it results in diabetes. If the pancreas secretes *too much* insulin, it results in hypoglycemia or low blood sugar. When a person has diabetes and experiences hypoglycemia symptoms (such as pale skin, hunger, dizziness, blurred vision), they often need to eat or drink carbohydrates immediately to increase their blood sugar level.

Your *thymus* is a small gland in your upper chest behind your breastbone (sternum) just in front of and above your heart. Researchers do not fully understand the way thymic hormones exert their effects, but hormones released by this gland are known to be essential to immune function. In fact, thymic hormones are used to treat many infections and certain autoimmune diseases (Thapa & Farber, 2019).

The *gonads* include the ovaries, located in the pelvis on either side of the uterus, and the testes, located in the scrotum. Both glands produce hormones related to sexual development and reproduction.

The Nervous System–Endocrine System Connection

Some hormones influence activity.

The endocrine system is not part of the brain. However, some of the hormones produced by endocrine glands influence brain activity by producing inhibitory or excitatory effects (Brady et al., 2005). The hypothalamus connects to *both* the nervous system and the endocrine system to control body activities (Fukushi et al., 2019).

For example, the hypothalamus influences the menstruation cycle by sending a signal to the pituitary gland. The pituitary gland then releases hormones that stimulate ovaries to develop an egg. During this process, the egg releases hormones that prepare the womb to receive a fertilized egg. If fertilized, the ovaries send hormonal feedback to the hypothalamus so that it will not stimulate further egg development.

Oxytocin also does double duty as both a neurotransmitter *and* a hormone. The hypothalamus makes oxytocin, but part of the pituitary gland stores and releases it into your bloodstream. The hypothalamus and the pituitary gland also communicate to maintain T3 and T4 balance in the thyroid gland.

The body's nervous systems and endocrine system perform an extraordinary chemical dance balancing your body and brain so you can enjoy life. You have an extraordinary, unique body and brain full of beauty, wonder, astonishment, and surprises. ●

Practice what you learn in **Knowledge Check 3.5**   **Sage** Vantage

CHAPTER REVIEW

Learning Objectives Summary

3.1   How do neurons communicate with each other and the body?

›› LO 3.1   Explain the nervous system, types of neurons, and their structure.

The central nervous system includes the brain and spinal cord, and the peripheral nervous system is made up of all the nerves and neurons not in the brain and spinal cord. Neurons are the messenger cells that receive, integrate, and transmit information using electrical impulses and chemical signals. There are three broad types of neurons. The structure of a neuron includes dendrites, the soma, the axon, and axon terminals. They fire in an all-or-none manner when they reach a charge called the action potential.

3.2   What are neurotransmitters, and how do they relate to drugs and disorders?

›› LO 3.2   Compare and contrast how different neurotransmitters and drugs affect the brain.

Neurotransmitters are chemical substances that allow neurons to communicate with each other throughout the body. Examples of neurotransmitters are acetylcholine, serotonin, dopamine, and more. Recreational drugs interfere with the natural communication process between neurons in various ways. Some disorders, such as multiple sclerosis, occur when that process is disrupted.

3.3   What are the different structures of the brain and what do they do?

›› LO 3.3   Identify major parts of the brain and their functions.

The brain has three major regions: the hindbrain, which coordinates functions that are fundamental to survival; the midbrain; and the forebrain, which allows us to think, perceive, and interpret the world around us.

3.4   How do we understand the location and/or function of different structures of the brain?

›› LO 3.4   Compare and contrast different brain neuroimaging techniques.

Various methods offer glimpses into the brain and its functions. These include CT, MRI, EEG, PET, and fMRI scans. Brain imagining has confirmed that while everyone's brain develops similarly, no two brains function just alike.

3.5   What is the endocrine system?

›› LO 3.5   Compare and contrast the nervous and endocrine systems and how they each affect behavior.

In the endocrine system, glands secrete chemicals called hormones, which travel to tissues and organs all over the body to communicate messages that influence biological functioning and behavior. Although the endocrine system is not part of the brain, some of the hormones produced by endocrine glands influence brain activity.

CRITICAL THINKING QUESTIONS

1. Look again at the list of neurotransmitters outlined in this chapter. Try to think of examples of when different neurotransmitters might be working to impact behavior, either in your own life or in the media (a person from a movie, TV show, or book). List three common things you do in your daily life and explain what neurotransmitters are involved and how.

2. Both prescription and recreational drugs influence behavior mainly by interfering with the work of neurotransmitters. Should a drug's impact on your nervous system help guide morality and/or legality of use? For example, consider the ways marijuana affects our nervous system and reflect on why you might disagree or agree with legalization efforts.

3. Your family invites you over for a cookout and card games. Describe how the following parts of the brain are involved during your afternoon of eating cookout food, socializing, and playing cards: hippocampus, hypothalamus, temporal lobes, and occipital lobes.

4. The number of people who could be described as neurodivergent is very high and continues to rise. What are three specific ways your college/university can be more neurodiversity-friendly?

REUTERS/Mike Blake

4

Identity, Sex, and Gender

You are complicated. Your age, hometown, family heritage, friends, ethnicity, and experiences all shape your identity. Each factor intersects with and influences the other factors. The end result is how you express your sense of self in the world. Often, how you see yourself matches how others see you—but not always.

This is a true story. Shannon was born in 1975 to Midwestern, conservative, lower-middle-class parents who were both military veterans. During her entire childhood, she thought of herself as a "tomboy," preferring short hair and jeans to more "feminine" fashion options. It wasn't until high school that Shannon finally admitted to herself that she was attracted to women. Unfortunately, when she revealed this to her mother, she was told never to step inside their house again. Shannon's mother even made her give her house keys back. Shannon worked on farms growing up and joined the Marines when she was 18.

Shannon left the military after a few years and drifted from job to job and from state to state. She used drugs and alcohol to dull the pain of her mother's rejection. She finally ended up in California and was invited to a "top party." She didn't know what that was until she arrived: The host was celebrating his breast removal surgery, an important step in his female-to-male gender transition. Shannon had an epiphany that night. Because of her sheltered childhood and growing up before the Internet age, she had never been exposed to the possibility of being transgender.

Shannon realized that this was the key to an elusive identity. Shannon changed his name to Patrick—both names honor his Irish ancestry—and started his gender transition process at the age of 41. It was a bumpy road.

The photo shown here is of another veteran transman—not Patrick, but Paolo Batista. Both men look similar today, with tattoos and beards, but we've elected not to use a photo of the real Patrick to help protect his identity and safety.

After reading this chapter, you will get answers to several questions you've been curious about:

Have You Ever Wondered?

4.1   How does our identity form?

4.2   What is the difference between sex and gender?

4.3   How is sexual orientation described in psychology?

4.4   How do culture and technology influence sexuality?

4.5   What is intersectionality?

Learning Objectives

LO 4.1   Describe theories that help explain how identity is formed.

LO 4.2   Analyze models of thinking about sex and gender.

LO 4.3   Compare and contrast the Kinsey and Storms models of sexual orientation.

LO 4.4   Explain ways that culture and technology influence sexual behaviors.

LO 4.5   Define intersectionality and analyze how it applies to your own life.

FORMING AN IDENTITY

>> **LO 4.1   Describe theories that help explain how identity is formed.**

Have You Ever Wondered?
4.1 How does our identity form?

Patrick's identity changed several times.

The characteristics and qualities that make you, well, *you* are not set at birth. A person's identity, that collection of distinctive traits that creates a sense of self, morphs and evolves over their lifetime. When you are in your 30s, you won't be quite the same person you were in your 20s. Even a single experience can change how we think about who we are. Patrick's identity slowly changed from (1) heterosexual woman to (2) lesbian woman to (3) heterosexual man. Patrick [a personal friend of Wind's who agreed to share his story for this chapter] often reflects on how much of his early life was spent trying to discover why he was so dissatisfied with the identities other people tried to put on him. He was asking the question most of us ask ourselves at different stages of our lives: Who am I?

It's a simple question, but sometimes a tough one to answer. The response represents our **self-concept**, the personal summary of who individuals believe they are. It includes our positive and negative qualities, relationships, group memberships, opinions, and previous behaviors—both public and private (Hewitt & Genest, 1990; Markus, 1977). For Patrick, his sexuality and gender aren't the only parts of his self-concept. He's also a wonderful chef, a Green Bay Packers fan, a military veteran, a home gardener, a husband, a stepfather, and a dog lover (among many other things). How does self-concept form in the first place?

Self-concept: The personal summary of who individuals believe they are, including qualities, relationships, group memberships, opinions, past actions, and more.

Social Identity Theory

You're complicated; we all are.

According to **social identity theory**, an individual's complicated self-concept comes from two sources: a personal identity and a social identity (Rivenburgh, 2000; Sherif, 1966; Tajfel, 1981, 1982; Tajfel & Turner, 1986):

Social identity theory: The idea that self-concept is composed of two parts: a personal identity, which includes personality and physical traits, and a social identity, made up of our group memberships, relationships, and culture.

- *Personal identity* includes our individual personality traits, physical traits, goals, and opinions.

- *Social identity* comes from our social relationships and group memberships, such as your family of origin, the family you choose to create as an adult, belonging to a choir, playing on a sports team, participating in a faith community, or declaring a specific academic major. Social identity also includes our culture and subcultures.

The Mirror Self-Recognition Test

Forming a personal identity might start with realizing you are you. If you look in a mirror and see something is stuck in your hair, then you'll reach for your own hair—not the hair in the reflection. Congratulations—you've just passed the **mirror self-recognition test** (sometimes called the mark test). It's a specific behavior indicating that you know the reflection is *you* and not some other person in the glass (Gallup, 1968). It might seem silly, but it's not as simple or as obvious as it might sound; for example, some people with advanced Alzheimer's disease cannot pass this test (Biringer & Anderson, 1992; Biringer et al., 1988).

Mirror self-recognition test: Marking an animal in a spot they cannot see without a mirror, to test if they recognize their reflection as themselves.

Gordon Gallup developed the mirror self-recognition test to test whether apes and monkeys have a sense of self. Gallup first anesthetized some chimpanzees, macaques,

Do nonhuman animals have a sense of self? A YouTube .com search for "animal self-recognition" results in videos of elephants, lions, chimpanzees, and others toying with their image in a mirror.

Michel Gunther/Science Source

Social comparison theory: We make assessments about who we are by comparing how we think or act to those around us.

and rhesus monkeys. Then he marked each animal with a nonodorous, nonirritating red dye just above the eyebrow (imagine a big red "X" on their foreheads). When the animals woke up, they didn't realize anything had happened. They could not see, smell, or feel the red dye without a mirror. To Gallup, the crucial behavior was whether the waking animals—upon looking in the mirror— would touch their own foreheads—a sign that they had a sense of self.

In Gallup's first study, the four chimpanzees (but not the other primates) touched the strange red mark on their own foreheads. Eureka! Since those original studies, the mirror self-recognition test has now provided evidence of a self-concept in other great apes (Parker, 1991), Asian elephants (Plotnik et al., 2006), killer whales (Delfour & Marten, 2001), dolphins (Marino, 2002), and magpies (Prior et al., 2008). Note, however, that the test may only indicate awareness of a *physical* self—our sense of our physical bodies as independent beings—not the complex psychological self we humans possess (e.g., Suddendorf & Butler, 2013). But it's a start to building a self-concept—which, it turns out, is influenced by many forces.

Social Comparison Theory

While we often look into a mirror (or at our own body, feelings, etc.) to develop a sense of our personal identity, we usually look to others to develop a social identity. **Social comparison theory** proposes that people assess how well they're doing by comparing themselves to others (Festinger, 1954). Being rich, shy, intelligent, or anything else only has meaning when those things are compared to others (Bachman & O'Malley, 1986; Marsh et al., 2001). High school and college students, for example, compare their body size and eating patterns to their peers or images they see in the media such as advertisements or on social media, which can affect body self-esteem (Bessenoff, 2006; Scott et al., 2023; Scully et al., 2020; Seekis et al., 2020; Tylka & Sabik, 2010).

The direction of these social comparisons has consequences:

- *Downward* social comparisons reference people and groups who are *worse* than us. If you got a C– on a test, but you compare yourself to a friend who failed it completely, then you feel pretty good! That downward social comparison boosts your self-esteem. Downward comparisons help people get through rough times and are a potential reminder of progress, even if they're not where they want to be yet. Of course, because it's almost always possible to find someone worse off, these downward comparisons can be used to justify bad behavior (e.g., "I'm not so bad, other people study less than I do").

- *Upward* social comparisons reference people and groups who are *better* than us. A C– is a passing grade, but why didn't you get an A like a few other students? That upward social comparison lowers self-esteem. If upward social comparisons lower self-esteem, then why do we do them? First, as social creatures, people can't stop comparing themselves to others. It's partly why social media is so appealing—envy seems to be built into us. That said, upward comparisons can be useful. They can help us learn and improve, and that growth yields long-term benefits to self-esteem. Mentors and coaches help fine-tune our thinking; they can inspire us and teach us how to do better next time.

A balance of upward and downward comparisons might be the best strategy.

WHAT'S MY SCORE?

Measuring Self-Esteem

Instructions: Below is a list of statements dealing with your general feelings about yourself. For each statement, write in a number indicating your agreement using this scale:

1	2	3	4
Strongly Disagree	Disagree	Agree	Strongly Agree

___ 1. On the whole, I am satisfied with myself.

___ 2. At times, I think I am no good at all.

___ 3. I feel that I have a number of good qualities.

___ 4. I am able to do things as well as most other people.

___ 5. I feel I do not have much to be proud of.

___ 6. I certainly feel useless at times.

___ 7. I feel that I'm a person of worth, at least on an equal plane with others.

___ 8. I wish I could have more respect for myself.

___ 9. All in all, I am inclined to feel that I am a failure.

___ 10. I take a positive attitude toward myself.

Scoring Instructions: Many surveys in psychology include something called "reserve scoring." It means that half of the items on a survey are in one direction (like indicating high self-esteem) while the other half are in the opposite direction (like indicating low self-esteem). By flipping half of the items, it makes it harder for people to manipulate their scores and requires them to pay more attention to what each item is asking.

To score this kind of survey, the first step is to reverse half of the answers—this makes it easier to add up responses so they're all in the same direction. For this particular survey, you need to "reverse score" items 2, 5, 6, 8, and 9.

That means if you wrote a "1" for these items, cross it off and write a "4" instead. Change a "2" response to a "3," change a "3" response to a "2," and finally, if you wrote a "4" response for any of these items, cross it off and write a "1" instead. For the other items, leave your original response as is.

Then, add up all 10 of your answers. Your total score should be between 10 and 40. The higher your score, the more positive your self-esteem. ●

Source: Rosenberg, Morris. 1989. *Society and the Adolescent Self-Image.* Revised edition. Middletown, CT: Wesleyan University Press.

Self-Discrepancy Theory: Three Selves in One Person

The self-concept is who we *are*—but what about who we *want* to be?

Patrick's parents wanted him to join the military. He did join for a while—but it didn't make him happy. He really wanted to be a chef. When he identified as a gay woman, his mother rejected him. Growing up, he was pulled in several directions. An interesting psychology theory was developed that tries to explain how we make choices based on how our identity and goals change over our lifetime. **Self-discrepancy theory** describes the forces acting on people as a struggle between *three* simultaneous selves: an actual self, an ideal self, and an ought self (Higgins, 1987, 2002; Kaye, 2023).

Self-discrepancy theory: The idea that we maintain three simultaneous selves (actual, ideal, and ought), and when they don't align, we have negative emotional reactions.

The *actual self* is our current self-concept, including positive and negative qualities, social comparisons, group memberships, and so on. It's everything we described earlier in terms of who we are, right now—all the good and bad. But that's only the start of the complicated self.

The *ideal self* is the person we hope to become in the future. The ideal self is the best version of our potential. It's who we could be if we added to or increased our positive qualities, eliminated anything about our actual self we don't like, and achieved all our goals and dreams. It's the person we strive to become, including secret desires we've never told anyone about or that we can't admit to anyone else. And there's one more.

The *ought self* is the person we think *other people* want us to become. It's what we think our family, friends, religious leaders, teachers, and everyone else wants us to be. It includes what our culture expects of us—including the pressure of social judgments or family traditions and values. The ought self is kind of like peer pressure, although it's influenced by more than just peers (our family, our culture, and so on).

Self-discrepancy theory notes that in a perfect world, these three selves would align like the Venn diagram in Figure 4.1. Each time the selves get closer together, the circles overlap more until only a single, perfect circle remains, because they are all the same self. This kind of perfect overlap is probably rare, maybe even impossible. And when discrepancies (mismatches) occur, the theory predicts specific negative outcomes.

When you fail to meet a personal goal, it means your actual self doesn't align with your ideal self. The theory predicts this discrepancy will result in *dejection-related emotions*, like disappointment, shame, and depression. For example, people who don't like their own physical body can experience depression and eating disorders (Heron & Smyth, 2013; Mason et al., 2022; Vartanian, 2012).

On the other hand, when you fail to meet a goal that someone else has provided for you through your ought self (in other words, maybe you're pursuing it out of obligation or social pressure), you feel differently. Self-discrepancy theory now says you're likely to experience *agitation-related emotions*, like guilt, fear, self-contempt, and anxiety (Higgins, 1987). Sometime immigrants to a new culture feel anxiety if

FIGURE 4.1

Self-Discrepancy Theory

How aligned are your three selves?

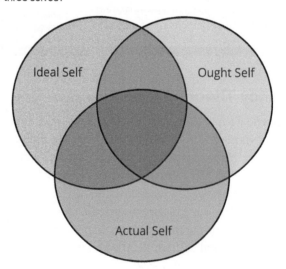

they don't believe they fit into the "ought" self that their new home may expect of them (Chakraborty & Chattaraman, 2022; Levinson & Rodebaugh, 2013). Many people find it hard to relax in social settings if you worry that you're not living up to social expectations, leading to social anxiety and phobias (Johns & Peters, 2012).

When Patrick was Shannon, she wanted to be a professional chef (her ideal self), but her parents both wanted her to join the military like they did (her ought self). She spent 4 years in the Marines—but she was miserable. As she started to suppress her attraction to women, she also started using drugs and alcohol to avoid the anxiety she felt building up in herself as she denied who she really was. The key for Shannon was the realization that, at least for her, her assigned sex and gender were more flexible than what society had taught her. Maybe she was really he.

The theories regarding identity, self-concept, and who we are or could be lead to interesting questions about how much of our selves are what psychologists call *social constructs*, subjective and abstract ideas with no objective reality. Social constructs only exist because human interactions have created shared meanings to understand them. For example, the idea that humans can or should be divided into different "races" is a social construct, because "race" has no objective or biological meaning. Another social construct is gender, which is not the same as sex.

Practice what you learn in **Knowledge Check 4.1**   Sage Vantage≻

SEX AND GENDER

>> **LO 4.2**   **Analyze models of thinking about sex and gender.**

How many sexes are there? How many genders?

Sex refers to our biological traits, such as chromosomes, hormones, internal reproductive systems, and genitals. In contrast, gender is a social construct relating to our sense of how masculine or feminine a person is. The easy, traditional answer to both questions is two: male and female. But what if the world's not so simple?

The research methods chapter introduced *continuous variables* that vary along a continuum or spectrum. Contrast this with *categorical variables* that fall into discrete and nonoverlapping categories. What college or university you attend is categorical (you're either enrolled in one or another), whereas your GPA at that school is continuous (it often ranges from 0.00 to 4.00). Most people consider sex and gender to be categorical, with only two categories.

Other people disagree. The idea of a sexual spectrum is that sex and gender are not always categorical variables with mutually exclusive groups (like "male" and "female"). Instead, maybe they range on a fluid, flexible continuum referred to as *gender expression*, how we present ourselves to others in terms of our masculinity or femininity. We acknowledge a spectrum of psychological gender whenever we observe masculine women and feminine men. It might be harder to think about sex, or the biological label given to us at birth, as continuous. Consider both sex and gender in more detail in the next two sections in terms of less traditional perspectives—and of course, ultimately, your view is up to you.

The Sexual Spectrum

Let's start with sex.

In middle school or high school, most of us learn the basics about what makes up sex. We learn what typically happens—and for most of us, that's the end of the lesson. Here, we'll review those basics so we have a foundation . . . but then we'll talk about things you might not have learned.

Have You Ever Wondered?
4.2 What is the difference between sex and gender?

Sex: Biological chromosomes, hormones, internal reproductive systems, and genitals.

Gender: A social construct regarding our sense of how masculine or feminine a person is.

Sexual spectrum: The idea that sex and gender are continuums, not distinct categorical groups with only two options.

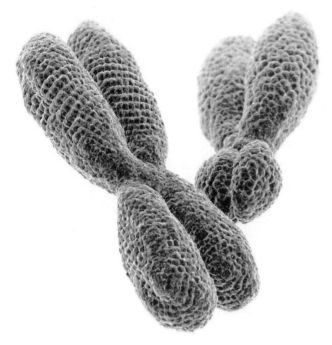

Biological sex is usually determined by chromosomes: XX is female and XY is male. But did you know there are other combinations?

iStock.com/laremenko

Estrogen: A type of hormone that promotes development of female body characteristics.

Androgen: A type of hormone that promotes development of male body characteristics.

Secondary sex characteristics: Physical aspects of the body that align with biological sex and emerge in puberty (such as breasts for girls and facial hair for boys).

Intersex: Conditions in which either chromosomes or hormones are neither traditionally "male" or "female" (also called disorders of sex development, or DSDs).

Typical Development: Two Sexes

For about 98% of people, sex is determined by two things: chromosomes and prenatal hormones. Most people get 23 chromosomes from their mother (on an egg) and 23 from their father (from whichever sperm fertilized the egg). Only one of the chromosome pairs is crucially important for determining the biological sex of the fetus. Usually, the egg contributes an X chromosome while the sperm contributes either another X chromosome (making an XX pair, a female) or a Y chromosome (making an XY pair, a male).

Once the chromosomes are determined, the fetus usually develops accordingly. An XX combination leads to the fetus being exposed to higher levels of feminine hormones like **estrogen**. This means the fetus will grow to have a clitoris, uterus, and ovaries. An XY combination usually leads the fetus to be exposed to higher levels of masculine hormones like testosterone (a kind of **androgen**), which usually leads to the development of a penis, vas deferens, and testes.

Further developmental changes happen in stages like puberty. During that time, which usually lasts from about ages 12 to 15, most people's bodies will develop **secondary sex characteristics**. These are physical aspects of our body that indicate our biological sex and prepare us for adulthood. Female secondary sex characteristics include wider hips and breasts; male secondary sex characteristics include deeper voices and growth of facial hair. In both boys and girls, hair grows in other new places as well (such as pubic hair and under the arms). Major transitions in puberty often include a boy's first ejaculation and a girl's first menstrual period (called *menarche*).

More Than Two: Intersex Individuals

When a baby is born, the first question many people are asked is whether it's a boy or a girl. What if the answer is neither, both, or we're not sure yet?

Some people are **intersex**; that is, they are born with what the modern biomedical world calls disorders of sex development (or DSDs). While estimates vary regarding how common intersex people are, they may be as many as 1.7% of the general population, making them about as common as having red hair (Fausto-Sterling, 2000). And just like red hair, some parts of the world have much higher proportions of intersex people, such as the Dominican Republic or New Guinea. There are about 30 different kinds of intersex situations with a very wide range of outcomes, including ambiguous genitals, unusual chromosome combinations (i.e., neither XX nor XY), and unusual levels of sex-relevant hormones like testosterone. Let's consider six biological intersex situations.

Unusual chromosome combinations. Two unusual chromosome combinations occur when people receive an extra chromosome, resulting in a fetus with either an XXY or an XYY combination. The XXY combination is called *Klinefelter syndrome* (Genetics Home Reference, 2021). It results in people who have a physical body that is a combination of traditional male and female characteristics. They're usually tall with small penises and small, firm testicles—but they can also grow small breasts, have wide hips, and develop a pattern of pubic hair more often found on women (Figure 4.2). They usually can't grow a beard or reproduce children. In addition, they often have cognitive challenges and are more likely to be diagnosed with learning disorders.

The *47, XYY syndrome* is sometimes called supermale syndrome because of the extra "Y" chromosome (Berglund et al., 2020). Supermales are more likely (than people with Klinefelter syndrome) to have normal-sized testicles and penises and can usually have children—but they also tend to have delayed motor skills (such as walking or athletic movements), weak muscle tone, and flat feet. Sometimes they are also more likely to have mental health concerns like attention-deficit/hyperactivity disorder (ADHD), depression, or anxiety. However, the origins of these problems are unclear (e.g., biological versus social or environmental).

A third unusual chromosome combination is called *Turner syndrome*, people born with a missing chromosome, leading to the combination represented as XO (where the 0 means neither X nor Y; Gravholt et al., 2019). People with Turner syndrome almost always "feel" female and self-identify as female, but their bodies have some unusual characteristics. They tend to be short (less than 5 feet) and their bodies typically don't

FIGURE 4.2

Klinefelter Syndrome

People born with Klinefelter syndrome have bodies that appear to be a combination of traditionally male characteristics (such as a penis) and female characteristics (such as breasts).

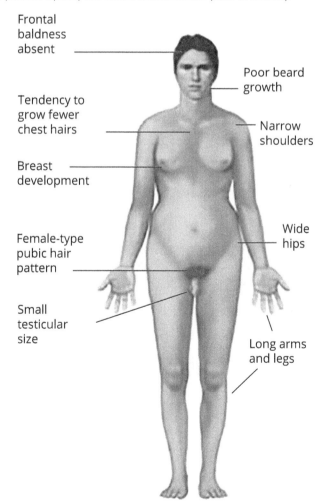

Frontal baldness absent

Poor beard growth

Tendency to grow fewer chest hairs

Narrow shoulders

Breast development

Female-type pubic hair pattern

Wide hips

Small testicular size

Long arms and legs

Source: Ahmad et al. (2010).

develop as most women's do—they never grow breasts and their hips don't widen. Usually, they don't menstruate and are infertile. Sometimes they can have extra folds of skin, and when these are visible at birth (in the form of a "webbed neck"), the folds are surgically removed. About one third of people with Turner syndrome have heart defects and/or kidney problems, but they seem to have normal intelligence levels (unlike those with Klinefelter or supermale syndrome).

Unusual hormone exposure. There are also intersex people who do have a typical XX or XY set of chromosomes, but something unusual happened in terms of the fetal exposure or reaction to prenatal hormones. The first situation is called *androgen insensitivity syndrome* or AIS (Batista et al., 2018). Here, despite the XY combination, the fetus doesn't respond when exposed to testosterone produced in the womb.

This means that the fetus's genitals remain in female form—a clitoris instead of a penis (Figure 4.3). AIS can range from "partial" to "complete," so babies with partial AIS can have genitals that are ambiguous: Is it a large clitoris or a small penis? Parents usually choose one sex or the other and raise their child accordingly. When the child reaches adulthood, they might want to adjust identities. This can mean changing not only a name, clothing, and so on but also hormone injections or even surgeries.

A second biological situation could be considered the "opposite" of AIS: CAH stands for *congenital adrenal hyperplasia* (Genetics Home Reference, 2023). While CAH can affect both XX and XY people, when it applies to someone with XX chromosomes, they are born with a traditionally "masculine" body, meaning they have a penis instead of a clitoris. They might still have ovaries and a uterus—but with a penis. Many XX people with CAH self-identify as feeling female, but they are also

FIGURE 4.3

Androgen Insensitivity Syndrome (AIS)

AIS individuals usually identify as female, despite their XY chromosomes.

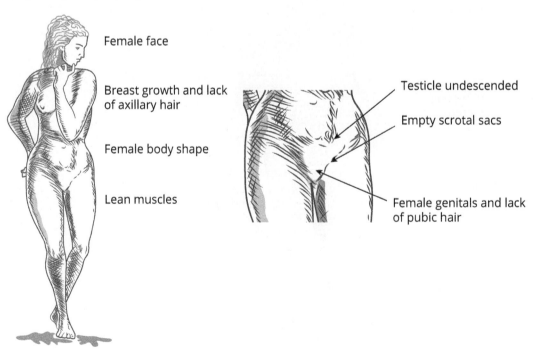

Female face

Breast growth and lack of axillary hair

Female body shape

Lean muscles

Testicle undescended

Empty scrotal sacs

Female genitals and lack of pubic hair

Source: Mendoza et al. (2017).

more likely to be sexually attracted to other women, compared to other XX women without CAH.

Finally, consider 5-alpha reductase deficiency (Nascimento et al., 2018). Here, fetuses with XY chromosomes don't convert their prenatal testosterone to a hormone called dihydrotestosterone (DHT). They are born with a traditionally female-looking body with a vagina and clitoris. Their gonads are testes instead of ovaries, but those testes remain undescended in the body. The most interesting aspect of 5-alpha reductase is that when they reach puberty, however, their body suddenly responds normally to testosterone, which means that they develop facial hair, the voice deepens, they grow taller and muscular, and both their scrotum and main sexual organ grow. In other words, their clitoris turns into a small penis when they're in middle school or junior high.

Often, these individuals are raised as girls throughout childhood, but they usually develop a male identity and live their adult lives as relatively "normal" men, marrying women (although they are often infertile). Interestingly, while this situation is very rare in the general population, there are some nations with larger-than-average incidents, such as in the Dominican Republic. There, the condition is so common that it has its own name: "guevedoces," which translates as "penis at twelve" (BBC, 2015).

All these biological variations signal that "male versus female" may be an oversimplified version of biological sex. Still, sex is biological and therefore relatively concrete and objective. Gender, on the other hand, is much more subjective.

Andrea Jenkins made history in 2017 as the first African American openly trans woman to be elected to office in the United States.

Dia Dipasupil/Staff/Getty Images Entertainment/via Getty Images

The Gender Spectrum

How masculine or feminine are you?

Recall that gender is our socially constructed psychological identity in terms of how masculine or feminine we are and how we express that to the world. When you think about *gender*, you may recognize personal variability in how masculine or feminine you feel and appear to others day to day, from outfit to outfit, or even from one minute to the next, usually depending on social and cultural factors.

Gender schema theory suggests that people raise children by training them to fit into culturally expected gender norms (Bem, 1972, 1984). Our **gender identity** is our internal and individual experience of gender, including how masculine or feminine we feel. Gender identity might also be more fluid than biological sex, with people who feel uncomfortable sticking to any given label or pronouns. But usually, people assimilate to what their culture demands.

Most societies cluster gender traits into "masculine" and "feminine." If you're "masculine," then you are expected to have traits like "assertive," "competitive," and "strong." In contrast, "feminine" traits are things like "kind," "sympathetic," and "delicate." But these categories and stereotypes limit everyone, pushing people into activities or careers that might not be right for them. It gives some people unfair opportunities and others unfair disadvantages.

Gender schema theory: The idea that when children are raised, they're trained to fit into culturally expected gender norms.

Gender identity: Each person's internal and individual experience of gender, which may be the same as or different from their birth-assigned sex.

FIGURE 4.4

Categories of Gender in Bem's Model

If you're high in both "feminine" and "masculine" traits, Bem's model (1972, 1974) gives you the label "androgynous."

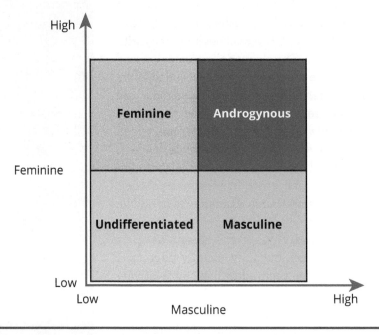

Source: Carver et al. (2013). Licensed under CC BY 4.0 DEED.

Psychological androgyny: The idea that some people will be high in both traditionally "masculine" and "feminine" traits at the same time.

However, if we see sex and gender as a spectrum of potential identities, then everyone has some mixture of masculine and feminine characteristics. This concept, called **psychological androgyny**, posits that we can simultaneously experience varied amounts of *both* masculinity and femininity (Bem, 1972, 1974). If you're high in one and low in the other, you might fall into the traditional categories of "masculine" or "feminine." But if you're high in *both* sets of traits, then you're considered "androgynous." Low in both is called "undifferentiated" in this model. See Figure 4.4 for how these all work together in a model created by psychologist Sandra Bem.

Bem spent most of her career studying psychological androgyny. She created a self-report scale that mapped individual androgyny scores onto the model in Figure 4.4 (Bem, 1974). Bem found that androgynous people were less likely to conform to gender-based conformity. Instead, they preferred to live authentically by throwing off social expectations. Androgynous men, for example, embraced the opportunity to play with a tiny kitten even though it wasn't considered a "masculine" choice from a variety of potential activities (Bem, 1975). Beyond some quality kitten time (who doesn't like kittens?), Bem also found that psychological androgyny is associated with many positive characteristics:

- Working effectively in different situations: Androgynous people can be aggressive and competitive in one situation, then switch to be nurturing and cooperative in another situation.

- They are more open-minded about possible careers and entertainment activities.

- They are less sexist when interacting with others.

- They have greater willingness to try a variety of tasks, regardless of their stereotypical nature.

- They have better mental health and adjustment.
- They have better physical health.

These positive characteristics are all associated with psychological androgyny (Alpert-Gillis & Connell, 1989; Antill & Cunningham, 1979; Ashmore, 1990; Bem & Lenney, 1967; Huston, 1983; Maheshwari & Kumar, 2008; Rose & Montemayor, 1994; Whitley, 1985). On the other hand, other researchers question these positive connections (see Martin et al., 2016; Spence & Hall, 1996; Whitley, 1983). Don't be shocked when research results point in different directions. Reconciling those different findings is how knowledge grows, and being a good scientist means keeping an open mind.

Patrick shows psychological androgyny when he balances his free time between gardening, lovingly brushing his dog's hair, building an extension onto his house, and baking perfect cheesecakes. At least for him, psychological androgyny has made him a much happier man.

The Transgender Experience

Of course, Patrick isn't just psychologically androgynous. He's trans.

Many people never feel comfortable in the sex assigned to them at birth, even with "typical" chromosomes and hormones. The respectful term for these people today is **transgender**, or simply trans. In contrast, **cisgender** refers to people who do feel comfortable with the sex assigned to them at birth and never wish to change it. Celebrities such as Lenya Bloom, Caitlyn Jenner, Hunter Schaefer, Carmen Carrera, Chaz Bono, and Elliot Page have received a lot of attention for their transgender status. Whether positive or negative, this attention has put transgender issues at the center of many cultural and political controversies.

Some trans people are also intersex; some others have brains that developed with receptor pathways more typical of people in a different biological sex than the one they were assigned at birth (e.g., Theisen et al., 2019). For others, exactly why they are trans remains unclear because they may choose not to undergo invasive medical testing. Being transgender has nothing to do with sexual orientation; trans people can be attracted to men, women, intersex people, other trans people—it's irrelevant to their own identity as male or female. For his entire adult life, Patrick has been attracted to women; that didn't change when he started his transition. Wind once asked him if he ever checked to see if he might have an intersex condition, just out of curiosity. He replied, "No—the reason I'm a man doesn't matter. I just am." Unfortunately, when he started his transition, he was married to a woman who identified as a lesbian person, and she didn't want to be married to a man. They divorced about a year after he started taking testosterone injections, which made his body and voice change in major ways.

Trans people are also increasingly seen in popular media. Just a few examples are the film *The Danish Girl* (2015) and the shows *Orange Is the New Black* (2013–2019), *Shameless* (2011–), *Euphoria* (2019–), and *Pose* (2018–), which stars several trans women. Many U.S. states are currently debating or have recently passed laws regarding transgender medical care, sports regulations, and so on. Colleges and universities are also grappling with trans issues on campuses, including questions such as where trans students should live (e.g., in traditionally male-only or female-only dorms), if gender-inclusive bathrooms are needed, which sports teams trans athletes will join, and so on. These are issues that will likely be discussed quite a bit over the next several years.

Transgender people: People who disagree with the sex assigned to them at birth, who later change their identity to a different sex.

Cisgender people: People who agree with the sex assigned to them at birth and who don't wish to change it.

SEXUAL ORIENTATION

? Have You Ever
Wondered?
4.3 How is sexual
orientation
described in
psychology?

>> **LO 4.3   Compare and contrast the Kinsey and Storms models of sexual orientation.**

For some people, college is an opportunity to explore sexuality for the first time.

The American College Health Association (2021) documented the wide variety of sexual experiences in a national survey of college and university students. There are several interesting findings from this 2019–2021 survey related to sexual identity. First, about 4.5% of college students identified as transgender or gender nonconforming. Second, the distribution of self-identified sexual orientation among the students is shown in Figure 4.5. As you can see, only 75% of students identified as heterosexual. The remaining students reported being bisexual, lesbian or gay, pansexual, asexual, queer, questioning, or other.

The Sexual Orientation Spectrum

Is sexual orientation also potentially on a spectrum?

What does it mean, for example, that only 75% of college students identified as strictly heterosexual? Traditionally, sexual orientation has been a categorical system of *heterosexual* (attraction to only the "opposite" sex) versus *gay or lesbian* (attraction to only the same sex). However, *bisexual*, attraction to both men and women, actually constitutes a larger fraction of the population than those who identify as gay or lesbian. *Pansexual* refers to people who don't focus on the sex or gender label when perceiving whether someone is physically attractive; it's a word similar to *bisexual* but intended to be more inclusive (i.e., to acknowledge trans and nonbinary people). In contrast,

---

FIGURE 4.5

College Student Sexual Orientations

Sexual orientations in college students, according to the American College Health Association (2021).

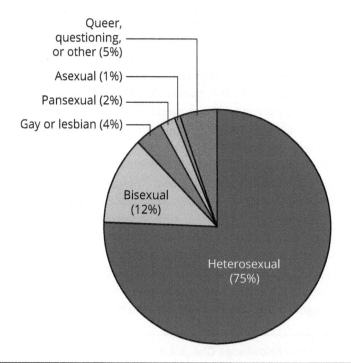

Source: Created using data from American College Health Association (2021).

---

asexual people are those who desire loving, intimate relationships with others but aren't very interested in engaging in sexual activities (see Bogaert, 2004; Hinderliter, 2009; Walton et al., 2016).

The boxes or categories like those shown in Figure 4.5 still may not describe the human experience that allows people to fluidly move back and forth (even a little bit) across relationships or over time. There are two alternatives that are truer to the idea of sexuality on a spectrum, if sexuality is on a spectrum. Let's consider each—but keep in mind that even scholars who think about this subject every day often disagree with each other. Just how sexuality works is still an academic debate, so consider some of these ideas and analyze what you think.

Scientifically Studying Sex: Pioneers on the Screen

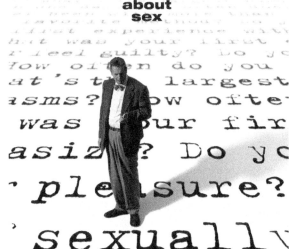

RGR Collection/Alamy Stock Photo

In the first half of the 1900s, studying human sexual behavior was quite controversial—even scandalous.

Alfred Kinsey, an American biologist, was probably the most controversial figure in the history of research on sex and intimate relationships. One part of his legacy are the terms *sexology* and *sexologist*, as he researched and developed university courses on human sexuality. Two of his views were the most controversial:

(1) that women were capable of several different kinds of orgasm (e.g., both from vaginal and clitoral stimulation), and

(2) that everyone is at least a little bit bisexual.

Those ideas were shocking in the 1930s to 1950s, and so were his methods for testing them. Kinsey interviewed prostitutes, prisoners, abuse victims, and gay men—populations that previously had been ignored in sex research. He also crossed the boundaries between objective observer and participant by engaging in sexual behaviors with his participants, graduate students, and colleagues on his research team. In 2004, Kinsey's fascinating life was made into a movie simply called *Kinsey*, starring Liam Neeson and Laura Linney (Coppola et al., 2004).

Following in Kinsey's footsteps were the famous pair William Masters (a gynecologist) and Virginia Johnson (his wife). They published research on human sexual behaviors over the entire second half of the 20th century. They also studied phases of sexuality and tried to understand the female orgasm, including how and why women can have multiple orgasms in a short period of time. Their lives and research have been fictionalized in the television series *Masters of Sex* that ran from 2013 to 2016 and starred Michael Sheen and Lizzy Caplan (Ashford, 2013–2016).

Though *Kinsey* and *Masters of Sex* are fictionalized depictions, they both offer insight into how scientists conduct sexuality research. Importantly, they both point out ethical breaches in early sex research that are carefully avoided now, due in part to ethical requirements from the American Psychological Association. ●

The Kinsey One-Dimensional Continuum

Are most people at least a little bit bisexual?

Over 70 years ago, Alfred Kinsey provided the first scientific model that proposed sexual orientation was continuous rather than categorical (Kinsey et al., 1948, 1953). He interviewed hundreds of people regarding their sexual histories, asking very personal questions about every detail of their fantasies and interactions. He then created the range you see in Figure 4.6, which goes from 0 (*exclusively heterosexual*) to 6 (*exclusively homosexual*). According to Kinsey, many people fall somewhere in the middle of the continuum even if they've never had an actual experience with someone of the same sex as themselves because they may have been attracted to someone from a different sex or fantasized about trying it, moving them away from zero (what some people might call "bi curious").

Kinsey recognized that there are people who don't self-identify as gay or lesbian but still have sexual experiences with people of the same sex. This was especially true when he was doing his research in the 1940s and 1950s. A term often used in scientific research is "men who have sex with men," or MSM (Sandfort & Dodge, 2009). These men don't label themselves as gay or even as bi- or pansexual, often because they live in cultures where homosexuality is not socially accepted or may even be illegal. So, people avoid the label but engage in the behavior anyway (e.g., Thaczuk, 2007). *Heteroflexibility* is the idea that people can experiment. For example, they might explore same-sex attractions or behaviors but still self-identify as heterosexual (Diamond, 2005).

The Storms Two-Dimensional Model

What about asexual people?

Kinsey believed that sexual orientation could be understood on a one-dimensional continuum. Michael Storms expanded that reasoning by adding a second dimension (Figure 4.7), with each continuum representing attraction to men or women (Storms,

---

FIGURE 4.6

The Kinsey Continuum of Sexual Orientation

Sex researcher Alfred Kinsey suggested that sexual orientation could be mapped on a one-dimensional continuum with heterosexuality on one end and homosexuality on the other.

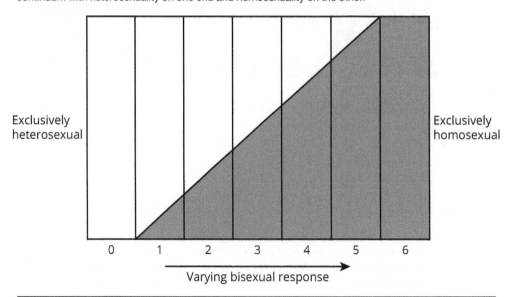

FIGURE 4.7

The Storms Model of Sexual Orientation

Storms expanded Kinsey's model by proposing two separate dimensions of sexual attraction that can each range in degree.

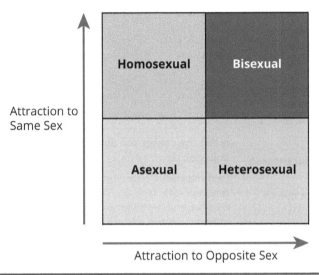

Source: Modified from Storms (1980).

1978, 1980). By separating the two traditional sexes onto different continuums, we add complexity to the model in an interesting way. Not only do we have the bisexuality range that Kinsey proposed, but we also have the potential range for asexuality. Although Figure 4.7 still shows these sexual orientations as four boxes or categories, the point is that either axis or dimension has a range, resulting in a wider spectrum of possibilities.

How do sex, gender, and sexual orientation all come together to inform identity? Table 4.1 summarizes five aspects of our sense of self. However, as stated earlier, these ideas remain controversial, so we encourage you to think critically and explore the research yourself.

TABLE 4.1

Aspects of Our Gender and Sexual Identity

Gender Identity	An internal sense of being male/masculine, female/feminine, neither, both, or other options.
Gender Expression	How you present your gender to the outside world through things like clothes, hairstyles, voice, body, and so on. How "masculine," "feminine," or androgynous you appear to others.
Sex Assigned at Birth	The biological sex classification label given to you on your birth certificate.
Physical Attraction	Your sexual orientation, or whom you find yourself physically interested in.
Emotional Attraction	Your romantic or emotional attraction, or whom you find appealing from a friendship or aesthetic perspective.

Source: Created using data from Trans Student Educational Resources (2015).

Meet Ian, Research Assistant at Rainbow Health

What is your career?

I am a research assistant intern with a Minneapolis-based health organization called Rainbow Health. They focus on the health needs of the LGBTQ+ community, conducting frequent research and surveying of the local community to identify needs for policy and programs. I develop survey materials, participate in data collection, and create the final write-up and statistical analysis.

How was studying psychology important for success in this career?

The position requires thorough knowledge of how to conduct a literature review of scholarly texts, establish methods, design materials, and collect, statistically analyze, and summarize the data. **My studies in psychology provided a much better context and starting point regarding the unique needs of the LGBTQ+ community, as well.**

How do concepts from this chapter help in this career?

We really wanted to understand how something universal to humanity—physical and mental

health—intersected with identity on myriad levels. **The organization is focused on how identifying with the LGBTQ+ community impacts various aspects of mental health (certain disorders, physical activity levels, etc.).** We also collect data on certain mental characteristics (self-esteem, body image, etc.) to examine the intersectionality between gender, sexual identity, physicality, and mental health.

Is this the career you always planned to have after college?

I actually anticipated becoming a high school English teacher. After taking a few psychology courses, I was hooked, and my intention after college was to attend graduate school and eventually become a professor. While that is still a path I'd like to pursue, there is a real feeling of connectedness to the work by being "on the ground," so to speak. There is a lot of good to be done in the nonprofit sector.

If you could give current college students one sentence of advice, what would it be?

Find a mentor, in anything you do, who will tell you the tough things you need to hear—and then listen. ●

Sage Vantage✌   Practice what you learn in **Knowledge Check 4.3**

SEXUALITY, CULTURE, AND TECHNOLOGY

?

Have You Ever Wondered?
4.4 How do culture and technology influence sexuality?

>> **LO 4.4** **Explain ways that culture and technology influence sexual behaviors.**

How many hours a day do you spend in front of a screen?

Technology has changed our lives, usually for the better. Many examples of this will be discussed throughout the book, but consider how you interact with the world through your phone. How do you share your identity through your use of social media? How do you form impressions of friends or make new friends, through technology? Social media only exists because of technology, and this technology allows for shared cultural experiences and messages.

So far, this chapter has discussed a lot of abstract concepts. Next, think about something a lot more concrete and specific—sexual behaviors. How do culture and technology interact with your sexual identity and behaviors?

Sexual Scripts

How do you decide how to act, sexually?

Havelock Ellis was an early researcher of sexual behaviors. An English physician in the Victorian era, Ellis suggested several ideas that were considered controversial at the time (Yarber & Sayad, 2016; see Goodfriend, 2012). He advocated for sexual diversity and wrote that people should be free to do what they want—as long as no one was getting hurt and everyone involved gave consent. He believed that sex between consenting adults could lead to positive results like decreased stress and anxiety (Yarber & Sayad, 2016), that homosexuality was a biological fact, and that each person's sexual expectations and behaviors were based on their culture growing up (Goodfriend, 2012).

Cultural expectations about sexual behaviors are called **sexual scripts** that communicate assumptions about what specific events will occur in sexual settings, and in what order. The metaphor of a script implies that these expectations are placed on us, like we're actors in our own lives: We live out the script our culture assigns to us (Gagnon & Simon, 1973; Laumann et al., 1994). That script comes from several sources: consuming mass media, parents giving us "the talk," and learning from more experienced peers. The traditional sexual script in the United States and other "Western" cultures goes something like this (Goodfriend, 2012):

Sexual scripts: Culture-based assumptions we make about what particular events will occur in sexual settings, and in what order.

- In middle school or high school, people start casually dating. The first exclusive relationship might begin, and engaging in sexual behaviors, such as kissing, occurs. The general script assumes everyone is heterosexual and that men should generally be the initiators of sexual behaviors (Blanc, 2001).

- In high school or college, true sexual exploration is initiated; many people "lose" their virginity at this time. People start looking for future spouses.

- Young people in their 20s find "true love" and get married. Again, the man asks the woman for marriage and pays for the ring, but her family pays for the wedding (the script tightly controls gender expectations).

- All couples engage in sex regularly and hope for children. Couples are expected to remain faithful, but everyone knows that many affairs happen. As the couple ages, sexual behaviors decline, and the couple members become more like friends.

Sexual scripts like this can govern many people's experiences—and they often lead to happiness. For example, one study asked college students to evaluate the relationship strength of a hypothetical couple based on traditional and nontraditional marriage proposals. Participants evaluated relationships as stronger when they conformed to traditional proposal scripts (Schweingruber et al., 2008). Scripts can be comforting because they tell us what to expect and what's "acceptable" in our culture. They give us a story we can live out and share with similar others who will likely be supportive. But scripts can also be limiting. The expectation that men should be aggressive initiators while women passively wait to be asked out, seduced, or asked to be married puts pressure on men and can lead to backlash against women who initiate but are then seen as "pushy" (Harrington & Maxwell, 2023; Infanger et al., 2016).

However, these traditional gendered expectations appear to be changing. For example, college men across a variety of ethnic backgrounds prefer more egalitarian scripts for both their relationships in general and sexual behaviors (Dworkin & O'Sullivan, 2005). Similarly, while some people maintain traditionally gendered sexual scripts, others have different ideas (Masters et al., 2013). They embrace two alternatives: "exception finding" (meaning a generally traditional arrangement but allowing occasional rule-breaking) and "transforming" (equal expectations for men and women—for example, either person might be on top during sex).

That said, most people follow a traditional or typical sexual script. Wind did a study in which college students answered questions about two things: (1) whether they personally would consider engaging in nontraditional sexual behaviors and (2) how socially acceptable these behaviors were, in general (Goodfriend, 2012). The students came from a small private school in the Midwest and were "WEIRD" (see Chapter 2), meaning they came from Western, Educated, Industrialized, Rich, Democratic backgrounds.

The survey results appear in Table 4.2. The scores ranged from 1 (*definitely not acceptable*) to 7 (*definitely acceptable*). Note some interesting patterns in the table. First, men's and women's ideas and preferences were pretty similar to each other—at least, in this sample. Second, people are more likely to personally consider doing things if they feel those actions are culturally accepted. Finally, the most popular option was "legal marriage with one person for life." Even though this option is happening less with each generation, most people still appear to consider it an ideal for their own sexual future. It is likely that their culture's sexual script influences this expectation.

TABLE 4.2

Sexual Scripts in U.S. Society

Men's and women's views on possible sexual paths, on a range from 1 (*definitely not acceptable*) to 7 (*definitely acceptable*).

	MEN'S AVERAGE	WOMEN'S AVERAGE
Legal marriage with one person for life		
I would personally consider.	6.47	6.65
Does society accept?	6.18	6.29
Cohabitation		
I would personally consider.	5.84	5.49
Does society accept?	4.95	5.18
Premarital sex		
I would personally consider.	5.58	5.35
Does society accept?	4.95	5.12
Casually dating several people		
I would personally consider.	4.87	5.51
Does society accept?	4.42	5.29
Masturbation		
I would personally consider.	5.58	4.43
Does society accept?	4.53	4.45
Single and sexually active for life		
I would personally consider.	3.79	3.00
Does society accept?	3.71	3.33
Bisexuality		
I would personally consider.	2.42	3.37
Does society accept?	3.29	3.47
Group marriage or polygamy		
I would personally consider.	2.31	1.27
Does society accept?	2.08	1.84

	MEN'S AVERAGE	WOMEN'S AVERAGE
Living in a sex commune		
I would personally consider.	1.87	1.39
Does society accept?	1.58	1.67
Prostitution		
I would personally consider.	1.92	1.29
Does society accept?	1.95	2.06

SPOTLIGHT ON RESEARCH METHODS

Sex Within Marriage

Couples who have more sex are happier. Seems obvious, right? But we never know until we gather research.

One longitudinal project started with public marriage records to recruit heterosexual couples from central Pennsylvania (Schoenfeld et al., 2017)—and then followed them for the next 13 years. Longitudinal research is expensive and requires a deep commitment by both researchers and participants. The research team followed participants' lives using a variety of techniques including surveys, diaries, and face-to-face interviews that allowed them to study a wide range of topics.

When researchers examined the connections between sex and relationship satisfaction, they focused on four main areas:

1. marital satisfaction,
2. sexual frequency,
3. sexual quality, and
4. interpersonal climate.

This last variable focused on behaviors directed toward one's partner that were either positive (like giving compliments, saying I love you, and being physically affectionate) or negative (like being impatient, annoying the partner, being angry, and dominating conversations). The 100 couples used in this sample provided data at three points in time in their marriages: 1 year, 2 years, and 13 years. Do you have any predictions?

First came a replication of others' research: Couples who had more sex also reported higher sexual satisfaction. No surprise there. But did more positive behaviors increase sexual frequency? Two answers: no, for wives; yes, for husbands. When husbands engaged in more positive behaviors, sex was more frequent. However, negative behaviors, from wives or husbands, did not relate to sexual frequency.

But remember the question we started with: Was there a connection between martial satisfaction and sexual frequency? In this study, there was *not*. Having more (or less) sex was *not* linked to marital satisfaction.

Here are two conclusions: (1) A more positive interpersonal climate from husbands was related to having more sex, but (2) more frequent intercourse did not necessarily benefit the couple's relationship satisfaction. Future research should investigate what does matter when it comes to martial satisfaction, because—at least according to this study—there's a lot more to it than just sex. And of course, there are more types of marriage than monogamous heterosexual ones, so this study could be replicated with different kinds of relationships. ●

Sexting, Social Media, and Dating Apps

"Swiping right" and cartoon eggplants.

The digital era has led to swift changes in how people meet, interact, and form sexual expectations. Many people using this book grew up with smartphones and touchscreens, but the frequency of sexting behaviors may still be surprising.

Sexting: Sending sexually explicit texts or photos to someone else.

According to one study, over 27% of teens have engaged in **sexting**, sending and/or receiving sexually explicit texts or photos (E. Rosenberg, 2018). And here's info that might be good to know: 23% of the time, people who receive a "sext" forward it to a few other people (Pew Research Internet Project, 2013).

Social media's influence on sexual attitudes, expectations, and opportunities can be a double-edged sword. While millions of people use social media to connect with friends and family members, and even to share photos and announcements about their relationship, it can lead to conflict as well. For example, sometimes couple members disagree about when to change their "relationship status" on social media or how often they should be posting about the relationship on each other's pages (Lane et al., 2016).

Online dating has exploded in popularity, across ages and socioeconomic backgrounds (Finkel et al., 2012; Valkenburg & Peter, 2007). Figure 4.8 shows data from a survey in 2013. At that time, a majority of people had gone on at least one date with someone they met online, and almost one in four had found a long-term partner or a spouse through a dating app. We can see Internet dating's growth by comparing information from 2013 to recent data estimates from the Pew Research Center reported in 2023 (Vogels & McClain, 2023). In 2023, overall use of online dating went up from 10% to 30%. LGBT+ people are more likely to use dating apps or websites than heterosexual people (51% vs. 28%), men are more likely than women (34% and 28%), and Tinder is the most popular app for adults under the age of 30. However, many users report mixed feelings about their experience.

There appear to be several advantages to online dating—and one distinct disadvantage. The advantages can be summed up by the unromantic term *efficiency*. Online dating allows (a) meeting a wider range of people; (b) replaces expensive and time-consuming methods like meeting at bars, social groups, or social events; and (c) immediately lets someone learn a lot about potential partners (Finkel et al., 2012).

If you know what you're looking for (e.g., level of education, whether they are a smoker, if they want kids, if they are interested in Netflix & chill), you can immediately select for those characteristics and, theoretically, be more efficient. Some dating

FIGURE 4.8

Experiences and Opinions About Dating Sites and Apps

According to survey results from the Pew Research Internet Project (2013), a lot of people use social media and some form of dating website or app to explore relationship options.

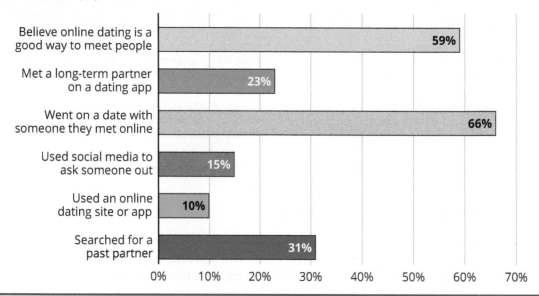

Source: Created using data from Pew Research Internet Project (2013).

services even boast computer algorithms that will do the "matching" work, allowing you to sit back and wait for the matches to roll in. But there is one disadvantage to online dating, and it's a big one: lying.

About 54% of people report that they've experienced a date in which the person they met "seriously misrepresented themselves in their profile" (Pew Research Internet Project, 2013). Studies investigating lying in online dating profiles found interesting sex differences (see Guadagno et al., 2012; Hitsch et al., 2010; Toma et al., 2008; Tooke & Camire, 1991):

- Men often admit that they present themselves as more dominant, more resourceful, and kinder than they really are.

- Women admit that they present themselves as being more physically attractive.

- Men admit they often lie about their height online.

- Women admit they lie about their weight.

- People change how they report personality traits to better fit into culturally approved gender norms.

Finally, some researchers argue that technology advances have changed cultural expectations about **sexual hookups**, relatively brief sexual encounters between people not in a committed relationship (Garcia et al., 2012). Of course, hooking up means different things to different people, from simply kissing to sexual intercourse. Hookups are increasingly ubiquitous in popular culture (movies, music, and so on), and dating apps like Tinder and Grindr make hookups both more convenient and (at least for some people) more socially acceptable.

Sexual hookups: Relatively brief sexual encounters between people not in a committed relationship.

College students report twice as many hookups as first dates (Bradshaw et al., 2010). That said, some people hook up because they believe it might lead to a real romantic relationship (Weitbrecht & Whitton, 2020). These changes in sexual scripts appear to create confusion among many people. The tension is between the pull of traditional, gendered expectations of slow, romantic dates versus modern expectations of casual sex almost immediately (Backstrom et al., 2012; Epstein et al., 2009; Phillips, 2000). It's a lot for people to navigate as they come of age sexually.

Pornography's Influence

What if your sexual script comes from pornography?

Technology has made pornography more accessible than ever before. One study that used a nationally representative sample of about 2,000 U.S. men and women (Herbenick et al., 2017) found that

- 57% of all men and 57% of all women have read erotic books or stories,

- 12% of men and 6% of women have used a porn phone app,

- 79% of men and 54% of women have looked at pornographic magazines, and

- 71% of men and 60% of women have watched sexually explicit videos or films.

Researchers have studied various effects of pornography usage, and the debate is strong about what exactly the effects are. Some studies indicate that prolonged use of pornography is harmful to users and to their relationships, including negative outcomes like unrealistic expectations or assumptions about what a partner will like (e.g., Bridges et al., 2003; Hilton & Watts, 2011; Kenrick et al., 1989; Wright, 2013). Some researchers believe that can contribute to positive, healthy sexual communication or exploration when used appropriately (e.g., Kohut et al., 2017; Komlenac & Hochleitner, 2022). However, many of these studies are correlational in nature, so causal conclusions can't be made. Other researchers say porn usage has no major effects on people at all.

When studies do identify troubling effects of using sexually explicit materials, these findings often relate to the *type* of materials and how they depict cultural ideas about gender, violence, and consent. For example, researchers in one study coded 400 porn videos available on mainstream Internet sites (like PornHub, xHamster, and YouPorn; Klaassen & Peter, 2015). They found that most of the videos showed consensual sex acts. However, sometimes disturbing images related to power appeared in the background of the action. For example, actresses were more often objectified through camera work such as close-ups of their individual body parts (compared to male actors). Men also received more oral sex than women. When movies depicted violence, women were far more likely to be the recipient of harm.

One response to concerns about violence and dominance toward women in porn is a movement called **femme porn**, erotic material designed to promote feminist values (Ryan, 2017). Female characters are leads in the storyline, lovers have personal or emotional intimacy, and there is more equality among the sexes for sexual motives and behaviors. In addition, femme porn tends to have more diversity in actors; shows different body types, races and ethnicities, ages, and sexual orientations; and includes gender queer people. From 2006 to 2015, there were even annual "feminist porn awards," given to films representing these ideas.

Femme porn: Erotic material designed to promote feminist values.

SageVantage Practice what you learn in **Knowledge Check 4.4**

INTERSECTIONALITY

? Have You Ever Wondered?
4.5 What is intersectionality?

>> **LO 4.5** **Define intersectionality and analyze how it applies to your own life.**

Patrick's life is complicated.

He grew up in a very conservative Midwestern household in the 1970s and early 1980s. At the time, he didn't realize there were other options besides continuing life as a cisgender, heterosexual female (Shannon). His local and family culture simply didn't expose him to alternatives. His attraction to girls and women was a secret he denied even to himself for years, until he simply couldn't deny his true self any longer. Years later, he had a parallel epiphany when he realized that his identity was a heterosexual man—but it cost Patrick his first wife, who wanted to be married to a woman. They divorced. One reason it took so long for Patrick to realize he identified as a transgender man was because he had never been exposed to the idea of transgender people until he moved to California as a young adult and started to have exposure to different subcultures of people.

Defining Intersectionality

Everyone's life is more complicated than it first appears.

That's because identity is a multifaceted mix that combines race, sex, gender, sexuality, socioeconomic status, and many other aspects of your self-concept depicted in Figure 4.9. Each of those pieces simultaneously influences how we interpret and interact with the world, as well as how others interpret and interact with you.

Meeting someone for the first time, you instantaneously form impressions of their age, gender, race, attractiveness, class, education level, physical ability, and much more. When considering these aspects of someone, it's impossible to focus on only a single part of who they are. Instead, the sense of their identity results from the combination of

FIGURE 4.9

Intersectionality

Intersectionality is the idea that our identity is simultaneously affected by multiple parts of our self and experience, not just one aspect at a time.

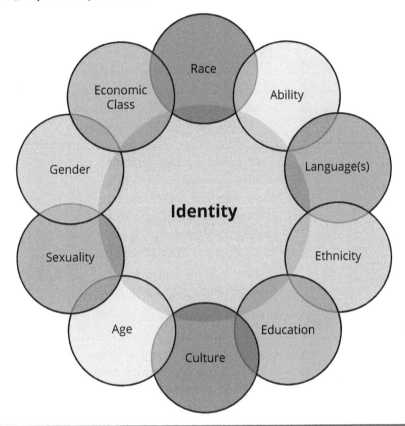

each individual part. Similarly, when you interview for a job, do hiring managers truly focus solely on your job qualifications? They should, but for better or worse, it can be impossible to ignore other aspects of your identity.

That's the essence of intersectionality, or the idea that an individual's lived experience of disadvantage and privilege—of opportunity and of oppression—is based on a unique combination of demographics and socially constructed categories (see Figure 4.9). For example, Patrick understands rural Midwestern life in a unique way, because he's lived most of his life with people treating him as a White lesbian woman living in a small town—but now people treat him as a White heterosexual man living in a different small town.

Consider how the idea of intersectionality emerged, some examples, and why it matters, including in the study of psychology.

Intersectionality: The idea that our lived experience of disadvantage and privilege is based on our unique combination of demographics and social categories.

Overlapping Identities

Almost all of us feel targeted or victimized at some point. An important aspect of intersectionality is that the frequency, kinds, and degree of discrimination we encounter vary depending on our combined identities. Different backgrounds can lead to different experiences. To explain, maybe it's best to give the example that started it all. Kimberlé Crenshaw is an African American woman and a law professor at both Columbia University and the University of California Los Angeles (UCLA). Her legal expertise is civil rights and employment. She first coined the term *intersectionality* in a paper arguing that racism and sexism combine in ways that harm some individuals (Crenshaw, 1989).

Legal professor Kimberlé Crenshaw coined the term *intersectionality* to discuss overlapping forms of discrimination.

RW3/Rachel Worth/WENN/ Newscom

Crenshaw focused on three big cases in which clients complained of discrimination. Five Black women who couldn't get hired sued the car company General Motors (GM). They lost the case. Why? The judge found that GM hired women, and they hired Black people. So the case was dismissed because GM couldn't be sexist or racist. But after the case had been dismissed, Crenshaw noted that GM hired only *men* to work in the factory (regardless of race) and only *White people* to work in the office (regardless of gender). So where could Black women work for GM? Nowhere.

It was the specific overlapping—or intersection—of their racial and gendered identities that caused the discrimination. Her term sparked controversy and inspired thousands of debates, research papers, and court cases; the word was added to the *Oxford English Dictionary* in 2015 (Coaston, 2019). To learn more about the history of the term, you can watch Crenshaw explain it herself in her TED talk online if you're interested.

Social Perceptions and Expectations

Is all this really still a problem?

Consider how intersectionality might apply to college and university athletes. We expect people with "masculine" traits to be more aggressive or violent. Some research indicates there's a stereotype that football players are particularly focused on a culture of traditional masculinity, which includes being competitive and aggressive (Foley, 2001; Steinfeldt et al., 2009). Does intersectionality mean anything on the football field?

A group of psychologists gathered 90 photographs of actual college quarterbacks from their online rosters (Wilson et al., 2017). Half the quarterbacks were Black men, and half were White men. Importantly, the researchers carefully chose photos in pairs such that on average, the Black players had the same physical size and weight as the White players (based on their published roster stats).

College student participants viewed the photos and rated each one on the athlete's physical size, how "formidable" and "intimidating" he appeared to be, and whether he seemed capable of harming the participant in a physical fight. Even though the selected photos showed Black and White players of roughly equal physical size, participants perceived Black football players in the photos as physically bigger, more intimidating, and more capable of causing harm in a fight. Further, the participants indicated how much physical force would be justified by police if the men in the photos committed a crime. As you might guess, they said that the police could justifiably use more force when responding to the masculine Black athletes, compared to the masculine White athletes (Wilson et al., 2017).

If we have stereotypes about "masculine" people being aggressive and about football players being aggressive, and if we grow up in a racist culture that teaches us that African American people are more likely to be aggressive than people from other races or ethnicities, then intersectionality might affect our perceptions of people. The results of this study indicate this possibility. There are now dozens of other examples of intersectionality coming from the world of psychology. For example, resources for survivors of domestic violence are particularly scarce if those survivors don't fit cultural expectations (e.g., if they are men or if they are in same-sex relationships; Allen-Collinson, 2009; Arnocky & Vaillancourt, 2014; Cruz, 2003; West, 1998). Women forced into sex trafficking are treated worse if they are women of color, compared to White women (Kara, 2009). There may be biases based on both age and sex of children in terms of diagnoses for disabilities such as ADHD (CHADD, 2021).

While intersectionality remains a controversial term, it is growing in popularity within psychology. Over the past two decades, several psychologists have studied how an intersectionality framework can help us understand the human experience in terms of discrimination, identity development, stereotypes, socialization of children, media messages, self-esteem, physical and mental health disparities, and more (for a review, see Rosenthal, 2016; see also Corrigan et al., 2004; Hatzenbuehler et al. 2013; Singh & Gudiño, 2023; Ummak et al., 2023). Figure 4.10 shows the number of times the word *intersectionality* is referenced within books, journal articles, or graduate school theses and dissertations listed in the psychology database PsycInfo over the past 25 years or so. In 1997, there was a single journal article with the word mentioned. In the year 2022, there were 777 separate psychology publications regarding intersectionality.

FIGURE 4.10

PsycInfo References to "Intersectionality" by Year (Total = 4,936)

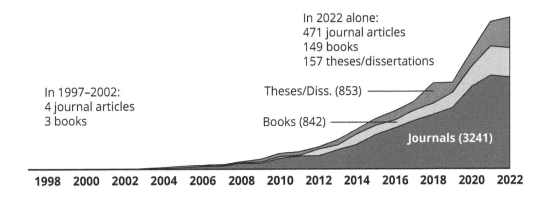

Source: Created using data from PsycInfo.

Our identity matters. Before Patrick realized he was Patrick—when he was Shannon—he struggled with anxiety and depression. He used drugs and alcohol to cope and escape from a world he didn't think accepted him, including rejection from his mother. Now that he's embraced his identity and is living as his true self, he's never been happier. He is newly married to a woman who knows his history and accepts it all. His life isn't perfect; he still struggles with paying for his medical needs and with people in the community who treat him badly because of who he is. His mother still refuses to talk to him. What's the next step? He recently completed a master's degree in counseling psychology and is working in a rural public school, helping the next generation of young adults crystallize their own unique identities.

How might intersectionality affect your own future, in both positive and potentially challenging ways? ●

Practice what you learn in **Knowledge Check 4.5**

Sage Vantage≯

Learning Objectives Summary

4.1   How does our identity form?

>> LO 4.1   Describe theories that help explain how identity is formed.

Our self-concept is our overall idea of who we are right now, including all aspects of the self. Self-esteem is our subjective evaluation, or whether we like ourselves. Self-discrepancy theory suggests that we all have three selves: an actual self (who we are now), an ideal self (who we'd like to be), and an ought self (who we think others want us to be).

4.2   What is the difference between sex and gender?

>> LO 4.2   Analyze models of thinking about sex and gender.

The sexual spectrum is the idea that biological sex might have more than two categories (male and female); intersex people are an example. Gender is a social construct, with psychological androgyny defined as high levels of masculinity and femininity in a single individual. Transgender people disagree with the sex assigned to them at birth.

4.3   How is sexual orientation described in psychology?

>> LO 4.3   Compare and contrast the Kinsey and Storms models of sexual orientation.

Two models of sexuality (by Kinsey and Storms) both suggest that sexual orientation may be a continuous variable rather than a categorical one. The Kinsey model suggests one continuum (with homosexuality at one end and heterosexuality at the other end) while the Storms model suggests two continuums (one for attraction to men and one for attraction to women), allowing space for bisexuality and asexuality.

4.4   How do culture and technology influence sexuality?

>> LO 4.4   Explain ways that culture and technology influence sexual behaviors.

Sexual scripts are culturally shaped expectations regarding how sexual interactions will occur; most of us conform to these scripts. Sexual expectations can also be shaped by technology (such as dating apps and social media) and by media messages (such as pornography).

4.5   What is intersectionality?

>> LO 4.5   Define intersectionality and analyze how it applies to your own life.

Intersectionality is the idea that our lived experience is based on the combination of our demographics (like age, gender, and ethnicity) and social categories. Still a controversial idea, many psychologists believe intersectionality is a helpful framework to understand human experiences of identity as well as discrimination, socialization of children, media messages, and more.

CRITICAL THINKING QUESTIONS

1. Self-discrepancy theory says we all have three selves: actual, ideal, and ought. Identify at least one way in which your "ideal" self (what you hope to achieve in your future) doesn't align with your "ought" self (what you think other people want for you, like your parents, friends, or culture in general). How does this discrepancy make you feel? Does your reaction match what Higgins predicted? Explain.

2. Watch two episodes of a show featuring gender or sexual minority celebrities or characters (e.g., *RuPaul's Drag Race*, *Queer Eye*, *Orange Is the New Black*, *Pose*, *Euphoria*, *Schitt's Creek*, etc.). Analyze whether the people featured are shown in positive, negative, or mixed ways. Does this show help or hurt stereotypes about the groups of people featured? In what ways?

3. Look up the American College Health Association statistics from 2019 to 2021 and focus on college students' sexual behaviors (via an online search). Pick out three specific findings from this research that you find the most interesting or surprising. Explain the three findings in your own words, then discuss why they struck you as interesting.

4. First, make a list of important aspects of your identity. Then, draw a pie graph in which you indicate how important each aspect you listed is to your daily life. Finally, write a paragraph in which you discuss how intersectionality does (or doesn't) seem to have an influence on your interactions with others, time in college, career plans, or anything else you think is important.

KEY TERMS

Androgen, 98
Cisgender people, 103
Estrogen, 98
Femme porn, 114
Gender, 97
Gender identity, 101
Gender schema theory, 101
Intersectionality, 115
Intersex, 98
Mirror self-recognition test, 93
Psychological androgyny, 102

Secondary sex characteristics, 98
Self-concept, 93
Self-discrepancy theory, 95
Sex, 97
Sexting, 112
Sexual hookups, 113
Sexual scripts, 109
Sexual spectrum, 97
Social comparison theory, 94
Social identity theory, 93
Transgender people, 103

iStock.com/SeanZeroThree

5

Stress, Health, and Happiness

It's your senior year of college!

That's right—it's the beginning of your final semester in school. Feelings of excitement and nervousness abound as you start making postgraduation plans. Unexpectedly, your academic advisor sends you an email notifying you that you are missing a required course for graduation. You think to yourself: Is the required course offered this semester? Will there be an open seat for enrollment? Will the course be difficult? You are officially a ball of stress.

This chapter focuses on stress and how we cope with it. Throughout your college years and beyond, you'll have plenty of challenges that will cause you stress. Overcoming them and learning from your mistakes will help you build lifelong success. We'll end the chapter by discussing ways to promote health and the psychology of happiness. Because what's life without experiences that make you happy?

After reading this chapter, you will get answers to several questions you've been curious about:

Have You Ever Wondered?

5.1   What is stress and what are different types of stressors?

5.2   What are the consequences of stress?

5.3   How do people cope with stress?

5.4   What promotes health and health behaviors?

5.5   What factors influence happiness?

Learning Objectives

LO 5.1   Define stress and compare and contrast types of stressors.

LO 5.2   Analyze the ways stress impacts the human body.

LO 5.3   Compare and contrast coping strategies.

LO 5.4   Describe behaviors that promote health and identify theories of health behavior.

LO 5.5   Analyze factors that impact happiness from a psychological approach.

STRESS: THE BAD AND THE GOOD

? Have You Ever Wondered?
5.1 What is stress and what are different types of stressors?

Stress: How we react when we feel a situation is threatening or challenging.

Stressors: Stress-causing events or situations.

>> **LO 5.1   Define stress and compare and contrast types of stressors.**

Stress is not inherently good or bad.

College can be stressful. Did you select the correct courses? How much are your textbooks? Will you be able to write a good paper? How difficult will your final exams be?

Stress occurs when we perceive a situation that threatens or challenges us. Most people experience some degree of stress daily. Car problems, paying bills, or the threat of a mass shooter incident are examples of **stressors**. Stressors range from merely irritating and annoying experiences, such as being stuck in traffic or temporarily losing your cellphone, to potentially fatal incidents such as armed robbery experience, military combat, or major car accidents. Certain life experiences, such as the death of a loved one, may be universally stressful, but the perception of stress for other situations may be person specific.

Certain times of life also predict stress—for example, 57% of college students in the United States reporting higher than average stress levels (American Psychological

Association, 2017). In fact, high levels of stress are found in students across countries and cultures (Pascoe et al., 2020). Still, stress is a personal experience. For someone who has attended class regularly, completed assigned readings, and studied carefully, the final exam may not be stressful. But for someone who missed classes, ignored assignments, and has not studied, the final exam might create significant stress. Table 5.1 categorizes common sources of stress among college students (Pitt et al., 2018).

TABLE 5.1

Common Sources of Stress in College

Common stressors in college are academic, financial, personal, and so on.

STRESSOR	TIMES STRESSOR REPORTED	% OF PARTICIPANTS REPORTING THIS STRESSOR
Academic	122	94.4
Assessments	34	83.3
Workload	27	55.6
Examinations	16	38.9
Time management	11	44.4
Being behind	9	44.4
Difficult university work	7	16.7
Waiting for results	5	22.2
Other	15	50
Finances/work	24	38.9
Finances	11	33.3
Work	8	16.7
University/work balance	5	22.2
Personal	23	50
Health	17	44.4
Other	6	11.1
Family related	19	50
Family related	14	38.9
University/family balance	5	22.2
University	17	66.7
Starting university	10	55.6
Other	7	22.2
Interpersonal	16	22.2
Partner	7	16.7
Other	9	11.1
Environment	10	22.8
Transport	7	22.2
Other	3	16.7

Source: Pitt et al. (2018).

Distress: Stress from unpleasant experiences (e.g., getting fired from work) or that causes negative outcomes (like anxiety).

Eustress: Stress from pleasant experiences (e.g., getting promoted at work) or that causes positive outcomes (like motivation).

Many people assume that stressors are only **distress**, or unpleasant experiences. But positive events are also stressors. Getting married, being promoted at work, or getting accepted into graduate school are positive events for most people, but they all require a significant amount of change in people's habits, duties, and lifestyle. Consequently, these events can create **eustress** (Selye, 1975). Researchers now think of eustress as the optimal amount of stress that people need to promote health and well-being (Le Fevre, 2003). Being a little anxious or stressed about your class presentation motivates you to prepare. Stress produces both positive and negative consequences.

However, eustress can feel like distress— nerves may abound, your heart might pound, and your thoughts might race. The difference is how you perceive these physical sensations. With distress, you may feel uncomfortable and overwhelmed, like trying to figure out if you will be able to register for the course you need for graduation. Eustress is associated with feelings of excitement or challenge, such as the anticipation of graduation and the new chapter of your life that will begin.

The excitement of a roller-coaster ride, a scary movie, or a fun challenge are all examples of eustress.

iStock.com/skynesher

Types of Stressors

Your life experience is full of stressors.

It isn't surprising that these stressors are not all harmful. In fact, some stressors can be good for you. Your perception and attitude toward both environmental and personal stressors is important for your mental health. Some stressors may play a role in the development of mental and physical diseases, such as cancer (Dai et al., 2020). In particular, chronic stress from stressors such as isolation, depression, loneliness, and adversity may be particularly damaging. Some researchers divide stressors into three major categories: catastrophes, major life events (both good and bad), and daily hassles.

Environmental Stressors

Both natural and human disasters can be catastrophic. **Catastrophes**, such as Hurricane Katrina, which caused over 1,800 fatalities and $125 billion in damage in late August 2005, can raise stress levels for a large population over an extended period of time. Among Hurricane Katrina survivors, distress declined over time after the hurricane but still remained high 43 to

Greenwood Avenue (or "Black Wall Street") was destroyed during the 1921 Tulsa Massacre, a major catastrophe in American history occurring years before psychologists measured stress levels.

Universal History Archive/Contributor/Universal Images Group/via Getty Images

Catastrophe: A stressor that occurs suddenly and typically affects many people at once.

54 months later (note, that's years later) and did not return to prehurricane levels (Paxson et al., 2012). The daughter of one of your authors [Tom] was missing for 2 weeks after barely escaping in a borrowed car already low on fuel. It was a scary experience for sure.

Personal Stressors: Hassles and Uplifts

Thankfully, most of us do not experience catastrophic stressors. However, **personal stressors** include negative and positive ordinary life experiences that require a person to adjust or change in a significant way, such as the death of a loved one, having a baby, or getting married. Typically, personal stressors cause some major, immediate reaction that generally fades with time. For example, the stress associated with the death of a loved one is typically strongest just after the death but gradually declines over time.

Taking care of a new baby can be a personal stressor.
iStock.com/DGLimages

Personal stressors: Ordinary life experiences that require a person to adjust or change in a significant way.

What about repeated minor life irritations? **Daily hassles** may result in an unpleasant mood or emotion but produce only minor stress. But daily hassles can "add up" to major stress, resulting in this type of stressor causing the most significant stress for many people in life. As daily hassles increase, mental and physical health problems such posttraumatic stress disorder, depression, chronic pain, and sleep disturbances increase as well (Burke et al., 2017; Herman et al., 2016; Kalmbach et al., 2018; Segerstrom & Miller, 2004). Think about this the next time you encounter a cranky customer service person who has likely been dealing with angry people all day for low pay—their job is highly stressful. And this is a problem that money doesn't solve. A good salary does not guarantee protection of workplace stressors like increases in workload, longer hours, poor physical conditions, and both deliberate and unintended hostility in general. The accumulation of hundreds of tiny emotional cuts can result in *burnout,* a form of exhaustion caused by constantly feeling swamped. College students may suffer from burnout when overwhelmed by readings, midterm papers, and exams.

Daily hassles: A source of stress involving irritating, frustrating, and distressing demands that people face on a day-to-day basis.

Fortunately, your daily life also includes **uplifts**: daily, positive, and joyful experiences (Kanner et al., 1981). Checking off items on our "to-do" lists or relating well to our romantic partners are uplifts associated with improved health. The more uplifts we experience, the fewer psychological and health problems we report later (Amiel Castro et al., 2020; Cooper et al., 2019; Hurley & Kwon, 2013).

Connecting with a romantic partner is an uplift.
iStock.com/Jlco—Julia Amaral

Uplifts: Daily, positive, and joyful experiences.

Meet Abby, Long-Term Care Administrator

What is your career?

I am a long-term care (LTC) administrator; I am responsible for running a skilled nursing and rehabilitation facility in Lincoln, Nebraska. We provide quality care to 104 seniors each day. I focus on ensuring the development of strong relationships with our residents, their families, and our team members. I am responsible for effective and economic operation of all departments in our facility and make sure facility goals are achieved day to day.

How was studying psychology important for success in this career?

Psychology is a great steppingstone to any career; I truly feel like I could put up a solid case for how it's relatable and necessary no matter which career path you take. **Psychology is so relevant when it comes to serving the elderly. It is such a difficult time for individuals when it comes time to move into a long-term care facility.** No one ever grows up thinking they can't wait to move into a nursing home someday and have people take care of them. Many of these folks are going through stages of grief for being at the point in life that they need additional care. You must truly be committed and passionate about wanting to meet people where they are at physically, mentally, and emotionally to provide the best care to them possible during such a difficult time.

How do concepts from this chapter help in this career?

Giving families the tools they need to continue meaningful relationships with their loved ones through stressful events is so important. Simple steps such as offering a gracious reminder for who you are when you talk in the room, using simple statements of seven words or less, and giving residents an endorphin boost before you leave helps us to maintain great relationships with our residents along with providing the best care possible to them.

Is this the career you always planned to have after college?

I absolutely did not plan on becoming a LTC administrator. My original game plan after graduating college was to become an occupational therapist. After one semester of graduate school, I took a job as a receptionist at a recruiting firm and I fell in love with human resources. From there, I combined my passion for recruiting with my passion for direct care and took a job at a nursing and rehabilitation center as the people development coordinator. I was in that role for 4½ years before taking the job as the administrator. I can't come up with a better job—I'm truly grateful to go to work each day.

If you could give current college students one sentence of advice, what would it be?

A degree in psychology is a degree without limits; you truly have every opportunity with this degree to do any job in the world. ●

Economic and Sociocultural Factors in Stress

Societal inequities can cause stress.

So far, you have learned that a wide variety of life events can cause stress—even happy and positive things, like having a baby or getting promoted at work. Additional sources of stress in everyday life come from issues within society and culture. While our discussion here doesn't list every possible cause of stress, next we discuss three important factors: poverty, acculturation, and racism.

Poverty Stress

The United States Census Bureau reported that 37.2 million people were living in poverty in 2020 (Kilduff, 2022).

Living in poverty is a chronic stressor: You don't have enough money to provide basic life necessities. Reduced access to resources that are needed to support a healthy quality of life, such as stable housing, healthy foods, accessible health care, and safe neighborhoods, contributes to worse health outcomes for people living in poverty (Khullar & Chokshi, 2018; Thompson et al., 2019). For example, people with limited finances may have more difficulty obtaining health insurance or paying for expensive procedures and medications (Thompson et al., 2019).

In addition, neighborhood factors, such as limited access to healthy foods and higher instances of violence, can affect health by influencing health behaviors and stress (Thompson et al., 2019). Research has also made it increasingly clear that one of the mechanisms through which poverty affects the health and well-being of children and adults is through the toxic effects of stress on the brain. In fact, effects of poverty on physiological and neurobiological development are likely central to poverty-related gaps in academic achievement and the well-documented lifelong effects of poverty on physical health (Feijó et al., 2023; Hair et al., 2015; Lawson et al., 2013).

Acculturation Stress

Acculturation stress is the mental and emotional challenges of adapting to a new culture. Short term, people sometimes call this "culture shock"—but long term, people who have transitioned to live in a new country or even region within a country often experience this kind of stress. For example, youth who are the only one in their family to attend college or people who move from the Midwest to the East Coast or from the East Coast to the West Coast are often surprised at the small differences they encounter (e.g., do you call fizzy caffeinated drinks "soda," "pop," "Coke," or something else? When you go to the grocery store, do you find the kinds of foods you're used to eating?). People who immigrate to a new country face a significant amount of acculturation stress and might enter the majority culture in several ways that influence stress.

As shown in Table 5.2 (Rudmin, 2003), acculturation can range from least to most stressful depending on the extent to which the new culture is adopted and the home culture is maintained:

- In *integration,* a person tries to maintain their original cultural identity while also trying to form a positive relationship with members of the majority culture. For example, an integrated person may maintain cultural traditions in the home but dress like the majority culture at work. Integration usually results in lower acculturation stress.

- In *assimilation,* a person gives up their old cultural identity and completely adopts the majority culture's ways. For example, an assimilated person may change their name to sound more "American." Assimilation leads to a moderate level of acculturation stress due to the loss of a person's own cultural identity.

- In *separation,* a person rejects the majority culture's ways and maintains their original cultural identity. Stress can be high if discrimination from the majority group forces the separation rather than self-imposed withdrawal from the majority culture.

> **Acculturation stress:** The mental and emotional challenges of adapting to a new culture.

The Chinatown district of San Francisco is full of rich culture. It's the oldest Chinatown in North America with a history stretching back to 1848.

iStock.com/SeanPavonePhoto

TABLE 5.2

Different Forms of Acculturation in People

How immigrants integrate their home and new culture affects stress levels.

		MAINTAINS HOME CULTURE	
		LOW	HIGH
ADOPTS NEW CULTURE	LOW	Marginalization	Separation
	HIGH	Assimilation	Integration

Source: Adapted from Rudmin (2003).

- In *marginalization,* people can't interact with their original culture and are also excluded from the majority culture. Essentially, they are relegated to the "margins" of both cultures and made invisible. Marginalization typically results in the greatest acculturation stress.

Entering a new culture is often a difficult experience. Even when it is a positive and chosen situation, it involves many changes.

Racism Stress

Racism stress: The psychological distress associated with experiences of racism.

Black, Indigenous, and other people of color (sometimes as a group referred to with the acronym BIPOC) may experience **racism stress**, or psychological or emotional distress associated with experiences of racism. Racist actions usually involve some form of racial bias and discrimination that can be overt, such as being targeted by racial slurs, or covert, for example, microaggressions.

Microaggressions are subtle, brief words and actions that communicate hostile, hurtful, or negative messages toward groups based on identity. For example, when Asian Americans and Latinx Americans are assumed to be foreign born—if people ask, "Where are you *really* from?" Not surprisingly, racism stress can lead to a long list of negative reactions: anger, anxiety, fear, frustration, depression, helplessness/ hopelessness, isolation, paranoia, resentment, self-blame, and self-doubt (Pieterse et al.,

Having a positive racial and ethnic identity, strong sense of self, and taking social action against injustice are ways to combat racial stress.

iStock.com/dragana991

2022). Racism stress is also associated with health concerns such as heart disease, hypertension, sleep disturbances, and dietary/digestive issues (Neblett, 2019; Williams et al., 2019).

THE CONSEQUENCES OF STRESS

>> **LO 5.2 Analyze the ways stress impacts the human body.**

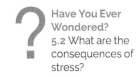

Have You Ever
Wondered?
5.2 What are the
consequences of
stress?

The pit inside your stomach comes from somewhere.

Remember from the start of the chapter—you have that pesky class that might get in the way of your graduation. You don't want to delay your future. If you get anxious about what might happen, you may start to sweat profusely, feel your heart racing, and feel the acid start to bubble away in your stomach. Stress has physical consequences.

General Adaptation Syndrome

Our bodies process different sources of stress in the same physiological way.

As illustrated in Figure 5.1, we experience a three-stage sequence of physiological reactions, known as **general adaptation syndrome (GAS)**, when responding to a stressor: alarm, resistance, and exhaustion.

Would you feel stressed if
your car's fuel gauge meter
showed you are almost out
of gas on a country road at
night?

iStock.com/kckate16

- *Alarm:* The stress from not knowing whether your graduation will be delayed can lead to a racing heart, sweating palms, and rising blood pressure. During this alarm stage, your body sends a distress signal to your brain. Your brain responds by sending a message to the body releasing "fight-or-flight" hormones such as adrenaline and cortisol. You may also experience reactions such as fever, nausea, and headache.

- *Resistance:* As the stress continues, your body tries to recover from the changes that occurred during the alarm stage. This typically occurs when the triggering event has stopped—such as being told that the course you need is indeed available before your graduation is supposed to happen (yay!). Your physiological symptoms begin to fade.

- *Exhaustion:* Prolonged stress can exhaust your body's physiological resources. The prolonged release of stress hormones increases risk for stress-related diseases, such as ulcers, high blood pressure, or a weakened immune system (Cohen et al., 2019).

**General adaptation
syndrome (GAS):** The three-
stage sequence of physiological
reactions the body goes
through when adapting to a
stressor: alarm, resistance, and
exhaustion.

The general adaptation syndrome begins the chain of physiological events shown in Figure 5.2. The **hypothalamic–pituitary–adrenocortical (HPA) axis** describes the interaction between the hypothalamus, pituitary gland, and adrenal glands that links stress to disease. The hypothalamus produces a corticotropin-releasing hormone (CRH), which stimulates the pituitary gland to release adrenocorticotropic hormone (ACTH). ACTH then stimulates the adrenal glands to release cortisol. Cortisol is the "stress hormone" that acts as nature's built-in alarm system that helps our bodies take quick action during the alarm stage.

Acute stress (sudden, stressful one-time events) can sometimes be adaptive because cortisol helps us take the necessary action, like fighting or fleeing, to avoid serious consequences in a stressful situation. Once the body has dealt with the stressor, cortisol levels typically return to normal. But there are consequences. Cortisol also suppresses the immune system, so even acute stressors can have a detrimental impact on health (Cohen et al., 2019).

**Hypothalamic–pituitary–
adrenocortical (HPA)
axis:** The interaction between
the hypothalamus, pituitary
gland, and adrenal glands; it
plays a major role in linking
stress to disease.

FIGURE 5.1

Selye's General Adaptation Syndrome

We experience a three-stage sequence of physiological reactions, known as general adaptation syndrome (GAS), when responding to a stressor: *alarm,* your body reacts to stress; *resistance,* the body begins to repair itself; and *exhaustion*, occurring during prolonged or chronic stress when the body's adaptation to higher stress levels starts to break down.

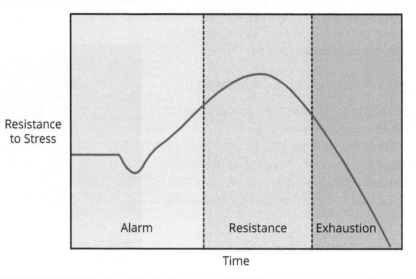

FIGURE 5.2

Hypothalamic–Pituitary–Adrenocortical (HPA) Axis

The hypothalamic–pituitary–adrenocortical (HPA) axis plays a major role in linking stress to disease.

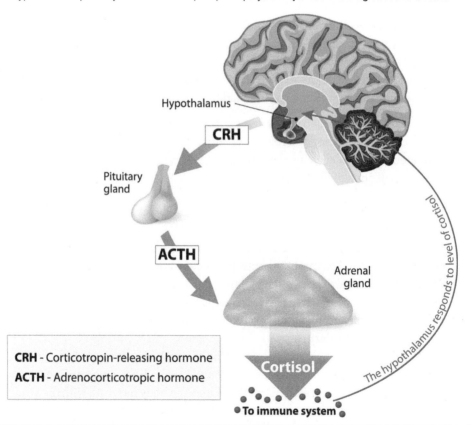

iStock.com/ttsz

Chronic stress is more likely to lead to long-term or permanent changes in our body. Chronic stress (such as caring for a parent with dementia) and brief events that continue to be experienced as overwhelming (such as experiencing a sexual assault) affect us long after they have ended. Under chronic stress, the body experiences prolonged or repeated activation of the HPA axis. This activation can interfere with a person's control of other physiological systems, such as the cardiovascular, metabolic, and immune systems, resulting in increased risk for disease (Juruena et al., 2020; Speer et al., 2019; Zänkert et al., 2019).

Stress and the Immune System

You may have experienced how stress harms your health.

Ever get sick immediately after a long period of stress, such as after end-of-term exams? Your immune system (the network of organs, cells, and proteins that defends the body against diseases and injuries) knows when you are stressed about work, family, finances, or current events and is sensitive to this stress, especially if it's chronic.

Psychoneuroimmunology studies the effects of psychological factors, such as stress and emotions, on the immune system (Ader, 2020; Irwin, 2008). Stress can lower the efficiency of the immune system, making a person more susceptible to disease (Schakel et al., 2019). Stress can also promote disease-producing processes or activate dormant viruses that weaken immune response (Capoccia et al., 2013; Perego et al., 2020). Experiencing stress doesn't guarantee poor health, but it does contribute to increases in the severity and progression of multiple illnesses, including depression, HIV/AIDS, asthma, autoimmune diseases, and cardiovascular diseases (Cohen et al., 2019).

Psychoneuroimmunology: The study of the effects of psychological factors, such as stress and emotions, on the immune system.

Sounds grim, right? On the bright side, most people who experience stressful events do not get sick. This is true for common stressful events, such as job loss or the end of an important relationship, and for less common traumatic events, such as direct exposure to violence or abuse. In one study, about 51% of participants who reported a stressful life event did *not* develop a cold. There is more to health (and happiness) than avoiding stress, and we'll talk more about keys to happiness at the end of this chapter.

Stress and Cardiovascular Disease (Heart Disease)

Stress can increase risk of cardiovascular disease through at least three overlapping paths.

The first is behavioral, where the combination of an unhealthy diet, reducing physical activity, and smoking forms a stress-related path to heart disease (Dar et al., 2019; Kivimäki & Steptoe, 2018; Lallukka et al., 2008). A second path involves developing metabolic diseases, such as Type 2 diabetes (Einarson et al., 2018; Isasi et al., 2015). A third stress-related path to cardiovascular disease takes a more roundabout route. While the body's "fight-or-flight" system is aroused during stress, the liver fails to activate, which means it isn't clearing fat and cholesterol from the bloodstream. The result? Clogged arteries.

The evidence that chronic stress is associated with heart disease is compelling and has been studied for 40 to 50 years (Bishop, 2016; Dar et al., 2019). An early study found that individuals with Type A personality behaviors that include being aggressive, competitive, hostile, short tempered, time conscious, preoccupied with deadlines, unable to relax, and cynical were prone to excessive stress (Friedman, 1977; Friedman & Rosenman, 1959). Follow-up studies zeroed in on cynical hostility as being the key part of that cluster of traits that seemed the most important link between stress and heart disease (e.g., Vassou et al., 2020). Why are hostility and anger so toxic? Hostility

Type A personality: Pattern of behaviors that are aggressive, competitive, hostile, short-tempered, time conscious, preoccupied with deadlines, unable to relax, and cynical; this pattern is positively correlated with heart disease.

and anger produce excessive arousal in stressful situations and over time take a toll on the heart (Myrtek, 2001).

Type B personality: Pattern of behaviors that are relaxed, easygoing, slow to anger, and less competitive; this pattern is negatively correlated with heart disease.

The same group of original researchers found that those with **Type B personality** behaviors, who tend to be relaxed, easygoing, slow to anger, and less competitive, have decreased risk of coronary artery disease. This finding suggests that altering your life from Type A to Type B behavior patterns after a heart attack can decrease the probability of heart attacks (Friedman et al., 1982).

The Type A and Type B approach is fairly well known, but because most studies have used male participants, there is no scientific consensus (Cooper et al., 1981; Petticrew et al., 2012). Not everyone who displays Type A personality will have coronary heart disease, and not everyone who has a heart attack has a Type A personality. However, anger and hostility are the most common behavioral components associated with this health issue (Espnes & Byrne, 2016; Sahoo et al., 2018).

Anger and hostility are the behavior components of Type A personality most consistently associated with coronary heart disease.

iStock.com/valentinrussanov

Type D personality: "Distressed" pattern of behaviors whereby a person experiences negative emotions over time and in different life situations; people who inhibit self-expression in social interactions.

A **Type D personality** may also be linked to coronary heart disease (Denollet, 2005; Denollet & Kupper, 2015). People with a Type D personality—short for "distressed"—tend to experience negative emotions over time across different life situations and inhibit self-expression in social interactions (Denollet, 2000). Higher cortisol responses, disruption of the hypothalamic–pituitary–adrenal axis, and exaggerated blood pressure and heart responses in relation to stressful events put people with a Type D personality at risk for cardiovascular disease (Denollet & Kupper, 2015; Lin et al., 2017; Molloy et al., 2008).

Stress and Cancer

There is still a lot to learn about what triggers cancer.

Cancer remains a leading cause of death, after cardiovascular diseases (World Health Organization, 2017). Normal cells divide, reproduce, and then stop dividing according to genetic instructions. But cancer cells multiply rapidly in an uncontrolled fashion and form tumors. These tumors, if left unchecked, destroy nutrients from healthy cells and body tissue and prevent the body's ability to function.

Natural killer (NK) cells play a critical role in the control of tumor growth, and chronic stress is associated with decreases in NK cell activity.

iStock.com/selvanegra

Recall that stress suppresses the immune system, which can make the unchecked growth of cancer more likely (Dai et al., 2020; Huntington et al., 2020). For instance, natural killer (NK) cells suppress viruses and destroy tumor cells. Stress depresses the release of NK cells, making it more difficult for the body to fight cancerous growths.

We, therefore, might expect to see a correlation between stress and cancer—and studies have linked chronic stress to cancer progression (Chiriac et al., 2018). However, some types of stress, like that experienced at work, do not appear to be directly linked to developing cancers of the colon, lungs, breasts, or prostate (Heikkilä et al., 2013).

Stress can also impact cancer treatments' effectiveness (Dai et al., 2020). One recent study suggests that stress hormones may wake up dormant cancer cells that remain in the body after treatment (Perego et al., 2020). In experiments with mice, a stress hormone triggered a chain reaction in immune cells that prompted dormant cancer cells to wake up and form tumors again. Yikes! That's a disturbing but possibly very important study.

SPOTLIGHT ON RESEARCH METHODS

Does Stress Make You Age More Quickly?

iStock.com/Renata Angerami

Stress can make you look worn out. But will stress give you gray hairs and wrinkles overnight? Most research evidence suggests the rate at which an individual turns gray depends on genetics (Trüeb, 2006). However, accumulated stress may relate to the causes of aging at the cellular level.

Your DNA "age" can be understood by the telomere length and telomerase levels. Telomeres are a protective casing at the end of a strand of DNA. Telomeres shorten each time your cells divide, and it is up to telomerase to correct this loss. Unfortunately, chronic stress and cortisol exposure decrease telomerase levels, which end up speeding the aging process. How does stress rank in terms of factors that affect telomere length? The two biggest factors are chronological aging and genetics, but stress is now on the map as one of the most consistent predictors of shorter telomere length (Yegorov et al., 2020). In short, people exposed to chronic stress age more rapidly.

But there is some good news: Researchers have identified some ways to slow down the stress-induced aging process. A study that evaluated blood samples from 444 young to middle-aged adults for age-related chemical changes and other markers of health

recently developed DNA epigenetic "clocks," which may provide a more accurate measure of biological age (Harvanek et al., 2021). Rather than using telomere length, they used recently developed DNA epigenetic "clocks," which may provide a more accurate measure of biological age (compared to your chronological age that you celebrate every birthday; Horvath & Raj, 2018; Levine et al., 2018). These clocks are built from a set of DNA markers that correlate with chronologic age and serve as molecular estimators of biological age in cells, tissues, and individuals (Bell et al., 2019). Epigenetic clocks have a significantly higher predictive value for mortality risk than previously used measures such as telomere length (Gao et al., 2018; Marioni et al., 2016) and chronologic age (Fries et al., 2017). Participants were also questioned regarding their stress levels, as well as their behavioral and psychological resilience (or the ability to adapt to difficulty).

Cumulative stress, insulin resistance, and lack of control over emotions were associated with accelerated epigenetic clocks and stress-related measures of adrenal sensitivity (Cortisol/ACTH ratio) and insulin resistance. Importantly, insulin resistance was also correlated with accelerated aging. Remarkably, psychological resilience factors of emotion regulation and self-control may have influenced these relationships. For participants with worse emotion regulation, there was greater stress-related age acceleration, while stronger emotion regulation prevented any significant effect of stress on aging, even while accounting for other factors such as race, smoking habits, and body mass index. High self-control blunted the relationship between stress and insulin resistance.

This study is the first one to identify a clear relationship between cumulative stress and age acceleration in a healthy population, which suggests stress may play a role in accelerated aging even prior to the onset of chronic diseases. ●

COPING WITH STRESS

? Have You Ever
Wondered?
5.3 How do people
cope with stress?

>> LO 5.3   Compare and contrast coping strategies.

Not everyone perceives the same events as stressful.

As you prepare to begin your last semester of college, you start to get anxious. You're not sure if you will apply for jobs or pursue another degree in graduate school. You notice that your friend who is also graduating this year seems to have it all figured out. In fact, they seem completely chill—excited instead of nervous. Though our bodies respond similarly to stressors, our interpretation of life events matters.

Cognitive Appraisal

In everyday life, we evaluate how events will impact us.

Before graduation, you likely arrive at a conclusion about how it will affect you. Cognitive appraisal is our interpretation of a situation, how it will affect us, and if we have the resources to effectively manage in the moment. Lazarus (1993) defined a two-step appraisal process. Primary appraisals happen first; here, you interpret a situation as (1) harmful or threatening, (2) a challenge to overcome, (3) benign, or (4) irrelevant. Lazarus believed that your friend perceiving graduation as an adventure rather than a threat is a good strategy for reducing stress.

Cognitive appraisal: A person's interpretation of a situation, how it will affect them, and if they have the resources to effectively manage.

Primary appraisals: Interpreting a situation as harmful or threatening, a challenge to overcome, benign, or irrelevant.

This child may perceive remote learning as a challenge to be met and not a harmful threat, which will help them manage stress.

iStock.com/Pikussi-Studio

Secondary appraisals happen next; now, you evaluate how to effectively manage the situation and consider resources for coping. Your friend may evaluate the resources they can use to successfully prepare for graduation. These include preparing their resume, obtaining an internship to develop hands-on skills, and applying for multiple jobs. In contrast, if you view the situation as threatening, you are less likely to do these activities, which may actually increase your stress levels.

Two Types of Coping

Secondary appraisals: Evaluation of how to effectively manage a situation if deemed stressful.

Coping: Trying to control, reduce, or tolerate threats and challenges that lead to stress.

Problem-focused coping: Directly facing your troubles and trying to solve them.

Emotion-focused coping: Seeking to reduce the negative emotional responses associated with stress.

Some people squarely face their troubles and others try to manage their emotions.

Cognitive appraisals help us with coping, or attempts to control, reduce, or tolerate threats and challenges that lead to stress. Lazarus and Susan Folkman (Folkman & Lazarus, 1988) identified two types of coping:

- **Problem-focused coping** involves directly facing troubles and trying to solve them. Strategies include generating alternative solutions, weighing their costs and benefits, and choosing between them. To cope with the stress of making sure you have graduation requirements, you promptly contact the registrar's office to see when you can enroll in the missing course noted by your academic advisor. You also consider contacting the course instructor to get more information about the course requirements, to get a head start.

- **Emotion-focused coping** involves trying to reduce the negative emotional responses associated with stress. Strategies include avoidance, minimizing the problem, trying to distance yourself from the problem, or eating and drinking. Meditating, exercising, journaling, and reframing are additional emotion-focused responses. Clearly, some strategies are healthier than others. You might avoid responding back to your academic advisor's email, tell yourself that your advisor made a mistake, or overeat and drink alcohol to dull the frustration. Alternatively, you may write down your feelings in a journal or talk it over with a friend or therapist, who helps you decide that taking an additional course will provide a learning opportunity.

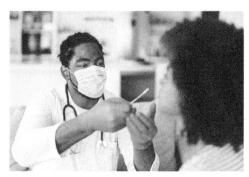 

Problem-focused coping leads to developing a plan of action to deal with stress, whereas emotion-focused coping seeks to change feelings about a problem.

iStock.com/pixelfit; iStock.com/yacobchuk

While using only one type of coping is better than nothing and results in moderate levels of stress (as opposed to high stress; Penley et al., 2002), the best strategy might be to use problem-focused and emotion-focused coping simultaneously. Some health care workers used both types of coping to manage stress associated with the coronavirus pandemic, and this was associated with positive mental and physical health outcomes (Labrague, 2021). Think about how you cope with stressful situations. To dive a bit deeper into this topic, check out the *What's My Score?* feature.

WHAT'S MY SCORE?

How Do You Cope?

Many studies on coping measure it through self-report scales. This scale measures how people cope with hardships in their life (Carver, 1997). How do you score?

Instructions: Read the statements and indicate how much you have been using each coping style to deal with a challenge in your life. Use the following scale for each question:

1	2	3	4
I haven't been doing this at all	A little bit	A medium amount	I've been doing this a lot

1. I've been concentrating my efforts on doing something about the situation I'm in.
2. I've been getting emotional support from others.
3. I've been learning to live with it.
4. I've been taking action to try to make the situation better.
5. I've been saying things to let my unpleasant feelings escape.
6. I've been getting help and advice from other people.
7. I've been criticizing myself.
8. I've been blaming myself for things that happened.
9. I've been trying to see it in a different light, to make it seem more positive.
10. I've been getting comfort and understanding from someone.
11. I've been trying to come up with a strategy about what to do.
12. I've been making jokes about it.
13. I've been looking for something good in what is happening.

(Continued)

(Continued)

14. I've been accepting the reality of the fact that it has happened.

15. I've been praying or meditating.

16. I've been trying to get advice or help from other people about what to do.

17. I've been expressing my negative feelings.

18. I've been thinking hard about what steps to take.

19. I've been trying to find comfort in my religion or spiritual beliefs.

20. I've been making fun of the situation.

Scoring instructions: In research, surveys with subscales often mix up the items. This helps ensure the people taking the survey carefully read each item, and sometimes it helps hide the purpose of the survey (when researchers try to avoid social desirability in responding). For this scale, sum your answers for the following subscales:

- Problem-focused coping: Total of Items 1, 4, 6, 9, 11, 13, 16, and 18
- Emotion-focused coping: Total of Items 2, 3, 5, 7, 8, 10, 12, 14, 15, 17, 19, and 20

When you consider your score, do you use problem-focused or emotion-focused coping? How do you think your coping style impacts your health? ●

Source: Carver (1997).

Learned Helplessness

If you love dogs, this may be a study you won't forget.

In 1967, researchers Martin Seligman and Steven Maier put three groups of dogs in separate cages with electric flooring.

- In Group 1, the dogs received no shock.
- In Group 2, the dogs received an electric shock—but they could stop it by pressing a panel with their noses.
- In Group 3, the dogs were restrained and had no way to stop the electric shock.

Learned helplessness: A state that occurs after someone has experienced a stressful situation repeatedly. They come to believe they are unable to control or change the situation, so they do not try—even when opportunities for change become available.

Later, the dogs were all put in another cage with a barrier in the middle and could escape the shock only by hopping over the barrier. Ninety percent of the dogs from the first two groups learned how to escape—but only one third of the dogs from the restrained group learned to escape. The rest huddled on the floor and waited for the shock to end.

The researchers believed the restrained group had learned in the first cage that their actions couldn't stop the shock. In other words, they **learned helplessness** and later didn't bother trying to escape, even when they had the opportunity.

People can learn helplessness by repeatedly experiencing a stressful situation. They come to believe that they are unable to control or change the situation, so they do not try—even when opportunities for change become available. For example, students who decide they are not good at statistics may not work hard in a required statistics course because they believe no matter the effort, they will never succeed. Sadly, their learned helplessness may ensure that they won't do well in the

Those who experience learned helplessness have concluded that there is no link between the responses they make and the outcomes that occur.

iStock.com/PeopleImages

course (Filippello et al., 2020). People with high amounts of learned helplessness experienced more mental health problems, like depression and stress, during the COVID-19 pandemic (Xue et al., 2023). And athletes in one study who had high levels of learned helplessness had *worse* performance over the course of their season, instead of improving; in the words of the researcher, "Despair is a frustrating factor of motivation" (Alwan, 2022, p. 93).

Successful Coping and Health

Better resources help people cope better with adversity.

Having to take more courses than originally anticipated can be a relatively good or bad experience, depending on the person's situation. The good news is that certain resources can help prevent stress and improve coping. We'll explore how specific internal and external resources contribute to successful coping: personality characteristics, exercising resilience, using religion and spirituality, and turning to others.

Personality Characteristics

When life gives lemons, some people make lemonade, sell it, turn it into a franchise business, and make millions! These people are equipped with **hardiness**, a set of personality characteristics that allow a person to thrive on stress instead of letting stress wear them down.

Hardiness: A set of personality characteristics that allow a person to thrive on stress instead of letting stress wear them down.

An original study on hardiness conducted at the Bell Telephone company examined when employees had to deal with massive layoffs and restructuring (Maddi & Kobasa, 1984). Many employees suffered, but others (the hardy ones) grew and even thrived from the stress. Hardy people have three common characteristics that act as a resource for coping with life's challenges (Maddi, 2002):

- They believe they can control events in their lives and what happens to them.

- They have a strong level of commitment and sense that their activities are important and meaningful.

- They can interpret problems as exciting challenges to personal growth rather than frightening difficulty.

Conscientiousness, or a tendency to be responsible and reliable, is also helpful for coping. Conscientious people are also more likely to use problem-focused coping strategies where they look to solve the root cause of what's troubling them (Bartley & Roesch, 2011; Connor-Smith & Flachsbart, 2007). Perhaps for these reasons, those with greater conscientiousness tend to live longer (Hagger-Johnson et al., 2012).

Bad things happen. We often can't control that. What we can control is our attitude and how we respond when those things occur. One important attitude is *optimism,* or the tendency to expect good experiences in the future. Even when faced with misfortune, optimists keep working to reach their goals or to find the "silver lining," whereas pessimists tend to give up. As a result, optimists are less likely to develop learned helplessness (Seligman, 2000).

Optimism can be protective against the negative effects of stress and help people cope with life's hassles.
iStock.com/Fokusiert

Successfully Adapting to Adversity

"I think I can . . . I think I can . . . I think I can."

This phrase is repeated as the little blue engine in the children's story *The Little Engine That Could* as it pulls a train full of toys over a large mountain. A quick summary of the plot: A train breaks down and a clown asks different engines for help to get over the mountain. The passenger, freight, and old rusty engines refuse. Only the little blue engine is willing to try and, saying "I think I can" over and over, the engine succeeds.

This tale's usual star is the little blue engine who kept saying, "I think I can." But the famous children's story's underrated character is the little clown. Despite repeated rejection, the little clown successfully copes with repeated failure/rejection and remains positive. The clown demonstrates **resilience**, the ability to adapt well in the face of adversity or stress.

Resilience: Adapting well in the face of adversity or stress.

Bouncing back from obstacles is how a person withstands, and perhaps even thrives, after profound stress. You may have had your share of challenging moments: failing a test, being rejected romantically, or being bullied because of who you are. You may have learned that you must keep trying, no matter what—that's resilience.

Resilience to stressful situations relates to structural differences in certain parts of the brain involved in executive control and emotional arousal, as show in Figure 5.3 (Gupta et al., 2017). These brain differences may be important markers for understanding who is and is not predisposed to psychological disorders when exposed to high levels of stress (Gupta et al., 2017).

Resilience is not as simple as it may seem. Some of us are disproportionately more sensitive to our curious world. The differential susceptibility model proposes that some individuals show greater sensitivity to the positive effects of supportive environments (e.g., nurturing caregivers; safe neighborhood) and the negative effects of adverse environments (e.g., harsh parenting; dangerous neighborhood; Belsky et al., 2022). Empirical support for differential susceptibility comes from both observational studies of Gene × Environment interactions and experimental research. Resilience may not be the only explanation for why some thrive and adapt effectively, and others don't.

FIGURE 5.3

Executive Control and Emotional Arousal in the Brain

Certain parts of the brain involved in executive control and emotional arousal might be related to resilience to stress.

Executive Control Network

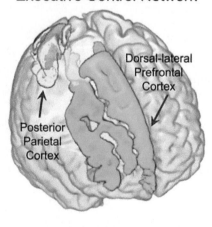

Emotional Arousal Network

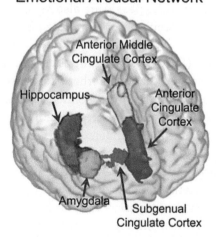

Source: Gupta et al. (2017).

Spirituality and Religion

Religious and spiritual practices have helped people cope with many obstacles, including health ailments (Ab Rahman et al., 2020; Amadi et al., 2016; Merluzzi & Philip, 2017) and racism (Copeland-Linder, 2006; Prosper et al., 2021). These practices may even help you live longer (Bagheri et al. 2021; Mann & Larimore, 2006).

Despite its benefits, religiosity can surprisingly also exacerbate stress. For example, it can sometimes expose people to negative forms of social interaction (Ellison et al., 2009; Krause et al., 2000) and create feelings of guilt over uncontrollable circumstances (Exline et al., 2000). Still, the average association of religion with coping outcomes is positive (Ano & Vasconcelles, 2005). One way religious practices can help people cope is through social support; a community of people who love and support you through hardship feels wonderful.

Meditation, once considered exclusively an Eastern practice associated with religion and spiritualism, can also help with coping (Behan, 2020; Travis et al., 2018). Meditation encourages a heightened state of awareness and refocuses attention to the present moment—thoughts, emotions, and sensations—whatever is happening. Meditative practices help with relaxation, lower blood pressure, calm anxiety, and restore immune function (Janusek et al., 2019; Krishnakumar et al., 2015). When properly meditating, brain waves change to include more theta and alpha waves, which suggest deep relaxation, but little to no delta waves, which would imply deep sleep (Krishnakumar et al., 2015; Nascimento et al., 2018). In short, people who regularly meditate might actually be changing their brains to help them be more resilient to stress (Lazar et al., 2000).

Whether visiting a synagogue to pray or receiving a spiritual reading from a traditional African healer, religion and spirituality can be great sources of comfort during times of stress.

iStock.com/coldsnowstorm; iStock .com/Sunshine Seeds

Social Support: The Gift of Others

Relationships with others can be a gift. For example, belonging to a faith community can give people access to others who are available during times of need. When there's a stressor, some people instinctively seek support from others. Shelley Taylor proposed the *tend and befriend* theory that explains that the value of social support, a network of others who provide love and care, gives us three types of gifts (Taylor, 2006).

Social support: A network of others who provide love and care.

- The gift of tangible aid: A social support network can provide goods and services in stressful circumstances. For example, food is given after the death of a loved one.

- The gift of information: People who extend support can provide information and advice about appropriate ways of dealing with stress. For example, your friend may notice that you are struggling with a class and suggests ways to better study and prepare for exams.

People who use animals for social support have been shown to recover quicker from illness and stress (O'Haire, 2010).

iStock.com/KatarzynaBialasiewicz

- The gift of emotional support: Social support people can help you feel valued and loved. For example, your family may reassure you that you are loved and cared for after experiencing a bad breakup.

Social support also affects our brains. One experiment found that there was less activation in areas of the brain reflecting stress when social support (being able to hold the hand of another person) was available (Coan et al., 2006). And while getting support from others is important, *giving* support also has coping benefits. Helping others may reduce stress hormones, which improves cardiovascular health and strengths our immune system (Schwartz et al., 2009).

Sage Vantage➤   Practice what you learn in **Knowledge Check 5.3**

PROMOTING HEALTH

?
Have You Ever Wondered?
5.4 What promotes health and health behaviors?

>> LO 5.4 **Describe behaviors that promote health and identify theories of health behavior.**

Our lifestyle choices directly impact our health.

Smoking cigarettes is the leading cause of preventable death in the United States, killing about 443,000 people per year (Stanford Research on the Impact of Tobacco Advertising, 2022). Even though people know tobacco is bad for their health, they continue to smoke. What makes someone engage in health-harming behaviors? How difficult is it to change unwanted health behaviors?

Health psychology explores behavioral and psychological characteristics that motivate people to prevent illness and embrace health promotion. In this section, we discuss the advantages of being physically active and eating healthy; then we describe what health psychologists have learned about making healthy behavioral changes.

Health psychology: The scientific study of behavioral and psychological characteristics that motivate people to prevent illness and embrace health promotion.

Being Physically Active

Imagine . . .

Before dishwashers, you had to scrub everything by hand.

Before the Internet, you had to travel to the library to research a topic of interest.

Before delivery services, you had to shop for your own groceries.

And thousands of people in the world still do these tasks without the benefit of machines or electricity. Advances in technology have benefited society but have also led to a substantial reduction in physical activity (Woessner et al., 2021). Physical activity previously performed as part of a workday (e.g., waiting tables) or as part of domestic duties around the home (e.g., vacuuming) has been reduced or replaced by technology (Figure 5.4). Just think how much the trend of working from home has

FIGURE 5.4

Correlation Between Technology and Obesity

While advancing medical technology and treatments have increased life expectancy (light blue line), health concerns related to lack of physical activity have also increased (dark blue line).

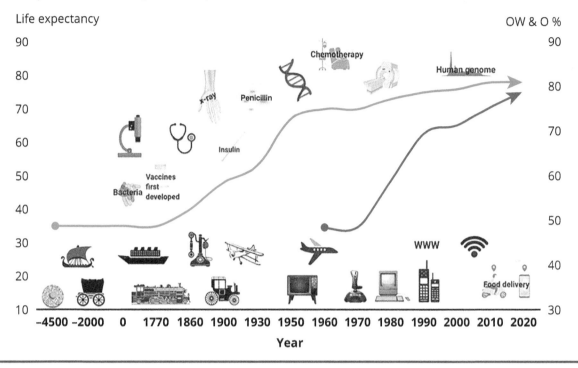

Source: Woessner et al. (2021).

decreased our daily step count. Here's the problem: Physical inactivity is strongly associated with health problems.

When we don't get enough exercise, there are a wide variety of potential issues—and these issues are increasing in the United States (Wang et al., 2020). Some of these include the onset of diabetes, hypertension and cardiovascular disease, depression, and other chronic diseases (Chu et al., 2018). Physically inactive middle-age and older adults risk muscle mass and strength loss, falls, fractures, cognitive decline, and hospitalizations (Bowden Davies et al., 2019; Cunningham et al., 2020).

Physical activity is a great way to maintain health. Taking the stairs instead of using the elevator, walking or biking to class instead of driving, or moving on the dance floor instead of sitting at the bar are simple choices that increase physical activity. Physical activity corresponds with lower risk of cardiovascular disease, positive coping with stress, and healthier aging, and it even offsets certain cancers (Amatriain-Fernández et al., 2020). Physical activity also reduces anxiety and depression, and it increases self-esteem.

Even a single exercise session can have a profound impact on the body. Researchers collected small tissue samples from participants before and after a single 400-calorie burning exercise cycle session (Barres et al., 2012). Researchers told some participants to exercise vigorously, while others were instructed to pedal gently. Changes in the DNA of the muscle cells occurred after only one workout! There was also evidence of "more pain, more gain" as the muscle cell changes were more pronounced among those who rode most vigorously—although of course, don't take the phrase literally; you shouldn't actually experience *pain.*

"Gamifying" exercise can improve motivation and make physical activity more frequent and effective.

iStock.com/eyesfoto

Physical activity also helps your brain. A meta-analytic study (one study that statistically combines the results of multiple studies) found that physical activity in children helped them with complex cognitive processes during laboratory tasks (Donnelly et al., 2016). This study also found physical activity was positively associated with academic achievement among school-aged kids. Essentially, being physically active is like investing in a wellness bank account! It pays off later.

What if we used technology to *encourage* physical activity? The pedometer provides quite the example. This technology has transitioned to a wearable activity tracker with the emergence of fitness bands and smartwatches that track steps, physical activity, heart rate, and other health-related data (examples are FitBits, iWatches, etc.). These devices have improved physical activity and mobility (Karapanos et al., 2016), though the long-term effects on behavior change have not been rigorously explored (Bravata et al., 2007). "Exergaming" and virtual reality technologies also present an intriguing opportunity to reimagine how to engage in physical activity using technology. Gamifying exercise through active video games and virtual reality can lead to reductions in cholesterol and body fat while increasing enjoyment and self-efficacy (McDonough et al., 2020).

Eating Healthy

Junk food or a salad?

When you're feeling bad, which would you likely reach for? Team junk food all the way. Makes sense, because sugary junk foods help us feel better. Stress increases eating, and in turn, eating reduces stress reactivity in the HPA axis (Dallman et al., 2005). When we eat in response to stress, reward pathways in the brain are stimulated, releasing endorphins, which make us feel better. This increases the likelihood that we will continue to eat foods high in sugar or other "comfort foods" to reduce stress. Temporarily, we feel better emotionally.

But no matter your preference—salty or sweet—eating right means selecting nutritious foods that maximize health and wellness. This means limiting sugar intake and eating foods high in vitamins, minerals, and fibers, such as fruits and vegetables. Why? Because what you eat has direct consequences for health. Consuming high-fiber foods such as whole grains and leafy vegetables can lessen the risk of cancer, provide more energy, and lower blood pressure (Randhawa et al., 2015). In contrast, eating saturated fats, or those found in animal-based foods like meat and dairy products, increases risk for heart disease (DiNicolantonio et al., 2016). Ultimately, choosing to eat too much fast food and too few well-balanced meals can result in long-term health problems (Lynch et al., 2014). In short, the comfort foods won't pay off in the long run.

The Psychology of Making Good Choices About Your Health

Making good choices about your health is not always easy.

Changing health behaviors might be even harder. Health psychologists help people identify and implement ways they can effectively change their behaviors for the better. In this section, we discuss how we come to engage in health behaviors and the stages for making changes to healthy behaviors.

Theories of Health Behaviors

Exercising, eating healthy, practicing safe sex, and keeping doctors' appointments all represent health behaviors or practices that impact health. The *health belief model* predicts health behaviors based on belief patterns. People who believe a health threat is severe or believe they are susceptible to a particular disease are motivated to make behavioral changes if they believe that the benefits of risk reduction outweigh the costs of performing the behaviors (Figure 5.5).

For example, you must first believe you are susceptible to acquiring a sexually transmitted infection (STI) and, second, that STIs are severe enough diseases that you want to prevent contracting them. Then the benefits of wearing or having a partner wear a condom (such as lowering the chances of contracting an STI) are weighed against the barriers and costs of condom use, which might be less pleasurable and result in awkward conversations, particularly if a partner doesn't want to use condom. A cue to action is typically necessary to trigger a health behavior. These cues can be internal, such as remembering that you have a symptom you think might be associated with an STI, or external, such as noticing a safe sex TV ad.

Many studies have used the health beliefs model to predict whether sexually active teenagers and young adults will use protection against STIs during sexual or oral intercourse (e.g., Downing-Matibag & Geisinger, 2009). Beliefs about barriers and benefits are the strongest predictors of health behaviors, whereas beliefs about disease severity are weakest (Carpenter, 2010).

In many instances, effective health behavior changes begin by changing attitudes. The *theory of reasoned action* suggests that effective change requires an *intention* to engage in a certain behavior. Intentions are predicted by *attitudes* and *subjective norms*. The more positively a person regards a behavior (attitudes) *and* the more they perceive the behavior as being important to their friends, family, or society (subjective norms), the more likely they are to form intentions to engage in the behavior.

Icek Azjen, a psychologist born in Poland, noted the importance of a sense of control. The *theory of planned behavior* is an extension of the theory of reasoned action and adds a person's perception of control over the outcome as an important requirement for effective health behavior change (Ajzen, 1991). These two theories

FIGURE 5.5

The Health Beliefs Model

Many beliefs affect our health behaviors.

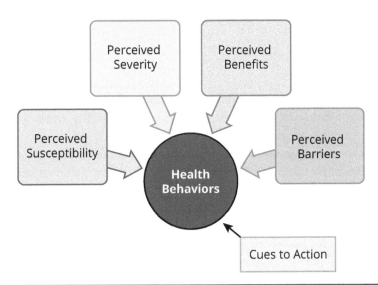

Theories of health behaviors can predict whether a person will engage in activities that prevent STIs.

iStock.com/CatLane

help explain changes to positive health behaviors, including HIV/AIDs prevention (Siuki et al., 2019), physical activity (Wing Kwan et al., 2009), cancer screening, preventing drug use and abuse (Zemore & Ajzen, 2014), and binge drinking (Cooke et al., 2016).

Like a sense of control, *self-efficacy* is a person's belief that they can master a situation and produce positive outcomes. Though self-efficacy theory was not developed as a theory of health behavior, it helps us understand and predict health behaviors (Figure 5.6). A person with low efficacy may doubt their ability to maintain a consistent exercise schedule. They don't attempt to begin an exercise regime. Their high efficacy counterpart sees themselves as fully capable of achieving their exercise goals and will likely be able to effectively problem-solve if any challenges arise.

High self-efficacy benefits exercising, weight loss, quitting smoking, condom use, and reducing substance use (Sheeran et al., 2016). Self-efficacy has also been linked to improved cardiovascular health. Individuals with high self-efficacy are less likely to suffer a second hospitalization due to heart failure and live longer (Maeda et al., 2013).

FIGURE 5.6

Self-Efficacy Theory

Self-efficacy beliefs are developed through knowledge, skills, practice, and social support.

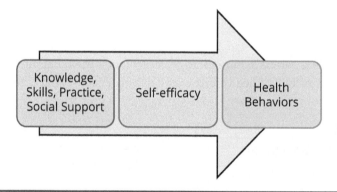

The Stages of Change Model

If you have ever made a New Year's resolution to eat better, exercise more, or stress less, you likely understand the difficulty of behavior change; most people don't keep their resolutions for very long. Change is hard because it usually involves a substantial commitment of time, effort, and emotion.

The stages of change model describes how individuals give up unhealthy habits and adopt healthier lifestyles. The model evolved through studies examining the experiences of smokers who quit on their own with those who required extensive support to quit (DiClemente & Prochaska, 1998). The model focuses on an individual's decision-making, but it assumes that people do not change behaviors overnight—even if that night is New Year's Eve. Rather, change in behavior occurs continuously through a cyclical process involving five stages:

1. *Precontemplation.* The precontemplation stage occurs when people are not thinking seriously about changing. People in this stage tend to defend their unhealthy habit and do not feel it is a problem: "I don't drink *that* much." They may be defensive in the face of other people's efforts to pressure them to change: "I'm not an alcoholic." At this stage, raising one's consciousness about the problem is important.

2. *Contemplation.* In the contemplation stage, people acknowledge the problem but are still weighing the pros and cons of modifying their behavior. Although they think about the negative aspects of their unhealthy habit and the positives associated with changing, they may doubt that the long-term benefits associated with change will outweigh the short-term costs. For example, how they will socialize with their friends if they stop drinking? Or how will they afford to cook healthier foods when fast food is so cheap and quick? It might take as little as a couple of weeks or as long as a lifetime to get through the contemplation stage.

3. *Preparation/Determination.* People in the preparation/determination stage have made a commitment to make a change and are ready to act. Their motivation for changing is reflected by statements such as, "I've got to do something about this—this is serious. Something must change. What can I do?" They gather information about what they will need to do to change their behavior. For example, they might explore local Alcoholics Anonymous meeting places and times. Too often, people skip this stage: They try to move directly from contemplation into action and struggle because they haven't adequately researched or accepted what it is going to take to make the major lifestyle change.

4. *Action/Willpower.* At the action/willpower stage, people are motivated to change their behavior and depend on their own willpower to enact a successful plan. They are making overt efforts to change the behavior and are at greatest risk for relapse (returning to former unhealthy patterns), which is a normal part of change. To support the new, healthy behavior pattern, a person may establish rewards or reinforcements for the new behavior. For example, they might treat themselves to a shopping spree for being 3 months sober. Using a social network of support (e.g., a friend group might all quit smoking at the same time) or focusing on alternate behaviors that replace unhealthy ones (e.g., participating in a fitness club instead of bar hopping on Thursday nights) can be used to deal with personal and external pressures that may lead to relapse.

5. *Maintenance.* In the maintenance stage, people successfully avoid temptations to return to the unhealthy habit and consistently pursue healthy behaviors. People in maintenance can anticipate the situations in which a relapse could occur and prepare coping strategies in advance. For example, a person wishing to remain sober may plan to sit farther away from the bar when dining out with friends. When a person has transcended, they are no longer consciously engaged in maintaining the healthy lifestyle because the lifestyle has become who they are. They are now nonsmokers, healthy eaters, or committed runners.

PURSUING HAPPINESS

>> LO 5.5 Analyze factors that impact happiness from a psychological approach.

"It's like the more money we come across the more problems we see...."

The lyrics to late The Notorious B.I.G.'s "Mo money, Mo problems" may be unrelatable to you because after all, money buys happiness. Or does it? To answer this question, in this section, we consider the elements of happiness, whether people are happy, and the characteristics of happy people.

Elements of Happiness

Imagine experiencing happiness.

You think about doing something you really enjoy, having a strong, positive connection with someone, accomplishing something great, or a moment you felt financially secure and safe. Certainly, finally graduating from college or university and moving on to the next part of your life should bring you happiness—right? How does happiness feel?

Can money buy happiness, or does more money cause problems?

iStock.com/Prostock-Studio

Happiness: An enduring state of mind consisting of joy, pleasure, contentment, and other positive emotions, plus the sense that one's life has meaning and value.

Happiness is defined differently depending on who you ask. Some people view happiness as a positive emotional experience ranging from contentment to intense joy. Some scientists refer to happiness as *hedonia* (the presence of pleasure, enjoyment, and comfort and the absence of negative emotions) and *eudimonia* (thriving and living well; Ryan & Deci, 2001).

Seligman (the same person who conducted the learned helplessness experiments) suggested that there are three types of happiness: the pleasant life, the good life, and the meaningful life (Seligman et al., 2004). The pleasant life is about experiencing day-to-day pleasures that add fun, joy, and excitement to our lives (e.g., eating a good meal or having a fulfilling sex life). The good life is about using your unique strengths and engaging these talents to enrich our lives. Those who achieve the good life often find themselves absorbed in their work or their recreational pursuits. The meaningful life is about a deep sense of fulfillment from using your strengths in the service of something that is bigger than you are and in ways that benefit the lives of others. In general, the happiest people tend to be those who pursue all three elements (see Figure 5.7; Seligman et al., 2004).

Happiness is an enduring state of mind consisting of joy, pleasure, contentment, and other positive emotions, plus the sense that one's life has meaning and value (Lyubomirsky, 2001). This implies that happiness is a long-term state, rather than a just a temporary positive mood we experience from time to time.

Are People Happy?

Most people tend to be relatively happy.

Positive psychology: The scientific study of human strengths, virtues, positive emotions, and achievements.

Psychology as a field has largely focused on understanding mental illness and how to fix problems in people's lives. In contrast, **positive psychology** changed that by focusing on human strengths, virtues, positive emotions, and achievements—things that make us happy.

On average, people experience more positive feelings than negative feelings (Diener et al., 2010). Also, while there are gender gaps in stressors—for example, women are more vulnerable to depression and anxiety, and men are more vulnerable to antisocial conduct and alcohol-use disorders—women and men express similar

FIGURE 5.7

Three Types of Happiness

Positive psychologists talk of three types of happiness.

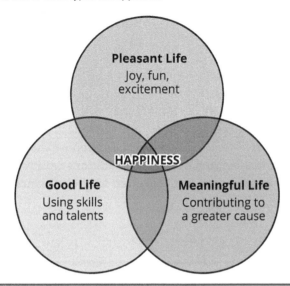

Source: Adapted from Seligman et al. (2004).

levels of life satisfaction and happiness. Happiness is also remarkably stable across the life span (Myers & Diener, 2018). People are *not* less happy during the stress-filled teenagers, midlife crisis, or later-life years.

In some circumstances, major life events permanently alter people's happiness (see Figure 5.8; Diener, 2012). One event you might expect to be a major happiness

FIGURE 5.8

Does Happiness Change?

In one study, participants adapted (or failed to adapt) to major life events.

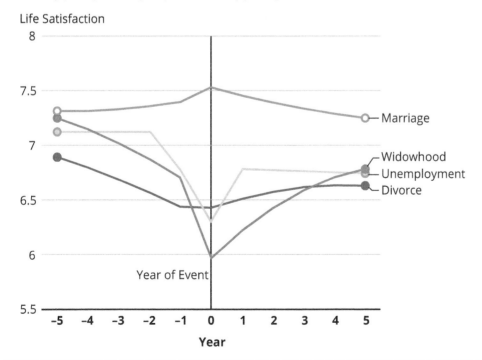

Source: Diener et al. (2006).

boost is marriage. But in one study, marriage produced only a brief happiness increase, followed by quick adaptation (Diener et al., 2006). In other words, marriage didn't provide the big emotional benefit that many might expect. That said, widows and those who had been laid off experienced sizable decreases in happiness that did not return to the level of happiness prior to those major life events. So long-term happiness levels can and do change for some people.

Figure 5.9 shows how happiness varies by country. Worldwide, the global average of happiness has been relatively stable even during the COVID-19 pandemic, and positive emotions have generally been twice as prevalent as negative ones (*World Happiness Report*, 2022). However, that gap has been narrowing over the past 10 years, with enjoyment and laughter on a negative trend in most regions and worry and sadness on rising trends. These global trends may be connected to the challenging economic conditions worldwide. Of course, this presumption implies happiness is closely tied to one's finances—and we haven't answered this question quite yet.

FIGURE 5.9

Happiness Varies by Country

Happiness rankings for the top 23 countries, based on the 2022 *World Happiness Report*.

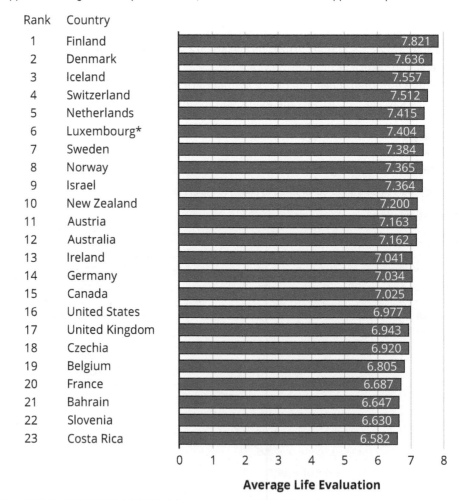

Rank	Country	Average Life Evaluation
1	Finland	7.821
2	Denmark	7.636
3	Iceland	7.557
4	Switzerland	7.512
5	Netherlands	7.415
6	Luxembourg*	7.404
7	Sweden	7.384
8	Norway	7.365
9	Israel	7.364
10	New Zealand	7.200
11	Austria	7.163
12	Australia	7.162
13	Ireland	7.041
14	Germany	7.034
15	Canada	7.025
16	United States	6.977
17	United Kingdom	6.943
18	Czechia	6.920
19	Belgium	6.805
20	France	6.687
21	Bahrain	6.647
22	Slovenia	6.630
23	Costa Rica	6.582

Source: Helliwell, J. F., Layard, R., Sachs, J. D., De Neve, J.-E., Aknin, L. B., & Wang, S. (Eds.). (2024). *World Happiness Report 2024.* University of Oxford: Wellbeing Research Centre.

*Data for Luxembourg is from 2019 alone, whereas for all the other countries shown the data are averaged from 2019, 2020, and 2021.

Positive Psychology Versus Pop Psychology: Placebo Effects

iStock.com/FranRodriguez

Don't confuse positive psychology with pop psychology.

Pop psychology refers to psychological fads: the application of untested therapies and beliefs that claim some psychological benefit. Want to improve your memory? Rub essential oils on your forehead. Feeling blue? Wave crystals beneath your nose. Interested in profiling mass murderers? Plan a career based on television crime dramas.

An alarming number of popular beliefs about psychology are myths, placebo effects, superstitions, and self-deceptions (see Lilienfeld, 2012). Pop psychology today is what "patent medicines" were a century earlier. Patent medicines were homemade concoctions that circulated freely through an unregulated society. Many contained just enough alcohol, cocaine, morphine, or other drugs to make you feel just fine (note, we don't suggest this "treatment"). Nonphysiological distractions can also produce temporary symptom relief. For example, jingling keys can often calm a crying infant (Stadlen, 2007). But it's not the keys that do the calming; it's the temporary distraction created by the sight and sound of clanking keys.

Pop psychology often invents untested (and untestable) beliefs and ideas. These ideas may sound exotic, but scratch the surface and you will discover empty, simplistic, wishful solutions to complex problems. Though the Ouija board phenomenon has been studied in psychology (e.g., Andersen et al., 2019; Burgess et al., 1998), the history of the Ouija board is nothing more than a tale of pranking preteens rather than mystical communications with the dead. These potentially dangerous ideas can achieve fad-like popularity for a simple reason: Sometimes they *appear* to work (Lynn et al., 2020; Patihis & Pendergrast, 2019). Pop psychology could potentially have a positive role helping people who can't afford therapy learn some of the skills they might need to better cope with problems. But why and how does a bogus treatment sometimes produce effects that seem like the real thing?

Placebo effects are based not on the treatment itself, but on *belief* in the treatment—and the expectations that you bring with you. Anything can be a placebo: a harmless pill, a nasty-tasting drink, a pleasant aroma, or even a spiritual gesture with supposed powers of healing. They all require one thing: your belief. Placebos may be useful in other ways, some of which raise complex ethical concerns (see Hill, 2003; Kayser, 2020).

However, placebo effects are limited by reality. Hundreds of thousands of people died from the COVID-19 virus even though many sincerely believed it was a political hoax. The virus, of course, did not care whether anyone believed in it. Physicist and science educator Neil deGrasse Tyson reminds us that "the good thing about science is that it's true whether or not you believe in it." ●

Factors Influencing Happiness

Helen Keller said we should "resolve to keep happy."

Positive psychologists help us with this resolve. Some factors influencing happiness involve biological processes: neurotransmitters, brain networks, and genes. Consistently perceiving and experiencing key life events in a more beneficial way is also important for happiness. Money and social media are important parts of our lives. But do we truly understand how they contribute to happiness? This section will explore the answer to this question and describe what influences happiness.

Biological and environmental factors contribute to happiness.

iStock.com/adamkaz

A Biological Perspective on Happiness

Biological processes in the human body are important for explaining experiences with happiness. Studies show that higher positive emotion is associated with higher levels of serotonin and lower levels of cortisol, whereas chronic immune system activity relates to lower levels of happiness (Dfarhud et al., 2014).

Research about brain areas involved in happiness has found that a more active default mode network, a large brain system including the medial prefrontal cortex, posterior cingulate cortex/precuneus, and angular gyrus, is related to lower happiness (Taruffi et al., 2017). This network is most active when a person focuses inward and ruminates, obsessively worrying or going over potential issues and problems. Instead, focusing on the outside world and distracting yourself can reduce the network's activity and increase happiness.

Some people are born with a set of genetic variants that makes it easier to feel happy, while others are less fortunate (Bartels, 2015; Lyubomirsky et al., 2005). Yet, most of our happiness is not determined by our genetics but by our experiences and our day-to-day lives. Genetic studies involving twin or family designs show that about 30% to 40% of the differences in happiness among individuals are accounted for by genetic differences, while the other 60% to 70% of differences result from the effect of environmental influences (Bartels, 2015; Layous & Lyubomirsky, 2014).

The PERMA Model of Happiness

Positive psychology also teaches us about practices that promote happiness. Gratitude exercises, such as writing down each day three things for which one is grateful, can increase happiness over time. Seligman (2018) also saw the value in gratitude for contributing to happiness. In addition to defining three types of happiness mentioned above, Seligman proposed five building blocks—PERMA—that contribute to happiness:

1. *Positive Emotion (**P**).* Positive emotions such as gratitude, hope, comfort, inspiration, and love are life-enhancing. A "dose" of positive emotion creates an upward spiral of positivity. Positive emotions can also undo the harmful effects of negative emotions and promote resilience (Cohn et al., 2009).

2. *Engagement (**E**).* Fully engaging in a situation, task, or project, allows us to experience flow: Time seems to stop, we lose our sense of self, and we concentrate intensely on the present. Research on engagement has found that individuals who tried to use their strengths in new ways each day for a week were happier and less depressed after six months (Seligman et al., 2005).

3. *Positive Relationships (**R**).* We are "social beings," and feeling supported, loved, and valued by others is essential for well-being. Sharing good news or celebrating success fosters strong bonds and better relationships, increasing happiness and life satisfaction (Siedlecki et al., 2014).

4. *Meaning (**M**).* Meaning comes from serving something larger than ourselves. It may be a religion or spirituality, a cause, or an overriding sense of purpose that we belong to something bigger. People who report having purpose in life live longer and have greater life satisfaction (Kashdan et al., 2009).

5. *Accomplishment/Achievement (**A**).* Mastering a skill or achieving one's goal is important for happiness. Having self-motivation to finish what you set out to do is rewarding and leads to larger gains in well-being than external goals such as fame or money (Seligman, 2018).

Money and Happiness

Speaking of money—can happiness buy it? When the question is carefully studied in scientific surveys, many believe the answer is yes (Myers & Diener, 2018). But is this commonsense assumption correct?

Globally, people are happy, but those living in rich rather than poor countries appear to be happ*ier* (see Figure 5.10). Variables such as a stable democracy, safety, and education are equally important for predicting happiness (Myers & Diener, 2018). Regions with greater inequality also tend to be less happy. Within any country, rich people are happier than not-so-rich people. Those driving a reliable car they own may be happier than those riding the bus. But money can only buy happiness up to about $100,000 in annual income, with variations by

"Being one with the music" or fully engaging in any task promotes happiness.

iStock.com/franckreporter

FIGURE 5.10

Can Money Buy Happiness?

While financial security may be a life goal, increase in income over time does not increase happiness. This figure from Myers and Diener (2018) shows U.S. personal income and happiness over time. The blue line shows per-person disposable personal income (left *y*-axis), and the red dots (with best-fitting regression line) show percentage of people who said they were "very happy" (right *y*-axis).

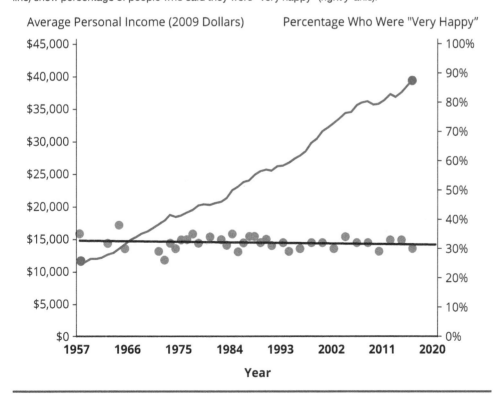

Source: Myers and Diener (2018).

Social media can facilitate or hinder happiness.

iStock.com/P.Kijsanayothin

region and sex. After that peak, income has no significant effect on happiness and actually begins to *reverse* above $250,000. How you spend your money also matters: Spending on others and on experiences lends to more happiness than money spent on material purchases.

Social Media and Happiness

Pursuing happiness through social means, such as spending more time with family and friends, is more likely to be effective than other methods, such as getting rich (Rohrer et al., 2018). But does this hold true for social media interactions?

There is some indication that social media *negatively* affects happiness. One study found that using social media more, having more "friends" on social media, and "liking" more people's posts on social media were all *negatively* correlated with life satisfaction (Stieger, 2019). This could be because constantly viewing people's "edited" lives—the versions they carefully chose to post online—makes us perceive that others' lives are more favorable than they really are. In contrast, having more real-world friends, feeling closer to those real-world friends, and having more frequent interactions with real-world friends are all associated with greater life satisfaction (Shakya & Chistakis, 2017).

Social media can also exacerbate "fear of missing out" (FOMO), or apprehension that others might be having rewarding experiences from which one is absent, threatening the happiness of those unable to unplug (Beyens et al., 2016; Dempsey et al., 2019; Gori et al., 2023; Park, 2022). The "always on" culture creates unreasonable expectations that users' time, attention, and mental energy constantly be attuned to digital connections. Despite these criticisms, social media can reinforce existing real-world relationships and facilitate access to social support, producing some positive benefits (Gilmour et al., 2020; Vaingankar et al., 2022; Valkenburg, 2022).

Health and Happiness

Even if you aren't rich, happiness leads to good ends.

Being happy doesn't just make us feel better; it improves our health. Happiness lowers risk for cardiovascular disease, lowers blood pressure, enables better sleep, improves consumption of healthy foods, and allows maintenance of healthy weight through regular exercise (Steptoe, 2019). Because happiness leads to healthier behaviors, such as exercising, wearing seat belts, and even using sunscreen, happier people tend to have stronger immune systems and live a longer life (Ngamaba et al., 2017).

Happy people also make for better citizens. For instance, happiness is a good predictor of civic engagement (working to make a difference in your community) during the transition to adulthood (Fang et al., 2018). Happiness also leads to career success, and it doesn't have to be "natural" happiness. Inducing positive emotions in an experimental design contributed to improved outcomes at work (Walsh et al., 2018). More research is needed on how different cultures and kinds of people define happiness, as much of the work so far has been done on WEIRD samples that define happiness in terms of financial or career satisfaction (see Sin & Ogn, 2023); this is an area where bright, curious new scholars are needed. ●

Practice what you learn in **Knowledge Check 5.5**

Learning Objectives Summary

5.1   What is stress and what are different types of stressors?

>> LO 5.1   **Define stress and compare and contrast types of stressors.**

Stress is the response that occurs when events are identified as threatening or challenging. Some stressors are unpleasant experiences and cause distress, whereas other stressors cause eustress or "good stress." Environmental and personal stressors can include both catastrophes and daily hassles as well as uplifts.

5.2   What are the consequences of stress?

>> LO 5.2   **Analyze the ways stress impacts the human body.**

The sequence of physiological reactions the body goes through when responding to a stressor is called the general adaption syndrome (GAS) and consists of three stages: alarm, resistance, and exhaustion. Chronic stress takes a toll on the body's immune system and is related to cardiovascular disease and particular cancers.

5.3   How do people cope with stress?

>> LO 5.3   **Compare and contrast coping strategies.**

Cognitive appraisal is a person's interpretation of a situation, how it will affect them, and if they have the resources to effectively cope. Some strategies for coping are problem focused, in that they address how to change the situation that caused the stress response, and others are emotion focused, aimed at reducing emotional distress. Personality characteristics, such as hardiness and conscientiousness, resilience, religion and spirituality, and social support, help with coping.

5.4   What promotes health and health behaviors?

>> LO 5.4   **Describe behaviors that promote health and identify theories of health behavior.**

Health psychology explores behavioral and psychological characteristics that motivate people to embrace health promotion. Being physically active and eating healthy promote health. Theories of health behaviors, such as the health beliefs model, theory of planned behavior, and self-efficacy, can be used to predict whether a person will engage in practices that promote health.

5.5   What factors influence happiness?

>> LO 5.5   **Analyze factors that impact happiness from a psychological approach.**

The happiest people are those who pursue a pleasant, good, and meaningful life. Biological factors and characteristics such as positive emotion, engagement, positive relationships, meaning and accomplishment/achievement contribute to happiness. Happiness is also a means to other good ends such as cardiovascular health, improved sleep, a stronger immune system, good citizenship, and a longer life.

CRITICAL THINKING QUESTIONS

1. Your friend just lost their job, which helped them cover tuition costs. Apply Lazarus' cognitive appraisal process and describe their potential reactions to the job loss. Be sure to describe the stressful event, primary appraisal, secondary appraisal, and stress response.

2. Think about a behavior you should change to improve your health. Use the stages of change model to discuss how you might go about changing the identified behavior. In your answer, be sure to provide an example of what each stage of the change process would look like for you.

3. Review the personality behavior patterns associated with stress and those personality characteristics that are associated with health and happiness. Reflect on your personality and whether you embrace behavior patterns associated more closely with stress, health and happiness, or a combination.

4. Social media can negatively impact happiness. What strategies might a positive psychologist suggest for using social media to promote happiness? Analyze your own use of social media and whether it seems to make you more happy, has less happy, or has no effect and why you think that pattern results.

5. Think of someone in your life who seems to be generally very happy and healthy and someone else in your life who seems to be generally unhealthy and/or unhappy. Write or discuss brief descriptions of these people and identify variables from this chapter that apply to each person, explaining the concepts and how they apply to the people you've identified in your own words.

KEY TERMS

Acculturation stress, 127
Catastrophe, 124
Cognitive appraisal, 134
Coping, 134
Daily hassles, 125
Distress, 124
Emotion-focused coping, 134
Eustress, 124
General adaptation
    syndrome (GAS), 129
Happiness, 146
Hardiness, 137
Health psychology, 140
Hypothalamic–pituitary–adrenocortical
    (HPA) axis, 129
Learned helplessness, 136

Personal stressors, 125
Positive psychology, 146
Primary appraisals, 134
Problem-focused coping, 134
Psychoneuroimmunology, 131
Racism stress, 128
Resilience, 138
Secondary appraisals, 134
Social support, 139
Stress, 122
Stressors, 122
Type A personality, 131
Type B personality, 132
Type D personality, 132
Uplifts, 125

iStock.com/gparusnikov

Sensation and Perception

What's better than an outdoor summer concert?

Whether you're attending a show in your hometown or making the trek to an outdoor festival, the journey might begin with your friends, the car windows down, and the radio volume up. Upon arrival, you stake out your tailgating location to hang out, take in the sights, and perhaps play a little corn hole (or "bags"). As you eat your snacks and sip your beverage, you can't help but notice the mix of odors wafting through the soft breeze.

When the concert starts, you're bombarded with lights, smoke, pyrotechnics, and huge video screens. Towers of speakers pump out bass notes that you feel in your heart and that will surely leave your ears ringing until the next morning. After the performer plays the obligatory encore, everyone leaves and pushes out to the parking lot to endure the drowsy trip home. Whether it's an outdoor music festival, a spoken word performance, or the ballet, many performers intentionally design their shows as multisensory events. How is it that we're able to take in everything going on and consciously make sense of it?

After reading this chapter, you will get answers to several questions you've been curious about:

Have You Ever Wondered?

6.1   What are the building blocks of sensation and perception?

6.2   How do we process visual information?

6.3   How do we process auditory information?

6.4   How do we process smell, taste, touch, and body movement information?

6.5   What are some perceptual mistakes, curiosities, and controversies?

Learning Objectives

LO 6.1   Explain how we detect and interpret sensory information from the outside world.

LO 6.2   Describe how the eye and brain process visual information to understand color, faces, size, and depth.

LO 6.3   Describe how the ear and brain process sound waves.

LO 6.4   Describe how we process smell, taste, touch, and body movement information.

LO 6.5   Analyze several ways that our perceptual processes lead to mistakes and why.

THE BUILDING BLOCKS OF SENSATION AND PERCEPTION

? Have You Ever Wondered? 6.1 What are the building blocks of sensation and perception?

>> **LO 6.1   Explain how we detect and interpret sensory information from the outside world.**

You're a data-processing machine, but perhaps not in the way you might think.

We don't mean your ability to make sense of numbers, memorize facts, or generate new ideas. Rather, much of your data-handling prowess happens automatically as you recognize and decipher an endless stream of sights, sounds, smells, tastes, and touches. That concert isn't going to be much fun if you don't see, hear, smell, taste, or touch anything while you're there.

Sensation is how the body detects, converts, and relays physical stimuli into information that the brain can then interpret and use. Just as a computer can receive information in multiple ways—with a keyboard, touchpad, USB drive, microphone, and camera—we also acquire data through multiple channels via our senses.

The brain, acting like the central processing unit (CPU) of the computer, receives all that information and puts it to use. While sensation is the process of detecting physical stimuli, **perception** is the process of recognizing, interpreting, and making sense of those sensations. Consider how each system works first (sensation and perception), before we then cover the five major senses. Finally, we'll discuss some controversies and curiosities, like illusions and whether mental telepathy (mind reading) is real.

Sensation: Picking Up Signals

To understand the world, you must let it in.

Into your body, and ultimately into your brain. Sensory receptors, such those in the ears and eyes, are merely the initial step toward helping you sense and perceive the world. You're armed with several key senses, each of which has an entire system of structures dedicated to helping detect and understand external stimuli. These structures provide the hardware that allow you to transmit everything to your brain. When those data arrive, your brain engages in **parallel processing** where it takes all the sensory information and processes it simultaneously.

Capturing all that sensory information must start somewhere. The progression starts far from the brain in the sensory receptors, nerve cells that respond to stimuli from outside the body. The process of **transduction** first transforms external stimuli into electrical impulses that are sent to the brain via the nervous system.

Specialized sensory receptors detect chemical stimulation (e.g., taste and smell) and physical stimulation (e.g., hearing and vision). Regardless of their specialization, those sensory receptors relay two different types of information to our brain:

- One type of information relates to the number of stimuli there are. Are we hearing one sound or a lot of different sounds?

- The other type of information reflects that stimulus intensity. Is the music loud or soft? Are the lights bright or dim?

When sufficiently stimulated, all sensory receptors trigger an impulse, or a signal (i.e., an action potential), that goes to the brain for processing.

Sensory Thresholds

How powerful are your sensory receptors?

Imagine you're alone on an outdoor concert stage, in absolute darkness and total silence. What's the tiniest noise you could notice under these circumstances? Figure 6.1 shows that we don't notice everything in our environment. Some stimuli go below our notice, like sounds too quiet to hear or an eyelash that falls on our cheek. Individual differences (like age—sometimes older people have trouble hearing) and the environment can influence our sensory detection abilities.

When we do notice a stimulus that's present in the environment, it's called *supraliminal* perception. When we don't notice a stimulus that's present in the environment, it's called *subliminal* perception. The tipping point, where we reach a 50/50 chance of correctly identifying that a given stimulus is present, is called the **absolute threshold** (as shown in Figure 6.1) (Swets, 1961). If you started the volume of a

Sensation: Process by which the body detects external physical stimuli and converts them into a format that the brain can use.

Perception: How we recognize, interpret, and make sense of sensory information.

Parallel processing: The brain takes all the sensory information from your world and processes it simultaneously.

Transduction: Process by which sensory receptor cells transform external stimuli into electrical impulses, then transmit signals to the brain via the nervous system.

Absolute threshold: The point at which a person correctly identifies a stimulus is present half (50%) of the time.

FIGURE 6.1

Absolute Thresholds

We don't notice everything in our environment. The absolute threshold is the point at which we correctly identify a stimulus's presence half (50%) of the time.

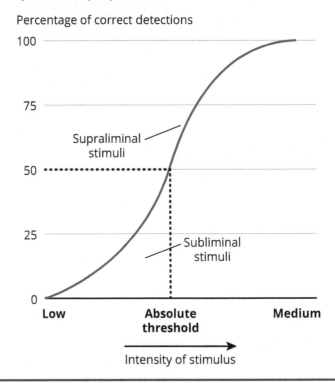

recorded concert at zero and very slowly turned the volume up, the absolute threshold would be the minimum strength of the stimulus when you'd have a 50% chance of registering that it is there.

The question most students want to know is usually whether **subliminal messages** can affect our attitudes or behavior—messages "hidden" under the surface of our conscious awareness. If you believe they can, you're not alone; 80% of college students believe in subliminal persuasion (Taylor & Kowalski, 2012). There have been several classic conspiracies over the years, such as that rock bands have hidden messages in songs played backward or that companies have visual embedded secret images within other, larger images.

A few studies have shown very small effects. For example, when a group of smokers watched a film that included subliminal images of smoking, the smokers had stronger cravings for a cigarette—even though they did not realize they saw the smoking images (Sargent et al., 2009). Similarly, students who saw subliminal images of letters spelling "Lipton Ice" later said they were more likely to drink it, compared to students who subliminally saw the same letters, but mixed up into nonsense words ("Npeic Tol"; Karremans et al., 2006; Strahan et al., 2002). But many more studies find no scientific evidence of their effectiveness at all, especially when replicated with large and diverse samples and with good scientific methodology (Trappey, 1996). For now, subliminal persuasion is likely more urban legend than reality.

Subliminal messages: Messages "hidden" under the surface of conscious awareness, supposedly in attempts to change the receiver's attitudes or behavior.

Signal Detection Theory

We can detect a lot with our senses, but we're not perfect.

Sometimes we pick up things that aren't really there, while other times we miss things that really are there. The world produces abundant stimulation, so it can be difficult to focus. At the concert, do we listen to the music, our ringing cell phone, our friend's off-key singing, or the couple fighting two rows behind us? In these cases, we must identify the *signal* or stimuli we want to attend to and screen out the *noise*, or anything that isn't the signal. Noise comes from all over. It could be something internal, such as the growling of our stomach, or external, such as noise from traffic outside the window when you're on a class video chat.

Signal detection theory explores our ability to detect whether the true or desired stimulus occurs amid other random or intervening stimuli (Macmillan & Creelman, 2005). In other words, can we accurately focus on what we want to when there's a lot of other background noise taking place? This is an important distinction in everyday life. Take, for example, the high-stakes idea of self-driving cars. Roadways are full of stimuli—and to successfully navigate that setting, the self-driving car must make clear distinctions about the visual imagery it receives (e.g., Kane, 2019). The cars need to avoid hitting people!

Sensing stimuli can lead to two kinds of successes and two kinds of errors, as shown in Figure 6.2. Here is how it works:

- When we get it right and say it's there, it's a *hit* (e.g., correctly identifying a person in the crosswalk).

- When we accurately say it wasn't there, it's a *correct rejection* (e.g., correctly identifying a clear crosswalk).

- When we fail to correctly identify the stimuli, it's a *miss* (e.g., there was a person in the crosswalk the car didn't detect).

- When we think it's there, but it isn't, it's a *false alarm* (e.g., thinking it's a person in the crosswalk, but it's a shadow).

While signal detection theory is meant to directly apply to physical stimuli in your environment, think about the same "getting it right and wrong" kind of detection with anything else in your life. Can you correctly identify the "signal" from the "noise" when it comes to choosing which classes to take, which people to date, which concerts to attend, and so on (in other words, which will successfully make you happy)? Our task is to cut through uncertainty by identifying which options are which, before we get overwhelmed with choices.

Signal detection theory: Our ability to detect a real or desired stimulus occurring amid other random or intervening stimuli.

FIGURE 6.2

Potential Outcomes of Signal Detection

Signal

	Present	Not Present
Yes	Hit	False Alarm
No	Miss	Correct Rejection

Response

Sensory Adaptation and Deprivation

Many professional drummers wear earplugs.

Sensory adaptation: When our sensory receptors become less receptive after repeated exposure.

Sometimes there is too much stimulation for us to fully handle. **Sensory adaptation** occurs when sensory receptors become less receptive after repeated exposure. In other words, over time, constant stimulation makes us less aware of stimuli (Webster, 2012). The music at a concert sounds loud at first, but eventually you get used to it. That oh-so-noticeable popcorn smell you detected earlier seemingly dissipates. In reality, you have become "noseblind" to it. Bad for delightful smells like cinnamon buns, but useful when others overdo their perfume or body spray.

Sensory deprivation: When our sensory receptors experience a lack of stimulation.

On the opposite end of the spectrum, **sensory deprivation** occurs when we experience little to no stimulation. This can have positive and negative effects. In the absence of sufficient stimulation, the brain will begin to hallucinate. In one study, a healthy 37-year-old woman wore a blindfold for 3 weeks (Sireteanu et al., 2008). As a result of the prolonged deprivation, the participant reported visual hallucinations, including flashes and moving patterns. Data from an fMRI scan indicated that visual areas in her brain became oversensitive due to the lack of visual input. Our brains like stimulation.

Sensory deprivation can also be beneficial. For example, in restricted environmental stimulation therapy (REST), participants enter a sensory deprivation tank filled with body-temperature saltwater that promotes easy floating (van Dierendonck & Te Nijenhuis, 2005). The chamber blocks all external light, sound, and smell—you are "free" from any outside input. A summary of many studies showed that those undergoing REST managed stress better and experienced lower blood pressure and cortisol, along with improved well-being and performance. A little understimulation may be helpful; maybe we could all use a little "rest" from the constant stimulation of life.

Perception: Understanding the Signals

Finding the signal is only half the battle.

We must also understand the information the signal contains. While the future will assuredly involve all kinds of artificial intelligence (some students may already be using AI to help write their papers), humans are particularly good at making sense of the wide variety of environmental stimuli that constantly bombard our senses (Rotenberg, 2013). If we weren't, it could have dire consequences for our survival—we might think that soft touch on our leg is a loose hair instead of a deadly spider.

How does human perception work?

Bottom-Up Versus Top-Down Processing

Interpreting sensory stimuli mimics the scientific method.

Some scientists start with a series of observations or sensations, then make a hypothesis about their meaning, test the hypothesis, revise understanding based on feedback, and form new conclusions. Other scientists approach a problem with a theory already in mind. They use that preformed idea to help identify a pattern they find in the data. These two approaches parallel the two ways our perceptual system processes information in two separate ways:

Bottom-up processing: Process by which we gather any physical sensations our sensory receptors register and form a conclusion based on our interpretation of the pieces.

- In **bottom-up processing**, we gather physical sensations from our sensory receptors, then form a conclusion based on our interpretation of the pieces. Think of bottom-up processing like assembling singular notes to form a melody. You have no idea what kind of music it will be. At first things are a bit confusing and disorganized, but then it starts to take shape. Once you recognize the pattern (hey, this sounds like "Watermelon Sugar" by Harry Styles), you identify a familiar tune. The smaller elements guide your larger concept.

- We can also process information in the exact opposite way. Just as scientists may start with theory to identify patterns in the data, **top-down processing** uses a larger concept to understand the elements. If you know you're at a Harry Styles concert, you already have a decent guess what songs might be played. That prediction helps you make sense of the first few notes, helping you identify songs and make conclusions. The larger concept and prediction guide how you interpret the smaller elements.

Top-down processing: When we start with an idea of what an experience will entail, then use that larger concept to understand the elements.

PSYCHOLOGY AND OUR CURIOUS WORLD

Top-Down Processing: Classic and Contemporary Examples

There are several examples of sensation and perception concepts in classic rock.

M.G.M./Album/Newscom; dcphoto/Alamy Stock Photo; Natallia Krechka/Alamy Stock Vector

When you think of classic rock, it's easy to think of guitars, record players, and your parents' music. But much of classic rock is not only timeless; it also crosses over into sensation and perception. Take, for example, Pink Floyd's bestselling album from 1973, *Dark Side of the Moon*. As legend has it, if you start playing the album exactly when the MGM lion roars the third time at the beginning of the 1939 classic film *The Wizard of Oz*, Pink Floyd's album plays like a soundtrack to the film. Believers have coined this pairing the "Dark Side of the Rainbow" or "The Wizard of Floyd."

Does it really work? Sort of. But it's really a classic case of top-down processing. If you go into the experience of pairing the album and expecting them to fit together, it seems like a great match. However, if you learned that the connection is fake, your perception will shift toward disbelief. So, was *Dark Side of the Moon* really written as a *Wizard of Oz* soundtrack? Doubtful. Or at least Pink Floyd did a pretty terrible job because their album is 43 minutes long, while the film extends over 100 minutes. If that one sent you over the rainbow, wait until you see how your expectations can even change how you perceive color.

It's difficult for a piece of clothing to become a viral phenomenon, but that's exactly what happened to a dress in the United Kingdom. It wasn't famous because of who wore it, how it was cut, or how much it cost. The color made it controversial mainly because it was hard to say what color it really was, at least based on a picture posted to Facebook. Kim Kardashian thought it was white and gold, Lady Gaga thought it was periwinkle and sand, while Taylor Swift thought it was blue and black. Millions of people had strongly held opposing views, perplexed by how anyone could see it differently, and the incident earned the hashtag #dressgate. Because the dress was intended for a wedding, many reasoned that the dress had to be white and gold. Their conclusion was based on a prior assumption or understanding of which colors were more appropriate for a wedding. While the fabric color was the same for everyone, some people's expectations affected their interpretation—and example of top-down processing. ●

The Gestalt Principles of Perception

Our brain's ability to take complex information and form a coherent representation isn't haphazard.

Whether we are processing information from the top down or the bottom up, our perpetual organization follows certain principles. Gestalt psychology is a subdiscipline that examines how we create a meaningfully organized whole from smaller parts of a stimulus. We often accomplish this through grouping elements together in predictable ways called the Gestalt principles of perception. You can see six common Gestalt principles illustrated and explained in Figure 6.3 and in Table 6.1.

FIGURE 6.3

Gestalt Principles of Perception

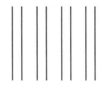

Proximity

Similarity

Figure-ground

Continuity

Closure

Connectedness

TABLE 6.1

Gestalt Principles of Perception

PRINCIPLE	DEFINITION	EXAMPLE
Similarity	Tendency to perceive elements that look similar as part of the same group.	At a concert, we recognize the security staff because they are all wearing the same "SECURITY" yellow vests.
Proximity	Tendency to categorize elements based on how physically close they are to each other.	We assume people standing close to each other at a concert know each other while people far from each other are strangers.
Connectedness	Tendency to group elements that touch each other.	We assume two people who are holding hands at a concert are dating each other.
Continuity	We tend to process information in a linear fashion rather than jump around randomly.	We look for people in a crowd by scanning in a given direction (e.g., starting in one corner and moving from left to right).
Closure	Our minds fill in missing parts of an incomplete stimulus to construct a more complete picture.	If the screen at a concert has a few broken pixels, we still recognize the image of a bird without needing every aspect of it to be there.
Figure-ground	We distinguish between a focal point (the "figure") and mentally fade out everything else, which becomes the background noise (the "ground").	The lead singer commands our attention during most of the concert. This can change upon mental command (e.g., the drummer can become the "figure" if they start a great solo performance).

These principles are also the foundation for many interesting optical illusions, such as that shown in Figure 6.4; this image has an organized shape that allows our attention to shift back and forth between "figure" and "ground." When we rely on Gestalt principles, we're making an intuitive leap—and they usually help us be efficient. They also lead to creative interpretations of stimuli, such as systems of constellations in the night sky based on patterns of stars and planets we see. But they can also lead to mistakes, something we'll discuss more at the end of the chapter when we talk more about illusions and perceptual errors.

FIGURE 6.4

An Example of a Figure-Ground Image

What do you see when you look at the logo on this sign? Can you see the white animals through the green trees? If you see the tree first, the tree is the figure and everything else is ground. If you see animals first, they're the figure, and the rest is the ground.

WoodsnorthPhotography/Alamy Stock Photo

Practice what you learn in **Knowledge Check 6.1**

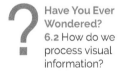

PROCESSING VISUAL INFORMATION

>> **LO 6.2** **Describe how the eye and brain process visual information to understand color, faces, size, and depth.**

What you see isn't all there is.

The amount of visual information sighted people take in is astounding. Our visual system processes all those colors and patterns in a myriad of light intensities, from as nearby as our nightstand to miles outside the window. In each case, we're capturing information from light waves.

Input: Light Waves

We don't capture the full picture because the visible spectrum humans can process makes up only a limited range on the electromagnetic spectrum spanning from gamma rays through radio waves (see Figure 6.5). We don't see the ultraviolet

Have You Ever Wondered?
6.2 How do we process visual information?

FIGURE 6.5

The Light Spectrum

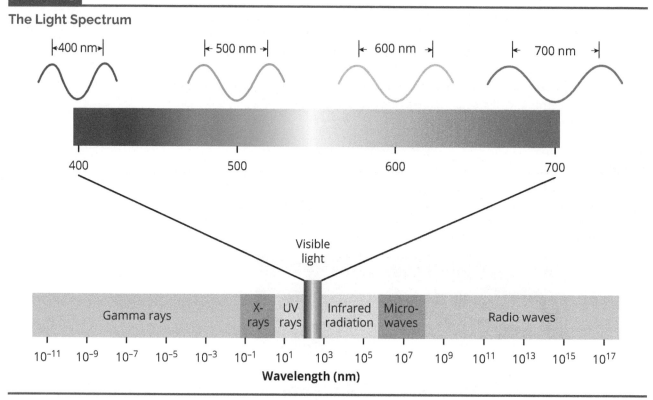

Source: Schwartz and Krantz (2024).

The colors in Monet's *Water Lilies* paintings suggest that he may have been able to detect ultraviolet light.

Peter van Evert/Alamy Stock Photo

rays that burn our skin or radio waves that come through our speaker. Each point on the electromagnetic spectrum corresponds to different wavelengths of light waves. We see a lot, but we miss a lot as well.

The light we see involves several key facets. Wavelengths of light determine hue or color. Saturation depends on how much white light is mixed in with a particular hue. More vivid colors have less white light and vice versa. Brightness depends on the light's intensity or the amplitude of the waves—how tall they are. The taller the wave, the brighter the light.

The human eye can reliably see wavelengths from around 700 nanometers (the color red), down to around 400 nanometers (the color violet). Wavelengths just above that range (infrared) become visible with night-vision goggles, while ultraviolet wavelengths (those just below violet) are accessible if the eye's lens is removed (don't try this at home). In fact, the famous painter Claude Monet developed such severe cataracts, he had his right eye's lens removed—which allowed him to see ultraviolet light. It's believed that because of this, his later paintings (e.g., *Water Lilies*) featured more blue and violet colors.

Structures: The Eye

Because vision is so important, your brain has an entire lobe (the occipital) dedicated to it.

You learned about the brain's lobes in another chapter. Of course, several other brain structures play a supporting role. Before light's information reaches your brain, it starts in your eyes. Light enters through the *cornea,* a thin transparent layer covering the front of the eye. Just beneath the cornea is the *pupil,* the dark portion at the eye's center. The *iris* surrounds the pupil and regulates how much light enters the eye. The iris also gives eyes their distinctive color such as brown, hazel, green, or blue. Beyond the pupil and iris is the *lens,* which focuses light onto the *retina,* a light-sensitive layer at the back of the eyeball.

The sclera is the supporting outside layer or wall that gives the eyeball its shape (see Figure 6.6). This shape is important. When functioning properly in a typically shaped eyeball, the images focused on the retina are clear and a person has nearly perfect vision. However, when the eye is a bit too long, the lens doesn't focus as well. The result is *myopia* or nearsightedness—a person can see clearly at close distances, but objects in the distance appear fuzzy. On the other hand, if the eyeball is slightly too short, the lens's focusing of the light overshoots its mark resulting in *hyperopia* or farsightedness. If your eyeball has this issue, then objects at a distance look clearer than those nearby. Most people wear glasses or contact lenses to correct the issue.

Transduction occurs in the retina when the light hits our photo receptors, triggering chemical changes that convert the light stimuli into electrical impulses that are transmitted to the bipolar cells, then the ganglion cells, and finally out to the brain through the *optic nerve.* The two types of photoreceptors, named for their shapes, are responsible for the different ways we see:

- *Cones* function primarily when there is a lot of light (day) and help us perceive fine details and color.

- *Rods* allow us to see when there isn't a lot of light (dim light, such as dusk or at night) but aren't very good at detecting small details.

Cones are found primarily near the *fovea,* an indented part of the retina near the eye's center where visual acuity is best. The fovea doesn't contain any rods, but at

FIGURE 6.6

The Eye's Key Structures

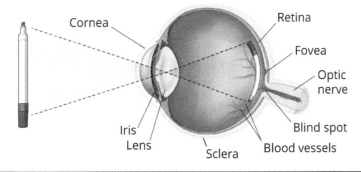

Carolina Hrejsa/Body Scientific Intl.

In many ways, camera lenses are similar to the eye; modern surveillance cameras can even automatically change focus from near to far as needed.

iStock.com/adventtr

the eye's periphery, there are more rods and fewer cones. As a result, when it's dark, we're more sensitive to light that falls on the fringes of our visual field.

The optic nerve is like a cord attached to the back of your eye. It transmits signals, so there isn't any room for photoreceptors to process light. You can't see if you can't process light. The result is that we have a *blind spot* at the point of attachment of the optic nerve to the back of your eye. You don't notice your own blind spot because your brain fills in the blank—but it's there. Check it out for yourself in Figure 6.7!

Here's the thing: Is it important for your future success that you've memorized parts of the eyeball or retinal structures like rods and cones? Probably not . . . unless, of course, you become some type of graphic artist, eye doctor, airline pilot, sign designer, printer, web designer, set designer, or interior decorator. But we do hope that you appreciate the "Wow!" of how beautifully your eyes process visual information. That beauty (and those career paths) is more relevant as we understand color.

FIGURE 6.7

Our Natural Blind Spot

Keeping your right eye closed, focus on the puppy. Move your head toward and away from the image and you'll see the kitten disappear. Now, with your left eye closed, focus on the kitten. Now moving your head toward and away from the image will make the puppy disappear.

iStock.com/Voren1; iStock.com/fotojagodka

Color Processing: Trichromatic and Opponent Process Theory

Color enriches our lives.

We may enjoy the experience of color during a nature hike, when shopping for clothes, or going to a concert. Color has three key characteristics (Camgöz et al., 2002):

- *Hue:* The nature of the light reflected from an object's surface (i.e., primary or secondary colors—red, yellow, blue, orange, green, and violet)

- *Saturation:* How deep and pure the hue appears (more saturated colors look more forceful)

- *Brightness:* Lightness related to the intensity of the reflected light

All that information comes together so we can experience the blue, red, purple, and white lights that appear onstage. And yet one of the key questions about vision is how structures like rods and cones make that possible. Spoiler alert: We don't fully know. But we have two main theories that, taken together, do a really nice job of providing answers—and demonstrate how scientific knowledge slowly increases.

The first is the Young–Helmholtz **trichromatic theory** of color vision (which Young first developed in 1802 and von Helmholz refined in 1850). It proposes that different cones are responsible for recognizing different wavelengths that we perceive as different colors. Some cones are dedicated to short, some to medium, and some to long wavelengths that correspond to blue-violet, green-yellow, and red-orange colors, respectively. Early research found evidence supporting the theory and it seemed like an adequate explanation for color vision.

However, it doesn't do a great job of explaining two interesting phenomena. The first is *color blindness*, which most commonly occurs when an individual has difficulty distinguishing between red and green (Loop et al., 2003; Sharpe et al., 2006). About 2% of men have this type of color blindness. If the trichromatic theory were entirely correct about specialized cones for different colors, then this kind of color blindness shouldn't really happen. A bigger problem for trichromatic theory is *afterimages*, the "ghost" colors you see after staring too long at one color. Try this. Stare (for about 30 seconds) at one of the images in Figure 6.8. Then, shift your gaze to a blank white space. You will see the same image, but the colors will change. If the original were blue and pink, then the afterimage would be yellow and green. Similarly, black becomes white. Trichromatic theory is helpful, but it doesn't explain some reliable observations.

These problems led to an update in 1892 by a physiologist named Hering called **opponent-process theory** that visual receptors are paired up to react to six main colors: blue–yellow, red–green, and black–white (see Strasburger et al., 2018). Within a pair, excessive firing of one color (e.g., staring at the color green) allows its paired opposite (red) to emerge. Opponent process theory explains both red-green color blindness and the afterimage experiences.

These theories are all very interesting if you want you to learn about your own eyeballs. However, we are most interested that you recognize the scientific process that helped these theories evolve to better explain vision. In 1802, color theory first proposed three photoreceptors. In 1850, scientists suggested which colors the cones detected. Finally, in 1892, in light of the failure of the tricolor theory to fully explain color blindness and afterimages, physiologists advanced opponent-process theory. Reliable observations that don't fit a theory are signposts that lead us to a better theory and a richer understanding of how we experience our curious world.

Trichromatic theory: Also known as the Young–Helmholtz theory, it suggests that different cones in the eye are responsible for recognizing different colors.

Opponent-process theory: A color vision theory that states that receptors are paired up so that they handle six main colors in three pairs (blue–yellow, red–green, black–white).

FIGURE 6.8

Afterimages

Stare at a single image for 30 seconds (it will seem like a long time). Then look away to a blank white space to see the afterimage.

Face Recognition

When you go to a show, you're there for more than just the colors.

You also need to recognize shapes so you can identify and distinguish between objects (e.g., "that's a guitar," "that's a drum," "look, guacamole and chips"). Of all the shapes you perceive, you're especially attuned to one: faces. Recognizing faces is so important that your brain evolved an entire area (the *fusiform gyrus*) dedicated to interpreting them (Haxby et al., 2000, 2002). As an infant, you quickly learned how to distinguish faces from other objects and your caregivers' faces from others, that is, unless you have the unusual disorder known as *prosopagnosia,* or face blindness, which means you are unable to recognize faces.

You also can become hypersensitive to faces. *Pareidolia* is the tendency to misperceive meaningful patterns where they don't really exist. A common form of pareidolia is seeing faces in places or objects such as an electrical outlet, household items, the side of a mountain, the front of a car, and so on (think of the "man in the moon"). One study even suggested that people who are lonelier have a greater tendency to see faces in inanimate objects (Epley et al., 2008), although others have been unable to replicate this effect (Sandstrom & Dunn, 2013).

Thanks to pareidolia, you're likely to see meaningful patterns like faces in inanimate objects.

Custom Life Science Images/Alamy Stock Photo; iStock.com/BitsAndSplits; Art Directors & TRIP/Alamy Stock Photo; iStock.com/oksanavg

Size and Shape Constancy

Of course, your visual system does more than recognize faces.

From the far-away lawn section, the lead singer at the concert looks small because the image projected onto your retina is small. As you walk toward the stage, the lead singer appears larger and larger as the image on your retina enlarges. However, you usually don't panic that the singer is suddenly growing into a monstrous size. There is a reason for that.

Size constancy: Our ability to perceive objects as maintaining their physical size, regardless of their size on our retina.

Size constancy is our ability to perceive objects as maintaining their physical size, regardless of the image's size on our retina. Similarly, if the lead singer happens to put on a hat and a pair of sunglasses or if we see them from the side instead of straight on, we're not suddenly confused by what we're seeing. Rather, thanks to shape constancy, we realize that objects maintain their physical shape, despite changes in how they temporarily appear.

Shape constancy: Our ability to perceive objects as maintaining their physical shape, despite changes in how they may temporarily appear.

Depth Perception

We don't live our life in two dimensions.

Another nice (and necessary) feature of our visual system is *depth perception.* This surely came in handy when our ancestors hunted for food—and for whomever drove the vehicle to the summer concert as they determined how close the other cars were on the road. Monocular cues involve only one eye, while binocular cues involve both of our eyes working together.

Common monocular cues involve objects' *relative size*—smaller objects seem farther away and larger objects seem closer. You may have experienced this if you've ever been hit in the face with a ball—that ball looks enormous at the last moment before impact. Binocular depth cues rely on using both eyes simultaneously. The *interocular distance* (a fancy way of saying how far apart your eyes are) between your two eyes produces *retinal disparity* because each eye's retina gets a slightly different image. The greater the retinal disparity, the closer the object.

Let's pause so you can try this out yourself. Find two objects, one partially in front of the other, that are a few feet away. First close both eyes, then quickly open one eye and then the other. (You'll feel like you are twitching.) You'll see the objects jump slightly from side to side. Fun!

Now do the same thing as you look at something much farther away. The object jumps around less or seemingly not at all. Both eyes look straight ahead for distant objects but turn inward for nearer objects. The amount of *convergence* for how much the muscles controlling the eyes turn in toward your nose lets us know how far away an object is. Binocular cues make playing sports much easier. Ask someone to toss you a crumpled-up piece of paper and try to catch it with one eye closed.

Practice what you learn in **Knowledge Check 6.2**   Sage Vantage➤

PROCESSING AUDITORY INFORMATION

» LO 6.3 Describe how the ear and brain process sound waves.

There are lots of reasons to go to a concert, but the best reason is listening to great music.

Your ear's superb ability to process sounds did not evolve just to entertain you. Sounds help orient us to potential danger and facilitate communication ("Look out! Bear!"). With the exception of vision, most people process more sensory information through hearing than from any of the other senses.

Have You Ever Wondered?
6.3 How do we process auditory information?

Input: Sound Waves

Hearing is all about waves.

Like vision, hearing relies on processing information from waves. When a guitarist strikes a chord, the air around the guitar strings vibrates. This produces sound waves that travel out, eventually reaching our ears. Those waves have two characteristics that affect the sound we hear:

- Wave *frequency,* or the number of up and down cycles that occur within 1 second, are typically measured as Hertz (Hz).

- Wave *amplitude,* or how high and low the waves are, corresponds to the wave's energy (see Figure 6.9).

Frequency and amplitude correspond to what sound we hear. Wavelengths with lower frequency have a deeper *pitch* or tone, and they sound like a lower note on a musical scale. Wavelengths with a higher frequency or more cycles have a higher pitch corresponding to higher notes on a musical scale. Either can vary in their *loudness* or intensity. A yappy dog bark might be high-pitched and have a large amplitude (loud and annoying), while a big dog might have a low-pitched bark but equally large amplitude (loud).

iStock.com/marochkina

FIGURE 6.9

Key Characteristics of Sound Waves

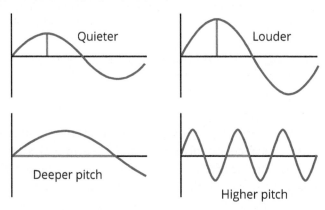

Structures: The Ear

At a concert, we don't want to miss a single note.

Our sensory receptors will process the physical sound waves, but how do we get the waves into our ears? The part of the ear we can see is the *pinna,* which is the outside structure that gathers soundwaves into the ear. Feel like you can't hear? You may cup your hand behind the pinna to enhance its functionality and capture more sound. The rest of the outer ear includes the *external auditory canal* or *meatus,* which funnels sounds waves to the *eardrum* (or *tympanic membrane*). When the waves hit the eardrum, it moves back and forth in response to pressure differences from the sound waves—like a drum that vibrates when you strike it (see Figure 6.10).

FIGURE 6.10

The Ear's Key Structures

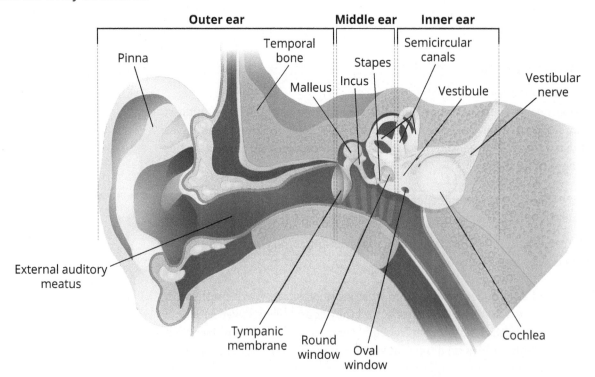

The eardrum's vibration passes into the *ossicles* in the middle ear. The ossicles are a set of three tiny bones: the *stirrup* (stapes), *hammer* (malleus), and *anvil* (incus). Their job is to stimulate the oval window. The *cochlea* is a snail-shaped structure containing a basilar membrane filled with fluid and hair cells; it carries out transduction. The vibration of the hair cells triggers neural impulses that ultimately transmit sound information to the brain.

Additional vibrations occur in the round window and are transmitted to the inner ear. There, the fluid-filled semicircular canals help provide spatial orientation information to the brain along with the vestibule and the vestibular nerve. All these structures are encased within the temporal bone, which protects the middle and inner ear.

Sound Processing

We need to make sense of all the sound information we gather.

Like color perception, there are competing theories about how we process a sound's pitch. *Place theory,* developed in 1857, suggests that the cochlea's basilar membrane plays a key role. Specifically, as a sound wave travels down the membrane, it stimulates distinct areas that correspond to particular sound intensities and frequencies. High-pitched sounds (waves with high frequency) cause vibrations near the beginning of the membrane while low-pitched sounds stimulate areas further down the membrane. That information then gets sent to the auditory cortex.

Frequency theory, developed several years later, suggests that a sound's pitch determines the frequency, or the number of neural signals in a given interval, sent to the brain. High-pitched sounds are higher frequency, so they will send more signals to the brain.

As with theories of color vision, neither theory can completely account for how we hear on its own. Place theory has a difficult time accounting for low-frequency tones (less than 120 Hz). Frequency theory can explain those low tones but has difficulty with the high ones because of limitations in the auditory nerve's firing speed. Both theories adequately account for moderate frequencies. Perhaps a third theory needs to be developed by a curious new scientist.

Making Sense of Sound

To our sensory system, sound waves are meaningless.

Those pressure signals only become sound when our perceptual system begins the interpretation process. Determining if a particular note came from a drum, guitar, violin, or saxophone is *perception,* as is deciding if the sounds form a certain song. Being able to pay attention to the meaning of that sound helps if you can focus.

Your focus will be enhanced if the volume isn't too soft or too loud. Volume is measured in *decibels* (dB). A loud rock concert registers around 120 dB, while a normal conversation is at about 60 dB. If the concert is too loud or you are positioned directly in front of a speaker, your ears are going to ring afterward, perhaps into the next day. Why? Those sound waves bent or even broke the fragile hair follicles in your cochlea. If you're lucky, your concert-induced ringing will be temporary, but why risk it? Our hearing ability naturally deteriorates over time, so you want to enjoy sounds as long as possible, even into advanced age. This is why professionals exposed to loud sounds on a regular basis (like drummers, construction workers, pilots, etc.) often wear ear plugs.

If you get lost in the concert crowd and hear your friends calling your name, you're also able to figure out where the sound is coming from due to *sound localization,* made possible because your two ears are spaced apart. Just as retinal disparity helps us perceive depth, each ear receives slightly different input. The sound intensity will differ, as will the timing of when the sound reaches the ear. If your friend is off to your right, your right ear will hear the calls more loudly and slightly before your left ear. Though we're often most aware of the sights and sounds, we also process the world around us using other senses.

SageVantage⸝   Practice what you learn in **Knowledge Check 6.3**

PROCESSING SMELL, TASTE, TOUCH, AND BODY MOVEMENT

? Have You Ever Wondered? 6.4 How do we process smell, taste, touch, and body movement information?

>> LO 6.4   Describe how we process smell, taste, touch, and body movement information.

Some people don't have five senses.

Thousands of people around the world live without sight or hearing. While this chapter started by covering the details of vision and hearing, the remaining senses are just as important—and even more so for some. Smell becomes immediately important if you can't stand someone's perfume. Taste is essential to enjoy the food at many holiday feasts. Touch and body movement are incredibly meaningful ways to bond with other people in intimate ways. How do these others senses work, in terms of sensation and perception?

Smell

Your nose, knows.

Olfaction: Our ability or sense of smell.

Whereas sound and light reach us via waves, your olfaction (sense of smell) relies on breaking down chemical compounds present in food, beverages, and odors. Smell is our oldest, most primitive sense—and it has a more direct pathway to the brain than most of the other senses.

We only need 40 to 50 molecules to identify a scent and can detect around 10,000 different scents. That's impressive. But our sense of smell isn't nearly as good as many other animals; a dog is 100,000 times better at scent identification. Our scent detection probably lagged that of other mammals because other parts of our brain were so well developed; smell became less important for humans compared to things like vision, language, and making weapons.

Still, it is powerful enough to smell a fellow concertgoer's overenthusiastic vaping or patchouli body spray. Here's how it works (see Figure 6.11):

- Aromatic odorants or molecules in the air enter your *nasal cavity,* where mucus helps the odorants make contact with the olfactory epithelium, a lining in the nose.

- That membrane contains the *olfactory neurons* or receptor cells that ultimately transmit information to the brain's *olfactory bulb* (a brain structure that processes smells).

- From there, information is sent to areas such as the limbic system, which allows you to identify specific scents (e.g., "That popcorn smells delicious").

We often have strong, emotional memories associated with odors that shape our reactions (Engen & Engen, 1997; Herz et al., 2004). That whiff of popcorn can transport you back to the fun memories of the carnival you attended when you were

FIGURE 6.11

The Nose's Key Structures

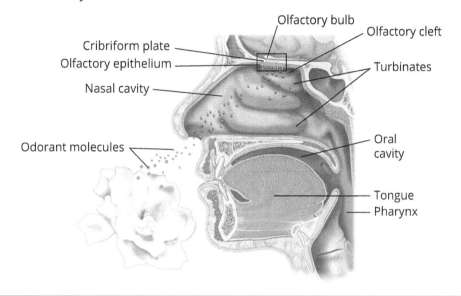

Source: Schwartz and Krantz (2024).

7 years old (Kostka & Bitzenhofer, 2022). Of course, if that smell is associated with a memory of food poisoning, then the same classical conditioning will induce a different reaction.

Taste

Thanks to your tongue, life can be pretty sweet.

Like smell, gustation—our sense of taste—also relies on breaking down chemical compounds present in food, beverages, and odors. From the moment a warm gooey brownie or cold brew hits your tongue, saliva immediately breaks down those substances to release their chemical compounds. The *papillae,* small bumps on the tongue, contain 8,000 to 10,000 *taste buds,* groups of sensory cells that detect taste. Each bud has a cluster of as many as 150 cells that can detect a wide range of tastes. These cells only last 10 to 14 days and are constantly replenished. This is the reason that burning your tongue on something hot only stunts your taste temporarily. In a week or so, a new group of taste cells is ready to go.

Gustation: Our ability or sense of taste.

Taste has long been thought to carry evolutionary significance and aided our survival by helping us detect the most nutrition-dense or high-calorie items like sweets (Callaway, 2012). Similarly, detecting sour tastes may have helped us avoid rotten or spoiled food, and even avoid ingesting poisonous items. In fact, humans have a collection of 24 to 25 different bitterness receptors that help identify toxic combinations of chemicals. But why do individual tastes differ—why do some people love hot and spicy foods while others love bland? Why do some people love chocolate while others love vanilla? Why do some people hate cilantro?

Some of the answer is habit, culture, and exposure; we get used to things. But it's also biology and physiology; each person's number of taste buds and cells is genetically determined. Those with fewer tastebuds are relatively indifferent to taste. People with abundant taste buds are discerning supertasters who can detect subtle differences in flavor (Bartoshuck et al., 1994); maybe they make for excellent chefs. On the other hand, they also may experience some foods and drinks as overly bitter, sweet, or salty. And some people have a genetic condition that makes coriander leaf (cilantro) taste like soap no matter how many times they're forced to "just try it!" (Spence, 2023). Interestingly, the cilantro/genetic connection might vary by ethnocultural group, as shown in Table 6.2.

TABLE 6.2

Dislike for Cilantro, by Ethnocultural Group

Do you like or dislike cilantro? Research indicates preference is at least partially genetically determined and varies by ethnocultural group; for some people, cilantro tastes like soap.

GROUP	PREVALENCE OF DISLIKING
East Asian	21%
White	17%
African	14%
South Asian	7%
Hispanic	4%
Middle Eastern	3%

Source: Created using data from Spence (2023).

Researchers previously believed that taste buds corresponding to basic tastes (bitter, salty, sour, sweet) resided on different regions of the tongue (Figure 6.12). However, subsequent research revealed that the different taste buds are more evenly distributed throughout the tongue (Lindemann, 2001). In addition, research shows there is a fifth basic taste known as *umami,* which in Japanese means "yummy" or "savory" (Barretto et al., 2015). Can you taste umami? Common foods that contain the flavor include soups, seaweeds, fish, tomatoes, kimchi, aged cheese, and soy sauce. Given that list, it's no surprise that so many people enjoy sushi.

FIGURE 6.12

The Original Idea of Tongue's Key Structures—Now Questioned

Research questions whether we have taste bud regions, as shown here, or if our taste buds are evenly distributed across the tongue.

iStock.com/MicrovOne

How you experience different tastes begins with the sensory information collected by the taste buds, which then gets sent to the thalamus (you'll recall from Chapter 5 that the thalamus is the brain's sensory relay station). Ultimately, your enjoyment of taste comes from previous experiences. Some of those start from before we're even born—babies show a preference for foods that their mothers ingested while the baby was still in the womb (Mennella et al., 2001).

Smell and taste are related because they both rely on processing chemical compounds. If you have had a severe cold and a stuffed-up nose, you may have a harder time tasting foods. A kid's best defense against eating "bad"-tasting food is to hold their nose while they (grudgingly) eat. And notice that before you eat or drink something delicious, you smell it first—that enhances the taste.

Touch and Body Movement

Touch is surprisingly complex and powerful.

Touch is just one aspect of somatosensation, the processes involved in conveying sensory information about the body and how it interacts with its surroundings. It is a *cutaneous* or *tactile* sense, which means that it occurs in the skin. That makes your skin the largest sensory receptor you have. It's got you covered—all over. If we look a little deeper into your skin, we'll find a network of structures that facilitate touch. The key receptors lie in the *epidermis*, which is the skin's outermost layer (the part you see), and in the *dermis*, which lies just beneath the epidermis and just above the *subcutaneous layer*. A tattoo artist injects ink into the dermis because that layer stays the same. The epidermis, however, regularly regenerates new but translucent skin cells that allow others to see the ink just below (see Figure 6.13).

The dermis has different *mechanoreceptors* that allow us to sense pain, vibration, and different types of pressure. The dermis also has *thermoreceptors* that register temperature. Like other senses, these receptors transmit information

Somatosensation: A collective term for all the processes involved in conveying sensory information about the body and how it interacts with its surroundings.

FIGURE 6.13

How Do Tattoos Work?

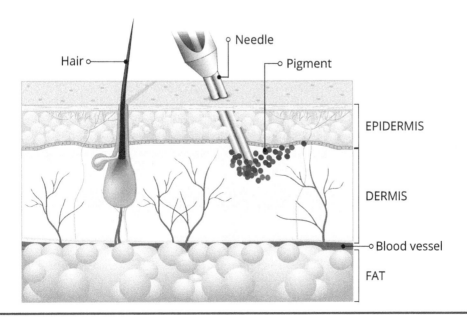

iStock.com/ttsz

FIGURE 6.14

The Sensory Homunculus

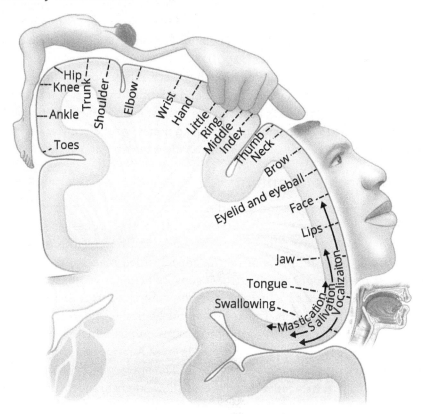

Source: Garrett and Hough (2022).

through the spinal cord to the brain. In the brain's parietal lobe, you have a *sensory homunculus,* which is a map-like structure specializing in processing sensory information from parts of our body (it's like an internal mini-me; see Figure 6.14). Interestingly, your more sensitive body parts (e.g., lips, fingers, etc.) have a larger area of the homunculus dedicated to it, compared to less sensitive body parts (e.g., calf, elbow, etc.).

How do we interpret that information? Consider touch sensitivity, pain, and balance.

Touch Sensitivity

You want to feel all the feels.

As the structure of the sensory homunculus suggests, our touch sensitivity varies depending on where it is on our body. When a confetti cannon from onstage shoots out into the crowd and a piece lands on your cheek, you're likely to feel it right away. But if it lands on your upper arm, you may not. Moreover, how much information your brain gets about the confetti varies. Simply feeling it is one thing, but your *touch acuity* involves being able to know the more precise nature of the touch. Was it one piece of confetti or two? How big is it?

You're able to make these judgments based on our touch acuity, which depends on the number of receptors in your skin. Your face has more than your upper arm. It also means that those sensitive areas are more susceptible to feeling tickle, temperature, itch, and pain.

You experience tickle from stimulation of nearby pressure sensors. However, there's more to it than mere sensation. You're more likely to be tickled when you don't know it's coming and when there is a social dynamic involved (e.g., you anticipate someone is about to tickle you!). This is why it's nearly impossible to tickle yourself (Blakemore et al., 2000).

To help feel temperature, you have fibers that react when you touch something warmer than your skin and different fibers when you touch something colder than your skin. Immersing your hand in icy water can confuse your receptors so that you may interpret the experience of ice as heat. Recently, studies have investigated the psychological benefits of cold baths or plunges. For example, one study found that after taking a cold bath (20°C/68°F), participants reported feeling less nervous and distressed, as well as more alert and active (Yankouskaya et al., 2023). Of course, extreme temperatures can be dangerous, so be careful.

Pain

Your skin operates like a gatekeeper.

It's the first line of defense alerting you to potential harm, whether from icy water or something more dangerous. Skin contains *nociceptors,* which allow you to sense noxious or harmful stimuli that cause pain (Dubin & Patapoutian, 2010). You have more of these free nerve ending receptors for detecting pain in more functionally important areas of the body (like your hands, feet, abdomen, and face). Pain comes in different forms, and you have different receptors to account for that. *Slow fibers* sense steady, dull, or chronic pain. *Fast fibers* sense sharp or urgent pain (Dickx et al., 2010) and are sensitive to rapid changes in temperature and pressure.

While it's helpful for our survival to sense pain, we also need to regulate it. As with the other senses, there are different theories about how we do this. According to the *gate-control theory,* we experience pain because small fibers send signals from the body to the brain. Larger fibers, however, control whether or not the pain signals go through (Melzack & Wall, 1996). When we experience muscle pain, we want to "close the gate." A common way to do that is by massaging those muscles to make them feel better (Ferrell-Torry & Glick, 1993). In fact, massage effectively lowers pain intensity and unpleasantness in a variety of contexts, including among patients who underwent cardiac surgery (Boitor et al., 2018) and to help reduce labor pain in pregnant women (Türkmen & Oran, 2021).

Pain is also a psychological phenomenon (Rainville, 2002). That is, maladies bother you more when you focus on them, which is why distraction and positive moods can effectively "close the gate." In contrast, people with childhood traumas or recent life stressors report more long-term physical pain (Kascakova et al., 2022). Sometimes, imagining pain when we're not feeling it ourselves can be difficult, which can sometimes lead to lack of empathy for people who need help—and some research indicates this problem might result in systemic inequalities in pain care (e.g., Berger & Baria, 2022; Mende-Siedlecki et al., 2022). You can explore your own ability to imagine pain in the *What's My Score?* feature.

Measuring Pain Sensitivity

Instructions: This questionnaire contains a series of questions in which you should imagine yourself in certain situations. Decide if these situations would be painful for you and, if yes, how painful they would be. Let 0 stand for no pain; 1 is an only just noticeable pain and 10 is the most severe pain that you can imagine or consider possible. Please indicate the number that is most true for you. Keep in mind that there are no "right" or "wrong" answers; only your personal assessment of the situation counts. Please try as much as possible not to allow your fear or aversion of the imagined situations affect your assessment of painfulness.

Not at All 0 1 2 3 4 5 6 7 8 9 10 Most Severe Pain
Painful   Imaginable

____ 1. Imagine you bump your shin badly on a hard edge, for example, on the edge of a glass coffee table. How painful would that be for you?

____ 2. Imagine you burn your tongue on a very hot drink.

____ 3. Imagine your muscles are slightly sore as the result of physical activity.

____ 4. Imagine you trap your finger in a drawer.

____ 5. Imagine you take a shower with lukewarm water.

____ 6. Imagine you have mild sunburn on your shoulders.

____ 7. Imagine you grazed your knee falling off your bicycle.

____ 8. Imagine you accidentally bite your tongue or cheek badly while eating.

____ 9. Imagine walking across a cool tiled floor with bare feet.

____ 10. Imagine you have a minor cut on your finger and inadvertently get lemon juice in the wound.

____ 11. Imagine you prick your fingertip on the thorn of a rose.

____ 12. Imagine you stick your bare hands in the snow for a couple of minutes or bring your hands in contact with snow for some time, for example, while making snowballs.

____ 13. Imagine you shake hands with someone who has a normal grip.

____ 14. Imagine you shake hands with someone who has a very strong grip.

____ 15. Imagine you pick up a hot pot by inadvertently grabbing its equally hot handles.

____ 16. Imagine you are wearing sandals and someone with heavy boots steps on your foot.

____ 17. Imagine you bump your elbow on the edge of a table ("funny bone").

Scoring instructions: Add up all 17 of your answers. Your total score should be between 0 and 170. The higher your score, the more sensitive to pain you are. In the original study, the average score was a 36.

Research using this scale found that participants' self-ratings of pain sensitivity were significantly related to their actual experience of pain on several measures (e.g., pinprick, heat and cold tolerance, and pressure).

Critical thinking: Do you believe that people who have more personal experience with physical pain are better EMTs, nurses, physicians' assistants, medical professionals, and so on because they can empathize with their patients more? Or not? Explain your answer and provide an example to support your argument if you can. ●

Source: Ruscheweyh et al. (2009).

Vestibular Sense

Your body's movements also provide sensory information.

Kinesthesis is the sense that provides information about your limbs' movement in space. Unlike other senses that gather information from outside the body, kinesthesis looks inward. You can feel a sense of stretch through receptors in our muscles called *muscle spindles*. Our joints and tendons also have receptors that allow you to sense their movements. You can thank kinesthesis for making it possible for you to walk, run, catch objects, and for your ability to play corn hole (also known as "bags" in some regions) while tailgating.

Kinesthesis works with your *vestibular sense* (your sense of balance, movement, and gravity), which comes from fluid-filled canals of the inner ear. When we move around, the fluid in our ears moves the hair follicles, which lets our brain know how our head is moving. Those movements help you maintain your posture and have a sense of your body's orientation in space. A roller coaster, for example, disrupts your vestibular system, resulting in dizziness. Your vestibular system is often the culprit for the miserable experience of motion sickness.

Interestingly, your vestibular sense may interact with your personality. Researchers had a group of participants with persistent dizziness view a roller-coaster simulator while undergoing an fMRI brain scan (Passamonti et al., 2018). Compared to a group of healthy controls, those with persistent dizziness who were also higher in neuroticism had greater activity and connectivity in their neural networks associated with attention to motion cues. In other words, they were more likely to notice (and ultimately be bothered by) movement. Anxiety and motion sickness may be connected; more research will help explain this potential link.

Thanks to your sense of balance, you have *proprioception,* awareness of your body's position in space relative to other objects. If you decide to dance at the concert, proprioception will help you calculate your distance from others and assess your own movements. Like all other senses, proprioception has survival value. It helps you avoid danger and embarrassment (e.g., dancing off the edge of the stage) and provides hand-eye coordination. Overall, it tends to decrease as we age; happily, training and practice can help older adults navigate their surroundings (Gabriel et al., 2022).

CAREER CORNER

Meet Alex, Slot Floor Person at a Casino

What is your career?

A slot floor person is an individual who assists all casino guests playing on slot machines around the casino floor. The job entails processing jackpots, dealing with guest disputes, and fixing machine errors. Guest disputes can involve money missing from a machine, misreading a slot pay line, another guest playing on a machine that already had money on it, promotional credits missing, and slot voucher thefts. Some guests come into the casino regularly enough that floor people become personally acquainted with them.

How was studying psychology important for success in this career?

Counseling classes assisted in conflict resolution and crisis management quite a bit on the casino floor. *Conflict resolution* also came in handy when one guest would put money into a machine without noticing that another guest had already had money in that machine. *Operant conditioning* in particular aided in dealing with some of the casino's regulars, by offering a free meal or promotional credits to keep them happy when a situation did not go the way they believed it should.

How do concepts from this chapter help in this career?

One way the machines keep the gamblers hooked is the lights and sounds that are triggered when they win. Usually, the sound that comes out of some of the older styles of machines sounds like coins hitting the metal tray at the bottom. Now this sound works on some of the older gamblers who were around when the machines still gave out actual coins, but it doesn't work on some of the younger gamblers, who go more for the computerized machines. Those machines use brightly colored characters and images of "luxury," such as gold bars and yachts. The bright flashing lights also work to keep the gambler playing and to entice others to gamble.

Is this the career you always planned to have after college?

This is a career that I had stumbled into after moving away after college. I decided to try this position out because it gave me an opportunity to observe people and use the knowledge gained during my psychology courses. This career was my chance to get paid to observe psychology in a real-world setting.

If you could give current college students one sentence of advice, what would it be?

Take your passions and make a career out of it. ●

PERCEPTUAL MISTAKES, CURIOSITIES, AND CONTROVERSIES

Have You Ever Wondered?
6.5 What are some perceptual mistakes, curiosities, and controversies?

>> **LO 6.5**   **Analyze several ways that our perceptual processes lead to mistakes and why.**

Your magnificent powers of perception help you navigate the world—but they can also deceive you.

The fact that we're able to process all the sensory stimuli in our world is amazing. But it's easy to take our capabilities for granted and ignore the times we mess up. It is often difficult to process so much information, especially when that information sends ambiguous or mixed signals. Many outside factors also impact perceptions. Can we see things that aren't really there? Why do optical illusions trick our senses? Can some people really tap into telepathy or telekinesis? We analyze these questions in the last sections of this chapter.

The Power of Suggestion

Sometimes, what influences your perception is hiding in plain sight.

Earlier, we discussed how Gestalt principles might help you figure out that the band's backdrop screen image was a bird, even if some parts were missing (Table 6.1). It might take a minute, or you might never figure it out. But if your friend says, "Hey, that looks like a bird," the simple suggestion virtually guarantees that you'll interpret the image that way. If your friend had suggested a rabbit, your interpretation might have been a rabbit instead.

What do you see? Random black dots, or a dog sniffing the curb?

Braga (2011)

Suggestions create expectations. You didn't necessarily expect to see anything in the backdrop—until you were told it looks like a bird. Then your brain started shaping your interpretation. This type of perceptual bias happens a lot when tasting new things. Concerts often have kiosks set up around the venue from local businesses. If you go past the local coffee shop's stand, they may offer you a chance to sample their newest coffee. As you prepare to sip, they will shape your taste experience with a sales pitch like this:

> This fair-trade coffee has been hand-selected from the Laguna de Ayarza region of southeast Guatemala. The organically grown bean comes from a family-owned farm and was naturally processed. This rare coffee has wine-like notes of ripe black cherry, dark chocolate, and hints of pipe tobacco.

As the warm liquid hits your tongue, you taste all of that. Of course, what you're tasting may be not-so-subtle notes of BS . . . which in this case stands for "basic sensation." That is, you taste ripe black cherry because the chemical compounds in the coffee did hit your taste buds and get interpreted by your brain—but the perception of cherry is likely because of the expectation.

Without that verbal nudge, you may have only tasted . . . coffee. In fact, research shows that descriptive menu labels like "succulent Italian seafood filet" were associated with more positive customer ratings of food, compared to when the exact same item was described simply as "seafood filet" (Wansink et al., 2005). The same thing happens with music. If you went to the concert expecting to hear good music, then you probably will. If you expected it to be bad, then your experience will match your expectations; top-down processing matters.

Perceptual Sets and Motivational-Emotional Factors

Our perceptions are easily biased.

A **perceptual set** is how current motivation or thought predisposes us to interpret (and react to) stimuli in particular ways. We get comfortable with our familiar perceptions and fall into a groove that enables us to interpret subsequent stimuli quickly and easily. If you're a huge "Swiftie" (i.e., fan of Taylor Swift) and she plays a brand-new, never-before-heard song, you're already inclined to like it because it's her. However, those in the crowd who aren't super fans may not have as favorable of a response.

Perceptual sets matter because they encourage us to organize stimuli in certain ways that are usually helpful but sometimes lead to mistakes (Vernon, 1955). Consider this example (please just try it): Say the following words *out loud* as quickly as you can.

Catch, Hatch, Snatch, Thatch, Batch, Match, Patch, Watch.

Didn't that last one sound a bit weird? Obviously, you all know how to properly pronounce "watch," yet you didn't. In this case, just going with the flow seems goofy, but innocent enough.

However, becoming predisposed to perceive the world in a certain way has larger implications. For example, police officers may unknowingly develop perceptual sets based on past experience, culture, or the setting (e.g., is it a "good" or "bad" neighborhood?) that lead them to perceive people differently. Those perceptions can then have implications for subsequent decision-making and behaviors. For example, research finds that contextual factors such as a neighborhood's unemployment rate and previous violent crime records are associated with police officers' use of force (Lee et al., 2010). Realizing how the process can start way back at the level of sensation and perception helps us avoid simply blaming individuals or labeling them as "bad apples." This insight can encourage more useful solutions to these problems, such as training and awareness programs.

When expectations come from our friend or a helpful barista, we can easily identify the source. That gives us a chance to realize what's happening and adjust accordingly. However, other influences on our perception aren't as obvious. Sometimes it's as simple as having a little bit of previous knowledge. Take something you've likely seen hundreds of times: the FedEx logo (see Figure 6.15).

Perceptual set: Our tendency to become predisposed to interpret and react to stimuli in a particular way.

FIGURE 6.15

A "Hidden" Symbol?

Is this just a logo, or is there a hidden symbol as well?

iStock.com/-Oxford-

Did you realize that between the E and the X there is a white arrow pointing to the right? If you had previous knowledge of it, you've seen the arrow each time you see the logo. However, if you never noticed the arrow before, from this point forward, you won't be able to miss it and each time will think fondly of the amazing book where you learned this important information. With just a little bit of prior knowledge, your perception has changed.

In addition to preexisting knowledge, personal preferences and motivations change our perceptions. If you learned that the song "Dragonfly" was about the lead singer's love of the show *Game of Thrones,* you'd like the song and band either more or less depending on your own view of that show. Security personnel searching concertgoers for less important but more common items (such as drinks people are trying to smuggle in so they don't have to pay for them inside) may cause the staff to miss more important items like fireworks or weapons (Biggs et al., 2015). Either way, previous experience affects our perceptions.

Two people can reach different conclusions based on the exact same physical stimuli. Head out to a home improvement store and grab a paint sample with a fancy name like Dusty Ocean or Buttermilk French Linen. Now ask each person to describe the color; their descriptions will vary even though the stimulus is identical. Table 6.3 summarizes the six motivational-emotional factors that influence how subjective perception can be (Allport, 1955; see also Sanford, 1936; Seibt et al., 2007). Each factor influences how individuals experience a concert. For someone to see the world exactly as you do, they would need to—at a minimum—have all six motivational-emotional factors in common. That's not going to happen, but it might explain why everyone's experience is so different.

TABLE 6.3

Motivational-Emotional Factors That Influence Perception

MOTIVATIONAL-EMOTIONAL FACTORS	EXAMPLE
Physiological needs	When you're hungry, you view food items more positively. Hunger also encourages you to see food-related images in ambiguous pictures.
Individual values	If you feel strongly about social justice, a band like U2 who has a strong social justice message will be more enjoyable.
Value of objects	If you place more value on an object like your favorite concert T-shirt that you stood in line for hours to get, you're going to think it looks cooler than someone else might.
Personality	If you're outgoing, you're likely to enjoy a crowded setting more than someone who is introverted.
Emotional state	If you had a terrible day at work before going out, that could make the whole evening seem worse—and a good mood will make it even better.
Rewards or punishments	If every time you went to a concert, you expected to twist your ankle, lose your phone, or wake up the next morning feeling sick (based on past experiences), then you wouldn't perceive concerts as so much fun.

Perceptual Illusions

Sometimes what you perceive isn't what you get.

In other words, our perceptual system plays tricks on us. A **perceptual illusion** occurs when we misread or misinterpret external physical stimuli. Illusions highlight our perceptual system's imperfections, but they also help us better understand how perception works (Carbon, 2014). Perception allows us to react to our physical world quickly and efficiently—but illusions show us that we can make mistakes.

One of the most common ways we're deceived is when perceiving size. In the well-known *Müller-Lyer illusion* (see Figure 6.16), two identical lines appear to be different lengths due to the diagonal lines at the end (Judd, 1905). Not convinced? Get your ruler out.

Perceptual illusion: These occur when we misread or misinterpret external physical stimuli.

FIGURE 6.16

Müller–Lyer Illusion

In the *Zöllner illusion* (see Figure 6.17), a series of long parallel lines appear to slant toward each other due to a series of small diagonal lines that bisect the parallel lines (Judd & Courten, 1905). Even when you know the long lines are parallel, it's hard to believe because it doesn't look that way.

FIGURE 6.17

Zöllner Illusion

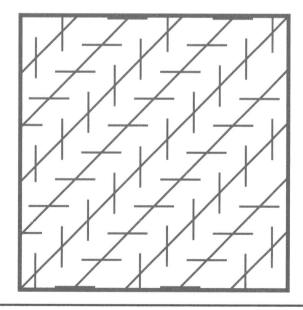

In the *Ebbinghaus illusion* (see Figure 6.18), two circles of identical size appear to be different due to the size of surrounding circles (Weintraub, 1979).

FIGURE 6.18

Ebbinghaus Illusion

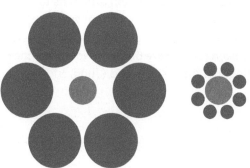

With each case, we're misperceiving reality due to contextual cues. These illusions may feel a bit contrived, so before you think "this couldn't happen in real life," rest assured it happens there as well. If you're lucky, you go to a concert on a clear night when there's a full moon. As night sets in, you get to witness the moon rise. If you catch it early enough, you'll notice that the moon appears gigantic—but it seems to shrink as it rises. This is the *moon illusion*. It's an illusion because, of course, the moon itself isn't getting smaller. Rather, we perceive the moon to be larger on the horizon because our visual system mistakes the distance between us and the moon (Kaufman & Kaufman, 2000).

Importantly, some of these illusions are a good example of being WEIRD (see Chapter 2; remember it stands for samples that are from primarily "Western," educated, industrialized, rich, and democratic cultures). Remember that early in this book, we cautioned that not all people think the same. It turns out that people from some cultures don't fall for these illusions. For example, several nomadic societies don't have trouble with the Müller–Lyer illusion (Sayood, 2018; see also Leibowitz, 1971; Masuda, 2009; Pani & Parida, 2000). One explanation is that WEIRD samples of people grew up in worlds of measured, carpentry-based right angles that are not particularly natural. Among Navajo people, there were even differences in line judgments between people living in round versus rectangular houses (Pederson & Wheeler, 1983). We experience the same world in different ways from even our closest neighbors.

The impossible figures in Figure 6.19 also demonstrate the subtle influence of contexts unrelated to culture. At first glance, the elephant image looks, well, like a regular elephant. But when you change the context by looking down its legs to its feet, you discover an impossibility: five feet! Your frustrated brain keeps returning to the image to interpret and organize it in a meaningful way—but the drawing keeps creating a perceptual paradox.

Visual illusions are most common, but your other senses can be tricked as well. If you've ever seen a marquee advertising a concert or theater with lights that appear to move or chase each other around a sign (but really they just turn on and off in a certain way), you've seen an illusion of movement called the *Phi phenomenon* (or stroboscopic motion; Dimmick, 1920).

The *parchment-skin illusion* occurs when a sound changes the way your skin feels (Jousmäki & Hari, 1998). Specifically, when you hear low-frequency sounds, your skin

FIGURE 6.19

Impossible Figures

Sources: Figures from Ros and Thomas (2002); elephant from Garrett and Hough (2022).

feels smooth when you rub your hands together. However, hearing high-frequency sounds makes your skin feel rough. Auditory illusions are also possible, and thanks to social media, two went viral: Search for the "Yanny-Laurel illusion" or "Brainstorm or Green Needle" to listen for yourself. Of course, just by seeing the names of the illusions we're setting your expectations.

SPOTLIGHT ON RESEARCH METHODS

Can You Increase Your Perceptual Abilities?

Who wouldn't want to improve their powers of perception? As with most things in life, practice leads to improvement. Perceptual learning can lead to improvements in a person's ability to detect motion, textures, patterns, and orientation in space.

The good news is that not only can these abilities be trained, but the resulting skills have real-world benefits such as improved accuracy in reading medical X-rays and for dermatologists who need to identify skin ailments (Marris et al., 2023).

The current study wanted to see if training could raise nonexperts' performance to an expert's level based on reading ultrasound images to detect fatty liver disease. The study also examined two types of perceptual training to determine if one was better. First is "traditional" training, where trainees see a single image and need to make a judgment (e.g., "Is there a hip fracture in this image?"), then immediately learn if they are correct. Second is "comparison" training, where the trainees see multiple images at the same time, need to identify which is abnormal, and then receive feedback. Finally, researchers wanted to see how much training was necessary.

In the first experiment, researchers compared a group doing "traditional" training to another group doing "comparison" training. They found that both groups showed significant posttraining improvement, but "traditional" was more effective. They also found that the meaningful improvements happened in the first training session. Importantly, though novice study participants showed improved perceptual abilities, their performance failed to reach expert level.

Overall, the findings show that, though not quite reaching expert levels, perceptual training can rapidly enhance performance on a challenging radiology task. In light of these improvements, it has to make you curious about what other applications perceptual training might have and which other skills it can help develop. ●

Extrasensory Perception (ESP)

Are there more than these five senses?

Extrasensory perception (ESP) is the idea that people can have perceptions beyond typical human physiology or from typical environmental stimuli. It sounds pretty mysterious—but Paul Kurtz, a founding member of the U.S. nonprofit group called the Committee for the Scientific Investigation of Claims of the Paranormal, argues that when humans can't explain something, they resort to belief in magic (Kurtz, 2023). He estimates that 80% of college students believe in the paranormal . . . until they take courses teaching critical thinking, when the number drops to around 15%. People who continue to believe in ESP also tend to fear death, believe in the power of intuition, and think that random chance controls their life (Brankovic, 2019).

There are potentially several different types of extrasensory perceptions:

- *Clairvoyance*—the ability to perceive information or "see things" about an event, location, object, or person beyond what is actually visible. If you find a wedding ring in the concert parking lot, you could use your clairvoyant powers to know who the ring belongs to.

- *Precognition*—the ability to know what will happen in the future. If you had a sense that your friend's phone was going to fall and break right before it did, that's precognition.

- *Psychokinesis* (or telekinesis)—the ability to move things with your mind. Did you drop your car keys on the far side of the field while you were walking to the stage? Just focus your psychokinesis and move them toward your hand with your mind.

- *Telepathy*—the ability to send thoughts to another person solely through the mind. Ready to leave the concert, but your friend is busy talking to some random guy? Send them a mental message.

All of this sounds cool, but there is one big problem: None of it holds up to scientific study.

None. There is no empirical or reliable support for these phenomena.

The "One Million Dollar Paranormal Challenge" has existed for decades, willing to award one million bucks to anyone who can prove a supernatural ESP ability. Many have tried, but none have succeeded. In each case, the alleged ability turned out to be a trick, a poorly designed attempt, a chance event, or an inflated claim. What looks like mental telepathy, for example, is often a subtle nonverbal signal between two people (like the flick of an eye or twitch of a nostril). The paranormal is cool enough to make for great films and shows, but that doesn't make it real.

What comes next is both cool and real—and a little disturbing.

Synesthesia and Misophonia

Can you smell a color?

Ideally, you should process visual experiences as visual information, sound stimuli as sound, and smell as smell. But that doesn't always happen. When sensory experiences get mixed up, the official term for it is *synesthesia* (Ramachandran & Hubbard, 2003). **Synesthesia**, which occurs in 2% to 4% of the population, is a neurological condition in which sensory stimulation from one sense (sound, smell, sight, touch, or taste) produces perceptions in a different sense (Simner et al., 2006).

Synesthesia: A neurological condition in which sensory stimulation from one sense (sound, smell, sight, touch, or taste) produces perceptions in a different sense.

For those with synesthesia, they may be able to smell the concert's light show or see a color when they taste something sweet in their drink. So when Skittles says, "Taste the rainbow," it sounds like clever marketing—but it's something a person with synesthesia might actually be able to do, in a way. Notably, synesthetes don't actually "taste" or "smell" a color. Rather, their sensory reaction to the light (in the retina, not nose or tongue) gets transmitted to the brain areas associated with taste or smell perception, rather than the area for vision.

Many people believe that the painter Vincent Van Gogh was a synesthete. Controversial "Harry Potter" author J. K. Rowling wrote a synesthesia-like tweet that "odd numbers are definitely female. You'll be saying Saturday isn't silver next" (Seaburg, 2020). The seemingly sincere suggestion that numbers are gendered, or that a day of the week links to a color, indicates that Rowling's processing of numbers and words may not be straightforward. Her curious perspective fits with other findings that synesthetes perceive numbers differently than nonsynesthetes (Ramachandran & Hubbard, 2003). Those higher in creativity are also more likely to experience synesthetic-like phenomena (Dailey et al., 1997).

And have you ever gotten weirdly angry when you hear someone chewing ice or whistling? **Misophonia** is a neurological condition in which specific sounds cause intense emotional responses—usually simultaneous and immediate rage, disgust, and/or anxiety (Taylor, 2017). Because misophonia has only recently been named and recognized by researchers, studies are only now being done that will determine whether it will be added as an official psychological disorder (e.g., Perez & Friedman, 2023) and how to best treat it (e.g., Mattson et al., 2023).

Misophonia: A neurological condition in which specific sounds cause intense emotional responses (usually rage, disgust, and/or anxiety).

Embodied Cognition

Sometimes we're not fully aware of how sensations affect us.

There is a longstanding controversy in philosophy and subsequently psychology about the connections between the body and mind. Back in the 1600s, the philosopher Descartes suggested that the mind and body were separate. Conversely, if the body connects to the mind, *embodied cognition,* or the ability for bodily sensations to influence how we think, becomes possible (Shapiro, 2011). We can see evidence of this connection in many of our common phrases: "When they met, sparks flew." "I'm feeling down today." "She has power over me." In each case, there is a physical sensation closely tethered to a thought or feeling. Dropping a mic on stage can be quite empowering.

There's also plenty of empirical evidence to support this type of mind–body connection. For example, after participants smelled clean scents, they were neater than when they ate a crumby biscuit (Holland et al., 2005). Similarly, participants in a cleaner-smelling room were willing to donate more money (Liljenquist et al., 2010). Temperature may also matter; when participants were outside on warm days or in a warm lab, they were more likely to believe in global warming (Risen & Critcher, 2011). Holding a cup of warm coffee may lead you to view someone as "warmer" and more caring than if you held an iced coffee (Williams & Bargh, 2008).

However, we have to say "may lead . . ." because several replications of these effects have failed. One research team tried three times with about 800 participants to replicate a study about holding hot or cold packs (Lynott et al., 2014). Likewise, research initially found that "power poses" (i.e., when you stand superhero-like with your hands on your hips with legs spread) could make a person feel more powerful and more risk tolerant (Carney et al., 2010). However, seven different studies could not replicate their findings (Jonas et al., 2017).

Failed replications promote good controversies: They push science forward. The good news is that once purely philosophical debates are now being tested with the open science methods described in Chapter 2 that can be examined, criticized, and improved. All of the ideas in the last section of this chapter need more research and attention from people with curious minds. ●

SageVantage🕊   Practice what you learn in **Knowledge Check 6.5**

CHAPTER REVIEW

Learning Objectives Summary

6.1   What are the building blocks of sensation and perception?

>> **LO 6.1   Explain how we detect and interpret sensory information from the outside world.**

Sensation is how the body detects, converts, and relays physical stimuli into information for the brain. Perception is how we recognize, interpret, and make sense of sensory information. Bottom-up processing starts with physical sensations, while top-down processing starts with a prior expectation. Gestalt principles often guide our perceptions by organizing and simplifying the world.

6.2   How do we process visual information?

>> **LO 6.2   Describe how the eye and brain process visual information to understand color, faces, size, and depth.**

Vision relies on processing light waves to extract information through the eye. In the eye, structures such as the lens, retina, and optic nerve help detect color, faces, size, shape, and depth. Color vision has two key explanations, trichromatic and opponent-process theory, that help explain afterimages and color blindness.

6.3   How do we process auditory information?

>> **LO 6.3   Describe how the ear and brain process sound waves.**

Hearing relies on processing sound waves through the ear. In the ear, structures such as the auditory canal, ear drum, and cochlea help detect pitch and loudness. Auditory processing has two key explanations, place theory and frequency theory, that help explain the full range of tones we hear.

6.4   How do we process smell, taste, touch, and body movement information?

>> **LO 6.4   Describe how we process smell, taste, touch, and body movement information.**

Our other senses are smell (olfaction), taste (gustation), touch (one aspect of somatosensation), and body movement. Each has unique physiological structures with important evolutionary implications.

6.5   What are some perceptual mistakes, curiosities, and controversies?

>> **LO 6.5   Analyze several ways that our perceptual processes lead to mistakes and why.**

Some of the ways we perceive the world are controversial. Perceptual processes like optical illusions, "impossible" visual images, extrasensory perception, synesthesia, misophonia, and embodied cognition are all relatively controversial and curious ideas that can lead to perceptual biases and errors.

1. You've been hired by Disney World to create their next indoor ride. They don't have a lot of room, so it must fit in a movie theater—but you have millions of dollars to create a multisense experience. How can you use your knowledge of sensation and perception to make the ride as immersive as possible? Describe a theme you would use (such as a popular movie franchise or adventure setting, like pirates) and how you would create experiences using at least three of the five major senses.

2. Explain how top-down and bottom-up processing might influence perceptions during job interviews (of the interviewer and interviewee) or of college courses (of the professor and students). Think of at least one specific way that top-down and one specific way that bottom-up processing might affect perceptions in your chosen context.

3. Virtual reality interfaces are getting more and more advanced. How might concepts from this chapter influence advancements in both hardware and software for virtual reality experiences?

4. Think of at least two examples of times when perceptual sets have affected your perceptions—once when the set helped your thinking and once when the set was problematic or led to some kind of bias or error.

5. What type of evidence would you need to believe that extrasensory perception is real? Pick one type of ESP and establish criteria for establishing its validity. Explain the procedure you'd use to test the validity of ESP in someone using concepts like random sampling, random assignment, control groups, reliability, replication, or other ideas from either Chapter 2 or from critical thinking in general.

KEY TERMS

Absolute threshold, 157
Bottom-up processing, 160
Gustation, 173
Misophonia, 187
Olfaction, 172
Opponent-process theory, 167
Parallel processing, 157
Perception, 157
Perceptual illusion, 183
Perceptual set, 181
Sensation, 157

Sensory adaptation, 160
Sensory deprivation, 160
Shape constancy, 168
Signal detection theory, 159
Size constancy, 168
Somatosensation, 175
Subliminal messages, 158
Synesthesia, 186
Top-down processing, 161
Transduction, 157
Trichromatic theory, 167

iStock.com/Oleksii Didok

7 Consciousness

You're exhausted and running on fumes.

Although being tired is standard, it's worse for you this week. Writing three papers and studying for four midterms doesn't help. You need to keep your grades up for your scholarship, so the stakes are high. It's even tougher if you have work and family obligations. Time to focus. If you have roommates, quality studying isn't going to happen when they are home. Why don't they seem to have as much work as you? You pull all-nighters; they pull the sheet over their head and sleep until noon.

You consider going to a coffee shop but ultimately decide to head to the library, where it will be easier to concentrate. There, you settle into your favorite semi-secluded spot—there is minimal foot traffic, relative quiet, and a window. You open your laptop and get to work.

After reading this chapter, you will get answers to several questions you've been curious about:

Have You Ever Wondered?

7.1	What is consciousness?
7.2	How does attention work?
7.3	Why do we sleep?
7.4	Why do we dream?
7.5	What are other ways to alter consciousness?
7.6	How do drugs impact consciousness?

Learning Objectives

LO 7.1	Explain different levels of consciousness and the survival advantages consciousness provides.
LO 7.2	Explain how our powers of attention help us both acquire and miss information.
LO 7.3	Summarize the importance and functions of sleep.
LO 7.4	Compare and contrast theories that attempt to explain the purpose of dreaming.
LO 7.5	Describe how flow, mindfulness, meditation, and hypnosis influence our consciousness.
LO 7.6	Describe the effects of using drugs to alter consciousness.

CONSCIOUSNESS

?

Have You Ever Wondered?
7.1 What is consciousness?

Consciousness: Your awareness of, and responsiveness to, your surroundings and mental processes.

>> **LO 7.1 Explain different levels of consciousness and the survival advantages consciousness provides.**

We all want to make sense of ourselves and the world around us.

To do that, you must be aware of what you're experiencing. That is, you must be fully present and cognizant of the sights, sounds, smells, touches, and tastes you encounter. That awareness all takes place in your conscious mind. **Consciousness** involves your awareness of, and responsiveness to, your surroundings and mental processes. If you just thought, "that sounds deep," thank your consciousness. It also allows you to acknowledge your own thoughts, feelings, and memories (Roth, 2000). Because of that, you're also conscious that you exist.

To fully understand consciousness, we need to discuss its roots, different levels, potential advantages, and consciousness in other animals.

Levels of Consciousness

When you think about it, your ability to contemplate your own thoughts is a little weird.

Even now, as you read these words, your brain is processing black and white symbols, perceiving them as meaningful letters, forming them into words, and then formulating thoughts. It's mind-blowing, really. Yet, for a long time in psychology, the prevailing belief from behaviorism was that the study of human behavior only needed to focus on stimuli and responses. These days, that type of strict exclusion of the conscious mind has fallen out of favor. That's because although thought processes are difficult to study, we recognize that consciousness factors into nearly everything we do.

We now recognize that consciousness is multifaceted. Consciousness involves what we know takes place, but there is a lot going on that we don't realize. For example, the *unconscious* involves thoughts and experiences we are not aware of and may be unable to access (Boag, 2017). We'll talk about this more in other chapters when we discuss many of Sigmund Freud's ideas.

There's also a sort of in-between consciousness level. The *preconscious* consists of those things we aren't thinking about currently but can easily call to mind (Boag, 2017). You weren't thinking about how comfortable these library chairs are—but now you are. That information was in your preconscious (or what some colloquially refer to as your subconscious) but easily retrievable into consciousness.

The preconscious has everyday implications. A recent study from China asked participants to look at a screen and indicate when a face first entered their consciousness (Wang et al., 2019). Researchers manipulated this by slowly decreasing each face's transparency, so that it faded in slowly. This meant that the face was there and potentially visible before participants acknowledged that they saw it. Results showed that some faces moved from preconscious to conscious more easily than others. Specifically, participants took longer to become consciously aware of neutral faces and were quicker to acknowledge both less and more trustworthy faces. This shows that information enters our consciousness at different rates depending on what we're perceiving and that consciousness may be tied to survival instincts and priorities like whom to trust.

Your consciousness also makes you attentive to your surroundings. From your library chair, you can consider what's going on in the minds of those looking for books in the stacks, contemplate where those walking down a path are coming from, or even ponder what your future holds. Being able to simultaneously navigate awareness of your internal and external worlds is a key component of a conscious being.

You're also *self-conscious* (Morin, 2006). Self-awareness allows you to know what you're doing (e.g., I'm sitting in a comfy chair reading psychology) and to know that you're the one doing it (e.g., "I'm the one responsible for turning pages and taking notes"). You're also self-aware about the fact that others are watching you, perhaps judging you, and forming their own thoughts and opinions (e.g., "that person's studying, they must be a serious student").

Survival Advantages

Why are we conscious?

It probably didn't evolve by accident. According to evolutionary psychologists, consciousness gives us an advantage: It helps us survive (Pinker, 1997). Because

Do our pets have the same kind of consciousness as humans?

iStock.com/Eva Blanco

we have *sentience,* the ability to know ourselves subjectively, we can seek out positive experiences that promote good feelings (happiness, contentment) and avoid negative ones. Like a time-traveler, you can conjure up experiences in your past, consider your present feelings about them, and then ponder what the future might bring. For example, we might think, "Because I studied in the library and did well on tests before, I should do well again." We can strategize (e.g., "In the morning, fewer people use the library, so it will be quieter"). Navigating a library certainly isn't a survival experience. But hopefully you can appreciate how consciousness provides evolutionary advantages that help us avoid danger, find resources, and keep us safe.

Animal Consciousness

It's easy to wonder what's going on in our pets' heads.

Do they know what they look like and that they're cute? Do they recognize loneliness or joy or other emotions? Can our pets remember traumas? Can they tell time?

Pet owners routinely marvel at their beloved pet's sleeping schedule, positions, and relative drowsiness throughout the day. But is your dog or cat self-aware? It's difficult to answer that question because animals can't self-report their internal experiences. Despite this obstacle, neuroscientists in Cambridge determined that "the weight of evidence indicates that humans are not unique in possessing the neurological substrates that generate consciousness" (Low, 2012). Some evidence of animals' self-awareness comes from the *sniff test,* in which dogs are able to recognize their own smell (Horowitz, 2017).

When considering which animals may have consciousness, it's easy to first think of apes (because of their similarity to us). However, research shows that crows, in addition to being clever, also display signs of consciousness (Nieder et al., 2020). Based on analyses of brain signals in response to a series of lights, scientists concluded that "the last common ancestors of humans and crows lived 320 million years ago. . . . It is possible that the consciousness of perception arose back then and has been passed down ever since" (University of Tübingen, 2020).

Sage Vantage   Practice what you learn in **Knowledge Check 7.1**

HOW ATTENTION WORKS

?

Have You Ever Wondered?
7.2 How does attention work?

>> **LO 7.2** **Explain how our powers of attention help us both acquire and miss information.**

The world is full of information.

Being able to focus is an increasingly valuable skill—so choosing to study in spaces like the library is probably a good idea if it means fewer distractions. Attention is focused consciousness. In high-stimulation settings like a concert, you may shift your awareness between the music, lyrics, instruments, listening to your friend, and wondering why the floor is so sticky. As you do, each aspect enters your consciousness and the rest recedes into the background. How does this happen?

Harnessing attention over time and maintaining focus is *attention span* (Levin & Bernier, 2011). Attention spans may be shifting. A recent study of older adults (ages 37–60) found those who preferred paper reading had longer attention spans than those who preferred digital/Internet reading (Medvedskaya, 2022). When teachers in Turkey gave their opinions about students' attention span, they thought that student attention spans are problematic and largely the students' fault (Cicekci & Sadik, 2019). Notably, the students themselves admitted their own role but also noted issues with the teacher and the surrounding environment.

The world is constantly engaging your senses (Domijan, 2003). But you have a filtering capability called **selective attention**. There's a lot going on around you, but not everything enters consciousness. We miss some things on purpose by focusing consciousness on what we consider most important. For example, at the library, you can selectively attend to what you study and ignore everything else (good choice). Later when you go to take your midterm, you'll need to ignore the sniffling and coughing of neighboring students, the buzz of the overhead lights, the uncomfortable chair, and the slamming of the door as each student leaves and pay attention only to the questions on the test. In each instance, you're precisely paying attention to one source of information while screening out the others. It's also true that we miss some things accidentally.

Selective attention: Intentional focusing of consciousness toward a particular stimulus, while filtering out the rest.

Consider a variety of interesting psychological phenomena related to how attention works.

The Cocktail Party Effect

Imagine yourself in a packed dining hall, party, or nightclub.

In those settings, it's difficult to fully hear or understand others, sometimes even when they're right next to you. But amid all the noise and conversation, if someone says your name, you hear it. This *cocktail party effect* demonstrates our unique ability to focus on our own name while screening out the rest. The selective hearing behind the cocktail party effect results from our brain processing the desired target and screening out the rest, a very useful form of selective attention (Mesgarani & Chang, 2012). So far, artificial intelligence has a difficult time mimicking this skill—which is why Siri and Alexa sometimes chime in when you didn't want them.

Technology like driving simulators can test people's ability to multitask.

iStock.com/NoSystem Images

Multitasking

Lots of people think they're good at multitasking.

Our powers of selective attention may give us a false sense of confidence. Research indicates overall, multitasking is quite difficult. For example, one study had participants simply look at digit-letter pairs (like "A4") and identify if the number was odd or even or decide if the letter was a vowel or consonant (Rogers & Monsell, 1995). Easy enough, right? When participants did only one of these two tasks in consecutive trials, they were quick. But if they switched back and forth from identifying odd numbers to vowels and consonants, they were 20% slower making their decisions. In other words, shifting attention between multiple tasks slowed them down.

A more relevant example to your life might be a second study that asked people to watch TV and use their computer simultaneously (Brasel & Gips, 2011). Have you ever tried it? Researchers found that (1) participants shifted their attention back and forth from the computer to the TV show an average of four times per minute, (2) they had no idea they were shifting attention so frequently, and (3) they only correctly recalled 12% of the changes in focus. So the TV show was much more distracting than they realized.

Here's the good news: Many people claim greater efficiency from multitasking. For students, checking their electronic device (phone, tablet, or laptop) during a lecture didn't hurt their comprehension of the material when tested *that same day*. In addition, multitasking across different forms of media (e.g., phone, music, computer, TV) may improve emotions. That sounds like a good excuse to use your phone during class.

But here's the bad news: Multitasking lowered *long-term* retention, which resulted in lower grades overall (Glass & Kang, 2019; Wang & Tchernev, 2012). This is why when you study or go to class, you should put your electronics away, to eliminate temptation.

Multitasking may feel good—but it isn't good for you, and you're not as good at it as you think. Multitasking overloads regions within the brain's frontal cortex, where critical decisions are made (Strayer et al., 2011). That is why talking or texting on your cell phone impairs driving in a way similar to legal intoxication. You're "out of it" because your attention is divided.

SPOTLIGHT ON RESEARCH METHODS

Multitasking on the Road

To make driving safer, applied psychology researchers navigate between tight ethical guardrails. We can't risk injury to participants. Fortunately, psychologists are a creative bunch, and when researchers can't have participants hit the road, they bring the road to the participants with driving simulators.

In one study, when participants sat down in their "1966 Ford Mustang," they saw a mock dashboard and looked out through a "windshield" and over the hood to reveal a blue sky dappled with white puffy clouds, mountains on the horizon, and the road outstretched in front of them (Nijboer et al., 2016). The simulator included an instrument panel, steering wheel, foot pedals, turn signals, and rearview mirror. This allowed researchers to dictate precise driving conditions and other cars' behavior. The simulator also recorded driving data for how well participants stayed in their lane, driving speed, steering, use of turn signals, and the beautifully euphemistic "contact with other cars" (crashes—they measured crashes.)

Researchers randomly assigned drivers to navigate either a traffic-free lane or a lane with substantial traffic that required drivers to pass other cars. Drivers in *both* conditions had to drive while performing a series of secondary tasks such as listening to the radio (a public radio talk show), answering questions via a radio quiz,

and using a tablet like an iPad to take a quiz. They also had a period where they drove without any secondary task. To incentivize good performance, participants received a financial reward for earning points on the quizzes.

Forty-eight participants "drove" for 2 hours. Driving performance was worst when they used the tablet and best when they listened to the radio or participated in the radio quiz. Using the tablet brought on all kinds of trouble: swerving, leaving their lane more, sharper steering corrections, slower driving, and—you guessed it—more crashes.

Surprisingly, listening to the radio helped driving. This result aligns with other research showing that listening to music increased driver arousal and improved their response times to a lead vehicle's changes in speed (Ünal et al., 2013). This suggests that listening can help break up the monotony of driving and keep the driver more engaged.

While it's unclear whether driving simulators are accurate and valid measures of actual, real-world driving (Caffò et al., 2020), they are the safest way to test for the potential dangers of texting while driving. This study indicates that while it's easy to convince ourselves that multitasking while driving is safe, it's not. ●

Inattentional Blindness

Even when we are not multitasking, we still miss things.

No one's perfect. But you may be surprised by just how much you can miss. You can even miss what's right in front of you. It's so bad that if you had to simply count the number of students walking back and forth on the path outside your window, you could completely miss the campus mascot running through. This phenomenon is known as **inattentional blindness**: the failure to detect unexpected objects, even when they are fully visible.

Inattentional blindness: The failure to detect unexpected objects, even though they are fully visible.

You will want to experience this for yourself. Take a moment to Google a short (< 2 minute) video called "The Monkey Business Illusion." (Trust us, it is worth it.) Count the number of times people on the same team pass a ball back and forth (Chabris & Simons, 2010). Simple? Yes, but you'll need to pay attention. They do make it a bit more challenging by having several people on screen at a time with some wearing black and others wearing white. Focus only on the passes by those wearing white. Try it before reading the next paragraph.

Welcome back:

- How many passes did you see? For "The Monkey Business Illusion," the correct answer is 16.

- How many apes did you see? The correct answer is 1.

Did you also notice that the curtain changed color, or that a player with a black shirt left the game? Probably not, even though those things happened in plain sight. This all happened when you were specifically asked to pay attention. Research shows inattentional blindness is even worse (90% of participants missed the unexpected event) when people are engaged in another activity, such as talking on a cell phone (Scholl et al., 2003). Recent research finds that even when participants indicate they did not see the key object, they do seem to notice it unconsciously, as indicated by participants being more accurate when taking guesses about the unexpected object (Kreitz et al., 2020).

In this famous video, many viewers miss obvious things the first time they watch it due to inattentional blindness.
Source: Simons and Chabris (1999).

Change Blindness

Are you shocked by how much you missed during that exercise?

Perhaps you're thinking exercises involving monkey suits and counting basketball passes are a bit artificial. Don't worry; we miss obvious changes in real life as well. *National Geographic* Channel's television show *Brain Games* tried this in an episode called "The Switcheroo." On the show, people approached a counter to fill out a form. Behind the counter, the person they were initially talking to ducks down to get a pen. When they pop back up, it's not the same person. Most people didn't notice the mid-conversation switch.

How does this happen? Researchers call this **change blindness**, a phenomenon where people fail to notice obvious variations in their environment (Levin & Baker, 2015). Though we may overestimate our individual ability to notice changes, when prompted, we are able to acknowledge that some details would be harder to track than others (Barnas & Ward, 2022). For example, change is easier to detect in objects but

Change blindness: The failure to notice obvious variations in their environment.

more difficult to detect in shadows, perhaps due to a shadow's ever-changing nature or because it typically falls toward the bottom of a scene (Hermens & Zdravković, 2022). Though we generally like to think that we completely and accurately notice everything in the world around us, knowing that we can make mistakes is useful.

Luckily, your notes aren't subject to change and your ability to pay attention comes in handy when you're studying. But all that focus can be tiring.

Sage Vantage

Practice what you learn in **Knowledge Check 7.2**

SLEEP

Have You Ever Wondered?
7.3 Why do we sleep?

>> **LO 7.3**   **Summarize the importance and functions of sleep.**

What happens when we're asleep and not fully conscious?

Most of the time, you're a fully present and active participant in your immediate experiences. Other times, when you're an hour into studying at the library—especially if you're staying up late—your mind wanders. You begin to think about the weekend, friends, and bed. Sure enough, you start to feel drowsy and feel yourself begin to slip away. Your immediate surroundings seem further and further away as you fall asleep. That transition, from being fully in the moment to allowing your mental focus to drift, shows how easily our awareness shifts. But what causes us to slip into sleep, and what happens to our brain?

Circadian Rhythm and Our Biological Clock

Do you ever feel like life falls into a certain rhythm?

Whether it's changing seasons or the daily shift from day to night, it's hard not to fall into a pattern. Who among us hasn't pulled an all-nighter, either for pleasure (traveling or a fun night out with friends) or out of necessity (a procrastination-inspired paper writing session)? Regardless of the reason, the next day was rough. You're not only extra tired because you didn't sleep, but you're now off your regular routine. Each of us has a default, internal schedule known as a **circadian rhythm**, which regulates bodily functions such as wakefulness, hormone levels, and body temperature across a 24-hour cycle (Monk, 2000).

This "biological clock" is set in part through light exposure. The brain's *suprachiasmatic nucleus*, which is located where the optic nerves cross in the brain, is light sensitive and helps regulate wakefulness (Pace-Schott & Hobson, 2002). However, even if you were placed into a cave or room without any light, sun exposure, or clocks, your circadian rhythms would still adhere roughly to the day's 24-hour cycle (Lavie, 2001). Circadian rhythms correspond with the geophysical day–night cycle in part due to melatonin, a darkness-induced hormone produced in the brain's pineal gland.

Circadian rhythm: The body's default schedule that regulates bodily functions such as wakefulness, hormone levels, and body temperature across a 24-hour cycle.

Early Birds Versus Night Owls

Individuals' circadian rhythms share common features.

For example, most people sleep between midnight and 6:00 a.m. However, some of us are night owls who are more alert in the evening, while others are early birds who are more energetic in the morning. Why? It's probably related to circadian rhythms associated with hormone levels and body temperature (Adan et al., 2012).

Being more of a morning or a night person has implications for behavior. On average, early birds are more punctual (Werner et al., 2015) and emotionally stable (Muro et al., 2009).

Night owls are more likely to engage in emotional eating (Konttinen et al., 2014) and have lower overall GPAs (Preckel et al., 2013), despite being more intelligent (Kanazawa & Perina, 2009).

Preference for morning or evening also correlates with personality (Lipnevich et al., 2017). Those who prefer the morning are more conscientious and less anxious; those who prefer the evening are more extraverted and open.

While circadian rhythm has a genetic component (Klei et al., 2005), your surroundings and peers can also impact your sleep schedule. Even the biggest "morning person" will become less so if their friends routinely encourage them to stay out past midnight. Either way, staying up late studying can lead to your eyes getting heavy. You sink down in your comfy library chair promising yourself to only close your eyes for a moment.

The Stages of Sleep

What happens to your brain when you fall asleep?

As you transition from awake toward sleep, you go through predictable stages. As you do, your brain waves change, which researchers detect with EEGs (see the chapter on the brain for EEGs in general [Chapter 3] and Figure 7.1 for EEGs during sleep):

- When you're fully awake and alert, your brain gives off *beta waves* (or sometimes gamma waves), high-frequency brain waves associated with intense attention (i.e., ideal study conditions).

- As you get more comfortable, drowsy, and begin to drift off to asleep, your brain shifts into *alpha waves.*

FIGURE 7.1

EEG Brain Waves

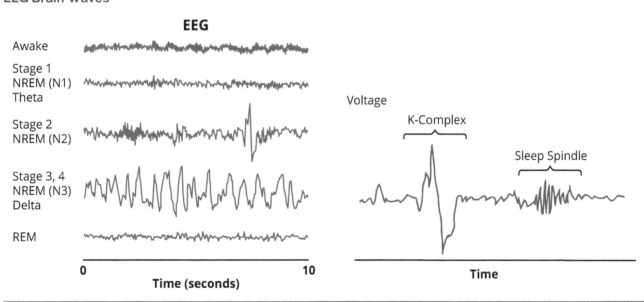

CORDELIA MOLLOY/Science Source

Stages 1 and 2: Progressing From Light to Deep Sleep

As you drift off, your EEG shows that you transition from the alpha waves of drowsiness to *theta waves* indicating Stage 1 of sleep. This is the lightest stage when you're most easily awakened. During this stage, you may experience an unintentional jerking of your limbs, called a *myoclonic twitch*. You may also feel like you're floating or falling, and you could experience brief auditory or visual hallucinations as cortical connectivity breaks down (Massimini et al., 2005). Although your brain is still quite active, each part is less in sync than it is while you're awake.

You spend very little time in Stage 1 and quickly move to Stage 2. There you fall into a deeper sleep where you're less aware of the outside world. Your EEG slows down and displays periodic bursts of small-wave *sleep spindles* and occasional large-wave *K-complexes* (Figure 7.1). Some speculate that sleep spindles and K-complexes (along with other mechanisms) operate as "guardians of sleep" that help screen out external stimuli (Parrino & Vaudano, 2018). No longer do noises or lights easily wake you up. Anyone who passes you in the library will easily notice that you're asleep.

Stages 3 and 4: Deep Sleep and REM

About an hour after falling asleep, you experience Stages 3 and 4, collectively known as either slow-wave or deep sleep. Here, the EEG registers slow *delta waves* between 2 and 4 Hertz. For a sense of just how slow this is, individuals in a coma register delta waves of 1 Hz. During this stage, you're very difficult to wake up. Despite the slow waves, your body experiences a lot of muscle activity, and you may talk in your sleep (a potentially embarrassing consequence of falling asleep in public—just hope you only mention your midterms!).

After hitting slow-wave sleep, you proceed back to Stage 1. The entire cycle takes about 90 minutes (shown in Figure 7.2).

After that first cycle of moving from Stage 1 to Stage 4 and back to Stage 1, you also experience **REM**, or a period of sleep characterized by rapid eye movements. During this period, an observer can easily see your eyes moving back and forth under your eyelids. Though your eyes experience a lot of movement, the rest of you is almost completely still. During REM, you experience *sleep paralysis* (Brooks & Peever, 2012), during which most of your muscles completely relax and you get a bit floppy. This

REM: A period of sleep characterized by rapid eye movements, a still body, and an active brain, including dreaming.

FIGURE 7.2

Stages of Sleep

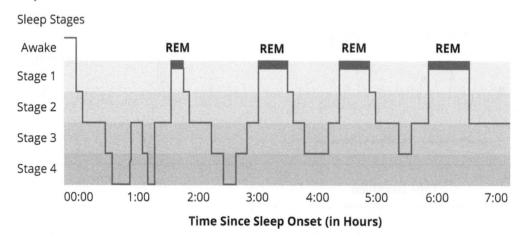

Source: Garrett and Hough (2022).

experience of *atonia,* or a lack of muscle control, leaves you drooling on your pillow and unable to engage in sleepwalking or other movement.

Therefore, people don't sleepwalk during REM; it's our body's way of making sure we don't physically act out our dreams. The only part of our body that defies this paralysis is our genitals. During REM, we experience erections or clitoral engorgement that are completely independent of any dream content.

Due to these contradictory processes, REM is often considered *paradoxical sleep.* During this time in REM sleep, your brain is in a state of alert wakefulness with EEGs showing beta waves of 19 to 23 Hz. Although your brain is active and likely dreaming, thanks to atonia, your body can't move.

Figure 7.2 shows that throughout the night, you'll experience between 4 and 5 REM periods about 90 minutes apart, with each period lasting around 20 minutes. If you experience insufficient REM sleep, either from not sleeping enough or not sleeping deeply enough, you will experience *REM rebound,* in which your REM periods get extended.

Following each REM period, you will cycle through the non-REM stages, all the way back to Stage 4, and then return to REM. Within this cycle, the best time to awaken is immediately after a REM period because your brain waves are most similar to when you're awake (both produce beta waves). The worst time to wake up is during deep slow-wave sleep. This is why sometimes we feel alert and rested when we wake up (from Stage 1 or from REM) and why we sometimes feel groggy and disoriented (from Stage 4, probably from an alarm clock).

Tracking Your Sleep

Do you get enough sleep?

As "wearable" technologies such as the Fitbit and Apple Watch have grown in popularity, so has interest in tracking a range of health-related outcomes, including sleep. Users typically wear these devices on their wrist and use them to gather data on time spent awake versus asleep, as well as how much time was spent in each sleep cycle. But are these devices accurate enough to be worthwhile?

First, it's useful to know that scientists measure sleep cycles with a *polysomnography* test, which involves attaching electrodes to the person's scalp and skin to measure eye movements and brain waves, in addition to gathering other data on breathing, blood oxygen levels, and heart rate (Gao et al., 2022). Compare that with actigraphy, which estimates sleep activity based on physical movements measured by a device's accelerometer, and you might expect the wearables to be less accurate. You would be correct (Tryon, 2004). In particular, wearable devices tend to underestimate the amount of deep sleep users get, in some cases by 46 minutes (Lee et al., 2019). Similarly, wearable monitors were only 38% accurate at tracking how long it took participants to fall asleep (Conley et al., 2019).

Though wearable actigraphy measures are understandably less accurate than a polysomnography test, wearables are not completely useless. Wearable sleep trackers accurately identify sleep versus wakefulness approximately 78% of the time (Conley et al., 2019). Accuracy goes up when the devices are

Can your watch really tell you how well you're sleeping?

iStock.com/YakobChukOlena

newer models that include heart rate and are better for night sleep than during the day (Gao et al., 2022; Roberts et al., 2020).

Finally, a word of caution when using these devices. How much sleep you get may not be as important as how much you *think* you're getting. One study varied the feedback participants received by manipulating the "sleep score" from their device (Gavriloff et al., 2018). One group was led to believe they had a bad night's sleep, while the other group thought they got a good night's sleep—when in reality, both groups were about equal. But the false feedback led the "bad sleep" group to report worse moods, more sleepiness, and less alertness the next day.

PSYCHOLOGY AND OUR CURIOUS WORLD

Sleep Paralysis and Frankenstein

iStock.com/PatriciaPix

If you're ever in Philadelphia with some free time, visit the Mütter Museum. It's devoted to historical medical instruments, strange cases, and physiological oddities. One of the first displays you might see is about the medical aspects of sleep paralysis and how the unnerving experience is tied to one of the most famous horror novels of all time: Mary Shelley's *Frankenstein*.

When we awake from REM, our mind might become alert while our body is still paralyzed—a scary feeling. We might feel like we can't breathe, and sometimes we even experience brief auditory or visual hallucinations (like mini-dreams). Before people had a scientific explanation, sometimes these spooky feelings were interpreted as supernatural or even demonic.

In the 1830 edition of *Frankenstein*, Shelley describes how her own experience of sleep paralysis inspired her imagination. She was terrified by the feeling of having a body she couldn't control and decided to frighten others in a similar way. This experience led to her classic novel about a scientist who creates a "monster" from stolen cadavers (although one of the important themes is the question of which is the real monster—the doctor or his creation).

Other famous authors have also vividly described waking but being unable to move; the list includes Herman Melville, F. Scott Fitzgerald, Ernest Hemingway, and more (Sharpless & Doghramji, 2015). ●

The Purpose of Sleep

Why is sleep important?

Here are four possible explanations for why we sleep:

- *Evolutionary adaptation:* Sleep allows us to conserve energy when we're not performing vital functions (e.g., looking for food). Sleep protects us from harm during a time of day that is potentially dangerous (e.g., nocturnal predators, it's colder outside).

- *Restoration:* Sleep gives our body and brain a chance to perform housekeeping and maintenance (Xie et al., 2013). During sleep, we're able to restore tissue, build up neurotransmitters, and replenish brain energy (Benington & Heller, 1995; Petit et al., 2015). The pituitary gland releases a hormone in deep sleep that supports growth (Van Cauter & Copinschi, 2000).

- *Learning:* Sleep consolidates memory with slow-wave processing and activates memory traces, and REM helps stabilize them (Diekelmann & Born, 2010). Participants had better recall of a list of foreign vocabulary words when they were able to sleep following learning (Mazza et al., 2016).

- *Feeds creative thinking:* Ever notice how you often wake up with the solution to a problem you were thinking about before falling asleep? There is evidence that sleep promotes creative thinking, in part due to memory replay (Lewis et al., 2018).

Regardless of the underlying explanation, we need to sleep . . . even if it's in an uncomfortable library chair.

Bad Sleep

When we don't get enough sleep, there are costs.

Sleep affects general health, cardiovascular health, metabolic health, immunological health, human performance, cancer, pain, mortality, and mental health (Watson et al., 2015). People who get lower-quality sleep report greater anger, anxiety, and stress (Minkel et al., 2012). Poor-quality sleep increases risk of motor vehicle accidents (Hershner & Chervin, 2014), depression (Dinis & Bragança, 2018), and pain sensitivity the next day (Rosseland et al., 2018). It may also worsen your mood at school, compromise learning (Hershner & Chervin, 2014), lower GPA, and decrease likelihood of graduating (Chen & Chen, 2019).

With that in mind, how much sleep do you need? It matters for your brain. A recent study found that those who got 6 to 8 hours of sleep had more gray matter volume (Tai et al., 2022). A joint recommendation from the American Academy of Sleep Medicine and the Sleep Research Society suggests that adults need 7 hours of sleep (Watson et al., 2015). Experts agree that less than 6 hours a night is problematic, and most experts think over 9 hours is unnecessary. That said, these are general guidelines and there is no absolute magic number for everyone. In fact, the idea that we need to sleep for 8 hours at night is a modern idea from postindustrial times. For most of human existence, it was not the norm. Instead, our ancestors likely had less regular sleep schedules that included frequent naps.

The Power of the Nap

If you don't get the recommended amount of nighttime sleep, that may explain napping at the library. Why do college students (along with many others, including intro psych textbook authors) nap? To find out, researchers asked a diverse group of 430 students, "When you nap, even if only very rarely, why do you choose to nap?" (Duggan et al., 2018). Within the hundreds of responses, five key themes emerged: catching up on sleep, working odd hours, because it's enjoyable, to refocus or boost attention, and to deal with mood or emotions.

Naps also help memory and learning. For example, when 3-month-old infants saw a cartoon face, they were better able to remember it later when they took a nap after seeing the face (Horváth et al., 2018). Similarly, when young adults learned factual knowledge and then took a 1-hour nap, they did better on a test 30 minutes later, compared to a group who took a break but not a nap (Cousins et al., 2019). Naps also lower your heart rate, which supports cardiovascular health (Whitehurst et al., 2018), and have physical and mental benefits for the elderly (Arakaki et al., 2019). Regular nappers may have advantages at some perceptual learning tasks (McDevitt et al., 2018), although they suffer more than nonnappers if forced to skip their usual nap (Ru et al., 2019).

Research indicates that "coffee naps" are more refreshing than either caffeine or naps alone.

iStock.com/ATHVisions

OK, let's get to the stuff you might really care about: Does science suggest how to take the *best* naps? Yes! They're called "coffee naps." This is the strategy:

- Immediately before you want to nap, get in bed and drink some caffeine.

- Then, sleep for no more than 20 minutes (set an alarm).

Why is this helpful? It takes caffeine about 20 minutes to get into your bloodstream and affect you. Plus, waking after only 20 minutes stops your brain from progressing to Stage 4 sleep, avoiding those slow delta waves. You should wake up energized and refreshed, just when the caffeine kicks in. Research shows the "coffee nap" is more effective than either caffeine alone or naps alone (Hayashi et al., 2003; Horne & Reyner, 1996).

Sleep Problems

Are you constantly tired?

Ideally, you would always get a full night's sleep, wake up rested, and ready to take on the day. That's not the reality for many people. Sleep deprivation, or times when you aren't getting enough sleep, is common and especially noticeable in the workplace (Munafo et al., 2018). There are negative physiological and psychological consequences: reduced brain gray matter, increased anxiety, and less adaptability to change, which can hurt job and academic performance (Goldstein-Piekarski et al., 2018; Honn et al., 2019).

These deficits have clear implications for paying attention in class. Studies find that better sleep quality is linked with better grades in college students (among other benefits; Okano et al., 2019). Importantly, the key determinant wasn't how well students slept the night before a test but rather their sleep quality over the previous month. Just like studying, cramming your sleep in the last minute isn't as effective as quality sleep spaced out over time.

Causes of sleep disruption:

- *Insomnia,* or the inability to fall asleep or stay asleep despite being tired. Approximately 30% to 40% of U.S. adults indicate symptoms of insomnia (Dopheide, 2020).

- *Sleep apnea,* a disorder where someone stops breathing for a period of time and often wakes up gasping for air. One review study found that an average of 17% of women and 22% of men suffer from sleep apnea (Franklin & Lindberg, 2015), and its impact on daytime sleepiness is much greater than snoring alone (Sánchez & Buela-Casal, 2007).

- *Night terrors,* where people flail their arms and scream in terror while in a deep sleep, then wake with little memory for it happening (Schredl, 2001). Night terrors are especially common in children and often relate to stressors such as school problems, parental divorce, and hospitalizations.

In contrast to difficulty sleeping, *narcolepsy* involves an uncontrollable and sudden onset of sleep. Someone afflicted with narcolepsy could fall asleep right in the middle of any activity, with little forewarning. Narcolepsy affects only 0.05% of the population and is more prevalent among first-degree relatives, which suggests a genetic component (Ohayon et al., 2005).

A more common and less severe sleep disorder is sleepwalking, known more formally as *somnambulism*. Sleepwalkers appear to be awake but are actually in deeply slow-wave sleep (not REM, as mentioned above). They can move around and even drive a car (Bollu et al., 2018) but are difficult to wake up or redirect to a different activity. Sleepwalking is more common in children, though adults are more prone to sleepwalking if they have other sleep issues (e.g., apnea) or are taking medication.

You can measure your own sleep problems with the *What's My Score?* feature.

WHAT'S MY SCORE?

Measuring Sleep Quality

Instructions: The following survey relates to the quality of sleep you had for the last month. Read the questions and indicate the closest answer.

0	1	2	3
Rarely, None, or 1–3 times a month	Sometimes, 1–2 times a week	Often, 3–5 times a week	Almost Always, or 6–7 times a week

____ 1. I have difficulty falling asleep.

____ 2. I fall into a deep sleep.

____ 3. I wake up while sleeping.

____ 4. I have difficulty getting back to sleep once I wake up in the middle of the night.

____ 5. I wake up easily because of noise.

____ 6. I toss and turn.

____ 7. I never go back to sleep after awakening during sleep.

____ 8. I feel refreshed after sleep.

____ 9. I feel unlikely to sleep again immediately after sleep.

____ 10. Poor sleep gives me headaches.

____ 11. Poor sleep makes me irritated.

____ 12. I would like to sleep more after waking up.

____ 13. My sleep hours are enough.

____ 14. Poor sleep makes me lose my appetite.

____ 15. Poor sleep makes it hard for me to think.

____ 16. I feel vigorous after sleep.

____ 17. Poor sleep makes me lose interest in work or others.

____ 18. My fatigue is relieved after sleep.

____ 19. Poor sleep makes me make mistakes at work.

____ 20. I am satisfied with my sleep.

____ 21. Poor sleep makes me forget things more easily.

____ 22. Poor sleep makes it hard to concentrate at work.

____ 23. Sleepiness interferes with my daily life.

____ 24. Poor sleep makes me lose desire in all things.

____ 25. I have difficulty getting out of bed.

____ 26. Poor sleep makes me easily tired at work.

____ 27. I have a clear head after sleep.

____ 28. Poor sleep makes my life painful.

Scoring instructions: First, reverse-score Items 8, 13, 16, 18, 20, and 27. That means if you wrote a "0" for these items, cross it off and write a "3" instead. Change a "1" response to a "2," change a "2" response to a "1," and finally, if you wrote a "3" response for any of these items, cross it off and write a "0" instead. For the other items, leave your original response as is.

Then, add up all 28 of your answers. Your total score should be between 0 and 84. The higher your score, the worse your sleep quality. In the study, insomniacs who had clear difficulty sleeping had an average score of 31.10 (*SD* = 13.61), while other "normal" subjects had an average score of 15.80 (*SD* = 9.06). While your score does not constitute a definitive diagnosis of sleep problems, if you have an elevated score, you may want to use the information in this chapter to help improve your sleeping habits. ●

Source: Yi et al. (2006).

Improve Your Sleep

You can take steps to sleep better.

Researchers have explored a variety of behaviors that can help sleep, from lifestyle changes to who you share a bed with.

Make Lifestyle Changes

There are activities you can do during your waking hours that benefit your sleep. Research studies show:

- Yoga improves sleep quality (Wang et al., 2020).

- Physical exercise improves college students' sleep quality (Li & Liu, 2013).

- Listening to music may matter; 62% of us report using music to help us fall asleep (Trahan et al., 2018). Note that what you listen to might matter—classical music seems to promote the best-quality sleep (Harmat et al., 2008).

Have you ever been tired, known you should go to bed, but find reasons to stay up anyway? Researchers call this *bedtime procrastination*. It's a key contributor to getting insufficient sleep, especially for those who struggle with controlling their own behavior (Kroese et al., 2014), who have more negative emotions and tend to ruminate (You et al., 2021), and who are more prone to boredom and fidgeting. All of these are tied to bedtime procrastination, which is often linked to smartphone addiction and lower sleep quality (Teoh et al., 2021; Zhang & Wu, 2020).

Avoid Electronics

The pattern has been replicated in countries around the world: Using your phone before (or while in) bed is associated with taking longer to fall asleep, having more sleep disturbances, getting worse sleep, and feeling worse the next day (Excelmans & Van den Bulck, 2016). For example, researchers found that for a sample of Iranian college students, late-night phone use was linked to insomnia as well as headaches, low energy, and tiredness the next day (Zarghami et al., 2015).

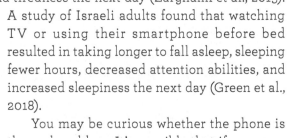

A study of Israeli adults found that watching TV or using their smartphone before bed resulted in taking longer to fall asleep, sleeping fewer hours, decreased attention abilities, and increased sleepiness the next day (Green et al., 2018).

You may be curious whether the phone is the real problem. It's possible that if you were doing something else, such as reading a book, it could have the same effect. Researchers tested this as well by comparing groups reading from an iPad versus a book. The iPad was more disruptive to sleep, perhaps because it emits light (Grønli et al., 2016). Studies show that light exposure hurts sleep quality and contributes to daytime sleepiness (Green et al., 2017). It wasn't the intensity of the light, but the wavelength, with short-wavelength light (i.e., blue light) being more problematic (Jniene et al., 2019; Silvani et al., 2022). This happens to be the type of light your device (phone, tablet, or laptop) is beaming toward you.

Do you listen to music or white/brown noise while trying to fall asleep?

iStock.com/sopradit

It's not just the light from your phone that's a problem; it's also what's on the screen. A systematic review of the literature found consistent evidence that social media use is associated with not only poor sleep quality but also poor mental health (Alonzo et al., 2021). Similarly, in a nationally representative sample of young adults from the United States, those who use social media before bed also had more disturbed sleep (Garett et al., 2018; Levenson et al., 2017). One study found that taking a break from social media increases well-being, in part due to better sleep quality (Graham et al., 2021). That's a simple way to improve sleep that you can easily implement tonight.

Consider Sleep Interventions

There is no shortage of sleep aids available to purchase, including pharmaceutical interventions like melatonin. Note that research on melatonin's efficacy is mixed, with very limited evidence regarding long-term implications (Besag et al., 2019; Costello et al., 2014; Kamkar et al., 2021).

There are also nonpharmacological options to improve sleep, such as noise machines and weighted blankets. White noise, a mix of random sound frequencies played at equal intensity, sounds like static, an electric fan, or heavy rain. To test whether white noise improves sleep, researchers had college students use white noise machines all night for a month (Forquer & Johnson, 2007). They found that students fell asleep quicker and woke up less frequently at night. Similar effects were found for patients of cardiac surgery (de Souza Machado et al., 2017). Some people also like "brown noise," which has a lower frequency and sounds more like wind or an airline jet; some research indicates it helps sleep quality and may improve concentration for people with conditions like attention-deficit/hyperactivity disorder (ADHD) as well (Pickens et al., 2018).

Preliminary research on weighted blankets' effectiveness looks promising for some, but not all, people. Some studies find no impact in children (France et al., 2018), while others found benefits (Lönn et al., 2023). Other studies with adults found weighted blankets helped with insomnia, allowing for a calmer and more refreshing night's sleep (Ackerley et al., 2015) and that it increased melatonin at bedtime (Meth et al., 2022). Among those diagnosed with ADHD and/or autism spectrum disorder, a weighted blanket helped people fall asleep, stay asleep throughout the night, and feel relaxed during the day (Bolic Baric et al., 2021).

Consider How You Sleep

You can also improve sleep without buying a thing. Obviously, slumbering in a library chair isn't the most comfortable sleep position imaginable. There are four main sleep positions people use: stomach/front, back, right side, and left side. College students mostly sleep on their right side (42.4%), followed by their left side (29.2%), stomach (17.8%), and back (10.6%; Arbinaga et al., 2018). Right-side sleepers reported worse sleep quality than left-side sleepers, while stomach sleepers reported more feelings of anger than other sleep positions.

Does your sleeping position influence how well you sleep at night?

iStock.com/Daria Golubeva

What about changing positions? Most people shift positions almost twice per hour, with women shifting less than men. Women are more likely to sleep on their right side than their back, while men are the opposite. And those who sleep on their stomach have dreams with more sexual content as well as more dreams about being locked up or tied up and unable to move (Yu, 2012).

Consider Who You Share Your Bed With

Of course, we don't always sleep alone, and our bed-sharing arrangements can affect sleep quality. Does having someone else in bed help or hurt sleep? To test this, researchers had individuals who regularly co-sleep with their partner alternate between sleeping together and sleeping alone, and then they compared their sleep quality (Drews et al., 2017). Participants reported sleeping better when their partner was with them, and this subjective feeling was supported by objective data showing more REM sleep and overall time asleep. A similar study replicated these results (Drews et al., 2020).

But wait…there's more. Those who considered their relationship a more significant part of their life experienced more synchronized sleep with their partner. In addition, when researchers compared married couples to a carefully matched group of never-married-but-living-together individuals (to make sure the groups were as similar as possible), they found that married participants had better REM sleep (Drews & Drews, 2021).

If you aren't sharing a bed with a relationship partner, perhaps a pet could be the next best thing! In fact, when researchers compared bed-sharing between parent/child pairs, adult couples, sibling pairs, and pet owners with their pets, they found that participants reported better sleep while sharing their bed—with no differences based on whom they slept with (Andre et al., 2021). That's encouraging because sharing a bed with a pet is common; in one study, 55% of people said they shared their bed with a dog and 31% shared with a cat (Hoffman et al., 2018). That same study found that, according to respondents, sleeping with a dog provided a sense of comfort and security. Cats, however, did not provide similar benefits [which Wind notes might be because they attack her in the morning when they decide it's time for breakfast!].

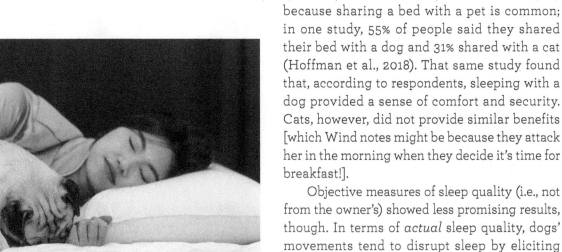

Should you let your dog sleep in bed with you?

iStock.com/Jomkwan

Objective measures of sleep quality (i.e., not from the owner's) showed less promising results, though. In terms of *actual* sleep quality, dogs' movements tend to disrupt sleep by eliciting movements from their human companions (Hoffman et al., 2020; Smith et al., 2018). Co-sleeping with a pet also makes it harder to fall asleep and increases the chances of waking up tired (Smith et al., 2014). So while people *report* better sleep with a pet in bed with them, likely due to emotional comfort, objective sleep measures indicate this might be a myth.

Check out Table 7.1 for a list of other common myths about our daily slumber.

TABLE 7.1

What Are Common Myths About Sleep?

TOP FIVE SLEEP MYTHS
1.   During sleep, the brain is not active.
2.   Being able to fall asleep "anytime, anywhere" is a sign of a healthy sleep system.
3.   Many adults need only 5 or fewer hours of sleep for general health.
4.   Your brain and body can learn to function just as well with less sleep.
5.   Lying in bed with your eyes closed is almost as good as sleeping.

Practice what you learn in **Knowledge Check 7.3**   Sage Vantage

DREAMS

>> **LO 7.4   Compare and contrast theories that attempt to explain the purpose of dreaming.**

To sleep, perchance to dream.

Although Shakespeare's Hamlet uttered these words in a state of worry, many of us look forward to our dreams, a collection of images and thoughts that take place during sleep. Some people think they don't dream because they can't remember their dreams. The ability to remember dreams varies, but waking up more frequently makes it easier to recall dreams (van Wyk et al., 2019). Dreams occur more frequently during REM sleep, with 80% of people reporting a dream when awakened during REM (Solms, 2003). Some dreams occur during slow-wave sleep, although less than half of participants report dreams during this time.

Types of Dreams

Not all dreams are the same.

Typically, dreams are illogical, provoke emotional and sensory response, and are out of your control—but not always. **Lucid dreaming** occurs when you become aware that you're dreaming and can then control your actions within the dream. With lucid dreaming, you get to choose your own adventure by deciding what to do next, like whether you want to fly or whether you want to wake up because the dream is too intense.

Lucid dreaming is common; about 73% of adults report having them (Stumbrys & Erlacher, 2016). When asked about the nature of their lucid dreams, most (83%) reported that they were trying to fulfill wishes or live out fantasies. Next most common was lucid dreaming to solve problems, overcome fears, and engage in mental/physical healing. Men were more likely to engage in wish fulfillment while women were more likely to overcome fears.

Do pets dream? We can't know for sure—but we do know that most mammals appear to experience some degree of REM sleep, although it varies by species

Have You Ever Wondered? 7.4 Why do we dream?

Lucid dreaming: A dream in which you become aware that you're dreaming and can then control your actions within the dream.

If you dreamt you were walking on a bridge, is there any hidden symbolic meaning to interpret?

iStock.com/baona

Manifest content: A dream's superficial content. What you actually see or experience in a dream.

Latent content: A dream's underlying or hidden meaning. The true meaning behind what you see or experience.

(Manger & Siegel, 2020). We'll probably never really know, but it would help if we understood the purpose of dreams in the first place. Psychologists have a few hypotheses.

Freud and Symbolism

If most of us dream, these dreams must serve a purpose (Eisner, 2005).

Though Freud gets a lot of credit for suggesting that dreams have special meaning, most cultures believe dreams have significance. People from both "Eastern" and "Western" cultures think it is possible to reveal hidden truths in dreams and that dreams can reveal insights into the world (Morewedge & Norton, 2009).

Freud's key contribution to the interpretation of dreams was the suggestion that dreams contain both **manifest content** that conveys the dream's obvious, superficial meaning and **latent content** or hidden, symbolic meaning. For example, when you dozed off in your library chair, you awoke from a dream where you were walking across a long narrow bridge and fell into the water. But that's the manifest content that masks the true meaning. The true meaning might be a parallel narrative that (a) you need to bring two sides together in your literature paper (hence the bridge), (b) you feel inadequate doing so (falling), and (c) you are hiding that you're emotionally overwhelmed and scared to fail (water).

This approach to understanding dreams relies heavily on symbolism to reveal the hidden unconscious and the person's repressed wishes. It leaves a lot up to interpretation. Freudian interpretations commonly evoke sexual symbolism where boxes, cases, chests, cupboards, ovens, and hollow objects symbolize a uterus, while anything phallic (i.e., pointy) such as a chimney, gun, pencil, pen, or sword symbolizes a penis. But others suggest that each person's symbols might be individual to them.

Brain Activity

Dreams may be more about function than fantasy.

If dream interpretation seems a bit far-fetched and anti-scientific, you're not alone. Many psychologists consider Freud's theory useful but highly speculative and in need of radical revision (e.g., Hobson, 1999). More modern theories have the benefit of new technology from neuropsychology. For example, *activation-synthesis theory* suggests that as we sleep, the brain experiences random neural signals (Hobson & McCarley, 1977). Dreams are our brain's attempt to make sense of that activation, but what form that interpretation takes is basically random and meaningless. It's also possible that dreams serve a basic physiological function and are simply providing the brain with the necessary stimulation for it to remain active.

More recently, *self-organization theory* suggests that dreams don't have an independent function but are a by-product of sleep in which the brain weaves different neuronal signals (i.e., pieces of a dream) into a narrative (Zhang & Guo, 2018). Dream content can include external stimuli and memories that need to be consolidated, or it can be a way to regulate emotions (Zhang, 2016). Thus, dreams are not symbolic or inherently meaningful, but rather represent a by-product of the sleeping person's recent mental and physical experiences.

Information Processing

Some days just feel like a lot to process.

Another hypothesis is that dreams facilitate *information processing* and help us add to our memories and organize them. Evidence for this idea is that dreams often include content relevant to what you did or thought about that day. For example, when participants in romantic relationships completed dream diaries for a week, those who were less secure about their relationship had dreams with more conflict, jealousy, anxiety, and stress (Selterman & Drigotas, 2009). World events can also impact our dream content; college students' dreams at the beginning of the COVID-19 pandemic included more virus-related themes (MacKay & DeCicco, 2020).

Dream content can influence our waking thoughts and behaviors as well. For example, participants who dreamt of a plane crash were more reluctant to fly, and those dreaming of a friend's betrayal expressed less affection toward that friend (Morewedge & Norton, 2009). If we *believe* our dreams have meaning, they can influence our waking world.

Emotion and Mood Regulation

Dreams may be therapeutic.

Pioneering sleep researcher Dr. Rosalind Cartwright also suggested that dreams play an important role in emotion and mood regulation. For example, in one of her studies, college students feeling a bit depressed (but not at clinical levels of depression) reported that over two nights, the content of their dreams became more positive—and so did their mood after sleep (Cartwright et al., 1998). Essentially, their dreams were therapeutic. Other researchers concur that while sleep is generally beneficial, it is time spent in REM sleep (dreaming) that primarily helps people deal with emotional or traumatic experiences (Walker & van der Helm, 2009).

Dreaming helps in other ways too. Dr. Cartwright found that when she gave college students problems to solve before and after sleeping or staying awake, those who slept and dreamed produced more successful solutions (Cartwright, 1974). Similarly, when researchers awakened sleeping participants during REM dreaming, they gained a 32% advantage in solving anagram puzzles compared to those awakened during non-REM periods (Walker et al., 2002). Taken together, these findings demonstrate the benefits of REM sleep and dreaming for emotion regulation and problem-solving.

Though sleep is the most recognizable and habitual way we shift consciousness, it is not the only one.

Dr. Rosalind Cartwright, an early pioneer on sleep research, was known as the "queen of dreams" until she passed away in 2021.

Rush University Medical Center Archives

Practice what you learn in **Knowledge Check 7.4**

Sage Vantage

ALTERED CONSCIOUSNESS

>> **LO 7.5 Describe how flow, mindfulness, meditation, and hypnosis influence our consciousness.**

Being awake or asleep aren't your only options.

As with many psychological phenomena, consciousness is not simply an either/or experience where you are fully awake or fully asleep. Rather, your consciousness at any

Have You Ever Wondered?
7.5 What are other ways to alter consciousness?

Altered consciousness: A state of consciousness that occurs any time you are outside of your typical mental state of being fully awake, aware, and alert.

moment resides on a continuum somewhere between those two extremes (Vaitl et al., 2005). This in between is where you experience altered consciousness, which occurs any time you are outside of your typical mental state of being fully awake, aware, and alert. Altered consciousness can happen slowly or spontaneously and from a range of experiences (Table 7.2).

TABLE 7.2

Causes of Altered Consciousness

CATEGORY	SOURCES
Disease	Coma, epilepsy, psychotic disorders, vegetative states
Pharmacological experiences	Drugs, fungi, plants
Physical experiences	Breathing/respiration, diet, extreme temperatures, sexual activity, starvation
Psychological experiences	Biofeedback, hypnosis, meditation, relaxation, rhythm-induced trance, sensory deprivation or overload
Spontaneous	Daydreaming, drowsiness, hypnagogic states, near-death experiences, sleep

Source: Adapted from Vaitl et al. (2005).

Daydreaming and Flow

Your consciousness can slip away, seemingly out of nowhere.

You've probably zoned out, or stopped paying attention, in boring class lectures (not in psychology, of course!) and imagined more fun things you could be doing. In that moment, you were *daydreaming,* which occurs when you spontaneously get lost in thought in a way that is unconnected to what you're doing or the immediate situation (Uleman & Bargh, 1989).

People often daydream unintentionally, but it can also result from a desire to deal with boredom or distress (Somer et al., 2016). Across multiple countries, the COVID-19 lockdown restrictions encouraged participants to spend more time fantasizing, which contributed to a stronger urge to daydream and more vivid daydreams (Somer et al., 2020). Interestingly, daydreaming coincides with worse cognitive performance and reading comprehension but may aid in problem-solving and planning (Mooneyham & Schooler, 2013).

Flow: A state that occurs when an individual becomes so fully immersed in an experience that everything else seems unimportant.

In the library, you also might find yourself locked in and completely focused on your notes—quite the opposite of daydreaming. That experience is flow, or a state that occurs when someone becomes so fully immersed in an experience that everything else fades away (Csikszentmihalyi, 2008). Mihaly Csikszentmihalyi (pronounced Me-high Cheek-sent-me-high-ee) suggests that flow is a highly enjoyable experience but can also lead people to persist in a task despite negative consequences.

Have you ever seen someone so focused on a game or activity on their phone that they accidentally run into something or trip? That's flow. If you've ever been working on a paper or project and lost track of time, that's flow as well. You can experience it playing sports, playing an instrument, reading, writing, playing video games, or simply thinking deeply.

Flow doesn't happen for everyone with the same level of ease. A study with over 10,000 twins from Sweden suggests that some individuals are more prone to flow than others (Ullén et al., 2016). While flow-proneness was not related to cognitive ability, it was correlated with conscientiousness, intrinsic motivation, emotional stability, extraversion, openness to experience, and agreeableness. You're also more likely to achieve flow as you get older.

Mindfulness

Be more mindful.

During your school's "De-Stress Fest" during finals last semester, you may have heard a lot about mindfulness, which involves becoming fully aware of and accepting of one's own thoughts, feelings, and bodily sensations in the present moment (Chu & Mak, 2020; Kristeller, 2019).

Mindfulness: A present-centered feeling achieved by being fully aware of and accepting of one's own thoughts, feelings, and bodily sensations.

Research on mindfulness's benefits is growing. Mindfulness helps people by increasing positive emotions, lowering stress, and helping people feel more aware, focused, relaxed, and well rested (Chu & Mak, 2020; Ramasubramanian, 2017; Sharma & Rush, 2014). When researchers compared mindfulness sessions to listening to an audiobook, mindfulness was more effective at lowering anxiety, depression, and stress (Strohmaier et al., 2021). Shorter 5-minute mindfulness sessions were more effective at decreasing stress than longer 20-minute sessions.

Like any intervention, mindfulness isn't universally positive. It's helpful up to a point but can backfire in excess (Britton, 2019). Furthermore, it might not be helpful to everyone. For example, it *increased* symptom distress in patients with cancer undergoing chemotherapy (Reynolds et al., 2017). Mindfulness researchers caution that though mindfulness has its benefits, the generalizability of its application is unknown (Van Dam et al., 2018).

Meditation can have positive mental and physical health benefits—and you can try it almost anywhere.

iStock.com/damircudic

There are several ways to encourage mindfulness (Davis & Hayes, 2011). For example, a body scan is a technique where you start at your feet and work upward toward your head, pausing along the way to focus on bodily sensations. Stretching or exercises like yoga and Pilates can also induce mindfulness, as can deep breathing.

Another common way to achieve mindfulness is through meditation.

Meditation

"Meditation: It's not what you think."

You saw that flier on the library's bulletin board, and you decide it can't hurt to give it a try. You close your eyes and focus your breath ... in ... out ... in ... out. ... You start to feel calm and focused.

This is the essence of meditation, or the deliberate practice of focused attention that promotes greater awareness. There are many different approaches, such as mindfulness (described above; Collier & Shi, 2020). Other forms of meditation require intense focus on a specific activity, object, sound, or thought. Techniques such as transcendental meditation have practitioners recite a mantra (specific words or phrases) for 20 minutes each day.

Meditation: The deliberate practice of focused attention that promotes greater awareness.

It's not clear what makes meditation effective, but we are fairly confident that its effects are real. Meditation can impact telomeres (the DNA structures that protect

You've probably seen hypnosis on TV or with stage performers—but can it really be used for anything in psychology?

iStock.com/redhumv

Hypnosis: A state of consciousness in which a person is highly susceptible to suggestion.

the ends of chromosomes from deterioration). These structures are positive biomarkers for health, and individuals who meditate more have longer telomeres (Schutte et al., 2020). Similarly, a meta-synthesis of randomized controlled trials including over 31,000 participants found that meditation had a significant effect on health, particularly in younger samples and for longer-term interventions (Rose et al., 2019). Those who achieved greater mindfulness experienced more positive emotions and fewer negative emotions.

Meditation is effective across cultures. MRI scans of adolescents' brains in California show that those who were trained in mindfulness meditation experienced changes in gray matter in areas related to emotional and physical awareness (Yuan et al., 2020). Among South African college students diagnosed with posttraumatic stress disorder (PTSD), those who practiced transcendental meditation had fewer symptoms of PTSD and depression (Bandy et al., 2020). Similarly, a research team from Iran found that transcendental meditation improved general health after a 12-week meditation course (Yunesian et al., 2008).

Meditation is something you can do by yourself for free, so it's a great option. The last option is a bit trickier.

Hypnosis

"Look into my eyes . . . you're getting sleepy."

At least, that's what hypnotists usually say on television and movies while dangling something shiny in front of someone's eyes. Actual **hypnosis**, which is a state of consciousness in which a person is highly susceptible to suggestion, is a bit less showy. At the initial induction stage, a therapist begins by helping someone quiet their mind and relax (Kubie & Margolin, 1944). Hypnosis's goal is an enhanced state of concentration that progressively eliminates sensation from the outside. This allows the inductee (the person getting hypnotized) to focus their attention on the therapist's directions, lose their anxiety, and be open to suggestions.

Is hypnosis real? An examination of cerebral blood flow with a positron emission tomography (PET) scan and brain electrical activity with an EEG found that hypnosis produced significant changes in both measures (Rainville et al., 1999). It has also been used to treat a range of issues. For example, when paired with cognitive behavioral therapy, those who underwent hypnosis lost nearly twice as much weight as those who did not have hypnosis, and they were able to keep the weight off at the 18-month follow-up (Kirsch et al., 1995). Hypnosis has also effectively reduced children's postoperative pain (Accardi & Milling, 2009) and can help people quit smoking (Carmody et al., 2008).

Though there are benefits to hypnosis, it shouldn't be considered a cure-all. First, some people are easier to hypnotize than others (Sheiner et al., 2016). It's also important to only seek treatments from licensed professionals. There are well-known cases where hypnosis has been misused (e.g., Kleinhauz & Beran, 1984). On a larger scale, the misuse of hypnosis was implicated in the "Satanic Panic" in the United States during the 1980s (Yuhas, 2021). At the time, a prevalent conspiracy theory conjectured that satanic cults were committing widespread child abuse, frequently in daycares. Several alleged pieces of evidence relied on "recovered memories" aided by hypnosis. However, research confirmed that hypnosis was fueling false "repressed" memories in highly suggestable patients (Coons, 1994; Loftus, 1996).

Of course, drugs are another way to experience altered consciousness; that's the topic of the final section of this chapter.

Practice what you learn in **Knowledge Check 7.5**   **Sage**Vantage**❯**

DRUGS AND CONSCIOUSNESS

>> **LO 7.6   Describe the effects of using drugs to alter consciousness.**

You may be using drugs and not even realize it.

Obvious drugs include alcohol, tobacco, sleeping aids, prescribed medication, or recreational drugs. However, any chemical compound that alters our consciousness, mood, or perception is a **psychoactive drug** (sometimes called "psychotropic"). The term *psychoactive* sounds intimidating, but you're ingesting a psychoactive drug in the iced coffee you brought with you to the library (caffeine).

You also have psychoactive drugs in your tea, soft drinks, energy drinks, chocolate, and over-the-counter medicines for a cold (NyQuil, Robitussin, etc.) or pain management (e.g., acetaminophen, aspirin). Of course, dosage for these substances plays a large role in their potential impact. But the fact remains that each substance affects your brain and subsequently how you interact with the world.

?
Have You Ever Wondered?
7.6 How do drugs impact consciousness?

Psychoactive drug: Any chemical compound that alters our consciousness, mood, or perception.

Types of Drugs

There are a lot of different drugs out there.

Let's cover some of the basics:

- *Depressants* ("downers") have a mellowing or calming effect that slows breathing and heart rate and are often used to facilitate sleep or relieve pain. When used excessively, these drugs (e.g., alcohol, barbiturates, benzodiazepines, toxic inhalants) can cause difficulty operating machinery, memory loss, brain damage, coma, or death. Doctors often prescribe depressants that are minor tranquilizers (e.g., Ativan, Valium, Xanax) to help alleviate anxiety.

- *Stimulants* ("uppers") boost energy, elevate mood, and suppress appetite. Stimulants are commonly used (e.g., caffeine, nicotine) and prescribed (e.g., Ritalin), but there are also illegal forms (like amphetamines, cocaine, MDMA/ecstasy, and methamphetamine). When users discontinue stimulants, they typically experience a "crash" that can be accompanied by irritability and headaches.

- *Opioids* are most used for pain management because they mimic the body's own endorphins. Opioids (e.g., codeine, heroin, morphine, and opium) have several severe side effects such as vomiting, headache, nausea, body ache, tremors, and severe abdominal pain.

- *Hallucinogens* (psychedelics) are drugs that promote hallucinations and otherwise alter consciousness. Hallucinogens (e.g., DMT/ayahuasca, LSD,

PCP, peyote, psilocybin/mushrooms, salvia) encourage distorted perceptions, feelings of altered time, and spiritual experiences. Side effects can include feelings of panic, fear, paranoia, or a prolonged sense of dread.

Some drugs are difficult to classify and may not fit neatly into a single category. For example, marijuana has properties of stimulants, depressants, and hallucinogens.

Marijuana

Once considered an illicit drug, views on marijuana have shifted considerably in the United States. Currently, marijuana is legal for medicinal purposes in most states, with a growing number allowing recreational use.

Marijuana is also commonly used for medical reasons, and proponents have substantial evidence for its effectiveness. For example, a review of clinical trial research concluded that marijuana was an effective treatment for pain, with initial evidence that it can reduce opioid use for pain (Hill et al., 2017). Other research has explored potential benefits of marijuana for conditions such as cancer (Zaki et al., 2018), traumatic brain injury (Hergert et al., 2021), migraines (Lochte et al., 2017), and lower back pain (First et al., 2020).

Though many consider marijuana a wonder drug, it's also a drug that can make you wonder where you put your keys. A review of 10 years of research found that long-term marijuana use impairs encoding, storage, and retrieval components of memory (Solowij & Battisti, 2008). Similarly, even a single dose of Δ9-THC (marijuana's active ingredient) can impair verbal and working memory (Schoeler & Bhattacharyya, 2013). In addition, longitudinal studies link greater marijuana use to lower motivation levels (Pacheco-Colón et al., 2018).

Alcohol

Alcohol also has a wide range of impacts on brain, cognitive, and motor functioning, including worse coordination, slower neural processing and reaction times, disruption of memory, reduced self-awareness, and lowered self-control (Sullivan et al., 2023).

Several factors impact how much a person drinks. For example, adolescents who thought more of their friends were drinking had greater alcohol use themselves a year later (Duell et al., 2022). Similarly, first-year college students who already drink or smoke *and* go to college in part because they want to party drink more in their first semester (Sher & Rutledge, 2007). On the other hand, more ambitious students focused on school are less likely to report drinking alcohol (Vaughan et al., 2009).

Students often wonder how marijuana use compares to alcohol use. At least one study found that compared to college students who smoke pot, those who drink alcohol engage in more negative behaviors—including taking risks, passing out, doing embarrassing things, driving dangerously, fighting, damaging property, and neglecting obligations (Mallett et al., 2019). Moreover, using *both* didn't result in more negative consequences than just drinking alone. As marijuana use becomes more common, it will be easier to research, which will help us better understand the implications of increased recreational use.

DMT/Ayahuasca

Ayahuasca is a psychoactive brew used in South America during rituals and ceremonies for its psychedelic and potentially therapeutic effects (Rossi et al., 2022). The active ingredient (DMT) has rapid onset and produces an intense psychedelic experience. Ayahuasca's pharmacological profile suggests that it could have potential use as an antidepressant. That said, at least one study conducted with participants in

Germany, the Netherlands, and Spain found that participants who took a pill reported improved anxiety, depression, and stress—regardless of whether they swallowed actual ayahuasca or a placebo (Uthaug et al., 2021). More research is needed.

Ayahuasca is often brewed as a drink that has psychedelic properties often used for ceremonies.

iStock.com/eskymaks

Coffee and Your Brain

Learning about all of this is making you feel drowsy again, so you decide to head over to the library's 24-hour coffee shop for a caffeine break. Research on coffee's benefits has a long history, with a study from 1936 showing that consumption of black coffee improved reaction times for several hours (Cheney, 1936). Even low to moderate doses of caffeine improves attention, alertness, and reaction time, although improvements in judgment and decision-making are less clear (McLellan et al., 2016). And there's that "coffee nap" we described earlier.

Like any drug, caffeine consumption has negative effects as well. For example, participants who consume caffeinated coffee have higher stress-induced heart rates and blood pressure (MacDougall et al., 1988). Caffeine is also addictive. Among those seeking treatment for caffeine addiction, 50% were coffee drinkers (Juliano et al., 2012). Participants sought treatment due to problems related to their health and no longer wanting to be dependent. Whether it's coffee, tea, soda, or Red Bull, caffeine impacts your brain and consciousness. But when thinking about drug use, we don't typically focus on those over-the-counter types of drugs.

Drug Use

"Everybody's doing it."

Is that really true? The University of Michigan conducted a nationwide survey of U.S. high school students to find out (Miech et al., 2023). You can see the prevalence data by grade in Table 7.3.

In the latest survey, 30.7% of high school seniors reported using marijuana, a level that was down from a prepandemic high of 35% to 36%. The pattern (similar to previous year, but down compared to prepandemic levels) was similar for alcohol use and for 8th and 10th graders.

TABLE 7.3

Drug Use Prevalence Data From the Monitoring the Future Study

	8TH GRADERS	10TH GRADERS	12TH GRADERS
Nicotine vaping	12.0%	20.5%	27.3%
Cannabis use	8.3%	19.5%	30.7%
Cannabis vaping	6.0%	15.0%	20.6%
Alcohol use	15.2%	31.3%	51.9%
Illicit drug use (nonmarijuana)	4.9%	5.7%	8.0%

Source: Created using data from Miech et al. (2023).

Many people assume that attending college encourages drug use. Attending college does seem to influence certain types of drug use, but not in the ways you might imagine. Among college students, only 6% report using marijuana daily, compared to 15% of young adults about the same age who are not in college. Cigarette smoking is also lower in college students (8%) compared to young adults who are not in college (16%). In contrast, college students appear to drink more, with 33% reporting binge drinking compared to just 22% of young adults not in college. The good news from the study is that cigarette smoking, prescription opioid, and amphetamine use all showed lower usage when compared to previous years.

Why People Use Drugs

Why would someone take a drug? Too often we answer that question by blaming individuals' biological factors (such as genes, ethnicity, gender, or stage of development) and ignoring systemic influences such as social norms. Youths' cigarette smoking has generally been on the decline, but less so for those from poorer and less educated homes (Johnston et al., 2012). Adolescent rates of drinking vary based on many factors, including race/ethnicity and community attachment (Patrick & Schulenberg, 2014).

Growing up with lower socioeconomic status also introduces other problems that can encourage drug use, such as struggling school systems (Gavurova et al., 2022), lack of parental supervision (Zucker et al., 2008), greater drug availability (Brook et al., 1999), and changing social roles (e.g., marriage, parenthood, divorce) at school or work (Staff et al., 2010). We observe these trends cross-culturally as well, with low-income individuals in Kenya more likely to abuse drugs and have a greater likelihood of dying (Were et al., 2022).

Broader systemic influences matter, but so does your immediate social circle. When students are around other binge drinkers, they are more likely to binge drink themselves (Clapp et al., 2006). This is especially true when there are more people drinking at an event, drinking games are in progress, and illicit drugs are available. Of course, there are individual differences as well. Adolescents who reach puberty earlier are more likely to abuse substances (Hedges & Korchmaros, 2016).

Some personalities predict drug use. Adolescent sensation-seekers are more likely to take risks—and to report smoking (Lydon & Geier, 2018). A review of factors associated with adolescent drug use found that high impulsivity, poor emotional regulation, experience of maltreatment, depression, easy access to drugs, low parental education, and having peers who use drugs all increased the likelihood of drug abuse (Nawi et al., 2021). Researchers also identified several factors that inhibited drug use, including optimism, greater mindfulness, school connectedness, structured activities, a desire for physical health, and strong religious beliefs.

Getting a handle on what promotes drug use, especially among youth, is critical because early drug use is a risk factor for using more dangerous drugs later in life (Lynskey et al., 2003).

Problematic Drug Use

No one thinks it's going to happen to them—but it does happen. In one year alone (January 2021–January 2022), over 107,000 people died in the United States from drug overdoses (American Medical Association, 2022). Overdoses can happen unintentionally when the person doesn't fully know what they're taking (e.g., marijuana laced with embalming fluid, fentanyl, or PCP). It can also occur from accidentally mixing drugs (e.g., forgetting you took cold medicine, then drinking alcohol).

Your authors enjoy a good concert or music festival. But concert day dealers who can disappear into a crowd will be less fussy about their product's quality or its impact on users. The result has been several concert-going drug-related deaths and hundreds of trips to emergency rooms (Ruest et al., 2018). In the category of unglamorous research, a study of the pooled urine collected at a popular Danish music festival found 77 drugs, including amphetamine, cocaine, methamphetamine/MDMA, THC, and ketamine (Hoegberg et al., 2018).

Some drugs are more dangerous than others. The *safety ratio* indicates how a drug's likely fatal dose compares to the typical dosage a person uses to experience the drug's effects (Gable, 2004). For drugs like heroin, the ratio is very low, indicating that a fatal dose is very similar to a typical dose, making overdose more likely. In contrast, the safety ratio of marijuana is very high, meaning there is less chance of a fatal overdose.

Overdoses are the extreme outcome. Repeated drug use also creates *tolerance,* which requires the user to increase their dosage to have a similar effect. The alertness you used to feel from a half cup of coffee now requires two cups. Without your regular coffee, you can experience *withdrawal* symptoms such as headaches, nausea, severe cravings for the drug, nervousness, trouble sleeping, loss of appetite, body aches, hallucinations, depression, or thoughts of self-harm. Symptoms vary depending on the drug being used and can occur a few hours after the last use.

Withdrawal is a sign of *dependence,* which is the need to regularly use a drug just to feel normal. Though similar, dependence is different from *addiction,* which is needing to continue use of a drug despite negative consequences to the self, close personal relationships, or at work. Addiction starts innocently enough (Volkow et al., 2016). At first, when the user experiences intoxication, it activates the brain's reward centers. These feelings of euphoria and pleasure become associated with the drug, as well as people, places, and things associated with the experience.

As use continues, the reward response diminishes, requiring greater amounts of the drug. Cravings begin, which encourages bingeing. The drug becomes less effective, yet the person craves the drug more. The miserable experience of withdrawal symptoms also leads to drug use, hoping to stop withdrawals. Drug use starting out as a pleasurable escape can swiftly shift to avoiding the negative feelings associated with not being intoxicated or high. No one starts out wanting to be a person with an addiction. ●

CAREER CORNER

Profiling Angus, Drug and Alcohol Counselor

What is your career?

I am a Certified Alcohol and Drug Counselor (CADC) in the state of Iowa. I function quite a bit like a traditional mental health therapist, but I specialize in people who suffer from addiction—typically alcohol or drugs but also process addictions such as gambling, food, shopping, and more.

How was studying psychology important for success in this career?

Through psychology, I learned not only therapeutic techniques but also up-to-date scientific information about the nature of disorders (what we know, what we don't). I learned the importance of positive regard and treating the whole person. More specifically, **I learned the latest theories and research on addiction** and how to treat it.

How do concepts from this chapter help in this career?

I learned the nature of tolerance and how it pertains to addiction. The information on the types of drugs and their effects, as well as psychopharmacological information, has been invaluable to my work.

(Continued)

(Continued)

Is this the career you always planned to have after college?

This is a second career for me but taking Introduction to Psychology helped me discover that I have skill as a clinician and as someone who can contribute to research and academia. The class allows students to explore various aspects of psychology in ways that spark their imagination and, hopefully, their desire to enter the field.

If you could give current college students one sentence of advice, what would it be?

This exploration into human nature and behavior—psychology—is the first step toward you becoming one of the many people who strive every day to better the world for our families and neighbors. ●

SageVantage Practice what you learn in **Knowledge Check 7.6**

CHAPTER REVIEW

Learning Objectives Summary

7.1   What is consciousness?

» LO 7.1 **Explain different levels of consciousness and the survival advantages consciousness provides.**

Consciousness requires awareness and responsiveness to our surroundings. Our consciousness operates on several levels, including the unconscious (things we can't easily access), preconscious (things just outside of awareness), and conscious (things we're aware of). We're also self-conscious and aware of our own actions and that others are perceiving us. These various types of consciousness have evolutionary advantages that aid our (and other animals') survival.

7.2   How does attention work?

» LO 7.2 **Explain how our powers of attention help us both acquire and miss information.**

There's a lot going on in our world, but it's impossible to pay attention to every single aspect. Our attention span is our ability to maintain focus and is impacted by the individual and the context. To focus, we need to selectively pay attention by screening out the extraneous, while focusing on the important pieces. But we miss more than we may realize, especially when multitasking.

7.3   Why do we sleep?

» LO 7.3 **Summarize the importance and functions of sleep.**

Our wakefulness follows a general pattern, though there is also room for individual differences such as being a morning or a night person. How we sleep, who with, and what we do before sleep all contribute to sleep quality. When we fall asleep, we proceed through a predictable series of stages, the most important of which may be REM sleep, all of which we can now monitor with wearable tracker devices.

7.4   Why do we dream?

» LO 7.4 **Compare and contrast theories that attempt to explain the purpose of dreaming.**

Dreams are a regular experience during sleep, for us and our pets. During lucid dreaming, we're aware that we're dreaming and can then control our actions. There are several potential reasons for why we dream and what those dreams mean, including symbolism, brain activity, information processing, and emotion/mood regulation.

7.5   What are other ways to alter consciousness?

>> LO 7.5   **Describe how flow, mindfulness, meditation, and hypnosis influence our consciousness.**

Consciousness occurs on a continuum, with many states in between awake and asleep. Experiences like daydreaming, flow, and mindfulness show how altered states impact us. Techniques such as meditation and hypnosis allow us to use altered consciousness to our benefit.

7.6   How do drugs impact consciousness?

>> LO 7.6   **Describe the effects of using drugs to alter consciousness.**

Because many drugs are common and legal, drugs affect our consciousness more than we may realize. There are many types of drugs, each with unique effects. Broad social factors (e.g., socioeconomic status) and peers both impact likelihood of using drugs. Drug use has numerous consequences in both the short and long term.

CRITICAL THINKING QUESTIONS

1. You're busy and feel like you have a million things to do. You have to study for a psychology test, maintain a social life by texting your friends, keep up with your new favorite show, write an English paper, and memorize this week's vocabulary words for your Spanish class. Given what you learned in this chapter, how should you approach getting all of this done? List three specific concepts from this chapter and explain how you can apply what you learned to help your daily life.

2. Find a peer-reviewed research article on "stage hypnosis." Summarize the article, then compare how hypnosis is used for therapy or counseling purposes versus for entertainment purposes.

3. Look at the sleep myths in Table 7.1. Which do you think is the most dangerous or unhealthy myth, and why?

4. Try to remember an interesting dream you had. Evaluate its purpose using each of the ideas in that section of this chapter. Then, analyze which explanation for the purpose of dreams you find the most and least persuasive and explain why.

5. Look up statistics on drug use for your own school, local city, or region. Point out three specific findings you think are interesting and explain why these data stood out to you. Then, provide an opinion on whether you think your school or region's current drug and/or alcohol policies are good or bad (should they be changed?) and why.

KEY TERMS

Altered consciousness, 212
Change blindness, 197
Circadian rhythm, 198
Consciousness, 192
Flow, 212
Hypnosis, 214
Inattentional blindness, 197
Latent content, 210

Lucid dreaming, 209
Manifest content, 210
Meditation, 213
Mindfulness, 213
Psychoactive drug, 215
REM, 200
Selective attention, 195

iStock.com/PeopleImages

8 Human Development

Being a human can be hard work.

Taking care of a human can also be difficult. There's a common high school assignment where students, either alone or with a partner, take care of an egg, a sack of flour, or even a sophisticated doll. The point is to learn firsthand how time-consuming caring for a baby can be, as well as the near round-the-clock dedication it takes. Just imagine what it must be like for real parents. This life is in your hands—it's a big responsibility.

You may already be a parent, or maybe you helped raise your siblings, or maybe you plan to be a parent one day in the future—or perhaps parenting isn't a part of your life plans. Parent or not, beginning to understand how humans develop is critical to understanding how people became who they are as they grow older. So play along with us as we imagine your life—in accelerated form from the moment you were conceived to old age, in the time it takes to read this chapter. What kind of changes will you experience? Will you succeed or fail when met with life's inevitable challenges? Your well-being depends on safely navigating through each stage of human development—so let's get started.

After reading this chapter, you will get answers to several questions you've been curious about:

Have You Ever Wondered?

8.1 How do psychologists study human life span development?

8.2 How do we change during prenatal development, infancy, and early childhood?

8.3 How do we change during middle childhood and adolescence?

8.4 How do we change in early and middle adulthood?

8.5 What is it like to be in late adulthood and to approach death?

Learning Objectives

LO 8.1 Compare and contrast five theoretical approaches to studying human development.

LO 8.2 Analyze the major competencies of the prenatal period and infancy and the milestones of biological, cognitive, and social development during early childhood.

LO 8.3 Summarize the biological, cognitive, and social changes experienced during middle childhood and adolescence.

LO 8.4 Explain the common milestones adults experience, including biological, cognitive, and social developments.

LO 8.5 Discuss the major biological, cognitive, and social transitions that characterize late adulthood and how we adjust to death.

THEORETICAL APPROACHES TO HUMAN DEVELOPMENT

?

Have You Ever Wondered?
8.1 How do psychologists study human life span development?

>> LO 8.1   Compare and contrast five theoretical approaches to studying human development.

The twists and turns of your pathway of change are what make you a unique individual.

As a college student, you already care about approaching life from an educated, thoughtful perspective. Psychologists who use theory and science to understand how humans change and grow over our life span are experts in developmental psychology. To best understand how your pathway of change is influenced by your biology, environment, and social interactions, let's start with considering theoretical approaches in human development.

Theoretical Lenses

Sometimes we're not aware of what drives us.

One of the earliest approaches to understanding human development comes from *psychoanalytic theories,* which suggest our mental drives, emotions, conflicts, and needs are sometimes outside of our awareness. Most psychologists use the term *unconscious* thoughts or drives (not *subconscious*) to refer to these mysterious pulls that psychoanalysis usually considers by-products of early childhood experiences.

Probably the most famous psychoanalytic concepts come from Sigmund Freud, who suggested that even infants have sexual and aggressive instincts (1940/1989). He believed we all go through five *psychosexual stages* (oral, anal, phallic, latent, genital) in which we explore different parts of our own body, feel sexual urges toward important others in life, and overcome attachment issues with our parents. During the oral stage, an infant gains pleasure from sucking on a pacifier or bottle and learns about their environment through their mouth. The genital stage, beginning at puberty and lasting into adulthood, marks the onset of romantic and sexual emotions, leading to the formation of intimate relationships. For Freud, a healthy personality came from parents who found a balance between pampering and neglect. Even in 1900s Europe, many of Freud's ideas were controversial, with both historical and modern psychologists criticizing him for being sexist (Aldridge et al., 2014).

Later, Erik Erikson (1950/1963, 1959) suggested that as we age, we must make important life decisions at crucial times. You've probably heard of a midlife crisis. Erikson's theory of identity development suggested we actually have *eight* crises. During each crisis, our development and identity—our self-concept—can become stunted if we make the wrong choice, or we can thrive and move forward, if we make the right decisions. Table 8.1 shows a summary of Erikson's stages.

Developmental psychology: A subfield focused on the study of how humans change and grow over our life span.

Erikson's theory of identity development: The idea that we move through eight decisions or "crises" that form our self-concept and views of the world.

TABLE 8.1

Erikson's Eight Stages of Identity Development

Erikson (1950/1963) thought everyone goes through eight stages, or "crises," of identity development. At each stage, choosing the first option leads to a happy, healthy life.

AGE	STAGE	WHAT'S HAPPENING	IDEAL VIRTUE OUTCOME
Birth–1 year	Trust vs. Mistrust	Infants learn to trust and rely on others, or lack confidence their needs will be met.	Hope
1–3 years	Autonomy vs. Doubt	Toddlers gain a sense of independence, or they develop self-doubts.	Will
3–6 years	Initiative vs. Guilt	Elementary school helps children develop curiosity and goal-setting, or feel guilt for disappointing others.	Purpose
6–12 years	Industry vs. Inferiority	Children develop good work habits and enjoy reaching goals, or establish low self-esteem.	Competence

(Continued)

(Continued)

AGE	STAGE	WHAT'S HAPPENING	IDEAL VIRTUE OUTCOME
Puberty–early adulthood	Identity vs. Role Confusion	Adolescents experiment with who they are in terms of talents, sexuality, and careers, or they never decide who they want to be.	Fidelity
Early adulthood	Intimacy vs. Isolation	Young adults form important intimate relationships with others, or feel loneliness and ostracism.	Love
Middle adulthood	Generativity vs. Stagnation	Adults contribute to the world and leave a legacy through family or work, or they feel lost and without purpose.	Care
Late adulthood	Integrity vs. Despair	Older adults look back on their life with pride and joy, or they regret choices and fear death.	Wisdom

While our unconscious mental urges, anxieties, and memories certainly influence us, other psychologists, like B. F. Skinner and John Watson, take a more direct approach: observable behavior. The *behaviorist* approach focuses on measurable actions we can see. We change and learn because experiences in the environment teach us how to predict what is going to happen next through classical and operant conditioning.

Similarly, *social learning* demonstrates that observing others and copying what they do also shapes our development. Notice how much children love to mimic their parents and teachers with toy lawn mowers, shopping carts, baby dolls, or games like "school." They practice the physical, cognitive, and emotional skills they need in their futures. The phrase "monkey see, monkey do" reminds us that many species rely on social learning. One of the most influential social learning theorists, Albert Bandura, noted an additional, important observation: While our environment shapes who we become, we also shape our environment—an idea called *reciprocal determinism* (Bandura, 2011).

How we all process, interpret, and remember the world we experience represents the *cognitive* approach to developmental psychology. As we progress from infancy to adulthood, our mental frameworks become more flexible and advanced. Compared to our childish view of the world, we have become fluent at considering multiple sides of a controversy, weighing evidence, and evaluating the consequences of your decisions. Cognitive theories of development identify stages of mental progression and identify key accomplishments, such as language development and critical thinking, that most of us make at various stages.

By contrast, *contextual theories* explore how social setting and culture influence our development. We don't develop alone; culture matters. Your family, your neighborhood, your religion and customs, and everything else in your social world impact how you think about yourself and your place in the world. Like Russian nesting dolls, each level of influence is embedded within the next, larger level—and they all influence us, simultaneously. These systems shift and overlap, according to **Bronfenbrenner's bioecological model** (Bronfenbrenner, 1977; Bronfenbrenner & Morris, 2006) portrayed in Figure 8.1.

The *microsystem* is our immediate environment, like our family and school. The *mesosystem* is how the microsystems interact, like whether our family encourages our schoolwork. Next, the *exosystem* represents larger influences in our life that we can't directly control. For example, through no fault of your own, your hometown's

Bronfenbrenner's bioecological model: The idea that our development is shaped by multiple interacting systems, such as our immediate environment and our larger culture.

FIGURE 8.1

Levels of Cultural Influence in Bioecological Systems Theory

In Bronfenbrenner's (1977) bioecological model, we're influenced by multiple social, contextual, and cultural systems simultaneously.

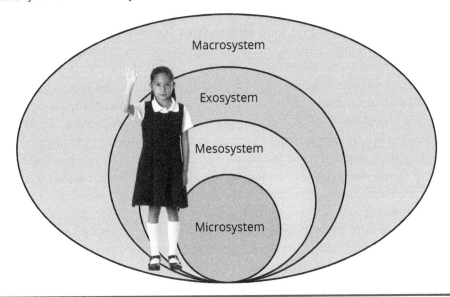

school budget has profoundly influenced your life. So does public transportation and neighborhood safety. Finally, the *macrosystem* is the larger national culture and society at large. While not shown in Figure 8.1, we're also part of the chronosystem, or how our influences change over time.

TABLE 8.2

Summary of Theoretical Lenses in Development

THEORETICAL LENS	WHAT INFLUENCES HUMAN DEVELOPMENT?
Psychoanalytic	Unconscious thoughts or drives
Behaviorist	Measurable actions we can see
Social learning	Observing others and copying what they do
Cognitive	Flexible mental frameworks
Contextual	Social settings and culture

The Science of Hereditary Influence

What exactly makes you, "you"?

Is it your *environment*—parents, siblings, family, friends, schooling, nutrition, and other experiences to which you are exposed—or is it *hereditary* factors—your genetic makeup—that impacts us most? Darwin famously suggested that we inherit our instincts from our ancestors and that the behaviors most helpful for survival and sexual reproduction are those that are most likely to be passed on to future generations.

We will see that the classic psychology question "nature versus nurture" isn't really an either/or proposition but actually a question of how *much* our biology versus our environment and upbringing influences us.

Behavioral geneticists who study the effects of hereditary influences on human behavior have found our genetic inheritance predisposes us to respond in particular ways to our environment (Ayorech et al., 2023; Rimfeld et al., 2019). For example, why are helpless babies (like little you!) so darn cute? Many humans are drawn toward "cute" things with the instinct to nurture and protect them; this surely helps babies survive their most vulnerable months of life.

Researchers use different approaches to learn about the relative effects of genetic and environmental factors. Family studies focus on the investigation of blood relatives to see how similar they are with respect to some trait (for example, the occurrence of a mental illness such as schizophrenia). Twin studies compare identical twins and fraternal twins for various similarities in appearance and behavior to see which traits or behaviors are affected by genetic makeup. In some cases when twins have been adopted into separate families, it is possible to expand the information and determine which traits are affected by environment rather than heredity. Studies of genetic defects (for example, certain types of developmental disabilities) also provide pertinent information on the effects of heredity and environment on traits and behavior.

Using these approaches, we know that your physical characteristics, such as height, weight, and athletic ability; intellectual characteristics, such as memory, intelligence, and language acquisition; and emotional characteristics, such as shyness, extraversion, and anxiety, are influenced significantly by genetic material or our *genotype*. Not only do genetic factors provide the potential for behaviors or traits to emerge, but heredity also places limitations on the emergence of these observable characteristics, or *phenotype* and specific traits. For example, genes define your physical abilities; regardless how much you practice, you simply cannot run at a speed of 70 miles per hour or grow as tall as 10 feet no matter the quality of your nutrition.

It may be easy to think of genes as a blueprint for a person. However, your pathway of development doesn't simply follow a genetic master plan. For each genotype, a range of phenotypes may be expressed, depending on the environment. A person might be born with the genes to be the next LeBron James, but without the necessary environmental factors such as access to a basketball court, adequate nutrition and health care, and good coaching, that potential might not ever be reached. Development is about the complex interactions of genes and experience that build the whole—both of which make their impact before birth.

The Music of Life

Music can have powerful effects.

For many of us, the music that was popular when we were certain ages (like when we were in high school) sticks with us as our favorite songs and artists for the rest of our life. Songs may also remind us of specific memories or serve as "our song" for intimate couples. Sometimes a song also highlights important rites of passage or shared experiences based on age groups in a given culture. The list of songs below associated with various times in life was compiled by Mandy Garcia, MS, adjunct psychology instructor at Virginia Western Community College.

TITLE	ARTIST/GROUP	CONNECTION
PRENATAL DEVELOPMENT		
Let's Get It Started	The Black-Eyed Peas	It starts with conception!
Small Bump	Ed Sheeran	Pregnancy bump
Push It	Salt N' Pepa	Birthing process
INFANCY & TODDLERHOOD		
With Arms Wide Open	Creed	Welcoming a child to life
I Want It Now	Willy Wonka	A common childhood phrase
Try Everything	Shakira	Every experience is new
CHILDHOOD		
Fireflies	Faith Hill	Imagination and play
I'll Be There for You	The Rembrandts	Importance of friendship
Family Portrait	Pink	Influence of family
ADOLESCENCE		
Shake It Off	Taylor Swift	Judgment from others
Boss of Me	They Might Be Giants	Teen rebellion
Titanium	David Guetta	Feeling invulnerable
EARLY & MIDDLE ADULTHOOD		
Piece by Piece	Kelly Clarkson	Intergenerational legacies
Let's Get Married	Jagged Edge	Intimacy and commitment
Forever Changed	Carrie Underwood	Being a parent
LATER LIFE		
Believe	Jennifer Hudson	Finding meaning in life
Seasons of Love	RENT cast	Importance of love in life
I'm Free	The Rolling Stones	Freedom (in retirement)

Critical thinking: The songs listed here are grouped by basic age categories. Take a moment to consider your life up to this point using Erikson's eight stages of identity development discussed earlier in the chapter. What songs would *you* select to be associated with various stages of your life? Carefully think about how each song you select might personally represent the corresponding stage of development for you. ●

Research Methods in Developmental Psychology

Human development is about growing and changing.

Researchers may desire to look at how people of various ages change over time and how they are different on certain characteristics. Two research designs that allow us to explore the pattern of continuity and change in human capabilities that occur throughout life are cross-sectional and longitudinal designs.

Consider this example. You want to understand how friendship interactions change over time. To do so, you decide to take one day to observe a group of a group of 6-year-olds, a group of 18-year-olds, a group of 35-year-olds, and a group of 60-year-olds interacting with their friends. This is an example of a cross-sectional design—a group of people are compared at one point in time. Cross-sectional studies provide information about differences in development between different age groups. However, we cannot be sure that differences we observe in friendship interactions are due to age differences alone. Instead, what we observe may reflect differences in the historical and social context of the time period in which each group was born and developed. For instance, 18-year-olds may be more likely to be distracted by cell phone use while interacting with their friends as compared to 60-year-olds.

To draw more definitive conclusions about human development, researchers may use a *longitudinal* design. Longitudinal designs study the behavior of one or more participants over time as they age. Consequently, this research design permits you to understand *changes* in behavior rather than simply assessing age *differences* as with the cross-sectional design. In our example, first we may observe a group of 6-year-olds as they interact with friends. We'd then come back 12 years later and observe them again at age 18. We'd then return to them again when they were 35 years old and again at 60 years old. If this seems like a lot of work, you're right! Longitudinal research can take a significant amount of time and resources. In addition, participants who begin a study at an early age may drop out, move away, or even die as the research continues.

As can be seen, cross-sectional and longitudinal designs both have pros and cons. These designs have allowed researchers to gain knowledge about the stages of human development.

Sage Vantage   Practice what you learn in **Knowledge Check 8.1**

PRENATAL, INFANCY, AND EARLY CHILDHOOD

?
Have You Ever
Wondered?
8.2 How do
we change
during prenatal
development,
infancy, and early
childhood?

>> **LO 8.2**   **Analyze the major competencies of the prenatal period and infancy and the milestones of biological, cognitive, and social development during early childhood.**

You've been quite busy. Even before birth.

You won't remember anything about it, but we go through rapid changes and are vulnerable as we start our developmental journey. It all starts with conception.

Before We Are Born

Ingredients: One egg, one sperm. Combine.

A conversation about human development begins with the ways we grow during the prenatal ("before birth") period. Development before birth is commonly divided into three distinct stages: germinal, embryonic, and fetal (Figure 8.2). The germinal stage begins at conception and lasts for 2 weeks. Beginning with fertilization, when a single sperm cell merges with the ovum (egg) to produce a zygote, astonishing changes occur! The zygote starts out as a microscopic, single cell with a total of 46 chromosomes. Normally, in a process called mitosis, the zygote will begin to divide, first into two cells, then four, then eight, and so on, with each new cell also having 46 chromosomes that copy themselves before each division.

Sometimes this division process doesn't work exactly like this, and the result is multiples. Early in the division process, if the mass of cells splits completely into two separate masses, each will develop into a separate zygote. These zygotes are referred to as monozygotic twins or "identical" twins, will be the same sex, and have the same features because they each possess the same set of 46 chromosomes. If two eggs are

FIGURE 8.2

Prenatal Development

The process of prenatal development occurs in three main stages: the germinal stage, the embryonic stage, and the fetal stage.

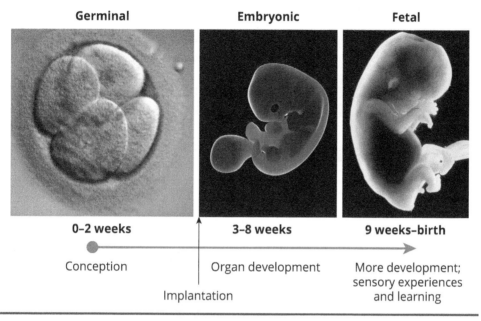

Jean-Paul Chassenet/Science Source; SCIEPRO/Science Source; GARRY WATSON/Science Source

fertilized, dizygotic twins (two zygotes) or possibly triplets or some other multiple number of zygotes will develop. Can you imagine being a sextuplet (one of 6!)?

If a fertilized egg attaches to a uterine wall, the embryonic stage of development begins—about 2 weeks after conception. It is in this stage where the nervous system and major organs such as heart, arms, legs, eyes, and external genitalia develop. Embryonic development continues until about 8 weeks after conception. The fetal stage is a period of tremendous growth lasting about 8 weeks from conception until birth. You're now referred to as a fetus with your length increasing about 20 times and your weight increasing from about 1 ounce to an average of over 7 pounds at birth. In addition, a lifetime's worth of brain neurons are produced.

What other major milestones occur during the fetal period? The age of viability, or the point at which the fetus can survive if born prematurely, is at about prenatal age 22 weeks. The fetus also passes through several sensitive periods when they are particularly susceptible to damage that may affect them if they are eventually born.

Physical Development

As an infant, you probably had four hobbies: eating, sleeping, crying, and going to the bathroom.

As soon as 1 minute after you were born, your health was assessed using the Apgar scale. The scale measures five health indicators (Apgar, 1952): appearance (is the color normal?), pulse (how's the heart rate?), grimace (facial expression and reflexes), activity (muscle tone), and respiration (breathing). Newborn, you pass with flying colors!

Maybe. Dr. Virginia Apgar recognized that the color assessment had problems. It was rated on a scale of 0 ("blue, pale"), 1 ("pink body, blue extremities"), or 2 ("pink all over"). But pink does not describe dark-skinned infants, a detail that slips past

Apgar scale: A quick assessment of a baby's health using five scales: appearance, pulse, grimace, activity, and respiration.

Lemurs aren't monkeys at all! They belong to different families of primates. How old do you need to be to distinguish between these two groups of primates?

iStock.com/PaulMaguire

many professionals caring for just-born babies (Grünebaum et al., 2023). If the original research had been conducted on infants of color, would "pink all over" still indicate "normal?" It's an example of implicit prejudice in science.

When we're born, we have most of the neurons we'll ever have—around 100 billion of them. Brain cells are important, but it's the *neural pathways* connecting the neurons that are crucial to our early development. These connections are being built faster in newborns than in any other age group, perhaps because everything is brand new. This rapid and amazing period of neural networking is necessary for newborns to gain the foundations for basic things like body movement, language, and memory. Our synaptic connections peak at age 3; after that, ones we use a lot become stronger while those we don't use eventually shrink and disappear—a process called *synaptic pruning*. As they say, "if you don't use it, you lose it."

During infancy, our mental structures and cultural learning are first formed as well. So next, let's explore of the most famous theories from developmental psychology, produced by Piaget, Kohlberg, and Vygotsky.

Cognitive Development

What's the difference between a monkey and a lemur?

When Wind went to the Omaha Zoo a few years ago, she saw a 3-year-old boy with his mom. As all three of them watched the ring-tailed lemurs jump around in their tree habitat, he exclaimed, "Look at the monkeys, mommy!" While his mother simply smiled, the scientist in Wind wondered when he would learn to distinguish lemurs from monkeys (although lemurs and monkeys are both primates, they belong to different groups).

Piaget's cognitive-developmental theory proposes that we are cognitive explorers, learning about our world and moving from simple, concrete ways of thinking to more abstract and complicated ones as we age (Piaget, 1930, 1932). As shown in Table 8.3, Piaget believed that all children move through four distinct stages of cognitive development. Each stage includes a significant mental achievement that would have been difficult for younger children, as well as increasingly complex and flexible cognitive schemas (or mental structures).

Piaget's cognitive-developmental theory: The idea that our mental abilities improve steadily and grow in complexity through infancy to adolescence.

TABLE 8.3

Piaget's Cognitive Development Theory

Piaget (1930, 1932) suggested four stages of cognitive development, punctuated by hallmark mental achievements.

AGE	STAGE	WHAT'S HAPPENING
Birth–2 years	Sensorimotor	• Mental development: Advances by exploring the world through senses and actions (touching, tasting, etc.) • Achievement: Object permanence
2–6 years	Preoperational	• Mental development: Can represent ideas and objects with words and images • Achievement: Language development
7–11 years	Concrete Operational	• Mental development: Logical thinking, concrete analogies, basic arithmetic • Achievements: Conservation, classification, reversibility
12 and up	Formal operational	• Mental development: Abstract thought and reasoning • Achievements: Critical thinking, moral reasoning

Infancy: Sensory Motor

At birth we're in Stage 1, what Piaget called the *sensorimotor stage*. As infants, we primarily interact with the world in two ways: through our senses (like putting something in our mouth or grabbing) and through motion (like kicking a string connected to a mobile over our crib). Combine "senses" and "motor movements" and you get "sensorimotor." Piaget said at this age, we can only understand the world through directly interacting with it. Infants also don't have developed memories or understanding of how the world works yet. So, one of their first achievements becomes *object permanence,* the understanding that objects still exist even if we can't see them.

How did Piaget determine if a baby developed object permanence? He observed infants' reactions when a favorite object or toy was presented and then was covered with a blanket or removed from sight. Try this experiment to find out! Experiment 1: If you put a toy behind a chair or under a blanket, babies don't appear to realize the object is still there but out of sight. As a baby, you may have played the game of "peekaboo" with a caregiver. If you were delighted with the surprise of seeing your caregiver come in and out of your vision, you were still early in Stage 1. As you developed, you likely became bored with the game, because you mastered object permanence (which usually happens around 8–12 months of age).

Early Childhood: Preoperational

As babies become a toddler (around age 2 years), they take some major mental leaps forward. Stage 2 is called *preoperational,* that basic language is mental symbolism. The words "bear" or "banana" or even "no!" become highly meaningful and represent specific objects or ideas. While these advancements are critical for young children, they still struggle with more advanced ideas. For example, they may have difficulty thinking about someone else's perspective or point of view due to *egocentrism.*

How did Piaget determine if a child displayed egocentrism? Piaget's classic experiment on egocentrism involved showing children a three-dimensional model of a mountain and asking them to describe what a doll that is looking at the mountain from a different angle might see. Children tend to choose a picture that represents their own view, rather than that of the doll. Try this experiment to find out! Experiment 2: If your caregiver wanted to test whether you displayed egocentrism as a child, they could put you on the phone (voice only) with their adult friend who asks you a series of yes or no questions. If you simply nod or shake your head, it's evidence that you don't realize your caregiver's friend can't see you—so it won't be an effective conversation.

Piaget's central idea (increasing cognitive complexity) has held up well over the decades, but there have been helpful criticisms. For example, he focused only on cognitive changes and didn't include other important developmental shifts like social needs, identity, and self-concept development or advances in moral and critical thinking (Crain, 2016). Others point out that he didn't take culture into account or acknowledge that people can move up and down in the stages, at least temporarily (Pakpahan & Saragih, 2022). That said, his theory is still hugely influential in psychology and in education and has led to hundreds of studies on child development that confirm many of his ideas (e.g., Lourenço & Machado, 1996).

Teaching children language is an essential step for them to understand cultural concepts.

iStock.com/monkeybusinessimages

Psychosocial Development

Easy. Difficult. Slow to warm up.

At the same time you're developing into a cognitive explorer, you also develop socially. For instance, you may demonstrate that you have a different personality from your sibling or other biological relative by your *temperament*. Believe it or not, your temperament is well established at birth, and as shown in Table 8.4, researchers identified three basic temperament styles of infants that are strongly influenced by heredity (Chess & Thomas, 1986). Of course, not all babies will fall neatly into one of these three patterns—some children may be a mix of two or even all three patterns of behavior (Chess & Thomas, 1986). Nonetheless, although these processes begin in infancy, early psychological and social development provides the foundation for social relationships that will last a lifetime.

TABLE 8.4

Three Types of Child Temperament

Chess and Thomas (1986) identified three basic temperament styles of infants that are strongly influenced by heredity.

EASY	DIFFICULT	SLOW TO WARM UP
• Adapts to change	• Does not easily adapt to change	• Can adjust slowly to new experiences
• Likes new experiences	• Does not like new experiences	• Observes before joining in
• Has a happy disposition	• Has especially big emotions	• Cautious in new situations
• Easygoing	• Has irregular daily routines	• Sensitive to others' emotions

Kohlberg's Stages of Moral Development

How do we decide what is right and what is wrong?

The answer depends on how old you are! Building on the work of Piaget, **Kohlberg's theory of moral development** suggests that children move through three increasingly advanced stages of thinking about morality and ethics (Kohlberg, 1969; Kohlberg et al., 1983; Kohlberg & Ryncarz, 1990). Each stage can be reached when a person reaches a certain age, though at times they do not reach said stage or level at all.

Kohlberg gave many dilemmas like the *"Heinz dilemma"* highlighted below to 75 young boys of different ages to investigate their moral reasoning (Kohlberg, 1969; see also Kohlberg et al., 1983; Kohlberg & Ryncarz, 1990). Using a longitudinal design, he followed the boys over time to test if their thinking would become more sophisticated, and eventually, he formulated three stages.

> What should Heinz do? Near death, a woman with cancer learns of a drug that may save her. The woman's husband, Heinz, approaches the druggist who created the drug, but the druggist refuses to sell the drug for anything less than $2,000, ten times what it cost him to make. After borrowing from everyone he knows, Heinz has only scraped together $1,000. Heinz asks the druggist to let him have the drug for $1,000 and he will pay him the rest later. The druggist says that it is his right to make money from the drug he developed and refuses to sell it to Heinz. Desperate for the drug, Heinz breaks into the druggist's store and steals the drug. Should Heinz have done that? Why or why not?

Kohlberg's theory of moral development: The idea that children move through three increasingly advanced stages of moral and ethical thinking.

Table 8.5 shows, in the first row, the *preconventional* stage (birth to age 9). In early childhood, we make decisions motivated by selfish thinking, such as what gets the most reward or least punishment for themselves. In the Heinz dilemma, a young child might say Heinz should steal the drug because if his wife dies, he'll be sad—or that he should *not* steal the drug because he might go to jail. An older child might say it's not wrong for Heinz to steal because human life must be preserved, and his wife's life is worth more than personal property or money. The Heinz dilemma doesn't have right or wrong answers per se. Instead, we use it as a tool to understand children's moral thinking behind their decision.

TABLE 8.5

Kohlberg's Theory of Moral Development

Kohlberg (1969) outlined how moral and ethical thinking develop in three major stages through childhood and adolescence.

AGE	STAGE	WHAT'S HAPPENING
Early childhood (before 9)	Preconventional	• Decisions based on getting rewards or avoiding punishments; generally selfish motivation
Early adolescence (9–11 years)	Conventional	• Follows rules to gain social acceptance and approval
Late adolescence (12 and up)	Postconventional	• Decisions based on abstract justice; rules can be broken for a higher purpose

The Influence of Culture and Society

Culture also affects cognitive development.

Piaget was criticized for paying little attention to culture and the social environment. In contrast, **Vygotsky's sociocultural theory** (1978) explores how different cultures and societies train children and solve problems. He said that the way we think is embedded within the concepts and assumptions we learned from birth.

Vygotsky's sociocultural theory: The idea that different cultures and societies train children to solve problems in different ways.

As little you learned about how families get and prepare food, did caregivers take you to the grocery store or to a dairy farm, start a garden in your backyard, or order fast food? Vygotsky emphasized that young children learn best when they are taught a task carefully through *guided participation*. This means an adult demonstrates how to do it but allows the child to help as an "apprentice," taking steps toward mastery and independence. At this point, your caregivers may have spent nights reading little you a bedtime story, showing you how books, letters, and words work and go with the pictures. The hope is that you start to pick up on some of the words yourself and get excited to read on your own.

The language you learned also influences cognitive complexity. For example, English nouns don't have a gender, but many other languages assign genders to nouns. In Spanish, *rosa* means "rose" and is considered female, while *libro* means "book" and is considered male. You can imagine how this kind of gendering might affect your assumptions about social roles, stereotypes, and the world. What's the takeaway? Active social and passive cultural experiences shape our cognitive development.

Feral Children

Social and cultural influences are important during childhood.

So important, that their absence can have serious consequences. I think we'd all agree that leaving little you alone in the wild would not be good for a caregiver to do.

Genie Wiley (the name given to protect her identity) was born in 1957 near Los Angeles and endured horrific abuse at the hands of her father as he kept her isolated in a room that was more akin to a prison cell for a little over 13 years. Most of the time, Genie was kept strapped into a toddler toilet, and sometimes she was even placed in an actual cage.

Feral children: Children who grew up without interaction or care from other people, usually through extreme neglect.

Most crucially, Genie had almost no interaction with anyone, had almost no stimulation of any kind, and was never allowed outside. In fact, the extent of her isolation prevented her from being exposed to any significant amount of speech, and as a result, she did not acquire language during her childhood. Though certainly extreme and unlikely, researchers have identified about 60 cases of **feral children**—or children who grew up without interaction or care from other humans, generally due to extreme neglect.

Like the heartbreaking case of Genie, after being rescued, other feral children had a problem with language (Di Sante et al., 2019; Niego & Benítez-Burraco, 2022). A girl named Oxana was abandoned by alcoholic parents and lived with a pack of dogs until she was 8. She really did show dog-like behavior at first but was able to learn language and eventually lived with other humans on a farm. Genie disproved the theory that a person could not learn a language after puberty, although she struggled with grammar.

In Genie's case, researchers desperately wanted to understand how extreme isolation in a person's formative years shaped their lives. In fact, scientists became highly interested in finding out what part social interaction has in a person's development. From 1971 to 1975, Genie was subjected to scientific experimentation and experts made some discoveries. In the end, many felt the experiments that Genie subjected to were too rigorous to be ethical, and eventually Genie would cease all contact with the researchers.

SPOTLIGHT ON RESEARCH METHODS

Components of Friendship

Do you have a "best friend"? If so, other than possibly sharing matching BFF necklaces, how is it different from all other friendships? You might be curious if your "best" friend relationship matches what psychological science predicts about it.

Researchers often build on each other's work, and friendship studies are a great example of this teamwork. In 1983, two scholars started this particular research by asking children to describe aspects of their friendships (Berndt & Perry, 1983). They interviewed children of all genders and asked them about the expectations and benefits they experienced in the friendship.

A decade later, a separate group of scholars thought about this qualitative work and decided to extend it with a quantitative measure of those same benefits and expectations (Bukowski et al., 1994). Their measure had five subcomponents: companionship, help, closeness, security, and conflict (see Table 8.6). Children said their best friendships had all these qualities. You might be surprised by the "conflict" factor—but friendships that can endure conflict and still be strong are sometimes the strongest ones (Laursen & Adams, 2018).

TABLE 8.6

Factors in Childhood Friendships

Companionship	Spending time together in playful activities
Help	Providing aid when needed and being an ally against bullies
Closeness	Feeling validated and accepted by each other
Security	Trusting each other, being honest, and listening to problems
Conflict	Getting through fights and still being friends

Notice how the research progressed from a foundation of qualitative interviews to quantifying what had been learned. The next step was to see whether these factors were tied to any interesting patterns in children's lives. Many studies have now used the friendship factors measure (Bukowski et al., 1994). Here is a small sample of what we've learned about childhood friendships:

- Children who are bullied at school but have strong friendships can buffer bullying's negative effects (Hodges et al., 1999; Lin, 2023).

- In interviews, children admitted that people they once thought of as friends bullied them (Smith et al., 2004).

- Children on the autism spectrum want friends, report feeling lonely, and indicate lower scores on the various friendship factors (Bauminger & Kassari, 2000; Sumiya & Senju, 2023).

- Children with happy, stable parental attachments report higher-quality friendships and less conflict (Lieberman et al., 1999).

Still curious about friendships? Enter "childhood friendships" in Google Scholar or PsycInfo at your college library's website. Psychology has learned a great deal about friendship by building on the foundation of previous work. Each study brings surprises and inspiration for the next new study. ●

Practice what you learn in **Knowledge Check 8.2**

Sage Vantage

MIDDLE CHILDHOOD AND ADOLESCENCE

>> **LO 8.3 Summarize the biological, cognitive, and social changes experienced during middle childhood and adolescence.**

You are going through some things.

Imagine that in sixth grade you arrive at home from school. Your caregiver asks that you complete some household chores. You slam the door and play overly loud music for several hours. Despite these signs of rebellion, you don't seem to be having trouble in school. Last weekend, you volunteered to spend some time with your grandparent—so maybe there's hope. But shifts in your behavior have been recently sudden and unexpected.

Adolescence is an extremely important time in our development. Psychologists have studied this age perhaps more than any other, and there are many theories about how puberty and adolescence change who we are. Even so, a child's developmental path in their middle childhood years (between 6 and 12 years of age) contributes substantially to the adolescent (and later adult) they will become. It is during middle childhood when we begin to spend more time away from our family, and events, such as starting school, bring children this age into regular contact with the larger world. In middle childhood and adolescence, social development is key, and friendships have a lot of influence.

Let's consider how physical and neural development affects us as we shift from children to adults and what we can learn about this age from Piaget's and Kohlberg's theories.

Have You Ever Wondered?
8.3 How do we change during middle childhood and adolescence?

Biological Development

You may now need several new grooming products and lots of time in the bathroom.

As we move through middle childhood and puberty, our bodies can seem out of control as we go through rapid physical and neurological changes.

The teenage years are a time of many physical changes marked by puberty.

iStock.com/NickyLloyd

Primary sex characteristics: Our reproductive organs and genitals.

Puberty

As we hit puberty, our bodies begin to change. Our **primary sex characteristics** are our reproductive organs and genitals. Most girls will experience *menarche,* their first menstruation (Kermanshahi & Gholami Fesharaki, 2023); most boys will experience *spermarche,* their first ejaculation containing living sperm (Brix et al., 2023). As puberty proceeds, our *secondary sex characteristics* also change, which are the outer physical indications of our biological sex. For girls, that's the development of breasts and hips; for boys, it's gaining muscle and lowering of the voice. People of all sexes experience hair growth, sometimes sudden height jumps, and changes in the skin (often, that means acne).

For many, these physical changes are exciting because they indicate imminent adulthood (Brooks-Gunn & Ruble, 2013). If we have older people (parents, siblings, cousins, friends) who can explain what everything means and give us resources, it helps us understand what's happening and not be afraid (Bosch et al., 2008; Frankel, 2002; Stidham-Hall et al., 2012). However, if the family environment is stressful, including family conflict and abuse at home, it can disrupt sexual development, resulting in irregular periods and reduced sperm production (Graber et al., 2010; Toufexis et al., 2014).

Body dissatisfaction can also reach a peak at this age. About half of children ages 6 to 12 say they don't like some aspect of their body and shape (Dion et al., 2016). Sometimes children this age even start dieting (e.g., Angraini et al. 2023). Girls with larger bodies are teased and bullied more at school, which leads to more body dissatisfaction (McVey et al., 2013; Williams et al., 2013). This can be a double psychological setback, with the combination of bullying and body dissatisfaction leading to lower self-esteem, depression, and anxiety (Dion et al., 2016).

Neural Development

Less visible at this age are the dramatic events in the brain. The rapid increase of hormones building up throughout puberty also leads to a burst of new and faster connections between neurons in the brain (Guyer et al., 2023; Sisk, 2017). The order of this brain development is also important, from the primitive brainstem to the frontal lobes, which are responsible for reasoning (Jensen & Nutt, 2015). The frontal lobes occupy about 40% of the mature human brain—and they are the last to develop, usually only fully connecting to the rest of the brain when people reach their early 20s.

Connections between different parts of the brain gradually become faster and stronger (Fuhrmann et al., 2015; Guyer et al., 2023). At the same time, our brain is going through the synaptic pruning mentioned earlier, the shrinking and eventual degradation of neural connections we no longer need. This is also good news, as it means our thinking becomes more efficient (Guyer et al., 2023; Zhou et al., 2015).

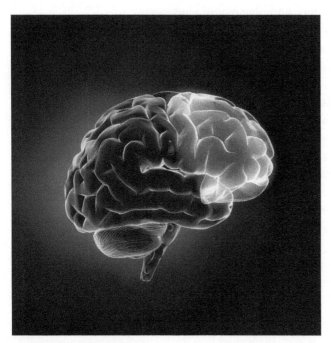

During adolescence, the brain goes through a lot of changes, including ongoing development of the frontal lobes.

iStock.com/janulla

So, at this stage of development, you are getting pretty good at rapid thinking. But there's another interesting neural change happening in our brain. Our limbic system—the area of our brain primarily known for our emotional responses—is also quickly blooming. In fact, limbic system development is slightly ahead of the prefrontal cortex (Shulman et al., 2016). For a while, this difference might lead teenagers to feel like their lives are slightly out of control. For example, adolescent brains have trouble processing other people's facial expressions, making it hard to feel like they relate to anyone (or vice versa; Yurgelun-Todd, 2007). Teens' own emotions seem dramatic, but they also have trouble seeing or understanding how anyone else is feeling.

One outcome of the neural shifting is increased risk-taking. Starting around fifth or sixth grade (ages 9–10), our brains start producing chemical rushes of serotonin, which stimulate thoughts, feelings, and behaviors that are full of great promise and unique hazards: impulsive decisions combined with a lack of inhibition and boredom combined with a need for novelty and immediate gratification (Jensen & Nutt, 2015; Luna et al., 2015; Mills et al., 2014).

These feelings accelerate through adolescence and help explain why teenagers make decisions they sometimes later regret, such as playing dangerous sports, experimenting with alcohol and drugs, or (in the case of one of Wind's high school friends) trying to invent and test new kinds of fireworks in the forest (Bava & Tapert, 2010; Geier, 2013; Spielberg et al., 2014). This pattern in adolescent behavior seems true all around the world: Sensation seeking steadily increases from around 10 to around age 19, then declining as people age (Steinberg et al., 2018).

Your loved ones may have worried about all this possible risk-taking during adolescence. So, consider this age-old advice: "Be good—and if you can't be good, be careful."

Cognitive Development

Logic and abstract thought are essential.

But as preteens, this kind of mental processing can be tough. If you had trouble grasping concepts in an algebra or physics class, you know that it can take time to stretch these mental muscles. As school challenges us and we move into our teenage years, our mental capacities quickly evolve to include logical thinking, basic arithmetic, and concrete analogies or comparisons.

Middle Childhood: Concrete Operational

Recall from Table 8.3 that Piaget's (1930, 1932) cognitive-developmental theory suggests that around age 6 or 7, we get to Stage 3, *concrete operational.* There are two major achievements we'll accomplish at this stage, and you have to get both of them down.

The first achievement is called *conservation.* Experiment 3: Imagine you are at a table with two rows of 10 pennies lined up with one row directly above the other in one-to-one correspondence. Someone takes one set of coins and spaces them further apart into a longer row. Then they ask, "Which row has the most pennies?" If you say they're still equal, then your little person has achieved conservation, the understanding that physical objects can change shape but still maintain their basic properties. It's like when you decide whether to cut your medium pizza into 8 pieces or 10 pieces—either way, you still have the same amount of pizza.

This is also the age when children can first grapple with *classifications* and *reversibility.* Classification means there are logical hierarchies, like general categories (dogs) and subcategories (poodles, beagles, chihuahuas, etc.). Children learn rules like "all poodles are dogs, but not all dogs are poodles." Reversibility means that some things can go back and forth, while others can't. In basic arithmetic, 2 + 5 = 7, and

7 − 5 = 2. Water can freeze into ice, and it can later melt back into water. But you can't unscramble an egg, and once grandpa passes away, he's not coming back (something that you may struggle to understand as a 6-year-old).

Adolescence: Formal Operations

Children reach Piaget's final stage of cognitive development around the age of 12, when puberty begins. Here, children slowly gain the ability to consider abstract ideas and hypothetical scenarios. For example, children can now use their minds to engage in intelligent debates such as

- Is it possible to have more than one "best" friend?
- Could there be life on other planets?
- The morality of forced labor in the home via chores

A big test of your development is whether you've gotten through all four of Piaget's stages. Piaget referred to Stage 4 as *formal operations* because children can now have meta-cognitions, the ability to think about how they think.

Experiment 4: Piaget created a kind of "final exam" for children past adolescence called the *pendulum problem* (Inhelder & Piaget, 1958). To test this, imagine you are brought to a table with a framework for swinging different pendulums (shown in Figure 8.3). You are asked how different properties of the pendulum will affect how

---

FIGURE 8.3

Piaget's Pendulum Problem

To test whether adolescents have completed all of Piaget's cognitive stages, they might be asked how different aspects of a pendulum (such as the length of string and weight at the end) will affect how quickly it swings.

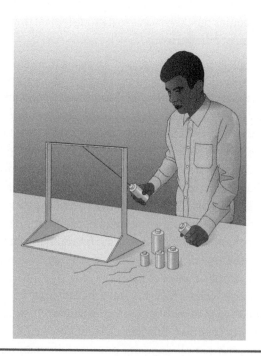

Source: Kuther (2023).

quickly it swings, including how long the string is, how much the bottom weighs, the height the pendulum is dropped from, and whether the pendulum is pushed or simply dropped. At this age, you can begin to imagine these scenarios in your head and make predictions.

WHAT'S MY SCORE?

Identity Versus Role Confusion

Erikson (1959) suggested that in our late teens and young adulthood, we explore our identity and social roles. How far are you in this process?

Instructions: Please answer the following questions regarding how you feel about yourself in general. Use the following scale for each question:

1	2	3	4
Never applies to me	Occasionally or seldom applies to me	Fairly often applies to me	Very often applies to me

____ 1. I wonder what sort of person I really am.

____ 2. People seem to change their opinion of me.

____ 3. I feel certain about what I should do with my life.

____ 4. I feel uncertain as to whether something is morally right or wrong.

____ 5. Most people seem to agree about what sort of person I am.

____ 6. I feel my way of life suits me.

____ 7. My worth is recognized by others.

____ 8. I feel freer to be my real self when I am away from those who know me very well.

____ 9. I feel that what I am doing in life is not really worthwhile.

____ 10. I feel I fit in well in the community in which I live.

____ 11. I feel proud to be the sort of person I am.

____ 12. People seem to see me very differently from the way I see myself.

____ 13. I feel left out.

____ 14. People seem to disapprove of me.

____ 15. I change my ideas about what I want from life.

____ 16. I am unsure as to how people feel about me.

____ 17. My feelings about myself change.

____ 18. I feel I am putting on an act or doing something for effect.

____ 19. I feel proud to be a member of the society in which I live.

Scoring instructions: First, reverse-score Items 1, 2, 4, 8, 9, 12, 13, 14, 15, 16, 17, and 18.

Then, add up all 19 of your responses. Your total score will be between 19 and 76, with higher numbers indicating more of an established identity. Lower scores indicate "identity confusion," meaning you are still exploring and experimenting with who you want to be. ●

Source: Ochse and Plug (1986).

Psychosocial Development

Uh oh—you got caught stealing at the mall.

You're livid because you're embarrassed and worry about what this means for your future. Your caregiver lectures you about "knowing better." Of course, you know that stealing is wrong, but you lowkey wanted to impress your friends. But what if that wasn't the case? What if you stole because you were starving and didn't have access to food otherwise? Or, what if you stole from someone who was extremely wealthy, yet stingy with their resources? And how would you feel if you were stealing in order to save someone's life?

We can even consider broad issues of social justice. Would you follow a corrupt law, or would you be willing to accept the consequences for breaking the law or protesting for it to be overturned? When is civil disobedience okay? Our answers to these complex questions are influenced by psychological factors and the surrounding social environment.

Kohlberg's Stages

According to Kohlberg's theory of moral development (Table 8.5), children enter the *conventional* stage between ages 9 and 11 and the *postconventional* stage from age 12 to young adulthood. In middle childhood (before completing adolescence), children have internalized more social norms and cultural rules. Here, children make decisions about what to do because they want to be socially accepted. They follow rules and conform. Remember the Heinz dilemma we discussed earlier? A child at this stage might think that Heinz should steal the drug because spouses ought to make sacrifices for each other—or that he shouldn't steal, because it's against the law and he should be "good."

Kohlberg found that in late adolescence and emerging adulthood, people think about moral and ethical dilemmas from a more philosophical view. That is, they could form opinions based on an understanding of the nuances and context of the situation. Maybe Heinz should not steal the drug because if vigilantes start doing whatever they want, chaos and anarchy will take over. On the other hand, other adolescents might see the value of civil disobedience and decide that if laws are unjust, maybe they can be broken.

There is evidence for Kohlberg's basic idea. Children do evolve in their moral thinking in the same basic stages he suggested (Edwards, 1981, 1982; Krebs & Denton, 2005; Krebs & Van Hesteren, 1994; Snarey, 1985). But, you might have noticed that we said Kohlberg did his original testing with a group of 75 *boys*. What about everyone else? Psychologist Carol Gilligan is a strong voice arguing that any theory based on such a limited view of humanity will have some biases (Gilligan, 1982). Her own research indicated that gender might affect how people see the world, at least partially, because parents and guardians raise boys and girls with such different expectations. She proposed that boys would likely make moral decisions using a "justice" orientation, focused on individual rights and what they thought was "fair," whereas girls would use a "care" orientation, focused on responsibility for all the relationships involved.

While Gilligan was justified in pointing out the sexist nature of Kohlberg's original work, others have since pointed out that maybe her modification was sexist itself, still emphasizing differences in genders. In a meta-analysis reviewing many studies on this question, only slight differences between boys and girls emerged (Jaffee & Hyde, 2000).

When you cross over from childhood to adulthood, many important life decisions and changes happen.

iStock.com/nirat

EARLY AND MIDDLE ADULTHOOD

>> **LO 8.4** **Explain the common milestones adults experience, including biological, cognitive, and social developments.**

You have to live in a van.

Imagine that you successfully graduated high school but couldn't decide on a college or even a future career. So, you bought a used van, converted the back into a bedroom, and struck out to tour national parks. It's unclear what that path would mean for your future.

Emerging adulthood is a time when we graduate from children to adults. In our early 20s, we experiment with our identity, relationships, and careers. As we move forward into our 30s, 40s, and 50s, each aspect of life evolves. For many, this can mean bad changes such as health risks—but it also can mean good changes, like finding a meaningful relationship partner or graduating from college. Let's consider biological, cognitive, and psychosocial development during this consequential stage of life.

Biological Development

You are young and healthy, and people around you encourage you to not take it for granted.

Our physical functioning peaks during emerging adulthood, so for now, you are perfectly happy with sleeping bags and long hikes. Sexual drive and exploration also peak in our 20s and 30s (King, 2019). Eventually, we all move on to senescence, a gradual decline in physical health through old age (Giannoula et al., 2023; Spini et al., 2016). People don't tend to really notice these changes until their 30s or 40s. Our strength decreases, unless we continually exercise, and we tend to put on weight. Vision and hearing are beginning to decline and by around age 40, and bifocal lenses may become necessary.

During this period, you also notice your skin is beginning to slightly wrinkle and that gray hairs are becoming more visible. Your height and sexual functioning don't go unscathed either! You may lose about a half inch for every 10 years past 40, although people who develop osteoporosis may lose up to 8 inches or more (Cummings & Melton, 2002). And while your sexual functioning may not decrease in middle adulthood, opportunities for sexual activity may be fewer as family responsibilities, finances, or career stress puts a damper on middle-age romance.

For many women around age 40, estrogen declines as the body's reproductive system prepares to cease that function. By about age 50, menopause will have begun and most women will have stopped ovulating and having a menstrual cycle. Most men also go through a time of sexual changes, but it is much more gradual. Andropause usually begins in the 40s with a decline in testosterone, which may result in physical symptoms such as fatigue, irritability, and potential problems in sexual functioning.

You will quickly learn that it is in middle adulthood that many health problems start to occur. The wear and tear from smoking, drinking alcohol, and/or staying up late during young adulthood may catch up to you in a major way! Common health problems of middle adulthood are high blood pressure, heart problems, arthritis, and obesity. Statistically, the most frequent causes of death in middle adulthood include heart disease, cancer, and stroke.

Have You Ever Wondered?
8.4 How do we change in early and middle adulthood?

Emerging adulthood: The transition from adolescence to young adulthood, when we experiment with identity, relationships, and careers.

Senescence: A gradual decline in physical health through old age.

Cognitive Development

Don't worry because all is not lost!

Despite physical declines, intelligence seems to increase from early to middle adulthood (up to about age 50; Deary, 2014). Of course, that depends on a lot of factors, such as how we define and measure intelligence, as well as individual differences (Schaie, 2013):

- *Fluid intelligence* is how well we can make connections between ideas or apply past experiences to new situations. It's how quickly we can solve problems and analyze what's going on. That kind of intelligence seems to decrease once we hit our 30s (Anderson & Craik, 2017; Hartshorne & Germine, 2015).

- The good news is that *crystallized intelligence* stays stable and even shows moderate gains through middle adulthood and older age (Schaie, 2013, 2016). Crystallized intelligence is our long-term memory accumulation of facts and knowledge. If you're a trivia whiz, your crystallized intelligence is high.

Psychosocial Development

Big decisions.

Career, relationships, and parenthood—these are the decisions that will affect your entire life. Yes, they are important … but you are allowed to change your mind. Trying things allows us to both satisfy curiosity and to see what seems right to us. Your path might be unique, and that's OK. Consider what psychology has to offer about this big time in your life.

Career Exploration

Sometimes our careers seem to choose us.

Think back. Maybe that year you lived in a van ended up working out. Your tour of national parks developed into a deep love of nature photography and an outstanding photo blog. It was published by an independent, boutique company and was the validation you needed to seriously start thinking about a career in photography. After working for a few years to save money, you took the leap and went back to college at the age of 27.

Just over two thirds of high school grads in the United States eventually go to college (Hussar et al., 2020). The experience can be transformational. Looking back, people remember their college years as extremely influential in shaping their beliefs, values, worldviews, ability to solve problems, and feel confident in their identity (King & Kitchener, 2016; Lapsley & Hardy, 2017; Patton et al., 2016). The more involved they are in extracurriculars and other parts of campus life, the more they feel a sense of belonging and satisfaction (Mayhew et al., 2016).

Unfortunately, college life is a privilege that isn't distributed equally. Not all high school graduates are able to afford college, a burden often felt by traditionally marginalized groups. When they do attend college, many are *first-generation students*, or the first person in their family to attend a 4-year college. First-generation students struggle more when the expectations of college are not aligned with students' home and personal responsibilities (Skomsvold, 2014; Tinto, 2012). Barriers to college completion are complex. For example, some students feel pressure to spend time helping at home and to spend any extra money on family needs, instead of relative luxuries like optional trips (Stephens et al., 2012; Vasquez-Salgado et al., 2015).

Student over the age of 22 often face similar pressures. These students experience challenges unfamiliar to many traditionally aged students. For example, paying for school while paying a mortgage, caring for children, and having a career adds multiple layers of stress (MacDonald, 2018). However, older students also tend to appreciate college more and take it more seriously in terms of career advancement (Cesnales et al., 2022).

Choosing a career is seldom easy even under ideal circumstances. One third of college students change their major at least once, and about 10% change it even more (National Center for Education Statistics, 2017). This exploration is understandable as we transition through developmental stages of life. Table 8.7 shows a model of five stages of occupational goals and the typical age range for each, at least in the United States (Super, 1980).

Of course, not everyone progresses through these ages or even successfully gets the chance to pursue their real dreams. Most adults have had nine different jobs or careers by the time they are middle aged (U.S. Bureau of Labor Statistics, 2015). If you're in college or university right now, we hope you are thrilled with your program of study and that you are thriving as you meet people with shared interests. When you consider the five stages in Table 8.7, where would you place yourself?

TABLE 8.7

Super's Five Stages of Occupational Goals

Super (1980) suggested five typical stages of career development.

AGE	STAGE	WHAT'S HAPPENING
14–18	Crystallization	Explore different careers and pick a tentative interest.
18–21	Specification	Identify a career choice and start pursuing it.
21–24	Implementation	Complete training or education and get an initial job.
24–35	Stabilization	Become established in a career; confirm your satisfaction.
35+	Consolidation	Advance with promotions and added responsibilities.

CAREER CORNER

Meet Mych'layla, Middle School and High School Teacher

What is your career?

I'm a charter school teacher (middle and high school). As a teacher, I've had the pleasure of creating individualized lesson plans, assisting children with emotional and social regulation, helping them developmentally as each child set out to learn the grade-level curriculum. I teach Spanish, English, Math, Social Studies, and Science.

How was studying psychology important for success in this career?

Psychology was important for success in this career because understanding what is developmentally appropriate for learning, understanding, and maintaining emotional and social well-being are all major factors in teaching the whole child. **Psychology enabled me to understand the importance of basic**

(Continued)

(Continued)

needs being met before the child can perform, academically, at their highest potential.

How do concepts from this chapter help in this career?

Piaget's cognitive theory speaks to the different stages that children go through as they learn. This essentially places some of the accountability for learning on the student, as they are active participants in the process (experimenting, making observations, utilizing curiosity as a guide, etc.) while focusing on how the students will learn best at that developmental stage. ***Vygotsky's theory*** also emphasized the need for scaffolding,

breaking down lesson plans into parts with a tool to assist in building understanding.

Is this the career you always planned to have after college?

Actually, no. I wanted to be a child psychologist. I burned out after 11 years in that field because I stopped loving the work. So I left and became a teacher. This is my dream job!

If you could give current college students one sentence of advice, what would it be?

Go with your heart; it's your purpose waiting to be fulfilled. ●

Intimate Relationships

For most young and middle-aged adults, forming close relationships is a critical support for their mental health and happiness (Busch & Hofer, 2012). The more confident we feel about ourselves and what we want in life, the more positive those relationships will be (Barry et al., 2009; Beyers & Seiffge-Krenke, 2010). This kind of intimacy doesn't have to come from a romantic or sexual partner; friendships can provide the same support (Gillespie et al., 2015; Hartup & Stevens, 1999; Wrzus et al., 2017). And adults who choose to be single can be equally happy. Unpartnered individuals face a curious prejudice called **singlism**: Most cultures *perceive* that single people will be unhappy. That said, over 90% of adults will be married or live with a partner at least once in their life (Connidis, 2001).

Singlism: The prejudiced belief that single adults are less happy and mature than adults in intimate relationships.

Over your life, you'll probably have a variety of relationships—friendships, life partners, and, of course, acquaintances like neighbors or work associates. You love a lot of people, but not all in the same way. As we mature, we sometimes prioritize our time and attention with relationships of different types. One way to think about how all the people in our life matter in different ways is a popular model called **Sternberg's triangular theory of love** (Sternberg, 1986). The theory is shown in Figure 8.4.

Sternberg's triangular theory of love: The idea that relationships can vary on three factors: intimacy, passion, and commitment.

Sternberg says that love is made up of three components, and the degree to which each component is present in each relationship determines its nature. The three components are

- *Intimacy:* Emotional closeness, connection, and bonding; shared respect and trust

- *Passion:* Sexual drive and physical intimacy

- *Commitment:* The thoughtful decision to maintain a relationship with this person, sometimes exclusively

If you barely know someone, you have none of the components; Sternberg calls this nonlove. Nonlove is the relationship you have with most people in your life (Sternberg, 1986), such as the crowds of people on the street or even those people at work where you can never remember their name. Companionate love refers to deep friendships. It doesn't include the sexual attraction of passion, but it has trust and emotional connection. In this model, the ideal intimate partnership has all three components. That's called consummate love, meaning it is complete or perfect. Again,

FIGURE 8.4

Sternberg's Triangular Theory of Love

In this theory (Sternberg, 1986), there are eight kinds of love that vary based on whether they have intimacy, commitment, and passion.

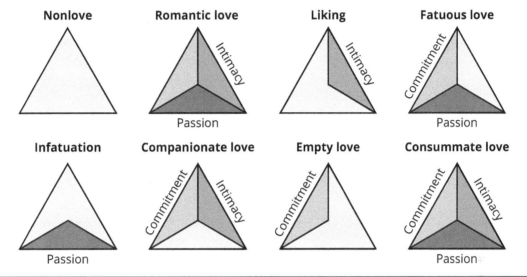

Source: Sternberg (1986).

you get to choose what kind of relationships you have in life, and what works for one person doesn't work for everyone. For some people, parenting is their most important relationships—let's explore that next.

Parenthood

Do you want to raise children?

The three top reasons people in the United States cite for why they choose to embark on parenthood are (O'Laughlin & Anderson, 2001)

1. wanting to feel the parent–child bond,

2. looking forward to the fun and growth that will occur, and

3. the hope of nurturing another person to achieve their own best potential.

Parenthood comes with challenges, like the loss of freedom, stress of dealing with problematic behavior, and expenses! Middle-income parents will spend an average of just under a quarter million dollars getting their little one to age 18 (U.S. Department of Agriculture, 2017). And that doesn't include college. New parents also experience many transitions:

- Changes in their identity and friendships

- Increased expenses

- Time management problems

- Additional chores

- Sleep deprivation

- Less time for hobbies or friendships

Having children can also contribute to lower self-esteem and lower mental health in new parents (Bleidorn et al., 2016; Nelson et al., 2014). These issues often affect new mothers more than new fathers. Mothers can experience postpartum (after childbirth) depression (Escribà-Agüir & Artazcoz, 2011). They are usually expected to perform more of the baby care and take a longer break from their career, especially in heterosexual couples (Katz-Wise et al., 2010; Nilsen et al., 2012). It may be that even in sexual-minority couples, including lesbian, gay, bisexual, transgender, queer, asexual, intersex, two-spirit, and other (LGBTQAI2S+) families, childcare duties are clustered together unequally (Goldberg, 2013; Goldberg et al., 2012). For example, in a study of 116 women and 128 men in sexual-minority relationships, Civettini (2015) showed that the division of labor is not shaped by gender per se but by levels of traditionally feminine and masculine traits. All genders also report more conflict in their relationships and marriages if they are parents, equating to lower satisfaction with their partner and less sex (Doss & Rhoades, 2017).

Older adulthood can have challenges, but many older people report great happiness and well-being.

iStock.com/monkeybusinessimages

OK, being a new parent is starting to sound awful. But new parents also claim that despite these challenges, parenthood is wonderful. They report loving their new identity as parents and that they have a greater sense of what's important in life (Brandel et al., 2018). There are also several different parenting styles, as shown in Figure 8.5 (see Baumrind, 1971). Each is associated with different outcomes, for both children and their parents (e.g., Allmann et al., 2022; Cheng & Deng, 2022; Dong et al., 2022). Which would be your ideal style of parenting? Which do you feel like your own caregivers used when raising you?

Usually, you need to be a parent to be a grandparent! Being a grandparent is typically very rewarding—even more than parenthood. It comes with positive mental

FIGURE 8.5

The Four Parenting Styles

Parenting does not come with a manual, but there are four general parenting styles.

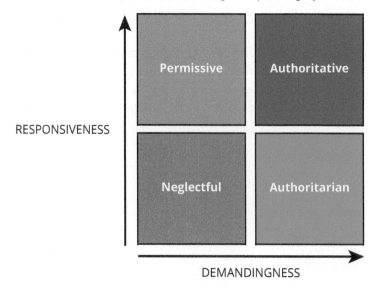

health and the feeling that you're leaving a real legacy behind when you eventually pass away (Coall & Hertwiz, 2011; Condon et al., 2018; Moore & Rosenthal, 2015). And that brings us to the final stage of life: late adulthood.

Practice what you learn in **Knowledge Check 8.4**   Sage Vantage

LATE ADULTHOOD

>> **LO 8.5   Discuss the major biological, cognitive, and social transitions that characterize late adulthood and how we adjust to death.**

What is your dream retirement?

Some people imagine being active; they want to travel the world, visit museums, and see their extended family. Others want peace and quiet, including time to read all the books on the shelf or finally catch up with streaming every show on your list. Some people want to live on their own, while others enjoy living in a community of other older people.

Any vision you have for yourself can be an ideal that you work toward. But you should also consider what psychological research predicts you'll experience as you enter and go through this last stage of life. Just like the earlier stages, you will probably go through physical, cognitive, and social changes.

Physical Aging

Napping, eating, walking, and conversing.

These might be your favorite pastimes during late adulthood. Interestingly, these might also some of your most frequent leisure activities as a college student. Although your leisure activities may be similar in some ways, late adulthood brings about many physical changes. Hair thinning and turning gray, skin wrinkling and folding, and continued loss of height due to loss of bone density are some of the most obvious physical changes. Sensory capabilities, such as vision, hearing, smell, and taste, become less sensitive and also decrease as a result of aging. Reaction time slows and physical stamina changes (Schilling & Diehl, 2015).

Even so, when people enter their 50s and 60s, there is a divergence between chronological, biological, and psychological age. Different gene pools, different biological effects of gene and environment interactions, and different psychological profiles make for very different 80-year-olds!

But exactly why do we physically decline as we age? Genetic programming theories of aging suggest that our longevity is primarily determined at conception and is largely reliant on our parents and their genes. These theories suggest that human cells have a built-in time limit to their reproduction and that they are no longer able to divide after a certain time, eventually becoming harmful to the body and self-destructing.

In contrast, wear-and-tear theories of aging suggest that aging is essentially an accident, an accumulation of damage and wear and tear to the body that eventually leads to death (Helgeson & Zajdel, 2017). In short, our body will eventually wear out like an old car. Research supports both the genetic programming and the wear-and-tear views, and it may be that both processes contribute to natural aging. Nonetheless, physical aging is not a disease but a natural biological process. On the bright side, some physical functions do not decline with age. For example, though sexual activity may decrease, it remains pleasurable well into old age.

Have You Ever Wondered?
8.5 What is it like to be in late adulthood and to approach death?

Cognitive Development

As we get older, we usually reflect on how well things turned out.

No life is perfect, but most older adults say their life is pretty darn good. They report positivity in terms of family, health, identity, personality, hobbies, and self-esteem (Freund, 1999; Ready et al., 2012). There is some research indicating that the way older adults may evaluate their lives may vary based on demographics. For example, Lee and colleagues (2020) found gender differences in reflections of quality of life among older adults such that a higher proportion of older men as compared to older women perceived their life as good or very good.

Even so, happy experiences are more likely when people focus on their successes and strengths—and for many, happiness just keeps going up as we get older (Darbonne et al., 2013; Jeste & Oswald, 2014). As Erikson predicted in his theory of important life stages (see Table 8.1 at the start of this chapter), you get a great sense of accomplishment from reflecting on your life with integrity and pride. After all, **subjective age** is the idea that we're only as "old" as we feel and that many adults feel younger, psychologically, than their chronological age implies.

Still, some declines in cognitive functioning during late adulthood do occur, as skills related to fluid intelligence, such as reasoning with new information and memory, show rapid declines in late adulthood (Bajpai et al., 2022).

Alzheimer's disease can be heartbreaking. In general, *dementia* is mental deterioration of mental abilities due to malfunctioning neural connections; it affects decision-making, emotions, memories, and emotion regulation (Alzheimer's Association, 2018). Probably the most well-known form of dementia is Alzheimer's disease, brain deterioration that causes problems in all the dementia categories (Agronin, 2014). The cause seems to be a buildup of proteins in the brain leading to clumps of dead neurons (called *amyloid plaques*) and tangled neural pathways called *neurofibrillary tangles* (Graham et al., 2017; Takahashi et al., 2017).

For most people, Alzheimer's moves through predictable steps. First comes memory problems, probably because of neural deterioration in the hippocampus (Guzmán-Vélez et al., 2016). We're all absent-minded sometimes (Where the heck did we park? Why did we walk into this room?), but it happens more as we get older, although more severely and rapidly for those with Alzheimer's. Attention span also declines (Huntley et al., 2017), making conversation harder. Confusion occurs more easily and vocabulary diminishes (Carson et al., 2015; Gollan et al., 2017). In the later stages, those with Alzheimer's might experience unpredictable emotions, including anger, paranoia, and depression (Agronin, 2014; Chi et al., 2014). Finally, there are larger memory issues (such as not recognizing friends and family) and loss of the ability to take care of themselves (Carson et al., 2015; Lavallée et al., 2016).

That's all pretty scary. Luckily, research is helping us understand how to prevent—or at least, slow down—Alzheimer's symptoms. First, different people have different risk levels: It's more common in women and people of color. Importantly, though, these differences aren't due to any biological differences; they seem instead to be due to differences in social determinants of health like where people live and work, level of education, and access to health care (Adkins-Jackson et al., 2023; Gurland et al., 1999). But Alzheimer's does run in families, showing that biological factors are relevant (Bettens et al., 2013).

What can you do to lower your chances of having Alzheimer's? You already have a head start: The higher the education level you achieve, the better neural health you'll have (Boots et al., 2015; Sattler et al., 2012; Seyedsalehi et al., 2023). College graduates are also likely to make more money, which means better access to health care (van de Vorst et al., 2016). Good nutrition seems to serve a protective role (Daviglus et al.,

Subjective age: How old we feel, psychologically (compared to our chronological age).

2010). Generally staying active also matters—get exercise (Tapia-Rojas et al., 2016). And keep learning new things (Hu, 2022)! Research indicates that playing a musical instrument and speaking more than one language are both great ways to decrease the onset of symptoms (Anderson et al., 2020; Walsh et al., 2021).

Social Changes

Getting old can be really great.

In retirement, we can focus on what we really care about, take vacations, and relax (Davies et al., 2017). All that being said, how we feel in older adulthood varies vastly from person to person, depending on a lot of variables. These include physical and mental health, social supports, economic stability, and positive relationships with friends and family. What remains true is that while late adulthood brings about significant challenges, for example, the death of a spouse, older adults often see themselves as functioning members of society (Wenger, 2021).

There is no single way to age successfully. However, the activity theory of aging suggests that successful aging is characterized by maintaining the interests, activities, and level of social interaction experienced during earlier stages of life. On the other hand, not all people in late adulthood need to engage as intensely with others on physical, psychological, or social levels. The disengagement theory of aging suggests that successful aging is characterized by a gradual withdrawal from the world. This disengagement is thought to provide an opportunity for increased reflectiveness and decreased emotional investment in others at a time in life when social relationships will inevitably end by death.

When you die, do you want to be buried, cremated, or something else? Does just thinking about this question make you change the way you think about your loved ones or your beliefs?

iStock.com/leezsnow

Death and Dying

There is nothing more inevitable in life than death.

As an older adult, you aren't just marking time until death. Rather, old age is a time of continued growth and development like any other important period in life. But at some time in your life, you will face death. The talk of death may be taboo, but preparing for death is a crucial developmental task, and awareness of its psychological aspects and consequences can make its inevitable arrival more understandable.

Managing Death Anxiety

Death is scary.

That's the basic premise of an intriguing idea called **terror management theory** (we'll call it TMT; Pyszczynski et al., 1996, 2003). As we get older, we're reminded of our own mortality in various ways, such as declining mental and physical health and an increasing number of funerals to attend. TMT is based on several basic premises, including

- All living things want to keep living.
- Humans are aware that we will not get to keep living forever.
- The thought of our eventual death is terrifying.

Terror management theory: The idea that when we're reminded of our own mortality, we comfort ourselves by clinging to worldviews or relationships.

We manage this death anxiety in two major ways: (1) trying to avoid thinking about it or (2) focusing on what we think makes life meaningful.

Ideally, we just don't think about it. TMT argues that how we spend our day, such as watching TV or engaging in any other hobby, is a distraction from our fears. But we can't escape death. Everyday occurrences like hearing an ambulance, walking past a funeral home, or seeing someone with a COVID-19 protective mask induces *mortality salience*, a reminder that death is coming for us (Greenberg et al., 2001). And according to the research, we respond to this anxiety in interesting ways.

One response is that we emphasize what we believe makes the world and life *matter*. This can be relatively healthy, such as when people become more devout in their religious beliefs and try to be more charitable toward others. But it can also take a darker direction. Research shows that when people are reminded of death, they also tend to become more prejudiced and aggressive toward others (Greenberg & Kosloff, 2008). Either way, these heightened beliefs seem to bring comfort to people who believe they are making the world a "better place."

Mortality salience is positively correlated with victim blaming and negatively correlated with compassion (Hirschberger, 2006; Hirschberger et al., 2005). Reminding people of death makes them recommend harsher penalties for crimes like prostitution (Jonas et al., 2008) and be more supportive of the military (Taubman-Ben-Ari & Findler, 2006). A theme in these findings is that people seem to strongly embrace whatever they believe about how the world works, because they want to approach death with the belief that their life meant something.

And this need for comfort also makes people cling to their relationships more than ever. For several months after the 9/11 terrorist attacks in the United States, the number of engagements, marriages, and babies born increased dramatically (Wisman & Goldenberg, 2005). We want the validation that we're loved and that our lives have included respect and connection with others. Being in love provides a happy distraction from death and makes us feel truly alive. Even so, psychological preparation for our own death often comes with acceptance of the inevitable.

Accepting Death

It's a fact: Everyone dies.

Kübler-Ross stages of dying theory: The idea that when we know we're close to death, we move through five stages: denial, anger, bargaining, depression, and acceptance.

The science of approaching and accepting death was pioneered by psychiatrist Elisabeth Kübler-Ross (1969). She interviewed hundreds of people who were terminally ill, many of whom were on *hospice care*, when health professionals focus on quality of life at the end stages. This qualitative research was the foundation for the **Kübler-Ross stages of dying theory** (see Table 8.8). She emphasized that throughout all five stages, hope was both possible and important.

TABLE 8.8

Kübler-Ross's Five Stages of Dying

Kübler-Ross (1969) suggested five psychological stages as we approach our own death.

STAGE	WHAT'S HAPPENING
Denial	Refusal to admit that death is imminent (rejecting a diagnosis, minimizing the severity of symptoms, etc.)
Anger	Emotional responses of anger toward others (blaming physicians, lack of trust in research, etc.)
Bargaining	Attempts to negotiate to find a way to avoid death (making a "deal" with a higher power, paying for experimental treatments, etc.)
Depression	Feeling a loss of control and hopelessness
Acceptance	Finding stability and closure; saying goodbye

Kübler-Ross's ideas have led to hundreds of research studies and interesting applications, such as whether these stages can be applied to going through a divorce (Gastil, 1996; Kruk, 1991), athletes accepting serious injuries (Van der Poel & Nel, 2011), or how we responded to the COVID-19 pandemic (Dzhurova, 2020; Tempski et al., 2020). That said, there have been numerous criticisms of the theory—so much that many scholars suggest it should be a historical framework more than a valid model for modern applications (Corr, 2021). Some have been even more critical, calling the theory "inadequate, superficial, and misleading" (Corr, 1993, p. 70).

For example, it's clear that not everyone who's approaching death goes through all five stages or that the order of stages experienced follows a consistent pattern (Corr et al., 2018; Kastenbaum, 2000, 2005, 2012). How we confront our death is individual and varies based on hundreds of variables, such as illness, relationships, and general situation. There are differences in how cultures understand death and what happens when a person dies. In some cultural traditions, death may be viewed as a transition to other forms of existence; some cultures propose a circular pattern of multiple deaths and rebirths, and yet other cultures view death as the final end with nothing afterward at all (Gire, 2014).

These different conceptions have a noticeable influence on people's lifestyles, readiness to die for a cause, the degree to which they fear death, expressions of grief and mourning, and the nature of funeral rituals (Gire, 2014). Regardless of how or where we were born, for most of us, what really matters as we help people transition toward death is that they can complete unfinished business, spend time with loved ones, are free of pain, and get the opportunity to feel at peace (Renz et al., 2018).

Despite the many criticisms of Kübler-Ross's model, we may be able to learn three basic lessons from it (as suggested by Corr, 1993):

- First, dying people aren't dead yet—listening to them and respecting their needs is paramount.

- Second, we cannot fully help them unless we develop empathy and focus on *their* needs, not our own.

- And finally, we should learn from their experiences, progressing on our own path toward understanding life and ourselves.

Perhaps we should fall back on what the ancient philosopher Socrates supposedly recommended (see Plato, 1962): that true wisdom is nothing, if not preparing for death. ●

Practice what you learn in **Knowledge Check 8.5**   Sage Vantage➤

CHAPTER REVIEW

Learning Objectives Summary

8.1 How do psychologists study human life span development?

>> LO 8.1 **Compare and contrast five theoretical approaches to studying human development.**

Developmental psychology is the study of how humans change and grow over our life span. Psychoanalytic theories, behaviorist and learning theories, cognitive theories, contextual theories, and evolutionary perspectives all suggest we change as we grow up—but each emphasizes different reasons why and variables that affect individual differences.

8.2   How do we change during prenatal development, infancy, and early childhood?

>> LO 8.2   Analyze the major competencies of the prenatal period and infancy and the milestones of biological, cognitive, and social development during early childhood.

Prenatal development progresses through the germinal, embryonic, and fetal periods. According to Piaget, cognitive development in infancy and early childhood is characterized by object permanence and language development. In early childhood, Kohlberg's theory of moral development proposed that morality and ethics are based on getting rewards or avoiding punishments.

8.3   How do we change during middle childhood and adolescence?

>> LO 8.3   Summarize the biological, cognitive, and social changes experienced during middle childhood and adolescence.

According to Piaget, cognitive development in middle childhood is characterized by conservation, classification, and reversibility. By adolescence, abstract thought appears. In middle childhood and adolescence, forming friendships becomes an important social task. Our biological development is also key during this stage of life; our neural development increases significantly.

8.4   How do we change in early and middle adulthood?

>> LO 8.4   Explain the common milestones adults experience, including biological, cognitive, and social developments.

Emerging adulthood is a time when we emphasize careers and whether we choose to commit to life partners. Our bodies also experience senescence, a graduate decline in physical health. Nonetheless, intelligence seems to increase from early to middle adulthood. Finally, Sternberg developed a theory that our relationships are made up of three major components: intimacy, passion, and commitment.

8.5   What is it like to be in late adulthood and to approach death?

>> LO 8.5   Discuss the major biological, cognitive, and social transitions that characterize late adulthood and how we adjust to death.

In late adulthood, many people experience neural declines that lead to conditions such as Alzheimer's disorder. Activity theory of aging and the disengagement theory of aging propose ways to age successfully. More controversial theories at this stage are terror management theory (the idea that we all look for ways to distract ourselves from our inevitable mortality) and Kübler-Ross's stages of grief theory, which has received several criticisms.

CRITICAL THINKING QUESTIONS

1.   Consider Erikson's eight stages of identity development (shown in Table 8.1). Think of three or four people you know personally who fit into different stages shown here. Explain who these people are and why you think they fit into the stages you've identified. Then, discuss where you think you are, right now, and why that stage seems to fit.

2.   A classic moral dilemma is the "trolley problem." Look it up online (you'll likely find several variations). Then, discuss what moral or ethical decision you believe a 10-year-old would make and a 16-year-old adolescent would make, given the variation you found. Finally, discuss what stage of Kohlberg's stage model each decision would fall in and why.

3.   Identify four celebrity couples. Based on what you have learned about each couple in the media, use Sternberg's triangular theory of love to discuss which one of the eight kinds of love you believe the couple represents and state why.

4.   Think of a time when you had to deal with a great personal loss. Can you relate to Kübler-Ross's stages of dying when navigating that loss? Compare and contrast your own experience with the stages she suggests. If you were going to update her theory, what would you add, subtract, or change?

KEY TERMS

Apgar scale, 231
Bronfenbrenner's bioecological
  model, 226
Developmental psychology, 225
Emerging adulthood, 243
Erikson's theory of identity
  development, 225
Feral children, 236
Kohlberg's theory of moral
  development, 234
Kübler-Ross stages of dying
  theory, 252

Piaget's cognitive-developmental
  theory, 232
Primary sex characteristics, 238
Senescence, 243
Singlism, 246
Sternberg's triangular
  theory of love, 246
Subjective age, 250
Terror management theory, 251
Vygotsky's sociocultural
  theory, 235

iStock.com/id-art

 Learning

Winter holidays smell like pecans and bourbon.

At least they do to Wind. When she was a kid, every year her mom baked pecan pies to give away and her dad set up an assembly line for their own little bourbon ball factory at home. Bourbon balls are little dough balls soaked in bourbon, a type of whisky likely invented in her parents' home state of Kentucky. For weeks, her house smelled like both desserts.

Now, years later, when she smells either pecan pie or bourbon, she immediately thinks of her parents and the holidays. The feelings that arise are happiness, excitement, and nostalgia. Whether it's Hanukah, Kwanza, Ramadan, Christmas, Diwali, or any other holiday, you know what smells, songs, rituals, and feelings are associated with it. Good or bad, these associations come from experiences in our past that we remember and that shape our reactions. The concepts in this chapter explain those reactions.

After reading this chapter, you will get answers to several questions you've been curious about:

Have You Ever Wondered?

9.1   What is classical conditioning?

9.2   What is operant conditioning?

9.3   What are cognitive and observational learning?

Learning Objectives

LO 9.1   Explain principles of classical conditioning, applications, and controversies.

LO 9.2   Explain principles of operant conditioning, applications, and controversies.

LO 9.3   Explain principles of cognitive and observational learning, applications, and controversies.

CLASSICAL CONDITIONING: STIMULUS AND RESPONSE

? Have You Ever Wondered?
9.1 What is classical conditioning?

>> LO 9.1   **Explain principles of classical conditioning, applications, and controversies.**

Can smells lead to feelings?

If you associate certain smells with memories (like holidays), you might have an emotional reaction to them. Similar experiences can happen with music, visual art, locations, and more. The associations and memories from our past make up our life experiences, which is how we learn. All of these associations, memories, and experiences change how we perceive the world and how we respond to it. In psychology, **learning** is a relatively long-term change in behavior or physiological responses, due to previous experiences.

Over the years, psychologists have identified several different forms of learning. We'll talk about each one in this chapter. For each major learning type, we'll identify basic principles and terms you should know, discuss classic research, go over some examples of how that kind of learning can be applied to your everyday world, and highlight an interesting controversy.

We'll begin by entering the glamorous world of . . . dog drool.

Learning: A relatively long-term change in behavior or physiological response, due to previous experiences.

Pavlov's Pioneering Research

Ivan Pavlov didn't start out as a psychologist.

He was trained as a physiologist and devoted the first part of his career to understanding how digestion works. In 1904, he earned the first Nobel Prize ever won by a Russian, in the field of Physiology and Medicine (not psychology). In the cold of St. Petersburg, Pavlov set up a research lab where he collected drool that trickled outside of dogs' mouths and was collected by a glass tube. He then measured how much they salivated when he gave them different kinds of food (Pavlov, 1927).

But Pavlov's experiments in digestion hit a big snag that turned out beautifully for psychology. He wanted to measure how much the dogs would drool at the precise moment (not before) the food he gave them touched their tongues. But the dogs quickly became familiar with his procedures. The dogs started to salivate at cues or signals in their environment that suggested the food was about to be served, including the sight of lab coats and the sound of someone coming down the hall.

According to Pavlov, the dogs had "psychic secretions" when they salivated early because they knew they were about to be fed. He was curious. This was a fascinating problem! The instinctive salivation reflex in response to food was an automatic, physiological response. But the reflex had transferred to other stimuli (such as lab coats and the sound of footsteps) that hinted at the food's imminent arrival. The dogs had learned how to predict what was about to happen.

Pavlov was hooked on the psychology behind this transfer of an instinctive, reflexive response. Now he needed a way to control it so he could also continue his work on digestion. He had to train the dogs to salivate on cue and not at any other time. He decided to train the dogs using various sound cues such as a metronome, whistle, tuning fork, and—yes—an electronic bell (Thomas, 1997).

At first, the dogs didn't salivate at all when they heard these noises. That's not surprising; there's no reason for a dog to salivate at the sounds of a tuning fork, metronome, or bell. But after repeatedly hearing the noise right before getting food, the dogs figured out the pairing. Now, they salivated at the noise in *anticipation* of what they assumed would happen next, based on their experiences.

They had learned. The kind of learning Pavlov studied is called **classical conditioning**. It occurs when a natural, instinctive, physiological response to one stimulus (like drooling because of food in your mouth) is transferred to another stimulus after the two have repeatedly been paired together (Figure 9.1). Classical

Ivan Pavlov pioneered research on classical conditioning when he trained dogs to salivate in response to a metronome, a whistle, a tuning fork, and other noise cues. While some people expressed doubt about whether he ever actually used a bell (Catania, 1994), Pavlov himself talked about the bell in lectures and a film (Thomas, 1997). Here, he's honored in a Russian stamp from 1991.

iStock.com/popovaphoto

One of Pavlov's actual dogs, preserved via taxidermy for over 100 years. You can see the tube used to measure salivation.

Rklawton via Wikimedia Commons. Licensed under CC BY-SA 3.0 DEED.

Classical conditioning: When a natural, physiological response to one stimulus is transferred to another because the two stimuli are associated with each other.

FIGURE 9.1

Pavlov's Famous Conditioning Research With Dogs

Pavlov trained dogs to salivate when they heard a certain noise. Salivation in response to a tuning fork is not a natural response. It only occurs after several conditioning trials in which the tuning fork is paired with presentation of food.

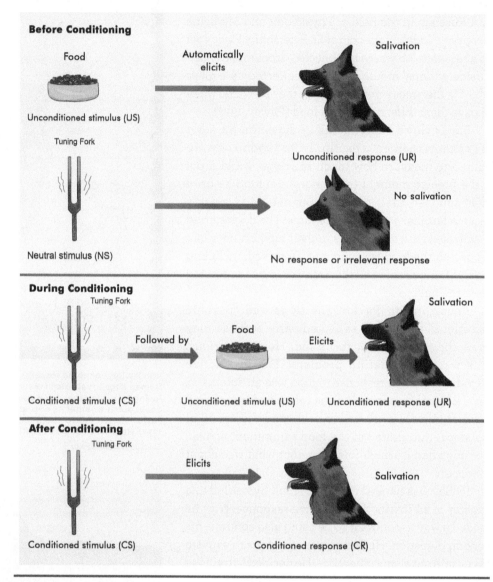

Illustrated by Sarah Yeh

conditioning involves anticipating what's about to happen because of a previous experience in the environment.

Types of Stimuli and Responses

Dogs aren't the only animals that can learn through classical conditioning.

To understand other examples, we first need to identify the types of stimuli and responses involved in Pavlov's experiment. There are a few terms that build the foundation of language around classical conditioning in psychology.

Before learning occurs:

- When we respond to something automatically and instinctively, we say that the stimulus (like food) is an **unconditioned stimulus**.

Unconditioned stimulus: An object, sound, smell, and so on in the environment that triggers an automatic, instinctive reaction.

- The reaction we have to that stimulus is an **unconditioned response**. Note that so far, no learning has occurred.

- The first time Pavlov hit a tuning fork and the dogs heard it, their ears might have moved, or their heads turned toward the sound—but they didn't salivate. This means that initially the sound was a **neutral stimulus**, one that doesn't cause any particular reaction.

Unconditioned response: The automatic, instinctive reaction caused by an unconditioned stimulus.

Neutral stimulus: An object, sound, smell, and so on in the environment that doesn't cause any particular reaction.

To do his digestion studies, Pavlov had to train the dogs. Over and over, he made a sound and then presented the dogs with food. Eventually, they learned the sound was a cue for what was about to happen.

After this learning occurs in classical conditioning, two additional terms come into play:

- After several trials of sound-then-food pairings, the dogs started salivating just from hearing the sound (see Figure 9.1). Now the sound was a **conditioned stimulus**: one that causes a reaction only after learning has occurred.

- Salivating to the sound is the **conditioned response**.

Conditioned stimulus: An object, sound, smell, and so on in the environment that causes an unnatural reaction only after learning has happened.

Conditioned response: The reaction caused by a conditioned stimulus, which occurs only after learning has happened.

That's classical conditioning.

Notice that the dogs don't control their environment—they simply respond to what's happening. A dog hears the sound and "begins to lick its lips vigorously," knowing the food is about to arrive (Pavlov, 1927, p. 22). Anyone who has a dog or cat can relate. Wind's dog gets *super* excited when she opens a certain drawer in her kitchen. Why? Because that's where she keeps the dog leash. He's learned to associate the sound of the drawer opening with going for a walk—so his excitement (a conditioned response) comes from the drawer (a conditioned stimulus) signaling what's about to happen, just like Pavlov's dogs learned to anticipate their food.

Table 9.1 has more classical conditioning examples of these different types of stimuli and responses.

TABLE 9.1

Examples of Classical Conditioning

Note that both the unconditioned response and the conditioned response are the same response, the same behavior or reaction. The difference is what caused this reaction. If the cause is natural and automatic, it's an unconditioned response. If the reaction is unnatural and only occurs because of previous association, it's a conditioned response and is evidence that learning has occurred.

SITUATION	UNCONDITIONED STIMULUS	UNCONDITIONED RESPONSE	CONDITIONED STIMULUS	CONDITIONED RESPONSE
A cat runs to the food bowl when it hears the can opener.	Cat food.	The cat running to the food bowl because there is food in it.	The sound of the can opener.	The cat running to the food bowl because of the sound.
A person's heartbeat increases when they hear a certain song because it was playing during their first kiss.	A kiss.	A person's heartbeat increasing due to the kiss.	The song.	The person's heartbeat increases when they hear the song.
A child feels fear in the waiting room at the dentist.	The pain of dental work.	Fear because of pain.	The dentist's waiting room.	The child feels fear as a result of sitting in the waiting room.
A person feels happiness when they smell pecan pie, because it was associated with a favorite family holiday growing up.	The favorite holiday.	Happiness about the holiday.	Smell of pecan pie.	Happiness when smelling pecan pie.

Classical Conditioning Phases

Learning usually takes time.

In fact, classical conditioning usually happens in three distinct phases.

Acquisition

Acquisition: In classical conditioning, it's when the association between two stimuli is first happening or is being strengthened with repeated pairings.

Acquisition is the phase of classical conditioning in which two stimuli are repeatedly paired together. It's the training phase. You know acquisition has happened when the conditioned response (like salivating in response to a sound) happens reliably.

There are many human examples of how acquisition can subtly affect everyday life. You may start drooling when you walk into a movie theater and smell the buttery popcorn or as you experience the sights and smells of holiday meals being prepared. After years of eating, acquisition has occurred when we pair food sights and smells with food tastes. You know just from the smell of popcorn what it's going to taste like (Gottfried & Dolan, 2003).

Here is another example. You've probably learned that the color red is associated with Valentine's Day, and some cultures use red during wedding ceremonies (Persaud & Bruggen, 2016). All these experiences seeing the color red paired with love and romance might change our perceptions and behavior. In one study, men sat closer to women and asked them more intimate questions when the women were wearing red, compared to green or blue (Niestra Kayser et al., 2010). Other studies show that photos of people are rated as more physically attractive when they're in front of a red background, compared to a white background—something to consider when you're creating your dating app profile (Elliot & Niestra, 2008; Schwarz & Singer, 2013).

Extinction

Extinction: In classical conditioning, it's when a conditioned response no longer occurs.

What would happen to Pavlov's salivating dogs if he kept making the sounds but stopped providing food? If you guessed the dogs would continue to drool for the first several trials, then slowly drool less each time until they stopped completely, then you would be right.

Extinction describes a conditioned response that no longer occurs because a previous association between two stimuli has stopped. Figure 9.2 shows you the steady rise and fall of responses during the first two phases (acquisition and extinction).

Spontaneous Recovery

Spontaneous recovery: In classical conditioning, it's when a conditioned response returns after a period of extinction.

After the dogs had experienced extinction, Pavlov discovered that if he left the dogs alone for several hours (for example, going home for the night and returning in the morning), the response would sometimes return if he played the sound again. This is shown on the right side of Figure 9.2, after the pause.

The return of a previously extinguished conditioned response is called **spontaneous recovery**. When it happens, the response will typically be weak; the dogs didn't salivate much. Spontaneous recovery probably happens after a break because the dogs aren't sure if the association has come back.

FIGURE 9.2

Acquisition, Extinction, and Spontaneous Recovery

Over acquisition trials, response to a conditioned stimulus (such as a sound) goes up each time. During extinction, response goes down because that conditioned stimulus is no longer associated with the unconditioned stimulus (such as food). However, if there is a pause, sometimes the response will come back; this is called spontaneous recovery.

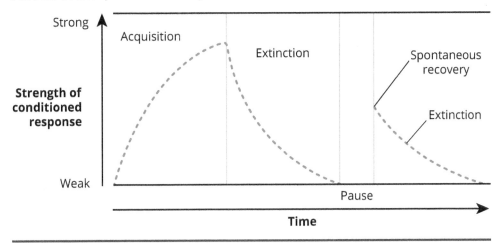

Source: Pavlov (1927).

Even a mild case of spontaneous recovery holds an exciting insight: Extinction is not *forgetting*. Yes, it might seem like the dogs forgot that a sound-signaled food was coming. But the fact that spontaneous recovery *does* occur in this example means that

- extinction is just another form of learning (not forgetting),
- dogs have a memory and can learn from it, and
- dogs hope.

Spontaneous recovery means that the dogs are aware, at some level, that there's a chance the association could come back—and they want to be ready if it does. Dogs are also smarter than some people give them credit for, which is important for the next topic, generalization and discrimination.

Generalization and Discrimination

1000 hertz (Hz).

It's the tone, close to a C note in the fifth octave, that Pavlov used a tuning fork to play to start training the dogs (Pavlov, 1927). Pavlov could produce precise tones like 1000 hertz because a tuning fork's original purpose is to help set musical instruments to specific pitches. In one of his studies, after acquisition had occurred, he then played tones the dogs had *never heard* before in the experiment. He was curious: What would happen when the dogs heard a new tone that had never previously been paired with food?

The dogs salivated in response to these new tones, but not as much as when they heard the original tone. In fact, the salivation amount was positively correlated to how close the new tone was to 1000 hertz. In other words, they salivated most to 900 hertz and to 1100 hertz, and salivation decreased as the new tone differed more from the original one. More saliva at 900 hertz, less at 500 hertz.

Generalization: In classical conditioning, it's when a conditioned response occurs because of a new stimulus that is similar to a previously learned conditioned stimulus.

When the dogs salivated to a tone that had never been paired with food, their behavior is what psychologists call generalization. **Generalization** occurs when a conditioned response (here, salivation in response to a sound) occurs because of a new stimulus that is similar to a previously learned conditioned stimulus. After acquisition, they had the tendency to respond to tones *in general*—although similarity to the original conditioned stimulus still mattered. Pavlov understood the evolutionary benefits of generalization. If an animal became sick after eating one group of mushrooms, generalization would help it steer clear of similar-looking mushrooms in the future.

Generalization can be seen in the everyday life of humans as well:

- Military veterans with combat-related posttraumatic stress disorder may experience increased physiological responses to noises similar to what they heard, such as the sounds and lights during fireworks displays (Pitman et al., 1987; Van der Kolk, 2022).

- Child abuse victims at home may generalize fear or anger responses toward anyone exhibiting cues they associate with abuse, such as facial expressions or raised voices (Lange et al., 2019; Pollak et al., 1998).

- Generalizing from a single negative encounter can also create a phobia (Cooper et al., 2022; Fraunfelter et al., 2022). One encounter with a nippy poodle can generalize and make someone afraid of all dogs and not just the particular dog that bit them.

All that said, there are times when generalization does *not* occur. Knowing the difference between one stimulus and other stimuli and responding only to a specific cue is called **discrimination (classical conditioning)**. Discrimination for Pavlov's dogs would be learning that only a tone of 1000 hertz yields food. If a poodle bites you and you now fear all poodles, then you've generalized your fear to the entire breed. But you've also displayed some discrimination by not fearing *all* dogs. A compromise between generalization and discrimination is often useful in everyday life. For example, if one person wrongs you, you wouldn't want to be permanently skeptical of all people.

Discrimination (classical conditioning): Responding only to a specific conditioned stimulus and not to other, similar stimuli.

If seeing a new roller coaster elicits feelings of either excitement or nausea based on your previous experiences with other roller coasters, you're experiencing generalization.

iStock.com/DougLemke

SPOTLIGHT ON RESEARCH METHODS

Pavlov's Trouble in the Lab

Even Nobel Prize winners have challenges in their research.

In Pavlov's (1927) book *Conditioned Reflexes,* he notes that psychology was a new field of study that hadn't determined how to apply truly scientific methods to mental processes. Being a physiologist, he noted a preference for objective, measurable behaviors as evidence of learning. Saliva is quantifiable—whereas guessing what's going on inside a person's (or a dog's) mind might just be "fantastic speculations" (p. 8). Still, Pavlov encountered problems just like any other researcher.

His original plan was to isolate each dog with a single experimenter in a research chamber. But almost immediately, he ran into problems. The experimenter's posture, breathing, and even "blinking of the eyelids" (p. 20) became cues to the dogs that food was coming,

which messed up his measurements. First, Pavlov tried placing the experimenter outside of the room, so the dog wouldn't get that information. That didn't work either; the dogs could hear people walking up and down the hallway and talking to each other—and again, they learned what signs meant food was coming. He finally had to acquire external funding to pay for an entirely new building with soundproof compartments. He also complained that the instruments in his lab weren't sensitive enough to measure subtle changes in the dogs' responses. First, he tried simply counting drops of saliva, but he had to switch to a complicated system of water displacement to ensure precision in his conclusions.

The bottom line: If you decide to pursue research in psychology or any other field, don't be discouraged if your study doesn't go perfectly the first time. Pavlov was frustrated, too. ●

Examples in Everyday Life

Classical conditioning might affect you more than you think.

We've touched on a few examples already, such as how smells or sounds might make you feel certain emotions because of their connection to memories. If bourbon and pecan pie aren't special to you, maybe it's the smell of a pine tree, the sight of lit candles in a menorah, a Buddhist alter and incense in your home, or ceremonial songs. Consider two more examples: marketing and food preferences.

Marketing

According to the advertising industry, the public loves three things: celebrities, music, and sex.

Marketing agencies understand classical conditioning. They manipulate us into buying products by pairing something we already love with whatever they're selling. They want our love for one thing to transfer to whatever they are selling.

For example, celebrity endorsements are a billion-dollar game just in the United States (Till et al., 2008; Wang & Liu, 2023). Taylor Swift loves Guitar Brand X! Samuel L. Jackson thinks Hamburger Brand Y is the best! Beloved celebrities will, they hope, improve customers' impressions of the brand. This pairing is especially effective if we see the celebrity as an expert on whatever is being sold. Taylor Swift selling guitars is more persuasive to us than Taylor Swift selling hunting rifles (Kamins, 1990; Till et al., 2008).

Music can also make us associate certain feelings with products (Rathee & Rajain, 2020; Worrachananun, 2022). The music is the unconditioned stimulus—it's something that already produces an emotional response. Marketers will pair a particular song with their product, hoping the product will become the conditioned stimulus that produces the same emotional response—and eventually a purchase. For example, research found that people preferred pens they had seen paired with liked music (in this case, a song from the musical *Grease*) compared to pens paired with disliked music (Gorn, 1982). The participants, however, didn't realize the music had any effect on their pen decision.

Finally, you've probably heard the classic marketing phrase "sex sells." Many companies incorporate sexuality into ads, even when the product, such as a hamburger or soft drink, is unrelated (Reichart & Lambiase, 2003; Stewart et al., 2022). The advertisers hope your unconditioned response (a positive reaction to the attractive model) will transfer to their product if you see the pairing often enough. Of course, they're likely using models that conform to socially accepted norms of what's considered "attractive." If you disagree, these ads won't work on you.

Taste Aversion

Is there a certain food that makes you sick, just by looking at it?

Taste aversion: The tendency to avoid certain foods after they have been paired with feeling sick, even after a single occurrence.

When Wind was about 10 years old, her family ate in a new restaurant. Her beloved cheeseburger came with onions on it, a topping she'd never had before. Later that day she got violently sick—and now she can't stand the sight or smell of onions. Has that happened to you? This experience is called **taste aversion** (also known as the Garcia effect): It happens when a single (but strong) pairing of a food and sickness makes us feel negative about that food for years (Bures et al., 1998; Rivi et al., 2021). In humans, this often happens when we're between 6 and 12 years old (Garb & Stunkard, 1974).

Taste aversion demonstrates how classical conditioning helps our survival. Getting sick after eating suggests the food was potentially poisonous, rotten, moldy, or otherwise harmful. Our bodies quickly learn to stay away. Even if the pairing was just a coincidence, it's powerful enough to really make an impact. The conditioned response of feeling nausea is enough to make us choose something else for dinner.

Biological preparedness: Our body's natural tendency to make some associations faster than others, especially when they are related to our biological needs.

Taste aversion also demonstrates how our bodies and minds can learn some associations faster than others. Our instincts and reflexes pay particular attention to pairings of pain, nausea, or sexual attraction because these physiological responses are biologically important to us (Bernstein, 1978; Clarke et al., 2023). **Biological preparedness** explains why our bodies learn some associations faster than others.

Classical Conditioning in TV and Movies

Learning through association—classical conditioning—is featured in a lot of films and TV shows. While writers don't usually use psychological terms, the idea of repeated pairings changing perceptions or behaviors is featured more often than you might realize. Here are some examples of classical conditioning on the big screen:

- In *Seabiscuit* (2003), we see a jockey training the famous racehorse. He starts by playing a bell (the neutral stimulus), which the horse initially ignores. Acquisition starts when the jockey repeatedly rings the bell, then whips the horse to make him run faster. The whip is the unconditioned stimulus, and running after being whipped is the unconditioned response. After several experiences, the horse learns that the bell (now the conditioned stimulus) is a cue that the whipping is about out happen, so the horse starts running at the sound (the conditioned response).

- In the cult classic *A Clockwork Orange* (1971), avant-garde film director Stanley Kubrick makes the novel come alive with teenager Alex gleefully committing crimes involving sexual assault and violence. After being sent to prison, he's subjected to an "experimental" technique in which he's injected with nausea-producing drugs and forced to watch dozens of films depicting sex and aggression in various forms. After only 2 weeks, Alex can no longer bear any kind of sexual or violent act, because it immediately induces nausea.

- In *South Park: Bigger, Longer, & Uncut* (1999), out-of-control youngster Eric Cartman is subjected to brain surgery in which an electronic chip is inserted and wired to send an electric shock to his body each time he swears. Quickly, Cartman learns to avoid swearing because it's now associated with these painful experiences.

- In the TV show *The Office* (2005–2013), salesman Jim plays a prank on his coworker Dwight. Jim repeatedly plays a sound on his computer, then immediately offers Dwight a mint. Eventually, Jim plays the sound and Dwight responds by holding his hand out and complaining of bad breath—without ever realizing how his behaviors have been trained into him.

In the first example, the unconditioned stimulus, unconditioned response, conditioned stimulus, and conditioned response were all identified for you. Can you identify these aspects of classical conditioning in the rest of the examples? ●

A Learning Controversy: Little Albert

What happened to Little Albert?

One of the most shocking and controversial studies in the history of psychology studied generalization and discrimination in an infant's fear development. Now called the "Little Albert" study, two researchers trained a baby to fear a white rat, then tested whether he would also be afraid of other white, furry things.

Over a century ago in 1920, two psychologists named John Watson and Rosalie Rayner were curious about the classical conditioning of fear. Their main question was whether fear could be taught to a human baby and whether that fear would be specifically contained to stimuli that had previously been associated with scary experiences. Their study design required a baby who started out with no fear—one who was always happy. Watson and Rayner worked for Johns Hopkins University, which included a daycare for employees' children. They "borrowed" an infant they called "Albert B." (to preserve his anonymity). They chose Albert because he was "stolid and unemotional" (Watson & Rayner, 1920, p. 313).

Get ready for some cruelty. Watson and Rayner presented Albert with a variety of stimuli they found in the university and hospital, such as cotton swabs, a rabbit, a dog, masks, and a white rat. He happily touched and played with all of them. "At no time did this infant ever show fear in any situation" (Watson & Rayner, 1920, p. 313). Here's where the study became unethical. To cause fear, the researchers removed all the stimuli, snuck up behind him while he was distracted, and struck a steel bar with a hammer. The noise was very loud and after hearing it three times in a row, Albert displayed crying and fear. They had an unconditioned stimulus (the loud noise) and an unconditioned response (fear because of the noise).

Now he fears even Santa Claus

A famously unethical study taught this baby to be afraid of rats.

John B. Watson, via the Akron Psychology Archives

They then put Albert through acquisition trials. They repeatedly put the white rat in front of him, waited a few seconds, then hit the steel bar with the hammer. After several trials, Albert began to lean away and cry as soon as he saw the white rat. Watson and Rayner interpreted this cruelty as a success! The white rat had become a conditioned stimulus that caused fear (the conditioned response) because it was associated with the scary noise. Little Albert had learned.

Their next step was to show Albert stimuli similar to the white rat such as a white rabbit, a dog, and white cotton balls. After learning to fear the rat, Albert's fear response was generalized—he showed fear and crying in response to all these stimuli. He even cried when Watson came into the room wearing a Santa Claus mask with a white, furry beard.

Watson and Rayner's original plan was to then teach Albert how to discriminate among the different stimuli. They were going to take him through several trials in which the white rat was always followed by the noise, but the other similar objects weren't. They anticipated that over time, Albert would only show fear to the rat (discrimination). They also planned to then finish the experiment by taking Albert through extinction trials in which they showed him the rat *without* the sound, with the hope that he would eventually get over his fear. If that didn't work, they planned to reverse his fear by pairing the rat with something positive— they suggested either giving Albert candy when the rat was presented or even stimulating his genitals!

Thankfully, they never had the chance to complete these next steps in their experiment. According to some sources, Albert's mother found out what they were doing, removed him from the study, and complained to the university's administrators (Powell et al., 2014). While those details are unclear, it is true that Watson and Rayner were having a sexual affair, which was against university policy. Either way, they were both fired, and the study ended earlier than they had planned (Beck et al., 2009).

Psychology students have often asked. "What happened to Little Albert later in life?" For example, did he retain his fear of white rats? Did the generalization stay as well, such that he lived a life in fear of all white, furry objects? The answer is unclear because Albert was never identified with certainty, and Watson burned all his records after being fired—but there are two possibilities.

One possibility is that Albert was really Douglas Merritte, who died of encephalitis at the age of 6, just a few years after the study (Beck et al., 2009). Other work suggests that Albert's name was really William Albert Barger, who lived into adulthood and had a lingering fear of dogs, barking, and even animals in general (Powell et al., 2014). It's possible that the results of Watson and Rayner's unethical procedures lingered for many years.

All over the world, holidays are celebrated with gifts and rewards. One example is the Chinese New Year, when children often get envelopes with money inside.

iStock.com/AsiaVision

OPERANT CONDITIONING: REWARDS AND PUNISHMENTS

>> **LO 9.2** **Explain principles of operant conditioning, applications, and controversies.**

? Have You Ever Wondered?
9.2 What is operant conditioning?

Several holidays around the world incorporate gifts and other rewards.

Ancient philosophy and religions from India suggest multiple types of karma; some types suggest that if you put good into the world, you'll be rewarded in turn. Observant Muslim people celebrate the holiday Eid al-Adha in part by giving gifts to children and cash to women in their family. Some people who participate in Halloween only give candy to children who first tell them a joke (the "trick" before the "treat"). In China, the Lunar New Year is a time of family reunions, feasts, and gift gifting. For those who celebrate the secular parts of Christmas, Santa keeps that list of who's naughty and nice to determine who will get a reward or a punishment. This last example—gifts if you're good, punishment if you've been bad—is the clearest example of the next type of learning: operant conditioning.

In classical conditioning, we learn to associate one thing in our environment with another. Classical conditioning relies on automatic, physiological, instinctive responses to learn how to *predict* what's about to happen. With this kind of learning, we're simply observing our environment and guessing what we think will happen next. We aren't *controlling* what happens next. Pavlov's dogs didn't control when he would make sounds or when he would give them food.

Operant conditioning is different: It's about trying to control what happens next, based on behavioral choices. Operant conditioning is learning to associate rewards or punishments with certain behaviors, based on what has followed those behaviors in the past. It relies on learning from experience by predicting, "If I do behavior A, then *this* will probably be my consequence . . . but if I do behavior B, then *that* will probably be my consequence." Operant conditioning is therefore more active that classical conditioning. As usual, there is a story about curious people—two people, in this case—behind the development of operant conditioning.

Operant conditioning:
Learning to associate rewards or punishments with certain behaviors, based on what has followed that behavior in the past.

Operant Conditioning's Pioneers

Animals like rewards, too.

Like Pavlov, the researchers who pioneered the theory of learning using rewards and punishments used animals for their research. But instead of drooling dogs, this research featured cats, rats, and pigeons.

Thorndike's Cats and the Law of Effect

While Pavlov was working with dogs in Russia around the year 1900, across the ocean in New York a man named Edward Thorndike was also studying animals. Like Pavlov, Thorndike was interested in how animals learn from experience, but his approach was different. He wanted animals to learn how to control their own environment to get rewards. To study this, he created simple cat escape rooms he called puzzle boxes (Thorndike, 1911).

Thorndike's wooden puzzle boxes included a series of pulleys, levers, and buttons for cats to manipulate to open the door. Thorndike first deprived cats of food for several hours to make sure they were

Edward Thorndike, one of psychology's operant conditioning pioneers.

HUMANITIES AND SOCIAL SCIENCES LIBRARY/NEW YORK PUBLIC LIBRARY/Science Source

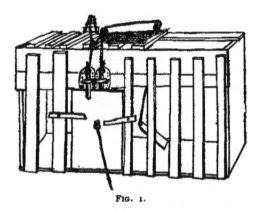

Examples of Thorndike's "puzzle boxes," in which cats had to figure out how to escape to get a food reward.

Thorndike (1911)

hungry. Then he put each cat in a box, with food next to the box that the cats could see and smell. Thorndike measured how long it took each cat to manipulate the box, escape, and get to the food.

Thorndike didn't think the cats were intelligent enough to logically work out exactly what to do in the box. Instead, he believed that the cats simply tried several things, "clawing all over the box" (Thorndike, 1911, p. 36), until something accidentally worked. This trial-and-error approach was not particularly efficient. However, after several trials in the same box, the cats knew what to do. Each time, the cats got out faster.

The cats had apparently determined that a specific behavior (tugging a string or pawing a button, for example) would lead to the reward of escape and food. The cats were *learning* from the consequences of their behavior.

Because a particular behavior had been rewarded, Thorndike called that behavior *strengthened* or more likely to occur. The opposite would probably also be true: If a behavior led to unpleasant consequences, such as a painful electric shock, then that behavior would be weakened or less likely to occur. Thorndike named his two most important observations:

- A pleasant consequence that follows a specific behavior is called **reinforcement**.

- An unpleasant consequence that follows a specific behavior is called **punishment**.

Reinforcement: Rewards for behavior that make the behavior more likely to occur in the future.

Punishment: Unpleasant consequences for behavior that make the behavior less likely to occur in the future.

Law of effect: Thorndike's theory that in general, behaviors followed by rewards will be strengthened while behaviors followed by punishments will be weakened.

Combining these two types of consequence—pleasant and unpleasant—led to what is now known as the **law of effect**, which states that behaviors that result in pleasant consequences (reinforcements) are more likely to occur again in the future, while behaviors that result in unpleasant consequences (punishments) are less likely to occur again in the future.

Skinner and the Operant Conditioning Chamber

Burrhus Frederic Skinner (known as B. F. Skinner) recognized the importance of operant conditioning's principles. Skinner was such a zealot that he believed there was no such thing as "free will." Instead, he believed that all our decisions, thoughts, and emotions were purely the products of past conditioning. He also believed that psychology should only study objective, observable behaviors, a trend that dominated much of psychology at that time (this is the school of behaviorism you learned about in Chapter 1).

Skinner expanded on Thorndike's research by creating boxes he called **operant conditioning chambers**. These mechanical boxes could produce rewards or punishments when an animal inside performed certain behaviors. Now, many people simply refer to operant conditioning chambers as "Skinner boxes," even though Skinner himself modestly didn't like that term (Skinner, 1959).

Operant conditioning chamber: A mechanical box in which animals can be trained using reinforcements and punishments.

Most of these research chambers were designed for two types of animals: rats and pigeons (see Figure 9.3). Most had a food tray, a water dispenser, an electric floor that could send shocks to the animal's feet, and either a series of lights and/or a speaker for sounds. Over time, the animals were trained to learn that certain behaviors (rats pushing a lever or pigeons pecking a button) led to rewards—usually a food pellet.

Skinner complicated the chambers in specific ways that tested the limits of the animals' ability to learn from consequences. For example, he could set up the chamber so that lever-pushing or button-pecking released food (a reward) when a *green* light was

FIGURE 9.3

Operant Conditioning Chambers

Two types of "operant conditioning chambers," also known as "Skinner boxes."

(a)

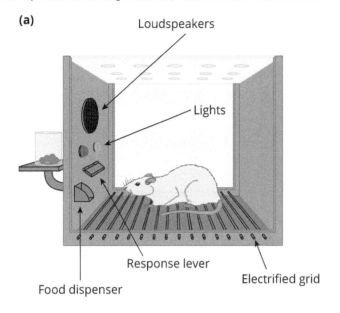

Loudspeakers

Lights

Response lever

Electrified grid

Food dispenser

(b)

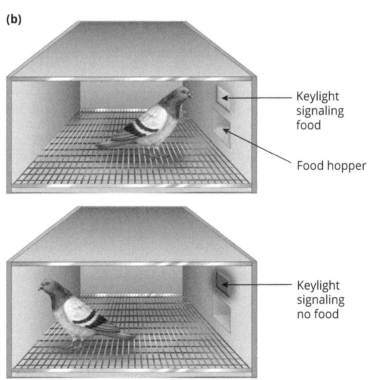

Keylight signaling food

Food hopper

Keylight signaling no food

(a) Created by AndreasJS, licensed under CC BY-SA 4.0 DEED; (b) Monica Wierzbicki/Body Scientific Intl.

on. But that same behavior led to an electric shock (a punishment) when the *red* light was on. Creating these research chambers opened the door for decades of research.

Check out the self-report scale in the *What's My Score?* feature. When seeking rewards and avoiding punishments is applied to humans, it gets even more complicated. Some people are motivated by the potential for rewards (such as money or attention), while others seem driven by a fear of punishment. Do either of these motivations apply to you more than the other?

Sensitivity to Rewards and Punishments

Instructions: For each item, simply circle "yes" or "no."

Yes No   1. Do you often refrain from doing something because you're worried it's illegal?

Yes No   2. Does the prospect of getting money motivate you to do some things?

Yes No   3. Do you prefer not to ask for something if you're not sure you'll get it?

Yes No   4. Are you often encouraged to act by the possibility of being valued at work, school, or at home?

Yes No   5. Are you often afraid of new or unexpected situations?

Yes No   6. Do you often meet people that you find physically attractive?

Yes No   7. Is it difficult for you to call someone on the phone you don't know?

Yes No   8. Do you like to take drugs because of the pleasure you get from them?

Yes No   9. Do you often give in to someone to avoid a quarrel or fight?

Yes No   10. Do you often do things to be praised?

Yes No   11. As a child, were you troubled by punishments at home or in school?

Yes No   12. Do you like being the center of attention at a party or meeting?

Yes No   13. Do you attach great importance to the possibility of failure?

Yes No   14. Do you spend a lot of time on obtaining a good image or reputation?

Yes No   15. Are you easily discouraged in difficult situations?

Yes No   16. Do you need people to show you affection all the time?

Scoring: Add all of the "yes" answers you circled for the odd-numbered questions; this is your sensitivity to punishment. Then, add all of the "yes" answers you circled for the even-numbered questions; this is your sensitivity to reward. For both subscales, the scores can range from 0 to 8, with higher numbers indicating greater sensitivity.

The full, original scale is longer—48 items instead of 16—and some of the items shown here have been edited slightly for length or clarification. When the authors (Torrubia et al., 2001) gave the scale to college students in Spain, they found that women are slightly more sensitive to punishment (compared to men), and men are slightly more sensitive to reward.

Critical thinking: Why do you think the authors found that college students in Spain showed slight gender differences, with men more sensitive to reward and women more sensitive to punishment? Do you think this finding would be true in other countries and cultures? What about people whose gender is nonbinary? When you consider your own scores on each subscale, is one score more extreme than the other? In what ways do your daily decisions seem motivated by either seeking reward or avoiding punishment? ●

Source: Torrubia et al. (2001).

Positive and Negative Reinforcement and Punishment

Addition and subtraction.

They're the foundation of childhood arithmetic, and they also apply to operant conditioning. You have learned that reinforcements make behaviors more likely to occur and punishments make behaviors less likely to occur. But there's more than one way to approach each.

In operant conditioning terms, "positive" indicates something that's added, given, or introduced, not that what's added is good or pleasant:

- **Positive reinforcement** occurs when a *pleasant* consequence is *added* or presented. When a rat in the operant conditioning chamber presses a lever and gets a food pellet, it's positive reinforcement because the pellet's been added and it should increase lever-pressing.

- **Positive punishment** happens when an *unpleasant* consequence is *added* or presented. If a rat in the chamber pressed the lever at the wrong time (say, when a red light was flashing), it might receive an electric shock. Importantly, in the world of operant conditioning, a "positive" can actually be quite painful. In this context, "positive" only means that something—pleasant or unpleasant—has been *added* or presented.

If "positive" only means that something has been added or presented, then, in operant conditioning terms, "negative" indicates something that's subtracted, removed, or taken away:

- **Negative reinforcement** occurs when a behavior is rewarded because something *unpleasant* is *removed* from the environment. For example, some operant conditioning chambers for rats add an exercise wheel and attach an electrode to each rat's tail. Electric shocks are sent to the rats through the electrodes at random times—but if they run on the exercise wheel, the shock stops. Running therefore quickly becomes a reward for the rat because the unpleasant shock goes away, thus reinforcing the running behavior. If you forget to buckle your seatbelt, then you will experience a loud, annoying sound. You put on the seatbelt to stop the sound—so buckling up is rewarded through negative reinforcement: removing the annoying sound. You're more likely to put your seatbelt on right away next time.

- **Negative punishment** occurs when a behavior is followed by a *pleasant* thing being *removed* from the environment. Children often experience negative punishment when their parents tell them that their naughty behavior has led to no dessert or a loss of their phone privileges. Something the child wanted has been taken away, and the parent hopes this means that the naughty behavior will stop as well.

These terms—positive and negative reinforcement and punishment—are often the most confusing terms in an entire Introduction to Psychology course. Students often mix them up because of the tendency to think of "positive" and "negative" as "good" and "bad." That's a mistake in this context! Think of "positive" as addition, like a plus sign in math—it means that something has been added to the environment. And "negative" as a minus sign, meaning subtraction.

To help you apply these terms to several more examples, go through Table 9.2 and make sure you understand each row. Remember, reinforcements are *always pleasant and make behaviors more likely to occur*. Reinforcements are always rewards. Punishments are *always unpleasant and make behaviors less likely to occur*.

Positive reinforcement: When a pleasant stimulus is added to the environment, rewarding behavior and making it more likely in the future.

Positive punishment: When an unpleasant stimulus is added to the environment, making behavior less likely in the future.

Negative reinforcement: When an unpleasant stimulus is removed from the environment, rewarding behavior and making it more likely in the future.

Negative punishment: When a pleasant stimulus is removed from the environment, making behavior less likely in the future.

TABLE 9.2

Examples of Positive and Negative Reinforcement and Punishment

EXAMPLE	REINFORCEMENT OR PUNISHMENT?	POSITIVE OR NEGATIVE?	FURTHER EXPLANATION
Zazzles the cat plays with ornaments on the Christmas tree until her owners spray her with water to make her stop.	Punishment (the behavior of playing with ornaments becomes weaker)	Positive (something has been added)	Zazzles is *less* likely to play with the ornaments because the water spray is *added* each time.
Reza's teacher gives them a gold star on the board every time they read a book.	Reinforcement (the behavior of reading becomes stronger)	Positive (something has been added)	Reza is *more* likely to read books because a star is *added* to the chart each time.
Monique's smoke detector makes annoying beeps until she replaces the batteries. The beeping immediately stops.	Reinforcement (the behavior of changing the batteries becomes stronger)	Negative (something has been subtracted)	Monique is more likely to change the batteries so that the annoying sound is *removed*.
Every time DeSean swears, his father subtracts $1 from his weekly allowance.	Punishment (the behavior of swearing becomes weaker)	Negative (something has been subtracted)	DeSean is *less* likely to swear because he knows money from his allowance will be *removed*.

When dogs successfully navigate obstacle courses, it's because their trainers used the operant conditioning process called shaping.

iStock.com/James Brey

Shaping: Learning through reinforcement over several, progressive stages.

Examples in Everyday Life

Just like classical conditioning, operant conditioning is all around you.

Consider a few examples, which also highlight a few additional important terms.

Shaping: Dog Obstacle Courses and More

All journeys start with a single step.

Have you ever been up late, browsing through channels on the TV, and started watching a show about dog obstacle courses? The dogs must go up and down ladders, weave in and out of cones, run through little tunnels…it's pretty amazing (and the Border Collies usually win!). This kind of animal agility training is possible because of shaping.

Shaping is learning through reinforcement over several stages, in which progressive steps toward a result receive rewards (Lazarus et al., 1965). At first, a dog might receive a treat if it stands next to a ladder and sniffs it. Then, it will only receive a treat if it places a front paw on the first step of the ladder. Next, it only gets a treat if it takes that step—and finally, the dog must climb the ladder to get a treat. Shaping requires patience, but if you string together enough steps, the result is pretty amazing.

Skinner used shaping to train his pigeons to do amazing things as well. For example, in their operant conditioning chambers, he would sometimes display a word like "TURN" or "PECK." Over many trials, the pigeons learned to associate each word with a given behavior in order to receive food. Essentially, Skinner had taught the pigeons how to read! He also trained them to play ping pong—you can find that video on YouTube. Others have used shaping to teach chimpanzees how to roller skate and train dolphins or whales to perform "tricks" like jumping through hoops (Coren, 1999; MacKellar et al., 2023).

Therapists use many of shaping's same basic principles when helping human clients (e.g., Pardo-Cebrian et al., 2022; Tanner, 2023). Sometimes children with autism have trouble with verbal communication, and shaping can help them in speech therapy settings (Lovaas, 1987). Here, the therapist will initially reward the children for any kind of vocalization, then slowly require the children to use increasingly advanced speech patterns (such as complete sentences or engaging in simple conversation) before receiving a reward. In a case study of a boy who refused to wear glasses, his therapists used shaping to get him to wear them for progressively longer periods of time in exchange for desired foods (Wolf, 2001).

You have experienced shaping yourself as you progress through school: You earn good grades, but—like leveling up in a video game—the expectations for your work get progressively harder and more complicated each year.

Schedules of Consequence: Gambling

Sometimes risks lead to rewards—but not always.

You might have learned that asking someone out sometimes leads to the reward of a first date—but sometimes not. Speeding sometimes leads to the punishment of an expensive ticket—but sometimes not. B. F. Skinner became intrigued with the idea that our behavior can be shaped over time not just by consequences but also by *how often or how consistently* those consequences occur. There are different schedules of consequence, or timetables regarding how often and how consistently reinforcements (rewards) or punishments occur after any given behavior.

Schedules can be continuous or partial. A **continuous schedule** occurs when the consequence (reinforcement or punishment) occurs *every time* the behavior is enacted: Maybe a rat gets a food pellet every time it pushes a lever. In many U.S. states, you get a nickel every time you return a soda can for the deposit. Maybe a child is punished consistently every time they display a bad behavior. Consistency is key. Continuous schedules are useful in training animals (including humans!) because they make learning happen quickly.

In **partial schedules** (sometimes called "intermittent" schedules), the consequence doesn't occur every single time. The following four schedules are all partial schedules, and they are more common than continuous schedules in the "real world," or outside of a lab setting.

Ratio schedules. Ratio schedules deliver a reinforcement or punishment based on the *number of times* a behavior has been performed. Skinner set up an operant conditioning chamber such that a rat had to push a lever five times before it received a food pellet (instead of only once). The rats took a little longer to learn that lever-pressing led to food—but once they learned that they had to push it several times, they adapted. There are two types of ratio schedules:

- If the number of times the behavior must occur is stable (say, always five times), it's called a **fixed ratio schedule**.

- Skinner could also make the required lever-pressing behavior unstable (an *average* of five times). Sometimes the rats got food after only two or three presses, and other times they'd have to wait until seven, eight, or nine presses. This kind of schedule is called a **variable ratio schedule**, one that is randomized but still based on an average number of behaviors.

Pause for a moment to think about the impact that either a fixed or variable ratio schedule might have on learning. Both schedules seem to instill tenacity and persistence in behavior. Both schedules teach the animal or human not to give up, because a reward is on its way! But these two schedules have slightly different effects on behavior.

Fixed ratio schedules tend to result in behaviors that happen in bursts ("powering up" in game speak), followed by a pause. Imagine you worked in a factory in which

Schedules of consequence: How often or consistently a reinforcement or punishment occurs after behavior is displayed.

Continuous schedule: When a reinforcement or punishment occurs every time a behavior occurs.

Partial schedule: Any schedule of consequence that is not continuous, meaning the consequence does not occur every time the behavior occurs.

Ratio schedules: When reinforcement or punishment occurs based on how often a behavior has been performed (regardless of how long that takes).

Fixed ratio schedule: When reinforcement or punishment consistently occurs after a set number of behaviors.

Variable ratio schedule: When reinforcement or punishment is based on a number of behaviors, but the exact amount of behaviors can change.

Slot machines, like most casinos, are set up on a variable ratio schedule of reinforcement. Each time you play, you might be reinforced with winning—and you never know for sure when that will happen.

iStock.com/mbbirdy

you were paid $100 every time you made 100 products. You might work hard to get to that 100th product, then collect your pay and take a break, knowing it's going to be a long time until you are paid again (due to the fixed ratio). However, with a *variable* ratio, you never know when you're about to get lucky! Each time you make the next product—it might be the 20th or the 30th or the 67th—the excitement grows. Maybe this is the one!

Variable ratio schedules help explain addictive gambling—and how casinos continue to make money from people who know the odds are against them. Like the lever rats press in Skinner boxes, slot machines were once called "one-armed bandits"—players really had to pull a lever to play again. Modern slot machines now require pressing a button—like pigeons pecking a disc.

Gamblers know that they can't win if they don't play. Under a variable schedule of reinforcement, each quarter deposited, lever pulled, or button pressed is a behavior filled with hope. This might be the one, so it's exciting every single time! When Skinner put his rats on variable ratio schedules to earn food pellets, their lever-pushing was the fastest and most consistent, compared to all other possible schedules. Those rats became furry little gamblers.

Interval schedules. There are two more possible schedules of consequence, both based on how much time has passed (think seconds, minutes, or days). They are called **interval schedules:**

Interval schedules: When reinforcement or punishment occurs based on how much time has passed (regardless of how many times the behavior was enacted).

Fixed interval schedule: When reinforcement or punishment consistently occurs after a set period of time.

- A **fixed interval schedule** is one in which a reinforcement or punishment can only happen once in each set time period. Skinner sometimes set up his chambers so that a food pellet would only be released once every 5 minutes. If the rat pressed the lever at least once in that 5-minute period, it would get food. For a slot machine, that would mean that the reward would come, for instance, every 14 minutes—no matter how many times someone pressed their button. Imagine what would happen if gamblers learned that casinos programmed their machines to kick out a reward every 14 minutes. No one would play for the first 13 minutes and then play furiously for the next 1 or 2 minutes.

Variable interval schedule: When reinforcement or punishment is based on time, but the exact amount of time can change.

- If the time period changes, it's called a **variable interval schedule.** Again, Skinner might set the machine to release a pellet *on average* every 5 minutes, but sometimes it would be sooner and sometimes later.

Many people experience a fixed interval schedule when getting paid at their jobs every 2 or 4 weeks. The time period is set. Someone might work more or less hard during any given period (in other words, work behaviors might go up or down), but the time period doesn't change. Fixed interval schedules can be very important in the world of medicine. A patient in a hospital might have a button they can push next to their bed that releases a dose of pain-managing medicine (like morphine). The machine has to be set to only release a certain amount of morphine every hour, no matter how many times they press that button.

Variable interval schedules are also common. When you put cookies or frozen pizza in the oven, you know you'll have to wait, but the length of time could be anywhere between 10 and 14 minutes. Checking the oven more won't make them cook faster—but you know you should start checking after a certain amount of time, and then you'd better check more frequently to make sure your treat doesn't burn.

Which schedule of reinforcement do you think would make the casino the most money: fixed ratio, variable ratio, fixed interval, or variable interval? Why?

A Learning Controversy: Spanking Children

Do you believe in spanking children?

Spanking is clearly a "positive punishment," in operant conditioning terms. The fear and pain of spanking are the added, unpleasant consequences designed to stop a specific behavior. But does it work? There are legitimate concerns about this kind of physical punishment. For example,

- Physical punishments such as spanking might stop the behavior immediately—but research suggests they are ineffective long term (Bucher & Lovaas, 1967; Heilmann et al., 2021). Physical punishments teach a child what *not* to do, but they do not show alternative, preferred behaviors.

- Fear of spankings creates anxiety in children that prevents them from learning (Avezum et al., 2022; Dobbs et al., 2006; Gershoff, 2010).

- Some children who are physically punished are more likely to later display aggression toward others. They've learned that physical violence is an acceptable solution to problems and that we can—and sometimes should—hit the people we love (Alampay et al., 2017; Bryan & Freed, 1982; Eron et al., 1971; Taylor et al., 2009).

What's a good alternative? A popular option with parents now is "time-out." In "time-out," parents have children sit quietly in an area with no stimulation or attention. It removes children from the situation, and it gives them an opportunity to calm down and consider why their behavior was not okay.

Some psychologists say that time-out is negative punishment; the child is not allowed to engage in regular activities, so it's like a miniature "grounding." No TV, no toys, and so on. Others argue that time-out is really extinction because it makes sure the child is not rewarded for bad behavior with responses like attention from their parents. Either way, time-out is much more effective at changing children's behaviors than spanking is (Culotta & McLain, 2019; Kostewicz, 2010), especially when the child is encouraged to use that time to self-soothe ("Positive Time Out," 2020).

CAREER CORNER

Profiling Kat, Youth Therapeutic Specialist

What is your career?

I am a therapeutic specialist at a youth psychiatric facility. We work with the youth in the facility to make sure that their needs are met. This may be preparing their meals, noticing warning signs, being conscious of their triggers, and being aware of their treatment goals. The treatment plan is individualized, so we cater to the youth's needs and maintain a structured environment where they can work on their treatment goals. We may need to help de-escalate a client from an escalated state, such as by using positive reinforcing words, sensory items, listening to them vent about their concerns, or directing them to their treatment coordinator.

(Continued)

(Continued)

How was studying psychology important for success in this career?

Studying psychology helped me get an overall idea on the different factors that would impact an individual's treatment. **By having a trauma-informed background or by learning about aspects of adolescent psychology, an individual will have a head start to this position.** At the facility, many of the youths that are admitted have experienced a trauma, so by having some understanding about the impact of trauma, people may be more likely to provide more informed care.

How do concepts from this chapter help in this career?

By studying operant conditioning in an educational environment, I am aware of some of the factors that could influence the efficacy of a reinforcer/ punishment, such as consistency. If a desired behavior is consistently given reinforcement, then moved to a variable ratio schedule, the individual may continue to exhibit the desired behavior even in the absence of a reinforcement.

Is this the career you always planned to have after college?

This is not the career that I planned, but I know that this is a great steppingstone to where I would like to be in the future. **This job may not be the end goal, but it provides me some great hands-on experience for the field.** I get to work directly with treatment coordinators and help clients work on their treatment goals, which is something I would like to do in a different way in the future.

If you could give current college students one sentence of advice, what would it be?

Even though you will hit bumps on the road throughout your academic career, you are capable of accomplishing whatever you set your mind to. ●

Toys like plastic lawn mowers are based on the principle that children naturally observe and copy behaviors they see in adults; this is the foundation for observational learning.

Steve Mason/Photodisc/via Getty Images

COGNITIVE AND OBSERVATIONAL LEARNING

>> **LO 9.3** **Explain principles of cognitive and observational learning, applications, and controversies.**

Have You Ever Wondered?
9.3 What are cognitive and observational learning?

What are your family's holiday traditions?

Many traditions are passed down from one generation to the next. Do you have certain foods that are always part of holiday celebrations? Do you have certain music you listen to, movies you watch on TV, dances, costumes, or behaviors like who gets to pass out or open gifts first? Usually these traditions are not taught explicitly; children learn them by observing their caregivers. Sometimes we're surprised to learn that our traditions are different from what other families do, because their traditions are not what we observed and experienced.

Classical and operant conditioning rely on observing what's happening around us, then responding. But other forms of learning are a little more subtle, which psychologists call cognitive and observational. In Wind's home, she and her three brothers made dozens of bourbon balls in their miniature assembly line at home. Wind learned how to roll the dough and place each ball neatly on the cooking sheets by watching her older brothers do it. This kind of learning is also key to our understanding of the world and our ability to successfully navigate it.

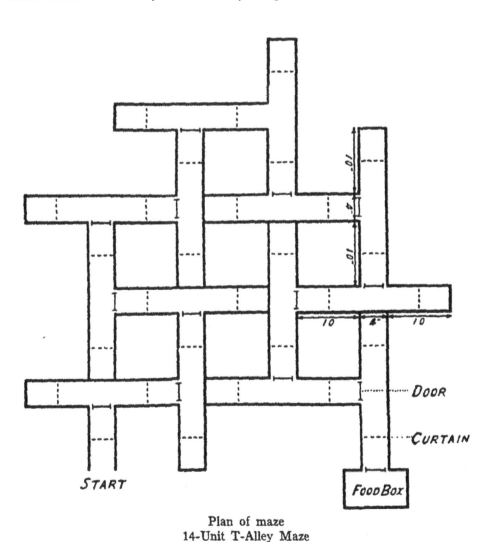

Plan of maze
14-Unit T-Alley Maze

Rats were put in mazes like the one shown here (Tolman, 1932, 1948; Tolman & Honzik, 1930). At first, they just got to run around without a food reward anywhere. Later, when they realized food was in a certain location, they showed that they already knew the layout of the maze from their previous experience; this is evidence of what psychologists call "latent learning."

Tolman (1948)

Cognitive Learning: Insights and Cognitive Maps

Hopefully, you're learning right now.

Your courses ask you to learn by reading textbooks and sitting through lectures, integrating new ideas with older assumptions. That kind of learning isn't classical or operant conditioning—so we need another term. **Cognitive learning** is a change in knowledge or understanding that occurs on a mental level.

We've all experienced cognitive learning through **insight**, finding a solution to a problem simply by thinking it through (as opposed to the trial and error used by Thorndike's cats). If you've never used a subway system before, the process can be intimidating. There will probably be a map of the different train lines posted, with different colors indicating each route. You might have to first find your current location on the map, determine where you need to go, then work out what color will get you there and whether you need to transfer lines. Using logic in this way is an essential skill that requires insight.

Maps are actually one of the early ways that psychologists studied cognitive learning. An early psychologist named Tolman put rats in mazes (Tolman, 1932; Tolman & Honzik, 1930). He sometimes put a rats in a maze and simply gave them time to explore all the paths and turns, without offering any kind of reward for getting to the end (Group A). Other rats ran the maze with food rewards at the end (Group B). Finally, he put all the rats in the maze for the final phase of his test, this time with food at the end, and timed how quickly they ran from start to finish across several trials. Once all the rats knew there was food available at the end, they all immediately ran to the end—and Group A rats were sometimes even faster than Group B.

Tolman concluded that the original rats had created a **cognitive map**, a mental representation of the layout of the area, in their mind. This was cognitive learning, because it was knowledge in the little rats' mind waiting to be used. Only when the food appeared did the rats show behavioral *evidence* of this learning—but the learning had already happened, without the reward. In this way, cognitive maps are an example of what's called **latent learning**, or knowledge gained that we can only observe indirectly or later. Here, the rats' ability to quickly get where they wanted to go (find the food!) was the observable proof of previous learning. To be clear, *all* the rats had created cognitive maps of the maze in their minds. There just wasn't evidence that Group A rats had done so until they showed evidence of it in the final phase of the study, when they ran immediately to the end of the maze once they had an incentive.

You have a cognitive map of your neighborhood, your campus, and other geographical areas you know well. That map sits in your head and is used each time you figure out the most efficient route to take from class to class (is there a shortcut?) and how long it will take (Epstein et al., 2017; Miller, 2021; Sholl, 1987). You might avoid signing up for back-to-back classes that are on different sides of campus, for example, because your cognitive map tells you it will be difficult to get to the second class on time.

Observational Learning: Modeling

Kids are smarter than they look.

Maybe the fastest way to learn is by watching someone else do it first. This can be good when traditions are passed down through generations to celebrate holidays. On the other hand, parents all over the world have been embarrassed when their toddlers yell swear words in public; it's awkward because everyone knows where they learned them. And kids seem to enjoy toys like plastic lawn mowers, kitchens, and tool sets because they want to copy what they see their caregivers doing. Children naturally observe and copy what they see in the world around them.

Cognitive learning: Change in knowledge or understanding on a mental level.

Insight: Working out a solution to a problem simply by thinking it through.

Cognitive map: A mental representation of the layout of a given geographical region or area.

Latent learning: Knowledge gained that can only be observed indirectly or later.

The instinct to observe and imitate is the foundation for the final type of learning. Observational learning occurs when we assume that we'll experience the same consequences that we've seen others experience. If Joan puts her hand on the stove and gets a burn, we assume we'll also get burned—we don't have to experience it for ourselves. If Mohammed receives praise in school for being polite, we assume we might get the same praise if we're polite, too.

Copying others' behaviors is called modeling. Modeling is helpful, even lifesaving. And just like classical and operant conditioning, there's a famous set of psychology studies that illustrate observational learning.

Bandura's Bobo Doll Studies

In the 1950s and early 1960s, many people were purchasing their first television sets. As TV became popular, so did its critics. Would these postwar "baby boomer" children imitate the violence they saw first in cartoons, then in "cowboy" dramas, and later during the antiwar and civil rights protests? How would this mass audience respond to violence on television?

Answering this question became the foundation for decades of research about observational learning. It could lead to both positive change (helping children learn to use household tools safely) and negative change (children becoming more aggressive). The "Bobo doll" studies by Albert Bandura used observational learning to test this important social question.

A Bobo doll is an inflatable plastic tube with a weighted bottom, such that someone can push or punch the top down and it will pop right back up again (like a standing punching bag). In the 1960s, this toy sometimes came with the image of a cartoon clown named Bobo on it. Bandura used it in his research on whether children would model aggression through observational learning.

Bandura's first major study was in 1961 and involved 72 children (36 boys, 36 girls) between 3 and 6 years old. Half the children were randomly assigned to the study's aggressive condition, and one child participated at a time:

This is a Bobo doll, an inflatable toy used by Bandura in his series of studies about aggression in children (Bandura et al., 1961).
Mirrorpix/Contributor/via Getty Images

Observational learning: When we change our behavior because we assume we'll experience the same consequences we've seen others experience for their behaviors.

Modeling: Imitating the behaviors of others, especially when we see them getting rewards.

- First, they were led into a room with several fun toys and told to sit at a table and draw a picture. While the children did this, they saw an adult in another part of the room play with different toys.

- The adult modeling aggressive behavior tipped Bobo on its side, sat on it, struck it with a plastic hammer, kicked it across the room, and punched it in the nose. The adult also yelled several phrases such as, "Sock him in the nose!" (Bandura et al., 1961, p. 577).

The other half of the children—the control group—saw the adult sitting quietly, playing with tinker toys (wooden building supplies like sticks and blocks).

In both groups, the children were then escorted into another room where they could play with whatever toys they wanted for several minutes. This new room included toys that could show aggression, such as dart guns, a mallet, and—of course—a Bobo doll. It also included nonaggressive toys such as stuffed bears and plastic farm animals. You can probably guess Bandura's hypothesis: The children who had observed aggression would imitate those behaviors. And he was right; physical and verbal aggression increased after children observed an adult being aggressive (Bandura et al., 1961).

Bandura (1965) used a similar procedure to explore how viewing different consequences of aggression influenced children's behavior. The children in this study viewed an adult beating up a Bobo doll on the TV—but this time the videos had three different possible endings. This was a more direct test of the effects of viewing aggression on television:

1. No Consequences Condition (a control condition): The video ended right after the aggressive behavior was displayed.

2. Reward Condition: The video showed a second adult rewarding the aggressive model with candy, soda pop, and praise for being a "strong champion!"

3. Punishment Condition: The video showed the aggressive model being chastised for being a bully and then spanked with a magazine.

Like the earlier study, the children in each experimental condition were then observed playing in a room with several toys, including the Bobo doll. You can probably guess the results: Compared to the other two conditions (see Figure 9.4), the children observing adults being punished for aggression (Ending 3) were less likely to display aggression themselves. This study demonstrated that children would observe and imitate—but much less if they think aggression might lead to punishment. Children are learning all the time, just by taking in the world around them.

Four Necessary Elements

Bandura's research continued for several decades. He proposed that observational learning will only be successful when four specific criteria are met:

- *Attention:* The observer needs to be paying attention to the behavior being modeled. If Bandura's children weren't watching the TV in his second study, they would not have known what to do (or not to do).

FIGURE 9.4

Average Number of Imitated Aggressive Behaviors in Bandura (1965)

Boys and girls both significantly decreased their aggressive behaviors if they had just watched an aggressive adult be punished. Adapted from Bandura (1965).

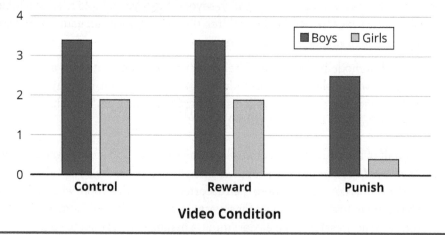

Source: Created using data from Bandura (1965).

- *Memory:* The observer must remember the behavior long enough to enact it when the time comes. If Bandura had waited 3 months before taking children into the room of toys, their behavior might have been different depending on children's latent learning.

- *Imitation:* The observer must be physically capable of copying the behavior. You can pay attention to and remember that fantastic acrobatic performance you saw last week, but you still might not be able to perform it yourself.

- *Desire:* Finally, the observer must have a reason to perform the behavior. Children were less likely to show aggression in the punishment condition. The final step of Bandura's 1965 study was to ask *all* the children to show him the aggression they had seen on TV, with the promise of a reward. Now, almost all of them easily did so. They just needed a reason to beat up the clown.

Observational learning can lead to both good and bad outcomes—consider both in the last few sections of this chapter.

Examples in Everyday Life

The instinct to learn through observation is strong, even from a very young age.

Imitation of simple acts such as facial expressions or hand gestures is observable in infants as young as 6 months (Elsner, 2007; Poulson et al., 1989). At 12 months, some babies can copy behaviors like rolling a ball or hitting a drum to make a sound (Fagard & Lockman, 2010). At 24 months, some toddlers start to copy simple manipulation of tools, such as using a stick to get something out of reach after seeing a parent do this (Nagell et al., 1993; for a review of articles on infant observational learning, see Fagard et al., 2016). Perhaps this is why humans have been so successful at taking over the world, despite the fact that we're not the strongest or fastest species. Our ability to observe, learn, and think critically gives us the advantage.

Improving Sports Performance

If you coach a sport, then you want your athletes to learn—and to learn quickly.

Want to improve your golf swing? Skilled golfers are better than novices at watching other golfers' swings and learning from them (D'Innocenzo et al., 2016). Similarly, a self-report survey measuring observational learning skills found higher scores for varsity athletes compared to athletes on junior varsity (Wesch et al., 2007). Observational learning can also help beginners. Novice golfers who had been trained in how to observe others' golf swings improved faster and remembered what they learned longer (D'Innocenzo et al., 2016).

Want to learn how to serve a volleyball correctly? Thirty students who didn't know how to serve were split into groups and assigned to one of three conditions:

1. Watch 10 demonstrations, then practice for several minutes.

2. Watch once, practice three times, watch again, and repeat (for a total of 10 demonstrations).

3. Watch five times, then alternate between practices and watching again (total of 10 demonstrations).

Observing properly executed sports moves, such as lifting weights, can help improve your own performance.

Viktor Cvetkovic/E+/via Getty Images

The final group led to the best results, and the authors concluded that "several modeling exposures before practice and several more exposures in the early stages of practice were optimal" (Weeks & Anderson, 2000, p. 259).

There are now over 50,000 published articles about the utility of observational learning in sports and athletics. Watching other people demonstrate techniques builds confidence and motivation, helps players develop strategy, and boosts performance, especially when that learning is guided by a coach (Capalbo et al., 2022; Cumming et al., 2005; Hall et al., 2009; Quinn et al., 2020; Wesch et al., 2007). Observational learning is not just for student-athletes. For individual sports like golf, swimming, or marathon running, observing others boosts confidence and strategy building. For team sports, modeling other players' behaviors is helpful in learning to manage mental states like staying positive and being confident (Kwon et al., 2022; Law & Hall, 2009; Lee et al., 2021).

Even if you are not now and have never considered yourself an athlete, you can still apply the principles of observational learning in everyday life.

College Success and Career Preparation

Observational learning is surprisingly powerful.

Learning by quietly observing what the most successful students do in class might help you succeed, too. Observational learning can help students struggling with critical thinking tasks (Krekling & Nordvik, 1992) or with memorizing information (Elworthy & Dutch, 1975). Students who watch videos of peers working out how to put together argumentative essays write better essays themselves (Couzijn, 1999; Raedts et al., 2007), and the same trend is found in students learning math concepts (Huang et al., 2020). Observation is especially instructive if the observers are encouraged to evaluate what seems to be working (Braaksma et al., 2006).

Observational learning can even help when performing creative tasks like writing poetry. Watching how other people approach the process, such as by creating steps to completing the task or how to edit your work, can be more helpful than simply practicing for hours by yourself (Groenendijk et al., 2013). We can even learn what *not* to do by observing other people's approaches to problem solving that fail (Hartmann et al., 2020).

Observational learning can also help your career preparation. In fact, the apprenticeship model of job training is based on observational learning (Wu & Xu, 2021). To demonstrate this, students in a management class were randomly divided into two groups (Hoover et al., 2012). One half negotiated and bargained over a starting salary without any practice. The other half first observed others go through the same exercise—and they learned a lot by just observing. Internships and job shadowing often revolve around watching others first, then trying things yourself.

Observational learning is an enduring, practical feature of the working world, and it can also be applied in therapeutic settings.

Modeling in Therapy

Learning from others can also help us grow.

Observational learning has been applied in a variety of therapeutic settings for decades. In 1972, 31 children with social anxiety received therapy to help them feel more comfortable interacting with others (O'Connor, 1972). Some participated in individual shaping therapy, reinforcing progressively better skills. Others viewed a 23-minute video depicting positive social behaviors and were then encouraged to try similar interactions. Children in the modeling condition improved their own behaviors faster, and these improvements lasted longer, compared to either the shaping-condition children or a control group.

Bandura himself used observational learning to help children overcome dog phobias (Bandura & Menlove, 1968). Children who were exposed to multiple videos of other children playing with dogs overcame their own fears more quickly than those who were exposed to single-session videos or control videos. The number of studies showing the utility of observational learning in therapeutic settings and to reduce anxiety is long, with many replications of the basic idea (e.g., Bilodeau-Houle et al., 2020; Karekar et al., 2019; Knell, 2022; Skversky-Blocq, Shmuel, & Cohen, et al., 2022; Skversky-Blocq, Shmuel, Waters, et al., 2022).

As a final question, consider this: Can you be your own role model? One creative study selected 18 children with relatively severe physical disabilities, such as cerebral palsy, muscular dystrophy, and spina bifida (Dowrick & Raeburn, 1995). The children were all asked to perform challenging behaviors, such as walking, balancing, and writing. The researchers videotaped these behaviors and then edited the tapes such that only the best parts of each child's behavior remained. When children watched tapes of *themselves* modeling perfect physical behaviors, their own behaviors improved dramatically. Many additional studies have shown the benefits of using yourself as your own model (for two reviews, see Dowrick, 1999, and Hitchcock et al., 2003). It's inspiring to see proof that you are capable of great things.

This combination of observational learning and believing in yourself might be the key to unlocking more of the potential in all of us.

A Learning Controversy: Violence in the Media

Hulk smash!

It's almost impossible these days to avoid encountering violence in the media, including movies, TV shows, video games, and even on our social media feeds. Blockbuster franchises like *The Avengers* (featuring the Hulk, a bulky green hero) depict epic battles of violence between individuals with superhuman powers of strength, fighting ability, suits with lasers, and so on. Videogames are also increasingly violent. Does all this violence make viewers more violent?

Bandura thought so. Dozens of studies followed Bandura's research on observational learning and aggression. They replicated his general findings that exposure to violence on TV is associated with more violent behavior and/or criminal action. One longitudinal study that followed 450 children over 15 years revealed that "childhood exposure to media violence predicts young adult aggressive behavior for both males and females" (Huesmann et al., 2003).

For example, violent videogames may make players less sensitive to real-world cruelty, less empathetic, more hostile, and more physically aggressive (Anderson & Dill, 2000; Arriaga et al., 2015; Bushman, 2016). Viewing aggressive crimes may also increase real aggression (Anderson et al., 2017). A generally consistent conclusion is that children exposed to violence in the media are more likely to display violent or aggressive behaviors (e.g., Anderson et al., 2010; Bushman & Huesman, 2006; Villani, 2001).

On the other hand, there are thousands of people who watch violent movies or play violent videogames and are personally nonviolent. A 2020 meta-analysis concluded the association between violent videogames and aggressive behavior was "negligible" and that links between videogames and aggressive thoughts and feelings was small (Ferguson et al., 2020). Other studies suggest possible positive effects of videogames (e.g., Halbrook et al., 2019). And remember that correlation does not imply causation; people who already had aggressive tendencies might prefer violent media, so the causal direction might be reversed.

While some textbooks portray this discussion as a debate, the research does seem to generally support conclusions that (1) exposure to violent media reinforces aggressive attitudes and thoughts, plus angry emotions, if they were already present in someone, and (2) the same exposure to violent media may impact aggressive behaviors through observational learning (Anderson & Bushman, 2023; Bushman & Anderson, 2023; Devilly et al., 2023). Of course, many factors play a role in personal violence. ●

Sage Vantage   Practice what you learn in **Knowledge Check 9.3**

CHAPTER REVIEW

Learning Objectives Summary

9.1   What is classical conditioning?

>> LO 9.1   **Explain principles of classical conditioning, applications, and controversies.**

Psychology identifies four major forms of learning, or how our behaviors change as a result of previous experiences. Classical conditioning occurs when a natural, instinctive response to one stimulus in our environment is transferred to another after repeated pairings. Pavlov famously trained dogs to learn that when he would play a certain sound, food would follow. Eventually the dogs salivated only from hearing the sound. Salivating from food was an unconditioned response to an unconditioned stimulus (it happened automatically). Here, the sound was originally a neutral stimulus but became a conditioned stimulus, causing salivation (a conditioned response). Classical conditioning applies to many settings, such as marketing and dislike of certain foods (taste aversion).

9.2   What is operant conditioning?

>> LO 9.2   **Explain principles of operant conditioning, applications, and controversies.**

Operant conditioning occurs when we learn to modify our behavior in order to gain rewards or avoid punishments. Thorndike's law of effect is the principle that behaviors that are rewarded are more likely to occur again, while behaviors that are punished are less likely to happen again. Skinner explored operant conditioning with rats, pigeons, and other animals through mechanical boxes he called operant conditioning chambers. Operant conditioning is also used in a wide variety of settings, such as casinos, animal training, and raising children.

9.3   What are cognitive and observational learning?

>> LO 9.3   **Explain principles of cognitive and observational learning, applications, and controversies.**

Learning can also happen through mentally working out solutions, called cognitive learning or insight. Finally, observational learning occurs when we watch what happens to other people when they perform certain behaviors. We assume that if someone else receives a reward or punishment, the same consequence will apply to us when we perform that behavior. The natural tendency for humans to imitate adults and each other is called modeling. Observational learning takes place and may be applied to almost any situation, including the worlds of sports, college success, and therapeutic settings.

CRITICAL THINKING QUESTIONS

1.   Have you experienced taste aversion for yourself? If so, describe your experience. Now that you know the psychology behind why you don't like that food, do you feel like you can try it again?

2.   Come up with your own examples of the following concepts, using human behaviors: positive reinforcement, positive punishment, negative reinforcement, and negative punishment.

3. Operant conditioning is often used in animal training. Explain how you've used rewards and punishments to train your own pets.

4. Most of the early researchers on classical and operant conditioning where White men, because in the early 1900s, people from diverse backgrounds were not given as many opportunities for education or research resources. Do an online search to identify an influential researcher in learning theory who is a woman or person of color. Describe their contributions.

5. This chapter described three controversies from learning research in psychology (the "Little Albert" study, use of physical punishment with children, and violence in the media). Which controversy do you find the most troubling, and why? How could researchers study similar questions in ethical ways?

Acquisition, 262
Biological preparedness, 266
Classical conditioning, 259
Cognitive learning, 280
Cognitive map, 280
Conditioned response, 261
Conditioned stimulus, 261
Continuous schedule, 275
Discrimination (classical conditioning), 264
Extinction, 262
Fixed interval schedule, 276
Fixed ratio schedule, 275
Generalization, 264
Insight, 280
Interval schedules, 276
Latent learning, 280
Law of effect, 270
Learning, 258
Modeling, 281

Negative punishment, 273
Negative reinforcement, 273
Neutral stimulus, 261
Observational learning, 281
Operant conditioning, 270
Operant conditioning chamber, 270
Partial schedule, 275
Positive punishment, 273
Positive reinforcement, 273
Punishment, 270
Ratio schedules, 275
Reinforcement, 269
Schedules of consequence, 275
Shaping, 274
Spontaneous recovery, 262
Taste aversion, 266
Unconditioned response, 261
Unconditioned stimulus, 260
Variable interval schedule, 276
Variable ratio schedule, 275

Jeffrey Isaac Greenberg 12+/Alamy Stock Photo

10

Memory

We spend a lot of money trying to improve ourselves.

Depending on how we define self-help—whether it includes coaching, podcasts, seminars, and so on, the self-help market may be worth over $43 billion (Grandview Research, 2023). Your local or online bookstore has an entire section dedicated to texts that tell you how to find career success, fix relationships, train children, manage finances, and boost self-esteem. Psychological scientists are trained to be healthy skeptics about such grandiose claims—but few of us would object to being stronger, smarter, better looking, or happier or having a better memory.

A better memory would be huge benefit for college students. It would decrease study time, increase understanding and grades, and give you more free time. A good book giving you tips for how to understand memory functioning and ways to improve your memory would be worth paying for! Guess what . . . you already own that book. It's the one you're reading right now. This chapter focuses on exactly that.

After reading this chapter, you will get answers to several questions you've been curious about:

Have You Ever Wondered?

10.1	How does memory work?
10.2	How can you improve memory encoding?
10.3	How can you improve memory storage?
10.4	How can you improve memory retrieval?
10.5	Why do you remember some things but forget others?
10.6	Can you remember things that never happened?
10.7	Can some memory loss be serious or intentional?

Learning Objectives

LO 10.1	Compare and contrast sensory, working, and long-term memory.
LO 10.2	Describe how we make new memories and how to improve that process.
LO 10.3	Summarize how to improve memory storage.
LO 10.4	Explain how to make memories easier to retrieve.
LO 10.5	Explain why we forget information.
LO 10.6	Describe the reasons for and implications of imperfect memory formation and retrieval.
LO 10.7	Analyze different types of memory loss and suppression.

THE NATURE OF MEMORY

?

Have You Ever Wondered?
10.1 How does memory work?

>> LO 10.1 Compare and contrast sensory, working, and long-term memory.

You may be curious why memory is even necessary these days.

You might think: I don't need a good memory—I have the Internet and a phone. Before letting them replace your brain, ask yourself what the point of doing anything really is. Without memory, you wouldn't recall your favorite experiences, you wouldn't build friendships, and you wouldn't improve and grow over time. **Memory** is how we make use of what we've learned in the past. It is a rich storehouse of images, information, events, and skills that we can recall as needed.

Memory also matters for your career. The U.S. Department of Labor has a database that gives each occupation a score for the importance of remembering information (McKay, 2019). Therapists need to remember what clients revealed in previous sessions. Sales professionals need to remember their products' features. Actors need to remember their lines; it would be downright embarrassing if George Washington forgot what to say in the middle of *Hamilton*. Certainly, your professors want you to remember class material on exams. It's also handy to remember your romantic partner's birthday, your friend's allergy and how to use an EpiPen, and all of your ever-changing passwords. A good memory can make nearly every aspect of your life better.

According to the *multistore* or *Atkinson–Shiffrin model* (Figure 10.1), memory can be broken down into three information-processing systems: sensory memory, working or short-term memory, and long-term memory (Atkinson & Shiffrin, 1968). The first section of this chapter explains each system.

This chapter also has a unique feature we hope will help you apply what you learn to everything you do. Throughout, when we (your authors) provide a tip regarding how to use your memory more effectively or efficiently based on psychological research, you'll see a "memory key" icon. There are 16 memory keys in total, summarized for you in Table 10.1. Here's the first memory key: Memory is a skill you develop through practice—meaning each section of this chapter will give you practical information you can use to improve how you make, keep, and retrieve memories. Like any skill, the more you practice, the better you'll get.

Memory: The process by which we store images, information, events, and skills, then recall them later.

FIGURE 10.1

The Multistore Model of Memory

The multistore model proposes three systems for memory (Atkinson & Shiffrin, 1968).

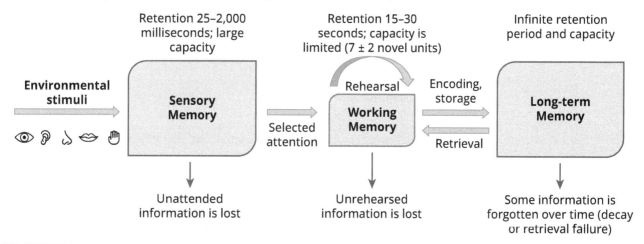

Sources: Adapted from Noushad and Khurshid (2019); icons from iStock.com/Alexey Yakovenko.

Before we get to more specific tips, first it's important to understand how your memory works.

	Memory Key:
	Memory is a skill
	you develop through practice.

Memory Key icon from iStock.com/chatchaisurakram

TABLE 10.1

Mastering the 16 Memory Keys

1.	Memory is a skill you develop through practice.
2.	Repetition is good, but not great.
3.	Go deeper and create connections to make info more meaningful.
4.	Tie memories to your self.
5.	Master the "Rule of 7": Combine info into larger chunks.
6.	Space out your study sessions: A bit each day > all at once.
7.	Overdo it: Once you "know it," keep going.
8.	Master mnemonics to memorize specific info and lists.
9.	Give yourself a break or a nap.
10.	Cues are clues: Give yourself lots to work with.
11.	Take yourself back both externally and internally.
12.	Mind the middle: Mix up the info's order.
13.	Put yourself to the test.
14.	Focus: Pay attention and avoid distractions.
15.	Be careful when studying similar topics together.
16.	Don't be tricked: Similar facts may sound right.

Sensory Memory

Where does memory start?

All memories start with something happening that you see, hear, feel, taste, or smell. **Sensory memory** briefly preserves physical features of sensations. Your senses gather information. Sensory memory holds that information only for a moment, often just 25 to 2,000 milliseconds, so you're often unaware of it happening. If you don't notice sensory information, it's quickly forgotten. In this case, forgetting is a good thing! You would be overwhelmed if you had to pay attention to all the information hitting your visual, auditory, and other senses. We learn to automatically filter what is and isn't important.

Consider two examples of specific forms of sensory memory: iconic and echoic.

Sensory memory: The ability to briefly preserve physical features of sensory stimuli.

FIGURE 10.2

Testing Iconic Memory

If you saw these letters for less than a second, how many could you recall?

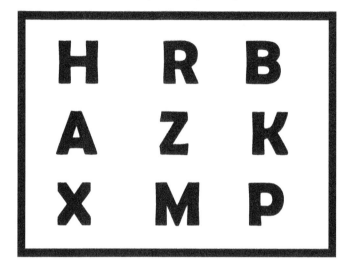

Iconic Memory

Have you ever tried to take a picture with your eyes? Perhaps you want a mental snapshot of your shopping list, the layout of a map, or a beautiful sunset. However, your visual memory doesn't work like the camera in your phone. The images you "take" with your eyes quickly fade. But that visual information is held there for a moment (about half a second) as an *iconic memory*, which allows us to picture an image in our mind after the physical object is no longer present.

Cognitive psychologist George Sperling (1960) created a clever demonstration of iconic memory by showing participants the rows of letters in Figure 10.2 for less than a second. Then, they reported what they had seen. Most recited only the first line, as if their iconic memory only gathered that much information. Sperling then asked the participants to look at the lines again. He paired the rows with unique sounds: the first row with a sound that had a low tone, the third row with a high tone, and the middle row with an in-between tone.

Once again, participants briefly saw the entire set of letters. When Sperling played one of the three tones and asked them to recall only the line that matched the sound, they could do it! The results suggested our iconic memory took a full picture of all the letters, but the image fades so quickly that we can only glance back at one part of our mental photo.

You may be curious about so-called photographic memory. *Eidetic memory* describes the ability to perfectly recall an image briefly viewed a single time. It sounds cool (test-taking made easy!), but most research done with rigorous testing indicates it's probably extremely rare and might be limited to children (Neath & Surprenant, 2003; Schwitzgebel, 2002). Usually, people with excellent memories use the tricks you'll learn by reading this chapter.

Echoic Memory

You've seen weddings or other ceremonies with vows. People are told, "repeat after me" and then given long phrases like, "I take this person to be my partner, to have and to hold from this day forward...." To complete this task, we must remember what the other person just said. Thanks to your *echoic memory,* you're able to retain auditory information for several seconds (Clark, 1987). Good thing, because if echoic memory were as brief as iconic memory, you'd barely make it past the first word. In echoic memory, a single sound enters memory, but that information is immediately replaced and updated—allowing us to monitor new information as it comes in (Kinukawa et al., 2019).

Working or Short-Term Memory

Working memory: A system that actively processes different types of information such as ideas, images, and sounds from multiple sources.

Short-term memory: See *working memory.*

Sensory memory is fragile, but your working memory is more stable.

Working memory (also called **short-term memory**) processes different types of information from multiple sources such as ideas, images, and sounds (Baddeley, 2002). Working memory has several important functions (Figure 10.3). For example, it selects, buffers, and holds some information, but it is still delicate, lasting only 15 to 30 seconds. Working memory helps to remember a security code from a website trying to verify your identity. You maintain that group of letters or numbers in your mind for a few seconds, enter it on the website, and then forget it. This is another case of good forgetting. No one wants a useless security code bouncing around their brain forever.

Other information sticks. Let's say you learned in high school history class that the American government poisoned industrial alcohol during Prohibition to make it unusable for bootleggers (true story). Thanks to working memory, that attention-getting information will be stickier in memory, partially because you also processed the context in which you learned it. You may have some recall of how your classmates reacted, your history teacher, or the associated sensations (smells, sounds, temperature in the room) when you learned the information. Each part of the memory is important and becomes a cue for the other parts.

FIGURE 10.3

The Characteristics of Working Memory

Working memory has several important functions.

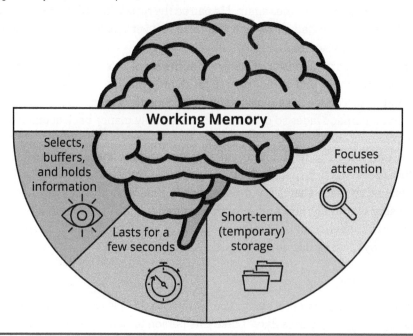

iStockPhoto.com/Ukususha; iStock.com/PeterSnow

FIGURE 10.4

Model of Working Memory

An overview of Baddeley's components of working memory.

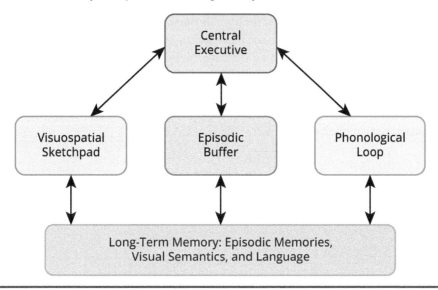

Source: McBride et al. (2023).

Working memory has different facets that are organized by a system called the *central executive* (Figure 10.4). It focuses attention, shifts between tasks, and combines processes as needed (Baddeley & Hitch, 1974). The central executive juggles three main parts of working memory.

One is the *visuospatial sketchpad,* a mental snapshot of a scene that you can refer to later. It's a general impression, not a perfect photo. For example, to remember where you parked your car, you might look back after you walk away, noting the yellow post directly above. When you want to find your car later, you look for the yellow post. Your visuospatial sketchpad is handy, but we use it like an erasable spot for temporary visual information.

There is a similar workspace for sounds called the *phonological loop.* If you're trying to remember something—a grocery list, a phone number, someone's name— and you say it out loud several times; that's the phonological loop. It also works if you rehearse sounds or speech-related information silently, but you hear your own voice in your head.

Another component, the *episodic buffer,* integrates auditory, spatial, and visual information with chronological order (Baddeley & Logie, 1999). Linking information chronologically creates coherent representations with a story structure that make it easier to remember information (Baddeley & Wilson, 2002). Think of the episodic buffer like "episodes" in a TV show: If you create a story, one piece of information can be a cue for the next, making the entire list more memorable.

Most people have a limited working memory that is capable of processing only a few ideas at a time (Luck & Vogel, 1997). This capacity can go up if we're good at screening out distractions (Fukuda & Vogel, 2009), but it can go down if our brains are hurt by something like drug use (Adam et al., 2020). Several phone apps offer "brain training" or memory aid games that promise help—but do they work? So far, the evidence is mixed (Owen et al., 2010; Simons et al., 2016). There is more evidence for the memory key strategies throughout this chapter (you'll see the next one in a few pages).

Long-Term Memory

Memories that last a lifetime.

That's what psychologists refer to as **long-term memory**, information that is retained relatively permanently. Unlike working memory, long-term memory may have limitless capacity. Long-term memories include personal history, phone numbers, your best friend's face, family, favorite bands, everything you've learned in school, plus all the peripheral information associated with each event (like what you were wearing on your first day of college). It can last decades, and it shapes how we think of ourselves.

Long-term memory is so rich with information that we can organize it into the different types summarized in Figure 10.5. Generally, psychologists break it into two major categories, implicit and explicit.

Long-term memory: Information that you retain in a lasting and relatively permanent way.

Explicit Long-Term Memory

Key moments from your life you want to cherish, forget, or when you learned something important are *explicit memories* (also known as declarative memories) that we consciously recall. There are two main types:

- *Semantic memory* focuses on concepts, facts, and other information that you consciously remember. It's like knowing that the chemical formula for water is H_2O. You might not remember exactly when and where you learned this fact, but it's solidly stored in your brain.

- *Episodic memories* are personal experiences such as that first kiss, a terrifying near-death accident, or some personal accomplishment. They're like "episodes" in the story of your life.

Some episodic memories seem more vivid than others. Many people have what psychologists call *flashbulb memories*, which are particularly strong, detailed recollections of emotional, meaningful, or surprising events (Brown & Kulik, 1977).

FIGURE 10.5

The Structure of Long-Term Memory

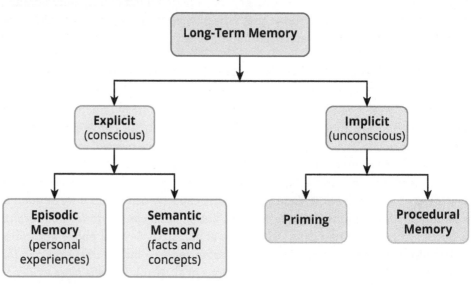

These can be personal nature, or they can be national or international events that are meaningful to an entire generation. People of a certain age might discuss their vivid memories of where they were when they watched TV coverage of astronauts first walking on the moon, for example; other generations might discuss flashbulb memories of the JFK assassination, the *Challenger* explosion, the 9/11 terrorist attacks, or Kobe Bryant's death.

While it *seems* like we perfectly remember every detail of our flashbulb memories, research tells a different story (Hirst et al., 2015; Hirst & Phelps, 2016). While people are quite confident their memories are accurate, *actual* accuracy is mediocre and inconsistent. Studies simply wait for a major event to occur, then have people write about it just a few days afterward (presumably, those memories are pretty accurate). The same individuals are then asked to write down their memories months or years later, and researchers can compare the reports (e.g., Neisser & Harsch, 1992; Schmolck et al., 2000). Even when people *think* they remember exactly what originally happened, major changes occur between their first and second account without the person realizing it.

Implicit Long-Term Memory

It's just like riding a bike. Sure, you haven't ridden for years, but you hop on, start pedaling, and it all comes back to you. This is an *implicit memory* because it's recalled automatically and is something you do without really thinking about it. You could substitute the word *implicit* here for *autopilot*—information in your memory you're not consciously aware of and maybe would find difficult to put into words, but it's there.

Physical skills such as riding a bike, driving, skiing, juggling, playing video games, and recalling all the moves in a TikTok dance rely on a specific type of implicit memory known as *procedural* or *motor memory*. When you're first learning them, they require thought and attention, but over time and with practice, you do them without a second thought—almost automatically. You don't need to explicitly recall each step; it's like your body takes over.

Implicit memory influences your daily experience in other ways. You've heard of Wind Goodfriend, right? The name sounds very Hollywood. It's not. Because of the *false fame effect,* names that you've heard or read before (like Wind Goodfriend, which you've seen on this book's cover) seem famous (Jacoby et al., 1989). If we have just a bit of prior experience with someone's name and then later can't place why it seems familiar, we make an implicit assumption: I've heard that name somewhere before, so it must be special.

Learning the latest TikTok dance requires the help of your procedural memory.

Georgijevic/E+/via Getty Images

What about that mysterious déjà vu experience of having previously lived through a moment? While it might be exciting to think you have psychic powers or have lived previous lives, those speculations can't be scientifically tested. What psychological science can tell us is that functional magnetic resonance imaging brain scans indicate memory conflicts during déjà vu (Urquhart et al., 2018). The odd feeling is probably simply recognition of a similar past experience, but the inability to identify when and where it happened (A. S. Brown, 2004).

Memory Is a Process

Memory is a process.

There are three basic steps (Figure 10.6):

- First, memories need to get into your brain, which you accomplish via encoding.

- Second, you need to retain those memories over time via storage.

- Third, you need to get the memories back out via retrieval.

Here is where you will start to see more of those memory keys. We'll cover each stage in depth in the next few sections of this chapter, and at each step, we'll discuss techniques that could make your memory work better.

Encoding: The process for getting memories into your brain.

Storage: A way to retain memories over time.

Retrieval: Recovering memories for use now.

FIGURE 10.6

The Stages of Memory

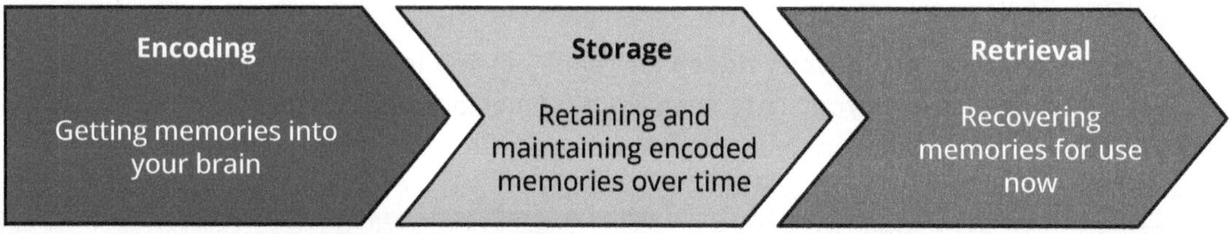

Encoding	Storage	Retrieval
Getting memories into your brain	Retaining and maintaining encoded memories over time	Recovering memories for use now

---

CAREER CORNER

Profiling Allen, Fight Master

What is your career?

I'm a fight master. I choreograph combat for theater, television, and film, working with actors and the creative team (director, set, lighting, and costume designers) to safely execute scenes involving intense physical moments.

How was studying psychology important for success in this career?

It helped me to quickly figure out different actors' abilities to learn and memorize complex and dangerous fight scenes. A good memory is essential for this work. Safety is paramount, so I use repetition to enhance muscle memory (implicit memory) and state-dependent rehearsal techniques. A sword fight, a stair fall, a carjacking, and a comedy pie fight all need to be memorized exactly by everyone involved so nothing goes wrong.

Is this the career you always planned to have after college?

I wanted to be a *National Geographic* photographer. But, in college, one of my professors altered the direction of my career into theater, as did a guest artist he hired during that time who was a fight director from the Stratford Festival in Canada. They helped me focus my goals.

If you could give current college students advice, what would it be?

Work hard and learn the empathy to read people and meet them where they are. **Encourage others' strengths and support them as they make their way.** Some will become famous, as many of my students did, and you can be proud you knew them and helped them along their path. ●

MAKING MEMORIES: ENCODING

>> **LO 10.2**   **Describe how we make new memories and how to improve that process.**

Encoding is how you begin the process of remembering.

Some memory tasks are basic life essentials, such as knowing your name, phone number, and where you live. Others are less practical—knowing the names of ancient Egyptian pharaohs in order, the noble gases on the periodic table of elements, the first five digits of pi, or the names of every Pokémon character. When committing information to memory, there are different *levels of processing* or ways to do it, some of which are deeper or more meaningful than others (Craik & Lockhart, 1972). In each case, the memory process begins with encoding: creating a new memory.

Have You Ever Wondered?
10.2 How can you improve memory encoding?

Rehearsal: Say It Again

Again and again.

You've probably had a coach or teacher tell you: You can't get better without practice. For memory research in psychology, *rehearsal* means practice or repetition with the goal of creating a new memory. Repetition is important, and how it happens can affect the quality of your memory. Hermann Ebbinghaus (1949) started early research on memory encoding and rehearsal using *nonsense syllables*, three-letter word fragments that aren't words (e.g., NUZ LEF TAK POB REJ WIV). Unlike familiar three-letter words such as DOG, CAT, TOP, or BAG, participants in Ebbinghaus's experiments had no prior exposure to nonsense syllables, so he could scientifically control their memories better in his research.

What have we learned about encoding and rehearsal since then?

Make Mental Connections With Elaborative Rehearsal

Not all rehearsal is created equal. The simplest way to commit information to memory is through repetition. If you had to remember a series of numbers such as 5-6-3-9-8-4-2-7-1, your go-to strategy may be simply saying the numbers over and over in your head. **Maintenance rehearsal** or *rote learning* is a memorization technique that involves purposeful verbal or mental repetition and review of material to encourage learning.

Maintenance rehearsal: Memorization technique that involves purposeful verbal or mental repetition and review of material to encourage learning.

Memory Key:

Repetition is good, but not great.

Memory Key icon from iStock.com/chatchaisurakram

Maintenance rehearsal can be a good strategy, but only for some tasks. Short-term memory can't hold onto information very long, but repeating information allows you to restart the clock. It's also beneficial because it forces you to focus your attention on the task that also blocks out other thoughts or activities that would inhibit encoding.

Imagine you want to remember Melissa's name and you just met her. Quietly repeating, "Melissa, Melissa, Melissa" would be maintenance rehearsal. A better strategy is to use **elaborative rehearsal** to add meaning to that name, forcing you to think more deeply while you encode the new memory. First say, "Nice to meet you, Melissa." Then think about how this Melissa plays the flute just like the performer

Elaborative rehearsal: Memorization technique that involves generating meaning as you repeat the information.

Lizzo, whose legal name is also Melissa, and you're much more likely to remember Melissa's name the next time you see her.

Memory Key:

Go deeper and create connections to make info more meaningful.

Memory Key icon from iStock.com/chatchaisurakram

Elaborative rehearsal takes advantage of levels of processing by encoding information in a more meaningful way. For example, consider this list:

- Strawberry

- Fairy

- Tree

- Gratitude

- Candy

- Light

- Smile

What method works better: repeating each word multiple times (maintenance rehearsal) or trying to create a story in which each word is followed by the next (elaborative rehearsal)? The storytelling approach. That's because it requires you to process each word more deliberately. Elaborative rehearsal helps both younger and older adults improve their encoding (Harris & Qualls, 2000).

Own the Idea: Using the Self-Reference Effect

Self-reference effect: The tendency to remember personally relevant information more easily.

Apply things to your own life. The **self-reference effect** describes the fact that memory is better for things that relate to the self (Symons & Johnson, 1997). Have you ever been in class and thought, "When am I ever going to use this information? Why should I possibly care—what does this have to do with me?" You probably had trouble remembering the information in that class. When you think of concepts in terms of yourself, your memory for those things improves.

Memory Key:

Tie memories to your self.

Memory Key icon from iStock.com/chatchaisurakram

Textbooks are full of examples, largely taken from the authors' lives. In this book, we (Wind, Gary, Charity, and Tom) use personal examples from time to time, just as we do in class. Our goal is to make concepts real and easier for you to recall them. But even better is if you can think of additional examples from *your* life. For example, do *you* have any flashbulb memories? Are you sure they're accurate?

The self-reference effect allows you elaborate on whatever information or memory you're encoding and place it in a context that is near and dear to your own experience

(Gillihan & Farah, 2005). The more you define terms in your own words and apply the concepts to your life, the deeper your level of processing and more lasting your memories.

Memory Span: Cooperate With Your Working Memory

When encoding information, you only have so much space to work with.

Working memory is temporary (aka "short term") and requires rehearsal just to keep information in place. It also has a limited capacity or *memory span* for the number of items that you can recall at any given time. If you've ever seen shows about tiny houses on HGTV, you know that it's not the size of the space you must work with, but how you use it that makes a difference. So, make friends with your working memory by accepting its limitations and getting creative to get the most out of it.

The Magic Number

Sometimes, less is more. Here's what we mean. First, try using maintenance rehearsal (just saying the numbers out loud) to memorize these numbers in order:

2 1 5 8 4 7 3 1 2 4 9 0

Do you know the order of planets in our solar system? How do you remember?

iStock.com/ChrisGorgio

Miller (1956) discovered that there was a "magic number" for most people's short-term memory span. When people try to memorize a list of numbers or letters, most can only recall a certain number of them. Want to know the magic number? First, without looking back, write down the numbers we asked you to memorize in the previous paragraph.

Miller's "magic number"—meaning what most people remember—is seven, plus or minus two. Most people's working memory span is between five and nine. Notice that the number seven keeps popping up . . . we can mostly recall

- the names of Snow White's seven dwarfs,

- the seven deadly sins,

- seven digits in a basic phone number, and

- the seven days of the week.

It's not a coincidence this chapter was split into seven major sections. But there's an easy way you can immediately expand your working memory's capacity, just like magic.

Chunking

Chunking is combining individual bits of information into fewer, larger pieces. For example, instead of memorizing 2 1 5 8 4 7 3 1 2 4 9 0 as 12 individual digits, try to remember four numbers: 215 847 312 490. Each group is a "chunk," and you've just multiplied your working memory.

Here's another example—you could try to memorize these 21 letters in order:

P A W A N B B F S D F Y O N F L L O P T A

Chunking: Combining and grouping smaller bits of information into larger pieces to increase memory capacity.

But that's a lot more than seven letters, so it's easier if you can reorganize them into six more familiar and meaningful chunks that represent sport leagues, text shorthand, and psychology terms:

N F L W N B A B F F Y O L O P T S D A P A

	**Memory Key:** Master the "Rule of 7": Combine info into larger chunks.

Memory Key icon from iStock.com/chatchaisurakram

It's even easier to remember items in chunks if you can find patterns or meaning. Many children in school learned the order of colors in the rainbow with a man named ROY G. BIV, the names of the U.S. Great Lakes with the acronym HOMES (Huron, Ontario, Michigan, Erie, and Superior), or the order of planets with the acrostic "My Very Elegant Mother Just Served Us Nine Pizzas"—where the first letter of each word reminds you that it's Mercury, Venus, Earth, Mars, Jupiter, Saturn, Uranus, Neptune, and Pluto (well, it used to be Pluto).

Time and Effort: Learn Faster by Learning Slower

More is better.

To enjoy the benefits of an effective memory, you need to give it the time and attention it deserves. If you're taking advantage of the memory keys we share in this chapter, then you'll stop wasting your time on unpleasant and ineffective strategies. You will learn *how* to learn faster by going slower and working smarter instead of harder.

Superficial Processing: Avoid Being Too Fast

Speed kills. Just as deeper, more meaningful processing helps encode memories, *superficial* or light, basic processing hurts encoding. Trying to speed-read usually means decreased accuracy, comprehension, and understanding (Rayner et al., 2016). If your goal is speed or a general overview, then skimming may be helpful. But most texts already do that for you with headings, subsections, and summaries of the main ideas. Highlighting while you read has some benefits but by itself doesn't accomplish much than make the words a different color; most students realize that deeper processing like taking notes while reading or making flashcards will better help memory (Blasiman et al., 2017).

The Spacing Effect

Spacing effect: Learning information across multiple sessions throughout a longer time span improves long-term memory.

Don't cram. Complicated information needs "time to sink in" (to a deeper level of processing). Ebbinghaus's early memory studies demonstrated a **spacing effect**, in which learning across multiple sessions throughout a longer time span improves encoding. For example, if you have 4 hours for studying, then you're better off breaking those hours up:

- Instead of one intense 4-hour session, do four 1-hour sessions.

- Better yet, study for eight sessions at 30 minutes each.

	Memory Key:
	Space out your study sessions: A bit each day > all at once.

Memory Key icon from iStock.com/chatchaisurakram

Surprise! This won't prolong the agony of studying. It will shorten your study time because you won't need all eight sessions, and learning will be more fun because you won't be exhausted. The spacing effect is why cramming for tests is less effective. For example, one study found that while most students *thought* cramming the day before a test was helpful, spacing studying out over time was better for 90% of them (Kornell, 2009).

Overlearning

Overdo it. Another tool for remembering is to fight the temptation to stop when you first "get it." You don't really "have it" until you can "keep it." **Overlearning** is continuing to practice material to secure and strengthen memory or skills, so they don't fade. Professional athletes are already great, but they still practice more than they compete. Many professions (like medical doctors, teachers, and social workers) are required to complete continuing education hours to maintain their licenses. Overlearning stabilizes knowledge (Shibata et al., 2017). One great way to keep a memory or skill up, by the way, is to teach it to someone else (Fiorella & Mayer, 2013).

Overlearning: Continual studying or practicing of material to strengthen memory.

	Memory Key:
	Overdo it: Once you "know it," keep going.

Memory Key icon from iStock.com/chatchaisurakram

Mnemonics: Make Remembering Fun Again

Overlearning has its benefits, but many people love a shortcut.

Like it or not, many of your college courses require memorization, so it's nice to have some "hacks" or memory tricks you can use. A **mnemonic** is a memory aid or technique to help remember specific information, especially lists. Mnemonics are especially useful aids for learning (Putnam, 2015), and they all share the same underlying feature: Depth of processing adds layers of meaning to otherwise obscure information. Try playing with some of these six specific memory strategies.

Mnemonic: A memory aid or technique to help remember specific information, especially lists.

	Memory Key:
	Master mnemonics to memorize specific info and lists.

Memory Key icon from iStock.com/chatchaisurakram

Music: There's Money in Memory

A successful commercial jingle is a musical earworm, a catchy tune that gets stuck in your head. Their purpose is usually straightforward: create a sticky memory to help sell some product. Songs are used to teach many children foundational information such as the alphabet (Cirigliano, 2013), and children learn information like phone numbers better when they are put to music (Wolfe & Hom, 1993). Depending on your generation, you may be able to name the company associated with these jingles:

- "I'm Lovin' It"
- "Five Dollar Foot Long"
- "Like a Good Neighbor"
- "Plop Plop Fizz Fizz"

Acronyms and Rhymes

You already learned about *acronyms* in the section about chunking (like HOMES for the Great Lakes). They are especially helpful if you need to remember something in a specific order, like the steps of mathematical operations, PEDMAS: parentheses, exponents, multiplication, division, addition, and subtraction. When you complete this section about mnemonics, you'll also be able to MARVEL (ha!) at your superhero-like ability to improve your memory through mnemonics.

Rhymes can also make facts easier to remember, which your elementary school teachers probably used to their advantage when explaining that Christopher Columbus "sailed the ocean blue" in "Fourteen-hundred-ninety-two." *Rhyming* links new ideas with a familiar cadence to make them more memorable. It's one more layer of processing.

Vivid Stories and Elaboration

Occasionally, you will have to recall what feels like trivial information in order. When I [Gary] was in school, I had to learn the order in which the U.S. states entered the union. That information hasn't proved life-altering, but the memory trick we learned has been. My teacher, Mr. Zebo, had our class create a fun *vivid story*. It was full of rich imagery and quirky details—and it worked.

Decades later, I still remember: We imagined taking a class trip to see the Delaware (#1) River; floating in the river were a bunch of huge pencils (Pennsylvania, #2) all wearing brand new shirts (New Jersey, #3) featuring pictures of George Bush (Georgia, #4) on them. But old George's hair had a fancy new cut (Connecticut, #5). It looked odd because his cheeks were puffy from his mouth being full of a massive wad of tobacco that he needed to spit (Massachusetts, #6). I'll spare you the rest, but you get the idea. Vivid, interactive, visual stories are easier to remember.

Elaboration creates multiple pathways to stored information. Play with the *keyword* technique by creating a mental image for each memory. For example, a dancing hippopotamus in the middle of your campus will help you remember the brain region that helps form new memories is the hippocampus. And knowing that *hippo* is the Greek word for "horse" will help you remember that the hippocampus is shaped a bit like a seahorse. Anything that shows connections helps elaborate on the information.

The Method of Loci

In his bestselling book *Moonwalking With Einstein,* journalist Joshua Foer (2012) describes how he used a mnemonic to become the record-setting U.S.A. Memory Champion. The *method of loci* is an ancient technique that attaches information to well-known physical spaces. One event at the memory championship is memorizing a full shuffled deck of 52 playing cards as quickly as possible: Ace of Spaces, 4 of Diamonds, 10 of Clubs, and so on.

The method of loci would be envisioning each card with a specific physical space that has a lot of spots in a certain order. Foer might visualize the ace of spades on his nightstand, the four of diamonds stuck to his alarm clock, the ten of clubs pinned to the bathroom mirror, and so on. With practice, you can quickly memorize an entire deck of cards in order (though perhaps not as quickly as the current world record of 12.74 seconds held by Shijir-Erdene Bat-Enkh).

The method of loci also has practical applications for those with depression (Dalgleish et al., 2013). Individuals with depression often struggle with recalling personal memories that are positive. To help with that, researchers trained some participants to use the method of loci to recall a set of positive memories, while another group learned how to chunk their positive memories. Both types of training helped with memory 1 week later, but 2 weeks later, those in the method of loci condition had an advantage.

Do you want to remember everything you've read in the section on mnemonics? Try to use an acronym to MARVEL at them, shown in Table 10.2, a mnemonic created by one of this book's authors [Gary].

TABLE 10.2

Mnemonics to Improve Memory

M.A.R.V.E.L. AT THE POWER OF MNEMONICS		
1.	**M**usic	Set key information to a song.
2.	**A**cronym	Take the first letter of items in a list to spell a word.
3.	**R**hyming	Link ideas with a rhyming cadence or tempo.
4.	**V**ivid **Stories**	Create a rich, detailed narrative tying everything together.
5.	**E**laborate	Give yourself extra information, perhaps by creating a mental image.
6.	**L**oci (**Method** of)	Attach information to places along a well-known physical path.

Practice what you learn in **Knowledge Check 10.2**

Sage Vantage➤

KEEPING MEMORIES: STORAGE

>> **LO 10.3** Summarize how to improve memory storage.

"This could go on your permanent record!"

This threat was how educators once warned misbehaving students. Perhaps your "permanent record" really is collecting dust in some rusty file cabinet in an old elementary school. But if your experiences survive the filtering processes of sensory and working/short-term memories, the relatively permanent record of your life is mentally stored in your long-term memory. How does storage work, and how can you improve it?

Have You Ever Wondered?
10.3 How can you improve memory storage?

Memory Storage's Structure

Memory storage isn't haphazard; it follows a system.

With apologies to those with a messy desk or office, it's easier to find what you need when there's an underlying organization. The same is true for memory; most

Because of schemas stored in your long-term memory, you have expectations for how weddings usually work.

iStock.com/Asia-Pacific Images Studio

Schemas: Existing collections of thoughts or knowledge that help you make sense of new information.

people organize their memories using meaningful relationships and groupings. These categories and concepts are called **schemas**, existing collections of thoughts or knowledge that help you make sense of new information. You have a schema for certain events (like a wedding—what to wear, the order of events, the expectation to bring a gift), types of professions, genres of music, international borders and politics, and more.

Any individual concept exists within a larger framework of related concepts, or *network of associations* (Collins & Loftus, 1975). Each concept or piece of information is a *node*, which connects with other related nodes. A fork is a node. Mentally, you probably have connections in your memory between the concept of "fork" and the related concepts of spoon, knife, plate, kitchen, food, and so on. *Spreading activation* refers to the idea that some connections will be closer than others; "fork" and "spoon" are probably connected more closely than "fork" and "hammer," for example, although both fork and screwdriver fall in the larger schema of "tools or utensils."

If our memory for an event is incomplete, we often rely on schemas to fill in the blanks. This is one way memories start to develop inaccuracies. For example, you have a schema for birthday parties that influences what you think typically happens. If someone asks you about a birthday party you attended weeks ago, you may remember there was a cake even if there wasn't—because it fits the schema.

Consolidation: Processing Memories

All that information must go somewhere.

Consolidation is the process that transforms temporary memories into more permanent memories (Hebb, 1949). But where does all that information go? The *engram* is the general physical location in your brain where a memory resides. Some research with case studies indicates that storage of long-term memories may involve the temporal lobes (Moriarity et al., 2001; Penfield & Perot, 1963; Squire et al., 2004), but it's tricky because a memory may not be in just one place (Lashley, 1930). Rather, *equipotentiality* suggests that memories are spread throughout your brain (Kleiner, 2011). If you removed pieces of the brain (do not try this at home), the impact on stored memories would depend more on the piece's size than its location.

Retaining and Relearning

What happens to all those facts you learn?

During elementary and high school, you stored lots of now-dusty information that you don't remember. It could be Spanish vocabulary words, the names of the U.S. presidents in order, state capitals, symbols on the periodic table of elements, or the lines of a poem. Have you really forgotten all that information? Research indicates the memories are still being stored somewhere in long-term memory, even if you haven't opened that mental file for a while.

The Retention Interval: For How Long?

How long is "a while"? The answer depends on the *retention interval,* how long you need to preserve the information:

- Where you parked your car at the mall: a few hours.

- Your hotel room number during spring break: a few days.

- The names of everyone you meet at a summer camp: a few months.

- Your high school locker combination: a few years.

The retention interval roughly corresponds to the information's importance. You may preserve personal details such as your parents' and pets' names for a lifetime. However, when the information is less personal, memory accuracy goes down as the retention interval goes up (i.e., memory erodes over time; Spearing & Wade, 2022).

But research indicates once something has been stored once, it's usually there permanently even if it doesn't *seem* like you can remember (retrieve) it. How do we know? Because if you have to now learn something again—*relearning*—the process will be faster than the first time (Nelson, 1985). If you took piano or guitar lessons as a kid, for example, then you'll pick it up in your 30s faster than someone who has never played.

Reconsolidation

Memory is malleable. Psychologists used to think that memories were stored in one spot, brought out to be used when needed, and put back in the same place afterward in the exact same condition (Alberini & LeDoux, 2013). This linear process is shown in the top half of Figure 10.7.

The more modern view from research is that memory is more malleable or fragile. In fact, after we retrieve a given memory from long-term storage, we then engage in *reconsolidation*—storing the memory all over again (as shown in the bottom half of Figure 10.7).

FIGURE 10.7

Two Theoretical Ways to Access Stored Long-Term Memories

Are long-term memories fixed, or do they change each time we use them?

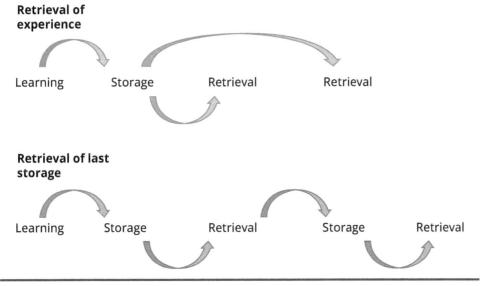

Source: Alberini and LeDox (2013).

Reconsolidation might benefit the memory; it provides an opportunity to strengthen it through things like practicing information or a skill. On the other hand, reconsolidation also means the memory can be altered from its original form. Your current state of mind, biases, and assumptions can start to color it slightly. We'll talk about these errors more later in the chapter.

	Memory Key:
	Give yourself a break or a nap.

Memory Key icon from iStock.com/chatchaisurakram

The Importance of Taking Breaks

Give yourself a break.

Want to avoid errors and improve good storage? Memory consolidation takes time, so give yourself some downtime after learning new information. Just like we discussed earlier with the spacing effect for encoding of new information, taking breaks during and immediately after storage of long-term memories can improve their processing and retention (Little et al., 2017; Seehagen et al., 2015; Tambini et al., 2010). Warning! These studies showed benefits of breaks and naps between 5 and 30 minutes—but "breaks" longer than that can be counterproductive excuses to just stop working.

Sage Vantage   Practice what you learn in **Knowledge Check 10.3**

USING MEMORIES: RETRIEVAL

Have You Ever Wondered?
10.4 How can you improve memory retrieval?

>> **LO 10.4**   **Explain how to make memories easier to retrieve.**

You're staring at an exam question that you know the answer to, but you don't remember it.

We've all been there. A memory could be perfectly encoded and stored, but if retrieval fails, you won't remember it. The memory exists, but you can't access it. Getting the memories out is a process, just like encoding and storage. According to the *two-stage theory*, memory retrieval begins with a search for the information (Stage 1), then checking to make sure it is correct (Stage 2; Tulving, 1976).

Prompts help us retrieve stored memories; the interaction between prompts and memory engrams is called *ecphory* (Frankland et al., 2019). Thanks to ecphory, you can retrieve stored memories from your childhood or for an upcoming chemistry test. In this section, we examine how different types of prompts (like recognition vs. recall) impact retrieval, then turn to some curious aspects of memory.

Recognition Versus Recall

Which is easier—multiple choice or fill-in-the-blank?

The two types of quiz questions rely on different types of retrieval. Multiple choice might be preferred because the menu of response options provides clues that might trigger retrieval of a useful memory. So multiple choice involves **recognition**, the ability to correctly identify information after seeing or experiencing it (Raaijmakers & Shiffrin, 1992). Fill-in-the-blank, however, relies on **recall**, or the

Recognition: The ability to remember information after seeing or experiencing it.

Recall: The ability to remember information without that information present.

ability to remember information without that information present. With recall, you have to retrieve a memory with few or without any clues, so it's a much harder task.

Memory Retrieval Cues

Cues are clues.

Memory cues (sometimes called retrieval cues) are stimuli or prompts that help you remember. The *encoding specificity principle* recognizes that it is easier to retrieve information when the circumstances during retrieval match the circumstances during encoding (Tulving & Thomson, 1973). For example, do you like to sit in the same spot every day in class—especially on the day of an exam? There's a good reason for that preference (keep reading!). Let us explain two types of especially powerful retrieval cues that might help you improve your memory retrieval: context and state.

Do you prefer to sit in the same spot for exams as wherever you sat when you learned the material? There's a good psychological reason to do so.

iStock.com/FatCamera

	Memory Key:
	Cues are clues:
	Give yourself lots to work with.

Memory Key icon from iStock.com/chatchaisurakram

Context-Dependent Memory

Context matters. Think of "context" here as the external environment when and where you encoded and stored a memory. *Context-dependent memory* recognizes that retrieval is improved when the context for encoding and retrieving matches. If you sit in a certain chair every day when you hear your biology lectures and put that information into your memory, you'll want to sit in the exact same chair on test day when it's time for memory retrieval.

Psychology researchers sometimes go to great lengths (or, in this case, underwater depths) to test a hypothesis (Godden & Baddely, 1975). In one study, researchers tested SCUBA divers' memories by asking them to learn lists of words on land and underwater, and then testing their recall in both environments. Divers who learned words underwater later recalled them more easily when they were underwater than when they were on land.

Context-dependent memory also works for smells. In another study, participants learned words in the presence of distinct smells such as pine and peppermint (Herz, 1997). When tested, they remembered the most words when the same scent was present at both encoding and retrieval. The sight and smell of Play-Doh might suddenly bring back specific childhood memories, and a whiff of perfume can stimulate memories of old family members or partners.

Not only can you smell this picture in your mind, but it can also conjure up childhood memories.

iStock.com/NoDerog

If you can't control your environment, you might be able to create your own context. For example, one study presented a set of images on a screen to people and asked participants to remember them (Wynn et al., 2018). Eye-tracking technology showed that during the retrieval test, participants whose eye movements on the screen repeated what they did during encoding had better memories.

	Memory Key:
	Take yourself back
	both externally and internally.

Memory Key icon from iStock.com/chatchaisurakram

State-Dependent Memory

While context-dependent memory is about your external environment, state-dependent memory is about your internal body sensations, which can also provide retrieval or memory cues. *State-dependent memory* occurs when your internal or physiological state at retrieval matches what it was at encoding. For example, if you're in a depressed mood when you made a memory, you might recall it more easily when you're depressed again (although research on mood, specifically, is a bit mixed; Eich, 1980).

Without fail, our students always want to know: Does state-dependent memory mean that if someone learns something while drunk, they'll remember it better later if they're drunk again?

Researchers are decades ahead of this question. The short answer is yes—but with warnings. First, state-dependent memory benefits of alcohol seem to vary quite a bit depending on what's being learned (Weingartner et al., 1976). And while material learned while drunk might be easier to remember if you get drunk again— the participants who do the best on memory tasks are the ones who never get drunk during the study at all (Goodwin et al., 1975).

Serial Position Curve

Order matters.

Retrieval, particularly for a list, doesn't happen haphazardly. Instead, there's a predictable pattern to what you're able to remember easily. Look back at the numbers you recalled during the chunking discussion (the 2 1 5 8 4 7 3 1 2 4 9 0 set). You probably got the first few numbers correct and some of the last few, as well. But the middle? Not so much. Thank the **serial position curve** for this, which is the tendency to have better recall for items at the beginning and end of a list.

Serial position curve: The tendency to have better recall for items at the beginning and end of a list.

Figure 10.8 shows that the serial position curve is shaped like a U. The y-axis (which is theoretical here, to give you a general idea) shows the likelihood that any given item from a list is recalled, and the x-axis is the order of items on the list. Memory is better for the first items in the list due to the *primacy effect*. We've had longer to rehearse those items, so they're easy to remember. It's also easy to remember the items at the end due to the *recency effect*. Those items are "fresher" because we recently encountered them, and there is less chance of something interfering with their encoding. We forget the stuff in the middle. You might notice this in class—you might zone out a bit in the middle of a lecture but feel more focused at the beginning and end.

	Memory Key:
	Mind the middle:
	Mix up the info's order.

Memory Key icon from iStock.com/chatchaisurakram

FIGURE 10.8

The Serial Position Curve

The serial position curve is the tendency for people to have better recall for things at the beginning and end of a list.

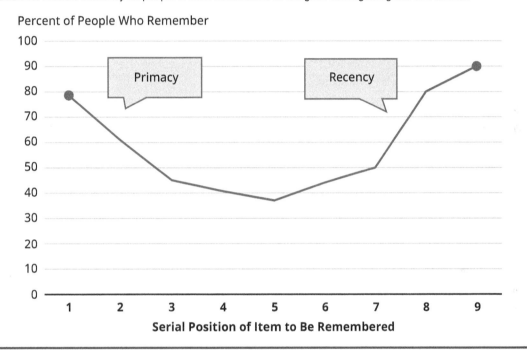

The key to defeating the serial position effect is to purposefully make the middle more memorable. You can do this by changing the order of the material when you study. If there is a test on Chapters 1 through 5 and you always study them in order, you might remember Chapters 1 and 5 best—so each time you study, start and end with a different chapter.

Practicing Retrieval With the Testing Effect

You might dislike tests.

	Memory Key:
	Put yourself to the test.

Memory Key icon from iStock.com/chatchaisurakram

Testing effect: Improving long-term memory by practicing retrieval while learning new information.

As a student, you rely on your memory to improve your test scores. But it goes the other way around, too: Tests help your memory improve. The **testing effect** demonstrates that you probably will have better long-term memory if you practice retrieving information while you're learning it (Roediger & Karpicke, 2006). Quizzes and exams are opportunities to practice retrieval, especially early in the learning process.

Yes, we know this sounds like a bunch of test-giving professors getting defensive. But it's also backed up by research. One study demonstrated the testing effect by dedicating the last 10 minutes of class to

- summarizing key lecture points,
- cueing recognition with multiple-choice questions, or
- cueing recall with short-answer essay questions (Greving & Richter, 2018).

The mini short answer tests (recall) were most effective. Students who prepare for their exams with practice tests both do better on the exams and decrease their stress levels (Smith et al., 2016).

Sage Vantage   Practice what you learn in **Knowledge Check 10.4**

FORGETTING

Have You Ever Wondered?
10.5 Why do you remember some things but forget others?

>> **LO 10.5   Explain why we forget information.**

We know your memory is great; here's a chance to prove it to yourself. Tell us:

- Your mom's maiden name
- Your city of birth
- The capital city of your home country
- The mascot of your high school

No, we're not trying to collect information to steal your passwords. But now that you recognize your routine memory abilities, it's safe to point out that your memory also has significant flaws. Knowing where things go wrong can help make sure they go right, starting now.

Everyday Forgetting

Your memory is good, but it's not perfect.

Everyone forgets things. We might go to the store to get something specific, but we come home with everything except what we went there for in the first place. Forgetting is a failure of the memory system at one of the three stages.

Encoding Failure

As computer programmers say, "Garbage in, garbage out." Sometimes the problem is how the information was originally encoded. A famous case study is the story of H. M., who we now know was Henry Molaison. At 27, Molaison underwent brain surgery to correct severe seizures. The seizures declined and his thinking abilities and intelligence remained intact, but his memory was disrupted in strange ways.

When Molaison was asked about his childhood or something he learned before the surgery, he was able to recall those details. But if he met someone new, moments after the introduction, Molaison would forget the person's name. And the next day, he would have no memory of meeting that person at all. Molaison's forgetting became pronounced because he appeared to have lost the ability to encode new memories after the surgery.

We all experience this on a smaller level when we're simply not paying attention and we lose focus, a state called *absentmindedness*. We lose focus, are distracted, or try to multitask with the result of missing a key piece of information like someone's name or a teacher's instruction (Madore et al., 2020; Robertson, 2003; Schacter, 2001). We forget because encoding never even got started. Sometimes this is no big deal, but sometimes the corresponding negative effects on memory can create emotional distress (Carriere et al., 2008). Measure your own absentmindedness with the *What's My Score?* feature.

WHAT'S MY SCORE?

Measuring Absentmindedness

Instructions: The Attention-Related Cognitive Errors Scale (ARCES) asks about common everyday situations where lack of attention could occur. Respond to each statement below with this scale:

1	2	3	4	5
Never				Very Often

____ 1. I have absent-mindedly placed things in unintended locations (e.g., putting milk in the pantry or sugar in the fridge).

____ 2. When reading I find that I have read several paragraphs without being able to recall what I read.

____ 3. I have misplaced frequently used objects, such as keys, pens, glasses, etc.

____ 4. I have found myself wearing mismatched socks or other apparel.

____ 5. I have gone into a room to get something, got distracted, and left without what I went there for.

____ 6. I fail to see what I am looking for even though I am looking right at it.

____ 7. I begin one task and get distracted into doing something else.

____ 8. I have absent-mindedly mixed up targets of my action (e.g., pouring or putting something in the wrong container).

____ 9. I make mistakes because I am doing one thing and thinking about another.

____ 10. I have gone to the fridge to get one thing (e.g., milk) and taken something else (e.g., juice).

____ 11. I have to go back to check whether I have done something or not (e.g., turning out lights, locking doors).

____ 12. I go into a room to do one thing (e.g., brush my teeth) and end up doing something else (e.g., brush my hair).

Scoring Instructions: Add up all 12 of your answers. Your total score should be between 12 and 60. The higher your score, the more absentminded you are. ●

Source: Cheyne et al. (2006).

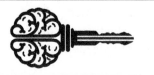

	Memory Key:
	Memory is a skill you develop through practice.

Memory Key icon from iStock.com/chatchaisurakram

Storage Failure: Decay and Interference

Time is memory's enemy. According to *decay theory,* the longer a memory is stored, the more that memory fades (J. Brown, 1958). Memory traces, or a change in the brain created by a new memory, tend to decay unless strengthened. But it's complicated; some memories decay over time while others stay strong for decades. Nevertheless, decay theory's central premise of time-based forgetting is well established (e.g., Ricker et al., 2020).

The older we get, the more memory decay affects us. But memory loss is not universal. A study of middle-aged and older individuals conducted over 9 years found that people who experience positive emotions like feeling enthusiastic, proud, and active have less memory loss (Hittner et al., 2020). Significantly, this study used statistical techniques to control for the effects of age, gender, education, depression, negative emotions, and an extraverted personality.

Storage-related memory failures are often related to two kinds of **interference**, which occurs when information gets in the way of other memories:

Interference: Information that gets in the way of other memories, either retroactively or proactively.

- *Retroactive interference* happens when learning something new makes it more difficult to recall old information. For example, taking a world geography class in college might make it harder to remember the geography class you took in high school about your home country.

- *Proactive interference occurs* when something that was learned in the past makes it hard to learn new information. If you previously encoded and stored someone's name as Devon, but they changed their name to Dakota, then encoding and storing the new information might be more difficult and you might accidentally make mistakes.

Interference is especially likely when you're getting a lot of information quickly, when you're distracted, or when your motivation to learn is low.

	Memory Key:
	Memory is a skill you develop through practice.

Memory Key icon from iStock.com/chatchaisurakram

Retrieval Failure: "It's on the Tip of My Tongue!"

Blocking: When memory is temporarily inaccessible because other information obstructs retrieval.

Information may be perfectly encoded and stored, and yet you're still unable to retrieve it. This can happen during **blocking**, when memory is temporarily inaccessible because different information obstructs retrieval. Try to think of your first-grade teacher's name. You may know it but can't retrieve it because you start recalling your friends at the time, the smell of the school cafeteria, or how your classroom looked. The other memories can block the memory you are trying to retrieve if they are stronger.

Blocking a memory can induce the *tip of the tongue phenomenon,* when the information remains just out of reach (Schwartz & Metcalfe, 2011). Information that only reaches the "tip of your tongue" is the result of an incomplete memory trace that got you most of the way to the desired information but did not complete the full journey (Schwartz, 1999). Since it's retrieval, you need more specific memory cues. Often, the information will pop into your head later when you are in a different context or state, because the needed retrieval cues are now there.

Source Amnesia: Forgetting Where Things Came From

Where did you learn that?

If you follow pop culture, then you may know the names of all the Kardashians, but you probably have no idea how, when, or where you learned those facts. Students especially have so much information going into memory that they often skip encoding *where* the information came from and experience source amnesia, which is remembering without knowing where or how something was learned (Schacter et al., 1984).

The main drawback of source amnesia is our susceptibility to encoding low-quality information. We might read some "fact" from social media or a conspiracy theory website and roll our eyes at it at the time—but if we have source amnesia, the fact might encode without the important note telling us not to trust the source. Later, then, we might mistakenly start to believe it.

Even worse is *cryptomnesia,* which is when we forget that a certain memory was taken from another source in the first place and we mistakenly believe we originated it ourselves. Now, we think we invented a gadget, wrote a song, or drafted an original story— but it's a kind of accidental plagiarism. It can even happen to professionals: Comedians Bill Burr and Bert Kreischer (from the BillBert podcast) describe their embarrassment when discovering they've been telling someone else's joke.

Aaron Fotheringham holds five Guinness world records for athletic stunts done in his wheelchair. If you know information (like this, for example) but can't place the source of the information (where, when, or how you learned it), it's called source amnesia.
James Devaney/Contributor/Getty Images Entertainment/via Getty Images

The study highlighted in the *Spotlight on Research Methods* feature found that dark chocolate can improve memory. Should you trust the findings? We encourage you to read more.
iStock.com/fcafotodigital

Source amnesia: Remembering information, but not being sure where or how you learned it.

Clickbait and Fake News: Dark Chocolate Can Improve Memory

At least that's what all the headlines claimed. It's exciting "news"—who doesn't like chocolate? But is it bogus? Psychologically, we want it to be true but . . . it also feels a little too good to be true. When a thoughtful person sees a clickbait headline, they evaluate it before buying several pounds of dark chocolate or pouring their life savings into a chocolate-making factory.

Go online and read the original article, "Enhancing Dentate Gyrus Function With Dietary Flavanols Improves Cognition in Older Adults" (Brickman et al., 2014). Older adults? Study participants were older adults in their 50s and 60s, a detail often dropped by media stories. Dig deeper, and you will note that the study used fewer than 40 people. Is that enough to make you skeptical?

Here's another detail. Science can be expensive, so articles often mention who helped pay for the study. In this case: Mars Inc. That's right—the study was supported by people who make and sell chocolate. Scientists are voluntarily bound by stringent ethical standards; the researchers wouldn't purposefully allow the funding source to impact their findings. But a funding source can bias the data in many ways, such as failing to publish contradictory results. Industry-pleasing outcomes would inspire the Mars public

relations department to share this wonderful news with the press.

Dosage also matters. In the case of these chocolate-induced memory gains, you'd need to eat about seven candy bars a day. That's a lot, even for the hungriest chocolate lover. At that dosage, chocolate's side effects (e.g., diabetes) likely outweigh the benefits for memory.

Let's summarize some of the "small" details that any critical thinker notices with less than a 5-minute glance at the original article:

- The study was limited to older adults.
- The sample size was small.
- The funders had a vested interest in the results.
- Dosage requirements are unrealistic.

It's not the study authors' fault that media coverage exaggerated their findings. The original research was peer-reviewed by other scientists who concluded the study warranted publication in a reputable journal. But fake news that sounds like clickbait on the Internet should not be believed without a fair-minded investigation. Your health, your beliefs, and your community participation are too important to take sensationalized headlines at face value. ●

Sage Vantage⍥ Practice what you learn in **Knowledge Check 10.5**

MEMORY'S IMPERFECTIONS

Have You Ever Wondered?
10.6 Can you remember things that never happened?

>> **LO 10.6** **Describe the reasons for and implications of imperfect memory formation and retrieval.**

Your memories aren't as accurate as you'd hope.

Although it's tough to admit, all of us are likely wrong about some—and perhaps much—of what we think we remember. Our sincere memory errors make us human. Unlike cell phone videos, memory is a reconstructive process that pieces together bits of information into a coherent whole. Along the way, we add interpretations, miss things, or fill in the blanks incorrectly. Each time we conjure up a memory, it can change slightly from the time before.

Memory researcher Schacter (1999) famously referred to the "seven sins of memory." Some mistakes are sins of omission—forgetting—and some are sins of commission, meaning we create a problem. Consider some interesting examples.

Memory Bias

You can be your memory's own worst enemy.

Memory looks backward into the past—but present experience can bias or influence those memories. We've long known that your current beliefs, expectations, and knowledge affect what you encode and retrieve (Bartlett, 1932). For example, when college students read and later recalled a brief story, they *sharpened* the story by focusing on some details while *leveling* or leaving out other pieces to shorten the story. Students also engaged in *assimilation* by shifting the facts to conform to their own worldviews. The result was that each student's recollection of a simple story was different. You might experience the same sort of thing when your memory of a family event is different from your sibling's or your parent's.

A specific example of memory bias is the **consistency bias**, which encourages us to overestimate how much our past attitudes and behaviors matched our current ones (Schacter, 1999). We misremember the past so that it matches up better with the present. One study examined this bias by asking couples how they felt about their relationship in the present, then asking them to compare that evaluation to how they reported feeling several months ago (McFarland & Ross, 1987). Participants typically recalled a great deal of consistency between the ratings, even though in reality, the two evaluations often didn't match. If the relationship had improved over the previous 2 months, participants recalled being more in love 2 months earlier than they really had been at the time. Similarly, if the relationship had soured, participants recalled having more negative feelings toward their partner 2 months ago than they really had.

Expectations also shape memory. One study randomly assigned participants to either an intense study-skills training group designed to improve grades or to a waitlist (Conway & Ross, 1984). Later, when participants assessed their skills' strength before the study, those who had been working on improving those skills recalled having worse skills than they actually did. Perhaps this bias allows us to feel even better about our hard work: Look how far we've come!

Memory bias might also keep people in mediocre romantic relationships. When researchers followed married couples over several decades, wives had a bias toward remembering the early years of marriage more negatively (Karney & Coombs, 2000). They were wrong; their relationship quality ratings were lower now than they had been. But the bias meant that they also reported being satisfied in their relationship because they *perceived* that it had gotten better over time.

Finally, memory bias can also affect how we judge other people. It's practically a tradition for older adults to regard current young people as somehow lacking compared to previous generations—the stereotypical hooligan "kids these days" (Protzko & Schooler, 2019). But the problem isn't kids—it's the older adults' memories. The memory bias is believing that they practiced their present-day qualities (e.g., being more responsible, conscientious, hardworking, mature) when they were young. OK, boomer.

Consistency bias: The tendency to overestimate how much our past attitudes and behaviors matched our current attitudes and behaviors, in a way that biases memory.

False Memory

Some of your memories never happened.

Memories can be sincere, *false memories* (sometimes called *confabulations*) when recall of an event or facts doesn't match up with reality, or it simply never happened at all (Loftus & Pickrell, 1995). False memories are easy to demonstrate. A common research method known as the *Deese–Roediger–McDermott (DRM) paradigm* is a simple two-step procedure.

- Step 1: Participants read a list of related words, such as *pet, treats, puppy, bowl, toy, kitten, leash, meow, bed, brush, bark,* and *cuddle.*

- Step 2: Participants are asked to list the words they just heard using free recall (Roediger & McDermott, 1995).

Often, participants' lists will mistakenly include words that never appeared but *seem* like they fit the category (in this case, *dog* or *cat*). Yet, participants will express confidence that they heard those words. The words are all connected to a concept that was never named, so a false memory is created.

	Memory Key:
	Memory is a skill
	you develop through practice.

Memory Key icon from iStock.com/chatchaisurakram

Did you correctly remember that C-3PO has a silver leg?

Ted Soqui/SIPA Photo USA/Sipa via AP Images

Misinformation effect: Occurs when overt suggestions, questions, or incorrect information alter an originally correct memory.

False memories, sometimes called the *Mandela effect,* can ripple through society. Many people mistakenly believe that the famous activist and politician Nelson Mandela died while imprisoned in South Africa. He didn't. He died in 2013, many years after his release. You probably have several of these Mandela effect false memories too. The peanut butter is Jif, not Jiffy. Kids' cartoons are Looney Tunes, not Looney Toons. For breakfast you eat Froot Loops, not Fruit Loops. And the beloved Star Wars character C-3PO isn't entirely gold; he has a silver leg. False memories don't mean lack of intelligence; they simply mean you're human.

The Misinformation Effect

You can also have mistaken memories implanted.

This is not science fiction from a popular television show. Unlike false memories, which are accidental, the **misinformation effect** occurs when overt suggestions, questions, or incorrect information alter an originally correct memory (Loftus, 1979). It when something happens between the original memory and the time of retrieval when you're exposed to something false about what happened, and that false information replaces the truth.

The psychologist most famous for research on the misinformation effect is Elizabeth Loftus, a pioneer in applied memory research. She completed a series of studies in which participants watched videos of realistic scenes, like car accidents, and were asked to simply report what they saw (Loftus, 1974, 1979; Loftus & Zanni, 1975; Loftus et al., 1978). The wording of the questions was critical in creating the misinformation effect and implanting false memories.

For example, she randomly assigned each participant to read one of these two questions:

- How fast was the white sports car going when it passed the barn while traveling along the country road?

- How fast was the white sports car going while traveling along the country road?

Importantly, the scene had *no barn* in the actual video—and note that students here aren't being asked if they saw a barn; the information is just mentioned casually, like a side note. The real question was about car speed (Loftus, 1975). All the participants came back 1 week later and, without seeing the original video again, were asked additional questions. The last question this time was, "Did you see a barn?" Participants who had received the misinformation in the earlier question were now much more likely (17.3%) to say yes, there was a barn, compared to participants who hadn't (only 2.7%).

You'd remember something as unique and vivid as going down in a helicopter crash, right? Not necessarily. Read the *Psychology and Our Curious World* feature if you're curious.

iStock.com/giocalde

It's easy to assume mistakes in recall only happen for minor details related to fake car crashes. However, it happens for more personal and meaningful events too. Have you ever been lost in the mall? In a more troubling study, Elizabeth Loftus convinced over 25% of participants that they had been lost in a mall as children, despite that it never actually happened (Loftus & Pickrell, 1995). There is some good news: Warning people about false information—like we've just done!—sometimes improves memory accuracy (Wahlheim et al., 2020).

Imagine the extremely important implications this research has for eyewitness testimony to crimes and how important it is to consider all the questions witnesses have been asked from the time of the original event to a trial (from reporters, police officers, lawyers, friends and family, and so on). That's the topic of the next section.

PSYCHOLOGY AND OUR CURIOUS WORLD

The Curious Case of the Helicopter Attack That Never Happened

"The story actually started with a terrible moment a dozen years back during the invasion of Iraq when the helicopter we were traveling in was forced down after being hit by an RPG. . . ."

A compelling story, but ultimately false. And it wasn't just anyone who made this claim. It was Brian Williams,

who at the time was the lead anchor for the *NBC Nightly News*, and he said it live on TV. This wasn't the first time either. He told a similar story as a guest on a late-night show. Both times, it was wrong. Williams later admitted to his error by saying, "I want to apologize. I said I was traveling in an aircraft that was hit by RPG [rocket-propelled grenade] fire. I was instead in a following aircraft" (Carroll, 2015).

(Continued)

(Continued)

Of course, Williams could have been purposefully lying to gain journalistic credibility and simply got caught. It's worth noting that Williams wasn't the only one who misremembered. His pilot from the day in question had corroborated parts of Williams's version and later recanted himself. Ultimately, it's entirely possible that Williams did legitimately "remember" the events he described, despite them never happening.

How? First, the incident had occurred 12 years ago. *Transience*, or forgetting what happens due to the passage of time, is natural (Schacter, 1999). Our memory misses things and "fills in the blanks" with other related information or experiences. The fact is, a helicopter was hit; it just wasn't the one that Williams was on, nor was it nearby. But the fact that a similar helicopter was involved in an attack made it easier for Williams to recall and then combine the two events. Still, if you were hit by a rocket-propelled grenade, you'd think your memory of that would be crystal clear. But we know that flashbulb memories aren't perfect either (Hirst & Phelps, 2016).

Another thing that contributed to Williams's error was the fact that he had told versions of the story over the past 12 years. At first, he got it right: Another helicopter was hit. A few years later, Williams was a bit vague about which helicopter it was. A blog he wrote at that time claimed, "We came under fire by what appeared to be Iraqi farmers with RPG's and AK-47's . . . we were forced down."

You can see where this is going. Each time he told the story, he got a little more directly involved. It might be intentional, or it might be reconsolidation—each time he told the story, it got slightly changed and reencoded with errors (Alberini & LeDoux, 2013). The next time he retrieved the memory, the mistakes could feel as authentic as any other memory.

It was likely an embarrassing yet honest mistake that ultimately cost Brian Williams his job. Perhaps rightfully so, but when you understand the nature of human memory, his error is a bit more understandable. Curious to learn more? Check out Malcolm Gladwell's *Revisionist History* podcast episode "Free Brian Williams." ●

Eyewitness Testimony

Could false memories send someone to jail?

The memory shortcomings discussed so far seem quirky and somewhat amusing. However, consider what slip-ups in your everyday memory mean when police are relying on your recollections to help solve a crime. In *The Seven Sins of Memory* (2001), Schacter provides the vivid example of the Oklahoma City bombing investigation of Timothy McVeigh. The FBI quickly and correctly identified McVeigh as the suspect, but they wasted a lot of time trying to find a nonexistent second person involved because an eyewitness falsely recalled two men renting the van involved instead of one. It turned out that the day before McVeigh rented his van, someone else who looked similar rented a different van—and that man had a second person with him.

There are other famous court cases involving false memories and eyewitness testimony. Jennifer Thompson, a rape survivor, received misinformation from the police about a suspect before the trial began, and her false memory sent an innocent man to prison for 11 years (Thompson-Cannino et al., 2009). Nadean Cool had false memories of being raised in a Satanic cult that led to a trial; her case was eventually settled for $2.4 million (Loftus, 1997). Research around false memories and the misinformation effect is fascinating and sometimes heartbreaking.

SERIOUS AND INTENTIONAL MEMORY LOSS

>> LO 10.7 **Analyze different types of memory loss and suppression.**

Sometimes your memory completely fails you.

But it's not your fault. Extreme memory irregularities can result from tragedy, personal trauma, illness, extreme stress, or substance abuse. These experiences disrupt the brain's typical functioning and produce notable changes to memory.

Amnesia

In some cases, it can seem like your memory has been erased.

More than just forgetting, amnesia is the inability to retrieve large amounts of information, often due to experiencing trauma (Bauer et al., 2003). You might also experience temporary amnesia following a head injury (e.g., a concussion) or excessive substance use (e.g., blackouts from drinking too much alcohol; Wetherill & Fromme, 2016).

Infantile Amnesia

Think back to when you were 1, 2, or 3 years old. How much do you remember? Likely not much. *Infantile amnesia* is adults' failure to retrieve memories from when they were young, especially before age 4 (Alberini & Travaglia, 2017). This isn't a sign that something's wrong, but rather a natural consequence of an underdeveloped brain that probably didn't store long-term memories the same way adults do. This is why some parents may jokingly suggest they shouldn't bother having lavish parties for their child's first birthday—is it pointless if their child won't remember it? (Again, this is usually meant as a joke.)

Retrograde and Anterograde Amnesia

Amnesia's memory loss generally takes two forms (Figure 10.9). Both are usually caused by physical injury or trauma, often to the brain area called the hippocampus.

Have You Ever Wondered?
10.7 Can some memory loss be serious or intentional?

Amnesia: The inability to retrieve large amounts of information, often due to experiencing trauma.

FIGURE 10.9

Two Types of Amnesia

Retrograde amnesia is when people can't remember events that happened before a physical injury or trauma. Anterograde amnesia is when people can't remember events that happened after an injury or trauma.

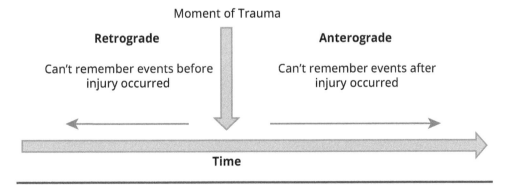

Can a major disaster, like the earthquake in 2011 Japan, cause severe memory loss?

Satoshi Takahashi/Contributor/LightRocket/via Getty Images

The first is *retrograde amnesia,* or the inability to remember things that happened before a certain time point or event (often, the point of injury).

In March 2011, Japan experienced a massive earthquake. Years later, a male patient came in for a medical examination and doctors discovered he had no memory of anything before the earthquake (Odagaki, 2017). His earliest memory was waking up under a collapsed wall of a house—he didn't know his name, where he was from, or his own age. The man had no trouble forming memories for everything that happened to him since waking up from the earthquake, but he remained unable to recall any events prior. His past had been wiped out by his brain trauma.

A second type of amnesia affects the ability to remember things *after* a trauma. Here, the problem doesn't seem to be encoding or storage as much as it is retrieval. *Anterograde amnesia* is the inability to retrieve new memories, while older memories remain intact. If you've ever seen the movies *50 First Dates* or *Memento,* that's anterograde amnesia.

Consider another real-life case study of a man known as M.S. After struggling with seizures for years, he had one that was so severe that it left him in a coma for 12 hours (Broman et al., 1997). When he finally woke up, M.S. could no longer retrieve new memories. He could clearly remember his elementary school, for example—no problem. But as an adult after his coma, he couldn't remember *new* people he met, and he had diminished language abilities and academic performance. Devastating consequences for sure—but there may be even scarier forms of amnesia.

Dissociative (Psychogenic) Amnesia

Dissociative amnesia: Loss of memory for personal or autobiographical information.

Imagine not knowing who you are, like the Japanese man who awoke from the earthquake (Odagaki, 2017). In **dissociative amnesia** (also known as psychogenic amnesia), a person loses memory for autobiographical memories or personal information related to the self.

While retrograde and anterograde amnesia are usually caused by physical brain damage, dissociative amnesia may be caused by psychological or social traumas that someone isn't able to cope with at the time. Because dissociative amnesia is psychological—not physical or physiological—exactly what parts of memory are lost tend to be tied to the person's family, relationships, finances, and/or employment; people with this issue also tend to suffer from more depression (Harrison et al., 2017).

Consider another example: the case of Mr. A (Sharma et al., 2015). Friends found Mr. A in a parking lot. He was 20 years old and perfectly healthy—but he had no idea how he got there. Earlier that day, his mom received a call from Mr. A's work supervisor, who said that Mr. A didn't seem to know his friends and had forgotten how to do his job. His mom took him to the emergency room, where doctors learned Mr. A had broken up with his boyfriend. Doctors thought the dissociative episode was an unconscious attempt to put his painful relationship behind him.

Extreme cases of dissociative amnesia may also be associated with *dissociative fugue,* in which a person flees suddenly by taking an unanticipated trip to a new location to establish a new identity. Though extreme, dissociative fugue is often reversible, with some research showing patients returning to normal after 3 to 6 months (Harrison et al., 2017).

Repression

Sometimes we just want to forget.

In a Freudian context, *repression* occurs when we hide traumatic memories in our unconscious, but we're unaware that we're doing so (Boag, 2006). The goal is to hide the trauma from ourselves; if we don't remember it, it won't cause us anxiety or depression.

Repressed memory is tricky to study, right? People who have successfully repressed memories won't know they have them. Psychologists and psychotherapists attempt to access repressed memories through a variety of techniques. One involves having clients sit with an old family photo album that may cue long-forgotten memories by bringing them to the surface (Lindsay et al., 2004).

We apologize if this baby shark image gets a song from your memory stuck in your head for the rest of the day.

iStock.com/Del_Mar

But there are ethical questions as well—will clients be better or worse if reminded of their past traumas? Repressed memories are also controversial given research on the reconstruction hypothesis, the misinformation effect, and the other memory biases discussed in this chapter; when people believe that they suddenly recall events from long ago, we can't discount the possibility that some of those memories may be false (Schacter, 1999). In fact, when researchers interviewed a group of memory experts (i.e., doctorates with a subspecialty in memory), most were highly skeptical about memory's reliability and repressed memories compared to the general public, students, and practitioners (Patihis et al., 2021).

Persistence: Unwanted Remembering

Sometimes you want to forget but can't.

We've spent a lot of time discussing all the ways memory can fail. However, memory *persistence* occurs when we keep recalling things we'd rather forget (Schacter, 1999). It could be the annoying song you can't stop singing to yourself (Baby Shark!) or a gross image you saw online that you can't get out of your head (don't Google "blackhead squeezing" . . . it's pure nightmare fuel). It could also be more serious.

For example, memories with strong emotional component are more likely to persist, in part due to the hormones linked to the emotional state (McGaugh, 2015). That's potentially problematic for negative memories. Intrusive and unwanted memories may significantly and negatively affect our well-being:

- When people "ruminate" (i.e., obsess) about negative past experiences, they also remember fewer positive life events and are more likely to suffer from depression (Lyubomirsky et al., 1998; Nolen-Hoeksema et al., 2008).

- About 97% of childhood sexual abuse survivors report persistent memories in the form of recalled thoughts, visions, smells, and physical sensations (Ehlers & Steil, 1995).

- Military veterans who experienced combat sometimes relive the experience through intrusive memories and flashbacks. Originally labeled "shell shock" after World War I, this general pattern has been expanded for anyone who suffers from recurring, unwanted memories of trauma that are accompanied by physical and emotional complications—a condition now called posttraumatic stress disorder or PTSD (Loughran, 2012).

That's troubling—so let's end on a more positive note: How can we rid ourselves of an intrusive, unwanted memory? You recognize the problem: If you consciously try to not think about something, then you're helping bring it to mind (Wang et al., 2020). Try this on yourself: Don't think of a purple elephant. And yet, you just did. It's the *ironic rebound effect of thought suppression* (Wegner, 1994). By identifying something you're trying to forget, you are forced to remember it.

But there is hope. There are multiple techniques for working through unwanted memories in safe and therapeutic ways (Vaverková et al., 2020). Techniques include using reconsolidation in your favor; each time you recall the painful memory, it might become less threatening. This process is tied to the concept of extinction we discussed in the chapter on learning (Chapter 9). There is also a pharmacological approach to reduce persistence. One study gave participants propranolol right before they remembered a personal fear (Soeter & Kindt, 2010). The participants failed to display a fear response (i.e., being startled) 24 hours later.

We all sometimes struggle with getting over a bad memory—the fact that we can't get it out of our head becomes maddening. While research is always exploring new techniques to help, different things work for different people, and curious minds drive the next innovations. ●

Sage Vantageꭗ   Practice what you learn in **Knowledge Check 10.7**

CHAPTER REVIEW

Learning Objectives Summary

10.1   How does memory work?

>> LO 10.1   **Compare and contrast sensory, working, and long-term memory.**

Memory is the process by which we store images, information, events, and skills, then recall them later. Psychology breaks memory up into three processes or types of memory. Sensory memory handles physical sensations, including auditory and visual stimuli. Working (sometimes called short-term) memory is a system that organizes information from different sources and holds it temporarily. Long-term memory holds onto information for longer periods of time.

10.2   How can you improve memory encoding?

>> LO 10.2   **Describe how we make new memories and how to improve that process.**

Your memory improvement plan starts when you initially commit facts to memory. To encode information, you typically use maintenance rehearsal but can improve upon that through elaborative rehearsal, chunking, spacing, overlearning, and mnemonics (specific memory-helping techniques).

10.3   How can you improve memory storage?

>> LO 10.3   **Summarize how to improve memory storage.**

You store those memories throughout the brain and can hold onto them for decades. After you take a memory from storage, you must reconsolidate or reencode the memory to place it back into storage after each time you use it. Storage is organized by meaningful concepts called schemas.

10.4   How can you improve memory retrieval?

>> LO 10.4   **Explain how to make memories easier to retrieve.**

Retrieval is critical to remembering anything, which we can assess through implicit memory tasks, recognition, and recall. When retrieving information, order matters and the more cues we have, including the state and context of where we learned the information, the more likely we are to remember.

10.5 Why do you remember some things but forget others?

>> LO 10.5 **Explain why we forget information.**

Forgetting happens due to failure at any of the three major steps (encoding, storage, or retrieval). Examples are absentmindedness (poor encoding due to being distracted), interference (when learning one thing makes it harder to learn a second thing), blocking (when a memory is temporarily inaccessible), and source amnesia (not remembering where you learned something).

10.6 Can you remember things that never happened?

>> LO 10.6 **Describe the reasons for and implications of imperfect memory formation and retrieval.**

Memory is a reconstructive process, and biases make it imperfect. The consistency bias overestimate how much our past matches our present. Sometimes we remember things incorrectly, as shown by phenomena labeled the Mandela effect and the misinformation effect. These errors are especially problematic in applications like eyewitness testimony for court trials.

10.7 Can some memory loss be serious or intentional?

>> LO 10.7 **Analyze different types of memory loss and suppression.**

Sometimes memory fails for large amounts of information, resulting in amnesia. Three types of amnesia are retrograde, anterograde, and dissociative (or psychogenic). While repression refers to putting unwanted traumatic memories into our unconscious mind, sometimes we experience the opposite: intrusive memories we wish would go away.

CRITICAL THINKING QUESTIONS

1. Imagine that you have a big test in a class coming up that requires you to learn 100 new vocabulary words, the geography of a country you've never visited, and the history of their political leaders. You want to do well on the exam. Choose three of the specific memory-boosting strategies described in this chapter and describe how you would use them to help boost your score as you study and practice for the exam.

2. You have an amazing idea and get to go on a show like *Shark Tank* to pitch your new invention and get potential investors. On the show, the panel listens to 10 ideas, then picks the ones they're most interested in. Based on what you know about memory, should you volunteer to give your pitch first, wait until after a few others go, or go last? What else from this chapter can you apply to your presentation that will help the panel positively remember your pitch? Apply terms from class.

3. Think back to your first day of college. What do you remember? Discuss at least three specific concepts from this chapter that suggest your memory of that day might not be accurate, and explain how the concept relates to your personal experience of this memory and your perception of it looking back now that you've read the chapter.

4. Imagine that the local authorities found a man wandering in the woods who appears to have a head injury. What questions could you ask to determine whether he has amnesia and, if so, which type?

5. Choose any of the famous case studies discussed in this chapter on amnesia, the misinformation effect, or eyewitness testimony and how problematic memory affected someone in the "real world." Find more information about that case study and discuss the details with a partner or in a small group. What happened to the people involved? What was the role of psychology or psychologists, if any?

KEY TERMS

Amnesia, 321
Blocking, 314
Chunking, 301
Consistency bias, 317
Dissociative amnesia, 322
Elaborative rehearsal, 299
Encoding, 298
Interference, 314
Long-term memory, 296
Maintenance rehearsal, 299
Memory, 291
Misinformation effect, 318
Mnemonic, 303
Overlearning, 303

Recall, 308
Recognition, 308
Retrieval, 298
Schemas, 306
Self-reference effect, 300
Sensory memory, 292
Serial position curve, 310
Short-term memory, 294
Source amnesia, 315
Spacing effect, 302
Storage, 298
Testing effect, 312
Working memory, 294

iStock.com/Anna Frank

11

Motivation and Emotion

"I love you."

These three words may be the most gratifying we can hear. The Greek philosopher Plato wrote, "Love is born into every human being . . . it tries to make one out of two and heal the wound of human nature" (from *Symposium,* circa 385 BCE). What exactly is love, though?

Defining it can be difficult. People have different kinds of loving relationships, such as love between parents and children, loving friendships, and we love our pets—but when someone you're dating says, "I love you," the meaning changes because of the specific context (Heshmati et al., 2019; Heshmati & Donaldson, 2020). Love could be a positive emotion between two people—but you might also "love" coffee in the morning, naps in the afternoon, or chocolate any time (Fredrickson, 2016). You might even "love" the thrill of a roller coaster or horror movie (Heshmati et al., 2019). Can we really "love" people, sleep, food, and even the experience of fear?

This chapter answers that question by exploring the complicated nature of human motivation and emotions. Whether it's love, fame, validation, security, or simple joy—what does science say about our fundamental needs and experiences?

After reading this chapter, you will get answers to several questions you've been curious about:

Have You Ever Wondered?

11.1	How do psychologists define and study motivation?
11.2	How does the psychology of motivation affect everyday life?
11.3	How do psychologists define and study emotion?
11.4	What are important research findings related to the psychology of emotion?

Learning Objectives

LO 11.1	Compare and contrast theories of motivation based on instincts, drive reduction, optimal arousal, incentives, self-determination, and a hierarchy of needs.
LO 11.2	Identify and explain examples of motivation, as well as various related subfields of psychology for work, school, and sports.
LO 11.3	Compare and contrast theories of emotion, including James–Lange, Cannon–Bard, Schachter–Singer, and cognitive appraisal.
LO 11.4	Explain psychology research on emotional expression, including cultural differences and lie detection, and on how emotions might benefit us.

THEORIES OF MOTIVATION

>> **LO 11.1**   **Compare and contrast theories of motivation based on instincts, drive reduction, optimal arousal, incentives, cognitive attribution, and a hierarchy of needs.**

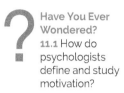

Have You Ever Wondered?
11.1 How do psychologists define and study motivation?

What motivates you?

Many people hope to fall in love at least once; the vast majority of cultures studied around the world experience romantic passion (Buss, 2006; Jankowiak & Fischer, 1992). Does this make love a basic life motivation? Some researchers say yes—just like the need for food, water, and sleep, love is a physiological motivation that encourages behaviors necessary for survival of the species (Burunat, 2019). Others disagree; they say that love is an emotion—a temporary (although sometimes strong) feeling or mental state (Ganji et al., 2021). So . . . motivation, or emotion?

Spoiler alert: We don't have the answer. The debate about the nature of "love" and how to operationalize it (define and measure it) in psychology and other academic fields continues (e.g., Isern-Mas & Gomila, 2022; Roland, 2021). Part of the controversy is in the precise definitions of terms like *motivation, need, goal, emotion, feeling,* and so on.

Love is just one example of the many motivations and emotions you'll experience over your lifetime. Still, you can probably see that some human experiences—like love, or loneliness, or fear—might seem like *both* motivation and emotion. This chapter combines them because many theoretical explanations acknowledge the overlap. Let's start by more thoroughly defining motivation and emotion.

Motivation is an inner drive that guides behavior toward achieving a specific goal. "I'm hungry, so I grab some tacos." Motivation typically has three stages: initial arousal, direction, and behavioral persistence. In other words, motivation leads to behavior with a beginning, a middle, and an end. A goal is set, causing related behavior to start—and typically, to accomplish a goal, the behavior must continue for at least some period of time. Once we accomplish the goal, the behavior can stop.

Emotion, on the other hand, is a pattern of inner thoughts and feelings, accompanied by physiological responses and sometimes behavioral expression. "Eating tacos makes me feel good." Just like motivation, emotions have multiple parts: a cognitive part (thoughts), a physiological part (arousal, such as a faster heartbeat), and usually—although not always—a behavioral part (an expression of the emotion, such as a smile or frown). Emotions are different from motivations in that they resist being neatly arranged into stages; all the components might happen simultaneously (Berridge, 2018; Buck, 1985; James, 1890; Mulligan, 2010). Emotions also aren't necessarily accomplishing a goal; happiness (for example) might *be* the goal.

Why are you in college or university classes—what is your primary motivation? What emotions have you had so far?

iStock.com/fstop123

Motivation: An inner drive that guides behavior toward achieving a specific goal; stages of motivation are initial arousal, direction, and behavioral persistence.

Emotion: A pattern of inner thoughts and feelings, accompanied by physiological responses and sometimes behavioral expression.

TABLE 11.1

Six Theories of Motivation

There are six major theories that explain motivation; some emphasize biological processes and some focus more on psychological processes. The last theory, Maslow's hierarchy of needs, incorporates both.

TYPE	NAME	EXPLANATION
Biological	Instinct theory	Evolution has resulted in certain innate impulses for all humans that help us survive and reproduce. We're motivated to do behaviors that match these impulses.
	Drive reduction theory	The idea that motivation operates like a thermostat that's sensitive to physiological discomfort, and we're driven to behaviors that bring our body back to homeostasis.
	Optimal arousal theory	We're motivated to achieve peak performance on tasks by maintaining a medium level of arousal.
Psychological	Incentive theory	The idea that motivation comes from external stimuli in the environment that push behaviors in certain directions, based on our goals.
	Self-determination theory	We're motivated to be personally satisfied individuals through three needs: autonomy, competence, and relatedness.
Both (biological and psychological)	Maslow's hierarchy of needs	Our motivation is based on priorities. Physiological needs are most important, followed by safety. If we fulfill these, as well as belongingness and esteem needs, we can then explore personal growth (self-actualization).

Life is complicated, which is one reason psychological research can be challenging. Psychologists have debated the nature of both motivation and emotion for decades, and those debates are still ongoing. There will always be room for new ideas from curious and innovative thinkers. In the first half of this chapter, we consider several theories and factors explaining the complicated nature of human motivation. Then, we'll do the same thing for emotions.

To start, compare and contrast six theories regarding human motivation (summarized in Table 11.1). Which theory best explains your own, personal life goals?

Biological Theories

We can't avoid basic biological needs.

One way to think about motivation is to realize that all living things appear to have some kind of motivation. Even plants show signs of motivation, if you count trees that lean toward the sunlight they crave because it helps them survive. Three major theoretical explanations have been offered for motivation that focus on our fundamental biological processes and needs.

Instinct Theory

Bears hibernate, slowing their metabolism during the cold winter when food is scarce. Baby ducks and geese imprint on their mothers (a kind of attachment), providing safety. Over multiple generations, monarch butterflies migrate across North America to follow patterns of temperature, food, and disease prevention (Reppert & de Roode, 2018). Each species is displaying motivational instincts.

Instinct theory explains motivation as evolutionary impulses that help a species survive and reproduce from one generation to the next. No individual within the species has to explicitly or consciously learn these motivations; they're built in from birth (Bernard, 1924; Dunlap, 1919; Krantz & Allen, 1967). Instincts lead to behaviors. For species like monarchs, the behaviors are simple and straightforward: fly, eat, mate. For humans, the specific behaviors can be much more complicated, but the idea is that basic instincts motivate all behavior (Freud, 1955).

For example, is going to the gym a human instinct? Getting on a treadmill at a gym is a specific behavior that couldn't have evolved thousands of years ago—but the instinct to be physically ready to fight, to be aggressive in order to protect ourselves against predators, or to fight for access to potential sexual mates might be an instinct (McDougall, 1918). How about buying a fancy car? Again, that exact behavior couldn't possibly be an evolutionary instinct. But if people's *motivation* behind car-buying behavior is driven by instincts such as gaining social status, which leads to more resources, more security, and more mating opportunities, it fits the theory.

Essentially, instinct theory says that all behaviors trace back to some basic instinct in this way. While most psychologists agree that instincts explain a lot of human behavior, many believe instincts might not explain *every* behavior. So, over the years, additional ideas have been added (Knopik et al., 2017).

Instinct theory: The idea that certain behaviors are motivated by innate evolutionary impulses.

Each year, the migration of monarch butterflies across North America occurs via instinct over multiple generations.

iStock.com/DebraLee Wiseberg

Drive Reduction Theory

We don't like to be uncomfortable. When all your biological and physiological needs are met, you feel perfectly satisfied and content. The temperature is ideal; you're not hungry or thirsty; you've gotten enough sleep; you feel relaxed and energetic. OK—most college students might not have felt like that for quite a while! But ultimately, it's what our body wants. That physiological state is called homeostasis: a steady state of healthy functioning and physiological balance in which all our biological needs are met.

Drive reduction theory proposes that motivation operates like a thermostat that is sensitive to discomfort (Hull, 1951). When any of our biological or physiological needs pop up because our body is too far away from the thermostat's set point, we experience discomfort. That discomfort results in an inner drive to feel better ("I need to warm up/cool down."). The drive creates the motivation to engage in behaviors that bring us back to homeostasis (e.g., using blankets or fans). Once our discomfort is gone, we stop doing the behavior until the need pops up again in a repetitive cycle (see Figure 11.1). It's why we turn the heat up or down, eat until we're full (and feel uncomfortable when we either are hungry or have stuffed ourselves), and why naps are so tempting when we're sleep deprived.

Drive reduction theory does a great job of explaining common behaviors like eating, drinking, and sleeping—but psychologists have noted two ways that it seems lacking (Berridge, 2018). First, it's mostly concerned with very immediate, short-term

Homeostasis: The steady state of healthy functioning and physiological balance in which all our biological needs are met.

Drive reduction theory: The idea that motivation operates like a thermostat that's sensitive to physiological discomfort, and we're driven to behaviors that bring our body back to homeostasis.

FIGURE 11.1

Drive Reduction Theory

Drive reduction theory suggests we're happy in a state of homeostasis, when our body's needs have been met. If a need arises—such as the need for sleep—we'll feel discomfort, which motivates behavior to meet that need. The behavior will end until we reach homeostasis again, and the cycle repeats.

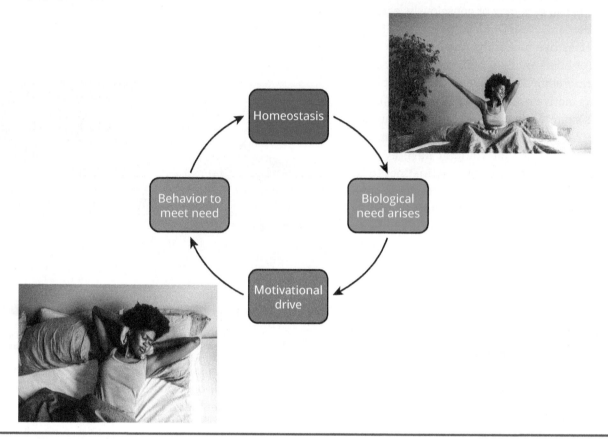

iStock.com/JulPo

needs. What about lifelong goals? Why do you study for each exam or write each paper? It might be to avoid some kind of hypothetical discomfort in the future if you don't get a good job, but that's pretty distant and abstract. Second, drive reduction focuses on avoiding *negative* biological states (discomfort due to lack of food, lack of sleep, etc.). What about motivation to seek out *positive* experiences—like happiness, success, and love? What explains behaviors like engaging in music, sports, and art?

We need more theories.

Optimal Arousal Theory

Think about the last time you had an important performance—it might have been in sports, music, theater, or a big speech or exam for one of your classes. You were probably a bit nervous. Is it possible that those nerves *helped* you do a better job?

Optimal arousal theory is the idea that we're motivated to achieve peak performance on tasks by maintaining a medium level of physiological arousal. When we engage in tasks we're motivated to do *well* on—we want to succeed. And performance seems to suffer when our body is either not aroused enough (indicating we're bored or apathetic) or when we're too aroused (indicating that we're so nervous it's distracting). You can see this pattern in Figure 11.2, a trend known as the *Yerkes-Dodson law* (Yerkes & Dodson, 1908).

FIGURE 11.2

The Yerkes–Dodson Law

The Yerkes–Dodson law says we'll do best on a task (like a test or performance) when we have a medium level of physiological arousal. Too little doesn't motivate us enough, and too much makes us anxious and distracted.

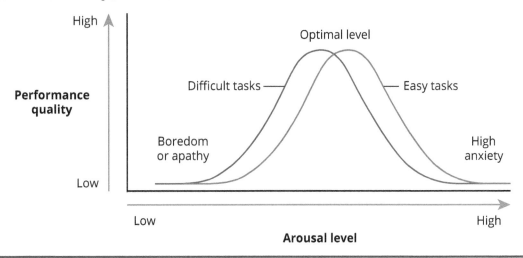

Source: Yerkes and Dodson (1908).

The Yerkes–Dodson law says that a moderate (medium) amount of arousal usually leads to peak performance on a task. Many studies find evidence for this basic pattern, in a wide variety of contexts. For example, a moderate amount of stress is associated with higher math scores (Wang et al., 2015), higher SAT scores (Shin et al., 2023), better performance from witnesses identifying crime suspects in line-ups (Gering et al., 2023), and friendlier and more cooperative driving (Yu et al., 2023). More difficult or new tasks require a bit less arousal (so, the peak of the curve shifts a bit to the left), but the overall pattern is still true (Hembree, 1988).

So the next time you've got a big test, first date/meetup, important speech, or any kind of public performance, it's OK to be a little nervous! Those nerves mean you care and might motivate you to work harder, as long as the anxiety doesn't overwhelm you.

Psychological Theories

Does it sound like love is a motivation?

Review the theories so far: Is love ...

- an innate instinct?

- part of physiological homeostasis?

- an experience where a moderate level leads to peak performance on tasks?

Again, we don't have the answer. So consider a few more theories that offer interesting insights into many of our behaviors regarding why we're motivated in all aspects of life.

Incentive Theory

How long would you experience discomfort if you got paid for it? The answer depends both on how much discomfort there will be and how much you're getting paid. Clearly, we're able to see past immediate biological or physiological needs, if the reward is

Incentive theory: The idea that motivation comes from external stimuli in the environment that push behaviors in certain directions, based on our goals.

substantial. We do things all the time that we don't enjoy if the incentive is strong enough. After all, very few of us would go to work if we didn't get paid.

Incentive theory is the idea that motivation comes from external stimuli in our environment that push behaviors in certain directions, based on our goals (Skinner, 1953). Incentives are based on the classical and operant conditioning principles we discussed in the chapter on learning (Chapter 9), such as reinforcements and punishments. The theory says we choose to engage in behaviors based on which incentives matter the most to us, based on what motivates us.

You might not like memorizing terms in classes outside of your academic major, but you do it if you're motivated to get a good grade because you want to get a good job or get into graduate school. On the other hand, if you have goals of increasing your social popularity, you'll likely skip all that memorizing and hang out with friends instead, hoping for social rewards. We can choose studying or partying based on which incentive is more personally appealing to us.

There's a common saying, "behaviors reveal priorities," which is to say our behaviors change based on our chosen goals and which incentives become our priority. Because incentive theory allows for much more individual choice and variation from one person to the next, it's definitely in the category of a psychological theory instead of a biological theory. If you're still curious about this kind of individual variation, don't worry; we'll discuss several more interesting factors in the next big section of this chapter.

Self-Determination Theory

You're probably heard this advice: If you do something you love, you never have to work a day in your life. When choosing your dream career, do you base it on that career's social status, earning potential, flexible benefits (like travel or schedule), ability to help others, because you're passionate or talented in that area, or something else? How do you decide what motivates you over your entire life?

Self-determination theory: The idea that psychological motivation to become satisfied individuals comes from three needs: autonomy, competence, and relatedness.

These "big picture" questions are addressed by **self-determination theory**, which suggests that our psychological motivation to become complete, satisfied individuals comes from three fundamental needs (Cameron et al., 2001; Gillison et al., 2019; Lepper & Henderlong, 2000; Ng et al., 2012; Ryan & Deci, 2020):

- *Autonomy*—initiative and feeling in control of our life, choices, and behaviors

- *Competence*—mastery, accomplishment, and personal growth

- *Relatedness*—a sense of social belonging; feeling connected and loved

Most research inspired by self-determination theory focuses on individual differences in how people prioritize autonomy, competence, and relatedness and how they affect our choices of things like relationship partners, college majors, and careers. But it's also interesting to see how culture and generational changes affect these needs and goals. The preface of this textbook noted that most people in college right now (that's Generation Z, or people born between 1997 and 2012), have different priorities than any previous generation in the United States (Nemeth, 2022). Specifically, Generation Z (overall) appears to believe that

1. salary at work is less important than benefits like flexible hours, vacation time, and healthy lifestyle;

2. work–life balance should be prioritized, and products used should reflect personal values;

3. companies should offer a mixture of at-home and virtual meeting and work options;

4. technology should be embraced, not feared; and

5. diversity is essential; labels, stereotypes, and assumptions get us nowhere.

As you can see, these priorities all map onto needs for autonomy, competence, and relatedness.

Maslow's Hierarchy of Needs

There are many pieces of the motivation puzzle.

To get the full picture of human motivation, we need to incorporate all the pieces together. One attempt to do this comes from the movement in the field called *humanistic psychology*. We discussed it in the chapter on personality (Chapter 13); it's an approach that emphasizes human potential, free will, growth, and self-esteem. Humanistic psychology produced Maslow's hierarchy of needs.

Maslow's hierarchy of needs suggests that motivation is set up as a prioritized system, as shown in Figure 11.3 (Maslow, 1943, 1954). Whatever needs are salient to us at the time drives our behavior, and we start at the bottom in terms of what we think is important. Maslow suggested that for everyone, our physiological needs will come first: We need the basics like air, food, and water. Next, we need to feel safe and secure. Our next priority is social; we want to fit in with others, have a community, and establish meaningful relationships. These social relationships allow us to establish self-esteem. Finally, once these lower needs are met, we can work on the top of the pyramid.

If a lower need is lacking, that becomes our priority. A child struggling with a lack of food or sleep due to challenges at home is going to care less about doing well on a test in school, for example, compared to a child who lives in relative comfort. Once the child achieves that comfort, they will be able to focus on higher motivations, such as art, music, and intellectual growth. We are curious and naturally driven to achieve the

> **Maslow's hierarchy of needs:** The idea that our motivation is based on priorities in a set order: physiological needs, safety, belongingness, esteem, and finally personal growth (called self-actualization).

FIGURE 11.3

Maslow's Hierarchy of Needs

Maslow believed we're motivated from the bottom up. If lower needs are satisfied, we can then work on the higher needs.

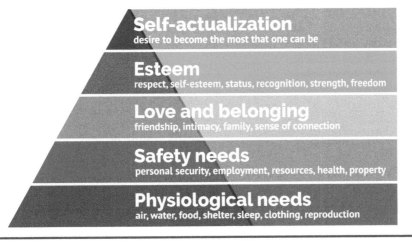

iStock.com/Plateresca

Self-actualization: According to Maslow's hierarchy of needs, it's the exploration of individual growth and achievement of our best personal potential self.

next need in the hierarchy once we fulfill the pyramid's bottom levels. The top of the pyramid is called **self-actualization**. It's when we can truly explore our own best self, our own potential, a spiritual or existential life that moves from *surviving* to *thriving*.

Maslow's theory has been criticized for some of the same problems as many of Freud's ideas. Many psychologists believe the concepts are hard to define and test (Wahba & Bridwell, 1976). He also developed the theory based on personal observations in the United States, and others have found that priorities are likely very different in other cultures (e.g., Gambrel & Cianci, 2003). Priorities might even shift based on sociocultural factors like age, gender, and socioeconomic status—so the universality (in other words, the generalizability) of the pyramid is certainly a debate (Yurdakul & Arar, 2023).

Despite these issues, the hierarchy of needs is extremely popular and has been applied (although not always successfully) to a wide range of situations. Just a few examples are motivating employees, helping immigrants, advancing adult education, supporting artists, furthering spiritual growth, understanding happiness despite hunger and homelessness, and making wiser decisions (Adler, 1977; Babula, 2023; Biswas-Diener & Diener, 2006; Shi & Lin, 2021; Sohail & Rafi, 2018).

Maslow's hierarchy of needs has even been used to help staff members at dog rescue shelters prioritize the needs of the dogs waiting to be adopted (Griffin et al., 2023). Are you curious whether dogs have the same needs as humans, or how this study even worked? To find out, read the *Spotlight on Research Methods* feature.

SPOTLIGHT ON RESEARCH METHODS

A Hierarchy of Needs for Dogs

iStock.com/GeorgePeters

Millions of dogs live in shelters every day, waiting to be adopted. The staff at most of these places probably cares deeply about giving them the best life possible—but are dogs' needs the same as humans'?

While we can never really know the answer for sure, psychology can at least give us a framework to try. One study (Griffin et al., 2023) started with Maslow's hierarchy of needs (for humans). Using the five major levels of needs listed there as inspiration (see Figure 11.4), they created a list of common needs dogs have in shelters, such as

- Healthy and appropriate amounts of food and water

- Regular visits with a veterinarian

- Appropriately sized and clean living spaces

- Training that emphasizes rewards for positive behavior (instead of punishment for negative behavior)

- Loving contact and attention from humans

- Socialization with other dogs

- Mental stimulation, such as enriched environments, variety (e.g., the ability to explore outdoor spaces), and toys

They eventually came up with over 30 different needs. The researchers put them in a spreadsheet and asked dog experts (including veterinarians, canine scientists, and managers of shelters) from six different countries to (1) confirm that the list of needs was valid, (2) put the list of needs in order in terms of priority, and (3) say where the needs should fall in terms of larger categories of motivation.

The final version based on the experts' consensus is shown in Figure 11.4. You can see that the first three levels of needs for dogs match those of the human needs identified by Maslow: physiological, safety, and social.

After that, though, the needs differ. According to this study, dogs in shelters next need what they called "integrity needs," a level focused on reinforcement of positive behaviors during training that would help the dogs get adopted by a family. The top level was "cognitive needs," in which the dogs' quality of life was enhanced with mental stimulation, variety, and toys. Interestingly, "cognitive needs" aren't explicitly included in Maslow's theory.

FIGURE 11.4

Results From Dog Expert Panel

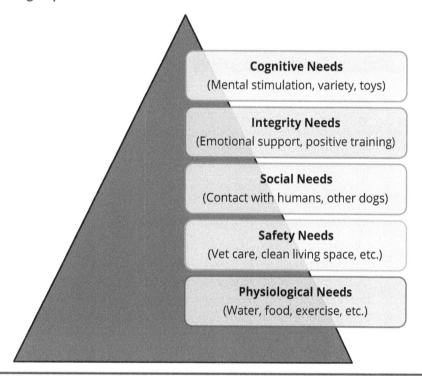

Source: Adapted from Griffin et al. (2023).

The researchers ended their paper by emphasizing that people who work in dog shelters and people who adopt dogs need to remember that for any pet, their needs might differ from ours. To maintain the best physical and mental happiness for us and for them, it's good to think about things from their perspective sometimes. ●

Practice what you learn in **Knowledge Check 11.1**

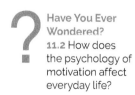

EXAMPLES AND APPLICATIONS OF MOTIVATION

>> **LO 11.2**   **Identify and explain examples of motivation, as well as various related subfields of psychology for work, school, and sports.**

What motivates us to eat chocolate—and why is it associated with love?

The motivation theories we just covered provide several possible answers. From a biological point of view, eating chocolate—or anything else—might fulfill physiological needs to satisfy hunger. Chocolate, in particular, might be appealing because of the

Have You Ever Wondered?
11.2 How does the psychology of motivation affect everyday life?

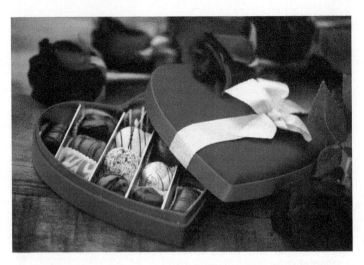

Do you like chocolate simply because of the taste?

iStock.com/Liliboas

sugar and caffeine it usually contains, satisfying innate instincts that crave both short- and long-term energy supplies (Nassar et al., 2011). But chocolate is also psychologically associated with love, romance, and luxury—a kind of classical conditioning (Benton & Nehlig, 2004). Chocolate might even serve as a substitute for needs like love and sex, due to the chemical and psychological nature of how we consume it and the cultural meanings we've put into it (Golomb et al., 2021).

Human motivation is clearly nuanced and complicated, and why we do any given behavior depends on a wide variety of factors. In this section, we take a deeper dive into several influences on motivation for examples of given behaviors. But keep in mind that just like when we eat chocolate, engage in loving and intimate behaviors with another person, or almost any other action, our reasons for doing so will be multifaceted—a combination of many, simultaneous influences and motivations. We'll end the section by naming specific subfields and careers that explore motivation in interesting ways.

Motivation for Hunger and Eating

Hunger is a good example of a complicated motivation.

We eat when we're hungry—but we also eat when we're bored, when we want to find comfort, when we feel insecure, or because many cultures use meals (such as feasts around holidays) as important social rituals (Abdulan et al., 2023; Braden et al., 2023; Frank et al., 2023). As hunger is fundamental to the human experience, we'll start this section using hunger as an example of how motivation comes from many different factors and influences.

Hormones and Homeostasis

The chapter on biology and your brain (Chapter 3) discussed that the hypothalamus maintains homeostasis by managing and monitoring hormones and chemicals in our body, mostly through the pituitary gland. When it comes to hunger, the hypothalamus monitors levels of *glucose*, a sugar our body uses as a primary energy source. If glucose is running low, the brain tells the body to release relevant hormones. For example, *ghrelin* is released in the stomach when it's empty, which causes it to contract and sometimes "growl" (Singh, 2023). After we eat, *insulin* (from the pancreas) and *leptin* (from fat cells) are detected by the hypothalamus, which signal it to decrease hunger.

When you're upset or depressed, what kind of food do you tend to eat?

iStock.com/fcafotodigital; iStock.com/ LauriPatterson

Basic homeostasis would predict that we eat only when we're hungry and that we stop eating when we're full. But of course, anyone who has been to a buffet or holiday feast knows that's not what happens. Many people have an unhealthy relationship with food, partially explained by psychological factors.

Obesity and Eating Disorders

When we're stressed or anxious, many of us prefer "junk" food over healthy food; it's even sometimes called "comfort" food (Dallmann et al., 2005). This is an ironic betrayal of our body, as it's a long-term unhealthy choice. If we chose things like bran muffins and spinach, the fiber and nutrients would lessen risks of cancer, increase energy, lower blood pressure, and decrease risk of heart disease; these foods are also associated with higher overall mental health (Brookie et al., 2018; DiNicolantonio et al., 2016; Lynch et al., 2014; Randhawa et al., 2015). But your authors are going to admit that when we're upset, we're not reaching for the kale and quinoa.

Obesity is typically defined as unhealthy and excessive body weight, measured by one's body mass index (BMI). BMI is calculated as weight (measured in kilograms) divided by height (in meters) squared; healthy BMI scores are usually recommended to be between 18.5 and 25.0. The number of people who qualify as "obese" in the United States has tripled over the past 50 years and is considered an "epidemic" due to the health concerns associated with it (Kranjac & Kranjac, 2023).

Obesity is an intersectional problem: Latinx and African American people in the United States—especially women and/or people with less money—are more likely to be obese than White people (Alemán et al., 2023; Lofton et al., 2023). Asian Americans are less likely to be obese than White people, but when they are obese, they are more likely to also have relevant problems like hypertension and sleep apnea (Li et al., 2023).

While some people suffer from the problems of obesity, others have a very different issue with eating and food. Eating disorders are mental illnesses in which someone's relationship with food causes them physical and psychological harm. While we discuss most of psychology's recognized mental illnesses in the last two chapters of this book, consider two of them right now:

- *Anorexia nervosa:* People inaccurately perceive themselves as "fat" and fear gaining weight. Sometimes people with this disorder also have a very high need for control and perfectionism. They are motivated to engage in dangerous weight-loss behaviors, including self-starvation and excessive exercise. The result is other health issues, including osteoporosis, bone fractures, and organ failure.

- *Bulimia nervosa:* To avoid gaining weight, people with this disorder allow themselves to eat very large amounts of food for the temporary comfort it brings ("binge") but will almost immediately attempt to get the food out of their system through vomiting, laxatives, or excessive exercise ("purge"). Again, resulting health issues are many but can include cardiac arrhythmia and digestive disorders, and the vomiting often leads to damage to the stomach, throat, and teeth.

Body Shaming and Body Positivity

What is the motivation behind eating disorders? This is a difficult question to answer, making eating disorder treatment very challenging. There may be heritability factors making some people more likely to develop eating disorders (Yilmaz et al., 2015). Some research suggests that personality traits such as perfectionism are associated with eating disorders—implying that many young people are motivated to be thin, but

Obesity: Unhealthy and excessive body weight, measured by one's body mass index (BMI).

Eating disorders: Mental illnesses in which someone's relationship with food causes them physical and psychological harm.

that those with eating disorders are the ones who can maintain the unhealthy tenacity required over extended periods of time (Longo et al., 2023; Stice, 2002).

Other studies suggest that eating disorders are the result of sexual and/or emotional abuse in childhood. Because these victims lost control of their bodies, the motivation for the eating disorder may be to regain control over their physical sense of self (Colle et al., 2023; Örge & Volkan, 2023). A less extreme version of emotional abuse is criticism some young people feel from their families or peers. Adolescents who perceive social hostility and have resulting low self-esteem are more likely to have eating disorders (Kluck, 2008; Polivy & Herman, 2002).

Another popular explanation is that mass media pushes the motivation to be thin on people (González, 2023; Slater et al., 2012). Fashion models and actresses have gotten increasingly thinner over the past several decades—and many companies profit off young people's desire to change their looks by selling products promising to do just that (Blodgett Salafia et al., 2015; Spettigue & Henderson, 2004). Access to social media appears to be only making the problem worse (Saul & Rodgers, 2018). In short, this research implies that people's motivation behind eating disorders is to fit in with others, to live up to what they perceive as social norms, and the hope that they will gain status or popularity if they weigh less.

Finally, motivation to diet, exercise, or use drugs like laxatives in extreme or unhealthy ways might come from social stigma regarding prejudice toward people with

FIGURE 11.5

Contributors and Consequences of Body Shaming

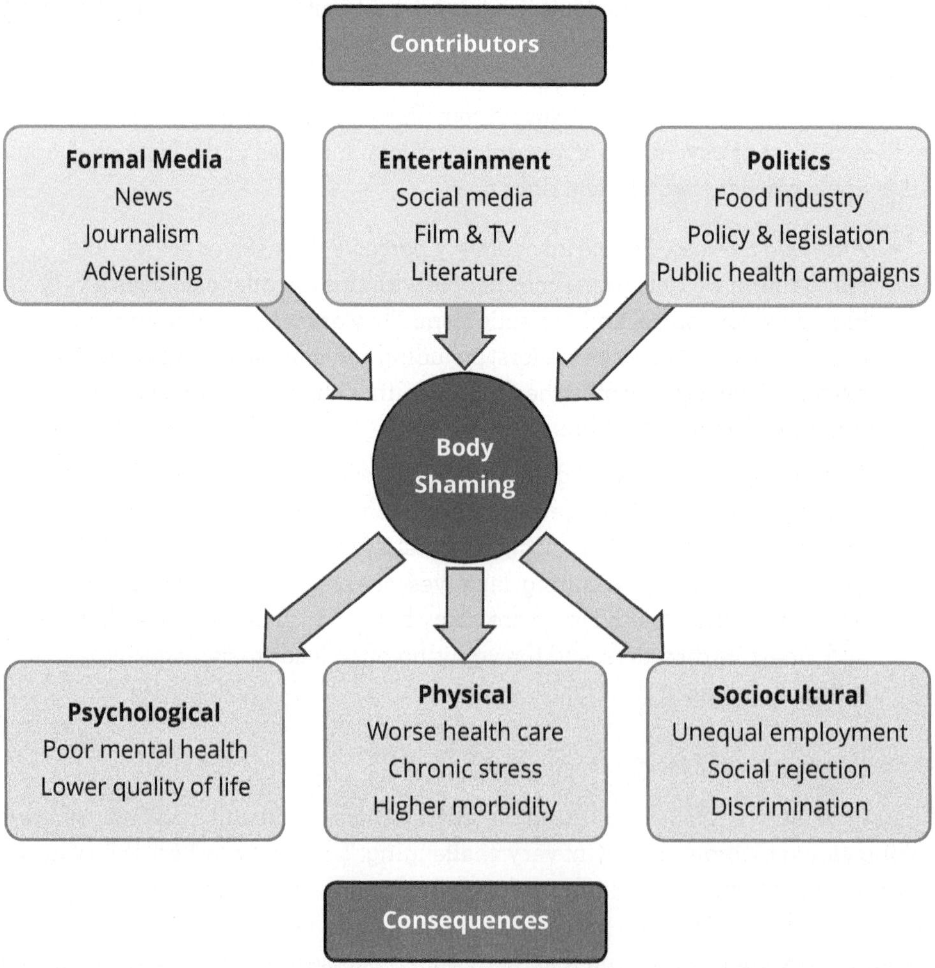

Source: Adapted from Westbury et al. (2023).

larger bodies. **Body shaming** refers to negative judgments, prejudice, and discrimination toward people based on their body size and shape, usually aimed at people labeled "fat" or overweight. In the model shown in Figure 11.5 (based on Westbury et al., 2023), cultural contributors to body shaming are formal media (e.g., journalism), the entertainment industry, and politics. Consequences are varied but include negative psychological, physical, and sociocultural effects.

Body shaming of people with big bodies is sometimes called by other names, including "fat shaming," "anti-fat bias," "obesity stigma," "weight stigma," "sizeism," and others. People who defend this behavior say shaming fat people will motivate them to be healthier—but research does not generally support this defense. First, people who experience body shaming are actually *less* motivated to engage in healthy eating and exercise habits, at least in part due to depression and anxiety (Emmer et al., 2020; Papadopoulos & Brennan, 2015; Pearl & Puhl, 2018). "Fat shaming" people *increases* their chances of long-term obesity (Westbury et al., 2023).

In addition, the *body positivity* movement argues that people can be physically healthy in bodies of all weights and sizes. For example, the "Health at Every Size" campaign attempts to fight "fat shaming" and highlights healthy behaviors as separate motivations and goals from body shape, size, or weight (Penney & Kirk, 2015). The body positivity perspective is associated with higher self-acceptance, increased self-esteem, *and* healthier attitudes and motivation toward food and eating behaviors (Nairn, 2023).

The body positivity movement emphasizes that health and happiness comes in bodies of all shapes and sizes.

Eugenio Marongiu/ImageSource/via Getty Images

Body shaming: Negative judgments, prejudice, and discrimination toward people based on their body size and shape, usually aimed at people labeled "fat" or overweight.

Intrinsic and Extrinsic Motivation

Why do you do the following things?

- Study for each of your classes
- Play sports
- Seek romantic partners

For each activity, there are many possible motivations—but for this section, we're going to group all possible motives into two major categories, following the system suggested by self-determination theory (Kruglankski et al., 2018; Ryan & Deci, 2000).

Intrinsic motivation is the desire to do something because the activity itself is rewarding or enjoyable. You might study because you simply like to learn new things; play sports because you enjoy the physical activity, team atmosphere, or like seeing yourself improve over time; and seek a romantic partner because it prevents loneliness or allows you to meet fun new people. Something is intrinsically motivating or rewarding when you *want* to do something simply because you enjoy doing it.

In contrast, **extrinsic motivation** is the desire to do something because the activity results in an external reward. These are behaviors you might feel you *have* to do, instead of that you *want* to do, because of the promised reward (or avoiding a punishment). The reward can be immediate or long term, abstract or concrete. You might study simply to get a good grade or play sports to maintain a scholarship, and there are even some people who seek romantic partners because they are paid to do so (professional escorts or sex workers).

Research on these two major categories of motivation indicates that *why* we do something has a huge effect on our attitude, how much we enjoy the task, how long we

Intrinsic motivation: The desire to do something because the activity itself is rewarding or enjoyable.

Extrinsic motivation: The desire to do something because the activity results in an external reward.

do it, how well we do it, and much more depending on the task and circumstances. For example, across three studies that investigated employees in a wide range of careers (including gas stations, banks, hospitals, and retail stores), people who had higher intrinsic motivation at work also had better work performance, higher commitment to their company, lower job burnout, lower intention to quit, and even lower work–family conflict (Kuvaas et al., 2017).

In short, people thrive more when they are in careers they love and are passionate about, regardless of the external rewards. One study measured intrinsic motivation at work with a survey asking people to rate items such as, "My job is so interesting that it is a motivation in itself" on a scale from 1 (*strongly disagree*) to 5 (*strongly agree*) (Arnulf et al., 2020). The results are shown in Figure 11.6. As you can see, from the careers they included, the five in which people reported the highest levels of intrinsic motivation were artist, photographer, CEO, priest, and dancer. The five lowest were cleaner, bouncer, magazine seller, sex worker, and stockbroker.

FIGURE 11.6

Intrinsic Motivation at Work, by Job Type

Intrinsic motivation (inherent love and interest in the job) is highest for artists and lowest for cleaners in this study.

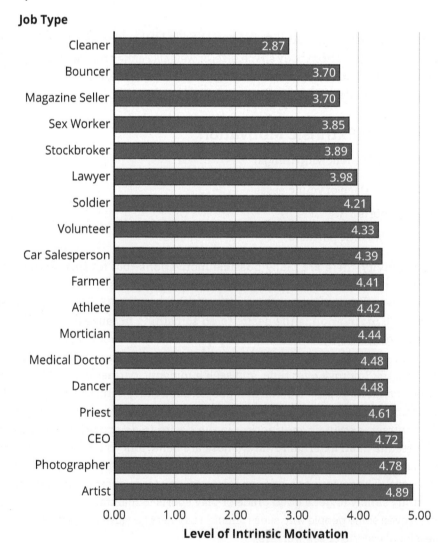

Source: Created using data from Arnulf et al. (2020).

Why Intrinsic Motivation Matters

Did you ever get paid for good grades when you were younger? Some parents try to boost children's motivation to study with this kind of incentive. The concern is that it will teach people to study only for the reward (extrinsic motivation), instead of to study simply because learning and getting smarter should be a reward in and of itself (intrinsic motivation).

Results on whether this tactic is a good idea are complicated and mixed. Most studies find that the extra boost will usually increase school performance—but with warnings, such as (1) be sure to use rewards for good work (e.g., money for getting As), not punishments for bad work (e.g., grounded for getting Fs); (2) be sure to set achievable, specific goals; and (3) it's better to reward *behaviors* [like time spent reading] than *outcomes* [like grades], as this helps people form healthy habits that might last over time (Covington & Müeller, 2001; Fryer, 2011; Putwain & Remedios, 2014).

How about for practicing and playing sports? Intrinsic motivation to play has been tied to several positive outcomes. Examples include more practice, increased persistence in the sport, better performance, more engagement during play, enhanced vitality, and higher overall well-being (for a review, see Standage, 2023). Coaches who emphasize intrinsic reasons to play (such as enjoyment, self-improvement, and teamwork) over extrinsic reasons (such as winning, competition, and trophies) may also improve their athletes' competence (Vallerand, 2007).

Motivation also seems to matter when it comes to dating and intimate relationships (La Guardia & Patrick, 2008). People with higher levels of intrinsic motivation in relationships report more honest and more deeply personal communication with their partners (Hodgins et al., 1996). They also tend to deal with relationship conflict in healthier ways (Knee et al., 2002). In married couples, intrinsic motivation is associated with greater affection and happiness (Blais et al., 1990; Knee et al., 2005).

When Play Becomes Work: The Overjustification Effect

What about when motivation to do something *changes?* College athletes enjoy their sport a little less after receiving a scholarship (Medic et al., 2007; Ryan, 1977). That's weird, right? They're finally getting rewarded for all those early morning practices, diets, and harsh training camps. But when compared to nonscholarship athletes, those receiving a financial incentive lose a little love for their sport. Worse, the effects appear to linger after their playing days are behind them (Moller & Sheldon, 2020).

Why? The **overjustification effect** refers to losing interest in an activity that was originally intrinsically rewarding after external rewards are offered for doing it (Deci et al., 1999; Lepper et al., 1973). The overjustification effect is also sometimes called the *undermining* effect. Basically, it's what happens when the fun gets sucked out of something because your reason for doing it changes. This is the danger of rewarding children for things like reading books over the summer (Henderlong & Lepper, 2002; Lepper et al., 2005). When children are offered candy, certificates, or even cash for doing so, their enjoyment and interest in reading for pleasure goes down.

The overjustification effect has been replicated in many settings and across many *meta-analyses* (statistical groupings across individual studies; for a review of all this research, see Ryan et al., 2022). That said, views on the overjustification effect are still debated in psychology. You can probably see why. If you love doing something, and you were told you could now do it professionally—would you really stop loving it?

The behaviorist model of psychology also argues that *more* rewards for any behavior should only reinforce those behaviors more, not less. Follow-up research points out that the effect might be strongest for activities that aren't *originally* inherently fun or interesting to begin with—so the external reward is needed to provide some kind of motivation (Cameron et al., 2001; Rigby et al., 2014).

Overjustification effect: When intrinsic motivation is undermined by providing a reward for something that originally didn't need to be rewarded.

Achievement Motivation

If you want to fall in love, is it because you want to find a caring life partner, or because you don't want to be lonely?

Either option of this multiple-choice question might sound like they boil down to the same goal, but psychology research finds that how we cognitively frame our motivation for life achievements—including falling in love—matters.

Achievement motivation (sometimes phrased as *need for achievement*) is the desire to work hard, master a skill or meet a goal, and do something useful with your life (McClelland, 1961, 1987). Generally, when you set goals for yourself, you can fantasize about all the glorious and wonderful things you'd like to achieve in the future—or you can worry about all the horrible things that might go wrong. Do you live your life based on hopes and dreams, or based on anxiety and fear?

In other words, research on achievement motivation breaks how we frame or position goals into different mindsets. There are two ways we can break goals down: (1) approach versus avoidance and (2) performance versus mastery.

- *Approach goals* are positively framed; they state what you want to achieve or accomplish *approach-mastery* (success).

- *Avoidance goals* are negatively framed; they state what you want to avoid or are afraid of (failure).

- *Performance goals* are based on doing a task for the extrinsic rewards (e.g., public recognition, popularity) or to avoid public punishment (e.g., embarrassment). These goals include competition to prove one is "better" than someone else.

- *Mastery goals* are based on doing a task for the intrinsic rewards (e.g., simply enjoying a task, wanting to improve, or pleasure in overcoming a challenge).

Combining these four categories together gets us the types of motivation shown in Figure 11.7 (Urdan & Kaplan, 2020). A snapshot of anyone's behavior from the outside won't tell you *why* they're doing it—but many studies now support the idea that

Achievement motivation:
The desire to work hard, master a skill or meet a goal, and do something useful with your life.

FIGURE 11.7

Four Types of Achievement Motivation

Here are examples of four types of motivation in the context of a sports performance.

Approach Performance
"I want to prove that I'm the best in my division."

Approach Mastery
"I want to play a perfect game."

Avoidance Performance
"I don't want to publicly embarrass myself."

Avoidance Mastery
"I want to avoid making any mistakes."

approach-mastery motivation mindsets toward goals lead to the best outcomes in a variety of settings, compared to the other three mindsets (Michou et al., 2016; Wigfield et al., 2021).

Another way to think about avoidance goals is as *fear of failure* (Chan et al., 2020; Cury et al., 2006; McGregor & Elliot, 2005). Often, fear of failure has negative effects on performance because it makes people afraid to take risks (Morgan & Sisak, 2016). However, that's not always the case. Sometimes, the haunting fear of failure makes people extra driven to succeed. Essentially, it is possible to have multiple kinds of motivation simultaneously when we strive to achieve excellence (Cacciotti et al., 2016).

Simone Biles is a shining example of achievement motivation. She has said, "I'm always trying to push myself to the limit to see what I can do . . . I always want to push myself to do better."

Laurence Griffiths/Staff/Getty Images Sport/via Getty Images

Applied Subfields and Careers

Motivation applies to every person, every day.

The examples and potential uses of the psychology of motivation are endless. We've already talked about some of them in other chapters, such as when we discussed *health psychology* in the chapter on stress, health, and happiness. If you've found yourself wanting to know more about the ideas in the current chapter, you might be a good fit for any of the following career opportunities.

Industrial/Organizational Psychology

Industrial/organizational psychology is a subfield focused on human dynamics in working environments. Most people in the field refer to it as "I/O psychology." It includes personnel selection, leadership, job satisfaction, consumer behavior, training, diversity efforts, and so much more. One important part of I/O psychology is employee motivation, such as how intrinsic motivation in careers often leads to better job outcomes. There are many job opportunities in the world of I/O psychology, especially for people with a master's degree.

Industrial/organizational psychology: A subfield focused on human dynamics in working environments (e.g., personnel selection and satisfaction, work motivation, and leadership).

School Psychology

School psychology is a subfield focused on assessment and intervention for children and adolescents in educational environments. While it can include mental health counseling, it is a separate job and requires separate graduate school education and licensure than school counselors. Instead, school psychologists are more interested in collaborating with teachers, parents, and administrators on what will make the school environment the best possible place for students to learn. This sometimes includes research on subjects like the ones discussed in this chapter, on kinds of motivation, goals, reinforcement, and so on.

School psychology: A subfield focused on assessment and intervention for children and adolescents in educational environments.

Sport Psychology

Sport psychology is a subfield devoted to players and coaches in athletic environments and how to make that environment as positive as possible. In this chapter, we've highlighted examples of how motivation changes athlete and coach behavior, but sport psychology encompasses many more areas of research. Careers include working with professional athletes who encounter challenges (such as injuries, addictions, or difficult social dynamics) and have to find ways to overcome them to succeed, as well as exploring the best way for athletes to practice, focus, maintain a positive attitude, and more.

Sport psychology: A subfield focused on the dynamics of players and coaches in athletic environments.

CAREER CORNER

Meet Mandie, Student Success Manager for an Online University

What is your career?

I am a Student Success Manager for an online university. I work with prospective students in the enrollment/admissions process and support them through graduation by monitoring their academic performance, assisting with course registration, and collaborating on strategies to balance school, work, family, and life in general.

How was studying psychology important for success in this career?

My overall education in psychology has definitely helped me to understand my students on a deeper level. Every student comes from a unique background and is in a different stage of their life—you can't effectively do this job if you treat every student the same way. **Studying psychology prepared me to identify relevant traits in my students and personalize my approach to best support each student in their own way.**

How do concepts from this chapter help in this career?

One of the biggest factors in effectively motivating students to succeed is the way in which they are motivated. Students fueled by extrinsic motivation may benefit from a quick message congratulating them on a good grade on a quiz or assignment, or they may need "tough love" from an outsider pointing out that they need to kick themselves back into gear. Students with intrinsic motivation may need to register for a class they will enjoy or excel in alongside a course in which they feel less comfortable.

Students often face obstacles in their lives and need help problem-solving to continue to succeed in school. **If a student's basic needs aren't met, they cannot prioritize their education.** Maslow's hierarchy of needs helped me to understand that I can't expect a student to put their basic and psychological needs to the side just to focus on school. We have to find a way for the student to both fulfill those needs and focus on their education.

Is this the career you always planned to have after college?

Absolutely not! I majored in psychology because I loved my Intro to Psych class and wanted to study something that I was passionate about and understood well. I still didn't know what I wanted to be when I grew up when I walked the stage at graduation! **I've found that the psychological concepts I studied in college are far more pervasive in the world than I had imagined, and my knowledge has helped me to excel in even the most unsuspecting of places.**

If you could give current college students one sentence of advice, what would it be?

If you don't know what you want to do as a career right now, that is okay—be open to new opportunities because you may find your passion when you least expect it! ●

The Wonderful World of Curiosity

Our curiosity also motivates us.

Curiosity: The intrinsic motivation to seek information about something unusual or interesting when there is no other incentive beyond simply wanting to know.

After we're reached homeostasis, as we're working toward big life goals like falling in love and reaching major achievements, curiosity is the intrinsic motivation to seek information about something unusual or interesting when there is no other incentive beyond simply wanting to know (Berlyne, 1966; Ryan et al., 2019; White, 1959; Yager & Kay, 2020).

To end the first half of this chapter—the half about motivation—we want to leave you with a word about curiosity because (as the name of the book suggests) it's one of our favorite ideas. There are two types (Reio, 2010). *Cognitive curiosity* encourages close observations that result in learning and problem-solving. It does have risks, like embarrassment if you make a public error. It's the kind of curiosity that you display if you bravely raise your hand to ask a question in class.

Sensory curiosity encourages thrill seeking and new physiological experiences. Because it requires seeking out new kinds of physical sensations, it risks physical dangers—and, when it goes wrong, can result in drug and alcohol abuse, risky sexual behaviors, and various kinds of accidents (Arnett, 1996; Harris et al., 2023; Wade et al., 2021).

So curiosity comes with risks; hence that famous warning about it killing the figurative cat. Safety and reasonable precautions are always a good idea. But we emphasize the joys and benefits of bold curiosity. Published reviews in psychology praise the benefits of curiosity across dozens of settings. The big picture is that curiosity enhances social relationships, job performance at work, a sense of belonging to clubs and organizations, tolerance for stress and trauma, meaning in life, and pure happiness (for a comprehensive summary of this research, see Yow et al., 2022). That's a lot of benefits.

Are you curious about how curious you are? If so, take the survey in the *What's My Score?* feature.

Curiosity has an unknown destination.

iStock.com/vgajic

WHAT'S MY SCORE?

Measuring Curiosity

Instructions: Using the scale below, indicate the extent to which you agree or disagree with each statement.

1	2	3	4	5
Strongly Disagree	Disagree	Neutral	Agree	Strongly Agree

___ 1. I actively seek as much information as I can in new situations.

___ 2. I am the type of person who really enjoys the uncertainty of everyday life.

___ 3. I am at my best when doing something that is complex or challenging.

___ 4. Everywhere I go, I am out looking for new things or experiences.

___ 5. I view challenging situations as an opportunity to grow and learn.

___ 6. I like to do things that are a little frightening.

___ 7. I am always looking for experiences that challenge how I think about myself and the world.

___ 8. I prefer jobs that are excitingly unpredictable.

___ 9. I frequently seek out opportunities to challenge myself and grow as a person.

___ 10. I am the kind of person who embraces unfamiliar people, events, and places.

Scoring Instructions: Find the total sum of your responses for your score, which should range from 10 to 50. The higher your score, the more curious you are. When the study was originally published, college students had an average score right around 33 across three samples. ●

Source: Kashdan et al. (2009).

Practice what you learn in **Knowledge Check 11.2**

Sage Vantage

THEORIES OF EMOTION

Have You Ever Wondered?
11.3 How do psychologists define and study emotion?

>> **LO 11.3** **Compare and contrast theories of emotion, including James–Lange, Cannon–Bard, Schachter–Singer, and cognitive appraisal.**

How do you know if you're in love?

There are different parts to the overall experience of emotion. The first is physiological. When people are passionately in love, heart rate increases, certain hormones are released, and breathing changes (among other things that can become aroused; Karandashev, 2022). Emotions are also cognitive. When people are in love, they often feel a commitment toward the other person and perceive them as part of their sense of self (Arriaga & Agnew, 2001). Emotions can also be abstract feelings that are hard to put into words. This elusive nature of the experience might be why love is the inspiration for centuries of poems, songs, and visual art.

The complicated nature of emotions has led to theoretical research and controversy regarding exactly how our body and mind process them. This section of the chapter introduces you to four theories developed by psychologists over time trying to explain how emotions work. Table 11.2 summarizes them, but spoiler alert (again): This is an ongoing debate in the field. It's likely that each theory holds one piece of the puzzle that is human emotion, and that only by understanding all of them will we get the full picture.

The first theory wasn't inspired by love. Instead, it was a bear.

TABLE 11.2

Four Theories on Emotion

Over time, psychologists have suggested four theories to explain the process of experiencing emotion. The bear represents seeing something in your environment to start the process (like seeing a bear). The icon of a body with a skeleton represents a physiological response. The icon of a brain represents a cognitive interpretation of what's happening, based on the context and environment. Not all theories include all components, and each theory suggests that the components occur in a different order.

THEORY NAME	ORDER OF EVENTS	EXPLANATION
James–Lange		Something in the environment causes our body to respond. We then have an emotion.
Cannon–Bard		Something in the environment causes two simultaneous and separate responses: Our body reacts and we have an emotion.
Schachter–Singer		Something in the environment causes two simultaneous responses: a physiological reaction and a cognitive label, based on the situational context. Our interpretation of both responses results in an emotion.
Cognitive–Mediational		Something in our environment causes us to put a cognitive label on the trigger, interpreting its meaning. We then have an emotion, and the emotion leads to our body's response.

James–Lange Theory

Imagine you see a bear.

What happens next? Would your body start to tremble, and would you feel afraid? One of the first major debates about emotion is how the timing and components of emotional reactions occur. The first famous theory is named for two people who came up with very similar ideas at almost the same time, independently. One was William James, who you learned about in Chapter 1 as one of the founders of psychology. He taught the first-ever psychology course in the United States, at Harvard in 1875. The other theorist was a physiologist and psychologist in Denmark named Carl Lange. To give credit to both of them, the theory now includes both of their names.

If you saw this bear, what would your emotional reaction be?

iStock.com/sarkophoto

James–Lange theory of emotion: Something in our environment causes our body to respond first; this physiological reaction is then interpreted as an emotion.

The **James–Lange theory of emotion** is that something in our environment causes our body to respond. This instinctive, physiological response will happen *first,* before anything else. It's the automatic "fight, flight, or freeze" reaction of our sympathetic nervous system. Next, this reaction in our body causes us to experience a relevant emotion.

James explained fear through the thought experiment of a hypothetical bear. He wrote that when we see a bear, "we feel afraid *because* we tremble," or "we are frightened *because* we run" (1884, p. 190). He and Lange both believed that our body responds first, then we interpret that physiological response as an emotion afterward. Their idea appears in the first row of Table 11.2.

The Facial Feedback Hypothesis

If the James–Lange theory has some degree of validity, you should be happier if you smile more. After all, emotions are supposed to *follow* physiological reactions. So, can we trick our mind into having certain emotions by manipulating our body into mimicking certain responses?

The **facial feedback hypothesis** proposes that the sensation of our facial expressions will influence our emotions (as the James–Lange theory suggests; Buck, 1985). To test the idea in an experiment, researchers first put participants into one of two conditions as shown in Figure 11.8 (Strack et al., 1988). They had to hold a pen in their mouth and extend it forward using only

Facial feedback hypothesis: Proposes that our emotions can be influenced by our facial expressions (in other words, facial expressions can happen first, then emotions).

a. the lips—forcing the face into a pouty frown, or

b. the teeth—forcing the face into a smile.

All participants then rated how funny a series of cartoons was. On average, participants whose faces were forced into smiles rated the cartoons as significantly funnier. It worked! While the facial feedback hypothesis hasn't always been replicated, these interesting results have been supported in several similar experiments (Soussignan, 2002; Wagenmakers et al., 2016).

FIGURE 11.8

Manipulating Facial Feedback

In the first image, the participant is forced into a frown. In the second image, the participant is forced into a smile. Will their emotional experiences follow accordingly?

© Sage Publishing

Limitations of James–Lange

The full James-Lange theory was a little more complicated than how we've presented it, but you now understand the basics. James had a student, Walter Cannon, who pointed out several limitations of the original conception (Cannon, 1927). First, it's possible for us to be physiologically aroused in a variety of ways with no particular emotional response, such as when we're exercising and we just zone out.

Second, if emotions always resulted from prior physiological responses, we'd have to have specific body reactions for each specific emotion—and Cannon doubted that was the case. Our sympathetic nervous system's "fight, flight, or freeze" response is general, but the emotion is specific. Again, does a racing heart mean love, or hate? It might be either. How are we supposed to figure out what emotion to feel?

And there's another problem, although it comes from interesting research that occurred after Cannon's career. If emotional responses always require interpretation of an initial physiological response, then people with severe injuries in their spinal cord should have restricted emotions. Interview study results have shown significant decreases in anger and fear, supporting the James-Lange theory—but the same people still had other emotions (Hohmann, 1966). And other studies of people with spinal cord injuries have found reports of *increased* depression, especially in the year or two after the injury (Craig et al., 1994; Kishi et al., 1994). Once again, we needed another theory.

Cannon–Bard Theory

Another physiologist named Philip Bard shared Cannon's concerns. Their combined ideas are now called the **Cannon–Bard theory of emotion**, which is that something in the environment can trigger two relatively *simultaneous* and *separate* responses. If surprised by a bear, then (a) the body produces a physiological reaction in our sympathetic nervous system, and (b) we have an emotional experience. The two

Cannon–Bard theory of emotion: The idea that we simultaneously experience physiological arousal and emotional experiences.

events are separate and independent (Friedman, 2010). Neither is dependent on the other, and they can happen in any order. Cannon believed that sometimes the physiological reaction would happen first, and sometimes it happens second—but they would be milliseconds apart, essentially simultaneous. The second row of Table 11.2 summarizes the theory.

Cannon and Bard showed that cats who had their sensory and motor cortexes surgically removed still appeared to experience emotions (Bard & Rioch, 1937; Cannon, 1927). This was evidence in their favor, because according to the James–Lange theory, the cats should not have experienced emotion because they would have first needed physiological response (Dalgleish, 2004). But other people still saw problems, the biggest being that neither theory made room for logic and interpretation of our environment. In other words, there wasn't much actual psychology, in terms of mental thought or processing, yet. Enter theory three.

Schachter–Singer Theory (Two-Factor Theory)

Think about that bear again.

A huge bear roaring right in front of you might get your heart pounding no matter what. But your precise emotional response will depend on the situational context. You'll have very different emotions if you're at the zoo, if you're seeing the bear on a movie screen, or if you're camping alone in the woods and the bear looks like it wants to attack you.

The Schachter–Singer theory of emotion proposed that something in the environment will trigger two relatively simultaneous things to occur, just like the previous theory. But this time, those two reactions are (a) physiological arousal in the body's sympathetic nervous system and (b) a cognitive label, based on the situational context. The final step is that our emotional experience is based on our interpretation of *both* that physiological arousal and the cognitive label (Cotton, 1981; Schachter & Singer, 1962). It's the interaction of the two that matters, which is why this theory is sometimes called two-factor theory of emotion. Table 11.3's third row summarizes it for you.

Consider two creative tests of this theory (don't worry—no humans or bears were harmed, but there were drugs involved).

Schachter–Singer theory of emotion: The idea that how we interpret both (a) our physiological arousal to something in our environment and (b) the situational context results in an emotional experience. Sometimes this idea is called "two-factor theory."

Two-factor theory of emotion: See *Schachter–Singer theory of emotion.*

Test 1: Drug Injections in the Lab

Stanley Schachter and Jerome Singer tested their theory in a now-famous study using drug injections (Schachter & Singer, 1962). The setup of the study is summarized for you in Table 11.3. It was even more complicated than what's shown, with a placebo group (a control group) as well, but we're providing the most important experimental conditions for you here.

TABLE 11.3

Schachter & Singer's Classic Study

In their 1962 study, there were two independent variables, meaning four possible conditions for participants.

INDEPENDENT VARIABLE 1: DRUG SIDE EFFECTS EITHER . . .	INDEPENDENT VARIABLE 2: CONFEDERATE ACTS EITHER . . .	
	HAPPY	ANGRY
Expected	Predicted emotion: Neutral	Predicted emotion: Neutral
Not expected	Predicted emotion: Happiness	Predicted emotion: Anger

Participants in the critical conditions were all given a shot of the drug epinephrine. This is similar to adrenaline, which causes people's sympathetic nervous system to have predictable responses: increased heart rates, rapid breathing, trembling, and so on. Importantly, *none* of the participants knew what was in the shot; researchers told them it was a "vitamin" to improve their vision.

The study had two independent variables, both based on random assignment. First, researchers told some of the participants to expect the real side effects of epinephrine and that they would start to feel those effects in a few minutes. Researchers told other participants that the "vitamin" would have no effects besides potentially improving vision.

The second independent variable involved the situation that happened next. All the participants waited in a room for about 20 minutes. They thought they were just waiting with another genuine participant, but there was some more deception here: That other person waiting with them was really a *confederate* (an actor). For some participants, the confederate acted excited and happy. For other confederates, the confederate acted angry, complaining about the study and refusing to comply with requests from the researchers.

The dependent variable was the real participants' emotions, which researchers measured with observations throughout and with self-report surveys. Note that Schachter and Singer had cleverly created a lab situation in which people's physiological arousal was up (due to the shot), but in a way they hoped could be pushed toward various emotions based on the situational context. If participants reported different emotions, it would support their theory.

Of course, that's what they found (or we wouldn't be talking about it in this book). Every participant was influenced by the most appropriate cognitive label, given the situational context. People who had been told to expect the adrenaline-like rush in their body reported fairly neutral emotions. They weren't swayed by the confederate because they knew their bodies were reacting to the shot and used that cognitive label to explain what was happening.

On the other hand, people in the control condition *didn't* expect those side effects. When their hearts and breathing started to race, Schachter and Singer believed that they looked around to figure out why. The best explanation was the other person in the room, who was making them feel either happy or angry. Participants in those conditions did, in fact, appear to feel happier or angrier, influenced by the situation. Which emotion they felt matched the confederate because it was the most convenient and logical cognitive label they had available.

Would walking over one bridge over the other lead your heart to beat faster? How about making you feel attraction toward the person you meet the moment you step off the bridge?

iStock.com/AlanMBarr; iStock.com/sasar

Test 2: Love in the Park (Misattribution of Arousal)

All this stuff about hypothetical bears and drug injections sounds pretty weird.

What happened to falling in love?

Enter the "shaky bridge study," which is another creative test of the Schachter-Singer "two-factor" theory of emotion. Researchers planned the whole thing around two bridges in a beautiful park located in Vancouver, Canada (Dutton & Aron, 1974). One bridge was low and sturdy, while the second was a high, shaky, 450-foot-long suspension bridge over a deep gorge. The idea was that people who had just walked across the shaky bridge would be a little scared and have their sympathetic nervous systems aroused, while those who had just walked across the sturdy bridge would not (a quasi-experimental design).

The researchers waited for young men who were by themselves to walk across either bridge. Immediately afterward, they were approached by a physically attractive young woman experimenter and asked to complete a survey. Then, she offered each man her phone number! Their hypothesis was that the men who had just crossed the shaky bridge might misinterpret their quickly beating hearts (from the bridge) as attraction to the woman, if she provided contextual cues such as flirting with him a little. This kind of misunderstanding the true origin of our own body's physiological arousal is now known as misattribution of arousal.

The experimenter gave two different (fake) names and numbers to the men, based on which bridge they had just crossed. Results showed that 50% of the men from the shaky bridge called her, compared to only 12.5% of the men from the sturdy bridge. The researchers concluded that the men who had just crossed the shaky bridge believed they were attracted to her because they misinterpreted their physiological response to the bridge as attraction to the woman, supporting the Schachter-Singer theory of emotion. They had physiological arousal, and they used the most obvious cognitive label available to them to feel an emotion.

Misattribution of arousal: Misunderstanding our body's physiological response to one environmental cue in the environment and thinking it is in response to something else.

Lazarus's Cognitive–Mediational Theory

There's one more piece to the puzzle.

The Schachter–Singer theory has gotten mixed reviews. Follow-up studies trying to replicate misattribution of arousal effects (sometimes called *excitation transfer*) are usually effective, but when they are done in naturalistic settings such as the park, confounding variables exist (Cotton, 1981). For example, in the shaky bridge study, it's possible that men who had just walked across the shaky bridge are simply more daring, and that explains both why they chose to walk across a scary bridge and why they were more willing to call a woman they had just met. So we're still missing some pieces.

The last theory (shown in the bottom row of Table 11.3) is the Lazarus cognitive–mediational theory of emotion, which says that something in our environment will cause us first to put a cognitive label on the trigger (Lazarus, 1982, 1984). The label we choose leads to a given emotion, which *then* leads to an appropriate physiological response. Think of these examples if you were walking in the woods:

Lazarus cognitive–mediational theory of emotion: The idea that something in our environment triggers a cognitive appraisal or label, which leads to an emotional experience, which leads to a physiological response.

- You suddenly see a bear. You immediately label it "threat!" Your emotion is fear. Your physiological response is a rush of adrenaline.

- You hear a rustling sound above you. You label it "just the wind in the trees." Your emotion is calm joy. Your physiological response is relaxation.

- You see the love of your life walking toward you. You immediately label them "my life partner." Your emotion is love. Your physiological response is an increased heart rate and rush of blood to your cheeks, causing you to blush.

Note that Lazarus believed emotions would always *start* with immediate, cognitive appraisal or label of the environmental trigger—is it a threat, or not? That appraisal leads to an emotion, which leads to the physiological response. In other words, the body's reaction happens *last,* unlike all the other theories shown in Table 11.3.

Psychologists acknowledge that none of the theories are fully comprehensive (e.g., Kunst-Wilson & Zajonc, 1980; LeDoux, 2012, 2016; Marcus, 2023). The good news is that the debate about how to operationalize emotion and how emotional experiences work has led to decades of fascinating research on many related topics. We summarize just a small sample of some of that work for you in the last section of this chapter.

Sage Vantage   Practice what you learn in **Knowledge Check 11.3**

EVERYDAY EMOTION: CULTURE, EXPRESSION, AND BENEFITS

Have You Ever Wondered?
11.4 What are important research findings related to the psychology of emotion?

>> **LO 11.4**   **Explain psychology research on emotional expression, including cultural differences and lie detection, and on how emotions might benefit us.**

Is the experience of love the same around the world?

While romantic love may not have been the main motivation for marriage alliances in most cultures for many centuries, the idea of falling in love is likely a universal and timeless human experience (Buss, 1988; Campbell & Ellis, 2015). That said, most cultures have rules about who is socially "acceptable" for us to fall in love with—and who is not—putting restrictions on our emotions and their expression (Berscheid & Walster, 1974; Winch, 1952). There are several benefits of love, including receiving social support (when the relationship is socially "acceptable"), release of pleasurable hormones, increases in self-esteem, and more (Deepak et al., 2019).

This final section of the chapter discusses several fascinating topics regarding the human emotional experience, tied around two topics: (1) how people express emotions, including whether that changes by culture and whether lies can be reliably detected, and (2) what the advantages and disadvantages are to having emotions.

Emotional Expression

Is emotional expression an inborn instinct?

No one has to teach infants how to smile, and it occurs even among unsighted newborns who have never seen others smile (Rogers & Puchalski, 1986). Infants around the world also make the same facial expressions to communicate food disgust (Ruba et al., 2017). This kind of similarity has been observed in other animal species, including elephants, chimpanzees, and rats, among others (Bering,

Instinct theory points out that infants don't need to be taught how to smile.

iStock.com/digitalskillet

2012; Bradshaw, 2004; King, 2013). If we express emotions automatically, then there shouldn't be much variation by culture, and it should be relatively difficult to cover up our emotions. Consider research on both of these ideas.

Emotion and Culture: The Universality Hypothesis

The **universality hypothesis** proposes that all humans, regardless of culture, have the same facial expressions for core emotions and can recognize them in others. It's an idea going all the way back to Charles Darwin, who wrote about the expression of emotions by people across cultures when he explored the world as a naturalist (Darwin, 1860, 1872/2005). He asked questions about the purpose of blushing, how people expressed contempt nonverbally, and whether frowns always convey defiance.

Years later, psychologists tested the hypothesis using photographs such as the ones in Figure 11.9. Paul Ekman showed photos of people displaying certain emotions to people from different cultures, including people in isolated areas of New Guinea in the 1970s who had relatively little influence from outsiders (Ekman, 1970, 1972; Ekman & Friesen, 1971; Ekman et al., 1971). This early work, as well as follow-up research, established that people from all over the world are relatively good at identifying seven basic facial expressions of emotion: fear, disgust, surprise, anger, sadness, contempt, and happiness.

While psychologists disagree on exactly how many "basic" emotions should be included in the list for the universality hypothesis, most generally agree that some facial expressions will be understood by anyone, anywhere. Ekman's research has been replicated with slight variations to the procedure and results, and researchers now argue for anywhere from 4 to 12 emotions in the "universal" list, but fear, anger, disgust, and surprise are consistently there—perhaps because of their importance to human survival (Izard, 1990, 2013; Jack et al., 2016; Plutchik, 2001; Tomkins, 2008).

Universality hypothesis: Proposes that all humans, regardless of culture, have the same facial expressions for core emotions and can recognize them in others.

FIGURE 11.9

"Universal" Facial Expressions of Emotion

Can you identify which face goes with which emotion from the following list? Fear, disgust, surprise, anger, sadness, contempt, and happiness.

 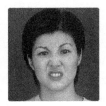  

Anger   Disgust   Fear   Surprise

Happiness   Sadness   Contempt

Courtesy of Paul Ekman

Display Rules

Not everyone agrees with the universality hypothesis (Jack et al., 2012). Even Paul Ekman, who did the pioneering research noted in the previous section, acknowledges that some variation in emotional expression will certainly happen from culture to culture in more nuanced, specific types of emotion. **Display rules** are socially learned, culture-specific norms for expressing emotions.

Display rules: Socially learned, culture-specific norms for expressing emotions.

Ekman (1972) observed that people from Japan and the United States who sat alone while watching a film about surgeries and accidents displayed the same facial expressions. But when an authority figure sat next to them, "the Japanese more than the Americans masked negative expressions with a smile" (Ekman, 2003, p. 4). This restraint matched Japanese cultural rules, which have more emphasis on formality and on appearing calm and collected in public compared to people in the United States (Ekman & Friesen, 1971). The public restraint on emotional expression in Japan has been replicated in many studies, extending even to more controlled and polite use of facial emojis in digital communication with people outside of one's family or close friends (Liu, 2023).

Here are a few other interesting examples of display rules for emotional expression:

- People in Latin America, Spain, and the Middle East often kiss and embrace when greeting each other as a sign of friendship (Axtell, 2007). This includes men kissing each other on the lips or cheeks, which would be considered quite strange in cultures such as the United States.

Did you know Wonder Woman and the first attempts at a working lie detector were both invented by a psychologist? It's why her magic lasso makes people tell the truth.

iStock.com/andylid

- People in Switzerland (specifically, Swiss citizens who speak German) display more emotions when grieving, compared to samples of people from China (Zhou et al., 2023). People from the Chinese sample in this study acknowledged the desire to display more emotions in public than they usually did.

- Young children in Nicaragua confused nonverbal expressions of prestige in the United States (expanded body, upward head tilt, and smile) for happiness (Witkower et al., 2023).

- Culture isn't always by country or region. For example, there appear to be display rules based on gender: Boys and men may be discouraged from talking about or expressing emotion as freely as girls and women, except that men are expected to express anger (Domagalski & Steelman, 2007; Polce-Lynch et al., 1998; Taylor et al., 2022).

- There can be even more specific display rules. In one Canadian prison, display rules appear to have formed between the cultures of prisoners versus guards, each emphasizing group solidarity (Fayter & Kilty, 2023). The article states that the display rules for each group are "scripts [that] become feeling rules that contour the emotion cultures that shape prison life" (p. 27).

Lie Detection

What do Wonder Woman and lie detectors have in common? Both were invented by a psychologist. William Moulton Marston was a psychology professor at Harvard along with William James (Lepore, 2015). Marston's wife inspired the lie detector when she told him that when she got particularly mad or excited, she noticed that her blood pressure went up. He spent years trying to create a functional machine to measure emotions and detect lies. While his version never quite worked, he did successfully create the Wonder Woman comic book series at the same time, and he incorporated her magic lasso—which forced her enemies to tell the truth when she caught them in it.

Modern research on lie detection is still controversial. In a summary across 247 samples, most people attempting to detect lies weren't any better than chance (in other words, 50/50; Bond & DePaulo, 2008). Still, there was variation, with a few people being quite good at it (and others, of course, being dismal). People particularly good at detecting lies have been labeled *truth wizards* by psychologists, and they sometimes find highly specialized jobs such as in the U.S. Secret Service (O'Sullivan & Ekman, 2004). Other psychologists argue that these "wizards" are *so* rare, though, that they might as well be called truth-detecting "unicorns" (O'Sullivan, 2007; Roulin & Ternes, 2019).

Here's a tip toward getting you closer to wizard status. One thing to look for is a Duchenne smile, a genuine, felt smile. Named after the French neurologist who first described it, a Duchenne smile is one that goes all the way to the eyes, producing "crow's feet" wrinkles and slightly lowered eyebrows. In contrast, false smiles given by liars who believe they might be getting away with something look more like smirks and don't reach the eyes; these smiles are called duping delight (Ekman & Frank, 1993).

Another common technique used during interviews (e.g., police interrogations) is to increase the interviewee's *cognitive load*—in other words, make the questions complicated (Lancaster et al., 2013; Vrij et al., 2011). If the questions are surprising or unanticipated, such as people being asked to draw a scenario or to explain the order of events backward, it's harder for liars to keep their fake story straight.

Duchenne smile: Genuine, felt smiles that reach the eyes and produce "crow's feet" wrinkles.

Duping delight: Fake smiles or smirks given by liars who believe they are getting away with their deception.

Benefits of Emotions

Certainly, there are pros and cons to having emotions.

The benefits of positive emotions are fairly obvious, but it's less clear for negative emotions. When we experience deep anger, grief, and sadness, it is truly debilitating. When this kind of emotional disruption causes severe damage to our lives and well-being for an extended period of time, it can be labeled a clinical psychological disorder. We will discuss mood disorders in much more detail in a later chapter of this book. For now, we encourage you to simply reflect on your personal experience with this kind of negative emotion and how much it affected your motivation, both short and long term.

Why would we ask you to focus on such a depressing topic? Because the last part of this chapter is going to focus on the advantages and disadvantages of having emotions—and we start with the idea that sometimes, maybe negative emotions are actually positive.

Survival Circuits

Could negative emotions have benefits? One possibility is that negative emotional experiences such as anger, threat, or sadness are important parts of the human

Does thinking about death make you feel fear? If so, how do you distract yourself?

iStock.com/Pears2295

Survival circuits: Finely tuned neural pathways tied to emotional experiences.

experience because they help us survive and learn about how to make changes to improve (LeDoux, 2012, 2016, 2022). **Survival circuits** are finely tuned neural pathways tied to emotional experiences that serve adaptive purposes.

For example, anger might actually provide three beneficial survival circuits:

1. a *defense* circuit that helps us protect the self from harm,

2. a *reproductive* circuit that helps us compete for sexual mates, and

3. a *feeding* circuit that helps us with predatory aggression.

In this way, having small to moderate levels of anger, fear, sadness, and anxiety aren't so bad; they help us stay vigilant, defensive, and may even help us learn from past mistakes. Perhaps these evolutionary benefits to seemingly negative states are one reason they are so pervasive and difficult to treat in therapy (Cain, 2023). Much of the future work on motivation, emotions, and how they tie together will likely come from ideas like this one, tied to neuropsychology and tested with technology now available, such as fMRI machines and virtual reality.

Facing Death: Terror Management Theory

"Briefly describe the emotions that the thought of your own death arouses in you." These are the instructions participants often receive when they are in a study about terror management theory, the idea that an awareness of our own eventual mortality terrifies us, leading us to cling to comforting beliefs and values (see Chapter 8; Pyszczynski et al., 1996, 1999, 2015). The usual experimental manipulation is to randomly assign some participants to write an essay about death, while other participants write about something also potentially painful and unpleasant but not life-ending (usually, the topic is dental pain).

Results across many studies show that people reminded of their own mortality respond in a variety of ways that appear to bring them comfort, usually by making life seem meaningful and important. This includes increased belief in religious faith, amplified commitment to personal relationships, and greater endorsement of cultural values. Studies have been done outside of lab settings as well, in which people's values and opinions become more extreme when they are reminded of death simply because they are standing next to a funeral home (Greenberg et al., 2008).

How does this benefit us, exactly? Awareness of our own mortality—and just a little bit of fear of death—can motivate us to have better physical health, live up to our own best standards for life, be more open-minded, and even give to charity (Vail et al., 2012). The COVID-19 pandemic made mortality more salient for many, with one study of emerging adults from India finding there were benefits such as increased focus on health maintenance and pursuing career goals (Paul & Vasudevan, 2021). In short, reminders of death help us make the best out of life—they motivate us to "have lives that are meaningful and significant" (Greenberg et al., 2014, p. 86).

PSYCHOLOGY AND OUR CURIOUS WORLD

Love, Death, and Pirates: "Our Flag Means Death"

iStock.com/Gwengoat

This illustration is of Captain Blackbeard, a famous pirate, drawn for a book about piracy in the 1700s. Blackbeard, whose real name was Edward Teach, lived from about 1680–1718. He quickly grew to fame in his time for his success and fearsome appearance, apparently in part due to tying lit fuses under his hat so his head would smoke when he attacked. At the same time in history, Stede Bonnet became famous as "The Gentleman Pirate." A wealthy landowner, Bonnet left his life of luxury to take up piracy. They met when Bonnet had to surrender his ship to Blackbeard due to Bonnet's lack of experience—but for a time, they worked together on a ship called *Queen Anne's Revenge.*

The HBO comedy series *Our Flag Means Death* imagines what their relationship might have been if Blackbeard and Bonnet had fallen in love during their time together. The show features many LGBTQ+ characters and storylines, as well as highlighting both the advantages and disadvantages of love, mortality salience, and a life of piracy. ●

Empathy

Finally, emotions may help us relate to others. **Empathy** is the tendency to feel what we perceive another person or animal is feeling. Emotional contagion happens in a variety of ways, such as mimicking the expressions, postures, and vocal tones of people around us (Ireland & Pennebaker, 2010). Moods appear to spread through groups (Totterdell et al., 1998).

Empathy also happens from one person to another, and it provides many benefits. For example, physicians and nurses with higher levels of individual empathy provide better care for their patients (Malbois & Hurst-Majno, 2023). Empathy also helps occupational therapists manage relationships with clients (de Klerk et al., 2023). Individuals with higher empathy show lower xenophobia and prejudice toward people from other cultures (Huisman, 2023).

Some psychologists suggest more specific types of empathy. For example, *cognitive empathy* refers to being able to understand someone else's mental state by imagining how they feel and by recognizing their emotions and perspective. In contrast, *affective empathy* is actually experiencing that emotional state—feeling it personally (Pang et al., 2022). The difference might translate into important outcomes. For example, some research suggests that certain kinds of criminals might specifically lack affective empathy but not cognitive empathy. Perhaps this is why they can *pretend* to get along with people well enough to con them, but then be comfortable harming others without remorse (Blair et al., 1996; Dolan & Fullam, 2004; Richell et al., 2003).

Empathy: The tendency to feel what we perceive another person or animal is feeling.

So the lack of empathy clearly causes harm. It also seems fairly clear that there are a lot of benefits to having empathy, even if it occasionally means that we feel uncomfortable when we sense others' pain. Empathy increases likeness and helps us bond with each other, and it is a driver of several positive mental and physical health outcomes (Chartrand & van Baaren, 2009; Worley, 2023). Higher empathy is also associated with motivation for engaging with global crises (Gates & Curwood, 2023). Empathy from teachers and professors toward students encourages learning in the classroom, and students can tell when it's sincere (Wynn et al., 2023). We hope the same is true regarding empathy from authors of psychology textbooks. ●

Sage Vantage⤲   Practice what you learn in **Knowledge Check 11.4**

CHAPTER REVIEW

Learning Objectives Summary

11.1   How do psychologists define and study motivation?

>> **LO 11.1   Compare and contrast theories of motivation based on instincts, drive reduction, optimal arousal, incentives, self-determination, and a hierarchy of needs.**

Instinct theory suggests that we're motivated to engage in behaviors that help us survive and reproduce. Drive reduction theory says we're motivated to maintain physiological homeostasis. Optimal arousal theory says peak performance is achieved when we have a medium level of physiological arousal. Incentive theory says we're motivated to get rewards and avoid punishments. Self-determination theory suggests we have three needs (autonomy, competence, and relatedness). Maslow's hierarchy of needs says that we prioritize our needs in order from physiological to safety/security, belongingness, esteem, and finally to self-actualization.

11.2   How does the psychology of motivation affect everyday life?

>> **LO 11.2   Identify and explain examples of motivation, as well as various related subfields of psychology for work, school, and sports.**

Hunger and eating is a good example of a motivation that comes from biological, psychological, and sociocultural factors. While obesity is a global concern, so are eating disorders and body shaming. A lot of research indicates that positive outcomes are more likely when behavior comes from intrinsic motivation (doing something because an activity is inherently pleasurable) instead of extrinsic motivation (doing something for an external reward). Applied areas of psychology such as industrial/organizational, school, and sport psychology offer interesting careers.

11.3   How do psychologists define and study emotion?

>> **LO 11.3   Compare and contrast theories of emotion, including James–Lange, Cannon–Bard, Schachter–Singer, and cognitive appraisal.**

James–Lange suggested that emotions occur after our body physiologically responds to an environmental trigger. Cannon–Bard added that the environmental trigger can cause both a physiological response and an emotional response that are essentially simultaneous but separate. Schachter–Singer's "two-factor" theory said that emotional responses are interpretations of both the body's physiological response and a cognitive label of contextual cues from the situation. Lazarus's cognitive–mediational model suggested that sometimes, the body's physiological response can happen last, after a cognitive label and emotional experience.

11.4   What are important research findings related to the psychology of emotion?

>> **LO 11.4   Explain psychology research on emotional expression, including cultural differences and lie detection, and on how emotions might benefit us.**

While research from the "universality hypothesis" suggests that between 4 and 12 emotions may be expressed and recognized in similar ways around the world in terms of facial expressions, more nuanced emotions vary by culture in what are called "display rules." Research is mixed on whether people are reliable at picking up on other people's attempts at deception. Finally, there are many advantages and disadvantages to emotions; advantages include survival circuits (specific neural pathways that help survival), motivation to make life meaningful, and empathy.

CRITICAL THINKING QUESTIONS

1. Many students are motivated to maintain "streaks" on social media apps like Snapchat. Evaluate this behavior using several of the theories of motivation discussed in the chapter.

2. Look again at Maslow's hierarchy of needs pyramid. Note that he suggests that "love and belonging" needs are a more fundamental need (a higher priority) than "esteem" needs. Do you agree? Do you think that people will prioritize relationships with other people before their view of themselves? Another debate about Maslow's hierarchy is that it doesn't explain why some people choose to sacrifice material goods (food, security) for art. In other words, some people would rather be "starving artists" if it means pursuing their dreams. How do you explain this kind of person? Do they negate Maslow's theory, or can they be incorporated into his theory? Explain your views.

3. Write three questions you think measure intrinsic and extrinsic motivation within academic majors at your college or university. Then, poll students at your school. Make a table showing your results. What kinds of patterns did you find? Analyze the results, discussing what kinds of patterns you found, as well as the potential limitations of your study based on things like sample size or other limitations of your procedure. Make sure to check with your course instructor to see if you need to get ethical approval before you do this activity.

4. This chapter mentioned three subfields of psychology: industrial/organizational, school, and sport. Do some online research to identify (a) what kind of education or licensure is usually required for people in those careers, (b) what the job market is like (are there current job openings in your area or on online job websites?), and (c) what salaries are like for those careers. Based on your information, are you interested in internships or careers in these subfields? Why or why not?

5. What is on your "bucket list"—your list of major accomplishments you'd like to achieve before you die? Identify at least five major goals you have and why these goals are important to you. After you make your list, analyze whether each goal is ultimately based on intrinsic or extrinsic motivation.

KEY TERMS

Achievement motivation, 344
Body shaming, 341
Cannon–Bard theory of emotion, 350
Curiosity, 346
Display rules, 356
Drive reduction theory, 331
Duchenne smile, 357
Duping delight, 357
Eating disorders, 339
Emotion, 329
Empathy, 359
Extrinsic motivation, 341
Facial feedback hypothesis, 349
Homeostasis, 331
Incentive theory, 334
Industrial/organizational psychology, 345
Instinct theory, 331

Intrinsic motivation, 341
James–Lange theory of emotion, 349
Lazarus cognitive–mediational theory of emotion, 353
Maslow's hierarchy of needs, 335
Misattribution of arousal, 353
Motivation, 329
Obesity, 339
Overjustification effect, 343
Schachter–Singer theory of emotion, 351
School psychology, 345
Self-actualization, 336
Self-determination theory, 334
Sport psychology, 345
Survival circuits, 358
Two-factor theory of emotion, 351
Universality hypothesis, 355

iStock.com/piovesempre

12

Cognition and Intelligence

Getting involved is essential.

You might have gotten that advice from friends and family about how to succeed in college. With that in mind, imagine you attend the Involvement Fair, where campus clubs have tables set up to describe what they do and recruit members. The Adventure Club can help you meet people outside of your major—and it moves you a bit beyond your comfort zone.

Six others signed up for the first event: The Great Escape (room). There's only one spot left, so you read the description: "Escape rooms are interactive adventures where your group is locked in a room and becomes immersed in a story. You have 60 minutes to explore the room, spot clues, make decisions, work on puzzles, communicate with your group, and use your smarts." Sounds intimidating, but it's only an hour. And it could be fun—especially if you get out.

After reading this chapter, you will get answers to several questions you've been curious about:

Have You Ever Wondered?

12.1 What is cognition?

12.2 How do we approach reasoning and decision-making, and how do we get it wrong?

12.3 How do we approach problem-solving, and how do we get it wrong?

12.4 How does our language relate to cognition?

12.5 What does it mean to be "smart"?

12.6 What is IQ, how has it been tested, and what are the issues with its use?

Learning Objectives

LO 12.1 Describe how mental representations, concepts, categories, prototypes, and schemas relate to thinking.

LO 12.2 Compare and contrast approaches to reasoning and decision-making.

LO 12.3 Compare and contrast problem-solving approaches.

LO 12.4 Explain the link between language and cognition.

LO 12.5 Analyze the key theories of intelligence and its association with creativity.

LO 12.6 Summarize the history, calculation, outcomes, and controversies related to IQ.

COGNITION

Have You Ever Wondered?
12.1 What is cognition?

Cognition: The process by which we focus on ideas, remember them, and work with them, involving decision-making, problem-solving, language, perception, and memory.

>> **LO 12.1** Describe how mental representations, concepts, categories, prototypes, and schemas relate to thinking.

You're going to be impressed by how wonderful your brain is.

We've used the word *cognition* several times in this book already, but let's really stop now to precisely define it. Psychologists refer to "thinking" as **cognition**: the process of focusing, remembering, and working with ideas. Cognition involves decision-making, problem-solving, and language, as well as perception, consciousness, and memory. It's not easy to study thinking, but when psychologists discovered ways to do it (in the 1950s), the effects were so far-reaching that it became known as "the cognitive revolution" in psychology.

Thoughts are *mental representations* that depict objects, memories, and ideas. For example, prior to stopping at the Adventure Club table, you had no idea what an escape room was—but the verbal description provided a string of clues that enabled you to imagine it. For example, the word *escape* induces several mental representations, including a convict fleeing from prison. These mental representations can originate from words or from visual images (e.g., a key, an open lock, or a picture of a prison cell with an open door). Visual images aren't exact replicas but can become icons or symbols, like the ones for your phone apps.

Concepts

Organization makes information easier to use.

New ideas consume a lot of mental energy as you try to understand and relate them to existing ideas. You organize incoming information into concepts that classify related images, ideas, information, events, and objects (Tversky & Hemenway, 1984). For example, you have a concept for what constitutes a "room." Those mental representations are varied (e.g., a bedroom, classroom, living room), but you can recognize shared characteristics of a typical room such as four walls, furniture that suggests its purpose, and at least one doorway.

> **Concepts:** The groupings or categories you use to classify related images, ideas, information, events, or objects based on their shared similarities.

Concepts such as "room" organize new information into useful categories. For example, each of these are also rooms: hearth, keeping, media, bunk, and parlor. Even if you have never heard of these room types, knowing that they fit within the concept of "room" gives you a way to start thinking about them (Mervis & Rosch, 1981).

Abstract concepts can be more difficult to organize than physical spaces and objects—yet, your brain still quickly makes sense of them. How? Two theories help us understand the psychological organization of concepts.

Prototypes

The first centers on the idea of a *prototype*, the best, shining example or representation of a concept (Rosch, 1975). We use prototypes as an ideal or benchmark that summarizes an entire category.

For example, when you consider the concept of a room, the prototype that comes to mind might be a living room or bedroom. All rooms fit the concept, but some room examples are better fits than others. For example, a "gift wrapping room" might seem a little weird (not to mention a bit bougie).

Your personal experience and memories will shape your prototype of a "room." If you are living on campus, then your prototypical room might be a dorm room or a classroom. When you were a kid, it could have been your bedroom. Concepts are flexible because your thinking changes with your experience.

The Exemplar Model

The second theory about how we form concepts is the *exemplar model*, which suggests each example within a group or category is a good representation of the concept (Nosofsky et al., 1992; Smith & Medin, 1981). Exemplars do not try to summarize the entire category. Instead, they use our memories of specific instances (i.e., exemplars) to make sense of the overall concept (Figure 12.1). For example, when you think of a room, you rely on all your memories of rooms to settle on what a room is—a kind of combined or smooshed together average of all the types that come to mind. Here, each example in the category is considered equally representative.

FIGURE 12.1

Theories of Cognition

What is a bird? Compare the prototype and exemplar theories.

Prototype Approach   **Exemplar Approach**

iStock.com/Elena Istomina

Is a hot dog a type of sandwich? How did you decide yes or no?

iStock.com/Haris Calkic

Categories

Some concepts just aren't clear-cut.

A "room" seems like an easy-to-understand concept. But is an elevator a room? It's got four walls, a door, and a purpose. How about an outdoor gazebo? A tent? Concepts get fuzzier around the edges when their categorization is unclear or if the categorization changes with context (Haack, 1996). But based on your representations of other rooms, you could still arrive at a determination.

When you meet up with your group at "The Great Escape," there are warm-up "conversation starter" cards for you to try while waiting. They're all interesting, but because you're a bit hungry, you pick one called "You Think You Know Food," which asks you to answer simple questions about foods.

For example, which of the following are sandwiches?

- Peanut butter and jelly
- Hoagie
- Panini
- Lettuce wrap
- Hot dog
- Taco

The conversation has started and it's clear that "sandwich" is a fuzzier concept than you thought. Eventually, you land on a shared concept whereby anything that bread wraps is a sandwich. Score one for the hot dog sandwich.

You flip the card over and see two more questions, "Is cereal a soup?" and "What is your team's name?" For team names, you consider three options: "Who-dinis" "The Escape Goats," or "Mission Cognition." Because everyone in the group comes from majors that focus on cognition (e.g., computer science, linguistics, mathematics, neuroscience, philosophy, and psychology), you settle on Mission Cognition as your team's name.

Part of what makes some concepts fuzzy is that every concept includes numerous individual characteristics. Some characteristics are shared with adjacent concepts (e.g., paninis and PB&J both used sliced bread), while others are unique (e.g., paninis are typically served warm, and PB&J isn't). There's a lot to manage. Thankfully, we organize the interrelation of concepts in a meaningful way by using hierarchical organization.

Any concept could be an instance of a broader category and have several subcategories under it. A sandwich is a subcategory of the common lunch foods, and under sandwich, you could imagine subcategories related to sliced bread, split bread/buns, and wraps. These hierarchical structures raise a larger point: We rarely use thoughts in isolation because individual concepts aren't terribly useful.

The sandwich category encompasses a wide variety of subcategories.

iStock.com/robynmac

Schemas

Combining concepts is an efficient way to organize your thoughts.

Human thinking automatically groups related concepts into larger *schemas*. We defined schemas in the chapter on memory (Chapter 10); you'll recall that the term refers to conceptual frameworks organized into clusters of knowledge that help you make sense of new information. You combine concepts into schemas about yourself, others, social situations, and events. Like concepts, schemas help you efficiently process large amounts of information.

For example, "The Great Escape" has three different themed rooms: London Library, Dig It, and Cockpit Chaos. Although you have never been in any of these escape rooms, your schemas shape your thoughts and perceptions about them. The group feels like they know more about libraries than archaeological digs or cockpits, so the London Library room is most appealing. But cockpits might be easier for a rural Alaskan student who learned to fly a plane before driving a car. Your culture, past experiences, learning, and memory influence how schemas are both unique to you yet also shared by others.

Schemas make thinking faster and easier—but with a downside: more errors. Combining related concepts into schemas can modify your memory, especially as events you've witnessed recede into the past and are absorbed by schemas (Kleider et al., 2008). This is a serious problem when juries rely on eyewitness testimonies in court. For example, when a group of eyewitnesses to a fatal shooting in Sweden recounted the event, they made consistent mistakes (Dahl et al., 2018). This was likely due to the shooting having atypical elements that were inconsistent with witness's schema-based expectations of what a typical shooting involves.

It's also important to recognize how schemas about other people may influence us. For example, research shows that something as simple as a person's name (e.g., Javier) was associated with implicit bias from online instructors, despite those instructors believing they were warm and accepting (Conaway & Bethune, 2015). A first name does not tell us much about a person, but it does activate broader schemas (e.g., stereotypes, a form of schema).

Brain Training

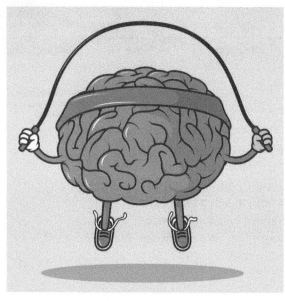

If you could improve your thinking by training your brain, would you?

iStock.com/Pedro Fernandes

Faster. Stronger. Better.

It's why you go to the gym. Run to get faster, weight-train to get stronger, both of which improve your health. If it's good enough for your body, what about your mind? For just a few dollars, you can download a brain-training app to your phone that exercises your brain through a series of fun games. Allegedly. Boosting brain power has clear appeal, but this is just another example of why it's important to examine the science before believing bold claims.

People believe in brain training. Surveys show that many people believe games and apps can boost memory, attention, and mood, as well as improve thinking (Sala et al., 2018; Torous et al., 2016). And why not? The apps boast millions of users and claim to be backed by science. There is some support. For example, a study of 4,715 people revealed that those who did brain training exhibited better memory, improved problem-solving, and quicker processing speeds, compared to those who did crossword puzzles (Hardy et al., 2015). Sounds good, but the study's authors were employed by a brain-training company, who also funded the study.

Other studies aren't as supportive. A review of existing brain-training research found little support for many alleged benefits of brain training (Simons et al., 2016). Even further, a meta-analysis (a systematic review of several studies on a given topic) found that brain training had minimal impact on cognitive skills (Sala & Gobet, 2019). Some of the studies showing results for the apps incorporated flawed methods (such as not using random assignment to groups). We all want to work smarter, not harder, but brain training is probably not the best way to enhance your thinking. ●

Sage Vantage   Practice what you learn in **Knowledge Check 12.1**

REASONING AND DECISION-MAKING

? Have You Ever Wondered?
12.2 How do we approach reasoning and decision-making, and how do we get it wrong?

>> LO 12.2 Compare and contrast approaches to reasoning and decision-making.

Ready or not, the next 10 years of your life are full of consequential life decisions.

Most of the big ones are probably in the not-too-distant future, such as what to major in. Learning how to make high-quality decisions is a complex skill with no guarantees—but you can load the decision dice in your favor.

Reasoning

Some thoughts are the result of random curiosities.

"Why do we drive on parkways, and park on driveways?" "Am I drinking enough water?" While these musings qualify as cognition, they're not what cognitive scientists typically study when they examine thinking. Instead, those scientists are more focused on **reasoning**, the purposeful use of facts and available information to form coherent thoughts, draw conclusions, and make progress toward goals (Lakin & Kell, 2020).

In an escape room, your goal is simple: Get out. The steps you take require reasoning. There are two key approaches to reasoning and generating ideas: inductive and deductive reasoning. The key difference is your starting point.

Reasoning: The purposeful use of facts and available information to form coherent thoughts, draw conclusions, and make progress toward goals.

Inductive Reasoning

As you enter the London Library room, you notice a quotation fastened to the door from Sir Arthur Conan Doyle's character Sherlock Holmes: *It is a capital mistake to theorize before you have all the evidence. It biases the judgment.* These words of wisdom advocate for *inductive reasoning,* which is a line of reasoning that uses the available facts to build a theory (Goel & Waechter, 2018). This "bottom-up" approach involves making generalizations from specifics. In the escape room game, an inductive reasoning approach to the London Library begins with a systematic search of the room to gather clues and information that you use to build a theory about the best course of action that will allow you escape in the next 60 minutes.

Deductive Reasoning

With the clock starting to count down, you need to be quick. Here, top-down *deductive reasoning* is using experience and existing knowledge to form a theory that allows you to interpret subsequent information and observations. For example, you use deductive reasoning by surmising that all libraries have books, and since this is a library room, the books are probably important and you start looking there. If your idea about books' importance is correct, all is well. But if that assumption was wrong, you'll waste time. The countdown clock is already at 58:32.

What's the best strategy for finding the combination to this lock?

iStock.com/webphotographer

Decision-Making

You must decide the best approach.

Inside the escape room, a desk drawer has a spinning combination lock requiring three numbers (this one goes from 0 to 9 for each spot), so you decide to work on that. **Decision-making** is the process by which you assess alternatives and select the best option (Beach & Connolly, 2005). Now you must decide the best way to open it. As with reasoning, there are a few ways to approach it.

Decision-making: The process by which you assess alternatives and select the best option.

Algorithms

An **algorithm** is a step-by-step procedure that systematically attempts all possible solutions. It will always work, eventually, but it takes time. With a typical three-number combination lock, you would start by trying 0-0-0, moving on to 0-0-1, then 0-0-2, and so on, using every permutation up to 9-9-9. Feeling the time pressure of the escape room, you decide an algorithm approach to the lock isn't going to work, so you consider other strategies.

Algorithm: A step-by-step procedure that systematically attempts all possible solutions.

Intuition or "Going With Your Gut"

Intuition: An instant sense of understanding that does not require reasoning.

Sometimes you just have a feeling about the right answer. In these cases, you're relying on your **intuition**, sometimes called "going with your gut."

According to the *somatic marker theory,* a gut feeling or instinct is an emotional reaction that manifests itself in the body and influences decisions and behavior (Damasio, 2008). You've probably met people who instantly made you feel an uneasy, nervous bodily sensation (i.e., a somatic marker). That sensation affects your decision-making and behaviors (such as avoiding the person). Knowing that you're not truly trapped in the room (it's just for fun) helps you manage your somatic markers in the escape room.

You tend to notice and remember when your intuition is correct and ignore, explain, or just plain forget when your intuition lets you down, giving you the impression that your intuition is right more than it really is. As your group members shout out gut feeling combinations like 9-1-1 and 1-2-3, each is wrong. You haven't solved the problem yet.

Heuristics

Heuristic: A guideline, mental shortcut, or "rule of thumb" designed to quicken thinking while making decisions.

The algorithmic approach of trying every combination takes too long. The intuitive approach feels haphazard, more like blind luck. But there is another strategy that people often use because it is convenient and relatively effective. A **heuristic** is a guideline, a mental shortcut or "rule of thumb" that helps decision-making. When you visit a new restaurant and need to use the restroom, there is always a moment of trepidation where you wonder where it is. You could ask the server, but you could also use a heuristic. Often, because of how buildings are constructed with their plumbing, the restroom will be adjacent to the kitchen. You also know it will probably be tucked into a back corner. That little shortcut saves you time and at least gets you started on finding the solution when you need it. Examples of heuristics are discussed more in the next section of this chapter.

How do you use heuristics in your escape room? Everyone searches the room for a set of three numbers or three objects. There's an old grandfather clock showing the time is 4:20—but those numbers don't open the lock. Another student notices the desk has a neat stack of three books, a pencil holder with eight pencils, and five pads of paper fanned out. Entering the combination 3-8-5 springs the lock open. The countdown clock now reads 46:22. But decision-making isn't always so easy.

Just how common are shark attacks? If you can easily think of examples, does that mean they are common?

iStock.com/ARTYuSTUDIO

Decision Aversion

Sometimes we experience *decision aversion,* or a reluctance to choose among available options (Beattie et al., 1994). Common reasons for decision aversion include

- Not wanting to feel responsible for a bad outcome
- Worrying about being fair with others
- Regretting a suboptimal choice

Decision aversion inspires some leaders to "pass the buck" by delegating responsibilities to others (Steffel et al., 2016). For example, if you were a regional manager of a paper company and had to decide on the best health care plan for your employees, you'd appoint a committee or let someone else pick (like the assistant to the regional manager) so you can avoid responsibility and blame. Decisions are aversive when the stakes are high and you think you may get it wrong.

Why We Make the Wrong Decisions

Most of us have made our fair share of bad decisions.

It could be a haircut (that mullet was not a good look), the person you never should have dated, the job you should have taken, or food you shouldn't have eaten with the already "expired by" date. Still, by learning about decision-making flaws, you can make better decisions next time. Back in the escape room, the desk is unlocked and reveals a poem:

To find your next clue,

Here's what to do.

Correctly answer the question below,

Time is short, so don't be slow.

In a world full of frights,

You'll want to get this right.

To avoid more distress,

Identify the leading cause of death in the U.S.:

1) Car Crashes, 2) Heart Disease, 3) Plane Crashes 4) Shark Attacks

A correct answer leads to your salvation in a book,

To find what you seek, look in every cranny and nook.

Overconfidence

Overconfidence is a common problem: We give ourselves too much credit for what we think we know, how well we know it, and for our good judgment (Moore & Healy, 2008). Ironically, the *Dunning–Kruger effect*, displayed in Figure 12.2, suggests that confidence is most likely when knowledge is either particularly high (we're an expert) or particularly low (we actually know almost nothing; Kruger & Dunning, 1999).

Overconfidence can also result from feeling a sense of power or control over an outcome (Fast et al., 2012). When those who felt powerful made decisions and predictions, they were more confident, despite being less accurate than those with less power. Power enhances perceived capability but undermines performance. So, you may not want the Adventure Club's president to make too many unilateral decisions in the escape room.

FIGURE 12.2

The Dunning–Kruger Effect

People are really confident when they know either a lot or almost nothing.

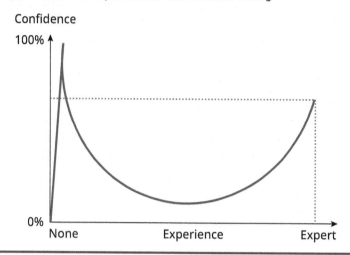

Source: Kruger and Dunning (1999).

Availability Heuristic

Many decisions are based on perceived probability of various outcomes using the **availability heuristic**, a guideline to how common something is based on how easily examples or cues come to mind (Tversky & Kahneman, 1973).

Consider the causes of death question from the escape room poem. How many examples do you know of people who have died of shark bites, car or plane crashes, or heart disease? If you are young, you may know more people who have been in car accidents than people with heart disease, and so choose car accidents. People also mistakenly think shark attacks and plane crashes are much more common than they really are, because when they happen, they get a lot of media attention. Yet, heart disease is consistently the number one cause of death (Kochanek et al., 2020). Here, the availability heuristic can lead you astray.

Representativeness Heuristic

Armed with the right answer, your group starts looking for "salvation in a book" related to heart disease. Everyone immediately gravitates to the large bookshelf. After all, what better nook is there for a book? Relying on a category's best example means you're using the **representativeness heuristic** (Tversky & Kahneman, 1972). But it doesn't always work. Some books are not on bookshelves, and none of the books on the bookshelf relate to heart disease.

Representativeness encourages you to focus too much on one type of example and ignore other pertinent information. Often you need to think "outside the box" by relying on less common examples. In this case, what else could be considered a nook? Perhaps a recess in a wall. Though the other side of the room has an alcove with a glass vase full of junk, it isn't big enough to fit an entire book.

Just then, you realize you're doing it again. You're allowing representativeness to cloud your decision-making. In fact, there is more than one kind of book. You notice the glass vase contains a matchbook with a heart. When you open it, where the matches would be, it says, "Have a heart, call your cardiologist at 795.03." Odd, because that

Availability heuristic: A guideline or mental shortcut that something must be common if examples easily come to mind.

Representativeness heuristic: A guideline or mental shortcut that depends on the best example of a category that comes to mind.

isn't a normal phone number. Now that you're embracing thinking outside of the box, you suggest it may be a book's call number. Sure enough, a scan of the bookshelf finds the book *Gambling Secrets From Monte Carlo* with the tag 795.03.

The countdown clock now reads 34:18.

The Gambler's Fallacy

A bookmark in the book opens to a page describing *the gambler's fallacy:* the mistaken belief that because something has previously happened less frequently, it is now more likely (Croson & Sundali, 2005). The book depicts a gambler spinning a roulette wheel marked with equal numbers of red and black spaces. After five consecutive red spins, the fallacy is assuming the next spin is more likely to land black.

It makes intuitive sense because if red and black have equal 50/50 chances, then many red spins in a row must mean black is due. However, chance has no memory. Each spin is its own independent event with no influence on the next spin.

In the margin, you see a handwritten note that reads: Young Einstein flips a coin 10 times. The first two times it lands tails, then lands heads the next eight times. On the 11th flip, what is most likely?

A) More likely tails because there have been more heads

B) More likely heads because this coin gives more heads

C) Impossible to say, other than it's a 50/50 chance of heads or tails

There are also three light switches, labeled ABC. Based on your answers to the quiz, you flip the C switch. The room instantly goes dark except for a glowing message on the far wall, "To progress, seek wisdom all around the world." Just as suddenly, the lights click back on.

If a coin comes up heads four times in a row, it's more likely to be tails on the next flip. Right? Wrong . . . that's the gambler's fallacy.

iStock.com/Jonathan Mauer

Law of Small Numbers

Taylor, the linguistics major in the group, explains how in a previous escape room, a wall message was a decoy. Really, they just needed to press on the wall. Sounds promising, but you must be careful to not fall for the *law of small numbers,* or the mistaken belief that limited or small samples represent the broader population (Tversky & Kahneman, 1971). That is, Taylor's experience is one example that may not generalize to how all escape rooms work. With a limited sample size, it could have been a fluke. This also is why psychology studies usually try to get as many people in the sample as possible; the more data we have, the better off we usually are.

Survivorship Bias

Relying too much on Taylor's suggestion of what worked before also has second problem. We may be succumbing to *survivorship bias,* giving too much credit to successes while undervaluing failures (Smith, 2014). Perhaps you've heard examples of successful individuals who never graduated college. Yes, it's true that Ellen DeGeneres, Ralph Lauren, Oprah Winfrey, and Mark Zuckerberg never got a college degree and have done well in their lives, at least financially. However, for most people, completing college leads to more opportunities for success and higher lifetime earnings. Focusing on exceptional successes can encourage bad decisions.

Confirmation Bias and Belief Perseverance

In the escape room, everyone is now convinced that the "around the world" message means they should check all around the room. You think differently and suggest that "around the world" might relate to maps or a geography book. However, your fellow group members are convinced about what they think they know. They are exhibiting *belief perseverance*, holding on to existing beliefs despite minimal or even contrary evidence (Festinger et al., 1956).

Like many of these mental shortcuts, belief perseverance is tightly connected to *confirmation bias*, which occurs when we seek out and prefer information that agrees with preconceived notions and then interpret information in a way that affirms existing beliefs (Nickerson, 1998). You've probably met people who strongly believe that their type of phone (e.g., iPhone or Android) is best—even after learning of the competitor's better features. That is because they seek out information that agrees with them (confirmation bias), while ignoring any facts that show their phone isn't the best.

You recognize that this might be happening to your group. Fortunately, you spot a globe covered in black smudges, and you do what everyone naturally does upon encountering a globe: You give it a spin. The smudges form letters. A faster spin reveals the message: "To learn more, check the screen by the door."

Framing and Anchoring

You tap the touchpad screen, which then reads, "Based on your progress you have an 80% chance of successfully escaping." Seems impressive until you realize you also have a 20% chance of not making it in time. Both percentages contain the same information, but somehow an 80% chance of success feels more encouraging than a 20% chance of failure. This is just one example of how *framing* influences how information is interpreted (Tversky & Kahneman, 1981).

Your starting point also influences decisions. We all rely on the *anchoring heuristic* where the original starting value exerts more influence than it should (Epley & Gilovich, 2006). We seldom drift very far from our initial decision. That first thought anchors even trivial decisions, especially when we are uncertain about the facts. For example, when participants in one study estimated vodka's freezing point, they anchored on water's freezing point of 32 degrees Fahrenheit. Vodka freezes at −20 (F) degrees, but participants' estimates clustered around 2 (F) degrees, much closer to the irrelevant information they knew about when water freezes.

The solution to anchoring is to not rely on initial information and instead seek out new and better data. With seeking in mind, you decide to focus on the most recent message: "To progress, seek wisdom all around the world." There must be more to it than a spinning globe. Perhaps it has to do with culture.

What temperature does vodka freeze at? Your knowledge about water's freezing point will likely anchor (and therefore might bias) your guess.

iStock.com/Miguel Tamayo Diaz

Culture's Role in Reasoning and Decision-Making

Culture influences how we think.

Culture is powerful partly because we take it for granted. Living, even briefly, in another culture helps you understand how profoundly culture influences decision-making, social structures, the size of social networks, and how people interact. For example, people from countries traditionally considered "Western" focus on the individual when reasoning about a decision, while those from traditionally Eastern cultures prioritize the group's welfare (Weber & Morris, 2010; Yates & de Oliviera, 2016):

- Individuals from Eastern cultures (e.g., Asia) were able to see both sides of contradictory proverbs (e.g., "keep your friends close but your enemies closer" and "beware of your friends not your enemies"). They also were more open to compromise between the contradictory positions.

- By contrast, individuals from Western cultures (e.g., U.S., Canadian, European) had a harder time understanding what the proverbs might mean (Peng & Nisbett, 1999; Yates & de Oliviera, 2016).

Culture can also encourage certain decision-making approaches. In one study, French and Danish decision-makers emphasized different parts of the decision-making process (Schramm-Nielsen, 2001):

- Danish managers focused on key pieces of information to make quicker decisions.

- French managers reviewed all potential options trying to reach complete certainty.

In a different study, managers in China were more willing to trust others and make risky decisions because of their large social networks (Weber & Morris, 2010). China's culture also provided people with higher status if they produced riskier decisions.

In this escape room, you're all from similar cultural backgrounds. That can make problem-solving more difficult if the next challenge in the escape room requires a solution that doesn't fit with the usual cultural habits or assumptions; it's a good example of why diversity helps most situations.

Practice what you learn in **Knowledge Check 12.2**

Sage Vantage🐦

PROBLEM-SOLVING STRATEGIES

>> LO 12.3 Compare and contrast problem-solving approaches.

You are a natural problem solver.

So were your ancestors (or you wouldn't be here). They encountered and solved some big problems: finding food, preparing it properly, avoiding predators, managing injuries, maintaining group harmony, and so on. Each challenge required a resolution. **Problem-solving** involves the mental processes used to assess and resolve complex problems and uncertain situations to reach a goal (Mayer, 2013). While it is like decision-making, problem-solving is a broader undertaking in which decision-making is a single step or action taken during the larger process (Table 12.1). Decision-making is like taking each step, while problem-solving is going up the entire staircase. You'll often need to make several correct decisions to solve a problem.

Have You Ever Wondered?
12.3 How do we approach problem-solving, and how do we get it wrong?

Problem-solving: The mental processes we use to assess and figure out complex issues or work out unclear situations to reach a goal.

TABLE 12.1

Distinguishing Decision-Making and Problem-Solving

DECISION-MAKING	PROBLEM-SOLVING
Analyze information to determine the best course of action from many possibilities	A series of choices and decisions leading to a solution for a complex problem or to reach a goal
Narrow	Broad and complex
Focused on single choice	Includes multiple steps
Deciding between known options	Dealing with known and unknown possibilities
Often one step within problem-solving	Usually requires decision-making

Problem-Solving Strategies

There's more than one way to cook an egg, catch a rabbit, make a bed, or bake a cake.

Much like decision-making, there are general strategies for problem-solving. Let's take a look—quickly, because the countdown clock reads 19:02.

Algorithmic Approaches

A *subgoal analysis* breaks a large problem into smaller steps (Ensen, 1987). You can't complete your college degree all at once. You must take it semester by semester, step by step, subgoal by subgoal. You probably have certain required classes in your major, perhaps in a certain order. You might have additional requirements outside of your major (often called "general education" courses) or things do to each year, like a senior thesis. Break each step down into smaller goals you then link together, to motivate your behavior.

To help identify subgoals, you might use a *backward search* by starting at the end and working back toward where you are right now. Not sure about a career? Find someone whose life and career you admire and ask them how they got there. They'll happily identify all the subgoals for you. Not sure what courses to take next semester? When you identify a career or social problem you'd like to solve, work backward from there to determine the right degree and major, and ultimately what courses you should take.

Working backward in the escape room leads you to consider going out the door you came in. Unfortunately, on this side, it's a sheet of flat metal. No handle, no lock, no way out. There must be another door. A *means-end analysis* focuses your attention on the goal and the best means of getting to it (Newell & Simon, 1972). However, you aren't sure what those steps might be.

Trial and Error

You and the Mission Cognition team fall back on perhaps the most basic problem-solving strategy, *trial and error*. You're hoping to get lucky using this quantity over quality tactic. It might work, but it also could waste time. As your group canvasses the room testing the wall for a secret switch, you're reminded of something Albert Einstein once said: "Insanity is doing the same thing over and over again and expecting a different result." With time running short, trial and error doesn't seem promising.

Restructuring by Finding an Analogy

So, you try something different: restructuring the problem so you can look at it in a new way, hoping to see new solutions (Fleck & Weisberg, 2013). You can do that by thinking of a similar or analogous situation to the current problem you're facing (Reeves & Weisberg, 1994). Analogical reasoning can also occur outside of your awareness (Gross & Greene, 2007) when a solution simply pops into your mind. You think of one: When your puppy was trapped in a playpen, she couldn't break through any of the walls—until she tried to go up instead of out.

Insight

That memory of your eager puppy sparks an *insight*, a sudden feeling of comprehension that leads to a solution (Chu & MacGregor, 2011). You usually must first work hard at solving a problem. But with insight, our mental lightbulb flicks on and the solution just comes to us. Your analogy has given your intuition something to work with.

In a classic study on insight in chimpanzees, Gestalt psychologist Wolfgang Köhler (1917/1925) placed bananas in a room where the chimps couldn't easily get to them. In one case, the bananas hung high from the ceiling in the middle of a room. Without any encouragement or external prompts, the chimps suddenly discovered that stacking boxes would allow them to grab the food. Their insight allowed them to reach their goal.

You have a similar problem. Your "a-ha" moment leads you to look up and discover a large balloon with a hoop attached nestled up on the 20-foot-tall ceiling. You look below and see a string poking out from under the rug. You pull on the string and a box underneath clicks open. It contains two paper clips, a feather, some coins, a large heavy iron key, and a bookmark wrapped in a bunch of string.

Imperfect Problem-Solving: Why We Get It Wrong

Sometimes the solution is obvious.

You have a key, and you're locked in a room. Clearly the key opens a lock that will spring you free. Or will it? No one has found a lock that matches the key. You're stuck.

The countdown clock now reads 17:13.

Functional Fixedness

Maybe you're looking at the objects in the box all wrong. Consider a classic study that provided participants with a box of tacks, a candle, and matches (Duncker, 1945). The participant's goal is to safely attach a burning candle to the wall. The most obvious starting point is to use the tacks to post the candle to the wall. But because the candle is round, it won't work. Another possibility is to use the matches to melt a side of the candle and stick the melted portion to the wall. While that may work, it isn't terribly safe.

Both solutions share the problem of functional fixedness, which occurs when we only consider the most common use of an object. Tacks are for puncturing and attaching items to something else. Matches are for creating fire, and candles are meant to be set aflame. All true, but also limiting because in the process, we forgot about the box holding the tacks. You could dump the tacks out, then tack the box to the wall and use it as a candle stand.

Interestingly, young children are less susceptible to functional fixedness because they haven't fully established objects' functions (German & Defeyter, 2000). If you can

Functional fixedness: Only considering an object's most common use.

The Broadway show *STOMP* broke free from functional fixedness to make percussive music and dance out of objects like garbage cans, buckets, and brooms.

Brad Barket/Stringer/Getty Images Entertainment/via Getty Images

be less rigid, it suggests new solutions. You reconsider the key's qualities and focus instead on its weight. That new function inspires you to tie the string to the key, then toss the key up to hook the balloon and pull it down. Free of functional fixedness, you unbend a paper clip and use the pointy end to pop the balloon, revealing a paper scrap inside that says "Complete the sequence: S-M-T-?-?-?-?".

Fixation

Huh? It's confusing because you're trying to determine what word starts with SMT. *Fixation* occurs when you focus too much on one aspect of a problem and fail to consider alternatives (Woodworth & Schlosberg, 1954). Fixation constrains thinking by providing a false sense of confidence (Storm & Hickman, 2015). Your initial solution gets in the way of thinking of novel solutions (Smith & Blankenship, 1991). To avoid this problem-solving trap in the escape room, you treat the letter sequence as an acronym. Counting . . . Months in a year? Zodiac signs? Days of the week? Yes! Sunday, Monday, Tuesday . . . etc. Great, but now what?

Mental Sets and the Power of Previous Experience

Mental set: The reliance on a strategy that previously worked to solve a similar problem.

Some parents were fond of saying, "If it ain't broke, don't fix it." True or not, we gravitate toward solutions that were successful in the past, relying on a **mental set** (also known as the *Einstellung effect*), or the reliance on a previously successful strategy to solve a similar problem (Luchins, 1942; Vallée-Tourangeau et al., 2011). Experience it for yourself in Figure 12.3. While sometimes helpful, sometimes mental sets can block creativity. Breaking your mental set worked earlier when the "book" clue turned out to be a matchbook.

Days of the week make you look at the desk's large date planner. Written in tiny faint handwriting is, *"Here in town, yearbook photos can be embarrassing so students 'opt in.' This year, 20% of the 800 eleventh- and twelfth-grade students opted in. The yearbook is on the shelf. If you randomly selected 110 people in the book, how many of them are unlisted?"* Instantly people start doing math, relying on their mental set. However, you realize it's a trick. Yearbooks only show who is listed, not who isn't. The answer is zero. You find a book with a strange call number of 000.00 and notice the subject of the book is language.

FIGURE 12.3

The Nine Dot Problem

Using no more than four lines, you must connect all nine dots by drawing straight lines (no curves) *without* picking up your pencil or pen. If you're able to avoid mental sets (simply drawing in lines along the rows or the columns), the solution will be easier to find. See the solution in Figure 12.6 at the end of the chapter.

LANGUAGE AND COGNITION

>> **LO 12.4** **Explain the link between language and cognition.**

"It's like an entirely different language."

That's a common phrase people utter when struggling to make sense of a confusing message. **Language** is a communication system consisting of symbols (usually words) and rules to systematically organize those symbols to convey information. As a result, language is generative, which means one set of finite rules is responsible for creating all sentences and linguistic expression.

Language Influences Thinking

Why are we talking about language in a chapter about thinking?

There is a long-held belief in **linguistic determinism** (also known as *linguistic relativity theory* or the *Sapir–Whorf hypothesis*), which suggests that the language structure you use dictates how you think (Hickmann, 2000).

Much of the support for linguistic determinism came from an interesting anecdote about the Inuit, who had more words for snow than others who live in less-snowbound environments (Nunberg, 1996). In other words, Inuits had separate words for fluffy snow, wet snow, snow in the air versus on the ground, and so on. The belief followed that language clearly dictates how we think about the world. If only we had more words for snow, we would start to appreciate all the subtleties and nuances that Inuits clearly saw.

Good story—but fake news. First, there isn't a single Inuit language. Second, within these several languages, the number of terms referring to snow is similar to the number in English (Pullum, 1991). Still, there is evidence that those in warmer climates have less linguistic differentiation of snow and ice (Regier et al., 2016). This suggests that the local context and needs do influence language use. Language is not necessary for thought; we know that infants and other animals lacking in linguistic abilities engage in intricate thought patterns (e.g., Coubart et al., 2014; Kelly & Lea, 2022).

Yet, language likely helps frame how we think. Language can reflect biases in one's culture and vice versa. For example, in work settings, men are more likely than women to be described as "mentors" and "leaders" (Stroi, 2020). "Western" cultures using English typically have words that shame women for having sex but praise men for the same behavior (e.g., "stud"), reflecting a double standard (Farvid et al., 2017). When people use language that reinforces a gender binary (e.g., "Hello, ladies and gentlemen" versus "Hello, everyone"), it perpetuates traditional views of gender (Bigler & Leaper, 2015).

Building Blocks of Language

You have to start somewhere.

The ideas expressed in every book, chapter, paragraph, poem, and sentence are built from basic units of language (see Figure 12.4). It begins with the raw sounds of language: *phonemes*. The "buh" sound in *book, bat,* and *bowl* is a phoneme. *Book* also has phonemes for the "oo" and "k" sounds.

Language groups phonemes into *morphemes*, the smallest unit of language that conveys meaning. *Book* is a single morpheme that combines several phonemes. The word *ebook* contains two morphemes, *e* and *book*, because each carries a unique meaning. Prefixes and suffixes are morphemes because they alter the original word's meaning (e.g., happy vs. unhappy). Put several morphemes together and you have a *lexicon*, or a collection of a language's morphemes.

Have You Ever Wondered?
12.4 How does our language relate to cognition?

Language: A communication system consisting of symbols (usually words) and rules to systematically organize those symbols to convey information.

Linguistic determinism: The theory that the language you use dictates your thoughts.

FIGURE 12.4

Basic Units of Language

Language conveys ideas based on several key pieces.

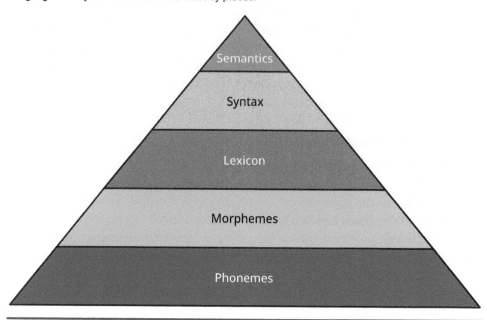

We use *syntax,* or how words combine, to create sentences and interpret them through *semantics,* which is the study of meaning within words (Fernández & Cairns, 2010). Grammar, the rules that guide word creation and sentence formation, helps you understand the differences between *their, they're,* and *there* or spoken sentences like, "If I marry Mary, all would be merry."

Language largely relies on written and spoken words, but it can also take other forms. For example, American Sign Language (ASL) is a system that relies on visual communication rather than auditory communication (Liddell & Johnson, 1989). Through a series of specific hand gestures, individuals communicate ideas, feelings, and information. Like other languages, American Sign Language has its own set of grammar rules.

Speaking of grammar, the language book in the escape room has a hidden compartment with six words: *SMART ARE WOW INCREDIBLY YOU SO.* Even if you never studied the rules of grammar, your brain still knows to rearrange the six words into a meaningful sentence: *"WOW, YOU ARE SO INCREDIBLY SMART."*

Acquiring Language

Language is complex, yet toddlers can do it.

Humans begin to acquire language early in their development. Babies can form phoneme sounds that they start to string together into babbling (e.g., ma and da become mama and dada). Around 1 year of age, children can create sounds meant to communicate meaning (i.e., morphemes) such as saying "more" or "no."

Two of these people are making gestures that might say "hi" while the third is a sign for "I love you." Language consists of layers of meaning.

iStock.com/kalig

Children's vocabulary grows quickly. However, their *receptive vocabulary* (what they understand) outpaces their *productive vocabulary* (what they can say; Webb, 2005). By age 3, children understand nearly 1,000 words.

Given this rapid proficiency of early language learning, it's easy to assume that you're built for language acquisition. Many have long believed in the *nativist perspective* that humans have a biological predisposition to learn language (Chomsky, 1965). In fact, some theorized that humans have a *critical period* during which language acquisition comes easily (Lenneberg, 1967). However, language acquisition is more subtle.

Critical periods vary for different aspects of language, with the critical period for syntax development ending around the first year (Friedmann & Rusou, 2015). An absence of learning during early childhood results in deficiencies, partially resulting from differences in how the brain represents language (Newport, 2002). This is evident from cases in which children were kept in isolation and not exposed to language until puberty.

In one famous and sad case, a social worker discovered a 13-year-old raised in severe isolation (Rolls, 2010). Genie (a pseudonym chosen to protect her identity) was forced by her father to live in one small room tied to a kid's potty chair. He would not speak to Genie and when she made noises, he would beat her. Psychologists set out to teach Genie language.

Early on, Genie seemed to make good progress. But after a year, Genie never experienced an explosion in her language like most young children do. Her vocabulary was good—hundreds of words—but her grammar and syntax were absent. Genie's case offers support for the nativist perspective of language acquisition and critical periods. However, it's important to note that Genie had several confounding factors (e.g., extreme abuse) that may have inhibited learning.

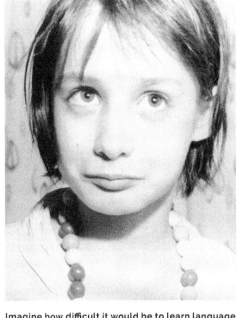

Imagine how difficult it would be to learn language when you're 13 years old, instead of when you were younger.

Bettmann/Contributor/Bettmann/via Getty Images

Animal Language

Can other animals use language? Honeybees dance, birds sing, wolves howl, dolphins squeak, and whales bellow, which all might count as rudimentary language (Janik, 2000; Marino, 2002; Miller & Bain, 2000). Dogs' spoken language is a little rough (ha!), but dogs can understand hundreds or even thousands of words. For example, Rico was a Border Collie who was able to make 200 links between words and their meaning (Kaminski et al., 2004). In another study, Chaser the Border Collie learned the names of 1,022 objects (Pilley & Reid, 2011). And chimpanzees and gorillas have learned sign language; they can sign for objects and basic commands, as well as put words together to form sentences (Gardner & Gardner, 1969; Terrace, 2019; Terrace et al., 1979).

Here, Koko the gorilla is taught American Sign Language.

San Francisco Chronicle/Hearst Newspapers/Contributor/via Getty Images

Multilingualism

Most people in the world are multilingual—that is, they speak more than one language (Diamond, 2010). It's a skill that has benefits starting in childhood: Bilingual children are better at complex processing tasks (Bialystok, 2010). Knowing more than one language appears to provide several benefits to adults:

- It facilitates switching attention between tasks (Prior & MacWhinney, 2010).
- It increases brain gray matter, integrity of white matter, and neuroplasticity (Li et al., 2014).
- It slows cognitive decline among older adults and eases symptoms of dementia like Alzheimer's (Bialystok et al., 2012; Kroll & Dussias, 2017).

Sarcasm

Sarcasm: The use of ironic or satirical wit to convey an alternate or opposite meaning.

"I am fluent in sarcasm."

Perhaps you've heard someone say this, almost like it's a form of multilingualism. It's not. But **sarcasm**, or the use of ironic or satirical wit, communicates an alternate or opposite meaning (Gibbs, 2007). Sarcasm relies less on what you say and more on how you say it. Understanding tone takes cognitive effort. You must understand the speaker's mental state, intentions, knowledge, and present attitude (McDonald, 1999).

When you rearranged the words in the escape room, it spelled out, *"WOW, YOU ARE SO INCREDIBLY SMART."* There are two ways to take that, depending on how it's said. (That's why it is risky to use sarcasm in texts.) Compliment or sarcasm? If sarcastic, maybe you should do something a little dumb; you risk embarrassment by reshelving the book backward and upside down. Somewhere in the world a librarian sheds a tear, but you hear a magnetic click and the bookcase swings open, revealing what looks like an old classroom.

SageVantage﹥ Practice what you learn in **Knowledge Check 12.4**

INTELLIGENCE

Have You Ever Wondered? 12.5 What does it mean to be "smart"?

» LO 12.5 Analyze the key theories of intelligence and its association with creativity.

Everyone wants to be smart.

But what does it really mean to be "smart" or "intelligent?" Answering that question is difficult because "intelligence" shows up in so many ways: knowing a random fact, solving a tricky math problem, delivering a well-timed joke, knowing the right thing to say when someone is sad, or inventing something new. In general terms, **intelligence** is the ability to learn from experience, adapt to, and shape environments (Sternberg, 2012). However, pinpointing the exact nature of intelligence is an age-old problem.

Intelligence: The ability to learn from experience, adapt to, and shape environments.

Sources of Intelligence

Some people are smarter (and better at escape rooms) than others.

But why? To better understand intelligence's origin, we need to explore two dichotomies: nature versus nurture and fixed versus growth mindset.

Is intelligence driven by nature (biological factors) or nurture (environmental factors)? Twin studies might offer insight.

kumacore/Moment/via Getty Images

Nature Versus Nurture

It's a classic dichotomy used to understand individual differences: nature versus nurture. Your intelligence could be the result of innate abilities (nature) or the result of your experiences, such as the education and training you've received so far (nurture). More likely, it could be both.

SPOTLIGHT ON RESEARCH METHODS

Nature Versus Nurture: Twin Studies of Intelligence

Good experimentation depends on control, which includes ensuring as many elements as possible are the same between the different conditions. Twins, especially identical or monozygotic twins, are as close to a perfect clone as possible because they share the same genetic material. If the identical twins are separated at birth because of their family's choice (not because of unethical psychologists!), researchers can study the influence of both *nature* (genetic and prenatal environmental effects) and *nurture* (environmental effects) on an outcome.

The Minnesota Twin project compared twins raised apart to those raised together. The conclusion was that identical twins were very similar, regardless of how they were raised (Bouchard et al., 1990). Similarly, a review of twin and adoption studies found that most psychological differences, including intelligence, are at least partially hereditary (Bouchard & McGue, 2003).

Another study, this time comparing Swedish identical and fraternal twins raised apart to those raised together, found general cognitive ability was heritable, but that association decreased over time—which suggests an environmental influence (Finkel et al., 1998). Other sibling, twin, and adoption studies also find that environment (e.g., parental education) plays a role in intelligence (Kirkpatrick et al., 2009). Though twin and adoption studies help establish the influence of genetics and environment to some extent, it's clear that definitively determining each factor's influence may be impossible (Sternberg & Grigorenko, 1997). ●

Maybe you're born with it. Thank (or blame) your parents for your grade in calculus, poetry skills, or musical ability. Twin studies demonstrate that genes contribute to intelligence (Bouchard, 2004). Two studies concluded that up to 50% of fluid intelligence is *heritable,* or highly transmissible, from parent to offspring (Davies et al., 2011; Plomin & von Stumm, 2018).

That said, there's also a case for environmental influence. For example, research found a link between being breastfed as a baby and intelligence (Brion et al., 2011; Victora et al., 2015). Education also plays a role, with parents' education level being positively correlated to their children's intelligence (Neiss & Rowe, 2000). Similarly, the more education a child receives, the higher their intelligence tends to be (Colom et al., 2002). Among wealthy children, genetic factors matter more than situational factors, but among children near poverty, environmental influences may be more important (Turkheimer et al., 2003).

A classic study of over 25,000 White and Black children found that the best predictors of a child's intelligence at age 4 were the mother's education level and the family's socioeconomic status (Broman et al., 1975). A more recent study replicated the pattern that higher family socioeconomic status positively correlated with intelligence and with improvements over time (von Stumm & Plomin, 2015).

Another classic study demonstrated how nature and nurture interact—but this time, with rats (Cooper & Zubek, 1958). The researchers started with two groups of lab rats who were genetically bred to be either "bright" or "dull" at the kind of problem-solving rats typically encounter, such as running mazes. Researchers randomly assigned the rats to either an enriched environment (basically a rat gymnasium/playground) or an unstimulating, boring environment. You can see the experimental setup in Table 12.2.

TABLE 12.2

The Experimental Setup to Test Nature Versus Nurture in Rat Learning

	GENETICALLY "BRIGHT" LAB RATS	GENETICALLY "DULL" LAB RATS
An enriched environment		
An impoverished environment		

Source: Adapted from Cooper and Zubek (1958).

The enriched environment helped the dull rats' learning but had no effect on the bright rats. Recent research suggests enriched environments provide stimulation that promotes greater neural plasticity (Han et al., 2022; van Praag et al., 2000). Similarly, research finds that engaging in physical activity can benefit thinking and brain function (Hillman et al., 2008). Consider what an enriched environment looks like for kids growing up. Maybe it is a home full of books, attention from parents, sophisticated conversations, exposure to complex ideas, rich vocabulary, and sufficient exercise. There may be thousands of bright children whose potential is never given the chance to bloom because they are not in a stimulating environment.

Fixed Versus Growth Mindset

While both nature and nurture can influence you, there's also a third factor of influence: your own attitude. Your *mindset* or belief system about the nature of intelligence has a big impact on your life, as described by psychologist Carol Dweck (2006):

Fixed mindset: The view that intelligence is stable and unchangeable.

- A **fixed mindset** believes in stable, unchangeable intelligence that defines your sense of self: I'm dumb (or smart). A fixed mindset discourages effort. Why bother? If you believe that "I'm just not a math person," then you're demonstrating a fixed mindset. You're also wrong. Only 20% of math ability is genetic; 80% is the result of other factors, such as practice (Skeide et al., 2020).

- In contrast, a **growth mindset** views intelligence as malleable. Intelligence is a quality to cultivate. Obstacles and challenges are opportunities for further development. The result is a willingness to put forth effort, a reluctance to quit, and an ability to draw inspiration from others' success.

Growth mindset: The view that intelligence is malleable and a quality to cultivate.

Mindset influences school performance (Blackwell et al., 2007). Seventh graders with a fixed mindset did not show academic improvement across 2 years of junior high school; students with a growth mindset did. Mindset continues to matter in college. Across several institutions and thousands of students, graduating high school seniors who learned about fixed versus growth mindset prior to college were more likely to go to college, had better grades, and felt like they belonged more (Yeager et al., 2016).

You can measure your own mindset with the *What's My Score?* feature.

WHAT'S MY SCORE?

Measuring Implicit Theories of Intelligence (Self-Theory) Scale

Instructions: The following questions explore students' beliefs about their personal ability to change their intelligence level. Using the scale below, indicate the extent to which you agree or disagree with the following statements.

1	2	3	4	5	6
Strongly Disagree	Disagree	Mostly Disagree	Mostly Agree	Agree	Strongly Agree

____1. I don't think I personally can do much to increase my intelligence.

____2. With enough time and effort I think I could significantly improve my intelligence level.

____3. My intelligence is something about me that I personally can't change very much.

____4. I believe I can always substantially improve on my intelligence.

____5. To be honest, I don't think I can really change how intelligent I am.

____6. Regardless of my current intelligence level, I think I have the capacity to change it quite a bit.

____7. I can learn new things, but I don't have the ability to change my basic intelligence.

____8. I believe I have the ability to change my basic intelligence level considerable over time.

Scoring Instructions: To get your fixed mindset score, add up all responses from the *odd*-numbered items.

To get your growth mindset score, add up all responses from the *even*-numbered items.

Your total score for each should be between 4 and 24. The higher your score, the more you have that mindset. ●

Source: De Castella and Byrne (2015).

Theories of Intelligence

Intelligence is a slippery concept.

Many psychologists have defined it differently over the years. Alfred Binet conceived of intelligence as a combination of skills like common sense, good judgment, taking initiative, and adaptability to circumstances (Binet & Simon, 1916). These sound like the skills you need in the escape room. You adapt to your current circumstance by thoroughly searching the room and are rewarded by finding a hidden slip of paper stuck in gum under a desk reading, "Getting out is as easy as pi."

Sternberg's Triarchic Theory of Intelligence

Intelligence isn't solely about solving math problems and knowing big words. Robert Sternberg's *triarchic theory of intelligence* combines analytical, creative, and practical abilities (Sternberg, 1988). *Analytical intelligence* works with information. *Creative intelligence* generates new ideas and materials. But out in the world, you need street smarts. That's *practical intelligence*, the ability to apply previous knowledge and skills to adapt to your environment (Sternberg & Grigorenko, 2000). Street smarts include soft survival skills: being aware of the surroundings, navigating public transportation, learning the unwritten social rules for dining out, knowing how to be a good neighbor, making friends with local merchants, and avoiding dangerous situations.

The Two-Factor Theory of Intelligence

Charles Spearman's *two-factor theory of intelligence* proposed that intelligence is the combination of two things (Spearman, 1904):

- general intelligence (g), a general factor that underlies all mental abilities, and
- specific skills (s), specific factors unique to each task.

An individual with high general intelligence (g) would demonstrate abilities across many domains but also have the skills (s) to apply those abilities to solve specific problems.

Spearman's theory has withstood most of its critics, and there appears to be a neural basis for general intelligence (Duncan et al., 2000; Sternberg, 2003). People with high g, for example, have greater working memory capacity (Conway et al., 2003); those with low g do worse in school (Deary et al., 2007) and tend to have worse physical health (Gottfredson, 2004). Cattell (1971) proposed an updated variation on Spearman's two general factors of intelligence:

Crystalized intelligence (gC): The ability to draw upon previous knowledge and experience.

Fluid intelligence (gF): The ability to understand new information, solve novel problems, decipher abstract relationships, and use logical reasoning in unfamiliar environments.

- Crystalized intelligence (gC) is the ability to draw upon previous knowledge and experience. gC helps you recall facts for a test or remember how to drive a car, for example.

- Fluid intelligence (gF) is your ability to understand new information, solve novel problems, decipher abstract relationships, and use logical reasoning in unfamiliar environments.

Fluid intelligence helps you know the clue's "easy as pi" may refer to the number "pi" (3.14). One of your teammates found scissors padlocked with another three-digit combo lock, a cloth bag, and a board with 16 empty slots. The combination 3-1-4 springs the scissors free so you can cut the bag open, revealing 16 blocks.

Gardner's Theory of Multiple Intelligences

Lewis Thurstone suggested that individuals possess a collection of primary mental abilities (Thurstone, 1938). After analyzing 56 mental ability tests, Thurstone identified seven primary mental abilities. While most psychologists don't use Thurstone's specific ideas today, they were an important precursor to more recent, similar ideas (Sternberg, 2003).

Howard Gardner's *theory of multiple intelligences* identifies eight key areas of intelligence (Gardner, 2011). As you can see in Table 12.3, this framework contains both traditional forms of intelligence (e.g., verbal, logical-mathematical) but also adds social intelligences (e.g., interpersonal, intrapersonal) and nontraditional areas like bodily-kinesthetic, musical, natural, and spatial. This broadened perspective allows for the possibility that a dancer, a computer coder, a poet, and a forest survivalist are all equally intelligent—just in different ways.

TABLE 12.3

Gardner's Multiple Intelligences

INTELLIGENCE	KEY SKILLS	POTENTIAL CAREERS
Bodily-Kinesthetic Intelligence The ability to control your body movements and skillfully handle objects	Acting, dancing, hand–eye coordination, playing sports, working with your hands	Acrobat, actor, athlete, craftsperson, dancer, firefighter, gymnast, personal trainer, physical education teacher
Interpersonal Intelligence Your ability to gauge others' feelings, moods, and motivations and respond appropriately	Conflict resolution, cooperation, communication, empathy, leadership, listening, reading nonverbal signals, taking perspective, understanding	Businessperson, counselor, leader, manager, minister, politician, psychologist, salesperson
Intrapersonal Intelligence Your ability to know yourself, to be self-aware and understand your emotions, motivations, beliefs, thought processes, and values	Assessment of personal strengths, awareness of feelings, introspection, self-reflection	Counselors, life coach, psychologists, researchers, scientists, philosophers, theorists, writers
Linguistic Intelligence Your ability to adeptly use language, including sensitivity to sounds and rhythms of words, and strong verbal skills	Debating, listening, reading, speaking, teaching, writing	Journalist, lawyer, orators, poet, politician, public relations, teacher, translator, writer
Logical-Mathematical Intelligence Ability to analyze problems, engage in abstract thinking, work conceptually, identify logical patterns, and work well with numbers	Experimentation, mathematical and logical problem-solving, scientific reasoning, solving equations and mathematical proofs	Accountants, actuary, coding/computer programmer, engineers, logicians, mathematicians, scientists
Musical Intelligence Your ability to think in rhythms, sounds, appreciate pitch and timber, and produce music	Composition of music, easily recognize and remember music, songs, and melodies, musical appreciation, musical performance (playing instruments, singing)	Composer, conductor, DJ, musician, music producer, music teacher, music therapist, singer
Naturalist Intelligence Your ability to be in tune with nature, engaging with the environment (e.g., hiking, camping), and interest in identifying animals, insects, and plants in nature	Appreciating your connection to nature, awareness of your surroundings, cataloging and categorizing information, finding patterns in nature	Conservationist, farmer, gardener, landscape architect, naturalist, oenologist (someone who specializes in wine making), park ranger, scientist (e.g., biologist, zoologist)
Spatial Intelligence Ability to accurately visualize complex and abstract forms, to think and work with pictures and images	Building and constructing, designing objects, drawing, fixing things, painting, puzzle creation and solving	Artist, architect, chess player, engineer, fashion designer, handyperson, inventor, jewelry maker, mechanic, pilot, sculptor, surgeon

Source: Adapted from Gardner (2011).

Gardner started with seven intelligences and later added naturalist—there may be more coming. For example, existential intelligence is the ability to ask and address profound questions about the meaning of life, human existence, human origins, and death. What about digital intelligence? That would capture individuals' ability to work with digital mediums, use technology effectively, and adapt to the digital world (Adams, 2004; Marnewick & Marnewick, 2021). Recently, others have also proposed cultural intelligence, or one's effectiveness at interacting with people from other cultures and dealing with problems related to cultural differences (Sternberg et al., 2022).

Intelligence isn't just about book smarts. What type of intelligence would help you survive?

iStock.com/simonkr

Gardner's theory of multiple intelligences is not without controversy (e.g., Klein, 1997). Some argue that it lacks empirical support (Waterhouse, 2006), while others criticize it as a feel-good approach that relabels skills and abilities as intelligence (Barnett et al., 2006; Morgan, 2021). Others believe Gardner's theory is useful because it helps us think more broadly and inclusively about what it means to be smart.

Back in the room, the 16 blocks obviously go in the two columns of eight slots. One column has a brain icon, the other a stick figure. The blocks contain either famous people's names or Gardner's eight intelligences. Your group quickly makes the matches shown in Table 12.4, and suddenly the bottom of a lectern opens, revealing a parchment.

TABLE 12.4

Examples of People With Different Kinds of Intelligence

🧠	🧍
Bodily-Kinesthetic	Simone Biles
Interpersonal	Mother Teresa
Intrapersonal	Brene Brown
Linguistic	Amanda Gorman
Logical-Mathematical	Katherine Johnson
Musical	Ariana Grande
Naturalist	Steve Irwin
Spatial	Kalpana Chawla

Source: Adapted from Gardner (2011).

Beyond Book Smarts: Other Forms of Intelligence

Someone (possibly Einstein) once said, "Everybody is a genius. But if you judge a fish by its ability to climb a tree, it will live its whole life believing that it is stupid."

Emotional Intelligence

Emotional intelligence: The social ability to detect, appraise, and express appropriate emotions in yourself and others.

Emotional intelligence is the social ability to detect, appraise, and express appropriate emotions in yourself and others (Mayer et al., 2000; Salovey & Mayer, 1990). Emotionally intelligent people display four abilities (Salovey & Grewal, 2005):

- Recognizing others' emotions
- Understanding others' emotional language
- Controlling their own emotions
- Using emotions to effectively guide their thinking and actions

Culture influences how we define and perceive intelligence (Cocodia, 2014). In several African societies, intelligence commonly emphasizes the importance of interpersonal skills (Ruzgis & Grigorenko, 1994). Within the United States, White and Asian people tend to focus more on cognitive abilities, whereas Latinx people are more likely to believe intelligence includes social skills (Okagaki & Sternberg, 1993). In a study that included people across nine different countries, researchers found that having a long-term orientation, wanting to avoid uncertainty, and collectivism (a culture that emphasizes the group over the individual) all had a positive association with emotional intelligence (Gunkel et al., 2014).

There are consequences for ignoring emotional intelligence. Men in college with lower emotional intelligence are more likely to abuse drugs and alcohol, engage in deviant behavior, and have troubled friendships (Brackett et al., 2004). Emotional intelligence is just one of several ways to be intelligent.

Creativity

We often label individuals as "creative geniuses." The label "creative genius" has been applied to Yo-Yo Ma, Frida Kahlo, Elon Musk, Oprah Winfrey, Joy Harjo, Bruce Lee, and Judit Polgar (among others). Quite a list, with each person's accomplishments occurring in very different areas. We commonly assume that creativity strongly relates to intelligence—although a meta-analysis using findings from over 45,000 participants found only a weak correlation (Kim, 2005). There's more to creativity than intelligence and vice versa.

What does it mean to be a creative genius like Delita Martin, who uses her art (the large piece on the right) to celebrate Black women's beauty, resilience, and strength?

Sean Drakes/Contributor/Getty Images Entertainment/via Getty Images

Creativity focuses more on *divergent thinking* (identifying many possible solutions) than on *convergent thinking* (identifying a single correct solution). Knowing trivia questions or vocabulary words is convergent thinking, while generating music, poetry, or funny captions for cartoons is divergent thinking (Price, 1953). Breaking free from functional fixedness (finding alternate uses for objects) is divergent creative thinking (Guilford, 1960).

The parchment from the escape room's lectern reads, "What's a book for? To remove all doubts, think of other uses for a book if you want to get out." There are 25 blank lines, so you start generating ideas: (1) paperweight, (2) bug killer, (3) staircase. . . . Huh. On a whim, you use books as a makeshift stepladder to reach up to adjust a flickering lightbulb in a wall sconce. It flicks on and a wall panel opens revealing a suitcase. Only 5:22 remaining.

Have you ever seen a funny picture with the challenge to "caption this"? Generating ideas successfully requires divergent thinking.

iStock.com/Claudiad

Improving Creativity: Brainstorming

Creativity is helpful in many ways: It helps speakers keep an audience engaged, counselors reach clients in new ways, and parents convince their child to eat vegetables. So how do we boost it?

The first step to improving creativity is realizing that it's not an innate personality factor but one that can be influenced and enhanced if the social and environmental influences are right (Amabile & Pillemer, 2012). The classic creativity promotion strategy is *brainstorming*, popularized in advertising during the 1950s (Osborn, 1963). There were only three basic rules to brainstorming:

(1) Suggest as many ideas as possible.

(2) Don't criticize any ideas.

(3) Emphasize unusual ideas.

Although a study from Kuwait found merits in brainstorming (AlMutairi, 2015), larger-scale analyses of multiple studies find that brainstorming is more popular than it is effective (Mullen et al., 1991).

Fortunately, training improves creativity (Scott et al., 2004). In one study, researchers trained city employees to enhance creativity and found that training increased new ideas by 55% (Epstein et al., 2008). There are significant practical benefits to tapping into employees' creativity: hundreds of thousands of dollars in new revenue and cost reductions. Yet the most important technique is perhaps the most boring: capturing and preserving ideas (Epstein & Phan, 2012). So, share your ideas and don't forget them.

Here are a few more ways to enhance creativity:

- Sleep on it: When participants in a research study thought about a problem prior to falling asleep, half reported having a dream that helped them generate new solutions to their problem (Barrett, 1993).

- Think like a kid: In another study, when participants imagined themselves as 7-year-olds, they were better at thinking creatively (Zabelina & Robinson, 2010).

- Go for a walk: When participants "gave their ideas some legs" by going for a walk, 81% of them increased creativity scores (Oppezzo & Schwartz, 2014).

- Take it outside: When researchers compared walking on a treadmill to walking outside, those who went outdoors produced more creative analogies (Oppezzo & Schwartz, 2014).

- Be in a good mood: While fear and anxiety are linked to less creativity, being in a happy and positive mood enhances creativity (Baas et al., 2008).

- Don't be afraid of AI: Harness the power of artificial intelligence (AI) to establish a "co-creativity" dynamic to explore and play with ideas (Wingström et al., 2022). Just make sure you do it ethically (Vinchon et al., 2023).

SageVantage Practice what you learn in **Knowledge Check 12.5**

MEASURING INTELLIGENCE

Have You Ever Wondered?
12.6 What is IQ, how has it been tested, and what are the issues with its use?

» LO 12.6 **Summarize the history, calculation, outcomes, and controversies related to IQ.**

"Put your intelligence to the test."

That was the bulletin board's message when you chose which escape room to attempt. Of course, your performance in an escape room may not be the best test of your intelligence. There are many ways to gauge how smart you are.

In fact, American culture is full of intelligence-related tests: the ACT, SAT, and GRE (when you apply to graduate school). Aspiring lawyers take the LSAT, medical doctors take the MCATs, and professional football players take the Wonderlic. You might have seen pseudo-challenges on TikTok like "Only people with IQ over 140 can do this" followed by a task that's really phishing for your passwords. Are any of these tests meaningful?

Early Intelligence Measures

We all like to see how we measure up.

Alfred Binet's first intelligence test measured French schoolchildren's current performance, not their intelligence (Binet & Simon, 1905). He and his colleague Theodore Simon started by designing a series of tasks for children at various ages. Their initial test focused on comprehension, judgment, language skills, memory, and reasoning. Binet and Simon concentrated on multiple abilities rather than a single number that could capture everything about a student's intellect.

Terman's Intelligence Quotient

There have been many revisions of this first famous intelligence test (Becker, 2003). The most significant revision occurred when Stanford University professor Lewis Terman (1916) adapted the questions for children in the United States. Terman's Stanford–Binet Intelligence Scale used the **intelligence quotient (IQ)**, a numeric representation of how a person's mental abilities compare to others of their same chronological age. IQ is still the most well-known index of intelligence.

Calculating IQ starts with a person's *chronological age*, how old someone is in years (imagine a 14-year-old). IQ then compares chronological age to their *mental age*, which is how old most people have to be before they can do whatever this individual is capable of doing. If this 14-year-old can do a complex puzzle that is typical for a 30-year-old, then their mental age is 30. These two numbers are simply put in a ratio and multiplied by 100 to get a nice round number. As you can see in Table 12.5, if your mental and chronological age match, your IQ will be exactly 100, which means you're as smart as you should be for your age—in other words, you have average intelligence. If your IQ is over 100, you're smarter than average. If your IQ is lower than 100, you're less intelligent than average. Most IQ tests are scored to have a standard deviation of about 15 points, meaning that most scores land between 85 and 115 (see Figure 12.5).

Intelligence quotient (IQ): The numeric representation of how a person's mental abilities compare to others of their same chronological age.

TABLE 12.5

Calculating IQ

	MENTAL AGE	CHRONOLOGICAL AGE	MA/CA	(MA/CA) × 100	IQ
Child 1	10	7	10/7 = 1.43	(1.43) × 100 = 143	143
Child 2	10	10	10/10 = 1.00	(1.00) × 100 = 100	100
Child 3	10	12	10/12 = 0.83	(0.83) × 100 = 83	83

Wechsler's Intelligence Measures

How does a suitcase fit into the history of psychology and intelligence? In 1939, David Wechsler believed that existing adult intelligence tests were asking too many verbal questions and neglected performance skills (Boake, 2002). He developed what is now known as the WAIS, or Wechsler Adult Intelligence Scale (Wechsler, 1981), and the materials all fit into a small suitcase.

FIGURE 12.5

Standard Range for IQ

Most IQ tests use standardization where the average score is 100 and the standard deviation is 15.

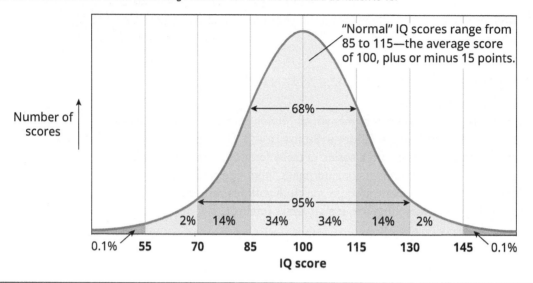

The revised editions include six traditional verbal question areas:

- arithmetic,
- comprehension,
- digit span (memorizing digits in order),
- information,
- similarities, and
- vocabulary.

Wechsler also included five performance subtests:

- block design (reproducing patterns of blocks),
- digit symbol (using symbols in place of numbers),
- object assembly (putting together pictures of common objects),
- picture arrangement (putting pictures in logical/chronological order to tell a story), and
- picture completion (identifying missing part of a picture).

These tasks provide test takers with a verbal IQ, performance IQ, and full IQ. Wechsler developed similar tests for children aged 4 to 6 and 6 to 17 (Wechsler & Psychological Corporation, 2012; Wechsler et al., 2014). In the escape room's suitcase, you find a note: "Don't despair, this test may not be fair. Now your escape requires a breath of fresh air."

Intelligence Testing's Dark History

Like that famous road to hell, intelligence testing started with good intentions.

Alfred Binet was trying to identify who was struggling in school and get those students extra help to succeed—a worthy goal with kind intentions (Binet & Simon, 1916). But intelligence tests have led to controversy and harm. The United States used early intelligence tests to transform millions of raw recruits into a working army (Terman,

1918). But those tests had clear racial and cultural biases favoring White soldiers. This led to a long line of problems disproportionally affecting people of color (Stern, 2020). Dr. Robert Lee Williams II and Dr. Mamie Phipps Clark both conducted pioneering research establishing systemic racial biases in testing and schools. Some of Phipps Clark's work was even used as evidence in the famous U.S. Supreme Court case *Brown v. Board of Education* that ended school segregation (Clark & Clark, 1939). Photos of Williams and Phipps Clark were shown in the opening chapter of this book.

It's a problem that still hasn't gone away. For example, school districts with more White students receive more funding—regardless of their socioeconomic status (Brandt, 2017). These types of racial biases are so deeply rooted that in some states, it is illegal to make educational decisions based on IQ tests (Walters, 2019). The SAT is not an IQ test, but it has similar problems—and a similar history.

The Wechsler intelligence tests have been used for decades and involve many different tasks.

Division of Medicine and Science, National Museum of American History, Smithsonian Institution

Carl Brigham, creator of the SAT, believed that intelligence tests from immigrants revealed (White) Nordic people's biological superiority (Brigham, 1923). Based on Brigham's book, the College Board asked him to create and launch the SAT in 1926 (Hammond, 2020). Even if the test creators were not being overly racist when designing the test, there were racial biases. The SAT may predict college success for White students, but not for students of color (Fleming, 2002). Modern IQ tests (and the SAT) have improved, especially in terms of measuring problem-solving skills, but many institutions are now "test optional," in part because of their biased history (Rubin & Canché, 2019).

CAREER CORNER

Profiling Justine, High School Art Teacher

What is your career?

I am a high school art teacher where I use design, administer, monitor, and evaluate the curriculum for art classes based on national and state standards. My classes include intro to studio art, art foundations, digital art, drawing, painting, ceramics, sculpture, design, and photography.

How was studying psychology important for success in this career?

Studying psychology gave me a background in how the brain learns, which translates very well to teaching. I also gained much better insight into classroom management strategies and relationship-building practices essential to teaching.

How do concepts from this chapter help in this career?

I focus on growth mindset in my teaching by having students keep a process portfolio while they are in art classes to allow them to look back and see their growth and improvement. I also focus on process and experimentation with art materials instead of just the expected outcomes. I find that one of the most

effective methods I have for teaching a growth mindset is by modeling it. I talk with my students about how I purposely seek out challenges in both teaching and in creating artwork. I remind them that I can do what I can do in art because I practice it regularly and have practiced it longer than they have.

Is this the career you always planned to have after college?

When I majored in art and psychology, I planned to get my master's in creative art therapy. My freshman advisor encouraged me to major in art education and psych, but I swore I would never be a teacher. My goal was to work with youth in a treatment facility. To gain experience, and because I half-heartedly applied to one grad school and was not accepted, I got a job in a youth foster care facility. While I was there, I realized that many of the girls at the facility needed an adult in their life that they could connect with.

If you could give current college students one sentence of advice, what would it be?

Challenge your comfort zone in ways that make you comfortable with being uncomfortable. ●

The Flynn Effect: Good News

Good news: Humans are getting smarter.

At least, that's true according to IQ measurements over the past decades. The **Flynn effect** is the finding that IQ scores at the societal level in industrialized nations have been steadily increasing (Flynn, 2007). According to a large meta-analysis, IQ scores are increasing approximately three points per decade, a finding that holds true across age groups and a variety of samples (Trahan et al., 2014).

Researchers have investigated whether the Flynn effect occurred in subgroups related to urbanization, household income, gender, race/ethnicity, and maternal education (Ang et al., 2010). Though there is evidence for a general increase in intelligence over generations, it was only clear in children from higher-income households and from more educated mothers. Again, it seems, a nurturing childhood matters. There are lots of potential methods for improving community IQ scores: improved global access to education, better health and nutrition, ensuring access to education for women, and improved support services.

Flynn effect: The finding that IQ scores at the societal level in industrialized nations have been steadily increasing over decades.

The Downside of High IQ: Cautionary News

Though higher IQs sound good, it's important to note that IQ doesn't guarantee success.

For example, it can make dating more difficult; some research finds that extremely high intelligence is less desirable (Gignac et al., 2018). Other research finds that students with high IQ can struggle in traditional schools (Frumau-van Pinxten et al., 2023). Here's another caution. Yes, intelligence can improve memory, abstract reasoning, and logical thinking. But intelligence doesn't always help with making rational decisions in real-life settings (Stanovich et al., 2016). Sometimes, very intelligent people do irrational things such as ignore science, embrace conspiracy theories, or believe in astrology and superstitions.

In the escape room, you have 2 minutes left. Stumped, you look in the mirror considering the final clue: "requires a breath of fresh air." It clicks. You breathe on the mirror revealing letters: Y Y U R Y Y U B I C U R Y Y 4 M E. Seems impossible. Someone points out the "two Ys" but you hear it at "too wise." That's all it took. You read the string out loud, practically shouting: Too Wise You Are, Too Wise You Be, I See You Are Too Wise For Me. Suddenly, a hidden door opens to the outside with a minute to spare. You escaped, and all it took was good decision-making, problem-solving, language skills, intelligence, and group effort.

Getting involved was not just essential; it opened doors. ●

Sage Vantage   Practice what you learn in **Knowledge Check 12.6**

CHAPTER REVIEW

Learning Objectives Summary

12.1   What is cognition?

>> **LO 12.1   Describe how mental representations, concepts, categories, prototypes, and schemas relate to thinking.**

We form mental representations of everything in our world. We organize those concepts by creating categories, using prototypes, and forming schemas.

12.2   How do we approach reasoning and decision-making, and how do we get it wrong?

>> LO 12.2   Compare and contrast approaches to reasoning and decision-making.

There are several ways to approach reasoning and decision-making. Algorithms involve systematic rules, intuition relies on a more intuitive process, while heuristics allow us to take shortcuts to save time. Unfortunately, these processes are imperfect and can produce errors.

12.3   How do we approach problem-solving, and how do we get it wrong?

>> LO 12.3   Compare and contrast problem-solving approaches.

Like decision-making, there are several key approaches to problem-solving, including heuristics, trial and error, using analogies, and insight. However, functional fixedness, fixation, and mental sets hinder effective problem-solving.

FIGURE 12.6

Solution to the Nine-Dot Problem

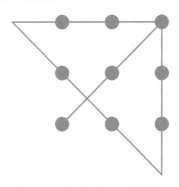

12.4   How does our language relate to cognition?

>> LO 12.4   Explain the link between language and cognition.

Humans are predisposed to acquiring and using language. Though animals use some facet of language, humans' ability far surpasses other animals. Our use of language involves working with phonemes, morphemes, syntax, and grammar, all of which help shape our thinking. Being multilingual has many benefits.

12.5   What does it mean to be "smart"?

>> LO 12.5   Analyze the key theories of intelligence and its association with creativity.

There are several theories that aim to explain intelligence. The most prominent is *g*, or the theory of general intelligence, suggesting that intelligence is one underlying ability. Other theories emphasize different competencies related to intelligence such as emotional ability, with some believing there are multiple intelligences. Creativity relates to intelligence, with research showing keys ways to cultivate creativity.

12.6   What is IQ, how has it been tested, and what are the issues with its use?

>> LO 12.6   Summarize the history, calculation, outcomes, and controversies related to IQ.

Although measures of intelligence were originally designed to identify children who would benefit from extra help, IQ tests have a long history of systemic biases. Still, some research indicates progressive improvement in IQ scores for some groups over time.

CRITICAL THINKING QUESTIONS

1. Schemas help us navigate new situations. Describe your schema for how to meet people at a party. Note some of the mental representations and concepts you're using (e.g., what kind of party?). Demonstrate the problem with unclear concepts using a question you might ask, like "Are you here with anyone?" Note how the concept of "with" could be taken two different ways.

2. You have a problem: You're leaving for Spring Break in 15 minutes and need to pack your bags. Describe how you'd use problem-solving heuristics to solve this problem.

3. Life is full of decisions. Highlight at least one key decision you will have to make and show how you could use different techniques to help.

4. The Internet is full of "challenges." One involves a $100 bill trapped underneath an upside-down bottle. Your goal is to remove the money without touching or knocking over the bottle. Explain how you can avoid problems such as functional fixedness, fixation, and mental set to grab the cash.

5. Several television shows have created entirely new languages (for aliens, fantasy species such as elves, fictional countries on *Game of Thrones*, and so on). If you wanted to create a new language, where would you start? What aspects of the relevant culture would be important to consider? What would you do differently if you wanted to teach the same language to animals like chimpanzees—or how would a language be different if it originated from those animals?

6. Intelligence is a construct that is difficult to pin down. Devise your own theory of what intelligence is and how you would measure it. What will people need to know? What should they be able to do? Be sure to point out how your test will be fair and unbiased.

7. Think about the influences in your own life that might have contributed to your intelligence, motivation in school, and personal interests. Identify at least two factors you think are tied to "nature" and at least two you think are tied to "nurture" and explain each.

KEY TERMS

Algorithm, 369
Availability heuristic, 372
Cognition, 364
Concepts, 365
Crystalized intelligence (*gC*), 386
Decision-making, 369
Emotional intelligence, 388
Fixed mindset, 384
Fluid intelligence (*gF*), 386
Flynn effect, 394
Functional fixedness, 377
Growth mindset, 385

Heuristic, 370
Intelligence, 382
Intelligence quotient (IQ), 391
Intuition, 370
Language, 379
Linguistic determinism, 379
Mental set, 378
Problem-solving, 375
Reasoning, 369
Representativeness heuristic, 372
Sarcasm, 382

iStock.com/Kerkez

13 Personality

It's job interview time.

Sure, you're nervous—but you walk in the room with confidence. Your internships, volunteer service, and college classes give you all the qualifications needed. It's a great company. They're flexible with your family needs, plus they offer great benefits. You crush the interview and think it's all locked up . . . but there's one more thing. They want you to take a personality test.

Many companies require personality tests to screen possible employees. They hope to learn many things: whether you'll be comfortable meeting new clients, whether you're better at working independently or as part of a team, whether you'll be a good leader, whether you're responsible—and even whether you're honest when taking a personality test.

As you prepare to learn the results of your application, the terms *test reliability* and *test validity* take on new meaning because now your income and career opportunities are at stake. We'll begin this chapter by introducing the theories behind psychological personality tests. By the end, you'll begin to appreciate the strengths, weaknesses, applications, and controversies around this fascinating subfield of psychology.

After reading this chapter, you will get answers to several questions you've been curious about:

Have You Ever Wondered?

13.1   What are some of the earliest psychological theories about personality?

13.2   How much of personality is biologically driven?

13.3   What is the trait approach to personality?

13.4   What are humanistic and social-cognitive theories of personality?

13.5   What are some current personality controversies?

Learning Objectives

LO 13.1   Explain early personality theories from the psychodynamic approach.

LO 13.2   Analyze research on biological drivers of personality.

LO 13.3   Explain how researchers from the trait approach measure personality and outline several contemporary trait examples.

LO 13.4   Compare and contrast humanistic and social-cognitive theories of personality.

LO 13.5   Analyze several controversies and debates when it comes to understanding the psychology of personality.

HISTORICAL APPROACHES TO PERSONALITY: PSYCHODYNAMIC THEORIES

>> **LO 13.1   Explain early personality theories from the psychodynamic approach.**

Have You Ever Wondered?
13.1 What are some of the earliest psychological theories about personality?

You head over to a private cubicle and open the personality test:

1. Rate how positive your childhood relationship was with your parents:

1	2	3	4	5
Terrible	Bad	Neutral	Good	Wonderful

2. What words or phrases come to mind when you look at these images?

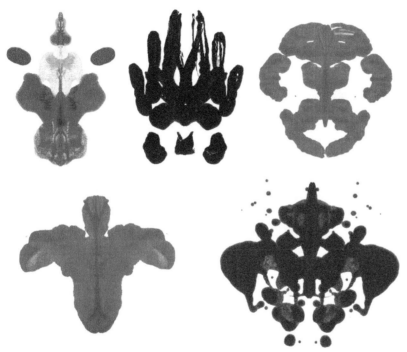

iStock.com/anankkml

3. Do you have any siblings? (check one answer)

_____ No, I'm an only child

_____ Yes, I'm the oldest

_____ Yes, I have older and younger siblings (I'm in the middle)

_____ Yes, I'm the youngest

4. What fictional character from movies, TV, or books do you relate to, and why?

_____

_____

5. Which of these sounds the most like you?

_____ I'm quite comfortable and trusting when it comes to other people.

_____ I often like others more than they like me.

_____ It's best to control other people, so they don't disappoint you.

_____ I prefer to work and live on my own.

Personality: How individuals consistently differ from each other, in terms of their perspectives and behavioral tendencies, across time and place.

Personality is how individuals consistently differ from each other, in terms of their perspectives and behavioral tendencies, across time and place. If you describe yourself as shy, for example, "shy" would only apply to your personality if you think that you're shy more often than not (consistency across time) and that you're shy in most situations (consistency across place).

In psychology, personality has been operationalized (defined and measured) in many different ways. The most famous theoretical approaches—the ones covered in this chapter, at least—are summarized in Table 13.1. Each approach makes distinctive contributions (strengths), and like most theories, each has unavoidable criticisms (weaknesses). Like most aspects of life, learning a little from each perspective might be best. Each idea in this first section of the chapter will tie to one of the five personality test questions you just saw in your employment interview.

TABLE 13.1

Five Theoretical Approaches to Personality

There are many ways to define and measure personality; here are five of the most popular approaches in psychology.

APPROACH	SUMMARY
Psychodynamic	Introduced by Freud, this approach focuses on unconscious anxieties and goals, often stemming from childhood experiences. Personality might be driven by inner conflicts, birth order, characters we play, and our attitude about other people.
Biological	This approach assumes at least part of our individual differences are tied to our genetics and brain anatomy.
Trait	The trait perspective focuses on aspects of personality that seem to predict behavior regardless of circumstance, time, or culture.
Humanistic	Humanistic personality psychologists focus on our self-concept, motivations, and personal potential; the goal is to empower you to be your best self.
Social-cognitive	This perspective proposes that our personality tendencies are a result of the interaction between our perceptions of the world and our environment at any given time.

"It goes back to being pulled out of the hat."

Freud suggested that our early childhood experiences—starting from birth—affect our personality.

iStock.com/andrewgenn

Freud and the Psychodynamic Approach

Who was Sigmund Freud, really?

He was named Sigismund Schlomo Freud in 1856 when his Jewish parents, Jakob and Amalia, welcomed him into the world (Whitebook, 2017). The family moved to Vienna, Austria, when Freud was 3 and a half years old. Freud did well in school, eventually earning a medical degree. He went on to become one of the most influential figures in all of psychology, although his life wasn't a happy one. He suffered from anti-Semitism during the rise of the Nazi party in Europe; his books were burned and many of his theories were dismissed simply due to prejudice. After decades of smoking cigars, he developed cancer and eventually died of physician-assisted suicide in 1939 at the age of 83.

Freud discovered a passion for understanding illnesses of the mind and focused most of his life developing what modern psychologists call his **psychodynamic approach to personality** (and to therapy). The psychodynamic approach assumes that we have unconscious anxieties and wishes that affect us, often due to childhood experiences.

Psychodynamic approach to personality: Studying personality with the assumption we all have unconscious anxieties and wishes that affect us, often due to childhood experiences.

Parts of the Mind: Id, Ego, and Superego

We live with conflict and anxiety.

Freud believed that we struggle for our entire life. We struggle between what our animal nature wants and how "proper" society expects us to behave. We struggle to rein in our anger and fears. We struggle between doing what's fun and what's disciplined. These struggles are all managed by three parts of our mind: the id, ego, and superego (Figure 13.1). Our personality is the result of our constant attempts to balance these competing demands (Freud, 1933).

The **id** is the only part of our personality we have when we're born. It's our primal, animal instincts of aggression, love, and desire. Our most childish nature, the id operates on what he called the *pleasure principle*—demanding immediate gratification. As we grow up, we still feel these pulls, but we might not be able to admit all of them to ourselves. Freud said that we often figuratively bury these instincts into our "unconscious" mind. (Note: For Freud, it was *unconscious*—not "subconscious.")

Id: According to Freud, it's our childlike, instinctive drives that operate on the pleasure principle (immediate gratification).

When we're about 2 years old, the second part of our mind forms: our **ego**. The ego's job is to find compromises with the id. We have to find pleasure, sure—but the ego figures out ways to have just enough pleasure to not get us into trouble, or helps us wait to enjoy the pleasure at an acceptable time. The ego operates on what Freud called the *reality principle*, satisfying the ego in reasonable ways.

Ego: According to Freud, it's the part of our mind that controls our id demands, operating on the reality principle (finding compromises).

Finally, the third part of our mind forms when we're 4 or 5 and we really enter the world outside of our own family or home. The last part is the **superego**, our sense of ethics, conscience, and what's culturally acceptable. The superego operates on the *idealistic principle*. As we grow up, we strive to fit in and get praise from others—and we feel guilt when we fall short. If you know people who have a very controlled, people-pleasing, perfectionist personality, Freud would say they have a very strong superego. On the other hand, people who have short tempers or are self-indulgent have strong ids.

Superego: According to Freud, it's our sense of ethics and wanting to please others based on cultural expectations, operating on the idealistic principle (being perfect).

This personality structure is a popular image in animations: The devilish id sits on one shoulder, the angelic superego on the other, and the indecisive person (you!) is stuck in the middle. But in Freud's world, the well-balanced, healthy personality has a strong, active, directing ego who sits in the middle deciding what to do.

FIGURE 13.1

Freud's Conceptualization of the Mind

Freud believed our mind is made up of three structures: the id, ego, and superego.

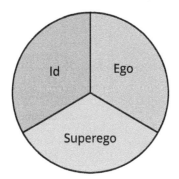

Five Psychosexual Stages

How do you feel about your parents?

The first question in your employment personality test asked you to rate your relationship with your parents on a scale from 1 to 5. Of course, this is a huge simplification and you probably struggled to answer it. Maybe you get along with one parent but not the other. Maybe you have multiple parental figures, or maybe only one. Maybe you have mixed feelings. Perhaps it depends on the day you're asked. For Freud, your childhood experiences and how well you bonded—or didn't—with the first people in charge of raising you shape much of your personality.

Just like the stage theories you learned about when we discussed human development in general, Freud created a set of five **psychosexual stages of development** (see Table 13.2). This is one of Freud's most controversial ideas, partially because it is tied to sexuality and partially because it is criticized for having sexist ideas by today's standards. He suggested that as we grow up, different body parts become integral at certain stages due to particular instincts or biological needs at that time.

For example, we start at birth in the *oral stage*. It's called that because our essential job is to breastfeed, so our mouth is the key to our survival. Next is the *anal stage*, tied to the potty training we all experienced around the age of 2 or 3. Third is the *phallic stage*, when children between the ages of 3 and 6 years are learning how their bodies work. Fourth is a period of rest called the *latency stage*, and finally as adults, Freud believed that healthy people would end in the *genital stage*.

Have you ever heard someone described as having an "anal" personality? This term comes from Freud's idea that psychologically, we can get "stuck" in any of the early stages.

Getting stuck is called "fixation," and Freud said it can happen from either enjoying that stage too much or feeling deprived at that age—leading to a constant need to revisit that childhood issue.

Consider the oral stage, where fixation can happen in two different ways. Depending on exactly how the mental fixation occurs, someone's resulting personality could be infantile and immature with them being either (a) overly mean, selfish, and sarcastic or (b) overly childish and needy. Freud believed that besides certain behaviors, a hallmark of an "oral fixation" would be shown by people constantly needing something in their mouth, such as excessive eating or drinking, smoking,

Psychosexual stages of development: Freud's theory that we move through five biological and psychological stages from infancy to adulthood that affect our personality.

TABLE 13.2

Freud's Psychosexual Stages of Development

Freud (1920/1966) believed everyone goes through five stages of personality development, each tied to a part of the body and a biological instinct or need at that age. For example, infants are in the "oral" stage because they are breastfeeding.

AGE	STAGE	WHAT'S HAPPENING
Birth–18 months	Oral	Infants are breastfeeding
18 months–3 years	Anal	Toddlers are potty training
3–6 years	Phallic	Young children are learning how to use their body
6 years–puberty	Latency	Children focus on school, peers, etc.
Puberty and on	Genital	Adults desire intimate relationships with others

or chewing of fingernails or the end of their pencil in class. Considering Freud's own addiction to cigars, it's an interesting idea.

What about that "anal" personality? Freud said getting fixated during potty training could also lead to two different kinds of personality. One is overly stingy, regulated, and scheduled—people who find it hard to relax. In other words, maybe they took the control of potty training a bit too far. On the other hand, maybe people who don't seem to have *any* control in their lives are also stuck in the anal stage, according to Freud—they're too "relaxed."

Perhaps the most criticized part of Freudian theory is his suggestions for trouble in the phallic stage, where he believed boys and girls would start to differentiate in their personality. Freud thought that boys in the *phallic stage* would experience the *"Oedipus complex."* Named for an ancient Greek play, he believed young boys would sexually desire their own mother. At the same time, they would fear their father discovering this desire and would end the rivalry by castrating them (ouch!). To avoid this clearly unpleasant outcome, boys "identify" with their fathers, befriending them and looking up to them as heroes and role models. Freud also suggested that around this age, girls would realize they were missing a penis—and would have immediate "penis envy," realizing they got the short end of the stick (pun intended). A healthy personality would result from children overcoming these anxieties by learning to fit in with their peers and follow culturally acceptable norms.

From today's perspective, many of Freud's ideas seem sexist, heterosexist, and/or just strange. While the psychosexual stages of development are generally rejected by most modern psychologists, Freud deserves credit for at least starting the idea of exploring how our childhoods and sexual development affect our personalities as adults.

Defense Mechanisms

That was a lot of (sometimes bizarre) information to take in.

If you don't remember going through these stages, Freud would have an answer for that, too. He believed we pushed much of these childhood anxieties, fears, and desires into the unconscious part of our mind. What are some specifics for how that happens?

He suggested that we manage our anxiety through a variety of **defense mechanisms**, mental tricks we play on ourselves to avoid guilt or having to admit things we don't like about ourselves (Freud, 1920/1966). Freud created a long list of different defense mechanisms, but here are just a few:

Defense mechanisms: According to Freud, these are mental tricks we play on ourselves to avoid anxiety from ideas, impulses, or experiences we don't want to admit to ourselves.

- *Denial:* Refusing to accept facts about ourselves or the world. For example, many alcohol and addiction therapies believe the first step toward recovery is to stop denying that there's a problem.

- *Regression:* Acting childishly to avoid dealing with adult responsibilities. Think of an adult having a temper tantrum rather than rationally discussing a disagreement.

- *Repression:* Moving a trauma-inducing memory into the unconscious part of our mind so that we don't consciously remember it ever happened. A controversial belief among some therapists is that victims of childhood traumas repress abusive memories until they are "recovered," usually in the context of therapy (Loftus & Ketcham, 1996).

- *Displacement:* Taking out our emotions on innocent, nonthreatening people or objects. If you're mad at your boss but fear getting fired, you might come home and yell at your family members instead.

- *Reaction formation:* Sometimes people twist a threatening urge into the opposite as a way of hiding what they can't admit. For example, some research indicates that highly homophobic people may actually have same-sex attractions that they don't want to acknowledge (e.g., Adams et al., 1996).

- *Projection:* If you have an impulse, fear, or desire that you can't admit to yourself, you might start to "see" it all around you. You may accuse your partner of flirting with others because you secretly want to cheat on them yourself. Projection describes some of the bizarre accusations made during heated political exchanges (Bell et al., 2021).

We can't test whether defense mechanisms arise from the unconscious impulses that Freud theorized. However, we all use a variety of strategies to avoid undesirable feelings; these defense mechanisms are a useful way to deal with them.

Defense Mechanisms and Projective Tests

What about those famous inkblots? The second question on the personality test asked what words or phrases come to mind when you look at these images:

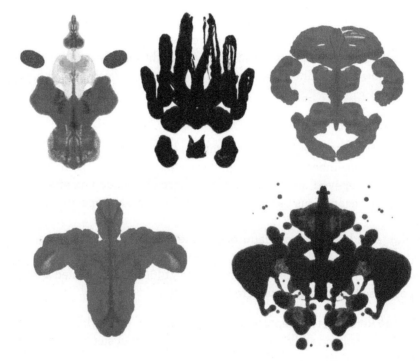

iStock.com/anankkml

Projective tests: A technique used to assess personality or in counseling in which people interpret ambiguous images like inkblots or drawings of people in a certain setting.

The last defense mechanism above, projection, probes into your personality through **projective tests** that ask you to report what you "see" in ambiguous images. The most famous projective tests are *Rorschach inkblots*, created by Swiss psychiatrist Hermann Rorschach (pronounced "roar-shock"). The *Thematic Apperception Test* is another picture-based projective test that shows people in various settings and prompts you to tell a story about the scene. In theory, your descriptions of others reveals your own unconscious anxieties, fears, or desires.

Interpreting projective tests like inkblots can be fun and entertaining—but they are extremely unreliable (Hunsley & Bailey, 1999; Lilienfeld et al., 2001; Sechrest et al., 1998; Wood et al., 2010). If your answers on a projective test mean you don't get the job and that feels unfair, it is. That said, they might have some uses in limited contexts. For example, some projective tests have greater reliability—and they might be a useful tool in therapy to start deeper conversations between a client and a counselor (Hojnoski et al., 2009).

Clearly, Freud's ideas about how personality forms and how to test it remain highly controversial. That said, he had an undeniable influence, partially because his ideas inspired others. To finish out this section on early personality theories, we'll quickly cover three people who expanded on what Freud started.

Is personality affected by birth order of siblings?

iStock.com/Image Source

Adler's Birth Order Theory

Are you an overachiever?

You may also be a middle child. Like a lot of attention? Classic only child. Question 3 in your test connects personality to birth order. Alfred Adler was one of Freud's most prominent students. A sickly child, Adler felt overlooked by his parents and that he could never live up to his siblings (Orgler, 1963). It seems that he was determined to prove his worth, haunted by feeling inferior.

Adler broke off from Freud by developing his own theory of how personality is influenced by **birth order** (Adler, 1928). Are you an only child, with no siblings at all? Adler suggests you are most likely to enjoy being the center of attention—it's what you're used to. You might have trouble sharing, because you never had to as a child. Because you were probably around adults a lot, you might also be particularly mature.

Adler pointed out that the oldest child in a family was once an only child—but then went through the anxiety of being "dethroned" when a little brother or sister came along. Suddenly no longer the center of attention, the oldest child often had the most responsibilities for taking care of their siblings. Adler suggested that oldest children might resent this and later develop personality problems like anxiety and maybe even criminal behavior.

What if you're the baby in the family? Adler said the youngest child is frequently spoiled and pampered. Their personality might stay relatively childish or immature, "getting away" with things and expecting special treatment. And what about the middle child or children? For Adler, anyone stuck in the middle is likely to be the highest achiever because they are desperate for praise and positive attention. They accomplish the most by always trying to prove themselves. But note ... Adler himself was a middle child, so he might have been a little biased.

As they have for many of Freud's theories, modern psychologists have a lot of doubts about birth order theories and think these ideas might reveal more about Adler than about anyone else. Lots of research shows that these patterns are not reliable (e.g., Botzet et al., 2021; Jefferson et al., 1998; Lejarraga et al., 2019; Pollet et al., 2010). And it's likely many other factors do matter, such as how much age difference there is among children, total family size, socioeconomic status, intelligence, and how ready parents are to have children (Lehmann et al., 2018; Rodgers et al., 2000).

Birth order: Whether you're an only child or the oldest, youngest, or middle child among siblings, Adler believed where you fall in comparison to siblings affects your personality.

Jung's Archetype Theory

Do you relate to any fictional characters?

We've all probably read books or seen movies with characters we can relate to. Another of Freud's famous students, Carl Jung, noticed that certain types of characters seem to be repeated across centuries and cultures (Jung, 1902/1961). These tropes from literature, mythology, ancient religion, and modern pop culture reflect important personality types and traits in Jung's theory, and he called them **archetypes**. The characters you chose for Question 4 in your personality test might reveal something about your identity and how you act across time and situations. Here are some of Jung's archetypes:

Archetypes: Common character types seen in myths and other stories across time and across cultures.

- *The Mother:* A powerful, curvy figure who can be fiercely protective ("mother bear") or generous and nurturing. Examples are Mother Earth, Mrs. Weasley from *Harry Potter*, and Circe from *Game of Thrones*.

- *The Hero:* A strong young man committed to saving others; he might have extraordinary powers and usually embodies virtue. Examples are Hercules, King David, and Captain America.

- *The Sage:* A wise older character who provides advice and seeks truth; they might be able to see the future but may be blind, underestimated, or not believed. Examples are Socrates, Yoda, and Dumbledore from *Harry Potter*.

- *The Trickster:* A magical and intelligent being with wizard-like powers who uses them to teach people lessons, usually for their own amusement. Examples are fairies, genies, leprechauns, coyotes in some Native American legends, and Loki from Norse mythology (and from *The Avengers*).

As you've probably surmised, Jung's theory of archetypes is used more in philosophy, literary analysis, and screenwriting than it is in modern psychology. But theories are supposed to help us better understand the world. It can be fun to analyze stories over time and from different parts of the world to see if you can identify common characters and themes.

Horney's Feminist Critique and Anxiety Theory

Do you basically trust other people?

Question 5 in the interview personality test asked how you generally relate to others. The last person we'll cover in the early psychodynamic perspective is Karen Horney (pronounced Horn-eye). Horney was deeply disturbed by the sexism in Freud's theories (Horney, 1945; see also Aldridge et al., 2014). In particular, she objected to his "penis envy" idea that little girls would realize their inferiority to boys and wish that they literally had a penis.

If little girls in Victorian Europe wanted to be boys, then it was most likely due to boys' extra opportunities and respect. She asked: Why not propose that boys and men experience "womb envy," the sadness in knowing they could never have the same physical bond with children that mothers could experience? Horney is now considered one of the first feminist psychologists.

Horney did much more than react to Freud's ideas; she came up with her own ideas of how personality is formed. She was particularly interested in interpersonal anxiety, or what she called "neurosis." Horney's neurosis focused on how children of parents who did not adequately provide for their needs develop one of three personalities, each which can lead to unhappy relationships (Horney, 1945, 1967).

First, *moving toward people* describes individuals who are desperate for love, attention, and validation from others. One way to get that attention is by attaching to the most powerful person they can find and presenting themselves as helpless. Second, *moving against people* describes socially anxious individuals who express hostility and aggression. They might bully others or lash out at their partners—they only feel comfortable if they have complete control. Third, *moving away from people* describes individuals who build figurative walls around themselves and live relatively isolated, independent lives. In Horney's words, they "build up a world of [their] own with nature, dolls, books, or dreams" (Horney, 1945, chap. 2). Do you know anyone who fits these patterns?

Practice what you learn in **Knowledge Check 13.1**   Sage Vantage ➤

THE BIOLOGICAL APPROACH

>> **LO 13.2**   **Analyze research on biological drivers of personality.**

The next part of your personality test seems a little strange.

But you go along with it because you want the job. They ask you for the following:

- Please ask a close genetic relative (bonus points if it's a biological parent) to write about (1) how you acted as a baby and (2) how your relative acts now. Please point out any similarities.

- Provide any photos—or even better, videos—of you when you were an infant.

- Finally, they ask you to sit in a chair and put on a strange-looking cap and chinstrap with wires sticking out of it. Then they hook you up to an EEG machine.

What does all of this have to do with your personality? Each might be connected to the next perspective to defining and measuring your individual differences. The biological approach to personality assumes that at least part of how you think and act is tied to your genetics, neural anatomy, and chemistry.

An Early Biological Theory: Phrenology

Do you have any weird bumps on your head?

One of the earliest examples of how people tried to tie personality to biology is the 19th-century theory of phrenology: Those bumps on your skull could reveal things about you like your intelligence or personality. People thought that parts of your brain were tied to different personality traits like "secretive" and "destructive." Those brain parts could get so big they would push against your skull and create bumps. It *sounded* scientific . . . if you were living in the 19th century. But there were a few problems with the theory.

First, the person most credited with the theory was a Viennese physician named Franz Joseph Gall. He developed his ideas by inspecting dead people's skulls and trying to figure out how the bumps he noticed were related to what he'd heard about the people before they died. This is a method ripe for experimenter bias. In other words, what Gall expected to find or wanted to find could have been tainting his conclusions.

Second—and this is a big problem—the theory was just wrong. The kinds of traits Gall "identified" aren't found in localized parts of the brain; thoughts and actions

---

? Have You Ever Wondered?
13.2 How much of personality is biologically driven?

Biological approach to personality: Studying personality with the assumption at least part of our individual differences is due to our genetics, neural anatomy, and chemistry.

Phrenology: The (now disproved) theory that bumps on your skull reveal things like your personality or intelligence.

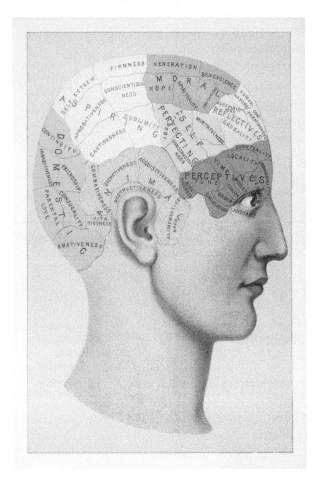

Phrenology was an early theory that proposed that your personality could be measured through the bumps on your head. Unfortunately, this theory had a lot of problems, including both lack of validity and lack of ethics.

iStock.com/THEPALMER

result from communication across many interconnected brain regions (Bressler, 2002; Edelman & Tononi, 2000). Various brain regions do have different general functions, but they don't poke out of your skull.

Third, the theory was used to promote prejudice. For example, because men are often physically bigger than women, their heads are also bigger. That could lead people to (incorrectly) believe that men are more intelligent than women. Charles Darwin's cousin, Francis Galton, tried to use phrenology as "scientific evidence" that some types of people were just inherently smarter and better than others. This led Galton to coin the term *eugenics*, an approach to selectively breed people like dogs so that "undesirable" traits would be eliminated from the gene pool (Paul, 2014). This inspired racist and homophobic pockets of 19th-century society to propose some people should be valued more—and that others should be sterilized.

Phrenology might have been a steppingstone to developing valid ideas about the biology behind personality, but it now lies in history's dustbin of falsified theories. Let's move on to theories with some scientific support.

Behavioral Genetics

Do you have the same personality as your biological parents?

What similarities do you see between yourself and your biological relatives, including any siblings? Is it possible there are certain aspects of personality that "run in the family"? Are some families naturally gifted in music, art, science, or athletics?

Do you have the same basic personality as your biological parents?

iStock.com/Alessandro Biascoli

Behavioral genetics: The study of how genes and heredity affect individual behavior.

Behavioral genetics studies how genes and heredity affect individual behavior. Biological factors like our genes may influences some traits more, while our experiences may have more impact on other traits (the classic "nature versus nurture" dichotomy). One interesting way to study these links is through *twin studies*.

Here's why twin studies are so helpful: Identical twins have the same genetics as each other. Of course, twins raised in the same family also share many experiences. So identical twins who are separated from each other and raised apart make for the most valuable studies, as now they have the same "nature" but different "nurture." Scientists also sometimes compare how similar twins are to other combinations of people with less genetic overlap, such as non-twin siblings, half-siblings, cousins, adopted siblings, and so on.

Consider one interesting example: It seems that there's a genetically heritable tendency for how much people watch TV. One early study found a correlation of $r = .49$ for identical twins and a lower correlation of $r = .38$ for nonidentical (fraternal) twins, a statistically significant difference (Loehlin & Nichols, 1976). Over 20 years later, other researchers replicated the general pattern by comparing adopted and biological children to their parents (Plomin et al., 1990). They estimated that about 20% of how much people watch TV is based on their childhood environment—meaning it's 80% due to your inherited genetics. Of course, there's probably not a "TV gene," considering that TV is such a recent invention. The authors suggest that people choose to watch an amount of TV that satisfies their need for comfort, sound, or pleasure that probably does have a genetic component.

Behavioral Genetics and Temperament

Why would baby pictures or videos help assess your personality?

If genetics influence your personality, then our personalities should stay pretty consistent as we grow up. That's why this personality test asked what you were like as a baby. **Temperament** refers to broad, general patterns of behavior and mood that can be observed in people of all ages, including newborn infants. The best approach is *longitudinal research* that observes personality features in babies and then follows them as they grow up.

How would you measure a baby's personality? Researchers have identified several key features (Buss & Plomin, 1984, 1986; Strelau & Zawadzki, 1995) such as

Temperament: Broad, general patterns of behavior and mood that can be observed in people of all ages, including infants.

- *Emotionality:* How intense are someone's emotional reactions? In infants, this might mean they cry a lot, show a startle response, or switch quickly from one emotion to another. The same patterns can be observed in adults who get upset easily, express anger in interpersonal relationships through yelling or aggression, or have unpredictable mood swings.

- *Activity:* How much energy does someone seem to have? Across people of all ages, this could be observed with how active they appear to be (e.g., amount of crawling, running, and exercise). Do people of older ages choose activities like sports or hiking in their spare time, or are they more sedentary ("couch potatoes")?

- *Sociability:* How comfortable is someone in social situations? Do they approach strangers with a smile? Do they seem to make friends quickly? Do they like parties? Or do they prefer alone time and seem awkward around others, especially new people?

- *Endurance:* Can someone focus on a single thing for an extended period of time, or is their attention span pretty short?

- *Briskness:* How quickly can someone react to their environment? Can you shift focus from one thing to another when needed?

If temperaments persist over time *and* place *and* among relatives *and* across generations, then you naturally suspect some genetic influence. Indeed, many studies find significant correlations among biological relatives' characteristics that imply heritability (Kandler et al., 2013; Mullineaux et al., 2009). One study indicated that even happiness (defined as experiencing positive emotional states) might be heritable (Bojanowska & Zalewska, 2018). On the other hand, some forms of mental illnesses may also be heritable: posttraumatic stress disorder, depression, impulse control, schizophrenia, antisocial personality, and more (Buthmann et al., 2018; DeLisi & Vaughn, 2014; Komasi et al., 2022; Trofimova & Christiansen, 2016; Zvereva et al., 2021).

Some proportion of your personality is likely due to biology—inherited tendencies that might be observed even when we're tiny babies. To learn more, check out the *What's My Score?* feature.

Temperament

Many studies on temperament measure it through observations, sometimes of infants. But for older participants, a self-report scale is much easier. Buss and Plomin (1984) developed this scale to measure three factors of temperament: emotionality, activity, and sociability. How do you score?

Instructions: Please answer the following questions regarding how typically feel. Use the following scale for each question:

1	2	3	4	5
Not at all characteristic of me		Neutral		Very characteristic of me

_____ 1. I like to be with people.

_____ 2. I usually seem to be in a hurry.

_____ 3. I am easily frightened.

_____ 4. I frequently get distressed.

_____ 5. When displeased, I let people know it right away.

_____ 6. I am something of a loner.

_____ 7. I like to keep busy all the time.

_____ 8. I am known as hot-blooded and quick-tempered.

_____ 9. I often feel frustrated.

_____ 10. My life is fast-paced.

_____ 11. Everyday events make me troubled and fretful.

_____ 12. I often feel insecure.

_____ 13. There are many things that annoy me.

_____ 14. When I get scared, I panic.

_____ 15. I prefer working with others rather than alone.

_____ 16. I get emotionally upset easily.

_____ 17. I often feel as if I'm bursting with energy.

_____ 18. It takes a lot to make me mad.

_____ 19. I have fewer fears than most people my age.

_____ 20. I find people more stimulating than anything else.

Scoring instructions: First, reverse-score items 6, 18, and 19. Remember, that means flipping your original responses so that if you wrote a 1 it becomes a 5, a 2 becomes a 4, a 3 stays a 3, a 4 becomes a 2, and a 5 becomes a 1.

Then, sum your answers for the following subscales:

- Distress: Total of items 4, 9, 11, and 16
- Fearfulness: Total of items 3, 12, 14, and 19
- Anger: Total of items 5, 8, 13, and 18
- Activity: Total of items 2, 7, 10, and 17
- Sociability: Total of items 1, 6, 15, and 20

Distress, fearfulness, and anger are all parts of the "Emotionality" factor. For all five of your scores, your sum should range from 4 to 20, with higher numbers meaning greater tendencies toward that part of temperament. When you consider your temperament today versus when you were younger, do you see consistency—or change? ●

Source: Buss and Plomin (1984).

Brain Activity and Hemispheric Lateralization

Remember that man with a hole through his brain?

Phineas Gage's historic accident demonstrated that personality was somehow linked to the brain's frontal lobes. There's been a lot of personality brain research since 1848. For example, the amygdala helps process our emotions—especially negative stimuli associated with anger and fear. Think of the many career paths in which managing anger and fear are critical parts of the job. Individuals who have damage to emotional brain regions might have difficulty recognizing, approaching, or avoiding new, threatening situations (Kagan, 1999; LeDoux, 1995, 1999).

It's not just the frontal lobes. Personality is also related to brain hemispheres. You might have heard the oversimplified myth that "right-brained people" are more creative and artistic whereas "left-brained people" are more analytical and logical (fake news! See Nielsen et al., 2013). If the two hemispheres didn't coordinate, managing your behavior would be like trying to guide a bicycle when the right and left pedals were turning at different speeds. No one is completely "right-brained" or "left-brained." However, there are intriguing hemispheric differences.

A more promising hypothesis is that our emotional tendencies are linked to hemispheric lateralization in the form of **cerebral asymmetry**, the difference in neural activity from the left to the right hemisphere. But instead of predicting "creative" versus "logical" thought patterns, the two hemispheres might influence our emotions; many of these studies are done with EEG machines.

Some studies have found evidence that positive emotions like happiness are processed more in the left hemisphere (Davidson et al., 1990). Similarly, negative emotions like fear and disgust might be processed more in the right side (Wheeler et al., 1993). When babies are picked up and held by their mother, when they laugh, and when they taste sweet foods, the left side of their brain is activated (Davidson & Fox, 1982, 1989; Fox & Davidson, 1987). Studies with adults find that people who show more activity in the left side of their brain are more likely to respond with happiness while watching movies like comedies, while people who are right-brain active show more fear and sadness when showing movies like tragedies (Davidson & Tomarken, 1989).

So, more responsiveness in one hemisphere or the other might be tied to emotional parts of our personality. Still, this information is relatively new, and exactly what it means remains to be seen for sure. Instead of mood, cerebral asymmetry may predict tendencies to approach (left-brain) or avoid (right-brain) experiences (Harmon-Jones & Allen, 1997; Pizzagalli et al., 2005). How these neural tendencies are linked to biology, human evolution, and personality is still under investigation, and we need more research (de Schotten & Beckmann, 2021; Esteves et al., 2020; Lukito et al., 2023; Palomero-Gallagher & Amunts, 2022; Rahmanian et al., 2023).

Cerebral asymmetry: The hypothesis that more brain activity in one hemisphere over the other predicts general patterns of emotion.

Practice what you learn in **Knowledge Check 13.2**   Sage Vantage ➤

THE TRAIT APPROACH

>> LO 13.3 **Explain how researchers from the trait approach measure personality and outline several contemporary trait examples.**

Have You Ever Wondered?
13.3 What is the trait approach to personality?

What's next in this unusual job interview?

You now unbuckle and remove your EEG headset, thinking this procedure really is pretty weird. Fortunately, the next part of your test seems more normal—it's back to typical survey questions. Consider what you would answer for the following questions, using this scale:

1	2	3	4	5	6	7
Not like me at all						Very much like me

_____ 1. I like to try new things and adventures.

_____ 2. I'm very responsible, detail-oriented, and perfectionistic.

_____ 3. I'm comfortable around new people and enjoy being in crowds.

_____ 4. I'm cooperative, a people-pleaser.

_____ 5. I'm a bit anxious and stressed; I'm emotionally responsive to my environment.

These five questions represent the most common way to define and measure personality. You are following the **trait approach to personality** if you describe yourself as "shy" or "outgoing"—behavioral tendencies that persist across time and place. The trait approach doesn't usually concern itself with *why* you are the way you are. Instead, it focuses on identifying and measuring which traits predict behavior.

Trait approach to personality: A focus on which aspects of personality predict behavior regardless of circumstance, time, or culture; it includes the "Big 5" model.

Identifying Important Traits: Factor Analysis

Just how many traits are there?

If you search for personality tests on any website—including "entertainment" sites like Buzzfeed—you'll discover that psychologists are defining, measuring, and testing hundreds of traits. It may seem overwhelming, but psychologists have a way of "playing favorites" in what they study. Favorites are usually chosen based on either someone's personal interests or because psychologists believe in scientific evidence for our claims . . . and that scientific evidence comes from statistical analysis.

Statistics are ways to satisfy your curiosity. And if the authors of this book (one of whom earned a D in high school algebra) can learn (and love) statistics, then you can, too. A favored approach in personality trait research is a technique called **factor analysis** that uses correlations to identify clusters of words or items. For example, consider the following adjectives and phrases:

Factor analysis: A statistical technique that uses correlation to identify clusters of items on a test that make up a reliable group or subscale.

1. Talkative

2. Helpful, unselfish

3. Comfortable around new people

4. A peacekeeper

5. Full of energy

6. Generally trusting

7. Tends to be loud

8. Warm and caring

If you asked 1,000 people to rate themselves on these eight items as a personality test, and you then correlated the ratings with each other, some of the words would probably cluster together. Here, the odd-numbered items are from a personality test measuring extraversion (John & Srivastava, 1999). Someone who's highly extraverted would probably put similar scores for these items (e.g., give them all a high score). The even-numbered items are from the same test, but they measure how cooperative and agreeable someone tends to be. A factor analysis test looks for this kind of clustering of subscales within a larger survey.

As a field, psychology debated just how many core psychology traits really mattered in terms of predicting behaviors. It took several decades for personality researchers to recruit, study, and analyze data from thousands of participants. But over hundreds of studies, the clusters (or factors) of traits gradually came into sharper focus. For example, early researchers used factor analysis to identify 16 traits initially thought to be important (Cattell, 1943; Cattell et al., 1970). Later, 16 was thought to be too many; maybe whittling it down to just 3 would be better (Eysenck, 1978).

Eventually, most people in the field today have agreed on five basic, universal personality traits in humans. Why five? Because the same five personality clusters keep reappearing across hundreds of studies using factor analysis tests (e.g., Digman, 1990; Fiske, 1949; Goldberg, 1992; McCrae & Costa, 1997, 2008). The "Big Five" have become widely accepted because they seem to predict people's behaviors in a wide variety of settings (validity) and have consistently emerged in studies by unrelated researchers over the decades across many different cultures (reliability). Importantly, the universality of the Big 5 model is somewhat debatable, and we'll finish the chapter by coming back to this question—but for now, understand that it's one of the most popular approaches to personality in all of psychology.

The Big 5 Model

Remember the OCEAN.

You can remember the Big 5 Model, sometimes called the "five-factor model," by using the mnemonic OCEAN for Openness, Conscientiousness, Extraversion, Agreeableness, and Neuroticism (see Figure 13.2). Each trait corresponds to the five job interview questions at the start of this section. You can also try rating yourself on each trait in Table 13.3.

It may also help you understand the Big 5 Model if you apply it to something you care about: success in college. Hundreds of studies have applied these traits to various outcomes for college and universities students (for a comprehensive review, see Kyllonen et al., 2014). For example, out of all five traits, openness to experience has the highest correlations with verbal intelligence (as measured by tests like the SAT);

Big 5 Model: A theory that there are five universally valid and reliable personality traits: openness to experience, conscientiousness, extraversion, agreeableness, and neuroticism.

FIGURE 13.2

The Big 5 Model of Personality

The Big 5 Model suggests there are five major and universal personality traits in everyone. You can remember the traits because the first letters of each can be arranged to spell the word "OCEAN."

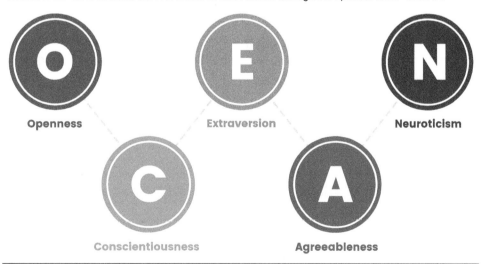

Openness
Extraversion
Neuroticism
Conscientiousness
Agreeableness

iStock.com/ribkhan

TABLE 13.3

Rate Yourself on the "Big 5" Traits

TRAIT	DESCRIPTION	RATING: 1–10
Openness to experience	Enjoyment of adventure, new experiences, independence, and curiosity	
Conscientiousness	Attention to detail, responsibility, self-discipline, high achievers	
Extraversion	Highly social, energetic, assertive, spontaneous	
Agreeableness	Cooperative, a peacemaker, compassionate toward other	
Neuroticism	Anxious, prone to stress, more likely to be depressed and socially insecure	

people high in openness also tend to have positive attitudes toward studying. Not surprisingly, conscientiousness—a trait tied to being responsible and disciplined—is consistently tied to doing well in college. There are less obvious links for extraversion, where context might matter. Some studies imply that extraverts might have an advantage in discussion-based classes, while introverts are better at writing essays. When it comes to agreeableness, scores on this subscale aren't directly tied to grades—but they are tied to college outcomes like social adjustment. And finally for neuroticism, high scores can be negatively correlated with college performance, but the relationship is weak; studies show that this trait only affects college life through other factors like motivation and impulsivity.

What about when it comes to careers and that interesting job interview? As you might expect, several research studies have found additional connections between personality traits, career paths, and other important life outcomes. For example, individuals high in

- openness to experience are often drawn to careers in science or art (Feist, 1998; Rubinstein & Strul, 2007), and they are more likely to try *and* benefit from therapy (Miller, 1991);

- conscientiousness tend to be better drivers (Arthur & Graziano, 1996) and live longer—probably because they are more aware of their health and make decisions based on long-term benefits instead of short-term pleasure (Friedman et al., 1995);

- extraversion have more friends and like to socialize more than introverts (Selfhout et al., 2010);

- agreeableness are more likely to help others in need (Habashi et al., 2016); and

- neuroticism people are more stressed out by daily challenges, as well as being more likely to experience anxiety and depression (Costa & McCrae, 1992; Gunthert et al., 1999).

Animal Personality

This is Thor on the day one of your authors [Wind] adopted him.

When Wind [one of your authors] saw a litter of wild kittens romping around in her neighbor's backyard, she couldn't resist their cuteness (despite being allergic to cats). Her partner and she agreed to adopt one of them and quickly decided on the little gray one who showed the most curiosity and boldness out of the four furballs. Now over a year old and quite huge, he continues to show these tendencies (they named him Thor).

Most pet owners and animal lovers agree: At least some species of animals have personalities. But we can't get them to complete self-report scales (their little paws just don't hold the pencils or hit the computer keys right!). So, research on animal personality relies on careful naturalistic observations of behaviors. Australia and New Zealand researchers (Litchfield et al., 2017) studied pet

cats by starting with a list of 52 possible traits previously observed in wild cats in Scotland. This list was provided to owners of 2,208 pet cats at least 1 year old and from a variety of breeds. Each human rated their cat on all 52 traits using a 1 to 7 scale ranging from *not at all* to *very much so*. Examples of items were "friendly to other cats" and "seems scared easily—jumpy and frightful in general." After the owners rated their own cat, a factor analysis looked for patterns.

Just like the Big 5 Model for personality in humans, the factor analysis revealed a "Feline 5" set of traits for the pet cats (Litchfield et al., 2017). Three of the factors ended up paralleling the same personality traits in humans: neuroticism (insecurity, anxiety), extraversion (bold, vocal, active), and agreeableness (affectionate, friendly). Two were a little different: dominance (aggressive, defiant, greedy) and impulsiveness (indecisive, clumsy, distractable).

Still curious about what other species of animals display unique personalities? Check it out on GoogleScholar, your library's database of psychology articles, or a summary about the social psychology of humans and their pets (Heinzen & Goodfriend, 2022). Typing "animal personality traits" will get you thousands of hits (use the quotation marks around the phrase to get specific results). Or, try coming up with your own list of possible personality traits in other animals, like dogs, birds, or horses. How would you test your ideas? ●

Philosophers Machiavelli (left) and Kant (right) both have personality traits named after them. One is much more positive than the other.

iStock.com/Grafissimo

The Dark and Light Triads of Personality

Should we really stop at five?

The Big 5 Model has been an enormous help, but your curiosity might compel you to explore the darker side of human behavior. For example—do you like true crime shows like *Law and Order, CSI,* or *Criminal Minds*? Are the five traits discussed in the section above adequate to understand the "dark side" of human behavior? What about abusive relationship partners, authoritarian dictators, and subversive political leaders who appear not to have a conscience? This kind of villainous character might be better described using a theory based on three other personality traits called the **dark triad**, which includes Machiavellianism, narcissism, and psychopathy (Paulhus & Williams, 2002).

The first trait, Machiavellianism, has a political context. An Italian diplomat, Niccolò Machiavelli (1469–1537), wrote *The Prince* as a practical guide for the ruthless application of political power (Dietz, 1986; Jackson & Grace, 2018). People high in *Machiavellianism* rely on lying, flattery, cheating, manipulation, and plotting. It combines distrust of others with a callous uncaring attitude toward friends and foes alike (Collison et al., 2018). For example, college students with Machiavellian impulses are more likely to cheat on tests—but only if they think they won't be caught (Barbaranelli et al., 2018). It won't surprise you that Machiavellianism is negatively correlated with agreeableness and with any kind of altruistic helping behaviors.

Extreme levels of the next two traits, narcissism and psychopathy, are clinical mental disorders—but don't need to be extreme to contribute to the dark triad. *Narcissism* involves feelings of entitlement, superiority to everyone around you, and the desire for dominance. *Psychopathy* refers to high impulsivity and thrill-seeking as well as low levels of empathy and anxiety. As part of the dark triad, people high in psychopathy enjoy taking risks and don't worry about the consequences, even when those risks might hurt others. People high in the dark triad traits tend to be bullies, but they can sometimes be charming bullies with a refined intuition for identifying vulnerable people whom they can victimize and con (Dåderman & Ragnestål-Impola, 2019; Gordon & Platek, 2009; Harrison et al., 2018; Lopes & Yu, 2017; Pruysers et al., 2019).

What about genuinely *good* people? They exist too! The **light triad** is a relatively new contribution to the trait perspective, suggesting a reciprocal cluster of traits (Kaufman et al., 2019). *Kantianism* (named after the German philosopher Immanuel Kant) is the tendency to treat relationships with people as a goal in and of itself, as opposed to thinking only about how to use people. *Humanism* is valuing the dignity and worth of others. Finally, *faith in humanity* is just as it sounds—believing in the fundamental goodness of humans. People who have high levels of these traits are happier, are healthier, and have better relationships with others.

If you were to profile world leaders in the past couple of decades—like Presidents Obama, Trump, or Vladimir Putin—where do you think they would fall on these traits? What about your favorite characters from books, movies, or TV shows?

Dark triad: A cluster of three traits thought to predict manipulation of others and criminal behavior; the traits are Machiavellianism, narcissism, and psychopathy.

Light triad: A cluster of three traits thought to predict positive relationships and quality of life; the traits are Kantianism, humanism, and faith in humanity.

THE HUMANISTIC AND SOCIAL COGNITIVE APPROACHES

>> **LO 13.4** **Compare and contrast humanistic and social-cognitive theories of personality.**

It's the last part of your interview!

To finish up the personality test, they ask you a few more questions in survey form. This time, you're asked to respond to the questions below with this scale:

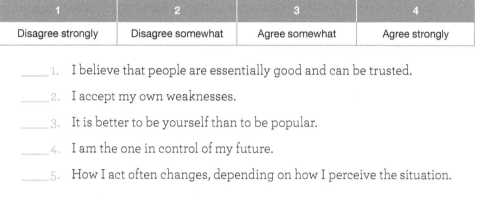

1	2	3	4
Disagree strongly	Disagree somewhat	Agree somewhat	Agree strongly

_____ 1. I believe that people are essentially good and can be trusted.

_____ 2. I accept my own weaknesses.

_____ 3. It is better to be yourself than to be popular.

_____ 4. I am the one in control of my future.

_____ 5. How I act often changes, depending on how I perceive the situation.

To review so far: The early, psychodynamic approach to personality says you are who you are because of your childhood experiences. The biological approach focuses on your genetic parents' influences. The trait approach measures your personality tendencies but doesn't really care where they came from. None of these perspectives has much room for you being in *control* of your personality. This is where the final two perspectives come in.

The **humanistic approach to personality** focuses on your self-concept, motivations, and personal potential; it assumes that what you find important in life shapes your thoughts and behaviors. It hopes to empower you and build your self-esteem. Finally, the **social-cognitive approach to personality** explores how your perceptions of what's going on at any given time influence your behavior: You can shift your personality depending on your environment. Both approaches place you more in the driver's seat of your own personality by acknowledging internal choice and motivation.

The Humanistic Approach

What would be the best version of you?

That question is key to the humanistic approach to personality, which we first introduced when we discussed motivation theories. What does it say about personality? Fulfilling your potential and achieving goals you set for yourself is one way to think about how to act across situations over time.

Peak Experiences

You already know about Maslow's (1943, 1962) hierarchy of needs from a previous chapter. The idea of fulfilling basic needs first, then working on self-actualization (achieving your best self) through extraordinary moments called peak experiences, can be inspiring. If you answered "3" or "4" to the first three questions on the personality test at the start of this section (modified from Jones & Crandall, 1986), then you're

? **Have You Ever Wondered?**
13.4 What are humanistic and social-cognitive theories of personality?

Humanistic approach to personality: Studying personality by focusing on self-concept, motivations, and personal potential.

Social-cognitive approach to personality: Studying personality by considering the interaction between perceptions of the world and the environment at any given time.

moving along Maslow's path toward your personal potential: You believe people are essentially good, you accept your own weaknesses, and you think it's more important to be authentic than popular (although they aren't mutually exclusive).

Some researchers suggest that one way to think about personality from a humanistic perspective would be to notice people who consistently appear particularly energetic, positive, and simply "alive," as if they never waste a moment of life. A term for this kind of personality could be *subjective vitality* (Ryan & Frederick, 1997). Other work shows that people who consistently pursue intrinsic goals (like better relationships and health) over extrinsic goals (like money and fame) have higher well-being and are happier overall (Bradshaw et al., 2023). Some scholars are working on a recent idea they're calling *emotion crafting*, the idea that people can both identify what makes us feel good and then proactively and consistently engage in behaviors to increase positive emotions over time and situations (van der Kaap-Deeder et al., 2023). Theoretically, people high in emotion crafting should therefore have better mental health and well-being as a function of their personality.

Personality and a Growth Mindset

Other psychologists have also built on the ideas of empowerment and free will. Recall from the chapter on cognition and intelligence (Chapter 12) Dweck's (2006) theory of growth versus fixed mindset. She proposed that people with a growth mindset believe our abilities and talents can improve over time, with practice and willpower. However, those with a fixed mindset believe that we are simply good or bad at things and helpless to change. How does mindset interact with personality?

One study asked over 11,000 young adults in Germany to complete survey measures of mindset and the Big 5 personality traits at two important moments in life: just before and just after graduating from school and moving away from home for the first time (De Vries et al., 2021). Results showed that for people with a fixed mindset, their personality didn't change between the first and second surveys. But for people with a growth mindset, their extraversion scores significantly increased. The researchers concluded that people with a growth mindset approach challenges like graduation and moving to a new community as opportunities to grow and adapt, resulting in an increase in extraversion. Note that none of the other Big 5 traits showed significant results. Do you agree with their conclusions, or do you think there are other ways to interpret what they found? Has being in college affected your personality?

If you're still curious about whether personality can change as you age, we'll come back to this question in the final section of the chapter.

A Fully Functioning Self

Fully functioning: Carl Rogers's term for a strong, empowered person who is living authentically.

Carl Rogers developed personality approaches to help his therapy clients overcome barriers to reaching their full potential—what he called a **fully functioning** person (Rogers, 1951, 1961, 1970) who was

- Open to new experiences; not afraid to try things

- Flexible and malleable in new circumstances rather than reliant on the comfort of routine

- Able to embrace life as it happens, understanding that even seemingly negative experiences can teach us lessons

- Trusting of their inner feelings and instincts

- Empowered to live authentically, even if that means going against social norms or expectations

- Nonconformist

- Capable of really *feeling* all emotions, good and bad, instead of avoiding them

Do these standards seem a bit out of reach—or do you aspire to live by them? Maslow, Dweck, and Rogers used different terms and images to explain their theories, but they had several things in common. The humanistic approach to personality suggests that we can always improve, learn from failure, that embracing our fully realized self leads to greater happiness and personal success, and that the courage of authentic nonconformity pushes society's boundaries. The core humanistic question might be: Who are you *really*—and who could you be if nothing were stopping you?

PSYCHOLOGY AND OUR CURIOUS WORLD

RuPaul and Nonconformity

Image Press Agency/Alamy Stock Photo; Album/Alamy Stock Photo

"If you can't love yourself, how can you love someone else?"

This catchphrase of well-known drag queen RuPaul has been modified to avoid controversial language. RuPaul is a hero in the LGBTQIA2S+ community for living by the humanistic ideal of authenticity. His popular competition show, *RuPaul's Drag Race*, chooses a drag queen contestant based on several personality traits along with talents like humor and grace.

RuPaul has received more Emmys than any other person of color for his pioneering work. He's also been named one of *Time* magazine's "most influential people in the world." One reason he's so beloved is that he encourages people to accept who they really are, even if their family doesn't. That said, his show has been controversial in the past for blurring the line between drag queens and trans women, for using terms not accepted by everyone in the LGBTQ+ community, and even for being transphobic. He has changed his show in response to such criticism. As a result, he might qualify as someone moving toward Maslow's description of someone who is "self-actualizing," Dweck's "growth" mindset, and Rogers's ideal of "fully functioning." Nonconformists will always be controversial . . . but they are the ones who pave the way for progress. ●

The Social-Cognitive Approach

Are you in control of your personality?

The psychodynamic, biological, and trait approaches assume adults are (more or less) stuck with their personality. However, a more empowered perspective is that we're thoughtful, intelligent beings with dynamic personalities that are always under construction. We can even modify our personality based on who we are with and social expectations of us in different situations. This flexibility is called **reciprocal determinism**: The environment shapes our thoughts and behaviors—and vice versa (see Figure 13.3) (Bandura, 1986, 1997, 2001).

For example, you normally might be a bit shy and tend to worry about how others judge you. But on a job interview, you *know* they're judging you. So, you smile, act friendly, and engage throughout the process. You can choose to bring out your inner

Reciprocal determinism: The idea that our thoughts and behaviors (including our personality) are shaped by the environment and vice versa.

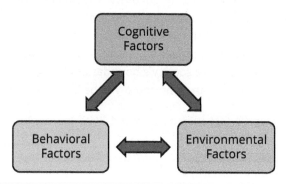

FIGURE 13.3

Reciprocal Determinism

Reciprocal determinism proposes that personality is the product of three interacting factors: (1) thoughts and perceptions (cognitive factors), (2) actions (behavioral factors), and (3) situations (environmental factors).

extravert, for example. Your circumstances (the environment) have influenced your thoughts and behaviors. At the same time, the reverse (or reciprocal) is also true. As you think optimistically and act confidently, the people around you shift as well to being more open and friendly. Your thoughts and behaviors have influenced the environment.

The social-cognitive approach to personality acknowledges that we have some control over ourselves and can bring out parts of our personality to suit the needs of the time and place. Two specific concepts, locus of control and self-monitoring, demonstrate how interactions between our chosen environments and our behavior shape our personalities.

Locus of Control

"I am the one in control of my future."

That was item 4 in the job interview personality test in this section of the chapter. It's inspired by a variable called **locus of control**, which is the degree to which you believe either that (a) you control your life (called an *internal locus*), or (b) your life is controlled by powerful external factors (called an *external locus*). External factors might be fate, random chance, a higher power, or even powerful people like your parents, professors, or boss (Rotter, 1966, 1990).

With an internal locus of control, you notice how your efforts and choices affect your life. You can take credit for successes like good grades, happy relationships, and job offers. But to be consistent, you must also take blame for failures. On the other hand, an external locus of control means you can blame your failures on external factors, such as mean professors and bad bosses. But to be consistent, you must also explain success as due to a lucky break. Locus of control has been applied to thousands of different situations across many cultures (e.g., Asante & Affum-Osei, 2019; Karkoulian et al., 2016; Nowicki & Duke, 2017).

The original locus of control scale (Rotter, 1966) required people to choose between two statements such as those in Table 13.4 ("a" or "b"). Circle the option you agree with more; the caption will help you interpret your answers. Hopefully, you can quickly see how locus of control is tied to personality. Whether you feel in control of your life has important effects on your approach to everything you do, including grades, social relationships, and physical and mental health (Lachman & Weaver, 1998;

Locus of control: Belief about whether your life is controlled by you (internal locus) or by outside factors (external locus).

TABLE 13.4

Example Items Measuring Locus of Control

For each pair of items, mark the one ("a" or "b") you agree with more. Then count your number of each. More "a" answers indicate an internal locus of control, while more "b" answers indicate an external locus of control.

1a.	People's misfortunes result from the mistakes they make.
1b.	Many of the unhappy things in people's lives are partly due to bad luck.
2a.	One of the major reasons why we have wars is because people don't take enough interest in politics.
2b.	There will always be wars, no matter how hard people try to prevent them.
3a.	In the long run, people get the respect they deserve in this world.
3b.	Unfortunately, an individual's worth often passes unrecognized no matter how hard they try.
4a.	The idea that teachers are unfair to students is nonsense.
4b.	Most students don't realize the extent to which their grades are influenced by accidental happenings.
5a.	Capable people who fail to become leaders have not taken advantage of their opportunities.
5b.	Without the right breaks, one cannot be an effective leader.
6a.	People who can't get others to like them don't understand how to get along with others.
6b.	No matter how hard you try, some people just don't like you.
7a.	It is one's experiences in life which determine what they're like.
7b.	Heredity plays the major role in determining one's personality.

Source: Adapted from Rotter (1966); the original scale had more items.

Miller et al., 1986; Nezlek, 2001; Tangney et al., 2018). A strong external locus of control can lead to feelings of helplessness—but acknowledging that some things really aren't your fault can be therapeutic.

A flexible balance between internal and external locus of control tendencies, interacting with particular circumstances, appears to be the healthiest approach.

Self-Monitoring

"How I act often changes, depending on the situation."

That was your job interview's last question. The social-cognitive approach recognizes that you can adjust your personality to fit your surroundings. Our ability to do this strategically in different situations is called **self-monitoring** (Snyder, 1974). People who are good at it—*high in self-monitoring*—are sometimes even called "social chameleons" (Kilduff & Day, 1994). They are often socially popular because they are good at reading the room and adjusting their behavior. People who *don't* change to fit in—people *low in self-monitoring*—act consistently regardless of their environments. They are always shy or loud or competitive or polite or sarcastic . . . no matter what. They don't "monitor"

Chameleons can change how they appear to fit into their surroundings. Can you?

iStock.com/bayshev

Self-monitoring: Individuals' ability to strategically notice and adjust their own behavior in different situations.

the situation or how they act because they (a) don't feel they have to, (b) don't know how, or (c) just don't care.

High self-monitors may gravitate to certain public careers, such as sales, politics, and acting; they tend to be more motivated by social status (Flynn et al., 2006). College students who are high self-monitors are generally more liked by their peers, and groups with high self-monitoring members often report better group cohesion (Qiongjing & Zhixue, 2018). High self-monitors are often chosen as group leaders (Eby et al., 2003). But be careful—people who change how they act can appear inauthentic, untrustworthy, and self-serving (Kleinbaum et al., 2015; Ogunfowora et al., 2013; Pillow et al., 2017). In sales, it can lead to unethical practices designed to deceive customers (Yang et al., 2019). At an extreme, high self-monitors might purposely hide who they really are (a classic example is the serial killer Ted Bundy!).

Do you think that you are a high or a low self-monitor—and is that working well for you?

CAREER CORNER

Meet Alec, Financial Advisor

What is your career?

I have worked in finance for 5 years, mostly in sales or management. As a financial advisor, it is my job to get to know my clients at a deeper level in order to help them articulate their goals, then create a holistic plan full of small, actionable steps that lead to success. This can include budgeting, debt repayment plans, investment advice, insurance, retirement planning, etc.

How was studying psychology important for success in this career?

I wanted a career path that was service oriented and allowed me to connect with people in a meaningful way. I know the finance world may not always seem "service oriented," but next to physical and mental health, financial well-being has one of the largest impacts on quality of life. **Understanding concepts like personality helps me bridge the gap between myself and a client when discussing highly emotional topics such as money.**

How do concepts from this chapter help in this career?

Most of my job as an advisor is helping clients change their behaviors. Building better money habits is normally the key to success, and that can be a tough pill for clients to swallow. **It requires buy-in and motivation from the client, which is where understanding the Big 5 personality traits is so important.** By trying to understand where my client falls on the spectrum for each trait, I can gain insight into the best way to approach them when suggesting changes in behavior. For example, the way I interact with someone who is high in conscientiousness and low in openness to experience would be very different from the client who is low in agreeableness and high in neuroticism.

Is this the career you always planned to have after college?

No—not at all. Thankfully, I had an internship with a company that showed me how much impact you can have on people's lives in this industry. **Mental, physical, and financial health all have enormous impacts on our lives and well-being.**

If you could give current college students one sentence of advice, what would it be?

Don't silo yourself to a title or job just because you chose a certain major when you were 17 or 18 years old; your passions and perspectives are going to change, so find ways to apply what you are learning any activity you find fulfilling. ●

PERSONALITY CONTROVERSIES

>> **LO 13.5** **Analyze several controversies and debates when it comes to understanding the psychology of personality.**

You got through the personality test for that job interview, but what does it *really* tell your potential employer?

Now that you know how most psychologists operationalize (define and measure) personality, you can form some science-based opinions about four interesting debates or controversies in the field. As you consider each, let your natural curiosity consider how you could learn more.

Controversy 1: Personality Versus the Situation

In most classrooms, everyone acts pretty much the same.

Does that mean personality doesn't really matter? Psychologist Walter Mischel famously wrote that most of the time, situations probably matter more (Mischel, 1968, 1973, 1990, 2009). If you look around a typical office, religious event, or party, pretty much everybody acts the same; personality isn't really noticeable. So why all the fuss about personality?

While Mischel's publications are often perceived as criticizing the very existence of personality, he denies that's what he meant. His point is that personality tests only predict a small variation of how people act across time and settings. Most personality tests only correlate around .20 to .40 (out of 1) with actual behaviors. He also notes that big events, like traumas or emergencies, can change our personality.

Consider one of the settings for which Mischel is most famous: his *marshmallow studies* (Mischel et al., 1972; Mischel & Ebbesen, 1970; Peake et al., 2002). Mischel brought preschool-aged kids to the lab and sat them down at a desk with a desired treat in front of them (marshmallows, pretzels, etc.). He then gave them a choice: You can have one treat now—or if you wait a few minutes without eating the treat, you can have *two* later (or sometimes they could get an even more preferred treat). The point was to test their self-control and ability to delay gratification. Follow-up studies years later showed that the kids who had self-control at age 4 did better in school, were more likely to get into college, and had better social relationships (Mischel et al., 1989).

This sounds like a personality trait—self-control—that's stable over time and predicts behavior, right? For Mischel, though, one of the most important *situational* elements of his studies often gets ignored: He made the waiting easier or harder for the child by having to wait with or without a distraction, or being able to hide (or not hide) the marshmallow from sight. These situational elements mattered—they helped the children resist temptation, regardless of personality (Mischel & Ebbesen, 1970).

These classic studies are now decades old, but the debate continues. Reciprocal determinism tells us that our thoughts, feelings, and behaviors are the result of constant interactions between personality and the environment, so it's perhaps the closest thing to a compromise in this controversy. Like most "either/or" questions, the answer isn't one or the other but degrees of both. In a classroom, most people generally act similarly—but there are still some people who talk more than others, for

Have You Ever Wondered?
13.5 What are some current personality controversies?

In a typical classroom, everyone acts the same as everyone else. Does that mean personality doesn't really matter much in terms of predicting behaviors?

iStock.com/pondsaksit

example. Personality produces *behavioral tendencies* that are an important part of how we humans explain our curious world—but personality is only part of the explanation.

Controversy 2: Personality Change Over Time

Does your personality ever change?

Some personality psychologists believe we're stable over our life span (e.g., Caspi, 2000). Others disagree, or at least think it's nuanced (e.g., Asendorph & van Aken, 1999; Atherton et al., 2021; Costa et al., 2019; Damian et al., 2019; Roberts & Del Vecchio, 2000). Even the biological approach, which generally implies relative stability, now has wiggle room. For example, in recent years, the study of *epigenetics* has clarified that the environment can influence the expression of genes (Kanherkar et al., 2014).

As Mischel suggested in the previous section, there is evidence that traumas can change your personality, in both positive and negative ways, but exactly how is pretty complicated (Jayawickreme et al., 2021). For example,

- neuroticism (anxiety) generally increases after traumas, especially if they happen early in life;

- stress in childhood is associated with higher openness to experience in adult men, but not in women; and

- traumas during adolescence were correlated with lower agreeableness and conscientiousness, but only when the traumas arose from the participants' own behaviors (something they controlled).

Fixed-role therapy: A counseling technique that encourages people to think and act in new ways, eventually changing their personality.

Many people who have experienced a trauma and now want to change their personality hope that therapy can help. **Fixed-role therapy** is a counseling technique in which clients imagine themselves as different kinds of people (more generous, less selfish, less aggressive, and so on), with the specific goal of eventually changing their personality (Kelly, 1955).

But perhaps the most direct way to test the question of whether personality changes over time is with *longitudinal* research, studies done over time. For example, one study asked 163 men to complete several surveys at two times: once at college graduation and again around age 67 (when many people retire; Soldz & Vaillant, 1999). They found that over the course of adulthood, people experience a wide variety of changes in their careers, relationships, mental health, political attitudes, and more . . . but personality was fairly stable.

Two researchers looked at 152 different longitudinal studies measuring personality and made two major conclusions, summarized in Figure 13.4 (Roberts & DelVecchio, 2000). First, scores on personality traits tend to be positively correlated with scores from the same people 7 years later. Second, as people age, those correlations got stronger—meaning personality stabilizes, probably reaching a plateau around age 50. Another way to say this is that personality is a bit more flexible in childhood, but it tends to crystalize more and more as we grow up. This compromised, middle-ground conclusion would explain inconsistencies in past research.

Controversy 3: Personality Tests at Work

Imagine this: You didn't get the job.

After all that strange testing! You'd probably be pretty upset—all that work for nothing! Many human resources departments really do ask potential or current employees to complete personality tests. One of the most popular is the Myers-Briggs assessment, a survey that puts responders into groups inspired by Jung's archetypes.

FIGURE 13.4

Stability of Personality as We Age

A review of 152 longitudinal studies found that personality is more flexible in childhood and stabilizes as we grow up.

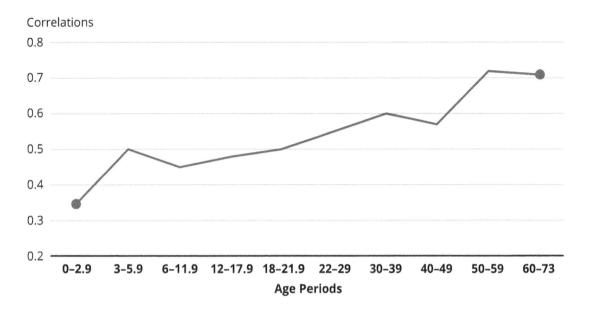

Source: Created using data from Roberts and DelVecchio (2000).

Despite the popularity of this test, there are many reasons why psychological scientists warn against it (Pittenger, 1993, 2005; Stein & Swan, 2019; Stromberg & Caswell, 2015). For example, the Myers–Briggs personality test

- was originally developed by a mother–daughter team who had no formal training in developing personality tests,

- ignores nuances (being an "introvert" or "extravert" isn't really a dichotomy— it's a spectrum or range with most people in the middle and rare exceptions at the outer fringes),

- is based on an untestable theory (Cherry, 2021; The Myers-Briggs Company, 2018), and

- forces personalities into 16 categories represented by four letters. For example, ENTJs are called "commanders" and supposedly make good leaders; ESTPs are called "persuaders" and are outgoing and friendly (Boyle, 1995; Stein & Swan, 2019).

Many psychologists criticize this test for another reason: When it puts people into the categories at the end, it provides vague descriptions of individuals in that category that produce a **Barnum effect**. A Barnum effect occurs for any personality test or similar type of survey when the results are so vague and general that they could apply to anyone. It's the criticism psychologists have for astrology: It's supposedly about you, but it's about *everyone*. Consider this example "personality profile":

> *You like to have a lot of information before you make a decision, but you also like to trust your instincts; you like to be noticed but are often worried about what people think of you.*

Barnum effect: When people believe the results of tests or surveys are supposedly for them individually, but don't realize the "results" are so broad and vague they apply to everyone.

Before you react with, "Amazing! That really describes me," realize...those words describe just about everyone. If something is true of everyone, then it can't distinguish anyone.

The official Myers–Briggs website now warns against using the test for hiring decisions. Several law firms also advertise that companies using these practices might be setting themselves up for discrimination lawsuits. And remember that people taking personality tests during job interviews might be under the influence of *social desirability* and *impression management;* their answers might not be entirely honest.

Controversy 4: WEIRD Biases and Non-"Western" Approaches

Are personality theories WEIRD?

There might be some bias built into the ideas in this chapter. Most of the researchers and studies in the history of personality theory are from WEIRD countries (recall that WEIRD stands for "Western," Educated, Industrialized, Rich, and Democratic). We already mentioned that phrenology was used for racist and homophobic purposes, as people tried to advance eugenics (selective human breeding). Here's another troubling example: Briggs and Briggs Myers, the creators of the Myers–Briggs test mentioned above, weren't trained psychologists—they were fiction writers. Their most controversial novel was published in 1934, a story some people believe has White supremacist overtones (Dahl, 2015; Emre, 2015; Spichak, 2021). (Note: The official test company's website defends the book and author, saying the characters were racist because the book was set in a racist time and place.)

Less sensational, but still important to consider, is the possibility that popular theories like the Big 5 Model are simply limited in terms of their generalizability. In personality research, scholars take one of two approaches (Sue, 1983). The "etic" approach generally assumes that there are core personality traits—like the Big 5— that matter to all humans, regardless of culture. In contrast, the "emic" approach emphasizes and values cultural differences. There are benefits and drawbacks to both perspectives, but several studies have now failed to replicate the Big 5 factor analysis results in certain parts of the world (for a nice review, see Thalmayer et al., 2022).

In fact, research with non-WEIRD samples finds not only that the Big 5 factor analysis structure fails to replicate in some cultures but that other, different personality traits might matter more when it comes to predicting behavior in those communities. Here are a few interesting examples:

- Research with the fishing, hunting, and farming Tsimane people of Bolivia suggested two new emic personality traits: prosociality (generosity, trustworthiness) and industriousness (ability to provide for one's family; Gurven et al., 2013).

- The emic personalities of indigenous Filipino participants showed variance in conscientiousness (an overlap with the Big 5), as well as six additional unique traits: concern for others, self-assuredness, temperamentality, intelligence, gregariousness, and "negative valence" (including uselessness, stupidity, cruelty, etc.; Guanzon-Lapeña et al., 1998).

- Emic personality traits in Chinese participants might be mental harmony, "Ren Qing" (a kind of social reciprocity), attitudes regarding tradition versus modernization, thrift versus extravagance in spending, "Ah-Q" (a sense of self-protection), and "face" (desire to enhance social standing; Cheung et al., 1996, 2001).

- In rural Kenya and Tanzania, the Maasai people are traditional herders and warriors. Their emic personality factor structure had five factors in one study: moral character, vulnerability, boldness, pride, and timidity (Thalmayer et al., 2020).

The more diversity we include in research, the more interesting our curious world becomes. ●

Practice what you learn in **Knowledge Check 13.5**   Sage Vantage➤

Learning Objectives Summary

13.1   What are some of the earliest psychological theories about personality?

≫ LO 13.1   **Explain early personality theories from the psychodynamic approach.**

Sigmund Freud started the psychodynamic approach to therapy and personality, which emphasizes unconscious anxieties and wishes that affect us, usually from childhood. He developed several theories regarding parts of our mind (called the id, ego, and superego) and defense mechanisms. Several people modified and updated his ideas, including Alder, Jung, and Horney.

13.2   How much of personality is biologically driven?

≫ LO 13.2   **Analyze research on biological drivers of personality.**

The biological approach to personality assumes at least part of our individual differences is driven by the genes we inherited and by our neural chemistry and anatomy. While early ideas were invalid and unethical (such as phrenology), more recent research has uncovered interesting links between personality, genetic heritability of behavioral tendencies, and neural activity.

13.3   What is the trait approach to personality?

≫ LO 13.3   **Explain how researchers from the trait approach measure personality and outline several contemporary trait examples.**

The trait approach attempts to identify factors or characteristics that predict behaviors across time and settings; some researchers believe these traits are universal regardless of culture. The most popular theory from this perspective is called the Big 5 Model, which identifies five important traits: openness to experience, conscientiousness, extraversion, agreeableness, and neuroticism. Other traits have also been suggested.

13.4   What are humanistic and social-cognitive theories of personality?

≫ LO 13.4   **Compare and contrast humanistic and social-cognitive theories of personality.**

The humanistic approach to personality focuses on your self-concept, motivations, and personal potential. The social-cognitive approach considers how your behaviors change due to an interaction between your thoughts/perceptions and the environment. Both approaches assume personality can change over time and emphasize control over your personality.

13.5   What are some current personality controversies?

≫ LO 13.5   **Analyze several controversies and debates when it comes to understanding the psychology of personality.**

Four current controversies in the science of personality are as follows: (1) Which predicts behaviors more—personality or the situation? (2) Does personality change as we age and grow? (3) What are the ethics of personality tests at work? and (4) Are current personality theories limited due to lack of diversity?

CRITICAL THINKING QUESTIONS

1. Look again at the list of Freudian defense mechanisms outlined in this chapter. Identify examples of at least three different mechanisms, either in your own life or in the media (like a movie, TV show, or book). Does using defense mechanisms seem to work out well for the person using it, both short term and long term? Why or why not?

2. Take an online personality test (pick one where you get your results). Describe and analyze each of the following:
   - What concepts the test is supposedly measuring and how the test is scored
   - Who created the test and whether they might have any personal biases or limitations based on what you know about them
   - Whether you think the results are reliable and valid, given (1) your knowledge of yourself compared to the results you got and (2) what these results might mean in the context of the Barnum effect (in other words, are the results specific? Vague? Etc.)
   - One strength of this test or concept
   - One weakness of test or concept (or one thing you think is missing, or something you think could be improved)

3. Choose an animal you know in real life (like a pet) and try to classify it on any three personality traits, characteristics, or concepts discussed in this chapter. To make this easier, rate each trait on a scale from 1 (*not at all*) to 10 (*completely*). Describe how you observed and rated the animal—what did you look for? Is your observation over a short or long period of time? What could you do to improve your observation technique?

4. Pick any of the four controversies discussed in the last section of this chapter. Find one article related to that controversy published within the past 5 years, then (1) summarize the article's main points and (2) analyze your personal views on this issue or controversy.

KEY TERMS

Archetypes, 406
Barnum effect, 425
Behavioral genetics, 408
Big 5 Model, 413
Biological approach to personality, 407
Birth order, 405
Cerebral asymmetry, 411
Dark triad, 416
Defense mechanisms, 403
Ego, 401
Factor analysis, 412
Fixed-role therapy, 424
Fully functioning, 418
Humanistic approach to personality, 417
Id, 401
Light triad, 416

Locus of control, 420
Personality, 400
Phrenology, 407
Projective tests, 404
Psychodynamic approach to personality, 401
Psychosexual stages of development, 402
Reciprocal determinism, 419
Self-monitoring, 421
Social-cognitive approach to personality, 417
Superego, 401
Temperament, 409
Trait approach to personality, 412

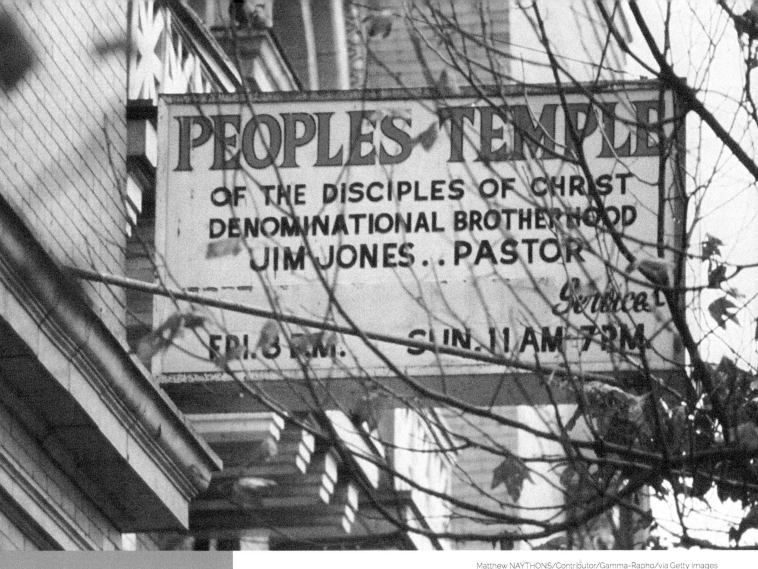

Matthew NAYTHONS/Contributor/Gamma-Rapho/via Getty Images

14

Social Psychology

When it started, Peoples Temple represented the best parts of humans living in a social world (Guinn, 2017). People who joined the church sincerely wanted to create a loving, altruistic community free of prejudice. It started in Indiana, stayed true to the mission when they moved to California, and was still their dream when they relocated to Guyana in South America.

In the end, it all went wrong. Peoples Temple ultimately represented the worst parts of humans living in a social world. Their leader, Jim Jones, used persuasion, conformity, obedience to authority, and old-fashioned lies to turn the group into his personal cult. The group named their settlement in Guyana Jonestown as Jones became increasingly paranoid and obsessed with power. Eventually, the story ended in tragedy: 909 members died in what is now called the largest mass suicide in history. But many psychologists believe it should be called murder, because of the psychological manipulation behind the scenes.

Even this tragedy has heroes. Some people survived and stood up to Jim Jones, including his own son, Stephan. Both the uplifting and troubling parts of this story relate to the fascinating topics within social psychology.

After reading this chapter, you will get answers to several questions you've been curious about:

Have You Ever Wondered?

14.1   How are attitudes formed, and how do people change their minds?

14.2   How does being in a group change people's behavior?

14.3   Why are stereotypes and prejudice so common in people?

14.4   When do we behave in altruistic and aggressive ways?

14.5   Why do people tend to conform to groups and obey authority figures?

Learning Objectives

LO 14.1   Explain how attitudes are formed, how they change, and how they can lead to biases.

LO 14.2   Analyze various ways group dynamics affect individual behavior.

LO 14.3   Explain the origins of stereotypes and prejudice, as well as research on how to reduce them.

LO 14.4   Describe theories that help explain altruism and aggression.

LO 14.5   Explain research on conformity, obedience, and rebellion.

ATTITUDES AND PERSUASION

**Have You Ever Wondered?
14.1** How are attitudes formed, and how do people change their minds?

>> **LO 14.1**   **Explain how attitudes are formed, how they change, and how they can lead to biases.**

Why do we find cults so intriguing?

Documentaries about cults continue to rise to the top of ratings and popularity on streaming services like Netflix and Hulu (Bryant, 2020). Perhaps the continued fascination is because thinking about the dynamics of cults and their leaders prompts us to wonder: How could all this happen? What kind of people were involved? What would I have done if I had been there?

When we think about people who have been labeled as villains—like Jim Jones and other cult leaders—and people who have been labeled as gullible followers, like the people who died in Guyana that evening in November 1978, it's easy to rely on assumptions and stereotypes. But there must have been powerful, complicated, and nuanced social and psychological forces at play that night—and not everyone acted the same.

Social psychology is a subfield that studies how people influence each other's thoughts, feelings, and behaviors. It includes many topics, and this chapter will focus on some of the most well-researched areas (shown in the opening table). To start, consider how you form attitudes about anything and then how you change your mind.

Social psychology: A subfield focused on how people influence each other's thoughts, feelings, and behaviors.

How Attitudes Are Formed

Young Jimmy Jones had a positive attitude toward Myrtle Kennedy.

As he was growing up in the small town of Lynn, Indiana (population just under 1,000 at the time, the 1930s and 1940s), he spent most afternoons and weekends wandering alone (Guinn, 2017). His parents both neglected him and told him he wasn't allowed in the house until the evening. Myrtle Kennedy, an older neighbor woman, took pity on him; she fed young Jimmy and took him to church with her, which he absolutely loved. He quickly decided to become a minister and to dedicate his life to helping other people who had been stigmatized and marginalized by society. He also recognized the social influence ministers had over their congregations.

Advertisers hope you form a positive attitude toward their product through classical conditioning when they pair it with attractive models.
RICHARD B. LEVINE/Newscom

Attitudes are judgments or evaluations of someone or something; they can be positive, negative, or mixed (Allport, 1935; Eagly & Chaiken, 2007; Smith & Nosek, 2011). Psychologists generally define attitudes as having three major components. They are partially *cognitive*, meaning attitudes are composed of our thoughts and assumptions about the person, idea, or object we're judging. Attitudes also include an *affective* component, which means an emotional response. Finally, attitudes often have a *behavioral* component, meaning they can drive our actual responses to whatever we're judging or evaluating.

Attitudes: Our judgments or evaluations of someone or something; they can be positive, negative, or mixed.

In adulthood, Jim Jones became a notorious cult leader who did terrible things (Guinn, 2017). But he always remembered the kindness of Myrtle Kennedy and retained his positive attitude toward her. We see the curious and complicated nature of humanity in the fact that this notorious man continued to send handwritten notes and cards to Kennedy, his "second mother," every week of his life. The notes expressed his hope that she was well and his gratitude to her.

Our attitudes come from our experiences, in several different ways.

Classical and Operant Conditioning

You already know that classical conditioning leads us to have automatic responses to things in our environment based on experience (see Chapter 9). Sometimes our attitudes are positive or negative because we associate the person, object, or idea with something else. Jim Jones associated Myrtle Kennedy with food, kindness, and a loving religious community (Guinn, 2017).

Classical conditioning as the basis for creating positive attitudes toward products is the foundation for many billion-dollar advertising campaigns (Reichart, 2019). They pair the product with an attractive model—the idea is that your automatic positive response to the model will be transferred to the product through classical conditioning after repeated pairings. Eventually, you'll have a positive attitude toward the product itself. In other words, "sex sells." The same idea uses humor in marketing and advertising, to put you in a positive mood and associate that good attitude with the product (Chung & Zhao, 2003; Gelb & Zinkhan, 1986; Lee & Mason, 1999; Strick et al., 2009).

We also form attitudes through operant conditioning—receiving rewards (reinforcement) or punishments. For example, consider many college students' attitudes about alcohol consumption. Research indicates that these attitudes are more positive in young people when they believe popularity and party invitations reward and reinforce drinking (Goldstein et al., 2013). Attitudes learned from operant conditioning tend to be particularly strong and persistent over time, showing our motivation for obtaining basic rewards and avoiding punishments like social ostracism (Davies, 1982; Guenther & Alicke, 2008; Slusher & Anderson, 1989).

Mere Exposure

We also tend to like things when they're comforting, familiar, and predictable. Psychologists call this *mere exposure*, the tendency to increasingly like things and people (in other words, have a positive attitude) the more we're around them or exposed to them (Monahan et al., 2000; Van Horn et al., 1997). Mere exposure was cleverly demonstrated in a now-classic study done on the campus of the Massachusetts Institute of Technology (MIT).

The researchers focused on the apartment buildings laid out as shown in Figure 14.1 (Festinger et al., 1950). At the beginning of the university term, the people assigned to live in each building were strangers. Months later, they completed surveys asking them to rate their neighbors in terms of who they were most likely to see socially. In other words, the survey measured their attitudes toward their neighbors.

Fairly consistently (across multiple buildings), the people who lived in Apartments 1 and 5 were liked the most, while people who lived in Apartments 6 and 10 were liked the least. Mere exposure explains these results: Residents in locations where their neighbors were more likely to pass by had higher chances of meeting, saying hi,

FIGURE 14.1

Apartments in Festinger et al. (1950)

Schematic diagram of the apartments in Festinger et al. (1950). When people in the buildings were asked to rate their neighbors, people in Apartments 1 and 5 were consistently liked the most, while people in Apartments 6 and 10 were liked the least.

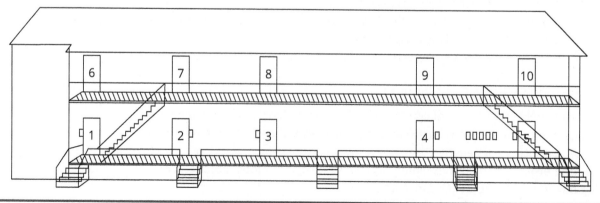

and getting to know each other—and therefore greater likelihood of forming a positive attitude.

Mere exposure effects have been replicated in many other ways, both in controlled lab experiments and in field studies (e.g., Echols & Graham, 2013; Kruse et al., 2016; Reis et al., 2011). The effect is more likely if an object is attractive and/or abstract, like a beautiful but blurry painting or well-designed advertisement (Cutting, 2020; Fang et al., 2007). Note that we don't *always* have increased positive attitudes after increased exposure; sometimes, we can end up *disliking* something the more we're around it. Increased exposure tends to lead to a positive attitude if our initial impression is positive or neutral. If our first impression is negative, however, we can quickly get even more annoyed.

And here's an interesting application of the mere exposure effect: Some researchers suggest the reason we prefer photos of ourselves that have been digitally reversed is because we're used to looking at ourselves in a mirror (Mita et al., 1977; Volpara et al., 2022). Most photos are backward from how we usually see ourselves, so they seem "off" without most people realizing why. If you're curious, there are apps and websites where you can try this for yourself.

We're used to looking at ourselves in a mirror—so we usually prefer photos of ourselves after they've been reversed. Our friends like the opposite, because it's what they're used to instead.

Kevin Mazur/Contributor/Getty Images Entertainment/via Getty Images

How Attitudes Are Changed

How often do you change your mind?

Jim Jones briefly changed his mind about becoming a minister twice; he considered being a pilot or a hospital orderly before eventually going back to his original plan of starting a church (Guinn, 2017). Once we form our attitudes and beliefs, it can be difficult to change them (Bensley, 2023; Kleinberg et al., 2023). There are two major paths to persuasion. External factors influence us when other people or things in our environment persuade us to change our minds. And sometimes, internal factors influence us— meaning we convince ourselves.

External Influence: Persuasion Techniques

Attempts to manipulate your attitudes are everywhere. Advertisers want you to buy things. Politicians want votes. Even your professors try to get you excited about the material in their own classes. The most blatant or obvious attempts we experience of people trying to persuade us come from the world of sales. Social psychologist Robert Cialdini studied sales persuasion techniques for years while he worked "under cover" at locations such as car dealerships and telemarking firms. He named several of these in his classic best-selling book, *Influence: The Psychology of Persuasion* (2006).

Do you take the free samples at stores? If so, do you then feel a little obligated to buy something?

Jeff Greenberg/Contributor/Universal Images Group/via Getty Images

Here are four examples, summarized for you in Table 14.1:

- *Lowballing:* When you agree to do or buy something under certain conditions, but then the deal is changed. People usually move forward anyway. Car dealerships are famous for offering "zero percent financing!" to get you in the door. But often, they later tell you that you "don't qualify" and offer you much steeper interest rates. Many people sign the contract anyway. Why? Cialdini says it's the psychology of *commitment*: Once we've mentally committed a positive attitude toward something (I like this car!), we like to follow through. By the time we're told about the change in the financing, we've already test driven the car, spent several hours at the dealership, imagined ourselves behind the wheel . . . so our positive attitude keeps up that momentum, despite the fact that the reason we went there in the first place is now gone.

- *Foot-in-the-door:* When people agree to an initial, small request, they are much more likely to then agree to a larger second request. If the person at the mall kiosk can get you to stop just for a few minutes to chat about your skin care routine, you might be willing to sit down for a brief demonstration . . . and before you know it, you're walking away with a bag full of scented lotion. Again, why? It's still commitment. If you care a little bit about whatever the initial topic, product, person, and so on is, then it's easy to convince you to care a little bit more.

- *Door-in-the-face:* When people say no to an initial, large request, they are much more likely to then agree to a smaller second request. After you graduate from college, your alumni association might ask you to donate a large amount of money. If you say no, they might politely reply, "No problem—what amount feels right?" People who just said no to a larger request sometimes feel obligated to say yes to a follow-up smaller one because of the *norm of reciprocity*, a social expectation that we return favors with favors.

- *Not-so-free:* When people accept a small free "gift," they often feel obligated to the person or company who provided it. You can probably see that this technique is also based on the norm of reciprocity; the organization is betting on the hope that you'll now purchase enough product that they'll still make a profit. Grocery stores do this all the time—and so did Jim Jones! After forming his churches in Indiana and later in California, when he wanted to influence a local politician, he would send them a cake and a card on their birthday, to make them feel obligated toward him (Guinn, 2017). He hoped the norm of reciprocity would persuade them to have a positive attitude toward him and maybe do him a favor if he ever needed one. He called it "cake diplomacy."

TABLE 14.1

Four Persuasion Techniques

These common sales techniques often get people to change their attitudes and behaviors.

TECHNIQUE NAME	DESCRIPTION	PSYCHOLOGY PRINCIPLE
Lowballing	When you agree to do or buy something under certain conditions, but then the deal is changed. People usually move forward anyway.	Commitment
Foot-in-the-door	When people agree to an initial, small request, they are much more likely to then agree to a larger second request.	Commitment
Door-in-the-face	When people say no to an initial, large request, they are much more likely to then agree to a smaller second request.	Norm of reciprocity
Not-so-free	When people accept a small free "gift," they often feel obligated to the person or company who provided the gift, so they purchase something (or equivalent return of "the favor").	Norm of reciprocity

Source: Created using data from Cialdini (2006).

Meet Brooke, Sales Associate—Financial Services

What is your career?

I am a sales associate at Farm Bureau Financial Services. We sell a variety of different types of insurance. I communicate with current clients, making updates or changes to their policies, and help quote other potential clients for new business.

How was studying psychology important for success in this career?

Psychology and sales go hand in hand. The way you talk to someone can make or break a sale. Are they the type of person who just wants the quote, or do you need to sit down with them and explain each part? It has a lot to do with understanding your client, and everyone is different.

How do concepts from this chapter help in this career?

Working as a team is very important to us. In terms of stereotypes and prejudice, people tend to dismiss me because I am young, new, and a female. **In terms of persuasion, everyone needs insurance—how much they need is the question.** Psychology ties into sales because you need to understand the person and what they want, and compare it to what they may need.

Is this the career you always planned to have after college?

I fully intended on going forward to get my master's degree in psychology. However, **after I graduated, the feeling of being done felt very good.** I think a lot of students go into college with one idea but come out with another for a variety of reasons. Just because you have one degree does not mean it will not help with other career choices. I love my psychology background, and I like that it fits in with many different careers.

If you could give current college students one sentence of advice, what would it be?

Every day is a new day, so get up, eat breakfast, and do what makes you happy. ●

Internal Influence: Cognitive Dissonance

The sales techniques just described involve someone else talking us into doing something—but we also talk *ourselves* into changing an attitude. We like to see ourselves as people who make good decisions, are intelligent and reasonable, and are generally reliable. Yet, we date the wrong people, procrastinate, eat junk food, and spend too much time on TikTok.

When our thoughts, feelings, or behaviors don't align with each other or even contradict each other it's an uncomfortable and anxiety-provoking experience. In short, we don't like to think of ourselves as hypocrites. This psychological discomfort is called **cognitive dissonance** (Festinger, 1957). It can motivate us to change our attitudes, in one way or another, to feel better and avoid guilt and anxiety.

Consider an example that might really matter to you: cheating in class. If you have a negative attitude about cheating, but you do it anyway—cognitive dissonance predicts you should feel guilt, anxiety, lower self-esteem, and so on. What can you do? One solution, of course, is simply not to cheat! But many people cheat anyway (McGrath, 2020; Romero, 2019; J. M. Stephens, 2017; S. Stephens, 2020; Vinski & Tryon, 2009). To get around the mental discomfort, they might persuade themselves that cheating isn't a big deal. After all:

Cognitive dissonance: A feeling of anxiety or discomfort if our thoughts and feelings aren't in alignment.

- Cheating in various forms is common in all sorts of species; it's an evolutionary advantage and the world is survival of the fittest, right (J. M. Stephens, 2017; Trivers, 2011)?

- Cheating just once or twice is probably no big deal, right (Harmon-Jones & Mills, 2019)?

- Cheating is something that everyone does, right? Even ancient Greek athletes did it (true story; S. Stephens, 2020)!

These justifications might allow someone to change their attitude toward cheating just enough to live with their own cheating behaviors without much guilt or anxiety from cognitive dissonance. Research on this phenomenon has been applied to dozens of different kinds of behaviors, but perhaps the most intriguing examples are the two original studies, now historical classics. One was a creative lab experiment conducted by social psychologists Leon Festinger and James Carlsmith in 1959 (see the *Spotlight on Research Methods* feature).

SPOTLIGHT ON RESEARCH METHODS

Creating Cognitive Dissonance

Leon Festinger's classic study on cognitive dissonance invented a clever methodology (Festinger & Carlsmith, 1959) that demonstrated how cognitive dissonance motivates attitude change. The procedure was:

- The experimenter asked college students to complete intentionally boring tasks for about an hour. One task was spending 30 minutes turning 48 square pegs in quarter turns over and over.

- The experimenter then asked the students for a favor: Would they mind telling the next participant (who was actually a confederate, a researcher pretending to be a participant) that the task was super exciting and fun?

- Participants were told they would be paid for telling the lie, but here's where the experimental manipulation came in (the independent variable): Half received $1 for telling the lie; the other half received $20. Keep in mind this was in 1959, so $20 seemed like a lot more money then. Almost everyone agreed to talk to the confederate, in both conditions ($1 and $20).

- After the participant spoke with the confederate, they were told the experiment was done and thanked for their help.

- They were then asked by a different person to report their genuine, true feelings about the task. How much fun was it really to turn those knobs, on a scale from −5 to +5?

Most people don't like to think of themselves as liars. But lying for $20? That was a great deal of money in the 1950s. Telling a simple, harmless lie for a welcome $20 represented what Festinger and Carlsmith called *sufficient justification*. In other words—totally worth it. There's little reason to actually believe—or even pretend to believe—our little lie because that $20 gives us a ready motivation: Cognitive dissonance is low.

However, if you're willing to lie for only $1, then what kind of person are you? Most of us wouldn't want to believe that we're willing to lie to another person for a measly $1. To Festinger and Carlsmith, the $1 lie represented *insufficient* justification—so, telling a lie for just $1 would generate high levels of cognitive dissonance.

The $1 liars found a simple solution to reduce this dissonance: Convince yourself it's not a lie. If you simply change your attitude about the task to believing it really was pretty fun after all, you avoid the guilt. The results showed that the participants paid only $1 reported that they really did like the task (an average rating of +1.35), while those paid $20 were honest about how they really didn't (an average rating of −0.45). ●

The other was a naturalistic field study Festinger did through participant observation (i.e., going "undercover") in 1954 when he joined a cult in Chicago (Festinger et al., 1956/2008). Their leader predicted that at midnight on Christmas Eve, aliens would arrive to save the group right before the rest of the world was destroyed. He observed as the cult members waited excitedly . . . and then nothing happened. Afterward, many of them demonstrated even *greater* commitment to the cult, and their attitude toward the leader became more positive than ever.

Why?

Festinger believed that these individuals had fully committed to the group; many of them had quit their jobs, publicly said goodbye to loved ones, and so on. Admitting to being wrong and changing their attitude toward the group now would conflict with those behaviors and cause a lot of cognitive dissonance. Instead, they doubled down on their positive attitude by convincing themselves that the prophecy had been a "test" of their faith and that the aliens decided that their purity had saved the world from destruction.

PSYCHOLOGY AND OUR CURIOUS WORLD

Documentaries About the Psychology of Cults

iStock.com/sqback

Have you seen any of the documentaries about groups labeled "cults"?

Start by watching *Going Clear: Scientology and the Prison of Belief*, then *Holy Hell*, *Waco*, followed by *Children of God*. The 2020 release of *The Vow* follows members of NXIVM, a group led by Keith Raniere who recruited successful young people into self-help seminars. Raniere claimed to be one of the smartest men in the world (with an IQ of 240—smarter than Einstein!), a gifted pianist, a teen judo champion, and more. He lied.

Raniere groomed underage girls to become his sex slaves and structured NXIVM as a sexual pyramid scheme: His chosen slaves each had to recruit six more slaves. After escaped members shared their stories in the *New York Times*, the FBI investigated in June 2019 and Raniere was found guilty of seven crimes: racketeering (including identity theft and extortion), racketeering conspiracy, forced labor conspiracy, wire fraud conspiracy, sex trafficking conspiracy, attempted sex trafficking, and sex trafficking.

The beliefs in each cult vary, but many of the social influence techniques are common: an idealistic vision, physical and social isolation, a leader with "divine" insight, conformity and obedience, and manipulating sincere but vulnerable individuals. ●

Practice what you learn in **Knowledge Check 14.1**

Sage Vantage➤

HOW GROUPS AFFECT OUR BEHAVIOR

>> LO 14.2   Analyze various ways group dynamics affect individual behavior.

Jim Jones seemed desperate for social approval.

Once he formed churches in Indianapolis and later in California—both which he called Peoples Temple—he worked tirelessly to recruit people (Guinn, 2017). When he was in front of his congregation, his energy seemed boundless. People remember his early charm, fantastic memory, and ability to convince people they were in the presence of someone truly special. But being in a group also brought out the worst in Jones; he was paranoid that other people were conspiring against him. His fears eventually led him to the decision that the only way to control his group was to isolate them in the jungle of Guyana in South America, where many of them moved in 1977 and started a new life in the village they named after him: Jonestown.

**? Have You Ever Wondered?
14.2** How does being in a group change people's behavior?

Caitlin Clark changed the popularity of women's college basketball when people noticed her fantastic skills on the court. In this case, being in a group makes effort and motivation go up.

Mitchell Layton/Contributor/Getty Images Sport/via Getty Images

Social facilitation: When the presence of others makes someone's individual performance on a task better.

Research from social psychology asks: How does being in a group setting change us? Most of us (fortunately) won't be in extreme situations like cults, but all of us experience hundreds of groups in our lives. Our cultures revolve around groups: Families, school divisions like grades or neighborhoods, and divisions at work are natural clusters that result in social cohesion, meaningful connections, and lifelong friendships (Boyer & Bergstrom, 2011; Dustin et al., 2019; Firestone et al., 1973; Gilbert, 2015; Schacter, 1959; Taylor, 2012). These cultural groups can also lead to biases, stereotypes, aggression, murder, and war (Buss & Duntley, 2006; Tajfel, 1970; Tajfel & Turner, 1979; Trivers, 2011). Why?

Social Facilitation

Some groups bring out the best in us.

Athletes, musicians, actors, and other performers know that when there's a large, excited audience, the energy in the room is electric. We might also be motivated to work harder in a group at school or work because we care about the product, are intrinsically motivated to learn, or like the other people involved. Social facilitation occurs when the presence of others makes someone's individual performance better.

Research on social facilitation started in 1898 with Norm Triplett, who is now considered the first sport psychologist. He noticed that bicycle racers were faster when racing against real people than when training by themselves. After replicating the effect with experiments in a lab, he concluded that the physical presence of others released physiological energy, boosting performance (Triplett, 1898).

Social facilitation is not unique to humans (Aiello & Douthitt, 2001); researchers have observed it among grazing cattle (Ralphs et al., 1994), lab rats (Galef, 1986), and capuchin monkeys (Dindo et al., 2009). In humans, it also happens across a wide variety of contexts—not just sports and games. For example, it occurs among

Are you ever in a group in which one member slacks off?

Image Source/via Getty Images

- donors who give more money to charity when others are watching (Izuma et al., 2010),

- airport security workers who do pat-downs more quickly when being observed (Yu & Wu, 2015), and

- diners who eat more in the presence of others (Ruddock et al., 2019).

There are two major theoretical explanations to explain why performance in some people increases when other people are present. The first is called *evaluation apprehension* (Geen, 1989; Henchy & Glass, 1968). Essentially, this is the argument that we work harder because we want to impress people—we either want to "show off" if we're good at a task, or we at least want to not embarrass ourselves if we're not great at something.

The second theoretical explanation came about because research showed that social facilitation occurs when there are others in the room, *even if those people aren't paying attention to us.* If that's the case, then they can't evaluate us—so why would we work harder? The alternative explanation is called *mere presence* (Zajonc, 1965). It's the idea that simply the presence of others causes physiological arousal in us, and this autonomic response improves our performance on simple tasks. Which explanation makes more sense is still a bit of a debate, and curious researchers may keep asking questions to learn more (Emmerich & Masuch, 2018; Halfmann et al., 2020; Lau et al., 2019; Neider et al., 2019; Strojny et al., 2018).

Social Loafing: Diffusion of Responsibility

Don't you just love group projects?

Just kidding. As professors, we know most students cringe when they are assigned to group projects, because they fear the opposite of social facilitation—that at least one person will use the group as an excuse to do no work at all. You might call them "slackers." Social loafing occurs when the presence of others makes someone reduce their individual effort, making their performance on a task worse (Jackson & Williams, 1985; Sanna, 1992).

Social loafing: When the presence of others makes someone reduce their individual effort on a task, making their performance worse.

Social loafers have both practical and personal justifications for avoiding work:

- Life is easier for loafers who take credit for others' work.

- Loafers think they can get away with it—and often do.

- Loafers usually don't care what others think because they are low in the personality traits of conscientiousness and agreeableness (Schippers, 2014). Therefore, they are low in evaluation apprehension.

Another important theoretical explanation for social loafing is called diffusion of responsibility. In a group, the amount of personal responsibility any individual feels for a task can be divided by the number of people present (Darley & Latané, 1968; Latané & Darley, 1970). Diffusion of responsibility leads people to think, "Someone else will do it—I don't have to." As noted above, people low in conscientiousness (they aren't particularly organized or detail oriented) and low in agreeableness (they don't particularly care about pleasing others) are especially likely to simply wait for someone else to do it.

Diffusion of responsibility: When the presence of others leads people to feel less personal responsibility for any given task, because they assume someone else will do it instead.

While social facilitation is the idea that groups make us work harder and better, social loafing is the idea that groups sometimes make us work less or worse. One interesting application of diffusion of responsibility occurs in settings when there's an emergency and a group of people witnesses it. Will diffusion of responsibility mean that, ironically, no one steps up to do anything? We'll discuss this more in the section on altruism later in this chapter.

Some groups require displays of behavior to be accepted; when this is publicly dangerous or humiliating, it's considered hazing. College fraternities and sororities are one example of where hazing is common.

Cristian Negroni/500px/500Px Plus/ via Getty Images

Committing to a Group: Loyalty Risks Abuse

Terri Buford joined Peoples Temple when she was 19 years old.

She was desperate to escape a mother who had assaulted and tried to kill her. She felt welcomed by the community and thought Jim Jones had psychic powers. She lived on the group property, worked for the cult, and earned two dollars a week. She quickly learned that Jones expected his employees to work up to 20 hours a day. At one point, seemingly satisfied with how loyal his cult had become, Buford says that Jones told her, "Keep them poor and keep them tired, and they'll never leave" (Guinn, 2017, p. 195).

Group dynamics can sometimes lead to strange outcomes and harmful psychological effects.

Hazing and the Initiation Effect

Hazing: A type of group initiation that requires humiliating or dangerous behaviors by new members.

Initiation effect: The increased commitment people have toward a group after enduring a tough initiation to become a member.

If a group requires humiliating or dangerous behaviors as part of an initiation to become a member or to be accepted, it's called **hazing**. On the surface, it seems like people would resent hazing and would dislike the group and its members after being put through such embarrassing treatment. But the opposite is true: Hazing is a specific example of what psychologists call the **initiation effect**, or the *increased* commitment people have toward a group after enduring difficult or embarrassing tasks to become a member (Keating et al., 2005; Martini, 1994).

Hazing occurs among Greek campus organizations, in athletic teams, in the military, and in workplaces (Kröger et al., 2023; O'Brien, 2023; Owen et al., 2008). It's even a tradition in higher education: Some people who get their doctorate degree feel that the process is a form of hazing (Lantsoght, 2021). Figure 14.2 shows a spectrum of possible group initiations. Team building can be positive and healthy—or it can cross the line to hazing, which easily slides to substance abuse, violence, and assault.

A 1959 experiment tested the spectrum of hazing activities and their effect on group loyalty (Aronson & Mills, 1959). During the 1950s, merely talking about sex with strangers was taboo—especially for "proper young ladies." They recruited college women and told them the study was about a small group that regularly met to discuss sex. Participants were randomly assigned to one of three groups (the independent variable) along a spectrum of hazing activities:

- Easy Initiation (control group): Simply asked participants to say they were willing to talk about sex.

- Mild Initiation (first experimental group): Asked participants to read aloud a mildly sexual passage that included words like *prostitute, virgin,* and *petting.*

- Severe Initiation (second experimental group): Asked participants to read aloud explicitly sexual material (essentially, written pornography).

FIGURE 14.2

Forms of Group Initiation

Different forms of group initiation can lead to team building and loyalty, but it can also lead to abuse.

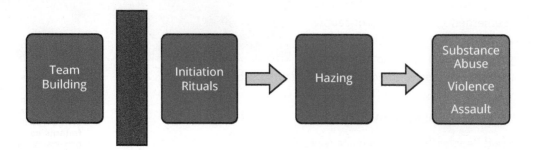

Source: Adapted from Jeckel et al. (2018).

Then all the women listened to a tape supposedly of the group's previous discussion. The trick of this study was that the women had been led to believe the group would talk about controversial, socially taboo subjects—but instead, they heard a purposely very *boring* discussion about the sexual behavior of insects. Researchers then measured how excited the women said they were to join the group and their interest in the discussion. This measurement—the dependent variable—was their loyalty to the group.

Figure 14.3 shows the results. With attitudes toward the group measured on a scale going up to 100, women who had gone through a severe initiation reported being significantly more excited and interested in the group, compared to the other two experimental conditions. The psychology behind hazing and the initiation effect is usually explained through effort justification, which is when we convince ourselves that a great deal of effort must have been worthwhile. Effort justification may be a form of cognitive dissonance (why would we go through all of that if we didn't really value this group?) and it might be a way to protect our self-esteem by trying to avoid looking foolish to others (Leary, 2019; Rosenfeld et al., 1984).

Patty Hearst was famously kidnapped but then appeared to join the cause of her kidnappers. Was she suffering from "Stockholm syndrome"?

Bettmann/Contributor/Bettmann/via Getty Images

Stockholm Syndrome

In 1973, four hostages in Stockholm, Sweden, resisted being rescued, defended the robbers holding them captive, and refused to testify against them. The term

Effort justification: When we convince ourselves that a great deal of effort must have been worthwhile.

FIGURE 14.3

The Initiation Effect

When a group is difficult to get into, we seem to like it more.

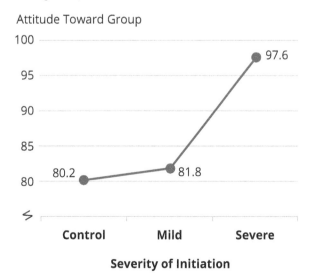

Attitude Toward Group

Severity of Initiation

Source: Adapted from Aronson and Mills (1959).

Stockholm syndrome: When hostages develop affection for their captors or agree with their captor's motives.

Stockholm syndrome came to describe situations in which individuals develop affection or empathy for their captors or abusers (West, 1993).

It's strange, but the effect has now been observed in a variety of settings, including prisoners of war, political prisoners, suicidal terrorists, and survivors of rape, sex trafficking, elder abuse, relationship violence, and more (Logan, 2018; Obeid & Hallit, 2018; Samant & Singh, 2022; Wallace, 2007). Karan and Hansen's (2018) study of female sex workers identified four conditions that help predict when Stockholm syndrome is more likely to occur:

1. Perceived threat to survival

2. Captor occasionally shows kindness (perhaps as a manipulation tactic)

3. Isolation from other perspectives

4. Perceived inability to escape

The FBI reports that about 8% of hostages end up agreeing with their captors, feeling friendship or romantic attraction, or supporting their motives (Martinez, 2001). In 1974, the U.S. newspaper heiress Patty Hearst was kidnapped by a small group of domestic terrorists who held her captive for months. She joined their cause and publicly helped them rob banks with a machine gun (Hearst & Moscow, 1988). When she was caught, she used Stockholm syndrome as her defense in court and was later pardoned by President Bill Clinton. Many years later, in 2001, British reporter Yvonne Ridley was held by the Taliban for 11 days before being released. Afterward, she converted to Islam, praised the Taliban, and denounced "Western" values. Ridley denied any influence of Stockholm syndrome (Adorjan et al., 2012).

Congressman Leo Ryan visited Jonestown, Guyana, in 1978. He was murdered by several of Jim Jones's cult members.

Bettmann/Contributor/Bettmann/via Getty Images

All four of the conditions listed above were true of the people living in Jonestown, Guyana, in 1978 when Congressman Leo Ryan visited them after hearing troubling reports from their friends and family members. When he arrived, almost everyone said they loved it and praised Jones as a loving father figure (Guinn, 2017). Perhaps some elements of Stockholm syndrome were present as the conditions were building toward their tragic end.

SageVantage   Practice what you learn in **Knowledge Check 14.2**

STEREOTYPES, PREJUDICE, AND DISCRIMINATION

Have You Ever Wondered?
14.3 Why are stereotypes and prejudice so common in people?

>> LO 14.3   Explain the origins of stereotypes and prejudice, as well as research on how to reduce them.

It's possible that Jim Jones sincerely wanted to end racism.

Much of his life was devoted to standing up to prejudice (Guinn, 2017). He and his wife, Marceline, adopted four children of color and called them their "rainbow family." He led peaceful sit-ins at segregated restaurants, and he encouraged people at his own church services to always sit next to someone of a different race. On the other hand, survivors have criticized Jones for being a hypocrite. He personally selected a few people for his church council—and only a token one or two members of that council were people of color.

More problematic was Jones's growing paranoia. He started to believe that his assistants were plotting against him and that the U.S. government was infiltrating the group with spies. His son Stephan remembered those years as filled with lessons that anyone not in Peoples Temple should not be trusted. Stephan said his father taught him, "If we can't convince you, you're the enemy." Jim Jones certainly believed that Congressman Leo Ryan was an enemy during his visit Jonestown in 1978.

An "us versus them" mentality is the fundamental basis of stereotypes, prejudice, and discrimination.

Components of Social Cognition: The ABC Model

Humans all over the world think in similar ways.

While we've emphasized the importance and influence of culture many times, there are some commonalities no matter where we grew up. One fundamental part of being human is that we all have the tendency to combine two basic ways of thinking: a relatively fast, automatic, *intuition* and a slower, more systematic *logic* (or like the famous book title suggests, *Thinking Fast and Slow*). When we combine these two processes to process social information, psychologists call it *social cognition* (Bargh & Williams, 2006; Kahneman, 2003; Sherman et al., 2014). We use social cognition when we think about and categorize other people, and it's the start of how we label and judge them.

Earlier in this chapter, we talked about how attitudes have three basic components: thoughts, emotions, and behaviors. We're going to apply those same three components to attitudes about people, and this is how psychologists distinguish among our three basic terms:

- **Stereotypes** are overgeneralized cognitive assumptions about groups (thoughts). They occur when we assume everyone in a group is basically the same.

- **Prejudice** is a judgment or evaluation of a group, either positive or negative (emotion).

- **Discrimination** occurs when our stereotypes and/or prejudices lead to unfair actions or behaviors.

Table 14.2 shows examples of stereotypes, prejudices, and discriminatory behaviors. Often, problems start with incorrect beliefs and assumptions (stereotypes). From there, we have emotional reactions (prejudice), and unfair responses follow.

Stereotypes: Believing that people in a certain group are all basically the same.

Prejudice: An emotional judgment or evaluation of a group, either positive or negative.

Discrimination: Unfair actions or behaviors based on stereotypes and/or prejudice.

TABLE 14.2

Distinctions Among Stereotypes, Prejudice, and Discrimination

Stereotypes can often lead to prejudiced feelings or judgments about a group, which can then lead to discriminatory behaviors.

TERM	COMPONENT	EXAMPLE	EXAMPLE	EXAMPLE
Stereotype	Beliefs (cognitive)	Belief that men wearing any kind of headscarf are Muslim	Belief that women are emotional	Belief that gay people are stylish
Prejudice	Feelings (affective)	Negative emotions toward Muslims; judgment that they are all "terrorists"	Negative judgment that women make for bad leaders	Positive judgment of gay people and their fashion sense
Discrimination	Actions (behavioral)	Refusing to board an airplane with anyone perceived to be Muslim	Not voting for female political candidates	Choosing a gay man as your hairdresser

Did you learn that pink was for girls and blue was for boys?

FatCamera/E+/via Getty Images

Adaptive categorization: The idea that stereotypes helped our ancestors survive through rapid categorization and labeling of people.

The column labeled "component" in the table shows that the three psychological pieces are the cognitive, affective, and behavioral drivers. If you take the first letter of each of those words and put them in a slightly different order, you'll see why some psychologists refer to this overall picture as the *ABC model* (or sometimes the *tripartite model*; Breckler, 1984; Perry et al., 2022; Zhang et al., 2021).

Origins of Stereotypes and Prejudice

We've probably all felt the hurt of prejudice.

If that's true, why do humans form stereotypes and prejudice in the first place? As usual, answering "why" questions can be complicated. Psychologists have offered many explanations for this question. Here are just a few of those ideas (summarized for you in Table 14.3).

Some psychologists believe stereotypes are so common, regardless of culture and throughout all human history, because they are simply human instinct. **Adaptive categorization** is an evolutionary explanation that proposes that rapid stereotyping into categories helped our ancestors survive—they needed to quickly label people as threats or nonthreats. While this is efficient, it also comes with built-in biases and leads to mistakes (Allport, 1954; Brewer, 1988; Devine & Sharp, 2009; Macrae et al., 1994). We automatically favor people in our *in-groups* (groups we're members of) and negatively evaluate those in *out-groups* (groups we're not members of; Fiske, 1989; Tajfel, 1970; Tajfel & Turner, 1979). It's the classic "us" versus "them." We're more comfortable around people who seem like ourselves because we believe they are safe.

The "us versus them" idea is a popular explanation; humans seem to naturally form groups, teams, or clusters of people who like each other or work together for some goal. Recall from an early chapter in the book that *social identity theory* proposes that our self-concept includes both our individual traits and our social groups (Tajfel & Turner, 1979). Research shows that we usually try to protect our own group, to the detriment of whomever is on the outside.

TABLE 14.3

Theories for the Origins of Stereotypes and Prejudice

Adaptive Categorization	Rapid stereotyping helped our ancestors survive; it's evolutionary instinct.
Social Identity	Our self-concept includes both individual traits and social groups; we naturally protect our own groups.
Realistic Conflict	We use stereotypes and prejudice as an excuse to fight other groups when we want a specific limited resource, like land.
Scapegoating	Prejudice occurs when we blame another group for our problems.
Social Learning	We learn stereotypes by imitating what we see other people doing, including cultural messages in the media.
Self-fulfilling Prophecies	Cultural expectations affect how we're treated, making those expectations more likely to come true, in turn perpetuating the stereotype.

This kind of social division also relates to the next idea. **Realistic conflict theory** suggests that we use stereotypes and prejudice as an excuse to fight other groups when our own group wants access to a specific and limited resource (Sherif, 1966; Sherif & Sherif, 1969; Zárate et al., 2004). The classic example is when colonizers dehumanize indigenous tribes of people and stereotype them as "savages" or "uncivilized" as justification for taking their land. Conflicts can happen between any two groups, though. One recent study used realistic conflict theory as a possible explanation for fighting that occurred between groups of local fishermen in Indonesia who both wanted access to declining fish catches (Widodo et al., 2022).

Maybe prejudice happens when we need someone to blame for our problems. When one group targets another and blames it for their recent troubles, it's called **scapegoating** (Allport, 1954; Dollard et al., 1939). Many historians believed the Nazis were able to rise to power after Germany's loss in World War I and the country's economic recession by blaming Jewish people and other marginalized groups (e.g., Zheng et al., 2022). As the COVID-19 pandemic continued, people in the United States were more likely to scapegoat unvaccinated over vaccinated people, and this blame was especially likely to come from politically liberal individuals (Graso et al., 2022).

Another idea is that stereotypes exist in each of us because we learned them from the previous generation. **Social learning theory** proposes that we naturally observe others and imitate what they do—and in this case, we will absorb and copy the prejudice we see. This might come from other people in our life, such as family members, or more abstractly through cultural messages (Bandura & Walters, 1977; Perry & Bussey, 1979). Cultural messages about what is expected of different groups are certainly portrayed in media messages; TV shows, movies, and videogames show stereotypes based on gender, ethnicity, sexual orientation, and more (e.g., Anderson, 2009; Annati & Ramsey, 2022; Huntley & Goodfriend, 2019; Seager, 2019; Shaheen, 2012).

Have you ever felt pressure to live up to stereotypes about your group? The final explanation is called is **self-fulfilling prophecies**. This is the idea that stereotypes create cultural expectations that affect people's behaviors in terms of how they treat people in a group, such that those expectations become more likely to become true, therefore reinforcing and perpetuating the stereotype (Dovidio et al., 2002; Klein & Snyder, 2003; McConnell & Leibold, 2001; Word et al., 1974). And the cycle just keeps going. If boys and girls are encouraged to play with gendered toys (think trucks versus Barbies), they may grow up thinking they are "supposed" to like and value different things. Research indicates such expectations in various kinds of social groups might contribute to stigmas or opportunities that translate into systemic privilege or problems for people based on race, gender, mental illness, physical attractiveness, and more (Almadi, 2022; Gentrup et al., 2020).

The Stereotype Content Model

Are all stereotypes created equal?

The last section discussed many reasons why we categorize, label, and dislike each other. There's probably some truth to each of the theories and ideas, and a full picture of discrimination will certainly be complex. One interesting idea that accounts for some of this nuance is the **stereotype content model** (Fiske et al., 2002). It acknowledges that our stereotypes about groups can include multiple judgments at once and that they might be a combination of positive and negative attitudes (see Table 14.4).

Specifically, the model breaks stereotype content into two major perceptions. The first is *warmth,* meaning our evaluation of whether the group is socially likable, friendly, and kind. The second is *competence,* meaning our evaluation of whether

Realistic conflict theory: The idea that we use stereotypes and prejudice as an excuse to fight other groups when we want a specific limited resource.

Scapegoating: The idea that prejudice occurs when we blame another group for our problems.

Social learning theory: The idea that we naturally observe others and imitate what they do (including prejudice).

Self-fulfilling prophecies: Expectations that affect how we're treated, such that the expectations are now more likely to come true.

Stereotype content model: The idea that two categories of perception (warmth and competence) interact to form four different types of prejudice about groups.

TABLE 14.4

The Stereotype Content Model

	LOW IN COMPETENCE	HIGH IN COMPETENCE
HIGH IN WARMTH	*Paternalistic prejudice* toward people who are low in status and do not compete with the in-group. Our emotional responses include pity and sympathy. Examples: Elderly people, people with disabilities, and housewives.	*Admiration prejudice* for people who have high status but do not compete with the in-group. Our emotional responses include pride and admiration. Examples: Our in-groups or allies.
LOW IN WARMTH	*Contemptuous prejudice* toward people with low status but who compete with the in-group. Our emotional responses include contempt, disgust, anger, and resentment. Examples: Welfare recipients and very poor people.	*Envious prejudice* toward people with high status and compete with the in-group. Our emotional responses include envy and jealousy. Examples: Asians, Jewish people, rich people, and feminists.

Source: Fiske et al. (2002).

the group is talented, intelligent, and capable. The combination of these two overall perceptions leads to four types of prejudice.

We can envy some groups, admire others, feel paternalistic (or condescending) about others, or even hold groups in contempt if we think they're neither likable nor competent. These prejudices lead to different types of discrimination.

Are women judged for putting careers before raising children? Are men judged if they choose to be "stay-at-home dads"?

iStock.com/Jose carlos Cerdeno;
iStock.com/Fly View Productions

Understanding Discrimination

Discrimination always hurts.

It's true that there have been great improvements in many cultures away from blatant, explicit discrimination such as segregated schools, clearly different opportunities for different kinds of people in education or jobs, or worse. Psychologists refer to this type of clear, unapologetic different treatment of groups *old-fashioned discrimination.* Of course, examples of it still do happen.

Psychologists have also identified that other forms of discrimination still exist but have gotten sneakier—and therefore more socially acceptable (Sears & Henry, 2005). For example, **benevolent discrimination** hides by using "positive" stereotypes to limit

Benevolent discrimination: Beliefs that use positively framed stereotypes to discriminate.

opportunities for certain groups (Glick & Fiske, 2001). It's "positive" (read: it sounds like a compliment) to say that women are naturally nurturing and good at taking care of children. But this kind of stereotype can harm women in various ways:

- Women are less likely to be selected as leaders (especially in business or politics) because they are seen as "nice" but therefore weak and emotional.

- Women are judged very harshly if they choose careers and jobs over raising children or if they struggle with motherhood.

- Women who put a lot of effort into raising children aren't given credit for it, because it's assumed they should just be naturally good at it.

Note this stereotype also hurts men! It implies that men are somehow deficient at being nurturing and taking care of children. This might damage father/child relationships, hurt child custody cases involving fathers, and lead to especially harsh treatment of stay-at-home fathers. Sexist cultural prejudices like this, that hurt the opportunities and mental well-being of men, are called **toxic masculinity**. Toxic masculinity also includes stereotypical ideas like men shouldn't ever ask for help, men shouldn't admit feeling pain, and men shouldn't express emotions (Saucier et al., 2016). Many studies show the harmful psychological effects this kind of pressure puts on men (for reviews, see Harianti, 2023; Watson et al., 2022).

Toxic masculinity: Sexist cultural prejudices that hurt opportunities for and well-being of men.

Ending Discrimination

So, what can be done to decrease stereotypes, prejudice, and discrimination?

Clearly, psychology has not found all the answers—but social psychologists around the world are constantly using their curiosity to test new ideas (Nordstrom & Goodfriend, 2021). Here are three promising ideas:

- When groups work together to achieve a common or *superordinate* goal, prejudice can decrease—especially when the group is successful (Aronson, 2002; Onyango, 2023; Sherif, 1966).

- Forming friendships with someone from a previously disliked group can lower prejudice, not only about that particular group—but sometimes even more generally (Binder et al., 2009; Killen et al., 2022).

- Sometimes, being reminded of what it feels like to be the target of discrimination can promote empathy, which then reduces prejudice (Miklikowska, 2018; Pashak et al., 2018).

For a famous and somewhat controversial example of that last idea—taking the perspective of the target of discrimination to be reminded of what it feels like—go online to watch the video footage of an elementary school teacher in Iowa named Jane Elliott. In the 1960s, she divided her students into two groups based on their eye color and treated one nicely and the other badly. The next day, she switched groups. The exercise got immediate attention, and the children still talk about what they learned.

Practice what you learn in **Knowledge Check 14.3**

SageVantage

ALTRUISM AND AGGRESSION

? Have You Ever Wondered?
14.4 When do we behave in altruistic and aggressive ways?

>> **LO 14.4** Describe theories that help explain altruism and aggression.

Many wonderful individuals joined Peoples Temple.

Tim Carter, a member for years and one of the very few survivors of Jonestown, remembered how the group allowed him to overcome previous prejudices (Guinn, 2017). He noted, "That was something good about the Temple—if you were part of it, you always had the opportunity to grow as a person, to be around and learn to accept, to appreciate, all different kinds of people" (p. 319).

But in the end, it represented aggression more than altruism. After Congressman Ryan visited Jonestown and several members tried to leave with him, Jim Jones couldn't stand his loss of control and the perceived betrayal. As Ryan, several news reporters, and 15 Jonestown members waited for a plane that was to take them back to the United States, they were all shot multiple times by loyal followers of Jones. When the gunmen returned to the village after their aggressive action, Jones decided it was time for his final act.

Theories of Altruism

Is there such a thing as a truly selfless act?

When people do community service, like Habitat for Humanity, what is their motivation?

iStock.com/Hispanolistic

Prosocial behavior: Behaviors that help others, regardless of one's motive for doing so.

Psychologists, philosophers, and others debate whether altruism even exists and—if so—how to define it (Beilin, 2013; Ottoni-Wilhelm et al., 2017). Is it really altruism if helping boosts our self-esteem? Don't you feel good when you help someone—and therefore get a reward?

Psychologists acknowledge this debate in multiple ways. First, most researchers have moved away from the term *altruism,* instead favoring the phrase **prosocial behavior** to refer to behaviors that help others, regardless of your motive for doing so (Bar-Tal, 1976; Pfattheicher et al., 2022). When they do talk about altruism, they make a distinction about what drives someone's actions.

Research has generally identified four theories for why people engage in prosocial behavior.

- *Kinship selection:* We generally prefer to help people related to us, or even who look like ourselves, as an evolutionary instinct to protect our own groups.

- *Reciprocity:* We help to build up some kind of altruism "karma," hoping that when we need help in the future, we're more likely to get it.

- *Negative state relief:* We know that if we don't help, we'll feel guilty or sad—so we help to avoid experiencing those negative feelings.

- *Empathy-altruism hypothesis:* Sometimes, some people genuinely help because we imagine ourselves in their situation. We help because we simply believe in doing the right thing.

Egoistic altruism: Helping others in exchange for some kind of personal benefit.

You can see all of this put together in Table 14.5. The top three rows are all considered forms of **egoistic altruism**, which refers to helping behaviors done in exchange for some kind of personal benefit (Bar-Tal, 1976; Pfattheicher et al., 2022). Yes, you're helping someone else—but you're also helping yourself in some way or

TABLE 14.5

Four Explanations for Prosocial Behavior

THEORY NAME	MOTIVATION FOR HELPING	TYPE OF ALTRUISM
Kinship Selection	Evolutionary instinct to help our group survive.	Egoistic
Reciprocity	Hope someone will help us sometime in the future.	Egoistic
Negative State Relief	Desire to avoid feeling bad or guilty if we didn't help.	Egoistic
Empathy–Altruism	Believe it's the right thing to do.	Pure

another. Only the last theoretical motive (the empathy-altruism hypothesis) is based on the idea of **pure altruism**, helping behaviors purely out of selfless concern for them and expecting absolutely nothing in return.

Pure altruism: Helping others with no expectation of reward.

Predictors of Helping

There's a famous story about helping in social psychology.

A young woman named Kitty Genovese was assaulted and murdered near the doorway to her New York City apartment building in the middle of the night. The case quickly got national attention when newspapers reported that 38 of her neighbors heard her cries for help and did nothing.

But it turns out that the case was more complicated than when it first appeared. The story was back in the headlines years later, thanks in part to her brother who decided to follow up with those 38 bystanders. He discovered that some had tried to intervene after all, including calling the police. One neighbor yelled at the attacker, who temporarily ran off (but came back later). Another neighbor held Genovese in her arms as she passed away (Kassin, 2017; Vyse, 2016).

Despite the misrepresentation of Kitty Genovese's story, it was part of the inspiration for the creation of the emergency 911 national phone number—and it led to decades of research on when and why people choose to help in an emergency (Hüffmeier et al., 2022; Vyse, 2016).

The Bystander Effect

While it turned out that a few people did actually help Genovese, several studies have established that ironically, a specific form of diffusion of responsibility can happen in the context of emergency situations.

The **bystander effect** occurs when *more* witnesses to an emergency lead to a *lower* probability that any one of the witnesses will help (Darley & Latané, 1968; Kassin, 2017; Latané & Darley, 1970). It seems they all assume someone else will do it, so they don't have to. The bystander effect has occurred when witnessing a theft, keeping quiet about cyberbullying, and even in the virtual world of multiplayer videogames (Obermaier et al., 2016; Stenico & Greitemeyer, 2015; van Bommel et al., 2014). An important application of the bystander effect is on college campuses if students see someone at risk for a potential sexual assault. Many reduction programs now emphasize the importance of stepping up to help if you see someone who might need help (Koss et al., 1987; Levine et al., 2020).

Bystander effect: A specific form of diffusion of responsibility, when more witnesses to an emergency lead to a lower probability any of them will help.

Note that not all situations lead to a bystander effect. Various factors about the environment can flip the odds, so that more observers or witnesses now lead to a great probability of helping (Fischer et al., 2011; Greitemeyer & Mügge, 2013, 2015; Liebst et al., 2019; van Bommel et al., 2014). This reverse effect can happen, for example, when

- the danger is violent aggression, making it immediately serious and urgent;

- people know they're being filmed; or

- multiple people are needed, such as lifting a heavy object.

Here's one more interesting variation. Researchers went to several bars in Amsterdam and acted like they needed help. The size of the bar's crowd had zero influence on helping—but what *did* matter was how much the people had been drinking. Drunker people were more likely to help (van Bommel et al., 2016). Who knew that a few Heinekens can make people more helpful?

The Five-Step Model of Helping

There are other factors that influence who and when will help. For example, people high in the trait of agreeableness express more empathy and help others more (Habashi et al., 2016; Krueger et al., 2001). On the other hand, people high in the "Dark Triad" personality traits are less likely to help—unless there's something in it for them (Djeriouat & Trémolière, 2014).

The situation also matters. For example, women are more likely to help in general—but less likely to help a stranger if the situation is perceived as dangerous, like stopping when someone appears stranded on the road (Eagly, 2009; Kumru et al., 2012). Likewise, people living in big cities are less likely to help strangers, but that might be simply because they are overwhelmed with how many needy people they encounter every day (Milgram, 1970).

Several psychologists pointed out that there are several legitimate reasons why perfectly nice, well-intentioned people might not help in each emergency situation. We've already mentioned several (such as assuming someone else would help, concerns over safety, and so on). This kind of thinking led to the development of the **Five-Step Model of Helping**, shown in Figure 14.4 (Latané & Darley, 1970).

It points out that for helping to occur, there must be five "yes" answers, one at every step along the way. At any of these steps, legitimate misunderstandings, diffusion of responsibility, or other problems might happen and some someone from deciding to help.

Five-Step Model of Helping: Suggests that helping will only occur in emergency situations if five criteria are met.

Theories of Aggression

What about hurting others?

The history of the world is certainly filled with plenty of examples of aggression. It runs the gambit from *micro-aggressions*—small looks, comments, or behaviors that indicate disapproval or disagreement—all the way up to genocide and war. To help break down this complex topic, consider the typology in Table 14.6, which identifies different forms of aggression (adapted from Buss, 1961). Do you consider some forms of aggression better or worse than others? If so, why?

While the typology above categorizes types of aggression, it doesn't explain *why* people aggress. Think about the last time you wanted to strike out at someone—what motivated your desire? Psychologists identify two very different kinds of aggression (Berkowitz, 1989; Dodge et al., 1997; Feshbach, 1964):

Hostile-reactive aggression: Impulsive, emotion-based reactions to perceived threats.

- **Hostile-reactive aggression** is an impulsive, emotion-based reaction to perceived threats. It's driven by feelings like jealousy, humiliation, or anger.

FIGURE 14.4

Latané and Darley's Five-Step Model of Helping

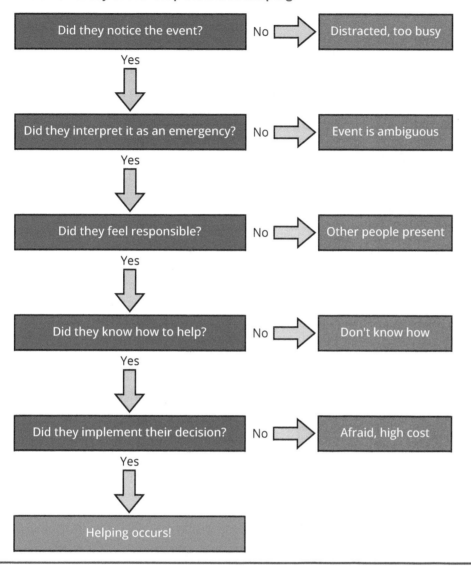

Source: Adapted from Latané and Darley (1970).

TABLE 14.6

A Typology of Eight Different Forms of Aggression

| | DIRECT | | INDIRECT | |
	ACTIVE	PASSIVE	ACTIVE	PASSIVE
Physical aggression	Hitting, stabbing, beating, etc.	Positioning your car to prevent someone else from changing lanes	Cheating in a competition or hiring a "hitman"	Refusing to stop the bleeding of an enemy soldier
Verbal aggression	Putdowns and insults	Giving someone the silent treatment to punish that person	Spreading mean rumors or negative gossip	Failing to defend someone who you know is being accused unfairly

Source: Adapted from Buss (1961).

Instrumental-proactive aggression: Thoughtful or reason-based decisions to harm others to gain resources.

- **Instrumental-proactive aggression** is a thoughtful or reason-based decision to harm others to gain resources such as territory, money, self-esteem, or social status.

Does "venting" your anger help reduce aggression, or is that just a myth?

iStock.com/jgroup

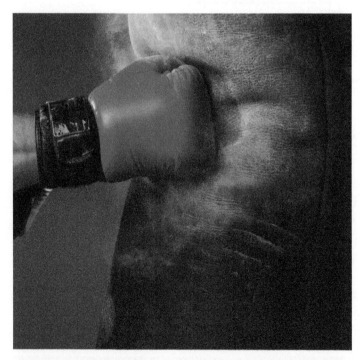

Does "venting" your anger help reduce aggression, or is that just a myth?

iStock.com/master1305

Catharsis hypothesis: The idea that "venting" a little bit of anger or frustration is an effective way to reduce aggression.

This distinction has resulted in interesting research. For example, people who engage in instrumental-proactive aggression are sometimes considered more "cold-blooded," cruel, and willing to do anything to reach their goals; they may also have lower resting heart rates (Belfry & Kolla, 2021). On the other hand, hostile-reactive aggression appears to be positively correlated to levels of impulsivity and may partially explain criminal behaviors (Vaughan et al., 2023).

Finally, researchers curious about why people decide to spend their time trolling others on social media found four motivations that divide into these categories (Mao et al., 2023). Some people troll online for "revenge" or "to maintain social justice" (which the researchers classified as hostile-reactive), while others troll for "thrill seeking" or "rebutting for disagreement" (which they classified as instrumental-proactive).

Reducing Aggression

What can reduce aggression?

Like the question of prejudice, psychological research has struggled to answer this question. An early idea is known as the **catharsis hypothesis**. If you've ever told yourself that you can "let off some steam" by playing violent videogames, punching a pillow, or trying axe-throwing, your behaviors suggest belief in this idea, which is that releasing a *little* aggression allows us to "vent" just enough frustration to prevent an explosion (Breuer & Freud, 1893/1955; Lee, 1993).

While it seems intuitively correct, and throwing axes is pretty fun, research indicates that it not only doesn't work—it might even make things worse. Angry participants became *more* hostile, for example, after hitting nails with a hammer for 10 minutes or pounding on a punching bag (Bushman, 2002; Hornberger, 1959; Shariff et al., 2017). That said, more recent research suggests that venting frustration might be effective if you get to choose how you want to "get it out" (Ferguson et al., 2018).

Getting "revenge" may be even worse: It just keeps the cycle of aggression going, and it may prompt other parties to escalate (Bushman et al., 1999, 2001; Guerin, 2001; Verona & Sullivan, 2008). Is there any hope? Yes. There are at least 25 cultures that specifically emphasize peaceful values, and they range all over the globe from the Arctic to Tahiti (Bonta, 1997). And there are a few studies showing that role models demonstrating helping and forgiveness toward others seem to lead children to later show more altruism and less aggression themselves (Baron, 1972; Crowder & Goodfriend, 2012; Donnerstein & Donnerstein, 1976; Vidyasagar & Mishra, 1993).

Practice what you learn in **Knowledge Check 14.4**   Sage Vantage ➤

CONFORMITY AND OBEDIENCE

>> **LO 14.5** **Explain research on conformity, obedience, and rebellion.**

"Don't drink the Kool-Aid."

You may not realize that phrase, which means not to follow the crowd when they're doing something unwise, comes from the mass deaths at Jonestown. After the murders of Ryan, the reporters, and the Jonestown members who tried to escape with them, Jim Jones gathered the members of his group and told them that the U.S. government would consider them all complicit, put the adults in jail or execute them, and persecute their children (Guinn, 2017). There was only one way out: Drink the cyanide that was now being passed out in paper cups filled with punch. It was actually another brand— Flavor Aid, not Kool-Aid—which he bought because it was cheaper.

Why did 909 people die that day?

Some went along voluntarily. They were sleep deprived, were scared, and had been manipulated for years into believing Jones was a messiah. Jones had also taken the group through several mass poisoning drills during the preceding weeks, desensitizing them to what was happening. Others drank because everyone else was doing it; their friends and family were all going to die within a few minutes. Some drank because they were afraid of the men standing along the perimeter of the village with machine guns, facing *in*—not out.

Conformity and obedience are core topics within social psychology.

Have You Ever Wondered?
14.5 Why do people tend to conform to groups and obey authority figures?

Understanding Conformity

There are two different reasons people conform to others.

Informational conformity occurs when we copy others to be "correct." If you notice everyone else at the deli counter grabbing a number to get in line, then you do it too. Whenever we're not sure of what do to in a social situation, we tend to look around to see what everyone else is doing. This kind of conformity has a very pragmatic motive, simply to figure out how to get something done.

Normative conformity, on the other hand, occurs when we copy others just to fit in. This is when we might compromise our better judgment and engage in behaviors we wouldn't do under other circumstances—it's the classic "peer pressure," or simply wanting social acceptance.

It explains dubious fashion choices—and that famous bridge parents warn children not to jump off.

Conformity is a powerful impulse. A glance at Figure 14.5 informs you that line "B" clearly matches the target line. Tested alone, people get the answer right 98% of the time. In Solomon Asch's (1951, 1952, 1955, 1956) experiments, all the participants around a table took turns reporting their perceptions of similar lines—until the third trial, when they all agreed that line "C" was correct. Why did this happen? Because everyone except the last person to respond were really *confederates*, people part of the experimenter's team just pretending to be real participants. The confederates had

Informational conformity: Behaving like others to perform "correct" behavior, to accomplish a task.

Normative conformity: Behaving like others to fit in and be socially accepted.

FIGURE 14.5

A Study of Conformity

Can you tell which line on the right matches the one on the left? It seems obvious, until the people sitting next to you all publicly state a different answer.

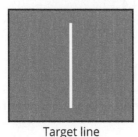 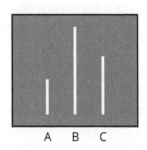

Target line   A   B   C

Source: Adapted from Asch (1952).

Do you think your culture praises nonconformists? It varies around the world.

Westend61/via Getty Images

all been trained to say the wrong line on purpose, just to see how the real participant would act. Under this kind of social pressure, 75% of the participants said the wrong answer at least once, giving in to conformity. Overall, they gave wrong answers about 37% of the time.

During debriefing, one of the participants captured the essence of normative conformity when he explained why he sometimes went along with the crowd's wrong answer (Asch, 1956, p. 34): "I was standing out . . . a sore thumb. I didn't particularly want to make a fool of myself . . . I felt I was definitely right [but] they might think I was peculiar."

There is variability in who decides to conform. After all, about 25% of the participants in Asch's study never gave in to the pressure—not even once (Asch, 1956). What predicts who conforms and who doesn't? While some variability is surely tied to personality or life experiences (Kosloff et al., 2017), other individual differences appear to be the result of cultural values (Triandis, 1989; Varnum & Grossmann, 2017).

When Asch's procedure was replicated in Kuwait, conformity rates were close to those in the United States: 33% (Amir, 1984). But Chandra (1973) found much higher rates of conformity (about 58%) in Fiji. A popular way to think about differences among world cultures is to divide them as generally fitting into one of these two categories (Hui & Triandis, 1986; Markus & Kitayama, 1994; Ramesh & Gelfand, 2010; Vishkin et al., 2023):

Individualistic cultures: Cultures centered on independence and promoting personal goals over group goals.

- **Individualistic cultures:** Views of the self are *independent* from the larger group. The self is based primarily on individual traits, abilities, rights, and feelings. While heroism and charity are admired, they are voluntary and should not be expected if they go against self-interest. The desire for rugged independence is valued and respected. These cultures are generally more common in Europe and North America (e.g., United States, Canada, Great Britain).

- **Collectivistic cultures**: Views of the self are *interdependent* with the larger group. They require adjusting to others, participating in actions that promote group welfare, and putting the group's needs in front of your own. The desire for independence is viewed as unnatural, immature, and selfish. These cultures are generally more common in Asia (e.g., Japan, Thailand, Korea).

Collectivistic cultures: Cultures centered on interdependence and promoting group goals over personal goals.

As you can see from these descriptions, people in collectivistic cultures not only tend to conform more than people in individualistic cultures—they also believe that conformity is a good thing. This value is explained well by representative from the Temne people of Sierra Leone on the West Coast of Africa: "When Temne people choose a thing, we must all agree with the decision—that is what we call cooperation" (Toffler, 1970, p. 273). In collectivist cultures, conforming isn't caving in; it's a virtuous social courtesy that puts the group's needs before your own. If you're curious about your own tendency to conform, you can try measuring it in the *What's My Score?* feature.

Measuring Conformity

Instructions: Please use the following scale to indicate the degree of your agreement or disagreement with each of the statements below. Try to describe yourself accurately and generally (that is, the way you are actually in most situations—not the way you would hope to be).

−4	−3	−2	−1	0	+1	+2	+3	+4
Very strong disagreement				Neutral				Very strong agreement

_____ 1. I often rely on, and act upon, the advice of others.

_____ 2. I would be the last one to change my opinion in a heated argument on a controversial topic.

_____ 3. Generally, I'd rather give in and go along for the sake of peace than struggle to have my way.

_____ 4. I tend to follow family tradition in making political decisions.

_____ 5. Basically, my friends are the ones who decide what we do together.

_____ 6. A charismatic and eloquent speaker can easily influence and change my ideas.

_____ 7. I am more independent than conforming in my ways.

_____ 8. If someone is very persuasive, I tend to change my opinion and go along with them.

_____ 9. I don't give in to others easily.

_____ 10. I tend to rely on others when I have to make an important decision quickly.

_____ 11. I prefer to make my own way in life rather than find a group I can follow.

Scoring: First, reverse-score items 2, 7, 9, and 11. For this scale, all you have to do is cross off the plus or minus in front of what you wrote and change it to the other sign (so, for example, a −3 becomes a +3). Zeros stay the same. Then, add up all the numbers to get your composite score, which should be between −44 and +44. Higher numbers mean more of a tendency to conform to others. ●

Source: Mehrabian and Stefl (1995).

Obedience to Authority: The Milgram Shock Studies

Stanley Milgram didn't expect the results he got.

Milgram wanted to understand why people are willing to do terrible things when an authority figure orders them to. The historical setting was the aftermath of the World War II Holocaust atrocities, when several of Hitler's henchmen claimed that they were not responsible for their war crimes because they were simply following orders. Milgram set up a study in which everyday people would get orders to harm an innocent person—and he expected that most of them would refuse. He was surprised by what happened.

"Persons Needed for a Study of Memory" was the purposely misleading newspaper announcement for what became a long series of studies under Milgram (1963, 1974). When participants arrived at Yale University, a researcher pretended to randomly assign the volunteers to be either the Teacher or the Learner (who was really a confederate). It wasn't really random; the participant always became the Teacher.

They were told that the Teacher's job was to review a series of word pairs with the Learner, then give the Learner a multiple-choice test. Any time the Learner made an error, the Teacher was ordered to give him an electric shock. The cover story (part of the deception) for why this was all happening was supposedly to see if having a motivation to learn (avoiding the punishing shocks) would help someone learn faster. A fake voltage-delivery machine displayed a row of switches with 15-volt increases ending at 450 volts with warnings of, "DANGER SEVERE SHOCK" and "X X X" (see Figure 14.6). The Teacher was told that each time a mistake was made, they should move up to the next-higher switch on the board and just keep going up.

The Teacher (the real participant), separated by a wall, could hear the Learner respond to the progressively higher voltages with groans, screams, declarations of a heart condition, and pleas to be released. These responses were scripted and recorded, played on a tape recorder so they were consistent for every participant—but they were disturbing to hear. You can read some examples of the scripted responses for each level of shock in Table 14.7.

FIGURE 14.6

Levels of Fake Electric Shock in Milgram's Famous Obedience Studies

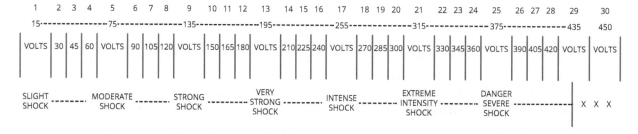

TABLE 14.7

The Learner's Scripted Responses in Milgram's Obedience Studies

SHOCK LEVEL	LEARNER'S SCRIPTED RESPONSE
75 volts	Ugh!
150 volts	Ugh!!! Experimenter! That's all. Get me out of here. I told you I had heart trouble. My heart's starting to bother me now. Get me out of here, please. My heart's starting to bother me. I refuse to go on. Let me out.
270 volts	[Agonized scream.] Let me out of here. Let me out of here. Let me out of here. Let me out. Do you hear? Let me out of here.
330 volts	[Intense and prolonged agonized scream.] Let me out of here. Let me out of here. My heart's bothering me. Let me out, I tell you. [Hysterically.] Let me out of here. Let me out of here. You have no right to hold me here. Let me out! Let me out! Let me out of here! Let me out! Let me out!
345–450 volts	[Silence]

Source: Milgram (1963).

If the participant hesitated to give the next shock, the experimenter (who stayed in the room with the participant) would prod them verbally to keep going up to four times:

- *Prod 1:* "Please continue" or "Please go on."
- *Prod 2:* "The experiment requires that you continue."
- *Prod 3:* "It is absolutely essential that you continue."
- *Prod 4:* "You have no other choice, you *must* go on."

The real purpose of the study was to test the limits of obedience to authority. How far would the Teacher go? Would a regular person off the street give what they thought were potentially painful (and maybe dangerous) shocks to a stranger they just met, simply because someone wearing a lab coat ordered them to do it?

Milgram himself expected most people to stop fairly early. But even he was surprised by what happened: A startling 26 out of 40 (65%) of the participants went all the way to 450 volts, a potentially dangerous level. Milgram himself replicated the study many times, trying to test various parts of the environment to see what would make obedience go up or down.

For example, he was curious how the same procedure might work with women as the participants. He thought maybe they would obey more, because American culture in the 1950s and 1960s had taught them to be docile. Or, perhaps women would obey less, because American culture had taught them to be kind and to care for the welfare of others. The women in his study obeyed at exactly the same rates as men; 65% went all the way up to 450 volts (Milgram, 1963). Rates of obedience did go down when he moved the study off the beautiful, prestigious Yale campus to a dumpy office building (but obedience rates remained high at 48%). When the Teacher had to sit in the same room as the Learner and watch him get the shocks, obedience rates went down again, to 40%. And when the Teacher had to physically hold the Learner's hand onto a metal plate to get the shocks (while the Teacher wore protective gloves), only 30% of the participants went all the way to 450 volts.

It is still pretty disturbing that about a third of the participants were willing to deliver shocks under those circumstances. Milgram has been criticized for conducting one of the most unethical series of studies in the history of psychology—but he didn't know how it would turn out when he planned it. Still, in contrast to what he originally reported, Milgram did not fully debrief all the participants before they left, and he could have done more to minimize the negative psychological consequences they experienced once he did the first couple of studies in the series (Brannigan, 2013; Nicholson, 2011, 2015; Perry, 2013).

Defiance and Rebellion

Some people refused to obey.

There were survivors of Jonestown. A few people managed to sneak past the armed guards and hid in the jungle. One man, Grover Davis, calmly walked past one of the guards while saying, "I don't want to die." The guard didn't stop him. Three of Jim Jones's sons were not in the village that day; they were in a nearby town with several other young men from Jonestown to play in an exhibition basketball game. Jones called them and ordered them to kill any possible enemies first, then themselves with knives. They all refused. Years later, Stephan Jones wrote an essay about his experiences during those tragic days (Jones, 2013):

> I watched my teammates ... I was okay. We would care for each other in our rebellion. Almost since we'd arrived in Georgetown, we'd been bucking the Temple system—if there truly was such a thing—and ignoring or blatantly

countermanding orders. . . . I never thought things would get as far as they had. . . . I had underestimated my father, and I was reeling. . . . I was nineteen years old, terrified and confused. . . . I thought I had time to stop Dad.

Stephan spent the rest of that night calling the police, driving to places like the U.S. Embassy, trying to save as many lives as possible.

Most psychology textbooks focus on the high number of participants in the Asch and Milgram studies who conformed and obeyed. We want to end this chapter by emphasizing that some people didn't. And while sometimes, conformity and obedience are good things (such as when putting the group's needs above your own indicate maturity and selflessness), sometimes the courage of defiance is needed if it helps us question authority and trust our own judgment, especially if we believe people are getting hurt.

While Milgram could have done more to protect the mental well-being of his participants, he did interview several of them during debriefing to understand their psychological state immediately afterward (Milgram, 1974). He gathered qualitative data regarding the motivation driving participants' choices both to obey and to rebel. To end this chapter, consider three examples of people who defied orders.

One participant was an industrial engineer who stopped delivering shocks at 255 volts. After Milgram's experimenter told him that he had no choice but to continue delivering the shocks, he asked (Milgram, 1974):

> Why don't have I have choice? I came here on my own free will. I thought I could help in a research project. But if I have to hurt somebody to do that, or if I was in his place, too, I wouldn't stay there. I can't continue. I'm very sorry. I think I've gone too far already, probably. (p. 51)

A professor of religion stopped at 150 volts. When the experimenter told him that he had to keep going, the professor responded, "If this were Russia maybe, but not in America" (Milgram, 1974, p. 48). Finally, a quiet woman stopped giving shocks after getting to 210 volts on the machine. When Milgram asked her why she had refused at that point, she politely said, "Perhaps we have seen too much pain" (p. 85). She had immigrated to the United States from Germany, where she had grown up as a former member of the Hitler youth program. ●

Sage Vantage   Practice what you learn in **Knowledge Check 14.5**

CHAPTER REVIEW

Learning Objectives Summary

14.1 How are attitudes formed, and how do people change their minds?

>> **LO 14.1 Explain how attitudes are formed, how they change, and how they can lead to biases.**

Attitudes are judgments or evaluations of someone or something that result from our experiences. We can change our attitudes either because of external influence (when we're persuaded by others, such as salespeople) or when we change our own minds. When we change our own attitudes to avoid mental discomfort, it's called cognitive dissonance.

14.2   How does being in a group change people's behavior?

>> LO 14.2   **Analyze various ways group dynamics affect individual behavior.**

The presence of others in a group sometimes makes an individual's performance on a task better; that's called social facilitation. When the opposite happens—the presence of others makes individual performance on a task worse—that's called social loafing. Social loafing is often due to diffusion of responsibility. A risk of joining groups is that group loyalty can be abused; examples are the initiation effect and Stockholm syndrome.

14.3   Why are stereotypes and prejudice so common in people?

>> LO 14.3   **Explain the origins of stereotypes and prejudice, as well as research on how to reduce them.**

Stereotypes are overgeneralized thoughts about groups; prejudice is a judgment or emotional evaluation of a group, and discrimination is unfair behavior toward someone because they are in a particular group. There are several psychological theories explaining why stereotypes and prejudice seem to be so pervasive in humans, as well as ideas on how to reduce them.

14.4   When do we behave in altruistic and aggressive ways?

>> LO 14.4   **Describe theories that help explain altruism and aggression.**

There are also different forms of aggression, and research is mixed on ways to effectively decrease aggression. Similarly, altruism (or helping behaviors) is complicated and might happen due to a variety of motivations. The Five-Step Model of Helping notes that helping will only occur under certain circumstances.

14.5   Why do people tend to conform to groups and obey authority figures?

>> LO 14.5   **Explain research on conformity, obedience, and rebellion.**

There are two major reasons why people conform: to accomplish a task correctly (informational conformity) and to be socially accepted (normative conformity). Conformity varies based on cultural values. A famous study by Stanley Milgram studied obedience to authority and found that many people are willing to follow orders, even if they think they are hurting someone, but that some people refuse.

CRITICAL THINKING QUESTIONS

1. The Asch line study and the Milgram obedience study both required a great deal of deception. Both have been criticized for being potentially unethical by today's standards for how participants should be treated. That said, if ethics were not a concern, what other kinds of changes to the people or environment would be interesting to test, to see how they would affect the results? Think of at least three variables that would be interesting and state your hypotheses for what you think the results might be.

2. Why do apparently normal, kind, intelligent people join groups that turn out to be cults? Do online research of another famous cult from history and profile (1) what group members thought it was, compared to what it turned out to be; (2) what kind of person the cult leader was; and (3) what kinds of people were drawn to join the group.

3. Think of a group that you've joined that had some kind of initiation. Describe the initiation, then analyze whether your commitment, loyalty, or perceptions of the group changed at all before and after you experienced the initiation. Did your experience match the initiation effect describe in the book? Explain.

4. Imagine you want to use the four persuasion strategies to influence your professor to do something for the class such as offering extra credit or a take-home final exam. Explain precisely how you could use each persuasion technique.

5. Find a recent example of people either helping or failing to help. Then, apply at least two concepts from this chapter to explain why people acted as they did.

KEY TERMS

Adaptive categorization, 444
Attitudes, 431
Benevolent discrimination, 446
Bystander effect, 449
Catharsis hypothesis, 452
Cognitive dissonance, 435
Collectivistic cultures, 455
Diffusion of responsibility, 439
Discrimination, 443
Effort justification, 441
Egoistic altruism, 448
Five-Step Model of Helping, 450
Hazing, 440
Hostile-reactive aggression, 450
Individualistic cultures, 454
Informational conformity, 453
Initiation effect, 440

Instrumental-proactive aggression, 452
Normative conformity, 453
Prejudice, 443
Prosocial behavior, 448
Pure altruism, 449
Realistic conflict theory, 445
Scapegoating, 445
Self-fulfilling prophecies, 445
Social facilitation, 438
Social learning theory, 445
Social loafing, 439
Social psychology, 431
Stereotype content model, 445
Stereotypes, 443
Stockholm syndrome, 442
Toxic masculinity, 447

Bob Daemmrich/Alamy Stock Photo

15

Psychological Disorders

Meet Nathan.

In fifth grade, a kick ball rolled right up to Nathan and bounced against his legs. He just stood there, frozen, right in the middle of an intense gym class battle. We shouted at him, but he didn't even try to pick up the ball, much less throw it at the runner. In middle school, Nathan navigated the hallways with one arm clinging magnet-like to the walls, staring out at the rest of us. We avoided him. And then, one day he was gone.

Those memories have reappeared across decades with a mixture of sadness and guilt—but also curiosity. Tom recalls thinking back then, "What's his problem?" Much later, Tom now wonders why everyone gave him the cold shoulder of schoolyard rejection. How might we have helped him instead? Nathan disappeared sometime during middle school; he lived only two blocks away.

This chapter is about psychological disorders. To really understand them, we have to start by asking how psychology defines mental health and mental illness in the first place, and why our culture allows even relatively naive fifth graders to stigmatize innocent people during their lives.

After reading this chapter, you will get answers to several questions you've been curious about:

Have You Ever Wondered?

15.1   How do psychologists define mental illness and psychological disorders, and what is mental illness stigma?

15.2   How are anxiety disorders different from typical worry or fear?

15.3   How do mood disorders connect to trauma, personality, and substance abuse?

15.4   What exactly are schizophrenia and multiple personality disorder, and do movies show them accurately?

Learning Objectives

LO 15.1   Describe various models of mental illness, then explain mental illness stigma.

LO 15.2   Compare and contrast different specific kinds of anxiety disorders.

LO 15.3   Compare and contrast different specific kinds of mood, personality, and substance abuse disorders.

LO 15.4   Analyze mass media portrayals of schizophrenia and dissociative disorders.

DEFINING MENTAL ILLNESS AND UNDERSTANDING STIGMA

?
Have You Ever
Wondered?
15.1 How do
psychologists define
mental illness and
psychological
disorders, and what
is mental illness
stigma?

>> LO 15.1   **Describe various models of mental illness, then explain mental illness stigma.**

In this chapter, you're going to meet several people with psychological disorders.

We've changed names and other identifying details, but many of them are people your authors have known personally. Their lives aren't perfect examples of psychological disorders, but they may feel familiar to you. All of us have encountered people in our lives who are currently living with symptoms related to mental illness,

FIGURE 15.1

The Mental Health Continuum

Mental Illness   Mental Health

whether we realized it or not. And this includes ourselves: Everyone occasionally feels depressed, anxious, paranoid, and fearful.

Mental health versus mental illness isn't a dichotomy or a binary system where it's one or the other with nothing in between. Instead, we all live somewhere along the mental health continuum in Figure 15.1.

According to the World Health Organization (WHO), **mental health** is a psychological state in which someone is aware of their own abilities, can cope with normal life stress, can work productively, and can contribute to their community (WHO, 2018). Most psychologists would probably add that mental health also includes a generally positive self-esteem and functioning social relationships with others.

In contrast, the other end of the continuum shown in Figure 15.1 is **mental illness**, which is experiencing one or more psychological disorders. **Psychological disorders** are syndromes that are significant enough to cause a major disturbance in an individual's mental and social functioning. By *syndrome*, we mean a collection of symptoms that consistently occur together.

For many people studying psychology, psychological disorders and therapy are the most fascinating topics in the entire course. This chapter is going to give you an outline of the major categories and types of psychological disorders, and the next chapter will discuss approaches to therapy and treatment. To get started in this very first section, we cover some questions that curious students usually want to know immediately:

- How do psychologists think about mental illness in general?

- How do they diagnose psychological disorders?

- How common is mental illness in general?

- Why do we treat mental illness differently than physical illness?

Models of Mental Illness

How do psychologists think about mental illness in general?

Over the years, psychology as a field has debated this question. Three major theoretical models have been considered, but none of them is adequate by itself. The best answer so far seems to be combining them into the fourth model. Consider each briefly.

The Biomedical Model

The **biomedical model** views mental illness as biologically based, often related to the brain. Certainly, some disorders have a strong tie to biological factors, as we'll discuss later; schizophrenia, depression, and substance abuse are examples. The causes and symptoms of these disorders seem to be linked more to biological issues (such as neurotransmitters) and less to factors such as someone's personality or culture. These disorders appear in parts of the world that have been very isolated from outside influence (Hacking, 1998; Murphy, 2001; Tan, 2019).

Mental health: A psychological state in which someone is aware of their own abilities, can cope with normal life stress, can work productively, and can contribute to their community.

Mental illness: Experiencing one or more psychological disorders.

Psychological disorders: Syndromes that are significant enough to cause a major disturbance in an individual's mental and social functioning.

Biomedical model: Views mental illness as biologically based and usually related to the brain.

The biomedical approach has a well-intended but harsh past, a rapidly evolving present, and a promising future. If disorders have biological causes, it implies biological treatments. Ancient Greek healers administered noxious plants to purge the body of evil spirits. A relatively kind version of the medical model led to creation of asylums intended to provide physical care in the 1700s and 1800s, but some of these well-intended efforts were diverted into cruelties such as chaining people to walls, forced bloodletting, and forced sterilizations (Bartlett, 2017; Hansen & King, 2013; Mitchell & Kirkby, 2014; Scull, 2019).

Today, though, biology-based breakthroughs have led to many effective diagnostic tools and treatments. For example, we benefit from neuroimaging that helps identify biomarkers associated with specific disorders (Rashid & Calhoun, 2020) and drugs that affect neurotransmitters helping depression and many other disorders (Fischer et al., 2019). Some disorders respond to surgery or—yes—even to electric shock treatments when done carefully and ethically.

The Psychological Model

It's not all biology.

As we'll discuss later in this chapter, while some people have symptoms of depression due to biological factors, others do because of difficult experiences such as a death, a breakup, or a personal trauma. So the biomedical model *alone* isn't enough to explain every mental illness for every person.

Psychological model: Views mental illness as based on mental factors such as personality, perceptions, cognitions, relationships, and so on.

The **psychological model** traces psychological disorders to mental factors such as someone's personality, unique perceptions, cognitive biases, internal self-deceptions, relationships, political or religious views, and so on (Amit et al., 2022; Kinderman, 2005; Minson & Dorison, 2022; Müller et al., 2022; Roberts et al., 2022). This model also accounts for personal experiences unique to the individual, both negative (like traumas) and positive (like achievements and overcoming challenges).

Personality matters. For example, the chapter on stress, health, and happiness discussed a personality trait called *resilience,* the ability to adapt well in the face of adversity or stress. People with high levels of resilience typically experience lower levels of stress, anxiety, and related psychological disorders; they are generally able to "bounce back" from trauma and adversity (Luthar et al., 2000; Vella & Pai, 2019).

Two models are better than one.

The Sociocultural Model

Do you believe the following statements about mental illness?

- Certain events are likely to be psychologically traumatic.

- Talking about our troubles and traumas is healthier than staying silent.

Those beliefs come from "Western" culture (which, as we've said in other chapters, usually refers to Western Europe, Canada, Australia, the United States, and similar cultures). But other cultures have different traditions and beliefs, and their views of mental illness vary.

Sociocultural model: The view that social and cultural forces shape our view of mental health and illness.

The **sociocultural model** recognizes that social and cultural forces can shape our understanding of and experience with mental illness. For example, anorexia and bulimia are eating disorders in some Western cultures in which people try to be thin. They were rare in Hong Kong, where the culture had no conception of valuing thinness as attractive. That changed when two things happened: Public schools, influenced by Western cultures, started eating disorder *prevention* programs, and the public saw a highly rated television interview with Princess Diana from England in which she talked about having bulimia (Watters, 2010). Suddenly, young people in Hong Kong realized they were expected to want to be thin—which became a self-fulfilling prophecy, increasing prevalence of the disorders.

Sociocultural factors can also affect treatment. Sometimes, well-meaning counselors from cultures accustomed to forms of therapy in which people talk about their traumas will rush to locations where a natural disaster has occurred, wanting to help survivors process the trauma. But if the local culture isn't used to "talking about their feelings," being forced to relive the experience by outsiders can become more traumatic than the disaster itself (Watters, 2010).

The sociocultural model also acknowledges that social and cultural forces can instill implicit bias in how we think about mental illness and that these biases can lead to stereotypes and discrimination. For example, many immigrants to the United States between 1892 and 1924 came through Ellis Island in New York and had to pass several tests, including the "mental deficiency test." It was supposed to test for mental illness—but really it asked questions biased against people not familiar with the majority culture or from lower socioeconomic backgrounds (Anemone, 2019; Bayor, 2014). Many of them were labeled "deficient" and not allowed into the country.

People experiencing poverty often have challenges in receiving help if they have mental disorders, which can make the disorders worse, negatively impacting both their quality of life and employability—a vicious circle (Slepecky et al., 2019). Culture also affects how people interpret and perceive "strange" behavior. Cultures that believe in demon possession will attribute very different causes to hearing voices or seizures, for example, than many psychologists from Western cultures (Furnham & Wong, 2007; Mercer, 2013). Occasionally, someone with a psychological disorder is celebrated as an eccentric genius instead of considered mentally ill—but that positive reputation is more likely if their family is also rich (Acar et al., 2018; Simonton, 2019).

So social factors and culture also matter—three models explain even more than two.

These pens in the Great Hall at Ellis Island held immigrants who had passed their first mental inspection.

The New York Public Library

Equine therapy can be helpful to a variety of psychological disorders, including autism spectrum disorder. From the biopsychosocial model, this kind of therapy can help a variety of outcomes, including motor skills (biological), sensory processing (psychological), and social skills (sociocultural).

iStock.com/martinedoucet

The Biopsychosocial Model

Due to the complex nature of mental illness, a complex theoretical model is needed. The **biopsychosocial model** views health and illness as part of a larger system and that both are the products of interactions among biological, psychological, and sociocultural factors (Gask, 2018; Grinker, 1966; Read et al., 2009; Sanders, 2006; Santos et al., 2021). Each individual person and each disorder exist in a world affected

Biopsychosocial model: Mental health and illnesses come from interactions between biological, psychological, and sociocultural factors.

Many mental health professionals use this book to diagnose psychological disorders.

OntheRun photo/Alamy Stock Photo

by millions of constantly changing subjective forces. This model embeds psychology in the health sciences by helping explain

- why pet therapy can be effective (Gee et al., 2021),
- how to prepare anxious patients for cardiac surgery (Saxena et al., 2022),
- why some people with social anxiety turn to cannabis (Buckner et al., 2021),
- ways to help youth recovering from burn injuries (Nelson et al., 2019),

and many more examples.

The biopsychosocial model helps unpack how all these factors work together. Equine therapy (working with horses) is a promising idea for people with autism spectrum disorder, for example (Madigand et al., 2023; McDaniel Peters & Wood, 2017; Srinivasan et al., 2018; Trzmiel et al., 2019). While some medical doctors tend to approach autism from a strictly neurological lens, equine therapy engages the biopsychosocial model by encouraging empathy between clients and the horses. It has been linked to several benefits for the riders, including increased fine motor skills (biological), sensory processing (psychological), and social skills (sociocultural; Malcolm et al., 2018).

In this chapter and the next, we will discuss many biological, psychological, and sociocultural factors tied to disorder symptoms, causes, outcomes, and treatments. It is important to understand how mental health and illness are multifaceted to gain a full understanding of these concepts.

Diagnostic and Statistical Manual of Mental Disorders

How do psychologists diagnose mental disorders?

Labels for disorders can be both helpful and harmful. They are helpful when mental health professionals can predict future behavior and decrease someone's pain, sometimes because a diagnosis means they now qualify for insurance that provides needed medications or therapy. But they are harmful when they oversimplify, promote name-calling, and encourage stereotypes. Understanding how different psychological disorders affect individual people requires

a. classifying syndromes in a systematic way,

b. documenting the prevalence of psychological disorders, and

c. developing theoretical models that help explain the disorders.

Diagnostic and Statistical Manual of Mental Disorders: A book that describes the categories and features of psychological disorders and assigns their numerical diagnostic codes.

Mental health professionals frequently look to a book called the *Diagnostic and Statistical Manual of Mental Disorders* (*DSM-5-TR*; American Psychiatric Association, 2022). It describes the categories and features of all the psychological disorders currently recognized by the American Psychiatric Association, and it provides numerical diagnostic codes for organization and insurance purposes. We're currently in the fifth major edition of the book, which everyone calls the "DSM" for short. You can see the major categories listed in the DSM in Table 15.1.

The DSM has changed from edition to edition as political culture shifted, research on various disorders advanced, and scientific compromises were debated (Blashfield

TABLE 15.1

Diagnostic Categories and Some of Their Disorders in the *DSM-5-TR*

CATEGORY OF DISORDER	SAMPLE DISORDERS WITHIN CATEGORY
1. Neurodevelopmental	Intellectual development, autism spectrum, attention-deficit/hyperactivity
2. Schizophrenias	Delusional disorder, brief psychosis, schizophrenia, schizoaffective
3. Bipolar Depression/Mania	Bipolar I (current/recent mania or depressive episodes), Bipolar II
4. Depressive	Disruptive mood, major depressive disorder, persistent depressive disorder
5. Anxiety	Separation, phobias, social anxiety, panic, agoraphobia, generalized anxiety
6. Obsessive-Compulsive	Obsessive-compulsive, body dysmorphia, hoarding, hair-pulling
7. Trauma and Stress	Reactive attachment, posttraumatic stress disorder, prolonged grief
8. Dissociative	Dissociative identity, dissociative amnesia, depersonalization
9. Somatic Symptoms	Somatic symptoms, illness anxiety, conversion
10. Feeding and Eating	Rumination, anorexia nervosa, bulimia nervosa, binge-eating
11. Elimination	Enuresis (nocturnal/diurnal), encopresis (with or without constipation)
12. Sleep–Wake	Sleep apnea, with/without opioid use, restless leg, delayed sleep
13. Sexual Dysfunctions	Arousal, premature/delayed ejaculation, female orgasmic, genito-pelvic pain
14. Gender Dysphoria	Sexual development, dysphoria in children, adolescents, adults, transition
15. Impulse and Conduct	Oppositional defiance, explosive, antisocial, pyromania, kleptomania
16. Substance Addictions	Alcohol, caffeine, cannabis, hallucinogens, opioids, sedatives, stimulants
17. Neurocognitive	Delirium, Alzheimer's, vascular, traumatic brain injury, Parkinson's
18. Personality	Paranoid, narcissistic, dependent, change due to medical condition
19. Paraphilic	Voyeuristic, exhibitionist, sexual masochism/sadism, pedophilia, fetish
20. Medication–Movement	Parkinson's, neuroleptic malignant, tardive dyskinesia, postural tremor
21. Abuse and Neglect	Of child, spouse/partner, relational/family problems, occupational

Source: Adapted from the American Psychiatric Association (2022).

et al., 2014; Child & Center, 2020; Clegg, 2012). It is always a work in progress, and there are still many controversies regarding what should—and shouldn't—be included (e.g., Aho, 2008; Frances, 2014; Zachar et al., 2017). Individual people may still be frustrated by the system as they encounter different diagnoses from different mental health professionals, insurance regulations that prevent them from access to medications, perceived political biases in the system, or other barriers to needed care.

For people who are not familiar with the world of psychological disorders, or if you've only encountered them through mass media such as television or movies, mental illness can seem scary at first. This may be because disorders and people who have them are often portrayed unrealistically and unfairly, a problem that increases stereotypes and prejudice. Consider the wise words of Marie Curie, the first woman to win a Nobel Prize. She is widely reported to have said, "Nothing in life is to be feared, it is only to be understood. Now is the time to understand more, so that we may fear less."

Now that we've discussed how to define disorders, you may be curious about their frequency—how many people have a disorder? And which disorders are most common?

Lifetime Prevalence and Comorbidity

How common is mental illness?

We can answer that question in a few different ways (WHO, 2022):

- About 970 million people in the world had at least one psychological disorder in 2019, before the COVID-19 pandemic. Frequency of disorders like anxiety went up during the pandemic, but that increase was probably a temporary spike.

- About 13% of the global population has at least one mental health disorder.

- Out of all the disorders diagnosed in the world, the most common are anxiety disorders (31%), followed by depression (29%), developmental disorders (11%), and attention-deficit/hyperactivity disorder (ADHD) (9%). All other categories combined make up the remaining 15% of disorders (see Figure 15.2).

FIGURE 15.2

Global Prevalence of Mental Disorders

Of all the psychological disorders diagnosed in the world, anxiety disorders are the most common.

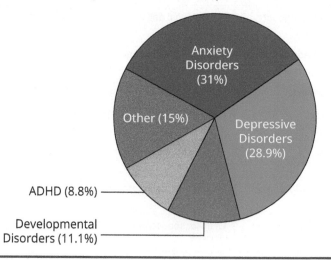

Source: Data from the WHO (2022).

The question of how many people might be dealing with a mental health issue at any given time is tricky (Lépine, 2002). At the simplest level, **lifetime prevalence rate** is the percentage of a population that has experienced any given psychological disorder at some point in life. The *DSM* and other sources can estimate the lifetime prevalence rate of each disorder. But some people can have an official diagnosis without currently experiencing any symptoms. Their disorder might not affect them all the time, or they might be taking medications that suppress symptoms, for example.

Another situation that complicates the frequency and prevalence question is called **comorbidity**, a term referring to patterns in which two or more health conditions often occur at the same time in a single person (see Figure 15.3). Some research indicates that comorbidity is so common that out of all the people diagnosed with one psychological disorder, *half* of them will qualify for at least one more (Newman et al., 1998; Solmi et al., 2023). For example, many people experience both depression *and* anxiety. It would be a mistake to ignore one set of symptoms and only count, diagnose, discuss, or treat the other set—so comorbidity makes mental illness even more interesting and complicated.

Lifetime prevalence rate: The percentage of a population that has experienced any given psychological disorder at some point in their lifetime.

Comorbidity: Patterns in which two or more health conditions often occur at the same time in a single person.

Stigma and the Language of Respect

Why do we treat mental illness differently than physical illness?

Many college courses and psychology textbooks used to call the part of psychology coursework tied to psychological disorders "abnormal" psychology. But given the prevalence rates just discussed, we know that having a disorder isn't that unusual. And what does the word *abnormal* imply? Table 15.2 shows important questions about mental health, mental illness, and psychological disorders. For example, if something is unusual, does that mean it's bad? Someone can be an Olympic athlete or a genius musician; those are both unusual (and therefore, by definition, "abnormal"), but they're praised in society. Behavior seen as extremely strange in one culture is perfectly acceptable in another culture.

FIGURE 15.3

Comorbidity

Comorbidity refers to patterns in which two or more health conditions often occur at the same time in a single person, such as both anxiety and depression.

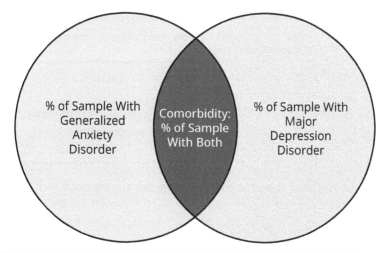

TABLE 15.2

What Is Mental Illness?

These questions can help mental health professionals decide if symptoms "count" as a mental illness or disorder—none of them are adequate by themselves.

DEFINING DESCRIPTION	CRITICAL QUESTION	CRITICAL EVALUATION: WHAT'S WRONG WITH THIS DEFINITION?
Abnormal behavior	Is the behavior normal?	• Is abnormal necessarily "bad"? An Olympic athlete is "different" and abnormal, but not bad or "crazy." • *Abnormal* is a general term that provides little useful information. • The label "abnormal" is sometimes used inappropriately, a fancier way of calling someone "crazy."
Statistical rarity	Is the disorder or behavior common?	• Mental illness is often underreported. For example, in many cultures, mental illnesses carry a social stigma that individuals try to hide, even from researchers. • Depression has been called the "common cold" of mental disorders—but if it's common, then it can't also be rare.
Personal distress	Do the symptoms cause distress?	• Sometimes symptoms can be exciting (such as the manic phase of bipolar depression). • A person with narcissistic personality disorder tends to be happily self-centered. • A person with an antisocial personality disorder is not distressed when others are harmed.
Maladaptive behavior	Does the behavior create problems in life?	• A maladaptive understanding of what it will be like to be married is not a psychological disorder, so not all behaviors qualify. • Some disorders (such as narcissism) are more maladaptive for people other than for the individual. • Some behaviors (such as aggression) provide short-term advantages but can be maladaptive in the long run (prison).
Social norm violations	Is the behavior different?	• Social norms are always evolving. The *DSM* once labeled same-sex attraction as a psychological disorder. • What is considered "different" depends on the situation. Dancing naked in a public fountain violates social norms for a 40-year-old but not for a 2-year-old. • Norm violations such as littering are selfish and rude, but not a psychological disorder. • Context also matters. Weeping on a park bench may signal depression, but it is relatively normal following the death of a loved one.
Biological malfunction	Is there a biological basis for the behavior?	• Some disorders are a mutation of a single gene (such as Mendelian disorders). • Similar genetic and environmental factors are implicated in multiple disorders, such as schizophrenia and bipolar disorder (Uher & Zwicker, 2017). • Environmental causes are more responsible for some psychological disorders, such as phobias.

Generally, psychologists have agreed that for symptoms or behavior to qualify as a disorder or as mental illness, they have to meet several of the rows in the table in terms of abnormality, deviance, and harm to an individual. Just matching one or two rows isn't enough.

When people suffer from a physical illness, we usually respond with empathy and kindness. Unfortunately, the response can be very different for people who have a psychological disorder. Many cultures have a **stigma** against mental illness, social disapproval and/or rejection based on stereotyped characteristics of a given group.

Stigma: Social disapproval and/or rejection based on stereotyped characteristics of a given group.

The stigma about mental illness includes false beliefs such as mental illness is a myth, people who have disorders simply want attention, that the symptoms are controllable, and that people with mental illnesses are dangerous or incompetent (Corrigan, 2000, 2004; Corrigan et al., 2014; Krendl & Freeman, 2019; Link & Phelan, 2001; Szasz, 1960, 1994, 2011).

As it was for Nathan, this stigma is well developed by middle school. When 400 fourteen-year-old students from five different schools described someone with mental illness in one study, they used about 250 mostly negative words such as "nuts," "disturbed," "psycho," "spastic," and "crazy" (Rose et al., 2007, p. 1; Volkow et al., 2021). This language matters. Beyond the bullying that many young people experience in school, language reflects how we think about people.

For example, tolerance and empathy go up when we describe "people with mental illness" rather than "the mentally ill" (Granello & Gibbs, 2016). This "person first" technique emphasizes that an illness is just one part of a person, not their entire being. Say "Roberto *has* depression" rather than "Roberto *is* depressed," just as you would say "Roberto has cancer" rather than "Roberto is cancerous."

Stigma regarding mental illness results in four major negative consequences that affect both the individuals involved and the larger culture (Kundert & Corrigan, 2021):

- *Avoidance:* People with mental illness are denied housing, jobs, accommodations in school, or equitable health care or avoided for friendships or intimate relationships.

- *Segregation:* Discrimination occurs in which people with mental illness are grouped together in facilities (e.g., low-income neighborhoods, institutions, government shelters) with low resources and "hidden" from others.

- *Coercion:* Stereotypes of incompetence result in unjust police intervention, mandatory medication, required medical and/or psychological treatments, or legal guardianship.

- *Discrimination:* Microaggressions (e.g., condescending or dismissive tones, laughter, questioning) and macroaggressions (e.g., physical assault) as well as traditional forms of discrimination occur, such as denial of access to stores and mistreatment.

When people grow up in a culture that teaches negative stereotypes, public stigma can become *self-stigma* when people realize they have a psychological disorder and the stereotypes turn inward (see Figure 15.4). Many people who experience symptoms of a disorder never tell anyone and never seek treatment that might help because they are embarrassed or worried how others will perceive them (Corrigan, 2004; Shee et al., 2023). Stigma is associated with delayed care and treatment, worse outcomes once treatment is started, and worse quality of life in general for people with psychological disorders (Ahad et al., 2023). Stigma has particularly negative effects on marginalized groups such as people of color and of low socioeconomic status, an example of intersectionality (Kapadia, 2023).

Do you ever try to avoid pavement cracks when you walk? If so, why?

iStock.com/wzfs1s

FIGURE 15.4

Two Kinds of Mental Illness Stigma

Stigma about mental illness can come from others or from inside the self.

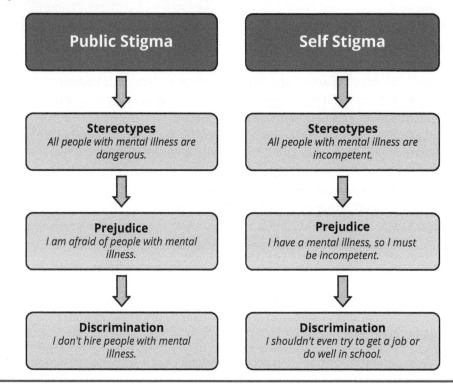

Source: Adapted from Corrigan (2004).

Fortunately, stigma about mental illness may be declining. Many celebrities have used their fame to publicly talk about and normalize having disorders. Actor Sterling Brown, NBA all-star Kevin Love, tennis champion Naomi Osaka, makeover artist Jeannie Mai, Olympic gymnast Simone Biles, and singers Billie Eilish and Taylor Swift have all publicly shared their struggles with mental illness, normalizing the idea that it's okay to not be okay (Killen, 2017).

PSYCHOLOGY AND OUR CURIOUS WORLD

Stigmatizing Mental Illness in Video Games

Some popular video games stigmatize people with mental illness. Ferrari et al. (2019) identified 100 recently released video games with content related to mental illness. Specifically, these games were published on Steam (a popular platform for computer games) and included descriptions using stigmatizing words like "insane," "psychos," "crazy," and "mental." Despite the games portraying mental illness in violent, demeaning ways, most players gave generally positive reviews to

the games—meaning they enjoyed playing the games and recommended them to others.

Here are some examples of specific games with stigmatizing content:

- *UltraGoodness* (2017): Psychosis is emphasized in a game involving "a fricking army of psychos" that "splatter blood all over the levels" (Ferrari et al., 2019, p. 5). Despite elements of comedy and satire, the game assumes a causal connection mental illness and violence.

- *Slayaway Camp* (2016): This killer puzzle game requires the player to "control Skullface, a psychotic slasher bent on slaughtering camp counsellors . . . this adorable murderer slides around isometric puzzle levels decapitating, squashing, and perforating his bloody victims." More stereotyping: Mental illness means violence.

- *The Hat Man: Shadow Ward* (2016): The plot tells "the real-life story of the events that took place at the Canton State Insane Asylum fifty years ago, as reported by those who survived . . . the asylum is being terrorized by supernatural beings." Using an asylum that really did exist with a troubled history perpetuated the idea that mental hospitals are scary, uncontrolled places.

Overall, 97% of the video games analyzed in the study portrayed mental illness negatively by associating it with violence, fear, "insanity," and hopelessness. Both mental illness and its treatment were portrayed as unpredictable, even supernatural, and with little hope of recovery. While celebrities are coming out about mental illnesses and trying to normalize them, the video game industry appears to be going backward by relying on harsh, negative, stigmatizing stereotypes.

But the news is not all bad. The developers of *Hellblade: Senua's Sacrifice* (2017) consulted with both psychiatrists and people living with psychosis, in an attempt to portray psychosis as realistically as possible, given the game's parameters. The developers of *Debris* (2017) created a game experience about coping with psychosis during a crisis and emphasized the larger social and cultural issues involved.

There's more good news. The annual conference *Games for Change* (G4C) demonstrates why video games have distinctive persuasive powers. G4C provides a network for people who are using the creative power of games for positive social purposes. ●

Practice what you learn in **Knowledge Check 15.1**

Sage Vantage➤

ANXIETY, WORRY, AND FEAR

>> **LO 15.2** **Compare and contrast different specific kinds of anxiety disorders.**

Meet Royal.

She was 10 years old when she started having anxiety problems. That childish saying, "Step on a crack and break your mother's back," made her adjust steps walking home from school. Sometimes she stepped right on a crack to get rid of the feeling but then had to make sure her next step with the other foot felt exactly the same through her shoe.

If her right arm naturally brushed against her body, then she had to balance it by brushing the left side—and to the same degree. And then to be balanced, the brushings had to happen in reverse order: right arm/left arm, followed by left arm/right arm. If one of those brushings was too hard or too soft, Royal had to start all over again. She worried that others noticed when she adjusted her steps and moved her arms in strange ways walking down the street.

Do you think Royal qualifies as having a psychological disorder?

The Origins of Anxiety

Anxiety seems to be a theme throughout history.

The terrifying creatures in the *Wizard of Oz* (witches and animals—in this case, flying monkeys) reflect images of beasts that our ancestors painted on cave walls.

? Have You Ever Wondered?
15.2 How are anxiety disorders different from typical worry or fear?

Religions might consolidate fears and death anxieties before resolving them with compulsive rituals that bring deep relief and reassurance. Philosophers describe existential anxiety—is there a higher purpose to life?—that motivated them to explore the meanings of existence (Horwitz, 2013; Weems et al., 2004).

Why is anxiety such a fundamental part of human life? Evolutionary psychology tries to explain human thought and behavior through universal instincts that helped our ancestors either survive longer or have more success in reproduction. From that perspective, anxiety isn't all that bad. In fact, it helps us detect potential threats in our environment and stay safe (Bateson et al., 2011; Nesse, 2022).

Imagine having *no* fear or anxiety at all—ever. You'd take unnecessary risks like walking into traffic, never wearing your seatbelt, eating raw chicken, going into dangerous situations . . . you get the idea. Small amounts of anxiety keep us alive. Moderate anxiety makes sense depending on the context. Anxiety only becomes a disorder when it becomes disruptive, maladaptive, and unrealistic. The *DSM-5-TR* includes several different forms of illness within the larger category of anxiety disorders.

Generalized Anxiety Disorder: Worry As a Way of Life

Royal was usually a pretty happy kid.

Generalized anxiety disorder (GAD): Nonspecific worries that are chronic, excessive, exaggerated, and extreme.

She didn't fit all the criteria for **generalized anxiety disorder (GAD)**: nonspecific worries that are chronic, excessive, exaggerated, and extreme. With GAD's "free-floating" anxiety, when one worry fades, a new one shows up as if waiting in line for its turn. Everyday situations cause anxiety, and it lasts for over 6 months. There are no specific triggers because everything can potentially make someone feel anxious. This leads to trouble with concentration and constantly feeling overwhelmed. Risk factors for GAD include being female, having low socioeconomic status, suffering from substance abuse, having a family history of anxiety, and being exposed to childhood adversity (Barlow et al., 2007; DeMartini et al., 2019; Rapee & Barlow, 2002). This variety of factors influencing someone's likelihood of having GAD is a good example of the biopsychosocial model.

As you can see in Figure 15.5, the lifetime prevalence rate of GAD was only around 3.7% (on average) for 26 different countries (Ruscio et al., 2017). During the COVID-19 pandemic, however, prevalence of GAD skyrocketed. The figure shows that in at least

---

FIGURE 15.5

The International Prevalence of Generalized Anxiety Disorder (GAD) Before and After the Start of COVID-19

The bottom line shows that in 26 countries before COVID-19, the lifetime prevalence of generalized anxiety disorder was only 3.7%. After COVID-19, prevalence rates in several countries increased significantly.

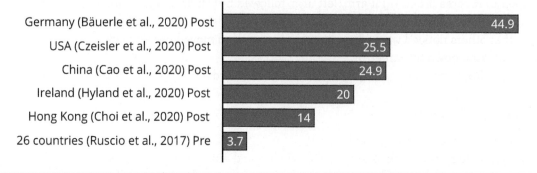

Germany (Bäuerle et al., 2020) Post	44.9
USA (Czeisler et al., 2020) Post	25.5
China (Cao et al., 2020) Post	24.9
Ireland (Hyland et al., 2020) Post	20
Hong Kong (Choi et al., 2020) Post	14
26 countries (Ruscio et al., 2017) Pre	3.7

five countries, between 14% and 45% of people experienced symptoms severe enough to qualify as having this psychological disorder (Huang & Zhao, 2020; Kessler et al., 2012; Ruscio et al., 2017; Wittchen, 2002). Current events affect anxiety, and it varies depending on local culture, perceptions, and so on.

Social Anxiety Disorder: Fear of Being Judged

Royal worried about what other people thought of her.

We've probably all had this concern from time to time. The discomfort is far more severe for people with **social anxiety disorder**, an intense fear of social situations in which people anticipate being negatively evaluated. This often translates into people becoming reluctant to leave their homes, where they don't risk that kind of social judgment (Leichsenring & Leweke, 2017). If they are in public, they might keep quiet or freeze in place if attention is drawn to them.

Social anxiety disorder: An intense fear of social situations in which the person anticipates being negatively evaluated.

Social anxiety in children leads to low school attendance, poor academic performance, unfulfilled relationships, and a greater risk for other clinical disorders (Leary & Kowalski, 1997; Pearcey et al., 2021). A study across seven countries (Brazil, China, Indonesia, Russia, Thailand, Vietnam, and the United States) used self-report surveys to measure symptoms in people between the ages of 16 and 29 (Jefferies & Ungar, 2020). They found that over one third of the participants (36%) qualified for social anxiety disorder, and approximately half of those individuals didn't realize they met the criteria for diagnosis.

Social anxiety could also be called sensitivity to social rejection. If you're curious about how you'd score on a measure of this quality, try the *What's My Score?* feature in this chapter. Remember that official diagnoses need to be made by professionals, but if you're concerned, most colleges and universities offer free counseling services.

WHAT'S MY SCORE?

Measuring Sensitivity to Social Rejection

Instructions: Consider each situation below and rate how concerned you would be that the other person involved would reject your request, using this scale:

1	2	3	4	5	6
Not at all					Very concerned

1. You ask someone in class if you can borrow their notes.
2. You ask your romantic partner to move in with you.
3. You ask your parents for help in deciding what academic programs to apply to.
4. You ask someone you don't know well out on a date.
5. Your romantic partner has plans to go out with friends tonight, but you really want to spend the evening with them, and you tell them so.
6. You ask your parents for extra money to cover living expenses.
7. After class, you tell your professor that you have been having some trouble with a section of the course and ask if they can give you some extra help.
8. You approach a close friend to talk after doing or saying something that seriously upset them.
9. You ask someone in one of your classes to coffee.

(Continued)

(Continued)

10. After graduation you can't find a job and you ask your parents if you can live at home for a while.

11. You ask a friend to go on vacation with you over Spring Break.

12. You call your romantic partner after a bitter argument to tell them you want to see them.

13. You ask a friend if you can borrow something of theirs.

14. You ask your parents to come to an occasion important to you.

15. You ask a friend to do you a big favor.

16. You ask your romantic partner if they really love you.

17. You go to a party and notice someone on the other side of the room, and then you ask them to dance.

18. You ask your romantic partner to come home to meet your parents.

Scoring Instructions: Find the sum by adding your ratings to find the total. You should get a score somewhere between 18 and 108. Higher scores mean that you're more sensitive (or anxious) about social rejection.

Note that this version of the survey has been modified slightly from the original in two ways. First, some of the items have slightly different wordings to be more gender inclusive. Second, the original scoring was more complicated because it included both ratings for how anxious each situation would make you and how likely it would be that each situation would turn out in a positive or negative way. Do you think these changes to the original version are helpful or not, and why? ●

Source: Downey, G., & Feldman, S. I. (1996). Implications of rejection sensitivity for intimate relationships. *Journal of Personality and Social Psychology, 70*(6), 1327–1343. https://doi.org/10.1037/0022-3514.70.6.1327

Phobias: Specific, Persistent, Unreasonable Fears

Have you heard of sewerkeyphobia?

Probably not—and Royal certainly didn't have it, because Tom invented it (so it's not in the *DSM* and doesn't exist anywhere except in his head). He made it up while walking through the parking lot, even though he never dropped his car keys into a sewer grate. But for some reason he started to worry about it—and little by little he began to widen his path around sewer openings, just in case. Mild fears are not unusual, but a **specific phobia** is a persistent, disabling fear that is excessive or unreasonable, associated with a specific object or situation, and that leads to personal distress and impaired functioning.

Most children have fears. Figure 15.6 shows how often these childhood fears become phobias that follow children into adulthood (Eaton et al., 2018). For example, in this study, almost 20% of children expressed some kind of fear of animals or of a particular animal, but only 5.7% of adults had any kind of animal phobia (including spiders, snakes, bugs, dogs, and so on).

Examples of specific phobias that *are* acknowledged by psychologists (unlike sewerkeyphobia) are acrophobia (fear of heights), aerophobia (flying), arachnophobia (spiders), ophidiophobia (snakes), cynophobia (dogs), trypanophobia (needles and injections), and mysophobia (dirt and germs).

Specific phobias can originate in many ways, including negative life experiences, such as unpredictable and uncontrollable events (especially if they resulted in physical harm), childhood abuse, and experiences tied to personal shame or blame (Magee, 1999; Zhou, 2023). One study (Tyson et al., 2023) found an exception to all of this, though, and identified a specific phobia that some people have despite never having a single negative experience with the feared thing: *coulrophobia*—the fear of clowns! Instead, coulrophobia is apparently driven by (1) clowns' unusual appearance,

Specific phobia: A persistent, disabling fear that is excessive or unreasonable and associated with a specific object or situation that leads to personal distress and impaired functioning.

(2) their unpredictable behavior, and (3) media portrayals of clowns as scary murderers.

Again—like anxiety—having a small, reasonable amount of fear isn't always a bad thing. A healthy amount of caution can keep us away from dangerous or risky situations. (Or murderous clowns.) So it's likely that some tendencies toward specific phobias have traveled through evolutionary instincts; our ancient phobias were once adaptive traits (see Table 15.3; Nesse, 2019). But when these fears become so maladaptive that they become a major disruption in life and prevent us from daily functioning, they become disorders (Davis et al., 2019; Eaton et al., 2018; Marks, 2002).

Do you have any persistent fears? The fear of clowns is officially called coulrophobia.

iStock.com/redhumv

FIGURE 15.6

Lifetime Percent Prevalence of Specific Childhood Fears That Become Phobias

Sometimes fears turn into phobias.

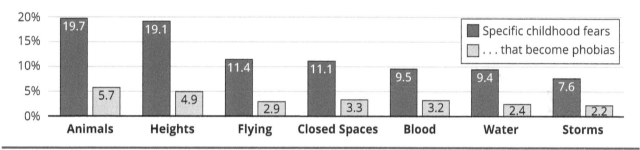

Source: Adapted from Eaton (2018).

TABLE 15.3

Phobias Related to Evolutionary Threats

The first column suggests possible threats to survival for ancient ancestors, which might have slowly turned into specific phobias for modern people—even if they are no longer useful.

DANGER TO ANCESTORS	MANIFESTS INTO MODERN SPECIFIC PHOBIAS
Poisonous or resource-devouring animals	Snakes, spiders, rodents
Natural environment	Storms, heights, darkness
Blood loss and infections	Vaccinations, blood draws, fainting, washing
Cornered by a predator	Small spaces, elevators, airplanes
Unusual and unexpected events	Clowns, loud noises, vomiting

Source: Adapted from Nesse (2019).

Obsessive-Compulsive Disorder: Intrusive Thoughts and Behaviors

We're getting closer to understanding Royal's anxiety.

In the *DSM-5-TR*, information about anxiety disorders is followed by a section describing obsessive-compulsive disorders. **Obsessions** are persistent, unwanted *thoughts* and urges accompanied by anxiety; **compulsions** are repetitive *behaviors* people feel driven to perform to relieve that anxiety, often according to rigid rules. When these obsessions and/or compulsions become so intrusive and maladaptive in your daily life that it's difficult to maintain normal functioning, the problem can qualify for a diagnosis of **obsessive-compulsive disorder (OCD)**.

The most common types of obsessions and compulsions include

- Cleaning (contamination obsessions, such as worry about germs and cleaning compulsions, such as washing hands over and over)

- Symmetry and checking (symmetry obsessions and repeating, counting, and ordering compulsions; checking, such as checking to make sure a door is locked)

- Forbidden or taboo thoughts (aggressive, sexual, or religious obsessions and related compulsions)

Symmetry compulsions were what most bothered Royal. It wasn't just right/left brushings and sidewalk crack-stepping. When it was her turn to do dishes, she insisted on arranging spoons, forks, and knives in the dishwasher in a certain way. She wasn't bothered by her often-messy bedroom, but when she did vacuum, she had to leave parallel vacuum lines. She was bothered because one of her friends casually parted her hair crooked. She carefully arranged any money so that the bills all faced the same way. There were many more rules she invented.

Prevalence data help us understand this disorder. Although the lifetime prevalence of OCD may be higher among women (Fawcett et al., 2020), estimates vary widely. For example, the lifetime prevalence around the world ranges fairly widely (Khan et al., 2021; Subramaniam et al., 2020):

- 3.3% in India

- 3.6% in Singapore

- 4.2% in Turkey

- 8.9% in Iran

The different prevalence estimates suggest two possibilities: (1) different ways of measuring OCD and (2) cultural influence. And again, a good example of how subjective perceptions of mental illness can be came during the COVID-19 pandemic. Wuhan, China, was the region of the initial devastating pattern of disease. Midway through the outbreak, the prevalence of symptoms qualifying for OCD in that part of the world surged to 18%; symptoms were things like obsessive worry about germs and

Obsessions: Persistent, unwanted thoughts and urges accompanied with anxiety.

Compulsions: Repetitive behaviors people feel driven to perform, often according to rigid rules.

Obsessive-compulsive disorder (OCD): The presence of extreme, intrusive, and maladaptive obsessions and/or compulsions.

hand-washing (Zheng et al., 2020). Did people really have OCD, or were they just trying not to get COVID? It's not clear.

Royal was mostly busy just being a normal 10-year-old. Her parents explained her sometimes odd behaviors as a teenager's growing pains. But her gradually increasing symptoms persisted toward her 11th birthday. The *DSM* notes that if symptoms persist beyond 6 months, the duration is enough that a diagnosis might be possible.

Posttraumatic Stress Disorder: Reliving a Trauma

Trauma can linger; anxiety is only one of its many consequences.

In World War I, "shell shock" was first identified in soldiers who endured 7 days of bombing in the Battle of the Somme. The same symptoms are now called posttraumatic stress disorder, or PTSD.

Pictorial Press Ltd./Alamy Stock Photo

Experiencing or witnessing a trauma can lead to **posttraumatic stress disorder (PTSD)**, a range of persistent psychiatric symptoms that often includes persistent anxiety. However, PTSD is officially categorized as a trauma-related disorder (not an anxiety disorder) because there are often other more prominent symptoms such as guilt, shame, and anger in response to trauma (Pai et al., 2017). What is now called PTSD was originally called "shell shock" and was first identified in World War I soldiers, whose military officials also referred to it as "war neurosis," "battle fatigue," or "soldier's heart," among other names.

For survivors of a trauma, routine life events can trigger a **flashback**, an intrusive reexperiencing of the initial trauma. The triggering events can be anything: a fireworks display, a rocking boat, or the color of a dress. PTSD flashbacks and associated fears can persist for decades (Levin-Aspenson et al., 2021). Consider the incredibly sad example of World War II survivors of the Holocaust; they not only endured their own traumatic experiences, but 78% of them also lost at least one close relative in the war (Kuch & Cox, 1992). Their most common PTSD symptoms were sleep disturbances, recurrent nightmares, and intense distress over reminders of their experience—including flashbacks triggered when they looked at the numerical arm tattoos they were forced to receive in concentration camps.

Simply being exposed to others' trauma can also be traumatic, making some careers difficult. The baseline prevalence of PTSD is about 4% of the U.S. population—but there are higher rates among ambulance staff (Kessler et al., 2007). Police specialists who work with victims of rape also experience **compassion fatigue** and become increasingly numb or indifferent to others' need for help (Turgoose et al., 2017). On the other hand, a little kindness seems to go a long way. Rape survivors are more likely to successfully take their offenders to court if the police demonstrate empathy (Maddox et al., 2011). If you're planning a career involving people who live with stress and trauma, it might be wise to consider how you plan to manage compassion fatigue and self care.

Posttraumatic stress disorder (PTSD): A range of persistent psychiatric symptoms, including anxiety, as a result of experiencing or witnessing a traumatic event.

Flashback: An intrusive reexperiencing of an initial trauma.

Compassion fatigue: When caregivers become increasingly numb or indifferent to others' need for help.

CAREER CORNER

Meet Greg, Psychiatric Technician at a Mental Health Hospital

What is your career?

Psychiatric technician. I work in a mental health hospital with units for children, adolescents, adults, and seniors. Each unit is staffed by one to three nurses, three to five psychiatric technicians (or one nurse and one tech during the night shift). Doctors and psychiatrists come and go as needed. The job of psychiatric technician is to monitor the unit and prevent patients from harming themselves or others. Each tech is also assigned three to four patients in a shift that we're responsible for monitoring more closely.

How was studying psychology important for success in this career?

You see firsthand the concepts you've studied. I recall one patient with psychosis and antisocial behavior, and prone to violence. He believed the government was tracking him through a chip implanted in his leg. **Patients rarely have a cut-and-dry presentation of their diagnosis.** I've worked with those in the manic phase of bipolar disorder, patients with schizophrenia, anxiety disorders, and crippling panic attacks. Patients with borderline personality disorder are some of the most difficult to work with, especially if there is more than one on the unit at the same time, as they will "compete" for attention.

How do concepts from this chapter help in this career?

Depression is the most common diagnosis I encounter. There is a lot of comorbidity: depression AND psychosis, or borderline personality disorder AND an eating disorder. **A knowledge of psychology helps you predict how these diagnoses might interact with each other and present themselves.** It gives you a richer understanding of the scholarly knowledge.

Is this the career you always planned to have after college?

Not this career exactly. **I've always been more "research" psychology-minded rather than clinical or abnormal psychology.** I found out about this job from a friend who suggested I might like it. They were right! It's been one of the most interesting and rewarding jobs I've had. It is sometimes periods of boredom, punctuated by moments of violence (e.g., you're chatting with a nurse behind the nurse's station when suddenly a chair goes flying over your head . . . true story).

If you could give current college students one sentence of advice, what would it be?

Always keep an open mind and try to view things through another person's perspective. Your experiences from childhood to now may be drastically different from your neighbor's experiences. We're all different, and that's a good thing! ●

SageVantage⌄   Practice what you learn in **Knowledge Check 15.2**

MOOD, PERSONALITY, AND SUBSTANCE ABUSE

?

Have You Ever Wondered?
15.3 How do mood disorders connect to trauma, personality, and substance abuse?

>> **LO 15.3** **Compare and contrast different specific kinds of mood, personality, and substance abuse disorders.**

Meet Alana.

She was 32 years old and had depression after her second marriage—to a famous radio news personality—started to crumble. She and her daughter stayed at a hotel, waiting for him to call her back, waiting for another apology and promises of better behavior, but in reality watching their money run out. Someone directed her to a pseudo-religious organization whose members gradually began taking over care of her daughter. After Alana and her daughter moved in with some of the church members, she kept trying to call her ex but, to her astonishment, most people in the group (a) didn't have phones and (b) seemed never to have heard of him.

They put her to work in a small basement factory in a farm town so rural it didn't have a streetlight. When she sliced her finger in the factory, the foreman put a large bandage on it, prayed over her, and sent her back to work. She didn't have the energy to figure a way out of her circumstances. She kept crying, pressing the foot pedal on the machine, wondering how she ended up there (Lasserre et al., 2022).

Mood Disorders

Mood disorders are a large, general category of emotional disorders.

They refer to any longstanding, intense emotional state that is chronically distorted, is inconsistent with circumstances, and interferes with daily function (Kessler et al., 2007; Tolliver & Anton, 2022). Many mood disorders are variations on depression and bipolar disorder (formerly called "manic depression") due to a general medical condition or substance use.

Mood disorders: A large, general category of emotional disorders that interfere with daily functioning.

Mood disorders disrupt daily functioning; sometimes it's hard to have any energy or hope.

iStock.com/valentinrussanov

Major Depressive Disorder

The *DSM-5-TR* definition of major depressive disorder fits many of Alana's symptoms. For several weeks, she lived in that strange world of depression that was more empty than sad and with cognitive changes that felt like being stuck in mud. Major depressive disorder (MDD) used to be called unipolar depression, to distinguish it from bipolar disorder (discussed below). MDD criteria specify that the depressive symptoms must last at least 2 weeks for diagnosis, but they often last much longer. In addition to simply feeling depressed, people with MDD experience changes in sleep, appetite, energy levels, or concentration and lower self-esteem. Sometimes, they have thoughts of suicide.

Major depressive disorder (MDD): A constant sense of despair and sadness, along with a loss of interest in most activities.

For Alana, moving through her symptoms was a gradual process. For months after leaving her husband, the depression was terrible. She lost herself in the repetitive factory work. Then, her nonfeeling sadness and crying episodes would transform for a while into boredom and hopelessness—and then suddenly, she would think of something that only she found funny. Her suffering wasn't over, but her depression was slowly starting to lift.

There are several types of depression based on relevant causes, and we don't have the ability to list all of them in an introductory chapter. Consider one specific type that often catches people by surprise: depression after having a baby. In postpartum depression, many women experience unanticipated but extreme biopsychosocial changes in their physiology, lifestyle, finances, and social support that produce

Postpartum depression: Feelings of sadness, exhaustion, and so on after women give birth due to rapid and extreme changes in their physiology, finances, social support, and more.

sadness, guilt, and exhaustion (Cheng et al., 2022). In severe cases of postpartum depression, mothers also fear harming their own baby. The arrival of a totally helpless human can feel overwhelming to someone who has underestimated the raw amount of work infants require (Habel et al., 2015; Schiller et al., 2015).

Several factors combine to make MDD more or less likely in any given person (Kendler, 2012; Nesse, 2019). Consider just a few of these factors:

- Gender: About half of women with MDD experience it only once, but women are more likely to reexperience depression and for longer periods of time than men (Eaton et al., 2000). Transgender and gender-nonconforming people also tend to experience elevated rates of both anxiety and depression, especially if they have internalized others' transphobia (Chodzen et al., 2019; Drescher, 2010; Monk et al., 2019).

- Biology: Depression may be influenced by genetics (Guffanti et al., 2016).

- Trauma: Survivors of traumas like child abuse or domestic violence are more likely to suffer from depression (Beydoun et al., 2012; Dillon et al., 2013; Rokach & Clayton, 2023).

- Comorbidity: Childhood depression can be a signal of comorbidity for other diagnoses later, such as bipolar disorder or schizophrenia (Burke et al., 1991; Power et al., 2015).

Postpartum depression can affect a new mother physically, emotionally, and cognitively.

iStock.com/PonyWang

The complexity of this disorder is why simple assessments (e.g., "It's just hormones") seldom work (Tabb et al., 2017) and why individuals with depression can't "just snap out of it." Depression's nuanced nature is also why well-meaning but naive messages like "just decide to be happy!" or "try smiling!" are now labeled *toxic positivity* and have been shown to actually cause *harm* to people with depression. This kind of messaging implies they chose to have symptoms of their disorder(s) and have control over them—stigma stereotypes that essentially blame people for their disorders (Bhattacharyya et al., 2021; Upadhyay et al., 2022).

Bipolar Disorder: Depression and Mania

Meet Jancie: She was a high school classmate of one of your authors. She was a drummer, increasingly unpredictable, and exuberant about life in general—sometimes too exuberant. One summer afternoon, Jancie crashed an outdoor party by swimming to a boat dock, running naked between invited guests, diving back into the water, and swimming away.

At some point, Jancie was diagnosed with **bipolar disorder**. Bipolar involves extreme mood swings, alternating between depression and mania, and shifts in a person's thinking and energy levels. A **manic episode** involves persistently elevated, expansive moods and increased goal-directed activity (e.g., hyperfocus on a given task). When people have bipolar disorder, they experience extreme emotions and energy levels like an unregulated thermostat—sometimes way too hot and then way too cold (Nesse, 2019). That was Jancie.

Jancie could be great fun when heading into a manic episode but would disappear during a depression. Medications helped stabilize her mood swings. She eventually grew up, settled down in a small town where her band's bus finally broke down, and

Bipolar disorder: Extreme mood swings, alternating between depression and mania, and shifts in someone's thinking and energy levels.

Manic episode: Abnormal and persistent elevated, expansive mood with increased goal-directed activity.

kept drumming in bars while living "off the grid" (no phone or mailing address). But Jancie's not hiding; you can find her if you know the name of the town and ask any shopkeeper if they know "Jancie, the drummer."

Jancie is a free spirit, a nonconformist, and a creative soul—but don't be too quick to endorse the romantic but stigmatizing stereotype that all the best artists must have psychological disorders or that all people with disorders are brilliant artists. Several review articles have investigated this hypothesis and found little supportive evidence (e.g., Cruz et al., 2022; Mishra et al., 2022). If anything, the pattern might be that severe cases of bipolar disorder usually have few "silver linings" in terms of creativity, compared to people who don't have bipolar disorder. On the other hand, it's possible that a milder condition called **cyclothymic disorder**, which is made up of more frequent but less intense mood swings, may be associated with some creativity advantages (Greenwood, 2020). Maybe Jancie's symptoms fit cyclothymic disorder better than bipolar.

Cyclothymic disorder: A milder version of bipolar disorder with more frequent but less intense mood swings.

While periods of mania can sometimes feel exciting, early childhood signals of bipolar disorder include sleep problems, depression, and anxiety (da Silva Costa et al., 2015; Goldstein et al., 2017). Like Jancie, for many people, symptoms start in late adolescence (Altemus et al., 2014; Rantala et al., 2021; Rubinow & Schmidt, 2019; Sasdelli et al., 2013). Bipolar disorder may be partially genetic (Fabbri, 2020; Gordovez & McMahon, 2020), but unlike MDD, prevalence rates do not vary with gender (Rubinow & Schmidt, 2019). Bipolar disorder does add significant economic and emotional strain on caregivers (Geddes & Miklowitz, 2013; Gordovez & McMahon, 2020; Kleine-Budde et al., 2014). Sadly, suicide occurs 15 to 20 times more frequently in people who have bipolar disorder compared to the general population (Yapici Eser et al., 2018).

Even though this paragraph occurs in the section about mood disorders, suicide is not always associated with any particular psychological disorder or mental health issue. Like mental health in general, there is a lot of stigma associated with people who die by suicide and even the word *suicide* itself (Nicholas et al., 2023; Sudak et al., 2008). People who have attempted suicide are often victims of social distancing and shaming, which can lead to embarrassment, reduced self-esteem, and increased likelihood of additional suicide attempts (Carpiniello & Pinna, 2017). Suicide is also often misunderstood, as it can occur in the absence of any disorder at all in cases such as dying to avoid severe pain from medical conditions. Like all social stigmas, education and empathy for others are important.

Personality Disorders

Meet Nikki.

Nikki was a college sophomore on academic probation, but she told her parents it was because her teachers didn't treat her fairly. One of your textbook authors remembers her quite well, because Nikki enjoyed coming to class a few minutes late, walking through the front doors of the large lecture hall, taking off her large fur coat, and sitting down in the front row wearing her string bikini in the middle of winter. She was known on campus as a young woman who was always ready to party, but she left school after punching another student in the kidney. Nikki might have had a personality disorder.

The general definition of personality (without a disorder) focuses on consistency across time and situations. You can compare that to a **personality disorder**, a chronic way of thinking, feeling, and behaving that violates social norms and causes distress or problems in functioning.

Personality disorder: A chronic way of thinking, feeling, and behaving that violates social norms and causes distress or problems in functioning.

In other words, most of the time with this category of mental illness, your personality gets in the way of fitting in with others. Your behaviors interfere with your relationships, career, or other aspects of life in a serious and maladaptive way. Often people with personality disorders don't acknowledge that *they* have a problem, though; they can blame other people or circumstances for any issues they encounter (Wilson et al., 2017).

Personality disorders are found in about 11% of the general population, but that percentage trends higher in wealthier countries (Volkert et al., 2018; Winsper et al., 2020). The idea of personality disorders isn't a new phenomenon or a by-product of "Western" psychiatry (Crocq, 2013; Dresser, 2023). That said, this category is subjective and very much based on cultural values and norms, making personality disorders one of the most controversial categories of mental illness (Chen et al., 2009; Fan et al., 2017; Wang & Wang, 2019).

The 10 different types of personality disorder listed in the *DSM* are shown in Table 15.4. They are organized into three "clusters" based on their similarities:

- **Cluster A:** The "odd and eccentric" personalities that may be socially awkward or withdrawn (American Psychiatric Association, 2022; Dammann, 2017; Triebwasser et al., 2012). Nathan and most of his fifth-grade classmates had been together since kindergarten in a small elementary school, yet none of us knew him very well. He may never have been to birthday parties or played in pickup games or organized sports. If he had a personality disorder, then it probably would be something like the Cluster A schizoid personality disorder with restricted emotional expression, preference for solitary activities, indifference to praise or criticism, disinterest in intimate relationships, and emotional coldness.

- **Cluster B:** The "dramatic and erratic," highly emotional personalities (Dinwiddie, 2015). Nikki may have had histrionic personality disorder; a common symptom is wearing sexually provocative clothes (Kellett, 2007). Her lack of empathy, impulsiveness, and aggression also may have qualified her for borderline and/or antisocial personality disorder (Barker et al., 2015; Liu, 2023). Nikki also appeared highly confident, manipulative, and charming—hallmarks of narcissistic personality disorder (Akhtar, 1989).

- **Cluster C:** The "anxious and fearful" personalities that are easily distracted (American Psychiatric Association, 2022; Diedrich & Voderholzer, 2015; Liggett et al., 2017). Royal probably qualified for OCD, but not obsessive-compulsive *personality* disorder (OCPD), the most common in Cluster C. The difference hinges on the lack of self-awareness for people who have OCPD. Often, adults with OCPD explain away their symptoms as simply being committed to work or as perfectionism (Atroszko et al., 2020; Burkauskas & Fineberg, 2020; Wheaton & Ward, 2020).

It is important to note that stigma toward people with mental illness may be particularly pervasive and harmful when it comes to personality disorders (Sheehan et al., 2016; Sheppard et al., 2023). This category is often perceived by others as the most controllable (e.g., "just stop being like that!") yet somehow simultaneously the least treatable (e.g., "they'll never change—just send them to prison"), an ironic paradox that results in discrimination and, sadly, suicide and self-harm in some people suffering from these disorders.

TABLE 15.4

Personality Disorders in the *DSM-5-TR*

NAME OF PERSONALITY DISORDER	DESCRIPTION: A PATTERN OF . . .
CLUSTER A: "ODD AND ECCENTRIC"	
Paranoid	Distrust and suspiciousness such that others' motives are interpreted as malevolent.
Schizoid	Detachment from social relationships and a restricted range of emotional expression.
Schizotypal	Acute discomfort in close relationships, cognitive or perceptual distortions, and eccentricities of behavior.
CLUSTER B: "DRAMATIC AND ERRATIC"	
Antisocial	Disregard for, and violation of, the rights of others. Criminal behaviors.
Borderline	Instability in interpersonal relationships, self-image, and emotions, plus marked impulsivity.
Histrionic	Excessive emotionality and attention seeking.
Narcissistic	Grandiosity, need for admiration, and lack of empathy.
CLUSTER C: "ANXIOUS AND FEARFUL"	
Avoidant	Social inhibition, feelings of inadequacy, and hypersensitivity to negative evaluation.
Dependent	Submissive and clinging behavior related to an excessive need to be taken care of.
Obsessive-compulsive	Preoccupation with orderliness, perfectionism, and control.

Source: American Psychiatric Association. (2022). *Diagnostic and statistical manual of mental disorders* (5th ed., text rev.). https://doi.org/10.1176/appi.books.9780890425787

Substance Abuse Addictions: Betrayed by Your Brain

Alana had somehow dodged severe alcohol and drug addiction.

But several of her friends had not. The biopsychosocial model helps explain why. They had shared and abused many of the same addictive substances together, but there are many factors that can influence how individual people react to drugs. The *DSM-5-TR* categorizes 10 classes of substances that might lead to addiction disorders:

1. Alcohol
2. Caffeine
3. Cannabis
4. Hallucinogens
5. Hypnotics and anxiolytics
6. Inhalants
7. Opioids

8. Sedatives

9. Stimulants

10. Tobacco

Many people who become addicted to drugs and/or alcohol also struggle with other psychological disorders—another example of comorbidity. Figure 15.7 shows the results of a study of 320 people ranging in age from 15 to 65 years with alcohol and opiate dependency (Casadio et al., 2014). Some of the participants had several disorders, so they could be represented in multiple bars shown in the figure.

As you can see, the most common comorbid disorder with substance abuse (at least in this study) was personality disorders, with over 62% of the sample qualifying for at least one personality disorder (the most common were borderline and antisocial). Other commonly comorbid disorders were mood disorders, followed by psychotic disorders (like schizophrenia) and anxiety. Comorbidity just means someone had multiple disorders; we don't know the timing of the symptoms, if one led to the other, or how they relate to each other. It's likely a complicated story for each individual person.

Memory: The Battleground of Addiction

Memories of pleasant drug experiences are the battleground on which many addiction struggles are won or lost (Das et al., 2019; Goldfarb & Sinha, 2018). There are two consequences when an addictive substance activates the brain's reward system (Cooper et al., 2017; McKendrick & Graziane, 2020):

1. Each drug activates its unique pharmacological mechanisms to play the same biological trick on the user: creating a psychological itch that only another dose will scratch.

FIGURE 15.7

Comorbidity of Substance Abuse and Other Disorders

In this study, patients getting treatment for substance abuse disorders often qualified for at least one additional disorder, most commonly a personality disorder.

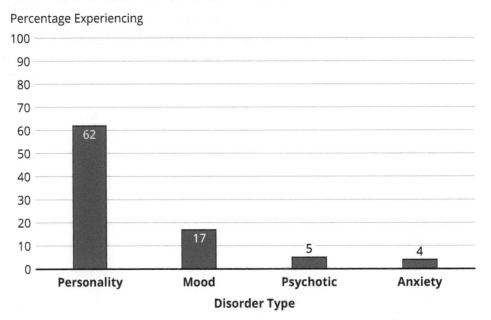

Source: Adapted from Casadio et al. (2014).

2. A pleasant first drug experience creates a vivid memory that people in rehab refer to as "chasing the first high" (Bornstein & Pickard, 2020; Childress et al., 1988).

The association between pleasure and the drug is fundamentally classical conditioning. The generalizing result of that conditioning is that even the drug paraphernalia (equipment, needles, lighters, etc.) gets associated with the pleasure. To someone with an addiction, just being around drug paraphernalia can stimulate cravings that deliver a brief expectancy high. People with an addiction can get "stoned on a memory" the same way your mouth may water at the sight or smell of a favorite food (Shi et al., 2023; Siegel et al., 1987). The result is one biopsychosocial part of that **addiction**: compulsive drug seeking and use, despite short- and long-term harmful effects on the user.

Research shows that just looking at drug paraphernalia can stimulate cravings once people suffer from addiction, partly due to classical conditioning.

iStock.com/monticello

Addiction: Compulsive drug seeking and use, despite short- and long-term harmful effects on the user.

Fortunately, psychologists know their way around the landscape of memory and are developing memory-retrieval "weapons" to fight drug-induced changes in brain circuits—even when they persist in memory after detoxification (Bornstein & Pickard, 2020; Phelps & Hofmann, 2019). Still, biopsychosocial treatments for drug addiction are a much-needed area for additional research and resources.

Menthols: Layers of Injustice

Parts of the prevalence data about smoking in the United States have been dubbed the "African American smoking paradox." Here's why: African Americans on average make *better* decisions than other groups about smoking but have *worse* health outcomes (Alexander et al., 2016). For example, African Americans on average have

- lower prevalence rates of smoking,
- wait to start smoking at an older age, and
- as adults smoke no more than any other smokers, in terms of amount.

These trends all seem to point toward better health. Nevertheless, Black individuals who smoke cigarettes in the United States

- are less likely to successfully quit,
- experience disproportionate disease burden, and
- are more likely to die from tobacco-related conditions.

Why?

The explanation for the paradox has an aroma: menthol. Figure 15.8 summarizes what the Food and Drug Administration (FDA, 2023) has concluded—yet another good example of the biopsychosocial model. First, menthol cigarettes enhance the effects of nicotine in the brain, making them more addictive (FDA, 2023; Henderson et al., 2017; Zhang et al., 2018). Second, cigarette companies skillfully market and shape perceptions of menthol cigarettes specifically in African American neighborhoods

FIGURE 15.8

The "African American Smoking Paradox"

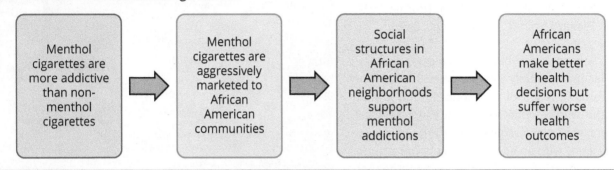

(Anderson, 2011). For example, free starter doses of the "minty poison" were delivered to Black neighborhoods in vans that resembled ice cream trucks (Romeo-Stuppy, 2021). Finally, cigarette companies target urban neighborhoods with a high density of tobacco outlets and lower rates of screening for health problems (Powers et al., 2023).

The result is a disproportionate number of deaths from smoking in African American communities. From 1980 to 2018, 1.5 million African Americans began smoking menthols that led to an estimated 157,000 premature deaths (Mendez & Le, 2022). Black middle school and high school students continue to start smoking menthols at an 8% higher rate than other cigarettes, a difference that gets worse over time (Centers for Disease Control and Prevention, 2023).

Sage Vantage⟩   Practice what you learn in **Knowledge Check 15.3**

SCHIZOPHRENIA AND DISSOCIATIVE DISORDERS

?

Have You Ever Wondered?
15.4 What exactly are schizophrenia and multiple personality disorder, and do movies show them accurately?

≫ **LO 15.4** **Analyze mass media portrayals of schizophrenia and dissociative disorders.**

Meet characters in the movies.

For the last two major categories of disorders covered in this chapter—schizophrenia and dissociative disorders—you'll "meet" people from popular Hollywood movies. Both movies were based on real people and resulted in Academy Awards, but the true stories were quite different from how they were shown on the big screen.

Mental Illness and Media Stereotypes

Movies usually get it wrong.

Filmmakers take a lot of liberties when it comes to mental illness—especially certain categories of disorder, including schizophrenia and dissociative disorders (such as what used to be called multiple personality disorder; Owen, 2012). Often, stigmas are passed from one generation to the next in a given culture through mass media.

Earlier, this chapter discussed how some video games stigmatize mental illness; movies often do the same thing. One study found that 6 out of 10 popular violent films for adolescents included a main character labeled with a mental illness (Sargent et al., 2002). Often these characters exhibit extreme violence, lower intelligence, poor social skills, and/or other negative stereotypes (Corrigan, 1998). Watching just portions of these films can significantly increase viewers' stigma ratings, even when the characters supposedly diagnosed with mental illnesses are likeable and comedic (Perciful & Meyer, 2017).

Mental illnesses portrayed in the movies usually reinforce two misconceptions: (1) All mentally ill people are violent and unpredictable, and (2) every mentally ill person is motivated by some deep, dark secret (Byrne, 2001). Filmmakers more interested in drama than accuracy tend to blur symptoms and write plots that rely on long-discarded theories and tropes.

As you consider the final two categories of disorder covered in this chapter, consider the movies you've seen that include characters who have a mental illness. Did the movies help or hurt your understanding and empathy?

SPOTLIGHT ON RESEARCH METHODS

Full Moons, Mental Illness, and the Legend of Lunacy

iStock.com/pasaven

A full moon seems like a strange explanation for temporary mental illness.

It's an old idea. *Luna* is Latin for "moon" and gives us the word *lunatic.* Greek myths and Hippocrates both suggested the moon affected mental health (White, 1914). Shakespeare added to the drama in *Othello* by writing that a moon too close to earth makes men [we'll say people] "mad."

It's sort of fun to believe in the moon myth, and it works well as a movie metaphor. The first werewolf film, *The Werewolf* (1914), was destroyed in a fire, so we can't see how the link between the moon and mental illness started in Hollywood. But in many subsequent films, werewolves were cast as some combination of our inner beast and split personalities that only appear during full moons (Mann, 2020; Sheppard, 2021). But a metaphor is, well, only a metaphor. So is there anything to the idea that people act strangely during a full moon?

One test of the moon myth in *The International Journal of Emergency Services* compared the number of incidents at five sites on full moon versus non–full moon nights (Greatbatch et al., 2019): no difference. There was a hint of correlational evidence related to traffic accidents during full moons (Templer et al., 1982). But then other researchers (Rotton & Kelly, 1985) asked, "How do you know that?" The correlation study only counted full moons on weekends, meaning there was also more traffic—and therefore more accidents (in other words, a confounding variable).

(Continued)

(Continued)

There appear to be no lunar effects in studies of suicides, psychiatric hospital admissions, dog bites, emergency room visits, ambulance runs, heart attacks, or emergency phone calls (see Lilienfeld et al., 2010). To sum it up, psychological research of archival data has found no reliable pattern of evidence that strange behavior increases when the moon is full.

So . . . what will you do the next time someone says, "Must be a full moon tonight!" to explain anything unusual? This is your moment to rise up as a critical thinker and share (politely, we suggest) your psychology knowledge. ●

Schizophrenia

Meet John Nash.

Nash was a real person, a Nobel Prize–winning mathematician with schizophrenia. His life became the inspiration for the movie *A Beautiful Mind* (2001). The film is riveting and won four Academy Awards—it's also quite inaccurate (Nasar, 1998; Suellentrop, 2001).

Most of the characters in the film are made up. The movie highlights Nash's enduring love and marriage with his wife. In reality, Nash had several affairs, some with other men. He was arrested for indecent exposure in a bathroom. He had a son with one of his mistresses that he never supported; that son had to live in foster care. Nash is shown as having visual hallucinations, which he never really had. The film portrays him as taking medication for his symptoms, which he refused to do for most of his life. The movie's climax shows Nash giving his Nobel acceptance speech, thanking his wife for her love and loyalty. In reality, he never gave a speech at all. In general, Hollywood movies are not reliable places to get accurate information.

What does schizophrenia really look like?

Psychosis occurs when someone loses touch with reality and cannot tell what's real from what's not. The mental illness most associated with psychosis is schizophrenia, a disorder that can lead to hallucinations, delusions, disorganized speech and thinking, and difficulty with routine self-care. *Hallucinations* are psychotic sensations or perceptions, most commonly auditory—such as hearing voices in your head. In contrast, *delusions* refer to psychotic beliefs. Common examples are conspiracy theories where someone believes they're being followed or watched, that they have special abilities (e.g., that they can fly), or that something has changed (when it hasn't).

You can see in Table 15.5 that psychologists sort the symptoms of schizophrenia into "positive" and "negative" (Marder & Galderisi, 2017). "Positive" here doesn't mean good or pleasant. Instead, just like with classical conditioning, positive means *addition*. So positive symptoms are additions to normal experience: exaggerated, distorted, and bizarre ideas, beliefs, perceptions, and behaviors (such as hallucinations and delusions). Negative symptoms are subtractions from normal experience: a lessening or absence of functional ideas, conversational skills, emotional expression, and body movements.

The most dangerous symptoms appear to be the rare combination of persecutory delusions and commanding hallucinations that create distress by justifying and then demanding compliance to commit harmful acts (Lamsma & Harte, 2015). These symptoms can be pretty scary, especially considering symptoms typically begin in late adolescence or early adulthood. While prevalence is low—less than 1% of the general population—it is associated with comorbid conditions, adverse medication effects, family stress, and higher rates of suicide (Charlson et al., 2018; McGrath et al., 2008).

Like many illnesses, early recognition and intervention can help people by reducing relapses, slowing disease progression, and encouraging therapy (Birchwood

Psychosis: Occurs when someone loses touch with reality; the individual typically experiences hallucinations and delusions.

Schizophrenia: A disorder that can lead to hallucinations, delusions, disorganized speech and thinking, and difficulty with routine self-care.

Positive symptoms: In schizophrenia, this refers to additions to "normal" experience (e.g., hallucinations, delusions).

Negative symptoms: In schizophrenia, this refers to subtractions from "normal" experience (e.g., lessening of conversational skills or body movements).

TABLE 15.5

Common Symptoms of Schizophrenia

POSITIVE SYMPTOMS	
Hallucinations: Experiencing sensory stimulations that others do not experience.	
TYPE	**EXAMPLE**
Auditory	Urgent demands from voices in the mind.
Visual	See things or people that are not really there.
Smell and taste	Believe can small or taste poison.
Tactile (touch)	Believe can feel bugs crawling on body.
Delusions: Bizarre, inaccurate beliefs that are illogical or easy to disprove.	
TYPE	**EXAMPLE**
Persecution	Believe someone is "after you" or "watching you."
Referential	Believe public events contain special messages for you alone.
Somatic	Believe you have a bizarre, rare disease.
Erotomatic	Believe something false about a romantic relationship.
Religious	Believe you are a deity or are possessed by a demon.
Grandiose	Believe your own importance or fame.
Disorganized thoughts and speech: Difficulty organizing and expressing thoughts, sometimes referred to as "word salad."	
Trouble concentrating: Not being able to follow an idea, such as a TV plot or conversation.	
Movement disorders: Displaying physical jumpiness, repetitive movements, or stillness.	
NEGATIVE SYMPTOMS	
Anhedonia/lack of pleasure: Loss of enjoyment in customary activities.	
Alogia/trouble with speech: Minimal talking or conveying ideas and feelings.	
Flat affect: Lack of expressing emotions (blank facial expression).	
Asociality/social withdrawal: Apathetic and limited interactions with others.	
Decline of self-care: Absence or decline of personal hygiene.	
Avolition/no follow-through: Difficulty getting started or completing basic tasks.	

Source: Adapted from Marder and Galderisi (2017).

et al., 2018; De Beradis et al., 2021; Hoffman et al., 2017; Murru & Carpiniello, 2018). But stigma stops or delays that early intervention. Despite what we see in movies, people with schizophrenia are usually no more dangerous to others than anyone else—especially if they have and are following an effective medication plan (Buchanan et al., 2019; Mørup et al., 2020).

In fact, by one estimate, people with schizophrenia are about 14 times more likely to be the *victims* rather than the perpetrators of violence (Brekke et al., 2001). And when public stigma turns into self-stigma, the danger is high; the estimated lifetime prevalence of suicide attempts (not completions) for people diagnosed with schizophrenia is about 27% (Lu et al., 2020).

Stereotypes in films and news media have contributed to the stereotype that people with schizophrenia are aggressive criminals (Gwarjanski & Parrott, 2018). One study that admittedly found evidence of increased violence in this population concluded that the causes of violence were stressors that might provoke most people and could arguably be linked to cultural stigmas about mental illness: unemployment, failure in school, separation from caregivers, and especially substance use (Kirchebner et al., 2022). So, these results might be because of discrimination against people with schizophrenia due to stigma; it's unclear because correlation does not imply causation.

Dissociative Disorders

Meet Christine Sizemore.

And meet Eve White—and Eve Black—and Jane. They're all the same person, a real person who was diagnosed with an illness called dissociative identity disorder (formerly known as multiple personality disorder in previous editions of the *DSM*). Sizemore's life was made into the film *The Three Faces of Eve* (1957), which—as you probably guessed—was not accurate (Bernstein, 2016).

Despite the film claiming to be 100% true, it just isn't. They never used her actual name. In reality, Sizemore witnessed three traumas within a few months of each other as a small child that she believes caused her disorder to start. In the film, they say the cause is that she had to kiss a dead body as a child. The film erases her son and shows only a daughter. It also portrays her being "cured" after seeing one therapist, instead of the eight she really saw. And perhaps most interestingly, the film shows Sizemore having a total of two alternate "personalities," as indicated by the name of the movie. In reality, she claimed 22.

Dissociative identity disorder might be the most popular mental illness on the big screen (Butler & Palesh, 2004). A partial list from each decade includes *Spellbound* (1945), *Three Faces of Eve* (1957), *The Manchurian Candidate* (1962), *The Deer Hunter* (1978), *Ordinary People* (1980), *Fight Club* (1999), *The Bourne Identity* (2002), *The Hulk* (2003), *Split* (2016), and *Memory* (2022). They are among the most outlandish and stigmatizing films that exist, partially adding to the controversy surrounding this category of disorders.

Dissociative disorders in general are a loss of connection between thoughts, perceptions, emotions, and memories that disrupt one's sense of self (Lynn et al., 2016; Swart et al., 2020). The *DSM-5-TR* organizes dissociative disorders into three major types:

Dissociative disorders: A loss of connection between thoughts, perceptions, emotions, and memories that disrupt one's sense of self.

1. *Depersonalization/derealization disorder:* Feeling detached from your self, your circumstances, and/or your feelings—as if you are observing yourself from the outside. There may be biological factors involved; people with this disorder have decreased automatic physiological responses when shown unpleasant images (Lynn et al., 2019; Phillips et al., 2001; Sierra et al., 2002).

2. *Dissociative amnesia:* The inability to recall important autobiographical information, usually after experiencing trauma (discussed earlier in the chapter on memory; Dalenberg et al., 2012; Mangiulli et al., 2022; Van Der Hart & Nijenhuis, 2001). This disorder is most likely psychologically driven, rather than biologically (unlike retrograde or anterograde amnesia).

3. **Dissociative identity disorder:** Experiencing two or more shifting but distinct personality states. The person's sense of self is markedly disrupted. Their behaviors, memories, perceptions, cognitions, sensory-motor functions, and so on change noticeably as they shift between personality states. The new identities are called "alters" and can appear when the original, legal person (called the "host") experiences distress or problems in their personal, social, or occupational environment.

Dissociative identity disorder: Experiencing two or more shifting but distinct personality states, accompanied by a disruption in the sense of self.

When people with dissociative identity disorder are tested, their alters differ in age, gender, preferences for music and food, handwriting, personality tests, and even IQ scores. Christine Sizemore famously had an alter that was allergic to nylon, when none of her other alters were. Often, the host will have trouble remembering what occurred when they were in an alter state (Nissen et al., 1988). This part of the disorder leads to an interesting question tied to several of the movies featuring this illness: If someone commits a crime as an alter personality, should the host be legally responsible? Most courts say yes (Kabene et al., 2022).

This category of mental illness is controversial, even among professional psychologists and psychiatrists—with some professionals who doubt it should even be included in the *DSM* at all (Blihar et al., 2020; Cormier & Thelen, 1998; Showalter, 1997; Utomo et al., 2023). One argument against it is a very low prevalence; the estimated rate for the dissociative category is about 1.5% for the entire population (although in private therapy centers, rates apparently go up to 10%-46%; Lynn et al., 2016; Lyssenco et al., 2018). Whether the category is "real" is a complex debate (Loewenstein, 2022; Reinders & Veltman, 2021; Saxena et al., 2023).

On one side of the argument, many mental health professionals believe that distinct "personality" states come from either (1) fantasy-prone individuals who have legitimately experienced trauma but are now conforming to a role they might have seen in the mass media that serves their needs or (2) counselors or therapists who rely on hypnosis, guided imagery, and leading questions and get overly excited about having a patient with this disorder (Cormier & Thelen, 1998; Dalenberg et al., 2012; Dimitrova et al., 2020; Lilienfeld et al., 1999; Showalter, 1997; Spanos et al., 1985).

On the other side, if there really are people suffering from these symptoms, we need the legitimization the *DSM* holds to reduce the stigma of their diagnosis, qualify them for insurance coverage, and get them to treatment. This is some evidence that people with this disorder show brain scan patterns that are different from other disorders, evidence of its validity (Blihar et al., 2021).

Some mental health practitioners have proposed that the experience of mental dissociation exists along a continuum that we all sometimes experience, like the one shown in Figure 15.9 (Loewenstein, 2022; Waller et al., 1996). We've probably all experienced mild dissociation when we let our mind wander, got lost in a great story, daydreamed, or drove for miles without realizing what happened between where we started and where we ended. So just like depression, anxiety, personality disorders, or substance abuse disorders, maybe dissociative disorders are on a continuum of experience, something most of us go through—at least, a little.

FIGURE 15.9

The Continuum of Dissociative Experiences

Normal Dissociative Experiences
(e.g., Spacing Out While Driving) → Pathological Dissociative Experiences
(Dissociative Identity Disorder)

Unlike most movies, there are no automatic happy endings no matter where we each live on the mental health continuum. However, we can embrace a compassionate attitude and a scientific approach to mental illnesses. The most important goal might be respect and empathy for each other's mental health. ●

Practice what you learn in **Knowledge Check 15.4**   Sage Vantage

CHAPTER REVIEW

Learning Objectives Summary

15.1 How do psychologists define mental illness and psychological disorders, and what is mental illness stigma?

>> LO 15.1 Describe various models of mental illness, then explain mental illness stigma.

Mental health and mental illness are on a continuum, with illness made up of several different psychological disorders. Psychologists categorize and define disorders using a system outlined in a book called the *Diagnostic and Statistical Manual of Mental Disorders*. A popular theoretical model of mental illness is the biopsychosocial model, which suggests that illnesses are influenced by biological, psychological, and social factors. Stigma is social disapproval based on stereotyped characteristics of a given group.

15.2 How are anxiety disorders different from typical worry or fear?

>> LO 15.2 Compare and contrast different specific kinds of anxiety disorders.

While small to moderate anxiety can help people avoid danger, it becomes a disorder when anxiety becomes disruptive, unrealistic, and maladaptive to everyday life. Some forms of anxiety disorder are generalized anxiety disorder, social anxiety disorder, phobias, and obsessive-compulsive disorder. Posttraumatic stress disorder also involves anxiety.

15.3 How do mood disorders connect to trauma, personality, and substance abuse?

>> LO 15.3 Compare and contrast different specific kinds of mood, personality, and substance abuse disorders.

Two common forms of mood disorder are major depressive disorder and bipolar disorder (swings between depression and mania). Personality disorders are chronic ways of thinking, feeling, and behaving that violate social norms and cause distress or problems in functioning; there are 10 specific types. Mood disorders, personality disorders, and substance abuse disorders are sometimes *comorbid*, a term referring to multiple disorders that often occur together in the same individual person.

15.4 What exactly are schizophrenia and multiple personality disorder, and do movies show them accurately?

>> LO 15.4 Analyze mass media portrayals of schizophrenia and dissociative disorders.

Two types of mental illness often portrayed inaccurately in movies are schizophrenia and dissociative disorders. Schizophrenia is a type of psychosis; symptoms include hallucinations, delusions, disorganized speech and thinking, and difficulty with routine self-care. One type of dissociative disorder is dissociative identity disorder, formerly known as multiple personality disorder.

CRITICAL THINKING QUESTIONS

1. Make a list of 10 resources available to people on your campus regarding mental health. At least three should be local (specific to your college, university, or town). For each, note if there is a cost or whether the resource is free, what services are offered, what the hours are when the resource is available, and who provides the resource (e.g., the company or organization).

2. Do you have any fears or anxieties that are small to moderate versions of specific phobias? If so, think back to where your fear started. Do you have a particular memory of an event that initially triggered the fear, or do you think it's a biological or evolutionary instinct gone wrong (or both)? If you could go through counseling or treatment for your fear, would you? If not, why not—and if so, what kinds of exercises do you think you'd find most useful?

3. Choose a celebrity who has publicly discussed having a psychological disorder. Find at least two online articles or interviews in which they talk about their symptoms, treatments, interactions with others, or any other aspect of their experience. What did you learn from these sources that you didn't already know from this chapter? Do you think this celebrity's portrayal of their experience has helped or hurt mental illness stigma in general and other people who are diagnosed with the same disorder—why and in what ways?

4. Watch a film with a main character who is portrayed as having a psychological disorder. Discuss how the disorder is shown in terms of whether symptoms are shown in an accurate manner, whether the film helps or hurts stigma toward mental illness, and what kind of impact you think this film might have on people who watch it in terms of how they think about this disorder. Note whether there are any psychologists in the film and how they are portrayed as well.

5. The last part of this chapter discussed the controversy regarding whether dissociative identity disorder is "real." Spend some time online looking for evidence for and against keeping this disorder in the *DSM* when it goes to the next edition. Provide links for at least two arguments in favor of keeping the disorder in the book and at least two links for arguments against; explain and summarize the evidence each link delivers. Then, analyze the debate for yourself. Write a brief paragraph or discuss with your classmates what your own opinion is on this controversy.

KEY TERMS

Addiction, 487
Biomedical model, 463
Biopsychosocial model, 465
Bipolar disorder, 482
Comorbidity, 469
Compassion fatigue, 479
Compulsions, 478
Cyclothymic disorder, 483
Diagnostic and Statistical Manual of Mental Disorders, 466
Dissociative disorders, 492
Dissociative identity disorder, 492
Flashback, 479
Generalized anxiety disorder (GAD), 474
Lifetime prevalence rate, 469
Major depressive disorder (MDD), 481
Manic episode, 482
Mental health, 463

Mental illness, 463
Mood disorders, 481
Negative symptoms, 490
Obsessions, 478
Obsessive-compulsive disorder (OCD), 478
Personality disorder, 483
Positive symptoms, 490
Postpartum depression, 481
Posttraumatic stress disorder (PTSD), 479
Psychological disorders, 463
Psychological model, 464
Psychosis, 490
Schizophrenia, 490
Social anxiety disorder, 475
Sociocultural model, 464
Specific phobia, 476
Stigma, 470

Courtesy of Lisa Rinzler

16

Mental Health: Therapy and Treatment

The suitcases are talking.

About 54,000 people passed through Willard State Mental Hospital during its 126 years, although historians recovered only 427 suitcases. President Lincoln approved the Willard State Mental Hospital only a few days before he was shot.

Mrs. Ethel Smalls was in her 40s during the Great Depression of the 1930s. She already had experienced a miscarriage, surgery for an ovarian tumor, the death of two infants, divorce from an abusive and alcoholic husband, and financial hardship. Yet she persevered. To survive, she traded her sewing skills for room and board and refused to leave after a financial dispute with her landlady. In what may have been a vengeful act, Smalls's landlady called the police to report that she had been laughing in the middle of the night.

On orders from a judge, Smalls was escorted by a nurse, a state trooper, and her doctor to Willard State Hospital. The items in Smalls's trunk were mostly infant clothing. It was easy to get into Willard but difficult to get out. Smalls lived there for 43 years, but historians discovered that she was never given proper treatment (Penney & Stastny, 2009).

That was a century ago; a lot has changed.

After reading this chapter, you will get answers to several questions you've been curious about:

Have You Ever Wondered?

16.1   How do professionals generally approach treatment?

16.2   What are biomedical therapy options?

16.3   What are the major approaches to talk therapies?

16.4   How did group and family therapies develop and what makes them effective?

Learning Objectives

LO 16.1   Explain various career paths for mental health professionals and different models of therapy.

LO 16.2   Identify various drugs and medical procedures used to improve mental health.

LO 16.3   Compare and contrast different psychotherapy approaches.

LO 16.4   Compare and contrast kinds of group therapy.

MODERN APPROACHES TO MENTAL HEALTH

**? Have You Ever Wondered?
16.1 How do professionals generally approach treatment?**

>> LO 16.1   **Explain various career paths for mental health professionals and different models of therapy.**

Only 18% of patients left Willard during its first 30 years.

Today, the average hospital stay for a patient with serious mental illness is 10 days (Adepoju et al., 2022). That's a big change. How did we get here? In the final chapter, we're going to discuss approaches to improving mental health, starting with career paths and philosophical models of therapy. Then we'll cover specific kinds of therapy or counseling, such as biological and "talk therapy" approach. As the field of psychology has advanced, more and better options have allowed for patients and clients with psychological disorders to get the help they need.

Of course, we know that people are still affected by mental illness, so continuing to (1) explore even more advances in research and (2) reduce the stigma against mental illness are both important priorities for the future of psychology. Access to counseling for people with fewer resources or in rural areas also remains an issue (Kazdin & Rabbitt, 2013).

We could use your help.

Counseling and Therapy Career Paths

The world needs more counselors and therapists.

You might be interested because you'd like to pursue this career path yourself—or you might be curious because you will see a counselor for therapy at some point in your life (if you haven't already). The various career path options for mental health professionals are complicated (Kuther & Morgan, 2019). Earning a professional counseling license in psychology requires four things:

1. A training program in their field

2. Supervised experience

3. A formal examination in their specialty

4. Ongoing continuing education each year afterward, to maintain the license

Part of the training will be ethical guidelines. Having a license doesn't guarantee professional behavior, but it greatly increases the likelihood of competence and ethical behavior.

Like other professions in the United States, the exams are national, but the license and other requirements are granted by the states. Additional certifications indicate that a professional has documented training in a particular technique. Although states use slightly different terms, Table 16.1 summarizes licenses related to providing mental health services (American Psychological Association [APA], 2021a).

There are many career paths for people interested in helping to promote mental health, such as school counseling.

iStock.com/SDI Productions

TABLE 16.1

Licensed Mental Health Professionals

The minimum academic requirements are what is shown plus additional specific training, such as residencies or supervised internships.

PROFESSIONAL TITLE	MINIMUM ACADEMIC REQUIREMENTS
Psychiatrist	Medical doctorate (MD or DO)
Licensed psychologist	Doctorate (PhD, PsyD, or EdD)
Nationally Certified School Psychologist	Master's plus NCSP
Advanced Nurse Practitioner	Master's plus ANP
Licensed Psychological Associate	Master's plus LPA
Licensed Professional Counselor	Master's plus LPC
Licensed Clinical Social Worker	Master's plus LCSW
Licensed Marriage and Family Therapist	Master's plus LMFT

Each career has different kinds of training, required education, and subsequent career options. For example, licensed psychiatrists first earn a medical degree, then complete a 3-year residency program. They can diagnose disorders and provide talk therapy, but because of their medical background, they can also prescribe medications (which many others listed in the table cannot). Specific rules and regulations vary from state to state in the United States.

Besides these paths, there are additional opportunities. There are mental health workers in schools, community health centers, jails, prisons, halfway houses, and court systems working on cases such as substance abuse, adoptions, divorce, custody arrangements, foster care, and violent offenders (Menkel-Meadow, 2018). Judges often call on psychologists to encourage therapy for juvenile offenders, hoping early intervention will help young people avoid bigger criminal issues later (Hachtel et al., 2019). School psychologists may provide counseling, but they also do mental testing, run prevention and antibullying programs, do data analysis for the school, and more (NASP, 2021). In contrast, school counselors focus more on individual counseling and working with families and administrators (American School Counselor Association [ASCA], 2021).

Many of the additional career paths are shown in Table 16.2. A few of these, such as pastoral counseling and life coaching, may have organizational certifications.

TABLE 16.2

Additional Mental Health Professionals

Counseling psychologists	Clinical psychologists	School psychologists
Neuropsychologists and clinical neuropsychologists	Industrial/organizational psychologists	Marriage and family therapists
Health care social workers	Mental health and substance abuse social workers	Child, family, and school social workers
Mental health counselors	Rehabilitation counselors	Substance abuse and behavioral disorder counselors
Educational and school counselors	Vocational and career counselors	Social and human service assistants
Psychiatric aides	Psychiatric technicians	Advanced practice psychiatric nurses
Arbitrators, mediators, and conciliators	Pastoral counselors	Life coaches

Source: Adapted from Hammer (2021).

CAREER CORNER

Meet Maya, In-Home Mental Health Therapist

What is your career?

I am an in-home mental health therapist working directly with children and their families to develop skills that improve daily functioning at home, school, and in the community. These skills include coping, focus, communication, emotional regulation, and many other skills.

How was studying psychology important for success in this career?

Studying psychology was imperative for this job, particularly in areas of how to understand mental health disorders and the ethics of treatment. Understanding mental health disorders allows me to focus my treatment plans on skills that can best improve daily functioning for clients. For example, a client dealing with depression may better benefit from skills involving positive affirmations than a client struggling with anxiety. Knowing the ethics of treatment made it much easier for me to understand federal laws and avoid violating client privacy.

How do concepts from this chapter help in this career?

Understanding concepts such as ethics of therapy and theoretical approaches are incredibly helpful in my career. Having a vast knowledge of theoretical approaches helps me to curate my treatment to each client differently, allowing me to adapt my approach depending on the client's needs and background.

Is this the career you always planned to have after college?

Yes and no. **I began working with children early in my career and have worked almost primarily with that demographic since.** Though I certainly enjoy the work that I do with children, I would like to eventually expand my services to help different demographics before I settle into a particular group I want to work with.

If you could give current college students one sentence of advice, what would it be?

Keep up the great work; it'll all be worth it! ●

Therapy Models

There are several ways to approach mental health therapy.

Modern mental health professionals generally rely on two models that work in tandem. The first is one we already discussed in the previous chapter: the biopsychosocial model, which recognizes that biology, psychology, and sociocultural factors jointly influence mental health (Ghaemi, 2009; Smith et al., 2013). The model identifies multiple possible entry points for therapy (e.g., prescription drugs, talking to a counselor) and recognizes that mental illnesses are complicated. One way to think about this model is shown in Figure 16.1. Psychological and social factors that might be relevant are shown in the top half of the figure, and biological and medical factors are in the bottom half, all clustered around the individual person (Engel, 1981).

For example, if you are drinking heavily, then you may enter therapy at the family level when a sibling or parent plans an intervention. You also could enter therapy at the community level by deciding to attend an Alcoholic Anonymous meeting. You also might enter therapy at the nervous system level when you consult with a physician about withdrawal side effects and take a medication designed to decrease negative reactions as you stop consuming alcohol. Treatment from multiple entry points might build the best support and success.

The second framework for therapeutic thinking is the science-practitioner model that applies scientific knowledge and reasoning to mental health problems. This model emphasizes that when working with people, a solid background and understanding of up-to-date research is needed to ethically provide evidence-based treatment (Frank, 1984; Knappe, 2021). At the same time, research should be informed by people who are doing real work within their applied practice. In this way, the field can continually improve.

Science-practitioner model: Application of scientific knowledge and reasoning to mental health problems.

The biopsychosocial and science-practitioner models cooperate with each other; a counselor can use both approaches simultaneously. Consider how they apply to three common problems today: diabetes, depression, and opioid addiction.

FIGURE 16.1

The Biopsychosocial Model

The biopsychosocial model identifies multiple entry points for mental health therapies. From the Hierarchy of Natural Systems.

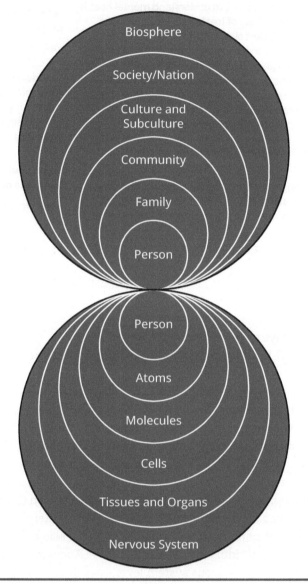

Biosphere

Society/Nation

Culture and Subculture

Community

Family

Person

Person

Atoms

Molecules

Cells

Tissues and Organs

Nervous System

Source: Adapted from Engel (1981).

Diabetes and Depression

In 2021, about 10.5% of people in the world had Type 2 diabetes, and by 2045, it's estimated to grow worse (Sun et al., 2022). In the United States alone, prevalence rose from 9.8% in 2000 to 14.3% in 2018 (Wang et al., 2021). Diabetes by itself is psychologically demanding; it requires stressful monitoring of glucose levels and eating habits. The condition is complicated by *comorbidity;* up to 84% of people with diabetes may have a mood disorder. People with depression and diabetes are more likely to be younger, be unemployed, and have thoughts of suicide, as each disease aggravates the other (Akena et al., 2015; Ogunsakin et al., 2021).

Figure 16.2 summarizes how one set of researchers organized the biopsychosocial model regarding the diabetes/depression problem (Habtewold et al., 2016).

FIGURE 16.2

The Biopsychosocial Model Applied to Diabetes and Depression

Diabetes and depression often go together; here are ways the biopsychosocial model might be relevant to both diseases.

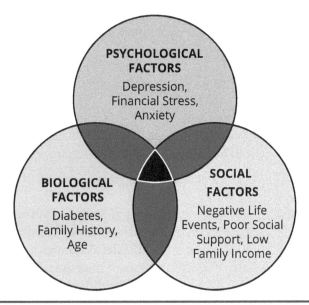

Source: Adapted from Habtewold et al. (2016).

Understanding the research behind causes and effective treatments for both diabetes and depression (the science-practitioner model) and approaching treatment or interventions for all three factors (biological, psychological, and psychosocial) can be highly effective in helping individuals and this larger public health concern.

The Opioid Epidemic

The opioid epidemic is also getting worse. In 2019, about 70,630 people died from it in the United States; the synthetic opioid death rate increased from 2013 to 2019 by over 1,000% (Mattson et al., 2021).

The usual short-term therapy begins with a biological intervention: detoxification. Unfortunately, relapse rates are pretty high because detoxification is a miserable experience. A biopsychological approach that combines tapering down drug use with counseling sessions appears more promising (Krambeer et al., 2001; Woody et al., 2008). After treatment, successes like employment and lower criminality are tied to sociocultural factors like personal background and family influence (Hater et al., 1984).

While this kind of therapy can be slow and expensive, it's cost-effective for a community when compared to the expenses of addiction, such as 30% more emergency health care services compared to the general population (McGeary & French, 2000; Morse & Bride, 2017; Zarkin et al., 2004, 2005).

Intersectionality and Transcultural Approach

Even the Rat Was White (Guthrie, 2004).

That simple book title crystallized the depth of institutionalized racism within psychology. It took far too long, but in 2021, the American Psychological Association (APA) formally apologized for its role in decades of prejudice (APA, 2021b). Just one part of this prejudice—which included racism, homophobia, sexism, and more—included treatment of people in mental hospitals and prisons (Cahalan, 2019; Felthous,

2015; Kessler et al., 2005; Konrad, 2002). In this way, intersectionality and stigma about mental illness are tied together, with marginalized communities often suffering from disorders and lack of resources the most (Ngui et al., 2010; Oexle & Corrigan, 2018; Torrey et al., 2010).

In response, the APA has made specific commitments to

- recruit and retain students of color in training and graduate programs,
- advocate for federal research,
- seek more funding from agencies and private foundations,
- research culturally responsive methods,
- promote collaborative opportunities in HBCUs (historically Black colleges/universities) and HSIs (Hispanic serving institutions), and
- develop partnerships with policymaking organizations.

The recognition of institutional bias is changing what happens inside the therapy room and group counseling. A **transcultural approach** in therapy emphasizes understanding of a client's background and belief system as it relates to their race, ethnicity, sexuality, gender, or other elements of their cultural identity (Friedman et al., 2010). Cultural sensitivity of people who are different from ourselves promotes a richer understanding of how someone is experiencing their life, which translates to more effective therapy. The future of therapy "respects cultural differences and invites collaboration with psychological and spiritual and religious traditions and practices from around the world" (Fleuridas & Krafcik, 2019, pp. 3–4).

Transcultural approach: Therapy that emphasizes greater awareness and sensitivity toward the role of culture in mental health.

SageVantage — Practice what you learn in **Knowledge Check 16.1**

BIOMEDICAL THERAPY

Have You Ever Wondered? 16.2 What are biomedical therapy options?

>> **LO 16.2** **Identify various drugs and medical procedures used to improve mental health.**

If a theory has lasted thousands of years, it's tempting to believe it must be true.

Resist that temptation. Consider two biomedical ideas regarding how to treat mental illness that appear to have been around that long—but are both completely bogus.

First: Hippocrates (460–370 BCE), who may have been the first person to propose that physicians "first, do no harm," seemed to believe the **theory of humors** (Herbst, 2013; Laios et al., 2015; Lloyd et al., 1983; Tsagkaris & Kalachanis, 2020). The theory was that an imbalance of four liquids in your body (blood, yellow bile, black bile, and phlegm) causes various problems. For example, too much black bile was tied to depression while too much blood was tied to aggression and mania. Treatment included suggestions like exercise, diet, and change to sexual behavior.

Second: An even older idea might be **trephination**, opening the skull to release demons or unfriendly gods to restore mental health. Skulls with carefully drilled holes apparently for this purpose from up to 12,000 years ago have been found all over the world: East Africa, South America, and France, with evidence that the practice continued into the 20th century (Liu & Apuzzo, 2003).

Theory of humors: Ancient Greek idea that four fluids maintain a healthy body and mind: blood, yellow bile, phlegm, and black bile.

Trephination: The ancient practice of drilling a hole in the skull to release demons or unfriendly gods to restore mental health.

Although discredited, these theories reflect some of the earliest attempts to connect mental illness to biology. **Biomedical theories of mental illness** look for biological or physiological explanations of mental illness, usually in the brain. While many early therapies unfortunately harmed thousands of patients, they eventually led to effective modern biomedical treatments used in psychology and psychiatry today.

Biomedical theories of mental illness: Focus mainly on biological or physiological explanations of mental illness, usually in the brain.

Electroconvulsive Therapy (ECT)

The history of shock therapy is embarrassing and brutal for psychology.

It started with inducing other kinds of "shocks" before electricity was an option. Early forms were bodily seizures caused by *insulin shock* (starting in hospitals in 1937) or *hydrotherapy*, which submerged "agitated" hospital patients for long periods in cold bath water—more of a punishment than a treatment (Penney & Stastny, 2009, p. 109).

These were replaced by shocks induced by electricity, what is still known as **electroconvulsive therapy (ECT)**. It administers electrical stimulation to the brain to purposely induce seizures that alter neural pathways. ECT has changed a lot from how it started to how it is used now.

Hallway of Willard State Psychiatric Hospital.
The New York State Archives

Electroconvulsive therapy (ECT): Careful delivery of electrical stimulation to the brain to induce seizures that alter neural pathways.

In 1942 alone, Willard State Hospital administered 1,443 shock treatments. Nancy Jaycot Caniff, a therapist at Willard, described how, "You had people trying to hold you down because the neck would arch up and they had this big thing they put in their mouth" (Penney & Stastny, 2009, p. 110). She was probably describing a protective device to ensure people didn't bite their tongues during the seizures. In the 1940s when ECT was new, institutions broadly tried it for substance abuse, depression, schizophrenia, hysteria, and anxiety—with few therapeutic benefits (Kim, 2018). In its early applications, ECT also caused forms of amnesia—sometimes erasing entire periods of a person's life. Journalists, possibly more than researchers, played a key role in reducing ECT's misuse (Maisel, 1946; Mayes & Horwitz, 2005).

Today, is it still used—but only for severe cases of long-term depression or bipolar disorder, and only when other treatments have failed. Properly administered, positive effects are almost immediate. Safety and side effects are controlled with careful monitoring, airway management, muscle sedatives, and so on (Kim, 2018). Patients experience minor electrical stimulation in very controlled areas of the brain and wake up after being anesthetized—a very different experience from what happened at Willard and other hospitals in the 1940s.

Typically, patients receive three treatments per week for 2 or more weeks. The most reliable side effect is minor: temporary loss of recent memories. Research indicates ECT probably works by encouraging brain plasticity via new growth and pruning of unused neural synapses—although more research is needed to be sure of exactly *why* it works (Bouckaert et al., 2014; Gbyl & Videbech, 2018; Li et al., 2020). Despite the benefits of ECT, it is still considered a last resort because researchers are still unsure of exactly why it works (Slade et al., 2017).

Therapeutic Drug Options

Many people rely on prescription drugs for mental illnesses.

"Big pharma," as the pharmaceutical industry is commonly known, started much of its spectacular growth by developing psychoactive drugs. While there is a lot of controversy around the use of drugs (including debates about whether they are overused, whether there is a stigma toward using them, whether they are overpriced, and so on), many people rely on access to therapeutic drugs to manage symptoms of psychological disorders.

These chemical interventions are usually designed to increase (*agonists*) or decrease (*antagonists*) neurotransmitters' activity. Table 16.3 summarizes how the National Institute of Mental Health (2021) organizes commonly prescribed psychoactive drugs into five types: antidepressants, anti-anxiety drugs, stimulants, antipsychotics, and mood stabilizers. We explain a bit about each next.

TABLE 16.3

Commonly Used Psychoactive Medications

Mixing drugs without careful medical oversight can produce harmful side effects.

CATEGORY AND BRAND NAMES	PURPOSE	SOME POSSIBLE SIDE EFFECTS	PRACTICAL INFORMATION
Antidepressants: SSRIs, SNRIs, bupropion Prozac, Celexa, Zoloft, Paxil, Lexapro, Cymbalta, Wellbutrin	Reduces symptoms of depression but sometimes used for anxiety, pain, and insomnia.	Vary with each individual and drug: suicidal ideation or attempts, worsening symptoms, agitation, aggression, impulsive behavior. Also nausea, vomiting, weight gain, sleepiness, and sexual problems.	1. Each drug addresses a unique symptom profile. 2. Individual reactions vary widely. 3. It takes about a month for most antidepressants to take effect.
Anti-anxiety drugs: benzodiazepines Klonopin, Xanax, Ativan	Reduces general and specific forms of anxiety such as panic attacks.	Drowsiness, dizziness, difficulty thinking, joint pain, blurred vision, increased salivation. Also, if taken with other drugs, such as an opiate, may cause life-threatening breathing problems.	1. Often used as a second-line drug after an SSRI. May be used to control side effects of antipsychotic medications. 2. Faster acting than SSRIs.
Stimulants: amphetamines Aderall	Primarily for treating attention-deficit/hyperactivity disorder; sometimes for narcolepsy.	Headaches, stomach pain, repetitive movements or sounds. Elevates heart rate and blood pressure. Also, difficulty falling or staying asleep, loss of appetite, feeling flat or without emotion, verbal tics.	1. Increase alertness, attention, and energy. 2. May cause sudden death among those with preexisting heart conditions.
Antipsychotics: *Typical (first generation):* Thorazine and Haldol *Atypical (second generation):* Risperdal, Zyprexa, Seroquel, Abilify, Latuda	Manages psychosis among people with symptoms of schizophrenia: hallucinations, delusions, and bipolar mania.	Drowsiness, dizziness, restlessness, weight gain, dry mouth, constipation, nausea, vomiting, blurred vision, low blood pressure, tics, seizures.	1. Atypical (second-generation) antipsychotics treat a broader spectrum of symptoms such as bipolar mania. 2. Agitation and hallucinations tend to decline in a few days; delusions may persist for 6 weeks.
Mood stabilizers: Tegretol, Lamictal, Trileptal	Reduces the swings between depression and mania in bipolar disorder. Also for disorders of impulse control.	Itching, rash, thirst, frequent urination, tremor, nausea, vomiting, slurred speech, seizures, hallucinations, swelling, loss of coordination.	1. Lithium is a well-known but now less prescribed medication for bipolar disorder. 2. Often used in conjunction with an antidepressant.

Source: Adapted from the National Institute of Mental Health (2021).

Note: SNRI = serotonin and norepinephrine reuptake inhibitor; SSRI = selective serotonin reuptake inhibitor.

Antidepressants

The first type of drugs used to treat depression were originally for tuberculosis, but in the 1950s it was discovered they also had a positive effect on mood. They became the first examples of *monoamine oxidase inhibitors (MAOIs)*. MAOIs block the activity of an enzyme whose primary function is to break down three neurotransmitters most involved in the control of mood: serotonin, norepinephrine, and dopamine. MAOIs increase the availability of these neurotransmitters, boosting mood. MAOIs are still used today, although less commonly due to dietary restrictions and potential interactions with other medications (Stahl, 2013).

In the late 1950s and early 1960s, *tricyclic antidepressants* were developed. Their name came because of the molecular structure consisting of three rings (cycles). These drugs block the reuptake of serotonin and norepinephrine, thereby increasing their levels in the brain. Both MAOIs and tricyclics can produce some unwanted side effects (commonly weight gain, constipation, dry mouth, dizziness, headaches, and some sexual arousal issues, among other effects), although these concerns often decrease with continued treatment (Stahl, 2013; Ulrich et al., 2020).

Still, research led to development of newer antidepressant options with fewer side effects. In the late 1980s, a breakthrough led to the introduction of *selective serotonin reuptake inhibitors*, better known as *SSRIs*. Common examples are fluoxetine (Prozac), sertraline (Zoloft), and paroxetine (Paxil). As their name says, SSRIs work by stopping the reuptake of only serotonin in the brain and are currently the most common form of drug therapy for depression.

For people with depression who don't respond well to SSRIs or other traditional antidepressants, other possibilities now are *serotonin norepinephrine reuptake inhibitors (SNRIs)* or ketamine, which has gained attention as a fast-acting anesthetic for people in crisis (Stahl, 2013).

Anti-Anxiety Drugs

Anti-anxiety drugs, also known as anxiolytics, are designed to help people manage excessive worry, fear, and anxiety (i.e., anxiety disorders, panic disorders, or generalized anxiety). They have a calming effect. The main category of anti-anxiety drugs is *benzodiazepines*. Examples are chlordiazepoxide (Librium), diazepam (Valium), and alprazolam (Xanax). They enhance the inhibitory neurotransmitter GABA.

While benzodiazepines (sometimes nicknamed "bennies") are typically very effective in the short term, they can be very addictive (Wilde et al., 2021). Therefore, SSRIs are usually prescribed for anxiety as well.

Stimulants

Think of stimulants as "brain organizers." They help the brain's attention systems work better, allowing you to concentrate on tasks, resist distractions, and stay alert as they increase the release and availability of dopamine and norepinephrine in the brain. Consequently, stimulants are commonly used to treat attention-deficit/hyperactivity disorder (ADHD) and, in some cases, narcolepsy (Beauti, 2023). Stimulant medications date back to the early 20th century; amphetamine (Adderall) was first synthesized in the 1920s. Later, methylphenidate (Ritalin) was developed in the 1950s as a treatment for hyperactivity and other attention problems.

Antipsychotics

Antipsychotic drugs are like the "reality-check" meds. They were first developed in the 1950s to help people with conditions like schizophrenia, where a person may have trouble distinguishing between what's real and what's not.

Antipsychotic drugs can be classified into two categories called "typical" and "atypical." The first drug to treat schizophrenia was chlorpromazine (called Thorazine), a *typical antipsychotic*. This type of drug works primarily by reducing the overactivity of dopamine, a neurotransmitter involved in mood and perception in specific parts of the brain that can cause hallucinations and delusions. However, there are many unwanted side effects, and prolonged use can lead to movement disorders similar to Parkinson's disease (Nguyen et al., 2022).

Atypical antipsychotics may also suppress dopamine, but they also block or partially block certain serotonin receptors. Many people who are unresponsive to typical antipsychotics have much better responses to atypical antipsychotics, with fewer symptoms of schizophrenia and fewer side effects of the drug itself (Stahl, 2013). Still, some side effects are common, including weight gain and changes in the electrical rhythms of the heart (Siafis et al., 2023; Tiihonen et al., 2020; Whitaker, 2010, 2020).

Mood Stabilizers

Mood stabilizers are like an emotional thermostat. They were first used to help people with bipolar disorder, to manage both depression and mania episodes. One of the earliest mood stabilizers was lithium, a natural element (Amare et al., 2023). Lithium affects the way sodium ions in neuron and muscle cells are transported, although it is not exactly clear how this affects moods. Anticonvulsant drugs (such as valproic acid, lamotrigine, and carbamazepine) are normally used to treat seizure disorders but have also been effective in controlling mood swings (Bowden et al., 2000; Thase & Sachs, 2000).

Controversies: Overprescribing and the Placebo Effect

Are we too reliant on drugs to fix our problems?

When someone is feeling depressed or anxious and we know it is due to recent, environmental concerns—not biological or physiological causes—should drugs still be used, or are they inappropriate? This question is a current debate, partially fueled by the pattern shown in Figure 16.3. The number of antidepressants prescribed per year

FIGURE 16.3

The Rising Use of Antidepressants in the United States

The number of antidepressants prescribed more than tripled over the past two decades.

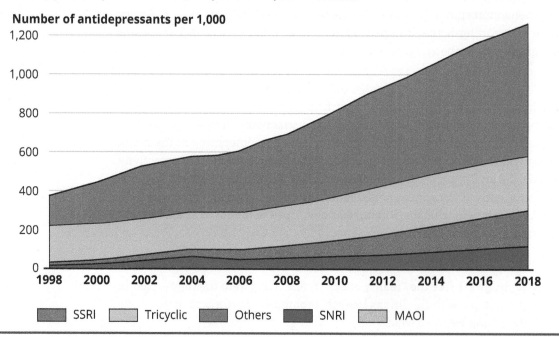

Source: Bogowicz et al. (2021). Licensed under CC BY 4.0.

more than tripled over the past two decades, from 18.4 million in 1998 to 70.9 million in 2018 (Bogowicz et al., 2021; see also Pratt et al., 2017).

Another major concern was a study that found six of the most popular antidepressants were only "marginally better" than placebo pills, which had no chemical effect at all (Kirsch et al., 2002). The result was replicated in a follow-up study that concluded, "Antidepressants and cognitive therapy fail to result in sustained positive effects for the majority of people who receive them" (Pigott et al., 2010). The placebo effect occurs when the mere expectation or belief in a drug or other type of intervention produces the same effect as an authentic treatment (Haas et al., 2020).

Combined, concerns about a global population overmedicated with drugs that (1) cause a lot of negative side effects but (2) show no better effectiveness than placebo pills have many people wondering whether the culture has become reliant on psychoactive drugs to fix our problems. That said, for the millions of people who truly believe using such prescriptions allows symptoms of their psychological disorders to be manageable, shame and guilt about drug use only adds to mental illness stigma (Sirey et al., 2001). The debate continues.

Placebo effect: When the mere expectation or a belief in a drug or other type of intervention produces the same effect as an authentic treatment.

Body-Based Approaches

There are other options.

While we don't have room to list every possible form of therapy, consider just a few more biomedical approaches to improving mental health.

EMDR

Sometimes when people survive a trauma (such as a car accident or sexual assault), the events can leave deep emotional scars that affect their mental health. *Eye movement desensitization and reprocessing* (EMDR) therapy was initially developed in 1987 for the treatment of posttraumatic stress disorder (PTSD; Shapiro, 2007). PTSD and similar disorders are believed to result from trauma memories that have not been adequately processed. The goal of EMDR is to change how the memories are stored in the brain, therefore eliminating problematic symptoms (like anxiety, flashbacks, nightmares, and depression).

During EMDR therapy, you talk to a therapist about the upsetting event(s) and your feelings. While you talk, the therapist helps you focus on something like their moving finger, a light, or a sound (this is the "eye movement" part). You might also hold something in your hands. In each session, you process the memory and emotions, making sense of them and reorganizing them in your long-term memory so they are less upsetting over time (Shapiro, 2007, 2017).

EMDR is somewhat controversial because researchers are not sure why eye movement helps process memory or improve mood, and some studies find it no more helpful than any other form of therapy in which traumatic memories are discussed with a counselor (e.g., Davidson & Parker, 2001). Other studies disagree, showing evidence of decreased depression and/or anxiety in both younger people (Matthijssen et al., 2020) and adults (Sepehry et al., 2021).

Biofeedback

You control some of your body's actions, like waving to a friend. Other body actions, like your heart rate or breathing patterns, are usually controlled involuntarily by your nervous system. *Biofeedback* is a form of therapy in which you attempt to gain more control over normally involuntary body functions that help promote relaxation, reduce stress, and/or manage mood (Patil et al., 2023; Ravada et al., 2023). To do this, you attach sensors to yourself that measure physiological functions such as heart rate, muscle tension, skin temperature, and brainwave activity in real time. You monitor the feedback of the data in various ways (e.g., lights or sounds).

A trained biofeedback therapist helps you practice relaxation exercises, which you fine-tune to control different body functions. For example, someone with an anxiety disorder who is feeling stress might experience an increased heart rate, tighter muscles, rising blood pressure, and sweating. As the biofeedback monitors shows these changes, the person learns to control their body and reduce their stress response. Success requires follow-up practice sessions without the equipment as well (Libo & Arnold, 1983).

How to Assess If Therapy Is Just a Con

Mindfulness-based meditation appears to be an effective way to reduce anxiety. Breath awareness is a common technique, but nearly any activity can be done mindfully.

iStock.com/lsbjorn

"Mindfulness" is a meditation therapy that encourages people to focus attention on the present moment (Baer et al., 2004). A specific technique is to be aware of each inhalation and exhalation of your breath, but just about any activity can be done mindfully: brushing your teeth, vacuuming the floor, yoga, walking, even sitting quietly (Germer, 2005). Although mindfulness comes from a Buddhist tradition, it isn't religious or even particularly philosophical—it shifts attention from "doing" to "being" (Germer, 2005; Kabat-Zinn, 1994).

Mindfulness meditation therapy is a hot trend in psychology right now. Meta-analyses indicate that it is legitimately effective, both short and long term (Chiesa & Serretti, 2009; Grossman et al., 2004; Zenner et al., 2014). But its meteoric jump in popularity and some unfortunate early misinformation on the Internet

(Van Dam et al., 2018) still make some people skeptical of it. Being scientifically doubtful about a new idea until enough evidence has been gathered is evidence of solid critical thinking. That's what science is, really.

Two researchers put together what they called the *Psychotherapy Hype List* (Meichenbaum & Lilienfeld, 2018). It's a checklist of red flags people can use to assess whether a new "therapy" should be trusted or whether it's just a lot of hype (in other words, you might be getting conned). We won't list all of the red flags here, but here are some of them:

- *Substantial exaggeration of claims of treatment effectiveness*
- *Excessive appeal to authorities or "gurus"*
- *Use of a slick sales pitch and extensive promotional efforts, including sale of paraphernalia (additional equipment you must purchase)*
- *Tendency of treatment followers to insulate themselves from criticism*
- *Extensive use of "psychobabble" or "neurobabble" (terms unique to the group)*
- *Extensive reliance on uncheckable stories and anecdotal evidence*
- *Claims that treatment is somehow special, "fits all," and works better than any others*

If any treatment program shows these signs, consider seeking help elsewhere (or maybe not investing so much in all those crystals). ●

Other Somatic Approaches

Light therapy, also known as phototherapy, is a common treatment for *seasonal affective disorder* (SAD), a type of depression that occurs seasonally, typically during the fall and winter months when there is less natural sunlight. This approach involves exposure to a bright light that mimics natural sunlight to stimulate the brain's production of serotonin and regulate the body's circadian rhythms. It helps reset the body's internal clock and improve mood. Light therapy can be highly effective for many individuals with SAD, with noticeable improvements in mood and reduced symptoms, although some studies suggest there may be placebo effects involved (Campbell et al., 2017; Nussbaumer-Streit et al., 2019).

A technique called *transcranial magnetic stimulation* (TMS) applies magnetic pulses to the brain's prefrontal cortex. This can help mood regulation (Brunelin et al., 2014), can treat the negative symptoms of schizophrenia (Hasan et al., 2017), and shows promise in treating obsessive-compulsive disorder (Mantovani et al., 2021). A typical TMS treatment course involves daily sessions over several weeks, with each session lasting around 20 to 40 minutes.

Another option is *deep brain stimulation* (DBS), a surgical procedure that involves implanting electrodes in specific areas of the brain to deliver electrical impulses to mood-regulating circuits (McIntyre & Anderson, 2016). Both TMS and DBS are usually considered only when other treatments for depression have been ineffective or when the condition is particularly severe (Brunelin et al., 2014; Zhang et al., 2013).

Exercise

Does exercise help or hurt your mental health? Research finds mixed results. Some studies indicate that physical exercise is associated with improved mental health, especially for people with mild (subclinical) levels of anxiety (Hughes, 1984; Salmon, 2001). Other studies show exercise might increase anxiety (Cameron & Hudson, 1986). The effects probably depend on many factors, as the biopsychosocial model would suggest.

For example, one factor might be the type of exercise. Mental health benefits might be highest if the activity (1) is rhythmic and aerobic exercise, (2) uses large muscle groups, (3) is at low to moderate intensity, and (4) is done about three times per week for 15 to 30 minutes—examples are jogging, swimming, cycling, and brisk walking (Guszkowska, 2004; Jayakody et al., 2014).

The biological mechanisms of exercise are well known, mostly involving endorphins, neurotransmitters, and increased blood supply to the brain. The psychological mechanisms are also well established: a greater sense of being in control of your life (self-efficacy) and simple distraction (McMurray, 2019; Mikkelsen et al., 2017). The social benefits come from the community of friends you make among other walkers, runners, soccer players, or people at the gym.

Other factors recently investigated include

- the effectiveness of combining exercise, medications, and psychotherapy with a counselor (Ströhle et al., 2018; Wegner et al., 2014);

The biopsychosocial model helps explain why exercise helps manage anxiety.

iStock.com/Kate_sept2004

- whether the effects of exercise vary depending on participant demographics, such as in older people (Kazeminia et al., 2020) and athletes (Arent et al., 2020); and

- how to maintain exercise benefits under isolation situations, such as during the COVID-19 pandemic (Hu et al., 2020).

Curiosity will surely lead to more research on additional important factors that make a difference.

Effectiveness of Biomedical Therapies

How effective are biomedical therapies?

It depends. Here are some examples of outcomes:

- ECT treatments are usually immediately effective for depression, but the benefits are brief (Tokutsu et al., 2013).

- Lithium is still widely used for bipolar disorder, but evidence for long-term effectiveness in treatment and prevention of severe symptoms is mixed (Carney & Goodwin, 2005; Reed et al., 2009; Volkmann et al., 2020).

- Antipsychotic drugs work fairly well for suppressing the positive symptoms of schizophrenia (e.g., hallucinations and delusions) but are generally less effective on negative symptoms (e.g., lack of emotional expression, cognitive confusion). Clozapine is more promising but may have serious side effects (Javitt & Coyle, 2004).

  - Antidepressants are effective in regulating mood—but may not be any more effective than placebo pills (see above).

  - Newer therapies such as transcranial magnetic stimulation and deep brain stimulation show promise in treating depression and other disorders but are complicated to implement (Schlaepfer, 2015).

There are many theoretical approaches to psychotherapy; it's important to find a counselor you feel comfortable with.

iStock.com/Prostock Studio

Many psychologists believe that biomedical therapies are effective—but are *most* effective when they are paired with regular sessions in which people talk about their symptoms and mental health challenges with a trained and licensed therapist or counselor. This kind of "talk therapy" is the subject of the next major section of the chapter.

 **Sage Vantage**   Practice what you learn in **Knowledge Check 16.2**

MAJOR APPROACHES TO PSYCHOTHERAPY

? Have You Ever Wondered? 16.3 What are the major approaches to talk therapies?

>> LO 16.3 Compare and contrast different psychotherapy approaches.

Psychotherapy is the general term for talking about your problems with a counselor or therapist.

Another term for the overall approach is **insight therapy**, because the goal is for clients to understand more about themselves to improve their mental health. Over the 126 years at Willard State Mental Hospital, specific forms of insight therapy would have changed as the staff, national culture, and field of psychology changed. Scholars often describe the development of different therapies as waves of influence (Pedersen, 2001; Peteet, 2018).

After all, the people providing these therapies received training at different times by different mentors. New ideas arise and are tested, and then we slowly come to know the extent to which they can be useful. When a new treatment approach arises, we hope it will solve all our previous problems. Research and experience gradually reveal strengths and weaknesses.

We're going to summarize the waves of therapy for you in this order:

- Psychoanalysis

- Psychodynamic

- Existential

- Humanistic

- Behavioral (or behaviorist)

- Cognitive and cognitive behavioral

Many now believe we're heading toward a new wave, as a rising generation of therapists adopt the *transcultural approach* that we discussed in the first section of the chapter (Friedlander et al., 2012; Pedersen, 2001). There are also a couple of specific techniques of interest to many counselors—art therapy and play therapy—that we'll touch on in this section. All of these forms of therapy have been more or less popular over the years, and they all still exist today. It's important for each person to find a therapist who provides counseling from an approach that matches their needs and makes them comfortable.

Today, many therapists know that they will have a variety of clients with different kinds of needs—they'll need to be professionally flexible. Most licenses prepare mental health professionals for an **eclectic approach** that tries to integrate whatever combinations of theories, techniques, and approaches seem most likely to work for a particular client.

Regardless of overall theoretical approach to psychotherapy, there are hundreds of different specific techniques. Despite this diversity of what might happen in any individual session, they all share four common things:

1. **The Therapeutic Relationship:** Central to psychotherapy is the relationship between the therapist and the client. This relationship is built on trust, empathy, and confidentiality. It's a safe space where you can openly discuss your thoughts, feelings, and concerns without fear of judgment.

2. **Goals and Objectives:** Psychotherapy typically has specific goals. These goals can vary widely depending on an individual person's needs and the type of therapy being used—but it will always focus on addressing psychological issues by changing their behavior and by facilitating a deeper self-awareness concerning their past, present, and future. Common goals include reducing symptoms of mental health issues, improving coping strategies, enhancing self-awareness, and developing healthier relationships.

Insight therapies: Counseling approaches that rely on talking about and understanding the self to improve mental health.

Eclectic approach: Therapy that integrates whatever theories, techniques, and approaches apply to meet the needs of a particular client.

3. **Progress and Evaluation:** Throughout therapy, clients and therapists regularly assess progress toward achieving the established goals. Adjustments to the treatment plan may be made as needed.

4. **Confidentiality:** One of the fundamental principles of psychotherapy is confidentiality. Therapists are legally and ethically bound to keep the content of sessions private. Exceptions to confidentiality may exist in cases where there is a risk of harm to the client or others.

Like the previous section on biomedical forms of therapy, this part of the chapter ends with a brief evaluation of the effectiveness of psychotherapy in general.

Psychoanalysis

For some therapeutic approaches, hidden thoughts and feelings are critical.

The first major insight therapy is credited to Sigmund Freud. His overall approach is called **psychoanalysis** and is treatment based on insight regarding the conscious and unconscious mind (remember, psychologists don't usually use the term *subconscious* for Freud). Freud proposed **dual instinct theory**, the idea that two contradictory impulses guide our behavior: A *life drive* attracts us to pleasure, sex, love, and cooperation, and a *death drive* explains why we perpetually feel aggression, competition, and go to war (Freud, 1921/2007). These two drives cause our conflicts, stress, and psychological problems—often outside of our awareness.

Psychoanalysis probes for these motives to explain our maladaptive behaviors with techniques intended to make the unconscious—our hidden dreams and fears—conscious. It assumes that a "talking cure" exposes the unconscious, repressed conflicts from experiences in early childhood. Once brought to awareness (i.e., once we have insight), it is easier to interpret them and change our behaviors.

You may have heard of the famous couch in Freud's therapy room. He thought that if people had to talk about hidden—and possibly shameful—childhood hopes or fears in front of a doctor, it would be difficult. He called them "patients" and he knew they might feel judged. To help them feel relaxed and comfortable, they laid on the couch. He sat behind them, at the head of the couch and out of view, so that while the patients talked, they would not see his reactions—ideally, making it easier for them to talk about anything.

Freudian psychologists encourage clients to use *free association*—a technique that encourages talking via stream of consciousness. Clients using free association say aloud whatever comes to mind, regardless of its apparent irrelevance or senselessness. Freud used this technique to attempt to recognize and label the connections between what a patient said and the patient's unconscious mind.

Freud also made use of dream interpretation to try to reveal the repressed information in his patients. *Dream interpretation* involves analyzing the elements within a patient's reported dream. Moving beyond the surface description of a dream (called the manifest content), Freud sought the dream's underlying meaning (called the latent content), which is thought to reveal the true unconscious meaning of the dream (Hill et al., 2013; Sandford, 2017).

Psychoanalysis: Treatment based on insight regarding the conscious and unconscious human mind.

Dual instinct theory: Freud's idea that humans have two contradictory impulses or drives: a death instinct and a life instinct.

Freud's famous couch is in his former home in London, where he lived at the end of his life after fleeing the Nazi occupation of Vienna. The house is now a museum. Psychoanalysis no longer dominates therapy, but it got things started (Johnston-Robledo & Barnack, 2004; Stepansky, 2009).

Tom Ferguson/Alamy Stock Photo

Free association and dream interpretation don't always move forward easily. Patients can show *resistance,* or an inability or unwillingness to discuss or reveal memories, thoughts, or motivations. For example, a patient may be discussing a childhood memory and suddenly forget what they were saying, or they may change the subject completely. Freud believed when this happened, it was a sign that the subject was actually quite important and they were unconsciously avoiding it for a reason—so the therapist should notice and focus on that topic or memory.

The relationship between a therapist and client is quite intimate and becomes emotionally charged. This makes *transference* more likely to occur. It's when a client feels false love or anger toward a therapist, because the feelings have actually been transferred from someone else in their life (such as a parental figure) and are unresolved. If unaddressed, transference is clearly an awkward problem—but Freud believed that when correctly identified by a trained therapist, transference could be used to help a client process past relationships that were psychologically difficult (Steiner, 2008; Turri, 2015).

Today, many people criticize some of Freud's wildest speculations. But when it comes to psychotherapy, he was like a pioneer without a map, exploring the world of mental illness from the confines of his own cultural experience. We may not have the techniques that exist today—or at least we'd be far behind—without him.

Psychodynamic Therapies

Traditional psychoanalysis can take years.

That long, expensive task has been largely replaced by **psychodynamic therapies,** which focus on gaining insights that connect current and childhood emotions, motivations, thoughts, and behaviors. Instead of hiding the therapist from view, psychodynamic therapies brought the person-therapist relationship to the forefront. In most counseling or therapy sessions today, the people involved sit comfortably facing each other, which is generally considered less artificial and more natural than Freud's couch setup.

Psychodynamic therapies: Insight approaches that help clients connect past and present emotions to motivations, thoughts, and behaviors.

Psychodynamic therapists also take a more active role than Freud would have prescribed, and they prompt and advise clients with considerable directness. Contemporary psychodynamic therapists put less emphasis on someone's history and childhood. Instead, they concentrate on a person's current relationships and specific concerns (Brafman, 2018; Driessen et al., 2017). Two famous psychodynamic therapists expanded the Freudian approach in important historical ways: Carl Jung and Karen Horney.

Freud had hoped that Carl Jung (1875–1961) would be his protégé—but Jung developed alternative ideas that strained their friendship. Jung expanded the description of the unconscious beyond repressed conflicts within a given individual. He proposed that humans across cultures shared a spiritual bond he described as the *collective unconscious* that responded to universal *archetypes* common across cultures—characters seen in

Karen Horney, the first well-known feminist psychologist.
Bettmann/Contributor/Bettmann/via Getty Images

every culture's myths, stories, and religions (as discussed in the personality chapter; Jung, 1936).

Karen Horney (1885–1952) is regarded as the founder of feminist psychology. Horney maintained her intellectual independence and became one of the few women of that era to be admitted to medical school. As you hopefully remember from the chapter on personality (Chapter 13), she rejected Freud's notion that all girls experience "penis envy"—the desire to have a penis and be a boy. It was more likely, Horney suggested, that men suffer from *womb envy*, sadness about not being able to bear children (Aldridge et al., 2014). She gradually replaced Freudian beliefs with a more humanistic and egalitarian description of human nature.

Existential Therapies

How do you find meaning in life during an atrocity?

One year before the Freud family fled Austria to escape the Nazis, the Jewish psychiatrist Viktor Frankl opened a private practice in Vienna in his sister's living room. The timing was risky, but Frankl and his wife Tilly remained to support his aging father. In September 1942, Viktor and Tilly were deported to the first of four concentration camps where Frankl experienced physical abuse, malnutrition, emotional humiliation, and torture. The experience deeply molded his philosophy of human nature (Bushkin et al., 2021).

Existential therapy:
Developed by Viktor Frankl; the idea that the search for personal meaning in life is a therapeutic motivation.

Existential therapy grew out of these experiences (Pytell, 2007), famously recorded in Frankl's (1959) book *Man's Search for Meaning*. There, Frankl suggested that the primary motivation in life—and the responsibility of each individual—is the search for meaning. Frankl observed that finding meaning was how many political prisoners transcended the horrors of the Nazi concentration camps. Surrounded by death, people somehow maintained hope and humanity as children and artists painted, actors performed, and musicians played.

Frankl developed this search for meaning into *logotherapy*, which assumes that some mental illnesses result when we don't have a meaningful purpose in life that drives us. In existential therapy, deciding how to live a meaningful life produces mental health even in a hostile environment. Techniques like *dereflection* focus attention away from yourself and toward others—in the process spending less mental energy on your own problems. *Paradoxical intention* is a technique that suggests wishing for the very thing you fear the most. If you fear being laughed at, then act silly and invite the laughter. That way, you conquer your fears.

The Humanistic Approach

No therapist can help you if you don't want to change.

Humanistic approach to therapy: Therapy techniques focused on building up individual free will, self-esteem, and personal potential.

Earlier techniques and ideas led to the **humanistic approach to therapy**, which focused on building up free will, self-esteem, and personal potential. Humanistic approaches to therapy draw on the philosophical perspective of personal responsibility in developing treatment techniques.

Gestalt therapy: A humanistic approach developed by Fritz Perls that seeks to make the client whole by focusing on present experience and the relationship between client and therapist.

German psychoanalyst Fritz Perls and colleagues (1951) developed **Gestalt therapy**, one example of the humanistic approach, which focused on the present (not the past or one's childhood). The goal was to integrate the dysfunctional, often anxious parts of a client's personality into a whole person. A phrase representing Gestalt philosophy is, "The whole is greater than the sum of its parts."

The most well-known Gestalt technique is the *empty chair role-playing* exercise. The client imagines and acts out a conversation with another person (or themselves) as if that person were sitting in the empty chair in front of the client. For example, a client might enact both sides of a marital argument. Taking the other person's point of view is facilitated by moving from one chair to another. The exercise encourages the client to see both someone else's perspective and how that person might be seeing them.

Another form of humanistic therapy was developed by American therapist Carl Rogers, who called his version **person-centered therapy** (Rogers, 1957). To be effective, Rogers said therapists must genuinely accept clients with *unconditional positive regard* that refuses to make negative judgments about a person's worth (Barry, 2002). In this way, clients trust their therapist and feel more comfortable being honest and sharing anything during sessions. Person-centered therapy's goal is self-actualization, maximizing the client's potential. Rogers emphasized genuine respect in sessions, and he is usually credited with the field's change from the word *patient* to the word *client* for anyone in therapy outside of a hospital setting (Kirschenbaum & Jourdan, 2005).

Person-centered therapy: A nonjudgmental, humanistic approach developed by Carl Rogers that relies on the therapist to convey unconditional positive regard for the client.

The guiding concept is *motivational interviewing*, creating conditions that make it easy for clients to change (Miller & Moyers, 2017; Miller & Rose, 2009). Rather than giving advice, the counselor seeks to use accurate empathy, warmth, and genuineness. For example, *skillful reflective listening* clarifies and amplifies the client's experience by facilitating accurate empathy (DiClemente & Velasquez, 2002). As a result, clients experience gradual therapeutic change.

Behavioral Therapies

Some versions of therapy focus on very specific problematic behaviors.

Carl Rogers leading group therapy.
Bettmann/Contributor/Bettmann/via Getty Images

If you have to fly for your job and you have a fear of flying, you might want a therapist to help you as efficiently as possible—and you might not really care about *why* the fear started in the first place. The same might be true if you have problematic behaviors in relationships; you might want to fix the behaviors without spending months (or years!) and hundreds (or thousands!) of dollars before you see improvements.

Rather than probe for root causes of psychological problems, **behavioral therapies** use techniques from learning principles to modify current behaviors so they are more adaptive (in other words, less problematic). In fact, some psychologists don't even consider behavioral therapies to be in the category of insight therapy at all and as a separate category all on their own. They rely on three familiar types of learning: *classical conditioning* (learning by association), *operant conditioning* (learning from consequences), and *social learning* (learning from observations).

Behavioral therapies: Techniques using learning principles to modify current behaviors so they are more adaptive (less problematic).

Classical Conditioning

Recall that classical conditioning is learning through association. For example, a person may develop agoraphobia, an intense and irrational fear of leaving the house, because the last time they left the house they got in a car accident. Now, they associate leaving the house and being in public (the conditioned stimulus) with fear, pain, and anxiety (the conditioned response).

Exposure therapies use classical conditioning to treat anxiety-related disorders such as obsessive-compulsive personality, posttraumatic stress disorder, and specific phobias like social phobias, fear of flying, and fear of heights. You could rename exposure therapy the "Nothing Bad Happened" or "Face Your Fears" therapy, because clients confront things to realize they aren't so bad after all. There are two kinds of exposure therapy.

Exposure therapies: Use of classical conditioning to treat disorders such as anxiety, specific phobias, and posttraumatic stress disorder.

The first approach is *systematic desensitization* (Wolpe, 1958; Wolpe & Lange, 1974/2017). It begins when the individual creates a personal *fear-avoidance hierarchy* by rank ordering the most disturbing situations related to, for example, fear of flying (shown in Figure 16.4). The therapist starts by using classical conditioning to train the individual in relaxation techniques during the least disturbing situation (looking at photos of planes).

FIGURE 16.4

A Fear Hierarchy for Flying

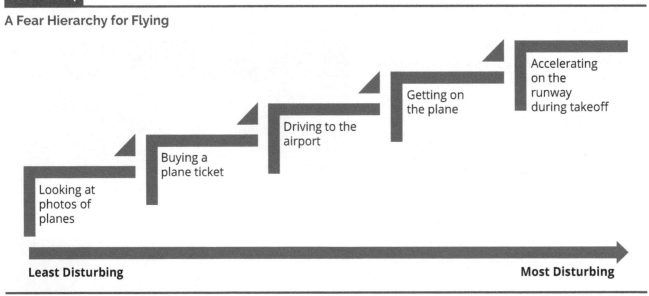

Looking at photos of planes

Buying a plane ticket

Driving to the airport

Getting on the plane

Accelerating on the runway during takeoff

Least Disturbing   **Most Disturbing**

When authentic relaxation has been conditioned at this least disturbing level, the therapist slowly moves up the hierarchy to something more anxiety provoking. They repeat the conditioning procedure to help the client feel relaxed when buying a plane ticket, driving to the airport, and so on. When conducted as a group therapy, the group may board a real plane parked in a hangar. The end goal, of course, is to experience feeling relaxed and comfortable while flying on a real airplane.

A second behavioral approach to treating phobias is *flooding* or *implosive therapy*. With this technique, a person confronts the most fear-inducing part of the hierarchy *first* and stays there for an extended time. If the person has a fear of heights, then the therapist takes them to the rooftop and they stay there until the individual makes the startling discovery that … nothing bad happened. To borrow a phrase from the famous speech by President Franklin Roosevelt, there was "nothing to fear but fear itself."

Which behavioral treatment for a phobia of spiders would you prefer: systematic desensitization, flooding, or virtual reality?

John K. Goodman/Moment Open/via Getty Images; iStock.com/izusek

Flooding seems like it would work a lot faster and more economically. But it can be a brutal therapy for someone truly terrified—and that can have consequences that can backfire. If the session goes badly, flooding may induce excessive anxiety resulting in long-lasting and harmful side effects (Boudewyns, 2012).

Like biomedical therapies, technology can help. Systematic desensitization and flooding may be accomplished more quickly—and perhaps more effectively—using virtual reality (Powers & Emmelcamp, 2008). Rather than standing on a rooftop, flying in an actual plane, or letting an actual spider crawl on you, you can simply do so virtually until you're ready for the real thing. For anxiety disorders, virtual reality appears to be equally effective to live treatment options (Opris et al., 2012).

Token economies give children small rewards, like gold stars, they can collect and then trade for larger rewards later.

iStock.com/Daisy-Daisy

Classical conditioning can also be used to reduce the frequency of undesirable behaviors, such as smoking. In *aversion therapy,* a therapist teaches their client that a behavior the client is trying to eliminate is now paired with an aversive (unpleasant) physiological response. For example, people struggling with alcohol addictions sometimes take a pill called Antabuse. If the client then chooses to drink, the chemical combination is a very violent reaction of sweating, heart palpitations, headache, painful vomiting, and more. The hope is that after only one or two experiences, this negative association will be so powerful, the client will avoid any more drinking.

Operant Conditioning

Thanks to operant conditioning, we know we're motivated by gaining rewards and avoiding punishments. That principle can be used in therapy to change maladaptive behaviors into healthier ones.

Applied behavior analysis (ABA) systematically rewards behaviors that improve social skills, reading, communication, and self-care skills (such as grooming, hygiene, and basic job skills; Alves et al., 2020). One example of ABA is a *token economy* that relies on systematic rewards to shape behaviors across a community. People in the community can save these small rewards and trade them for larger rewards later. It allows the therapists to provide immediate positive rewards for the behavior and usually allows the individuals earning the small rewards to choose a larger reward of personal interest, ensuring that they care about the goal and therefore have motivation to do the desired behavior.

Applied behavior analysis (ABA): Use of operant conditioning to systematically reduce maladaptive behaviors and increase adaptive behaviors.

Many elementary school teachers create token economies by rewarding appropriate behaviors with stickers that students later exchange for other rewards such as candy, extra recess, or a homework pass (Filcheck et al., 2004). Think of gold stars or smiley-faces your elementary school teachers used to give you. If you could save those up and trade them for rewards, you were in a token economy. Even the points you earn on assignments in college classes could be considered a token economy: You don't really care about the points themselves. You want to save them up, trade them for a grade, and hope that you can trade enough grades for a desired career at some point in the future (Doll et al., 2013).

These techniques show promise in a variety of contexts. Token economies help change behaviors in school settings, institutional homes, mental hospitals, and more (Glowacki et al., 2016; Kim et al., 2022). *Gamification,* encouraging behaviors through healthy competition and rewards, can increase motivation and learning rates in computer-mediated environments. Children with autism might play computer games in which they practice reading people's facial expressions and what emotions go with what faces; the reward might be simply "leveling up" with success (Goosen, 2022; Millslagle & Goodfriend, 2019).

Social Learning Therapies

Social learning began with Albert Bandura's observations of children learning aggression by noticing others behave aggressively. Children who witnessed an adult hitting a doll were likely to show aggression, too. Similar to what they observed in the adults' behaviors, the children kicked the doll, hit it with a mallet, and threw it in the air. They even came up with new ways to hurt the doll, such as throwing darts or aiming a toy gun at it. This kind of social imitation and learning begins early in life (DeMayo et al., 2019; Rogers et al., 2022).

Therapeutic modeling: A social learning therapy that helps people develop adaptive behaviors through observation and practice.

Social learning is the basis of **therapeutic modeling**, in which observing others with similar issues work through them or as successful role models serves as the basis for one's own recovery. For example, this can help people recovering from a stroke, experiencing speech difficulties, or controlling some body movements from Parkinson's disease and cerebral palsy.

Observational learning may also help treat obsessive-compulsive disorder and specific phobias (Oouchida et al., 2013). Watching someone else successfully overcome their fear of heights helps the viewer believe it can be done. Social learning therapies can also develop "softer" clinical skills. In marriage therapy, couples first observe and then practice communication skills and problem-solving strategies (Jacobsen & Margolin, 2019).

Cognitive and Cognitive Behavioral Therapies

Many people hope therapy will change their negative thought patterns and perspectives.

Cognitive therapy: Changing irrational and unhealthy thought patterns that cause someone problems.

Cognitive therapy focuses on changing irrational and unhealthy thought patterns that cause someone problems. Maybe you experience fear, depression, anxiety, low self-esteem, or problematic relationships because of unhealthy thoughts like "I'm not good enough" or "Nobody likes me." Cognitive therapy helps you identify these thoughts, points out how they are unrealistic, and helps you replace them with healthier ones. Table 16.4 gives examples of the negative cognitive profile of several common psychological disorders that might be addressed in therapy sessions.

TABLE 16.4

Cognitive Profile of Common Psychological Disorders

DISORDER	DYSFUNCTIONAL THINKING
Depression	Negative view of self, experience, or future
Mania	Inflated view of self and future
Anxiety disorders	Sense of physical or psychological danger
Panic disorder	Catastrophic interpretation of bodily/mental experiences
Phobias	Sense of danger in specific, avoidable situations
Paranoia	Attribution of bias to others
Obsessions	Repeated warning or doubts about safety
Compulsions	Rituals to ward off perceived threat
Suicidal behavior	Hopelessness and deficiencies in problem-solving
Anorexia nervosa	Fear of being fat
Hypochondriasis	Attribution of serious medical disorder

Source: Adapted from Beck and Weishaar (1989).

Many effective therapies (and therapists) combine techniques, and most counselors and therapists acknowledge that our thinking patterns affect our decisions and actions. So one of the most common approaches to psychotherapy today is called **cognitive behavioral therapy (CBT)**. It involves helping clients replace dysfunctional, irrational thoughts with healthier patterns that lead to adaptive behaviors (Ratnayake, 2022).

There are three reasons for the wide acceptance of these techniques. First, there is substantial scientific evidence that supports their effectiveness (discussed later). Second, they are relatively short-term, immediate techniques—which also means that they are relatively inexpensive and accessible to more people. Third, they specify practical behaviors that help clients take control of their own mental health. This pragmatic and empowering approach is very appealing to many people today.

While many psychologists have contributed to research and development regarding CBT, consider just two important people who influenced the field.

Cognitive behavioral therapy (CBT): Helps clients replace dysfunctional, irrational thoughts with healthier patterns that lead to adaptive behaviors.

Ellis's Therapy

For Albert Ellis, many unhealthy behaviors in life are driven by *irrational beliefs* (Ellis, 1991). His approach to cognitive behavioral therapy is summarized as the ABCDE model presented in Figure 16.5. An activating event (A) leads to automatic beliefs (B). Those beliefs have consequences (C) that either promote or discourage mental health. The therapist then actively disputes (D) irrational, harmful beliefs to produce a positive mental health effect (E) (David et al., 2005).

Beck's Therapy

For Aaron Beck, unhealthy and problematic mental processes were better described as *dysfunctional beliefs*, because sometimes irrational beliefs served an adaptive purpose (Beck & Weishaar, 1989). Beck specified that therapy should only target beliefs that were dysfunctional (otherwise, if they are irrational but not causing any harm—or even potentially helping in some cases—they could be left alone).

To address dysfunctional beliefs, clients should

- *Monitor* negative, automatic thoughts (cognitions).

- *Recognize* connections among cognition, affect (emotions), and behavior.

FIGURE 16.5

Albert Ellis's ABCDE Model of Cognitive Behavioral Therapy

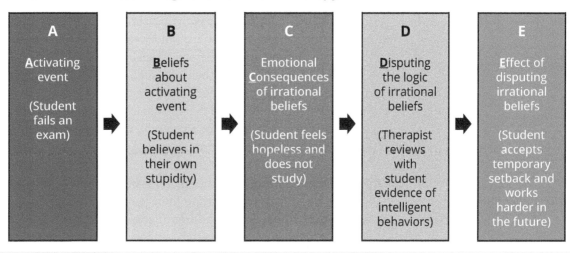

A	B	C	D	E
Activating event (Student fails an exam)	**B**eliefs about activating event (Student believes in their own stupidity)	Emotional **C**onsequences of irrational beliefs (Student feels hopeless and does not study)	**D**isputing the logic of irrational beliefs (Therapist reviews with student evidence of intelligent behaviors)	**E**ffect of disputing irrational beliefs (Student accepts temporary setback and works harder in the future)

- *Examine* the evidence for and against distorted automatic thoughts.

- *Substitute* more reality-oriented interpretations for biased cognitions.

- *Learn* to *identify* and *alter* beliefs that predispose them to distort their experiences.

The cognitive and behavioral techniques developed by Ellis and Beck are summarized in Table 16.5.

TABLE 16.5

Techniques in Cognitive Behavioral Therapy

COGNITIVE TECHNIQUES	BEHAVIORAL TECHNIQUES
Automatic thoughts are identified and tested by direct evidence or by logical analysis.	*Homework* gives patients the opportunity to apply cognitive principles between sessions.
Maladaptive assumptions are identified through active therapeutic interactions.	*Hypothesis testing* forms a personal, testable hypothesis such as "I am not a good student."
Decatastrophizing ("what if") helps clients emotionally prepare for feared consequences.	*Self-monitoring* records behaviors related to the hypothesis, to test its validity.
Reattribution techniques explore alternative causes of events.	*Behavioral rehearsal* practices skills needed to achieve therapeutic goals.
Redefining clarifies when a problem is—or is not—beyond the individual's control.	*Diversion* reduces negative thinking by adding activities, social contact, work, and play.
Decentering helps the individual understand that they are not the focus of everyone's attention.	*Activity scheduling* structures time and specifies goals that make it easier to evaluate outcomes.

Source: Adapted from Beck and Weishaar (1989).

Modern Insight Therapy Techniques: Art and Play

Dmytre Zarchuk was already artistically inclined when he arrived at Willard.

He was transferred to another facility when the mental hospital was closed, but his suitcase from Willard was discovered years later. It contained photos from his wedding, booklets in three languages, paper patterns, and wood carvings of animals. Zarchuk died in 2001 at the age of 84, and one of his paintings was later displayed in an American Psychiatric Association exhibit in Washington, D.C.

Zarchuk probably explored his artistic hobbies relatively independently. When he lived at Willard, it was long before psychologists would develop **art therapy**, which encourages reflection and personal insight by expressing difficult feelings or memories through artistic creation. Art therapy typically relies on painting, drawing, or sculpture to allow clients to explore their physical, mental, and emotional well-being. Sessions occur under the guidance of a professional trained in the use of art materials, psychological functioning, and therapeutic intervention (Brady et al., 2017).

Art therapists recognize that art can be a powerful way to communicate thoughts and feelings too difficult to put into words, especially for children (AATA, 2021; Edwards, 2014; Malchiodi, 2011). Most art therapists have master's degrees, ensuring they are prepared to help clients process the emotions involved in the artistic process.

Getting kids to talk and clearly describe their feelings is a challenge. Another option is **play therapy**, which allows children (usually less than 12 years old) to communicate difficult-to-express emotions through their desire to explore and engage

Art therapy: Encourages reflection and insight by expressing difficult feelings or memories through artistic creation (e.g., painting, drawing).

Play therapy: Enables children to express difficult-to-articulate feelings in their natural language of play.

with toys (Landreth, 2012). They might express family frustrations or fears while playing with dolls, for example. Children might experience play therapy under a variety of conditions, such as being observed through one-way glass, with other children, or with an adult using strategic interventions in hopes of discovering relevant psychological information.

What's the next insight therapy horizon? Technology. Telehealth now offers flexible and digital sessions to people at any time of day and in rural areas. Perhaps more controversially, *therapeutic chatbots* appear to be gaining acceptance: artificial intelligence–powered interactive apps you can carry on your phone for immediate feedback. Currently, they're most popular for screening and training, but they're also used for depression and autism (Bendig et al., 2019). Chatbots' effectiveness for therapy right now is limited by the software interface (Abd-Alrazaq et al., 2019; Bell et al., 2019; Jang et al., 2021). Clearly, technology is going to be part of the future's high demand for psychological services (Kazdin, 2015).

Techniques like play therapy are helpful when working with children.

iStock.com/PeopleImages

Effectiveness of Psychotherapy

Psychotherapy can be used for self-development and for treatment.

Freudian psychoanalysis is largely criticized today because it is time-consuming, is expensive, and often focuses on people's childhoods instead of current issues (Eagle, 2007). Many modern psychologists also believe Freudian theory had little basis in science-backed evidence. That said, there are significant differences between pretests and posttests in symptom levels for people in this form of therapy across many studies (for a meta-analysis, see de Maat et al., 2013).

Criticisms of psychodynamic therapy are similar to psychoanalysis, and reports of effectiveness vary. Again, though, it remains helpful for some people; it may be particularly beneficial for individuals who are highly communicative and verbal (Anestis et al., 2011; Sell et al., 2017; Thase, 2013).

Clients who want a particularly supportive environment respond well to humanistic and/or existential forms of psychotherapy that build on their empowerment and self-esteem (Cooper, 2007). A meta-analysis of 91 separate studies indicated that humanistic-existential therapy was particularly effective for helping people improve their relationships and decrease self-damaging activities (Elliott et al., 2021). However, these forms of treatment have been criticized for lacking specificity and precision.

Behavioral therapy works especially well for eliminating anxiety disorders, treating phobias and compulsions, and learning social skills to replace maladaptive behavior (e.g., Abdalla, 2023; Çiller et al., 2022; Weitlauf et al., 2014). Arguably, more than any other therapeutic approach, behavior therapy provides techniques that a variety of people can use in many different settings and contexts (schools, hospitals, private homes, and so on). Critics of behavior therapy believe that because it emphasizes changing external behavior, it ignores people's inner thoughts and anxieties—preventing them from needed insight for long-term change. Even so, evidence shows that behavioral treatments can produce changes in brain functioning, suggesting significant impacts (Schnell & Herpertz, 2007).

Cognitive approaches to therapy are successful in dealing with a broad range of psychological disorders, especially when sessions address issues not caused by biomedical factors. Most cognitive therapists are willing to incorporate eclectic techniques to serve their clients' needs (Beck & Rector, 2005; Bhar et al., 2008; Fresco, 2013). Critics of cognitive therapies note that helping people to think more rationally ignores the fact that life and people can sometimes be irrational—so changing one's assumptions to make them more logical may not always be helpful.

Cognitive behavioral therapy is the most popular approach to counseling today, along with a general eclectic perspective. The number of studies supporting the effectiveness of CBT is so numerous, it would take books and books to list them, so we chose just a few examples (Ahrens et al., 2023; Barlattani et al., 2023; Carey, 2021; Öst et al., 2023). A small minority of clients do have negative responses to CBT, although that's the case for all forms of therapy (Rozental & Powers, 2023).

Sage Vantage   Practice what you learn in **Knowledge Check 16.3**

GROUP THERAPY

? Have You Ever Wondered? 16.4 How did group and family therapies develop and what makes them effective?

Group therapy: A pragmatic, economical approach that uses group interactions to teach members more adaptive responses.

>> **LO 16.4**   **Compare and contrast kinds of group therapy.**

Willard State Mental Hospital often had the residents work together in groups.

They spent time together doing recreational and craft activities, maintaining the grounds and growing food together in a garden. It's unclear today how much these group times were meant as therapeutic or were simply the staff using the patients as free labor. Willard overall "offered very little that could be called mental health treatment during its first seventy-five years" (Penney & Stastny, 2009, p. 102). Fortunately, there is much more to group therapy now.

In **group therapy**, people with shared problems or interests talk about their needs, challenges, and successes. The first group therapies were created to be very pragmatic: They were meant to be accessible, inexpensive, and immediately helpful. One therapist can help multiple clients at the same time (Brabender et al., 2004). These benefits endure as group therapies are still very popular.

Group therapies developed as pragmatic, effective responses to a wide range of psychological needs.

iStock.com/SDI Productions

Common themes are substance abuse, other addictions (like gambling), grief, a particular illness, or personal growth. Sometimes the groups are led by a therapist or counselor, and sometimes not. Group therapy simultaneously provides support for the given problem and reduces stigma for it because everyone there shares and understands the issue and can affirm each other's experiences (Chen et al., 2020).

Groups vary greatly in terms of the theoretical approach they use; there are psychoanalytic groups, humanistic groups, and others. In some groups, a therapist directs and sets rules; in others, members of the group set their own agenda and everyone has equal status (Arlo, 2017).

Psychologists believe group therapy provides unique advantages to help participants heal, including (Yalom & Leszcz, 2020)

1. *installation of hope:* sharing and supporting others in the belief that their acute concerns will not be permanent;

2. *universality:* being with others in ways that communicate that they are not alone in their challenges;

3. *imparting information:* timely sharing (rather than advice giving) about how they have coped with challenges;

4. *altruism:* selflessness that shows interest and concern for others without expectation of something in return;

5. *development of socializing skills:* routine communications of support and participation; and

6. *learning from one another:* observing and imitating those who are further along in the process.

In successful groups, members stick together. We refer to the bonds among group members as *group cohesion,* which raises the collective self-esteem of the group and its individual members and does not depend on any particular theoretical approach (Burlingame et al., 2018; Marmarosh et al., 2005). Group cohesion can be a great experience, like being part of a great band or sports team.

The last part of this chapter covers a few specific kinds of group therapy and evaluates its effectiveness. As we conclude the chapter on therapy in general, you can measure your own readiness to start any form of psychological counseling in the *What's My Score?* feature.

WHAT'S MY SCORE?

Readiness for Therapy Questionnaire (RTQ)

Answer the questions using this scale:

1 = Strongly disagree

2 = Disagree

3 = Undecided

4 = Agree

5 = Strongly agree

___1.   It's essential that I work on my problems now because they affect my quality of life.

___2.   I like to do things the way I've always done them and I don't want to change.

___3.   If I'm skeptical about something, I'm not willing to try it.

___4.   Even if therapy becomes difficult, I will stick with it to the end.

___5.   In between sessions, I will dedicate time to regularly practice the things I learn in therapy.

___6.   I won't attend therapy if I have something more pressing or interesting planned.

Instructions: Reverse-score Items 2, 3, and 6, then add up your total. Higher scores indicate more readiness for therapy and change. ●

Source: Adapted from Ghomi et al. (2021).

Family and Couples Therapy

Family cohesion can be disrupted—or maybe it never existed.

In **family therapy**, a therapist meets with family members to observe and improve their interactions and dynamics. Unlike most group therapy settings, in which group members typically only interact during sessions, family members are part of a *system.* A system, in this context, means that everyone in the group affects everyone else in regular life, so their interactions outside of the therapy sessions must be accounted for. Systems exist in families, at work, in neighborhoods, and so on.

Family therapy: When a therapist meets with family members together, to observe and improve interactions and dynamics.

Within any system, members have evolved ways of interacting that assign social roles to each individual. One member act as a leader, making all the decisions; others might act as supporters, rebels, or bystanders. A given family might have established unhealthy roles or patterns of behavior (Conoley et al., 2015; Sori, 2012). These behaviors may express themselves as symptoms associated with mental illness, such as depression, or they may exacerbate a symptom. Because family therapy focuses on the family as a whole system of interacting "parts," no one person is seen as the "problem." The entire dynamic is addressed from a global perspective (Colapinto, 2019).

Dysfunctional family dynamics may also result in conflict or in members assuming undesirable roles. One sibling might be "the athlete" or "the brain" and another "the dumb one" or "the scapegoat" (APA, 2019; Brabender et al., 2004; Minuchin & Fishman, 1981). A family member who feels ignored may engage in negative behaviors simply to get attention. Social roles and labels matter, and therapy can find healthier ways for all members to support each other.

A family system has a life cycle of its own, displayed in Table 16.6 (Carter & McGoldrick, 1988). It's a good way to examine many experiences you will likely have in the future.

TABLE 16.6

The Family Life Cycle

STAGE IN LIFE	EMOTIONAL TRANSITION PROCESS	TASKS ESSENTIAL FOR DEVELOPMENTAL PROGRESS
Leaving home	Accepting emotional and financial responsibility for self	Differentiating self from the family of origin Developing adult-to-adult relationships with parents Developing intimate relationships Beginning a career and moving toward financial independence Establishing self in a community and society
Forming a couple	Committing to a new system	Selecting a partner and forming a long-term relationship Developing ways to live together Realigning couple's relationships with others to include partners
Families with young children	Accepting new members into the system	Adjusting couple system to make space for children Arranging child, housekeeping, and financial responsibilities Realigning relationships with families of origin to include parent and grandparenting roles Realigning family relationships with community and society to accommodate new family structure
Families with adolescents	Increasing flexibility of family boundaries to accommodate adolescents' independence and grandparents' constraints	Adjusting parent–child relationships to allow adolescents more autonomy Adjusting family relationships as couple accepts responsibility for aging parents Realigning family relationships with community and society to accommodate adolescents increasing autonomy and grandparents' increasing constraints
Launching children and moving into midlife	Accepting many exits from and entrances into the family system	Adjusting to living as a couple again Addressing couple's midlife issues and opportunities for new interests and projects Parents and grown children negotiating adult-to-adult relationships Adjusting to include in-laws and grandparents within the family circle Dealing with disabilities and death of couple's aging parents Realigning family relationships with community and society to accommodate new family structure and relationships

STAGE IN LIFE	EMOTIONAL TRANSITION PROCESS	TASKS ESSENTIAL FOR DEVELOPMENTAL PROGRESS
Families with parents in late middle age	Accepting new generational roles	Maintaining couple's functioning and interests, and exploring new family and social roles while coping with physiological decline
		Adjusting to children taking a more central role in family maintenance
		Making room for the wisdom and experience of the aging couple
		Supporting the older generation to live as independently as possible
		Realigning family relationships with community and society to accommodate new family structure and relationships
Families with parents nearing the end of life	Accepting the constraints of aging and the reality of death, and the completion of one cycle of life	Dealing with loss of partner, siblings, and peers
		Preparing for death with life review and integration
		Adjusting to reversal of roles where children care for parents
		Realigning family relationships with community and society to accommodate changing family relationships

Source: Adapted from Carter and McGoldrick (1988).

Couples therapy can be considered a form of group therapy involving intimate couples who want to address problems within their relationship. Alcohol abuse, jealousy, sexual issues, infidelity, gender roles, two-career families, divorce, remarriage, and blended families are issues often addressed in couples therapy (Suddeath et al., 2017). Communication is a common problem within intimate couples, and physical and emotional abuse is perceived as the most damaging concern (Doss et al., 2004; Whisman et al., 1997).

Family therapists use specific training and view families as a system.

iStock.com/Oleh Veres

Self-Help and Support Groups

A trained leader isn't always necessary.

Self-help and support groups can provide intimate knowledge, experience, and sympathy about particular needs. When people are new to caring for children, support groups can be very helpful (Cook et al., 2004; Strozier, 2012). Support groups for people with breast cancer know the best places to buy wigs, exchange recipes that minimize nausea, and share tips that might not occur to someone unfamiliar with that disease (Guidry et al., 1997). Technology has made access to support groups easier than ever with options like Zoom or Teams meetings from home for people from rural areas, people with mobility issues, without transportation, in hospice care, or during the COVID-19 pandemic (Armstrong & Alliance, 2019; Benson et al., 2020).

The most famous self-help groups are probably Alcoholics Anonymous (AA) and Narcotics Anonymous (NA). Studies on whether AA and NA are effective are famously controversial, with mixed results on whether they are any better than other programs (Kaskutas, 2009; Kelly et al., 2020; Zenmore et al., 2017). Part of the controversy is the required faith or religious nature of the "twelve steps" embedded in these programs, which will likely help some members and not help others (Dermatis & Galanter, 2016). Like all forms of therapy, many factors matter.

Stream to Boost Your Mood

Self-care is important.

You work hard, and everyone deserves a break sometimes. Psychotherapist Elaine Slater conducted a survey with participants on what TV shows and movies helped boost their mood, especially when they were feeling the effects of seasonal affective disorder (see Steber, 2019). She tried to identify choices that inspire hope, a character who overcomes challenges, and shows that include messages and themes about belonging to a community. Options also made the list if they were just fun to watch.

The shows and movies on her list (in no particular order, but limited to Netflix and Amazon Prime) were

- Legally Blonde
- Friends

- Queer Eye
- Pitch Perfect
- The Big Bang Theory
- Sex Education
- Modern Family
- The Good Place
- Dumplin
- Love and Other Drugs
- Catastrophe
- Grace and Frankie
- The Marvelous Mrs. Maisel
- Good Will Hunting
- About a Boy ●

Evaluating Group Therapy

There are several reasons to be hopeful about group therapies.

The long list of positive evaluations applies across psychological problems. Here are just a few examples:

- A cognitive-existential group therapy for depression appeared to increase life expectancy among people living in a nursing home (Khezri Moghadam et al., 2018).

- A group therapy treatment for depression worked well, even when several of the therapists were trainees or relatively inexperienced (McDermut et al., 2001).

- Group therapy for women experiencing postpartum depression had mostly positive results (Goodman & Santangelo, 2011).

- A meta-analysis of four studies showed family therapy helped adolescents who were having thoughts of suicide (Waraan et al., 2023).

There can be drawbacks to groups as well. Highly cohesive groups can use undue influence to control members' thoughts, feelings, and behaviors; they lack the one-on-one attention inherent in individual therapy, and especially shy or withdrawn individuals may not receive needed attention (DuBrow-Mashall & DuBrow-Marshall, 2015). Dropout rates from group therapies range from about 16% to 28% (Dixon & Linardon, 2020; Lewis et al., 2020; Ong et al., 2018), and they don't work for all problems.

There is no simple solution to mental illness. We need more research, more resources, and more curious minds to continue learning and providing better options and answers. ●

Learning Objectives Summary

16.1   How do professionals generally approach treatment?

>> **LO 16.1   Explain various career paths for mental health professionals and different models of therapy.**

There are many ways to enter the mental health professions, including psychiatrists, clinical and counseling psychologists, and a wide variety of certifications for those with master's degrees. Almost all professions require licenses, national exams, and certifications. The two general frameworks for thinking about mental health are the biopsychosocial model and the science-practitioner model. The transcultural approach is increasingly popular and important.

16.2   What are biomedical therapy options?

>> **LO 16.2   Identify various drugs and medical procedures used to improve mental health.**

Biomedical therapy is biologically based and relies on drugs and medical procedures to improve mental illness. Medical procedures to improve mental health include electroconvulsive therapy and body-based approaches, such as EMDR, biofeedback, meditation, and yoga. Different classes of drugs to treat improve mental health include mood stabilizers, antipsychotic drugs, antidepressants, anti-anxiety drugs, and stimulants.

16.3   What are the major approaches to talk therapies?

>> **LO 16.3   Compare and contrast different psychotherapy approaches.**

Another term for *psychotherapy* is *insight therapy.* Major approaches over time include psychoanalysis, psychodynamic, existential, humanistic, behavioral, cognitive, and cognitive behavioral. Many modern therapists are trained to use a variety of techniques depending on their clients' needs, which is called an eclectic approach.

16.4   How did group and family therapies develop and what makes them effective?

>> **LO 16.4   Compare and contrast kinds of group therapy.**

Group therapies emerged as pragmatic solutions; they are often less expensive, are faster, and can help many people at once. Various specific forms of group therapy include family therapy, couples therapy, and self-help support groups. All forms of therapy have various rates of effectiveness based on multiple factors; having many options available is ideal.

CRITICAL THINKING QUESTIONS

1. Choose two specific psychoactive drugs commonly prescribed for psychological disorders today. Using online resources, find information about (1) what kinds of symptoms they are intended to treat, (2) how they work chemically, and (3) what kinds of side effects they have. Analyze the advantages and disadvantages of each drug you have chosen to investigate.

2. The section on exercise noted that some studies find that it helps mental health, while other studies find that it can hurt; it depends on biopsychosocial factors, like what kind of exercise is done, a sense of self-control, and friendship groups. Identify at least one additional biological factor, psychological factor, and sociocultural factor that you think might relate to the positive or negative effects of exercise on mental health. Write out specific hypotheses for each of the three factors you've identified, then explain why you came up with your ideas.

3. Which of the various methods of therapy do you find the most personally appealing? If you were going to start therapy with a new mental health professional, what kind of therapy would you be most likely to try? Then, consider each of the following challenges and describe why you would recommend a particular form of therapy for each: substance abuse addiction, depression, and recovery from childhood trauma.

4. What do you think is the future of mental health therapies? Will telehealth, therapy phone apps, and virtual reality take off? How can technology be more creative at developing effective therapies? What are the benefits and potential drawbacks of thinking about culture in a therapy setting? What challenges are important but were not covered by this chapter?

5. Should mental health therapies be free to anyone requesting services, or is there some benefit if people have to pay? What should insurance cover, or not cover, and why? If federal taxes paid for everyone to have free access to social workers, mental health therapy, and psychoactive drugs to prevent symptoms of mental illness, do you think it would actually save the country money in the long run by preventing the costs of the negative effects of mental illness? Why or why not?

KEY TERMS

Applied behavior analysis (ABA), 519
Art therapy, 522
Behavioral therapies, 517
Biomedical theories of
    mental illness, 505
Cognitive behavioral therapy
    (CBT), 521
Cognitive therapy, 520
Dual instinct theory, 514
Eclectic approach, 513
Electroconvulsive therapy (ECT), 505
Existential therapy, 516
Exposure therapies, 517
Family therapy, 525

Gestalt therapy, 516
Group therapy, 524
Humanistic approach to therapy, 516
Insight therapies, 513
Person-centered therapy, 517
Placebo effect, 509
Play therapy, 522
Psychoanalysis, 514
Psychodynamic therapies, 515
Science-practitioner model, 501
Theory of humors, 504
Therapeutic modeling, 520
Transcultural approach, 504
Trephination, 504

GLOSSARY

Absolute threshold: The point at which a person correctly identifies a stimulus is present half (50%) of the time.

Acculturation stress: The mental and emotional challenges of adapting to a new culture.

Achievement motivation: The desire to work hard, master a skill or meet a goal, and do something useful with your life.

Acquisition: In classical conditioning, it's when the association between two stimuli is first happening or is being strengthened with repeated pairings.

Action potential: The sudden arrival of positive ions that reverses the charge of the cell from negative to positive, abiding by the all-or-nothing principle.

Adaptive categorization: The idea that stereotypes helped our ancestors survive through rapid categorization and labeling of people.

Addiction: Compulsive drug seeking and use, despite short- and long-term harmful effects on the user.

Agonists: Recreational drugs that mimic neurotransmitters' effects.

Algorithm: A step-by-step procedure that systematically attempts all possible solutions.

Altered consciousness: A state of consciousness that occurs any time you are outside of your typical mental state of being fully awake, aware, and alert.

American Psychological Association: The largest professional organization for psychologists in North America, including over 50 subdivisions or interest groups.

Amnesia: The inability to retrieve large amounts of information, often due to experiencing trauma.

Amygdala: A structure of the limbic system involved in fear responses.

Analysis of variance: Statistical analysis that compares the outcomes of three or more groups, to see if they are different from each other.

Androgen: A type of hormone that promotes development of male body characteristics.

ANOVA: See *analysis of variance*.

Antagonists: Recreational drugs that block neurotransmitters' effects.

Apgar scale: A quick assessment of a baby's health using five scales: appearance, pulse, grimace, activity, and respiration.

Applied behavior analysis (ABA): Use of operant conditioning to systematically reduce maladaptive behaviors and increase adaptive behaviors.

Archetypes: Common character types seen in myths and other stories across time and across cultures.

Archival studies: Research using materials originally created for some other purpose, like police records or social media posts.

Art therapy: Encourages reflection and insight by expressing difficult feelings or memories through artistic creation (e.g., painting, drawing).

Attitudes: Our judgments or evaluations of someone or something; they can be positive, negative, or mixed.

Autonomic nervous system: Part of the peripheral nervous system that controls involuntary muscles, organs, and glands that support processes such as breathing, heart rate, and digestion.

Availability heuristic: A guideline or mental shortcut that something must be common if examples easily come to mind.

Axon: Part of the neuron that the electrical impulse travels through.

Axon terminals: Small sacs at the end of the neuron that contain chemicals that communicate with other neurons.

Barnum effect: When people believe the results of tests or surveys are supposedly for them individually, but don't realize the "results" are so broad and vague they apply to everyone.

Behavioral genetics: The study of how genes and heredity affect individual behavior.

Behavioral therapies: Techniques using learning principles to modify current behaviors so they are more adaptive (less problematic).

Behaviorist approach: Studying psychology with the belief that the only truly scientific approach to the field is to measure only objective, observable behaviors in humans and other animals.

Benevolent discrimination: Beliefs that use positively framed stereotypes to discriminate.

Big 5 Model: A theory that there are five universally valid and reliable personality traits: openness to experience, conscientiousness, extraversion, agreeableness, and neuroticism.

Biological approach: Studying psychology in terms of how thoughts and behaviors are influenced by biological factors in the body (genes, hormones, etc.).

Biological approach to personality: Studying personality with the assumption at least part of our individual differences is due to our genetics, neural anatomy, and chemistry.

Biological preparedness: Our body's natural tendency to make some associations faster than others, especially when they are related to our biological needs.

Biomedical model: Views mental illness as biologically based and usually related to the brain.

Biomedical theories of mental illness: Focus mainly on biological or physiological explanations of mental illness, usually in the brain.

Biopsychosocial model: Mental health and illnesses come from interactions between biological, psychological, and sociocultural factors.

Bipolar disorder: Extreme mood swings, alternating between depression and mania, and shifts in someone's thinking and energy levels.

Birth order: Whether you're an only child or the oldest, youngest, or middle child among siblings, Adler believed where you fall in comparison to siblings affects your personality.

Blocking: When memory is temporarily inaccessible because other information obstructs retrieval.

Body shaming: Negative judgments, prejudice, and discrimination toward people based on their body size and shape, usually aimed at people labeled "fat" or overweight.

Bottom-up processing: Process by which we gather any physical sensations our sensory receptors register and form a conclusion based on our interpretation of the pieces.

Bronfenbrenner's bioecological model: The idea that our development is shaped by multiple interacting systems, such as our immediate environment and our larger culture.

Bystander effect: A specific form of diffusion of responsibility, when more witnesses to an emergency lead to a lower probability any of them will help.

Cannon–Bard theory of emotion: The idea that we simultaneously experience physiological arousal and emotional experiences.

Catastrophe: A stressor that occurs suddenly and typically affects many people at once.

Catharsis hypothesis: The idea that "venting" a little bit of anger or frustration is an effective way to reduce aggression.

Central nervous system: The brain and the spinal cord.

Cerebellum: A structure of the hindbrain that controls movement, balance, and coordination.

Cerebral asymmetry: The hypothesis that more brain activity in one hemisphere over the other predicts general patterns of emotion.

Change blindness: The failure to notice obvious variations in their environment.

Chunking: Combining and grouping smaller bits of information into larger pieces to increase memory capacity.

Circadian rhythm: The body's default schedule that regulates bodily functions such as wakefulness, hormone levels, and body temperature across a 24-hour cycle.

Cisgender people: People who agree with the sex assigned to them at birth and who don't wish to change it.

Classical conditioning: When a natural, physiological response to one stimulus is transferred to another because the two stimuli are associated with each other.

Cognition: The process by which we focus on ideas, remember them, and work with them, involving decision-making, problem-solving, language, perception, and memory.

Cognitive appraisal: A person's interpretation of a situation, how it will affect them, and if they have the resources to effectively manage.

Cognitive approach: Studying psychology with a focus on inner mental processes such as memory, decision-making, and thought structures.

Cognitive behavioral therapy (CBT): Helps clients replace dysfunctional, irrational thoughts with healthier patterns that lead to adaptive behaviors.

Cognitive dissonance: A feeling of anxiety or discomfort if our thoughts and feelings aren't in alignment.

Cognitive learning: Change in knowledge or understanding on a mental level.

Cognitive map: A mental representation of the layout of a given geographical region or area.

Cognitive therapy: Changing irrational and unhealthy thought patterns that cause someone problems.

Collectivistic cultures: Cultures centered on interdependence and promoting group goals over personal goals.

Comorbidity: Patterns in which two or more health conditions often occur at the same time in a single person.

Compassion fatigue: When caregivers become increasingly numb or indifferent to others' need for help.

Compulsions: Repetitive behaviors people feel driven to perform, often according to rigid rules.

Concepts: The groupings or categories you use to classify related images, ideas, information, events, or objects based on their shared similarities.

Conditioned response: The reaction caused by a conditioned stimulus, which occurs only after learning has happened.

Conditioned stimulus: An object, sound, smell, and so on in the environment that cause an unnatural reaction only after learning has happened.

Confounding variables: Other explanations for why the outcome of study happened, besides what the researcher is testing.

Consciousness: Your awareness of, and responsiveness to, your surroundings and mental processes.

Consistency bias: The tendency to overestimate how much our past attitudes and behaviors matched our current attitudes and behaviors, in a way that biases memory.

Construct: An abstract concept or variable within a research study.

Construct validity: The degree to which tests, surveys, and so on chosen for a study really measure what we think they're measuring.

Continuous schedule: When a reinforcement or punishment occurs every time a behavior occurs.

Control group: A neutral or baseline group in a study, used as a comparison to what is being tested.

Coping: Trying to control, reduce, or tolerate threats and challenges that lead to stress.

Correlation analysis: Statistical analyses testing whether two variables are systematically tied to each other.

Crystalized intelligence (gC): The ability to draw upon previous knowledge and experience.

Curiosity: The intrinsic motivation to seek information about something unusual or interesting when there is no other incentive beyond simply wanting to know.

Cyclothymic disorder: A milder version of bipolar disorder with more frequent but less intense mood swings.

Daily hassles: A source of stress involving irritating, frustrating, and distressing demands that people face on a day-to-day basis.

Dark triad: A cluster of three traits thought to predict manipulation of others and criminal behavior; the traits are Machiavellianism, narcissism, and psychopathy.

Decision-making: The process by which you assess alternatives and select the best option.

Defense mechanisms: According to Freud, these are mental tricks we play on ourselves to avoid anxiety from ideas, impulses, or experiences we don't want to admit to ourselves.

Dendrites: Thick treelike fibers that receive messages from other neurons.

Dependent variable: The measured outcome at the end of a study, to see how the groups in an experiment had different results.

Developmental psychology: A subfield focused on the study of how humans change and grow over our life span.

Diagnostic and Statistical Manual of Mental Disorders: A book that describes the categories and features of psychological disorders and assigns their numerical diagnostic codes.

Diffusion of responsibility: When the presence of others leads people to feel less personal responsibility for any given task, because they assume someone else will do it instead.

Discrimination: Unfair actions or behaviors based on stereotypes and/or prejudice.

Discrimination (classical conditioning): Responding only to a specific conditioned stimulus and not to other similar stimuli.

Display rules: Socially learned, culture-specific norms for expressing emotions.

Dissociative amnesia: Loss of memory for personal or autobiographical information.

Dissociative disorders: A loss of connection between thoughts, perceptions, emotions, and memories that disrupt one's sense of self.

Dissociative identity disorder: Experiencing two or more shifting but distinct personality states, accompanied by a disruption in the sense of self.

Distress: Stress from unpleasant experiences (e.g., getting fired from work) or that causes negative outcomes (like anxiety).

Drive reduction theory: The idea that motivation operates like a thermostat that's sensitive to physiological discomfort, and we're driven to behaviors that bring our body back to homeostasis.

Dual instinct theory: Freud's idea that humans have two contradictory impulses or drives: a death instinct and a life instinct.

Duchenne smile: Genuine, felt smiles that reach the eyes and produce "crow's feet" wrinkles.

Duping delight: Fake smiles or smirks given by liars who believe they are getting away with their deception.

Eating disorders: Mental illnesses in which someone's relationship with food causes them physical and psychological harm.

Eclectic approach: Therapy that integrates whatever theories, techniques, and approaches apply to meet the needs of a particular client.

Effort justification: When we convince ourselves that a great deal of effort must have been worthwhile.

Ego: According to Freud, it's the part of our mind that controls our id demands, operating on the reality principle (finding compromises).

Egoistic altruism: Helping others in exchange for some kind of personal benefit.

Elaborative rehearsal: Memorization technique that involves generating meaning as you repeat the information.

Electroconvulsive therapy (ECT): Careful delivery of electrical stimulation to the brain to induce seizures that alter neural pathways.

Emerging adulthood: The transition from adolescence to young adulthood, when we experiment with identity, relationships, and careers.

Emotion: A pattern of inner thoughts and feelings, accompanied by physiological responses and sometimes behavioral expression.

Emotional intelligence: The social ability to detect, appraise, and express appropriate emotions in yourself and others.

Emotion-focused coping: Seeking to reduce the negative emotional responses associated with stress.

Empathy: The tendency to feel what we perceive another person or animal is feeling.

Encoding: The process for getting memories into your brain.

Endocrine system: A complex network of glands and organs that release chemicals directly into the bloodstream to communicate messages that influence biological functioning *and* behavior.

Erikson's theory of identity development: The idea that we move through eight decisions or "crises" that form our self-concept and views of the world.

Estrogen: A type of hormone that promotes development of female body characteristics.

Eustress: Stress from pleasant experiences (e.g., getting promoted at work) or that causes positive outcomes (like motivation).

Existential therapy: Developed by Viktor Frankl; the idea that the search for personal meaning in life is a therapeutic motivation.

Experimental group: The group (or groups) in a study that experiences an intervention or change, to see how that change affects the participants.

Experiments: Research designs in which researchers compare two or more groups to see how groups differ by the end of the study.

Exposure therapies: Use of classical conditioning to treat disorders such as anxiety, specific phobias, and posttraumatic stress disorder.

External validity: The extent to which results of any single study could apply to other people or settings (see *generalizability*).

Extinction: In classical conditioning, it's when a conditioned response no longer occurs.

Extrinsic motivation: The desire to do something because the activity results in an external reward.

Facial feedback hypothesis: Proposes that our emotions can be influenced by our facial expressions (in other words, facial expressions can happen first, then emotions).

Factor analysis: A statistical technique that uses correlation to identify clusters of items on a test that make up a reliable group or subscale.

Family therapy: When a therapist meets with family members together, to observe and improve interactions and dynamics.

Femme porn: Erotic material designed to promote feminist values.

Feral children: Children who grew up without interaction or care from other people, usually through extreme neglect.

Five-Step Model of Helping: Suggests that helping will only occur in emergency situations if five criteria are met.

Fixed interval schedule: When reinforcement or punishment consistently occurs after a set period of time.

Fixed mindset: The view that intelligence is stable and unchangeable.

Fixed ratio schedule: When reinforcement or punishment consistently occurs after a set number of behaviors.

Fixed-role therapy: A counseling technique that encourages people to think and act in new ways, eventually changing their personality.

Flashback: An intrusive reexperiencing of an initial trauma.

Flow: A state that occurs when an individual becomes so fully immersed in an experience that everything else seems unimportant.

Fluid intelligence (gF): The ability to understand new information, solve novel problems, decipher abstract relationships, and use logical reasoning in unfamiliar environments.

Flynn effect: The finding that IQ scores at the societal level in industrialized nations have been steadily increasing over decades.

Frontal lobes: Lobes located in the front of the brain and are responsible for higher-order functions such as attention, planning, impulse control, problem solving, creativity, social interaction, and motor function.

Fully functioning: Carl Rogers's term for a strong, empowered person who is living authentically.

Functional fixedness: Only considering an object's most common use.

Functionalism: Studying psychology by focusing on the purpose of mental processes and behaviors.

Gender: A social construct regarding our sense of how masculine or feminine a person is.

Gender identity: Each person's internal and individual experience of gender, which may be the same as or different from their birth-assigned sex.

Gender schema theory: The idea that when children are raised, they're trained to fit into culturally expected gender norms.

General adaptation syndrome (GAS): The three-stage sequence of physiological reactions the body goes through when adapting to a stressor: alarm, resistance, and exhaustion.

Generalizable: A term describing studies in which the sample of participants represents the diversity in the larger population of interest.

Generalization: In classical conditioning, it's when a conditioned response occurs because of a new stimulus that is similar to a previously learned conditioned stimulus.

Generalized anxiety disorder (GAD): Nonspecific worries that are chronic, excessive, exaggerated, and extreme.

Gestalt therapy: A humanistic approach developed by Fritz Perls that seeks to make the client whole by focusing on present experience and the relationship between client and therapist.

Group therapy: A pragmatic, economical approach that uses group interactions to teach members more adaptive responses.

Growth mindset: The view that intelligence is malleable and a quality to cultivate.

Gustation: Our ability or sense of taste.

Happiness: An enduring state of mind consisting of joy, pleasure, contentment, and other positive emotions, plus the sense that one's life has meaning and value.

Hardiness: A set of personality characteristics that allow a person to thrive on stress instead of letting stress wear them down.

Hazing: A type of group initiation that requires humiliating or dangerous behaviors by new members.

Health psychology: The scientific study of behavioral and psychological characteristics that motivate people to prevent illness and embrace health promotion.

Heuristic: A guideline, mental shortcut, or "rule of thumb" designed to quicken thinking while making decisions.

Hippocampus: A structure of the limbic system responsible for formation and storage of memories.

Homeostasis: The steady state of healthy functioning and physiological balance in which all our biological needs are met.

Hormones: Chemical messengers released in the endocrine system.

Hostile-reactive aggression: Impulsive, emotion-based reactions to perceived threats.

Humanistic approach: Studying psychology by exploring how individuals can achieve their personal potential and positive self-esteem.

Humanistic approach to personality: Studying personality by focusing on self-concept, motivations, and personal potential.

Humanistic approach to therapy: Therapy techniques focused on building up individual free will, self-esteem, and personal potential.

Hypnosis: A state of consciousness in which a person is highly susceptible to suggestion.

Hypothalamic–pituitary–adrenocortical (HPA) axis: The interaction between the hypothalamus, pituitary gland, and adrenal glands; it plays a major role in linking stress to disease.

Hypothalamus: A structure of the brain that maintains homeostasis and regulates hunger, thirst, temperature, and sexual desires.

Hypothesis: A specific statement about the expected outcome of a study.

Id: According to Freud, it's our childlike, instinctive drives that operate on the pleasure principle (immediate gratification).

Inattentional blindness: The failure to detect unexpected objects, even though they are fully visible.

Incentive theory: The idea that motivation comes from external stimuli in the environment that push behaviors in certain directions, based on our goals.

Independent variable: A variable that's manipulated at the beginning of the study, creating groups that will be compared to each other.

Individualistic cultures: Cultures centered on independence and promoting personal goals over group goals.

Industrial/organizational psychology: A subfield focused on human dynamics in working environments (e.g., personnel selection and satisfaction, work motivation, and leadership).

Informational conformity: Behaving like others to perform "correct" behavior, to accomplish a task.

Initiation effect: The increased commitment people have toward a group after enduring a tough initiation to become a member.

Insight: Working out a solution to a problem simply by thinking it through.

Insight therapies: Counseling approaches that rely on talking about and understanding the self to improve mental health.

Instinct theory: The idea that certain behaviors are motivated by innate evolutionary impulses.

Instrumental-proactive aggression: Thoughtful or reason-based decisions to harm others to gain resources.

Intelligence: The ability to learn from experience, adapt to, and shape environments.

Intelligence quotient (IQ): The numeric representation of how a person's mental abilities compare to others of their same chronological age.

Interference: Information that gets in the way of other memories, either retroactively or proactively.

Internal validity: Confidence that a study was designed correctly and the results mean what we think they mean.

Intersectionality: The idea that our lived experience of disadvantage and privilege is based on our unique combination of demographics and social categories.

Intersex: Conditions in which either chromosomes or hormones are neither traditionally "male" or "female" (also called disorders of sex development, or DSDs).

Interval schedules: When reinforcement or punishment occurs based on how much time has passed (regardless of how many times the behavior was enacted).

Intrinsic motivation: The desire to do something because the activity itself is rewarding or enjoyable.

Introductory Psychology Initiative: The APA's suggested approach to teaching high-quality initial, general psychology courses for the college level.

Intuition: An instant sense of understanding that does not require reasoning.

James–Lange theory of emotion: Something in our environment causes our body to respond first; this physiological reaction is then interpreted as an emotion.

Kohlberg's theory of moral development: The idea that children move through three increasingly advanced stages of moral and ethical thinking.

Kübler-Ross stages of dying theory: The idea that when we know we're close to death, we move through five stages: denial, anger, bargaining, depression, and acceptance.

Language: A communication system consisting of symbols (usually words) and rules to systematically organize those symbols to convey information.

Latent content: A dream's underlying or hidden meaning. The true meaning behind what you see or experience.

Latent learning: Knowledge gained that can only be observed indirectly or later.

Law of effect: Thorndike's theory that in general, behaviors followed by rewards will be strengthened while behaviors followed by punishments will be weakened.

Lazarus cognitive–mediational theory of emotion: The idea that something in our environment triggers a cognitive appraisal or label, which leads to an emotional experience, which leads to a physiological response.

Learned helplessness: A state that occurs after someone has experienced a stressful situation repeatedly. They come to believe they are unable to control or change the situation, so they do not try—even when opportunities for change become available.

Learning: A relatively long-term change in behavior or physiological response, due to previous experiences.

Lifetime prevalence rate: The percentage of a population that has experienced any given psychological disorder at some point in their lifetime.

Light triad: A cluster of three traits thought to predict positive relationships and quality of life; the traits are Kantianism, humanism, and faith in humanity.

Linguistic determinism: The theory that the language you use dictates your thoughts.

Locus of control: Belief about whether your life is controlled by you (internal locus) or by outside factors (external locus).

Long-term memory: Information that you retain in a lasting and relatively permanent way.

Lucid dreaming: A dream in which you become aware that you're dreaming and can then control your actions within the dream.

Maintenance rehearsal: Memorization technique that involves purposeful verbal or mental repetition and review of material to encourage learning.

Major depressive disorder (MDD): A constant sense of despair and sadness, along with a loss of interest in most activities.

Manic episode: Abnormal and persistent elevated, expansive mood with increased goal-directed activity.

Manifest content: A dream's superficial content. What you actually see or experience in a dream.

Maslow's hierarchy of needs: The idea that our motivation is based on priorities in a set order: physiological needs, safety, belongingness, esteem, and finally personal growth (called self-actualization).

Meditation: The deliberate practice of focused attention that promotes greater awareness.

Medulla oblongata: A structure of the hindbrain that controls processes such as breathing, blood pressure, and heart rate.

Memory: The process by which we store images, information, events, and skills, then recall them later.

Mental health: A psychological state in which someone is aware of their own abilities, can cope with normal life stress, can work productively, and can contribute to their community.

Mental illness: Experiencing one or more psychological disorders.

Mental set: The reliance on a strategy that previously worked to solve a similar problem.

Mindfulness: A present-centered feeling achieved by being fully aware of and accepting of one's own thoughts, feelings, and bodily sensations.

Mirror self-recognition test: Marking an animal in a spot they cannot see without a mirror, to test if they recognize their reflection as themselves.

Misattribution of arousal: Misunderstanding our body's physiological response to one environmental cue in the environment and thinking it is in response to something else.

Misinformation effect: Occurs when overt suggestions, questions, or incorrect information alter an originally correct memory.

Misophonia: A neurological condition in which specific sounds cause intense emotional responses (usually rage, disgust, and/or anxiety).

Mnemonic: A memory aid or technique to help remember specific information, especially lists.

Modeling: Imitating the behaviors of others, especially when we see them getting rewards.

Mood disorders: A large, general category of emotional disorders that interfere with daily functioning.

Motivation: An inner drive that guides behavior toward achieving a specific goal; stages of motivation are initial arousal, direction, and behavioral persistence.

Myelin sheath: The coating of fat and protein surrounding axons that protects and speeds communications.

Naturalistic observation: Watching and recording people's behaviors where they would have happened anyway, but for research purposes.

Negative punishment: When a pleasant stimulus is removed from the environment, making behavior less likely in the future.

Negative reinforcement: When an unpleasant stimulus is removed from the environment, rewarding behavior and making it more likely in the future.

Negative symptoms: In schizophrenia, this refers to subtractions from "normal" experience (e.g., lessening of conversational skills or body movements).

Neurodiversity: The idea that there are a variety of ways people's brains process information, function, and lead to behaviors.

Neurons: Messenger cells that receive, integrate, and transmit information through the body.

Neuroplasticity: The brain's ability to adopt new functions, reorganize itself, or make new neural connections as a function of experience.

Neurotransmitters: Chemical substances that are stored in tiny synaptic sacs and allow neurons to communicate with each other throughout the body.

Neutral stimulus: An object, sound, smell, and so on in the environment that don't cause any particular reaction.

Normative conformity: Behaving like others to fit in and be socially accepted.

Obesity: Unhealthy and excessive body weight, measured by one's body mass index (BMI).

Observational learning: When we change our behavior because we assume we'll experience the same consequences we've seen others experience for their behaviors.

Obsessions: Persistent, unwanted thoughts and urges accompanied with anxiety.

Obsessive-compulsive disorder (OCD): The presence of extreme, intrusive, and maladaptive obsessions and/or compulsions.

Occipital lobes: Lobes located in the back of the brain and are responsible for processing visual information.

Olfaction: Our ability or sense of smell.

Open science: A movement to make science more transparent, cooperative, reproducible, and honest.

Operant conditioning: Learning to associate rewards or punishments with certain behaviors, based on what has followed that behavior in the past.

Operant conditioning chamber: A mechanical box in which animals can be trained using reinforcements and punishments.

Operationalization: Specifying how a construct will be defined and measured in a given study.

Opponent-process theory: A color vision theory that states that receptors are paired up so that they handle six main colors in three pairs (blue–yellow, red–green, black–white).

Overjustification effect: When intrinsic motivation is undermined by providing a reward for something that originally didn't need to be rewarded.

Overlearning: Continual studying or practicing of material to strengthen memory.

Parallel processing: The brain takes all the sensory information from your world and processes it simultaneously.

Parasympathetic division: Part of the autonomic nervous system that calms the body.

Parietal lobes: Lobes located at the top/back of the brain and are responsible for understanding body position and movement as well as sensation and perception of touch.

Partial schedule: Any schedule of consequence that is not continuous, meaning the consequence does not occur every time the behavior occurs.

Participant observation: A technique used during naturalistic observation where researchers covertly disguise themselves as people belonging in an environment.

Perception: How we recognize, interpret, and make sense of sensory information.

Perceptual illusion: These occur when we misread or misinterpret external physical stimuli.

Perceptual set: Our tendency to become predisposed to interpret and react to stimuli in a particular way.

Peripheral nervous system: All the nerve cells in the body outside the central nervous system.

Personal stressors: Ordinary life experiences that require a person to adjust or change in a significant way.

Personality: How individuals consistently differ from each other, in terms of their perspectives and behavioral tendencies, across time and place.

Personality disorder: A chronic way of thinking, feeling, and behaving that violates social norms and causes distress or problems in functioning.

Person-centered therapy: A nonjudgmental, humanistic approach developed by Carl Rogers that relies on the therapist to convey unconditional positive regard for the client.

Phrenology: The (now disproved) theory that bumps on your skull reveal things like your personality or intelligence.

Piaget's cognitive-developmental theory: The idea that our mental abilities improve steadily and grow in complexity through infancy to adolescence.

Placebo effect: When the mere expectation or a belief in a drug or other type of intervention produces the same effect as an authentic treatment.

Play therapy: Enables children to express difficult-to-articulate feelings in their natural language of play.

Pons: A structure of the hindbrain that transmits information to coordinate motor movements.

Positive psychology: The scientific study of human strengths, virtues, positive emotions, and achievements.

Positive punishment: When an unpleasant stimulus is added to the environment, making behavior less likely in the future.

Positive reinforcement: When a pleasant stimulus is added to the environment, rewarding behavior and making it more likely in the future.

Positive symptoms: In schizophrenia, this refers to additions to "normal" experience (e.g., hallucinations, delusions).

Postpartum depression: Feelings of sadness, exhaustion, and so on after women give birth due to rapid and extreme changes in their physiology, finances, social support, and more.

Posttraumatic stress disorder (PTSD): A range of persistent psychiatric symptoms, including anxiety, as a result of experiencing or witnessing a traumatic event.

Prejudice: An emotional judgment or evaluation of a group, either positive or negative.

Primary appraisals: Interpreting a situation as harmful or threatening, a challenge to overcome, benign, or irrelevant.

Primary sex characteristics: Our reproductive organs and genitals.

Problem-focused coping: Directly facing your troubles and trying to solve them.

Problem-solving: The mental processes we use to assess and figure out complex issues or work out unclear situations to reach a goal.

Projective tests: A technique used to assess personality or in counseling in which people interpret ambiguous images like inkblots or drawings of people in a certain setting.

Prosocial behavior: Behaviors that help others, regardless of one's motive for doing so.

Psychoactive drug: Any chemical compound that alters our consciousness, mood, or perception.

Psychoanalysis: Treatment based on insight regarding the conscious and unconscious human mind.

Psychodynamic approach: Studying psychology by focusing on how our mental processes are affected by childhood and by thoughts and fears (which we are often unaware of).

Psychodynamic approach to personality: Studying personality with the assumption we all have unconscious anxieties and wishes that affect us, often due to childhood experiences.

Psychodynamic therapies: Insight approaches that help clients connect past and present emotions to motivations, thoughts, and behaviors.

Psychological androgyny: The idea that some people will be high in both traditionally "masculine" and "feminine" traits at the same time.

Psychological disorders: Syndromes that are significant enough to cause a major disturbance in an individual's mental and social functioning.

Psychological model: Views mental illness as based on mental factors such as personality, perceptions, cognitions, relationships, and so on.

Psychology: The scientific study of mental processes (perceptions, thoughts, and feelings) and behaviors.

Psychoneuroimmunology: The study of the effects of psychological factors, such as stress and emotions, on the immune system.

Psychosexual stages of development: Freud's theory that we move through five biological and psychological stages from infancy to adulthood that affect our personality.

Psychosis: Occurs when someone loses touch with reality; the individual typically experiences hallucinations and delusions.

Punishment: Unpleasant consequences for behavior that make the behavior less likely to occur in the future.

Pure altruism: Helping others with no expectation of reward.

Quasi-experiments: Research designs that compare preexisting groups to see how or if they differ in response to something in the study.

Racism stress: The psychological distress associated with experiences of racism.

Random assignment: Putting participants into experimental groups by a purely chance method (like flipping a coin).

Random sampling: Method of choosing who will participate in a study from the larger group of interest in an unbiased, random way.

Ratio schedules: When reinforcement or punishment occurs based on how often a behavior has been performed (regardless of how long that takes).

Reactivity: When people change their behaviors because they realize they're being watched.

Realistic conflict theory: The idea that we use stereotypes and prejudice as an excuse to fight other groups when we want a specific limited resource.

Reasoning: The purposeful use of facts and available information to form coherent thoughts, draw conclusions, and make progress toward goals.

Recall: The ability to remember information without that information present.

Reciprocal determinism: The idea that our thoughts and behaviors (including our personality) are shaped by the environment and vice versa.

Recognition: The ability to remember information after seeing or experiencing it.

Refractory period: The brief span of time a neuron cannot fire immediately after an action potential.

Reinforcement: Rewards for behavior that make the behavior more likely to occur in the future.

Reliability: Whether the measures in a study are consistent over time and place.

REM: A period of sleep characterized by rapid eye movements, a still body, and an active brain, including dreaming.

Replication: Getting the same findings over and over again, with different participants, in different settings, and with different researchers.

Replication crisis: The controversial finding that only 40% of several classic psychology studies replicated years later.

Representativeness heuristic: A guideline or mental shortcut that depends on the best example of a category that comes to mind.

Resilience: Adapting well in the face of adversity or stress.

Resting potential: The state when a neuron is not transmitting information; positively charged sodium ions are outside of the cell and negatively charged potassium ions are largely contained inside.

Reticular formation: A network of nerves in the midbrain that regulates the sleep–wake cycle and plays a major role in alertness, fatigue, and motivation to perform various activities.

Retrieval: Recovering memories for use now.

Sarcasm: The use of ironic or satirical wit to convey an alternate or opposite meaning.

Scapegoating: The idea that prejudice occurs when we blame another group for our problems.

Scatterplot: A graph used to show a pattern between two continuous variables (a correlation).

Schachter–Singer theory of emotion: The idea that how we interpret both (a) our physiological arousal to something in our environment and (b) the situational context results in an emotional experience. Sometimes this idea is called "two-factor theory."

Schedules of consequence: How often or consistently a reinforcement or punishment occurs after behavior is displayed.

Schemas: Existing collections of thoughts or knowledge that help you make sense of new information.

Schizophrenia: A disorder that can lead to hallucinations, delusions, disorganized speech and thinking, and difficulty with routine self-care.

School psychology: A subfield focused on assessment and intervention for children and adolescents in educational environments.

Science-practitioner model: Application of scientific knowledge and reasoning to mental health problems.

Scientific method: A series of objective steps for empirically testing an idea.

Secondary appraisals: Evaluation of how to effectively manage a situation if deemed stressful.

Secondary sex characteristics: Physical aspects of the body that align with biological sex and emerge in puberty (such as breasts for girls and facial hair for boys).

Selective attention: Intentional focusing of consciousness toward a particular stimulus, while filtering out the rest.

Self-actualization: According to Maslow's hierarchy of needs, it's the exploration of individual growth and achievement of our best personal potential self.

Self-concept: The personal summary of who individuals believe they are, including qualities, relationships, group memberships, opinions, past actions, and more.

Self-determination theory: The idea that psychological motivation to become satisfied individuals comes from three needs: autonomy, competence, and relatedness.

Self-discrepancy theory: The idea that we maintain three simultaneous selves (actual, ideal, and ought), and when they don't align, we have negative emotional reactions.

Self-fulfilling prophecies: Expectations that affect how we're treated, such that the expectations are now more likely to come true.

Self-monitoring: Individuals' ability to strategically notice and adjust their own behavior in different situations.

Self-reference effect: The tendency to remember personally relevant information more easily.

Senescence: A gradual decline in physical health through old age.

Sensation: Process by which the body detects external physical stimuli and converts them into a format that the brain can use.

Sensory adaptation: When our sensory receptors become less receptive after repeated exposure.

Sensory deprivation: When our sensory receptors experience a lack of stimulation.

Sensory memory: The ability to briefly preserve physical features of sensory stimuli.

Serial position curve: The tendency to have better recall for items at the beginning and end of a list.

Sex: Biological chromosomes, hormones, internal reproductive systems, and genitals.

Sexting: Sending sexually explicit texts or photos to someone else.

Sexual hookups: Relatively brief sexual encounters between people not in a committed relationship.

Sexual scripts: Culture-based assumptions we make about what particular events will occur in sexual settings, and in what order.

Sexual spectrum: The idea that sex and gender are continuums, not distinct categorical groups with only two options.

Shape constancy: Our ability to perceive objects as maintaining their physical shape, despite changes in how they may temporarily appear.

Shaping: Learning through reinforcement over several, progressive stages.

Short-term memory: See *working memory.*

Signal detection theory: Our ability to detect a real or desired stimulus occurring amid other random or intervening stimuli.

Singlism: The prejudiced belief that single adults are less happy and mature than adults in intimate relationships.

Size constancy: Our ability to perceive objects as maintaining their physical size, regardless of their size on our retina.

Social anxiety disorder: An intense fear of social situations in which the person anticipates being negatively evaluated.

Social comparison theory: We make assessments about who we are by comparing how we think or act to those around us.

Social desirability: The tendency for participants to provide dishonest survey answers because they want to look good to the researchers or to themselves.

Social facilitation: When the presence of others makes someone's individual performance on a task better.

Social identity theory: The idea that self-concept is composed of two parts: a personal identity, which includes personality and physical traits, and a social identity, made up of our group memberships, relationships, and culture.

Social learning theory: The idea that we naturally observe others and imitate what they do (including prejudice).

Social loafing: When the presence of others makes someone reduce their individual effort on a task, making their performance worse.

Social psychology: A subfield focused on how people influence each other's thoughts, feelings, and behaviors.

Social support: A network of others who provide love and care.

Social-cognitive approach to personality: Studying personality by considering the interaction between perceptions of the world and the environment at any given time.

Sociocultural approach: Studying psychology by considering how social dynamics and culture interact in our everyday lives.

Sociocultural model: The view that social and cultural forces shape our view of mental health and illness.

Soma: The main body of a neuron cell.

Somatic nervous system: Part of the peripheral nervous system that controls voluntary movements through sensory and motor pathways.

Somatosensation: A collective term for all the processes involved in conveying sensory information about the body and how it interacts with its surroundings.

Source amnesia: Remembering information, but not being sure where or how you learned it.

Spacing effect: Learning information across multiple sessions throughout a longer time span improves long-term memory.

Specific phobia: A persistent, disabling fear that is excessive or unreasonable and associated with a specific object or situation that leads to personal distress and impaired functioning.

Spontaneous recovery: In classical conditioning, it's when a conditioned response returns after a period of extinction.

Sport psychology: A subfield focused on the dynamics of players and coaches in athletic environments.

Stereotype content model: The idea that two categories of perception (warmth and competence) interact to form four different types of prejudice about groups.

Stereotypes: Believing that people in a certain group are all basically the same.

Sternberg's triangular theory of love: The idea that relationships can vary on three factors: intimacy, passion, and commitment.

Stigma: Social disapproval and/or rejection based on stereotyped characteristics of a given group.

Stockholm syndrome: When hostages develop affection for their captors or agree with their captor's motives.

Storage: A way to retain memories over time.

Stress: How we react when we feel a situation is threatening or challenging.

Stressors: Stress-causing events or situations.

Structuralism: An early approach to psychology in which people attempted to break down sensation and perception experiences into their smaller parts.

Subjective age: How old we feel, psychologically (compared to our chronological age).

Subliminal messages: Messages "hidden" under the surface of conscious awareness, supposedly in attempts to change the receiver's attitudes or behavior.

Superego: According to Freud, it's our sense of ethics and wanting to please others based on cultural expectations, operating on the idealistic principle (being perfect).

Survey: Asking questions directly to participants in order to collection information.

Survival circuits: Finely tuned neural pathways tied to emotional experiences.

Sympathetic division: Part of the autonomic system that responds to stress and arouses the body for action in response to threats.

Synapse: The tiny gap where the axon of a presynaptic neuron communicates with the dendrite of a postsynaptic neuron.

Synesthesia: A neurological condition in which sensory stimulation from one sense (sound, smell, sight, touch, or taste) produces perceptions in a different sense.

Taste aversion: The tendency to avoid certain foods after they have been paired with feeling sick, even after a single occurrence.

Temperament: Broad, general patterns of behavior and mood that can be observed in people of all ages, including infants.

Temporal lobes: Lobes located right behind the ears and are responsible for processing auditory information.

Terror management theory: The idea that when we're reminded of our own mortality, we comfort ourselves by clinging to worldviews or relationships.

Testing effect: Improving long-term memory by practicing retrieval while learning new information.

Thalamus: The "triage" system of the brain that processes sensory information before sending it on to the part of the forebrain that deals with that kind of sensation.

Theory of humors: Ancient Greek idea that four fluids maintain a healthy body and mind: blood, yellow bile, phlegm, and black bile.

Therapeutic modeling: A social learning therapy that helps people develop adaptive behaviors through observation and practice.

Top-down processing: When we start with an idea of what an experience will entail, then use that larger concept to understand the elements.

Toxic masculinity: Sexist cultural prejudices that hurt opportunities for and well-being of men.

Trait approach to personality: A focus on which aspects of personality predict behavior regardless of circumstance, time, or culture; it includes the "Big 5" model.

Transcultural approach: Therapy that emphasizes greater awareness and sensitivity toward the role of culture in mental health.

Transduction: Process by which sensory receptor cells transform external stimuli into electrical impulses, then transmit signals to the brain via the nervous system.

Transgender people: People who disagree with the sex assigned to them at birth, who later change their identity to a different sex.

Trephination: The ancient practice of drilling a hole in the skull to release demons or unfriendly gods to restore mental health.

Trichromatic theory: Also known as the Young–Helmholtz theory, it suggests that different cones in the eye are responsible for recognizing different colors.

True experiments: Research designs that compare groups created by the researcher using random assignment.

t-**test:** Statistical analysis that compares the outcomes of two groups, to see if they are different from each other.

Two-factor theory of emotion: See *Schachter–Singer theory of emotion*.

Type A personality: Pattern of behaviors that are aggressive, competitive, hostile, short-tempered, time conscious, preoccupied with deadlines, unable to relax, and cynical; this pattern is positively correlated with heart disease.

Type B personality: Pattern of behaviors that are relaxed, easygoing, slow to anger, and less competitive; this pattern is negatively correlated with heart disease.

Type D personality: "Distressed" pattern of behaviors whereby a person experiences negative emotions over time and in different life situations; people who inhibit self-expression in social interactions.

Unconditioned response: The automatic, instinctive reaction caused by an unconditioned stimulus.

Unconditioned stimulus: An object, sound, smell, and so on in the environment that trigger an automatic, instinctive reaction.

Universality hypothesis: Proposes that all humans, regardless of culture, have the same facial expressions for core emotions and can recognize them in others.

Uplifts: Daily, positive, and joyful experiences.

Variable interval schedule: When reinforcement or punishment is based on time, but the exact amount of time can change.

Variable ratio schedule: When reinforcement or punishment is based on a number of behaviors, but the exact amount of behaviors can change.

Vygotsky's sociocultural theory: The idea that different cultures and societies train children to solve problems in different ways.

Wilhelm Wundt: Considered by many to be the founder of psychology as a separate scientific field of study.

Working memory: A system that actively processes different types of information such as ideas, images, and sounds from multiple sources.

REFERENCES

AATA. (2021). *Art therapy in action: Adolescents.* https://arttherapy .org/art-therapy-action/

Ab Rahman, Z., Kashim, M. I. A. M., Mohd Noor, A. Y., Saari, C. Z., Hasan, A. Z., Ridzuan, A. R., Ashaari, M. F., Kassim, S. B. M., & Norhayati Rafida, A. R. (2020). Critical review of religion in coping against the COVID-19 pandemic by former COVID-19 Muslim patients in Malaysia. *International Journal of Critical Reviews, 7*(5), 219–229. https://doi.org/10.31838/jcr.07.05.219

Abdalla, S. A. (2023). The effectiveness of behavioral therapy programs in improving social interaction for children with attention deficit hyperactivity disorder (ADHD) in kindergarten. *Halabja University Journal, 8*(1), 91–105. https://doi.org/ 10.32410/huj-10450

Abd-Alrazaq, A. A., Alajlani, M., Alalwan, A. A., Bewick, B. M., Gardner, P., & Househ, M. (2019). An overview of the features of chatbots in mental health: A scoping review. *International Journal of Medical Informatics, 132,* Article 103978. https://doi .org/10.1016/j.ijmedinf.2019.103978

Abdulan, I. M., Popescu, G., Maştaleru, A., Oancea, A., Costache, A. D., Cojocaru, D. C., Cumpăt, C.-M., Ciuntu, B. M., Rusu, B., & Leon, M. M. (2023). Winter holidays and their impact on eating behavior—A systematic review. *Nutrients, 15*(19), Article 4201. https://doi.org/10.3390/nu15194201

Acar, S., Chen, X., & Cayirdag, N. (2018). Schizophrenia and creativity: A meta-analytic review. *Schizophrenia Research, 195,* 23–31. https://doi.org/10.1016/j.schres.2017.08.036

Accardi, M. C., & Milling, L. S. (2009). The effectiveness of hypnosis for reducing procedure-related pain in children and adolescents: A comprehensive methodological review. *Journal of Behavioral Medicine, 32*(4), 328–339. https://doi.org/10.1007/ s10865-009-9207-6

Ackerley, R., Badre, G., & Olausson, H. (2015). Positive effects of a weighted blanket on insomnia. *Journal of Sleep Medicine & Disorders, 2*(3), 1–7.

Adam, K. C. S., Doss, M. K., Pabon, E., Vogel, E. K., & de Wit, H. (2020). Δ9-Tetrahydrocannabinol (THC) impairs visual working memory performance: A randomized crossover trial. *Neuropsychopharmacology, 45*(11), 1807–1816. https://doi .org/10.1038/s41386-020-0690-3

Adams, H. E., Wright, L. W., Jr., & Lohr, B. A. (1996). Is homophobia associated with homosexual arousal? *Journal of Abnormal Psychology, 105*(3), 440–445. https://doi.org/10.1037/0021-843X.105.3.440

Adams, N. B. (2004). Digital intelligence fostered by technology. *Journal of Technology Studies, 30*(2), 93–97.

Adan, A., Archer, S. N., Hidalgo, M. P., Di Milia, L., Natale, V., & Randler, C. (2012). Circadian typology: A comprehensive review. *Chronobiology International, 29*(9), 1153–1175. https://doi.org/10 .3109/07420528.2012.719971

Adelman, C. (1993). Kurt Lewin and the origins of action research. *Educational Action Research, 1*(1), 7–24. https://doi.org/ 10.1080/0965079930010102

Adelman, C. (2004). *The empirical curriculum: Changes in postsecondary course-taking, 1972–2000.* U.S. Department of Education.

Adepoju, O. E., Kim, L. H., & Starks, S. M. (2022). Hospital length of stay in patients with and without serious and persistent mental illness: Evidence of racial and ethnic differences. *Healthcare, 10*(6), Article 1128. https://doi.org/10.3390/healthcare10061128

Ader, R. (2020). Historical perspectives on psychoneuroimmunology. In H. Friedman, T. W. Klein, & A. L. Friedman (Eds.), *Psychoneuroimmunology, stress, and infection* (pp. 1–24). CRC Press. https://doi.org/10.1201/9780367812522

Adkins-Jackson, P. B., George, K. M., Besser, L. M., Hyun, J., Lamar, M., Hill-Jarrett, T. G., Bubu, O. M., Flatt, J. D., Heyn, P. C., Cicero, E. C., Kraal, A. Z., Zanwar, P. P., Peterson, R., Kim, B., Turner, R. W., II, Viswanathan, J., Kulick, E. R., Zuelsdorff, M., Stites, S. D., Renteria, M. A., . . . Babulal, G. (2023). The structural and social determinants of Alzheimer's disease related dementias. *Alzheimer's & Dementia, 19*(7), 3171–3185. https://doi.org/10.1002/alz.13027

Adler, A. (1928). Characteristics of the first, second and third child. *Children, 3*(5), 14–52.

Adler, S. (1977). Maslow's need hierarchy and the adjustment of immigrants. *International Migration Review, 11*(4), 444–451. https://doi.org/10.1177/019791839701100402

Adorjan, M., Christensen, T., Kelly, B., & Pawluch, D. (2012). Stockholm syndrome as vernacular resource. *The Sociological Quarterly, 53*(3), 454–474. https://doi.org/10.1111/j.1533-8525.2012.01241.x

Agronin, M. E. (2014). *Alzheimer disease and other dementias: A practical guide.* Lippincott Williams & Wilkins.

Ahad, A. A., Sanchez-Gonzalez, M., & Junquera, P. (2023). Understanding and addressing mental health stigma across cultures for improving psychiatric care: A narrative review. *Cureus, 15*(5), 1–8. https://doi.org/10.7759/cureus.39549

Ahmad, M., Silvera-Redondo, C., & Hamdan Rodriguez, M. (2010). Nondisjunction and chromosomal anomalies / La no disyunción y las anomalias cromosómicas. *Salud Uninorte, 26*(1), 117–133.

Aho, K. (2008). Medicalizing mental health: A phenomenological alternative. *Journal of Medical Humanities, 29*(4), 243–259. https://doi.org/10.1007/s10912-008-9065-1

Ahrens, J., Shao, R., Blackport, D., Macaluso, S., Viana, R., Teasell, R., & Mehta, S. (2023). Cognitive-behavioral therapy for managing depressive and anxiety symptoms after stroke: A systematic review and meta-analysis. *Topics in Stroke Rehabilitation, 30*(4), 368–383. https://doi.org/10.1080/1074935 7.2022.2049505

Aiello, J. R., & Douthitt, E. A. (2001). Social facilitation from Triplett to electronic performance monitoring. *Group Dynamics: Theory, Research, and Practice, 5*(3), 163–180. https://doi.org/ 10.1037/1089-2699.5.3.163

Ajzen, I. (1991). The theory of planned behavior. *Organizational Behavior and Human Decision Processes, 50*(2), 179–211. https:// doi.org/10.1016/0749-5978(91)90020-T

Akena, D., Kadama, P., Ashaba, S., Akello, C., Kwesiga, B., Rejani, L., Okello, J., Mwesiga, E. K., & Obuku, E. A. (2015). The association between depression, quality of life, and the health care expenditure of patients with diabetes mellitus in Uganda. *Journal of Affective Disorders, 174,* 7–12. https://doi .org/10.1016/j.jad.2014.11.019

Akhtar, S. (1989). Narcissistic personality disorder: Descriptive features and differential diagnosis. *Psychiatric Clinics of North America, 12*(3), 505–529. https://doi.org/10.1016/S0193-953X(18)30411-8

Alampay, L. P., Godwin, J., Lansford, J. E., Bombi, A. S., Bornstein, M. H., Chang, L., Deater-Deckard, K., Di Giunta, L., Dodge, K. A., Malone, P. S., Oburu, P., Pastorelli, C., Skinner, A. T., Sorbring, E., Tapanya, S., Uribe Tirado, L. M., Zelli, A., Al-Hassan, S. M., & Bacchini, D. (2017). Severity and justness do not moderate the relation between corporal punishment and negative child outcomes: A multicultural and longitudinal study. *International Journal of Behavioral Development, 41*(4), 491–502. https://doi.org/10.1177/0165025417697852

Alberini, C. M., & LeDoux, J. E. (2013). Memory reconsolidation. *Current Biology, 23*(17), R746–R750. https://doi.org/10.1016/j.cub.2013.06.046

Alberini, C. M., & Travaglia, A. (2017). Infantile amnesia: A critical period of learning to learn and remember. *The Journal of Neuroscience, 37*(24), 5783–5795. https://doi.org/10.1523/JNEUROSCI.0324-17.2017

Aldridge, J., Kilgo, J. L., & Jepkemboi, G. (2014). Four hidden matriarchs of psychoanalysis: The relationship of Lou von Salome, Karen Horney, Sabina Spielrein and Anna Freud to Sigmund Freud. *International Journal of Psychology and Counselling, 6*(4), 32–39. https://doi.org/10.5897/IJPC2014.0250

Alemán, J. O., Almandoz, J. P., Frias, J. P., & Galindo, R. J. (2023). Obesity among Latinx people in the United States: A review. *Obesity, 31*(2), 329–337. https://doi.org/10.1002/oby.23638

Alexander, L. A., Trinidad, D. R., Sakuma, K. L., Pokhrel, P., Herzog, T. A., Clanton, M. S., Moolchan, E. T., & Fagan, P. (2016). Why we must continue to investigate menthol's role in the African American smoking paradox. *Nicotine & Tobacco Research, 18*(Suppl. 1), S91–S101. https://doi.org/10.1093/ntr/ntv209

Allen-Collinson, J. (2009). A marked man: A case of female-perpetrated intimate partner abuse. *International Journal of Men's Health, 8*(1), 22–40. http://dx.doi.org/10.3149/jmh.0801.22

Allmann, A. E., Klein, D. N., & Kopala-Sibley, D. C. (2022). Bidirectional and transactional relationships between parenting styles and child symptoms of ADHD, ODD, depression, and anxiety over 6 years. *Development and Psychopathology, 34*(4), 1400–1411. https://doi.org/10.1017/S0954579421000201

Allport, F. H. (1955). *Theories of perception and the concept of structure.* Wiley.

Allport, G. W. (1935). Attitudes. In C. Murchison (Ed.), *Handbook of social psychology* (Vol. 2, pp. 798–844). Clark University Press.

Allport, G. W. (1954). *The nature of prejudice.* Addison.

Almadi, S. (2022). The meta-narrative of self-fulfilling prophecy in the different research areas. *Society and Economy, 44*(2), 251–269. https://doi.org/10.1556/204.2022.00001

AlMutairi, A. (2015). The effect of using brainstorming strategy in developing creative problem solving skills among male students in Kuwait: A field study on Saud Al-Kharji School in Kuwait City. *Journal of Education and Practice, 6*(3), 136–145.

Alonzo, R., Hussain, J., Stranges, S., & Anderson, K. K. (2021). Interplay between social media use, sleep quality, and mental health in youth: A systematic review. *Sleep Medicine Reviews, 56,* Article 101414. http://doi.org/10.1016/j.smrv.2020.101414

Alpert-Gillis, L. J., & Connell, J. P. (1989). Gender and sex-role influences on children's self-esteem. *Journal of Personality, 57*(1), 97–114. https://doi.org/10.1111/j.1467-6494.1989.tb00762.x

Altemus, M., Sarvaiya, N., & Epperson, C. N. (2014). Sex differences in anxiety and depression clinical perspectives. *Frontiers in Neuroendocrinology, 35*(3), 320–330. https://doi.org/10.1016/j.yfrne.2014.05.004

Alves, F. J., De Carvalho, E. A., Aguilar, J., De Brito, L. L., & Bastos, G. S. (2020). Applied behavior analysis for the treatment of autism: A systematic review of assistive technologies. *IEEE Access, 8,* 118664–118672. https://doi.org/10.1109/ACCESS.2020.3005296

Alwan, S. A. (2022). Role of the learned helplessness in diminishing the precision of jump shooting for young basketball players. *Revista Iberoamericana de Psicología del Ejercicio y El Deporte, 17*(3), 91–93.

Alzheimer's Association. (2018). *2018 Alzheimer's disease facts and figures.* https://www.alz.org/media/homeoffice/facts%20and%20figures/facts-and-figures.pdf

Amabile, T. M., & Pillemer, J. (2012). Perspectives on the social psychology of creativity. *Journal of Creative Behavior, 46*(1), 3–15. https://doi.org/10.1002/jocb.001

Amadi, K. U., Uwakwe, R., Odinka, P. C., Ndukuba, A. C., Muomah, C. R., & Ohaeri, J. U. (2016). Religion, coping and outcome in outpatients with depression or diabetes mellitus. *Acta Psychiatrica Scandinavica, 133*(6), 489–496. https://doi.org/10.1111/acps.12537

Amare, A. T., Thalamuthu, A., Schubert, K. O., Fullerton, J. M., Ahmed, M., Hartmann, S., Papiol, S., Heilbronner, U., Degenhardt, F., Tekola-Ayele, F., Hou, L., Hsu, Y., Shekhtman, T., Adli, M., Akula, N., Akiyama, K., Ardau, R., Arias, B., Aubry, J., Hasler, R., & Stamm, T. (2023). Association of polygenic score and the involvement of cholinergic and glutamatergic pathways with lithium treatment response in patients with bipolar disorder. *Molecular Psychiatry.* Advance online publication. https://doi.org/10.1038/s41380-023-02149-1

Amatriain-Fernández, S., Murillo-Rodríguez, E. S., Gronwald, T., Machado, S., & Budde, H. (2020). Benefits of physical activity and physical exercise in the time of pandemic. *Psychological Trauma: Theory, Research, Practice, and Policy, 12*(S1), S264–S266. https://doi.org/10.1037/tra0000643

American College Health Association. (2021). *American College Health Association–National College Health Assessment III: Undergraduate student reference group.*

American Medical Association. (2022). *Issue brief: Nation's drug-related overdose and death epidemic continues to worsen.* Advocacy Resource Center. https://www.ama-assn.org/system/files/issue-brief-increases-in-opioid-related-overdose.pdf

American Psychiatric Association (APA). (2022). *Diagnostic and statistical manual of mental disorders* (5th ed., text rev.).

American Psychological Association (APA). (2013). *APA guidelines for the undergraduate psychology major: Version 2.0.* https://www.apa.org/ed/precollege/about/psymajor-guidelines.pdf

American Psychological Association (APA). (2014). *Strengthening the common core of the introductory psychology course.* http://www.apa.org/ed/governance/bea/intro-psych-report.pdf

American Psychological Association (APA). (2017). *2017: APA member profiles.* http://www.apa.org/workforce/publications/17-member-profiles

American Psychological Association (APA). (2019, October 31). *Psychotherapy: Understanding group therapy.* https://www.apa.org/topics/psychotherapy/group-therapy

American Psychological Association (APA). (2021). Apology to people of color for APA's role in promoting, perpetuating, and failing to challenge racism, racial discrimination, and human hierarchy in U.S. https://www.apa.org/about/policy/racism-apology

American Psychological Association (APA). (2021a). *Licensure and practice.* https://www.apa.org/support/licensure

American Psychological Association (APA). (2021b). *Apology to people of color.* https://www.apa.org/about/policy/racism-apology

American Psychological Association (APA). (2022). *APA adopts racial equity action plan.* https://www.apa.org/news/press/releases/2022/08/racial-equity-action-plan

American Psychological Association (APA). (2023). APA guidelines for the undergraduate psychology major version 3.0: Empowering people to make a difference in their lives and communities. https://www.apa.org/about/policy/undergraduate-psychology-major.pdf

American Psychological Association. (2017). *Stress in America: The state of our nation.* https://www.apa.org/news/press/releases/stress/2017/state-nation.pdf

American School Counselor Association (ASCA). (2021). *The role of the school counselor.* https://www.schoolcounselor.org/

getmedia/ee8b2e1b-d021-4575-982c-c84402cb2cd2/Role-Statement.pdf

Amiel Castro, R. T., Ehlert, U., Dainese, S. M., Zimmerman, R., & Marca-Ghaemmaghami, L. (2020). Psychological predictors of gestational outcomes in second trimester pregnant women: Associations with daily uplifts. *Archives of Gynecology and Obstetrics, 301*, 869–874. https://doi.org/10.1007/s00404-020-05506-5

Amir, T. (1984). The Asch conformity effect: A study in Kuwait. *Social Behavior and Personality, 12*(2), 187–190. https://doi.org/10.2224/sbp.1984.12.2.187

Amit, A. M. L., Pepito, V. C. F., Sumpaico-Tanchanco, L., & Dayrit, M. M. (2022). COVID-19 vaccine brand hesitancy and other challenges to vaccination in the Philippines. *PLoS Global Public Health, 2*(1), e0000165. https://doi.org/10.1371/journal.pgph.0000165

Andersen, M., Nielbo, K. L., Schjoedt, U., Pfeiffer, T., Roepstorff, A., & Sørensen, J. (2019). Predictive minds in Ouija board sessions. *Phenomenology and the Cognitive Sciences, 18*, 577–588. https://doi.org/10.1007/s11097-018-9585-8

Anderson, C. A., & Bushman, B. J. (2023). Straw men, bogus claims, and misinformation about media violence: Reply to comment by Devilly et al. (2023). *Psychology of Popular Media, 12*(3), 373–382.

Anderson, C. A., & Dill, K. E. (2000). Video games and aggressive thoughts, feelings, and behavior in the laboratory and in life. *Journal of Personality and Social Psychology, 78*(4), 772–790. https://doi.org/10.1037/0022-3514.78.4.772

Anderson, C. A., Lazard, D. S., & Hartley, D. E. (2017). Plasticity in bilateral superior temporal cortex: Effects of deafness and cochlear implantation on auditory and visual speech processing. *Hearing Research, 343*, 138–149. https://doi.org/10.1016/j.heares.2016.07.013

Anderson, C. A., Shibuya, A., Ihori, N., Swing, E. L., Bushman, B. J., Sakamoto, A., Rothstein, H. R., & Saleem, M. (2010). Violent video game effects on aggression, empathy, and prosocial behavior in Eastern and Western countries. *Psychological Bulletin, 136*(2), 151–173. https://psycnet.apa.org/doi/10.1037/a0018251

Anderson, C. A., Suzuki, K., Swing, E. L., Groves, C. L., Gentile, D. A., Prot, S., Lam, C. P., Sakamoto, A., Horiuchi, Y., Krahe, B., Jelic, M., Liuqing, W., Toma, R., Warburton, W. A., Zhang, X-M., Tajima, S., Qing, F., & Petrescu, P. (2017). Media violence and other aggression risk factors in seven nations. *Personality and Social Psychology Bulletin, 43*(7), 986–998. https://doi.org/10.1177/0146167217703064

Anderson, E. D. (2009). The maintenance of masculinity among the stakeholders of sport. *Sport Management Review, 12*(1), 3–14. https://doi.org/10.1016/j.smr.2008.09.003

Anderson, J. A., Hawrylewicz, K., & Grundy, J. G. (2020). Does bilingualism protect against dementia? A meta-analysis. *Psychonomic Bulletin & Review, 27*(5), 952–965. https://doi.org/10.3758/s13423-020-01736-5

Anderson, N. D., & Craik, F. I. (2017). 50 years of cognitive aging theory. *The Journals of Gerontology: Series B, 72*(1), 1–6. https://doi.org/10.1093/geronb/gbw108

Anderson, S. J. (2011). Marketing of menthol cigarettes and consumer perceptions: A review of tobacco industry documents. *Tobacco Control, 20*(Suppl. 2), ii20–ii28. http://doi.org/10.1136/tc.2010.041939

Andre, C. J., Lovallo, V., & Spencer, R. (2021). The effects of bed sharing on sleep: From partners to pets. *Sleep Health.* Advance online publication. https://doi.org/10.1016/j.sleh.2020.11.011

Anemone, R. L. (2019). *Race and human diversity: A biocultural approach.* Routledge.

Anestis, M. D., Anestis, J. C., & Lilienfeld, S. O. (2011). When it comes to evaluating psychodynamic therapy, the devil is in the details. *American Psychologist, 66*(2), 149–151. https://psycnet.apa.org/doi/10.1037/a0021190

Ang, S., Rodgers, J., & Wänström, L. (2010). The Flynn effect within subgroups in the U.S.: Gender, race, income, education, and urbanization differences in the NLSY-Children Data. *Intelligence, 38*(4), 367–384. https://doi.org/10.1016/j.intell.2010.05.004

Angraini, D. I., Izzah, A. N., Nisa, K., & Zuraida, R. (2023). Factors influencing the selection of healthy and unhealthy diet behavior in adolescent girls in Bandar Lampung. *International Journal of Advanced Health Science and Technology, 3*(2), 72–78. https://doi.org/10.35882/ijahst.v3i2.216

Annati, A., & Ramsey, L. R. (2022). Lesbian perceptions of stereotypical and sexualized media portrayals. *Sexuality & Culture, 26*(1), 312–338. https://doi.org/10.1007/s12119-021-09892-z

Ano, G. G., & Vasconcelles, E. B. (2005). Religious coping and psychological adjustment to stress: A meta-analysis. *Journal of Clinical Psychology, 61*(4), 461–480. https://doi.org/10.1002/jclp.20049

Antheunis, M. L., & Schouten, A. P. (2011). The effects of other-generated and system-generated cues on adolescents' perceived attractiveness on social network sites. *Journal of Computer-Mediated Communication, 16*(3), 391–406. https://doi.org/10.1111/j.1083-6101.2011.01545.x

Antill, J. K., & Cunningham, J. D. (1979). Self-esteem as a function of masculinity in both sexes. *Journal of Consulting and Clinical Psychology, 47*(4), 783–785. https://doi.org/10.1037/0022-006X.47.4.783

Apgar, V. (1952). A proposal for a new method of evaluation of the newborn. *Classic Papers in Critical Care, 32*, 260–267. https://doi.org/10.1007/978-1-84800-145-9

Apple, D. M., Fonseca, R. S., & Kokovay, E. (2017). The role of adult neurogenesis in psychiatric and cognitive disorders. *Brain Research, 1655*, 270–276. https://doi.org/10.1016/j.brainres.2016.01.023

Arakaki, F. H., Tufik, S., & Andersen, M. L. (2019). Naps and exercise: Reinforcing a range of benefits for elderly health. *Chronobiology International, 36*(7), 886–887. https://doi.org/10.1080/07420528.2019.1602050

Arancibia-Cárcamo, I. L., Ford, M. C., Cossell, L., Ishida, K., Tohyama, K., & Attwell, D. (2017). Node of Ranvier length as a potential regulator of myelinated axon conduction speed. *Elife, 6*, 1–6. https://doi.org/10.7554/eLife.23329

Arbinaga, F., Tornero-Quiñones, I., & Fernández-Ozcorta, E. (2018). Sleeping position, expression of anger and subjective sleep quality in university students. *Sleep and Hypnosis, 20*(4), 267–274. https://dx.doi.org/10.5350/Sleep.Hypn.2018.20.0161

Arent, S. M., Walker, A. J., & Arent, M. A. (2020). *Handbook of sport psychology* (4th ed.). John Wiley.

Arlo, C. (2017). Group therapy and dialectical behavior therapy: An integrative response to a clinical case. *International Journal of Group Psychotherapy, 67*(Suppl. 1), S13–S23. https://doi.org/10.1080/00207284.2016.1218773

Armstrong, M. J., & Alliance, S. (2019). Virtual support groups for informal caregivers of individuals with dementia: A scoping review. *Alzheimer Disease & Associated Disorders, 33*(4), 362–369. https://doi.org/10.1097/WAD.0000000000000349

Arnett, J. J. (1996). Sensation seeking, aggressiveness, and adolescent reckless behavior. *Personality and Individual Differences, 20*(6), 693–702. https://doi.org/10.1016/0191-8869(96)00027-X

Arnett, J. J. (2009). The neglected 95%, a challenge to psychology's philosophy of science. *American Psychologist, 64*(6), 571–574. https://doi.org/10.1037/a0016723

Arnocky, S., & Vaillancourt, T. (2014). Sex differences in response to victimization by an intimate partner: More stigmatization and less help-seeking among males. *Journal of Aggression, Maltreatment & Trauma, 23*(7), 705–724. https://doi.org/10.1080/10926771.2014.933465

Arnulf, J. K., Nimon, K., Larsen, K. R., Hovland, C. V., & Arnesen, M. (2020). The priest, the sex worker, and the CEO: Measuring motivation by job type. *Frontiers in Psychology*, *11*, Article 1321. https://doi.org/10.3389/fpsyg.2020.01321

Aronson, E. (2002). Building empathy, compassion, and achievement in the jigsaw classroom. In J. Aronson (Ed.), *Improving academic achievement* (pp. 209–225). Academic Press. https://doi.org/10.1016/B978-012064455-1/50013-0

Aronson, E., & Mills, J. (1959). The effect of severity of initiation on liking for a group. *Journal of Abnormal and Social Psychology*, *59*(2), 177–181. https://doi.org/10.1037/h0047195

Arriaga, P., Adrião, J., Madeira, F., Cavaleiro, I., Maia e Silva, A., Barahona, I., & Esteves, F. (2015). A "dry eye" for victims of violence: Effects of playing a violent video game on pupillary dilation to victims and on aggressive behavior. *Psychology of Violence*, *5*(2), 199–208. https://psycnet.apa.org/doi/10.1037/a0037260

Arriaga, X. B., & Agnew, C. R. (2001). Being committed: Affective, cognitive, and conative components of relationship commitment. *Personality and Social Psychology Bulletin*, *27*(9), 1190–1203. https://doi.org/10.1177/0146167201279011

Arthur, W., Jr., & Graziano, W. G. (1996). The five-factor model, conscientiousness, and driving accident involvement. *Journal of Personality*, *64*(3), 593–618. https://doi.org/10.1111/j.1467-6494.1996.tb00523.x

Asante, E. A., & Affum-Osei, E. (2019). Entrepreneurship as a career choice: The impact of locus of control on aspiring entrepreneurs' opportunity recognition. *Journal of Business Research*, *98*, 227–235. https://doi.org/10.1016/j.jbusres.2019.02.006

Asch, S. E. (1951). Effects of group pressure upon the modification and distortion of judgments. In H. Guetzkow & H. Guetzkow (Eds.), *Groups, leadership and men; research in human relations* (pp. 177–190). Carnegie Press.

Asch, S. E. (1952). Effects of group pressure on the modification and distortion of judgments. In G. E. Swanson, T. M. Newcomb, & E. L. Hartley (Eds.), *Readings in social psychology* (2nd ed.). Holt.

Asch, S. E. (1955). Opinions and social pressure. *Scientific American*, *193*(5), 33–35. https://doi.org/10.1038/scientificamerican1155-31

Asch, S. E. (1956). Studies of independence and conformity: I. A minority of one against a unanimous majority. *Psychological Monographs: General and Applied*, *70*(9), 1–70. https://doi.org/10.1037/h0093718

Asendorpf, J. B., & van Aken, M. A. (1999). Resilient, overcontrolled, and undercontrolled personality prototypes in childhood: Replicability, predictive power, and the trait-type issue. *Journal of Personality and Social Psychology*, *77*(4), 815–832. https://doi.org/10.1037/0022-3514.77.4.815

Ashford, M. (Creator, Writer). (2013–2016). *Masters of sex* [Television series]. Showtime.

Ashmore, R. D. (1990). Sex, gender, and the individual. In L. A. Pervin (Ed.), *Handbook of personality theory and research* (pp. 486–525). Guilford.

Atherton, O. E., Grijalva, E., Roberts, B. W., & Robins, R. W. (2021). Stability and change in personality traits and major life goals from college to midlife. *Personality and Social Psychology Bulletin*, *47*(5), 841–858. https://doi.org/10.1177/0146167220949362

Atkinson, R. C., & Shiffrin, R. M. (1968). Human memory: A proposed system and its control processes. In K. W. Spence & J. T. Spence (Eds.), *The psychology of learning and motivation* (Vol. 2, pp. 89–195). Academic Press.

Atroszko, P. A., Demetrovics, Z., & Griffiths, M. D. (2020). Work addiction, obsessive-compulsive personality disorder, burn-out, and global burden of disease: Implications from the ICD-11. *International Journal of Environmental Research and Public Health*, *17*(2), Article 660. https://doi.org/10.3390/ijerph17020660

Aulinas, A. (2019). Physiology of the pineal gland and melatonin. *Endotext* [online]. https://europepmc.org/article/NBK/nbk550972

Avezum, MDM de Melo, Altafim, E. R. P., & Linhares, M. B. M. (2022). Spanking and corporal punishment parenting practices and child development: A systematic review. *Trauma, Violence, & Abuse*, *24*(5), 3094–3111. https://doi.org/10.1177/15248380221124243

Axtell, R. E. (2007). *Essentials do's and taboos: The complete guide to international business and leisure time travel*. Wiley.

Ayorech, Z., Baldwin, J. R., Pingault, J. B., Rimfeld, K., & Plomin, R. (2023). Gene-environment correlations and genetic confounding underlying the association between media use and mental health. *Scientific Reports*, *13*(1), Article 1030. https://doi.org/10.1038/s41598-022-25374-0

Baas, M., De Dreu, C. K. W., & Nijstad, B. A. (2008). A meta-analysis of 25 years of mood-creativity research: Hedonic tone, activation, or regulatory focus? *Psychological Bulletin*, *134*(6), 779–806. https://doi.org/10.1037/a0012815

Babula, M. (2023). The association of prayer frequency and Maslow's hierarchy of needs: A comparative study of the USA, India and Turkey. *Journal of Religion and Health*, *62*(3), 1832–1852. https://doi.org/10.1007/s10943-022-01649-8

Bache, R. M. (1895). Reaction time with reference to race. *Psychological Review*, *2*(5), 475–486. https://doi.org/10.1037/h0070013

Bachman, J. G., & O'Malley, P. M. (1986). Self-concepts, self-esteem, and educational experiences: The frog pond revisited (again). *Journal of Personality and Social Psychology*, *50*(1), 35–46. https://doi.org/10.1037/0022-3514.50.1.35

Backstrom, L., Armstrong, E. A., & Puentes, J. (2012). Women's negotiation of cunnilingus in college hookups and relationships. *Journal of Sex Research*, *49*(1), 1–12. https://doi.org/10.1080/00224499.2011.585523

Baddeley A. D., & Wilson, B. A. (2002). Prose recall and amnesia: Implications for the structure of working memory. *Neuropsychologia*, *40*(10), 1737–1743. https://doi.org/10.1016/S0028-3932(01)00146-4

Baddeley, A. D. (2002). Is working memory still working? *European Psychologist*, *7*(2), 85–97. https://doi.org/10.1027/1016-9040.7.2.85

Baddeley, A. D., & Hitch, G. J. (1974). Working memory. In G. A. Bower (Ed.), *The psychology of learning and motivation: Advances in research and theory* (Vol. 8, pp. 47–89). Academic Press.

Baddeley, A. D., & Logie, R. H. (1999). Working memory: The multiple-component model. In A. Miyake & P. Shah (Eds.), *Models of working memory: Mechanisms of active maintenance and executive control* (pp. 28–61). Cambridge University Press.

Baer, R. A., Smith, G. T., & Allen, K. B. (2004). Assessment of mindfulness by self-report: The Kentucky Inventory of Mindfulness Skills. *Assessment*, *11*(3), 191–206. https://doi.org/10.1177/1073191104268029

Bagheri, L., Safouraei, S., & Safouraei, M. M. (2021). The resilience prediction of patients with corona disease based on life expectancy, religious coping style, spiritual intelligence and self-compassion. *Journal of Quran and Medicine*, *5*(4), 1–10.

Bajpai, S., Upadhayay, A. D., Banerjee, J., Chakrawarthy, A., Chatterjee, P., Lee, J., & Dey, A. B. (2022). Discrepancy in fluid and crystallized intelligence: An early cognitive marker of dementia from the LASI-DAD cohort. *Dementia and Geriatric Cognitive Disorders Extra*, *12*(1), 51–59. https://doi.org/10.1159/000520879

Banaji, M. R., Bhaskar, R., & Brownstein, M. (2015). When bias is implicit, how might we think about repairing harm? *Current Opinion in Psychology*, *6*, 183–188. https://doi.org/10.1016/j.copsyc.2015.08.017

Bandura, A. (1965). Influence of models' reinforcement contingencies on the acquisition of imitative responses. *Journal of Personality and Social Psychology, 1*(6), 589–595. https://psycnet.apa.org/doi/10.1037/h0022070

Bandura, A. (1977). *Social learning theory*. General Learning Press.

Bandura, A. (1986). *Social foundations of thought and action: A social-cognitive theory*. Prentice-Hall.

Bandura, A. (1997). *Self-efficacy: The exercise of control*. Freeman.

Bandura, A. (2001). Social cognitive theory: An agentic perspective. *Annual Review of Psychology, 52*, 1–26. https://doi.org/10.1146/annurev.psych.52.1.1

Bandura, A. (2011). But what about that gigantic elephant in the room? In A. Robert (Ed.), *Most underappreciated 50 prominent social psychologists describe their most unloved work* (pp. 51–59). Oxford University Press.

Bandura, A., & Menlove, F. L. (1968). Factors determining vicarious extinction of avoidance behavior through symbolic modeling. *Journal of Personality and Social Psychology, 8*(2, Pt. 1), 99–108. https://psycnet.apa.org/doi/10.1037/h0025260

Bandura, A., & Walters, R. H. (1977). *Social learning theory* (Vol. 1). Prentice Hall.

Bandura, A., Ross, D., & Ross, S. A. (1961). Transmission of aggression through imitation of aggressive models. *Journal of Abnormal and Social Psychology, 63*(3), 575–582. https://psycnet.apa.org/doi/10.1037/h0045925

Bandy, C. L., Dillbeck, M. C., Sezibera, V., Taljaard, L., Wilks, M., Shapiro, D., de Reuck, J., & Peycke, R. (2020). Reduction of PTSD in South African university students using transcendental meditation practice. *Psychological Reports, 123*(3), 725–740. https://doi.org/10.1177/0033294119828036

Bao, Y., Zhang, H., Bruera, E., Portenoy, R., Rosa, W. E., Reid, M. C., & Wen, H. (2023). Medical marijuana legalization and opioid-and pain-related outcomes among patients newly diagnosed with cancer receiving anticancer treatment. *JAMA Oncology, 9*(2), 206–214. https://doi:10.1001/jamaoncol.2022.5623

Barbaranelli, C., Farnese, M. L., Tramontano, C., Fida, R., Ghezzi, V., Paciello, M., & Long, P. (2018). Machiavellian ways to academic cheating: A mediational and interactional model. *Frontiers in Psychology, 9*, Article 695. https://doi.org/10.3389/fpsyg.2018.00695

Bard, P., & Rioch, D. M. (1937). A study of four cats deprived of neocortex and additional portions of the forebrain. *The Johns Hopkins Medical Journal, 60*, 73–153.

Bargh, J. A., & Williams, E. L. (2006). The automaticity of social life. *Current Directions in Psychological Science, 15*(1), 1–4.

Barker, V., Romaniuk, L., Cardinal, R. N., Pope, M., Nicol, K., & Hall, J. (2015). Impulsivity in borderline personality disorder. *Psychological Medicine, 45*(9), 1955–1964. https://doi.org/10.1017/S0033291714003079

Barlattani, T., D'Amelio, C., Cavatassi, A., De Luca, D., Di Stefano, R., Di Berardo, A., Mantenuto, S., Minutillo, F., Leonardi, V., Renzi, G., Russo, A., Rossi, A., & Pacitti, F. (2023). Autism spectrum disorders and psychiatric comorbidities: A narrative review. *Journal of Psychopathology, 29*, 3–24. https://doi.org/10.36148/2284-0249-N281

Barlow, D. H., Allen, L. B., & Basden, S. L. (2007). Psychological treatments for panic disorders, phobias, and generalized anxiety disorder. In P. E. Nathan & J. M. Gorman (Eds.), *A guide to treatments that work* (pp. 351–394). Oxford University Press.

Barnas, A. J., & Ward, E. J. (2022). Metacognitive judgements of change detection predict change blindness. *Cognition, 227*, 1–13. https://doi.org/10.1016/j.cognition.2022.105208

Barnett, S. M., Ceci, S. J., & Williams, W. M. (2006). Is the ability to make a bacon sandwich a mark of intelligence? and other issues: Some reflections on Gardner's theory of multiple intelligences. In J. A. Schaler (Ed.), *Howard Gardner under fire: The rebel psychologist faces his critics* (pp. 95–114). Open Court.

Baron, R. A. (1972). Aggression as a function of ambient temperature and prior anger arousal. *Journal of Personality and Social Psychology, 21*(2), 183–189. https://doi.org/10.1037/h0032892

Barres, R., Yan, J., Egan, B., Treebak, J. T., Rasmussen, M., Fritz, T., Caidahl, K., Krook, A., O'Gorman, D., & Zierath, J. R. (2012). Acute exercise remodels promoter methylation in human skeletal muscle. *Cell Metabolism, 15*(3), 405–411. https://doi.org/10.1016/j.cmet.2012.01.001

Barrett, D. (1993). The "committee of sleep": A study of dream incubation for problem solving. *Dreaming, 3*(2), 115–122. https://doi.org/10.1037/h0094375

Barretto, R. P. J., Gillis-Smith, S., Chandrashekar, J., Yarmolinsky, D. A., Schnitzer, M. J., Ryba, N. J. P., & Zuker, C. S. (2015). The neural representation of taste quality at the periphery. *Nature, 517*(7534), 373–376. https://doi.org/10.1038/nature13873

Barry, C. M., Madsen, S. D., Nelson, L. J., Carroll, J. S., & Badger, S. (2009). Friendship and romantic relationship qualities in emerging adulthood: Differential associations with identity development and achieved adulthood criteria. *Journal of Adult Development, 16*(4), 209–222. https://doi.org/10.1007/s10804-009-9067-x

Barry, C. T., Doucette, H., Loflin, D. C., Rivera-Hudson, N., & Herrington, L. L. (2017). "Let me take a selfie": Associations between self-photography, narcissism, and self-esteem. *Psychology of Popular Media Culture, 6*(1), 48–60. https://doi.org/10.1037/ppm0000089

Barry, P. (2002). *Mental health and mental illness* (7th ed.). Lippincott.

Bar-Tal, D. (1976). *Prosocial behavior: Theory and research*. Academic Press.

Bartels, M. (2015). Genetics of wellbeing and its components satisfaction with life, happiness, and quality of life: A review and meta-analysis of heritability studies. *Behavior Genetics, 45*(2), 137–156. https://doi.org/10.1007/s10519-015-9713-y

Bartlett, F. C. (1932). *Remembering*. Cambridge University Press.

Bartlett, S. C. (2017). A path towards abuse—the decline of moral treatment in the Utica Lunatic Asylum. *Global Tides, 11*(1), Article 1.

Bartley, C. E., & Roesch, S. C. (2011). Coping with daily stress: The role of conscientiousness. *Personality and Individual Differences, 50*(1), 79–83. https://doi.org/10.1016/j.paid.2010.08.027

Bartoshuck, L. M., Duffy, V. B., & Miller, I. J., (1994). PTS/PROP tasting: Anatomy, psychophysics and sex effects. *Physiology & Behavior, 56*(6), 1165–1171. https://doi.org/10.1016/0031-9384(94)90361-1

Basedow, L. A., Riemer, T. G., Reiche, S., Kreutz, R., & Majić, T. (2021). Neuropsychological functioning in users of serotonergic psychedelics—A systematic review and meta-analysis. *Frontiers in Pharmacology, 12*, 1–16. https://doi.org/10.3389/fphar.2021.739966

Bateson, M., Brilot, B., & Nettle, D. (2011). Anxiety: An evolutionary approach. *The Canadian Journal of Psychiatry, 56*(12), 707–715. https://doi.org/10.1177/070674371105601202

Batista, R. L., Costa, E. M. F., Rodrigues, A. D. S., Gomes, N. L., Faria, J. A., Jr., Nishi, M. Y., Prado Arnhold, I. J., Domenice, S., & de Mendonca, B. B. (2018). Androgen insensitivity syndrome: A review. *Archives of Endocrinology and Metabolism, 62*, 227–235. https://doi.org/10.20945/2359-3997000000031

Bauer, R. M., Grande, L., & Valenstein, E. (2003). Amnesic disorders. In K. M. Heilman & E. Valenstein (Eds.), *Clinical neuropsychology* (4th ed., pp. 495–573). Oxford University Press.

Bäuerle, A., Teufel, M., Musche, V., Weismüller, B., Kohler, H., Hetkamp, M., Dörrie, N., Schweda, A., & Skoda, E. M. (2020). Increased generalized anxiety, depression and distress during the COVID-19 pandemic: A cross-sectional study in Germany. *Journal of Public Health, 42*(4), 672–678. https://doi.org/10.1093/pubmed/fdaa106

Bauminger, N., & Kasari, C. (2000). Loneliness and friendship in high-functioning children with autism. *Child Development, 71*(2), 447–456. https://doi.org/10.1111/1467-8624.00156

Baumrind, D. (1971). Current patterns of parental authority. *Developmental Psychology, 4*(1, Pt. 2), 1–103. https://doi.org/10.1037/h0030372

Bava, S., & Tapert, S. F. (2010). Adolescent brain development and the risk for alcohol and other drug problems. *Neuropsychology Review, 20*(4), 398–413. https://doi.org/10.1007/s11065-010-9146-6

Bayor, R. H. (2014). *Encountering Ellis Island: How European immigrants entered America.* JHU Press.

BBC. (2015). *The extraordinary case of the Guevedoces.* https://www.bbc.com/news/magazine-34290981

Beach, L. R., & Connolly, T. (2005). *The psychology of decision making: People in organizations.* Sage.

Beattie, J., Baron, J., Hershey, J. C., & Spranca, M. D. (1994). Psychological determinants of decision attitude. *Journal of Behavioral Decision Making, 7*(2), 129–144. https://doi.org/10.1002/bdm.3960070206

Beauti, A. (2023). The long-term effect of stimulant medication on the ADHD brain. *Lynchburg Journal of Medical Science, 5*(1), Article 73.

Beck, A. T., & Rector, N. A. (2005). Cognitive approaches to schizophrenia: Theory and therapy. *Annual Reviews of Clinical Psychology, 1*, 577–606. https://doi.org/10.1146/annurev.clinpsy.1.102803.144205

Beck, A. T., & Weishaar, M. (1989). Cognitive therapy. In A. Freeman, K. M. Simon, L. E. Beutler, & H. Arkowitz (Eds.), *Comprehensive handbook of cognitive therapy* (pp. 21–36). Springer. https://doi.org/10.1016/0272-7358(91)90115-B

Beck, H. P., Levinson, S., & Irons, G. (2009). Finding little Albert: A journey to John B. Watson's infant laboratory. *American Psychologist, 64*(7), 605–614. https://psycnet.apa.org/doi/10.1037/a0017234

Becker, K. A. (2003). *History of the Stanford-Binet intelligence scales: Content and psychometrics* (5th ed.). Riverside Publishing.

Becker, M. P., Collins, P. F., Schultz, A., Urošević, S., Schmaling, B., & Luciana, M. (2018). Longitudinal changes in cognition in young adult cannabis users. *Journal of Clinical and Experimental Neuropsychology, 40*(6), 529–543. https://doi.org/10.1080/13803395.2017.1385729

Behan, C. (2020). The benefits of meditation and mindfulness practices during times of crisis such as COVID-19. *Irish Journal of Psychological Medicine, 37*(4), 256–258. https://doi.org/10.1017/ipm.2020.38

Beilin, H. (2013). *The development of prosocial behavior.* Academic Press.

Bekkali, S., Youssef, G. J., Donaldson, P. H., Albein-Urios, N., Hyde, C., & Enticott, P. G. (2021). Is the putative mirror neuron system associated with empathy? A systematic review and meta-analysis. *Neuropsychology Review, 31*(1), 14–57. https://doi.org/10.1007/s11065-020-09452-6

Belfry, K. D., & Kolla, N. J. (2021). Cold-blooded and on purpose: A review of the biology of proactive aggression. *Brain Sciences, 11*(11), Article 1412. https://doi.org/10.3390/brainsci11111412

Bell, A. C., Eccleston, C. P., Bradberry, L. A., Kidd, W. C., Mesick, C. C., & Rutchick, A. M. (2021). Ingroup projection in American politics: An obstacle to bipartisanship. *Social Psychological and Personality Science, 13*(5), 906–915. https://doi.org/10.1177/19485506211046788

Bell, C. G., Lowe, R., Adams, P. D., Baccarelli, A. A., Beck, S., Bell, J. T., Christensen, B. C., Gladyshev, V. N., Heijmans, B. T., Horvath, S., Ideker, T., Issa, J.-P., J., Kelsey, K. T., Marioni, R. E., Reik, W., Relton, C. L., Schalkwyk, L. C., Teschendorff, A. E., Wagner, W., Zhang, K., & Rakyan, V. K. (2019). DNA methylation aging clocks: Challenges and recommendations. *Genome Biology, 20*(1), 1–24. https://doi.org/10.1186/s13059-019-1824-y

Bell, S., Wood, C., & Sarkar, A. (2019, May). Perceptions of chatbots in therapy. In *Extended Abstracts of the 2019 CHI Conference on Human Factors in Computing Systems* (pp. 1–6). https://doi.org/10.1145/3290607.3313072

Belsky, J., Zhang, X., & Sayler, K. (2022). Differential susceptibility 2.0: Are the same children affected by different experiences and exposures? *Development and Psychopathology, 34*(3), 1025–1033. https://doi.org/10.1017/S0954579420002205

Bem, S. L. (1972). Psychology looks at sex roles: Where have all the androgynous people gone? Paper presented at the UCLA Symposium on Sex Roles, Los Angeles.

Bem, S. L. (1974). The measurement of psychological androgyny. *Journal of Consulting and Clinical Psychology, 42*(2), 155–162. https://doi.org/10.1037/h0036215

Bem, S. L. (1975). Sex role adaptability: One consequence of psychological androgyny. *Journal of Personality and Social Psychology, 31*(4), 634–643. https://doi.org/10.1037/h0077098

Bem, S. L. (1984). Androgyny and gender schema theory: A conceptual and empirical integration. In Nebraska Symposium on Motivation: Psychology and Gender (Vol. 32, pp. 179–226). University of Nebraska Press.

Bem, S. L., & Lenney, E. (1976). Sex typing and the avoidance of cross-sex behavior. *Journal of Personality and Social Psychology, 33*(1), 48–54. https://doi.org/10.1037/h0078640

Bendig, E., Erb, B., Schulze-Thuesing, L., & Baumeister, H. (2019). The next generation: Chatbots in clinical psychology and psychotherapy to foster mental health<@151>a scoping review. *Verhaltenstherapie.* Advance online publication. https://doi.org/10.1159/000501812

Benington, J. H., & Heller, H. C. (1995). Restoration of brain energy metabolism as the function of sleep. *Progress in Neurobiology, 45*(4), 347–360. https://doi.org/10.1016/0301-0082(94)00057-O

Benjamin, L. T., & Crouse, E. M. (2004). The American Psychological Association's response to Brown v. Board of Education: The case of Kenneth B. Clark. *American Psychologist, 57*(1), 38–50. https://doi.org/10.1037/10812-013

Bensley, D. A. (2023). Critical thinking, intelligence, and unsubstantiated beliefs: An integrative review. *Journal of Intelligence, 11*(11), Article 207. https://doi.org/10.3390/jintelligence11110207

Benson, J. J., Oliver, D. P., Washington, K. T., Rolbiecki, A. J., Lombardo, C. B., Garza, J. E., & Demiris, G. (2020). Online social support groups for informal caregivers of hospice patients with cancer. *European Journal of Oncology Nursing, 44*, Article 101698. https://doi.org/10.1016/j.ejon.2019.101698

Benton, D., & Nehlig, A. (2004). The biology and psychology of chocolate craving. In A. Nehlig (Ed.), *Coffee, tea, chocolate, and the brain* (pp. 206–219). CRC Press.

Berger, S. E., & Baria, A. T. (2022). Assessing pain research: A narrative review of emerging pain methods, their technosocial implications, and opportunities for multidisciplinary approaches. *Frontiers in Pain Research, 3*, Article 896276. https://doi.org/10.3389/fpain.2022.896276

Berglund, A., Stochholm, K., & Gravholt, C. H. (2020). Morbidity in 47, XYY syndrome: A nationwide epidemiological study of hospital diagnoses and medication use. *Genetics in Medicine, 22*(9), 1542–1551. https://doi.org/10.1038/s41436-020-0837-y

Bering, J. (2012). The rat that laughed. *Scientific American, 307*(1), 74–77. https://www.jstor.org/stable/26016001

Berkowitz, L. T. (1989). Frustration-aggression hypothesis: Examination and reformulation. *Psychological Bulletin, 106*(1), 59–73. https://doi.org/10.1037/0033-2909.106.1.59

Berlyne, D. E. (1966). Curiosity and exploration: Animals spend much of their time seeking stimuli whose significance raises problems for psychology. *Science, 153*(3731), 25–33. https://doi .org/10.1126/science.153.3731.25

Bernard, L. L. (1924). *Instinct: A study in social psychology.* Holt.

Berndt, T. J., & Perry, B. (1983). *Benefits of friendship interview.* Unpublished paper, University of Oklahoma, Norman.

Bernstein, A. (2016, July 29). Chris Sizemore, whose many personalities were the real "Three Faces of Eve," dies at 89. *The Washington Post.* https://www.washingtonpost.com/national/ health-science/chris-sizemore-whose-multiple-personality-disorder-was-filmed-as-the-three-faces-of-eve-dies-at-89/2016/07/29/3ed468e2-55b4-11e6-bbf5-957ad17b4385_ story.html

Bernstein, I. L. (1978). Learned taste aversions in children receiving chemotherapy. *Science, 200*(4347), 1302–1303. https://doi.org/ 10.1126/science.663613

Berridge, K. C. (2018). Evolving concepts of emotion and motivation. *Frontiers in Psychology, 9*, Article 1647. https://doi.org/10.3389/ fpsyg.2018.01647

Berscheid, E., & Walster, E. (1974). A little bit about love. *Foundations of Interpersonal Attraction, 1*, 356–381.

Besag, F. M. C., Vasey, M. J., Lao, K. S. J., & Wong, I. C. K. (2019). Adverse events associated with melatonin for the treatment of primary or secondary sleep disorders: A systematic review. *CNS Drugs, 33*(12), 1167–1186. https://doi.org/10.1007/s40263-019-00680-w

Bessenoff, G. R. (2006). Can the media affect us? Social comparison, self-discrepancy, and the thin ideal. *Psychology of Women Quarterly, 30*(3), 239–251.

Bettens, K., Sleegers, K., & Van Broeckhoven, C. (2013). Genetic insights in Alzheimer's disease. *The Lancet Neurology, 12*(1), 92–104. https://doi.org/10.1016/S1474-4422(12)70259-4

Beydoun, H. A., Beydoun, M.A., Kaufman, J. S., Lo, B., & Zonderman, A. B. (2012). Intimate partner violence against adult women and its association with major depressive disorder, depressive symptoms and postpartum depression: A systematic review and meta-analysis. *Social Science & Medicine, 75*(6), 959–975. https://doi.org/10.1016/j.socscimed.2012.04.025

Beyens, I., Frison, E., & Eggermont, S. (2016). "I don't want to miss a thing": Adolescents' fear of missing out and its relationship to adolescents' social needs, Facebook use, and Facebook related stress. *Computers in Human Behavior, 64*, 1–8. https:// doi.org/10.1016/j.chb.2016.05.083

Beyers, W., & Seiffge-Krenke, I. (2010). Does identity precede intimacy? Testing Erikson's theory on romantic development in emerging adults of the 21st century. *Journal of Adolescent Research, 25*(3), 387–415. https://doi.org/ 10.1177/0743558410361370

Bhandarkar, A. M., Pandey, A. K., Nayak, R., Pujary, K., & Kumar, A. (2021). Impact of social media on the academic performance of undergraduate medical students. *Medical Journal Armed Forces India, 77*(Suppl. 1), S37–S41. https://doi.org/10.1016/ j.mjafi.2020.10.021

Bhar, S. S., Brown, G. K., & Beck, A. T. (2008). Dysfunctional beliefs and psychopathology in borderline personality disorder. *Journal of Personality Disorders, 22*(2), 165–177. https://doi.org/ 10.1521/pedi.2008.22.2.165

Bhattacharyya, R., Bhattacharyya, M. N., & Sharaff, M. S. (2021). Toxic positivity and mental health—it is ok to not be ok. *Design Engineering, 8*, 5109–5127.

Bialystok, E. (2010). Global-local and trail-making tasks by monolingual and bilingual children: Beyond inhibition. *Developmental Psychology, 46*(1), 93–105. https://doi.org/ 10.1037/a0015466

Bialystok, E., Craik, F. I., & Luk, G. (2012). Bilingualism: Consequences for mind and brain. *Trends in Cognitive Sciences, 16*(4), 240–250. https://doi.org/10.1016/j.tics.2012.03.001

Biggs, A. T., Adamo, S. H., Dowd, E. W., & Mitroff, S. R. (2015). Examining perceptual and conceptual set biases in multiple-target visual search. *Attention, Perception, & Psychophysics, 77*(3), 844–855. https://doi.org/10.3758/s13414-014-0822-0

Bigler, R. S., & Leaper, C. (2015). Gendered language: Psychological principles, evolving practices, and inclusive policies. *Policy Insights From the Behavioral and Brain Sciences, 2*(1), 187–194. https://doi.org/10.1177/2372732215600452

Bilodeau-Houle, A., Bouchard, V., Morand-Beaulieu, S., Herringa, R. J., Milad, M. R., & Marin, M. F. (2020). Anxiety sensitivity moderates the association between father-child relationship security and fear transmission. *Frontiers in Psychology, 11*, Article 579514. https://doi.org/10.3389/fpsyg.2020.579514

Binder, J., Zagefka, H., Brown, R., Funke, F., Kessler, T., Mummendey, A., Maquil, A., Demoulin, S., & Leyens, J.-P. (2009). Does contact reduce prejudice or does prejudice reduce contact? A longitudinal test of the contact hypothesis among majority and minority groups in three European countries. *Journal of Personality and Social Psychology, 96*(4), 843–856. https://doi .org/10.1037/a0013470

Binet, A., & Simon, T. (1905). New methods for the diagnosis of the intellectual level of subnormals. In H. H. Goddard (Ed.), *Development of intelligence in children (the Binet-Simon Scale)* (pp. 191–244). Williams & Wilkins.

Binet, A., & Simon, T. (1916). *The development of intelligence in children.* Williams & Wilkins.

Birchwood, M., Dunn, G., Meaden, A., Tarrier, N., Lewis, S., Wykes, T., Davies, L., Michail, M., & Peters, E. (2018). The COMMAND trial of cognitive therapy to prevent harmful compliance with command hallucinations: Predictors of outcome and mediators of change. *Psychological Medicine, 48*(12), 1966–1974. https:// doi.org/10.1017/S0033291717003488

Biringer, F., & Anderson, J. R. (1992). Self- recognition in Alzheimer's disease: A mirror and video study. *Journal of Gerontology, 47*(6), 385–388. https://doi.org/10.1093/geronj/47.6.P385

Biringer, F., Anderson, J. R., & Strubel, D. (1988). Self-recognition in senile dementia. *Experimental Aging Research, 14*(4), 177–180. https://doi.org/10.1080/03610738808259745

Bishop, G. D. (2016). Personality and cardiovascular disease: Overview. In M. E. Alvarenga & D. Byrne (Eds.), *Handbook of psychocardiology* (pp. 631–643). Springer Science + Business Media. https://doi.org/10.1007/978-981-287-206-7_28

Biswas-Diener, R., & Diener, E. D. (2006). The subjective well-being of the homeless, and lessons for happiness. *Social Indicators Research, 76*(2), 185–205. https://doi.org/10.1007/s11205-005-8671-9

Blackwell, L. S., Trzesniewski, K. H., & Dweck, C. S. (2007). Implicit theories of intelligence predict achievement across an adolescent transition: A longitudinal study and an intervention. *Child Development, 78*(1), 246–263. https://doi.org/10.1111/ j.1467-8624.2007.00995.x

Blair, J., Sellars, C., Strickland, I., Clark, F., Williams, A., Smith, M., & Jones, L. (1996). Theory of mind in the psychopath. *Journal of Forensic Psychiatry, 7*(1), 15–25. https://doi.org/10.1080/ 09585189608409914

Blais, M. R., Sabourin, S., Boucher, C., & Vallerand, R. (1990). Toward a motivational model of couple happiness. *Journal of Personality and Social Psychology, 59*(5), 1021–1031. https://doi .org/10.1037/0022-3514.59.5.1021

Blakemore, S.-J., Wolpert, D., & Frith, C. (2000). Why can't you tickle yourself? *NeuroReport: For Rapid Communication of Neuroscience Research, 11*(11), R11–R16. http://dx.doi.org/ 10.1097/00001756-200008030-00002

Blakeslee, S. (2004). The CRAAP test. *Loex Quarterly, 31*(3), 4–5.

Blanc, A. K. (2001). The effect of power in sexual relationships on sexual and reproductive health: An examination of the evidence. *Studies in Family Planning, 32*(3), 189–213. https://doi .org/10.1111/j.1728-4465.2001.00189.x

Blashfield, R. K., Keeley, J. W., Flanagan, E. H., & Miles, S. R. (2014). The cycle of classification: DSM-I through DSM-5. *Annual Review of Clinical Psychology, 10*, 25–51. https://doi.org/10.1146/annurev-clinpsy-032813-153639

Blasiman, R. N., Dunlosky, J., & Rawson, K. A. (2017). The what, how much, and when of study strategies: Comparing intended versus actual study behaviour. *Memory, 25*(6), 784–792. https://doi.org/10.1080/09658211.2016.1221974

Bleidorn, W., Buyukcan-Tetik, A., Schwaba, T., Van Scheppingen, M. A., Denissen, J. J., & Finkenauer, C. (2016). Stability and change in self-esteem during the transition to parenthood. *Social Psychological and Personality Science, 7*(6), 560–569. https://doi.org/10.1177/1948550616646428

Blihar, D., Crisafio, A., Delgado, E., Buryak, M., Gonzalez, M., & Waechter, R. (2021). A meta-analysis of hippocampal and amygdala volumes in patients diagnosed with dissociative identity disorder. *Journal of Trauma & Dissociation, 22*(3), 365–377. https://doi.org/10.1080/15299732.2020.1869650

Blihar, D., Delgado, E., Buryak, M., Gonzalez, M., & Waechter, R. (2020). A systematic review of the neuroanatomy of dissociative identity disorder. *European Journal of Trauma & Dissociation, 4*(3), 100148. https://doi.org/10.1016/j.ejtd.2020.100148

Blodgett Salafia, E. H., Jones, M. E., Haugen, E. C., & Schaefer, M. K. (2015). Perceptions of the causes of eating disorders: A comparison of individuals with and without eating disorders. *Journal of Eating Disorders, 3*, Article 32. https://doi.org/10.1186/s40337-015-0069-8

Blumenthal, A. (1998). Leipzig, Wilhelm Wundt, and psychology's gilded age. In G. A. Kimble & M. Wertheimer (Eds.), *Portraits of pioneers in psychology* (Vol. 3, pp. 31–50). American Psychological Association.

Boag, S. (2006). Freudian repression, the common view, and pathological science. *Review of General Psychology, 10*(1), 74–86. https://doi.org/10.1037/1089-2680.10.1.74

Boag, S. (2017). Conscious, preconscious, and unconscious. In V. Zeigler-Hill & T. Shackelford (Eds.), *Encyclopedia of personality and individual differences* (pp. 1–8). Springer. https://doi.org/10.1007/978-3-319-28099-8_1370-1

Boake, C. (2002). From the Binet-Simon to the Wechsler-Bellevue: Tracing the history of intelligence testing. *Journal of Clinical and Experimental Neuropsychology, 24*(3), 383–405. https://doi.org/10.1076/jcen.24.3.383.981

Bogaert, A. F. (2004). Asexuality: Prevalence and associated factors in a national probability sample. *Journal of Sex Research, 41*(3), 279–287. https://doi.org/10.1080/00224490409552235

Bogowicz, P., Curtis, H. J., Walker, A. J., Cowen, P., Geddes, J., & Goldacre, B. (2021). Trends and variation in antidepressant prescribing in English primary care: A retrospective longitudinal study. *BJGP Open, 5*(4), 1–12. https://doi.org/10.3399/BJGPO.2021.0020

Boitor, M., Martorella, G., Maheu, C., Laizner, A. M., & Gélinas, C. (2018). Effects of massage in reducing the pain and anxiety of the cardiac surgery critically ill—A randomized controlled trial. *Pain Medicine, 19*(12), 2556–2569. https://doi.org/10.1093/pm/pny055

Bojanowska, A., & Zalewska, A. M. (2018). Temperamental predictors of subjective well-being from early adolescence to mid-life: The role of temporal and energetic regulation. *International Journal of Psychology, 53*(6), 458–467. https://doi.org/10.1002/ijop.12414

Bolic Baric, V., Skuthälla, S., Pettersson, M., Gustafsson, P. A., & Kjellberg, A. (2021). The effectiveness of weighted blankets on sleep and everyday activities—A retrospective follow-up study of children and adults with attention deficit hyperactivity disorder and/or autism spectrum disorder. *Scandinavian Journal of Occupational Therapy.* Advance online publication. https://doi.org/10.1080/11038128.2021.1939414

Bollu, P. C., Goyal, M. K., Thakkar, M. M., & Sahota, P. (2018). Sleep medicine: Parasomnias. *Missouri Medicine, 115*(2), 169–175.

Bond, C. F., Jr., & DePaulo, B. M. (2008). Individual differences in judging deception: Accuracy and bias. *Psychological Bulletin, 134*(4), 477–492. https://doi.org/10.1037/0033-2909.134.4.477

Bonini, L., Rotunno, C., Arcuri, E., & Gallese, V. (2022). Mirror neurons 30 years later: Implications and applications. *Trends in Cognitive Sciences, 26*(9), 767–781. https://doi.org/10.1016/j.tics.2022.06.003

Bonta, B. D. (1997). Cooperation and competition in peaceful societies. *Psychological Bulletin, 121*(2), 299–320. https://doi.org/10.1037/0033-2909.121.2.299

Boots, E. A., Schultz, S. A., Almeida, R. P., Oh, J. M., Koscik, R. L., Dowling, M. N., Gallagher, C. L., Carlsson, C. M., Rowley, H. A., Bendlin, B. B., Asthana, S., Sager, M. A., Hermann, B. P., Johnson, S. C., & Okonkwo, O. C. (2015). Occupational complexity and cognitive reserve in a middle-aged cohort at risk for Alzheimer's disease. *Archives of Clinical Neuropsychology, 30*(7), 634–642. https://doi.org/10.1093/arclin/acv041

Bornstein, A. M., & Pickard, H. (2020). "Chasing the first high": Memory sampling in drug choice. *Neuropsychopharmacology, 45*(6), 907–915. https://doi.org/10.1038/s41386-019-0594-2

Borroto-Escuela, D. O., Ambrogini, P., Chruścicka, B., Lindskog, M., Crespo-Ramirez, M., Hernández-Mondragón, J. C., Perez de la Mora, M., Schellekens, H., & Fuxe, K. (2021). The role of central serotonin neurons and 5-HT heteroreceptor complexes in the pathophysiology of depression: A historical perspective and future prospects. *International Journal of Molecular Sciences, 22*(4), 1–13. https://doi.org/10.3390/ijms22041927

Bosch, A. ., Hutter, I., & van Ginneken, J. . (2008). Perceptions of adolescents and their mothers on reproductive and sexual development in Matlab, Bangladesh. *International Journal of Adolescent Medicine and Health, 20*(3), 329–342. https://doi.org/10.1515/IJAMH.2008.20.3.329

Botella, C., Fernández-Álvarez, J., Guillén, V., García-Palacios, A., & Baños, R. (2017). Recent progress in virtual reality exposure therapy for phobias: A systematic review. *Current Psychiatry Reports, 19*(7), article 42. https://doi.org/10.1007/s11920-017-0788-4

Boto, T., & Tomchik, S. M. (2019). The excitatory, the inhibitory, and the modulatory: Mapping chemical neurotransmission in the brain. *Neuron, 101*(5), 763–765. https://doi.org/10.1016/j.neuron.2019.02.021

Botzet, L. J., Rohrer, J. M., & Arslan, R. C. (2021). Analysing effects of birth order on intelligence, educational attainment, big five and risk aversion in an Indonesian sample. *European Journal of Personality, 35*(2), 234–248. https://doi.org/10.1002/per.2285

Bouchard, T. J. (2004). Genetic influence on human psychological traits: A survey. *Compensation & Benefits Review, 13*(4), 12–27. https://doi.org/10.1111/j.0963-7214.2004.00295.x

Bouchard, T. J., & McGue, M. (2003). Genetic and environmental influences on human psychological differences. *Journal of Neurobiology, 54*(1), 4–45. https://doi.org/10.1002/neu.10160

Bouchard, T. J., Lykken, D. T., McGue, M., Segal, N. L., & Tellegen, A. (1990). Sources of human psychological differences: The Minnesota Study of Twins Reared Apart. *Science, 250*(4978), 223–228. https://doi.org/10.1126/science.2218526

Bouckaert, F., Sienaert, P., Obbels, J., Dols, A., Vandenbulcke, M., Stek, M., & Bolwig, T. (2014). ECT: Its brain enabling effects—a review of electroconvulsive therapy–induced structural brain plasticity. *The Journal of ECT, 30*(2), 143–151. https://doi.org/10.1097/YCT.0000000000000129

Boudewyns, P. A. (Ed.). (2012). *Flooding and implosive therapy: Direct therapeutic exposure in clinical practice.* Springer Science & Business Media.

Bowden Davies, K. A., Pickles, S., Sprung, V. S., Kemp, G. J., Alam, U., Moore, D. R., Tahrani, A. A., & Cuthbertson, D. J. (2019). Reduced physical activity in young and older adults: Metabolic and musculoskeletal implications. *Therapeutic Advances in Endocrinology and Metabolism, 10,* 1–15. https://doi.org/10.1177/2042018819888824

Bowden, C. L., Calabrese, J. R., McElroy, S. L., Gyulai, L., Wassef, A., Petty, F., Pope, H. G., Jr, Chou, J. C. Y., Keck Jr, P. E., Rhodes, L. J., Swann, A. C., Hirschfeld, R. M. A., & Wozniak, P. J. (2000). A randomized, placebo-controlled 12-month trial of divalproex and lithium in treatment of outpatients with Bipolar I Disorder. *Archives of General Psychiatry, 57*(5), 481–489. https://doi.org/10.1001/archpsyc.57.5.481

Bowden-Green, T., Hinds, J., & Joinson, A. (2021). Understanding neuroticism and social media: A systematic review. *Personality and Individual Differences, 168*(1), 110344. https://doi.org/10.1016/j.paid.2020.110344

Boyer, P., & Bergstrom, B. (2011). Threat-detection in child development: An evolutionary perspective. *Neuroscience & Biobehavioral Reviews, 35*(4), 1034–1041. https://doi.org/10.1016/j.neubiorev.2010.08.010

Boyle, G. J. (1995). Myers-Briggs type indicator (MBTI): Some psychometric limitations. *Australian Psychologist, 30*(1), 71–74. https://doi.org/10.1111/j.1742-9544.1995.tb01750.x

Braaksma, M. A. H., Rijlaarsdam, G., Van den Bergh, H., & Van Hout-Wolters, B. H. A. M. (2006). What observational learning in writing courses entails: A multiple case study. *Educational Studies in Language and Literature, 6*(1), 31–62. https://doi.org/10.17239/L1ESLL-2006.06.01.05

Brabender, V. M., Smolar, A. I., & Fallon, A. E. (2004). *Essentials of group therapy.* John Wiley.

Brackett, M. A., Mayer, J. D., & Warner, R. M. (2004). Emotional intelligence and its relation to everyday behavior. *Personality and Individual Differences, 36*(6), 1387–1402. https://doi.org/10.1016/S0191-8869(03)00236-8

Braden, A., Barnhart, W. R., Kalantzis, M., Redondo, R., Dauber, A., Anderson, L., & Tilstra-Ferrell, E. L. (2023). Eating when depressed, anxious, bored, or happy: An examination in treatment-seeking adults with overweight/obesity. *Appetite, 184,* Article 106510. https://doi.org/10.1016/j.appet.2023.106510

Bradshaw, C., Kahn, A. S., & Saville, B. K. (2010). To hook up or date: Which gender benefits? *Sex Roles, 62*(9–10), 661–669. https://doi.org/10.1007/s11199-010-9765-7

Bradshaw, E. L., Conigrave, J. H., Steward, B. A., Ferber, K. A., Parker, P. D., & Ryan, R. M. (2023). A meta-analysis of the dark side of the American dream: Evidence for the universal wellness costs of prioritizing extrinsic over intrinsic goals. *Journal of Personality and Social Psychology, 124*(4), 873–899. https://doi.org/10.1037/pspp0000431

Bradshaw, I. G. (2004). Not by bread alone: Symbolic loss, trauma, and recovery in elephant communities. *Society & Animals, 12*(2), 143–158. https://doi.org/10.1163/1568530041446535

Brady, C., Moss, H., & Kelly, B. D. (2017). A fuller picture: Evaluating an art therapy programme in a multidisciplinary mental health service. *Medical Humanities, 43*(1), 30–34. http://dx.doi.org/10.1136/medhum-2016-011040

Brady, S., Siegel, G., Albers, R. W., & Price, D. L. (Eds.). (2005). *Basic neurochemistry: Molecular, cellular and medical aspects.* Elsevier.

Brafman, A. H. (2018). *Fostering independence: Helping and caring in psychodynamic therapies.* Routledge.

Braga, B. (2011). *Cognitive effective instance diagram design.* https://www.researchgate.net/publication/257236013_Cognitive_effective_instance_diagram_design

Brandel, M., Melchiorri, E., & Ruini, C. (2018). The dynamics of eudaimonic well-being in the transition to parenthood: Differences between fathers and mothers. *Journal of Family Issues, 39*(9), 2572–2589. https://doi.org/10.1177/0192513X18758344

Brandt, E. (2017, April 15). Studies show racial bias in Pennsylvania school funding. *The Times Herald.* https://www.timesherald.com/news/studies-show-racial-bias-in-pennsylvania-school-funding/article_903428ec-c472-5886-b3d6-621f21b3edfe.html

Brankovic, M. (2019). Who believes in ESP: Cognitive and motivational determinants of the belief in extra-sensory perception. *European Journal of Psychology, 15*(1), 120–139. https://doi.org/10.5964/ejop.v15i1.1689

Brannigan, A. (2013). Stanley Milgram's obedience experiments: A report card 50 years later. *Society, 50*(6), 623–628. https://doi.org/10.1007/s12115-013-9724-3

Brasel, S. A., & Gips, J. (2011). Media multitasking behavior: Concurrent television and computer usage. *Cyberpsychology, Behavior, and Social Networking, 14*(9), 527–534. https://doi.org/10.1089/cyber.2010.0350

Bravata, D. M., Smith-Spangler, C., Sundaram, V., Gienger, A. L., Lin, N., Lewis, R., Stave, C. D., Olkin, I., & Sirard, J. R. (2007). Using pedometers to increase physical activity and improve health: A systematic review. *Journal of the American Medical Association, 298*(19), 2296–2304. https://doi.org/10.1001/jama.298.19.2296

Breckler, S. J. (1984). Empirical validation of affect, behavior, and cognition as distinct components of attitude. *Journal of Personality and Social Psychology, 47,* 1191–1205. https://doi.org/10.1037/0022-3514.47.6.1191

Brekke, J. S., Prindle, C., Bae, S. W., & Long, J. D. (2001). Risks for individuals with schizophrenia who are living in the community. *Psychiatric Services, 52*(10), 1358–1366. https://doi.org/10.1176/appi.ps.52.10.1358

Bressler, S. L. (2002). Understanding cognition through large-scale cortical networks. *Current Directions in Psychological Science, 11*(2), 58–61. https://doi.org/10.1111/1467-8721.00168

Breuer, J., & Freud, S. (1955). *Studies on hysteria* (Standard ed., Vol. II). Hogarth. (Original work published 1893)

Brewer, M. B. (1988). A dual-process model of impression formation. In T. K. Srull & R. S. Wyer (Eds.), *Advances in social cognition* (Vol. 1, pp. 1–36). Erlbaum.

Breyer, N. L., & Allen, G. J. (1975). Effects of implementing a token economy on teacher attending behavior. *Journal of Applied Behavior Analysis, 8*(4), 373–380. https://doi.org/10.1901/jaba.1975.8-373

Brickman, A., M., Khan, U. A., Provenzano, F. A., Yeung, L., Suzuki, W., Schroeter, H., Wall, M., Sloan, R. P., & Small, S. A. (2014). Enhancing dentate gyrus function with dietary flavanols improves cognition in older adults. *Nature Neuroscience, 17*(12), 1798–1803. https://doi.org/10.1038/nn.3850

Bridges, A. J., Bergner, R. M., & Hesson-McInnis, M. (2003). Romantic partners use of pornography: Its significance for women. *Journal of Sex & Marital Therapy, 29*(1), 1–14. https://doi.org/10.1080/713847097

Brigham, C. C. (1923). *A study of American intelligence.* Princeton University Press.

Brion, M. J., Lawlor, D. A., Matijasevich, A., Horta, B., Anselmi, L., Araújo, C. L., Menezes, A. M., Victora, C. G., & Smith, G. D. (2011). What are the causal effects of breastfeeding on IQ, obesity and blood pressure? Evidence from comparing high-income with middle-income cohorts. *International Journal of Epidemiology, 40*(3), 670–680. https://doi.org/10.1093/ije/dyr020

Britton, W. B. (2019). Can mindfulness be too much of a good thing? The value of a middle way. *Current Opinion in Psychology, 28,* 159–165. https://doi.org/10.1016/j.copsyc.2018.12.011

Brix, N., Gaml-Sørensen, A., Ernst, A., Arendt, L. H., Lunddorf, L. L. H., Toft, G., Tøttenborg, S. S., Hærvig, K. K., Høyer, B., B., Hougaard, K. S., Bonde, J. P. E., & Ramlau-Hansen, C. H. (2023). Timing of puberty in relation to semen characteristics, testicular volume, and reproductive hormones: A cohort study. *Fertility and Sterility.* Advance online publication. https://doi.org/10.1016/j.fertnstert.2023.05.164

Brody, H., Rip, M. R., Vinten-Johansen, P., Paneth, N., & Rachman, S. (2000). Map-making and myth-making in Broad Street: The London cholera epidemic, 1854. *The Lancet, 356*(9223), 64–68. https://doi.org/10.1016/S0140-6736(00)02442-9

Broman, M., Rose, A. L., Hotson, G., & Casey, C. M. (1997). Severe anterograde amnesia with onset in childhood as a result of anoxic encephalopathy. *Brain: A Journal of Neurology, 120*(3), 417–433. https://doi.org/10.1093/brain/120.3.417

Broman, S. H., Nichols, P. L., & Kennedy, W. A. (1975). *Preschool IQ: Prenatal and early developmental correlates.* Lawrence Erlbaum.

Bronfenbrenner, U. (1977). Toward an experimental ecology of human development. *American Psychologist, 32*(7), 513–531. https://doi.org/10.1037/0003-066X.32.7.513

Bronfenbrenner, U., & Morris, P. (2006). The bioecological model of human development. In W. Damon & R. M. Lerner (Eds.), *Handbook of child psychology: Vol. 1. Theoretical models of human development* (6th ed., pp. 793–828). John Wiley.

Brook, J. S., Kessler, R. C., & Cohen, P. (1999). The onset of marijuana use from preadolescence and early adolescence to young adulthood. *Development and Psychopathology, 11*(4), 901–914. https://doi.org/10.1017/S0954579499002370

Brookie, K. L., Best, G. I., & Conner, T. S. (2018). Intake of raw fruits and vegetables is associated with better mental health than intake of processed fruits and vegetables. *Frontiers in Psychology, 9*, Article 487. https://doi.org/10.3389/fpsyg.2018.00487

Brooks, P. L., & Peever, J. H. (2012). Identification of the transmitter and receptor mechanisms responsible for REM sleep paralysis. *The Journal of Neuroscience, 32*(29), 9785–9795. https://doi.org/10.1523/JNEUROSCI.0482-12.2012

Brooks-Gunn, J., & Ruble, D. N. (2013). Developmental processes in the experience of menarche. In J. E. S. A. Baum, J. E. Sin, & A. Baum (Eds.), *Issues in child health and adolescent health: Handbook of psychology and health* (pp. 124–154). Psychology Press.

Brown, A. S. (2004). The déjà vu illusion. *Current Directions in Psychological Science, 13*(6), 256–259. https://doi.org/10.1111/j.0963-7214.2004.00320.x

Brown, J. (1958). Some tests of the decay theory of immediate memory. *The Quarterly Journal of Experimental Psychology, 10*(1), 12–21. https://doi.org/10.1080/17470215808416249

Brown, R., & Kulik, J. (1977). Flashbulb memories. *Cognition, 5*(1), 73–79. https://doi.org/10.1016/0010-0277(77)90018-X

Brunelin, J., Jalenques, I., Trojak, B., Attal, J., Szekely, D., Gay, A., Januel, D., Haffen, E., Schott-Pethelaz, Brault, C., & STEP Group. (2014). The efficacy and safety of low frequency repetitive transcranial magnetic stimulation for treatment-resistant depression: The results from a large multicenter French RCT. *Brain Stimulation, 7*(6), 855–863. https://doi.org/10.1016/j.brs.2014.07.040

Bryan, J. W., & Freed, F. W. (1982). Corporal punishment: Normative data and sociological and psychological correlates in a community college population. *Journal of Youth and Adolescence, 11*(2), 77–87. https://doi.org/10.1007/BF01834705

Bryant, J. (2020, May 28). *Why are we obsessed with cults right now?* Pacific San Diego. https://www.pacificsandiego.com/arts-culture/tv/story/2020-05-28/waco-wild-wild-country-cult-tv-shows

Buchanan, A., Sint, K., Swanson, J., & Rosenheck, R. (2019). Correlates of future violence in people being treated for schizophrenia. *American Journal of Psychiatry, 176*(9), 694–701. https://doi.org/10.1176/appi.ajp.2019.18080909

Bucher, B., & Lovaas, O. I. (1967). Use of aversive stimulation in behavior modification. In M. R. Jones (Ed.), *Miami symposium on the prediction of behavior* (pp. 77–145). University of Miami Press.

Buck, R. (1985). Prime theory: An integrated view of motivation and emotion. *Psychological Review, 92*(3), 389–413. https://doi.org/10.1037/0033-295X.92.3.389

Buckner, J. D., Morris, P. E., Abarno, C. N., Glover, N. I., & Lewis, E. M. (2021). Biopsychosocial model social anxiety and substance use revised. *Current Psychiatry Reports, 23*(Article 35), 1–9. https://doi.org/10.1007/s11920-021-01249-5

Bukowski, W. M., Hoza, B., & Boivin, M. (1994). Measuring friendship quality during pre- and early adolescence: The development and psychometric properties of the friendship qualities scale. *Journal of Social & Personal Relationships, 11*(3), 471–484. https://doi.org/10.1177/0265407594113011

Bullock, W. A., & Gilliland, K. (1993). Eysenck's arousal theory of introversion-extraversion: A converging measures investigation. *Journal of Personality and Social Psychology, 64*(1), 113–123. https://psycnet.apa.org/doi/10.1037/0022-3514.64.1.113

Bures, J., Bermúdez-Rattoni, F., & Yamamoto, T. (1998). *Conditioned taste aversion: Memory of a special kind.* Oxford University Press.

Burgess, A. (1962). *A clockwork orange.* William Heinemann.

Burgess, C. A., Kirsch, I., Shane, H., Niederauer, K. L., Graham, S. M., & Bacon, A. (1998). Facilitated communication as an ideomotor response. *Psychological Science, 9*(1), 71–74. https://doi.org/10.1111/1467-9280.00013

Burkauskas, J., & Fineberg, N. A. (2020). History and epidemiology of OCPD. In J. E. Grant, A. Pinto, & S. R. Chamberlain (Eds.), *Obsessive-compulsive personality disorder* (pp. 1–26). American Psychiatric Association.

Burke, K. C., Burke, J. D., Rae, D. S., & Regier, D. A. (1991). Comparing age at onset of major depression and other psychiatric disorders by birth cohorts in five US community populations. *Archives of General Psychiatry, 48*(9), 789–795. https://doi.org/10.1001/archpsyc.1991.01810330013002

Burke, N. N., Finn, D. P., McGuire, B. E., & Roche, M. (2017). Psychological stress in early life as a predisposing factor for the development of chronic pain: Clinical and preclinical evidence and neurobiological mechanisms. *Journal of Neuroscience Research, 95*(6), 1257–1270. https://doi.org/10.1002/jnr.23802

Burlingame, G. M., McClendon, D. T., & Yang, C. (2018). Cohesion in group therapy: A meta-analysis. *Psychotherapy, 55*(4), 384–398. https://doi.org/10.1037/pst0000173

Burunat, E. (2019). Love is a physiological motivation (like hunger, thirst, sleep or sex). *Medical Hypotheses, 129*, Article 109225. https://doi.org/10.1016/j.mehy.2019.05.011

Busch, H., & Hofer, J. (2012). Self-regulation and milestones of adult development: Intimacy and generativity. *Developmental Psychology, 48*(1), 282–293. https://doi.org/10.1037/a0025521

Bushkin, H., van Niekerk, R., & Stroud, L. (2021). Searching for meaning in chaos: Viktor Frankl's story. *Europe's Journal of Psychology, 17*(3), 233–242. https://doi.org/10.5964/ejop.5439

Bushman, B. J. (2002). Does venting anger feed or extinguish the flame? Catharsis, rumination, distraction, anger, and aggressive responding. *Personality and Social Psychology Bulletin, 28*(6), 724–731. https://doi.org/10.1177/0146167202289002

Bushman, B. J. (2016). Violent media and hostile appraisals: A meta-analytic review. *Aggressive Behavior, 42*(6), 605–613. https://doi.org/10.1002/ab.21655

Bushman, B. J., & Anderson, C. A. (2023). Solving the puzzle of null violent media effects. *Psychology of Popular Media, 12*(1), 1–9. https://doi.org/10.1037/ppm0000361

Bushman, B. J., & Huesman, L. R. (2006). Short-term and long-term effects of violent media on aggression in children and adults. *Archives of Pediatrics & Adolescent Medicine, 160*(4), 348–352. https://doi.org/10.1001/archpedi.160.4.348

Bushman, B. J., Baumeister, R. F., & Phillips, C. M. (2001). Do people aggress to improve their mood? Catharsis beliefs, affect regulation opportunity, and aggressive responding.

Journal of Personality and Social Psychology, 81(1), 17–32. https://doi.org/10.1037/0022-3514.81.1.17

Bushman, B. J., Baumeister, R. F., & Stack, A. D. (1999). Catharsis, aggression, and persuasive influence: Self-fulfilling or self-defeating prophecies? *Journal of Personality and Social Psychology, 76*(3), 367–376. https://doi.org/10.1037/0022-3514.76.3.367

Buss, A. H. (1961). *The psychology of aggression.* John Wiley & Sons.

Buss, A. H., & Plomin, R. (1984). *Temperament: Early developing personality traits.* Psychology Press.

Buss, A. H., & Plomin, R. (1986). The EAS approach to temperament. In R. Plomin & J. Dunn (Eds.), *The study of temperament: Changes, continuities and challenges* (pp. 67–79). Erlbaum.

Buss, D. M. (1988). Love acts: The evolutionary biology of love. In R. J. Sternberg & M. L. Barnes (Eds.), *The psychology of love* (pp. 100–118). Yale University Press.

Buss, D. M. (2006). The evolution of love. In R. J. Sternberg & K. Weis (Eds.), *The new psychology of love* (pp. 65–86). Yale University Press.

Buss, D. M., & Duntley, J. D. (2006). The evolution of aggression. In M. Schaller, J. A. Simpson, & D. T. Kenrick (Eds.), *Evolution and social psychology* (pp. 263–286). Psychology Press.

Buthmann, J., Finik, J., & Nomura, Y. (2018). Sex differences in the relations between infant temperament and electrodermal responses in early childhood. *International Journal of Behavioral Development, 42*(6), 535–542. https://doi.org/10.1177/0165025418757705

Butler, L. D., & Palesh, O. (2004). Spellbound: Dissociation in the movies. *Journal of Trauma & Dissociation, 5*(2), 61–87. https://doi.org/10.1300/J229v05n02_04

Byrne, P. (2001). The butler(s) DID it—dissociative identity disorder in cinema. *Medical Humanities, 27*(1), 26–29. http://doi.org/10.1136/mh.27.1.26

Cacciotti, G., Hayton, J. C., Mitchell, J. R., & Giazitzoglu, A. (2016). A reconceptualization of fear of failure in entrepreneurship. *Journal of Business Venturing, 31*(3), 302–325. https://doi.org/10.1016/j.jbusvent.2016.02.002

Caffò, A. O., Tinella, L., Lopez, A., Spano, G., Massaro, Y., Lisi, A., Stasolla, F., Catanesi, R., Nardulli, F., Grattagliano, I., & Bosco, A. (2020). The drives for driving simulation: A scientometric analysis and a selective review of reviews on simulated driving research. *Frontiers in Psychology, 11*, Article 917. https://doi.org/10.3389/fpsyg.2020.00917

Cahalan, S. (2019). *The great pretender: The undercover mission that changed our understanding of madness.* Hachette UK.

Cain, C. K. (2023). Beyond fear, extinction, and freezing: Strategies for improving the translational value of animal conditioning research. In M. R. Milad & S. D. Norrholm (Eds.), *Fear extinction: Current topics in behavioral neurosciences* (pp. 19–57). Springer. https://doi.org/10.1007/7854_2023_434

Cairo, A. H., Green, J. D., Forsyth, D. R., Behler, A. M. C., & Raldiris, T. L. (2020). Gray (literature) matters: Evidence of selective hypothesis reporting in social psychological research. *Personality and Social Psychology Bulletin, 46*(9), 1344–1362. https://doi.org/10.1177/0146167220903896

Calkins, M. W. (1893). Statistics of dreams. *The American Journal of Psychology, 5*(3), 311–343. https://www.jstor.org/stable/1410996

Callaway, E. (2012). Evolutionary biology: The lost appetites. *Nature, 486*, S16–S17. https://doi.org/10.1038/486S16a

Camerer, C. F., Dreber, A., Holzmeister, F., Ho, T. H., Huber, J., Johannesson, M., Kirchler, M., Nave, G., Nosek, B. A., Pfeiffer, T., Altmejd, A., Buttrick, N., Chan, T., Chen, Y., Forsell, E., Gampa, A., Heikensten, E., Hummer, L., Imai, T., . . . Wu, H. (2018). Evaluating the replicability of social science experiments in Nature and Science between 2010 and 2015. *Nature Human Behaviour, 2*(9), 637–644. https://doi.org/10.1038/s41562-018-0399-z

Cameron, J., Banko, K. M., & Pierce, W. D. (2001). Pervasive negative effects of rewards on intrinsic motivation: The myth continues. *The Behavior Analyst, 24*(1), 1–44. https://doi.org/10.1007/BF03392017

Cameron, O. G., & Hudson, C. J. (1986). Influence of exercise on anxiety level in patients with anxiety disorders. *Psychosomatics, 27*(10), 720–723. https://doi.org/10.1016/S0033-3182(86)72622-4

Camgöz, N., Yener, C., & Güvenç, D. (2002). Effects of hue, saturation, and brightness on preference. *Color Research and Application, 27*(3), 199–207. https://doi.org/10.1002/col.10051

Campbell, L., & Ellis, B. J. (2015). Commitment, love, and mate retention. In D. Buss (Ed.), *The handbook of evolutionary psychology* (pp. 419–442). John Wiley.

Campbell, P. D., Miller, A. M., & Woesner, M. E. (2017). Bright light therapy: Seasonal affective disorder and beyond. *Einstein Journal of Biology and Medicine, 32*, E13–E25.

Cannon, W. B. (1927). The James-Lange theory of emotions: A critical examination and an alternative theory. *The American Journal of Psychology, 39*(1/4), 106–124. https://doi.org/10.2307/1415404

Cao, W., Fang, Z., Hou, G., Han, M., Xu, X., Dong, J., & Zheng, J. (2020). The psychological impact of the COVID-19 epidemic on college students in China. *Psychiatry Research, 287*, Article 112934. https://doi.org/10.1016/j.psychres.2020.112934

Capalbo, A., Miltenberger, R. G., & Cook, J. L. (2022). Training soccer goalkeeping skills: Is video modeling enough? *Journal of Applied Behavior Analysis, 55*(3), 958–970. https://doi.org/10.1002/jaba.937

Capoccia, S., Berry, A., Bellisario, V., Vacirca, D., Ortona, E., Alleva, E., & Cirulli, F. (2013). Quality and timing of stressors differentially impact on brain plasticity and neuroendocrine-immune function in mice. *Neural Plasticity, 2013*, 1–9. https://doi.org/10.1155/2013/971817

Carbon, C.-C. (2014). Understanding human perception by human-made illusions. *Frontiers in Human Neuroscience, 8*, 1–6. https://doi.org/10.3389/fnhum.2014.00566

Carey, B. (2021, November 1). Dr. Aaron Beck, developer of cognitive therapy, dies at 100. *New York Times.* https://doi.org/10.1161/01.CIR.100.1.14

Carlisle, J. E., & Patton, R. C. (2013). Is social media changing how we understand political engagement? An analysis of Facebook and the 2008 presidential election. *Political Research Quarterly, 66*(4), 883–895. https://doi.org/10.1177/1065912913482758

Carmody, T. P., Duncan, C., Simon, J. A., Solkowitz, S., Huggins, J., Lee, S., & Delucchi, K. (2008). Hypnosis for smoking cessation: A randomized trial. *Nicotine & Tobacco Research, 10*(5), 811–818. https://doi.org/10.1080/14622200802023833

Carney, D. R., Cuddy, A. J. C., & Yap, A. J. (2010). Power posing: Brief nonverbal displays affect neuroendocrine levels and risk tolerance. *Psychological Science, 21*(10), 1363–1368. https://doi.org/10.1177/0956797610383437

Carney, S. M., & Goodwin, G. M. (2005). Lithium<@151>a continuing story in the treatment of bipolar disorder. *Acta Psychiatrica Scandinavica, 111*, 7–12. https://doi.org/10.1111/j.1600-0447.2005.00521.x

Carpenter, C. J. (2010). A meta-analysis of the effectiveness of health belief model variables in predicting behavior. *Health Communication, 25*(8), 661–669. https://doi.org/10.1080/10410236.2010.521906

Carpiniello, B., & Pinna, F. (2017). The reciprocal relationship between suicidality and stigma. *Frontiers in Psychiatry, 8*, Article 35. https://doi.org/10.3389/fpsyt.2017.00035

Carriere, J. S., Cheyne, J. A., & Smilek, D. (2008). Everyday attention lapses and memory failures: The affective consequences of mindlessness. *Consciousness and Cognition, 17*(3), 835–847. https://doi.org/10.1016/j.concog.2007.04.008

Carroll, L. (February 5, 2015). Timeline of Brian Williams' statements on Iraqi helicopter attack. *Politifact*. https://www.politifact.com/article/2015/feb/05/timeline-brian-williams-statements-iraqi-helicopte/

Carson, V. B., Vanderhorst, K. J., & Koenig, H. G. (2015). *Care giving for Alzheimer's disease: A compassionate guide for clinicians and loved ones*. Springer.

Carter, B. E., & McGoldrick, M. E. (1988). *The changing family life cycle: A framework for family therapy*. Gardner Press.

Carter, R. (1998). *Mapping the mind*. University of California Press.

Cartwright, R. (1974). Problem solving: Waking and dreaming. *Journal of Abnormal Psychology, 83*(4), 451–455. https://doi.org/10.1037/h0036811

Cartwright, R., Luten, A., Young, M., Mercer, P., & Bears, M. (1998). Role of REM sleep and dream affect in overnight mood regulation: A study of normal volunteers. *Psychiatry Research, 81*(1), 1–8. https://doi.org/10.1016/S0165-1781(98)00089-4

Carver, C. S. (1997). You want to measure coping but your protocol's too long: Consider the brief cope. *International Journal of Behavioral Medicine, 4*(1), 92–100. https://doi.org/10.1207/s15327558ijbm0401_6

Carver, L., Vafaei, A., Guerra, R., Freire, A., & Phillips, S. P. (2013). Gender differences: Examination of the 12-Item Bem Sex Role Inventory (BSRI-12) in an older Brazilian population. *PLoS ONE, 8*(10), e76356. 10.1371/journal.pone.0076356.

Casadio, P., Olivoni, D., Ferrari, B., Pintori, C., Speranza, E., Bosi, M., Belli, V., Baruzzi, L., Pantieri, P., Ragazzini, G., Rivola, F., & Atti, A. R. (2014). Personality disorders in addiction outpatients: Prevalence and effects on psychosocial functioning. *Substance Abuse: Research and Treatment, 8*, SART-S13764. https://doi.org/10.4137/SART.S13764

Caspi, A. (2000). The child is father of the man: Personality continuities from childhood to adulthood. *Journal of Personality and Social Psychology, 78*(1), 158–172. https://doi.org/10.1037/0022-3514.78.1.158

Catania, A. C. (1994, June 7). Query: Did Pavlov's research ring a bell? *Psycholoquy Newsletter*.

Cattell, R. B. (1933). *Psychology and social progress: Mankind and destiny from the standpoint of a scientist*. C. W. Daniel.

Cattell, R. B. (1943). The description of personality: Basic traits resolved into clusters. *Journal of Abnormal and Social Psychology, 38*(4), 476–507. https://doi.org/10.1037/h0054116

Cattell, R. B. (1971). *Abilities: Their structure, growth, and action*. Houghton Mifflin.

Cattell, R. B. (1972). *A new morality from science: Beyondism*. Pergamon Press.

Cattell, R. B., Eber, H. W., & Tatsuoka, M. (1970). *Handbook for the Sixteen Personality Factor Questionnaire*. Institute for Personality and Ability Testing.

Center for Open Science. (2021). *Registered reports*. https://www.cos.io/initiatives/registered-reports

Centers for Disease Control and Prevention (CDC). (2023). *Menthol smoking and related health disparities*. https://www.cdc.gov/tobacco/basic_information/menthol/related-health-disparities.html#

Cera, N., Vargas-Cáceres, S., Oliveira, C., Monteiro, J., Branco, D., Pignatelli, D., & Rebelo, S. (2021). How relevant is the systemic oxytocin concentration for human sexual behavior? A systematic review. *Sexual Medicine, 9*(4), 1–11. https://doi.org/10.1016/j.esxm.2021.100370

Cesnales, N. I., Dauenhauer, J. A., & Heffernan, K. (2022). Everything gets better with age: Traditional college-aged student perspectives on older adult auditors in multigenerational classrooms. *Journal of Intergenerational Relationships, 20*(3), 265–276. https://doi.org/10.1080/15350770.2020.1835781

Chabris, C., & Simons, D. (2010). *The invisible gorilla: And other ways our intuitions deceive us*. Harmony Publishers.

CHADD. (2021). Women and girls. *Children and adults with Attention Deficit/Hyperactivity Disorder*. https://chadd.org/for-adults/women-and-girls/

Chakraborty, S., & Chattaraman, V. (2022). Acculturative stress and consumption-based coping strategies among first-generation Asian-Indian immigrants in the United States. *International Journal of Consumer Studies, 46*(3), 831–849. https://doi.org/10.1111/ijcs.12731

Chan, A. P., Nwaogu, J. M., & Naslund, J. A. (2020). Mental ill-health risk factors in the construction industry: Systematic review. *Journal of Construction Engineering and Management, 146*(3), Article 04020004.

Chandra, S. (1973). The effects of group pressure in perception: A cross-cultural conformity study. *International Journal of Psychology, 8*(1), 37–39. https://doi.org/10.1080/00207597308247059

Charlson, F. J., Ferrari, A. J., Santomauro, D. F., Diminic, S., Stockings, E., Scott, J. G., McGrath, J. J., & Whiteford, H. A. (2018). Global epidemiology and burden of schizophrenia: Findings from the Global Burden of Disease Study 2016. *Schizophrenia Bulletin, 44*(6), 1195–1203. https://doi.org/10.1093/schbul/sby058

Chartrand, T. L., & van Baaren, R. (2009). Human mimicry. *Advances in Experimental Social Psychology, 41*, 219–274. https://doi.org/10.1016/S0065-2601(08)00405-X

Chawla, M., & Garrison, K. A. (2018). Neurobiological considerations for tobacco use disorder. *Current Behavioral Neuroscience Reports, 5*(4), 238–248. https://doi.org/10.1007/s40473-018-0168-3

Chen, E. C., Boyd, D. M., & Cunningham, C. A. (2020). Demarginalizing stigmatized identities of transgender and gender nonconforming individuals through affirmative group therapy. *International Journal of Group Psychotherapy, 70*(4), 552–578. https://doi.org/10.1080/00207284.2020.1755291

Chen, W., & Chen, J. (2019). Consequences of inadequate sleep during the college years: Sleep deprivation, grade point average, and college graduation. *Preventive Medicine, 124*, 23–28. https://doi.org/10.1016/j.ypmed.2019.04.017

Chen, Y., Nettles, M. E., & Chen, S. W. (2009). Rethinking dependent personality disorder: Comparing different human relatedness in cultural contexts. *The Journal of Nervous and Mental Disease, 197*(11), 793–800. https://doi.org/10.1097/NMD.0b013e3181be76ae

Cheney, R. H. (1936). Reaction time behavior after caffeine and coffee consumption. *Journal of Experimental Psychology, 19*(3), 357–369. https://doi.org/10.1037/h0062397

Cheng, B., Roberts, N., Zhou, Y., Wang, X., Li, Y., Chen, Y., Zhao, Y., Deng, P., Meng, Y., Deng, W., & Wang, J. (2022). Social support mediates the influence of cerebellum functional connectivity strength on postpartum depression and postpartum depression with anxiety. *Translational Psychiatry, 12*(1), Article 54. https://doi.org/10.1038/s41398-022-01781-9

Cheng, S., & Deng, M. (2022). Psychological stress and parenting styles predict parental involvement for children with intellectual disabilities during the COVID-19. *Journal of Child and Family Studies, 32*, 122–131. https://doi.org/10.1007/s10826-022-02485-w

Cheng, T., Wallace, D. M., Ponteri, B., & Tuli, M. (2018). Valium without dependence? Individual GABAA receptor subtype contribution toward benzodiazepine addiction, tolerance, and therapeutic effects. *Neuropsychiatric Disease and Treatment, 14*, 1351–1361. https://doi.org/10.2147/NDT.S164307

Cherry, K. (2021). *An overview of the Myers-Briggs Type Indicator*. Verywellmind.com. https://www.verywellmind.com/the-myers-briggs-type-indicator-2795583#toc-the-mbti-types

Chess, S., & Thomas, A. (1986). Longitudinal study: From infancy to early adult life. In R. Plomin & J. Dunn (Eds.), *The study of temperament: Changes, continuities, and challenges* (pp. 39–52). Lawrence Erlbaum.

Chételat, G., Lutz, A., Arenaza-Urquijo, E., Collette, F., Klimecki, O., & Marchant, N. (2018). Why could meditation practice help promote mental health and well-being in aging? *Alzheimer's Research & Therapy, 10*(1), 1–4. https://doi.org/10.1186/s13195-018-0388-5

Cheung, F. M., Leung, K., Fan, R. M., Song, W. Z., Zhang, J. X., & Zhang, J. P. (1996). Development of the Chinese Personality Assessment Inventory. *Journal of Cross-Cultural Psychology, 27*, 181–199. https://doi.org/10.1177/0022022196272003

Cheung, F. M., Leung, K., Zhang, J. X., Sun, H. F., Gan, Y. Q., Song, W. Z., & Xie, D. (2001). Indigenous Chinese personality constructs: Is the five-factor model complete? *Journal of Cross-Cultural Psychology, 32*(4), 407–433. https://doi.org/10.1177/0022022101032004003

Cheyne, J. A., Carriere, J. S. A., & Smilek, D. (2006). Absent-mindedness: Lapses of conscious awareness and everyday cognitive failures. *Consciousness and Cognition, 15*(3), 578–592. https://doi.org/10.1016/j.concog.2005.11.009

Chi, S., Yu, J. T., Tan, M. S., & Tan, L. (2014). Depression in Alzheimer's disease: Epidemiology, mechanisms, and management. *Journal of Alzheimer's Disease, 42*(3), 739–755. https://doi.org/10.3233/JAD-140324

Chiao, J. Y. (2009). Cultural neuroscience: A once and future discipline. *Progress in Brain Research, 178*, 287–304. https://doi.org/10.1016/S0079-6123(09)17821-4

Chiesa, A., & Serretti, A. (2009). Mindfulness-based stress reduction for stress management in healthy people: A review and meta-analysis. *The Journal of Alternative and Complementary Medicine, 15*(5), 593–600. https://doi.org/10.1089/acm.2008.0495

Child, S. O., & Center, F. G. (2020). A primer for clinicians on alternatives to the Diagnostic and Statistical Manual of Mental Disorders. *Professional Psychology: Research and Practice, 52*(2), 91–103. https://doi.org/10.1037/pro0000327

Childress, A. R., McLellan, A. T., Ehrman, R., & O'Brien, C. P. (1988). Classically conditioned responses in opioid and cocaine dependence: A role in relapse? In B. A. Ray (Ed.), *Learning factors in substance abuse* (pp. 25–43). Alcohol, Drug Abuse, and Mental Health Administration.

Chiriac, V. F., Baban, A., & Dumitrascu, D. L. (2018). Psychological stress and breast cancer incidence: A systematic review. *Clujul Medical, 91*(1), 18–26. https://doi.org/10.15386/cjmed-924

Chodzen, G., Hidalgo, M. A., Chen, D., & Garofalo, R. (2019). Minority stress factors associated with depression and anxiety among transgender and gender-nonconforming youth. *Journal of Adolescent Health, 64*(4), 467–471. https://doi.org/10.1016/j.jadohealth.2018.07.006

Choi, K. R., Heilemann, M. V., Fauer, A., & Mead, M. (2020). A second pandemic: Mental health spillover from the novel coronavirus (COVID-19). *Journal of the American Psychiatric Nurses Association, 26*(4), 340–343. https://doi.org/10.1177/1078390320919803

Chomsky, N. (1965). *Aspects of the theory of syntax*. MIT Press.

Chu, D. T., Nguyet, N. T. M., Dinh, T. C., Lien, N. V. T., Nguyen, K. H., Ngoc, V. T. N., Tao, Y., Son, L. H., Le, D-H., Nga, V. B., Jurgonski, A., Tran, Q-H., Tu, P. V., & Pham, V. H. (2018). An update on physical health and economic consequences of overweight and obesity. *Diabetes & Metabolic Syndrome: Clinical Research & Reviews, 12*(6), 1095–1100. https://doi.org/10.1016/j.dsx.2018.05.004

Chu, S. T.-W., & Mak, W. W. S. (2020). How mindfulness enhances meaning in life: A meta-analysis of correlational studies and randomized controlled trials. *Mindfulness, 11*(1), 177–193. https://doi.org/10.1007/s12671-019-01258-9

Chu, Y., & MacGregor, J. N. (2011). Human performance on insight problem solving: A review. *The Journal of Problem Solving, 3*(2), 119–150. https://doi.org/10.7771/1932-6246.1094

Chung, H., & Zhao, X. (2003). Humour effect on memory and attitude: Moderating role of product involvement. *International Journal of Advertising, 22*(1), 117–144. https://doi.org/10.1080/02650487.2003.11072842

Cialdini, R. B. (2006). *Influence: The psychology of persuasion* (Rev. ed.). Harper Business.

Cicekci, M.A., & Sadık, F. (2019). Teachers' and students' opinions about students' attention problems during the lesson. *Journal of Education and Learning, 8*(6), 15–30. https://doi.org/10.5539/jel.v8n6p15

Çiller, A., Köskün, T., & Akca, A. Y. E. (2022). Post traumatic stress disorder and behavioral therapy intervention techniques used in treatment. *Psikiyatride Güncel Yaklaşımlar, 14*(4), 499–509. https://doi.org/10.18863/pgy.1096518

Cirigliano, M. M. (2013). Musical mnemonics in health science: A first look. *Medical Teacher, 35*(3), e1020–e1026. https://doi.org/10.3109/0142159X.2012.733042

Civettini, N. (2015). Gender display, time availability, and relative resources: Applicability to housework contributions of members of same-sex couples. *International Social Science Review, 91*(1), 1–36. https://www.jstor.org/stable/intesociscierevi.91.1.01

Clapp, J. D., Reed, M. B., Holmes, M. R., Lange, J. E., & Voas, R. B. (2006). Drunk in public, drunk in private: The relationship between college students, drinking environments and alcohol consumption. *The American Journal of Drug and Alcohol Abuse, 32*(2), 275–285. https://doi.org/10.1080/00952990500481205

Clare, K., Pan, C., Kim, G., Park, K., Zhao, J., Volkow, N. D., Lin, Z., & Du, C. (2021). Cocaine reduces the neuronal population while upregulating dopamine D2-receptor-expressing neurons in brain reward regions: Sex-effects. *Frontiers in Pharmacology, 12*, 1–15. https://doi.org/10.3389/fphar.2021.624127

Clark, K. B., & Clark, M. K. (1939). The development of consciousness of self and the emergence of racial identification in Negro preschool children. *Journal of Social Psychology, 10*(4), 591–599. https://doi.org/10.1080/00224545.1939.9713394

Clark, T. (1987). Echoic memory explored and applied. *Journal of Services Marketing, 1*(2), 41–48. https://doi.org/10.1108/eb024707

Clarke, E., Pugh, G., van den Heuvel, E., Kavanagh, E., Cheung, P., Wood, A., Winstanley, M., Braakhuis, A., & Lovell, A. L. (2023). Navigating nutrition as a childhood cancer survivor: Understanding patient and family needs for nutrition interventions or education. *Nutrition & Dietetics, 80*, 494–510. https://doi.org/10.1111/1747-0080.12803

Clegg, J. W. (2012). Teaching about mental health and illness through the history of the DSM. *History of Psychology, 15*(4), 364–370. https://doi.org/10.1037/a0027249

Coall, D. A., & Hertwig, R. (2011). Grandparental investment: A relic of the past or a resource for the future? *Current Directions in Psychological Science, 20*(2), 93–98. https://doi.org/10.1177/0963721411403269

Coan, J. A., Schaefer, H. S., & Davidson, R. J. (2006). Lending a hand: Social regulation of the neural response to threat. *Psychological Science, 17*(12), 1032–1039. https://doi.org/10.1111/j.1467-9280.2006.01832.x

Coaston, J. (2019, May 28). The intersectionality wars. *Vox*. https://www.vox.com/the-highlight/2019/5/20/18542843/intersectionality-conservalism-law-race-gender-discrimination

Cocodia, E. A. (2014). Cultural perceptions of human intelligence. *Journal of Intelligence, 2*, 180–196. https://doi.org/10.3390/jintelligence2040180

Cohen, S., & Williamson, G. (1988). Perceived stress in a probability sample of the United States. In S. Spacapan & S. Oskamp (Eds.),

The social psychology of health: Claremont Symposium on Applied Social Psychology (pp. 31–67). Sage.

Cohen, S., Murphy, M. L., & Prather, A. A. (2019). Ten surprising facts about stressful life events and disease risk. *Annual Review of Psychology, 70*, 577–597. https://doi.org/10.1146/annurev-psych-010418-102857

Cohn, M. A., Fredrickson, B. L., Brown, S. L., Mikels, J. A., & Conway, A. M. (2009). Happiness unpacked: Positive emotions increase life satisfaction by building resilience. *Emotion, 9*(3), 361–368. https://doi.org/10.1037/a0015952

Colapinto, J. (2019). Structural family therapy. In J. Lebow, A. Chambers, & D. Breunlin (Eds.), *Encyclopedia of couple and family therapy* (pp. 2820–2828). Springer. https://doi.org/10.1007/978-3-319-49425-8_334

Colle, L., Hilviu, D., Boggio, M., Toso, A., Longo, P., Abbate-Daga, G., Garbarini, F., & Fossataro, C. (2023). Abnormal sense of agency in eating disorders. *Scientific Reports, 13*, Article 14176. https://doi.org/10.1038/s41598-023-41345-5

Collier, W. G., & Shi, X. (2020). Mindfulness, meditation, and belief in free will/determinism. *Psychological Reports, 123*(5), 1724–1752. https://doi.org/10.1177/0033294119892884

Collins, A. M. & Loftus, E. F. (1975). A spreading activation theory of semantic processing. *Psychological Review, 82*(6), 407–428. https://doi.org/10.1037/0033-295X.82.6.407

Collison, K. L., Vize, C. E., Miller, J. D., & Lynam, D. R. (2018). Development and preliminary validation of a five factor model measure of Machiavellianism. *Psychological Assessment, 30*(10), 1401–1407. https://doi.org/10.1037/pas0000637

Colom, R., Abad, R. J., Garcia, L. F., & Juan-Espinosa, M. (2002). Education, Wechsler's Full Scale IQ, and g. *Intelligence, 30*(5), 449–462. https://doi.org/10.1016/S0160-2896(02)00122-8

Conaway, W., & Bethune, S. (2015). Implicit bias and first name stereotypes: What are the implications for online instruction? *Online Learning, 19*(3), 162–178. http://dx.doi.org/10.24059/olj.v19i3.452

Condon, J., Luszcz, M., & McKee, I. (2018). The transition to grandparenthood: A prospective study of mental health implications. *Aging & Mental Health, 22*(3), 336–343. https://doi.org/10.1080/13607863.2016.1248897

Conley, S., Knies, A., Batten, J., Ash, G., Miner, B., Hwang, Y., Jeon, S., & Redeker, N. S. (2019). Agreement between actigraphic and polysomnographic measures of sleep in adults with and without chronic conditions: A systematic review and meta-analysis. *Sleep Medicine Reviews, 46*, 151–160. https://doi.org/10.1016/j.smrv.2019.05.001

Connidis, I. A. (2001). *Family ties and aging.* Sage.

Connor-Smith, J. K., & Flachsbart, C. (2007). Relations between personality and coping: A meta-analysis. *Journal of Personality and Social Psychology, 93*(6), 1080–1107. https://doi.org/10.1037/0022-3514.93.6.1080

Conoley, C. W., Plumb, E. W., Hawley, K. J., Spaventa-Vancil, K. Z., & Hernández, R. J. (2015). Integrating positive psychology into family therapy: Positive family therapy. *The Counseling Psychologist, 43*(5), 703–733. https://doi.org/10.1177/0011000015575392

Conway, A. R. A., Kane, M. J., & Engle, R. W. (2003). Working memory capacity and its relation to general intelligence. *Trends in Cognitive Sciences, 7*(12), 547–552. https://doi.org/10.1016/j.tics.2003.10.005

Conway, M., & Ross, M. (1984). Getting what you want by revising what you had. *Journal of Personality and Social Psychology, 47*(4), 738–748. https://doi.org/10.1037/0022-3514.47.4.738

Cook, J. A., Boxer, A. M., Burke, J., Cohen, M. H., Weber, K., Shekarloo, P., Lubin, H., & Mock, L. O. (2004). Child care arrangements of children orphaned by HIV/AIDS: The importance of grandparents as kinship caregivers. *Journal of HIV/AIDS & Social Services, 2*(2), 5–20. https://doi.org/10.1300/J187v02n02_02

Cooke, R., Dahdah, M., Norman, P., & French, D. P. (2016). How well does the theory of planned behaviour predict alcohol consumption? A systematic review and meta-analysis. *Health Psychology Review, 10*(2), 148–167. https://doi.org/10.1080/17437199.2014.947547

Coons, P. M. (1994). Reports of satanic ritual abuse: Further implications about pseudomemories. *Perceptual and Motor Skills, 78*(3, Pt 2), 1376–1378. https://doi.org/10.2466/pms.1994.78.3c.1376

Cooper, J. M. (2007). *Cognitive dissonance: 50 years of a classic theory.* Sage.

Cooper, J. N., Corral, M. D., Macaulay, C. D., Cooper, M. S., Nwadike, A., & Mallery, M., Jr. (2019). Collective uplift: The impact of a holistic development support program on black male former college athletes' experiences and outcomes. *International Journal of Qualitative Studies in Education, 32*(1), 21–46. https://doi.org/10.1080/09518398.2018.1522011

Cooper, R. M., & Zubek, J. P. (1958). Effects of enriched and restricted early environments on the learning ability of bright and dull rats. *Canadian Journal of Psychology, 12*(3), 159–164. https://doi.org/10.1037/h0083747

Cooper, S. E., van Dis, E. A. M., Hagenaars, M. A., Krypotos, A-M., Nemeroff, C. B., Lissek, S., Engelhard, I. M., & Dunsmoor, J. E. (2022). A meta-analysis of conditioned fear generalization in anxiety-related disorders. *Neuropsychopharmacology, 47*, 1652–1661. https://doi.org/10.1038/s41386-022-01332-2

Cooper, S., Robison, A. J., & Mazei-Robison, M. S. (2017). Reward circuitry in addiction. *Neurotherapeutics, 14*(3), 687–697. https://doi.org/10.1007/s13311-017-0525-z

Cooper, T., Detre, T., & Weiss, S. M. (1981). Coronary-prone behavior and coronary heart disease: A critical review. *Circulation, 63*(6I), 1199–1215. https://doi.org/10.1161/01.cir.63.6.1199

Copeland-Linder, N. (2006). Stress among black women in a South African township: The protective role of religion. *Journal of Community Psychology, 34*(5), 577–599. https://doi.org/10.1002/jcop.20116

Coppola, F. F., & Mutrux, G. (Producers), & Condon, B. (Director). (2004). *Kinsey* [Motion picture]. Fox Searchlight.

Coren, S. (1999). Psychology applied to animal training. In A. Stec & D. Bernstein (Eds.), *Psychology: Fields of application*. Houghton Mifflin.

Cormier, J. F., & Thelen, M. H. (1998). Professional skepticism of multiple personality disorder. *Professional Psychology: Research and Practice, 29*(2), 163–167. https://doi.org/10.1037/0735-7028.29.2.163

Corr, C. A. (1993). Coping with dying: Lessons that we should and should not learn from the work of Elisabeth Kübler-Ross. *Death Studies, 17*(1), 69–83. https://doi.org/10.1080/07481189308252605

Corr, C. A. (2021). Elisabeth Kübler-Ross and the "five stages" model in a sampling of recent textbooks published in 10 countries outside the United States. *OMEGA—Journal of Death and Dying, 83*(1), 33–63. https://doi.org/10.1177/0030222819840476

Corr, C. A., Corr, D. M., & Doka, K. J. (2018). *Death and dying, life and living.* Cengage Learning.

Corrigan, P. (1998). The impact of stigma on severe mental illness. *Cognitive and Behavioral Practice, 5*, 201–222. https://doi.org/10.1016/S1077-7229(98)80006-0

Corrigan, P. W. (2000). Mental health stigma as social attribution: Implications for research methods and attitude change. *Clinical Psychology: Science and Practice, 7*(1), 48–67. https://doi.org/10.1093/clipsy.7.1.48

Corrigan, P. W. (2004). How stigma interferes with mental health care. *American Psychologist, 59*(7), 614–625. https://doi.org/10.1037/0003-066X.59.7.614

Corrigan, P. W., Druss, B. G., & Perlick, D. A. (2014). The impact of mental illness stigma on seeking and participating in mental health care. *Psychological Science in the Public Interest*, *15*(2), 37–70. https://doi.org/10.1177/1529100614531398

Corrigan, P. W., Markowitz, F. E., & Watson, A. C. (2004). Structural levels of mental illness stigma and discrimination. *Schizophrenia Bulletin*, *30*, 481–491. http://dx.doi.org/10.1093/oxfordjournals.schbul.a007096x

Costa, P. T., & McCrae, R. R. (1992). Normal personality assessment in clinical practice: The NEO Personality Inventory. *Psychological Assessment*, *4*(1), 5–13. http://dx.doi.org/10.1037/1040-3590.4.1.5

Costa, P. T., Jr., McCrae, R. R., & Löckenhoff, C. E. (2019). Personality across the life span. *Annual Review of Psychology*, *70*, 423–448. https://doi.org/10.1146/annurev-psych-010418-103244

Costello, R. B., Lentino, C. V., Boyd, C. C., O'Connell, M. L., Crawford, C. C., Sprengel, M. L., & Deuster, P. A. (2014). The effectiveness of melatonin for promoting healthy sleep: A rapid evidence assessment of the literature. *Nutrition Journal*, *13*, Article 106. https://doi.org/10.1186/1475-2891-13-106

Cotton, J. L. (1981). A review of research on Schachter's theory of emotion and the misattribution of arousal. *European Journal of Social Psychology*, *11*(4), 365–397. https://doi.org/10.1002/ejsp.2420110403

Coubart, A., Izard, V., Spelke, E. S., Marie, J., & Streri, A. (2014). Dissociation between small and large numerosities in newborn infants. *Developmental Science*, *17*(1), 11–22. https://doi.org/10.1111/desc.12108

Cousins, J. N., Wong, K. F., Raghunath, B. L., Look, C., & Chee, M. W. L. (2019). The long-term memory benefits of a daytime nap compared with cramming. *Sleep: Journal of Sleep and Sleep Disorders Research*, *42*(1), 1–7. https://doi.org/10.1093/sleep/zsy207

Couzijn, M. (1999). Learning to write by observation of writing and reading processes: Effects on learning and transfer. *Learning and Instruction*, *9*(2), 109–142. https://doi.org/10.1016/S0959-4752(98)00040-1

Covington, M. V., & Müeller, K. J. (2001). Intrinsic versus extrinsic motivation: An approach/avoidance reformulation. *Educational Psychology Review*, *13*, 157–176. https://doi.org/10.1023/A:1009009219144

Craig, A. R., Hancock, K. M., & Dickson, H. G. (1994). Spinal cord injury: A search for determinants of depression two years after the event. *British Journal of Clinical Psychology*, *33*(2), 221–230. https://doi.org/10.1111/j.2044-8260.1994.tb01116.x

Craik, F. I., & Lockhart, R. S. (1972). Levels of processing: A framework for memory research. *Journal of Verbal Learning & Verbal Behavior*, *11*(6), 671–684. https://doi.org/10.1016/S0022-5371(72)80001-X

Crain, W. C. (2016). *Theories of development: Concepts and applications* (4th ed.). Routledge.

Cramblet Alvarez, L. D., Jones, K. N., Walljasper-Schuyler, C., Trujillo, M., Weiser, M. A., Rodriguez, J. L., Ringler, R. L., & Leach, J. L. (2019). Psychology's hidden figures: Undergraduate psychology majors' (in)ability to recognize our diverse pioneers. *Psi Chi Journal of Psychological Research*, *24*, 84–96. https://doi.org/10.24839/2325-7342.JN24.2.84

Crenshaw, K. (1989). Demarginalizing the intersection of race and sex: A Black feminist critique of antidiscrimination doctrine, feminist theory and antiracist politics. In K. Maschke (Ed.), *Feminist legal theories* (pp. 139–167). Routledge.

Crocq, M. A. (2013). Milestones in the history of personality disorders. *Dialogues in Clinical Neuroscience*, *15*(2), 147–153. https://doi.org/10.31887/DCNS.2013.15.2/macrocq

Croson, R., & Sundali, J. (2005). The gambler's fallacy and the hot hand: Empirical data from casinos. *Journal of Risk and Uncertainty*, *30*, 195–209. https://doi.org/10.1007/s11166-005-1153-2

Crowder, K., & Goodfriend, W. (2012). Good monkey see, good monkey do: Children's imitative prosocial behavior. *Journal of Psychological Inquiry*, *17*(2), 7–16.

Crowne, D. P., & Marlowe, D. (1960). A new scale of social desirability independent of psychopathology. *Journal of Consulting Psychology*, *24*(4), 349–354. https://doi.org/10.1037/h0047358

Cruz, J. M. (2003). "Why doesn't he just leave?" Gay male domestic violence and the reasons victims stay. *The Journal of Men's Studies*, *11*(3), 309–323. https://doi.org/10.3149/jms.1103.309

Cruz, T. N. D., Camelo, E. V., Nardi, A. E., & Cheniaux, E. (2022). Creativity in bipolar disorder: A systematic review. *Trends in Psychiatry and Psychotherapy*, *44*, 1–9. https://doi.org/10.47626/2237-6089-2021-0196

Csikszentmihalyi, M. (2008). *Flow: The psychology of optimal experience*. Harper Perennial.

Culotta, P., & McLain, T. (2019). Corporal punishment. In A. P. Giardino, M. A. Lyn, & E. R. Giardino (Eds.), *A practical guide to the evaluation of child physical abuse and neglect* (3rd ed., pp. 431–443). Springer.

Cumming, J., Clark, S. E., Ste-Marie, D.M., McCullagh, P., & Hall, C. (2005). The functions of observational learning. *Psychology of Sport and Exercise*, *6*(5), 517–537. https://doi.org/10.1016/j.psychsport.2004.03.006

Cummings, N., & Cummings, D. (2022). Historical chronology: Examining psychology's contributions to the belief in racial hierarchy and perpetuation of inequality for people of color in the U.S. https://www.apa.org/about/apa/addressing-racism/historical-chronology.pdf

Cummings, S. R., & Melton, L. J. (2002). Epidemiology and outcomes of osteoporotic fractures. *The Lancet*, *359*(9319), 1761–1767. https://doi.org/10.1016/S0140-6736(02)08657-9

Cunningham, C., O'Sullivan, R., Caserotti, P., & Tully, M. A. (2020). Consequences of physical inactivity in older adults: A systematic review of reviews and meta-analyses. *Scandinavian Journal of Medicine & Science in Sports*, *30*(5), 816–827. https://doi.org/10.1111/sms.13616

Cury, F., Elliot, A. J., Da Fonseca, D., & Moller, A. C. (2006). The social-cognitive model of achievement motivation and the 2×2 achievement goal framework. *Journal of Personality and Social Psychology*, *90*(4), 666–679. https://doi.org/10.1037/0022-3514.90.4.666

Cutting, J. E. (2020). The mere exposure effect and aesthetic preference. In P. Locher, C. Martindale, & L. Doftman (Eds.), *New directions in aesthetics, creativity, and the arts* (pp. 33–46). Routledge.

Czeisler, M. É., Lane, R. I., Petrosky, E., Wiley, J. F., Christensen, A., Njai, R., Weaver, M. D., Robbins, R., Facer-Childs, E. R., Barger, L. K., Czeisler, C. A., Howard, M. E., & Rajaratnam, S. M. (2020). Mental health, substance use, and suicidal ideation during the COVID-19 pandemic—United States, June 24–30, 2020. *Morbidity and Mortality Weekly Report*, *69*(32), 1049–1057. https://doi.org/10.1016/j.jpsychires.2021.05.080

D'Innocenzo, G., Gonzalez, C. C., Williams, A. M., & Bishop, D. T. (2016). Looking to learn: The effects of visual guidance on observational learning of the golf swing. *PLoS ONE*, *11*(5), Article e0155442. https://doi.org/10.1371/journal.pone.0155442

da Silva Costa, L., Alencar, Á. P., Neto, P. J. N., dos Santos, M. D. S. V., da Silva, C. G. L., Pinheiro, S. D. F. L., Silveira, R. T., Vieira Bianco, B. A., Fontenelle Pinheiro, R. F., Jr., Pereira de Lima, M. A., Advincula Reis, A. O., & Neto, M. L. R. (2015). Risk factors for suicide in bipolar disorder: A systematic review. *Journal of Affective Disorders*, *170*, 237–254. https://doi.org/10.1016/j.jad.2014.09.003

Dåderman, A. M., & Ragnestål-Impola, C. (2019). Workplace bullies, not their victims, score high on the dark triad and extraversion, and low on agreeableness and honesty-humility. *Heliyon*, *5*(10), e02609. https://doi.org/10.1016/j.heliyon.2019.e02609

Dahl, M. (2015). *Isabel Briggs Myers co-created the famed personality test. But who was she?* The Cut. https://www.thecut.com/2015/10/who-was-isabel-briggs-myers.html

Dahl, M., Granér, S., Fransson, P.-A., Bertilsson, J., & Fredriksson, P. (2018). Analysis of eyewitness testimony in a police shooting with fatal outcome—Manifestations of spatial and temporal distortions. *Cogent Psychology, 5*(1), Article 1487271. https://doi.org/10.1080/23311908.2018.1487271

Dai, S., Mo, Y., Wang, Y., Xiang, B., Liao, Q., Zhou, M., Li, X., Li, Y., Xiong, W., Li, G., Guo, C., & Zeng, Z. (2020). Chronic stress promotes cancer development. *Frontiers in Oncology, 10*(1492), 1–10. https://doi.org/10.3389/fonc.2020.01492

Dailey, A., Martindale, C., & Borkum, J. (1997). Creativity, synesthesia, and physiognomic perception. *Creativity Research Journal, 10*(1), 1–8. https://doi.org/10.1207/s15326934crj1001_1

Dalenberg, C. J., Brand, B. L., Gleaves, D. H., Dorahy, M. J., Loewenstein, R. J., Cardeña, E., Frewen, P. A., Carlson, E. B., & Spiegel, D. (2012). Evaluation of the evidence for the trauma and fantasy models of dissociation. *Psychological Bulletin, 138*(3), 550–588. https://doi.org/10.1037/a0027447

Dalgleish, T. (2004). The emotional brain. *Nature Reviews Neuroscience, 5*(7), 583–589. https://doi.org/10.1038/nrn1432

Dalgleish, T., Navrady, L., Bird, E., Hill, E., Dunn, B. D., & Golden, A. M. (2013). Method-of-loci as a mnemonic device to facilitate access to self-affirming personal memories for individuals with depression. *Clinical Psychological Science, 1*(2), 156–162. https://doi.org/10.1177/2167702612468111

Dallman, M. F., Pecoraro, N. C., & la Fleur, S. E. (2005). Chronic stress and comfort foods: Self-medication and abdominal obesity. *Brain, Behavior, and Immunity, 19*(4), 275–280. https://doi.org/10.1016/j.bbi.2004.11.004

Dallman, M. F., Pecoraro, N. C., & la Fleur, S. E. (2005). Chronic stress and comfort foods: Self-medication and abdominal obesity. *Brain, Behavior, and Immunity, 19*(4), 275–280. https://doi.org/10.1016/j.bbi.2004.11.004

Damasio, A. R. (2008). *Descartes' error: Emotion, reason and the human brain.* Random House.

Damian, R. I., Spengler, M., Sutu, A., & Roberts, B. W. (2019). Sixteen going on sixty-six: A longitudinal study of personality stability and change across 50 years. *Journal of Personality and Social Psychology, 117*(3), 674–695. https://doi.org/10.1037/pspp0000210

Dammann, G. (2017). Schizoid personality disorder. *Psychosomatic Medicine and General Practice, 2*(4), e020484. https://doi.org/10.26766/PMGP.V2I4.84

Daprati, E., Sirigu, A., & Nico, D. (2010). Body and movement: Consciousness in the parietal lobes. *Neuropsychologia, 48*(3), 756–762. https://doi.org/10.1016/j.neuropsychologia.2009.10.008

Dar, T., Radfar, A., Abohashem, S., Pitman, R. K., Tawakol, A., & Osborne, M. T. (2019). Psychosocial stress and cardiovascular disease. *Current Treatment Options in Cardiovascular Medicine, 21*(5), 1–17. https://doi.org/10.1007/s11936-019-0724-5

Darbonne, A., Uchino, B. N., & Ong, A. D. (2013). What mediates links between age and well-being? A test of social support and interpersonal conflict as potential interpersonal pathways. *Journal of Happiness Studies, 14*(3), 951–963. https://doi.org/10.1007/s10902-012-9363-1

Darley, J. M., & Latané, B. (1968). Bystander intervention in emergencies: Diffusion of responsibility. *Journal of Personality and Social Psychology, 8*(4), 377–383. https://doi.org/10.1037/h0025589

Darwin, C. (1860). *A naturalist's voyage round the world.* Journal of Researches, W. Clowes and Sons.

Darwin, C. (2005). *The expression of emotion in man and animals.* Appleton. (Original work published 1872)

Das, R. K., Gale, G., Walsh, K., Hennessy, V. E., Iskandar, G., Mordecai, L. A., Brandner, B., Kindt, M., Curran, H. V., & Kamboj, S. K. (2019). Ketamine can reduce harmful drinking by pharmacologically rewriting drinking memories. *Nature Communications, 10*(1), Article 5187. https://doi.org/10.1038/s41467-019-13162-w

David, D., Szentagotai, A., Eva, K., & Macavei, B. (2005). A synopsis of rational-emotive behavior therapy (REBT): Fundamental and applied research. *Journal of Rational-Emotive & Cognitive-Behavior Therapy, 23*(3), 175–221. https://doi.org/10.1007/s10942-005-0011-0

Davidson, P. R., & Parker, K. C. H. (2001). Eye movement desensitization and reprocessing (EMDR): A meta-analysis. *Journal of Consulting and Clinical Psychology, 69*(2), 305–316. https://doi.org/10.1037/0022-006X.69.2.305

Davidson, R. J., & Fox, N. A. (1982). Asymmetrical brain activity discriminates between positive and negative affective stimuli in human infants. *Science, 218*(4578), 1235–1237. https://doi.org/10.1126/science.7146906

Davidson, R. J., & Fox, N. A. (1989). Frontal brain asymmetry predicts infants' response to maternal separation. *Journal of Abnormal Psychology, 98*(2), 127–131. https://doi.org/10.1037/0021-843X.98.2.127

Davidson, R. J., & Tomarken, A. J. (1989). Laterality and emotion: An electrophysiological approach. *Handbook of Neuropsychology, 3*, 419–441.

Davidson, R. J., Ekman, P., Saron, C. D., Senulis, J. A., & Friesen, W. V. (1990). Approach-withdrawal and cerebral asymmetry: Emotional expression and brain physiology. *Journal of Personality and Social Psychology, 58*(2), 330–341. https://doi.org/10.1037/0022-3514.58.2.330

Davies, E. M., Van der Heijden, B. I., & Flynn, M. (2017). Job satisfaction, retirement attitude and intended retirement age: A conditional process analysis across workers' level of household income. *Frontiers in Psychology, 8*, Article 891. https://doi.org/10.3389/fpsyg.2017.00891

Davies, G., Tenesa, A., Payton, A., Yang, J., Harris, S. E., Liewald, D., Ke, X., Le Hellard, S., Christoforou, A., Luciano, M., McGhee, K., Lopez, L., Gow, A. J., Corley, J., Redmond, P., Fox, H. C., Haggarty, P., Whalley, L. J., McNeill, G., Goddard, M. E., . . . Deary, I. J. (2011). Genome-wide association studies establish that human intelligence is highly heritable and polygenic. *Molecular Psychiatry, 16*(10), 996–1005. https://doi.org/10.1038/mp.2011.85

Davies, M. F. (1982). Self-focused attention and belief perseverance. *Journal of Experimental Social Psychology, 18*(6), 595–605. https://doi.org/10.1016/0022-1031(82)90075-0

Daviglus, M. L., Bell, C. C., Berrettini, W., Bowen, P. E., Connolly, E. S., Jr., Cox, N. J., Dunbar-Jacob, J. M., Granieri, E. C., Hunt, G., McGarry, K., Patel, D., Potosky, A. L., Sanders-Bush, E., Silberberg, D., & Trevisan, M. (2010). National Institutes of Health State-of-the-Science Conference statement: Preventing Alzheimer disease and cognitive decline. *Annals of Internal Medicine, 153*(3), 176–181. https://doi.org/10.7326/0003-4819-153-3-201008030-00260

Davis, D. M., & Hayes, J. A. (2011). What are the benefits of mindfulness? A practice review of psychotherapy-related research. *Psychotherapy, 48*(2), 198–208. https://doi.org/10.1037/a0022062

Davis, T. E., III, Ollendick, T. H., & Öst, L. G. (2019). One-session treatment of specific phobias in children: Recent developments and a systematic review. *Annual Review of Clinical Psychology, 15*, 233–256. https://doi.org/10.1146/annurev-clinpsy-050718-095608

De Berardis, D., De Filippis, S., Masi, G., Vicari, S., & Zuddas, A. (2021). A neurodevelopment approach for a transitional model of early onset schizophrenia. *Brain Sciences, 11*(2), Article 275. https://doi.org/10.3390/brainsci11020275

De Castella, K., & Byrne, D. (2015). My intelligence may be more malleable than yours: The Revised Implicit Theories of Intelligence (Self-Theory) Scale is a better predictor of achievement, motivation, and student disengagement. *European Journal of Psychology of Education, 30*(3), 245–267. https://doi.org/10.1007/s10212-015-0244-y

De Klerk, L. M., Kramer, M., Pieterse, B., Smith, K. A., van Tiddens, A., Jansen, A., & Aluko, O. (2023). Empathy and associated influencing factors in occupational therapy students: A cross-sectional study. *South African Journal of Occupational Therapy, 53*(2), 32–42. http://dx.doi.org/10.17159/2310-3833/2023/vol53n2a4

de la Rubia Ortí, J. E., Fernández, D., Platero, F., & García-Pardo, M. P. (2021). Can ketogenic diet improve Alzheimer's disease? Association with anxiety, depression, and glutamate system. *Frontiers in Nutrition, 8*, 1–8. https://doi.org/10.3389/fnut.2021.744398

de Maat, S., de Jonghe, F., de Kraker, R., Leichsenring, F., Abbass, A., Luyten, P., Barber, J. P., Van, R., & Dekker, J. (2013). The current state of the empirical evidence for psychoanalysis: A meta-analytic approach. *Harvard Review of Psychiatry, 21*(3), 107–137. https://doi.org/10.1097/HRP.0b013e318294f5fd

de Schotten, M. T., & Beckmann, C. F. (2021). Asymmetry of brain structure and function: 40 years after Sperry's Nobel Prize. *Brain Structure & Function, 227*, 421–424. https://doi.org/10.1007/s00429-021-02426-1

de Souza Machado, F., da Silva Souza, R. C., Brito Poveda, V., & Siqueira Costa, A. L. (2017). Non-pharmacological interventions to promote the sleep of patients after cardiac surgery: A systematic review. *Revista Latino-Americana de Enfermagem, 25*, 1–10. https://doi.org/10.1590/1518-8345.1917.2926

De Vries, J. H., Spengler, M., Frintrup, A., & Mussel, P. (2021). Personality development in emerging adulthood—How the perception of life events and mindset affect personality trait change. *Frontiers in Psychology, 12*, Article 671421. https://doi.org/10.3389/fpsyg.2021.671421

Deary, I. J. (2014). The stability of intelligence from childhood to old age. *Current Directions in Psychological Science, 23*(4), 239–245. https://doi.org/10.1177/0963721414536905

Deary, I. J., Strand, S., Smith, P., & Fernandes, C. (2007). Intelligence and educational achievement. *Intelligence, 35*(1), 13–21. https://doi.org/10.1016/j.intell.2006.02.001

Deci, E. L., Koestner, R., & Ryan, R. M. (1999). A meta-analytic review of experiments examining the effects of extrinsic rewards on intrinsic motivation. *Psychological Bulletin, 125*(6), 627–668. https://doi.org/10.1037/0033-2909.125.6.627

Deepak, S., Bhatia, H., & Chadha, N. K. (2019). A psychological study on the positive impacts of experiencing love. *IAHRW International Journal of Social Sciences Review, 7*(3), 513–518.

Delfour, F., & Marten, K. (2001). Mirror image processing in three marine mammal species: Killer whales (Orcinus orca), false killer whales (Pseudorca crassidens) and California sea lions (Zalophus californianus). *Behavioural Processes, 53*(3), 181–190. https://doi.org/10.1016/S0376-6357(01)00134-6

DeLisi, M., & Vaughn, M. G. (2014). Foundation for a temperament-based theory of antisocial behavior and criminal justice system involvement. *Journal of Criminal Justice, 42*(1), 10–25. https://doi.org/10.1016/j.jcrimjus.2013.11.001

DeMartini, J., Patel, G., & Fancher, T. L. (2019). Generalized anxiety disorder. *Annals of Internal Medicine, 170*(7), ITC49–ITC64. https://doi.org/10.7326/AITC201904020

DeMayo, M. M., Young, L. J., Hickie, I. B., Song, Y. J. C., & Guastella, A. J. (2019). Circuits for social learning: A unified model and application to autism spectrum disorder. *Neuroscience & Biobehavioral Reviews, 107*, 388–398. https://doi.org/10.1016/j.neubiorev.2019.09.034

Dempsey, A. E., O'Brien, K. D., Tiamiyu, M. F., & Elhai, J. D. (2019). Fear of missing out (FoMO) and rumination mediate relations between social anxiety and problematic Facebook use.

Addictive Behaviors Reports, 9, 1–7. https://doi.org/10.1016/j.abrep.2018.100150

Denollet, J. (2000). Type D personality: A potential risk factor refined. *Journal of Psychosomatic Research, 49*(4), 255–266. https://doi.org/10.1016/s0022-3999(00)00177-x

Denollet, J. (2005). DS14: Standard assessment of negative affectivity, social inhibition, and Type D personality. *Psychosomatic Medicine, 67*(1), 89–97. https://doi.org/10.1097/01.psy.0000149256.81953.49

Denollet, J., & Kupper, N. (2015). Stress and the heart: The role of Type D personality in personalized care. *European Heart Journal, 36*(28), 1783–1785.

Dermatis, H., & Galanter, M. (2016). The role of twelve-step-related spirituality in addiction recovery. *Journal of Religion and Health, 55*, 510–521. https://doi.org/10.1007/s10943-015-0019-4

Devilly, G. J., Drummond, A., Sauer, J. D., Copenhaver, A., Kneer, J., & Ferguson, C. J. (2023). Directional is the new null? A comment on Bushman & Anderson (2023). *Psychology of Popular Media, 12*(3), 364–372. https://doi.org/10.1037/ppm0000361

Devine, P. G., & Sharp, L. B. (2009). Automaticity and control in stereotyping and prejudice. In T. D. Nelson (Ed.), *Handbook of prejudice, stereotyping, and discrimination* (pp. 61–87). Taylor & Francis.

Dfarhud, D., Malmir, M., & Khanahmadi, M. (2014). Happiness & health: The biological factors-systematic review article. *Iranian Journal of Public Health, 43*(11), 1468–1477.

Di Sante, M., Sylvestre, A., Bouchard, C., & Leblond, J. (2019). The pragmatic language skills of severely neglected 42-month-old children: Results of the ELLAN study. *Child Maltreatment, 24*(3), 244–253. https://doi.org/10.1177/1077559519828838

Diamond, J. (2010). The benefits of multilingualism. *Science, 330*(6002), 332–333. https://doi.org/10.1126/science.1195067

Diamond, L. M. (2005). "I'm straight, but I kissed a girl": The trouble with American media representations of female-female sexuality. *Feminism & Psychology, 15*(1), 104–110.

Dickx, N., Cagnie, B., Achten, E., Vandemaele, P., Parlevliet, T., & Danneels, L. (2010). Differentiation between deep and superficial fibers of the lumbar multifidus by magnetic resonance imaging. *European Spine Journal, 19*(1), 122–128. https://doi.org/10.1007/s00586-009-1171-x

DiClemente, C. C., & Prochaska, J. O. (1998). Toward a comprehensive, transtheoretical model of change: Stages of change and addictive behaviors. In W. R. Miller & N. Heather (Eds.), *Treating addictive behaviors* (pp. 3–24). Plenum. https://doi.org/10.1007/978-1-4899-1934-2_1

DiClemente, C. C., & Velasquez, M. M. (2002). Motivational interviewing and the stages of change. In W. R. Miller & S. Rollnick (Eds.), *Motivational interviewing: Preparing people for change* (pp. 201–216). Guilford.

Diedrich, A., & Voderholzer, U. (2015). Obsessive–compulsive personality disorder: A current review. *Current Psychiatry Reports, 17*(2), Article 2. https://doi.org/10.1007/s11920-014-0547-8

Diekelmann, S., & Born, J. (2010). The memory function of sleep. *Nature Reviews Neuroscience, 11*(2), 114–126. https://doi.org/10.1038/nrn2762

Diener, E. (2012). New findings and future directions for subjective well-being research. *American Psychologist, 67*(8), 590–597. https://doi.org/10.1037/a0029541

Diener, E., & Biswas-Diener, R. (2019). The replication crisis in psychology. *NOBA.* https://nobaproject.com/modules/the-replication-crisis-in-psychology

Diener, E., Lucas, R. E., & Scollon, C. N. (2006). Beyond the hedonic treadmill: Revising the adaptation theory of well-being. *American Psychologist, 61*(4), 305–314. https://doi.org/10.1037/0003-066X.61.4.305

Diener, E., Ng, W., Harter, J., & Arora, R. (2010). Wealth and happiness across the world: Material prosperity predicts life evaluation, whereas psychosocial prosperity predicts positive feeling. *Journal of Personality and Social Psychology, 99*(1), 52–61. https://doi.org/10.1037/a0018066

Dietz, M. G. (1986). Trapping the prince: Machiavelli and the politics of deception. *American Political Science Review, 80*(3), 777–799. https://doi.org/10.2307/1960538

Digman, J. M. (1990). Personality structure: Emergence of the five-factor model. *Annual Review of Psychology, 41*(1), 417–440. https://doi.org/10.1146/annurev.ps.41.020190.002221

Dillon, G., Hussain, R., Loxton, D., & Rahman, S. (2013). Mental and physical health and intimate partner violence against women: A review of the literature. *International Journal of Family Medicine, 2013*, Article 313909. https://doi.org/10.1155/2013/313909

Dimitrova, L., Fernando, V., Vissia, E. M., Nijenhuis, E. R., Draijer, N., & Reinders, A. A. (2020). Sleep, trauma, fantasy and cognition in dissociative identity disorder, post-traumatic stress disorder and healthy controls: A replication and extension study. *European Journal of Psychotraumatology, 11*(1), Article 1705599. https://doi.org/10.1080/20008198.2019.1705599

Dimmick, F. L. (1920). An experimental study of visual movement and the Phi phenomenon. *The American Journal of Psychology, 31*, 317–332. https://doi.org/10.2307/1413667

Dindo, M., Whiten, A., & de Waal, F. B. (2009). Social facilitation of exploratory foraging behavior in capuchin monkeys (Cebus apella). *American Journal of Primatology: Official Journal of the American Society of Primatologists, 71*(5), 419–426. https://doi.org/10.1002/ajp.20669

DiNicolantonio, J. J., Lucan, S. C., & O'Keefe, J. H. (2016). The evidence for saturated fat and for sugar-related to coronary heart disease. *Progress in Cardiovascular Diseases, 58*(5), 464–472. https://doi.org/10.1016/j.pcad.2015.11.006

DiNicolantonio, J. J., Lucan, S. C., & O'Keefe, J. H. (2016). The evidence for saturated fat and for sugar related to coronary heart disease. *Progress in Cardiovascular Diseases, 58*(5), 464–472. https://doi.org/10.1016/j.pcad.2015.11.006

Dinis, J., & Bragança, M. (2018). Quality of sleep and depression in college students: A systematic review. *Sleep Science, 11*(4), 290–301. https://doi.org/10.5935/1984-0063.20180045

Dinwiddie, S. H. (2015). Psychopathy and sociopathy: The history of a concept. *Psychiatric Annals, 45*(4), 169–174. https://doi.org/10.3928/00485713-20150401-04

Dion, J., Hains, J., Vachon, P., Plouffe, J., Laberge, L., Perron, M., McDuff, P., Kalinova, E., & Leone, M. (2016). Correlates of body dissatisfaction in children. *The Journal of Pediatrics, 171*, 202–207. https://doi.org/10.1016/j.jpeds.2015.12.045

Dixon, L. J., & Linardon, J. (2020). A systematic review and meta-analysis of dropout rates from dialectical behaviour therapy in randomized controlled trials. *Cognitive Behaviour Therapy, 49*(3), 181–196. https://doi.org/10.1080/16506073.2019.1620324

Djeriouat, H., & Trémolière, B. (2014). The dark triad of personality and utilitarian moral judgment: The mediating role of honesty/humility and harm/care. *Personality and Individual Differences, 67*, 11–16. https://doi.org/10.1016/j.paid.2013.12.026

Dobbs, T. A., Smith, A. B., & Taylor, N. J. (2006). "No, we don't get a say, children just suffer the consequences": Children talk about family discipline. *International Journal of Children's Rights, 14*(2), 137–156. https://doi.org/10.1163/157181806777922694

Dobrean, A., & Pǎsǎrelu, C. R. (2016). Impact of social media on social anxiety: A systematic review. *New Developments in Anxiety Cisorders* [open access chapter]. https://www.intechopen.com/books/new-developments-in-anxiety-disorders/impact-of-social-media-on-social-anxiety-a-systematic-review

Dodge, K. A., Lochman, J. E., Harnish, J. D., Bates, J. E., & Pettit, G. S. (1997). Reactive and proactive aggression in school children and psychiatrically impaired chronically assaultive youth. *Journal of Abnormal Psychology, 106*(1), 37–51. https://doi.org/10.1037/0021-843X.106.1.37

Dolan, M., & Fullam, R. (2004). Theory of mind and mentalizing ability in antisocial personality disorders with and without psychopathy. *Psychological Medicine, 34*(6), 1093–1102. https://doi.org/10.1017/S0033291704002028

Doll, C., McLaughlin, T. F., & Barretto, A. (2013). The token economy: A recent review and evaluation. *International Journal of Basic and Applied Science, 2*(1), 131–149.

Dollard, J., Miller, N. E., Doob, L. W., Mowrer, O. H., & Sears, R. R. (1939). *Frustration and aggression.* Yale University Press.

Domagalski, T. A., & Steelman, L. A. (2007). The impact of gender and organizational status on workplace anger expression. *Management Communication Quarterly, 20*(3), 297–315. https://doi.org/10.1177/0893318906295681

Domijan, D. (2003). A neural model for visual selection of grouped spatial arrays. *NeuroReport: For Rapid Communication of Neuroscience Research, 14*(3), 367–370. http://dx.doi.org/10.1097/00001756-200303030-00014

Dong, Y., Lin, J., Li, H., Cheng, L., Niu, W., & Tong, Z. (2022). How parenting styles affect children's creativity: Through the lens of self. *Thinking Skills and Creativity, 45*, Article 101045. https://doi.org/10.1016/j.tsc.2022.101045

Donnelly, J. E., Hillman, C. H., Castelli, D., Etnier, J. L., Lee, S., Tomporowski, P., Lambourne, K., & Szabo-Reed, A. N. (2016). Physical activity, fitness, cognitive function, and academic achievement in children: A systematic review. *Medicine and Science in Sports and Exercise, 48*(6), 1197–1222. https://doi.org/10.1249/MSS.0000000000000901

Donnerstein, E., & Donnerstein, M. (1976). Research in the control of interracial aggression. In R. G. Green & E. C. O'Neal (Eds.), *Perspectives on aggression* (pp. 133–168). Academic Press.

Dopheide J. A. (2020). Insomnia overview: Epidemiology, pathophysiology, diagnosis and monitoring, and nonpharmacologic therapy. *The American Journal of Managed Care, 26*(4, Suppl.), S76–S84. https://doi.org/10.37765/ajmc.2020.42769

Doss, B. D., & Rhoades, G. K. (2017). The transition to parenthood: Impact on couples' romantic relationships. *Current Opinion in Psychology, 13*, 25–28. https://doi.org/10.1016/j.copsyc.2016.04.003

Doss, B. D., Simpson, L. E., & Christensen, A. (2004). Why do couples seek marital therapy? *Professional Psychology: Research and Practice, 35*(6), 608–614. https://doi.org/10.1037/0735-7028.35.6.608

Douaud, G., Lee, S., Alfaro-Almagro, F., Arthofer, C., Wang, C., McCarthy, P., Lange, F., Andersson, J. L. R., Griffanti, L., Duff, E., Jdabdi, S., Taschler, B., Keating, P., Winkler, A. M., Collins, R., Matthews, P. M., Allen, N., Miller, K. L., Nichols, T. E., & Smith, S. M. (2022). SARS-CoV-2 is associated with changes in brain structure in UK Biobank. *Nature, 604*(7907), 697–707. https://doi.org/10.1038/s41586-022-04569-5

Dovidio, J. F., Kawakami, K., & Gaertner, S. L. (2002). Implicit and explicit prejudice and interracial interaction. *Journal of Personality and Social Psychology, 82*(1), 62–68. https://doi.org/10.1037/0022-3514.82.1.62

Downing-Matibag, T. M., & Geisinger, B. (2009). Hooking up and sexual risk taking among college students: A health belief model perspective. *Qualitative Health Research, 19*(9), 1196–1209. https://doi.org/10.1177/1049732309344206

Dowrick, P. W., & Raeburn, J. M. (1995). Self-modeling: Rapid skill training for children with physical disabilities. *Journal of Developmental and Physical Disabilities, 7*(1), 25–37. https://doi.org/10.1007/BF02578712

Drescher, J. (2010). Queer diagnoses: Parallels and contrasts in the history of homosexuality, gender variance, and the Diagnostic and Statistical Manual. *Archives of Sexual Behavior, 39*, 427–460. https://doi.org/10.1007/s10508-009-9531-5

Dresser, S. (2023). *Chinese philosophy has long known that mental health is communal*. Psyche. https://psyche.co/ideas/chinese-philosophy-has-long-known-that-mental-health-is-communal

Drews, H. J., & Drews, A. (2021). Couple relationships are associated with increased REM sleep-a proof-of-concept analysis of a large dataset using ambulatory polysomnography. *Frontiers in Psychiatry, 12*, Article 641102. https://doi.org/10.3389/fpsyt.2021.641102

Drews, H. J., Wallot, S., Brysch, P., Berger-Johannsen, H., Weinhold, S., Mitkidis, P., Baier, P., Lechinger, J., Roepstorff, A., & Göder, R. (2020). Bed-sharing in couples is associated with increased and stabilized REM sleep and sleep-stage synchronization. *Frontiers in Psychiatry, 11*, 1–12. https://doi.org/10.3389/fpsyt.2020.00583

Drews, H. J., Wallot, S., Weinhold, S. L., Mitkidis, P., Baier, P. C., Roepstorff, A., & Göder, R. (2017). "Are we in sync with each other?" Exploring the effects of cosleeping on heterosexual couples' sleep using simultaneous polysomnography: A pilot study. *Sleep Disorders*, Article 8140672. https://doi.org/10.1155/2017/8140672

Driessen, E., Van, H. L., Peen, J., Don, F. J., Twisk, J. W., Cuijpers, P., & Dekker, J. J. (2017). Cognitive-behavioral versus psychodynamic therapy for major depression: Secondary outcomes of a randomized clinical trial. *Journal of Consulting and Clinical Psychology, 85*(7), 653–663. https://psycnet.apa.org/doi/10.1037/ccp0000207

Dubin, A. E., & Patapoutian, A. (2010). Nociceptors: The sensors of the pain pathway. *The Journal of Clinical Investigation, 120*(11), 3760–3772. http://dx.doi.org/10.1172/JCI42843

Dubrow-Marshall, R. P., & Dubrow-Marshall, L. (2015). Cults and mental health. In H. S. Friedman (Ed.), *Encyclopedia of mental health* (2nd ed., pp. 393–401). Academic Press. https://doi.org/10.1016/B978-0-12-397045-9.00153-1

Duell, N., Clayton, M. G., Telzer, E. H., & Prinstein, M. J. (2022). Measuring peer influence susceptibility to alcohol use: Convergent and predictive validity of a new analogue assessment. *International Journal of Behavioral Development, 46*(3), 190–199. https://doi.org/10.1177/0165025420965729

Duggan, K. A., McDevitt, E. A., Whitehurst, L. N., & Mednick, S. C. (2018). To nap, perchance to DREAM: A factor analysis of college students' self-reported reasons for napping. *Behavioral Sleep Medicine, 16*(2), 135–153. https://doi.org/10.1080/15402002.2016.1178115

Duman, R. S., Sanacora, G., & Krystal, J. H. (2019). Altered connectivity in depression: GABA and glutamate neurotransmitter deficits and reversal by novel treatments. *Neuron, 102*(1), 75–90. https://doi.org/10.1016/j.neuron.2019.03.013

Dumitru, E.-A. (2020). Testing children and adolescents' ability to identify fake news: A combined design of quasi-experiment and group discussions. *Societies, 10*(3), article 71. https://doi.org/10.3390/soc10030071

Duncan, J., Seitz, R. J., Kolodny, J., Bor, D., Herzog, H., Ahmed, A., Newell, F. N., & Emslie, H. (2000). A neural basis for general intelligence. *Science, 289*(5478), 457–460. https://doi.org/10.1126/science.289.5478.457

Duncker, K. (1945). On problem-solving. *Psychological Monographs, 58*(5, Whole No. 270). https://doi.org/10.1037/h0093599

Dunlap, K. (1919). Are there any instincts? *Journal of Abnormal Psychology, 14*(5), 307–311. https://doi.org/10.1037/h0074215

Dustin, D. L., Wright, B., Harper, J., Lamke, G., Murphy, J., & McDonald, C. (2019). Travel hopefully: The obvious and not so obvious dividends from professional investments. *SCHOLE: A Journal of Leisure Studies and Recreation Education, 34*(1), 62–68. https://doi.org/10.1080/1937156X.2019.1589812

Dutton, D. G., & Aron, A. P. (1974). Some evidence for heightened sexual attraction under conditions of high anxiety. *Journal of*

Personality and Social Psychology, 30(4), 510–517. https://doi.org/10.1037/h0037031

Duverne, S., & Koechlin, E. (2017). Rewards and cognitive control in the human prefrontal cortex. *Cerebral Cortex, 27*(10), 5024–5039. https://doi.org/10.1093/cercor/bhx210

Dweck, C. S. (2006). *Mindset: The new psychology of success*. Random House.

Dworkin, S. L., & O'Sullivan, L. (2005). Actual versus desired initiation patterns among a sample of college men: Tapping disjunctures within traditional male sexual scripts. *The Journal of Sex Research, 42*, 150–158. https://doi.org/10.1080/00224490509552268

Dzhurova, A. (2020). Symbolic politics and government response to a national emergency: Narrating the COVID-19 crisis. *Administrative Theory & Praxis, 42*(4), 571–587. https://doi.org/10.1080/10841806.2020.1816787

Eagle, M. N. (2007). Psychoanalysis and its critics. *Psychoanalytic Psychology, 24*(1), 10–24. https://doi.org/10.1037/0736-9735.24.1.10

Eagly, A. H. (2009). The his and hers of prosocial behavior: An examination of the social psychology of gender. *American Psychologist, 64*(8), 644–658. https://doi.org/10.1037/0003-066X.64.8.644

Eagly, A. H., & Chaiken, S. (2007). The advantages of an inclusive definition of attitude. *Social Cognition, 25*(5), 582–602. https://doi.org/10.1521/soco.2007.25.5.582

Eaton, W. W., Bienvenu, O. J., & Miloyan, B. (2018). Specific phobias. *The Lancet Psychiatry, 5*(8), 678–686. https://doi.org/10.1016/S2215-0366(18)30169-X

Eaton, W. W., Neufeld, K., Chen, L. S., & Cai, G. (2000). A comparison of self-report and clinical diagnostic interviews for depression: Diagnostic interview schedule and schedules for clinical assessment in neuropsychiatry in the Baltimore epidemiologic catchment area follow-up. *Archives of General Psychiatry, 57*(3), 217–222. https://doi.org/10.1001/archpsyc.57.3.217

Ebbinghaus, H. (1949). Experiments in memory. In W. Dennis (Ed.), *Readings in general psychology* (pp. 225–230). Prentice-Hall. https://doi.org/10.1037/11352-033

Eby, L. T., Cader, J., & Noble, C. L. (2003). Why do high self-monitors emerge as leaders in small groups? A comparative analysis of the behaviors of high versus low self-monitors. *Journal of Applied Social Psychology, 33*, 1457–1479. https://doi.org/10.1111/j.1559-1816.2003.tb01958.x

Echols, L., & Graham, S. (2013). Birds of a different feather: How do cross-ethnic friends flock together? *Merrill-Palmer Quarterly, 59*(4), 461–488. https://doi.org/10.13110/merrpalmquar1982.59.4.0461

Edelman, G. M., & Tononi, G. (2000). *A universe of consciousness: How matter becomes imagination*. Basic Books.

Edlund, J. E., Cuccolo, K., Irgens, M. A., Wagge, J. R., & Zlokovich, M. S. (in press). Saving science through replication studies. *Perspectives on Psychological Science*.

Edwards, C. P. (1981). The comparative study of the development of moral judgment and reasoning. In R. H. Munroe, R. L. Munroe, & B. B. Whiting (Eds.), *Handbook of cross-cultural human development* (pp. 501–528). Garland.

Edwards, C. P. (1982). Moral development in comparative cultural perspective. In D. A. Wagner & H. W. Stevenson (Eds.), *Cultural perspectives on child development* (pp. 248–279). Freeman.

Edwards, D. (2014). *Art therapy*. Sage.

Ehlers, A., & Steil, R. (1995). Maintenance of intrusive memories in posttraumatic stress disorder: A cognitive approach. *Behavioural and Cognitive Psychotherapy, 23*(3), 217–249. https://doi.org/10.1017/S135246580001585X

Eich, J. E. (1980). The cue-dependent nature of state-dependent retrieval. *Memory and Cognition, 8*(2), 157–173. https://doi.org/10.3758/BF03213419

Einarson, T. R., Acs, A., Ludwig, C., & Panton, U. H. (2018). Prevalence of cardiovascular disease in type 2 diabetes: A systematic literature review of scientific evidence from across the world in 2007–2017. *Cardiovascular Diabetology, 17*(1), 1–19. https://doi .org/10.1186/s12933-018-0728-6

Eisner, A. S. (2005). Physiology and psychology of dreams. *Seminars in Neurology, 25*(1), 97–105. https://doi.org/10.1055/ s-2005-867078

Ekman, P. (1970). Universal facial expressions of emotions. *California Mental Health Research Digest, 8*(4), 151–158.

Ekman, P. (1972). Universal and cultural differences in facial expression of emotion. In J. R. Cole (Ed.), *Nebraska Symposium on Motivation, 1971* (pp. 207–283). Nebraska University Press.

Ekman, P. (2003). *Emotions revealed.* Holt.

Ekman, P., & Frank, M. G. (1993). Lies that fail. In M. Lewis & C. Saarni (Eds.), *Lying and deception in everyday life* (pp. 184–200). Guilford.

Ekman, P., & Friesen, W. V. (1971). Constants across cultures in the face and emotion. *Journal of Personality and Social Psychology, 17*(2), 124–129. https://doi.org/10.1037/h0030377

Ekman, P., Friesen, W. V., & Tomkins, S. S. (1971). Facial affect scoring technique: A first validity study. *Semiotica, 3*, 37–58. https://doi .org/10.1515/semi.1971.3.1.37

Eliot, L. (2019). Neurosexism: The myth that men and women have different brains. *Nature, 566*(7745), 453–455.

Elkins, R. L. (1991). An appraisal of chemical aversion (emetic therapy) approaches to alcoholism treatment. *Behaviour Research and Therapy, 29*(5), 387–413. https://doi.org/ 10.1016/0005-7967(91)90123-K

Elliot, A. J., & Niesta, D. (2008). Romantic red: Red enhances men's attraction to women. *Journal of Personality & Social Psychology, 95*(5), 1150–1164. https://psycnet.apa.org/doi/10.1037/0022- 3514.95.5.1150

Elliott, R., Watson, J. C., Timulak, L., & Sharbanee, J. (2021). Research on humanistic-experiential psychotherapies: Updated review. In M. Barkham, W. Lutz, & L. G. Castonguay (Eds.), *Bergin and Garfield's handbook of psychotherapy and behavior change* (7th ed, pp. 421–467). Wiley.

Ellis, A. (1991). The revised ABC's of rational-emotive therapy (RET). *Journal of Rational-Emotive and Cognitive-Behavior Therapy, 9*(3), 139–172. https://doi.org/10.1007/BF01061227

Ellison, C. G., Zhang, W., Krause, N., & Marcum, J. P. (2009). Does negative interaction in the church increase psychological distress? Longitudinal findings from the Presbyterian Panel Survey. *Sociology of Religion, 70*(4), 409–431. https://doi.org/ 10.1093/socrel/srp062

Elsner, B. (2007). Infants' imitation of goal-directed actions: The role of movements and action effects. *Acta Psychologica, 124*(1), 44–59. https://doi.org/10.1016/j.actpsy.2006.09.006

Elworthy, J. E., & Dutch, J. (1975). The influence of errors and decision-making on learning by performance and learning by observation. *Australian Journal of Psychology, 27*(1), 41–46. https://doi.org/10.1080/00049537508255238

Emmer, C., Bosnjak, M., & Mata, J. (2020). The association between weight stigma and mental health: A meta-analysis. *Obesity Reviews, 21*(1), Article e12935. https://doi.org/10.1111/obr.12935

Emmerich, K., & Masuch, M. (2018, April). Watch me play: Does social facilitation apply to digital games? In Proceedings of the 2018 CHI Conference on Human Factors in Computing Systems (p. 100). ACM.

Emre, M. (2015). *Uncovering the secret history of Myers-Briggs.* Digg. https://digg.com/2015/myers-briggs-secret-history

Engel, G. L. (1981). The clinical application of the biopsychosocial model. *Journal of Medicine and Philosophy: A Forum for Bioethics and Philosophy of Medicine, 6*(2), 101–124. https://doi.org/ 10.1093/jmp/6.2.101

Engen, T., & Engen, É. A. (1997). Relationship between development of odor perception and language. *Enfance, 1*, 125–140. http:// dx.doi.org/10.3406/enfan.1997.3052

Ensen, R. (1987). Stuck? Don't give up! Subgoal-generation strategies in problem solving. *The Mathematics Teacher, 80*(8), 614–634. https://doi.org/10.5951/MT.80.8.0614

Epley, N., & Gilovich, T. (2006). The anchoring-and-adjustment heuristic: Why the adjustments are insufficient. *Psychological Science, 17*(4), 311–318. https://doi.org/10.1111/j.1467- 9280.2006.01704.x

Epley, N., Akalis, S., Waytz, A., and Cacioppo, J. T. (2008). Creating social connection through inferential reproduction: Loneliness and perceived agency in gadgets, gods, and greyhounds. *Psychological Science, 19*(2), 114–120. https://doi.org/10.1111/ j.1467-9280.2008.02056.x

Epstein, M., Calzo, J. P., Smiler, A. P., & Ward, L. M. (2009). "Anything from making out to having sex": Men's negotiations of hooking up and friends with benefits scripts. *Journal of Sex Research, 46*(5), 414–424. https://doi.org/10.1080/00224490902775801

Epstein, R., & Phan, V. (2012). Which competencies are most important for creative expression? *Creativity Research Journal, 24*(4), 278–282. https://doi.org/10.1080/10400419.2012.726579

Epstein, R., Schmidt, S. M., & Warfel, R. (2008). Measuring and training creativity competencies: Validation of a new test. *Creativity Research Journal, 20*(1), 7–12. https://doi.org/ 10.1080/10400410701839876

Erikson, E. H. (1959). Identity and the life cycle. *Psychological Issues, 1*, 1–171.

Erikson, E. H. (1963). *Childhood and society* (2nd ed.). Norton. (Original work published 1950)

Eron, L. D., Walder, L. O., & Lefkowitz, M. M. (1971). *Learning of aggression in children.* Little, Brown.

Escribà-Agüir, V., & Artazcoz, L. (2011). Gender differences in postpartum depression: A longitudinal cohort study. *Journal of Epidemiology & Community Health, 65*(4), 320–326. http://dx.doi .org/10.1136/jech.2008.085894

Espnes, G. A., & Byrne, D. (2016). Type A behavior and cardiovascular disease. In M. E. Alvarenga & D. Byrne (Eds.), *Handbook of psychocardiology* (pp. 645–664). Springer Science + Business Media. https://doi.org/10.1007/978-981-287-206- 7_30

Esteves, M., Lopes, S. S., Almeida, A., Sousa, N., & Leite-Almeida, H. (2020). Unmasking the relevance of hemispheric asymmetries— Break on through (to the other side). *Progress in Neurobiology, 192*, Article 101823. https://doi.org/10.1016/j.pneurobio .2020.101823

Exelmans, L., & Van den Bulck, J. (2016). Bedtime mobile phone use and sleep in adults. *Social Science & Medicine, 148*, 93–101. https://doi.org/10.1016/j.socscimed.2015.11.037

Exline, J. J., Yali, A. M., & Sanderson, W. C. (2000). Guilt, discord, and alienation: The role of religious strain in depression and suicidality. *Journal of Clinical Psychology, 56*(12), 1481–1496. https://doi.org/10.1002/1097-4679(200012)56:12<1481::AID- 1>3.0.CO;2-A

Eysenck, H. J. (1978). Superfactors P, E and N in a comprehensive factor space. *Multivariate Behavioural Research, 13*(4), 475–481. https://doi.org/10.1207/s15327906mbr1304_7

Fabbri, C. (2020) The role of genetics in bipolar disorder. In A. H. Young & M. F. Juruena (Eds.), *Bipolar disorder: From neuroscience to treatment* (pp. 41–60). Springer.

Fagard, J., & Lockman, J. J. (2010). Change in imitation for object manipulation between 10 and 12 months of age. *Developmental Psychobiology, 52*(1), 90–99. https://doi.org/10.1002/dev.20416

Fagard, J., Rat-Fischer, L., Esseily, R., Somogyi, E., & O'Regan, J. K. (2016). What does it take for an infant to learn how to use a tool by observation? *Frontiers in Psychology, 7*, 1–11. https://doi .org/10.3389/fpsyg.2016.00267

Fan, H., Zhang, B., & Wang, W. (2017). Family functions in relation to behavioral and psychological disorders in Chinese culture. *The Family Journal, 25*(2), 130–136. https://doi.org/10.1177/1066480717697681

Fancher, R. E., & Rutherford, A. (2012). *Pioneers of psychology: A history* (4th ed.). W. W. Norton.

Fang, S., Galambos, N. L., Johnson, M. D., & Krahn, H. J. (2018). Happiness is the way: Paths to civic engagement between young adulthood and midlife. *International Journal of Behavioral Development, 42*(4), 425–433. https://doi.org/10.1177/0165025417711056

Fang, X., Singh, S., & Ahluwalia, R. (2007). An examination of different explanations for the mere exposure effect. *Journal of Consumer Research, 34*(1), 97–103. https://doi.org/10.1086/513050

Farvid, P., Braun, V., & Rowney, C. (2017). "No girl wants to be called a slut!": Women, heterosexual casual sex and the sexual double standard. *Journal of Gender Studies, 26*(5), 544–560. https://doi.org/10.1080/09589236.2016.1150818

Fast, N. J., Sivanathan, N., Mayer, N. D., & Galinsky, A. D. (2012). Power and overconfident decision-making. *Organizational Behavior and Human Decision Processes, 117*(2), 249–260. https://doi.org/10.1016/j.obhdp.2011.11.009

Fausto-Sterling, A. (2000). *Sexing the body: Gender politics and the construction of sexuality.* Basic Books.

Fawcett, E. J., Power, H., & Fawcett, J. M. (2020). Women are at greater risk of OCD than men: A meta-analytic review of OCD prevalence worldwide. *The Journal of Clinical Psychiatry, 81*(4), 13075.

Fayter, R., & Kilty, J. M. (2023). Walking an emotional tightrope: Examining the carceral emotion culture(s) of federal prisons for women in Canada. *The Prison Journal, 104*(1), 24–45. https://doi.org/10.1177/00328855231212438

Feijó, D. M., Pires, J. F., Gomes, R. M. R., Carlo, E. J. F., Viana, T. N. de L., Magalhães, J. R., Santos, A. C. T., Rodrigues, L. D., Oliveira, L. F., & dos Santos, J. C. C. (2023). The impact of child poverty on brain development: Does money matter? *Dementia & Neuropsychologia, 17*, 1–10. https://doi.org/10.1590/1980-5764-DN-2022-0105

Feist, G. J. (1998). A meta-analysis of personality in scientific and artistic creativity. *Personality and Social Psychology Review, 2*(4), 290–309. https://doi.org/10.1207/s15327957pspr0204_5

Feldman, R., & Bakermans-Kranenburg, M. J. (2017). Oxytocin: A parenting hormone. *Current Opinion in Psychology, 15*, 13–18. https://doi.org/10.1016/j.copsyc.2017.02.011

Felthous, A. R. (2015). Enforced medication in jails and prisons: The new asylums. *Albany Government Law Review, 8*, 563–613.

Ferguson, C. J., Copenhaver, A., & Markey, P. (2020). Reexamining the findings of the American Psychological Association's 2015 Task Force on Violent Media: A meta-analysis. *Perspectives on Psychological Science, 15*(6), 1423–1443. https://doi.org/10.1177/1745691620927666

Ferguson, C. J., Maguire, R., & Lemar, S. (2018). Pick your poison: Choice of activity determines mood management following a stressful task. *Journal of Aggression, Maltreatment & Trauma, 27*(3), 332–346. https://doi.org/10.1080/10926771.2017.1322656

Ferguson, G. O. (1916). The psychology of the Negro: An experimental study. *Archives of Psychology, 36*, 1–138. https://www.jstor.org/stable/2763478

Fernández, E., & Cairns, H. (2010). *Fundamentals of psycholinguistics.* Wiley-Blackwell.

Ferrari, M., McIlwaine, S. V., Jordan, G., Shah, J. L., Lal, S., & Iyer, S. N. (2019). Gaming with stigma: Analysis of messages about mental illnesses in video games. *JMIR Mental Health, 6*(5), e12418. https://doi.org/10.2196/12418

Ferrell-Torry, A. T., & Glick, O. J. (1993). The use of therapeutic massage as a nursing intervention to modify anxiety and the perception of cancer pain. *Cancer Nursing, 16*(2), 93–101.

Feshbach, S. (1964). The function of aggression and the regulation of aggressive drive. *Psychological Review, 71*(4), 257–272. https://doi.org/10.1037/h0043041

Festinger, L. (1954). A theory of social comparison processes. *Human Relations, 7*(2), 117–140. https://doi.org/10.1177/001872675400700202

Festinger, L. (1957). *A theory of cognitive dissonance.* Stanford University Press.

Festinger, L., & Carlsmith, J. M. (1959). Cognitive consequences of forced compliance. *Journal of Abnormal and Social Psychology, 58*(2), 203–210. https://doi.org/10.1037/h0041593

Festinger, L., Riecken, H. W., & Schachter, S. (1956). *When prophecy fails.* University of Minnesota Press.

Festinger, L., Riecken, H. W., & Schachter, S. (2008). *When prophecy fails: A social and psychological study of a modern group that predicted the destruction of the world.* University of Minnesota Press. (Original work published 1956)

Festinger, L., Schachter, S., & Back, K. W. (1950). *Social pressures in informal groups: A study of human factors in housing.* Harper & Bros.

Filcheck, H. A., McNeil, C. B., Greco, L. A., & Bernard, R. S. (2004). Using a whole-class token economy and coaching of teacher skills in a preschool classroom to manage disruptive behavior. *Psychology in the Schools, 41*(3), 351–361. https://doi.org/10.1002/pits.10168

Filippello, P., Buzzai, C., Costa, S., Orecchio, S., & Sorrenti, L. (2020). Teaching style and academic achievement: The mediating role of learned helplessness and mastery orientation. *Psychology in the Schools, 57*(1), 5–16. https://doi.org/10.1002/pits.22315

Finkel, D., Pedersen, N. L., Plomin, R., & McClearn, G. E. (1998). Longitudinal and cross-sectional twin data on cognitive abilities in adulthood: The Swedish Adoption/Twin Study of Aging. *Developmental Psychology, 34*(6), 1400–1413. https://doi.org/10.1037/0012-1649.34.6.1400

Finkel, E. J., Eastwick, P. W., Karney, B. R., Reis, H. T., & Sprecher, S. (2012). Online dating: A critical analysis from the perspective of psychological science. *Psychological Science in the Public Interest, 13*(1), 3–66. https://doi.org/10.1177/1529100612436522

Fiorella, L., & Mayer, R. E. (2013). The relative benefits of learning by teaching and teaching expectancy. *Contemporary Educational Psychology, 38*(4), 281–288. https://doi.org/10.1016/j.cedpsych.2013.06.001

Firestone, I. J., Kaplan, K. J., & Russell, J. C. (1973). Anxiety, fear, and affiliation with similar-state versus dissimilar-state others: Misery sometimes loves nonmiserable company. *Journal of Personality and Social Psychology, 26*(3), 409–414. https://doi.org/10.1037/h0034455

First, L., Douglas, W., Habibi, B., Singh, J. R., & Sein, M. T. (2020). Cannabis use and low-back pain: A systematic review. *Cannabis and Cannabinoid Research, 5*(4), 283–289. https://doi.org/10.1089/can.2019.0077

Fischer, P., Krueger, J. I., Greitemeyer, T., Vogrincic, C., Kastenmüller, A., Frey, D., Heene, M., Wicher, M., & Kainbacher, M. (2011). The bystander-effect: A meta-analytic review on bystander intervention in dangerous and non-dangerous emergencies. *Psychological Bulletin, 137*(4), 517–537. https://doi.org/10.1037/a0023304

Fischer, S., Ehlert, U., & Castro, R. A. (2019). Hormones of the hypothalamic-pituitary-gonadal (HPG) axis in male depressive disorders—A systematic review and meta-analysis. *Frontiers in Neuroendocrinology, 55*, Article 100792. https://doi.org/10.1016/j.yfrne.2019.100792

Fiske, D. W. (1949). Consistency of the factorial structures of personality ratings from different sources. *The Journal of Abnormal and Social Psychology, 44*(3), 329–344. https://doi.org/10.1037/h0057198

Fiske, S. T. (1989). Examining the role of intent: Toward understanding its role in stereotyping and prejudice. In J. S. Uleman & J. A. Bargh (Eds.), *Unintended thought* (pp. 253–286). Guilford.

Fiske, S. T., Cuddy, A. J., Glick, P., & Xu, J. (2002). A model of (often mixed) stereotype content: Competence and warmth respectively follow from perceived status and competition. *Journal of Personality and Social Psychology, 82*(6), 878–902. https://doi.org/10.1037//0022-3514.82.6.878

Flack, K., Pankey, C., Ufholz, K., Johnson, L., & Roemmich, J. N. (2019). Genetic variations in the dopamine reward system influence exercise reinforcement and tolerance for exercise intensity. *Behavioural Brain Research, 375*, 1–7. https://doi.org/10.1016/j.bbr.2019.112148

Fleck, J., & Weisberg, R. (2013). Insight versus analysis: Evidence for diverse methods in problem solving. *Journal of Cognitive Psychology, 25*(4), 436–463. https://doi.org/10.1080/20445911.2013.779248

Fleming, J. (2002). Who will succeed in college? When the SAT predicts Black students' performance. *The Review of Higher Education, 25*(3), 281–296. https://doi.org/10.1353/rhe.2002.0010

Fleuridas, C., & Krafcik, D. (2019). Beyond four forces: The evolution of psychotherapy. *Sage Open, 9*(1), 2158244018824492. https://doi.org/10.1177/2158244018824492

Flynn, F. J., Reagans, R. E., Amanatullah, E. T., & Ames, D. R. (2006). Helping one's way to the top: Self-monitors achieve status by helping others and knowing who helps whom. *Journal of Personality and Social Psychology, 91*(6), 1123–1137. https://doi.org/10.1037/0022-3514.91.6.1123

Flynn, J. (2007). *What is intelligence? Beyond the Flynn effect.* Cambridge University Press.

Foer, J. (2012). *Moonwalking with Einstein.* Penguin Books.

Foley, D. E. (2001). The great American football ritual: Reproducing race, class, and gender inequality. In A. Yiannakis & M. J. Melnick (Eds.), *Contemporary issues in sociology of sport.* Human Kinetics.

Folkman, S., & Lazarus, R. S. (1988). Coping as a mediator of emotion. *Journal of Personality and Social Psychology, 54*(3), 466–475. https://doi.org/10.1037/0022-3514.54.3.466

Food and Drug Administration (FDA). (2023). *Scientific review of the effects of menthol in cigarettes on tobacco addiction: 1980-2021.* https://www.fda.gov/media/157642/

Forquer, L. M., & Johnson, C. M. (2007). Continuous white noise to reduce sleep latency and night wakings in college students. *Sleep and Hypnosis, 9*(2), 60–66.

Fox, N. A., & Davidson, R. J. (1987). Electroencephalogram asymmetry in response to the approach of a stranger and maternal separation in 10-month-old infants. *Developmental Psychology, 23*(2), 233–240. https://doi.org/10.1037/0012-1649.23.2.233

France, K. G., McLay, L. K., Hunter, J. E., & France, M. L. S. (2018). Empirical research evaluating the effects of non-traditional approaches to enhancing sleep in typical and clinical children and young people. *Sleep Medicine Reviews, 39*, 69–81. https://doi.org/10.1016/j.smrv.2017.07.004

Frances, A. (2014). *Saving normal: An insider's revolt against out-of-control psychiatric diagnosis, DSM-5, big pharma, and the medicalization of ordinary life.* William Morrow.

Frank, G. (1984). The Boulder Model: History, rationale, and critique. *Professional Psychology: Research and Practice, 15*(3), 417–435. https://doi.org/10.1037/0735-7028.15.3.417

Frank, M. L., Sprada, G. B., Hultstrand, K. V., West, C. E., Livingston, J. A., & Sato, A. F. (2023). Toward a deeper understanding of food insecurity among college students: Examining associations with emotional eating and biological sex. *Journal of American College Health, 71*(5), 1463–1471. https://doi.org/10.1080/07448481.2021.1936536

Frankel, L. (2002). "I've never thought about it": Contradictions and taboos surrounding American males' experiences of first ejaculation (semenarche). *The Journal of Men's Studies, 11*(1), 37–54. https://doi.org/10.3149/jms.1101.37

Frankl, V. E. (1959). *Man's search for meaning.* Beacon.

Frankland, P. W., Josselyn, S. A., & Köhler, S. (2019). The neurobiological foundation of memory retrieval. *Nature Neuroscience, 22*(10), 1576–1585. https://doi.org/10.1038/s41593-019-0493-1

Franklin, K. A., & Lindberg, E. (2015). Obstructive sleep apnea is a common disorder in the population-a review on the epidemiology of sleep apnea. *Journal of Thoracic Disease, 7*(8), 1311–1322. https://doi.org/10.3978/j.issn.2072-1439.2015.06.11

Franz, D. (2014). *A naturalist observation of social media use in public spaces by adult couples.* Unpublished paper. GoogleScholar.

Fraunfelter, L., Gerdes, A. B. M., & Alpers, G. W. (2022). Fear one, fear them all: A systematic review and meta-analysis of fear generalization in pathological anxiety. *Neuroscience & Biobehavioral Reviews, 139*, Article 104707. https://doi.org/10.1016/j.neubiorev.2022.104707

Fredrickson, B. L. (2016). Love: Positivity resonance as a fresh, evidence-based perspective on an age-old topic. In L. F. Barrett, M. Lewis, & J. M. Haviland-Jones (Eds.), *Handbook of emotions* (4th ed., pp. 847–858). Guilford.

Fresco, D. M. (2013). Tending the garden and harvesting the fruits of behavior therapy. *Behavior Therapy, 44*(2), 177–179. https://doi.org/10.1016/j.beth.2013.02.003

Fresco, D. M., Coles, M. E., Heimberg, R. G., Liebowitz, M. R., Hami, S., Stein, M. B., & Goetz, D. (2001). The Liebowitz Social Anxiety Scale: A comparison of the psychometric properties of self-report and clinician-administered formats. *Psychological Medicine, 31*(6), 1025–1035. https://doi.org/10.1017/S0033291701004056

Freud, S. (1933). *New introductory lectures on psychoanalysis.* Carlton House.

Freud, S. (1955). Beyond the pleasure principle. In *The standard edition of the complete psychological works of Sigmund Freud, Volume XVIII (1920-1922): Beyond the pleasure principle, group psychology and other works* (pp. 1–64). Hogarth.

Freud, S. (1966). *Introductory lectures on psychoanalysis.* Liveright. (Original work published 1920)

Freud, S. (1989). *An outline of psychoanalysis.* W. W. Norton. (Original work published 1940)

Freud, S. (2007). *Group psychology and the analysis of the ego.* Duke University Press. (Original work published 1921)

Freund, A. M. (1999). Methodological comment: Temporal stability of older person's spontaneous self-definition. *Experimental Aging Research, 25*(1), 95–107. https://doi.org/10.1080/036107399244165

Freund, K., & Blanchard, R. (1993). Erotic target location errors in male gender dysphorics, paedophiles, and fetishists. *The British Journal of Psychiatry, 162*(4), 558–563. https://doi.org/10.1192/bjp.162.4.558

Friedlander, M. L., Pieterse, A., Lambert, J. E. (2012). The evolution of theory in counseling psychology. In N. A. Fouad, J. A. Carter, & L. M. Subich (Eds.), *APA handbook of counseling psychology: Vol. 2. Practice, interventions, and applications* (pp. 31–58). American Psychological Association. https://psycnet.apa.org/doi/10.1037/13754-002

Friedman, B. H. (2010). Feelings and the body: The Jamesian perspective on autonomic specificity of emotion. *Biological Psychology, 84*(3), 383–393. https://doi.org/10.1016/j.biopsycho.2009.10.006

Friedman, H. L., Krippner, S., Riebel, L., & Johnson, C. (2010). Transpersonal and other models of spiritual development. *International Journal of Transpersonal Studies, 29*(1), 279–294. http://dx.doi.org/10.24972/ijts.2010.29.1.79

Friedman, H. S., Tucker, J. S., Schwartz, J. E., Tomlinson-Keasey, C., Martin, L. R., Wingard, D. L., & Criqui, M. H. (1995). Psychosocial and behavioral predictors of longevity: The aging and death of the "Termites." *American Psychologist, 50*(2), 69–78. http://dx.doi.org/10.1037/0003-066X.50.2.69

Friedman, M. (1977). Type A behavior pattern: Some of its pathophysiological components. *Bulletin of the New York Academy of Medicine, 53*(7), 593.

Friedman, M., & Rosenman, R. H. (1959). Association of specific overt behavior pattern with blood and cardiovascular findings: Blood cholesterol level, blood clotting time, incidence of arcus senilis, and clinical coronary artery disease. *Journal of the American Medical Association, 169*(12), 1286–1296. https://doi.org/10.1001/jama.1959.03000290012005

Friedman, M., Thoresen, C. E., Gill, J. J., Ulmer, D. I. A. N. E., Thompson, L., Powell, L. Y. N. D. A., Price, V., Elek, S. R., Rabin, D. D., Breall, W. S., Piaget, G., Dixon, T., Bourg, E., Levy, R. A., & Tasto, D. L. (1982). Feasibility of altering type A behavior pattern after myocardial infarction. Recurrent Coronary Prevention Project Study: Methods, baseline results and preliminary findings. *Circulation, 66*(1), 83–92. https://doi.org/10.1161/01.cir.66.1.83

Friedmann, N., & Rusou, D. (2015). Critical period for first language: The crucial role of language input during the first year of life. *Current Opinion in Neurobiology, 35*, 27–34. https://doi.org/10.1016/j.conb.2015.06.003

Fries, G. R., Bauer, I. E., Scaini, G., Wu, M. J., Kazimi, I. F., Valvassori, S. S., Zunta-Soares, G., Walss-Bass, C., Soares, J. C., & Quevedo, J. (2017). Accelerated epigenetic aging and mitochondrial DNA copy number in bipolar disorder. *Translational Psychiatry, 7*(12), 1–10. https://doi.org/10.1038/s41398-017-0048-8

Frumau-van Pinxten, W. L., Derksen, J. J. L., & Peters, W. A. M. (2023). The psychological world of highly gifted young adults: A follow-up study. *Trends in Psychology.* Advance online publication. https://doi.org/10.1007/s43076-023-00313-8

Fryer, R. G., Jr. (2011). Financial incentives and student achievement: Evidence from randomized trials. *The Quarterly Journal of Economics, 126*(4), 1755–1798. https://doi.org/10.1093/qje/qjr045

Fudin, J. (2018, January 6). *Opioid agonists, partial agonists, antagonists: Oh my!* Pharmacytimes.com. https://www.pharmacytimes.com/contributor/jeffrey-fudin/2018/01/opioid-agonists-partial-agonists-antagonists-oh-my

Fuhrmann, D., Knoll, L. J., & Blakemore, S. J. (2015). Adolescence as a sensitive period of brain development. *Trends in Cognitive Sciences, 19*(10), 558–566. https://doi.org/10.1016/j.tics.2015.07.008

Fukuda, K., & Vogel, E. K. (2009). Human variation in overriding attentional capture. *The Journal of Neuroscience, 29*(27), 8726–8733. https://doi.org/10.1523/JNEUROSCI.2145-09.2009

Fukushi, I., Yokota, S., & Okada, Y. (2019). The role of the hypothalamus in modulation of respiration. *Respiratory Physiology & Neurobiology, 265*, 172–179. https://doi.org/10.1016/j.resp.2018.07.003

Furnham, A., & Wong, L. (2007). A cross-cultural comparison of British and Chinese beliefs about the causes, behaviour manifestations and treatment of schizophrenia. *Psychiatry Research, 151*(1–2), 123–138. https://doi.org/10.1016/j.psychres.2006.03.023

Fuss, J., Steinle, J., Bindila, L., & Gass, P. (2015). A runner's high depends on cannabinoid receptors in mice. *Neuroscience, 112*(42), 13105–13108. https://doi.org/10.1073/pnas.1514996112

Gable, R. S. (2004). Comparison of acute lethal toxicity of commonly abused psychoactive substances. *Addiction, 99*(6), 686–696. https://doi.org/10.1111/j.1360-0443.2004.00744.x

Gabriel, G. A., Harris, L. R., Henriques, D. Y. P., Pandi, M., & Campos, J. L. (2022). Multisensory visual-vestibular training improves visual heading estimation in younger and older adults. *Frontiers in Aging Neuroscience, 14*, Article 816512. https://doi.org/10.3389/fnagi.2022.816512

Gagnon, J., & Simon, W. (1973). *Sexual conduct: The social sources of human sexuality.* Aldine.

Galef, B. G. (1986). Social interaction modifies learned aversions, sodium appetite, and both palatability and handling-time induced dietary preference in rats (Rattus norvegicus). *Journal of Comparative Psychology, 100*(4), 432–439. https://doi.org/10.1037/0735-7036.100.4.432

Gallup, G. J. (1968). Mirror-image stimulation. *Psychological Bulletin, 70*(6, Pt.1), 782–793. https://doi.org/10.1037/h0026777

Gambrel, P. A., & Cianci, R. (2003). Maslow's hierarchy of needs: Does it apply in a collectivist culture. *Journal of Applied Management and Entrepreneurship, 8*(2), 143–161.

Ganji, M., Mousavi, S. K., & Vahedian, M. (2021). Semantic development of love and romantic action procedure in the context of online communication experience in social networks. *Strategic Research on Social Problems in Iran, 10*(3), 1–22. https://doi.org/10.22108/srspi.2021.132061.1765

Gao, C., Li, P., Morris, C. J., Zheng, X., Ulsa, M. C., Gao, L., Scheer, F. A. J. L., & Hu, K. (2022). Actigraphy-based sleep detection: Validation with polysomnography and comparison of performance for nighttime and daytime sleep during simulated shift work. *Nature and Science of Sleep, 14*, 1801–1816. https://doi.org/10.2147/NSS.S373107

Gao, X., Zhang, Y., Mons, U., & Brenner, H. (2018). Leukocyte telomere length and epigenetic-based mortality risk score: Associations with all-cause mortality among older adults. *Epigenetics, 13*(8), 846–857. https://doi.org/10.1080/15592294.2018.1514853

Garb, J. L., & Stunkard, A. J. (1974). Taste aversions in man. *American Journal of Psychiatry, 131*(11), 1204–1207.

Garcia, J. R., Reiber, C., Massey, S. G., & Merriwether, A. M. (2012). Sexual hookup culture: A review. *Review of General Psychology, 16*(2), 161–176. https://doi.org/10.1037/a0027911

Gardner, H. (2011). *Frames of mind: The theory of multiple intelligences.* Hachette United Kingdom.

Gardner, R. A., & Gardner, B. T. (1969). Teaching sign language to a chimpanzee. *Science, 165*(3894), 664–672. http://www.jstor.org/stable/1727877

Garett, R., Liu, S., & Young, S. D. (2018). The relationship between social media use and sleep quality among undergraduate students. *Information, Communication & Society, 21*(2), 163–173. https://doi.org/10.1080/1369118X.2016.1266374

Garrett, B., & Hough, G. (2022). *Brain & behavior: An introduction to behavioral neuroscience.* Sage.

Garrett, B., & Hough, G. (2022). *Brain & behavior: An introduction to behavioral neuroscience* (6th ed.). Sage.

Gask, L. (2018). In defence of the biopsychosocial model. *The Lancet Psychiatry, 5*(7), 548–549. https://doi.org/10.1016/S2215-0366(18)30165-2

Gastil, R. W. (1996). *The process of divorce recovery: A review of the research.* Doctoral dissertation, Biola University. https://files.eric.ed.gov/fulltext/ED397365.pdf

Gates, E., & Curwood, J. S. (2023). A world beyond self: Empathy and pedagogy during times of global crisis. *The Australian Journal of Language and Literacy, 46*, 195–209. https://doi.org/10.1007/s44020-023-00038-2

Gavriloff, D., Sheaves, B., Juss, A., Espie, C. A., Miller, C. B., & Kyle, S. D. (2018). Sham sleep feedback delivered via actigraphy biases daytime symptom reports in people with insomnia: Implications for insomnia disorder and wearable devices. *Journal of Sleep Research, 27*(6), Article e12726. https://doi.org/10.1111/jsr.12726

Gavurova, B., Popesko, B., & Ivankova, V. (2022). Socioeconomic status and drug use among students. In V. B. Patel & V. R. Preedy (Eds.), *Handbook of substance misuse and addictions* (pp. 1–26). Springer. https://doi.org/10.1007/978-3-030-67928-6_18-1

Gazzaniga, M. S., Bogen, J. E., & Sperry, R. W. (1962). Some functional effects of sectioning the cerebral commissures in man. *Proceedings of the National Academy of Sciences, 48*(10), 1765–1769. https://doi.org/10.1073/pnas.48.10.1765

Gbyl, K., & Videbech, P. (2018). Electroconvulsive therapy increases brain volume in major depression: A systematic review and meta-analysis. *Acta Psychiatrica Scandinavica, 138*(3), 180–195. https://doi.org/10.1111/acps.12884

Geddes, J. R., & Miklowitz, D. J. (2013). Treatment of bipolar disorder. *The Lancet, 381*(9878), 1672–1682. https://doi.org/10.1016/S0140-6736(13)60857-0

Gee, N. R., Rodriguez, K. E., Fine, A. H., & Trammell, J. P. (2021). Dogs supporting human health and well-being: A biopsychosocial approach. *Frontiers in Veterinary Science, 8*, 630465. https://doi.org/10.3389/fvets.2021.630465

Geen, R. G. (1989). Alternative conceptions of social facilitation. In P. B. Paulus (Ed.), *Psychology of group influence* (2nd ed., pp. 15–51). Erlbaum.

Geier, C. F. (2013). Adolescent cognitive control and reward processing: Implications for risk taking and substance use. *Hormones and Behavior, 64*(2), 333–342. https://doi.org/10.1016/j.yhbeh.2013.02.008

Gelb, B. D., & Zinkhan, G. M. (1986). Humor and advertising effectiveness after repeated exposures to a radio commercial. *Journal of Advertising, 15*(2), 15–34. https://doi.org/10.1080/00913367.1986.10673000

Genetics Home Reference. (2021). Klinefelter syndrome. https://ghr.nlm.nih.gov/condition/klinefelter-syndrome

Genetics Home Reference. (2023). Congenital adrenal hyperplasia due to 11-beta-hydroxylase deficiency. https://ghr.nlm.nih.gov/condition/congenital-adrenal-hyperplasia-due-to-11-beta-hydroxylase-deficiency

Gentrup, S., Lorenz, G., Kristen, C., & Kogan, I. (2020). Self-fulfilling prophecies in the classroom: Teacher expectations, teacher feedback and student achievement. *Learning and Instruction, 66*, Article 101296. https://doi.org/10.1016/j.learninstruc.2019.101296

Gering, M., Johnson, T., & Tredoux, C. (2023). Non-linear effects of stress on eyewitness memory. *South African Journal of Science, 119*(3–4), 1–8. http://dx.doi.org/10.17159/sajs.2023/12102

German, T. P., Defeyter, M. A. (2000). Immunity to functional fixedness in young children. *Psychonomic Bulletin & Review, 7*(4), 707–712. https://doi.org/10.3758/BF03213010

Germer, C. K. (2005). Teaching mindfulness in therapy. In C. K. Germer, R. D. Siegel, & P. R. Fulton (Eds.), *Mindfulness and psychotherapy* (pp. 113–129). Guilford.

Gershoff, E. T. (2010). More harm than good: A summary of scientific research on the intended and unintended effects of corporal punishment on children. *Law and Contemporary Problems, 73*(31), 154–157.

Ghaemi, S. N. (2009). The rise and fall of the biopsychosocial model. *The British Journal of Psychiatry, 195*(1), 3–4. https://doi.org/10.1192/bjp.bp.109.063859

Ghomi, M., Wrightman, M., Ghaemian, A., Grey, N., Pickup, T., & Richardson, T. (2021). Development and validation of the Readiness for Therapy Questionnaire (RTQ). *Behavioural and Cognitive Psychotherapy, 49*(4), 413–425. https://doi.org/10.1017/S1352465820000764

Giannoula, Y., Kroemer, G., & Pietrocola, F. (2023). Cellular senescence and the host immune system in aging and age-related disorders. *Biomedical Journal, 46*(3), Article 100581. https://doi.org/10.1016/j.bj.2023.02.001

Gibbs, R. W., Jr. (2007). On the psycholinguistics of sarcasm. In R. W. Gibbs Jr. & H. L. Colston (Eds.), *Irony in language and thought: A cognitive science reader* (pp. 173–200). Lawrence Erlbaum.

Gignac, G. E., Darbyshire, J., & Ooi, M. (2018). Some people are attracted sexually to intelligence: A psychometric evaluation of sapiosexuality. *Intelligence, 66*, 98–111. https://doi.org/10.1016/j.intell.2017.11.009

Gilbert, P. (2015). The evolution and social dynamics of compassion. *Social and Personality Psychology Compass, 9*(6), 239–254. https://doi.org/10.1111/spc3.12176

Gillespie, B. J., Lever, J., Frederick, D., & Royce, T. (2015). Close adult friendships, gender, and the life cycle. *Journal of Social and Personal Relationships, 32*(6), 709–736. https://doi.org/10.1177/0265407514546977

Gilligan, C. (1982). *In a different voice: Psychological theory and women's development.* Harvard University Press.

Gillihan, S. J., & Farah, M. J. (2005). Is self special? A critical review of evidence from experimental psychology and cognitive neuroscience. *Psychological Bulletin, 131*(1), 76–97. https://doi.org/10.1037/0033-2909.131.1.76

Gillison, F. B., Rouse, P., Standage, M., Sebire, S. J., & Ryan, R. M. (2019). A meta-analysis of techniques to promote motivation for health behaviour change from a self-determination theory perspective. *Health Psychology Review, 13*(1), 110–130. https://doi.org/10.1080/17437199.2018.1534071

Gilmour, J., Machin, T., Brownlow, C., & Jeffries, C. (2020). Facebook-based social support and health: A systematic review. *Psychology of Popular Media, 9*(3), 328–346. https://doi.org/10.1037/ppm0000246

Gire, J. (2014). How death imitates life: Cultural influences on conceptions of death and dying. *Online Readings in Psychology and Culture, 6*(2), Article 3. http://dx.doi.org/10.9707/2307-0919.1120

Glass, A. L., & Kang, M. (2019). Dividing attention in the classroom reduces exam performance. *Educational Psychology, 39*(3), 395–408. https://doi.org/10.1080/01443410.2018.1489046

Glick, P., & Fiske, S. T. (2001). An ambivalent alliance: Hostile and benevolent sexism as complementary justifications for gender inequality. *American Psychologist, 56*(2), 109–118. https://doi.org/10.1037/0003-066X.56.2.109

Glowacki, K., Warner, G., & White, C. (2016). The use of a token economy for behaviour and symptom management in adult psychiatric inpatients: A critical review of the literature. *Journal of Psychiatric Intensive Care, 12*(2), 119–127. https://doi.org/10.20299/jpi.2016.009

Godden, D. R., & Baddely, A. D. (1975). Context-dependent memory in two natural environments: On land and underwater. *The British Journal of Psychology, 66*(3), 325–331. https://doi.org/10.1111/j.2044-8295.1975.tb01468.x

Goel, V., & Waechter, R. (2018). Inductive and deductive reasoning: Integrating insights from philosophy, psychology, and neuroscience. In L. J. Ball & V. A. Thompson (Eds.), *The Routledge international handbook of thinking and reasoning* (pp. 218–247). Routledge/Taylor & Francis Group.

Goldberg, A. E. (2013). "Doing" and "undoing" gender: The meaning and division of housework in same-sex couples. *Journal of Family Theory & Review, 5*(2), 85–104. https://doi.org/10.1111/jftr.12009

Goldberg, A. E., Smith, J. Z., & Perry-Jenkins, M. (2012). The division of labor in lesbian, gay, and heterosexual new adoptive parents. *Journal of Marriage and Family, 74*(4), 812–828. https://doi.org/10.1111/j.1741-3737.2012.00992.x

Goldberg, L. R. (1992). The development of markers for the Big-Five factor structure. *Psychological Assessment, 4*(1), 26–42. https://doi.org/10.1037/1040-3590.4.1.26

Goldfarb, E. V., & Sinha, R. (2018). Drug-induced glucocorticoids and memory for substance use. *Trends in Neurosciences, 41*(11), 853–868. https://doi.org/10.1016/j.tins.2018.08.005

Goldstein, A. L., Wall, A. M., Wekerle, C., & Krank, M. (2013). The impact of perceived reinforcement from alcohol and involvement in leisure activities on adolescent alcohol use. *Journal of Child & Adolescent Substance Abuse, 22*(4), 340–363. https://doi.org/10.1080/1067828X.2012.735190

Goldstein, B. I., Birmaher, B., Carlson, G. A., DelBello, M. P., Findling, R. L., Fristad, M., Kowatch, R. A., Miklowitz, D. J., Nery, F. G., Perez-Algorta, G., Van Meter, A., Zeni, C. P., Correll, C. U., Kim, H-W., Wozniak, J., Chang, K. D., Hillegers, M., & Youngstrom, E. A. (2017). The International Society for Bipolar Disorders Task Force report on pediatric bipolar disorder: Knowledge to date and directions for future research. *Bipolar Disorders, 19*(7), 524–543. https://doi.org/10.1111/bdi.12556

Goldstein-Piekarski, A. N., Greer, S. M., Saletin, J. M., Harvey, A. G., Williams, L. M., & Walker, M. P. (2018). Sex, sleep deprivation, and the anxious brain. *Journal of Cognitive Neuroscience, 30*(4), 565–578. https://doi.org/10.1162/jocn_a_01225

Gollan, T. H., Stasenko, A., Li, C., & Salmon, D. P. (2017). Bilingual language intrusions and other speech errors in Alzheimer's disease. *Brain and Cognition, 118*, 27–44. https://doi.org/10.1016/j.bandc.2017.07.007

Golomb, B. A., Berg, B. K., & Berg, B. (2021). Chocolate consumption and sex-interest. *Cureus, 13*(2), Article e13310. https://doi.org/10.7759/cureus.13310

González, J. J. L. (2023). Mass media, social networks and eating disorders: Image, perfection and death. In I. Jáuregui-Lobera & J. V. Martínez-Quiñones (Eds.), *Eating—pathology and causes* (pp. 1–91). InTechOpen. https://doi.org/10.5772/intechopen.1002270

Goodfriend, W. (2012). Sexual script or sexual improv? Nontraditional sexual paths. In M. Paludi (Ed.), *The psychology of love* (Vol. 1, pp. 59–71). Praeger.

Goodman, J. H., & Santangelo, G. (2011). Group treatment for postpartum depression: A systematic review. *Archives of Women's Mental Health, 14*(4), 277–293. https://doi.org/10.1007/s00737-011-0225-3

Goodwin, D. W., Crane, J. B., & Guze, S. B. (1975). Alcoholic "blackouts": A review and clinical study of 100 alcoholics. *American Journal of Psychiatry, 126*(2), 191–198. https://doi.org/10.1176/ajp.126.2.191

Goosen, L. (2022). Assistive technologies for children and adolescents with autism spectrum disorders. In F. Stasolla (Ed.), *Assistive technologies for assessment and recovery of neurological impairments* (pp. 1–24). IGI Global. https://doi.org/10.4018/978-1-7998-7430-0.ch001

Gordon, D. S., & Platek, S. M. (2009). Trustworthy? The brain knows: Implicit neural responses to faces that vary in dark triad personality characteristics and trustworthiness. *Journal of Social, Evolutionary, and Cultural Psychology, 3*(3), 182–200. http://dx.doi.org/10.1037/h0099323

Gordovez, F. J. A., & McMahon, F. J. (2020). The genetics of bipolar disorder. *Molecular Psychiatry, 25*(3), 544–559. https://doi.org/10.1038/s41380-019-0634-7

Gori, A., Topino, E., & Griffiths, M. D. (2023). The associations between attachment, self-esteem, fear of missing out, daily time expenditure, and problematic social media use: A path analysis model. *Addictive Behaviors, 141*, 1–8. https://doi.org/10.1016/j.addbeh.2023.107633

Gorn, G. J. (1982). The effects of music in advertising on choice behavior: A classical conditioning approach. *Journal of Marketing, 46*(1), 94–101. https://doi.org/10.1177/002224298204600109

Gottfredson, L. S. (2004). Intelligence: Is it the epidemiologists' elusive "fundamental cause" of social class inequalities in health? *Journal of Personality and Social Psychology, 86*(1), 174–199. https://doi.org/10.1037/0022-3514.86.1.174

Gottfried, J. A., & Dolan, R. J. (2003). The nose smells what the eye sees: Crossmodal visual facilitation of human olfactory perception. *Neuron, 39*(2), 375–386. https://doi.org/10.1016/S0896-6273(03)00392-1

Gotts, S. J., Jo, H. J., Wallace, G. L., Saad, Z. S., Cox, R. W., & Martin, A. (2013). Two distinct forms of functional lateralization in the human brain. *Proceedings of the National Academy of Sciences, 110*(36), E3435–E3444. https://doi.org/10.1073/pnas.1302581110

Graber, J. A., Nichols, T. R., & Brooks-Gunn, J. (2010). Putting pubertal timing in developmental context: Implications for prevention. *Developmental Psychobiology, 52*(3), 254–262. https://doi.org/10.1002/dev.20438

Graham, S., Mason, A., Riordan, B., Winter, T., & Scarf, D. (2021). Taking a break from social media improves wellbeing through sleep quality. *Cyberpsychology, Behavior, and Social Networking, 24*(6), 421–425. http://doi.org/10.1089/cyber.2020.0217

Graham, W. V., Bonito-Oliva, A., & Sakmar, T. P. (2017). Update on Alzheimer's disease therapy and prevention strategies. *Annual Review of Medicine, 68*, 413–430. https://doi.org/10.1146/annurev-med-042915-103753

Grandview Research. (2023). *Personal development market size, share & trends analysis report by instrument (books, e-platforms), by focus area (mental health, physical health), by region, and segment forecasts, 2023–2030.* https://www.grandviewresearch.com/industry-analysis/personal-development-market

Granello, D. H., & Gibbs, T. A. (2016). The power of language and labels: "The mentally ill" versus "people with mental illnesses." *Journal of Counseling & Development, 94*(1), 31–40. https://doi.org/10.1002/jcad.12059

Graso, M., Chen, F. X., & Aquino, K. (2022). *Scapegoating of the unvaccinated and the role of political ideology.* https://ssrn.com/abstract=4056613 or http://dx.doi.org/10.2139/ssrn.4056613

Gravholt, C. H., Viuff, M. H., Brun, S., Stochholm, K., & Andersen, N. H. (2019). Turner syndrome: mechanisms and management. *Nature Reviews Endocrinology, 15*(10), 601–614. https://doi.org/10.1210/endrev/bnac016

Greatbatch, I., Koester, R. J., & Kleinsmith, A. L. (2019). Rescue responses during a full moon and Friday 13th. *International Journal of Emergency Services, 8*(2), 108–121. https://doi.org/10.1108/IJES-12-2017-0066

Green, A., Cohen-Zion, M., Haim, A., & Dagan, Y. (2017). Evening light exposure to computer screens disrupts human sleep, biological rhythms, and attention abilities. *Chronobiology International, 34*(7), 855–865. https://doi.org/10.1080/07420528.2017.1324878

Green, A., Dagan, Y., & Haim, A. (2018). Exposure to screens of digital media devices, sleep, and concentration abilities in a sample of Israel adults. *Sleep and Biological Rhythms, 16*(3), 273–281. https://doi.org/10.1007/s41105-018-0150-1

Greenberg, J., & Kosloff, S. (2008). Terror management theory: Implications for understanding prejudice, stereotyping, intergroup conflict, and political attitudes. *Social and Personality Psychology Compass, 2*(5), 1881–1894. https://doi.org/10.1111/j.1751-9004.2008.00144.x

Greenberg, J., Arndt, J., Schimel, J., Pyszczynski, T., & Solomon, S. (2001). Clarifying the function of mortality salience-induced worldview defense: Renewed suppression or reduced accessibility of death-related thoughts? *Journal of Experimental Social Psychology, 37*(1), 70–76. https://doi.org/10.1006/jesp.2000.1434

Greenberg, J., Solomon, S., & Arndt, J. (2008). A basic but uniquely human motivation: Terror management. In J. Y. Shah & W. L. Gardner (Eds.), *Handbook of motivation science* (pp. 114–134). Guilford.

Greenberg, J., Vail, K., & Pyszczynski, T. (2014). Terror management theory and research: How the desire for death transcendence drives our strivings for meaning and significance. *Advances in Motivation Science, 1*, 85-134. https://doi.org/10.1016/bs.adms.2014.08.003

Greenwood, J. (2017). Psychologists go to war. *Behavioral Scientist.* https://behavioralscientist.org/psychologists-go-war/

Greenwood, T. A. (2020). Creativity and bipolar disorder: A shared genetic vulnerability. *Annual Review of Clinical*

Psychology, 16, 239–264. https://doi.org/10.1146/annurev-clinpsy-050718-095449

Greitemeyer, T., & Mügge, D. O. (2013). Rational bystanders. *British Journal of Social Psychology, 52*(4), 773–780. https://doi.org/10.1111/bjso.12036

Greitemeyer, T., & Mügge, D. O. (2015). "Video games do affect social outcomes: A meta-analytic review of the effects of violent and prosocial video game play": Corrigendum. *Personality and Social Psychology Bulletin, 41*(8), 1164. https://doi.org/10.1177/0146167215591992

Greving, S., & Richter, T. (2018). Examining the testing effect in university teaching: Retrievability and question format matter. *Frontiers in Psychology, 9,* Article 2412. https://doi.org/10.3389/fpsyg.2018.02412

Griffin, K. E., Arndt, S. S., & Vinke, C. M. (2023). The adaptation of Maslow's hierarchy of needs to the hierarchy of dogs' needs using a consensus building approach. *Animals, 13*(16), Article 2620. https://doi.org/10.3390/ani13162620

Grinker, R. R. (1966). "Open-system" psychiatry. *American Journal of Psychoanalysis, 26*(2), 115–128. https://doi.org/10.1007/bf01873427

Groenendijk, T., Janssen, T., Rijlaarsdam, G., & van den Bergh, H. (2013). The effect of observational learning on students' performance, processes, and motivation in two creative domains. *British Journal of Educational Psychology, 83*(1), 3–28. https://doi.org/10.1111/j.2044-8279.2011.02052.x

Grønli, J., Byrkjedal, I. K., Bjorvatn, B., Nødtvedt, Ø., Hamre, B., & Pallesen, S. (2016). Reading from an iPad or from a book in bed: The impact on human sleep. A randomized controlled crossover trial. *Sleep Medicine, 21,* 86–92. https://doi.org/10.1016/j.sleep.2016.02.006

Gross, W. L., & Greene, A. J. (2007). Analogical inference: The role of awareness in abstract learning. *Memory, 15*(8), 838–844. https://doi.org/10.1080/09658210701715469

Grossman, P., Niemann, L., Schmidt, S., & Walach, H. (2004). Mindfulness-based stress reduction and health benefits: A meta-analysis. *Journal of Psychosomatic Research, 57*(1), 35–43. https://doi.org/10.1016/S0022-3999(03)00573-7

Grünebaum, A., Bornstein, E., Dudenhausen, J. W., Lenchner, E., Jones, M. D. F., Varrey, A., Lewis, D., & Chervenak, F. A. (2023). Hidden in plain sight in the delivery room—the Apgar score is biased. *Journal of Perinatal Medicine, 51*(5), 628–633. https://doi.org/10.1515/jpm-2022-0550

Guadagno, R. E., Okdie, B. M., & Kruse, S. A. (2012). Dating deception: Gender, online dating, and exaggerated self-presentation. *Computers in Human Behavior, 28*(2), 642–647. https://doi.org/10.1016/j.chb.2011.11.010

Guanzon-Lapeña, M. A., Church, A. T., Carlota, A. J., & Katigbak, M. S. (1998). Indigenous personality measures: Philippine examples. *Journal of Cross-Cultural Psychology, 29*(1), 249–270. https://doi.org/10.1177/0022022198291013

Guenther, C. L., & Alicke, M. D. (2008). Self-enhancement and belief perseverance. *Journal of Experimental Social Psychology, 44*(3), 706–712. https://doi.org/10.1016/j.jesp.2007.04.010

Guerin, B. (2001). Replacing catharsis and uncertainty reduction theories with descriptions of historical and social context. *Review of General Psychology, 5*(1), 44–61. https://doi.org/10.1037/1089-2680.5.1.44

Guffanti, G., Gameroff, M. J., Warner, V., Talati, A., Glatt, C. E., Wickramaratne, P., & Weissman, M. M. (2016). Heritability of major depressive and comorbid anxiety disorders in multigenerational families at high risk for depression. *American Journal of Medical Genetics Part B: Neuropsychiatric Genetics, 171*(8), 1072–1079. https://doi.org/10.1002/ajmg.b.32477

Guidry, J. J., Aday, L. A., Zhang, D., & Winn, R. J. (1997). The role of informal and formal social support networks for patients with cancer. *Cancer Practice, 5*(4), 241–246.

Guilford, J. P. (1960). *Alternate uses, Form A.* Sheridan Supply.

Guinn, J. (2017). *The road to Jonestown: Jim Jones and Peoples Temple.* Simon & Schuster.

Gunkel, M., Schlägel, C., & Engle, R. L. (2014). Culture's influence on emotional intelligence: An empirical study of nine countries. *Journal of International Management, 20,* 256–274. https://doi.org/10.1016/j.intman.2013.10.002

Gunthert, K. C., Cohen, L. H., & Armeli, S. (1999). The role of neuroticism in daily stress and coping. *Journal of Personality and Social Psychology, 77*(5), 1087–1100. http://dx.doi.org/10.1037/0022-3514.77.5.1087

Guo, H., & Zhang, Y. (2020). Resting state fMRI and improved deep learning algorithm for earlier detection of Alzheimer's disease. *IEEE Access, 8,* 115383–115392. https://doi.org/10.1109/ACCESS.2020.3003424

Gupta, A., Love, A., Kilpatrick, L. A., Labus, J. S., Bhatt, R., Chang, L., Tillisch, K., Naliboff, B., & Mayer, E. A. (2017). Morphological brain measures of cortico-limbic inhibition related to resilience. *Journal of Neuroscience Research, 95*(9), 1760–1775. https://doi.org/10.1002/jnr.24007

Gurland, B. J., Wilder, D. E., Lantigua, R., Stern, Y., Chen, J., Killeffer, E. H., & Mayeux, R. (1999). Rates of dementia in three ethnoracial groups. *International Journal of Geriatric Psychiatry, 14*(6), 481–493. https://doi.org/10.1002/(SICI)1099-1166(199906)14:6<481::AID-GPS959>3.0.CO;2-5

Gurven, M., Von Rueden, C., Massenkoff, M., Kaplan, H., & Lero Vie, M. (2013). How universal is the Big Five? Testing the five-factor model of personality variation among forager–farmers in the Bolivian Amazon. *Journal of Personality and Social Psychology, 104*(2), 354–370. https://doi.org/10.1037/a0030841

Guszkowska, M. (2004). Effects of exercise on anxiety, depression and mood. *Psychiatria Polska, 38*(4), 611–620.

Guthrie, R. V. (2004). *Even the rat was white: A historical view of psychology* (2nd ed.). Allyn and Bacon.

Guthrie, R. V. (2004). *Even the rat was white: A historical view of psychology.* Pearson Education.

Guyer, A. E., Beard, S. J., & Venticinque, J. S. (2023). Brain development during adolescence and early adulthood. In L. J. Crockett, G. Carlo, & J. E. Schulenberg (Eds.), *APA handbook of adolescent and young adult development* (pp. 21–37). American Psychological Association.

Guzmán-Vélez, E., Warren, D. E., Feinstein, J. S., Bruss, J., & Tranel, D. (2016). Dissociable contributions of amygdala and hippocampus to emotion and memory in patients with Alzheimer's disease. *Hippocampus, 26*(6), 727–738. https://doi.org/10.1002/hipo.22554

Gwarjanski, A. R., & Parrott, S. (2018). Schizophrenia in the news: The role of news frames in shaping online reader dialogue about mental illness. *Health Communication, 33*(8), 954–961. https://doi.org/10.1080/10410236.2017.1323320

Haack, S. (1996). *Deviant logic, fuzzy logic: Beyond the formalism.* University of Chicago Press.

Haas, J. W., Rief, W., Glombiewski, J. A., Winkler, A., & Doering, B. K. (2020). Expectation-induced placebo effect on acute sadness in women with major depression: An experimental investigation. *Journal of Affective Disorders, 274,* 920–928. https://doi.org/10.1016/j.jad.2020.05.056

Habashi, M. M., Graziano, W. G., & Hoover, A. E. (2016). Searching for the prosocial personality: A Big Five approach to linking personality and prosocial behavior. *Personality and Social Psychology Bulletin, 42*(9), 1177–1192. https://doi.org/10.1177/0146167216652859

Habashi, M. M., Graziano, W. G., & Hoover, A. E. (2016). Searching for the prosocial personality: A big five approach to linking personality and prosocial behavior. *Personality and Social Psychology Bulletin, 42*(9), 1177–1192. https://doi.org/10.1177/0146167216652859

Habel, C., Feeley, N., Hayton, B., Bell, L., & Zelkowitz, P. (2015). Causes of women's postpartum depression symptoms: Men's and women's perceptions. *Midwifery*, *31*(7), 728–734. https://doi.org/10.1016/j.midw.2015.03.007

Habtewold, T. D., Islam, M. A., Radie, Y. T., & Tegegne, B. S. (2016). Comorbidity of depression and diabetes: An application of biopsychosocial model. *International Journal of Mental Health Systems*, *10*(1), 1–9. https://doi.org/10.1186/s13033-016-0106-2

Hachtel, H., Vogel, T., & Huber, C. G. (2019). Mandated treatment and its impact on therapeutic process and outcome factors. *Frontiers in Psychiatry*, *10*, Article 219. https://doi.org/10.3389/fpsyt.2019.00219

Hacking, I. (1998). *Mad travelers: Reflections on the reality of transient mental illnesses*. University of Virginia Press.

Hagger-Johnson, G., Sabia, S., Nabi, H., Brunner, E., Kivimaki, M., Shipley, M., & Singh-Manoux, A. (2012). Low conscientiousness and risk of all-cause, cardiovascular and cancer mortality over 17 years: Whitehall II cohort study. *Journal of Psychosomatic Research*, *73*(2), 98–103. https://doi.org/10.1016/j.jpsychores.2012.05.007

Hair, N. L., Hanson, J. L., Wolfe, B. L., & Pollak, S. D. (2015). Association of child poverty, brain development, and academic achievement. *JAMA Pediatrics*, *169*(9), 822–829. https://doi.org/10.1001/jamapediatrics.2015.1475

Halbrook, Y. J., O'Donnell, A. T., & Msetfi, R. M. (2019). When and how video games can be good: A review of the positive effects of video games on well-being. *Perspectives on Psychological Science*, *14*(6), 1096–1104. https://doi.org/10.1177/1745691619863807

Halfmann, E., Bredehöft, J., & Häusser, J. A. (2020). Replicating roaches: A preregistered direct replication of Zajonc, Heingartner, and Herman's (1969) social-facilitation study. *Psychological Science*, *31*(3), 332–337. https://doi.org/10.1177/0956797620902101

Hall, C. R., Munroe-Chandler, K. J., Cumming, J., Law, B., Ramsey, R., & Murphy, L. (2009). Imagery and observational learning use and their relationship to sport confidence. *Journal of Sports Sciences*, *27*(4), 327–337. https://doi.org/10.1080/02640410802549769

Hall, G. S. (1904). *Adolescence: Its psychology and its relation to physiology, anthropology, sociology, sex, crime, religion, and education* (Vol. 1). D. Appleton and Company.

Hall, G. S. (1905). *Adolescence: Its psychology and its relation to physiology, anthropology, sociology, sex, crime, religion, and education* (Vol. 2). D. Appleton and Company.

Hall, G. S., & Motora, Y. (1887). Dermal sensitiveness to gradual pressure changes. *The American Journal of Psychology*, *1*(1), 72–98. https://doi.org/10.2307/1411232

Hammer, J. (2021). *Counseling psychology vs. clinical psychology*. http://drjosephhammer.com/psych-grad-school/counseling-psychology-vs-clinical-psychology/

Hammond, B. G. (2020, August 17). *The SAT and systemic racism*. InsideHigherEd. https://www.insidehighered.com/admissions/views/2020/08/17/history-sat-reflects-systemic-racism-opinion

Han, Y., Yuan, M., Guo, Y. S., Shen, X. Y., Gao, Z. K., & Bi, X. (2022). The role of enriched environment in neural development and repair. *Frontiers in Cellular Neuroscience*, *16*, Article 890666. https://doi.org/10.3389/fncel.2022.890666

Hansen, R., & King, D. (2013). *Sterilized by the state: Eugenics, race, and the population scare in twentieth-century North America*. Cambridge University Press.

Hardy, J. L., Nelson, R. A., Thomason, M. E., Sternberg, D. A., Katovich, K., Farzin, F., & Scanlon, M. (2015). Enhancing cognitive abilities with comprehensive training: A large, online, randomized, active-controlled trial. *PLoS ONE*, *10*(9), e0134467. https://doi.org/10.1371/journal.pone.0134467

Harianti, W. S. (2023). Social construct of masculinity towards mental health: A literature review. *European Journal of Behavioral Sciences*, *6*(3), 69–83. https://doi.org/10.33422/ejbs.v6i3.1103

Harmat, L., Takács, J., & Bódizs, R. (2008). Music improves sleep quality in students. *Journal of Advanced Nursing*, *62*(3), 327–335. https://doi.org/10.1111/j.1365-2648.2008.04602.x

Harmon-Jones, E., & Allen, J. J. (1997). Behavioral activation sensitivity and resting frontal EEG asymmetry: Covariation of putative indicators related to risk for mood disorders. *Journal of Abnormal Psychology*, *106*(1), 159–163. http://dx.doi.org/10.1037/0021-843X.106.1.159

Harmon-Jones, E., & Mills, J. (2019). An introduction to cognitive dissonance theory and an overview of current perspectives on the theory. In E. Harmon-Jones (Ed.), *Cognitive dissonance: Reexamining a pivotal theory in psychology* (pp. 3–24). American Psychological Association. https://doi.org/10.1037/0000135-001

Harrington, A. G., & Maxwell, J. A. (2023). It takes two to tango: Links between traditional beliefs about both men's and women's gender roles and comfort initiating sex and comfort refusing sex. *Sex Roles*, *88*, 514–528. https://doi.org/10.1007/s11199-023-01366-w

Harris, B., McCredie, M. N., Truong, T., Regan, T., Thompson, C. G., Leach, W., & Fields, S. A. (2023). Relations between adolescent sensation seeking and risky sexual behaviors across sex, race, and age: A meta-analysis. *Archives of Sexual Behavior*, *52*(1), 191–204. https://doi.org/10.1007/s10508-022-02384-7

Harris, J. L., & Qualls, C. D. (2000). The association of elaborative or maintenance rehearsal with age, reading comprehension and verbal working memory performance. *Aphasiology*, *14*(5–6), 515–526. https://doi.org/10.1080/026870300401289

Harrison, A., Summers, J., & Mennecke, B. (2018). The effects of the dark triad on unethical behavior. *Journal of Business Ethics*, *153*(1), 53–77. https://doi.org/10.1007/s10551-016-3368-3

Harrison, N. A., Johnston, K., Corno, F., Casey, S. J., Friedner, K., Humphreys, K., Jaldow, E. J., Pitkanen, M., & Kopelman, M. D. (2017). Psychogenic amnesia: Syndromes, outcome, and patterns of retrograde amnesia. *Brain: A Journal of Neurology*, *140*(9), 2498–2510. https://doi.org/10.1093/brain/awx186

Hartmann, C., van Gog, T., & Rummel, N. (2020). Do examples of failure effectively prepare students for learning from subsequent instruction? *Applied Cognitive Psychology*, *34*(4), 879–889. https://doi.org/10.1002/acp.3651

Hartshorne, J. K., & Germine, L. T. (2015). When does cognitive functioning peak? The asynchronous rise and fall of different cognitive abilities across the life span. *Psychological Science*, *26*(4), 433–443. https://doi.org/10.1177/0956797614567339

Hartup, W. W., & Stevens, N. (1999). Friendships and adaptation across the life span. *Current Directions in Psychological Science*, *8*(3), 76–79. https://doi.org/10.1111/1467-8721.00018

Harvanek, Z. M., Fogelman, N., Xu, K., & Sinha, R. (2021). Psychological and biological resilience modulates the effects of stress on epigenetic aging. *Translational Psychiatry*, *11*(1), 1–9. https://doi.org/10.1038/s41398-021-01735-7

Hasan, A., Wobrock, T., Guse, B., Langguth, B., Landgrebe, M., Eichhammer, P., Frank, E., Cordes, J., Wowler, W., Musso, E., Winterer, G., Gaebal, W., Hajak, G., Ohmann, C., Verde, P. E., Rietschel, M., Ahmed, R., Honer, W. G., Dechent, P., Malchow, B., & Koutsouleris, N. (2017). Structural brain changes are associated with response of negative symptoms to prefrontal repetitive transcranial magnetic stimulation in patients with schizophrenia. *Molecular Psychiatry*, *22*(6), 857–864. https://doi.org/10.1038/mp.2016.161

Hashash, M., Abou Zeid, M., & Moacdieh, N. M. (2019). Social media browsing while driving: Effects on driver performance and attention allocation. *Transportation Research Part F: Traffic*

Psychology and Behaviour, 63, 67–82. https://doi.org/10.1016/j.trf.2019.03.021

Hater, J. J., Singh, B. K., & Simpson, D. D. (1984). Influence of family and religion on long-term outcomes among opioid addicts. *Advances in Alcohol & Substance Abuse, 4*(1), 29–40. https://doi.org/10.1300/J251v04n01_04

Hatzenbuehler, M. L., Phelan, J. C., & Link, B. G. (2013). Stigma as a fundamental cause of population health inequalities. *American Journal of Public Health, 103*, 813–821. http://dx.doi.org/10.2105/AJPH.2012.301069

Haxby, J. V., Hoffman, E. A., & Gobbini, M. I. (2000). The distributed human neural system for face perception. *Trends in Cognitive Sciences, 4*(6), 223–233. https://doi.org/10.1016/S1364-6613(00)01482-0

Haxby, J. V., Hoffman, E. A., & Gobbini, M. I. (2002). Human neural systems for face recognition and social communication. *Biological Psychiatry, 51*(1), 59–67. https://doi.org/10.1016/S0006-3223(01)01330-0

Hayashi, M., Masuda, A., & Hori, T. (2003). The alerting effects of caffeine, bright light and face washing after a short daytime nap. *Clinical Neurophysiology, 114*(12), 2268–2278. https://doi.org/10.1016/S1388-2457(03)00255-4

Hearst, P. C., & Moscow, A. (1988). *Patty Hearst: Her own story.* Avon Books.

Hebb, D. O. (1949). *The organization of behavior.* Wiley & Sons.

Hedges, K., & Korchmaros, J. D. (2016). Pubertal timing and substance abuse treatment outcomes: An analysis of early menarche on substance use patterns. *Journal of Child & Adolescent Substance Abuse, 25*(6), 598–605. https://doi.org/10.1080/1067828X.2016.1171186

Heikkilä, K., Nyberg, S. T., Theorell, T., Fransson, E. I., Alfredsson, L., Bjorner, J. B., Bonenfant, S., Borritz, M., Bouillon, K., Burr, H., Dragano, N., Geuskens, G. A., Goldberg, M., Hamer, M., Hooftman, W. E., Houtman, I. L., Joensuu, M., Knutsson, A., Koskenvuo, M., Koskinen, A., . . . Kivimäki, M. (2013). Work stress and risk of cancer: meta-analysis of 5700 incident cancer events in 116 000 European men and women. *BMJ, 346*, 1–10. https://doi.org/10.1136/bmj.f165

Heilmann, A., Mehay, A., Watt, R. G., Kelly, Y., Durrant, J. E., van Turnhout, J., & Gershoff, E. T. (2021). Physical punishment and child outcomes: A narrative review of prospective studies. *The Lancet, 398*(10297), 355–364. https://doi.org/10.1016/S0140-6736(21)00582-1

Heinzen, T., & Goodfriend, W. (2022). *Social psychology* (2nd ed.). Sage.

Helgeson, V. S., & Zajdel, M. (2017). Adjusting to chronic health conditions. *Annual Review of Psychology, 68*(1), 545–571. https://doi.org/10.1146/annurev-psych-010416-044014

Hembree, R. (1988). Correlates, causes, effects, and treatment of test anxiety. *Review of Educational Research, 58*(1), 47–77. https://doi.org/10.3102/00346543058001047

Henchy, T., & Glass, D. C. (1968). Evaluation apprehension and the social facilitation of dominant and subordinate responses. *Journal of Personality and Social Psychology, 10*(4), 446–454. https://doi.org/10.1037/h0026814

Henderlong, J., & Lepper, M. R. (2002). The effects of praise on children's intrinsic motivation: A review and synthesis. *Psychological Bulletin, 128*(5), 774–795. https://doi.org/10.1037/0033-2909.128.5.774

Henderson, B. J., Wall, T. R., Henley, B. M., Kim, C. H., McKinney, S., & Lester, H. A. (2017). Menthol enhances nicotine reward-related behavior by potentiating nicotine-induced changes in nAChR function, nAChR upregulation, and DA neuron excitability. *Neuropsychopharmacology, 42*(12), 2285–2291. https://doi.org/10.1038/npp.2017.72

Hengartner, M. P., Amendola, S., Kaminski, J. A., Kindler, S., Bschor, T., & Plöderl, M. (2021). Suicide risk with selective serotonin reuptake inhibitors and other new-generation antidepressants in adults: A systematic review and meta-analysis of observational studies. *Journal of Epidemiology & Community Health, 75*(6), 523–530. https://doi.org/10.1136/jech-2020-214611

Henle, M., & Hubbell, M. B. (1938). "Egocentricity" in adult conversation. *Journal of Social Psychology, 9*(2), 227–234. https://doi.org/10.1080/00224545.1938.9921692

Herbenick, D., Bowling, J., Fu, T. C. J., Dodge, B., Guerra-Reyes, L., & Sanders, S. (2017). Sexual diversity in the United States: Results from a nationally representative probability sample of adult women and men. *PLoS One, 12*(7), e0181198. https://doi.org/10.1371/journal.pone.0181198

Herbst, J. (2013). *Germ theory* (Rev. ed.). Twenty-First Century Books.

Hergert, D. C., Robertson-Benta, C., Sicard, V., Schwotzer, D., Hutchison, K., Covey, D. P., Quinn, D. K., Sadek, J. R., McDonald, J., & Mayer, A. R. (2021). Use of medical cannabis to treat traumatic brain injury. *Journal of Neurotrauma.* Advance online publication. https://doi.org/10.1089/neu.2020.7148

Herholz, K., Langen, K. J., Schiepers, C., & Mountz, J. M. (2012). Brain tumors. *Seminars in Nuclear Medicine, 42*(6), 356–370. https://doi.org/10.1053/j.semnuclmed.2012.06.001

Herman, J. P., McKlveen, J. M., Ghosal, S., Kopp, B., Wulsin, A., Makinson, R., Scheimann, J., & Myers, B. (2016). Regulation of the hypothalamic-pituitary-adrenocortical stress response. *Comprehensive Physiology, 6*(2), 603–621. https://doi.org/10.1002/cphy.c150015

Hermens, D. F., & Lagopoulos, J. (2018). Binge drinking and the young brain: A mini review of the neurobiological underpinnings of alcohol-induced blackout. *Frontiers in Psychology, 9*, 1–7. https://doi.org/10.3389/fpsyg.2018.00012

Hermens, F., & Zdravković, S. (2022). Visual attention in change blindness for objects and shadows. *Perception, 51*(9), 605–623. https://doi.org/10.1177/03010066221109936

Heron, K. E., & Smyth, J. M. (2013). Body image discrepancy and negative affect in women's everyday lives: An ecological momentary assessment evaluation of self discrepancy theory. *Journal of Social and Clinical Psychology, 32*(3), 276–295. https://doi.org/10.1521/jscp.2013.32.3.276

Hershner, S., & Chervin, R. (2014). Causes and consequences of sleepiness among college students. *Nature and Science of Sleep, 6*, 73–84. https://doi.org/10.2147/NSS.S62907

Herz, R. (1997). The effects of cue distinctiveness on odor-based context-dependent memory. *Memory & Cognition, 25*(3), 375–380. https://doi.org/10.3758/BF03211293

Herz, R. S., Beland, S. L., & Hellerstein, M. (2004). Changing odor hedonic perception through emotional associations in humans. *International Journal of Comparative Psychology, 17*(4), 315–338. https://doi.org/10.46867/ijcp.2004.17.04.05

Heshmati, S., & Donaldson, S. I. (2020). The science of positive relationships and love. In S. I. Donaldson, M. Csikszentmihalyi, & J. Nakamura (Eds.), *Positive psychological science: Improving everyday life, well-being, work, education, and societies around the globe* (2nd ed., pp. 52–63). Routledge. https://doi.org/10.4324/9780203731833

Heshmati, S., Oravecz, Z., Pressman, S., Batchelder, W. H., Muth, C., & Vandekerckhove, J. (2019). What does it to feel loved: Cultural consensus and individual differences in felt love. *Journal of Social and Personal Relationships, 36*(1), 214–243. https://doi.org/10.1177/0265407517724600

Hettich, P. (2014). *APA guidelines for the undergraduate psychology major, version 2.0: Your covert career counselor.* https://www.apa.org/ed/precollege/psn/2014/09/career-counselor#:~:text=Goal%201%3A%20knowledge%20base%20in,%2C%202013%2C%20p%2017

Hewer, M. (2015). *Why should psychological science care about diversity?* https://www.psychologicalscience.org/observer/why-should-psychological-science-care-about-diversity

Hewitt, P. L., & Genest, M. (1990). The ideal self: Schematic processing of perfectionistic content in dysphoric university students. *Journal of Personality and Social Psychology*, 59(4), 802–808. https://doi.org/10.1037/0022-3514.59.4.802

Hickmann, M. (2000). Linguistic relativity and linguistic determinism: Some new directions. *Linguistics*, 38(2), 409–434. https://doi.org/10.1515/ling.38.2.409

Higgins, E. T. (1987). Self-discrepancy: A theory relating self and affect. *Psychological Review*, 94(3), 319–340. https://doi.org/10.1037/0033-295X.94.3.319

Higgins, E. T. (2002). How self-regulation creates distinct values: The case of promotion and prevention decision making. *Journal of Consumer Psychology*, 12(3), 177–191. https://doi.org/10.1207/S15327663JCP1203_01

Hill, C. E., Gelso, C. J., Gerstenblith, J., Chui, H., Pudasaini, S., Burgard, J., Baumann, E., & Huang, T. (2013). The dreamscape of psychodynamic psychotherapy: Dreams, dreamers, dream work, consequences, and case studies. *Dreaming*, 23(1), 1–45. https://doi.org/10.1037/a0032207

Hill, J. (2003). Placebos in clinical care: For whose pleasure? *The Lancet*, 362(9379), Article 254. https://doi.org/10.1016/S0140-6736(03)13940-2

Hill, K. P., Palastro, M. D., Johnson, B., & Ditre, J. W. (2017). Cannabis and pain: A clinical review. *Cannabis and Cannabinoid Research*, 2(1), 96–104. https://doi.org/10.1089/can.2017.0017

Hillman, C., Erickson, K., & Kramer, A. (2008). Be smart, exercise your heart: Exercise effects on brain and cognition. *Nature Reviews: Neuroscience*, 9(1), 58–65. https://doi.org/10.1038/nrn2298

Hilton, D. L., Jr., & Watts, C. (2011). Pornography addiction: A neuroscience perspective. *Surgical Neurology International*, 2, 19. https://doi.org/10.4103/2152-7806.76977

Hinderliter, A. C. (2009). Methodological issues for studying asexuality. *Archives of Sexual Behavior*, 38(5), 619–621. https://doi.org/10.1007/s10508-009-9502-x

Hines, T. (1987). Left brain/right brain mythology and implications for management and training. *Academy of Management Review*, 12(4), 600–606. https://doi.org/10.5465/amr.1987.4306708

Hirschberger, G. (2006). Terror management and attributions of blame to innocent victims: Reconciling compassionate and defensive responses. *Journal of Personality and Social Psychology*, 91(5), 832–844. https://doi.org/10.1037/0022-3514.91.5.832

Hirschberger, G., Florian, V., & Mikulincer, M. (2005). Fear and compassion: A terror management analysis of emotional reactions to physical disability. *Rehabilitation Psychology*, 50(3), 246–257. https://doi.org/10.1037/0090-5550.50.3.246

Hirst, W., & Phelps, E. A. (2016). Flashbulb memories. *Current Directions in Psychological Science*, 25(1), 36–41. https://doi.org/10.1177/0963721415622487

Hirst, W., Phelps, E. A., Meksin, R., Vaidya, C. J., Johnson, M. K., Mitchell, K. J., Buckner, R. L., Budson, A. E., Gabrieli, J. D. E., Lustig, C., Mather, M., Ochsner, K. N., Schacter, D., Simons, J. S., Lyle, K. B., Cuc, A. F., & Olsson, A. (2015). A ten-year follow-up of a study of memory for the attack of September 11, 2001: Flashbulb memories and memories for flashbulb events. *Journal of Experimental Psychology: General*, 144(3), 604–623. https://doi.org/10.1037/xge0000055

Hitchcock, C. H., Dowrick, P. W., & Prater, M. A. (2003). Video self-modeling intervention in school-based settings: A review. *Remedial and Special Education*, 24(1), 36–45. https://doi.org/10.1177/074193250302400104

Hitsch, G. J., Hortaçsu, A., & Ariely, D. (2010). What makes you click? Mate preferences in online dating. *Quantitative Marketing and Economics*, 8(4), 393–427. https://doi.org/10.1007/s11129-010-9088-6

Hittner, E. F., Stephens, J. E., Turiano, N. A., Gerstorf, D., Lachman, M. E., & Haase, C. M. (2020). Positive affect is associated with less memory decline: Evidence from a 9-year longitudinal study. *Psychological Science*, 31(11), 1386–1395. https://doi.org/10.1177/0956797620953883

Hlavinka, E. (2019, July 2). 60 years on, twin/triplet study still raises questions. *Medpage Today*. https://www.medpagetoday.com/psychiatry/generalpsychiatry/80829

Hobson, J. A. (1999). The new neuropsychology of sleep: Implications for psychoanalysis. *Neuropsychoanalysis*, 1(2), 157–183. https://doi.org/10.1080/15294145.1999.10773258

Hobson, J. A., & McCarley, R. W. (1977). The brain as a dream state generator: An activation-synthesis hypothesis of the dream process. *The American Journal of Psychiatry*, 134(12), 1335–1348. https://doi.org/10.1176/ajp.134.12.1335

Hoche, F., Guell, X., Sherman, J. C., Vangel, M. G., & Schmahmann, J. D. (2016). Cerebellar contribution to social cognition. *The Cerebellum*, 15(6), 732–743. https://doi.org/10.5465/amr.1987.4306708

Hodges, E. V., Boivin, M., Vitaro, F., & Bukowski, W. M. (1999). The power of friendship: Protection against an escalating cycle of peer victimization. *Developmental Psychology*, 35(1), 94–101. https://doi.org/10.1037/0012-1649.35.1.94

Hodgins, H. S., Koestner, R., & Duncan, N. (1996). On the compatibility of autonomy and relatedness. *Personality and Social Psychology Bulletin*, 22(3), 227–237. https://doi.org/10.1177/0146167296223001

Hoegberg, L. C. G., Christiansen, C., Soe, J., Telving, R., Andreasen, M. F., Staerk, D., Christrup, L. L., & Kongstad, K. T. (2018). Recreational drug use at a major music festival: Trend analysis of anonymised pooled urine. *Clinical Toxicology*, 56(4), 245–255. https://doi.org/10.1080/15563650.2017.1360496

Hoffman, C. L, Stutz, K., & Vasilopoulos, T. (2018). An examination of adult women's sleep quality and sleep routines in relation to pet ownership and bedsharing. *Anthrozoös*, 31(6), 711–725. https://doi.org/10.1080/08927936.2018.1529354

Hoffman, C. L., Browne, M., & Smith, B. P. (2020). Human-animal co-sleeping: An actigraphy-based assessment of dogs' impacts on women's nighttime movements. *Animals (Basel)*, 10(2), Article 278. https://doi.org/10.3390/ani10020278

Hoffmann, A., Sportelli, V., Ziller, M., & Spengler, D. (2017). Epigenomics of major depressive disorders and schizophrenia: Early life decides. *International Journal of Molecular Sciences*, 18(8), Article 1711. https://doi.org/10.3390/ijms18081711

Hohmann, G. W. (1966). Some effects of spinal cord lesions on experienced emotional feelings. *Psychophysiology*, 3(2), 143–156. https://doi.org/10.1111/j.1469-8986.1966.tb02690.x

Holland, R. W., Hendriks, M., & Aarts, H. (2005). Smells like clean spirit: Nonconscious effects of scent on cognition and behavior. *Psychological Science*, 16(9), 689–693. https://doi.org/10.1111/j.1467-9280.2005.01597.x

Honn, K. A., Hinson, J. M., Whitney, P., & Van Dongen, H. P. A. (2019). Cognitive flexibility: A distinct element of performance impairment due to sleep deprivation. *Accident Analysis and Prevention*, 126, 191–197. https://doi.org/10.1016/j.aap.2018.02.013

Hoover, J. D., Giambatista, R. C., & Belkin, L. Y. (2012). Eyes on, hands on: Vicarious observational learning as an enhancement of direct experience. *Academy of Management Learning & Education*, 11(4), 591–608. https://doi.org/10.5465/amle.2010.0102

Hornberger, R. H. (1959). The differential reduction of aggressive responses as a function of interpolated activities. *American Psychologist*, 14(7), 354.

Horne, J. A., & Reyner, L. A. (1996). Counteracting driver sleepiness: Effects of napping, caffeine, and placebo. *Psychophysiology*, 33(3), 306–309. https://doi.org/10.1111/j.1469-8986.1996.tb00428.x

Horney, K. (1945). *Our inner conflicts: A constructive theory of neurosis.* W. W. Norton.

Horney, K. (1967). *Feminine psychology.* W. W. Norton.

Horowitz, A. (2017). Smelling themselves: Dogs investigate their own odours longer when modified in an "olfactory mirror" test. *Behavioural Processes, 143,* 17–24. https://doi.org/10.1016/j.beproc.2017.08.001

Horváth, K., Hannon, B., Ujma, P. P., Gombos, F., & Plunkett, K. (2018). Memory in 3-month-old infants benefits from a short nap. *Developmental Science, 21*(3), 1–9. https://doi.org/10.1111/desc.12587

Horvath, S., & Raj, K. (2018). DNA methylation-based biomarkers and the epigenetic clock theory of ageing. *Nature Reviews Genetics, 19*(6), 371–384. https://doi.org/10.1038/s41576-018-0004-3

Horwitz, A. V. (2013). *Anxiety: A short history.* JHU Press.

Hu, S., Tucker, L., Wu, C., & Yang, L. (2020). Beneficial effects of exercise on depression and anxiety during the COVID-19 pandemic: A narrative review. *Frontiers in Psychiatry, 11,* Article 587557. https://doi.org/10.3389/fpsyt.2020.587557

Hu, Y., Zhang, Y., Zhang, H., Gao, S., Wang, L., Wang, T., Han, Z., Sun, B., & Liu, G. (2022). Cognitive performance protects against Alzheimer's disease independently of educational attainment and intelligence. *Molecular Psychiatry, 27*(10), 4297–4306. https://doi.org/10.1038/s41380-022-01695-4

Huang, M. C. L., Chou, C. Y., Wu, Y. T., Shih, J. L., Yeh, C. Y., Lao, A. C., Fong, H., Lin, Y-F., & Chan, T. W. (2020). Interest-driven video creation for learning mathematics. *Journal of Computers in Education, 7*(3), 395–433. https://doi.org/10.1007/s40692-020-00161-w

Huang, Y., & Zhao, N. (2020). Generalized anxiety disorder, depressive symptoms and sleep quality during COVID-19 outbreak in China: A web-based cross-sectional survey. *Psychiatry Research, 288,* Article 112954. https://doi.org/10.1016/j.psychres.2020.112954

Huesmann, L. R., Moise-Titus, J., Podolski, C. L., & Eron, L. D. (2003). Longitudinal relations between children's exposure to TV violence and their aggressive and violent behavior in young adulthood: 1977–1992. *Developmental Psychology, 39*(2), 201–221. https://doi.org/10.1037/0012-1649.39.2.201

Hüffmeier, J., Hertel, G., Torka, A. K., Nohe, C., & Krumm, S. (2022). In field settings group members (often) show effort gains instead of social loafing. *European Review of Social Psychology, 33*(1), 131–170. https://doi.org/10.1080/10463283.2021.1959125

Hughes, A. N. (2021). Glial cells promote myelin formation and elimination. *Frontiers in Cell and Developmental Biology, 9,* 1–16. https://doi.org/10.3389/fcell.2021.661486

Hughes, J. R. (1984). Psychological effects of habitual aerobic exercise: A critical review. *Preventive Medicine, 13*(1), 66–78. https://doi.org/10.1016/0091-7435(84)90041-0

Hui, C. H., & Triandis, H. C. (1986). Individualism-collectivism: A study of cross-cultural researchers. *Journal of Cross-Cultural Psychology, 17*(2), 225–248. https://doi.org/10.1177/0022002186017002006

Huisman, J. (2023, June). Cultural empathy in international contexts: Successes and pitfalls. Paper presented at the Conference Proceedings: The Future of Education, New York, NY.

Hull, C. L. (1951). *Essentials of Behavior.* Yale University Press.

Humphreys, L. (1970). Tearoom trade. *Trans-action, 7,* 10–24.

Hunsley, J., & Bailey, J. M. (1999). The clinical utility of the Rorschach: Unfulfilled promises and an uncertain future. *Psychological Assessment, 11*(3), 266–277. https://doi.org/10.1037/1040-3590.11.3.266

Hunt, M. (1993). *The story of psychology.* Doubleday.

Huntington, N. D., Cursons, J., & Rautela, J. (2020). The cancer–natural killer cell immunity cycle. *Nature Reviews Cancer, 20*(8), 437–454. https://doi.org/10.1038/s41568-020-0272-z

Huntley, J. D., Hampshire, A., Bor, D., Owen, A. M., & Howard, R. J. (2017). The importance of sustained attention in early Alzheimer's disease. *International Journal of Geriatric Psychiatry, 32*(8), 860–867. https://doi.org/10.1002/gps.4537

Huntley, M., & Goodfriend, W. (2019). Feminism in the Legend of Zelda. In A. Bean (Ed.), *Psychology of Zelda* (pp. 219–243). BenBella Books.

Hurley, D. B., & Kwon, P. (2013). Savoring helps most when you have little: Interaction between savoring the moment and uplifts on positive affect and satisfaction with life. *Journal of Happiness Studies, 14,* 1261–1271. https://doi.org/10.1007/s10902-012-9377-8

Hussar, B., Zhang, J., Hein, S., Wang, K., Roberts, A., Cui, J., Smith, M., Mann, F. B., Barmer, A., Dilig, R., Nachazel, T., Barnett, M., & Purcell, S. (2020). *The condition of education 2020: NCES 2020-144.* National Center for Education Statistics.

Huston, A. C. (1983). Sex typing. In E. M. Hetherington (Ed.), *Handbook of child psychology: Socialization, personality, and social development* (4th ed., Vol. 4, pp. 387–467). Wiley.

Hyland, P., Shevlin, M., McBride, O., Murphy, J., Karatzias, T., Bentall, R. P., Martinez, A., & Vallières, F. (2020). Anxiety and depression in the Republic of Ireland during the COVID-19 pandemic. *Acta Psychiatrica Scandinavica, 142*(3), 249–256. https://doi.org/10.1111/acps.13219

Infanger, M., Rudman, L. A., & Sczesny, S. (2016). Sex as a source of power? Backlash against self-sexualizing women. *Group Processes & Intergroup Relations, 19*(1), 110–124. https://doi.org/10.1177/1368430214558312

Inhelder, B., & Piaget, J. (1958). *The growth of logical thinking: From childhood to adolescence.* Basic Books.

Iovino, L., Tremblay, M. E., & Civiero, L. (2020). Glutamate-induced excitotoxicity in Parkinson's disease: The role of glial cells. *Journal of Pharmacological Sciences, 144*(3), 151–164. https://doi.org/10.1016/j.jphs.2020.07.011

Ireland, M. E., & Pennebaker, J. W. (2010). Language style matching in writing: Synchrony in essays, correspondence, and poetry. *Journal of Personality and Social Psychology, 99*(3), 549–571. https://doi.org/10.1037/a0020386

Irwin, M. R. (2008). Human psychoneuroimmunology: 20 years of discovery. *Brain, Behavior, and Immunity, 22*(2), 129–139. https://doi.org/10.1016/j.bbi.2007.07.013

Isasi, C. R., Parrinello, C. M., Jung, M. M., Carnethon, M. R., Birnbaum-Weitzman, O., Espinoza, R. A., Penedo, F. J., Perreira, K. M., Schneiderman, N., Stores-Alvarez, D., Van Horn, L., & Gallo, L. C. (2015). Psychosocial stress is associated with obesity and diet quality in Hispanic/Latino adults. *Annals of Epidemiology, 25*(2), 84–89. https://doi.org/10.1016/j.annepidem.2014.11.002

Isern-Mas, C., & Gomila, A. (2022). Love, friendship, and moral motivation. *Journal of Theoretical and Philosophical Psychology, 42*(2), 93–107. https://doi.org/10.1037/teo0000166

Izard, C. E. (1990). The substrates and functions of emotion feelings: William James and current emotion theory. *Personality and Social Psychology Bulletin, 16*(4), 626–635. https://doi.org/10.1177/0146167290164004

Izard, C. E. (2013). *Human emotions.* Springer.

Izuma, K., Saito, D. N., & Sadato, N. (2010). Processing of the incentive for social approval in the ventral striatum during charitable donation. *Journal of Cognitive Neuroscience, 22*(4), 621–631. https://doi.org/10.1162/jocn.2009.21228

Jack, R. E., Garrod, O. G., Yu, H., Caldara, R., & Schyns, P. G. (2012). Facial expressions of emotion are not culturally universal. *Proceedings of the National Academy of Sciences, 109*(19), 7241–7244. https://doi.org/10.1073/pnas.1200155109

Jack, R. E., Sun, W., Delis, I., Garrod, O. G. B., & Schyns, P. G. (2016). Four not six: Revealing culturally common facial expressions of emotion. *Journal of Experimental Psychology: General, 145*(6), 708–730. https://doi.org/10.1037/xge0000162

Jackson, J. M., & Williams, K. D. (1985). Social loafing on difficult tasks: Working collectively can improve performance. *Journal of Personality and Social Psychology, 49*(4), 937–942. https://doi.org/10.1037/0022-3514.49.4.937

Jackson, J. P., & Winston, A. S. (2021). The mythical taboo on race and intelligence. *Review of General Psychology, 25*(1), 3–26. https://doi.org/10.1177/1089268020953622

Jackson, M., & Grace, D. (2018). *Machiavelliana*. Brill Rodopi.

Jacobson, N. S., & Margolin, G. (2019). *Marital therapy: Strategies based on social learning and behavior exchange principles*. Routledge.

Jacoby, L. L., Kelley, C., Brown, J., & Jasechko, J. (1989). Becoming famous overnight: Limits on the ability to avoid unconscious influences of the past. *Journal of Personality and Social Psychology, 56*(3), 326–338. https://doi.org/10.1037/0022-3514.56.3.326

Jaffee, S., & Hyde, J. S. (2000). Gender differences in moral orientation: A meta-analysis. *Psychological Bulletin, 126*(5), 703–726. https://doi.org/10.1037/0033-2909.126.5.703

James, W. (1884). What is an emotion? *Mind, 9*, 188–205. https://doi.org/10.1093/mind/os-IX.34.188

James, W. (1890). *The principles of psychology*. Holt.

James, W. (1894). Discussion: The physical basis of emotion. *Psychological Review, 1*(5), 516–529. https://doi.org/10.1037/h0065078

Jang, S., Kim, J. J., Kim, S. J., Hong, J., Kim, S., & Kim, E. (2021). Mobile app-based chatbot to deliver cognitive behavioral therapy and psychoeducation for adults with attention deficit: A development and feasibility/usability study. *International Journal of Medical Informatics, 150*, Article 104440. https://doi.org/10.1016/j.ijmedinf.2021.104440

Janik, V. M. (2000). Whistle matching in wild bottlenose dolphins (Tursiops truncatus). *Science, 289*(5483), 1355–1357. https://doi.org/10.1126/science.289.5483.1355

Jankowiak, W. R., & Fischer, E. F. (1992). A cross-cultural perspective on romantic love. *Ethnology, 31*(2), 149–155. https://doi.org/10.2307/3773618

Janusek, L. W., Tell, D., & Mathews, H. L. (2019). Mindfulness based stress reduction provides psychological benefit and restores immune function of women newly diagnosed with breast cancer: A randomized trial with active control. *Brain, Behavior, and Immunity, 80*, 358–373. https://doi.org/10.1016/j.bbi.2019.04.012

Javitt, D. C., & Coyle, J. T. (2004). Decoding schizophrenia. *Scientific American, 290*(1), 48–55. https://www.jstor.org/stable/26172654

Jayakody, K., Gunadasa, S., & Hosker, C. (2014). Exercise for anxiety disorders: Systematic review. *British Journal of Sports Medicine, 48*(3), 187–196. http://dx.doi.org/10.1136/bjsports-2012-091287

Jayawickreme, E., Infurna, F. J., Alajak, K., Blackie, L. E., Chopik, W. J., Chung, J. M., Dorfman, A., Fleeson, W., Forgeard, M. J. C., Frazier, P., Furr, R. M., Grossmann, I., Heller, A. S., Laceulle, O. M., Lucas, R. E., Luhmann, M., Luong, G., Meijer, L., McLean, R. E., Park, C. L. . . . Zonneveld, R. (2021). Post-traumatic growth as positive personality change: Challenges, opportunities, and recommendations. *Journal of Personality, 89*(1), 145–165. https://doi.org/10.1111/jopy.12591

Jeckel, A. S., Copenhaver, E. A., & Diamond, A. B. (2018). The spectrum of hazing and peer sexual abuse in sports: A current perspective. *Sports Health, 10*(6), 558–564. https://doi.org/10.1177/1941738118797322

Jefferies, P., & Ungar, M. (2020). Social anxiety in young people: A prevalence study in seven countries. *PLoS One, 15*(9), e0239133. https://doi.org/10.1371/journal.pone.0239133

Jefferson, T., Jr., Herbst, J. H., & McCrae, R. R. (1998). Associations between birth order and personality traits: Evidence from self-reports and observer ratings. *Journal of Research in Personality, 32*(4), 498–509. https://doi.org/10.1006/jrpe.1998.2233

Jensen, F. (2015). *The teenage brain*. Harper.

Jensen, F. E., & Nutt, A. E. (2015). *The teenage brain: A neuroscientist's survival guide to raising adolescents and young adults*. HarperCollins.

Jeste, D. V., & Oswald, A. J. (2014). Individual and societal wisdom: Explaining the paradox of human aging and high well-being. *Psychiatry: Interpersonal and Biological Processes, 77*(4), 317–330. https://doi.org/10.1521/psyc.2014.77.4.317

Jniene, A., Errguig, L., El Hangouche, A. J., Rkain, H., Aboudrar, S., El Ftouh, M., & Dakka, T. (2019). Perception of sleep disturbances due to bedtime use of blue light-emitting devices and its impact on habits and sleep quality among young medical students. *BioMed Research International, 2019*, Article 7012350. https://doi.org/10.1155/2019/7012350

John, O. P., & Srivastava, S. (1999). The big five trait taxonomy. In L. A. Pervin & O. P. John (Eds.), *Handbook of personality: Theory and research* (2nd ed., pp. 102–138). Guilford.

John, R. A., Liu, F., Chien, N. A., Kulkarni, M. R., Zhu, C., Fu, Q., Basu, A., Liu, Z., & Mathews, N. (2018). Synergistic gating of electro-iono-photoactive 2D chalcogenide neuristors: Coexistence of Hebbian and homeostatic synaptic metaplasticity. *Advanced Materials, 30*(25), Article 1800220. https://doi.org/10.1002/adma.201800220

Johns, A., & Peters, L. (2012). Self-discrepancies and the situational domains of social phobia. *Behaviour Change, 29*(2), 109–125. https://doi.org/10.1017/bec.2012.1

Johnson, W., Boehmler, R. M., Dahlstrom, W. G., Darley, F. L., Goodstein, L. D., Kools, J. A., Neeley, J. N., Prather, W. F., Sherman, D., Thurman, C. G., Trotter, W. D., Williams, D., & Young, M. A. (1959). *The onset of stuttering: Research findings and implications*. University of Minnesota Press.

Johnston, L. D., O'Malley, P. M., Bachman, J. G., & Schulenberg, J. E. (2012). *Monitoring the Future national results on adolescent drug use: Overview of key findings, 2011*. Institute for Social Research, University of Michigan.

Johnston-Robledo, I., & Barnack, J. (2004). Psychological issues in childbirth: Potential roles for psychotherapists. *Women & Therapy, 27*(3–4), 133–150. https://doi.org/10.1300/J015v27n03_10

Jonas, E., Martens, A., Niesta Kayser, D., Fritsche, I., Sullivan, D., & Greenberg, J. (2008). Focus theory of normative conduct and terror-management theory: The interactive impact of mortality salience and norm salience on social judgment. *Journal of Personality and Social Psychology, 95*(6), 1239–1251. https://doi.org/10.1037/a0013593

Jonas, K. J., Cesario, J., Alger, M., Bailey, A. H., Bombari, D., Carney, D., Dovidio, J. F., Duffy, S., Harder, J. A., van Huistee, D., Jackson, B., Johnson, D. J., Keller, V. N., Klaschinski, L., LaBelle, O., LaFrance, M., Latu, I. M., Morssinkhoff, M., Nault, K., Pardal, V., . . . Tybur, J. M. (2017). Power poses—where do we stand? *Comprehensive Results in Social Psychology, 2*(1), 139–141. https://doi.org/10.1080/23743603.2017.1342447

Jones, A., & Crandall, R. (1986). Validation of a short index of self-actualization. *Personality and Social Psychology Bulletin, 12*(1), 63–73. https://doi.org/10.1177/0146167286121007

Jones, S. (2013). *Death's night*. https://jonestown.sdsu.edu/?page_id=40172

Jousmäki, V., & Hari, R. (1998). Parchment-skin illusion: Sound-biased touch. *Current Biology, 8*(6), R190. https://doi.org/10.1016/S0960-9822(98)70120-4

Judd, C. H. (1905). The Müller-Lyer illusion. *The Psychological Review: Monograph Supplements, 7*(1), 55–81.

Judd, C. H., & Courten, H. C. (1905). The Zöllner illusion. *The Psychological Review: Monograph Supplements, 7*(1), 112–139.

Juergensmeyer, M. (2017). *Terror in the mind of God: The global rise of religious violence* (Vol. 13). University of California Press.

Juliano, L. M., Evatt, D. P., Richards, B. D., & Griffiths, R. R. (2012). Characterization of individuals seeking treatment for caffeine dependence. *Psychology of Addictive Behaviors*, *26*(4), 948–954. https://doi.org/10.1037/a0027246

Jung, C. (1961). *The collected works of Carl Jung* (Vols. *1–17*). Princeton University Press. (Original work published 1902)

Jung, C. G. (1936). The concept of the collective unconscious. *Collected Works*, *9*(1), 99–104.

Juruena, M. F., Eror, F., Cleare, A. J., Young, A. H. (2020). The role of early life stress in HPA axis and anxiety. In Y. K. Kim (Ed.), *Anxiety disorders: Advances in experimental medicine and biology* (pp. 141–153). Springer. https://doi.org/10.1007/978-981-32-9705-0_9

Kaasinen, V., Vahlberg, T., Stoessl, A. J., Strafella, A. P., & Antonini, A. (2021). Dopamine receptors in Parkinson's disease: A meta-analysis of imaging studies. *Movement Disorders*, *36*(8), 1781–1791. https://doi.org/10.1002/mds.28632

Kabat-Zinn, J. (1994). *Wherever you go, there you are: Mindfulness meditation in everyday life*. Hyperion.

Kabene, S. M., Balkir Neftci, N., & Papatzikis, E. (2022). Dissociative identity disorder and the law: Guilty or not guilty? *Frontiers in Psychology*, *13*, Article 891941. https://doi.org/10.3389/fpsyg.2022.891941

Kagan, J. (1999). Born to be shy. In R. Conlan (Ed.), *States of mind* (pp. 29–51). Wiley.

Kahneman, D. (2003). A perspective on judgment and choice: Mapping bounded rationality. *American Psychologist*, *58*(9), 697–720.

Kahneman, D. (2011). *Thinking, fast and slow*. Farrar, Straus and Giroux.

Kalmbach, D. A., Anderson, J. R., & Drake, C. L. (2018). The impact of stress on sleep: Pathogenic sleep reactivity as a vulnerability to insomnia and circadian disorders. *Journal of Sleep Research*, *27*(6), 1–21. https://doi.org/10.1111/jsr.12710

Kamins, M. A. (1990). An investigation into the "match-up" hypothesis in celebrity advertising: When beauty may be only skin deep. *Journal of Advertising*, *19*(1), 4–13. https://doi.org/10.1080/00913367.1990.10673175

Kaminski, J., Call, J., & Fischer, J. (2004). Word learning in a domestic dog: Evidence for "fast mapping." *Science*, *304*(5677), 1682–1683. https://doi.org/10.1126/science.1097859

Kamkar, M. Z., Mahyar, M., Maddah, S. A., Khoddam, H., & Modanloo, M. (2021). The effect of melatonin on quality of sleep in patients with sleep disturbance admitted to post coronary care units: A randomized controlled trial. *BioMedicine*, *11*(1), 34–40. https://doi.org/10.37796/2211-8039.1123

Kanazawa, S., & Perina, K. (2009). Why night owls are more intelligent. *Personality and Individual Differences*, *47*(7), 685–690. https://doi.org/10.1016/j.paid.2009.05.021

Kandler, C., Riemann, R., & Angleitner, A. (2013). Patterns and sources of continuity and change of energetic and temporal aspects of temperament in adulthood: A longitudinal twin study of self-and peer reports. *Developmental Psychology*, *49*(9), 1739–1753. https://doi.org/10.1037/a0030744

Kane, P. J. (2019). Signal detection theory and automotive imaging. *Electronic Imaging*, *31*, 1–7. https://doi.org/10.2352/ISSN.2470-1173.2019.15.AVM-027

Kanherkar, R. R., Bhatia-Dey, N., & Csoka, A. B. (2014). Epigenetics across the human lifespan. *Frontiers in Cell and Developmental Biology*, *2*, Article 49. https://doi.org/10.3389/fcell.2014.00049

Kanner, A. D., Coyne, J. C., Schaefer, C., & Lazarus, R. S. (1981). Comparison of two modes of stress measurement: Daily hassles and uplifts versus major life events. *Journal of Behavioral Medicine*, *4*(1), 1–39. https://doi.org/10.1007/BF00844845

Kapadia, D. (2023). Stigma, mental illness & ethnicity: Time to centre racism and structural stigma. *Sociology of Health & Illness*, *45*(4), 855–871. https://doi.org/10.1111/1467-9566.13615

Kara, S. (2009). *Sex trafficking: Inside the business of modern slavery*. Columbia University Press.

Karan, A., & Hansen, N. (2018). Does the Stockholm syndrome affect female sex workers? The case for a "Sonagachi syndrome." *BMC International Health and Human Rights*, *18*(1), 1–3. https://doi.org/10.1186/s12914-018-0148-4

Karandashev, V. (2022). *Cultural typologies of love*. Springer International Publishing. https://doi.org/10.1007/978-3-031-05343-6_3

Karapanos, E., Gouveia, R., Hassenzahl, M., & Forlizzi, J. (2016). Wellbeing in the making: Peoples' experiences with wearable activity trackers. *Psychology of Well-Being*, *6*(4), 1–17. https://doi.org/10.1186/s13612-016-0042-6

Karekar, P., Bijle, M. N., & Walimbe, H. (2019). Effect of three behavior guidance techniques on anxiety indicators of children undergoing diagnosis and preventive dental care. *Journal of Clinical Pediatric Dentistry*, *43*(3), 167–172. https://doi.org/10.17796/1053-4625-43.3.4

Karkoulian, S., Srour, J., & Sinan, T. (2016). A gender perspective on work-life balance, perceived stress, and locus of control. *Journal of Business Research*, *69*(11), 4918–4923. https://doi.org/10.1016/j.jbusres.2016.04.053

Karney, B. R., & Coombs, R. H. (2000). Memory bias in long-term close relationships: Consistency or improvement? *Personality and Social Psychology Bulletin*, *26*(8), 959–970. https://doi.org/10.1177/01461672002610006

Karremans, J. C., Stroebe, W., & Claus, J. (2006). Beyond Vicary's fantasies: The impact of subliminal priming and brand choice. *Journal of Experimental Social Psychology*, *42*(6), 792–798. https://doi.org/10.1016/j.jesp.2005.12.002

Kascakova, N., Furstova, J., Trnka, R., Hasto, J., Geckova, A. M., & Tavel, P. (2022). Subjective perception of life stress events affects long-term pain: The role of resilience. *BMC Psychology*, *10*(1), Article 54. https://doi.org/10.1186/s40359-022-00765-0

Kashdan, T. B., Gallagher, M. W., Silvia, P. J., Winterstein, B. P., Breen, W. E., Terhar, D., & Steger, M. F. (2009). The Curiosity and Exploration Inventory-II: Development, factor structure, and psychometrics. *Journal of Research in Personality*, *43*(6), 987–998. https://doi.org/10.1016/j.jrp.2009.04.011

Kashdan, T. B., Mishra, A., Breen, W. E., & Froh, J. J. (2009). Gender differences in gratitude: Examining appraisals, narratives, the willingness to express emotions, and changes in psychological needs. *Journal of Personality*, *77*(3), 691–730. https://doi.org/10.1111/j.1467-6494.2009.00562.x

Kaskutas, L. A. (2009). Alcoholics Anonymous effectiveness: Faith meets science. *Journal of Addictive Diseases*, *28*(2), 145–157. https://doi.org/10.1080/10550880902772464

Kassin, S. M. (2017). The killing of Kitty Genovese: What else does this case tell us? *Perspectives on Psychological Science*, *12*(3), 374–381. https://doi.org/10.1177/1745691616679465

Kastenbaum, R. (2000). Death attitudes and aging in the 21st century. In A. Tomer (Ed.), *Death attitudes and the older adult* (pp. 257–280). Brunner-Routledge.

Kastenbaum, R. (2005). Is death better in utopia? *Illness, Crisis & Loss*, *13*(1), 31–48. https://doi.org/10.1177/105413730501300104

Kastenbaum, R. (2012). *Death, society, and human experience*. Routledge.

Katz-Wise, S. L., Priess, H. A., & Hyde, J. S. (2010). Gender-role attitudes and behavior across the transition to parenthood. *Developmental Psychology*, *46*(1), 18–28. https://doi.org/10.1037/a0017820

Kaufman, L., & Kaufman, J. H. (2000). Explaining the moon illusion. *Proceedings of the National Academy of Sciences of the United*

States of America, 97(1), 500–505. https://doi.org/10.1073/pnas.97.1.500

Kaufman, S. B., Yaden, D. B., Hyde, E., & Tsukayama, E. (2019). The light vs. dark triad of personality: Contrasting two very different profiles of human nature. *Frontiers in Psychology*, 10, Article 467. https://doi.org/10.3389/fpsyg.2019.00467

Kaye, D. (2023). The effect of self-discrepancies on emotions and life satisfaction. *Biomedical Science and Clinical Research*, 2(1), 94–99. https://doi.org/10.33140/BSCR

Kayser, B. (2020). Why are placebos not on WADA's Prohibited List? *Performance Enhancement & Health*, 8(1), Article 100163. https://doi.org/10.1016/j.peh.2020.100163

Kazdin, A. E. (2015). Technology-based interventions and reducing the burdens of mental illness: Perspectives and comments on the special series. *Cognitive and Behavioral Practice*, 22(3), 359–366. https://doi.org/10.1016/j.cbpra.2015.04.004

Kazdin, A. E., & Rabbitt, S. M. (2013). Novel models for delivering mental health services and reducing the burdens of mental illness. *Clinical Psychological Science*, 1(2), 170–191. https://doi.org/10.1177/2167702612463566

Kazeminia, M., Daneshkhah, A., Jalali, R., Vaisi-Raygani, A., Salari, N., & Mohammadi, M. (2020). The effect of exercise on the older adult's blood pressure suffering hypertension: Systematic review and meta-analysis on clinical trial studies. *International Journal of Hypertension*, 2020, Article 2786120. https://doi.org/10.1155/2020/2786120

Keating, C. F., Pomerantz, J., Pommer, S. D., Ritt, S. J., Miller, L. M., & McCormick, J. (2005). Going to college and unpacking hazing: A functional approach to decrypting initiation practices among undergraduates. *Group Dynamics: Theory, Research, Practice*, 9(2), 104–126. https://doi.org/10.1037/1089-2699.9.2.104

Keles, B., McCrae, N., & Grealish, A. (2020). A systematic review: The influence of social media on depression, anxiety and psychological distress in adolescents. *International Journal of Adolescence and Youth*, 25(1), 79–93. https://doi.org/10.1080/02673843.2019.1590851

Kellett, S. (2007). A time series evaluation of the treatment of histrionic personality disorder with cognitive analytic therapy. *Psychology and Psychotherapy: Theory, Research and Practice*, 80(3), 389–405. https://doi.org/10.1348/147608306X161421

Kelly, D. M., & Lea, S. E. G. (2022). Animal cognition, past present and future, a 25th anniversary special issue. *Animal Cognition*, 26, 1–11. https://doi.org/10.1007/s10071-022-01738-x

Kelly, G. A. (1955). *The psychology of personal constructs*. Norton.

Kelly, J. F., Humphreys, K., & Ferri, M. (2020). Alcoholics Anonymous and other 12-step programs for alcohol use disorder: A distillation of a 2020 Cochrane Review for clinicians and policy makers. *Alcohol and Alcoholism*, 55(6), 641–651. https://doi.org/10.1093/alcalc/agaa050

Kendler, K. S. (2012). The dappled nature of causes of psychiatric illness: Replacing the organic–functional/hardware–software dichotomy with empirically based pluralism. *Molecular Psychiatry*, 17(4), 377–388. https://doi.org/10.1038/mp.2011.182

Kenrick, D. T., Gutierres, S. E., & Goldberg, L. L. (1989). Influence of popular erotica on judgments of strangers and mates. *Journal of Experimental Social Psychology*, 25(2), 159–167. https://doi.org/10.1016/0022-1031(89)90010-3

Kermanshahi, M. K., & Gholami Fesharaki, M. (2023). Investigating the relationship between demographic factors and adolescent girls' pubertal health performance. *Journal of Pediatric Nursing*, 9(4), 64–73. http://jpen.ir/article-1-695-en.html

Kessler, R. C., Chiu, W. T., Demler, O., & Walters, E. E. (2005). Prevalence, severity, and comorbidity of 12-month DSM-IV disorders in the National Comorbidity Survey Replication. *Archives of General Psychiatry*, 62(6), 617–627. https://doi.org/10.1001/archpsyc.62.6.617

Kessler, R. C., Merikangas, K. R., & Wang, P. S. (2007). Prevalence, comorbidity, and service utilization for mood disorders in the United States at the beginning of the twenty-first century. *Annual Review of Clinical Psychology*, 3, 137–158. https://doi.org/10.1146/annurev.clinpsy.3.022806.091444

Kessler, R. C., Petukhova, M., Sampson, N. A., Zaslavsky, A. M., & Wittchen, H. U. (2012). Twelve-month and lifetime prevalence and lifetime morbid risk of anxiety and mood disorders in the United States. *International Journal of Methods in Psychiatric Research*, 21(3), 169–184. https://doi.org/10.1002/mpr.1359

Kevles, D. J. (1968). Testing the Army's intelligence: Psychologists and the military in World War I. *The Journal of American History*, 55(3), 565–581. https://doi.org/10.2307/1891014

Khan, A. S., Alalawi, A. H., Alalawi, M. H., Alsahaf, H. A., Albahrani, M. S., & Alhasawi, F. A. (2021). Screening for depression, anxiety, and obsessive–compulsive disorders among secondary school students in Al-Hasa Region, Saudi Arabia. *Journal of Family & Community Medicine*, 28(1), 28–34. https://doi.org/10.4103/jfcm.JFCM_386_20

Khan, G. F., Swar, B., & Lee, S. K. (2014). Social media risks and benefits: A public sector perspective. *Social Science Computer Review*, 32(5), 606–627. https://doi.org/10.1177/0894439314524701

Khezri Moghadam, N., Vahidi, S., & Ashormahani, M. (2018). Efficiency of cognitive-existential group therapy on life expectancy and depression of elderly residing in nursing home. *Iranian Journal of Ageing*, 13(1), 62–73. https://doi.org/10.21859/sija.13.1.62

Khullar, D., & Chokshi, D. A. (2018). *Health, income, & poverty: Where we are & what could help*. Health Affairs Health Policy Brief. https://doi.org/10.1377/hpb20180817.901935

Kidwell, M. C., Lazarević, L. B., Baranski, E., Hardwicke, T. E., Piechowski, S., Falkenberg, L. S., Kennett, C., Slowik, C., Hess-Holden, C., Errington, T. M., Fiedler, S., & Nosek, B. A. (2016). Badges to acknowledge open practices: A simple, low-cost, effective method for increasing transparency. *PLoS Biology*, 14(5), e1002456. https://doi.org/10.1371/journal.pbio.1002456

Kilduff, L. (2022). *How and why poverty in the United States is measured and why it matters*. Population Reference Bureau. https://www.prb.org/resources/how-poverty-in-the-united-states-is-measured-and-why-it-matters/

Kilduff, M., & Day, D. V. (1994). Do chameleons get ahead? The effects of self-monitoring on managerial careers. *Academy of Management Journal*, 37(4), 1047–1060. https://doi.org/10.5465/256612

Killen, A. (2017). Psychiatry and its visual culture in the modern era. In G. Eghigian (Ed.), *The Routledge history of madness and mental health* (pp. 172–190). Routledge.

Killen, M., Luken Raz, K., & Graham, S. (2022). Reducing prejudice through promoting cross-group friendships. *Review of General Psychology*, 26(3), 361–376. https://doi.org/10.1177/10892680211061262

Kim, H. H. (2018). Electroconvulsive therapy: A historical and legal perspective. *American Journal of Psychiatry*, 13(3), 10–11. https://doi.org/10.1176/appi.ajp-rj.2018.130305

Kim, J. Y., Fienup, D. M., Oh, A. E., & Wang, Y. (2022). Systematic review and meta-analysis of token economy practices in K-5 educational settings, 2000 to 2019. *Behavior Modification*, 46(6), 1460–1487. https://doi.org/10.1177/01454455211058077

Kim, K. H. (2005). Can only intelligent people be creative? A meta-analysis. *Journal of Secondary Gifted Education*, 16(-3), 57–66. https://doi.org/10.4219/jsge-2005-473

Kinderman, P. (2005). A psychological model of mental disorder. *Harvard Review of Psychiatry*, 13(4), 206–217. https://doi.org/10.1080/10673220500243349

King, B. J. (2013). *How animals grieve*. University of Chicago Press.

King, B. M. (2019). *Human sexuality today*. Pearson.

King, L. A. (2001). The health benefits of writing about life goals. *Personality and Social Psychology Bulletin, 27*(7), 798–807. https://doi.org/10.1177/0146167201277003

King, L. A., & Smith, N. G. (2004). Gay and straight possible selves: Goals, identity, subjective well-being, and personality development. *Journal of Personality, 72*(5), 967–994. https://doi.org/10.1111/j.0022-3506.2004.00287.x

King, P. M., & Kitchener, K. S. (2016). Cognitive development in the emerging adult. In J. J. Arnett (Ed.), *The Oxford handbook of emerging adulthood* (pp. 205–225). Oxford University Press.

Kinsey, A. C., Pomeroy, W. B., & Martin, C. E. (1948). *Sexual behavior in the human male*. Indiana University Press.

Kinsey, A. C., Pomeroy, W. B., Martin, C. E., & Gebhard, P. H. (1953). *Sexual behavior in the human female*. Indiana University Press.

Kinukawa, T., Takeuchi, N., Sugiyama, S., Nishihara, M., Nishiwaki, K., & Inui, K. (2019). Properties of echoic memory revealed by auditory-evoked magnetic fields. *Scientific Reports, 9*, Article 12260. https://doi.org/10.1038/s41598-019-48796-9

Kirchebner, J., Sonnweber, M., Nater, U. M., Günther, M., & Lau, S. (2022). Stress, schizophrenia, and violence: A machine learning approach. *Journal of Interpersonal Violence, 37*(1–2), 602–622. https://doi.org/10.1177/0886260520913641

Kirkpatrick, R. M., McGue, M., & Iacono, W. G. (2009). Shared-environmental contributions to high cognitive ability. *Behavior Genetics, 39*(4), 406–416. https://doi.org/10.1007/s10519-009-9265-0

Kirsch, I., Montgomery, G., & Sapirstein, G. (1995). Hypnosis as an adjunct to cognitive-behavioral psychotherapy: A meta-analysis. *Journal of Consulting and Clinical Psychology, 63*(2), 214–220. https://doi.org/10.1037/0022-006X.63.2.214

Kirsch, I., Moore, T. J., Scoboria, A., & Nicholls, S. S. (2002). The emperor's new drugs: An analysis of antidepressant medication data submitted to the US Food and Drug Administration. *Prevention & Treatment, 5*(1), Article 23. http://dx.doi.org/10.1037/1522-3736.5.1.523a

Kirschenbaum, H., & Jourdan, A. (2005). The current status of Carl Rogers and the person-centered approach. *Psychotherapy: Theory, Research, Practice, Training, 42*(1), 37–51. https://doi.org/10.1037/0033-3204.42.1.37

Kishi, Y., Robinson, R. G., & Forrester, A. W. (1994). Prospective longitudinal study of depression following spinal cord injury. *The Journal of Neuropsychiatry and Clinical Neurosciences, 6*(3), 237–244. https://doi.org/10.1176/jnp.6.3.237

Kivimäki, M., & Steptoe, A. (2018). Effects of stress on the development and progression of cardiovascular disease. *Nature Reviews Cardiology, 15*(4), 215–229. https://doi.org/10.1038/nrcardio.2017.189

Klaassen, M. J., & Peter, J. (2015). Gender (in) equality in Internet pornography: A content analysis of popular pornographic Internet videos. *Journal of Sex Research, 52*(7), 721–735. https://doi.org/10.1080/00224499.2014.976781

Klei, L., Reitz, P., Miller, M., Wood, J., Maendel, S., Gross, D., Waldner, T., Eaton, J., Monk, T. H., & Nimgaonkar, V. L. (2005). Heritability of morningness-eveningness and self-report sleep measures in a family based sample of 521 Hutterites. *Chronobiology International, 22*(6), 1041–1054. https://doi.org/10.1080/07420520500397959

Kleider, H. M., Pezdek, K., Goldinger, S. D., & Kirk, A. (2008). Schema-driven source misattribution errors: Remembering the expected from a witnessed event. *Applied Cognitive Psychology, 22*(1), 1–20. https://doi.org/10.1002/acp.1361

Klein, O., & Snyder, M. (2003). Stereotypes and behavioral confirmation: From interpersonal to intergroup perspectives. *Advances in Experimental Social Psychology, 35*, 153–234. https://doi.org/10.1016/S0065-2601(03)01003-7

Klein, P. (1997). Multiplying the problems of intelligence by eight: A critique of Gardner's theory. *Canadian Journal of Education/Revue Canadienne De L'éducation, 22*(4), 377–394. https://doi.org/10.2307/1585790

Kleinbaum, A. M., Jordan, A. H., & Audia, P. G. (2015). An altercentric perspective on the origins of brokerage in social networks: How perceived empathy moderates the self-monitoring effect. *Organization Science, 26*(4), 941–1261. https://doi.org/10.1287/orsc.2014.0961

Kleinberg, S., Korshakova, E., & Marsh, J. K. (2023). How beliefs influence perceptions of choices. In *Proceedings of the Annual Meeting of the Cognitive Science Society* (Vol. 45, No. 45). https://escholarship.org/content/qt2f9840bx/qt2f9840bx_noSplash_981fb2a3968a4c32871a99e5c957758f.pdf?t=rxyb4g

Kleine-Budde, K., Touil, E., Moock, J., Bramesfeld, A., Kawohl, W., & Rössler, W. (2014). Cost of illness for bipolar disorder: A systematic review of the economic burden. *Bipolar Disorders, 16*(4), 337–353. https://doi.org/10.1111/bdi.12165

Kleiner, J. S. (2011). Equipotentiality. In J. S. Kreutzer, J. DeLuca, & B. Caplan (Eds.), *Encyclopedia of clinical neuropsychology*. Springer.

Kleinhauz, M., & Beran, B. (1984). Misuse of hypnosis: A factor in psychopathology. *The American Journal of Clinical Hypnosis, 26*(4), 283–290. https://doi.org/10.1080/00029157.1984.10402577

Kluck, A. S. (2008). Family factors in the development of disordered eating: Integrating dynamic and behavioral explanations. *Eating Behaviors, 9*(4), 471–483. https://doi.org/10.1016/j.eatbeh.2008.07.006

Knappe, S. (2021). Learning and teaching in clinical psychology. In J. Zumbach, D. Bernstein, S. Narciss, & G. Marsico (Eds.), *International handbook of psychology learning and teaching* (pp. 1–23). Springer International Publishing. https://doi.org/10.1007/978-3-030-26248-8_3-2

Knee, C. R., Lonsbary, C., Canevello, A., & Patrick, H. (2005). Self-determination and conflict in romantic relationships. *Journal of Personality and Social Psychology, 89*(6), 997–1009. https://doi.org/10.1037/0022-3514.89.6.997

Knee, C. R., Patrick, H., Vietor, N. A., Nanayakkara, A., & Neighbors, C. (2002). Self-determination as growth motivation in romantic relationships. *Personality and Social Psychology Bulletin, 28*(5), 609–619. https://doi.org/10.1177/0146167202288005

Knell, S. M. (2022). Cognitive behavioral play therapy. In R. D. Friedberg & E. V. Rozmid (Eds.), *Creative CBT with youth* (pp. 65–82). Springer. https://doi.org/10.1007/978-3-030-99669-7_5

Knopik, V. S., Neiderhiser, J. M., DeFries, J. C., & Plomin, R. (2017). *Behavioral genetics*. Worth.

Kochanek, K. D., Xu, J. Q., & Arias, E. (2020). *Mortality in the United States, 2019* (NCHS Data Brief No. 395). National Center for Health Statistics. https://www.cdc.gov/nchs/fastats/leading-causes-of-death.htm

Kohlberg, L. (1969). Stage and sequence: The cognitive-developmental approach to socialization. In D. A. Goslin (Ed.), *Handbook of socialization* (pp. 347–480). Rand McNally.

Kohlberg, L., & Ryncarz, R. A. (1990). Beyond justice reasoning: Moral development and consideration of a seventh stage. In C. N. Alexander & E. J. Langer (Eds.), *Higher stages of human development: Perspectives on adult growth* (pp. 191–207). Oxford University Press.

Kohlberg, L., Levine, C., & Hewer, A. (1983). Moral stages: A current formulation and a response to critics. *Contributions to Human Development, 10*, 174.

Köhler, W. (1925). *The mentality of apes*. Routledge & Kegan Paul. (Original work published 1917)

Kohls, N., & Benedikter, R. (2010). The origins of the modern concept of "neuroscience": Wilhelm Wundt between empiricism, and idealism: Implications for contemporary neuroethics. In J. J. Giodano & B. Gordijn (Eds.), *Scientific and philosophical perspectives in neuroethics* (pp. 37–65). Cambridge University Press.

Kohut, T., Fisher, W. A., & Campbell, L. (2017). Perceived effects of pornography on the couple relationship: Initial findings of open-ended, participant-informed, "bottom-up" research. *Archives of Sexual Behavior*, *46*(2), 585–602. https://doi.org/10.1007/s10508-016-0783-6

Komasi, S., Rezaei, F., Hemmati, A., Rahmani, K., Amianto, F., & Miettunen, J. (2022). Comprehensive meta-analysis of associations between temperament and character traits in Cloninger's psychobiological theory and mental disorders. *Journal of International Medical Research*, *50*(1), 1–27. https://doi.org/10.1177/03000605211070766

Komlenac, N., & Hochleitner, M. (2022). Associations between pornography consumption, sexual flexibility, and sexual functioning among Austrian adults. *Archives of Sexual Behavior*, *51*, 1–14. https://doi.org/10.1007/s10508-021-02201-7

Konrad, N. (2002). Prisons as new asylums. *Current Opinion in Psychiatry*, *15*(6), 583–587. http://dx.doi.org/10.1097/00001504-200211000-00004

Konttinen, H., Kronholm, E., Partonen, T., Kanerva, N., Männistö, S., & Haukkala, A. (2014). Morningness-eveningness, depressive symptoms, and emotional eating: A population-based study. *Chronobiology International*, *31*(4), 554–563. https://doi.org/10.3109/07420528.2013.877922

Kornell, N. (2009). Optimising learning using flashcards: Spacing is more effective than cramming. *Applied Cognitive Psychology*, *23*(9), 1297–1317. https://doi.org/10.1002/acp.1537

Kosloff, S., Irish, S., Perreault, L., Anderson, G., & Nottbohm, A. (2017). Assessing relationships between conformity and meta-traits in an Asch-like paradigm. *Social Influence*, *12*(2–3), 90–100. https://doi.org/10.1080/15534510.2017.1371639

Koss, M. P., Gidycz, C. A., & Wisniewski, N. (1987). The scope of rape: Incidence and prevalence of sexual aggression and victimization in a national sample of higher education students. *Journal of Consulting and Clinical Psychology*, *55*(2), 162–170. https://doi.org/10.1037/0022-006X.55.2.162

Kostewicz, D. E. (2010). A review of timeout ribbons. *The Behavior Analyst Today*, *11*(2), 95–104. https://doi.org/10.1037/h0100693

Kostka, J. K., & Bitzenhofer, S. H. (2022). How the sense of smell influences cognition throughout life. *Neuroforum*, *28*(3), 177–185. https://doi.org/10.1515/nf-2022-0007

Krambeer, L. L., Krambeer, L., Von McKnelly, W., Gabrielli, W., & Penick, E. C. (2001). Methadone therapy for opioid dependence. *American Family Physician*, *63*(12), 2404–2411.

Kramer, A. D. I., Guillory, J. E., & Hancock, J. T. (2014). Experimental evidence of massive-scale emotional contagion through social networks. *Proceedings of the National Academy of Sciences of the United States of America*, *111*(24), 8788–8790. https://doi.org/10.1073/pnas.1320040111

Kranjac, A. W., & Kranjac, D. (2023). Explaining adult obesity, severe obesity, and BMI: Five decades of change. *Heliyon*, *9*(5), Article e16210. https://doi.org/10.1016/j.heliyon.2023.e16210

Krantz, D. L., & Allen, D. (1967). The rise and fall of McDougall's instinct doctrine. *Journal of the History of the Behavioral Sciences*, *3*(4), 326–338. https://doi.org/10.1002/1520-6696(196710)3:4<326::AID-JHBS2300030403>3.0.CO;2-6

Krause, N., Chatters, L. M., Meltzer, T., & Morgan, D. L. (2000). Negative interaction in the church: Insights from focus groups with older adults. *Review of Religious Research*, *41*(4), 510–533. https://doi.org/10.2307/3512318

Krebs, D. L., & Denton, K. (2005). Toward a more pragmatic approach to morality: A critical evaluation of Kohlberg's model. *Psychological Review*, *112*(3), 629–649. https://doi.org/10.1037/0033-295X.112.3.629

Krebs, D. L., & Van Hesteren, F. (1994). The development of altruism: Toward an integrative model. *Developmental Review*, *14*(2), 103–158. https://doi.org/10.1006/drev.1994.1006

Kreitz, C., Pugnaghi, G., & Memmert, D. (2020). Guessing right: Preconscious processing in inattentional blindness. *The Quarterly Journal of Experimental Psychology*, *73*(7), 1055–1065. https://doi.org/10.1177/1747021820911324

Krekling, S., & Nordvik, H. (1992). Observational training improves adult women's performance on Piaget's water-level task. *Scandinavian Journal of Psychology*, *33*(2), 117–124. https://doi.org/10.1111/j.1467-9450.1992.tb00891.x

Krendl, A. C., & Freeman, J. B. (2019). Are mental illnesses stigmatized for the same reasons? Identifying the stigma-related beliefs underlying common mental illnesses. *Journal of Mental Health*, *28*(3), 267–275. https://doi.org/10.1080/09638237.2017.1385734

Krishnakumar, D., Hamblin, M. R., & Lakshmanan, S. (2015). Meditation and yoga can modulate brain mechanisms that affect behavior and anxiety: A modern scientific perspective. *Ancient Science*, *2*(1), 13–19. https://doi.org/10.14259/as.v2i1.171

Kristeller, J. L. (2019). Mindfulness. In C. D. Llewellyn, S. Ayers, C. McManus, S. Newman, K. J. Petrie, T. A. Revenson, & J. Weinman (Eds.), *The Cambridge handbook of psychology, health and medicine* (3rd ed., pp. 283–288). Cambridge University Press.

Krizman, J., Lindley, T., Bonacina, S., Colegrove, D., White-Schwoch, T., & Kraus, N. (2020). Play sports for a quieter brain: Evidence from Division I collegiate athletes. *Sports Health*, *12*(2), 154–158. https://doi.org/10.1177/1941738119892275

Kroese, F. M., De Ridder, D. T. D., Evers, C., & Adriaanse, M. A. (2014). Bedtime procrastination: Introducing a new area of procrastination. *Frontiers in Psychology*, *5*, Article 611. https://doi.org/10.3389/fpsyg.2014.00611

Kröger, C., Venema, N., & van Baarle, E. (2023). Hazing in the military: A scoping review. *Journal of Military, Veteran and Family Health*, *9*(4), 2–18. https://doi.org/10.3138/jmvfh-2023-0016

Kroll, J. F., & Dussias, P. E. (2017). The benefits of multilingualism to the personal and professional development of residents of the US. *Foreign Language Annals*, *50*(2), 248–259. https://doi.org/10.1111/flan.12271

Krueger, R. F., Hicks, B. M., & McGue, M. (2001). Altruism and antisocial behavior: Independent tendencies, unique personality correlates, distinct etiologies. *Psychological Science*, *12*(5), 397–402. https://doi.org/10.1111/1467-9280.00373

Kruger, J., & Dunning, D. (1999). Unskilled and unaware of it: How difficulties in recognizing one's own incompetence lead to inflated self-assessments. *Journal of Personality and Social Psychology*, *77*(6), 1121–1134. https://doi.org/10.1037/0022-3514.77.6.1121

Kruglanski, A. W., Fishbach, A., Woolley, K., Bélanger, J. J., Chernikova, M., Molinario, E., & Pierro, A. (2018). A structural model of intrinsic motivation: On the psychology of means-ends fusion. *Psychological Review*, *125*(2), 165–182. https://doi.org/10.1037/rev0000095

Kruk, E. (1991). The grief reaction of noncustodial fathers subsequent to divorce. *Men's Studies Review*, *8*(2), 17–21.

Kruse, H., Smith, S., van Tubergen, F., & Maas, I. (2016). From neighbors to school friends? How adolescents' place of residence relates to same-ethnic school friendships. *Social Networks*, *44*, 130–142. https://doi.org/10.1016/j.socnet.2015.07.004

Kubie, L. S., & Margolin, S. (1944). The process of hypnotism and the nature of the hypnotic state. *The American Journal of Psychiatry*, *100*(5), 611–622. https://doi.org/10.1176/ajp.100.5.611

Kübler-Ross, E. (1969). *On death and dying*. Touchstone.

Kubrick, S. (Producer & Director). (1971). *A clockwork orange* [Motion picture]. Warner Bros.

Kuch, K., & Cox, B. J. (1992). Symptoms of PTSD in 124 survivors of the Holocaust. *American Journal of Psychiatry*, *149*(3), 337–340.

Kumru, A., Carlo, G., Mestre, M. V., & Samper, P. (2012). Prosocial moral reasoning and prosocial behavior among Turkish and Spanish adolescents. *Social Behavior and Personality, 40*(2), 205–214. https://doi.org/10.2224/sbp.2012.40.2.205

Kundert, C., & Corrigan, P. W. (2021). Honest, Open, Proud (HOP): A program to combat the stigma of mental illness with strategic disclosure. In A. H. Nordstrom & W. Goodfriend (Eds.), *Innovative stigma and discrimination reduction programs across the world* (pp. 43–55). Routledge.

Kunst-Wilson, W. R., & Zajonc, R. B. (1980). Affective discrimination of stimuli that cannot be recognized. *Science, 207*(4430), 557–558. https://doi.org/10.1126/science.7352271

Kurtz, P. (2023). Reflections on the "transcendental temptation." In K. Frazier (Ed.), *The hundredth monkey* (Vol. 3, pp. 13–16). Prometheus Books.

Kuther, T. L. (2023). *Lifespan development lives in context* (3rd ed.). Sage.

Kuther, T. L., & Morgan, R. D. (2019). *Careers in psychology: Opportunities in a changing world*. Sage.

Kuvaas, B., Buch, R., Weibel, A., Dysvik, A., & Nerstad, C. G. (2017). Do intrinsic and extrinsic motivation relate differently to employee outcomes? *Journal of Economic Psychology, 61*, 244–258. https://doi.org/10.1016/j.joep.2017.05.004

Kwok, Y. L. A., Gralton, J., & McLaws, M. L. (2015). Face touching: A frequent habit that has implications for hand hygiene. *American Journal of Infection Control, 43*(2), 112–114. https://doi.org/10.1016/j.ajic.2014.10.015

Kwon, T., Shin, S., & Shin, M. (2022). The effect of observational learning on self-efficacy by sport competition condition, performance level of team members, and whether you win or lose. *International Journal of Environmental Research and Public Health, 19*(16), Article 10148. https://doi.org/10.3390/ijerph191610148

Kyllonen, P. C., Lipnevich, A. A., Burrus, J., & Roberts, R. D. (2014). Personality, motivation, and college readiness: A prospectus for assessment and development. *ETS Research Report Series, 2014*(1), 1–48. https://doi.org/10.1002/ets2.12004

La Guardia, J. G., & Patrick, H. (2008). Self-determination theory as a fundamental theory of close relationships. *Canadian Psychology/Psychologie Canadienne, 49*(3), 201–209. https://doi.org/10.1037/a0012760

Labrague, L. J. (2021). Psychological resilience, coping behaviours and social support among health care workers during the COVID-19 pandemic: A systematic review of quantitative studies. *Journal of Nursing Management, 29*(7), 1893–1905. https://doi.org/10.1111/jonm.13336

Lachman, M. E., & Weaver, S. L. (1998). The sense of control as a moderator of social class differences in health and well-being. *Journal of Personality and Social Psychology, 74*(3), 763–773. http://dx.doi.org/10.1037/0022-3514.74.3.763

Laios, K., Tsoucalas, G., Kontaxaki, M. I., Karamanou, M., Sgantzos, M., & Androutsos, G. (2015). Mental health and sexual activity according to ancient Greek physicians. *Psychiatrike = Psychiatriki, 26*(3), 198–203.

Lakin, J. M., & Kell, H. J. (2020). Intelligence and reasoning. In R. J. Sternberg (Ed.), *The Cambridge handbook of intelligence* (2nd ed., pp. 528–552). Cambridge University Press.

Lallukka, T., Lahelma, E., Rahkonen, O., Roos, E., Laaksonen, E., Martikainen, P., Head, J., Brunner, E., Mosdol, A., Marmot, M., Sekine, M., Nasermoaddeli, A., & Kagamimori, S. (2008). Associations of job strain and working overtime with adverse health behaviors and obesity: Evidence from the Whitehall II Study, Helsinki Health Study, and the Japanese Civil Servants Study. *Social Science & Medicine, 66*(8), 1681–1698. https://doi.org/10.1016/j.socscimed.2007.12.027

Lamsma, J., & Harte, J. M. (2015). Violence in psychosis: Conceptualizing its causal relationship with risk factors. *Aggression and Violent Behavior, 24*, 75–82. https://doi.org/10.1016/j.avb.2015.05.003

Lancaster, G. L., Vrij, A., Hope, L., & Waller, B. (2013). Sorting the liars from the truth tellers: The benefits of asking unanticipated questions on lie detection. *Applied Cognitive Psychology, 27*(1), 107–114. https://doi.org/10.1002/acp.2879

Landis, C. (1924). Studies of emotional reactions II: General behavior and facial expression. *Journal of Comparative Psychology, 4*(5), 447–510. https://doi.org/10.1037/h0073039

Landreth, G. L. (2012). *Play therapy: The art of the relationship*. Routledge.

Lane, B. L., Piercy, C. W., & Carr, C. T. (2016). Making it Facebook official: The warranting value of online relationship status disclosures on relational characteristics. *Computers in Human Behavior, 56*, 1–8. https://doi.org/10.1016/j.chb.2015.11.016

Lange, I., Goossens, L., Bakker, J., Michielse, S., Van Winkel, R., Lissek, S., Leibold, N., Marcelis, M., Wichers, M., van Os, J., van Amelsvoort, T., & Schruers, K. (2019). Neurobehavioural mechanisms of threat generalization moderate the link between childhood maltreatment and psychopathology in emerging adulthood. *Journal of Psychiatry and Neuroscience, 44*(3), 185–194. https://doi.org/10.1503/jpn.180053

Lantsoght, E. O. (2021). Students' perceptions of doctoral defense in relation to sociodemographic characteristics. *Education Sciences, 11*(9), Article 519. https://doi.org/10.3390/educsci11090519

Lapsley, D., & Hardy, S. A. (2017). Identity formation and moral development in emerging adulthood. In L. M. Padilla-Walker & L. J. Nelson (Eds.), *Flourishing in emerging adulthood: Positive development during the third decade of life* (Vol. 1, pp. 14–39). Oxford University Press.

Lashley, K. S. (1930). Basic neural mechanisms in behavior. *Psychological Review, 37*(1), 1–24. https://doi.org/10.1037/h0074134

Lasserre, A. M., Imtiaz, S., Roerecke, M., Heilig, M., Probst, C., & Rehm, J. (2022). Socioeconomic status, alcohol use disorders, and depression: A population-based study. *Journal of Affective Disorders, 301*, 331–336. https://doi.org/10.1016/j.jad.2021.12.132

Latané, B., & Darley, J. (1970). *The unresponsive bystander: Why doesn't he help? Century psychology series*. Appleton-Century Crofts.

Latif, S., Jahangeer, M., Razia, D. M., Ashiq, M., Ghaffar, A., Akram, M., Allam, A. E., Bouyahya, A., Garipova, L., Shariati, M. A., Thiruvengadam, M., & Ansari, M. A. (2021). Dopamine in Parkinson's disease. *Clinica Chimica Acta, 522*, 114–126. https://doi.org/10.1016/j.cca.2021.08.009

Lau, A., Schwarz, J., & Stoll, O. (2019). Influence of social facilitation on learning development using a Wii Balanceboard. *German Journal of Exercise and Sport Research, 49*(1), 97–102. https://doi.org/10.1007/s12662-018-0562-8

Laumann, E. O., Gagnon, J. H., Michael, R. T., & Michaels, S. (1994). *The social organization of sexuality: Sexual practices in the United States*. University of Chicago Press.

Laursen, B., & Adams, R. (2018). Conflict between peers. In W. M. Bukowski, B. Laursen, & K. H. Rubin (Eds.), *Handbook of peer interactions, relationships, and groups* (pp. 265–283). Guilford.

Lavallée, M. M., Gandini, D., Rouleau, I., Vallet, G. T., Joannette, M., Kergoat, M. J., Busigny, T., Rossion, B., & Joubert, S. (2016). A qualitative impairment in face perception in Alzheimer's disease: Evidence from a reduced face inversion effect. *Journal of Alzheimer's Disease, 51*(4), 1225–1236. https://doi.org/10.3233/JAD-151027

Lavie, P. (2001). Sleep-wake as a biological rhythm. *Annual Review of Psychology, 52*(1), 277–303. https://doi.org/10.1146/annurev.psych.52.1.277

Law, B., & Hall, C. (2009). Observational learning use and self-efficacy beliefs in adult sport novices. *Psychology of Sport and*

Exercise, 10(2), 263–270. https://doi.org/10.1016/j .psychsport.2008.08.003

Lawson, G. M., Duda, J. T., Avants, B. B., Wu, J., & Farah, M. J. (2013). Associations between children's socioeconomic status and prefrontal cortical thickness. *Developmental Science, 16*(5), 641–652. https://doi.org/10.1111/desc.12096

Layous, K. T. I. N., & Lyubomirsky, S. (2014). The how, why, what, when, and who of happiness. In J. Gruber & J. W. Mosowitz (Eds.), *Positive emotion: Integrating the light sides and dark sides* (pp. 473–495). Oxford University Press. https://doi.org/10.1093/ acprof:oso/9780199926725.003.0025

Lazar, S. W., Bush, G., Gollub, R. L., Fricchione, G. L., Khalsa, G., & Benson, H. (2000). Functional brain mapping of the relaxation response and meditation. *Neuroreport, 11*(7), 1581–1585.

Lazarus, A. A., Davison, G. C., & Polefka, D. A. (1965). Classical and operant factors in the treatment of a school phobia. *Journal of Abnormal Psychology, 70*(3), 225–229. https://doi.org/10.1037/ h0022130

Lazarus, R. S. (1982). Thoughts on the relations between emotion and cognition. *American Psychologist, 37*, 1019–1024. https://doi .org/10.1037/0003-066X.37.9.1019

Lazarus, R. S. (1984). On the primacy of cognition. *American Psychologist, 39*, 124–129. https://doi.org/10.1037/0003- 066X.39.2.124

Lazarus, R. S. (1993). From psychological stress to the emotions: A history of changing outlooks. *Annual Review of Psychology, 44*(1), 1–22.

Le Fevre, M., Matheny, J., & Kolt, G. S. (2003). Eustress, distress, and interpretation in occupational stress. *Journal of Managerial Psychology, 18* (7), 726–744. https://doi.org/10.1108/ 02683940310502412

Leary, M. R. (2019). *Self-presentation: Impression management and interpersonal behavior.* Routledge.

Leary, M. R., & Kowalski, R. M. (1997). *Social anxiety.* Guilford.

LeDoux, J. (2012). Rethinking the emotional brain. *Neuron, 73*(4), 653–676. https://doi.org/10.1016/j.neuron.2012.02.004

LeDoux, J. (2016). *Anxious: Using the brain to understand and treat fear and anxiety.* Penguin.

LeDoux, J. E. (1995). Emotion: Clues from the brain. *Annual Review of Psychology, 46*(1), 209–235. https://doi.org/10.1146/annurev .ps.46.020195.001233

LeDoux, J. E. (1999). The power of emotions. In R. Conlan (Ed.), *States of mind* (pp. 123–149). Wiley.

LeDoux, J. E. (2022). As soon as there was life, there was danger: The deep history of survival behaviours and the shallower history of consciousness. *Philosophical Transactions of the Royal Society B, 377*(1844), 20210292. https://doi.org/10.1098/ rstb.2021.0292

Lee, H., Jang, H., Yun, I., Lim, H., Tushaus, D. W. (2010). An examination of police use of force utilizing police training and neighborhood contextual factors: A multilevel analysis. *Policing: An International Journal of Police Strategies & Management, 33*(4), 681–702. http://dx.doi.org/10.1108/13639511011085088

Lee, J. (1993). *Facing the fire: Experiencing and expressing anger appropriately.* Bantam Books.

Lee, K. H., Xu, H., & Wu, B. (2020). Gender differences in quality of life among community-dwelling older adults in low-and middle-income countries: Results from the Study on global AGEing and adult health (SAGE). *BMC Public Health, 20*, 1–10. https://doi.org/10.1186/s12889-020-8212-0

Lee, S., Kwon, S., & Ahn, J. (2021). The effect of modeling on self-efficacy and flow state of adolescent athletes through role models. *Frontiers in Psychology, 12*, Article 661557. https://doi .org/10.3389/fpsyg.2021.661557

Lee, X. K., Chee, N. I. Y. N., Ong, J. L., Teo, T. B., van Rijn, E., Lo, J. C., & Chee, M. W. L. (2019). Validation of a consumer sleep wearable device with actigraphy and polysomnography in adolescents across sleep opportunity manipulations. *Journal of Clinical Sleep Medicine, 15*(9), 1337–1346. https://doi.org/10.5664/ jcsm.7932

Lee, Y. H., & Mason, C. (1999). Responses to information incongruency in advertising: The role of expectancy, relevancy, and humor. *Journal of Consumer Research, 26*(2), 156–169. https://doi.org/10.1086/209557

Lee, Y., & Kim, Y. K. (2021). Understanding the connection between the gut–brain axis and stress/anxiety disorders. *Current Psychiatry Reports, 23*(5), 1–7. https://doi.org/10.1007/s11920- 021-01235-x

Lehmann, J. Y. K., Nuevo-Chiquero, A., & Vidal-Fernandez, M. (2018). The early origins of birth order differences in children's outcomes and parental behavior. *Journal of Human Resources, 53*(1), 123–156. https://doi.org/10.3368/jhr.53.1.0816-8177

Leibowitz, H. W. (1971). Sensory, learned, and cognitive mechanisms of size perception. *Annals of the New York Academy of Sciences, 188*(1), 47–62. https://doi.org/10.1111/j.1749-6632.1971.tb13089.x

Leichsenring, F., & Leweke, F. (2017). Social anxiety disorder. *New England Journal of Medicine, 376*(23), 2255–2264. https://doi .org/10.1056/NEJMcp1614701

Leisman, G., & Melillo, R. (2012). The development of the frontal lobes in infancy and childhood: Asymmetry and the nature of temperament and affect. In A. E. Cavanna (Ed.), *Frontal lobe: Anatomy, functions and injuries* (pp. 1–48). Nova Scientific Publishers.

Lejarraga, T., Frey, R., Schnitzlein, D. D., & Hertwig, R. (2019). No effect of birth order on adult risk taking. *Proceedings of the National Academy of Sciences, 116*(13), 6019–6024. https://doi .org/10.1073/pnas.1814153116

Lenneberg, E. H. (1967). *Biological foundations of language.* Wiley.

Lent, R., Azevedo, F. A., Andrade-Moraes, C. H., & Pinto, A. V. (2012). How many neurons do you have? Some dogmas of quantitative neuroscience under revision. *European Journal of Neuroscience, 35*(1), 1–9. https://doi.org/10.1111/j.1460-9568.2011.07923.x

Lépine, J. P. (2002). The epidemiology of anxiety disorders: Prevalence and societal costs. *Journal of Clinical Psychiatry, 63*(Suppl. 14), 4–8.

Lepore, J. (2015). *The secret history of Wonder Woman.* Vintage.

Lepper, M. R., & Henderlong, J. (2000). Turning "play" into "work" and "work" into "play": 25 years of research on intrinsic versus extrinsic motivation. In C. Sansone & J. M. Harackiewicz (Eds.), *Intrinsic and extrinsic motivation: The search for optimal motivation and performance* (pp. 257–307). Academic Press. https://doi.org/10.1016/B978-012619070-0/50032-5

Lepper, M. R., Corpus, J. H., & Iyengar, S. S. (2005). Intrinsic and extrinsic motivational orientations in the classroom: Age differences and academic correlates. *Journal of Educational Psychology, 97*(2), 184–196. https://doi.org/10.1037/0022- 0663.97.2.184

Lepper, M. R., Greene, D., & Nisbett, R. E. (1973). Undermining children's intrinsic interest with extrinsic reward: A test of the "overjustification" hypothesis. *Journal of Personality and Social Psychology, 28*(1), 129–137. https://doi.org/10.1037/h0035519

Levenson, J. C., Shensa, A., Sidani, J. E., Colditz, J. B., & Primack, B. A. (2017). Social media use before bed and sleep disturbance among young adults in the United States: A nationally representative study. *Sleep: Journal of Sleep and Sleep Disorders Research, 40*(9), 1–7. https://doi.org/10.1093/sleep/zsx113

Levin, D., & Baker, L. (2015). Change blindness and inattentional blindness. In J. M. Fawcett, E. F. Risko, A. Kingstone, J. M. Fawcett, E. F. Risko, A. Kingstone (Eds.), *The handbook of attention* (pp. 199–231). MIT Press.

Levin, E., & Bernier, J. (2011). Attention span. In S. Goldstein & J. A. Naglieri (Eds.), *Encyclopedia of child behavior and development.* Springer. https://doi.org/10.1007/978-0-387-79061-9_226

Levin-Aspenson, H. F., Watson, D., Ellickson-Larew, S., Stanton, K., & Stasik-O'Brien, S. M. (2021). Beyond distress and fear: Differential psychopathology correlates of PTSD symptom clusters. *Journal of Affective Disorders, 284*, 9–17. https://doi.org/10.1016/j.jad.2021.01.090

Levine, M. E., Lu, A. T., Quach, A., Chen, B. H., Assimes, T. L., Bandinelli, S., Hou, L., Baccarelli, A. A., Stewart, J. D., Li, Y., Whitsel, E. A., Wilson, J. G., Reiner, A. P., Aviv, A., Lohman, K., Liu, Y., Ferrucci, L., & Horvath, S. (2018). An epigenetic biomarker of aging for lifespan and healthspan. *Aging, 10*(4), 573–591. https://doi.org/10.18632/aging.101414

Levine, M., Philpot, R., & Kovalenko, A. G. (2020). Rethinking the bystander effect in violence reduction training programs. *Social Issues and Policy Review, 14*(1), 273–296. https://doi.org/10.1111/sipr.12063

Levingson, S. (Creator, Director). 2019. *Euphoria* [Television series]. HBO.

Levinson, C. A., & Rodebaugh, T. L. (2013). Anxiety, self-discrepancy, and regulatory focus theory: Acculturation matters. *Anxiety, Stress & Coping: An International Journal, 26*(2), 171–186. https://doi.org/10.1080/10615806.2012.659728

Lewin, K. (1946). Action research and minority problems. *Journal of Social Issues, 2*(4), 34–46. https://doi.org/10.1037/10269-013

Lewis, C., Roberts, N. P., Gibson, S., & Bisson, J. I. (2020). Dropout from psychological therapies for post-traumatic stress disorder (PTSD) in adults: Systematic review and meta-analysis. *European Journal of Psychotraumatology, 11*(1), Article 1709709. https://doi.org/10.1080/20008198.2019.1709709

Lewis, P. A., Knoblich, G., & Poe, G. (2018). How memory replay in sleep boosts creative problem-solving. *Trends in Cognitive Sciences, 22*(6), 491–503. https://doi.org/10.1016/j.tics.2018.03.009

Li, L., & Liu, X. (2013). Experimental studies of physical exercises to improve students sleep quality and mental health. In A. M. Columbus (Ed.), *Advances in psychology research* (Vol. 98, pp. 109–116). Nova Science Publishers.

Li, M., Yao, X., Sun, L., Zhao, L., Xu, W., Zhao, H., Xu, W., Zhao, H., Zhao, F., Zou, X., Cheng, Z., Li, B., Yang, W., & Cui, R. (2020). Effects of electroconvulsive therapy on depression and its potential mechanism. *Frontiers in Psychology, 11*, Article 80. https://doi.org/10.3389/fpsyg.2020.00080

Li, P., Legault, J., & Litcofsky, K. A. (2014). Neuroplasticity as a function of second language learning: Anatomical changes in the human brain. *Cortex, 58*, 301–324. https://doi.org/10.1016/j.cortex.2014.05.001

Li, Z., Daniel, S., Fujioka, K., & Umashanker, D. (2023). Obesity among Asian American people in the United States: A review. *Obesity, 31*(2), 316–328. https://doi.org/10.1002/oby.23639

Libo, L. M., & Arnold, G. E. (1983). Relaxation practice after biofeedback therapy: A long-term follow-up study of utilization and effectiveness. *Biofeedback and Self-Regulation, 8*, 217–227. https://doi.org/10.1007/BF00998852

Liddell, S., & Johnson, R. (1989). American Sign Language: The phonological base. *Sign Language Studies, 64*, 195–278.

Lieberman, M., Doyle, A. B., & Markiewicz, D. (1999). Developmental patterns in security of attachment to mother and father in late childhood and early adolescence: Associations with peer relations. *Child Development, 70*(1), 202–213. https://doi.org/10.1111/1467-8624.00015

Liebowitz, M. R. (1987). Social phobia. *Modern Problems in Pharmacopsychiatry, 22*, 141–173. https://doi.org/10.1159/000414022

Liebst, L. S., Philpot, R., Heinskou, M. B., & Lindegaard, M. R. (2019). Bystander intervention in street violence: Current evidence and implications for practice. *Samfundsøkonomen, 4*, 1–10. https://doi.org/10.31235/osf.io/7m9uv

Liggett, J., Sellbom, M., & Carmichael, K. L. (2017). Examining the DSM-5 Section III criteria for obsessive-compulsive personality disorder in a community sample. *Journal of Personality Disorders, 31*(6), 790–809. https://doi.org/10.1521/pedi_2017_31_281

Lilienfeld, S. O. (2012). Public skepticism of psychology: Why many people perceive the study of human behavior as unscientific. *American Psychologist, 67*(2), 111–129. https://doi.org/10.1037/a0023963

Lilienfeld, S. O. (2017). Psychology's replication crisis and the grant culture: Righting the ship. *Perspectives on Psychological Science, 12*(4), 660–664. https://doi.org/10.1177/1745691616687745

Lilienfeld, S. O., Kirsch, I., Sarbin, T. R., Lynn, S. J., Chaves, J. F., Ganaway, G. K., & Powell, R. A. (1999). Dissociative identity disorder and the sociocognitive model: Recalling the lessons of the past. *Psychological Bulletin, 125*(5), 507–523. https://doi.org/10.1037/0033-2909.125.5.507

Lilienfeld, S. O., Lynn, S. J., Ruscio, J., & Beyerstein, B. L. (2009). *50 great myths of popular psychology: Shattering widespread misconceptions about human behavior.* John Wiley.

Lilienfeld, S. O., Wood, J. M., & Garb, H. N. (2001). What's wrong with this picture? *Scientific American, 284*(5), 80–87. https://www.jstor.org/stable/26059212

Lilienfeld, S., Lynn, S., Ruscio, J. & Beyerstein, B. (2010). *50 Great myths of popular psychology.* Wiley-Blackwell.

Liljenquist, K., Zhong, C., & Galinsky, A. (2010). The smell of virtue: Clean scents promote reciprocity and charity. *Psychological Science, 21*(3), 381–383. https://doi.org/10.1177/0956797610361426

Lin, I. M., Wang, S. Y., Chu, I. H., Lu, Y. H., Lee, C. S., Lin, T. H., & Fan, S. Y. (2017). The association of Type D personality with heart rate variability and lipid profiles among patients with coronary artery disease. *International Journal of Behavioral Medicine, 24*(1), 101–109. https://doi.org/10.1007/s12529-016-9571-x

Lin, J. (2023). Protective and risk factors of peer victimization among adolescents: A perspective from victims. *Journal of Education, Humanities and Social Sciences, 11*, 273–281. https://doi.org/10.54097/ehss.v11i.7674

Lindemann, B. (2001). Receptors and transduction in taste. *Nature, 413*(6852), 219–225. https://doi.org/10.1038/35093032

Lindsay, D. S., Hagen, L., Read, J. D., Wade, K. A., & Garry, M. (2004). True photographs and false memories. *Psychological Science, 15*(3), 149–154. https://doi.org/10.1111/j.0956-7976.2004.01503002.x7(3)

Link, B. G., & Phelan, J. C. (2001). Conceptualizing stigma. *Annual Review of Sociology, 27*(1), 363–385. https://doi.org/10.1146/annurev.soc.27.1.363

Lipnevich, A. A., Credè, M., Hahn, E., Spinath, F. M., Roberts, R. D., & Preckel, F. (2017). How distinctive are morningness and eveningness from the Big Five factors of personality? A meta-analytic investigation. *Journal of Personality and Social Psychology, 112*(3), 491–509. https://doi.org/10.1037/pspp0000099

Litchfield, C. A., Quinton, G., Tindle, H., Chiera, B., Kikillus, K. H., & Roetman, P. (2017). The "Feline Five": An exploration of personality in pet cats (Felis catus). *PLoS One, 12*(8), e0183455. https://doi.org/10.1371/journal.pone.0183455

Little, D. F., Zhang, Y. & Wright, B. A. (2017). Disruption of perceptual learning by a brief practice break. *Current Biology, 27*(23), 3699–3705. https://doi.org/10.1016/j.cub.2017.10.032

Liu, C. Y., & Apuzzo, M. L. (2003). The genesis of neurosurgery and the evolution of the neurosurgical operative environment: Part I—Prehistory to 2003. *Neurosurgery, 52*(1), 3–19. https://doi.org/10.1227/0006123-200301000-00001

Liu, M. (2023). Are you really smiling? Display rules for emojis and the relationship between emotion management and psychological well-being. *Frontiers in Psychology, 14*, Article 1035742. https://doi.org/10.3389/fpsyg.2023.1035742

Liu, R. (2023). The relationship between empathic deficits and risk of antisocial personality disorder. *Journal of Education, Humanities and Social Sciences, 8*, 152–157. https://doi.org/10.54097/ehss.v8i.4241

Lloyd, G., Chadwick, J., & Mann, W. N. (1983). *Introduction to Hippocratic writings*. Penguin.

Lochte, B. C., Beletsky, A., Samuel, N. K., & Grant, I. (2017). The use of cannabis for headache disorders. *Cannabis and Cannabinoid Research, 2*(1), 61–71. https://doi.org/10.1089/can.2016.0033

Loehlin, J. C., & Nichols, R. C. (1976). *Heredity, environment and personality*. University of Texas Press.

Loewenstein, R. J. (2022). Dissociation debates: Everything you know is wrong. *Dialogues in Clinical Neuroscience, 20*(3), 229–242. https://doi.org/10.31887/DCNS.2018.20.3/rloewenstein

Lofton, H., Ard, J. D., Hunt, R. R., & Knight, M. G. (2023). Obesity among African American people in the United States: A review. *Obesity, 31*(2), 306–315. https://doi.org/10.1002/oby.23640

Loftus, E. F. (1974). Reconstructing memory: The incredible eyewitness. *Psychology Today, 8*, 116–119.

Loftus, E. F. (1975). Leading questions and the eyewitness report. *Cognitive Psychology, 7*(4), 560–572. https://doi.org/10.1016/0010-0285(75)90023-7

Loftus, E. F. (1979). The malleability of human memory. *American Scientist, 67*(3), 312–320. https://www.jstor.org/stable/27849223

Loftus, E. F. (1996). The myth of repressed memory and the realities of science. *Clinical Psychology: Science and Practice, 3*(4), 356–362. https://doi.org/10.1111/j.1468-2850.1996.tb00089.x

Loftus, E. F. (1997). Creating false memories. *Scientific American, 277*(3), 70–75. https://www.jstor.org/stable/24995913

Loftus, E. F., & Pickrell, J. E. (1995). The formation of false memories. *Psychiatric Annals, 25*(12), 720–725. https://doi.org/10.3928/0048-5713-19951201-07

Loftus, E. F., & Zanni, G. (1975). Eyewitness testimony: The influence of the wording of a question. *Bulletin of the Psychonomic Society, 5*(1), 86–88. https://doi.org/10.3758/BF03336715

Loftus, E. F., Miller, D. G., & Burns, H. J. (1978). Semantic integration of verbal information into a visual memory. *Journal of Experimental Psychology: Human Learning and Memory, 4*(1), 19–31. https://doi.org/10.1037/0278-7393.4.1.19

Loftus, E., & Ketcham, K. (1996). *The myth of repressed memory: False memories and allegations of sexual abuse*. Macmillan.

Logan, M. H. (2018). Stockholm syndrome: Held hostage by the one you love. *Violence and Gender, 5*(2), 67–69. https://doi.org/10.1089/vio.2017.0076

Lohani, D. C., & Rana, B. (2023). ADHD diagnosis using structural brain MRI and personal characteristic data with machine learning framework. *Psychiatry Research: Neuroimaging, 334*, 1–17. https://doi.org/10.1016/j.pscychresns.2023.111689

Longo, M. R., Trippier, S., Vagnoni, E., & Lourenco, S. F. (2015). Right hemisphere control of visuospatial attention in near space. *Neuropsychologia, 70*, 350–357. https://doi.org/10.1016/j.neuropsychologia.2014.10.035

Longo, P., Bevione, F., Amodeo, L., Martini, M., Panero, M., & Abbate-Daga, G. (2023). Perfectionism in anorexia nervosa: Associations with clinical picture and personality traits. *Clinical Psychology & Psychotherapy, 31*(1), Article e2931.https://doi.org/10.1002/cpp.2931

Lönn, M., Svedberg, P., Nygren, J., Jarbin, H., Aili, K., & Larsson, I. (2023). The efficacy of weighted blankets for sleep in children with attention-deficit/hyperactivity disorder—A randomized controlled crossover trial. *Journal of Sleep Research*. Advance online publication. https://doi.org/10.1111/jsr.13990

Loop, M. S., Shows, J. F., Mangel, S. C., & Kuyk, T. K. (2003). Colour thresholds in dichromats and normals. *Vision Research, 43*(9), 983–992. https://doi.org/10.1016/S0042-6989(03)00074-9

Lopes, B., & Yu, H. (2017). Who do you troll and why: An investigation into the relationship between the Dark Triad Personalities and online trolling behaviours towards popular and less popular Facebook profiles. *Computers in Human Behavior, 77*, 69–76. https://doi.org/10.1016/j.chb.2017.08.036

Loughran, T. (2012). Shell shock, trauma, and the first world war: The making of a diagnosis and its histories. *Journal of the History of Medicine and Allied Sciences, 67*(1), 94–119. https://doi.org/10.1093/jhmas/jrq052

Lourenço, O., & Machado, A. (1996). In defense of Piaget's theory: A reply to 10 common criticisms. *Psychological Review, 103*(1), 143–164. https://doi.org/10.1037/0033-295X.103.1.143

Lovaas, O. I. (1987). Behavioral treatment and normal educational and intellectual functioning in young autistic children. *Journal of Consulting and Clinical Psychology, 55*(1), 3–9. https://doi.org/10.1037/0022-006X.55.1.3

Low, P. (2012). The Cambridge Declaration on Consciousness Publicly proclaimed in Cambridge, UK, on July 7, 2012, at the Francis Crick Memorial Conference on Consciousness in Human and non-Human Animals. http://fcmconference.org/img/CambridgeDeclarationOnConsciousness.pdf

Lu, L., Dong, M., Zhang, L., Zhu, X. M., Ungvari, G. S., Ng, C. H., Wang, G., & Xiang, Y. T. (2020). Prevalence of suicide attempts in individuals with schizophrenia: A meta-analysis of observational studies. *Epidemiology and Psychiatric Sciences, 29*, Article e39. https://doi.org/10.1017/S2045796019000313

Luchins, A. S. (1942). Mechanization in problem solving: The effect of Einstellung. *Psychological Monograph, 54*(Whole No. 248).

Luck, S. J., & Vogel, E. K. (1997). The capacity of visual working memory for features and conjunctions. *Nature, 390*(6657), 279–281. https://doi.org/10.1038/36846

Lukito, S., Fortea, L., Groppi, F., Wykret, K. Z., Tosi, E., Oliva, V., Damiani, S., Radua, J., & Fusar-Poli, P. (2023). Should perception of emotions be classified according to threat detection rather than emotional valence? An updated meta-analysis for a whole-brain atlas of emotional faces processing. *Journal of Psychiatry and Neuroscience, 48*(5), E376–E389. https://doi.org/10.1503/jpn.230065

Luna, B., Marek, S., Larsen, B., Tervo-Clemmens, B., & Chahal, R. (2015). An integrative model of the maturation of cognitive control. *Annual Review of Neuroscience, 38*, 151–170. https://doi.org/10.1146/annurev-neuro-071714-034054

Luthar, S. S., Cicchetti, D., & Becker, B. (2000). The construct of resilience: A critical evaluation and guidelines for future work. *Child Development, 71*(3), 543–562. https://doi.org/10.1111/1467-8624.00164

Lydon, S. D. M., & Geier, C. F. (2018). Age-varying associations between cigarette smoking, sensation seeking, and impulse control through adolescence and young adulthood. *Journal of Research on Adolescence, 28*(2), 354–367. https://doi.org/10.1111/jora.12335

Lynch, A., Elmore, B., & Kotecki, J. (2014). *Choosing health*. Pearson Higher Ed.

Lynn, S. J., Kirsch, I., Terhune, D. B., & Green, J. P. (2020). Myths and misconceptions about hypnosis and suggestion: Separating fact and fiction. *Applied Cognitive Psychology, 34*(6), 1253–1264. https://doi.org/10.1002/acp.3730

Lynn, S. J., Lilienfeld, S. O., Merckelbach, H., Maxwell, R., Baltman, J., & Giesbrecht, T. (2016). *Dissociative disorders*. Routledge/Taylor & Francis.

Lynn, S. J., Maxwell, R., Merckelbach, H., Lilienfeld, S. O., van Heugten-van der Kloet, D., & Miskovic, V. (2019). Dissociation and its disorders: Competing models, future directions, and a way forward. *Clinical Psychology Review, 73*, Article 101755. https://doi.org/10.1016/j.cpr.2019.101755

Lynott, D., Corker, K. S., Wortman, J., Connell, L., Donnellan, M. B., Lucas, R. E., & O'Brien, K. (2014). Replication of "Experiencing physical warmth promotes interpersonal warmth" by Williams and Bargh (2008). *Social Psychology*, *45*(3), 216–222. https://doi.org/10.1027/1864-9335/a000187

Lynskey, M. T., Heath, A. C., Bucholz, K. K., Slutske, W. S., Madden, P. A. F., Nelson, E. C., Statham, D. J., & Martin, N. G. (2003). Escalation of drug use in early-onset cannabis users vs co-twin controls. *JAMA: Journal of the American Medical Association*, *289*(4), 427–433. https://doi.org/10.1001/jama.289.4.427

Lyssenko, L., Schmahl, C., Bockhacker, L., Vonderlin, R., Bohus, M., & Kleindienst, N. (2018). Dissociation in psychiatric disorders: A meta-analysis of studies using the dissociative experiences scale. *American Journal of Psychiatry*, *175*(1), 37–46. https://doi.org/10.1176/appi.ajp.2017.17010025

Lyubomirsky, S. (2001). Why are some people happier than others? The role of cognitive and motivational processes in well-being. *American Psychologist*, *56*(3), 239–249. https://doi.org/10.1037/0003-066X.56.3.239

Lyubomirsky, S., Caldwell, N. D., & Nolen-Hoeksema, S. (1998). Effects of ruminative and distracting responses to depressed mood on retrieval of autobiographical memories. *Journal of Personality and Social Psychology*, *75*(1), 166–177. https://doi.org/10.1037/0022-3514.75.1.166

Lyubomirsky, S., Sheldon, K. M., & Schkade, D. (2005). Pursuing happiness: The architecture of sustainable change. *Review of General Psychology*, *9*(2), 111–131. https://doi.org/10.1037/1089-2680.9.2.111

Ma, K. G., & Qian, Y. H. (2019). Alpha 7 nicotinic acetylcholine receptor and its effects on Alzheimer's disease. *Neuropeptides*, *73*, 96–106. https://doi.org/10.1016/j.npep.2018.12.003

MacDonald, K. (2018). A review of the literature: The needs of nontraditional students in postsecondary education. *Strategic Enrollment Management Quarterly*, *5*(4), 159–164. https://doi.org/10.1002/sem3.20115

MacDougall, J. M., Musante, L., Castillo, S., & Acevedo, M. C. (1988). Smoking, caffeine, and stress: Effects on blood pressure and heart rate in male and female college students. *Health Psychology*, *7*(5), 461–478. https://doi.org/10.1037/0278-6133.7.5.461

MacKay, C., & DeCicco, T. L. (2020). Pandemic dreaming: The effect of COVID-19 on dream imagery, a pilot study. *Dreaming*, *30*(3), 222–234. https://doi.org/10.1037/drm0000148

MacKellar, M. E., Robeck, T. R., Staggs, L., Wilson, S., Hieneman, M., MacKellar, D., & Cumella, E. (2023). Behavior skills training with zoological staff to increase killer whale attending behavior. *Behavior Analysis in Practice*, *16*(1), 266–283. https://doi.org/10.1007/s40617-022-00719-3

Macmillan, M. (2002). *An odd kind of fame: Stories of Phineas Gage*. MIT Press.

Macmillan, N. A., & Creelman, C. D. (2005). *Detection theory: A user's guide* (2nd ed.). Lawrence Erlbaum.

Macrae, C. N., Milne, A. B., & Bodenhausen, G. V. (1994). Stereotypes as energy-saving devices: A peek inside the cognitive toolbox. *Journal of Personality and Social Psychology*, *66*(1), 37–47. https://doi.org/10.1037/0022-3514.66.1.37

Maddi, S. R. (2002). The story of hardiness: Twenty years of theorizing, research, and practice. *Consulting Psychology Journal: Practice and Research*, *54*(3), 173–185. https://doi.org/10.1037/1061-4087.54.3.173

Maddi, S. R., & Kobasa, S. C. (1984). *The hardy executive: Health under stress*. Dorsey Press. https://lccn.loc.gov/83073088

Maddox, B. (2003). The double helix and the "wronged heroine." *Nature*, *421*, 407–408. https://doi.org/10.1038/nature01399

Maddox, L., Lee, D., & Barker, C. (2011). Police empathy and victim PTSD as potential factors in rape case attrition. *Journal of Police and Criminal Psychology*, *26*(2), 112–117. https://doi.org/10.1007/s11896-010-9075-6

Madigand, J., Rio, M., & Vandevelde, A. (2023). Equine assisted services impact on social skills in autism spectrum disorder: A meta-analysis. *Progress in Neuro-Psychopharmacology and Biological Psychiatry*, *125*, Article 110765. https://doi.org/10.1016/j.pnpbp.2023.110765

Madore, K. P., Khazenzon, A. M., Backes, C. W., Jiang, J., Uncapher, M., Norcia, A. M., & Wagner, A. D. (2020). Memory failure predicted by attention lapsing and media multitasking. *Nature*, *587*(7832), 87–91. https://doi.org/10.1038/s41586-020-2870-z

Maeda, U., Shen, B. J., Schwarz, E. R., Farrell, K. A., & Mallon, S. (2013). Self-efficacy mediates the associations of social support and depression with treatment adherence in heart failure patients. *International Journal of Behavioral Medicine*, *20*(1), 88–96. https://doi.org/10.1007/s12529-011-9215-0

Magee, W. J. (1999). Effects of negative life experiences on phobia onset. *Social Psychiatry and Psychiatric Epidemiology*, *34*, 343–351. https://doi.org/10.1007/s001270050154

Maheshwari, N., & Kumar, V. (2008). Personal effectiveness as a function of psychological androgyny. *Industrial Psychiatry Journal*, *17*(1), 39–45.

Maisel, A. Q. (1946). Bedlam 1946: Most US mental hospitals are a shame and a disgrace. *Life Magazine*, *20*(18), 102–118.

Malbois, E., & Hurst-Majno, S. (2023). Empathy is not so perfect! For a descriptive and wide conception of empathy. *Medicine, Health Care and Philosophy*, *26*(1), 85–97. https://doi.org/10.1007/s11019-022-10124-w

Malchiodi, C. A. (Ed.). (2011). *Handbook of art therapy*. Guilford.

Malcolm, R., Ecks, S., & Pickersgill, M. (2018). "It just opens up their world": Autism, empathy, and the therapeutic effects of equine interactions. *Anthropology & Medicine*, *25*(2), 220–234. https://doi.org/10.1080/13648470.2017.1291115

Mallett, K. A., Turrisi, R., Trager, B. M., Sell, N., & Linden-Carmichael, A. N. (2019). An examination of consequences among college student drinkers on occasions involving alcohol-only, marijuana-only, or combined alcohol and marijuana use. *Psychology of Addictive Behaviors*, *33*(3), 331–336. https://doi.org/10.1037/adb0000458

Manger, P. R., & Siegel, J. M. (2020). Do all mammals dream? *Journal of Comparative Neurology*, *528*(17), 3198–3204. https://doi.org/10.1002/cne.24860

Mangiulli, I., Otgaar, H., Jelicic, M., & Merckelbach, H. (2022). A critical review of case studies on dissociative amnesia. *Clinical Psychological Science*, *10*(2), 191–211. https://doi.org/10.1177/21677026211018194

Mankiewicz, R. (2000). *The story of mathematics*. Princeton University Press.

Mann, C. I. (2020). *Phases of the moon: A cultural history of the werewolf film*. Edinburgh University Press.

Mann, J. R., & Larimore, W. (2006). Impact of religious attendance on life expectancy. *The Journal of the American Board of Family Medicine*, *19*(4), 429–430. https://doi.org/10.3122/jabfm.19.4.429

Mantovani, A., Neri, F., D'Urso, G., Mencarelli, L., Tatti, E., Momi, D., Menardi, A., Sprugnoli, G., Santarnecchi, E., & Rossi, S. (2021). Functional connectivity changes and symptoms improvement after personalized, double-daily dosing, repetitive transcranial magnetic stimulation in obsessive-compulsive disorder: A pilot study. *Journal of Psychiatric Research*, *136*, 560–570. https://doi.org/10.1016/j.jpsychires.2020.10.030

Mao, Y., Xu, T., & Kim, K. J. (2023). Motivations for proactive and reactive trolling on social media: Developing and validating a four-factor model. *Social Media + Society*, *9*(4), 1–14. https://doi.org/10.1177/20563051231203682

Marcus, G. E. (2023). Evaluating the status of theories of emotion in political science and psychology. *Frontiers in Political Science*, *4*, Article 1080884. https://doi.org/10.3389/fpos.2022.1080884

Marder, S. R., & Galderisi, S. (2017). The current conceptualization of negative symptoms in schizophrenia. *World Psychiatry, 16*(1), 14–24. https://doi.org/10.1002/wps.20385

Marino, L. (2002). Convergence of complex cognitive abilities in cetaceans and primates. *Brain, Behavior and Evolution, 59*(1–2), 21–32.

Marino, L. (2002). Convergence of complex cognitive abilities in cetaceans and primates. *Brain, Behavior and Evolution, 59*(1–2), 21–32. https://doi.org/10.1159/000063731

Marioni, R. E., Harris, S. E., Shah, S., McRae, A. F., von Zglinicki, T., Martin-Ruiz, C., Wray, N. R., Visscher, P. M., & Deary, I. J. (2016). The epigenetic clock and telomere length are independently associated with chronological age and mortality. *International Journal of Epidemiology, 45*(2), 424–432. https://doi.org/10.1093/ije/dyw041

Marks, I. M. (2002). Innate and learned fears are at opposite ends of a continuum of associability. *Behaviour Research and Therapy, 40*(2), 165–167. https://doi.org/10.1016/S0005-7967(01)00048-1

Markus, H. R. (1977). Self-schemata and processing information about the self. *Journal of Personality and Social Psychology, 35*(2), 63–78. https://doi.org/10.1037/0022-3514.35.2.63

Markus, H. R., & Kitayama, S. (1994). A collective fear of the collective: Implications for selves and theories of selves. *Personality and Social Psychology Bulletin, 20*(5), 568–579. https://doi.org/10.1177/0146167294205013

Marmarosh, C., Holtz, A., & Schottenbauer, M. (2005). Group cohesiveness, group-derived collective self-esteem, group-derived hope, and the well-being of group therapy members. *Group Dynamics: Theory, Research, and Practice, 9*(1), 32–44. https://doi.org/10.1037/1089-2699.9.1.32

Marnewick, C., & Marnewick, A. (2021). Digital intelligence: A must-have for project managers. *Project Leadership and Society, 2*, Article 100026. https://doi.org/10.1016/j.plas.2021.100026

Marris, J. E., Perfors, A., Mitchell, D., Wang, W., McCusker, M. W., Lovell, T. J. H., Gibson, R. N., Gaillard, F., & Howe, P. D. L. (2023). Evaluating the effectiveness of different perceptual training methods in a difficult visual discrimination task with ultrasound images. *Cognitive Research: Principles and Implications, 8*(1), Article 19. https://doi.org/10.1186/s41235-023-00467-0.

Marsh, H. W., Köller, O., & Baumert, J. (2001). Reunification of East and West German school systems: Longitudinal multilevel modeling study of the big-fish-little-pond effect on academic self-concept. *American Educational Research Journal, 38*(2), 321–350.

Martin, C. L., Andrews, N. C. Z., England, D., Zosuls, K., & Ruble, D. N. (2016). A dual identity approach for conceptualizing and measuring children's gender identity. *Child Development, 88*(1), 167–182. https://doi.org/10.1111/cdev.12568

Martinez, J. (2001). *Hostages in the home: Domestic violence as seen through its parallel, the Stockholm syndrome.* Minnesota Center Against Violence and Abuse. http://www.mincava.umn.edu/documents/clergybook/clergybook.html

Martini, M. (1994). Peer interactions in Polynesia: A view from the Marquesas. In J. Roopnarine, J. E. Johnson, & F. H. Hooper (Eds.), *Children's play in diverse cultures* (pp. 74–122). State University of New York Press.

Maruta, N., Kolyadko, S., Fedchenko, V., & Yavdak, I. (2021). Features of the influence of hereditary factors on the clinical manifestations of depressive disorders. *European Psychiatry, 64*(S1), S331. https://doi.org/10.1192/j.eurpsy.2021.888

Maslow, A. H. (1943). A theory of human motivation. *Psychological Review, 50*(4), 370–396. https://doi.org/10.1037/h0054346

Maslow, A. H. (1954). *Motivation and personality.* Harper & Row.

Maslow, A. H. (1962). Lessons from the peak-experiences. *Journal of Humanistic Psychology, 2*(1), 9–18.

Mason, T. B., Smith, K. E., Crosby, R. D., Dvorak, R., Engel, S. G., Crow, S., Wonderlich, S. A., & Peterson, C. B. (2022). Self-discrepancy as a predictor of eating disorder symptoms: Findings from two ecological momentary assessment studies of adults with binge eating. *Cognitive Therapy and Research, 46*(3), 580–589. https://doi.org/10.1007/s10608-021-10279-5

Massimini, M., Ferrarelli, F., Huber, R., Esser, S. K., Singh, H., & Tononi, G. (2005). Breakdown of cortical effective connectivity during sleep. *Science, 309*(5744), 2228–2232. https://doi.org/10.1126/science.1117256

Masters, N. T., Casey, E., Wells, E. A., & Morrison, D. M. (2013). Sexual scripts among young heterosexually active men and women: Continuity and change. *Journal of Sex Research, 50*(5), 409–420. https://doi.org/10.1080/00224499.2012.661102

Masuda, T. (2009). Cultural effects on visual perception. In E. B. Goldstein (Ed.), *SAGE encyclopedia of perception* (Vol. 1, pp. 339–343). Sage.

Matthijssen, S. J., Lee, C. W., de Roos, C., Barron, I. G., Jarero, I., Shapiro, E., Hurley, E. C., Schubert, S., Baptist, J., Amann, B. L., Moreno-Alcázar, A., Tesarz, J., & de Jongh, A. (2020). The current status of EMDR therapy, specific target areas, and goals for the future. *Journal of EMDR Practice and Research, 14*(4), 241–284. https://doi.org/10.1891/EMDR-D-20-00039

Mattson, C. L., Tanz, L. J., Quinn, K., Kariisa, M., Patel, P., & Davis, N. L. (2021). Trends and geographic patterns in drug and synthetic opioid overdose deaths—United States, 2013–2019. *Morbidity and Mortality Weekly Report, 70*(6), 202–207. https://doi.org/10.15585/mmwr.mm7006a4

Mattson, S. A., D'Souza, J., Wojcik, K. D., Guzick, A. G., Goodman, W. K., & Storch, E. A. (2023). A systematic review of treatments for misophonia. *Personalized Medicine in Psychiatry, 39*, Article 100104. https://doi.org/10.1016/j.pmip.2023.100104

Mayer, J. D., Salovey, P., & Caruso, D. (2000). Emotional intelligence. In R. J. Sternberg (Ed.), *Handbook of intelligence* (pp. 396–421). Cambridge University Press.

Mayer, R. E. (2013). *Problem solving.* In D. Reisberg (Ed.), *The Oxford handbook of cognitive psychology* (pp. 769–778). Oxford University Press.

Mayes, R., & Horwitz, A. V. (2005). DSM-III and the revolution in the classification of mental illness. *Journal of the History of the Behavioral Sciences, 41*(3), 249–267. https://doi.org/10.1002/jhbs.20103

Mayhew, M. J., Rockenbach, A. N., Bowman, N. A., Seifert, T. A., & Wolniak, G. C. (2016). *How college affects students: 21st century evidence that higher education works* (Vol. 1). John Wiley.

Mazza, S., Gerbier, E., Gustin, M.-P., Kasikci, Z., Koenig, O., Toppino, T. C., & Magnin, M. (2016). Relearn faster and retain longer: Along with practice, sleep makes perfect. *Psychological Science, 27*(10), 1321–1330. https://doi.org/10.1177/0956797616659930

McBride, D. M., Cutting, J. C., & Zimmerman, C. (2023). *Cognitive psychology: Theory, process, and methodology.* Sage.

McClelland, D. C. (1961). *The achieving society.* The Free Press.

McClelland, D. C. (1987). *Human motivation.* Cambridge University Press.

McConnell, A. R., & Leibold, J. M. (2001). Relations among the Implicit Association Test, discriminatory behavior, and explicit measures of racial attitudes. *Journal of Experimental Social Psychology, 37*(5), 435–442. https://doi.org/10.1006/jesp.2000.1470

McCrae, R. R., & Costa, P. T., Jr. (1997). Personality trait structure as a human universal. *American Psychologist, 52*(5), 509–516. https://doi.org/10.1037/0003-066X.52.5.509

McCrae, R. R., & Costa, P. T., Jr. (2008). The five-factor theory of personality. In O. P. John, R. W. Robins, & L. A. Pervin (Eds.), *Handbook of personality* (3rd ed., pp. 159–181). Guilford.

McCutcheon, R. A., Abi-Dargham, A., & Howes, O. D. (2019). Schizophrenia, dopamine and the striatum: From biology to symptoms. *Trends in Neurosciences, 42*(3), 205–220. https://doi .org/10.1016/j.tins.2018.12.004

McDaniel Peters, B. C., & Wood, W. (2017). Autism and equine-assisted interventions: A systematic mapping review. *Journal of Autism and Developmental Disorders, 47*, 3220–3242.

McDermut, W., Miller, I. W., & Brown, R. A. (2001). The efficacy of group psychotherapy for depression: A meta-analysis and review of the empirical research. *Clinical Psychology: Science and Practice, 8*(1), 98–116. https://doi.org/10.1093/clipsy.8.1.98

McDevitt, E. A., Sattari, N., Duggan, K., Cellini, N., Whitehurst, L. N., Perera, C., Reihanabad, N., Granados, S., Hernandez, L. T., & Mednick, S. (2018). The impact of frequent napping and nap practice on sleep-dependent memory in humans. *Scientific Reports, 8*, Article 15053. https://doi.org/10.1038/s41598-018-33209-0

McDonald, S. (1999). Exploring the process of inference generation in sarcasm: A review of normal and clinical studies. *Brain and Language, 68*(3), 486–506. https://doi.org/10.1006/brln.1999.2124

McDonough, D. J., Pope, Z. C., Zeng, N., Liu, W., & Gao, Z. (2020). Comparison of college students' blood pressure, perceived exertion, and psychosocial outcomes during virtual reality, exergaming, and traditional exercise: An exploratory study. *Games for Health Journal, 9*(4), 290–296. https://doi .org/10.1089/g4h.2019.0196

McDougall, W. (1918). *An introduction to social psychology* (13th ed.). John W. Luce & Company.

McFarland, C., & Ross, M. (1987). The relation between current impressions and memories of self and dating partners. *Personality and Social Psychology Bulletin, 13*(2), 228–238. https://doi.org/10.1177/0146167287132008

McGaugh, J. L. (2015). Consolidating memories. *Annual Review of Psychology, 66*, 1–24. https://doi.org/10.1146/annurev-psych-010814-014954

McGeary, K. A., & French, M. T. (2000). Illicit drug use and emergency room utilization. *Health Services Research, 35*(1, Pt. 1), 153–169.

McGrath, A. (2020). Bringing cognitive dissonance theory into the scholarship of teaching and learning: Topics and questions in need of investigation. *Scholarship of Teaching and Learning in Psychology, 6*(1), 84–90. https://doi.org/10.1037/stl0000168

McGrath, J., Saha, S., Chant, D., & Welham, J. (2008). Schizophrenia: A concise overview of incidence, prevalence, and mortality. *Epidemiologic Reviews, 30*(1), 67–76. https://doi.org/10.1093/epirev/mxn001

McGregor, H. A., & Elliot, A. J. (2005). The shame of failure: Examining the link between fear of failure and shame. *Personality and Social Psychology Bulletin, 31*(2), 218–231. https://doi.org/10.1177/0146167204271420

McIntyre, C. C., & Anderson, R. W. (2016). Deep brain stimulation mechanisms: The control of network activity via neurochemistry modulation. *Journal of Neurochemistry, 139*, 338–345. https://doi.org/10.1111/jnc.13649

McKay, D. R. (2019, November 20). *Careers for people with good memory*. Liveabout.com. https://www.liveabout.com/careers-that-require-the-ability-to-memorize-information-525682

McKendrick, G., & Graziane, N. M. (2020). Drug-induced conditioned place preference and its practical use in substance use disorder research. *Frontiers in Behavioral Neuroscience, 14*, Article 582147. https://doi.org/10.3389/fnbeh.2020.582147

McLellan, T. M., Caldwell, J. A., & Lieberman, H. R. (2016). A review of caffeine's effects on cognitive, physical and occupational performance. *Neuroscience and Biobehavioral Reviews, 71*, 294–312. https://doi.org/10.1016/j.neubiorev.2016.09.001

McMurray, R. G. (2019). Exercise, mood states, and neuroendocrinology. In L. Diamant (Ed.), *Mind-body maturity* (pp. 237–254). Taylor & Francis.

McVey, G. L., Levine, M. P., Piran, N., & Ferguson, H. B. (Eds.). (2013). *Preventing eating-related and weight-related disorders: Collaborative research, advocacy, and policy change*. Wilfrid Laurier University Press.

Medic, N., Mack, D. E., Wilson, P. M., & Starkes, J. L. (2007). The effects of athletic scholarships on motivation in sport. *Journal of Sport Behavior, 30*, 292–306. https://doi.org/10.1037/t55190-000

Medvedskaya, E. I. (2022). Features of the attention span in adult Internet users. *RUDN Journal of Psychology and Pedagogics, 19*(2), 304–319. https://doi.org/10.22363/2313-1683-2022-19-2-304-319

Mehrabian, A., & Stefl, C. A. (1995). Basic temperament components of loneliness, shyness, and conformity. *Social Behavior and Personality: An International Journal, 23*(3), 253–263.

Meichenbaum, D., & Lilienfeld, S. O. (2018). How to spot hype in the field of psychotherapy: A 19-item checklist. *Professional Psychology: Research and Practice, 49*(1), 22–30. https://doi .org/10.1037/pro0000172

Melzack, R., & Wall, P. (1996). *The challenge of pain*. Penguin.

Mende-Siedlecki P., Goharzad, A., Tuerxuntuoheti, A., Reyes, P., Lin, J., & Drain, A. (2022). Assessing the speed and spontaneity of racial bias in pain perception. *Journal of Experimental Social Psychology, 101*, Article 104315. https://doi.org/10.1016/j .jesp.2022.104315

Mendez, D., & Le, T. T. (2022). Consequences of a match made in hell: The harm caused by menthol smoking to the African American population over 1980–2018. *Tobacco Control, 31*(4), 569–571. http://doi.org/10.1136/tobaccocontrol-2021-056748

Mendoza, N., Rodriguez-Alcalá, C., Motos, M. A., & Salamanca, A. (2017). Androgen insensitivity syndrome: An update on the management of adolescents and young people. *Journal of Pediatric and Adolescent Gynecology, 30*(1), 2–8. http://doi.org/10.1016/j.jpag.2016.08.013

Menkel-Meadow, C. (Ed.). (2018). *Mediation: Theory, policy and practice*. Routledge.

Mennella, J. A., Jagnow, C. P., & Beauchamp, G. K. (2001). Prenatal and postnatal flavor learning by human infants. *Pediatrics, 107*(6), Article E88. https://doi.org/10.1542/peds.107.6.e88

Mercer, J. (2013). Deliverance, demonic possession, and mental illness: Some considerations for mental health professionals. *Mental Health, Religion & Culture, 16*(6), 595–611. https://doi.org/10.1080/13674676.2012.706272

Merluzzi, T. V., & Philip, E. J. (2017). "Letting go": From ancient to modern perspectives on relinquishing personal control—A theoretical perspective on religion and coping with cancer. *Journal of Religion and Health, 56*(6), 2039–2052. https://doi .org/10.1007/s10943-017-0366-4

Mervis, C., & Rosch, E. (1981). Categorization of natural objects. *Annual Review of Psychology, 32*, 89–115. https://doi.org/10.1146/annurev.ps.32.020181.000513

Mesgarani, N., & Chang, E. F. (2012). Selective cortical representation of attended speaker in multi-talker speech perception. *Nature, 485*(7397), 233–236. https://doi.org/10.1038/nature11020

Meth, E. M. S., Brandão, L. E. M., van Egmond, L. T., Xue, P., Grip, A., Wu, J., Adan, A., Andersson, F., Pacheco, A. P., Uvnäs-Moberg, K., Cedernaes, J., & Benedict, C. (2022). A weighted blanket increases pre-sleep salivary concentrations of melatonin in young, healthy adults. *Journal of Sleep Research*. Advance online publication. https://doi.org/10.1111/jsr.13743

Metrik, J., Kahler, C. W., McGeary, J. E., Monti, P. M., & Rohsenow, D. J. (2011). Acute effects of marijuana smoking on negative and positive affect. *Journal of Cognitive Psychotherapy, 25*(1), 31–46. https://doi.org/10.1891/0889-8391.25.1.31

Micheva, K. D., Wolman, D., Mensh, B. D., Pax, E., Buchanan, J., Smith, S. J., & Bock, D. D. (2016). A large fraction of neocortical myelin ensheathes axons of local inhibitory neurons. *elife, 5*, 1–29. https://doi.org/10.7554/eLife.15784.001

Michou, A., Matos, L., Gargurevich, R., Gumus, B., & Herrera, D. (2016). Building on the enriched hierarchical model of achievement motivation: Autonomous and controlling reasons underlying mastery goals. *Psychologica Belgica, 56*(3), 269–287. https://doi.org/10.5334/pb.281

Micozzi, M. S. (2018). *Fundamentals of complementary, alternative, and integrative medicine.* Elsevier.

Middlemist, R. D., Knowles, E. S., & Matter, C.F. (1976). Personal space invasions in the lavatory: Suggestive evidence for arousal. *Journal of Personality and Social Psychology, 33*(5), 541–546. https://doi.org/10.1037/0022-3514.33.5.541

Miech, R. A., Johnston, L. D., Patrick, M.E., O'Malley, P. M., Bachman, J. G., & Schulenberg, J. E., (2023). *Monitoring the future: National survey results on drug use, 1975–2022: Secondary school students.* Institute for Social Research, The University of Michigan. https://monitoringthefuture.org/wp-content/uploads/2022/12/mtf2022.pdf

Mikkelsen, K., Stojanovska, L., Polenakovic, M., Bosevski, M., & Apostolopoulos, V. (2017). Exercise and mental health. *Maturitas, 106*, 48–56. https://doi.org/10.1016/j.maturitas.2017.09.003

Miklikowska, M. (2018). Empathy trumps prejudice: The longitudinal relation between empathy and anti-immigrant attitudes in adolescence. *Developmental Psychology, 54*(4), 703–717. https://doi.org/10.1037/dev0000474

Milgram, S. (1963). Behavioral study of obedience. *Journal of Abnormal and Social Psychology, 67*(4), 371–378. https://doi.org/10.1037/h0040525

Milgram, S. (1970). The experience of living in cities. *Science, 167*(3924), 1461–1468. https://doi.org/10.1126/science.167.3924.1461

Milgram, S. (1974). *Obedience to authority: An experimental view.* Harper & Row.

Miller, B. L., & Cummings, J. L. (Eds.). (2017). *The human frontal lobes: Functions and disorders.* Guilford.

Miller, G. A. (1956). The magical number seven, plus or minus two: Some limits on our capacity for processing information. *Psychological Review, 63*(2), 81–97. https://doi.org/10.1037/h0043158

Miller, M. B., Merrill, J. E., DiBello, A. M., & Carey, K. B. (2018). Distinctions in alcohol-induced memory impairment: A mixed methods study of en bloc versus fragmentary blackouts. *Alcoholism: Clinical and Experimental Research, 42*(10), 2000–2010. https://doi.org/10.1111/acer.13850

Miller, N. (2021). Taking shortcuts in the study of cognitive maps. *Learning & Behavior, 49*(3), 261–262. https://doi.org/10.3758/s13420-020-00461-2

Miller, P. C., Lefcourt, H. M., Holmes, J. G., Ware, E. E., & Saleh, W. E. (1986). Marital locus of control and marital problem solving. *Journal of Personality and Social Psychology, 51*(1), 161–169. https://doi.org/10.1037/0022-3514.51.1.161

Miller, P. J., & Bain, D. E. (2000). Within-pod variation in the sound production of a pod of killer whales, Orcinus orca. *Animal Behaviour, 60*(5), 617–628. https://doi.org/10.1006/anbe.2000.1503

Miller, T. R. (1991). The psychotherapeutic utility of the five-factor model of personality: A clinician's experience. *Journal of Personality Assessment, 57*(3), 415–433. https://doi.org/10.1207/s15327752jpa5703_3

Miller, W. R., & Moyers, T. B. (2017). Motivational interviewing and the clinical science of Carl Rogers. *Journal of Consulting and Clinical Psychology, 85*(8), 757–766. https://doi.org/10.1037/ccp0000179

Miller, W. R., & Rose, G. S. (2009). Toward a theory of motivational interviewing. *American Psychologist, 64*(6), 527–537. https://doi.org/10.1037/a0016830

Mills, K. L., Goddings, A. L., Clasen, L. S., Giedd, J. N., & Blakemore, S. J. (2014). The developmental mismatch in structural brain maturation during adolescence. *Developmental Neuroscience, 36*(3–4), 147–160. https://doi.org/10.1159/000362328

Millslagle, M., & Goodfriend, W. (2019). Recognition of facial affect: Do training, autism, sex, extraversion, and age matter? *Journal of Psychological Inquiry, 23*, 5–14.

Minkel, J. D., Banks, S., Htaik, O., Moreta, M. C., Jones, C. W., McGlinchey, E., Simpson, N., & Dinges, D. (2012). Sleep deprivation and stressors: Evidence for elevated negative affect in response to mild stressors when sleep deprived. *Emotion, 12*(5), 1015–1020. https://doi.org/10.1037/a0026871

Minson, J. A., & Dorison, C. A. (2022). Why is exposure to opposing views aversive? Reconciling three theoretical perspectives. *Current Opinion in Psychology, 47*, Article 101435. https://doi.org/10.1016/j.copsyc.2022.101435

Minuchin, S., & Fishman, H. C. (1981). *Family therapy techniques.* Harvard University Press.

Mischel, W. (1968). *Personality and assessment.* Wiley.

Mischel, W. (1973). Toward a cognitive social learning reconceptualization of personality. *Psychological Review, 80*(4), 252–283. https://doi.org/10.1037/h0035002

Mischel, W. (1990). Personality dispositions revisited and revised: A view after three decades. In L. A. Pervin (Ed.), *Handbook of personality: Theory and research* (pp. 111–134). Guilford.

Mischel, W. (2009). From personality and assessment (1968) to personality science 2009. *Journal of Research in Personality, 43*(2), 282–290. https://doi.org/10.1016/j.jrp.2008.12.037

Mischel, W. (2014). *The marshmallow test: Understanding self-control and how to master it.* Little, Brown.

Mischel, W., & Ebbesen, E. (1970). Attention in delay of gratification. *Journal of Personality and Social Psychology, 16*(2), 329–337. https://doi.org/10.1037/h0029815

Mischel, W., & Ebbesen, E. B. (1970). Attention in delay of gratification. *Journal of Personality and Social Psychology, 16*(2), 329–337. https://doi.org/10.1037/h0029815

Mischel, W., Ebbesen, E. B., & Raskoff Zeiss, A. (1972). Cognitive and attentional mechanisms in delay of gratification. *Journal of Personality and Social Psychology, 21*(2), 204–218. https://doi.org/10.1037/h0032198

Mischel, W., Shoda, Y., & Rodriguez, M. L. (1989). Delay of gratification in children. *Science, 244*(4907), 933–938. https://doi.org/10.1126/science.2658056

Mishra, A., Sil, R., Patel, V., Devanathan, Y., & Vyas, M. (2022). Two sides of a coin: A review of literature on the relationship between bipolar disorder and creativity. *IAHRW International Journal of Social Sciences Review, 10*(3), 360–365.

Mita, T. H., Dermer, M., & Knight, J. (1977). Reversed facial images and the mere-exposure hypothesis. *Journal of Personality and Social Psychology, 35*(8), 597–601. https://doi.org/10.1037/0022-3514.35.8.597

Mitchell, P. B., & Kirkby, K. C. (2014). Biological therapies before the introduction of modern psychotropic drugs. In F. Lopez-Munoz, C. Alamo, & E. F. Domino (Eds.), *History of pharmacology* (pp. 327–347). NPP Books.

Moller, A. C., & Sheldon, K. M. (2020). Athletic scholarships are negatively associated with intrinsic motivation for sports, even decades later: Evidence for long-term undermining. *Motivation Science, 6*(1), 43–48. https://doi.org/10.1037/mot0000133

Molloy, G. J., Perkins-Porras, L., Strike, P. C., & Steptoe, A. (2008). Type-D personality and cortisol in survivors of acute coronary syndrome. *Psychosomatic Medicine, 70*(8), 863–868. https://doi.org/10.1097/PSY.0b013e3181842e0c

Monahan, J. L., Murphy, S. T., & Zajonc, R. B. (2000). Subliminal mere exposure: Specific, general, and diffuse effects. *Psychological Science, 11*(6), 462–466. https://doi.org/10.1111/1467-9280.00289

Monk, J. D., Giglio, E., Kamath, A., Lambert, M. R., & McDonough, C. E. (2019). An alternative hypothesis for the evolution of same-sex sexual behaviour in animals. *Nature Ecology & Evolution, 3*(12), 1622–1631. https://doi.org/10.1038/s41559-019-1019-7

Monk, T. H. (2000). Circadian rhythms: An overview. In A. E. Kazdin (Ed.), *Encyclopedia of psychology* (Vol. 2, pp. 83–85). American Psychological Association.

Mooneyham, B. W., & Schooler, J. W. (2013). The costs and benefits of mind-wandering: A review. *Canadian Journal of Experimental Psychology, 67*(1), 11–18. https://doi.org/10.1037/a0031569

Moore, D. A., & Healy, P. J. (2008). The trouble with overconfidence. *Psychological Review, 115*(2), 502–517. https://doi.org/10.1037/0033-295X.115.2.502

Moore, S. M., & Rosenthal, D. A. (2015). Personal growth, grandmother engagement and satisfaction among non-custodial grandmothers. *Aging & Mental Health, 19*(2), 136–143. https://doi.org/10.1080/13607863.2014.920302

Morewedge, C. K., & Norton, M. I. (2009). When dreaming is believing: The (motivated) interpretation of dreams. *Journal of Personality and Social Psychology, 96*(2), 249–264. https://doi.org/10.1037/a0013264

Morgan, H. (2021). Howard Gardner's multiple intelligences theory and his ideas on promoting creativity. In F. Reisman (Ed.), *Celebrating giants and trailblazers: A-Z of who's who in creativity research and related fields* (pp.124–141). KIE Publications.

Morgan, J., & Sisak, D. (2016). Aspiring to succeed: A model of entrepreneurship and fear of failure. *Journal of Business Venturing, 31*(1), 1–21. https://doi.org/10.1016/j.jbusvent.2015.09.002

Moriarity, J. L., Boatman, D., Krauss, G. L., Storm, P. B., & Lenz, F. A. (2001). Human "memories" can be evoked by stimulation of the lateral temporal cortex after ipsilateral medial temporal lobe resection. *Journal of Neurology, Neurosurgery & Psychiatry, 71*(4), 549–551. http://dx.doi.org/10.1136/jnnp.71.4.549

Morin, A. (2006). Levels of consciousness and self-awareness: A comparison and integration of various neurocognitive views. *Consciousness and Cognition, 15*(2), 358–371. https://doi.org/10.1016/j.concog.2005.09.006

Morse, S., & Bride, B. E. (2017, September). Decrease in healthcare utilization and costs for opioid users following residential integrated treatment for co-occurring disorders. *Healthcare, 5*(3), Article 54. https://doi.org/10.3390/healthcare5030054

Mørup, M. F., Kymes, S. M., & Oudin Åström, D. (2020). A modelling approach to estimate the prevalence of treatment-resistant schizophrenia in the United States. *PLoS One, 15*(6), e0234121. https://doi.org/10.1371/journal.pone.0234121

Motora, Y. (1905). Conflict of religion and science: A Japanese point of view. *The Monist, 15*(3), 398–408. https://www.jstor.org/stable/27899608

Mueller, P. A., & Oppenheimer, D. M. (2014). The pen is mightier than the keyboard: Advantages of longhand over laptop note taking. *Psychological Science, 25*(6), 1159–1168. https://doi.org/10.1177/0956797614524581

Mullen, B., Johnson, C., & Salas, E. (1991). Productivity loss in brainstorming groups: A meta-analytic integration. *Basic and Applied Social Psychology, 12*(1), 3–23. https://doi.org/10.1207/s15324834basp1201_1

Müller, J., Tellier, A., & Kurschilgen, M. (2022). Echo chambers and opinion dynamics explain the occurrence of vaccination hesitancy. *Royal Society Open Science, 9*(10), Article 220367. https://doi.org/10.1098/rsos.220367

Mulligan, K. (2010). Emotions and values. In P. Goldie (Ed.), *The Oxford handbook of philosophy of emotion* (pp. 475–500). Oxford University Press. https://doi.org/10.1093/oxfordhb/9780199235018.003.0022

Mullineaux, P. Y., Deater-Deckard, K., Petrill, S. A., Thompson, L. A., & DeThorne, L. S. (2009). Temperament in middle childhood: A behavioral genetic analysis of fathers' and mothers' reports. *Journal of Research in Personality, 43*(5), 737–746. https://doi.org/10.1016/j.jrp.2009.04.008

Munafo, D., Loewy, D., Reuben, K., Kavy, G., & Hevener, B. (2018). Sleep deprivation and the workplace: Prevalence, impact, and solutions. *American Journal of Health Promotion, 32*(7), 1644–1646. https://doi.org/10.1177/0890117118790621e

Muro, A., Gomà-i-Freixanet, M., & Adan, A. (2009). Morningness-eveningness, sex, and the alternative five factor model of personality. *Chronobiology International, 26*(6), 1235–1248. https://doi.org/10.3109/07420520903240491

Murphy, D. (2001). Hacking's reconciliation: Putting the biological and sociological together in the explanation of mental illness. *Philosophy of the Social Sciences, 31*(2), 139–162. https://doi.org/10.1177/004839310103100201

Murru, A., & Carpiniello, B. (2018). Duration of untreated illness as a key to early intervention in schizophrenia: A review. *Neuroscience Letters, 669*, 59–67. https://doi.org/10.1016/j.neulet.2016.10.003

Myers, D. G., & Diener, E. (2018). The scientific pursuit of happiness. *Perspectives on Psychological Science, 13*(2), 218–225. https://doi.org/10.1177/1745691618765171

Myrtek, M. (2001). Meta-analyses of prospective studies on coronary heart disease, Type A personality, and hostility. *International Journal of Cardiology, 79*(2–3), 245–251. https://doi.org/10.1016/S0167-5273(01)00441-7

Nagell, K., Olguin, R. S., & Tomasello, M. (1993). Processes of social learning in the tool use of chimpanzees (Pan troglodytes) and human children (Homo sapiens). *Journal of Comparative Psychology, 107*(2), 174–186. https://doi.org/10.1037/0735-7036.107.2.174

Nairn, R. (2023, February 20). *Health at every size: A concept to reduce weight-centric thinking and to promote body positivity.* Johns Hopkins University. https://wellbeing.jhu.edu/blog/2023/02/20/health-at-every-size/

Nannoni, S., de Groot, R., Bell, S., & Markus, H. S. (2021). Stroke in COVID-19: A systematic review and meta-analysis. *International Journal of Stroke, 16*(2), 137–149. https://doi.org/10.1177/1747493020972922

Nasar, S. (1998). *A beautiful mind: A biography of John Forbes Nash.* Simon & Schuster.

Nascimento, R. L. P., de Andrade Mesquita, I. M., Gondim, R., Dos Apóstolos, R. A. A. C., Toralles, M. B., De Oliveira, L. B., Cangucu-Campinho, A. K., & Barroso, U., Jr. (2018). Gender identity in patients with 5-alpha reductase deficiency raised as females. *Journal of Pediatric Urology, 14*(5), 419e1–419e6. https://doi.org/10.1016/j.jpurol.2018.08.021

Nascimento, S. S., Oliveira, L. R., & DeSantana, J. M. (2018). Correlations between brain changes and pain management after cognitive and meditative therapies: A systematic review of neuroimaging studies. *Complementary Therapies in Medicine, 39*, 137–145. https://doi.org/10.1016/j.ctim.2018.06.006

Nasir, M., Trujillo, D., Levine, J., Dwyer, J. B., Rupp, Z. W., & Bloch, M. H. (2020). Glutamate systems in DSM-5 anxiety disorders: Their role and a review of glutamate and GABA psychopharmacology. *Frontiers in Psychiatry, 11*, 1–17. https://doi.org/10.3389/fpsyt.2020.548505

NASP. (2021). *Who are school psychologists?* https://www.nasponline.org/about-school-psychology/who-are-school-psychologists

Nasser, J. A., Bradley, L. E., Leitzsch, J. B., Chohan, O., Fasulo, K., Haller, J., Jaeger, K., Szulanczyk, B., & Del Parigi, A. (2011). Psychoactive effects of tasting chocolate and desire for more chocolate. *Physiology & Behavior, 104*(1), 117–121. https://doi.org/10.1016/j.physbeh.2011.04.040

National Center for Education Statistics. (2017). *Percentage of 2011–12 first time postsecondary students who had ever* declared a major in an associate's or bachelor's degree program within 3 years of enrollment, by type of degree program and control of first institution: 2014. Institute of Education Sciences, U.S. Department of Education. https://nces.ed.gov/pubs2018/2018434.pdf

National Institute of Mental Health (NIMH). (2021). *Mental health medications*. https://www.nimh.nih.gov/health/topics/mental-health-medications

Nawi, A. M., Ismail, R., Ibrahim, F., Hassan, M. R., Manaf, M. R. A., Amit, N., Ibrahim, N., & Shafurdin, N. S. (2021). Risk and protective factors of drug abuse among adolescents: A systematic review. *BMC Public Health, 21*(1), Article 2088. https://doi.org/10.1186/s12889-021-11906-2

Neath, I., & Surprenant, A. M. (2003). *Human memory: An introduction to research, data, and theory* (2nd ed.). Thomson/Wadsworth.

Neblett, E. W., Jr. (2019). Racism and health: Challenges and future directions in behavioral and psychological research. *Cultural Diversity and Ethnic Minority Psychology, 25*(1), 12–20. https://doi.org/10.1037/cdp0000253

Neider, D. P., Fuse, M., & Suri, G. (2019). Cockroaches, performance, and an audience: Reexamining social facilitation 50 years later. *Journal of Experimental Social Psychology, 85*, Article 103851. https://doi.org/10.1016/j.jesp.2019.103851

Neiss, M., & Rowe, D. C. (2000). Parental education and child's verbal IQ in adoptive and biological families in the National Longitudinal Study of Adolescent Health. *Behavior Genetics, 30*(6), 487–495. https://doi.org/10.1023/A:1010254918997

Neisser, U., & Harsch, N. (1992). Phantom flashbulbs: False recollections of hearing the news about Challenger. In E. Winograd & U. Neisser (Eds.), *Affect and accuracy in recall: Studies of "flashbulb" memories* (pp. 9–31). Cambridge University Press. https://doi.org/10.1017/CBO9780511664069.003

Nelson, B. (1968). Black psychologists' association makes proposals to APA. *Science, 162*(3850), 243. https://doi.org/10.1126/science.162.3850.243

Nelson, S. K., Kushlev, K., & Lyubomirsky, S. (2014). The pains and pleasures of parenting: When, why, and how is parenthood associated with more or less well-being? *Psychological Bulletin, 140*(3), 846–895. https://doi.org/10.1037/a0035444

Nelson, S., Conroy, C., & Logan, D. (2019). The biopsychosocial model of pain in the context of pediatric burn injuries. *European Journal of Pain, 23*(3), 421–434. https://doi.org/10.1002/ejp.1319

Nelson, T. O. (1985). Ebbinghaus's contribution to the measurement of retention: Savings during relearning. *Journal of Experimental Psychology: Learning, Memory, and Cognition, 11*(3), 472–478. https://doi.org/10.1037/0278-7393.11.3.472

Nemeth, D. (2022, August 18). Authentically Gen Z: The values, aspirations & drivers that will re-define the future of work. *Work Design Magazine*. https://www.workdesign.com/2022/08/authentically-gen-z-the-values-aspirations-drivers-that-will-re-define-the-future-of-work/

Neniskyte, U., & Gross, C. (2017). Errant gardeners: Glial-cell-dependent synaptic pruning and neurodevelopmental disorders. *National Review of Neuroscience, 18*, 658–670. https://doi.org/10.1038/nrn.2017.110

Nesse, R. M. (2019). *Good reasons for bad feelings: Insights from the frontier of evolutionary psychiatry*. Penguin.

Nesse, R. M. (2022). Anxiety disorders in evolutionary perspective. In R. Abed & P. St John-Smith (Eds.), *Evolutionary psychiatry: Current perspectives on evolution and mental health* (pp. 101–116). Cambridge University Press. https://dx.doi.org/10.7302/6996

Newell, A., & Simon, H. A. (1972). *Human problem solving*. Prentice-Hall.

Newman, D. L., Moffitt, T. E., Caspi, A., & Silva, P. A. (1998). Comorbid mental disorders: Implications for treatment and sample selection. *Journal of Abnormal Psychology, 107*(2), 305–311. https://doi.org/10.1037/0021-843X.107.2.305

Newport, E. L. (2002). Critical periods in language development. In L. Nadel (Ed.), *The encyclopedia of cognitive science* (pp. 737–740). Macmillan.

Nezlek, J. B. (2001). Daily psychological adjustment and the planfulness of day-to-day behavior. *Journal of Social and Clinical Psychology, 20*(4), 452–475. http://dx.doi.org/10.1521/jscp.20.4.452.22398

Ng, J. Y., Ntoumanis, N., Thøgersen-Ntoumani, C., Deci, E. L., Ryan, R. M., Duda, J. L., & Williams, G. C. (2012). Self-determination theory applied to health contexts: A meta-analysis. *Perspectives on Psychological Science, 7*(4), 325–340. https://doi.org/10.1177/1745691612447309

Ngamaba, K. H., Panagioti, M., & Armitage, C. J. (2017). How strongly related are health status and subjective well-being? Systematic review and meta-analysis. *The European Journal of Public Health, 27*(5), 879–885. https://doi.org/10.1093/eurpub/ckx081

Ngui, E. M., Khasakhala, L., Ndetei, D., & Roberts, L. W. (2010). Mental disorders, health inequalities and ethics: A global perspective. *International Review of Psychiatry, 22*(3), 235–244. https://doi.org/10.3109/09540261.2010.485273

Nguyen, T. P. P., Thibault, D., Hamedani, A. G., Weintraub, D., & Willis, A. W. (2022). Atypical antipsychotic use and mortality risk in Parkinson disease. *Parkinsonism & Related Disorders, 103*, 17–22. https://doi.org/10.1016/j.parkreldis.2022.08.013

Nicholas, A., Haregu, T., Henderson, C., & Armstrong, G. (2023). Suicide stigma measures: A scoping review. *Journal of Affective Disorders, 321*, 114–125. https://doi.org/10.1016/j.jad.2022.10.023

Nicholson, I. A. M. (2011). "Torture at Yale": Experimental subjects, laboratory torment and the "rehabilitation" of Milgram's "obedience to authority." *Theory & Psychology, 21*(6), 737–761. https://doi.org/10.1177/0959354311420199

Nicholson, I. A. M. (2015). The normalization of torment: Producing and managing anguish in Milgram's "Obedience" laboratory. *Theory & Psychology, 25*(5), 639–656. https://doi.org/10.1177/0959354315605393

Nickerson, R. S. (1998). Confirmation bias: A ubiquitous phenomenon in many guises. *Review of General Psychology, 2*(2), 175–220. https://doi.org/10.1037/1089-2680.2.2.175

Nieder, A., Wagener, L., & Rinnert, P. (2020). A neural correlate of sensory consciousness in a corvid bird. *Science, 369*(6511), 1626–1629. https://doi.org/10.1126/science.abb1447

Niego, A., & Benítez-Burraco, A. (2022). Revisiting the case for "feral" humans under the light of the human self-domestication hypothesis: focusing on language. *Biolinguistics, 16*, 1–55. https://doi.org/10.5964/bioling.9319

Nielsen, J. A., Zielinski, B. A., Ferguson, M. A., Lainhart, J. E., & Anderson, J. S. (2013). An evaluation of the left-brain vs. right-brain hypothesis with resting state functional connectivity magnetic resonance imaging. *PLoS ONE, 8*(8), e71275. https://doi.org/10.1371/journal.pone.0071275

Niesta Kayser, D., Elliot, A. J., & Feltman, R. (2010). Red and romantic behavior in men viewing women. *European Journal of Social Psychology, 40*(6), 901–908. https://doi.org/10.1002/ejsp.757

Nijboer, M., Borst, J. P., van Rijn, H., & Taatgen, N. A. (2016). Driving and multitasking: The good, the bad, and the dangerous. *Frontiers in Psychology, 7*, 1–16. https://doi.org/10.3389/fpsyg.2016.01718

Nilsen, A. B. V., Waldenström, U., Hjelmsted, A., Rasmussen, S., & Schytt, E. (2012). Characteristics of women who are pregnant with their first baby at an advanced age. *Acta Obstetricia et Gynecologica Scandinavica, 91*(3), 353–362x. https://doi.org/10.1111/j.1600-0412.2011.01335.x

Nissen, M. J., Ross, J. L., Willingham, D. B., Mackenzie, T. B., & Schacter, D. L. (1988). Memory and awareness in a patient with multiple personality disorder. *Brain and Cognition, 8*(1), 117–134. https://doi.org/10.1016/0278-2626(88)90043-7

Nolen-Hoeksema, S., Wisco, B. E., & Lyubomirsky, S. (2008). Rethinking rumination. *Perspectives on Psychological Science*, *3*(5), 400–424. https://doi.org/10.1111/j.1745-6924.2008.00088.x

Nordstrom, A., & Goodfriend, W. (Eds.). (2021). *Innovative stigma and discrimination reduction programs across the world*. Routledge.

Nosek, B. A., Ebersole, C. R., DeHaven, A. C., & Mellor, D. T. (2017, June 16). *The preregistration revolution*. https://doi.org/10.1073/pnas.1708274114

Nosofsky, R. M., Kruschke, J. K., & McKinley, S. C. (1992). Combining exemplar-based category representations and connectionist learning rules. *Journal of Experimental Psychology: Learning, Memory, and Cognition*, *18*(2), 211–233. https://doi.org/10.1037/0278-7393.18.2.211

Noushad, B., & Khurshid, F. (2019). Facilitating student learning: An instructional design perspective for health professions educators. *Research and Development in Medical Education*, *8*(2), 69–74. https://doi.org/10.15171/rdme.2019.014

Nowicki, S., & Duke, M. P. (2017). Foundations of locus of control. In J. W. Reich & F. J. Infurna (Eds.), *Perceived control: theory, research, and practice in the first 50 years* (pp. 147–170). Oxford University Press.

Nunberg, G. (1996). Snowblind. *Natural Language and Linguistic Theory*, *14*(1), 205–213. https://www.jstor.org/stable/4047883

Nussbaumer-Streit, B., Forneris, C. A., Morgan, L. C., Van Noord, M. G., Gaynes, B. N., Greenblatt, A., Wipplinger, J., Lux, L. J., Winkler, D., & Gartlehner, G. (2019). Light therapy for preventing seasonal affective disorder. *Cochrane Database of Systematic Reviews*, *3*, Article CD011269. https://doi.org/10.1002/14651858.CD011269.pub3

Nwosu, K. C., Ikwuka, O. I., Onyinyechi, M. U., & Unachukwu, G. C. (2020). Does the association of social media use with problematic internet behaviours predict undergraduate students' academic procrastination? *Canadian Journal of Learning and Technology*, *46*(1), n1.

O'Brien, T. (2023). Heed warnings gleaned from hazing case at Northwestern. *College Athletics and the Law*, *20*(6), 1–7. https://doi.org/10.1002/catl.31215

O'Connor, R. D. (1972). Relative efficacy of modeling, shaping, and the combined procedures for modification of social withdrawal. *Journal of Abnormal Psychology*, *79*(3), 327–334. https://doi.org/10.1037/h0033226

O'Haire, M. (2010). Companion animals and human health: Benefits, challenges, and the road ahead. *Journal of Veterinary Behavior*, *5*(5), 226–234. https://doi.org/10.1016/j.jveb.2010.02.002

O'Laughlin, E. M., & Anderson, V. N. (2001). Perceptions of parenthood among young adults: Implications for career and family planning. *American Journal of Family Therapy*, *29*(2), 95–108. https://doi.org/10.1080/01926180125728

O'Sullivan, M. (2007). Unicorns or Tiger Woods: Are lie detection experts myths or rarities? A response to on lie detection "wizards" by Bond and Uysal. *Law and Human Behavior*, *31*, 117–123. https://doi.org/10.1007/s10979-006-9058-4

O'Sullivan, M., & Ekman, P. (2004). The wizards of deception detection. In P.-A. Granhag & L. Strömwall (Eds.), *The detection of deception in forensic contexts* (pp. 269–286). Cambridge University Press. https://doi.org/10.1017/CBO9780511490071.012

Obeid, S., & Hallit, S. (2018). Correlation of the Stockholm syndrome and early maladaptive schemas among Lebanese women victims of beating into domestic/marital violence. *Couple and Family Psychology: Research and Practice*, *7*(3–4), 171–182. https://doi.org/10.1037/cfp0000106

Obermaier, M., Fawzi, N., & Koch, T. (2016). Bystanding or standing by? How the number of bystanders affects the intention to intervene in cyberbullying. *New Media & Society*, *18*(8), 1491–1507. https://doi.org/10.1177/1461444814563519

Ochse, R., & Plug, C. (1986). Cross-cultural investigation of the validity of Erikson's theory of personality development. *Journal of Personality and Social Psychology*, *50*(6), 1240–1252. http://doi.org/10.1037/0022-3514.50.6.1240

Odagaki, Y. (2017). A case of persistent generalized retrograde autobiographical amnesia subsequent to the great east Japan earthquake in 2011. *Case Reports in Psychiatry*, *2017*, Article 5173605. https://doi.org/10.1155/2017/5173605

Oexle, N., & Corrigan, P. W. (2018). Understanding mental illness stigma toward persons with multiple stigmatized conditions: Implications of intersectionality theory. *Psychiatric Services*, *69*(5), 587–589. https://doi.org/10.1176/appi.ps.201700312

Ogunfowora, B., Bourdage, J. S., & Nguyen, B. (2013). An exploration of the dishonest side of self-monitoring: Links to moral disengagement and unethical business decision making. *European Journal of Personality*, *27*(6), 532–544. https://doi.org/10.1002/per.1931

Ogunsakin, R. E., Olugbara, O. O., Moyo, S., & Israel, C. (2021). Meta-analysis of studies on depression prevalence among diabetes mellitus patients in Africa. *Heliyon*, *7*(5), e07085. https://doi.org/10.1016/j.heliyon.2021.e07085

Ohayon, M. M., Ferini-Strambi, L., Plazzi, G., Smirne, S., & Castronovo, V. (2005). Frequency of narcolepsy symptoms and other sleep disorders in narcoleptic patients and their first-degree relatives. *Journal of Sleep Research*, *14*(4), 437–445. https://doi.org/10.1111/j.1365-2869.2005.00476.x

Okagaki, L., & Sternberg, R. J. (1993). Parental beliefs and children's school performance. *Child Development*, *64*(1), 36–56. https://doi.org/10.1111/j.1467-8624.1993.tb02894.x

Okano, K., Kaczmarzyk, J., Dave, N., Gabrieli, J., & Grossman, J. (2019). Sleep quality, duration, and consistency are associated with better academic performance in college students. *NPJ Science of Learning*, *4*, Article 16. https://doi.org/10.1038/s41539-019-0055-z

Ong, C. W., Lee, E. B., & Twohig, M. P. (2018). A meta-analysis of dropout rates in acceptance and commitment therapy. *Behaviour Research and Therapy*, *104*, 14–33. https://doi.org/10.1016/j.brat.2018.02.004

Onyango, V. C. (2023). Reflections on the Robbers Cave Experiment: Finding lessons on political conflict, racism, xenophobia, and business environments. *American Journal of Human Psychology*, *1*(1), 34–38. https://doi.org/10.54536/ajhp.v1i1.2092

Oouchida, Y., Suzuki, E., Aizu, N., Takeuchi, N., & Izumi, S. (2013). Applications of observational learning in neurorehabilitation. *International Journal of Physical Medicine & Rehabilitation*, *1*(5), Article 1000146. https://doi.org/10.4172/2329-9096.1000146

Open Science Collaboration. (2017). Maximizing the reproducibility of your research. In S. O. Lilienfeld & I. D. Waldman (Eds.), *Psychological science under scrutiny: Recent challenges and proposed solutions*. Wiley.

Oppezzo, M., & Schwartz, D. L. (2014). Give your ideas some legs: The positive effect of walking on creative thinking. *Journal of Experimental Psychology: Learning, Memory, and Cognition*, *40*(4), 1142–1152. https://doi.org/10.1037/a0036577

Opriş, D., Pintea, S., Garcia-Palacios, A., Botella, C., Szamosközi, Ş., & David, D. (2012). Virtual reality exposure therapy in anxiety disorders: A quantitative meta-analysis. *Depression and Anxiety*, *29*(2), 85–93. https://doi.org/10.1002/da.20910

Örge, E., & Volkan, E. (2023). Effect of childhood traumas on eating disorders: Systematic review. *Psikiyatride Güncel Yaklaşımlar*, *15*(4), 652–664. https://doi.org/10.18863/pgy.1216836

Orgler, H. (1963). *Alfred Adler: The man and his work*. Liveright.

Osborn, A. F. (1963). *Applied imagination: Principles and procedures of creative problem-solving*. Charles Scribner's Sons.

Ose Askvik, E., Van der Weel, F. R., & van der Meer, A. L. (2020). The importance of cursive handwriting over typewriting for learning in the classroom: A high-density EEG study of 12-year-old children and young adults. *Frontiers in Psychology, 11,* 1–16. https://doi.org/10.3389/fpsyg.2020.01810

Öst, L.-G., Enebrink, P., Finnes, A., Ghaderi, A., Havnen, A., Kvale, G., Salomonsson, S., & Wergeland, G. J. (2023). Cognitive behavior therapy for adult anxiety disorders in routine clinical care: A systematic review and meta-analysis. *Clinical Psychology: Science and Practice, 30*(3), 272–290. https://doi.org/10.1037/cps0000144

Ottoni-Wilhelm, M., Vesterlund, L., & Xie, H. (2017). Why do people give? Testing pure and impure altruism. *American Economic Review, 107*(11), 3617–3633. https://doi.org/10.1257/aer.20141222

Owen, A. M., Hampshire, A., Grahn, J. A., Stenton, R., Dajani, S., Burns, A. S., Howard, R. J., & Ballard, C. G. (2010). Putting brain training to the test. *Nature, 465*(7299), 775–778. https://doi.org/10.1038/nature09042

Owen, P. R. (2012). Portrayals of schizophrenia by entertainment media: A content analysis of contemporary movies. *Psychiatric Services, 63*(7), 655–659. https://doi.org/10.1176/appi.ps.201100371

Owen, S. S., Burke, T. W., & Vichesky, D. (2008). Hazing in student organizations: Prevalence, attitudes, and solutions. *Oracle: The Research Journal of the Association of Fraternity/Sorority Advisors, 3*(1), 40–58. https://doi.org/10.25774/7s24-ez41

Pace-Schott, E. F., & Hobson, J. A. (2002). The neurobiology of sleep: Genetics, cellular physiology and subcortical networks. *Nature Reviews Neuroscience, 3*(8), 591–605. https://doi.org/10.1038/nrn895

Pacheco-Colón, I., Limia, J. M., & Gonzalez, R. (2018). Nonacute effects of cannabis use on motivation and reward sensitivity in humans: A systematic review. *Psychology of Addictive Behaviors, 32*(5), 497–507. https://doi.org/10.1037/adb0000380

Pai, A., Suris, A. M., & North, C. S. (2017). Posttraumatic stress disorder in the DSM-5: Controversy, change, and conceptual considerations. *Behavioral Sciences, 7*(1), 1–7. https://doi.org/10.3390/bs7010007

Pakpahan, F. H., & Saragih, M. (2022). Theory of cognitive development by Jean Piaget. *Journal of Applied Linguistics, 2*(1), 55–60. https://doi.org/10.52622/joal.v2i2.79

Palomero-Gallagher, N., & Amunts, K. (2022). A short review on emotion processing: A lateralized network of neuronal networks. *Brain Structure and Function, 227,* 673–682. https://doi.org/10.1007/s00429-021-02331-7

Pang, Y., Song, C., & Ma, C. (2022). Effect of different types of empathy on prosocial behavior: Gratitude as mediator. *Frontiers in Psychology, 13,* Article 768827. https://doi.org/10.3389/fpsyg.2022.768827

Pani, M., & Parida, S. K. (2000). Effect of culture on cognitive development. *Psycho-Lingua, 30*(1), 51–55.

Papadopoulos, S., & Brennan, L. (2015). Correlates of weight stigma in adults with overweight and obesity: A systematic literature review. *Obesity, 23*(9), 1743–1760. https://doi.org/10.1002/oby.21187

Pardo-Cebrian, R., Virues-Ortega, J., Calero-Elvira, A., & Guerrero-Escagedo, M. C. (2022). Toward an experimental analysis of verbal shaping in psychotherapy. *Psychotherapy Research, 32*(4), 497–510. https://doi.org/10.1080/10503307.2021.1955418

Park, G., Yaden, D. B., Schwartz, H. A., Kern, M. L., Eichstaedt, J. C., Kosinski, M., Stillwell, D., Ungar, L. H., & Seligman, M. E. (2016). Women are warmer but no less assertive than men: Gender and language on Facebook. *PloS One, 11*(5), e0155885. https://doi.org/10.1371/journal.pone.0155885

Park, H. J. (2022). Impact of Facebook usage intensity on fear of missing out and depression: moderated mediating effect of Facebook usage behaviour. *Telematics and Informatics, 74,* 1–11. https://doi.org/10.1016/j.tele.2022.101878

Parker, S. T. (1991). A developmental approach to the origins of self-recognition in great apes. *Human Evolution, 6*(5–6), 435–449. https://doi.org/10.1007/BF02435535

Parker, T., & Stone, M. (Producers), & Parker, T. (Director). (1999). *South Park: Bigger, longer, & uncut* [Motion picture]. Paramount.

Parrino, L., & Vaudano, A. E. (2018). The resilient brain and the guardians of sleep: New perspectives on old assumptions. *Sleep Medicine Reviews, 39,* 98–107. https://doi.org/10.1016/j.smrv.2017.08.003

Parrott, A. C. (2013). MDMA, serotonergic neurotoxicity, and the diverse functional deficits of recreational "Ecstasy" users. *Neuroscience & Biobehavioral Reviews, 37*(8), 1466–1484. https://doi.org/10.1016/j.neubiorev.2013.04.016

Pascoe, M. C., Hetrick, S. E., & Parker, A. G. (2020). The impact of stress on students in secondary school and higher education. *International Journal of Adolescence and Youth, 25*(1), 104–112. https://doi.org/10.1080/02673843.2019.1596823

Pashak, T. J., Conley, M. A., Whitney, D. J., Oswald, S. R., Heckroth, S. G., & Schumacher, E. M. (2018). Empathy diminishes prejudice: Active perspective-taking, regardless of target and mortality salience, decreases implicit racial bias. *Psychology, 9*(6), Article 1340.

Passamonti, L., Riccelli, R., Lacquaniti, F., Staab, J. P., & Indovina, I. (2018). Brain responses to virtual reality visual motion stimulation are affected by neurotic personality traits in patients with persistent postural-perceptual dizziness. *Journal of Vestibular Research: Equilibrium & Orientation, 28*(5–6), 369–378. https://doi.org/10.3233/VES-190653

Patihis, L., & Pendergrast, M. H. (2019). Reports of recovered memories of abuse in therapy in a large age-representative US national sample: Therapy type and decade comparisons. *Clinical Psychological Science, 7*(1), 3–21. https://doi.org/10.1177/2167702618773315

Patihis, L., Ho, L. Y., Loftus, E. F., & Herrera, M. E. (2021). Memory experts' beliefs about repressed memory. *Memory, 29*(6), 823–828. https://doi.org/10.1080/09658211.2018.1532521

Patil, A. U., Lin, C., Lee, S. H., Huang, H. W., Wu, S. C., Madathil, D., & Huang, C. M. (2023). Review of EEG-based neurofeedback as a therapeutic intervention to treat depression. *Psychiatry Research: Neuroimaging, 329,* Article 111591. https://doi.org/10.1016/j.pscychresns.2023.111591

Patrick, M. E., & Schulenberg, J. E. (2014). Prevalence and predictors of adolescent alcohol use and binge drinking in the United States. *Alcohol Research: Current Reviews, 35*(2), 193–200.

Patton, L. D., Renn, K. A., Guido, F. M., & Quaye, S. J. (2016). *Student development in college: Theory, research, and practice.* John Wiley.

Paul, D. B. (2014). What was wrong with eugenics? Conflicting narratives and disputed interpretations. *Science & Education, 23*(2), 259–271. https://doi.org/10.1007/s11191-012-9556-3

Paul, D., & Vasudevan, M. H. (2021). Exploring mortality salience and pandemic impact in the context of COVID-19. *OMEGA—Journal of Death and Dying, 88*(3), 889–907. https://doi.org/10.1177/00302228211056221

Paulhus, D. L., & Williams, K. M. (2002). The dark triad of personality: Narcissism, Machiavellianism and psychopathy. *Journal of Research in Personality, 36*(6), 556–563. https://doi.org/10.1016/S0092-6566(02)00505-6

Pavlov, I. P. (1927). *Conditioned reflexes: An investigation of the physiological activity of the cerebral cortex.* Oxford University Press.

Paxson, C., Fussell, E., Rhodes, J., & Waters, M. (2012). Five years later: Recovery from post traumatic stress and psychological distress among low-income mothers affected by Hurricane Katrina. *Social Science & Medicine, 74*(2), 150–157. https://doi.org/10.1016/j.socscimed.2011.10.004

Peake, P. K., Hebl, M., & Mischel, W. (2002). Strategic attention deployment for delay of gratification in working and waiting situations. *Developmental Psychology, 38*(2), 313–326. https://doi.org/10.1037/0012-1649.38.2.313

Pearcey, S., Gordon, K., Chakrabarti, B., Dodd, H., Halldorsson, B., & Creswell, C. (2021). Research review: The relationship between social anxiety and social cognition in children and adolescents: A systematic review and meta-analysis. *Journal of Child Psychology and Psychiatry*, *62*(7), 805–821. https://doi .org/10.1111/jcpp.13310

Pearl, R. L., & Puhl, R. M. (2018). Weight bias internalization and health: A systematic review. *Obesity Reviews*, *19*(8), 1141–1163. https://doi.org/10.1111/obr.12701

Pedersen, D. M., & Wheeler, J. (1983). The Müller-Lyer illusion among Navajos. *Journal of Social Psychology*, *121*(1), 3–6. https://doi.org/10.1080/00224545.1983.9924459

Pedersen, P. B. (2001). Multiculturalism and the paradigm shift in counselling: Controversies and alternative futures. *Canadian Journal of Counselling and Psychotherapy*, *35*(1), 15–25.

Penfield, W., & Perot, P. (1963). The brain's record of auditory and visual experience: A final summary and discussion. *Brain: A Journal of Neurology*, *86*(4), 595–696. https://doi.org/10.1093/ brain/86.4.595

Peng, K., & Nisbett, R. E. (1999). Culture, dialectics, and reasoning about contradiction. *American Psychologist*, *54*(9), 741–754. https://doi.org/10.1037/0003-066X.54.9.741

Penley, J. A., Tomaka, J., & Wiebe, J. S. (2002). The association of coping to physical and psychological health outcomes: A meta-analytic review. *Journal of Behavioral Medicine*, *25*(6), 551–603. https://doi.org/10.1023/A:1020641400589

Penney, D., & Stastny, P. (2009). *The lives they left behind: Suitcases from a state hospital attic*. Bellevue Literary Press.

Penney, T. L., & Kirk, S. F. (2015). The health at every size paradigm and obesity: Missing empirical evidence may help push the reframing obesity debate forward. *American Journal of Public Health*, *105*(5), e38–e42. https://doi.org/10.2105%2 FAJPH.2015.302552

Perciful, M. S., & Meyer, C. (2017). The impact of films on viewer attitudes towards people with schizophrenia. *Current Psychology*, *36*(3), 483–493. https://doi.org/10.1007/s12144-016- 9436-0

Perego, M., Tyurin, V. A., Tyurina, Y. Y., Yellets, J., Nacarelli, T., Lin, C., Nefedova, Y., Kossenkov, A., Liu, Q., Sreedhar, S., Pass, H., Roth, J., Vogl, T., Feldser, D., Zhang, R., Kagan, V., & Gabrilovich, D. I. (2020). Reactivation of dormant tumor cells by modified lipids derived from stress-activated neutrophils. *Science Translational Medicine*, *12*(572), 1–16. https://doi.org/10.1126/scitranslmed. abb5817

Perez, V. W., & Friedman, A. (2023). Misophonia matters: A case study of the role of brain imaging in debates over new diagnoses. *Sociology of Health & Illness*, *46*, 1–18. https://doi .org/10.1111/1467-9566.13679

Perls, F., Hefferline, G., & Goodman, P. (1951). *Gestalt therapy*. Julian Press.

Perry, D. G., & Bussey, K. (1979). The social learning theory of sex differences: Imitation is alive and well. *Journal of Personality and Social Psychology*, *37*(10), 1699–1712. https://doi. org/10.1037/0022-3514.37.10.1699

Perry, G. (2013). *Behind the shock machine: The untold story of the notorious Milgram psychology experiments*. New Press.

Perry, L. R., Moorhouse, T. P., Jacobsen, K., Loveridge, A. J., & Macdonald, D. W. (2022). More than a feeling: Cognitive beliefs and positive—but not negative—affect predict overall attitudes toward predators. *Conservation Science and Practice*, *4*(2), Article e584. https://doi.org/10.1111/csp2.584

Persaud, R., & Bruggen, P. (2016, February 14). Does the color red hold the secret to attraction? *Psychology Today*. https://www .psychologytoday.com/blog/slightly-blighty/201602/does- the-color-red-hold-the-secret-attraction

Peteet, J. R. (2018). A fourth wave of psychotherapies: Moving beyond recovery toward well-being. *Harvard Review*

of *Psychiatry*, *26*(2), 90–95. https://doi.org/10.1097/ HRP.0000000000000155

Petit, J.-M., Burlet-Godinot, S., Magistretti, P. J., & Allaman, I. (2015). Glycogen metabolism and the homeostatic regulation of sleep. *Metabolic Brain Disease*, *30*(1), 263–279. https://doi.org/10.1007/ s11011-014-9629-x

Petticrew, M. P., Lee, K., & McKee, M. (2012). Type A behavior pattern and coronary heart disease: Philip Morris's "crown jewel." *American Journal of Public Health*, *102*(11), 2018–2025. https:// doi.org/10.2105/AJPH.2012.300816

Pew Research Internet Project. (2013). Online dating and relationships. http://www.pewinternet.org/2013/10/21/online- dating-relationships/

Pfattheicher, S., Nielsen, Y. A., & Thielmann, I. (2022). Prosocial behavior and altruism: A review of concepts and definitions. *Current Opinion in Psychology*, *44*, 124–129. https://doi .org/10.1016/j.copsyc.2021.08.021

Phelps, E. A., & Hofmann, S. G. (2019). Memory editing from science fiction to clinical practice. *Nature*, *572*(7767), 43–50. https://doi .org/10.1038/s41586-019-1433-7

Phillips, L. M. (2000). *Flirting with danger*. New York University Press.

Phillips, M. L., Medford, N., Senior, C., Bullmore, E. T., Suckling, J., Brammer, M. J., Andrew, C., Sierra, M., Williams, S. C. R., & David, A. S. (2001). Depersonalization disorder: Thinking without feeling. *Psychiatry Research: Neuroimaging*, *108*(3), 145–160. https://doi.org/10.1016/S0925-4927(01)00119-6

Piaget, J. (1930). *The child's conception of physical causality*. Routledge & Kegan Paul.

Piaget, J. (1932). *The moral judgment of the child*. Harcourt, Brace & World.

Pickens, T. A., Khan, S. P., & Berlau, D. J. (2018). White noise as a possible therapeutic option for children with ADHD. *Complementary Therapies in Medicine*, *42*, 151–155. https://doi .org/10.1016/j.ctim.2018.11.012

Pieterse, A. L., Roberson, K. L., Garcia, R., & Carter, R. T. (2022). Racial discrimination and trauma symptoms: Further support for the Race-Based Traumatic Stress Symptom Scale. *Cultural Diversity and Ethnic Minority Psychology*, *29*(3), 332–338. https://doi .org/10.1037/cdp0000544

Pigott, H. E., Leventhal, A. M., Alter, G. S., & Boren, J. J. (2010). Efficacy and effectiveness of antidepressants: Current status of research. *Psychotherapy and Psychosomatics*, *79*(5), 267–279. https://doi.org/10.1159/000318293

Piliavin, J. A., & Piliavin, I. M. (1972). Effect of blood on reactions to a victim. *Journal of Personality and Social Psychology*, *23*(3), 353–361. https://doi.org/10.1037/h0033166

Pilley, J., & Reid, A. (2011). Border collie comprehends object names as verbal referents. *Behavioural Processes*, *86*(2), 184–195. https://doi.org/10.1016/j.beproc.2010.11.007

Pillow, D. R., Hale, W. J., Jr., Crabtree, M. A., & Hinojosa, T. L. (2017). Exploring the relations between self-monitoring, authenticity, and well-being. *Personality and Individual Differences*, *116*, 393–398. https://doi.org/10.1016/j.paid.2017.04.060

Pinker, S. (1997). *How the mind works*. Norton.

Pinter, A. T., Scheuerman, M. K., & Brubaker, J. R. (2021). Entering doors, evading traps: Benefits and risks of visibility during transgender coming outs. *Proceedings of the ACM on Human-Computer Interaction*, *4*(CSCW3), 1–27. https://doi .org/10.1145/3434181

Pitman, R. K., Orr, S. P., Forgue, D. F., de Jong, J. B., & Claiborn, J. M. (1987). Psychophysiologic assessment of posttraumatic stress disorder imagery in Vietnam combat veterans. *Archives of General Psychiatry*, *44*(11), 970–975. https://doi.org/10.1001/ archpsyc.1987.01800230050009

Pitt, A., Oprescu, F., Tapia, G., & Gray, M. (2018). An exploratory study of students' weekly stress levels and sources of stress during the semester. *Active Learning in Higher Education*, *19*(1), 61–75. https://doi.org/10.1177/1469787417731194

Pittenger, D. J. (1993). Measuring the MBTI . . . and coming up short. *Journal of Career Planning and Employment*, *54*(1), 48–52.

Pittenger, D. J. (2005). Cautionary comments regarding the Myers-Briggs Type Indicator. *Consulting Psychology Journal: Practice and Research*, *57*(3), 210–221. https://doi.org/10.1037/1065-9293.57.3.210

Pizzagalli, D. A., Sherwood, R. J., Henriques, J. B., & Davidson, R. J. (2005). Frontal brain asymmetry and reward responsiveness: A source-localization study. *Psychological Science*, *16*(10), 805–813. https://doi.org/10.1111/j.1467-9280.2005.01618.x

Plato. (1962). Phaedo. In E. Hamilton & H. Cairns (Eds.), *The collected dialogues of Plato, including the letters* (pp. 40–98). Pantheon Books.

Plomin, R., & von Stumm, S. (2018). The new genetics of intelligence. *Genetics*, *19*(3), 148–159. https://doi.org/10.1038/nrg.2017.104

Plomin, R., Corley, R., DeFries, J. C., & Fulker, D. W. (1990). Individual differences in television viewing in early childhood: Nature as well as nurture. *Psychological Science*, *1*(6), 371–377. https://doi.org/10.1111/j.1467-9280.1990.tb00244.x

Plotnik, J. M., de Waal, F. M., & Reiss, D. (2006). Self-recognition in an Asian elephant. *PNAS Proceedings of the National Academy of Sciences of the United States of America*, *103*(45), 17053–17057. https://doi.org/10.1073/pnas.0608062103

Plutchik, R. (2001). The nature of emotions: Human emotions have deep evolutionary roots, a fact that may explain their complexity and provide tools for clinical practice. *American scientist*, *89*(4), 344–350. https://www.jstor.org/stable/27857503

Polce-Lynch, M., Myers, B. J., Kilmartin, C. T., Forssmann-Falck, R., & Kliewer, W. (1998). Gender and age patterns in emotional expression, body image, and self-esteem: A qualitative analysis. *Sex Roles*, *38*(11–12), 1025–1048. https://doi.org/10.1023/A:1018830727244

Polivy, J., & Herman, C. P. (2002). Causes of eating disorders. *Annual Review of Psychology*, *53*(1), 187–213. https://doi.org/10.1146/annurev.psych.53.100901.135103

Pollak, S., Cicchetti, D., & Klorman, R. (1998). Stress, memory, and emotion: Developmental considerations from the study of child maltreatment. *Development and Psychopathology*, *10*(4), 811–828. https://doi.org/10.1017/S0954579498001886

Pollet, T. V., Dijkstra, P., Barelds, D. P., & Buunk, A. P. (2010). Birth order and the dominance aspect of extraversion: Are firstborns more extraverted, in the sense of being dominant, than laterborns? *Journal of Research in Personality*, *44*(6), 742–745. https://doi.org/10.1016/j.jrp.2010.10.002

Pons-Espinal, M., Gasperini, C., Marzi, M. J., Braccia, C., Armirotti, A., Pötzsch, A., Walker, T. L., Fabel, K., Nicassio, F., Kempermann, G., & Tonelli, D. D. P. (2019). MiR-135a-5p is critical for exercise-induced adult neurogenesis. *Stem Cell Reports*, *12*(6), 1298–1312. https://doi.org/10.1016/j.stemcr.2019.04.020

Popper, K. R. (1963). Science as falsification. *Conjectures and Refutations*, *1*, 33–39.

Positive Time Out. (2020). *Positive discipline: Creative respectful relationships in homes and schools*. https://www.positivediscipline.com/articles/positive-time-out

Poulson, C. L., Nunes, L. R., & Warren, S. F. (1989). Imitation in infancy: A critical review. *Advances in Child Development and Behavior*, *22*, 271–298. https://doi.org/10.1016/S0065-2407(08)60417-6

Powell, R. A., Digdon, N., Harris, B., & Smithson, C. (2014). Correcting the record on Watson, Rayner, and Little Albert: Albert Barger as "Psychology's lost boy." *American Psychologist*, *69*(6), 600–611. https://doi.org/10.1037/a0036854

Power, R. A., Steinberg, S., Bjornsdottir, G., Rietveld, C. A., Abdellaoui, A., Nivard, M. M., Johannesson, M., Galesloot, T. E.,

Hottenga, J. J., Willemsen, G., Cesarini, D., Benjamin, D. J., Magnusson, P. K. E., Ullen, F., Tiemeier, H., Hofman, A., van Rooij, F. J. A., Walters, G. B., Sigurdsson, E., Thorgeirsson, T. E., . . . Stefansson, K. (2015). Polygenic risk scores for schizophrenia and bipolar disorder predict creativity. *Nature Neuroscience*, *18*(7), 953–955. https://doi.org/10.1038/nn.4040

Powers, J. M., Zale, E. L., Deyo, A. G., Rubenstein, D., Terry, E. L., Heckman, B. W., & Ditre, J. W. (2023). Pain and menthol use are related to greater nicotine dependence among Black adults who smoke cigarettes at wave 5 (2018–2019) of the Population Assessment of Tobacco and Health (PATH) Study. *Journal of Racial and Ethnic Health Disparities*, *10*(5), 2407–2416. https://doi.org/10.1007/s40615-022-01419-y

Powers, M. B., & Emmelkamp, P. M. (2008). Virtual reality exposure therapy for anxiety disorders: A meta-analysis. *Journal of Anxiety Disorders*, *22*(3), 561–569. https://doi.org/10.1016/j.janxdis.2007.04.006

Praszkier, R. (2016). Empathy, mirror neurons and SYNC. *Mind & Society*, *15*(1), 1–25. https://doi.org/10.1007/s11299-014-0160-x

Pratt, L. A., Brody, D. J., & Gu, Q. (2017). *Antidepressant use among persons aged 12 and over: United States, 2011-2014* (NCHS Data Brief No. 283). National Center for Health Statistics.

Praveen, S. K., Ganesha, K. S., & Sinnoor, G. B. (2020). Social media addiction and youths. *4th International Conference on Marketing, Technology & Society*. https://iimk.ac.in/research/markconf20/Proceedings/64.pdf

Preckel, F., Lipnevich, A. A., Boehme, K., Brandner, L., Georgi, K., Könen, T., Mursin, K., & Roberts, R. D. (2013). Morningness-eveningness and educational outcomes: The lark has an advantage over the owl at high school. *British Journal of Educational Psychology*, *83*(1), 114–134. https://doi.org/10.1111/j.2044-8279.2011.02059.x

Price, R. (1953). *Droodles*. Simon & Schuster.

Prior, A., & MacWhinney, B. (2010). A bilingual advantage in task switching. *Bilingualism: Language and Cognition*, *13*(2), 253–262. https://doi.org/10.1017/S1366728909990526

Prior, H., Schwarz, A., & Güntürkün, O. (2008). Mirror-induced behavior in the magpie (Pica pica): Evidence of self-recognition. *PLoS Biology*, *6*(8), e202. https://doi.org/10.1371/journal.pbio.0060202

Prosper, T., Gushue, G. V., & Lee, T. R. (2021). Promoting African American activism: Experiences of racism-related stress and spirituality. *Journal of Black Psychology*, *47*(8), 657–668. https://doi.org/10.1177/00957984211034949

Protzko, J., & Schooler, J. W. (2019). Kids these days: Why the youth of today seem lacking. *Science Advances*, *5*(10), 1–6. https://doi.org/10.1126/sciadv.aav5916

Pruysers, S., Blais, J., & Chen, P. G. (2019). Who makes a good citizen? The role of personality. *Personality and Individual Differences*, *146*, 99–104. https://doi.org/10.1016/j.paid.2019.04.007

Pullum, G. (1991). *The great Eskimo vocabulary hoax and other irreverent essays on the study of language*. University of Chicago Press.

Putnam, A. L. (2015). Mnemonics in education: Current research and applications. *Translational Issues in Psychological Science*, *1*(2), 130–139. https://doi.org/10.1037/tps0000023

Putwain, D., & Remedios, R. (2014). The scare tactic: Do fear appeals predict motivation and exam scores? *School Psychology Quarterly*, *29*(4), 503–516. https://doi.org/10.1037/spq0000048

Pyszczynski, T., Greenberg, J., & Solomon, S. (1999). A dual-process model of defense against conscious and unconscious death-related thoughts: An extension of terror management theory. *Psychological Review*, *106*(4), 835–845. https://doi.org/10.1037/0033-295X.106.4.835

Pyszczynski, T., Solomon, S., & Greenberg, J. (2003). *In the wake of 9/11*. American Psychological Association.

Pyszczynski, T., Solomon, S., & Greenberg, J. (2015). Thirty years of terror management theory: From genesis to revelation. *Advances in Experimental Social Psychology, 52*, 1–70. https://doi.org/10.1016/bs.aesp.2015.03.001

Pyszczynski, T., Wicklund, R. A., Floresku, S., Koch, H., Gauch, G., Solomon, S., & Greenberg, J. (1996). Whistling in the dark: Exaggerated consensus estimates in response to incidental reminders of mortality. *Psychological Science, 7*(6), 332–336. https://doi.org/10.1111/j.1467-9280.1996.tb00384.x

Pyszczynski, T., Wicklund, R. A., Floresku, S., Koch, H., Gauch, G., Solomon, S., & Greenberg, J. (1996). Whistling in the dark: Exaggerated consensus estimates in response to incidental reminders of mortality. *Psychological Science, 7*(6), 332–336. https://doi.org/10.1111/j.1467-9280.1996.tb00384.x

Pytell, T. (2007). Extreme experience, psychological insight, and Holocaust perception: Reflections on Bettelheim and Frankl. *Psychoanalytic Psychology, 24*(4), 641–657. https://doi.org/10.1037/0736-9735.24.4.641

Qiongjing, H., Xi, L., & Zhixue, Z. (2018). Self-monitoring in group context: Its indirect benefits for individual status attainment and group task performance. *Acta Psychologica Sinica, 50*(10), 1169–1179. https://doi.org/10.3724/SP.J.1041.2018.01169

Quinn, M., Narozanick, T., Miltenberger, R., Greenberg, L., & Schenk, M. (2020). Evaluating video modeling and video modeling with video feedback to enhance the performance of competitive dancers. *Behavioral Interventions, 35*(1), 76–83. https://doi.org/10.1002/bin.1691

Raaijmakers, J. G., & Shiffrin, R. M. (1992). Models for recall and recognition. *Annual Review of Psychology, 43*, 205–234. https://doi.org/10.1146/annurev.ps.43.020192.001225

Raedts, M., Rijlaarsdam, G., Van Waes, L., & Daems, F. (2007). Observational learning through video-based models: Impact on students' accuracy of self-efficacy beliefs, task knowledge and writing performances. In G. Rijlaarsdam (Series Ed.), & P. Boscolo, & S. Hidi (Vol Eds.), *Studies in writing: Vol. 19. Writing and motivation* (pp. 219–238). Elsevier.

Rahmanian, M., Hassani, J., & Zamani, M. (2023). The assessment of frontal EEG asymmetry according to neuroticism and extraversion dimensions. *Neuropsychology, 8*(4), 1–11.

Rainville, P. (2002). Brain mechanisms of pain affect and pain modulation. *Current Opinion in Neurobiology, 12*(2), 195–204. https://doi.org/10.1016/S0959-4388(02)00313-6

Rainville, P., Hofbauer, R. K., Paus, T., Duncan, G. H., Bushnell, M. C., & Price, D. D. (1999). Cerebral mechanisms of hypnotic induction and suggestion. *Journal of Cognitive Neuroscience, 11*(1), 110–125. https://doi.org/10.1162/089892999563175

Rajmohan, V., & Mohandas, E. (2007). The limbic system. *Indian Journal of Psychiatry, 49*(2), 132–139. https://doi.org/10.4103/0019-5545.33264

Ralphs, M. H., Graham, D., & James, L. F. (1994). Social facilitation influences cattle to graze locoweed. *Rangeland Ecology & Management/Journal of Range Management Archives, 47*(2), 123–126. https://doi.org/10.2307/4002819

Ramachandran, V. S., & Hubbard, E. M. (2003). Hearing colors, tasting shapes. *Scientific American, 288*(5), 53–59. https://www.jstor.org/stable/26060283

Ramasubramanian, S. (2017). Mindfulness, stress coping and everyday resilience among emerging youth in a university setting: A mixed methods approach. *International Journal of Adolescence and Youth, 22*(3), 308–321. https://doi.org/10.1080/02673843.2016.1175361

Ramesh, A., & Gelfand, M. J. (2010). Will they stay or will they go? The role of job embeddedness in predicting turnover in individualistic and collectivistic cultures. *Journal of Applied Psychology, 95*(5), 807–823. https://doi.org/10.1037/a0019464

Randhawa, M. A., Khan, A. A., Javed, M. S., & Sajid, M. W. (2015). Green leafy vegetables: A health promoting source. In R. R. Watson (Ed.), *Handbook of fertility* (pp. 205–220). Academic Press. https://doi.org/10.1016/B978-0-12-800872-0.00018-4

Randhawa, M. A., Khan, A. A., Javed, M. S., & Sajid, M. W. (2015). Green leafy vegetables: A health promoting source. In R. R. Watson (Ed.), *Handbook of fertility* (pp. 205–220). Academic Press.

Rantala, M. J., Luoto, S., Borráz-León, J. I., & Krams, I. (2021). Bipolar disorder: An evolutionary psychoneuroimmunological approach. *Neuroscience & Biobehavioral Reviews, 122*, 28–37. https://doi.org/10.1016/j.neubiorev.2020.12.031

Rapee, R. M., & Barlow, D. H. (2002). Generalized anxiety disorders, panic disorders, and phobias. In H. E. Adams & P. B. Sutker (Eds.), *Comprehensive handbook of psychopathology* (pp. 131–154). Springer.

Rashid, B., & Calhoun, V. (2020). Towards a brain-based predictome of mental illness. *Human Brain Mapping, 41*(12), 3468–3535. https://doi.org/10.1002/hbm.25013

Rathee, R., & Rajain, P. (2020). Influence of music on consumer behaviour: An experimental study. *Abhigyan, 38*(1), 30–39.

Ratnayake, S. (2022). It's been utility all along: An alternate understanding of cognitive behavioral therapy and the depressive realism hypothesis. *Philosophy, Psychiatry, & Psychology, 29*(2), 75–89. https://doi.org/10.1353/ppp.2022.0013

Ravada, V. A., Lahari, K. V. S., Reddipogu, H. T., Vuyyuru, L. P., Konda, C., & Pinjar, M. J. (2023). Reducing stress and anxiety in first-year undergraduates through biofeedback-assisted relaxation training. *Cureus, 15*(11), Article e48200. https://doi.org/10.7759/cureus.48200

Rayner, K., Schotter, E. R., Masson, M. E. J., Potter, M. C., & Treiman, R. (2016). So much to read, so little time: How do we read, and can speed reading help? *Psychological Science in the Public Interest, 17*(1), 4–34. https://doi.org/10.1177/1529100615623267

Read, B., & Hughes-Hallett, G. (Producers), & Wardle, T. (Director). (2018). *Three identical strangers* [Motion picture]. CNN Films.

Read, J., Bentall, R. P., & Fosse, R. (2009). Time to abandon the bio-bio-bio model of psychosis: Exploring the epigenetic and psychological mechanisms by which adverse life events lead to psychotic symptoms. *Epidemiology and Psychiatric Sciences, 18*(4), 299–310. https://doi.org/10.1017/S1121189X00000257

Ready, R. E., Carvalho, J. O., & Åkerstedt, A. M. (2012). Evaluative organization of the self-concept in younger, midlife, and older adults. *Research on Aging, 34*(1), 56–79. https://doi.org/10.1177/0164027511415244

Reed, C., Novick, D., Gonzalez-Pinto, A., Bertsch, J., & Haro, J. M. (2009). Observational study designs for bipolar disorder—What can they tell us about treatment in acute mania? *Progress in Neuro-Psychopharmacology and Biological Psychiatry, 33*(4), 715–721. https://doi.org/10.1016/j.pnpbp.2009.03.024

Reeves, L., & Weisberg, R. W. (1994). The role of content and abstract information in analogical transfer. *Psychological Bulletin, 115*(3), 381–400. https://doi.org/10.1037/0033-2909.115.3.381

Regier, T., Carstensen, A., & Kemp, C. (2016). Languages support efficient communication about the environment: Words for snow revisited. *PLoS ONE, 11*(4), Article e0151138. https://doi.org/10.1371/journal.pone.0151138

Reichart, T., & Lambiase, J. (Eds.). (2003). *Sex in advertising: Perspectives on the erotic appeal.* Routledge.

Reichert, T. (Ed.). (2019). *Investigating the use of sex in media promotion and advertising.* Routledge.

Reinders, A. A., & Veltman, D. J. (2021). Dissociative identity disorder: Out of the shadows at last? *The British Journal of Psychiatry, 219*(2), 413–414. https://doi.org/10.1192/bjp.2020.168

Reio, T. G., Jr. (2010). What about adolescent curiosity and risk taking? In J. L. DeVitis & L. Irwin-DeVitis (Eds.), *Adolescent education: A reader* (pp. 99–109). Peter Lang.

Reis, H. T., Maniaci, M. R., Caprariello, P. A., Eastwick, P. W., & Finkel, E. J. (2011). Familiarity does indeed promote attraction in live interaction. *Journal of Personality and Social Psychology*, *101*(3), 557–570. https://doi.org/10.1037/a0022885

Rekers, G. A., & Lovaas, O. I. (1974). Behavioral treatment of deviant sex-role behaviors in a male child. *Journal of Applied Behavior Analysis*, *7*(2), 173–190. https://doi.org/10.1901/jaba.1974.7-173

Renkewitz, F., & Heene, M. (2019). The replication crisis and open science in psychology. *Open Science in Psychology*, *227*(4), eISSN: 2151–2604. https://doi.org/10.1027/2151-2604/a000389

Renz, M., Reichmuth, O., Bueche, D., Traichel, B., Mao, M. S., Cerny, T., & Strasser, F. (2018). Fear, pain, denial, and spiritual experiences in dying processes. *American Journal of Hospice and Palliative Medicine*, *35*(3), 478–491. https://doi.org/10.1177/1049909117725271

Reppert, S. M., & de Roode, J. C. (2018). Demystifying monarch butterfly migration. *Current Biology*, *28*(17), R1009–R1022. https://doi.org/10.1016/j.cub.2018.02.067

Reynolds, L. M., Bissett, I. P., Porter, D., & Consedine, N. S. (2017). A brief mindfulness intervention is associated with negative outcomes in a randomised controlled trial among chemotherapy patients. *Mindfulness*, *8*(5), 1291–1303. https://doi.org/10.1007/s12671-017-0705-2

Richell, R. A., Mitchell, D. G., Newman, C., Leonard, A., Baron-Cohen, S., & Blair, R. J. R. (2003). Theory of mind and psychopathy: Can psychopathic individuals read the "language of the eyes"? *Neuropsychologia*, *41*(5), 523–526. https://doi.org/10.1016/S0028-3932(02)00175-6

Ricker, T. J., Sandry, J., Vergauwe, E., & Cowan, N. (2020). Do familiar memory items decay? *Journal of Experimental Psychology: Learning, Memory, and Cognition*, *46*(1), 60–76. https://doi.org/10.1037/xlm0000719

Rigby, C. S., Schultz, P. P., & Ryan, R. M. (2014). Mindfulness, interest-taking, and self-regulation: A self-determination theory perspective on the role of awareness in optimal functioning. In A. Ie, C. T. Ngnoumen, & E. J. Langer (Eds.), *Wiley Blackwell handbook of mindfulness* (pp. 216–235). John Wiley.

Rimfeld, K., Malanchini, M., Spargo, T., Spickernell, G., Selzam, S., McMillan, A., Dale, P. S., Eley, T. C., & Plomin, R. (2019). Twins early development study: A genetically sensitive investigation into behavioral and cognitive development from infancy to emerging adulthood. *Twin Research and Human Genetics*, *22*(6), 508–513. https://doi.org/10.1017/thg.2019.56

Risen, J. L., & Critcher, C. R. (2011). Visceral fit: While in a visceral state, associated states of the world seem more likely. *Journal of Personality and Social Psychology*, *100*(5), 777–793. https://doi.org/10.1037/a0022460

Rivenburgh, N. K. (2000). Social identity theory and news portrayals of citizens involved in international affairs. *Media Psychology*, *2*(4), 303–329.

Rivi, V., Batabyal, A., Juego, K., Kakadiya, M., Benatti, C., Blom, J. M., & Lukowiak, K. (2021). To eat or not to eat: A Garcia effect in pond snails (Lymnaea stagnalis). *Journal of Comparative Physiology A*, *207*, 479–495. https://doi.org/10.1007/s00359-021-01491-5

Rizzolatti, G., Fadiga, L., Gallese, V., & Fogassi, L. (1996). Premotor cortex and the recognition of motor actions. *Cognitive Brain Research*, *3*(2), 131–141. https://doi.org/10.1016/0926-6410(95)00038-0

Roberts, B. W., & DelVecchio, W. F. (2000). The rank-order consistency of personality traits from childhood to old age: A quantitative review of longitudinal studies. *Psychological Bulletin*, *126*(1), 3–25. http://dx.doi.org/10.1037/0033-2909.126.1.3

Roberts, D. M., Schade, M. M., Mathew, G. M., Gartenberg, D., & Buxton, O. M. (2020). Detecting sleep using heart rate and motion data from multisensor consumer-grade wearables, relative to wrist actigraphy and polysomnography. *Sleep*, *43*(7), Article zsaa045. https://doi.org/10.1093/sleep/zsaa045

Roberts, H. A., Clark, D. A., Kalina, C., Sherman, C., Brislin, S., Heitzeg, M. M., & Hicks, B. M. (2022). To vax or not to vax: Predictors of anti-vax attitudes and COVID-19 vaccine hesitancy prior to widespread vaccine availability. *PLoS One*, *17*(2), e0264019. https://doi.org/10.1371/journal.pone.0264019

Robertson, I. H. (2003). The absent mind attention and error. *The Psychologist*, *16*(9), 476–479.

Rodgers, J. L., Cleveland, H. H., Van Den Oord, E., & Rowe, D. C. (2000). Resolving the debate over birth order, family size, and intelligence. *American Psychologist*, *55*(6), 599–612. https://doi.org/10.1037/0003-066X.55.6.599

Roediger, H. L. & Karpicke, J. D. (2006). Test-enhanced learning: Taking memory tests improves long-term retention. *Psychological Science*, *17*(3), 249–255. https://doi.org/10.1111/j.1467-9280.2006.01693.x

Roediger, H. L., & McDermott, K. B. (1995). Creating false memories: Remembering words not presented in lists. *Journal of Experimental Psychology: Learning, Memory, and Cognition*, *21*(4), 803–814.

Rogers, C. R. (1951). *Client-centered therapy: Its current practice, implications, and theory*. Houghton Mifflin.

Rogers, C. R. (1957). The necessary and sufficient conditions of therapeutic personality change. *Journal of Consulting Psychology*, *21*(2), 95–103. https://doi.org/10.1037/h0045357

Rogers, C. R. (1961). *On becoming a person: A therapist's view of psychotherapy*. Houghton Mifflin.

Rogers, C. R. (1970). *Carl Rogers on encounter groups*. Harper & Row.

Rogers, C. R., Fry, C. M., Lee, T. H., Galvan, M., Gates, K. M., & Telzer, E. H. (2022). Neural connectivity underlying adolescent social learning in sibling dyads. *Social Cognitive and Affective Neuroscience*, *17*(11), 1007–1020. https://doi.org/10.1093/scan/nsac025

Rogers, R. D., & Monsell, S. (1995). Costs of a predictable switch between simple cognitive tasks. *Journal of Experimental Psychology: General*, *124*(2), 207–231. https://doi.org/10.1037/0096-3445.124.2.207

Rogers, S. J., & Puchalski, C. B. (1986). Social smiles of visually impaired infants. *Journal of Visual Impairment & Blindness*, *80*(7), 863–865. https://doi.org/10.1177/0145482X8608000712

Rogler, L. H. (1983). *A conceptual framework for mental health research on Hispanic populations* (No. 10). Hispanic Research Center, Fordham University.

Rohrer, J. M., Richter, D., Brümmer, M., Wagner, G. G., & Schmukle, S. C. (2018). Successfully striving for happiness: Socially engaged pursuits predict increases in life satisfaction. *Psychological Science*, *29*(8), 1291–1298. https://doi.org/10.1177/0956797618761660

Rokach, A., & Clayton, S. (2023). The consequences of child abuse. *Healthcare*, *11*(11), Article 1650. https://doi.org/10.3390/healthcare11111650

Roland, M. (2021). Love, motivation, and reasons: The case of the drowning wife. In S. Cushing (Ed.), *New philosophical essays on love and loving* (pp. 215–239). Palgrave Macmillan. https://doi.org/10.1007/978-3-030-72324-8_11

Rollema, H., & Hurst, R. S. (2018). The contribution of agonist and antagonist activities of 42° nAChR ligands to smoking cessation efficacy: A quantitative analysis of literature data. *Psychopharmacology*, *235*(9), 2479–2505. https://doi.org/10.1007/s00213-018-4921-9

Rolls, G. (2010). *Classic case studies in psychology* (2nd ed.). Hodder Arnold.

Romeo-Stuppy, K., Huber, L., Phelps, N., Jefferson, D., & McGruder, C. (2021). Why menthol bans protect African Americans. *Tobacco Induced Diseases*, *19*, Article 87. https://doi.org/10.18332%2Ftid%2F142932

Romero, F. (2019). Philosophy of science and the replicability crisis. *Philosophy Compass*, *14*(11), e12633. https://doi.org/10.1111/phc3.12633

Ros, L., & Thomas, F. (2002). Overcoming superstrictness in line drawing interpretation. *IEEE Transactions on Pattern Analysis and Machine Intelligence, 24*(4), 456–466. https://doi.org/10.1109/34.993554

Rosch, E. (1975). Cognitive representations of semantic categories. *Journal of Experimental Psychology: General, 104*(3), 192233. https://doi.org/10.1037/0096-3445.104.3.192

Rose, A. J., & Montemayor, R. (1994). The relationship between gender role orientation and perceived self-competency in male and female adolescents. *Sex Roles, 31*, 579–595.

Rose, D., Thornicroft, G., Pinfold, V., & Kassam, A. (2007). 250 Labels used to stigmatise people with mental illness. *BMC Health Services Research, 7*(1), 1–7. https://doi.org/10.1186/1472-6963-7-97

Rose, S., Zell, E., & Strickhouser, J. E. (2019). The effect of meditation on health: A metasynthesis of randomized controlled trials. *Mindfulness, 11*(2), 507–516. https://doi.org/10.1007/s12671-019-01277-6

Rosenberg, E. (2018, February 27). One in four teens are sexting, a new study shows. Relax, researchers say, it's mostly normal. *The Washington Post.*https://www.washingtonpost.com/news/the-switch/wp/2018/02/27/a-new-study-shows-one-in-four-teens-are-sexting-relax-experts-say-its-mostly-normal/

Rosenberg, M. (1965). *Society and the adolescent self-image.* Princeton University Press.

Rosenfeld, P., Giacalone, R. A., & Tedeschi, J. T. (1984). Cognitive dissonance and impression management explanations for effort justification. *Personality and Social Psychology Bulletin, 10*(3), 394–401. https://doi.org/10.1177/0146167284103007

Rosenthal, L. (2016). Incorporating intersectionality into psychology: An opportunity to promote social justice and equity. *American Psychologist, 71*(6), 474–485. https://doi.org/10.1037/a0040323

Rosseland, R., Pallesen, S., Nordhus, I. H., Matre, D., & Blågestad, T. (2018). Effects of sleep fragmentation and induced mood on pain tolerance and pain sensitivity in young healthy adults. *Frontiers in Psychology, 9*, Article 2089. https://doi.org/10.3389/fpsyg.2018.02089

Rossi, G. N., Guerra, L. T. L., Baker, G. B., Dursun, S. M., Saiz, J. C. B., Hallak, J. E. C., & dos Santos, R. G. (2022). Molecular pathways of the therapeutic effects of ayahuasca, a botanical psychedelic and potential rapid-acting antidepressant. *Biomolecules, 12*, Article 1618. https://doi.org/10.3390/biom12111618

Rotenberg, V. S. (2013). Moravec's paradox: Consideration in the context of two brain hemisphere functions. *Activitas Nervosa Superior, 55*, 108–111. https://doi.org/10.1007/BF03379600

Roth, G. (2000). The evolution and ontogeny of consciousness. In T. Metzinger (Ed.), *Neural correlates of consciousness: Empirical and conceptual questions* (pp. 77–97). MIT Press.

Rotter, J. B. (1966). Generalized expectancies for internal versus external control of reinforcement. *Psychological Monographs: General and Applied, 80*(1), 1–28. https://doi.org/10.1037/h0092976

Rotter, J. B. (1990). Internal versus external control of reinforcement: A case history of a variable. *American Psychologist, 45*(4), 489–493. https://doi.org/10.1037/0003-066X.45.4.489

Rotton, J., & Kelly, I. W. (1985). Much ado about the full moon: A meta-analysis of lunar-lunacy research. *Psychological Bulletin, 97*(2), 286–306. https://doi.org/10.1037/0033-2909.97.2.286

Roulin, N., & Ternes, M. (2019). Is it time to kill the detection wizard? Emotional intelligence does not facilitate deception detection. *Personality and Individual Differences, 137*, 131–138. https://doi.org/10.1016/j.paid.2018.08.020

Rowhani-Farid, A., Allen, M., & Barnett, A. G. (2017). What incentives increase data sharing in health and medical research? A systematic review. *Research Integrity and Peer Review, 2*, 1–10. https://doi.org/10.1186/s41073-017-0028-9

Rozental, A., & Powers, M. (2023). Cognitive behaviour therapy: 50th anniversary. *Cognitive Behaviour Therapy, 52*(3), 163–175. https://doi.org/10.1080/16506073.2023.2189794

Ru, T., Chen, Q., You, J., & Zhou, G. (2019). Effects of a short midday nap on habitual nappers' alertness, mood and mental performance across cognitive domains. *Journal of Sleep Research, 28*(3), 1–11. https://doi.org/10.1111/jsr.12638

Ruba, A. L., Johnson, K. M., Harris, L. T., & Wilbourn, M. P. (2017). Developmental changes in infants' categorization of anger and disgust facial expressions. *Developmental Psychology, 53*(10), 1826–1832. https://doi.org/10.1037/dev0000381

Rubin, P. G., & Canché, M. S. G. (2019). Test-flexible admissions policies and student enrollment demographics: Examining a public research university. *The Review of Higher Education, 42*(4), 1337–1371. https://doi.org/10.1353/rhe.2019.0068

Rubinow, D. R., & Schmidt, P. J. (2019). Sex differences and the neurobiology of affective disorders. *Neuropsychopharmacology, 44*(1), 111–128. https://doi.org/10.1038/s41386-018-0148-z

Rubinstein, G., & Strul, S. (2007). The Five Factor Model (FFM) among four groups of male and female professionals. *Journal of Research in Personality, 41*(4), 931–937. https://doi.org/10.1016/j.jrp.2006.09.003

Ruddock, H. K., Brunstrom, J. M., Vartanian, L. R., & Higgs, S. (2019). A systematic review and meta-analysis of the social facilitation of eating. *The American Journal of Clinical Nutrition, 110*(4), 842–861. https://doi.org/10.1093/ajcn/nqz155

Rudmin, F. W. (2003). Critical history of the acculturation psychology of assimilation, separation, integration, and marginalization. *Review of General Psychology, 7*(1), 3–37. https://doi.org/10.1037/1089-2680.7.1.3

Ruest, S. M., Stephan, A. M., Masiakos, P. T., Biddinger, P. D., Camargo, C. A., & Kharasch, S. (2018). Substance use patterns and in-hospital care of adolescents and young adults attending music concerts. *Addiction Science & Clinical Practice, 13*(1), Article 1. https://doi.org/10.1186/s13722-017-0105-x

Ruscheweyh, R., Marziniak, M., Stumpenhorst, F., Reinholz, J., & Knecht, S. (2009). Pain sensitivity can be assessed by self-rating: Development and validation of the Pain Sensitivity Questionnaire. *Pain, 146*(1–2), 65–74. https://doi.org/10.1016/j.pain.2009.06.020.

Ruscio, A. M., Hallion, L. S., Lim, C. C., Aguilar-Gaxiola, S., Al-Hamzawi, A., Alonso, J., Andrade, L. H., Borges, G., Bromet, E. J., Bunting, B., Caldas de Almeida, J. M., Demyttenaere, K., Flurescu, S., de Girolama, G., Gureje, O., Haro, J. M., He, Y., Hinkov, H., Hu, C., de Jonge, P., . . . Scott, K. M. (2017). Cross-sectional comparison of the epidemiology of DSM-5 generalized anxiety disorder across the globe. *JAMA Psychiatry, 74*(5), 465–475. https://doi.org/10.1001/jamapsychiatry.2017.0056

Rushton, J. P. (1988). Race differences in behaviour: A review and evolutionary analysis. *Personality and Individual Differences, 9*(6), 1009–1024. https://doi.org/10.1016/0191-8869(88)90135-3

Ruzgis, P., & Grigorenko, E. L. (1994). Cultural meaning systems, intelligence, and personality. In R. J. Sternberg & P. Ruzgis (Eds.), *Personality and intelligence* (pp. 248–270). Cambridge University Press.

Ryan, E. D. (1977). Attribution, intrinsic motivation, and athletics. In L. I. Gedvilas & M. E. Kneer (Eds.), Proceedings of the National Association for Physical Education of College Men National Conference Association for Physical Education of College Women National Conference. University of Illinois at Chicago.

Ryan, P. (2017, June 7). Can porn be feminist? These female directors say "yes." *USA Today*, p. 2D.

Ryan, R. M., & Deci, E. L. (2000). When rewards compete with nature: The undermining of intrinsic motivation and self-regulation. In C. Sansone & J. M. Harackiewicz (Eds.), *Intrinsic and extrinsic motivation* (pp. 13–54). Academic Press. https://doi.org/10.1016/B978-012619070-0/50024-6

Ryan, R. M., & Deci, E. L. (2001). On happiness and human potentials: A review of research on hedonic and eudaimonic well-being. *Annual Review of Psychology, 52,* 141–166. https://doi.org/10.1146/annurev.psych.52.1.141

Ryan, R. M., & Deci, E. L. (2020). Intrinsic and extrinsic motivation from a self-determination theory perspective: Definitions, theory, practices, and future directions. *Contemporary Educational Psychology, 61,* Article 101860. https://doi.org/10.1016/j.cedpsych.2020.101860

Ryan, R. M., & Frederick, C. (1997). On energy, personality, and health: Subjective vitality as a dynamic reflection of well-being. *Journal of Personality, 65*(3), 529–565. https://doi.org/10.1111/j.1467-6494.1997.tb00326.x

Ryan, R. M., Duineveld, J. J., Di Domenico, S. I., Ryan, W. S., Steward, B. A., & Bradshaw, E. L. (2022). We know this much is (meta-analytically) true: A meta-review of meta-analytic findings evaluating self-determination theory. *Psychological Bulletin, 148*(11–12), 813–842. https://doi.org/10.1037/bul0000385

Ryan, R., Bradshaw, E., & Deci, E. (2019). A history of motivation theories in psychology. In R. Sternberg & W. E. Pickren (Eds.), *The Cambridge handbook for the intellectual history of psychology* (pp. 391–411). Cambridge University Press.

Sahoo, S., Padhy, S. K., Padhee, B., Singla, N., & Sarkar, S. (2018). Role of personality in cardiovascular diseases: An issue that needs to be focused too! *Indian Heart Journal, 70,* S471–S477. https://doi.org/10.1016/j.ihj.2018.11.003

Sala, G., & Gobet, F. (2019). Cognitive training does not enhance general cognition. *Trends in Cognitive Sciences, 23*(1), 9–20. https://doi.org/10.1016/j.tics.2018.10.004

Sala, G., Tatlidil, K. S., & Gobet, F. (2018). Video game training does not enhance cognitive ability: A comprehensive meta-analytic investigation. *Psychological Bulletin, 144*(2), 111–139. https://doi.org/10.1037/bul0000139

Salmon, P. (2001). Effects of physical exercise on anxiety, depression, and sensitivity to stress: A unifying theory. *Clinical Psychology Review, 21*(1), 33–61. https://doi.org/10.1016/S0272-7358(99)00032-X

Salovey, P., & Grewal, D. (2005). The science of emotional intelligence. *Current Directions in Psychological Science, 14*(6), 281–285. https://doi.org/10.1111/j.0963-7214.2005.00381.x

Salovey, P., & Mayer, J. D. (1990). Emotional intelligence. *Imagination, Cognition, and Personality, 9*(3), 185–211. https://doi.org/10.2190/DUGG-P24E-52WK-6CDG

Samant, T., & Singh, M. (2022, May 30). *Stockholm syndrome in Indian organizational culture.* The Leap Blog. https://blog.theleapjournal.org/2020/05/stockholm-syndrome-in-indian.html

Sánchez, A. I., & Buela-Casal, G. (2007). Assessment of daytime symptoms in snoring subjects and obstructive sleep apnea patients. *Salud Mental, 30*(1), 9–15.

Sanders, P. (2006). Why person-centred therapists must reject the medicalisation of distress. *Self & Society, 34*(3), 32–39. https://doi.org/10.1080/03060497.2006.11083918

Sandford, S. (2017). Freud, Bion and Kant: Epistemology and anthropology in The Interpretation of Dreams. *The International Journal of Psychoanalysis, 98*(1), 91–110. https://doi.org/10.1111/1745-8315.12564

Sandfort, T. G. M., & Dodge, B. (2009). Homosexual and bisexual labels and behaviors among men: The need for clear conceptualizations, accurate operationalizations, and appropriate methodological designs. In V. Reddy, T. G. M. Sandfort, & R. Rispel (Eds.), *Perspectives on same-sex sexuality, gender and HIV/AIDS in South Africa: From social silence to social science* (pp. 51–57). Human Sciences Research Council.

Sandstrom, G. M., & Dunn, E. W. (2013). Replication of "Creating social connection through inferential reproduction: Loneliness and perceived agency in gadgets, Gods, and greyhounds" by Nick Epley, Scott Akalis, Adam Waytz, and John T. Cacioppo (2008, Psychological Science). https://osf.io/m5a2c/

Sanford, R. N. (1936). The effects of abstinence from food upon imaginal processes: A preliminary experiment. *Journal of Psychology: Interdisciplinary and Applied, 2*(1), 129–136. https://doi.org/10.1080/00223980.1936.9917447

Sanna, L. J. (1992). Self-efficacy theory: Implications for social facilitation and social loafing. *Journal of Personality and Social Psychology, 62*(5), 774–786. https://doi.org/10.1037/0022-3514.62.5.774

Santos, H. P., Jr., Adynski, H., Harris, R., Bhattacharya, A., Rodriguez, A. C. I., Cali, R., Torres Yabar, A., Nephew, B. C., & Murgatroyd, C. (2021). Biopsychosocial correlates of psychological distress in Latina mothers. *Journal of Affective Disorders, 282,* 617–626. https://doi.org/10.1016/j.jad.2020.12.193

Sargent, J. D., Dalton, M. A., Beach, M. L., Mott, L. A., Tickle, J. J., Ahrens, B. M., & Heatherton, T. F. (2002). Viewing tobacco use in movies: Does it shape attitudes that mediate adolescent smoking? *American Journal of Preventive Medicine, 22,* 137–145. https://doi.org/10.1016/S0749-3797(01)00434-2

Sargent, J. D., Morgenstern, M., Isensee, B., & Hanewinkel, R. (2009). Movie smoking and urge to smoke among adult smokers. *Nicotine & Tobacco Research, 11*(9), 1042–1046. https://doi.org/10.1093/ntr/ntp097

Sarlo, G. L., & Holton, K. F. (2021). Brain concentrations of glutamate and GABA in human epilepsy: A review. *Seizure, 91,* 213–227. https://doi.org/10.1016/j.seizure.2021.06.028

Sasdelli, A., Lia, L., Luciano, C. C., Nespeca, C., Berardi, D., & Menchetti, M. (2013). Screening for bipolar disorder symptoms in depressed primary care attenders: Comparison between Mood Disorder Questionnaire and Hypomania Checklist (HCL-32). *Psychiatry Journal, 2013,* Article 548349. https://doi.org/10.1155/2013/548349

Sato, T., & Sato, T. (2005). The early 20th century: Shaping the discipline of psychology in Japan. *Japanese Psychological Research, 47*(2), 52–62. https://doi.org/10.1111/j.1468-5884.2005.00273.x

Sattler, C., Toro, P., Schönknecht, P., & Schröder, J. (2012). Cognitive activity, education and socioeconomic status as preventive factors for mild cognitive impairment and Alzheimer's disease. *Psychiatry Research, 196*(1), 90–95. https://doi.org/10.1016/j.psychres.2011.11.012

Saucier, D. A., Stanford, A. J., Miller, S. S., Martens, A. L., Miller, A. K., Jones, T. L., McManus, J. L., & Burns, M. D. (2016). Masculine honor beliefs: Measurement and correlates. *Personality and Individual Differences, 94,* 7–15. https://doi.org/10.1016/j.paid.2015.12.049

Saul, J. S., & Rodgers, R. F. (2018). Adolescent eating disorder risk and the online world. *Child and Adolescent Psychiatric Clinics, 27*(2), 221–228. https://doi.org/10.1016/j.chc.2021.09.004

Saxena, A., Paredes-Echeverri, S., Michaelis, R., Popkirov, S., & Perez, D. L. (2022). Using the biopsychosocial model to guide patient-centered neurological treatments. *Seminars in Neurology, 42,* 80–87. https://doi.org/10.1055/s-0041-1742145

Saxena, M., Tote, S., & Sapkale, B. (2023). Multiple personality disorder or dissociative identity disorder: Etiology, diagnosis, and management. *Cureus, 15*(11), Article e49057. https://doi.org/10.7759/cureus.49057

Sayood, K. (2018). Information theory and cognition: A review. *Entropy, 20*(9), Article 706. https://doi.org/10.3390/e20090706

Scammell, T. E., Arrigoni, E., & Lipton, J. O. (2017). Neural circuitry of wakefulness and sleep. *Neuron, 93*(4), 747–765. http://dx.doi.org/10.1016/j.neuron.2017.01.014

Schachter, S. (1959). *The psychology of affiliation: Experimental studies of the sources of gregariousness.* Stanford University Press.

Schachter, S., & Singer, J. (1962). Cognitive, social, and physiological determinants of emotional state. *Psychological Review*, *69*(5), 379–399. https://doi.org/10.1037/h0046234

Schacter, D. L. (1999). The seven sins of memory: Insights from psychology and cognitive neuroscience. *American Psychologist*, *54*(3), 182–203. https://doi.org/10.1037/0003-066X.54.3.182

Schacter, D. L. (2001). *The seven sins of memory: How the mind forgets and remembers*. Houghton-Mifflin.

Schacter, D. L., Harbluk, J. L., & McLachlen, D. R. (1984). Retrieval without recollection: An experimental analysis of source amnesia. *Journal of Verbal Learning and Verbal Behavior*, *23*(5), 593–611. https://doi.org/10.1016/S0022-5371(84)90373-6

Schaie, K. W. (2013). *Developmental influences on adult intelligence: The Seattle Longitudinal Study*. Oxford University Press.

Schaie, K. W. (2016). The longitudinal study of adult cognitive development. In R. J. Sternberg, S. T. Fiske, & D. J. Foss (Eds.), *Scientists making a difference: One hundred eminent behavioral and brain scientists talk about their most important contributions* (pp. 218–222). Oxford University Press.

Schakel, L., Veldhuijzen, D. S., Crompvoets, P. I., Bosch, J. A., Cohen, S., van Middendorp, H., Joosten, S. A., Ottenhoff, T. H. M., Visser, L. G., & Evers, A. W. (2019). Effectiveness of stress-reducing interventions on the response to challenges to the immune system: A meta-analytic review. *Psychotherapy and Psychosomatics*, *88*(5), 274–286. https://doi.org/10.1159/000501645

Schiller, C. E., Meltzer-Brody, S., & Rubinow, D. R. (2015). The role of reproductive hormones in postpartum depression. *CNS Spectrums*, *20*(1), Article 48. https://doi.org/10.1017/S1092852914000480

Schilling, O. K., & Diehl, M. (2015). Psychological vulnerability to daily stressors in old age. *Zeitschrift für Gerontologie und Geriatrie*, *48*(6), 517–523. https://doi.org/10.1007/s00391-015-0935-7

Schippers, M. C. (2014). Social loafing tendencies and team performance: The compensating effect of agreeableness and conscientiousness. *Academy of Management Learning & Education*, *13*(1), 62–81. https://doi.org/10.5465/amle.2012.0191

Schlaepfer, T. E. (2015). Deep brain stimulation for major depression—steps on a long and winding road. *Biological Psychiatry*, *78*(4), 218–219. https://doi.org/10.1016/j.biopsych.2015.06.020

Schmolck, H., Buffalo, E. A., & Squire, L. R. (2000). Memory distortions develop over time: Recollections of the OJ Simpson trial verdict after 15 and 32 months. *Psychological Science*, *11*(1), 39–45. https://doi.org/10.1111/1467-9280.00212

Schnell, K., & Herpertz, S. C. (2007). Effects of dialectic-behavioral-therapy on the neural correlates of affective hyperarousal in borderline personality disorder. *Journal of Psychiatric Research*, *41*(10), 837–847. https://doi.org/10.1016/j.jpsychires.2006.08.011

Schoeler, T., & Bhattacharyya, S. (2013). The effect of cannabis use on memory function: An update. *Substance Abuse and Rehabilitation*, *4*, 11–27. https://doi.org/10.2147/SAR.S25869

Schoenfeld, E. A., Loving, T. J., Pope, M. T., Huston, T. L., & Štulhofer, A. (2017). Does sex really matter? Examining the connections between spouses' nonsexual behaviors, sexual frequency, sexual satisfaction, and marital satisfaction. *Archives of Sexual Behavior*, *46*(2), 489–501. https://doi.org/10.1007/s10508-015-0672-4

Scholl, B. J., Noles, N. S., Pasheva, V., & Sussman, R. (2003). Talking on a cellular telephone dramatically increases "sustained inattentional blindness" [Abstract]. *Journal of Vision*, *3*(9), 156–156a. https://doi.org/10.1167/3.9.156

Schooler, J. W. (2014). Metascience could rescue the "replication crisis". *Nature News*, *515*(7525), 9. https://doi.org/10.1038/515009a

Schramm-Nielsen, J. (2001). Cultural dimensions of decision-making: Denmark and France compared. *Journal of Managerial Psychology*, *16*(6), 404–423. https://doi.org/10.1108/02683940110402389

Schredl, M. (2001). Night terrors in children: Prevalence and influencing factors. *Sleep and Hypnosis*, *3*(2), 68–72.

Schutte, N. S., Malouff, J. M., & Keng, S.-L. (2020). Meditation and telomere length: A meta-analysis. *Psychology & Health*, *35*(8), 901–915. https://doi.org/10.1080/08870446.2019.1707827

Schwartz, B. L. (1999). Sparkling at the end of the tongue: The etiology of tip-of-the-tongue phenomenology. *Psychonomic Bulletin & Review*, *6*(3), 379–393. https://doi.org/10.3758/BF03210827

Schwartz, B. L., & Krantz, J. H. (2024). *Sensation and perception* (3rd ed.). Sage.

Schwartz, B. L., & Metcalfe, J. (2011). Tip-of-the-tongue (TOT) states: Retrieval, behavior, and experience. *Memory & Cognition*, *39*(5), 737–749. https://doi.org/10.3758/s13421-010-0066-8

Schwartz, C. E., Keyl, P. M., Marcum, J. P., & Bode, R. (2009). Helping others shows differential benefits on health and well-being for male and female teens. *Journal of Happiness Studies*, *10*(4), 431–448. https://doi.org/10.1007/s10902-008-9098-1

Schwarz, S., & Singer, M. (2013). Romantic red revisited: Red enhances men's attraction to young, but not menopausal women. *Journal of Experimental Social Psychology*, *49*(1), 161–164. https://doi.org/10.1016/j.jesp.2012.08.004

Schweingruber, D., Cast, A. D., & Anahita, S. (2008). "A story and a ring": Audience judgments about engagement proposals. *Sex Roles*, *58*(3–4), 165–178. https://doi.org/10.1007/s11199-007-9330-1

Schwitzgebel, E. (2002). How well do we know our own conscious experience? The case of visual imagery. *Journal of Consciousness Studies*, *9*(5–6), 35–53.

Scott, G. G., Pinkosova, Z., Jardine, E., & Hand, C. J. (2023). "Thinstagram": Image content and observer body satisfaction influence the when and where of eye movements during Instagram image viewing. *Computers in Human Behavior*, *138*, Article 107464. https://doi.org/10.1016/j.chb.2022.107464

Scott, G., Leritz, L. E., & Mumford, M. D. (2004). The effectiveness of creativity training: A quantitative review. *Creativity Research Journal*, *16*(4), 361–388. https://doi.org/10.1080/10400410409534549

Scull, A. (2019). The asylum, the hospital, and the clinic. In A. Scull (Ed.), *Psychiatry and its discontents* (pp. 38–53). University of California Press.

Scully, M., Swords, L., & Nixon, E. (2020). Social comparisons on social media: Online appearance-related activity and body dissatisfaction in adolescent girls. *Irish Journal of Psychological Medicine*, *41*(1), 31–42. https://doi.org/10.1017/ipm.2020.93

Seaburg, M. (2020, May 1). Could J. K. Rowling be a synesthete? *Psychology Today*. https://www.psychologytoday.com/us/blog/sensorium/202005/could-jk-rowling-be-synesthete

Seager, M. (2019). From stereotypes to archetypes: An evolutionary perspective on male help-seeking and suicide. In J. A. Barry, R. Kingerlee, M. Seager, & L. Sullivan (Eds.), *The Palgrave handbook of male psychology and mental health* (pp. 227–248). Palgrave Macmillan.

Sears, D. O., & Henry, P. J. (2005). Over thirty years later: A contemporary look at symbolic racism. In M. P. Zanna (Ed.), *Advances in experimental social psychology* (Vol. 37, pp. 95–150). Academic Press.

Sechrest, L., Stickle, T. R., & Stewart, M. (1998). The role of assessment in clinical psychology. In A. Bellack & M. Hersen (Series Eds.) & C. R. Reynolds (Vol. Ed.), *Comprehensive Clinical Psychology: Vol. 4: Assessment* (pp. 1–32). Pergamon.

Seehagen, S., Konrad, C., Herbert, J. S., & Schneider, S. (2015). Sleep serves memory consolidation in infants. *Proceedings of the National Academy of Sciences*, *112*(5), 1625–1629. https://doi.org/10.1073/pnas.1414000112

Seekis, V., Bradley, G. L., & Duffy, A. L. (2020). Appearance-related social networking sites and body image in young women: Testing an objectification-social comparison model. *Psychology of Women Quarterly, 44*(3), 377–392. https://doi .org/10.1177/0361684320920826

Segerstrom, S. C., & Miller, G. E. (2004). Psychological stress and the human immune system: A meta-analytic study of 30 years of inquiry. *Psychological Bulletin, 130*(4), 601–630. https://doi .org/10.1037/0033-2909.130.4.601

Seibt, B., Häfner, M., & Deutsch, R. (2007). Prepared to eat: How immediate affective and motivational responses to food cues are influenced by food deprivation. *European Journal of Social Psychology, 37*(2), 359–379. https://doi.org/10.1002/ejsp.365

Selfhout, M., Burk, W., Branje, S., Denissen, J., Van Aken, M., & Meeus, W. (2010). Emerging late adolescent friendship networks and Big Five personality traits: A social network approach. *Journal of Personality, 78*(2), 509–538. https://doi.org/10.1111/ j.1467-6494.2010.00625.x

Seligman, M. (2018). PERMA and the building blocks of well-being. *The Journal of Positive Psychology, 13*(4), 333–335. https://doi.org /10.1080/17439760.2018.1437466

Seligman, M. E. (2000). Optimism, pessimism, and mortality. *Mayo Clinic Proceedings, 75*(2), 133–134. https://doi .org/10.4065/75.2.133

Seligman, M. E. P., Steen, T. A., Park, N., & Peterson, C. (2005). Positive psychology progress: Empirical validation of interventions. *American Psychologist, 60*(5), 410–421. https://doi .org/10.1037/0003-066X.60.5.410

Seligman, M. E., & Maier, S. F. (1967). Failure to escape traumatic shock. *Journal of Experimental Psychology, 74*(1), 1–9. https://doi .org/10.1037/h0024514

Seligman, M. E., Parks, A. C., & Steen, T. (2004). A balanced psychology and a full life. *Philosophical Transactions of the Royal Society of London. Series B: Biological Sciences, 359*(1449), 1379–1381. https://doi.org/10.1098/rstb.2004.1513

Sell, C., Möller, H., & Taubner, S. (2017). Effectiveness of integrative imagery- and trance-based psychodynamic therapies: Guided imagery psychotherapy and hypnopsychotherapy. *Journal of Psychotherapy Integration, 28*(1), 90–113. https://doi .org/10.1037/int0000073

Selterman, D., & Drigotas, S. (2009). Attachment styles and emotional content, stress, and conflict in dreams of romantic partners. *Dreaming, 19*(3), 135–151. https://doi.org/10.1037/ a0017087

Selye, H. (1975). Stress and distress. *Comprehensive Therapy, 1*(8), 9–13. https://doi.org/10.1037/0033-2909.130.4.601

Senan, S., Ali, M. S., Vadivel, R., & Arik, S. (2017). Decentralized event-triggered synchronization of uncertain Markovian jumping neutral-type neural networks with mixed delays. *Neural Networks, 86*, 32–41. https://doi.org/10.1016/j .neunet.2016.10.003

Sepehry, A. A., Lam, K., Sheppard, M., Guirguis-Younger, M., & Maglio, A. S. (2021). EMDR for depression: A meta-analysis and systematic review. *Journal of EMDR Practice and Research, 15*(1), 2–17. https://doi.org/10.1891/EMDR-D-20-00038

Seyedsalehi, A., Warrier, V., Bethlehem, R. A., Perry, B. I., Burgess, S., & Murray, G. K. (2023). Educational attainment, structural brain reserve and Alzheimer's disease: A Mendelian randomization analysis. *Brain, 146*(5), 2059–2074. https://doi.org/10.1093/ brain/awac392

Shaheen, J. G. (2012). *Guilty: Hollywood's verdict on Arabs after 9/11.* Interlink Publishing.

Shakya, H. B., & Christakis, N. A. (2017). Association of Facebook use with compromised well-being: A longitudinal study. *American Journal of Epidemiology, 185*(3), 203–211. https://doi.org/ 10.1093/aje/kww189

Shapiro, F. (2007). EMDR, adaptive information processing, and case conceptualization. *Journal of EMDR Practice and Research, 1*, 68–87. https://doi.org/10.1891/1933-3196.1.2.68

Shapiro, F. (2017). *Eye movement desensitization and reprocessing (EMDR) therapy: Basic principles, protocols and procedures* (3rd ed.). Guilford.

Shapiro, L. (2011). Standard cognitive science. In L. Shapiro (Ed.), *Embodied cognition: New problems of philosophy* (pp. 7–27). Routledge.

Shariff, M., Rahim, A., Javed, S., Salimin, N., & Abdul Majid, N. (2017). Aggression in the sporting: Catharsis and social support. *Science International, 29*(1), 259–263.

Sharma, M., & Rush, S. E. (2014). Mindfulness-based stress reduction as a stress management intervention for healthy individuals: A systematic review. *Journal of Evidence-Based Complementary & Alternative Medicine, 19*(4), 271–286. https:// doi.org/10.1177/2156587214543143

Sharma, P., Guirguis, M., Nelson, J., & McMahon, T. (2015). A case of dissociative amnesia with dissociative fugue and treatment with psychotherapy. *The Primary Care Companion for CNS Disorders, 17*(3). https://doi.org/10.4088/PCC.14l01763

Sharpe, L. T., de Luca, E., Hansen, T., Jägle, H., & Gegenfurtner, K. R. (2006). Advantages and disadvantages of human dichromacy. *Journal of Vision, 6*(3), 213–223. https://doi.org/10.1167/6.3.3

Sharpless, B. A., & Doghramji, K. (2015). *Sleep paralysis: Historical, psychological, and medical perspectives.* Oxford University Press. https://doi.org/10.1093/med/9780199313808.001.0001

Shaughnessy, J. J., Zechmeister, E. B., & Zechmeister, J. S. (2009). *Research methods in psychology* (8th ed.). McGraw-Hill.

Shee, H., & Huntley, M., & Goodfriend, W. (2023). A cross-cultural study on attitudes towards mental illness and willingness to seek professional help among Japanese and U.S. college students. *Journal of Psychological Inquiry, 27*(2), 5–17.

Sheehan, L., Nieweglowski, K., & Corrigan, P. (2016). The stigma of personality disorders. *Current Psychiatry Reports, 18*, 1–7. https:// doi.org/10.1007/s11920-015-0654-1

Sheeran, P., Maki, A., Montanaro, E., Avishai-Yitshak, A., Bryan, A., Klein, W. M., Miles, E., & Rothman, A. J. (2016). The impact of changing attitudes, norms, and self-efficacy on health-related intentions and behavior: A meta-analysis. *Health Psychology, 35*(11), 1178–1188. https://doi.org/10.1037/hea0000387

Sheiner, E. O., Lifshitz, M., & Raz, A. (2016). Placebo response correlates with hypnotic suggestibility. *Psychology of Consciousness: Theory, Research, and Practice, 3*(2), 146–153. https://doi.org/10.1037/cns0000074

Sheppard, H., Bizumic, B., & Calear, A. (2023). Prejudice toward people with borderline personality disorder: Application of the prejudice toward people with mental illness framework. *International Journal of Social Psychiatry, 69*(5), 1065–1298. https://doi.org/10.1177/0020764023115505

Sheppard, R. (2021). *The year of the wolf—1981 and the Hollywood lycanthrope boom.* Unpublished master's thesis, University of East Anglia.

Sher, K. J., & Rutledge, P. C. (2007). Heavy drinking across the transition to college: Predicting first-semester heavy drinking from precollege variables. *Addictive Behaviors, 32*(4), 819–835. https://doi.org/10.1016/j.addbeh.2006.06.024

Sherif, M. & Sherif, C. W. (1969). Ingroup and intergroup relations: Experimental analysis. In M. Sherif & C. W. Sherif (Eds.), *Social psychology* (pp. 221–266). Harper & Row.

Sherif, M. (1966). *In common predicament: Social psychology of intergroup conflict and cooperation.* Houghton Mifflin.

Sherman, J. W., Gawronski, B., & Trope, Y. (2014). *Dual-process theories of the social mind.* Guilford.

Shi, Y., & Lin, X. (2021, October). A test of Maslow's hierarchy of needs concept by a correlational model among adult learners.

Paper presented at the American Association for Adult and Continuing Education Conference. Online.

Shi, Z., Wang, A. L., Fairchild, V. P., Aronowitz, C. A., Lynch, K. G., Loughead, J., & Langleben, D. D. (2023). Addicted to green: Priming effect of menthol cigarette packaging on brain response to smoking cues. *Tobacco Control*, *32*(e1), e45–e52. http://dx.doi.org/10.1136/tobaccocontrol-2021-056639

Shibata, K., Sasaki, Y., Bang, J., Walsh, E. G., Machizawa, M. G., Tamaki, M., Chang, L., & Watanabe, T. (2017). Overlearning hyperstabilizes a skill by rapidly making neurochemical processing inhibitory-dominant. *Nature Neuroscience*, *20*(3), 470–475. https://doi.org/10.1038/nn.4490

Shin, J., Lee, H. J., Park, H., Hong, Y., Song, Y. K., Yoon, D. U., & Oh, S. (2023). Perfectionism, test anxiety, and neuroticism determines high academic performance: A cross-sectional study. *BMC Psychology*, *11*(1), Article 410. https://doi.org/10.1186/s40359-023-01369-y

Sholl, M. J. (1987). Cognitive maps as orienting schemata. *Journal of Experimental Psychology: Learning, Memory, and Cognition*, *13*(4), 615–628. https://doi.org/10.1037/0278-7393.13.4.615

Showalter, E. (1997). *Hystories: Hysterical epidemics and modern media* (Vol. 2). Columbia University Press.

Shulman, E. P., Smith, A. R., Silva, K., Icenogle, G., Duell, N., Chein, J., & Steinberg, L. (2016). The dual systems model: Review, reappraisal, and reaffirmation. *Developmental Cognitive Neuroscience*, *17*, 103–117. https://doi.org/10.1016/j.dcn.2015.12.010

Siafis, S., Wu, H., Wang, D., Burschinski, A., Nomura, N., Takeuchi, H., Scheider-Thoma, J., Davis, J. M., & Leucht, S. (2023). Antipsychotic dose, dopamine D2 receptor occupancy and extrapyramidal side-effects: A systematic review and dose-response meta-analysis. *Molecular Psychiatry*, *28*, 3267–3277. https://doi.org/10.1038/s41380-023-02203-y

Siedlecki, K. L., Salthouse, T. A., Oishi, S., & Jeswani, S. (2014). The relationship between social support and subjective well-being across age. *Social Indicators Research*, *117*(2), 561–576. https://doi.org/10.1007/s11205-013-0361-4

Siegel, S., Krank, M. D., & Hinson, R. E. (1987). Anticipation of pharmacological and nonpharmacological events: Classical conditioning and addictive behavior. *Journal of Drug Issues*, *17*(1), 83–110. https://doi.org/10.1177/002204268701700106

Sierra, M., Senior, C., Dalton, J., McDonough, M., Bond, A., Phillips, M. L., O'Dwyer, A. M., & David, A. S. (2002). Autonomic response in depersonalization disorder. *Archives of General Psychiatry*, *59*(9), 833–838. https://doi.org/10.1001/archpsyc.59.9.833

Silvani, M. I., Werder, R., & Perret, C. (2022). The influence of blue light on sleep, performance and wellbeing in young adults: A systematic review. *Frontiers in Physiology*, *13*, Article 943108. https://doi.org/10.3389/fphys.2022.943108

Silverman, F. H. (1988). The "monster" study. *Journal of Fluency Disorders*, *13*(3), 225–231. https://doi.org/10.1016/0094-730X(88)90049-6

Simner, J., Sagiv, N., Mulvenna, C., Tsakanikos, E., Witherby, S. A., Fraser, C., Scott, K., & Ward, J. (2006). Synaesthesia: The prevalence of atypical cross-modal experiences. *Perception*, *35*(8), 1024–1033. https://doi.org/10.1068/p5469

Simons, D. J., & Chabris, C. F. (1999). Gorillas in our midst: Sustained inattentional blindness for dynamic events. *Perception*, *28*(9), 1059–1074. https://doi.org/10.1068/p281059

Simons, D. J., Boot, W. R., Charness, N., Gathercole, S. E., Chabris, C. F., Hambrick, D. Z., & Stine-Marrow, E. A. L. (2016). Do "brain-training" programs work? *Psychological Science in the Public Interest*, *17*(3), 103–186. https://doi.org/10.1177/1529100616661983

Simons, D. J., Boot, W. R., Charness, N., Gathercole, S. E., Chabris, C. F., Hambrick, D. Z., & Stine-Marrow, E. A. L. (2016). Do "brain-training" programs work? *Psychological Science in the Public*

Interest, *17*(3), 103–186. https://doi.org/10.1177/1529100616661983

Simonton, D. K. (2019). Creativity and psychopathology: The tenacious mad-genius controversy updated. *Current Opinion in Behavioral Sciences*, *27*, 17–21. https://doi.org/10.1016/j.cobeha.2018.07.006

Sin, N. L., & Ong, L. Q. (2023). Considerations for advancing the conceptualization of well-being. *Affective Science*, *4*, 45–48. https://doi.org/10.1007/s42761-022-00149-y

Singal, J. (2017, April 25). How should we talk about Amy Cuddy, death threats, and the replication crisis? *TheCut.com*. https://www.thecut.com/2017/04/amy-cuddy-death-threats.html

Singh, A. (2023). *Sleep to heal: 7 simple steps to better sleep*. Humanix Books.

Singh, M. N., & Gudiño, O. G. (2023). Translating liberation psychology for children and adolescents from historically marginalized racial and ethnic backgrounds: A synthesis of the literature. *Clinical Child and Family Psychology Review*, *26*(1), 65–81. https://doi.org/10.1007/s10567-022-00416-1

Sireteanu, R., Oertel, V., Mohr, H., Linden, D., & Singer, W. (2008). Graphical illustration and functional neuroimaging of visual hallucinations during prolonged blindfolding: A comparison to visual imagery. *Perception*, *37*(12), 1805–1821. https://doi.org/10.1068/p6034

Sirey, J. A., Bruce, M. L., Alexopoulos, G. S., Perlick, D. A., Friedman, S. J., & Meyers, B. S. (2001). Stigma as a barrier to recovery: Perceived stigma and patient-rated severity of illness as predictors of antidepressant drug adherence. *Psychiatric Services*, *52*(12), 1615–1620. https://doi.org/10.1176/appi.ps.52.12.1615

Sisk, C. L. (2017). Development: Pubertal hormones meet the adolescent brain. *Current Biology*, *27*(14), R706–R708. https://doi.org/10.1016/j.cub.2017.05.092

Siuki, H. A., Peyman, N., Vahedian-Shahroodi, M., Gholian-Aval, M., & Tehrani, H. (2019). Health education intervention on HIV/AIDS prevention behaviors among health volunteers in healthcare centers: An applying the theory of planned behavior. *Journal of Social Service Research*, *45*(4), 582–588. https://doi.org/10.1080/01488376.2018.1481177

Skeide, M. A., Wehrmann, K., Emami, Z., Kirsten, H., Hartmann, A. M., & Rujescu, D. (2020). Neurobiological origins of individual differences in mathematical ability. *PLoS Biology*, *18*(10), Article e3000871. https://doi.org/10.1371/journal.pbio.3000871

Skinner, B. F. (1953). *Science and human behavior*. Macmillan.

Skinner, B. F. (1954, November). Critique of psychoanalytic concepts and theories. *Scientific Monthly*, pp. 77–87. https://www.jstor.org/stable/21512

Skinner, B. F. (1959). *Cumulative record*. B. F. Skinner Foundation.

Skomsvold, P. (2014). *Profile of undergraduate students: 2011-12*. National Center for Education Statistics. https://files.eric.ed.gov/fulltext/ED581717.pdf

Skversky-Blocq, Y., Shmuel, S., Cohen, O., & Shechner, T. (2022). Looking fear in the face: Adults but not adolescents gaze at social threat during observational learning. *International Journal of Psychophysiology*, *182*, 240–247. https://doi.org/10.1016/j.ijpsycho.2022.11.004

Skversky-Blocq, Y., Shmuel, S., Waters, A. M., & Shechner, T. (2022). Observational extinction reduces fear and its retention among adolescents and adults. *Behaviour Research and Therapy*, *159*, Article 104207. https://doi.org/10.1016/j.brat.2022.104207

Slade, E. P., Jahn, D. R., Regenold, W. T., & Case, B. G. (2017). Association of electroconvulsive therapy with psychiatric readmissions in US hospitals. *JAMA Psychiatry*, *74*(8), 798–804. https://doi.org/10.1001/jamapsychiatry.2017.1378

Slater, A., Tiggemann, M., Firth, B., & Hawkins, K. (2012). Reality check: An experimental investigation of the addition of warning labels to fashion magazine images on women's mood and body dissatisfaction. *Journal of Social and Clinical Psychology*, *31*(2), 105–122. https://doi.org/10.1521/jscp.2012.31.2.105

Slepecky, M., Clark, D. M., Sefarova, I., Prasko, J., Zatkova, M., Popelkova, M., Kotianova, A., Basistova, A., Jandova, K., & Saffova, S. (2019). The role of effective treatment of mental illness in the fight against poverty. *Ceskoslovneska Psychologie*, *63*(1), 67–79.

Slusher, M. P., & Anderson, C. A. (1989). Belief perseverance and self-defeating behavior. In R. C. Curtis (Ed.), *Self-defeating behaviors: Experimental research, clinical impressions, and practical implications* (pp. 11–40). Plenum Press.

Smith, A. M., Floerke, V. A., & Thomas, A. K. (2016). Retrieval practice protects memory against acute stress. *Science*, *354*(6315), 1046–1048. https://doi.org/10.1126/science.aah5067

Smith, B. P., Browne, M., Mack, J., & Kontou, T. G. (2018). An exploratory study of human–dog co-sleeping using actigraphy: Do dogs disrupt their owner's sleep? *Anthrozoös*, *31*(6), 727–740. https://doi.org/10.1080/08927936.2018.1529355

Smith, B. P., Thompson, K., Clarkson, L., & Dawson, D. (2014). The prevalence and implications of human–animal co-sleeping in an Australian sample. *Anthrozoös*, *27*(4), 543–551. https://doi.org/10.2752/089279314X14072268687880

Smith, C. T., & Nosek, B. A. (2011). Affective focus increases the concordance between implicit and explicit attitudes. *Social Psychology*, *42*(4), 300–313. https://doi.org/10.1027/1864-9335/a000072

Smith, E. E., & Medin, D. L. (1981). *Categories and concepts*. Harvard University Press.

Smith, G. (2014). *Standard deviations: Flawed assumptions, tortured data, and other ways to lie with statistics*. Abrams Press.

Smith, P. K., Talamelli, L., Cowie, H., Naylor, P., & Chauhan, P. (2004). Profiles of non-victims, escaped victims, continuing victims and new victims of school bullying. *British Journal of Educational Psychology*, *74*(4), 565–581. https://doi.org/10.1348/0007099042376427

Smith, R. C., Fortin, A. H., Dwamena, F., & Frankel, R. M. (2013). An evidence-based patient-centered method makes the biopsychosocial model scientific. *Patient Education and Counseling*, *91*(3), 265–270. https://doi.org/10.1016/j.pec.2012.12.010

Smith, S., & Blankenship, S. (1991). Incubation and the persistence of fixation in problem solving. *American Journal of Psychology*, *104*(1), 61–87. https://doi.org/10.2307/1422851

Snarey, J. R. (1985). Cross-cultural universality of social-moral development: A critical review of Kohlbergian research. *Psychological Bulletin*, *97*(2), 202–232. https://doi.org/10.1037/0033-2909.97.2.202

Snow, J. (1854). *On the mode of communication of cholera*. C. F. Cheffins, Lith, Southhampton Buildings.

Snyder, M. (1974). Self-monitoring of expressive behavior. *Journal of Personality and Social Psychology*, *30*(4), 526–537. https://doi.org/10.1037/h0037039

Soeter, M., & Kindt, M. (2010). Dissociating response systems: Erasing fear from memory. *Neurobiology of Learning and Memory*, *94*(1), 30–41. https://doi.org/10.1016/j.nlm.2010.03.004

Soga, T., Teo, C. H., & Parhar, I. (2021). Genetic and epigenetic consequence of early-life social stress on depression: Role of serotonin-associated genes. *Frontiers in Genetics*, *11*, 1–8. https://doi.org/10.3389/fgene.2020.601868

Sohail, R., & Rafi, S. (2018). Discourse historical approach towards "Killing hunger with entertainment": A street art. *Linguistics and Literature Review*, *4*(2), 135–143. https://ssrn.com/abstract=3825422

Soldz, S., & Vaillant, G. E. (1999). The Big Five personality traits and the life course: A 45-year longitudinal study. *Journal of*

Research in Personality, *33*(2), 208–232. https://doi.org/10.1006/jrpe.1999.2243

Solmi, M., Soardo, L., Kaur, S., Azis, M., Cabras, A., Censori, M., Fausti, L., Bensana, F., Salazar de Pablo, G., & Fusar-Poli, P. (2023). Meta-analytic prevalence of comorbid mental disorders in individuals at clinical high risk of psychosis: The case for transdiagnostic assessment. *Molecular Psychiatry*, *28*, 2291–2300. https://doi.org/10.1038/s41380-023-02029-8

Solms, M. (2003). Dreaming and REM sleep are controlled by different brain mechanisms. In E. F. Pace-Schott, M. Solms, M. Blagrove, & S. Harnad (Eds.), *Sleep and dreaming: Scientific advances and reconsiderations* (pp. 51–58). Cambridge University Press.

Solowij, N., & Battisti, R. (2008). The chronic effects of cannabis on memory in humans: A review. *Current Drug Abuse Reviews*, *1*(1), 81–98. https://doi.org/10.2174/1874473710801010081

Somer, E., Abu-Rayya, H. M., Schimmenti, A., Metin, B., Brenner, R., Ferrante, E., Göçmen, B., & Marino, A. (2020). Heightened levels of maladaptive daydreaming are associated with covid-19 lockdown, pre-existing psychiatric diagnoses, and intensified psychological dysfunctions: A multi-country study. *Frontiers in Psychiatry*, *11*, Article 587455. https://doi.org/10.3389/fpsyt.2020.587455

Somer, E., Somer, L., & Jopp, D. S. (2016). Parallel lives: A phenomenological study of the lived experience of maladaptive daydreaming. *Journal of Trauma & Dissociation*, *17*(5), 561–576. https://doi.org/10.1080/15299732.2016.1160463

Sørensen, A., Ruhé, H. G., & Munkholm, K. (2022). The relationship between dose and serotonin transporter occupancy of antidepressants—a systematic review. *Molecular Psychiatry*, *27*(1), 192–201. https://doi.org/10.1038/s41380-021-01285-w

Sori, C. F. (Ed.). (2012). *Engaging children in family therapy: Creative approaches to integrating theory and research in clinical practice*. Routledge.

Soussignan, R. (2002). Duchenne smile, emotional experience, and autonomic reactivity: A test of the facial feedback hypothesis. *Emotion*, *2*(1), 52–74. https://doi.org/10.1037/1528-3542.2.1.52

Spanos, N. P., Weekes, J. R., & Bertrand, L. D. (1985). Multiple personality: A social psychological perspective. *Journal of Abnormal Psychology*, *94*(3), 362–376. https://doi.org/10.1037/0021-843X.94.3.362

Spearing, E. R., & Wade, K. A. (2022). Long retention intervals impair the confidence–accuracy relationship for eyewitness recall. *Journal of Applied Research in Memory and Cognition*, *11*(3), 384–391. https://doi.org/10.1037/mac0000014

Spearman, C. (1904). "General intelligence," objectively determined and measured. *American Journal of Psychology*, *15*(2), 201–293. https://doi.org/10.1037/11491-006

Speer, K. E., Semple, S., Naumovski, N., D'Cunha, N. M., & McKune, A. J. (2019). HPA axis function and diurnal cortisol in post-traumatic stress disorder: A systematic review. *Neurobiology of Stress*, *11*, 1–10. https://doi.org/10.1016/j.ynstr.2019.100180

Spence, C. (2023). Coriander (cilantro): A most divisive herb. *International Journal of Gastronomy and Food Science*, *33*, Article 100779. https://doi.org/10.1016/j.ijgfs.2023.100779

Spence, J. T., & Hall, S. K. (1996). Children's gender-related self-perceptions, activity preferences, and occupational stereotypes: A test of three models of gender constructs. *Sex Roles*, *35*, 659–691. https://doi.org/10.1007/BF01544086

Sperling, G. (1960). The information available in brief visual presentations. *Psychological Monographs: General and Applied*, *74*(11), 1–29. https://doi.org/10.1037/h0093759

Spettigue, W., & Henderson, K. A. (2004). Eating disorders and the role of the media. *The Canadian Child and Adolescent Psychiatry Review*, *13*(1), 16–19. https://pubmed.ncbi.nlm.nih.gov/19030149/

Spichak, S. (2021). The racist origin of the popular Myers-Briggs Test. *History of Yesterday*. https://historyofyesterday.com/the-racist-origin-of-the-popular-myers-briggs-test-49c735da660a

Spielberg, J. M., Olino, T. M., Forbes, E. E., & Dahl, R. E. (2014). Exciting fear in adolescence: Does pubertal development alter threat processing? *Developmental Cognitive Neuroscience, 8*, 86–95. https://doi.org/10.1016/j.dcn.2014.01.004

Spini, D., & Jopp, D., Pin, S., & Stringhini, S. (2016). The multiplicity of aging: Lessons for theory and conceptual development from longitudinal studies. In V. L. Bengtson & R. A. Settersten (Eds.), *Handbook of theories of aging* (3rd ed., pp. 669–690). Springer.

Squire, L. R., & Kandel, E. R. (2009). *Memory: From mind to molecules* (2nd ed.). Roberts & Company.

Squire, L. R., Stark, C. E. L., & Clark, R. E. (2004). The medial temporal lobe. *Annual Review of Neuroscience, 27*, 279–306. https://doi.org/10.1146/annurev.neuro.27.070203.144130

Srinivasan, S. M., Cavagnino, D. T., & Bhat, A. N. (2018). Effects of equine therapy on individuals with autism spectrum disorder: A systematic review. *Review Journal of Autism and Developmental Disorders, 5*, 156–175. https://doi.org/10.1007/s40489-018-0130-z

Stadlen, N. (2007). *What mothers do especially when it looks like nothing*. Penguin.

Staff, J., Schulenberg, J. E., Maslowsky, J., Bachman, J. G., O'Malley, P. M., Maggs, J. L., & Johnston, L. D. (2010). Substance use changes and social role transitions: Proximal developmental effects on ongoing trajectories from late adolescence through early adulthood. *Development and Psychopathology, 22*(4), 917–932. https://doi.org/10.1017/S0954579410000544

Stafford, B. K., & Huberman, A. D. (2017). Signal integration in thalamus: Labeled lines go cross-eyed and blurry. *Neuron, 93*(4), 717–720. http://dx.doi.org/10.1016/j.neuron.2017.02.020

Stahl, S. M. (2013). *Stahl's essential psychopharmacology: Neuroscientific basis and practical applications* (4th ed.). Cambridge University Press.

Standage, M. (2023). Self-determination theory applied to sport. In R. M. Ryan (Ed.), *The Oxford handbook of self-determination theory* (pp. 702–723). Oxford University Press. https://doi.org/10.1093/oxfordhb/9780197600047.013.35

Stanford Research on the Impact of Tobacco Advertising. (2022). *Collection: Truth Campaign*. https://tobacco.stanford.edu/antismoking/anti-industry/truth-campaign/

Stanovich, K. E., West, R. F., & Toplak, M. E. (2016). *The rationality quotient: Toward a test of rational thinking*. Boston Review.

Steber, C. (2019, March 7). *Therapist says these 15 shows & movies on Netflix & Amazon Prime can boost people's moods*. Bustle. https://www.bustle.com/p/therapists-found-these-15-shows-movies-on-netflix-amazon-prime-dramatically-boost-peoples-moods-16765038

Steffel, M., Williams, E. F., & Perrmann-Graham, J. (2016). Passing the buck: Delegating choices to others to avoid responsibility and blame. *Organizational Behavior and Human Decision Processes, 135*, 32–44. https://doi.org/10.1016/j.obhdp.2016.04.006

Stein, R., & Swan, A. B. (2019). Evaluating the validity of Myers-Briggs Type Indicator theory: A teaching tool and window into intuitive psychology. *Social and Personality Psychology Compass, 13*(2), e12434. https://doi.org/10.1111/spc3.12434

Steinberg, L., Icenogle, G., Shulman, E. P., Breiner, K., Chein, J., Bacchini, D., Chang, L., Chaudhary, N., Di Giunta, L., Dodge, K. A., Fanti, K. A., Lansford, J. E., Malone, P. S., Oburu, P., Pastorelli, C., Skinner, A. T., Sorbring, E., Tapanya, S., Uribe Tirado, L. M., Alampay, L. P., . . . Takash, H. M. (2018). Around the world, adolescence is a time of heightened sensation seeking and immature self-regulation. *Developmental Science, 21*(2), e12532. https://doi.org/10.1111/desc.12532

Steiner, J. (2008). Transference to the analyst as an excluded observer. *The International Journal of Psychoanalysis, 89*(1), 39–54. https://doi.org/10.1111/j.1745-8315.2007.00005.x

Steinfeldt, J. A., Steinfeldt, M. C., England, B., & Speight, Q. L. (2009). Gender role conflict and stigma toward help-seeking among college football players. *Psychology of Men & Masculinities, 10*(4), 261–272. https://doi.org/10.1037/a0017223

Stenico, C., & Greitemeyer, T. (2015). "The others will help: The presence of multiple video game characters reduces helping after the game is over": Corrigendum. *Journal of Social Psychology, 154*(2), 101–104. https://doi.org/10.1080/00224545.2013.864595

Stepansky, P. E. (2009). *Psychoanalysis at the margins*. Other Press.

Stephens, J. M. (2017). How to cheat and not feel guilty: Cognitive dissonance and its amelioration in the domain of academic dishonesty. *Theory Into Practice, 56*(2), 111–120. https://doi.org/10.1080/00405841.2017.1283571

Stephens, N. M., Fryberg, S. A., Markus, H. R., Johnson, C. S., & Covarrubias, R. (2012). Unseen disadvantage: How American universities' focus on independence undermines the academic performance of first-generation college students. *Journal of Personality and Social Psychology, 102*(6), 1178–1197. http://dx.doi.org/10.1037/a0027143

Stephens, S. (2020). Cheating and gaming the system in ancient athletics. *Journal of the Philosophy of Sport, 47*(3), 391–402. https://doi.org/10.1080/00948705.2020.1811110

Steptoe, A. (2019). Happiness and health. *Annual Review Public Health, 40*(1), 339–359. https://doi.org/10.1146/annurev-publhealth-040218-044150

Stern, A., (2020, September 23). *Forced sterilization policies in the US targeted minorities and those with disabilities—and lasted into the 21st century*. Michigan Institute for Healthcare Policy & Innovation. https://ihpi.umich.edu/news/forced-sterilization-policies-us-targeted-minorities-and-those-disabilities-and-lasted-21st

Sternberg R. J. (2012). Intelligence. *Dialogues in Clinical Neuroscience, 14*(1), 19–27.

Sternberg, R. J. (1986). A triangular theory of love. *Psychological Review, 93*(2), 119–135. http://dx.doi.org/10.1037/0033-295X.93.2.119

Sternberg, R. J. (1988). *The triarchic mind: A new theory of human intelligence*. Viking.

Sternberg, R. J. (2003). Contemporary theories of intelligence. In W. M. Reynolds & G. E. Miller (Eds.), *Handbook of psychology: Educational psychology* (Vol. 7, pp. 23–45). John Wiley & Sons.

Sternberg, R. J., & Grigorenko, E. L. (2000). Practical intelligence and its development. In R. Bar-On & J. D. A. Parker (Eds.), *The handbook of emotional intelligence: Theory, development, assessment, and application at home, school, and in the workplace* (pp. 215–243). Jossey-Bass.

Sternberg, R. J., & Grigorenko, E. L. (Eds.). (1997). *Intelligence, heredity, and environment*. Cambridge University Press.

Sternberg, R. J., Siriner, I., Oh, J., & Wong, C. H. (2022). Cultural intelligence: What is it and how can it effectively be measured? *Journal of Intelligence, 10*(3), Article 54. https://doi.org/10.3390/jintelligence10030054

Stetson, G. R. (1897). Some memory tests of Whites and Blacks. *Psychological Review, 4*(3), 285–289. https://doi.org/10.1037/h0069814

Steuer, F. B., & Ham, K. W., II. (2008). Psychology textbooks: Examining their accuracy. *Teaching of Psychology, 35*, 160–168. https://doi.org/10.1080/00986280802189197

Stewart, K., Dalakas, V., & Eells, D. (2022). Does sex sell? Examining the effect of sex appeals in social media ads on engagement with the ad and actual purchase. *Journal of Marketing Communications, 29*(7), 701–714. https://doi.org/10.1080/13527266.2022.2072367

Stice, E. (2002). Risk and maintenance factors for eating pathology: A meta-analytic review. *Psychological Bulletin, 128*(5), 825–848. https://doi.org/10.1037/0033-2909.128.5.825

Stidham-Hall, K., Moreau, C., & Trussell, J. (2012). Patterns and correlates of parental and formal sexual and reproductive health communication for adolescent women in the United States, 2002–2008. *Journal of Adolescent Health, 50*(4), 410–413. https://doi.org/10.1016/j.jadohealth.2011.06.007

Stieger, S. (2019). Facebook usage and life satisfaction. *Frontiers in Psychology, 10*, 1–9. https://doi.org/10.3389/fpsyg.2019.02711

Stigler, S. M. (1989). Francis Galton's account of the invention of correlation. *Statistical Science, 4*(2), 73–79. https://www.jstor.org/stable/2245329

Storm, B. C., & Hickman, M. L. (2015). Mental fixation and metacognitive predictions of insight in creative problem solving. *Quarterly Journal of Experimental Psychology, 68*(4), 802–813. https://doi.org/10.1080/17470218.2014.966730

Storms, M. D. (1978). Sexual orientation and self-perception. In P. Pliner, K. R. Blanstein, I. M. Spigel, T. Alloway, & L. Krames (Eds.), *Advances in the study of communication and affect: Vol. 5, Perception of emotion in self and others* (pp. 165–180). Plenum.

Storms, M. D. (1980). Theories of sexual orientation. *Journal of Personality & Social Psychology, 38*(5), 783–792. https://doi.org/10.1037/0022-3514.38.5.783

Strack, F., Martin, L. L., & Stepper, S. (1988). Inhibiting and facilitating conditions of the human smile: A nonobtrusive test of the facial feedback hypothesis. *Journal of Personality and Social Psychology, 54*(5), 768–777. https://doi.org/10.1037/0022-3514.54.5.768

Strahan, E. J., Spencer, S. J., & Zanna, M. P. (2002). Subliminal priming and persuasion: Striking while the iron is hot. *Journal of Experimental Social Psychology, 38*(6), 556–568. https://doi.org/10.1016/S0022-1031(02)00502-4

Strasburger, H., Huber, J., & Rose, D. (2018). Ewald Hering's (1899) On the limits of visual acuity: A translation and commentary. *i-Perception, 9*(3), 1–14. http://dx.doi.org/10.1177/2041669518763675

Strayer, D. L., Watson, J. M., & Drews, F. A. (2011). Cognitive distraction while multitasking in the automobile. In B. Ross (Ed.) *The psychology of learning and motivation* (Vol. 54, pp. 29–58). Academic Press.

Strelau, J., & Zawadzki, B. (1995). The formal characteristics of behaviour—Temperament inventory (FCB–TI): Validity studies. *European Journal of Personality, 9*(3), 207–229. https://doi.org/10.1002/per.2410090304

Strick, M., van Baaren, R. B., Holland, R. W., & van Knippenberg, A. (2009). Humor in advertisements enhances product liking by mere association. *Journal of Experimental Psychology: Applied, 15*(1), 35–45. https://doi.org/10.1037/a0014812

Ströhle, A., Gensichen, J., & Domschke, K. (2018). The diagnosis and treatment of anxiety disorders. *Deutsches Ärzteblatt International, 115*(37), 611–620. https://doi.org/10.3238/arztebl.2018.0611

Strohmaier, S., Jones, F. W., & Cane, J. E. (2021). Effects of length of mindfulness practice on mindfulness, depression, anxiety, and stress: A randomized controlled experiment. *Mindfulness, 12*(1), 198–214. https://doi.org/10.1007/s12671-020-01512-5

Stroi, O. O. (2020). Gender-biased language of the workplace. *Discourse, 5*(6), 120–131. https://doi.org/10.32603/2412-8562-2019-5-6-120-131

Strojny, P., Strojny, A., Kałwak, W., & Bańbura, A. (2018). Take your eyes off me: The effect of the presence of witnesses on the conduct of rescue operations. *Bezpieczeństwo i Technika Pożarnicza, 49*, 14–22. http://doi.org/10.12845/bitp.49.1.2018.1

Stromberg, J., & Caswell, E. (2015). Why the Myers-Briggs test is totally meaningless. http://www.vox.com/2014/7/15/5881947/myers-briggs-personality-test-meaningless

Strozier, A. L. (2012). The effectiveness of support groups in increasing social support for kinship caregivers. *Children and Youth Services Review, 34*(5), 876–881. https://doi.org/10.1016/j.childyouth.2012.01.007

Stumbrys, T., & Erlacher, D. (2016). Applications of lucid dreams and their effects on the mood upon awakening. *International Journal of Dream Research, 9*(2), 146–150. https://doi.org/10.11588/ijodr.2016.2.33114

Subramaniam, M., Abdin, E., Vaingankar, J., Shafie, S., Chang, S., Seow, E., Chua, B. Y., Jeyagurunathan, A., Heng, D., Kwok, K. W., & Chong, S. A. (2020). Obsessive-compulsive disorder in Singapore: Prevalence, comorbidity, quality of life and social support. *Annals, Academy of Medicine, Singapore, 49*(1), 15–25.

Sudak, H., Maxim, K., & Carpenter, M. (2008). Suicide and stigma: A review of the literature and personal reflections. *Academic Psychiatry, 32*, 136–142. https://doi.org/10.1176/appi.ap.32.2.136

Suddeath, E. G., Kerwin, A. K., & Dugger, S. M. (2017). Narrative family therapy: Practical techniques for more effective work with couples and families. *Journal of Mental Health Counseling, 39*(2), 116–131. https://doi.org/10.17744/mehc.39.2.03

Suddendorf, T., & Butler, D. L. (2013). The nature of visual self-recognition. *Trends in Cognitive Sciences, 17*(3), 121–127. https://doi.org/10.1016/j.tics.2013.01.004

Sue, S. (1983). Ethnic minority issues in psychology: A reexamination. *American Psychologist, 38*, 583–592. https://doi.org/10.1037/0003-066X.38.5.583

Suellentrop, C. (2001, December 21). *A real number: A Beautiful Mind's John Nash is nowhere near as complicated as the real one.* Culturebox. https://slate.com/culture/2001/12/a-beautiful-mind-s-john-nash-is-less-complex-than-the-real-one.html

Sullivan, E. V., Lannoy, S., Le Berre, A.-P., Fama, R., & Pfefferbaum, A. (2023). Alcohol drinking and alcohol use disorder across the ages: Dynamic effects on the brain and function. In G. G. Brown, T. Z. King, K. Y. Haaland, & B. Crosson (Eds.), *APA handbook of neuropsychology: Vol. 1. Neurobehavioral disorders and conditions: Accepted science and open questions* (pp. 569–607). American Psychological Association. https://doi.org/10.1037/0000307-027

Sumiya, M., & Senju, A. (2023). Influence of friendship on loneliness among adolescents with Autism Spectrum Disorders in Japan. *Journal of Autism and Developmental Disorders.* Advance online publication. https://doi.org/10.1007/s10803-023-05958-z

Sun, H., Saeedi, P., Karuranga, S., Pinkepank, M., Ogurtsova, K., Duncan, B. B., Stein, C., Basit, B., Chan, J. C. N., Mbanya, J. C., Pavkov, M. E., Ramachandaran, A., Wild, S. H., James, S., Herman, W. H., Zhang, P., Bommer, C., Kuo, S., Boyko, E. K., & Magliano, D. J. (2022). IDF Diabetes Atlas: Global, regional and country-level diabetes prevalence estimates for 2021 and projections for 2045. *Diabetes Research and Clinical Practice, 183*, Article 109119. https://doi.org/10.1016/j.diabres.2021.109119

Super, D. E. (1980). A life-span, life-space approach to career development. *Journal of Vocational Behavior, 16*(3), 282–298. https://doi.org/10.1016/0001-8791(80)90056-1

Swart, S., Wildschut, M., Draijer, N., Langeland, W., & Smit, J. H. (2020). The dissociative subtype of posttraumatic stress disorder or PTSD with comorbid dissociative disorders: Comparative evaluation of clinical profiles. *Psychological Trauma: Theory, Research, Practice, and Policy, 12*(1), 38–45. https://doi.org/10.1037/tra0000474

Swets, J. A. (1961). Is there a sensory threshold? *Science, 134*(3473), 168–177. https://doi.org/10.1126/science.134.3473.168

Symons, C. S. & Johnson, B. T. (1997). The self-reference effect in memory: A meta-analysis. *Psychological Bulletin, 121*(3), 371–394. https://doi.org/10.1037/0033-2909.121.3.371

Szasz, T. (1960). The myth of mental illness. *American Psychologist, 15*(2), 113–118. https://doi.org/10.1037/h0046535

Szasz, T. (1994). Mental illness is still a myth. *Society, 31*(4), 34–39. https://doi.org/10.1007/BF02693245

Szasz, T. (2011). The myth of mental illness: 50 years later. *The Psychiatrist, 35*(5), 179–182. https://doi.org/10.1192/pb.bp.110.031310

Tabb, K., Schaffner, K. F., Kendler, K. S., & Parnas, J. (2017). Causal pathways, random walks and tortuous paths: Moving from the descriptive to the etiological in psychiatry. In K. S. Kendler & J. Parnas (Eds.), *Philosophical issues in psychiatry IV: Psychiatric nosology* (pp. 342–360). Oxford University Press.

Tai, X. Y., Chen, C., Manohar, S., & Husain, M. (2022). Impact of sleep duration on executive function and brain structure. *Communications Biology, 5*, Article 201. https://doi.org/10.1038/s42003-022-03123-3

Tajfel, H. M. (1970). Experiments in intergroup discrimination. *Scientific American, 223*(5), 96–102. https://doi.org/10.1038/scientificamerican1170-96

Tajfel, H. M. (1981). *Human groups and social categories: Studies in Social Psychology.* CUP Archive.

Tajfel, H. M. (1982). Social psychology of intergroup relations. *Annual Review of Psychology, 33*(1), 1–39. https://doi.org/10.1146/annurev.ps.33.020182.000245

Tajfel, H. M., & Turner, J. C. (1979). An integrative theory of intergroup conflict. *The Social Psychology of Intergroup Relations, 33*(47), 33–47.

Tajfel, H. M., & Turner, J. C. (1986). The social identity theory of intergroup behavior. In S. Worchel & W. G. Austin, (Eds.), *Psychology of intergroup relations* (pp. 7–24). Nelson-Hall.

Takahashi, R. H., Nagao, T., & Gouras, G. K. (2017). Plaque formation and the intraneuronal accumulation of -amyloid in Alzheimer's disease. *Pathology International, 67*(4), 185–193. https://doi.org/10.1111/pin.12520

Takeda, T., Ando, M., & Kumagai, K. (2015). Attention deficit and attention training in early twentieth-century Japan. *ADHD Attention Deficit and Hyperactivity Disorders, 7*, 101–111. https://doi.org/10.1007/s12402-014-0157-7

Tambini, A., Ketz, N., & Davachi, L. (2010). Enhanced brain correlations during rest are related to memory for recent experiences. *Neuron, 65*(2), 280–290. https://doi.org/10.1016/j.neuron.2010.01.001

Tan, J. C. (2019). Perspectives of psychopathology across cultures and among indigenous societies. In K. D. Keith (Ed.), *Cross-cultural psychology: Contemporary themes and perspectives* (pp. 467–481). Wiley.

Tangney, J. P., Boone, A. L., & Baumeister, R. F. (Eds.). (2018). *High self-control predicts good adjustment, less pathology, better grades, and interpersonal success.* Routledge.

Tanner, A. E. (2023). Shaping, systematic desensitization, and graduated exposure. In J. H. Cihon, L. Tereshko, K. B. Marshall, & M. J. Weiss (Eds.), *Behavior analytic approaches to promote enjoyable mealtimes for autistics/individuals diagnosed with autism and their families* (pp. 153–182). Vernon Press.

Tapia-Rojas, C., Aranguiz, F., Varela-Nallar, L., & Inestrosa, N. C. (2016). Voluntary running attenuates memory loss, decreases neuropathological changes and induces neurogenesis in a mouse model of Alzheimer's disease. *Brain Pathology, 26*(1), 62–74. https://doi.org/10.1111/bpa.12255

Taruffi, L., Pehrs, C., Skouras, S., & Koelsch, S. (2017). Effects of sad and happy music on mind-wandering and the default mode network. *Scientific Reports, 7*(1), 1–10. https://doi.org/10.1038/s41598-017-14849-0

Taubman-Ben-Ari, O., & Findler, L. (2006). Motivation for military service: A terror management perspective. *Military Psychology, 18*(2), 149–159. https://doi.org/10.1207/s15327876mp1802_4

Taylor, A. K., & Kowalski, P. (2012). Students' misconceptions in psychology: How you ask matters...sometimes. *Journal of the Scholarship of Teaching and Learning, 12*(3), 62–77. https://doi.org/10.1007/bf03395459

Taylor, C. A., Fleckman, J. M., & Lee, S. J. (2009). Attitudes, beliefs, and perceived norms about corporal punishment and related training needs among members of the "American Professional Society on the Abuse of Children." *Child Abuse and Neglect, 71*, 56–68. https://doi.org/10.1016/j.chiabu.2017.04.009

Taylor, C. L., Ivcevic, Z., Moeller, J., Menges, J. I., Reiter-Palmon, R., & Brackett, M. A. (2022). Gender and emotions at work: Organizational rank has greater emotional benefits for men than women. *Sex Roles, 86*(1–2), 127–142. https://doi.org/10.1007/s11199-021-01256-z

Taylor, S. (2017). Misophonia: A new mental disorder? *Medical Hypotheses, 103*, 109–117. https://doi.org/10.1016/j.mehy.2017.05.003

Taylor, S. E. (2006). Tend and befriend: Biobehavioral bases of affiliation under stress. *Current Directions in Psychological Science, 15*(6), 273–277. https://doi.org/10.1111/j.1467-8721.2006.00451.x

Taylor, S. E. (2012). Tend and befriend theory. *Handbook of Theories of Social Psychology, 1*, 32–49. https://doi.org/10.4135/9781446249215

Templer, D. I., Veleber, D. M., & Brooner, R. K. (1982). Geophysical variables and behavior: VI. Lunar phase and accident injuries: A difference between night and day. *Perceptual and Motor Skills, 55*(1), 280–282. https://doi.org/10.2466/pms.1982.55.1.280

Tempski, P., Danila, A. H., Arantes-Costa, F. M., Siqueira, M. A., Torsani, M. B., & Martins, M. A. (2020). The COVID-19 pandemic: Time for medical teachers and students to overcome grief. *Clinics, 75*, e2206. https://doi.org/10.6061/clinics/2020/e2206

Teoh, A. N., Ooi, E. Y. E., & Chan, A. Y. (2021). Boredom affects sleep quality: The serial mediation effect of inattention and bedtime procrastination. *Personality and Individual Differences, 171*, Article 110460. https://doi.org/10.1016/j.paid.2020.110460

Terman, L. M. (1916). *The measurement of intelligence.* Houghton, Mifflin and Company.

Terman, L. M. (1918). The use of intelligence tests in the army. *Psychological Bulletin, 15*(6), 177–187. https://doi.org/10.1037/h0071532

Terrace, H. (2019). *Why chimpanzees can't learn language and only humans can.* Columbia University Press.

Terrace, H. S., Petitto, L. A., Sanders, R. J., & Bever, T. G. (1979). Can an ape create a sentence? *Science, 206*(4421), 891–902. https://doi.org/10.1126/science.504995

Thaczuk, D. (2007, June 28). MSM in Africa: Highly stigmatised, vulnerable and in need of urgent HIV prevention. *AIDSmap.* Retrieved from https://web.archive.org/web/20070701184934/http://www.aidsmap.com:80/en/news/16F65073-E5CE-40B9-B189-50763B6B8E06.asp.

Thalmayer, A. G., Saucier, G., & Rotzinger, J. S. (2022). Absolutism, relativism, and universalism in personality traits across cultures: The case of the big five. *Journal of Cross-Cultural Psychology, 53*(7–8), 935–956. https://doi.org/10.1177/00220221221111813

Thalmayer, A. G., Saucier, G., Ole-Kotikash, L., & Payne, D. (2020). Personality structure in east and west Africa: Lexical studies of personality in Maa and Supyire-Senufo. *Journal of Personality and Social Psychology, 119*(5), 1132–1152. https://doi.org/10.1037/pspp0000264

Thapa, P., & Farber, D. L. (2019). The role of the thymus in the immune response. *Thoracic Surgery Clinics, 29*(2), 123–131. https://doi.org/10.1016/j.thorsurg.2018.12.001

Thase, M. E. (2013). Comparative effectiveness of psychodynamic psychotherapy and cognitive-behavioral therapy: It's about time, and what's next? *American Journal of Psychiatry, 170*(9), 953–956. https://doi.org/10.1176/appi.ajp.2013.13060839

Thase, M. E., & Sachs, G. S. (2000). Bipolar depression: Pharmacotherapy and related therapeutic strategies. *Biological Psychiatry, 48*(6), 558–572. https://doi.org/10.1016/S0006-3223(00)00980-X

The Myers-Briggs Company. (2018). Myers-Briggs Type Indicator (MBTI)—A positive framework for life-long people development. https://www.themyersbriggs.com/en-US/Products-and-Services/Myers-Briggs

Theisen, J. G., Sundaram, V., Filchak, M. S., Chorich, L. P., Sullivan, M. E., Knight, J., Kim, H-G., & Layman, L. C. (2019). The use of whole exome sequencing in a cohort of transgender individuals to identify rare genetic variants. *Scientific Reports*, 9(1), 1–11. https://doi.org/10.1038/s41598-019-53500-y

Thomas, R. K. (1997). Correcting some Pavloviana regarding "Pavlov's bell" and Pavlov's "mugging." *American Journal of Psychology*, 110(1), 115–125. https://doi.org/10.2307/1423704

Thompson, T., McQueen, A., Croston, M., Luke, A., Caito, N., Quinn, K., Funaro, J., & Kreuter, M. W. (2019). Social needs and health-related outcomes among Medicaid beneficiaries. *Health Education & Behavior: The Official Publication of the Society for Public Health Education*, 46(3), 436–444. https://doi.org/10.1177/1090198118822724

Thompson-Cannino, J., Cotton, R., & Torneo, E. (2009). *Picking cotton*. St. Martins Grifin.

Thorndike, E. L. (1911). *Animal intelligence: Experimental studies*. Macmillan.

Thurstone, L. L. (1938). *Primary mental abilities*. University of Chicago Press.

Tiihonen, J., Taipale, H., & Correll, C. U. (2020). Commentary on Robert Whitaker's viewpoint. *Psychological Medicine*, 50(16), 2653–2654. https://doi.org/10.1017/S0033291720003591

Till, B. D., Stanley, S. M., & Priluck, R. (2008). Classical conditioning and celebrity endorsers: An examination of belongingness and resistance to extinction. *Psychology & Marketing*, 25(2), 179–196. https://doi.org/10.1002/mar.20205

Tillage, R. P., Foster, S. L., Lustberg, D., Liles, L. C., McCann, K. E., & Weinshenker, D. (2021). Co-released norepinephrine and galanin act on different timescales to promote stress-induced anxiety-like behavior. *Neuropsychopharmacology*, 46(8), 1535–1543. https://doi.org/10.1038/s41386-021-01011-8

Tinto, V. (2012). *Completing college: Rethinking institutional action*. University of Chicago Press.

Tinto, V. (2017). Through the eyes of students. *Journal of College Student Retention: Research, Theory & Practice*, 19(3), 254–269. https://doi.org/10.1177/1521025115621917

Titchener, E. B. (2009). An outline of psychology. In B. Gentile & B. O. Miller (Eds.), *Foundations of psychological thought: A history of psychology* (pp. 219–236). SAGE. (Original work published 1896)

Toffler, A. (1970). *Future shock*. Random House.

Tokutsu, Y., Umene-Nakano, W., Shinkai, T., Yoshimura, R., Okamoto, T., Katsuki, A., Hori, H., Ikenouchi-Sugita, A., Hayashi, K., Atake, K., & Nakamura, J. (2013). Follow-up study on electroconvulsive therapy in treatment-resistant depressed patients after remission: A chart review. *Clinical Psychopharmacology and Neuroscience*, 11(1), 34–38. https://doi.org/10.9758/cpn.2013.11.1.34

Tolliver, B. K., & Anton, R. F. (2022). Assessment and treatment of mood disorders in the context of substance abuse. *Dialogues in Clinical Neuroscience*, 17(2), 181–190. https://doi.org/10.31887/DCNS.2015.17.2/btolliver

Tolman, E. C. (1932). *Purposive behavior in animals and men*. Century.

Tolman, E. C. (1948). Cognitive maps in rats and men. *Psychological Review*, 55(4), 189–208. https://doi.org/10.1037/h0061626

Tolman, E. C., & Honzik, C. H. (1930). Introduction and removal of reward, and maze performance in rats. *University of California Publications in Psychology*, 4, 257–275.

Toma, C. L., Hancock, J. T., & Ellison, N. B. (2008). Separating fact from fiction: An examination of deceptive self-presentation in online dating profiles. *Personality and Social Psychology Bulletin*, 34(8), 1023–1036. https://doi.org/10.1177/0146167208318067

Tomkins, S. S. (2008). *Affect imagery consciousness: The complete edition*. Springer.

Tooke, W., & Camire, L. (1991). Patterns of deception in intersexual and intrasexual mating strategies. *Ethology and Sociobiology*, 12(5), 345–364. https://doi.org/10.1016/0162-3095(91)90030-T

Torous, J., Staples, P., Fenstermacher, E., Dean, J., & Keshavan, M. (2016). Barriers, benefits, and beliefs of brain training smartphone apps: An internet survey of younger us consumers. *Frontiers in Human Neuroscience*, 10, Article 180. https://doi.org/10.3389/fnhum.2016.00180

Torrey, E. F., Kennard, A. D., Eslinger, D., Lamb, R., & Pavle, J. (2010). *More mentally ill persons are in jails and prisons than hospitals: A survey of the states*. Treatment Advocacy Center.

Torrubia, R., Avila, C., Moltó, J., & Caseras, X. (2001). The Sensitivity to Punishment and Sensitivity to Reward Questionnaire (SPSRQ) as a measure of Gray's anxiety and impulsivity dimensions. *Personality and Individual Differences*, 31(6), 837–862. https://doi.org/10.1016/S0191-8869(00)00183-5

Totterdell, P., Kellett, S., Teuchmann, K., & Briner, R. B. (1998). Evidence of mood linkage in work groups. *Journal of Personality and Social Psychology*, 74(6), 1504–1515. https://doi.org/10.1037/0022-3514.74.6.1504

Toufexis, D., Rivarola, M. A., Lara, H., & Viau, V. (2014). Stress and the reproductive axis. *Journal of Neuroendocrinology*, 26(9), 573–586. https://doi.org/10.1111/jne.12179

Trahan, L. H., Stuebing, K. K., Fletcher, J. M., & Hiscock, M. (2014). The Flynn effect: A meta-analysis. *Psychological Bulletin*, 140(5), 1332–1360. https://doi.org/10.1037/a0037173

Trahan, T., Durrant, S. J., Müllensiefen, D., & Williamson, V. J. (2018). The music that helps people sleep and the reasons they believe it works: A mixed methods analysis of online survey reports. *PLoS ONE*, 13(11), Article e0206531. https://doi.org/10.1371/journal.pone.0206531

Trans Student Educational Resources. (2015). *The gender unicorn*. www.transstudent.org/gender

Trappey, C. (1996). A meta-analysis of consumer choice and subliminal advertising. *Psychology and Marketing*, 13(5), 517–530. https://doi.org/10.1002/(SICI)1520-6793(199608)13:5<517::AID-MAR5>3.0.CO;2-C

Travis, F., Valosek, L., Konrad IV, A., Link, J., Salerno, J., Scheller, R., & Nidich, S. (2018). Effect of meditation on psychological distress and brain functioning: A randomized controlled study. *Brain and Cognition*, 125, 100–105. https://doi.org/10.1016/j.bandc.2018.03.011

Triandis, H. C. (1989). The self and social behavior in differing cultural contexts. *Psychological Review*, 96(3), 506–520. https://doi.org/10.1037/0033-295X.96.3.506

Triebwasser, J., Chemerinski, E., Roussos, P., & Siever, L. J. (2012). Schizoid personality disorder. *Journal of Personality Disorders*, 26(6), 919–926. https://doi.org/10.1521/pedi.2012.26.6.919

Triplett, N. (1898). The dynamogenic factors in pacemaking and competition. *American Journal of Psychology*, 9(4), 507–533. https://doi.org/10.2307/1412188

Trivers, R. (2011). *The folly of fools: The logic of deceit and self-deception in human life*. Basic Books.

Trofimova, I., & Christiansen, J. (2016). Coupling of temperament with mental illness in four age groups. *Psychological Reports*, 118(2), 387–412. https://doi.org/10.1177/0033294116639430

Trüeb, R. M. (2006). Pharmacologic interventions in aging hair. *Clinical Interventions in Aging*, 1(2), 121–129. https://doi.org/10.2147/ciia.2006.1.2.121

Tryon, W. W. (2004). Issues of validity in actigraphic sleep assessment. *Sleep*, 27(1), 158–165. https://doi.org/10.1093/sleep/27.1.158

Trzmiel, T., Purandare, B., Michalak, M., Zasadzka, E., & Pawlaczyk, M. (2019). Equine assisted activities and therapies in children with autism spectrum disorder: A systematic review and a meta-analysis. *Complementary Therapies in Medicine*, 42, 104–113. https://doi.org/10.1016/j.ctim.2018.11.004

Tsagkaris, C., & Kalachanis, K. (2020). The Hippocratic account of mental health: Humors and human temperament. *Mental*

Health: Global Challenges Journal, 3(1), 33–37. https://doi.org/10.32437/mhgcj.v3i1.83

Tulving, E. (1976). Ecphoric processes in recall and recognition. In J. Brown (Ed.), *Recall and recognition* (pp. 37–73). Wiley.

Tulving, E., & Thomson, D. M. (1973). Encoding specificity and retrieval processes in episodic memory. *Psychological Review, 80*(5), 352–373. https://doi.org/10.1037/h0020071

Turgoose, D., Glover, N., Barker, C., & Maddox, L. (2017). Empathy, compassion fatigue, and burnout in police officers working with rape victims. *Traumatology, 23*(2), 205–213. https://doi.org/10.1037/trm0000118

Turkheimer, E., Haley, A., Waldron, M., D'Onofrio, B., & Gottesman, I. I. (2003). Socioeconomic status modifies heritability of IQ in young children. *Psychological Science, 14*(6), 623–628. https://doi.org/10.1046/j.0956-7976.2003.psci_1475.x

Türkmen, H., & Oran, N. T. (2021). Massage and heat application on labor pain and comfort: A quasi-randomized controlled experimental study. *Explore, 17*(5), 438–445. https:// doi.org/10.1016/j.explore.2020.08.002

Turri, M. G. (2015). Transference and katharsis, Freud to Aristotle. *The International Journal of Psychoanalysis, 96*(2), 369–387. https://doi.org/10.1111/1745-8315.12243

Tversky, A., & Kahneman, D. (1971). Belief in the law of small numbers. *Psychological Bulletin, 76*(2), 105–110. https://doi.org/10.1037/h0031322

Tversky, A., & Kahneman, D. (1972). Subjective probability: A judgment of representativeness. *Cognitive Psychology, 3*(3), 430–454. https://doi.org/10.1016/0010-0285(72)90016-3

Tversky, A., & Kahneman, D. (1973). Availability: A heuristic for judging frequency and probability. *Cognitive Psychology, 5*(2), 207–232. https://doi.org/10.1016/0010-0285(73)90033-9

Tversky, A., & Kahneman, D. (1981). The framing of decisions and the psychology of choice. *Science, 211*(4481), 453–458. https://doi.org/10.1007/978-1-4613-2391-4_2

Tversky, B., & Hemenway, K. (1984). Objects, parts, and categories. *Journal of Experimental Psychology: General, 113*(2), 169–197. https://doi.org/10.1037/0096-3445.113.2.169

Tylka, T. L., & Sabik, N. J. (2010). Integrating social comparison theory and self-esteem within objectification theory to predict women's disordered eating. *Sex Roles, 63*(1–2), 18–31. https://doi.org/10.1007/s11199-010-9785-3

Tyson, P. J., Davies, S. K., Scorey, S., & Greville, W. J. (2023). Fear of clowns: An investigation into the aetiology of coulrophobia. *Frontiers in Psychology, 14*, Article 1109466. https://doi.org/10.3389/fpsyg.2023.1109466

U.S. Bureau of Labor Statistics. (2015). *Number of jobs held, labor market activity, and earnings growth among the youngest baby boomers: Results from a longitudinal study.* https://www.bls.gov/news.release/archives/nlsoy_03312015.pdf

U.S. Department of Agriculture. (2017). *Families projected to spend an average of $233,610 raising a child born* in 2015. https://www.usda.gov/media/press-releases/2017/01/09/families-projected-spend-average-233610-raising-child-born-2015

Uher, R., & Zwicker, A. (2017). Etiology in psychiatry: Embracing the reality of poly-gene-environmental causation of mental illness. *World Psychiatry, 16*(2), 121–129. https://doi.org/10.1002/wps.20436

Uhls, Y. T., Ellison, N. B., & Subrahmanyam, K. (2017). Benefits and costs of social media in adolescence. *Pediatrics, 140*(Suppl. 2), S67–S70. https://doi.org/10.1542/peds.2016-1758E

Uleman, J. S., & Bargh, J. A. (Eds.). (1989). *Unintended thought.* Guilford.

Ullén, F., Harmat, L., Theorell, T., & Madison, G. (2016). Flow and individual differences—A phenotypic analysis of data from more than 10,000 twin individuals. In L. Harmat, F. Ø. Andersen, F. Ullén, J. Wright, & G. Sadlo (Eds.), *Flow experience: Empirical research and applications* (pp. 267–288). Springer International Publishing AG. https://doi.org/10.1007/978-3-319-28634-1_17

Ulrich, S., Ricken, R., Buspavanich, P., Schlattmann, P., & Adli, M. (2020). Efficacy and adverse effects of tranylcypromine and tricyclic antidepressants in the treatment of depression: A systematic review and comprehensive meta-analysis. *Journal of Clinical Psychopharmacology, 40*(1), 63–74. https://doi.org/10.1097/JCP.0000000000001153

Ummak, E., Türken, S., & Keles, S. (2023). Where to belong: Being a sexual and ethnic minority group member in Norway. *Sex Roles, 89*, 35–47. https://doi.org/10.1007/s11199-023-01370-0

Ünal, A. B., de Waard, D., Epstude, K., & Steg, L. (2013). Driving with music: Effects on arousal and performance. *Transportation Research Part F: Traffic Psychology and Behaviour, 21*, 52–65. https://doi.org/10.1016/j.trf.2013.09.004

University of Tübingen. (2020). *Tübingen researchers show conscious processes in birds' brains for the first time* [Press release]. https://uni-tuebingen.de/en/university/news-and-publications/press-releases/press-releases/article/tuebingen-researchers-show-conscious-processes-in-birds-brains-for-the-first-time/

Upadhyay, I. S., Srivatsa, K. A., *& Mamidi, R.* (2022, July). Towards toxic positivity detection. *In Proceedings of the Tenth International Workshop on Natural Language Processing for Social Media (pp.* 75–82). Association for Computational Linguistics.

Urdan, T., & Kaplan, A. (2020). The origins, evolution, and future directions of achievement goal theory. *Contemporary Educational Psychology, 61*, Article 101862. https://doi.org/10.1016/j.cedpsych.2020.101862

Urquhart, J. A., Sivakumaran, M. H., Macfarlane, J. A., & O'Connor, A. R. (2018). fMRI evidence supporting the role of memory conflict in the déjà vu experience. *Memory, 29*(7), 1–12. https://doi.org/10.1080/09658211.2018.1524496

Urry, H. L., Crittle, C. S., Floerke, V. A., Leonard, M. Z., Perry, C. S., Akdilek, N., Albert, E. R., Block, A. J., Bollinger, C. A., Bowers, E. M., Brody, R. S., Burk, K. C., Burnstein, A., Chan, A. K., Chan, P. C., Chang, L. J., Chen, E., Chiarawongse, C. P., Chin, G., . . . Zarrow, J. (2021). Don't ditch the laptop just yet: A direct replication of Mueller and Oppenheimer's (2014) study 1 plus mini-meta-analyses across similar studies. *Psychological Science, 32*(3), 326–339. https://doi.org/10.1177/0956797620965541

Uthaug, M. V., Mason, N. L., Toennes, S. W., Reckweg, J. T., de Sousa Fernandes Perna, E. B., Kuypers, K. P. C., van Oorsouw, K., Riba, J., & Ramaekers, J. G. (2021). A placebo-controlled study of the effects of ayahuasca, set and setting on mental health of participants in ayahuasca group retreats. *Psychopharmacology, 238*(7), 1899–1910. https://doi.org/10.1007/s00213-021-05817-8

Utomo, Y. P., Luthfi Adnan, M., & Putri Susanti, E. A. (2023). Understanding dissociative identity disorder: A literature review. *Archives of Psychiatry Research: An International Journal of Psychiatry and Related Sciences, 59*(2), 305–310. https://doi.org/10.20471/dec.2023.59.02.14

UvnäsMoberg, K., Ekström-Bergström, A., Buckley, S., Massarotti, C., Pajalic, Z., Luegmair, K., Kotlowska, A., Lengler, L., Olza, I., Gryllka-Baeschlin, S., Leahy-Warren, P., Hadjigeorgiu, E., Villarmea, S., & Dencker, A. (2020). Maternal plasma levels of oxytocin during breastfeeding—A systematic review. *PLoS One, 15*(8), 1–38. https://doi.org/10.1371/journal.pone.0235806

Vail, K. E., III, Juhl, J., Arndt, J., Vess, M., Routledge, C., & Rutjens, B. T. (2012). When death is good for life: Considering the positive trajectories of terror management. *Personality and Social Psychology Review, 16*(4), 303–329. https://doi.org/10.1177/1088868312440046

Vaingankar, J. A., Van Dam, R. M., Samari, E., Chang, S., Seow, E., Chua, Y. C., Luo, N., Verma, S., & Subramaniam, M. (2022). Social media–driven routes to positive mental health among youth: Qualitative enquiry and concept mapping study. *JMIR Pediatrics and Parenting, 5*(1), 1–14. https://doi.org/10.2196/32758

Vaitl, D., Birbaumer, N., Gruzelier, J., Jamieson, G. A., Kotchoubey, B., Kübler, A., Lehmann, D., Miltner, W. H. R., Ott, U., Pütz, P., Sammer, G., Strauch, I., Strehl, U., Wackermann, J., & Weiss, T. (2005). Psychobiology of altered states of consciousness. *Psychological Bulletin, 131*(1), 98–127. https://doi.org/10.1037/0033-2909.131.1.98

Valkenburg, P. M. (2022). Social media use and well-being: What we know and what we need to know. *Current Opinion in Psychology, 45*, Article 101294. https://doi.org/10.1016/j.copsyc.2021.12.006

Valkenburg, P. M., & Peter, J. (2007). Who visits online dating sites? Exploring some characteristics of online daters. *CyberPsychology & Behavior, 10*(6), 849–852. https://doi.org/10.1089/cpb.2007.9941

Vallée-Tourangeau, F., Euden, G., & Hearn, V. (2011). Einstellung defused: Interactivity and mental set. *Quarterly Journal of Experimental Psychology, 64*(10), 1889–1895. https://doi.org/10.1080/17470218.2011.605151

Vallerand, R. J. (2007). Intrinsic and extrinsic motivation in sport and physical activity: A review and a look at the future. In G. Tenenbaum & R. C. Eklund (Eds.), *Handbook of sport psychology* (3rd ed., pp. 59–83). John Wiley.

van Bommel, M., van Prooijen, J. W., Elffers, H., & Van Lange, P. A. M. (2014). Intervene to be seen: The power of a camera in attenuating the bystander effect. *Social Psychological and Personality Science, 5*(4), 459–466. https://doi.org/10.1177/1948550613507958

van Bommel, M., van Prooijen, J. W., Elffers, H., & Van Lange, P. A. M. (2016). The lonely bystander: Ostracism leads to less helping in virtual bystander situations. *Social Influence, 11*(3), 141–150. https://doi.org/10.1080/15534510.2016.1171796

Van Cauter, E., & Copinschi, G. (2000). Interrelationships between growth hormone and sleep. *Growth Hormone & IGF Research, 10*(Suppl. B), S57–S62. https://doi.org/10.1016/s1096-6374(00)80011-8

Van Dam, N. T., van Vugt, M. K., Vago, D. R., Schmalzl, L., Saron, C. D., Olendzki, A., Meissner, T., Lazar, S. W., Kerr, C. E., Gorchov, J., Fox, K. C. R., Field, B. A., Britton, W. B., Brefczynski-Lewis, J. A., & Meyer, D. E. (2018). Mind the hype: A critical evaluation and prescriptive agenda for research on mindfulness and meditation. *Perspectives on Psychological Science, 13*(1), 36–61. https://doi.org/10.1177/1745691617709589

Van Dam, N. T., Van Vugt, M. K., Vago, D. R., Schmalzl, L., Saron, C. D., Olendzki, A., Meissner, T., Lazar, S. W., Kerr, C. E., Gorchov, J., Fox, K. C. R., Field, B. A., Britton, W. B., Brefczynski-Lewis, J. A., & Meyer, D. E. (2018). Mind the hype: A critical evaluation and prescriptive agenda for research on mindfulness and meditation. *Perspectives on Psychological Science, 13*(1), 36–61. https://doi.org/10.1177/1745691617709589

van de Vorst, I. E., Koek, H. L., Stein, C. E., Bots, M. L., & Vaartjes, I. (2016). Socioeconomic disparities and mortality after a diagnosis of dementia: Results from a nationwide registry linkage study. *American Journal of Epidemiology, 184*(3), 219–226. https://doi.org/10.1093/aje/kwv319

Van Der Hart, O., & Nijenhuis, E. (2001). Generalized dissociative amnesia: Episodic, semantic and procedural memories lost and found. *Australian & New Zealand Journal of Psychiatry, 35*(5), 589–600. https://doi.org/10.1080/0004867010060506

van der Kaap-Deeder, J., Wichstrøm, L., Mouratidis, A., Matos, L., & Steinsbekk, S. (2023). Emotion crafting: Individuals as agents of their positive emotional experiences. *Motivation and Emotion, 47*, 870–886. https://doi.org/10.1007/s11031-023-10035-0

Van der Kolk, B. (2022). Posttraumatic stress disorder and the nature of trauma. *Dialogues in Clinical Neuroscience, 2*(1), 1–16. https://doi.org/10.31887/DCNS.2000.2.1/bvdkolk

Van der Poel, J., & Nel, P. (2011). Relevance of the Kübler-Ross model to the post-injury responses of competitive athletes. *South African Journal for Research in Sport, Physical Education and Recreation, 33*(1), 151–163. https://hdl.handle.net/10520/EJC108933

van Dierendonck, D., & Te Nijenhuis, J. (2005). Flotation restricted environmental stimulation therapy (REST) as a stress-management tool: A meta-analysis. *Psychology & Health, 20*(3), 405–412. https://doi.org/10.1080/08870440412331337093

Van Horn, K. R., Arnone, A., Nesbitt, K., Desilets, L., Sears, T., Giffin, M., & Brudi, R. (1997). Physical distance and interpersonal characteristics in college students' romantic relationships. *Personal Relationships, 4*(1), 25–34. https://doi.org/10.1111/j.1475-6811.1997.tb00128.x

van Praag, H., Kempermann, G., & Gage, F. H. (2000). Neural consequences of environmental enrichment. *Nature Reviews: Neuroscience, 1*(3), 191–198. https://doi.org/10.1038/35044558

van Wyk, M., Solms, M., & Lipinska, G. (2019). Increased awakenings from non-rapid eye movement sleep explain differences in dream recall frequency in healthy individuals. *Frontiers in Human Neuroscience, 13*, 1–9. https://doi.org/10.3389/fnhum.2019.00370

Vannucci, A., Flannery, K. M., & Ohannessian, C. M. (2017). Social media use and anxiety in emerging adults. *Journal of Affective Disorders, 207*(1), 163–166. https://doi.org/10.1016/j.jad.2016.08.040

Varnum, M. E., & Grossmann, I. (2017). Cultural change: The how and the why. *Perspectives on Psychological Science, 12*(6), 956–972. https://doi.org/10.1177/1745691617699971

Vartanian, L. R. (2012). Self-discrepancy theory and body image. In T. F. Cash (Ed.), *Encyclopedia of body image and human appearance* (pp. 711–717). Elsevier.

Vásquez, J. A., & Gold, C. (1981). *Counseling and minorities: A bibliography.* National Clearinghouse for Bilingual Education, InterAmerica Research Associates.

Vasquez, M. T., & Lopez, S. (2002). Martha E. Bernal (1931-2001): Obituary. *American Psychologist, 57*(5), 362–363. https://doi.org/10.1037/0003-066X.57.5.362

Vasquez-Salgado, Y., Greenfield, P. M., & Burgos-Cienfuegos, R. (2015). Exploring home-school value conflicts: Implications for academic achievement and well-being among Latino first-generation college students. *Journal of Adolescent Research, 30*(3), 271–305. https://doi.org/10.1177/0743558414561297

Vassou, C., D'Cunha, N. M., Naumovski, N., & Panagiotakos, D. B. (2020). Hostile personality as a risk factor for hyperglycemia and obesity in adult populations: A systematic review. *Journal of Diabetes & Metabolic Disorders, 19*, 1659–1669. https://doi.org/10.1007/s40200-020-00551-y

Vaughan, E. L., Corbin, W. R., & Fromme, K. (2009). Academic and social motives and drinking behavior. *Psychology of Addictive Behaviors, 23*(4), 564–576. https://doi.org/10.1037/a0017331

Vaughan, E. P., Speck, J. S., Frick, P. J., Walker, T. M., Robertson, E. L., Ray, J. V., Wall Myers, T. D., Thornton, L. C., Steinberg, L., & Cauffman, E. (2023). Proactive and reactive aggression: Developmental trajectories and longitudinal associations with callous–unemotional traits, impulsivity, and internalizing emotions. *Development and Psychopathology.* Advance online publication. https://doi.org/10.1017/S0954579423000317

Vaverková, Z., Milton, A. L., & Merlo, E. (2020). Retrieval-dependent mechanisms affecting emotional memory persistence: Reconsolidation, extinction, and the space in between. *Frontiers in Behavioral Neuroscience, 14*, Article 574358. https://doi.org/10.3389/fnbeh.2020.574358

Vella, S. L. C., & Pai, N. B. (2019). A theoretical review of psychological resilience: Defining resilience and resilience research over the decades. *Archives of Medicine and Health Sciences, 7*(2), 233–239. https://doi.org/10.4103/amhs.amhs_119_19

Vernon, M. D. (1955). The functions of schemata in perceiving. *Psychological Review, 62*(3), 180–192. https://doi.org/10.1037/h0042425

Verona, E., & Sullivan, E. A. (2008). Emotional catharsis and aggression revisited: Heart rate reduction following aggressive responding. *Emotion, 8*(3), 331–340. https://doi.org/10.1037/1528-3542.8.3.331

Victora, C. G., Horta, B. L., Loret de Mola, C., Quevedo, L., Pinheiro, R. T., Gigante, D. P., Gonçalves, H., & Barros, F. C. (2015). Association between breastfeeding and intelligence, educational attainment, and income at 30 years of age: A prospective birth cohort study from Brazil. *The Lancet: Global Health, 3*(4), e199–e205. https://doi.org/10.1016/S2214-109X(15)70002-1

Vidyasagar, P., & Mishra, H. (1993). Effect of modeling on aggression. *Indian Journal of Clinical Psychology, 20*(1), 50–52.

Vigen, T. (2015). *Spurious correlations.* Hachette Books.

Vijay, A., Cavallo, D., Goldberg, A., de Laat, B., Nabulsi, N., Huang, Y., Krishnan-Sarin, S., & Morris, E. D. (2018). PET imaging reveals lower kappa opioid receptor availability in alcoholics but no effect of age. *Neuropsychopharmacology, 43*(13), 2539–2547. https://doi.org/10.1038/s41386-018-0199-1

Villani, S. (2001). Impact of media on children and adolescents: A 10-year review of the research. *Journal of the American Academy of Child & Adolescent Psychiatry, 40*(4), 392–401. https://doi.org/10.1097/00004583-200104000-00007

Vinchon, F., Lubart, T., Bartolotta, S., Gironnay, V., Botella, M., Bourgeois-Bougrine, S., Burkhardt, M., Bonnardel, N., Corazza, G. E., Glăveanu, V., Hanson, M. H., Ivcevic, Z., Karwowski, M., Kaufman, J. C., Okada, T., Reiter-Palmon, R., & Gaggioli, A. (2023). Artificial intelligence & creativity: A manifesto for collaboration. *The Journal of Creative Behavior, 57*(4), 472–484. https://doi.org/10.1002/jocb.597

Vinski, E. J., & Tryon, G. S. (2009). Study of a cognitive dissonance intervention to address high school students' cheating attitudes and behaviors. *Ethics & Behavior, 19*(3), 218–226. https://doi.org/10.1080/10508420902886692

Vishkin, A., Kitayama, S., Berg, M. K., Diener, E., Gross-Manos, D., Ben-Arieh, A., & Tamir, M. (2023). Adherence to emotion norms is greater in individualist cultures than in collectivist cultures. *Journal of Personality and Social Psychology, 124*(6), 1256–1276. https://doi.org/10.1037/pspi0000409

Vogels, E. A., & McClain, C. (2023). Key findings about online dating in the U.S. *Pew Research Center.* https://www.pewresearch.org/short-reads/2023/02/02/key-findings-about-online-dating-in-the-u-s/#:~:text=Online%20dating%20is%20more%20common,of%20those%2065%20and%20older

Volkert, J., Gablonski, T. C., & Rabung, S. (2018). Prevalence of personality disorders in the general adult population in Western countries: Systematic review and meta-analysis. *The British Journal of Psychiatry, 213*(6), 709–715. https://doi.org/10.1192/bjp.2018.202

Volkmann, C., Bschor, T., & Köhler, S. (2020). Lithium treatment over the lifespan in bipolar disorders. *Frontiers in Psychiatry, 11*(377), 1–11. https://doi.org/10.3389/fpsyt.2020.00377

Volkow, N. D., Gordon, J. A., & Koob, G. F. (2021). Choosing appropriate language to reduce the stigma around mental illness and substance use disorders. *Neuropsychopharmacology, 46*, 2230–2232. https://doi.org/10.1038/s41386-021-01069-4

Volkow, N. D., Koob, G. F., & McLellan, A. T. (2016). Neurobiologic advances from the brain disease model of addiction. *The New England Journal of Medicine, 374*(4), 363–371. https://doi.org/10.1056/NEJMra1511480

Volkow, N. D., Swanson, J. M., Evins, A. E., DeLisi, L. E., Meier, M. H., Gonzalez, R., Bloomfield, M. A. P., MRCPsych, Curran, H. V., & Baler, R. (2016). Effects of cannabis use on human behavior, including cognition, motivation, and psychosis: A review. *JAMA Psychiatry, 73*(3), 292–297. https://doi:10.1001/jamapsychiatry.2015.3278

Volpara, G., Nani, A., & Cauda, F. (2022). The reflected face as a mask of the self: An appraisal of the psychological and neuroscientific research about self-face recognition. *Topoi, 41*(4), 715–730. https://doi.org/10.1007/s11245-022-09815-z

von Stumm, S., & Plomin, R. (2015). Socioeconomic status and the growth of intelligence from infancy through adolescence. *Intelligence, 48*, 30–36. https://doi.org/10.1016/j.intell.2014.10.002

Vrij, A., Granhag, P. A., Mann, S., & Leal, S. (2011). Outsmarting the liars: Toward a cognitive lie detection approach. *Current Directions in Psychological Science, 20*(1), 28–32. https://doi.org/10.1177/0963721410391245

Vygotsky, L. S. (1978). *Mind in society: The development of higher psychological processes.* Harvard University Press.

Vyse, S. (July 21, 2016). *Kitty Genovese: Revising the parable of the bad Samaritan.* Skeptical Inquirer. https://skepticalinquirer.org/exclusive/kitty-genovese-revising-the-parable-of-the-bad-samaritan/

Wade, N. E., Palmer, C. E., Gonzalez, M. R., Wallace, A. L., Infante, M. A., Tapert, S. F., Jacobus, J., & Bagot, K. S. (2021). Risk factors associated with curiosity about alcohol use in the ABCD cohort. *Alcohol, 92*, 11–19. https://doi.org/10.1016/j.alcohol.2021.01.002

Wagenmakers, E. J., Beek, T., Dijkhoff, L., Gronau, Q. F., Acosta, A., Adams, R. B., Jr., Albohn, D. N., Allard, E. S., Benning, S. D., Blouin-Hudon, E. M., Bulnes, L. C., Caldwell, T. L., Calin-Jageman, R. J., Capaldi, C. A., Carfagno, N., S., Chasten, K. T., Cleeremans, A., Connell, L., DeCicco, J. M., . . . Zwaan, R. A. (2016). Registered replication report: Strack, Martin, & Stepper (1988). *Perspectives on Psychological Science, 11*(6), 917–928. https://doi.org/10.1177/1745691616674458

Wahba, M. A., & Bridwell, L. G. (1976). Maslow reconsidered: A review of research on the need hierarchy theory. *Organizational Behavior and Human Performance, 15*(2), 212–240. https://doi.org/10.1016/0030-5073(76)90038-6

Wahlheim, C. N., Alexander, T. R., & Peske, C. D. (2020). Reminders of everyday misinformation statements can enhance memory for and beliefs in corrections of those statements in the short term. *Psychological Science, 31*(10), 1325–1339. https://doi.org/10.1177/0956797620952797

Walker, M. P., & van der Helm, E. (2009). Overnight therapy? The role of sleep in emotional brain processing. *Psychological Bulletin, 135*(5), 731–748. https://doi.org/10.1037/a0016570

Walker, M. P., Liston, C., Hobson, J. A., & Stickgold, R. (2002). Cognitive flexibility across the sleep-wake cycle: REM-sleep enhancement of anagram problem solving. *Brain Research: Cognitive Brain Research, 14*(3), 317–324. https://doi.org/10.1016/s0926-6410(02)00134-9

Wallace, P. (2007). How can she still love him? Domestic violence and the Stockholm syndrome. *Community Practitioner, 80*(10), 32–35.

Waller, N., Putnam, F. W., & Carlson, E. B. (1996). Types of dissociation and dissociative types: A taxometric analysis of dissociative experiences. *Psychological Methods, 1*(3), 300–321. https://doi.org/10.1037/1082-989X.1.3.300

Walsh, L. C., Boehm, J. K., & Lyubomirsky, S. (2018). Does happiness promote career success? Revisiting the evidence. *Journal of Career Assessment, 26*(2), 199–219. https://doi.org/10.1177/1069072717751441

Walsh, S., Causer, R., & Brayne, C. (2021). Does playing a musical instrument reduce the incidence of cognitive impairment and dementia? A systematic review and meta-analysis. *Aging & Mental Health, 25*(4), 593–601. https://doi.org/10.1080/13607863.2019.1699019

Walters, P. (Senior Ed.). (2019, June 7). G: The Miseducation of Larry P [Audio podcast]. In *Radiolab.* WNYC Studios. https://www.wnycstudios.org/podcasts/radiolab/articles/g-miseducation-larry-p

Walton, M. T., Lykins, A. D., & Bhullar, N. (2016). Beyond heterosexual, bisexual, and homosexual: A diversity in sexual identity expression. *Archives of Sexual Behavior*, *45*(7), 1591–1597. https://doi.org/10.1007/s10508-016-0778-3

Wang, D., Hagger, M. S., & Chatzisarantis, N. L. D. (2020). Ironic effects of thought suppression: A meta-analysis. *Perspectives on Psychological Science*, *15*(3), 778–793. https://doi.org/10.1177/1745691619898795

Wang, H., Tong, S., Shang, J., & Chen, W. (2019). The role of gender in the preconscious processing of facial trustworthiness and dominance. *Frontiers in Psychology*, *10*, Article 2565. https://doi.org/10.3389/fpsyg.2019.02565

Wang, J., & Wang, W. (2019). Cultural contribution to personality disorders in China. In W. Wang (Ed.), *Chinese perspectives on cultural psychiatry: Psychological disorders in "A dream of red mansions" and contemporary society* (pp. 75–91). Springer. https://doi.org/10.1007/978-981-13-3537-2_5

Wang, L., Li, X., Wang, Z., Bancks, M. P., Carnethon, M. R., Greenland, P., Feng, Y-Q., Wang, H., & Zhong, V. W. (2021). Trends in prevalence of diabetes and control of risk factors in diabetes among US adults, 1999-2018. *JAMA*, *326*(8), 704–716. https://doi.org/10.1001/jama.2021.9883

Wang, S., & Liu, M. T. (2023). Celebrity endorsement in marketing from 1960 to 2021: A bibliometric review and future agenda. *Asia Pacific Journal of Marketing and Logistics*, *35*(4), 849–873.

Wang, W.-L., Chen, K.-H., Pan, Y.-C., Yang, S.-N., & Chan, Y.-Y. (2020). The effect of yoga on sleep quality and insomnia in women with sleep problems: A systematic review and meta-analysis. *BMC Psychiatry*, *20*, Article 195. https://doi.org/10.1186/s12888-020-02566-4

Wang, Y., Beydoun, M. A., Min, J., Xue, H., Kaminsky, L. A., & Cheskin, L. J. (2020). Has the prevalence of overweight, obesity and central obesity levelled off in the United States? Trends, patterns, disparities, and future projections for the obesity epidemic. *International Journal of Epidemiology*, *49*(3), 810–823. https://doi.org/10.1093/ije/dyz273

Wang, Z., & Tchernev, J. M. (2012). The "myth" of media multitasking: Reciprocal dynamics of media multitasking, personal needs, and gratifications. *Journal of Communication*, *62*(3), 493–513. https://doi.org/10.1111/j.1460-2466.2012.01641.x

Wang, Z., Lukowski, S. L., Hart, S. A., Lyons, I. M., Thompson, L. A., Kovas, Y., Mazzocco, M. M., Plomin, R., & Petrill, S. A. (2015). Is math anxiety always bad for math learning? The role of math motivation. *Psychological Science*, *26*(12), 1863–1876. https://doi.org/10.1177/0956797615602471

Wansink, B., Ittersum, K. V., & Painter, J. E. (2005). How descriptive food names bias sensory perceptions in restaurants. *Food Quality and Preference*, *16*, 393–400. https://doi.org/10.1016/j.foodqual.2004.06.005

Waraan, L., Siqveland, J., Hanssen-Bauer, K., Czjakowski, N. O., Axelsdóttir, B., Mehlum, L., & Aalberg, M. (2023). Family therapy for adolescents with depression and suicidal ideation: A systematic review and meta-analysis. *Clinical Child Psychology and Psychiatry*, *28*(2), 831–849. https://doi.org/10.1177/13591045221125005

Waterhouse, L. (2006). Multiple intelligences, the Mozart effect, and emotional intelligence: A critical review. *Educational Psychologist*, *41*(4), 207–225. https://doi.org/10.1207/s15326985ep4104_1

Watson, C., Poulter, D., Ventriglio, A., & Bhugra, D. (2022). Masculinity, male roles, mental illnesses, and social psychiatry. In D. Bhugra, D. Moussaoui, & T. J. Craig (Eds.), *Oxford textbook of social psychiatry* (pp. 219–231). Oxford University Press.

Watson, J. (1968). *The double helix: A personal account of the discovery of the structure of DNA*. Atheneum.

Watson, J. B. (1913). Psychology as the behaviorist views it. *Psychological Review*, *20*(2), 158–177. https://doi.org/10.1037/h0074428

Watson, J. B., & Rayner, R. (1920). Conditioned emotional reactions. *American Psychologist*, *55*(3), 313–317. https://doi.org/10.1037/h0069608

Watson, J. B., & Rayner, R. (1920). Conditioned emotional reactions. *American Psychologist*, *55*(3), 313–317. https://doi.org/10.1037/0003-066X.55.3.313

Watson, N. F., Badr, M. S., Belenky, G., Bliwise, D. L., Buxton, O. M., Buysse, D., Dinges, D. F., Gangwisch, J., Grandner, M. A., Kushida, C., Malhotra, R. K., Martin, J. L., Patel, S. R., Quan, S. F., & Tasali, E. (2015). Recommended amount of sleep for a healthy adult: A joint consensus statement of the American Academy of Sleep Medicine and Sleep Research Society. *Sleep*, *38*(6), 843–844.

Watters, E. (2010). *Crazy like us: The globalization of the American psyche*. Simon & Schuster.

Watts, T. W., Duncan, G. J., & Quan, H. (2018). Revisiting the marshmallow test: A conceptual replication investigating links between early delay of gratification and later outcomes. *Psychological Science*, *29*(7), 1159–1177. https://doi.org/10.1177/0956797618761661

Webb, S. (2005). Receptive and productive vocabulary learning: The effects of reading and writing on word knowledge. *Studies in Second Language Acquisition*, *27*(1), 33–52. https://doi.org/10.1017/S0272263105050023

Weber, E. U., & Morris, M. W. (2010). Culture and judgment and decision making: The constructivist turn. *Perspectives on Psychological Science*, *5*(4), 410–419. https://doi.org/10.1177/1745691610375556

Webster, M. A. (2012). Evolving concepts of sensory adaptation. *F1000 Biology Reports*, *4*(21), 1–7. https://doi.org/10.3410/B4-21

Wechsler, D. (1981). *WAIS-R: Wechsler Adult Intelligence Scale-Revised*. Psychological Corporation.

Wechsler, D., & Psychological Corporation. (2012). *WPPSI-IV: Wechsler preschool and primary scale of intelligence* (4th ed.). Pearson.

Wechsler, D., Pearson Education, Inc., & Psychological Corporation. (2014). *WISC-V: Wechsler Intelligence Scale for Children*. NCS Pearson, Inc.

Weeks, D. L., & Anderson, P. L. (2000). The interaction of observational learning with overt practice: Effects on motor skill learning. *Acta Psychologica*, *104*(2), 259–271. https://doi.org/10.1016/S0001-6918(00)00039-1

Weems, C. F., Costa, N. M., Dehon, C., & Berman, S. L. (2004). Paul Tillich's theory of existential anxiety: A preliminary conceptual and empirical examination. *Anxiety, Stress & Coping*, *17*(4), 383–399. https://doi.org/10.1080/10615800412331318616

Wegner, D. M. (1994). Ironic processes of mental control. *Psychological Review*, *101*(1), 34–52. https://doi.org/10.1037/0033-295X.101.1.34

Wegner, M., Helmich, I., Machado, S., E Nardi, A., Arias-Carrion, O., & Budde, H. (2014). Effects of exercise on anxiety and depression disorders: Review of meta-analyses and neurobiological mechanisms. *CNS & Neurological Disorders-Drug Targets*, *13*(6), 1002–1014.

Weimann, G. (2016). Why do terrorists migrate to social media? In A. Aly, S. Macdonald, L. Jarvis, & T. Chen (Eds.), *Violent extremism online: New perspectives on terrorism and the internet* (pp. 67–84). Routledge.

Weingartner, H., Adefras, W., Eich, J. E., & Murphy, D. L. (1976). Encoding-imagery specificity in alcohol state-dependent learning. *Journal of Experimental Psychology: Human Learning and Memory*, *2*(1), 83–87. https://doi.org/10.1037/0278-7393.2.1.83

Weintraub, D. J. (1979). Ebbinghaus illusion: Context, contour, and age influence the judged size of a circle amidst circles. *Journal of Experimental Psychology: Human Perception and Performance*, *5*(2), 353–364. https://doi.org/10.1037/0096-1523.5.2.353

Weitbrecht, E. M., & Whitton, S. W. (2020). College students' motivations for "hooking up": Similarities and differences in motives by gender and partner type. *Couple and Family Psychology: Research and Practice, 9*(3), 123–142. https://doi .org/10.1037/cfp0000138

Weitlauf, A. S., McPheeters, M. L., Peters, B., Sathe, N., Travis, R., Aiello, R., Williamson, E., Veenstra-VanderWeele, J., Krishnaswami, S., Jerome R., & Warren, Z. (2014). *Therapies for children with autism spectrum disorder: Behavioral interventions update.* Agency for Healthcare Research and Quality.

Welsh, M. C., & Pennington, B. F. (1988). Assessing frontal lobe functioning in children: Views from developmental psychology. *Developmental Neuropsychology, 4*(3), 199–230. https://doi .org/10.1080/87565648809540405

Wenger, G. C. (2021). *The supportive network: Coping with old age.* Routledge.

Were, V. O., Okoyo, C. O., Araka, S. B., Kanyi, H. M., Echoka, E. E., Mwandawiro, C. S., & Njomo, D. W. (2022). Socioeconomic disparities in the uptake of substances of abuse: Results from a household cross-sectional survey in Murang' a County, Kenya. *Discover Social Science and Health, 2*(5), 1–10. https://doi .org/10.1007/s44155-022-00008-y

Werner, L., Geisler, J., & Randler, C. (2015). Morningness as a personality predictor of punctuality. *Current Psychology, 34*(1), 130–139. https://doi.org/10.1007/s12144-014-9246-1

Wesch, N., Law, B., & Hall, C. (2007). The use of observational learning by athletes. *Journal of Sport Behavior, 30*(2), 219–231.

West, C. M. (1998). Leaving a second closet: Outing partner violence in same-sex couples. In J. L. Jasinski & L. M. Williams (Eds.), *Partner violence: A comprehensive review of 20 years of research* (pp. 163–183). SAGE.

West, L. J. (1993). A psychiatric overview of cult-related phenomenon. *Journal of the American Academy of Psychoanalysis, 21*(1), 1–19. https://doi.org/10.1521/ jaap.1.1993.21.1.1

Westbury, S., Oyebode, O., Van Rens, T., & Barber, T. M. (2023). Obesity stigma: Causes, consequences, and potential solutions. *Current Obesity Reports, 12*(1), 10–23. https://doi.org/10.1007/ s13679-023-00495-3

Westby, C. (2019). The myth of learning styles. *Word of Mouth, 31*(2), 4–7. https://doi.org/10.1177/1048395019879966a

Wetherill, R. R., & Fromme, K. (2016). Alcohol-induced blackouts: A review of recent clinical research with practical implications and recommendations for future studies. *Alcoholism: Clinical and Experimental Research, 40*(5), 922–935. https://doi. org/10.1111/acer.13051

Wheaton, M. G., & Ward, H. E. (2020). Intolerance of uncertainty and obsessive-compulsive personality disorder. *Personality Disorders: Theory, Research, and Treatment, 11*(5), 357–364. https://doi.org/10.1037/per0000396

Wheeler, R. E., Davidson, R. J., & Tomarken, A. J. (1993). Frontal brain asymmetry and emotional reactivity: A biological substrate of affective style. *Psychophysiology, 30*(1), 82–89. https://doi .org/10.1111/j.1469-8986.1993.tb03207.x

Whisman, M. A., Dixon, A. E., & Johnson, B. (1997). Therapists' perspectives of couple problems and treatment issues in couple therapy. *Journal of Family Psychology, 11*(3), 361–366. https://doi.org/10.1037/0893-3200.11.3.361

Whitaker, R. (2010). *Anatomy of an epidemic: Magic bullets, psychiatric drugs, and the astonishing rise of mental illness in America.* Random House Digital, Inc.

Whitaker, R. (2020). Do antipsychotics protect against early death? A critical view. *Psychological Medicine, 50*(16), 1–10. https://doi .org/10.1017/S003329172000358X

White, R. W. (1959). Motivation reconsidered: The concept of competence. *Psychological Review, 66*(5), 297–333. https://doi .org/10.1037/h0040934

White, W. A. (1914). Moon myth in medicine: The moon as libido symbol. *Psychoanalytic Review, 1*(3), 241–256.

Whitebook, J. (2017). *Freud: An intellectual biography.* Cambridge University Press.

Whitehurst, L. N., Naji, M., & Mednick, S. C. (2018). Comparing the cardiac autonomic activity profile of daytime naps and nighttime sleep. *Neurobiology of Sleep and Circadian Rhythms, 5*, 52–57. https://doi.org/10.1016/j.nbscr.2018.03.001

Whitley, B. E. (1983). Sex role orientation and self-esteem: A critical meta-analytic review. *Journal of Personality and Social Psychology, 44*(4), 765–778. https://doi.org/10.1037/0022-3514.44.4.765

Whitley, B. E. (1985). Sex-role orientation and psychological well-being: Two meta-analyses. *Sex Roles, 12*, 207–225. https://doi .org/10.1007/BF00288048

Wichowski, D. E., & Kohl, L. E. (2013). Establishing credibility in the information jungle: Blogs, microblogs, and the CRAAP test. In L. Johnston (Managing director), *DigitalCommons@ BryantUniversity* (pp. 229–251). IGI Global.

Widodo, P., Saragih, H. J., Sukendro, A., Madjid, M. A., Ky, I. G. S., Samudro, E. G., & Maysarah, M. M. (2022). The conflict resolution and prevention between fishermen in Panipahan, Riau Province, Indonesia. *Resmilitaris, 12*(4), 1568–1577.

Wigfield, A., Muenks, K., & Eccles, J. S. (2021). Achievement motivation: What we know and where we are going. *Annual Review of Developmental Psychology, 3*, 87–111. https://doi .org/10.1146/annurev-devpsych-050720-103500

Wilbanks, B., Maher III, L. J., & Rodriguez, M. (2019). Glial cells as therapeutic targets in progressive multiple sclerosis. *Expert Review of Neurotherapeutics, 19*(6), 481–494. https://doi.org/10.1 080/14737175.2019.1614443

Wilde, M., Auwärter, V., & Moosmann, B. (2021). New psychoactive substances—Designer benzodiazepines. *Wiley Interdisciplinary Reviews: Forensic Science, 3*(6), 1–23. https://doi.org/10.1002/ wfs2.1416

Williams, D. R., Lawrence, J., & Davis, B. (2019). Racism and health: Evidence and needed research. *Annual Review of Public Health, 40*, 105–125. https://doi.org/10.1146/annurev-publhealth-040218-043750

Williams, L. E., & Bargh, J. A. (2008). Experiencing physical warmth promotes interpersonal warmth. *Science, 322*(5901), 606–607. https://doi.org/10.1126/science.1162548

Williams, N. A., Fournier, J., Coday, M., Richey, P. A., Tylavsky, F. A., & Hare, M. E. (2013). Body esteem, peer difficulties and perceptions of physical health in overweight and obese urban children aged 5 to 7 years. *Child: Care, Health and Development, 39*(6), 825–834. https://doi.org/10.1111/j.1365-2214.2012.01401.x

Williams, R. L. (1975). *Ebonics: The true language of Black folks.* Institute of Black Studies.

Wilson, J. P., Hugenberg, K., & Rule, N. O. (2017). Racial bias in judgments of physical size and formidability: From size to threat. *Journal of Personality and Social Psychology, 113*(1), 59–80. https://doi.org/10.1037/pspi0000092

Wilson, S., Stroud, C. B., & Durbin, C. E. (2017). Interpersonal dysfunction in personality disorders: A meta-analytic review. *Psychological Bulletin, 143*(7), 677–734. https://doi.org/10.1037/ bul0000101

Winch, R. F. (1952). *The modern family.* Holt.

Winerman, L. (2005). The mind's mirror. *Monitor on Psychology, 36*(9), 48–49.

Wing Kwan, M. Y., Bray, S. R., & Martin Ginis, K. A. (2009). Predicting physical activity of first-year university students: An application of the theory of planned behavior. *Journal of American College Health, 58*(1), 45–55. https://doi.org/10.3200/JACH.58.1.45-55

Wingström, R., Hautala, J., & Lundman, R. (2022). Redefining creativity in the era of AI? Perspectives of computer scientists and new media artists. *Creativity Research Journal.* Advance online publication. https://doi.org/10.1080/10400419.2022.2107850

Winsper, C., Bilgin, A., Thompson, A., Marwaha, S., Chanen, A. M., Singh, S. P., & Furtado, V. (2020). The prevalence of personality disorders in the community: A global systematic review and meta-analysis. *The British Journal of Psychiatry*, *216*(2), 69–78. https://doi.org/10.1192/bjp.2019.166

Winston, A. S. (1998). Science in the service of the far right: Henry E. Garrett, the IAAEE, and the Liberty Lobby. *Journal of Social Issues*, *54*(1), 179–210. https://doi.org/10.1111/j.1540-4560.1998.tb01212.x

Wisman, A., & Goldenberg, J. L. (2005). From the grave to the cradle: Evidence that mortality salience engenders a desire for offspring. *Journal of Personality and Social Psychology*, *89*(1), 46–61. https://doi.org/10.1037/0022-3514.89.1.46

Witkower, Z., Hill, A. K., Pun, A., Baron, A. S., Koster, J., & Tracy, J. L. (2023). Nonverbal displays of dominance and prestige: Evidence for cross-cultural and early-emerging recognition. *Journal of Experimental Psychology: General*. *Journal of Experimental Psychology: General*, *153*(2), 282–292. https://doi.org/10.1037/xge0001481

Wittchen, H. U. (2002). Generalized anxiety disorder: Prevalence, burden, and cost to society. *Depression and Anxiety*, *16*(4), 162–171. https://doi.org/10.1002/da.10065

Woessner, M. N., Tacey, A., Levinger-Limor, A., Parker, A. G., Levinger, P., & Levinger, I. (2021). The evolution of technology and physical inactivity: The good, the bad, and the way forward. *Frontiers in Public Health*, *9*, 1–7. https://doi.org/10.3389/fpubh.2021.655491

Wolf, M. M. (2001). Application of operant conditioning procedures to the behavior problems of an autistic child: A 25-year follow-up and the development of the teaching family model. In W. T. O'Donohue, D. A. Henderson, S. C. Hayes, J. E. Fisher, & L. J. Hayes (Eds.), *A history of the behavioral therapies: Founders' personal histories* (pp. 289–294). Context Press.

Wolfe, D. E., & Hom, C. (1993). Use of melodies as structural prompts for learning and retention of sequential verbal information by preschool students. *Journal of Music Ttherapy*, *30*(2), 100–118. https://doi.org/10.1093/jmt/30.2.100

Wolman, D. (2012). The split brain: A tale of two halves. *Nature*, *483*, 260–263. https://doi.org/10.1038/483260a

Wolpe, J. (1958). *Psychotherapy by reciprocal inhibition*. Stanford University Press.

Wolpe, J., & Lang, P. J. (2017). A fear survey schedule for use in behavior therapy. In E. J., Thomas (Ed.), *Behavior modification procedure: A sourcebook* (pp. 228–232). Routledge. (Original work published 1974)

Wood, J. M., Lilienfeld, S. O., Nezworski, M. T., Garb, H. N., Allen, K. H., & Wildermuth, J. L. (2010). Validity of Rorschach Inkblot scores for discriminating psychopaths from nonpsychopaths in forensic populations: A meta-analysis. *Psychological Assessment*, *22*(2), 336–349. https://doi.org/10.1037/a0018998

Wood, S. K., & Valentino, R. J. (2017). The brain norepinephrine system, stress and cardiovascular vulnerability. *Neuroscience & Biobehavioral Reviews*, *74*, 393–400. https://doi.org/10.1016/j.neubiorev.2016.04.018

Woodmansee, W. W. (2019). Pituitary disorders in pregnancy. *Neurologic Clinics*, *37*(1), 63–83. https://doi.org/10.1016/j.ncl.2018.09.009

Woodworth, R. S., & Schlosberg, H. (1954). *Experimental psychology* (Rev. ed.). Holt.

Woody, G. E., Poole, S. A., Subramaniam, G., Dugosh, K., Bogenschutz, M., Abbott, P., Patkar, A., Publicker, M., McCain, K., Sharpe Potter, J., Forman, R., Vetter, V., McNicholas, L., Blaine, J., Lynch, K. G., & Fudala, P. (2008). Extended vs short-term buprenorphine-naloxone for treatment of opioid-addicted youth: A randomized trial. *Journal of the American Medical Association*, *300*(17), 2003–2011. https://doi.org/10.1001/jama.2008.574

Word, C. O., Zanna, M. P., & Cooper, J. (1974). The nonverbal mediation of self-fulfilling prophecies in interracial interaction. *Journal of Experimental Social Psychology*, *10*(2), 109–120. https://doi.org/10.1016/0022-1031(74)90059-6

World Happiness Report. (2022). happiness-report.s3.amazonaws.com/2022/WHR+22.pdf

World Health Organization (WHO). (2018, March 30). *Mental health: Strengthening our response*. https://www.who.int/news-room/fact-sheets/detail/mental-health-strengthening-our-response

World Health Organization (WHO). (2022). *World mental health report: Transforming mental health for all*.

World Health Organization. (2017). *First WHO report details devastating impact of hypertension and ways to stop it*. https://www.who.int/news/item/19-09-2023-first-who-report-details-devastating-impact-of-hypertension-and-ways-to-stop-it

Worley, J. A. (2023). Empathy as a wellness driver in the workplace. In J. Marques (Ed.), *The Palgrave handbook of fulfillment, wellness, and personal growth at work* (pp. 231–250). Palgrave Macmillan. https://doi.org/10.1007/978-3-031-35494-6_12

Worrachananun, M. (2022). The effect of music in destination marketing on tourists' attitudes and intentions to visit secondary-tier destinations in the northern part of Thailand. *Social Space*, *22*(1), 345–363.

Wright, P. J. (2013). US males and pornography, 1973–2010: Consumption, predictors, correlates. *Journal of Sex Research*, *50*(1), 60–71. https://doi.org/10.1080/00224499.2011.628132

Wrzus, C., Zimmermann, J., Mund, M., & Neyer, F. J. (2017). Friendships in young and middle adulthood: Normative patterns and personality differences. In M. Hojjat & A. Moyer (Eds.), *The psychology of friendship* (pp. 21–38). Oxford University Press.

Wu, K., & Xu, F. (2021). The dissemination of vocational technology and influencing factors under modern apprenticeship. *Open Journal of Social Sciences*, *9*(6), 32–42. https://doi.org/10.4236/jss.2021.96004

Wynn, C. E., Ziff, E., & Snyder, A. H. (2023). Understanding, experiencing, connecting: The benefits of empathy in the classroom. In J. Chin & M. L. Kozimor (Eds.), *Emerging stronger* (pp. 41–57). Routledge. https://doi.org/10.4324/9781003316336

Wynn, J. S., Olsen, R. K., Binns, M. A., Buchsbaum, B. R., & Ryan, J. D. (2018). Fixation reinstatement supports visuospatial memory in older adults. *Journal of Experimental Psychology: Human Perception and Performance*, *44*(7), 1119–1127. https://doi.org/10.1037/xhp0000522

Xie, L., Kang, H., Xu, Q., Chen, M. J., Liao, Y., Thiyagarajan, M., O'Donnell, J., Christensen, D. J., Nicholson, C., Iliff, J. J., Takano, T., Deane, R., & Nedergaard, M. (2013). Sleep drives metabolite clearance from the adult brain. *Science*, *342*(6156), 373–377. https://doi.org/10.1126/science.1241224

Xue, S., Gu, Q., Zhu, K., & Jiang, J. (2023). Self-compassion buffers the impact of learned helplessness on adverse mental health during COVID-19 lockdown. *Journal of Affective Disorders*, *327*, 285–291. https://doi.org/10.1016/j.jad.2023.01.099

Yager, J., & Kay, J. (2020). Clinical curiosity in psychiatric residency training: Implications for education and practice. *Academic Psychiatry*, *44*(1), 90–94. https://doi.org/10.1007/s40596-019-01131-w

Yalom, I. D., & Leszcz, M. (2020). *The theory and practice of group psychotherapy* (6th ed.). Basic Books.

Yang, J., Yu, K. H. F., & Huang, C. J. (2019). Service employees' concurrent adaptive and unethical behaviors in complex or non-routine tasks: The effects of customer control and self-monitoring personality. *Asia Pacific Journal of Management*, *36*(1), 245–273. https://doi.org/10.1007/s10490-018-9567-y

Yankouskaya, A., Williamson, R., Stacey, C., Totman, J. J., & Massey, H. (2023). Short-term head-out whole-body cold-water immersion facilitates positive affect and increases interaction between large-scale brain networks. *Biology*, *12*(2), Article 211. https://doi.org/10.3390/biology12020211

Yapici Eser, H., Kacar, A. S., Kilciksiz, C. M., Yalçinay-Inan, M., & Ongur, D. (2018). Prevalence and associated features of anxiety disorder comorbidity in bipolar disorder: A meta-analysis and meta-regression study. *Frontiers in Psychiatry, 9*, Article 229. https://doi.org/10.3389/fpsyt.2018.00229

Yarber, W. L., & Sayad, B. (2016). *Human sexuality: Diversity in contemporary America* (9th ed.). McGraw-Hill.

Yates, J. F., & de Oliveira, S. (2016). Culture and decision making. *Organizational Behavior and Human Decision Processes, 136*, 106–118. https://doi.org/10.1016/j.obhdp.2016.05.003

Yeager, D. S., Walton, G. M., Brady, S. T., Akcinar, E. N., Paunesku, D., Keane, L., Kamentz, D., Ritter, G., Duckworth, A. L., Urstein, R., Gomez, E. M., Markus, H. R., Cohen, G. L., & Dweck, C. S. (2016). Teaching a lay theory before college narrows achievement gaps at scale. *PNAS Proceedings of the National Academy of Sciences of the United States of America, 113*(24), E3341–E3348. https://doi.org/10.1073/pnas.1524360113

Yegorov, Y. E., Poznyak, A. V., Nikiforov, N. G., Sobenin, I. A., & Orekhov, A. N. (2020). The link between chronic stress and accelerated aging. *Biomedicines, 8*(7), 198–184. https://doi.org/10.3390/biomedicines8070198

Yerkes, R. M. (1921). Psychological examining in the U.S. Army. *Memoirs of the National Academy of Sciences, No. 15*. National Academy of Sciences.

Yerkes, R. M., & Dodson, J. D. (1908). The relation of strength of stimulus to rapidity of habit-formation. *Journal of Comparative Neurology and Psychology, 18*(5), 459–482. https://doi.org/10.1002/cne.920180503

Yi, H., Shin, K., & Shin, C. (2006). Development of the sleep quality scale. *Journal of Sleep Research, 15*(3), 309–316.

Yi, J. H., Whitcomb, D. J., Park, S. J., Martinez-Perez, C., Barbati, S. A., Mitchell, S. J., & Cho, K. (2020). M1 muscarinic acetylcholine receptor dysfunction in moderate Alzheimer's disease pathology. *Brain Communications, 2*(2), 1–13. https://doi.org/10.1093/braincomms/fcaa058

Yilmaz, Z., Hardaway, J. A., & Bulik, C. M. (2015). Genetics and epigenetics of eating disorders. *Advances in Genomics and Genetics, 5*, 131–150. https://doi.org/10.2147/AGG.S55776

Yoder, R. M., Chan, J. H., & Taube, J. S. (2017). Acetylcholine contributes to the integration of self-movement cues in head direction cells. *Behavioral Neuroscience, 131*(4), 312–324. https://psycnet.apa.org/doi/10.1037/bne0000205

Yong, E. (2018). Psychology's replication crisis is running out of excuses. *The Atlantic*. https://www.theatlantic.com/science/archive/2018/11/psychologys-replication-crisis-real/576223/

You, Z., Li, X., Ye, N., & Zhang, L. (2021). Understanding the effect of rumination on sleep quality: A mediation model of negative affect and bedtime procrastination. *Current Psychology: A Journal for Diverse Perspectives on Diverse Psychological Issues*. Advance online publication. https://doi.org/10.1007/s12144-020-01337-4

Yow, Y. J., Ramsay, J. E., Lin, P. K., & Marsh, N. V. (2022). Dimensions, measures, and contexts in psychological investigations of curiosity: A scoping review. *Behavioral Sciences, 12*(12), Article 493. https://doi.org/10.3390/bs12120493

Yu, C. K.-C. (2012). The effect of sleep position on dream experiences. *Dreaming, 22*(3), 212–221. https://doi.org/10.1037/a0029255

Yu, R. F., & Wu, X. (2015). Working alone or in the presence of others: Exploring social facilitation in baggage X-ray security screening tasks. *Ergonomics, 58*(6), 857–865. https://doi.org/10.1080/00140139.2014.993429

Yu, Z., Yu, T., Ge, Y., & Qu, W. (2023). The effect of perceived global stress and altruism on prosocial driving behavior, yielding behavior, and yielding attitude. *Traffic Injury Prevention, 24*(5), 402–408. https://doi.org/10.1080/15389588.2023.2191765

Yuan, J. P., Connolly, C. G., Henje, E., Sugrue, L. P., Yang, T. T., Xu, D., & Tymofiyeva, O. (2020). Gray matter changes in adolescents participating in a meditation training. *Frontiers in Human Neuroscience, 14*, Article 319. https://doi.org/10.3389/fnhum.2020.00319

Yuhas, A. (2021, March 3). It's time to revisit the satanic panic. *The New York Times*. https://www.nytimes.com/2021/03/31/us/satanic-panic.html

Yunesian, M., Aslani, A., Vash, J. H., & Yazdi, A. B. (2008). Effects of transcendental meditation on mental health: A before-after study. *Clinical Practice and Epidemiology in Mental Health, 4*, Article 25. https://doi.org/10.1186/1745-0179-4-25

Yurdakul, G., & Arar, T. (2023). Revisiting Maslow's hierarchy of needs: Is it still universal content? *Journal of Human Behavior in the Social Environment, 33*(8), 1103–1130. https://doi.org/10.1080/10911359.2023.2177227

Yurgelun-Todd, D. (2007). Emotional and cognitive changes during adolescence. *Current Opinion in Neurobiology, 17*(2), 251–257. https://doi.org/10.1016/j.conb.2007.03.009

Zabelina, D. L., & Robinson, M. D. (2010). Child's play: Facilitating the originality of creative output by a priming manipulation. *Psychology of Aesthetics, Creativity, and the Arts, 4*(1), 57–65. https://doi.org/10.1037/a0015644

Zachar, P., First, M. B., & Kendler, K. S. (2017). The bereavement exclusion debate in the DSM-5: A history. *Clinical Psychological Science, 5*(5), 890–906. https://doi.org/10.1177/2167702617711284

Zajonc, R. B. (1965). Social facilitation. *Science, 149*(3681), 269–274. https://doi.org/10.1126/science.149.3681.269

Zaki, P., Blake, A., Wolt, A., Chan, S., Zhang, L., Wan, A., Lam, H., Deangelis, C., Slaven, M., Shaw, E., Ganesh, V., Malek, L., Chow, E., & O'Hearn, S. (2018). The use of medical cannabis in cancer patients. *Journal of Pain Management, 10*(4), 353–362.

Zald, D. H., & Treadway, M. (2017). Reward processing, neuroeconomics, and psychopathology. *Annual Review of Clinical Psychology, 13*, 471–495. https://doi.org/10.1146/annurev-clinpsy-032816-044957

Zänkert, S., Bellingrath, S., Wüst, S., & Kudielka, B. M. (2019). HPA axis responses to psychological challenge linking stress and disease: What do we know on sources of intra-and interindividual variability. *Psychoneuroendocrinology, 105*, 86–97. https://doi.org/10.1016/j.psyneuen.2018.10.027

Zárate, M. A., Garcia, B., Garza, A. A., & Hitlan, R. T. (2004). Cultural threat and perceived realistic group conflict as dual predictors of prejudice. *Journal of Experimental Social Psychology, 40*(1), 99–105. https://doi.org/10.1016/S0022-1031(03)00067-2

Zarghami, M., Khalilian, A., Setareh, J., & Salehpour, G. (2015). The impact of using cell phones after light-out on sleep quality, headache, tiredness, and distractibility among students of a university in north of Iran. *Iranian Journal of Psychiatry and Behavioral Sciences, 9*(4), Article e2010. https://doi.org/10.17795/ijpbs-2010

Zarkin, G. A., Dunlap, L. J., & Homsi, G. (2004). The substance abuse services cost analysis program (SASCAP): A new method for estimating drug treatment services costs. *Evaluation and Program Planning, 27*(1), 35–43. https://doi.org/10.1016/j.evalprogplan.2003.09.002

Zarkin, G. A., Dunlap, L. J., Belenko, S., & Dynia, P. A. (2005). A benefit-cost analysis of the Kings County District Attorney's Office drug treatment alternative to prison (DTAP) program. *Justice Research and Policy, 7*(1), 1–25. https://doi.org/10.3818/JRP.7.1.2005.1

Zemore, S. E., & Ajzen, I. (2014). Predicting substance abuse treatment completion using a new scale based on the theory of planned behavior. *Journal of Substance Abuse Treatment, 46*(2), 174–182. https://doi.org/10.1016/j.jsat.2013.06.011

Zemore, S. E., Kaskutas, L. A., Mericle, A., & Hemberg, J. (2017). Comparison of 12-step groups to mutual help alternatives for AUD in a large, national study: Differences in membership characteristics and group participation, cohesion, and satisfaction. *Journal of Substance Abuse Treatment*, *73*, 16–26. https://doi.org/10.1016/j.jsat.2016.10.004

Zenner, C., Herrnleben-Kurz, S., & Walach, H. (2014). Mindfulness-based interventions in schools—a systematic review and meta-analysis. *Frontiers in Psychology*, *5*, Article 603. https://doi.org/10.3389/fpsyg.2014.00603

Zhang, B., Zhang, Y., & Zhou, P. (2021). Consumer attitude towards sustainability of fast fashion products in the UK. *Sustainability*, *13*(4), Article 1646. https://doi.org/10.3390/su13041646

Zhang, M. X., & Wu, A. M. S. (2020). Effects of smartphone addiction on sleep quality among Chinese university students: The mediating role of self-regulation and bedtime procrastination. *Addictive Behaviors*, *111*, Article 106552. https://doi.org/10.1016/j.addbeh.*2020*.106552.

Zhang, M., Harrison, E., Biswas, L., Tran, T., & Liu, X. (2018). Menthol facilitates dopamine releasing effect of nicotine in rat nucleus accumbens. *Pharmacology, Biochemistry and Behavior*, *175*, 47–52. https://doi.org/10.1016/j.pbb.2018.09.004

Zhang, W. (2016). A supplement to self-organization theory of dreaming. *Frontiers in Psychology*, *7*, Article 332. https://doi.org/10.3389/fpsyg.2016.00332

Zhang, W. N., Chang, S. H., Guo, L. Y., Zhang, K. L., & Wang, J. (2013). The neural correlates of reward-related processing in major depressive disorder: A meta-analysis of functional magnetic resonance imaging studies. *Journal of Affective Disorders*, *151*(2), 531–539. https://doi.org/10.1016/j.jad.2013.06.039

Zhang, W., & Guo, B. (2018). Freud's dream interpretation: A different perspective based on the self-organization theory of dreaming. *Frontiers in Psychology*, *9*, Article 1553. https://doi.org/10.3389/fpsyg.2018.01553

Zheng, L., Su, Z., Yu, Y., Zhuang, D., Ma, J., Xue, C., & Zhou, J. (2022). Research of social group prejudice after Germany's defeat during the World War via the investigation of prejudice against domestic Communists and Jews. *International Journal of Social Science and Education Research*, *5*(8), 591–598. https://doi.org/10.6918/IJOSSER.202208_5(8).0084

Zheng, Y., Xiao, L., Xie, Y., Wang, H., & Wang, G. (2020). Prevalence and characteristics of obsessive-compulsive disorder among urban residents in Wuhan during the stage of regular control of coronavirus disease-19 epidemic. *Frontiers in Psychiatry*, *11*, Article 594167. https://doi.org/10.3389/fpsyt.2020.594167

Zhong, B., Huang, Y., & Liu, Q. (2021). Mental health toll from the coronavirus: Social media usage reveals Wuhan residents' depression and secondary trauma in the COVID-19 outbreak. *Computers in Human Behavior*, *114*, 106524. https://doi.org/10.1016/j.chb.2020.106524

Zhou, D., Lebel, C., Treit, S., Evans, A., & Beaulieu, C. (2015). Accelerated longitudinal cortical thinning in adolescence. *Neuroimage*, *104*, 138–145. https://doi.org/10.1016/j.neuroimage.2014.10.005

Zhou, N., Smith, K. V., Stelzer, E., Maercker, A., Xi, J., & Killikelly, C. (2023). How the bereaved behave: A cross-cultural study of emotional display behaviours and rules. *Cognition and Emotion*, *5*, 1023–1039. https://doi.org/10.1080/02699931.2023.2219046

Zhou, S. (2023). A comparative analysis of arachnophobia and claustrophobia. *Journal of Education, Humanities and Social Sciences*, *8*, 1190–1194.

Zhu, H., Wang, N., Yao, L., Chen, Q., Zhang, R., Qian, J., Hou, Y., Guo, W., Fan, S., Liu, S., Zhao, Q., Du, F., Zuo, X., Guo, Y., Xu, Y., Li, J., Xue, T., Zhong, K., . . . Xiong, W. (2018). Moderate UV exposure enhances learning and memory by promoting a novel glutamate biosynthetic pathway in the brain. *Cell*, *173*(7), 1716–1727. https://doi.org/10.1016/j.cell.2018.04.014

Zucker, R. A., Donovan, J. E., Masten, A. S., Mattson, M. E., & Moss, H. B. (2008). Early developmental processes and the continuity of risk for underage drinking and problem drinking. *Pediatrics*, *121*(Suppl. 4), S252–S272. https://doi.org/10.1542/peds.2007-2243B

Zvereva, N., Zvereva, M., & Pyatnitskaya, L. (2021). Temperament profiles of children and adolescents with psychotic and mood disorders. *Neuropsychobiology*, *80*(2), 176–184. https://doi.org/10.1159/000511108

Zwan, M. D., Bouwman, F. H., Konijnenberg, E., Van Der Flier, W. M., Lammertsma, A. A., Verhey, F. R., Aalten, P., van Berckel, B. N. M., & Scheltens, P. (2017). Diagnostic impact of [18F] flutemetamol PET in early-onset dementia. *Alzheimer's Research & Therapy*, *9*(1), 1–8. https://doi.org/10.1186/s13195-016-0228-4

AUTHOR INDEX

McLaws, M. L., 31
McLay, L. K., 207
McLean, R. E., 424
McLellan, A. T., 69, 219, 487
McLellan, T. M., 217
McMahon, F. J., 483
McMahon, T., 322
McManus, J. L., 447
McMillan, A., 228
McMurray, R. G., 511
McNeil, C. B., 519
McNeill, G., 383
McNicholas, L., 503
McPheeters, M. L., 523
McQueen, A., 126, 127
McRae, A. F., 133
McVey, G. L., 238
Mead, M., 474
Meaden, A., 490–491
Medic, N., 343
Medin, D. L., 365
Mednick, S., 203
Medvedskaya, E. I., 195
Meeus, W., 414
Mehlum, L., 528
Mehrabian, A., 455
Mehta, S., 524
Meichenbaum, D., 510
Meier, M. H., 69, 219
Meijer, L., 424
Meissner, T., 213, 510
Melchiorri, E., 248
Melillo, R., 77
Melton, L. J., 243
Meltzer, T., 139
Meltzer-Brody, S., 482
Melzack, R., 177
Memmert, D., 197
Menardi, A., 511
Mencarelli, L., 511
Menchetti, M., 483
Mende-Siedlecki, P., 177
Mendez, D., 488
Mendonca, B. B., 100
Mendoza, N., 100
Menezes, A. M., 384
Meng, Y., 482
Menges, J. I., 356
Menkel-Meadow, C., 500
Menlove, F. L., 285
Mennecke, B., 416
Mennella, J. A., 175
Mensh, B. D., 64, 69
Mercer, J., 465
Mercer, P., 211
Merikangas, K. R., 479, 481
Merlo, E., 324
Merluzzi, T. V., 139
Merrill, J. E., 68
Merriwether, A. M., 113
Mervis, C., 365
Mesgarani, N., 195
Mesick, C. C., 404
Mestre, M. V., 450
Metcalfe, J., 315
Meth, E. M. S., 207
Metin, B., 212
Metrik, J., 69
Meyer, C., 489
Meyer, D. E., 213, 510
Meyers, B. S., 509

Michael, R. T., 109
Michaelis, R., 466
Michaels, S., 109
Michail, M., 490–491
Michalak, J., 466
Micheva, K. D., 64, 69
Michielse, S., 264
Michou, A., 345
Micozzi, M. S., 66
Middlemist, R. D., 49
Miech, R. A., 217
Miettunen, J., 409
Mikels, J. A., 150
Miklikowska, M., 447
Miklowitz, D. J., 483
Mikuliner, M., 252
Milad, M. R., 285
Miles, E., 144
Miles, S. R., 467, 468
Milgram, S., 450, 456–458
Miller, A. M., 511
Miller, B. L., 77
Miller, C. B., 202
Miller, D. G., 318
Miller, G. A., 301
Miller, G. E., 125
Miller, I. J., 173–174
Miller, I. W., 528
Miller, J. D., 416
Miller, K. L., 80
Miller, M., 199
Miller, M. B., 68
Miller, N., 280, 445
Miller, P. J., 381
Miller, T. R., 414
Miller, W. R., 517
Milling, L. S., 214
Mills, J., 435, 440
Mills, K. L., 239
Millslagle, M., 520
Milne, A. B., 444
Miloyan, B., 476–478
Miltenberger, R., 284
Miltner, W. H. R., 212
Milton, A. L., 324
Min, J., 141, 324
Miner, B., 201
Minkel, J. D., 203
Minson, J. A., 464
Minuchin, S., 526
Minutillo, F., 524
Mischel, W., 45, 423
Mishra, A., 150, 483
Mishra, H., 453
Mita, T. H., 433
Mitchell, D., 185
Mitchell, D. G., 359
Mitchell, J. R., 345
Mitchell, P. B., 464
Mitchell, S. J., 66
Mitkidis, P., 246
Mitroff, S. R., 182
Mo, Y., 124, 132–133
Moacdieh, N. M., 26
Mock, L. O., 527
Modanloo, M., 207
Moeller, J., 356
Moffitt, T. E., 469
Mohammadi, M., 512
Mohandas, E., 74
Mohr, H., 160

Moise-Titus, J., 285
Molinario, E., 341
Moller, A. C., 34, 345
Möller, H., 523
Molloy, G. J., 132
Moltó, J., 272
Momi, D., 511
Monahan, J. L., 432
Monk, J. D., 482
Monk, T. H., 198, 199
Mons, U., 133
Monsell, S., 10, 195
Montanaro, E., 144
Monteiro, J., 67
Montemayor, R., 103
Montgomery, G., 214
Monti, P. M., 69
Moolchan, E. T., 487
Mooneyham, B. W., 212
Moore, D. A., 371
Moore, D. R., 141
Moore, S. M., 249
Moore, T. J., 509
Moosmann, B., 507
Mora, M., 66
Morand-Beaulieu, S., 285
Mordecai, L. A., 486
Moreau, C., 238
Moreno-Alcázar, A., 509
Moreta, M. C., 203
Morewedge, C. K., 210, 211
Morgan, D. L., 139
Morgan, H., 388
Morgan, J., 345
Morgan, L. C., 511
Morgan, R. D., 499
Morgenstern, M., 158
Moriarity, J. L., 306
Morin, A., 193
Morris, C. J., 201
Morris, E. D., 81
Morris, M. W., 375
Morris, P., 226, 466
Morrison, D. M., 109
Morssinkhoff, M., 187
Mørup, M. F., 491
Moscow, A., 442
Mosdol, A., 131
Moss, H., 218, 522
Motora, Y., 17
Motos, M. A., 100
Mott, L. A., 489
Mountz, J. M., 81
Mousavi, S. K., 329
Mowrer, O. H., 445
Moyers, T. B., 517
Moyo, S., 502
Msetfi, R. M., 285
Müeller, K. J., 343
Mueller, P. A., 46
Muenks, K., 345
Mügge, D. O., 450
Mullen, B., 390
Müllensiefen, D., 206
Müller, J., 464
Mulligan, K., 329
Mullineaux, P. Y., 409
Mulvenna, C., 186–187
Mumford, M. D., 390
Mummendey, A., 447
Munafo, D., 204

SUBJECT INDEX

Self-determination theory, 334–335
  autonomy, 334
  competence and relatedness, 334
Self-discrepancy theory, 95–97, 96 (figure)
Self-efficacy theory, 144, 144 (figure)
Self-esteem, 95
Self-fulfilling prophecies, 445
Self-help, 527
Self-monitoring, 421–422
Self-organization theory, 210
Self-reference effect, 300–301
Self-stigma, 471
Self-theory, 385
Semantic memory, 296
Senescence, 243
Sensation, 157
  adaptation and deprivation, 160
  parallel processing, 157
  sensory receptors, 157–158
  signal detection theory, 158–159, 159 (figure)
  transduction, 157
Sensory adaptation, 160
Sensory curiosity, 347
Sensory deprivation, 160
Sensory homunculus, 77, 176, 176 (figure)
Sensory memory, 292–294
Sensory motor, 233
Sensory neurons, 59
Serial position curve, 310–311, 311 (figure)
Serotonin, 66
Serotonin norepinephrine reuptake inhibitors (SNRIs), 507
Sex, 97
  within marriage, 111
Sexting, 112
Sex trafficking, 437
Sexual hookups, 113
Sexually transmitted infection (STI), 143
Sexual orientations, 104
  college students, 104–105, 104 (figure)
  Kinsey continuum, 106, 106 (figure)
  Storms model, 106–107, 107 (figure)
Sexual scripts, 108–110, 110–111 (table)
Sexual spectrum, 97
  intersex individuals, 98–101
  typical development, 98
Shape constancy, 168
Shaping, 274–275
Short-term memory. *See* Working memory
Short-term therapy, 503
Signal detection theory, 158–159, 159 (figure)
Singlism, 246
Situational elements, 423
Size constancy, 168
Skillful reflective listening, 517
Sleep, 198
  avoid electronics, 206–207
  bad, 203–205
  bed-sharing, 208
  circadian rhythm and biological clock, 198
  early birds *vs.* night owls, 198–199
  interventions, 207
  lifestyle changes, 206
  myths, 208, 209 (table)
  paralysis, 302
  positions, 207–208
  purpose of, 202–203
  quality, 205
  stages of, 199–201, 200 (figure)
  tracking, 201–202
Sleep apnea, 204
Smell, 172–173, 173 (figure)

Sociability, 409
Social adjustment, 414
Social anxiety disorder, 475
Social chameleons, 421
Social cognition, 443–444
Social-cognitive approach to personality, 417, 419
Social comparison theory, 94–95
Social constructs, 97
Social desirability, 33
Social facilitation, 438–439
Social identity theory, 93–95, 444
Social learning theory, 226, 445, 517, 520
Social loafing, 439
Social media, 35, 112
  Facebook, 50
  and happiness, 152
Social psychology, 431, 438, 449
Social support, 139–140
Sociocultural approach, 13
Sociocultural factors, 5, 336, 464–466
Soma, 61
Somatic marker theory, 370
Somatic nervous system, 58
Somatosensation, 175
Somnambulism, 205
Sound waves, 169, 170 (figure)
Source amnesia, 315
Spacing effect, 302–303
Spanking children, 277
Specific phobia, 477
Split brain research, 75, 76 (figure)
Spontaneous recovery, 262–263, 263 (figure)
Sport psychology, 345
Spreading activation, 306
State-dependent memory, 310
Stereotypes
  and prejudice, 443–445, 443 (table), 444 (table)
  stereotype content model, 445–446, 446 (table)
Sternberg's triangular theory of love, 246–247, 247 (figure)
Stigma, 470–472, 472 (figure)
Stimulants, 215, 507
Stockholm syndrome, 441–442
Storage, 298, 298 (figure)
  consolidation, 306
  failure, 314
  importance, taking breaks, 308
  reconsolidation, 307–308
  retention interval, 306–307
  schemas, 306
  structure, 305–306
Storms two-dimensional model, sexual orientations, 106–107, 107 (figure)
Stress, 122
  acculturation, 127–128, 128 (table)
  cancer, 132–133
  cardiovascular disease, 131–132
  common sources, 123, 123 (table)
  coping strategies, 134–140
  general adaptation syndrome (GAS), 129–131, 130 (figure)
  immune system, 131
  poverty, 126–127
  racism, 128
Stressors, 122
  environmental, 124–125
  personal, 125
Structuralism, 11
Subgoal analysis, 376
Subjective age, 250
Subjective vitality, 418